THE
ROYAL DESCENTS OF
900 IMMIGRANTS

Volume II

Descents from Kings or Sovereigns Who Died before 1200,
with Supplemental Material, Abbreviations, and Index
[pp. 735-1611]

Edward III, King of England (1312–1377, reigned 1327–1377), a central figure of this work (see pages 107–93), from a rubbing of the Hastings Brass in Elsing Church, Norfolk, as published in Joseph Foster, *Some Feudal Coats of Arms* (James Parker and Co., Oxford and London, 1902), p. 78. Note that the king's tunic features his coat-of-arms, post 1340, as depicted also on the front cover.

THE
ROYAL DESCENTS
OF
900 IMMIGRANTS

to the American Colonies, Quebec,
or the United States

Who Were Themselves Notable
or Left Descendants
Notable in American History

Volume II

Gary Boyd Roberts

Computerized (from Manuscript) and Indexed
by Julie Helen Otto,
Who Also Undertook Research

Proofread by Margaret Foye Mill

Baltimore, 2018

For, among others, my four major contributors:

John C. Brandon
John Anderson Brayton
John Blythe Dobson
Douglas Richardson

Copyright © 2018
Gary Boyd Roberts
All Rights Reserved.
No part of this publication may be reproduced, in any form
or by any means, including electronic reproduction or
reproduction via the Internet, except by permission of the author.

Published by Genealogical Publishing Company
Baltimore, Maryland
2018

Library of Congress Preassigned Control Number 2018935565

ISBN, the two-volume set: 9780806320748
ISBN, Volume II: 9780806320762

Front cover: Shield of Edward III, King of England (died 1377), post 1340, with the arms of England (three lions) in the second and third quarters and those of France (fleurs-de-lis) in the first and fourth quarters, as drawn from the king's tomb at Westminster Abbey and published by C. S. Scott-Giles, *Looking at Heraldry* (rev. ed., Phoenix House, 1967), p. 7.

THE ROYAL DESCENTS OF 900 IMMIGRANTS

Volume II

Descents from Kings or Sovereigns Who Died before 1200, with Supplemental Material, Abbreviations, and Index
[pp. 735-1611]

The Royal Descents of 900 Immigrants

1. Frederick I Barbarossa, Holy Roman Emperor, d. 1190 = (2) Beatrix of Burgundy

2. Otto of Hohenstaufen, Palatine Count of Burgundy = Margaret of Blois, daughter of Theobald V, Count of Blois, and Alix of France, daughter of Louis VII, King of France, d. 1180, and Eleanor of Aquitaine (who = [2] Henry II, King of England)

3. Beatrix of Burgundy = Otto I, Duke of Meran, Count Palatine of Burgundy

4. Adelaide of Burgundy = Hugh de Châlon, Count Palatine of Burgundy

5. Hypolite of Burgundy = Aymar III de Poitiers, Count of Valentinois. They were patrilineal ancestors of Diane de Poitiers, Duchess of Valentinois, SETH, mistress of Henry II, King of France.

6. Constance de Poitiers = Hugh III Adhémar, Seigneur de la Garde

7. Lambert III Adhémar, co-Seigneur de Monteil = Douce Gaucelme

8. Hugh IV Adhémar, Seigneur de la Garde = Mabile du Puy

9. Louis Adhémar, co-Seigneur de Monteil = Dauphine de Glandevez

10. Marguerite Adhémar = Berthold di Baschi, Seigneur en parti di Vitozzo

11. Thadée de Baschi, Seigneur de Saint-Estève = Jeanne de Barras

12. Louis de Baschi, Seigneur de Saint-Estève = Melchionne de Matheron

13. Louis de Baschi, Seigneur d'Auzet = Louise de Varas

14. Balthazard de Baschi, Seigneur de Saint-Estève = Marguerite du Faur

15. Louis de Baschi, Baron d'Aubais = Anne de Rochemore

16. Louise de Baschi = Jacques des Vignolles, Seigneur de Prades

17. Charles des Vignolles, Seigneur de Prades = Gabrielle de Sperandieu (generations 17-19 were, before Louis Nicola's immigration to Pa., Huguenot refugees in Ireland)

18. Charlotte des Vignolles = Charles Nicola (or Nicholas)

19. **Louis Nicola** (c. 1717-1807) of Pa., revolutionary soldier, public official, editor, merchant = (1) Christiana D'Oyly; (2) Jane Bishop.

Sources: *TAG* 57 (1981): 139-44, and sources cited therein and listed on p. 144. The accent marks are from the late W.A. Reitwiesner's original draft of this article.

The Royal Descents of 900 Immigrants

1. Henry II, King of England, d. 1189 = Eleanor of Aquitaine

2. (illegitimate by Ida de Toeni, later wife of Roger Bigod, 2nd Earl of Norfolk) William Longespee, Earl of Salisbury = Ela, Countess of Salisbury, daughter of William Fitz Patrick, Earl of Salisbury (and Eleanor de Vitré), son of Patrick, Earl of Salisbury, and Ela Talvas, daughter of William III Talvas, Count of Alençon and Ponthieu, and Alice of Burgundy, SETH (see *AR8*, lines 108, 101)

3. Ida de Longespee = William de Beauchamp

4. Beatrice de Beauchamp = Sir Thomas FitzOtho or FitzOtes

5. Maud (or Matilda) FitzThomas = John de Botetourte, 1st Baron Botetourte, formerly thought to be an illegitimate son of Edward I, King of England, d. 1307, but see *TAG* 63 (1988): 145-53

6. Elizabeth de Botetourte = William le Latimer, 3rd Baron Latimer

7. Elizabeth le Latimer = Sir John Camoys

8. Thomas Camoys, 1st Baron Camoys = Elizabeth Louches (he married secondly, Elizabeth Mortimer, widow of Sir Henry "Hotspur" Percy)

9. Sir Richard Camoys = Joan Poynings, daughter of Richard Poynings, 3rd Baron Poynings, and Isabel FitzPayn, for whom see *RD600*, p. 479

10. Margaret Camoys = Ralph Radmylde

11. Margaret Radmylde = John Goring

12. John Goring = Joan Hewster

13. John Goring = Constance Dyke

14. Constance Goring = Sir John Kingsmill

15. Mary Kingsmill = Edward Goddard

16. Bridget Goddard = 17. William Cordray, see below. Their son, John Cordray, married firstly Sarah —— and left two sons, William and Samuel Cordray, who immigrated to Virginia, as did Eleanor Cordray, John and Anna's sister. William and probably Eleanor died unmarried; Samuel Cordray left two sons but no NDTPS.

17. **Anna Cordray** of Va. = Richard **Bernard** of Va., ARD, SETH.

17, 18. Bridget Cordray = Samuel Ironmonger. Two of their younger children, Martha Ironmonger, wife of Robert Jones, and Cordray Ironmonger, who married Mrs. Mary —— Field, also immigrated to Va., but left no NDTPS.

18, 19. **Francis Ironmonger** of Va. = Elizabeth ——.

18, 19. **William Ironmonger** of Va. = Elizabeth Jones.

    15. Alice Kingsmill (sister of Mary) = James Pilkington, Bishop of Durham

    16. Deborah Pilkington = Walter Dunch

    17. **Deborah Dunch**, known as **Lady Deborah Moody** (d. c. 1659), founder of a colony at Gravesend, L.I. = **Sir Henry Moody**, 1st Bt.

    11. Elizabeth Radmylde (sister of Margaret) = Nicholas Lewknor, son of Sir Thomas Lewknor and (2) Elizabeth Echyngham, SETH

    12. Edward Lewknor = (1) Margaret ——, SETH, (3) Anne Everard

    13. (by 3) Eleanor Lewknor = Sir William Wroughton

    14. Sir Thomas Wroughton = Anna Berwick

    15. Gertrude Wroughton = Sir Ralph Gibbs

    16. Sir Henry Gibbs = Elizabeth Temple

    17. **Robert Gibbs** of Mass. = Elizabeth Sheafe.

    10. Eleanor Camoys (sister of Margaret) = Sir Roger Lewknor, son of Sir Thomas Lewknor above and (1) Philippa Dalyngridge, SETH

    11. Elizabeth Lewknor = John Wroth

    12. John Wroth = Joan (Newdigate?)

    13. Robert Wroth = Jane Hawte

    14. Sir Thomas Wroth = Mary Rich

    15. Elizabeth Wroth = George Mynne

The Royal Descents of 900 Immigrants

16. Anne Mynne = George Calvert, 1st Baron Baltimore (c. 1578/9-1632), promoter of Md.

17. **Cecil Calvert**, 2nd **Baron Baltimore** (1605-1675), proprietor of Md. = Hon. Anne Arundell, ARD, SETH.

17. **Hon. Leonard Calvert** (1606-1647), colonial governor of Md. = ——. Note: Hon. Grace and Hon. Helen or Ellen Calvert, daughters of George Calvert, 1st Baron Baltimore and Anne Mynne, married respectively Sir Robert Talbot, 2nd Bt., and James Talbot, and left sons Sir William Talbot, 3rd Bt. (son of Grace), secretary of Md. (= Anne Nugent) and George Talbot (son of Helen), surveyor general of Md. (= Sarah ——). Both returned to Ireland; Sir William died childless and George left no NDTPS.

15. Mary Wroth (sister of Elizabeth) = John Hussey

16. John Hussey = Anne Denne

17. **Thomas Hussey** of Md. = Joanna ——

16. Nathaniel Hussey (brother of John) = Mary Catlin/Catelyn

17. **Elizabeth Hussey** of Mass. = Robert **Scott**.

1. Henry I, King of England, d. 1135 = Matilda of Scotland

2. (illegitimate by Sybil Corbet) Reginald FitzRoy or de Mortain, Earl of Cornwall = Mabel FitzWilliam

3. Maud FitzReginald = Robert de Beaumont, Count of Meulan, great-great-grandson of Henry I, King of France, d. 1060, and Anne of Kiev (see *AR8*, lines 53, 50)

4. Maud de Beaumont = William de Vernon, 5th Earl of Devon

5. Mary de Vernon = Sir Robert Courtenay

6. Sir John Courtenay = Isabel de Vere

7. Sir Hugh Courtenay = Eleanor le Despencer

8. Isabel Courtenay = John St. John, 1st Baron St. John

The Royal Descents of 900 Immigrants

9. Margaret St. John = John Beauchamp, 2nd Baron Beauchamp of Hatch

10. Cecily Beauchamp = Sir Roger Seymour

11. William Seymour = Margaret Brockbury

12. Roger Seymour = Maud Estumy

13. Sir John Seymour = Isabel William

14. Roger Seymour = Sybil Harden

15. Jane Seymour = Thomas Cordray

16. Thomas Cordray = Jane Morris

17. William Cordray = 16. Bridget Goddard, above

Sources: *RA* 3: 400-2 (Ironmonger, Cordray, Seymour), 4: 611-21 (Seymour, Beauchamp), 4: 8-10 (Vivonne), 2: 561-64 (Ferrers), 4: 319-20 (St. John), 2: 317-23 (Courtenay), 5: 276-78 (Vernon, Beaumont), 1: 8-18 (Henry I and Reginald FitzRoy), 2: 263 (Radmylde), 2: 69-72 (Camoys), 5: 159-60 (le Latimer), 1: 448-56 (Botetourte, FitzThomas, FitzOtho, Beauchamp), 3: 599-610 (Longespee), 2: 63-65 (Calvert, Mynne), 5: 400-2 (Wroth), 3: 571-74 (Lewknor); *TAG* 73 (1998): 181-93, 294-311 (Cordray, Ironmonger) (Paul C. Reed), *TG* 1 (1980): 113, 124, 2 (1981): 249, 255, *VGE*, pp. 414-15, *LDBR* 1, pp. 642-43, and *LDBR* 3, pp. 42-44 (Sir Richard Camoys and Joan Poynings to William and Francis Ironmonger); W.H. Rylands, ed., *Visitations of Hampshire, 1530, 1575, 1622 and 1634* (*HSPVS*, vol. 64, 1913), p. 168 (Goddard); *Berry's Hants*, pp. 44-45 (Kingsmill); *BP* (Goring, baronets and Camoys); *CP* (Camoys, le Latimer, Botetourte, Beauchamp of Hatch); *AR8*, lines 50, 121 and *TG* 9 (1988): 226-27; *NAW* (Lady Deborah Moody), *CB* (Moody of Garesdon), *MGH*, 3rd ser., 2 (1898): 43 (Dunch), and John Pilkington, *History of the Pilkington Family of Lancashire*, 3rd ed. (1912), pp. 104-110, 268-72, 297 and chart in pocket at end; Walter Kendall Watkins, *The Robert Gibbs House, Boston* (1932, excerpt from *Old-Time New England* 22 [1931-32]: 193-96), *NEHGR* 19 (1865): 208-9, *Heraldic Journal* 3 (1867): 165-66 (Gibbs), Josiah Willard Gibbs, *Memoir of the Gibbs Family of Warwickshire, England, and [the] United States of America* (1879), pp. 12-13, 48-49 and G.D. Squibb, *Wiltshire Visitation Pedigrees, 1623* (*HSPVS*, vol. 105-6, 1954), pp. 219-20 (Wroughton); *AP&P* 4: 1: 468-72, *MG* 1:

132-38, 143-44 (Calvert, Mynne), *DAB* (Leonard Calvert); *TAG* 89 (2017): 31-41, 128-36 (Leslie Mahler and John C. Brandon) plus sources cited therein, esp. *MGH*, 5th *Ser.* 5 (1923-25): 71 and the 1656 and 1646 wills of, respectively, Rev. John Hussey of Harbey, Lincolnshire and his mother Mary (Wroth) Hussey of London, which mention both sons above (John and Nathaniel), plus grandchildren Elizabeth Scott and Thomas Hussey, son of John (Hussey, Scott); *Mary Isaac*, pp. 177-78, *Archaeologia Cantiana* 12 (1878): 315, F.W. Weaver, *Visitations of Somerset, 1531 and 1573* (1885), p. 93, and J.C. Wedgwood, *History of Parliament: Biographies of Members of the Commons House, 1439-1509* (1936), p. 974 (Wroth), plus *Lewes*, pp. 149-53 (Lewknor); *Foundations* 3 (2009-11): 217-27 (Seymour, generations 10-12 above). The Cordray line to Henry I is included in part because *RA* does not treat Goring and Kingsmill and because Mrs. Anna Cordray Bernard is an ancestor of H.M. the late Queen Elizabeth The Queen Mother and thus the present British royal family. In addition John Seymour, brother of Roger Seymour at generation 14 above, married Elizabeth Coker and was the father of John Seymour, who married Elizabeth Darrell, SETH. These last were grandparents of Queen Jane Seymour, third wife of Henry VIII, King of England, and mother of Edward VI, King of England.

Note that all immigrant descendants of Henry II charted herein are through a single illegitimate son, William Longespee, Earl of Salisbury, and all except Mrs. Thomasine Ward Buffum through Longespee's son, Stephen Longespee, or the two daughters Ida. For "Countess Ida," mistress of Henry II and mother of William Longespee, Earl of Salisbury, above and on various following charts, see *NEHGR* 10 (1856): 262 and *TAG* 77 (2002): 137-49.

The Royal Descents of 900 Immigrants

1. Henry II, King of England, d. 1189 = Eleanor of Aquitaine
2. (illegitimate by Ida de Toeni, later wife of Roger Bigod, 2nd Earl of Norfolk) William Longespee, Earl of Salisbury = Ela, Countess of Salisbury, SETH
3. Stephen Longespee = Emmeline de Riddleford
4. Ela Longespee = Sir Roger la Zouche
5. Alan la Zouche, 1st Baron Zouche of Ashby = Eleanor de Segrave
6. Maud la Zouche = Robert Holand, 1st Baron Holand
7. Elizabeth Holand = Sir Henry FitzRoger
8. John FitzRoger = Alice ——
9. Elizabeth FitzRoger = (1) John Bonville; (2) Richard Stukeley
10. (by 1) William Bonville, 1st Baron Bonville = (1) Margaret Grey; (2) Elizabeth Courtenay
11. (illegitimate by Isabella Kirkby) John Bonville = Alice Dennis
12. Isabella Bonville = Edmund Larder
13. Ursula Larder = William Hull
14. Henry Hull = ——
15. Ursula Hull = Peter Colleton
16. Sir John Colleton, 1st Bt. = Katherine Amy
17. **James Colleton**, colonial governor of S.C. = Anne Kendall.

17. Anne Colleton (sister of Gov. James Colleton of S.C.) = Humphrey Selwood
18. **Katherine Selwood**, almost certainly of S.C. = John **Moore** (1659-1732), colonial official of S.C. and Pa. Katherine apparently left no NDTPS; Moore's large progeny was derived through second wife Rebecca Axtell.

17. Thomas Colleton of Barbados, landgrave of S.C. (brother of James Colleton, colonial governor of S.C., and of Anne) = —— Mead.

18. Elizabeth Colleton = Thomas Garth

19. Mary Garth = Charles Boone

20. **Thomas Boone** (c. 1730-1812), governor of N.J. and N.C. = Mrs. Sarah Anne Tatnall Peronneau.

12. Cecily Bonville (sister of Isabella) = Morris Moore

13. Ellen Moore = Bartholomew Fortescue, son of John Fortescue (and Jacquetta St. Leger), son of Martin Fortescue (and Elizabeth Deynsell), son of Sir John Fortescue (and Isabella Jamys), son of Sir John Fortescue (and Eleanor Norris), son of William Fortescue and Elizabeth Beauchamp, SETH

14. Elizabeth Fortescue = Lewis Hatch

15. Jane Hatch = John Walrond

16. Cecily Walrond = John Greene

17. **Jane Greene** of Mass. = William **Poole** of Mass., ARD, SETH.

10. (by 2) Hugh Stukeley (half-brother of the 1st Baron Bonville) = Katherine de Affeton

11. Nicholas Stukeley = Thomasine Cockworthy

12. Joan Stukeley = Philip Baynard

13. Robert Baynard = Anne Blake

14. Thomas Baynard = Elizabeth Barnes

15. Henry Baynard = Anne Hobbes

16. Thomas Baynard = Martha Prickman

17. Thomas Baynard = Mary Bennett

18. **John Baynard** of Md. = Elizabeth Blackwell.

11. Alice Stukeley (sister of Nicholas) = Sir Thomas Beaumont
12. Hugh Beaumont = Thomasine Wise
13. Margaret Beaumont = John Chichester
14. Elizabeth Chichester = Nicholas Pyne
15. John Pyne = Honor Penfound
16. George Pyne = Joan Darte
17. John Pyne = Anstice Rich
18. John Pyne = Alice ——
19. John Pyne = Charity White
20. John Pyne = Mary Hammett
21. John Pyne = Mary Craze
22. **Thomas Pyne** of N.Y. = (1) Sarah Gainesford; (2) Anna Rivington.

16. John Pyne (brother of George) = ——
17. Josias Pyne = Christian Heydon
18. Philip Pyne = Anne ——, widow of James Oxenham
19. John Pyne = Joan Hunt
20. Cornelius Pyne = Margaret Markham
21. John Pyne = Isabella Pyne
22. **John Pyne** of S.C. = Honora Smith.

Sources: *SCG* 2: 3-7 and *Pennsylvania Genealogical Magazine* 44 (2005-6): 101-21 (Colleton, Selwood, Moore, by Terri Bradshaw O'Neill), *VD*, pp. 218 (Colleton), 492 (Hull), 524 (Larder), 101-3 (Bonville), 572-73 (Moore), 352-54 (Fortescue), 456 (Hatch), *NGSQ* 59 (1971): 254-62, 60 (1972): 25-35 (FitzRoger, Holand); John W. Raimo, *Biographical Directory of American Colonial and Revolutionary Governors, 1607-1789* (1980), p. 438 (Thomas Boone), *Parliament, 1715-1754*, 1: 471-72 (Charles Boone), 2: 59 (John Garth, brother of Mary), and *Surtees*, vol. 4, pt. 1, p. 29 (Garth), plus *English Historical Review* 54 (1939): 443-70 ("Charles

The Royal Descents of 900 Immigrants

Garth and His Connections"); *RA* 3: 9-11 (Greene, Walrond, Hatch, Fortescue), 4: 515-16 (Moore, Bonville), 1: 432-35 (Bonville, FitzRoger), 3: 292-96 (Holand), 5: 474-77 (la Zouche), 3: 595-610 (Longespee), *AR8*, lines 261, 30-32, *CP* (Bonville) and *MCS5*, lines 90-90A, 142, 144; Burton W. Spear, *Search for the Passengers of the Mary & John, 1630*, vol. 19 (1993), pp. 139-40 (Pole/Poole, Greene), F.T. Colby, *Visitation of the County of Somerset in the Year 1623* (1876), p. 43 (Greene), *Transactions of the Devonshire Association for the Advancement of Science, Literature and Art* 39 (1907): 264-66 (Walrond, including Bridget [sister of Cecily], wife of Rev. Theophilus Gale and mother of another Rev. Theophilus Gale, a book donor to Harvard, and of Katherine Gale, wife of Walter Northcott; Hatch) and *GGE*, pp. 661-62, 931 (wills of Theophilus Gale [Jr.] and his sister Katherine Northcott, in the latter of which a bequest is left to "kinswoman Mrs. Jane Poole of Boston in New England" and "her son Theophilus"); *NGSQ* 71 (1983): 37-40 (Baynard) and sources cited in both, esp. G.D. Squibb, ed., *Wiltshire Visitation Pedigrees, 1623* (*HSPVS*, vol. 105-6, 1954), pp. 15-16 (Baynard) and *VD*, p. 721 (Stucley); M. Taylor Pyne, *Memorials of the Pyne Family* (1919), pp. 120-26, 170-203, 228-54, F.W. Pyne, *The John Pyne Family in America, Being the Comprehensive Genealogical Record of the Descendants of John Pyne (1766-1813) of Charleston, South Carolina* (1992), pp. 16-35, 180-83 esp., *BLG*, 1939 ed., p. 2875, 1952 ed., p. 2103 (Pyne), and *VD*, pp. 632 (Pyne), 173 (Chichester), 65 (Beaumont). The line for Gov. Thomas Boone was developed and brought to my attention by John C. Brandon, and that of Mrs. Jane Greene Poole was developed by Douglas Richardson, John C. Brandon, and John Higgins.

The Royal Descents of 900 Immigrants

1. Henry II, King of England, d. 1189 = Eleanor of Aquitaine
2. (illegitimate by Ida de Toeni, later wife of Roger Bigod, 2nd Earl of Norfolk) William Longespee, Earl of Salisbury = Ela, Countess of Salisbury
3. Stephen Longespee = Emmeline de Riddleford
4. Ela Longespee = Sir Roger la Zouche
5. Alan la Zouche, 1st Baron Zouche of Ashby = Eleanor de Segrave
6. Elena la Zouche = Alan de Charlton
7. Alan de Charlton = Margery FitzAer
8. Thomas de Charlton = ──
9. Anna de Charlton = William de Knightley
10. Thomas de Knightley de Charlton = Elizabeth Francis
11. Robert Charlton = Mary Corbet, daughter of Robert Corbet and Margaret ── (who later married Sir William Malory, son of Sir Anketil Malory and Alice de Driby, SETH; thus the Bulkeleys below are *not* of Malory, Driby, or Gaveston descent).
12. Richard Charlton = Anne Mainwaring
13. Anne Charlton = Randall Grosvenor, son of Randall Grosvenor and Margaret Mainwaring, daughter of Randall Mainwaring and Margaret Savage, SETH
14. Elizabeth Grosvenor = Thomas Bulkeley
15. Edward Bulkeley = Olive Irby
16. **Rev. Peter Bulkeley** (1582/3-1658/9) of Mass., Puritan clergyman, a founder and first minister of Concord, Mass. = (1) Jane Allen (died in England), ARD, SETH; (2) Grace Chetwode of Mass., ARD, SETH.
17. (by 1) Edward Bulkeley = Lucian ──
18. Peter Bulkeley = Rebecca Wheeler
19. Rebecca Bulkeley = Jonathan Prescott, Jr.

The Royal Descents of 900 Immigrants

20. Abel Prescott = Abigail Brigham
21. Lucy Prescott, sister of Dr. Samuel Prescott, who completed Paul Revere's "Midnight Ride" of 19 Apr. 1775 = Jonathan Fay, Jr.
22. Samuel Prescott Phillips Fay = Harriet Howard
23. Samuel Howard Fay = Susan Shellman
24. Harriet Eleanor Fay = James Smith Bush
25. Samuel Prescott Bush = Flora Sheldon
26. Prescott Sheldon Bush, U.S. senator = Dorothy Walker
27. George Herbert Walker Bush (b. 1924), 41st U.S. President = Barbara Pierce, SETH
28. George Walker Bush (b. 1946), 43rd U.S. President = Laura Lane Welch, SETH

16. **Elizabeth Bulkeley** of Mass. = (1) Richard **Whittingham**; (2) Atherton **Haugh**.
16. **Martha Bulkeley** of Mass. = Abraham **Mellowes**.
16. Sarah Bulkeley = Oliver St. John, son of Henry St. John (and Jane Neale), son of Alexander St. John (and Jane Dalison), son of Sir John St. John and Sybil ferch Morgan ap Jenkin, SETH
17. **Elizabeth St. John** of Mass. = Rev. Samuel **Whiting**.
18. Samuel Whiting, Jr. = Dorcas Chester
19. Samuel Whiting (III) = Elizabeth Read
20. Katherine Whiting = John Lane, Jr.
21. Susanna Lane = Nathaniel Davis
22. Nathaniel Davis, Jr. = Lydia Harwood
23. Mary Davis = John Moor
24. Hiram D. Moor = Abigail Franklin
25. Victoria Josephine Moor = John Calvin Coolidge

26. (John) Calvin Coolidge (Jr.) (1872-1933), 30th U.S. President = Grace Anna Goodhue

16. Dorcas Bulkeley = Anthony Ingoldsby
17. Olive Ingoldsby = Rev. Thomas James, sometime of Charlestown, Mass., and New Haven, Conn.
18. **Rev. Thomas James**, first minister of East Hampton, L.I., N.Y. = (1) Ruth Jones; (2) Katherine Blux.

Sources: *RA* 2: 8-10 (Bulkeley [and Ingoldsby and James], Grosvenor), 5: 474-80 (Charlton, Knightly, la Zouche), 3: 599-606 (Longespee, Salisbury), 2: 292 (Corbet), 4: 523-36 (St. John, Beauchamp); *AR8,* lines 31, 30, 85, 203, *NEXUS* 13 (1996): 128, second column, and items listed in *NEHGR* 141 (1987): 100, esp. *Blackman,* pp. 57, 60, 62-134, 138-58. See also *Bulkeley,* pp. 2-36, and *Hawes, Freeman and James,* plus *GM* 16 (1969-71): 93-96, 244 and *TAG* 34 (1958): 15-17, 175, 46 (1970): 256 (St. John).

The Royal Descents of 900 Immigrants

1. Henry II, King of England, d. 1189 = Eleanor of Aquitaine
2. (illegitimate by Ida de Toeni, later wife of Roger Bigod, 2nd Earl of Norfolk) William Longespee, Earl of Salisbury = Ela, Countess of Salisbury
3. Ida Longespee = Sir Walter FitzRobert
4. Ela FitzRobert = Sir William de Odingsells
5. Ida de Odingsells = (1) Sir Roger de Herdeburgh; (2) John de Clinton, 1st Baron Clinton
6. (by 1) Ela de Herdeburgh = (2) William le Boteler, 1st Baron Boteler of Wem
7. Ankaret le Boteler = John le Strange, 2nd Baron Strange of Blackmere
8. Eleanor le Strange = Reginald de Grey, 2nd Baron Grey of Ruthyn
9. Reginald de Grey, 3rd Baron Grey of Ruthyn = Joan Astley
10. John Grey = Elizabeth ——
11. Reynold (Reginald) Grey = Beatrice ——
12. Thomas Grey = Bennett Launcelyn
13. Reynold (Reginald) Grey = Elizabeth Isaac
14. Anne Grey = Simon Digby, son of William Digby (and Rose Prestwiche or Perwyche), son of Sir John Digby and Catherine Griffin, SETH
15. Everard Digby = Katherine Stockbridge
16. Elizabeth Digby = Enoch Lynde
17. **Simon Lynde** of Mass. = Hannah Newgate.

10. Robert Grey (brother of John) = Eleanor Lowe
11. Humphrey Grey = Anne Fielding
12. Sir Edward Grey = Joyce Hoord

13. Agnes Grey = Richard Mitton

14. Elizabeth Mitton = Nicholas Grosvenor

15. Eleanor Grosvenor = Jasper Lodge

16. Elizabeth Lodge = John Kenrick

17. Matthew Kenrick = Rebecca Percival

18. Elizabeth Kenrick = David Clarkson

19. **Matthew Clarkson**, provincial secretary of N.Y. = Katherine Van Schaick.

12. Mary Grey (sister of Sir Edward) = John Dixwell

13. William Dixwell = Elizabeth Knight

14. Charles Dixwell = Abigail Herdson

15. William Dixwell = Elizabeth Brent

16. **John Dixwell** (c. 1607-1688/9), English regicide and Cromwellian politician, later a resident of New Haven, Conn. = (1) Mrs. Joanna —— Ling; (2) Bathsheba Howe.

14. Humphrey Dixwell (brother of Charles) = Ellen Lowe (their daughter Elizabeth Dixwell was the first wife of Sampson Erdeswick, historian of Staffordshire).

15. Anne Dixwell = Edward Broughton

16. Edward Broughton = Helen Pell

17. **Thomas Broughton** of Mass. = Mary Biscoe.

Sources: *RA* 3: 680-83 (Lynde, Digby), 3: 414-16 (Grey of Kempston), 3: 125-30 (Grey of Ruthyn), 1: 371-75 (Strange, Boteler), 2: 259-63 (Herdeburgh), 4: 272-73 (Odingsells), 2: 650-51 (FitzRobert), 3: 599-610 (Longespee), 2: 215-18 (Clarkson, Kenrick, Lodge, Grosvenor, Mitton, Grey of Enville); *AR8*, lines 99, 94, 93, 170, E.E. Salisbury, *Family Histories and Genealogies*, vol. 1, part II (1892), pp. 359-471 (Lynde, Digby, Griffin), vol. 3 (*Supplement*), pedigree VIII (Lynde), and *CP* (Grey de Ruthyn, Strange, Boteler, Clinton, Salisbury, Latimer), *Nichols*, vol. 4, p. 48 (Grey of Kempston), and *Mary Isaac*, p. 25; *NYGBR* 127 (1996): 193-201 and sources cited therein, esp. George Grazebrook and J.P. Rylands, eds., *Visitations of Shropshire, 1623, Part II* (*HSPVS*, vol. 29, 1889), pp. 284-85 (Kenrick), plus *AR8*, lines 93A, 93, 170 (for Clarkson); *DAB*, *Oxford DNB* and *EB*, pp. 161-62 (Dixwell), John Fetherston, ed., *Visitation of Warwickshire, 1619* (*HSPVS*, vol. 12, 1877), pp. 43 (Grey), 297, 41 (Dixwell), *Shaw*, vol. 2, p. 268 (Grey of Enville) (for Dixwell); *Salt* 5, pt. 2 (1884) (which is H.S. Grazebrook, ed., *Heraldic Visitations of Staffordshire, 1614 and 1663-64*), p. 61, Sir G.J. Armytage and W.H. Rylands, eds., *Staffordshire Pedigrees, 1664-1700* (*HSPVS*, vol. 63, 1912), p. 38, *NEHGR* 40 (1886): 106, and *GDMNH*, p. 113 (Broughton).

The Royal Descents of 900 Immigrants

1. Henry II, King of England, d. 1189 = Eleanor of Aquitaine
2. (illegitimate by Ida de Toeni, later wife of Roger Bigod, 2nd Earl of Norfolk) William Longespee, Earl of Salisbury = Ela, Countess of Salisbury
3. Stephen Longespee = Emmeline de Riddleford
4. Ela Longespee = Sir Roger la Zouche
5. Alan la Zouche, 1st Baron Zouche of Ashby = Eleanor de Segrave
6. Maud la Zouche = Robert Holand, 1st Baron Holand
7. Maud Holand = Sir Thomas Swinnerton
8. Sir Robert Swinnerton = Elizabeth Beke
9. Maud Swinnerton = Sir John Savage
10. Sir John Savage = Eleanor Brereton
11. Margaret Savage = Randall Mainwaring
12. Margery Mainwaring = Thomas Davenport
13. Thomas Davenport = Katherine Radcliffe
14. Thomas Davenport = Elizabeth Fitton
15. Katherine Davenport = William Leversage
16. William Leversage = Eleanor Sheffield
17. Eleanor Leversage = John Weld
18. Jane Weld = John Lowndes
19. Charles Lowndes = Sarah ——
20. **Charles Lowndes** of S.C. = Ruth Rawlins.

19. Richard Lowndes (brother of Charles) = Alice ——
20. Richard Lowndes = Margaret Poole
21. **Christopher Lowndes** of Md. = Elizabeth Tasker, daughter of Benjamin Tasker, president of the council (and act. gov.) of Md., and Anne Bladen, daughter of William Bladen of Md.,

colonial publisher and attorney-general of Md., ARD, SETH, and Anne Van Swearingen.

21. Charles Lowndes (brother of Christopher of Md.) = Eleanor Baldwin
22. Richard Lowndes = Susannah Dobson
23. William Lowndes = Elizabeth Byerley
24. Richard Lowndes = Anne Stuart Byrth
25. **Mary Elizabeth Lowndes** (1863-1947) of Conn., headmistress of Rosemary Hall (a girls' preparatory school), author, d. unm.

Sources: *NEHGR* 30 (1876): 141-46, *MG* 2: 187-88, *BLG*, 18th ed., vol. 3 (1972), pp. 553-54 (Lowndes of Hassall), *WWWA*, vol. 2, *1943-1950* (1950), p. 331 (Mary E. Lowndes) and John Parsons Earwaker, *The History of the Ancient Parish of Sandbach* (1890), pp. 121-23 (Weld, Lowndes), 102-3 (Leversage); *Ormerod*, vol. 3, pp. 707-8 (Davenport of Henbury), 80 (Mainwaring of Kermincham) and vol. 1, pp. 712-13 (Savage, plus vol. 3, p. 89 for Eleanor or Elizabeth Brereton as the wife of Sir John Savage); *RA* 4: 554-57 (Savage, with no husband for Margaret Savage), 3: 292-96 (Holand), 5: 474-77 (la Zouche), 3: 599-610 (Longespee) and *AR8*, lines 30-32.

The Royal Descents of 900 Immigrants

1. Henry II, King of England, d. 1189 = Eleanor of Aquitaine
2. (illegitimate by Ida de Toeni, later wife of Roger Bigod, 2nd Earl of Norfolk) William Longespee, Earl of Salisbury = Ela, Countess of Salisbury
3. Ida Longespee = Sir Walter FitzRobert
4. Ela FitzRobert = Sir William de Odingsells
5. Ida de Odingsells = (1) Sir Roger de Herdeburgh; (2) John de Clinton, 1st Baron Clinton
6. (by 1) Ela de Herdeburgh = William le Boteler, 1st Baron Boteler of Wem
7. Alice le Boteler = Sir Nicholas Longford
8. Sir Nicholas Longford = Alice Deincourt
9. Sir Nicholas Longford = Margery (or Margaret) Solney
10. Alice Longford = Sir Robert Neville
11. Thomas Neville = Elizabeth Babington
12. William Neville = Katherine Palmer
13. Thomas Neville = Isabel Griffin, daughter of Nicholas Griffin and Catherine Curzon, SETH
14. Thomas Neville = Alice Wauton
15. Anne Neville, illegitimately by Sir John St. John (husband of Margaret Waldegrave, SETH) had
16. Cresset St. John = John Boteler
17. John Boteler = Jane Elliott
18. **Thomas Boteler (Butler)** of Md. = Mrs. Joan Christopher Mountstephen.
18. **Elizabeth Boteler** of Va. = William **Claiborne** (1600-c. 1677/8), dep. gov. and secretary of state for Va. John Boteler (Butler), a brother of Thomas and Elizabeth, also came to Md., but left no NDPTS.

12. Ellen Neville (sister of William) = John St. Paul

13. William St. Paul = —— Tyrwhit

14. Joyce St. Paul = Robert Dighton

15. Elizabeth Dighton = Sir William Dalison

16. William Dalison = Silvester Deane

17. Sir Maximilian Dalison = Mary Spencer, daughter of Sir William Spencer and Susan Knightley (patrilineal ancestors of British Prime Minister Sir Winston [Leonard Spencer-] Churchill and the late Diana [Frances Spencer], Princess of Wales), daughter of Sir Richard Knightley (and Joan Skenard), son of Sir Richard Knightley and Eleanor Throckmorton, daughter of Sir John Throckmorton and Eleanor Spinney, SETH

18. William Dalison = Elizabeth Oxenden

19. Maximilian Dalison = Frances Stanley

20. Mary Dalison = Thomas Kerrill

21. Elizabeth Kerrill = Jeffrey Amherst

22. **Jeffrey Amherst, 1st Baron Amherst of Holmesdale and Montréal** (1716/7-1797), commander-in-chief of British forces in North America, governor of Virginia = (1) Jane Dalison, ARD, SETH; (2) Elizabeth Cary, ARD, SETH.

Sources: *RA* 1: 384-87 (Boteler, St. John), 3: 615-19 (Neville, Longford), 1: 371-73 (Boteler), 2: 259-63 (Herdeburgh), 4: 272-73 (Odingsells), 2: 650-51 (FitzRobert), 3: 599-610 (Longespee), *MCS5*, line 61 (Thomas Boteler and Mrs. Claiborne), *VHG*, pp. 18-26, 36-39 and *VM* 56 (1948): 458-60; F.A. Blaydes, ed., *Visitations of Bedfordshire, 1566, 1582, and 1634* (*HSPVS*, vol. 19, 1884), pp. 53 (St. John), 168-69 (Neville of Holt); George F. Farnham, *Leicestershire Medieval Pedigrees* (1925), p. 36 (Neville of Holt); *Foundations* 1 (2003-5): 213-23 (Longford); Walter C. Metcalfe, ed., *Visitations of Northamptonshire, 1564 and 1618-19* (1887), pp. 23-24 (Griffin). For Amherst see F.A. Crisp, *Visitation of England and Wales, Notes*, vol. 10 (1913), pp. 157-58 (Amherst), *BLG* 1952, p. 596 and *Archaeologia Cantiana* 15 (1883): 402 (Kerrill, Dalison), and *Lincolnshire Pedigrees* 1: 301-2 (Dighton), 3: 844 (St. Paul); *Baker*, vol. 1, pp. 381-82

The Royal Descents of 900 Immigrants

(Knightley), 109, 752 (Spencer), and *Throckmorton*, pp. 43-51. The "improved" descent for Amherst was brought to my attention by John C. Brandon of Columbia, S.C.

The Royal Descents of 900 Immigrants

1. Henry II, King of England, d. 1189 = Eleanor of Aquitaine
2. (illegitimate by Ida de Toeni, later wife of Roger Bigod, 2nd Earl of Norfolk) William Longespee, Earl of Salisbury = Ela, Countess of Salisbury
3. Ida Longespee = Sir Walter FitzRobert
4. Ela FitzRobert = Sir William de Odingsells
5. Ida de Odingsells = (1) Sir Roger de Herdeburgh; (2) John de Clinton, 1st Baron Clinton
6. (by 1) Ela de Herdeburgh = William le Boteler, 1st Baron Boteler of Wem
7. Alice le Boteler = Sir Nicholas Longford
8. Alice Longford = William FitzHerbert
9. Henry FitzHerbert = —— Downes
10. Nicholas FitzHerbert = Alice Booth
11. Ralph FitzHerbert = Elizabeth Marshall
12. Dorothy FitzHerbert = Thomas Comberford
13. Mary Comberford = John Revell
14. John Revell = Margaret Beighton
15. Robert Revell = Anne Knowles
16. **Anne Revell** of N.J. = John **Curtis**.

11. Joan FitzHerbert (sister of Ralph) = John Cotton
12. Margaret/Margery Cotton = Richard Belgrave
13. Dorothy Belgrave = William Saunders
14. Mary Saunders = John Sharpe
15. Bridget Sharpe = Leonard Chester
16. John Chester = Dorothy Hooker, sister of Rev. Thomas Hooker, founder of Hartford, Conn.
17. **Leonard Chester** of Conn. = Mary Wade.

18. Dorcas Chester = Samuel Whiting, Jr.

19. Samuel Whiting (III) = Elizabeth Read

20. Katherine Whiting = John Lane, Jr.

21. Susanna Lane = Nathaniel Davis

22. Nathaniel Davis, Jr. = Lydia Harwood

23. Mary Davis = John Moor

24. Hiram D. Moor = Abigail Franklin

25. Victoria Josephine Moor = John Calvin Coolidge

26. (John) Calvin Coolidge (Jr.), 1872-1933, 30th U.S. President = Grace Anna Goodhue

Sources: *NGSQ* 61 (1973): 84-85 (Curtis); G.D. Squibb, ed., *Visitation of Derbyshire, 1662-1664* (*HSPVS*, new ser. 8, 1989), p. 83 (Revell, including Anne [Revell] Curtis, husband John and eldest son Thomas Curtis), *FMG*, vol. 1, p. 399 (with earlier Revell generations) and the 1568 PCC will (proved 1576/7) of the elder John Revell, which mentions his brother-in-law Henry Comberford; John Fetherston, ed., *Visitation of Warwick, 1619* (*HSPVS*, vol. 12, 1877), p. 35 (Comberford); John Burke, *A Genealogical and Heraldic History of the Commoners of Great Britain and Ireland*, vol. 1 (1836, repr. 1977), p. 79 (FitzHerbert, listing the daughters and sons-in-law of Nicholas FitzHerbert and Alice Booth and of Ralph FitzHerbert and Elizabeth Marshall, including Dorothy and Thomas Comberford) and *BP* (Stafford, which includes FitzHerbert); *RA* 3: 615 (Longford), 1: 371-73 (le Boteler), 2: 259-63 (Herdeburgh), 4: 272-73 (Odingsells), 2: 650-51 (FitzRobert), 3: 599-610 (Longespee); *Staffordshire Parish Register Society*, vol. 1, *Hamstall Ridware* (1904), p. 2 (Cotton, naming the 15 children of John Cotton and Joan[na] FitzHerbert) and *Shaw*, vol. 1, p. *157 (Cotton); *Nichols*, vol. 3, pp. 177, 261 (Belgrave, Saunders, Sharpe), vol. 4, pt. 1, p. 52 (Chester); Walter C. Metcalfe, *Visitations of Northamptonshire, 1564, 1618-19* (1887), p. 44 (Saunders), the 1583 PCC will of Clement Saunders, which names his "cousins" (nephew and nieces) Nicholas, Bridget, and Dorothy Sharpe, and the 1612-14 will of this Nicholas Sharpe, which mentions Saunders kinsmen and Chester relatives at Blaby. The line of Mrs. Curtis was developed by Robert Allen Wolfe and Janet (Paulette Chevalley) Wolfe, of Ann Arbor, Mich., and brought to my attention by Don Charles Stone. The line for Leonard Chester was developed by John C. Brandon and Leslie Mahler, and brought to my attention by the former. Mr. Brandon and Mr. Mahler have also collected various other printed and documentary sources that cover the above FitzHerbert to Chester descent, esp. I.S. Leadam, ed., *Select Cases Before the King's Council in the Star Chamber*, vol. 2 (*A.D. 1509-1544*) (Selden Society Publications, 1911), p. 53, which discusses the Saunders-Belgrave marriage.

The Royal Descents of 900 Immigrants

1. Henry II, King of England, d. 1189 = Eleanor of Aquitaine
2. (illegitimate by Ida de Toeni, later wife of Roger Bigod, 2nd Earl of Norfolk) William Longespee, Earl of Salisbury = Ela, Countess of Salisbury
3. Stephen Longespee = Emmeline de Riddleford
4. Ela Longespee = Sir Roger la Zouche
5. Alan la Zouche, 1st Baron Zouche of Ashby = Eleanor de Segrave
6. Maud la Zouche = Robert Holand, 1st Baron Holand
7. Maud Holand = Sir Thomas Swinnerton
8. Sir Robert Swinnerton = Elizabeth Beke
9. Maud Swinnerton = Sir William Ipstones, for whom see *RD600*, pp. 875-76
10. Alice Ipstones = Sir Randall Brereton
11. Randall Brereton = Katherine Bulkeley
12. Randall Brereton = Emma Carrington
13. Sir Randall Brereton = Eleanor Dutton
14. John Brereton = Alicia ——
15. William Brereton = Elizabeth Green
16. Cuthbert Brereton = Joan House or Howes
17. **Rev. John Brereton** or **Brierton** (fl. 1572-1619) of Maine, explorer, author of the first English work dealing with New England = Margaret ——.

Sources: *DAB* and Robert Maitland Brereton, *The Breretons of Cheshire, 1100 to 1904 A.D.* (1904), pp. 97-98, 112-13 esp.; Walter Rye, ed., *Visitations of Norfolk, 1563, 1589, and 1613* (*HSPVS*, vol. 32, 1891), p. 53 and *Ormerod*, vol. 2, pp. 686-87 (Brereton); *Salt* 7, pt. 2 (1886), pp. 24, 36-47 (Ipstones, Swinnerton); *RA* 1: 521-23 (Brereton, to the first John), 4: 554-56 (Ipstones, Swinnerton), 3: 292-96 (Holand), 5: 474-77 (la Zouche), 3: 599-610 (Longespee) and *AR8*, lines 30-32.

The Royal Descents of 900 Immigrants

1. Henry II, King of England, d. 1189 = Eleanor of Aquitaine
2. (illegitimate by Ida de Toeni, later wife of Roger Bigod, 2nd Earl of Norfolk) William Longespee, Earl of Salisbury = Ela, Countess of Salisbury
3. Sir William Longespee = Idoine de Camville
4. Ela Longespee = James de Audley
5. Hugh de Audley, 1st Baron Audley = Isolde (Mortimer?)
6. Alice de Audley = Ralph Neville, 2nd Baron Neville
7. John Neville, 3rd Baron Neville = Maud Percy
8. Eleanor Neville = Ralph Lumley, 1st Baron Lumley
9. Katherine Lumley = Sir John Chidiock
10. Katherine Chidiock = Sir John Arundell
11. Margaret Arundell = Sir William Capel
12. Sir Giles Capel = Isabel Newton
13. Margaret Capel = Robert Ward
14. Henry Ward = Margaret Ugges
15. Tobias Ward = Thomasine Fisher
16. (very likely) George Ward = Dionis Burrow
17. **Thomasine Ward** of Mass. = (1) John **Thompson**; (2) Robert **Buffum**.

Sources: Owen A. Perkins, *Buffum Family, Volume II* (1983), pp. 1-5 and *Davis* 1: xiii-xiv, 3:405-8; Walter Rye, *Norfolk Families* (1913), p. 988, Walter Rye, ed., *Visitations of Norfolk, 1563, 1589, and 1613* (*HSPVS*, vol. 32, 1891), pp. 305-6 and Rev. G.H. Dashwood, ed., *Visitation of Norfolk, 1563*, vol. 1 (1878), pp. 31-33 (Ward); Walter C. Metcalfe, ed., *Visitations of Essex, 1552, 1558, 1570, 1612 and 1634*, vol. 1 (*HSPVS*, vol. 13, 1878), p. 171 (Capel); J.J. Howard and H.S. Hughes, *Genealogical Collections Illustrating the History of Roman Catholic Families of England, Based on the Lawson Manuscript, Part III: Arundell* (1887?), pp. 224, 226-27 (Arundell, Chidiock). *RA* 2: 165-68 (Capel, Arundell, Chidiock), 3: 671-73 (Lumley), 4: 228-32 (Neville), 5: 75-79 (Audley),

The Royal Descents of 900 Immigrants

3: 599-613 (Longespee). The descent of Mrs. Buffum was first developed (and brought to my attention) by Michael J. Wood of London. Clinching proof of George Ward's parentage, asserted by Rye in *Norfolk Families* and highly probable from naming patterns and chronology alone, but doubted by W.G. Davis, would be welcome.

The Royal Descents of 900 Immigrants

1. Henry II, King of England, d. 1189 = Eleanor of Aquitaine
2. (illegitimate by Ida de Toeni, later wife of Roger Bigod, 2nd Earl of Norfolk) William Longespee, Earl of Salisbury = Ela, Countess of Salisbury
3. Ida Longespee = William Beauchamp
4. Beatrice de Beauchamp = Sir Thomas FitzOtho or FitzOtes
5. Maud (or Matilda) FitzThomas = John de Botetourte, 1st Baron Botetourte, formerly thought to be an illegitimate son of Edward I, King of England, d. 1307, but see *TAG* 63 (1988): 145-53
6. Ada de Botetourte = Sir John de St. Philibert
7. Maud de St. Philibert = Sir Warin Trussell, son of Sir William Trussell and Matilda de Mainwaring, daughter of Warin Mainwaring (and Agnes Arderne), son of Sir Thomas de Mainwaring (and ——), son of Roger de Mainwaring (and ——), SETH
8. Maud Trussell = John Hastang
9. Maud Hastang = Ralph Stafford
10. Sir Humphrey Stafford = Elizabeth Burdet
11. Sir Humphrey Stafford = Eleanor Aylesbury, daughter of Sir Thomas Aylesbury and Katherine Pabenham, SETH
12. Humphrey Stafford = Katherine Fray
13. Sir Humphrey Stafford = Margaret Fogge
14. Sir Humphrey Stafford = Margaret Tame
15. Ellen Stafford = Thomas Barlow
16. Stafford Barlow = —— (possibly father or uncle of a Stafford Barlow of Va., for whom I can find no later history or NDTPS)
17. **Audrey Barlow** of R.I. = William Almy.
18. Anne Almy = John Greene, Jr.
19. Philip(pa) Greene = Caleb Carr
20. Caleb Carr, Jr. = Joanna Slocum

The Royal Descents of 900 Immigrants

21. Patience Carr = Joseph Slocum, a cousin
22. Sarah Slocum = William Tripp
23. Phoebe Tripp = Amos Harding
24. George Tryon Harding = Elizabeth Madison
25. Charles Alexander Harding = Mary Ann Crawford
26. George Tryon Harding = Phoebe Elizabeth Dickerson
27. Warren Gamaliel Harding (1865-1923), 29th U.S. President = Mrs. Florence Mabel Kling DeWolfe

18. Christopher Almy (brother of Anne) = Elizabeth Cornell
19. Elizabeth Almy = Lewis Morris
20. Richard Morris = ———
21. Sarah Morris = Joseph Burdg
22. Jacob Burdg = Judith Smith
23. Jacob Burdg, Jr. = Miriam Matthews
24. Oliver Burdg = Jane M. Hemingway
25. Almira Park Burdg = Franklin Milhous
26. Hannah Milhous = Francis Anthony Nixon
27. Richard Milhous Nixon (1913-1994), 37th U.S. President = Thelma Catherine (Pat) Ryan

21. Job Morris (brother of Sarah) = Mary Ansley
22. Lydia Morris = Abel Ansley, a cousin
23. Ann Ansley = Wiley Carter
24. Littleberry Walker Carter = Mary Ann Diligent Seals
25. William Archibald Carter = Nina Pratt
26. James Earl Carter = Bessie Lillian Gordy

The Royal Descents of 900 Immigrants

27. James Earl Carter, Jr., b. 1924, 39th U.S. President = (Eleanor) Rosalynn Smith, SETH

Sources: *RA* 3: 236-44 (Almy, Barlow, Stafford, Hastang), 4: 541-44 (Trussell, St. Philibert), 1: 448-56 (Botetourt, FitzThomas, Beauchamp), 3: 599-607 (Longespee), *GM*, vol. 1 (1999), pp. 42-47, esp. 44 (1626 marriage license for William Almy and Audrey Barlow, both aged 26, with the consent of Audrey's father, Stafford Barlow of Lutterworth, Leics.); *Notes and Queries*, 4th ser., 6 (July-Dec. 1870): 250-51 (generations 14-16); *TG*, new ser., 31 (1915): 175-76 (Stafford of Blatherwick) (generations 9-14). For Stafford Barlow of Va., under-sheriff of Henrico Co. in 1640, see *VM* 11 (1903-4): 279-80. This line was developed by John C. Brandon and Leslie Mahler and posted on *soc.genealogy.medieval* in November 2007. A monograph on the Lutterworth and Va. Stafford Barlows would be welcome. See also *TAG* 61 (1985-86): 178 and *AAP* (2009, 2012), pp. 253-54, 270, 275-77, 346-47, 491.

The Royal Descents of 900 Immigrants

1. Henry II, King of England, d. 1189 = Eleanor of Aquitaine

2. (illegitimate by Ida de Toeni, later wife of Roger Bigod, 2nd Earl of Norfolk) William Longespee, Earl of Salisbury = Ela, Countess of Salisbury

3. Ida Longespee = William de Beauchamp

4. Beatrice de Beauchamp = Sir Thomas FitzOtho or FitzOtes

5. Maud (or Matilda) FitzThomas = John de Botetourte, 1st Baron Botetourte, formerly thought to be an illegitimate son of Edward I, King of England, d. 1307, but see *TAG* 63 (1988): 145-53.

6. Sir John Botetourte = Margaret ——

7. Sir John Botetourte = Joan Gernon

8. Joan Botetourte = Sir Robert Swinborne

9. Alice Swinborne = John Helion

10. Elizabeth Helion = John Warner

11. Elizabeth Warner = John Worthy

12. Elizabeth Worthy = Thomas Golding

13. John Golding (father by first wife Elizabeth Towe of Margery Golding, wife of John de Vere, 16th Earl of Oxford, and mother of Elizabethan scholar and poet Edward de Vere, 17th Earl of Oxford) = Ursula Marston

14. Arthur Golding, Elizabethan scholar = Ursula Roydon

15. Percival Golding = ——

16. Percival Golding of Bermuda = ——

17. **Ephraim Golding** of L.I., N.Y. = Rebecca Gibbs.

Sources: *NEHGR* 87 (1933): 27-34 (Arthur to Ephraim Golding) and L.T. Golding, *An Elizabethan Puritan* (1937), *passim*, plus *Oxford DNB* (Arthur Golding); Joanne McCree Sanders, *Barbados Records: Wills and Administrations, Volume II, 1681-1700* (1980), pp. 136-37 (will of Gideon Golding, brother of Percival [Jr.] of Bermuda); Walter C. Metcalfe, ed., *Visitations of Essex, 1552, 1558, 1570, 1612, 1634, Part I*

(*HSPVS*, vol. 13, 1878), p. 55, and *Part II* (*HSPVS*, vol. 14, 1879), p. 580 (Helion, Warner, Worthy, Golding); *RA* 3: 276-78 (Helion, Swinborne, which does not, however, list Elizabeth, wife of John Warner, as a daughter of John Helion and Alice Swinborne), 1: 448-56 (Botetourte, FitzOtho, Beauchamp), 3: 599-610 (Longespee). This line was developed from printed sources and shown to me by Henry Bainbridge Hoff. William Golding of Brooklyn and John Golding of Huntington, L.I., possibly father and son but for whom I cannot readily find descendants, were probably agnate kin of Ephraim and may share the Worthy-Warner-Helion-Swinborne-Botetourte ancestry outlined above.

The Royal Descents of 900 Immigrants

1. Henry II, King of England, d. 1189 = Eleanor of Aquitaine
2. (illegitimate by Ida de Toeni, later wife of Roger Bigod, 2nd Earl of Norfolk) William Longespee, Earl of Salisbury = Ela, Countess of Salisbury
3. Ida Longespee = William de Beauchamp
4. Beatrice de Beauchamp = Sir Thomas FitzOtho or FitzOtes
5. Maud (or Matilda) FitzThomas = John de Botetourte, 1st Baron Botetourte, formerly thought to be an illegitimate son of Edward I, King of England, d. 1307, but see *TAG* 63 (1988): 145-53
6. Ada de Botetourte = Sir John de St. Philibert
7. Maud de St. Philibert = Sir Warin Trussell, son of Sir William Trussell and Matilda de Mainwaring, daughter of Warin Mainwaring (and Agnes Arderne), son of Sir Thomas de Mainwaring (and ——), son of Roger de Mainwaring (and ——), SETH
8. Lawrence Trussell = Matilda de Charnells
9. Sir William Trussell = Margery Ludlow
10. Isabel Trussell = Thomas Wodhull, a descendant of David of Scotland, Earl of Huntingdon, via Wahul/Wodhull, de Pinkney, and de Lindsay
11. John Wodhull = Joan Etwell
12. Fulk Wodhull = Anne Newenham
13. Lawrence Wodhull = Elizabeth Hall
14. Fulk Wodhull = Alice Wickliffe
15. Thomas Wodhull = Margaret ——
16. Alice Wodhull = William Elkington
17. Joseph Elkington = Ann ——
18. **George Elkington** of N.J. = (1) ——; (2) Mrs. Mary Humphries Core
19. (by 2) Elizabeth Elkington = Thomas Ballinger

20. Samuel Ballinger = Elizabeth Groff

21. Joshua Ballinger = Sarah Jones

22. Sarah Ballinger = Allen Haines

23. Jonathan Haines = Mary Jane Sprague

24. Sarah Haines = Jacob Marion Flickinger

25. Lula Dell Flickinger = James Edgar Robinson

26. Pauline Robinson = Marvin Pierce

27. Barbara Pierce = George Herbert Walker Bush (b. 1924), 41st U.S. President, SETH

28. George Walker Bush (b. 1946), 43rd U.S. President = Laura Lane Welch, SETH

Sources: *RA* 2: 490-92 (Elkington, Wodhull), 2: 154-57 (Wodhull, Wahul), 4: 541-45 (Trussell, St. Philibert), 1: 448-56 (Botetourt, FitzThomas, FitzOtho, Beauchamp), 3: 599-610 (Longespee), 4: 381-82 (de Pinkney, de Lindsay, Scotland); *TG* 7-8 (1986-87): 4-127, esp. 34-41, 48-68, 96-101, 107-22, *TAG* 75 (2000): 277-92 (both by Col. Charles M. Hansen), which correct Arthur Adams, *The Elkington Family of England and America, Being the Ancestry and Descendants of George Elkington of Burlington County, New Jersey* (1945); *AR8*, lines 216, 122A, 30 (generations 1-5). See also Charles M. Hansen, *Ancestor Table: Hansen* (2017), *passim*, for the entire English and Scottish royal descents (generations 8-18 are included in the AT, and the earlier generations are outlined on pp. 199-202).

The Royal Descents of 900 Immigrants

1. Henry II, King of England, d. 1189 = Eleanor of Aquitaine
2. (illegitimate by Ida de Toeni, later wife of Roger Bigod, 2nd Earl of Norfolk) William Longespee, Earl of Salisbury = Ela, Countess of Salisbury
3. Ida Longespee = William de Beauchamp
4. Beatrice de Beauchamp = Sir Thomas FitzOtho or FitzOtes
5. Maud (or Matilda) FitzThomas = John de Botetourte, 1st Baron Botetourte, formerly thought to be an illegitimate son of Edward I, King of England, d. 1307, but see *TAG* 63 (1988): 145-53
6. Ada de Botetourte = Sir John de St. Philibert
7. Maud de St. Philibert = Sir Warin Trussell, son of Sir William Trussell and Matilda de Mainwaring, daughter of Warin Mainwaring (and Agnes Arderne), son of Sir Thomas de Mainwaring (and ——), son of Roger de Mainwaring (and ——), SETH
8. Lawrence Trussell = Matilda de Charnells
9. Sir William Trussell = Margery Ludlow
10. Joan Trussell = Eustace Whitney
11. Sir Robert Whitney = Elizabeth Vaughan
12. Eleanor Whitney = John Puleston, son of John Puleston (and Alswn Fechan ferch Hywel), son of Madog Puleston (and Angharad ferch Davydd), son of Robert Puleston and Lowri ferch Gruffudd Fychan, SETH
13. Sir Robert Puleston = Jane ferch Richard Thomas
14. Margaret Puleston = Lewys Owen
15. Robert Owen = Elsbeth ferch Robert ap Morgan
16. Humphrey Owen = ——
17. **Robert Owen** of Pa. = Jane Vaughan of Pa., ARD, SETH, his second cousin once removed.

The Royal Descents of 900 Immigrants

Sources: *WFP* 1, pedigree V, pp. 50-56 and chart facing p. 50, and *PACF*, p. 275 (Puleston), both corrected by *Bartrum 1*, p. 741 and *Bartrum 2*, p. 1454 (Puleston); *RA* 1: 354-55 (Whitney), 4: 541-45 (Trussell, St. Philibert), 1: 448-56 (Botetourt, FitzThomas, Beauchamp), 3: 599-607 (Longespee). Note also *TG* 7-8 (1986-87): 35, 61-68, 96-97, 115-22 (Trussell, Mainwaring, Meschines, Chester and Gloucester, by Col. Charles M. Hansen).

The Royal Descents of 900 Immigrants

1. Henry II, King of England, d. 1189 = Eleanor of Aquitaine
2. (illegitimate by Ida de Toeni, later wife of Roger Bigod, 2nd Earl of Norfolk) William Longespee, Earl of Salisbury = Ela, Countess of Salisbury
3. Stephen Longespee = Emmeline de Riddleford
4. Ela Longespee = Sir Roger la Zouche
5. Alan la Zouche, 1st Baron Zouche of Ashby = Eleanor de Segrave
6. Maud la Zouche = Robert Holand, 1st Baron Holand
7. Maud Holand = Sir Thomas Swinnerton
8. Sir Robert Swinnerton = Elizabeth Beke
9. Maud Swinnerton = Sir William Ipstones, for whom see *RD600*, pp. 875-76
10. Alice Ipstones = Sir Randall Brereton
11. Sir William Brereton = Catherine Wylde
12. Edward Brereton = Elizabeth Roydon
13. John Brereton = Margaret ferch Richard ab Ievan ap David ab Ithel Fychan
14. Owen Brereton = Elizabeth Salisbury
15. John Brereton = Margaret Wynn
16. Dorothy Brereton = Peter Wood
17. **Elizabeth Wood** of Va. = Charles **Barcroft**.
18. Jane Barcroft = George Moore
19. Magdalene Moore = Thomas Carter (III)
20. (probably) Moore Carter = Jane ——
21. Isaac Carter = Sarah Browne
22. Kindred Carter = ——
23. James Carter = Eleanor Duckworth

24. Wiley Carter = Ann Ansley

25. Littleberry Walker Carter = Mary Ann Diligent Seals

26. William Archibald Carter = Nina Pratt

27. James Earl Carter = Bessie Lillian Gordy

28. James Earl Carter, Jr., b. 1924, 39th U.S. President = (Eleanor) Rosalynn Smith, SETH

Sources: Joseph Foster, ed., *Alumni Oxonienses...1500-1714*, vol. 1 (1891), p. 68 (for Charles Barcroft, aged 17 in 1626); PRs of St. Mary Whitechapel, Middlesex (FHL #94691) (1618 baptism and 1634 marriage of Elizabeth Wood [to Charles Barcroft]); J.L. Chester and G.J. Armitage, eds., *Allegations for Marriage Licences Issued by the Bishop of London, 1611 to 1828*, vol. 2 (*HSPVS*, vol. 26, 1887), p. 58 (1617/8 licence for Peter Wood and Dorothy Brereton) and vol. 1 (*HSPVS*, vol. 25, 1887), p. 141 (1585 licence for John Brereton and Margaret Kempton, widow), will (PCC 1657, Ruthen Quire, fo. 519) of Dorothy Wood naming Barcroft grandchildren and sisters Elizabeth "Buckley" (Bulkeley) and Janet Lloyd; 1612 funeral certificate for John "Bruerton" (Harleian MS, 2041, f. 109), which mentions wife Margaret (Gwyn) Kempton and daughters Elizabeth, wife of Thomas Bulkeley, Janet (then wife of John "Facknallt") and Dorothy; R.M. Brereton, *The Breretons of Cheshire, 1100 to 1904 A.D.* (1904), pp. 42-44, *Bartrum 2*: 278 (generations 11-14) and *Parliament, 1558-1603*, vol. 1, pp. 482-83 (Owen Brereton); *RA* 1: 521-22 (Brereton, to Sir William), 4: 554-56 (Ipstones, Swinnerton), 3: 292-96 (Holand), 5: 474-77 (la Zouche), 3: 599-610 (Longespee). See also B.A. Chapman, *Marriages of Isle of Wight County, Virginia, 1628-1800* (1933, "improved" reprint 1976), pp. 33 (George Moore and Jane Barecroft, daughter of Charles Barecroft, 1661), 9 (Thomas Carter and Magdalen Moore, daughter of George Moore, 1673 [*sic?*]) and *Wills and Administrations of Isle of Wight County, Virginia, 1647-1800* (1975), pp. 3, 60, 54 (Charles Barcroft and George Moore). This line was developed and contributed by John Anderson Brayton of Memphis, Tenn., who, doubtful of the Holand-Swinnerton descent, also developed the alternative in *RD600*, pp. 875-76.

The Royal Descents of 900 Immigrants

1. Louis VII, King of France, d. 1180 = (1) Eleanor of Aquitaine (who = (2) Henry II, King of England)
2. Marie of France = Henry I, Count of Champagne
3. Marie of Champagne = Baldwin IX, Count of Flanders, Emperor of Constantinople, d. 1205
4. Margaret of Flanders = Bouchard d'Avesnes
5. John I, Count of Hainault = Adelaide of Holland, a great-great-granddaughter of Stephen, King of England, d. 1154, and Matilda of Boulogne, and of Henry of Scotland, Earl of Huntingdon, and Ada de Warenne, SETH (see *AR8*, lines 100, 170, 155, 165, 169)
6. Guy of Avesnes, Bishop of Utrecht (great-uncle of Philippa of Hainault, wife of Edward III, King of England)
7. (illegitimate by ——) William (Willem) de Cuser = Ida van Oosterwijk
8. Coenraad Cuser van Oosterwijk = Clementia Gerrit Boelendochter
9. Ida Cuser van Oosterwijk = Jan Herpertsz. van Foreest
10. Catryn van Foreest = Frank van der Meer
11. Arend van der Meer = Jacomina Jacob Claesdr. van Ruyven
12. Pieter van der Meer = Liedewey de Wilt van Bleyswyck
13. Frank van der Meer = Clara van Berendrecht. Their son, Willem van der Meer van Berendrecht, married Anna Sandelin and left a son, Willem van der Meer van Berendrecht, who married Anna Campe and left a daughter, Cornelia van der Meer van Berendrecht, who married Herman Anthonisz. de Huybert. Their son, Anthony Hermansz. de Huybert, married Helena van Zyll and left a son, Herman Anthonisz. de Huybert, who immigrated to N.Y., married Lucretia Roodenburgh, but left no NDTPS. See *NYGBR* 56 (1925): 227, 71 (1940): 241-42.
14. Joost van der Meer van Berendrecht = Machteld van der Dussen
15. Sophia van der Meer van Berendrecht = Cornelis van Lodensteyn

16. Jan van Lodensteyn = Geertruy (Gertrude) Jansdr. van Ilpendam
17. **Sophia van Lodensteyn** of N.Y. = Carel **de Beauvois** or **Debevoise**.

Sources: *NYGBR* 66 (1935): 376-83, 122 (1991): 161; *Genealogisches Bijdragen Leiden en Omgeving* 7 (1992): 476-79 (Ilpendam); *Gens Nostra* 45 (1990), 10/11: 370-72, 380-81, 423-24, 434, 437, 440, 443 (generations 2-16), Adriaan Willem Eliza Dek, *Genealogie der Graven van Holland* (1954?), pp. 29-31, 40-41 esp., and *RA* 3: 187-90 (Cuser, Hainault, Flanders), corrected for the parentage of Cuser by *De Nederlandsche Leeuw* 133 (2016): 57-63 (Bert den Hertog); *RA* 1: 392-93 (Champagne). For the ancestry of John I, Count of Hainault, and Adelaide of Holland, see George Andrews Moriarty, "The Plantagenet Ancestry of King Edward III and Queen Philippa," mss. at NEHGS and elsewhere, and Ernest Flagg Henderson III, *Ancient, Medieval and More Recent Ancestors of Ernest Flagg Henderson IV and Roberta Campbell Henderson* (2013), esp. vol. 4.

The Royal Descents of 900 Immigrants

1. Louis VII, King of France, d. 1180 = (1) Eleanor of Aquitaine (who = (2) Henry II, King of England)

2. Marie of France = Henry I, Count of Champagne

3. Marie of Champagne = Baldwin IX, Count of Flanders, Emperor of Constantinople, d. 1205

4. Margaret of Flanders = Bouchard d'Avesnes

5. John I, Count of Hainault = Adelaide of Holland, a great-great-granddaughter of Stephen, King of England, d. 1154, and Matilda of Boulogne, and of Henry of Scotland, Earl of Huntingdon, and Ada de Warenne, SETH (see *AR8*, lines 100, 170, 155, 165, 169)

6. Guy of Avesnes, Bishop of Utrecht (great-uncle of Philippa of Hainault, wife of Edward III, King of England)

7. (illegitimate by ——) Maria of Avesnes = Arnoud van Amstel van Ijsselstein, knight

8. Catharina van Amstel = Daniel van Goor, knight

9. Johan van Goor = —— van Hameland?

10. William van Goor = Christina van Giessen

11. Balthasar van Goor = Elisabeth van Rijswick

12. Jan van Goor = (2) Margriet van Goor, a likely cousin

13. Balthasar van Goor = Geertken van Giessen

14. (very probably) Willemke van Goor = Sander Reijnersz. van Tuyl

15. Jan Sandersz. van Tuyl = Marijke Otten van Oever

16. Ott Jansz. van Tuyl = Neelken Geerlof Aertsdr.

17. **Jan Otten van Tuyl** of N.Y. = Geertruijt Jansdr. van Lent.

Sources: *New Netherland Connections* 7 (2002): 1-4 (Henry Bainbridge Hoff), based largely on Rory L. Van Tuyl and Jan N.A. Groenendijk, *A Van Tuyl Chronicle* (1996): 505-10, 589-90; *Genealogisch Tijdschrift voor Midden-en West-Noord-Brabant* 11 (1987): 101-7, 17 (1993): 202-3 (Goor); *Gens Nostra* 45 (1990), 10/11: 370-72, 468-69, 492-93 (generations 2-12), *RA* 3: 187-88 (Hainault, to Guy of Avesnes), 1: 392-93

(Champagne). The above Willemke, daughter of a Balthasar van Goor and wife of Sander Reijnersz. van Tuyl, certainly belonged to this family and shared the above *RD* via Avesnes and Amstel, regardless of the identity of her father.

The Royal Descents of 900 Immigrants

1. David I, King of Scotland, d. 1153 = Matilda of Northumberland, widow of Simon de St. Liz, SETH
2. Henry of Scotland, Earl of Huntingdon = Ada de Warenne, a great-granddaughter of Henry I, King of France, d. 1060, and Anne of Kiev, see *AR8*, lines 89, 50, 53
3. David of Scotland, Earl of Huntingdon (brother of Malcolm IV and William the Lion, Kings of Scotland) = Maud de Meschines, daughter of Hugh Kevelioc, 3rd Earl of Chester, SETH, and Bertrade de Montfort
4. Ada of Scotland = Sir Henry Hastings
5. Hilaria Hastings = Sir William Harcourt
6. Sir Richard Harcourt = Margaret Beke
7. Sir John Harcourt = Ellen la Zouche
8. Matilda Harcourt = Henry Crispe
9. John Crispe = Anne Phillips (or Fettiplace)
10. Henry Crispe = Joan Dyer
11. John Crispe = Joan Sevenoaks
12. John Crispe = Agnes Queke
13. John Crispe = Avice Denne
14. Margaret Crispe = (1) John Crayford; (2) John Blechynden
15. (by 1) Edward Crayford = Mary Atsea
16. Sir William Crayford = Anne Norton
17. Anne Crayford = John Warren
18. William Warren = Catherine Gookin, niece of Daniel Gookin of Newport News, Va.
19. **Thomas Warren** of Va. = Jane ———.

15. (by 2) Alice Blechynden (half-sister of Edward Crayford) = Thomas Tournay
16. Jane Tournay = Stephen Gibbes

17. Robert Gibbes of Barbados = Mary Coventry

18. **Robert Gibbes**, colonial governor of S.C. = ―― Davis.

18. **Thomas Gibbes** of S.C. = Elizabeth ――.

18. Basil Gibbes = Ann Murrey

19. **John Gibbes**, very probably the immigrant to Goose Creek, S.C. = Elizabeth ――.

Sources: *PSECD* 3: 308-11 and *LDBR* 1, pp. 186-89 (Thomas Warren); *VHG*, pp. 232-49 (Warren, Crayford), *HSF* 2: 87-90 (Crispe); Brice McAdoo Clagett, "The Gibbes Family of St. Andrew Parish, Barbados: Its English Ancestry in Kent, England, and its Beginnings in South Carolina" (1987), unpublished mss. sent to the author, data incorporated into Mr. Clagett's *Seven Centuries: Ancestors for Twenty Generations of John Brice de Treville Clagett and Ann Calvert Brooke Clagett*, mss. sent to various scholars in Brice's lifetime; *RA* 3: 205-7 (Harcourt, to Sir John, without naming daughters), 3: 249-52 (Hastings), 1: 223-28 (Huntingdon), 4: 578-83 (Scotland) and *AR8*, lines 93, 170. See also W. Bruce Bannerman, ed., *Visitations of Kent, 1574 and 1592* (*HSPVS*, vol. 75, 1924), p. 146 (Torney or Tournay) and F.A. Crisp, *Collections Relating to the Family of Crispe,* new ser. (1913), vol. 1, p. 34 (Blechynden) and *passim* (Crispe).

Note that all immigrant descendants charted herein of David I, King of Scotland, are through his son Henry of Scotland, Earl of Huntingdon, and all except George Sandys, Lady Margaret (Sandys) Wyatt and Gov. Thomas Greene are via Henry's son David of Scotland, Earl of Huntingdon (and Maud de Meschines). The above Simon de St. Liz as noted on pp. 879 and 919 but not above or on the other charts treating descendants of David I, King of Scotland, is generally recognized as Earl of Huntingdon and Earl of Northampton, two of the three earldoms of his father-in-law. The earldom of Huntingdon was later held by Henry of Scotland as shown above.

The Royal Descents of 900 Immigrants

1. David I, King of Scotland, d. 1153 = Matilda of Northumberland, widow of Simon de St. Liz, SETH

2. Henry of Scotland, Earl of Huntingdon = Ada de Warenne, a great-granddaughter of Henry I, King of France, d. 1060, and Anne of Kiev, see *AR8*, lines 89, 50, 53

3. David of Scotland, Earl of Huntingdon (brother of Malcolm IV and William the Lion, Kings of Scotland) = Maud de Meschines, daughter of Hugh Kevelioc, 3rd Earl of Chester, SETH, and Bertrade de Montfort

4. Margaret of Scotland = Alan, lord of Galloway

5. Devorguilla of Galloway = John Baliol

6. Cecily Baliol (sister of John Baliol, King of Scotland 1292-96) = Sir John de Burgh

7. Hawise de Burgh = Sir Robert de Grelle

8. Joan de Grelle = John La Warre, 2nd Baron La Warre

9. Catherine La Warre = Warin le Latimer, 2nd Baron Latimer of Braybrooke, son of Thomas le Latimer, 1st Baron Latimer of Braybrooke, and Lora Hastings, daughter of Sir Henry Hastings (and Joan de Cantilupe), son of Sir Henry Hastings and Ada of Scotland, daughter of David of Scotland, Earl of Huntingdon, and Maud de Meschines, above

10. Elizabeth le Latimer = Sir Thomas Griffin

11. Richard Griffin = Anna Chamberlain

12. Nicholas Griffin = Margaret Pilkington

13. Nicholas Griffin = Catherine Curzon

14. Catherine Griffin = Sir John Digby

15. Elizabeth Digby = Humphrey Hercy. Their daughter Anne Hercy married Nicholas Denman; their son Francis Denman married Anne Blount; their daughter Anne Denman married Sir Thomas Aylesbury, 1st Bt.; their daughter Frances Aylesbury married Edward Hyde, 1st Earl of Clarendon, statesman and historian; and their daughter Anne Hyde, Duchess of York, was the first

wife of James II, King of England, and mother of Mary II and Anne, Queens of England.

16. Alice Hercy = Henry Hatfield

17. Elizabeth Hatfield = Thomas Whalley

18. Richard Whalley = Frances Cromwell, aunt of Oliver Cromwell, the Lord Protector

19. **Edward Whalley** (d. 1674 or 1675), English army officer and regicide, later a resident of Mass. and Conn. = (1) Judith Duffell; (2) Mary Middleton. Frances Whalley, a daughter of Judith, married William Goffe, also an English army officer and regicide and later a resident of Mass. and Conn.

19. **Jane Whalley**, sometime of Mass. and Conn. = William **Hooke**, 1600/1-1678, Independent minister.

16. Barbara Hercy (sister of Alice) = George Neville

17. John Neville = Gertrude Whalley

18. Hercy Neville = Bridget Saville

19. Gilbert Neville = Margaret Bland

20. Edward Neville = Mary Scott

21. Mary Neville = William Lovelace

22. **John Lovelace, 4th Baron Lovelace**, colonial governor of N.Y. = Charlotte Clayton, ARD, SETH.

Sources: *Oxford DNB* (Whalley, Hooke, and Lovelace), Mark Noble, *Memoirs of the Protectoral House of Cromwell*, 3rd ed., vol. 2 (1787), pp. 139-41, 143-53 (Whalley), G.W. Marshall, ed., *Visitations of the County of Nottingham, 1569 and 1614* (*HSPVS*, vol. 4, 1871), pp. 117-18 (Whalley, Hatfield), 15 (Hercy), 65-66 (Neville), *Thoroton*, vol. 3, pp. 262-63 (Neville), *CP* (Lovelace) and *NYGBR* 51 (1920): 179, footnote 1; Walter C. Metcalfe, *Visitations of Northamptonshire, 1564 and 1618-19* (1887), pp. 23-24 (Griffin); E.E. Salisbury, *Family Histories and Genealogies*, vol. I, part II (1892), pp. 427-71 (Digby, Griffin); *RA* 3: 680-81 (Digby), 3: 141-45 (Griffin, Latimer), 3: 457-60 (de la Warre, de Grelle, de Burgh), 1: 223-32 (Baliol, Huntingdon), 4: 578-83 (Scotland),

The Royal Descents of 900 Immigrants

AR8, lines 99, 94, 93, 170, 89, 50, 53 and *CP* (Latimer, de la Warre, Hastings). See also *Nichols*, vol. 2, p. 261*** (Digby) and *TG*, new ser., 8 (1892): 44 (Hercy to Anne Hyde).

The Royal Descents of 900 Immigrants

1. David I, King of Scotland, d. 1153 = Matilda of Northumberland, widow of Simon de St. Liz, SETH

2. Henry of Scotland, Earl of Huntingdon = Ada de Warenne, a great-granddaughter of Henry I, King of France, d. 1060, and Anne of Kiev, see *AR8*, lines 89, 50, 53

3. Margaret of Scotland = Humphrey IV de Bohun, hereditary constable of England

4. Henry de Bohun, 1st Earl of Hereford = Maud FitzGeoffrey, Countess of Essex

5. Humphrey de Bohun, 2nd Earl of Hereford = Maud (de Lusignan) of Eu

6. Alice de Bohun = Roger V de Toeni

7. Ralph VII de Toeni = Mary ——

8. Alice de Toeni = Guy de Beauchamp, 10th Earl of Warwick

9. Maud de Beauchamp = Geoffrey de Say, 2nd Baron Say

10. Joan de Say = Sir William Fiennes

11. Sir William Fiennes = Elizabeth Batisford

12. James Fiennes, 1st Baron Saye and Sele = Joan ——

13. Elizabeth Fiennes = William Cromer

14. Sir James Cromer = Catherine Cantilupe (Cantelow)

15. Anne Cromer = William Whetenhall

16. Rose Whetenhall = Thomas Wilsford

17. Cecily Wilsford = Edwin Sandys, Archbishop of York

18. **George Sandys** (1577/8-1643/4), poet, treasurer of Va., d. unm.

18. Sir Samuel Sandys = Mercy Colepepper/Culpeper, daughter of Martin Colepepper/Culpeper (and Lettice Clarke), son of Walter Colepepper/Culpeper and Cecily Barrett, SETH

19. **Margaret Sandys** of Va. = Sir Francis **Wyatt** (1588-1644), colonial governor of Va., ARD, SETH.

The Royal Descents of 900 Immigrants

Sources: *RA* 1: 260-62 (Sandys, Wilsford), 2: 348-52 (Whetenhall, Cromer, Fiennes), 2: 579-80 (Fiennes), 4: 570-72 (Say), 1: 287-93 (Beauchamp), 5: 174-78 (Toeni), 1: 404-15 (Bohun), 4: 578-83 (Scotland), 2: 368-69 (Colepepper/Culpeper, plus *Sussex Archaeological Collections*, vol. 47 [1904], esp. chart following p. 72); *PCF Lancashire* (Sandys pedigree); *Berry's Kent*, p. 134 (Wilsford); W.B. Bannerman, ed., *Visitations of Kent, 1530-1, 1574, and 1592*, vol. 2 (*HSPVS*, vol. 75, 1924), p. 116 (Whetenhall), vol. 1 (*HSPVS*, vol. 74, 1923), p. 43 (Cromer); *Collins*, vol. 7, pp. 17-19 (Say and Fiennes); *CP* (Say and Sele, Say, Warwick, Tony, Hereford, Essex, Huntingdon) and *AR8*, lines 86, 98, 97, 96, 170.

The Royal Descents of 900 Immigrants

1. David I, King of Scotland, d. 1153 = Matilda of Northumberland, widow of Simon de St. Liz, SETH

2. Henry of Scotland, Earl of Huntingdon = Ada de Warenne, a great-granddaughter of Henry I, King of France, d. 1060, and Anne of Kiev, see *AR8*, lines 89, 50, 53

3. David of Scotland, Earl of Huntingdon (brother of Malcolm IV and William the Lion, Kings of Scotland) = Maud de Meschines, daughter of Hugh Kevelioc, 3rd Earl of Chester, SETH, and Bertrade de Montfort

4. Ada of Scotland = Sir Henry Hastings

5. Sir Henry Hastings = Joan de Cantilupe

6. John Hastings, 1st Baron Hastings = Isabel de Valence, daughter of William de Valence, Earl of Pembroke (and Joan Munchensy), son of Hugh X de Lusignan, Count of la Marche, and Isabel of Angoulême, widow of John "Lackland," King of England, SETH

7. Elizabeth Hastings = Roger de Grey, 1st Baron Grey of Ruthyn

8. Mary de Grey = Sir William Disney

9. Sir William Disney = Lucy Felton

10. John Disney = Katherine Leake

11. Richard Disney = Jane Middleton

12. Emeline Disney = Hamon Sutton

13. Mary Sutton = Thomas Yorke

14. Mary Yorke = Thomas Randes

15. Mary Randes = George Merriton (Meriton, Meryton), Dean of York, chaplain of Anne of Denmark, Queen of James I, King of England

16. Anne Merriton = Francis Wright

17. **Richard Wright** of Va. = Anne Mottrom.

The Royal Descents of 900 Immigrants

Sources: *PSECD* 3: 284-85 (undocumented) and Timothy Field Beard, *How to Find Your Family Roots* (1977), p. 174 (Richard Wright), *DVY*, vol. 3, p. 456 (Wright), vol. 2, pp. 485-86 (Meryton), *Lincolnshire Pedigrees*, pp. 810 (Randes), 1125 (Yorke), 940 (Sutton), vol. 1 (*HSPVS*, vol. 50, 1902), p. 303 (Disney), *RA* 3: 124-25 (Grey of Ruthyn, but no daughter Mary is given for the 1st Baron and Elizabeth Hastings), 3: 249-58 (Hastings), 1: 223-28 (Huntingdon), 4: 578-83 (Scotland), 4: 48-55 (Valence), 1: 43-48, 58 (Lusignan).

The Royal Descents of 900 Immigrants

1. David I, King of Scotland, d. 1153 = Matilda of Northumberland, widow of Simon de St. Liz, SETH

2. Henry of Scotland, Earl of Huntingdon = Ada de Warenne, a great-granddaughter of Henry I, King of France, d. 1060, and Anne of Kiev, see *AR8*, lines 89, 50, 53

3. David of Scotland, Earl of Huntingdon (brother of Malcolm IV and William the Lion, Kings of Scotland) = Maud de Meschines, daughter of Hugh Kevelioc, 3rd Earl of Chester, SETH, and Bertrade de Montfort

4. Isabel of Scotland = Robert Bruce, lord of Annandale

5. Robert Bruce, lord of Annandale = Isabel de Clare

6. Robert Bruce, Earl of Carrick = Marjorie of Carrick (parents of Robert I, King of Scotland)

7. Margaret Bruce = Sir William Carlyle

8. Sir John Carlyle = ——

9. William Carlyle = ——

10. (probably) Sir John Carlyle = ——

11. William Carlyle of Torthorwald = Elizabeth Kirkpatrick

11. Catherine Carlyle = Simon Carruthers

12. Adam Carlyle = ——

13. Adam Carlyle = 12. Ellen Carruthers

13, 14. Alexander Carlyle of Bridekirk = ——

14, 15. Adam Carlyle of Lymekilns = ——

15, 16. Herbert Carlyle of Bridekirk = Margaret Cunningham

16, 17. Lancelot Carlyle = Barbara Johnston

17, 18. Mary Carlyle = John Gale

18, 19. **George Gale** (1671-1712) of Va. and Md., Maryland colonial official = (1) Mrs. Mildred Warner Washington, ARD, SETH (paternal grandmother of President George Washington); (2) Elizabeth Denwood.

The Royal Descents of 900 Immigrants

Sources: Edward C. Papenfuse, et al., *A Biographical Dictionary of the Maryland Legislature, 1635-1789*, 2 vols. (1979-85), pp. 334-38 (the immigrant, three of his sons, one grandson, and two great-grandsons, all Gales); *TCWAAS*, new ser., 8 (1908), chart opposite p. 382 (Gale), which erroneously states that the immigrant George Gale died without issue (before 1714); C.L. Johnstone, *The Historical Families of Dumfriesshire and the Border Wars*, 2nd ed. (1912), pp. 129 etc., Scottish National Archives: Dumfries, Register of Sasines, 1617-1671, vol. 4, pp. 108-110a (generations 15/16 and 16/17) and *SP* 2: 377-82 (Carlyle, the latter source from Margaret Bruce to Adam Carlyle and Ellen Carruthers), *RA* 1: 588-605 (Carlyle, to 8. Sir John; Bruce), 1: 223-28 (Huntingdon), 4: 578-83 (Scotland). This line was developed and contributed by John Anderson Brayton of Memphis, Tenn.

The Royal Descents of 900 Immigrants

1. David I, King of Scotland, d. 1153 = Matilda of Northumberland, widow of Simon de St. Liz, SETH

2. Henry of Scotland, Earl of Huntingdon = Ada de Warenne, a great-granddaughter of Henry I, King of France, d. 1060, and Anne of Kiev, see *AR8*, lines 89, 50, 53

3. David of Scotland, Earl of Huntingdon (brother of Malcolm IV and William the Lion, Kings of Scotland) = Maud de Meschines, daughter of Hugh Kevelioc, 3rd Earl of Chester, SETH, and Bertrade de Montfort

4. Isabel of Scotland = Robert Bruce, lord of Annandale

5. Robert Bruce, lord of Annandale = Isabel de Clare

6. Robert Bruce, Earl of Carrick = Marjorie of Carrick (parents of Robert I, King of Scotland)

7. Mary Bruce = Sir Alexander Fraser of Philorth

7. Maud Bruce = Hugh Ross, 4th Earl of Ross, SETH (he = (2) Margaret Graham)

8. Sir William Fraser of Philorth = Margaret Moray

8. William Ross, 5th Earl of Ross = Mary of the Isles

9. Sir Alexander Fraser of Philorth = 9. Joanna Ross

10. Sir William Fraser of Philorth = Eleanor Douglas

11. Agnes Fraser = Sir William Forbes of Pitsligo

12. Sir Alexander Forbes of Pitsligo = Maria Hay

13. William Forbes of Pitsligo = Mariota Ogilvy

14. William Forbes of Daach = Elizabeth Forbes of Brux

15. Alexander Forbes of Newe = Jean Lumsden

16. William Forbes of Newe = Margaret Gordon

17. John Forbes of Newe = Isabel Burnett

18. Alexander Forbes of Newe = Janet Robertson   18. William Forbes of Culquhonny = Isabel Gordon

19. William Forbes of Newe = 19. Helen Forbes of Culquhonny

20. John Forbes of Deskrie = Margaret Farquharson

21. Archibald Forbes of Deskrie = Agnes Lumsden

22. **Rev. John Forbes** (c. 1740-1783), Anglican clergyman and magistrate in East Florida = Dorothy Murray, daughter of James Murray of N.C. and Mass. and Mrs. Barbara Bennet Murray of N.C., both ARD, SETH.

Sources: *Forbes*, pp. 345-46, 365-66, 384, 388; *SP* (Forbes of Pitsligo, Saltoun [Fraser], Carrick) and *CP* (Ross, Carrick); *RA* 1: 588-605 (Bruce, to Sir William Fraser), 1: 223-28 (Huntingdon), 4: 578-83 (Scotland).

The Royal Descents of 900 Immigrants

1. Boleslaw III, King of Poland, d. 1138 (son of Wladislaw I, King of Poland, d. 1102, and Judith of Bohemia, his first wife) = (2) Salome of Berg-Schelklingen

2. Casimir II, Prince of Sandomir and Krakow, Kujamien and Masovia = Helena of Znaim

3. ____ of Poland (daughter) = Vsevelod III, Grand Prince of Kiev

4. (St.) Michael, Prince of Chernigov, Grand Prince of Kiev = Maria of Halicz

5. Maria of Chernigov = Vassilko, Prince of Rostov

6. Boris, Prince of Rostov = Maria of Murom

7. Constantine II, Prince of Rostov and Uglich = ____ (first wife)

8. Vassili, Prince of Rostov = ____

9. Constantine III, Prince of Rostov = Maria of Moscow, daughter of Ivan I, Grand Prince of Moscow (and Helene ____), son of Daniel, Prince of Perejaslavl (and ____), son of Alexander Nevsky, Grand Prince of Kiev and (Grand Prince of) Vladimir, the Russian hero, and Praskovya of Polotsk

10. Anna of Rostov = Dimitri IV, Prince of Suzdal and Vladimir

11. Semyon, Prince of Suzdal = Alexandra ____

11. Maria of Suzdal = Nicholas Veliaminov

12. Vassili, Prince Shuisky = ____

12. Xenia Veliaminov = Ivan, Prince Vsevoloje

13. Ivan, Prince Gorbaty-Shuisky = ____

13. Ivan, Prince Vsevoloje = ____

14. Ivan, Prince Gorbaty-Shuisky = ____

14. Vassilissa, Princess Vsevoloje = Daniel, Prince Kholmsky

15. Boris, Prince Gorbaty-Shuisky = ____

15. Anna, Princess Kholmsky = Ivan Golovine

16. Peter Golovine = Maria, Princess Odoevsky

16. Alexander, Prince Gorbaty-Shuisky = 17. Anastasia Golovine

791

The Royal Descents of 900 Immigrants

17, 18. Eudoxia, Princess Gorbaty-Shuisky = Nikita Romanov, brother of Anastasia Romanov, first wife of Ivan IV, the Terrible, Czar of Russia. Fedor Romanov, son of Nikita and Eudoxia, married Xenia Chestov and was the father of Michael III, Czar of Russia, d. 1645.

18, 19. Anastasia Romanov = Boris, Prince Lykov-Obolensky

19, 20. Elena, Princess Lykov-Obolensky = Fedor, Prince Khvorostinine

20, 21. Maria, Princess Khvorostinine = Boris, Prince Golitsyn, Russian minister under Peter the Great, son of Alexei, Prince Golitsyn and Irina, Princess Khilkov, SETH. Alexei, Prince Golitsyn, son of Maria and Boris, married Anna Soukine; their daughter, Maria, Princess Golitsyn, married Vassili, Count Saltykov, and was the mother of Sergei, Count Saltykov, paramour of Catherine (II) the Great, Czarina of Russia and, some authorities think, likely father of Paul, Czar of Russia.

21, 22. Anastasia, Princess Golitsyn = Andrei, Prince Romodanovsky

22, 23. Ekaterina, Princess Romodanovsky = Ivan Ladyjensky

23, 24. Anastasia Ladyjensky = Vassili, Prince Dolgoroukov

24, 25. Paul, Prince Dolgoroukov = Henriette Adolfina de Bandré-du Plessis

25, 26. Elena, Princess Dolgoroukov = Andrei Fadeev (their daughter, Ekaterina Fadeev, married Julius von Witte and was the mother of Sergei, Count Witte, the Russian statesman)

26, 27. Elena Fadeev, writer and woman of letters (as "Zinaïde R—sky") = Peter Hahn von Rotherhahn

27, 28. **Helena Petrovna Hahn**, known as **Madame Blavatsky** (1831-1891), founder of the Theosophical movement, a resident of New York City from 1873 to 1878 = (1) Nikifor Vassilievitch **Blavatsky**; (2) Mikheil C. **Betaneli**.

23, 24. Anna Ladyjensky (sister of Anastasia) = Sergei, Prince Troubetskoy

24, 25. Petr, Prince Troubetskoy = (1) Daria, Princess Gruzinski; (2) Maria Kromin

25, 26. (by 1) Alexander, Prince Troubetskoy = Louise Rościszewski

26, 27. Petr, Prince Troubetskoy = Elizabeth von Moeller

27, 28. Sergei, Prince Troubetskoy = Olga Demidov

28, 29. Sergei, Prince **Troubetskoy**, sometime of Va. = **Dorothy Livingston Ulrich**, 1914-2003, known as Ulrich Troubetzkoy, Virginia newspaperwoman, magazine writer, and biographer of Edward Arlington Robinson.

25, 26. (by 1) Petr, Prince Troubetskoy = Elisabeth Bachmetev

26, 27. Daria, Princess Troubetskoy = Dimitri, Prince Obolensky

27, 28. Maria, Princess Obolensky = Andrei, Prince Gagarin

28, 29. **Sergei, Prince Gagarin**, of N.Y. = Ekaterina Chonkhov. Their son, Andrei, Prince Gagarin, married Jamie Porter and was the father of Michael, Prince Gagarin, b. 1942, professor of classics at the University of Texas at Austin, who married Donna Dean Carter.

25, 26. (by 2) Nikita, Prince Troubetskoy (half-brother of Petr) = Alexandra Nelidov

26, 27. Ekaterina, Princess Troubetskoy = Paul, Prince Galitzine/ Golitsyn

27, 28. Paul, Prince Galitzine/Golitsyn = Alexandra, Princess Mestchersky

28, 29. **Nicholas, Prince Galitzine** (1903-1981), of Ill., utilities executive and civic leader = Josephine Dennehy.

28, 29. **Alexandra, Princess Galitzine** of Ill. = (1) Rostislav, Grand Duke of Russia, SETH (and was the mother of Rostislav, Grand Duke of Russia, known as Rostislav Romanoff, 1938-1999, vice-president and head of international banking at Northern Trust Co., Chicago, who married Stephena Verdel Cook); (2) Lester **Armour** (1895-1970), Chicago banker, son of Philip

The Royal Descents of 900 Immigrants

Danforth Armour, Jr. (and May Elizabeth Lester), son of meatpacking tycoon Philip Danforth Armour and Malvina Belle Ogden.

21, 22. Sergei, Prince Golitzin (brother of Anastasia) = Maria Miloslavsky

22, 23. Boris, Prince Golitzin = Natalie, Princess Dolgorukov

23, 24. Maria, Princess Golitzin = Peter Almazov

24, 25. Varvara Almazov = Sergei, Count Cheremetev

25, 26. Anna, Countess Cheremetev = Dimitri, Count Cheremetev, a cousin

26, 27. Sergei, Count Cheremetev = Catherine, Princess Wiazemsky

27, 28. Dimitri, Count Cheremetev = Irina, Countess Vorontzov-Dachkov, see below

28, 29. Vassili, Count Cheremetev = Daria Tatistchev

29, 30. **Catherine, Countess Cheremetev** of N.Y. = **Daniel Pomeroy Davison** (1925-2010), banker, president and CEO of U.S. Trust, chairman of Christie's (auction house).

20, 21. Anastasia, Princess Khvorostinine (sister of Maria) = Youri, Prince Odoevsky

21, 22. Vassili, Prince Odoevsky = Maria, Princess Lykov-Obolensky

22, 23. Ivan, Prince Odoevsky = Praskovia, Countess Tolstoy

23, 24. Varvara, Princess Odoevsky = Dimitri, Prince Troubetskoy

24, 25. Ekaterina, Princess Troubetskoy = Nicholas, Prince Volkonsky

25, 26. Maria, Princess Volkonsky = Nicholas, Count Tolstoy

26, 27. Leo, Count Tolstoy, the Russian novelist and seer, author of *War and Peace* and *Anna Karenina* = Sophia A. Behrs

27, 28. **Alexandra, Countess Tolstoy**, known as **Alexandra Leo Tolstoy** (1884-1979) of N.Y., author, lecturer, co-founder of the Tolstoy Foundation, d. unm.

19, 20. Feodosia, Princess Lykov-Obolensky (sister of Elena) = Semen, Prince Ourrossov

20, 21. Petr, Prince Ourrossov = Eudoxia Sokovnine

21, 22. Anastasia, Princess Ourrossov = Jakov (Jacob), Prince Lobanov-Rostovsky

22, 23. Ivan, Prince Lobanov-Rostovsky = ——

23, 24. Ivan, Prince Lobanov-Rostovsky = Ekaterina, Princess Kurakin

24, 25. Jakov (Jacob), Prince Lobanov-Rostovsky = Alexandra Saltykov

25, 26. Marie, Princess Lobanov-Rostovsky = Kyrill Naryshkin

26, 27. Alexandra Naryshkin = Ivan, Count Vorontzov-Dachkov

27, 28. Hilarion, Count Vorontzov-Dachkov = Elizabeth, Princess Shuvalov. Their son, Ivan, Count Vorontzov-Dachkov, married Varvara Orlov and left a daughter, Sophia, Countess Vorontzov-Dachkov, who married Vladimir, Prince Wiazemsky. Ivan, Prince Wiazemsky, a son of these last, married Marie-Thérèse Mauriac, daughter of François Mauriac, the French man of letters, and was the father of Anne-Françoise-Sophie, Princess Wiazemsky, wife of Jean-Luc Godard, the film director, SETH.

28, 29. Irina, Countess Vorontzov-Dachkov = Dimitri, Count Cheremetev, see above.

Sources: *DAB* (Mme. Blavatsky); *DGA*, vol. 1 (1939), p. 297 (Sergei, Count Witte, first cousin of Mme. Blavatsky); *ES2*: 3: 5: 837 (Dolgoroukov), 2: 23: 1, 3 (Golitsyn), 2: 24: 122 (Saltykov), 2: 3: 5: 897 (Lykov-Obolensky), 2: 24: 137 (Romanov), 2: 23: 28 (Golovine), 2: 2: 147 (Suzdal and Gorbaty-Shuisky to Ivan, son of Vassili and to Maria of Suzdal, wife of Nicholas Veliaminov), 2: 2: 141-42 (Rostow), 2: 2: 131 ([Ts]Chernigow, Grand Prince of Kiev), 2: 2: 120, 122 (Poland); Ikonnikov, *La Noblesse de Russie*, 1st ed. (at least) 11 vols. (1933-40), and 2nd ed., 26 vols. (1957-66), esp. for Ladyjensky, Romodanovsky, Khvorostine, Vsevoloje, Veliaminov, and descendants of Rurik and Gedymin) (and note 2nd ser., vol. D1, Fadeev, #s 12, 23, 25); *Prince*

The Royal Descents of 900 Immigrants

Charles, #s M1057-58 (p. 70), N2115-16 (pp. 104-5), O4229, 4231-32 (p. 152), P8457, 8461-62 (p. 224), Q16913, 16923-24 (p. 344) (generations 12-17 for Gorbaty-Shuisky, 13-18 for Veliaminov-Vsevoloje-Kholmsky-Golovine). For (Dorothy Livingston) Ulrich (Princess) Troubetzkoy see *WWAW*, 5th ed., *1968-1969* (1967), p. 1230, and *ES2*: 24: 153-56 (Troubetskoy). For Sergei, Prince Gagarin, see *WWA* 2006 (2005), p. 1610 (Michael, Prince Gagarin), *ES2*: 3: 5: 853-54 (Gagarin), 2: 3: 5: 905-6 (Obolensky). For Nicholas, Prince Galitzine and Mrs. Armour see *WWWA*, vol. 8, *1982-1985* (1985), p. 147 (N. Galitzine), *NCAB* 56 (1975): 520-21 (Lester Armour), *ES2*: 23: 17 (Galitzine, Golitsin), *BRFW1*, p. 473 (Russia). For Mrs. Davison see *WWWA*, vol. 21, *2009-2010* (2010), p. 52, *ES2*: 24: 140, 144 (Cheremetev, there spelled Scheremetjew) and 2: 23: 1, 3, 8 (Galatzine, Golitsin). For Alexandra Leo Tolstoy see *WWWA*, vol. 7, *1977-1981* (1981), p. 573 and, as reported in *American Ancestors* 13 (2012), 3: 41-42, *ES2*: 25: 36-37 (Tolstoy), 2: 3: 5: 989 (where the children of Nicholas, Prince Volkonsky and Ekaterina, Princess Troubetskoy, although indicated elsewhere, are by an oversight not carried forward), 2: 24: 153, 164 (Troubetskoy), 2: 3: 5: 911-12 (Odoevsky). For the second Cheremetev line, via Vorontzov-Dachkov, see *ES* 2: 25: 143-44 (Vorontzov), 2: 24: 3 (Narys[c]hkin), 2: 3: 5: 878-79 (Lobanov-Rostovsky), Nicolas Ikonnikov, as above, 1st ser., vol. E2 (1940), princes Ourrossov, #s 25, 27, 32a (with Anastasia [not N.N.] Ourrossov identified in the above *ES* 2: 3: 5: 878) and Jacques Ferrand, *Les Familles Princières d'Ancien Empire de Russie*, 2nd ed., vol. 1 (1997), pp. 364-65 (Wiazemsky) and *Les Familles Comtales d'Ancien Empire de Russie*, 2nd ed., vol. 1 (1997), pp. 37-39 (Cheremetev) (I also sometimes used the works by Ferrand to check recent generations covered as well in *ES2*). As these charts show, a considerable number of Russian nobles were cousins of the Romanov czars, these last of Romanov descent through either Peter III, Czar of Russia, or Sergei, Count Saltykov.

The Royal Descents of 900 Immigrants

1. Bolesław III, King of Poland, d. 1138 (son of Władisław I, King of Poland, d. 1102, and Judith of Bohemia, his first wife) = (2) Salome of Berg-Schelklingen

2. Casimir II, Prince of Sandomir and Krakow, Kujamien and Mazovia = Helena of Znaim

3. —— of Poland = Vsevelod III, Grand Prince of Kiev

4. (St.) Michael, Prince of Chernigov, Grand Prince of Kiev = Maria of Halicz

5. Maria of Chernigov = Vassilko, Prince of Rostov

6. Boris, Prince of Rostov = Maria of Murom

7. Constantine II, Prince of Rostov and Uglich = —— (first wife)

8. Vassili, Prince of Rostov = ——

9. Constantine III, Prince of Rostov = Maria of Moscow, daughter of Ivan I, Grand Prince of Moscow (and Helene ——), son of Daniel, Prince of Perejaslavl (and ——), son of Alexander Nevsky, Grand Prince of Kiev and Vladimir, the Russian hero, and Praskovya of Polotsk

10. Anna of Rostov = Dimitri IV, Prince of Suzdal and Vladimir

11. Eudoxia of Suzdal = Dimitri IV, Grand Prince of Moscow, son of Ivan II, Grand Prince of Moscow (and Alexandra ——), brother of Maria of Moscow, wife of Constantine III, Prince of Rostov, SETH. Basil II, Grand Prince of Moscow, son of Dimitri and Eudoxia, married Sophie of Lithuania and was the father of Basil III, Grand Prince of Moscow, who married Maria of Borovsk and was the father in turn of Ivan III, first Czar of Russia, d. 1505.

12. Anna of Moscow = Youri, son of Patrick (and Helena ——), son of Narimond, Prince of Pinsk (son of Gedymin, Grand Duke of Lithuania, and Eva), allegedly by Maria, daughter of Toktai, Khan of the Golden Horde (a great-great-great-grandson of Genghis Khan) and Maria Palaeologina, illegitimate daughter of Andronicus II Palaeologus, Byzantine Emperor

13. Vassili Patrikeev = Maria ——

13. Ivan Grozdj Patrikeev = Eudoxia Khovrine

The Royal Descents of 900 Immigrants

14. Ivan Boulgak Patrikeev = 14. Xenia, Princess Vsevoloje, daughter of 13. Ivan, Prince Vsevoloje (and ——), SETH

15. Michael, Prince Golitsyn = ——

16. Youri, Prince Golitsyn = Xenia ——

17. Ivan, Prince Golitsyn = Eudoxia ——

18. Andrei, Prince Golitsyn = Anna ——

19. Andrei, Prince Golitsyn = Euphemia Piliemanov-Sabourov

14. Irina Patrikeev = Semen Khripoun, Prince Riapolovsky

15. Fedor, Prince Riapolovsky = ——

16. Ivan Khrilek, Prince Riapolovsky = ——

17. Dimitri, Prince Khilkov = ——

18. Vassili, Prince Khilkov = ——

19. Andrei, Prince Khilkov = ——

20. Fedor, Prince Khilkov = ——

20. Alexei, Prince Golitsyn = 21. Irina, Princess Khilkov

21, 22. Ivan, Prince Golitsyn = Anastasia, Princess Prozorovsky

22, 23. Alexei, Prince Golitsyn = Daria, Princess Gagarin

23, 24. Dimitri, Prince Golitsyn = Adelaide Amalia, Countess von Schmettau

24, 25. **Demetrius Augustine, Prince Golitzin** (or **Gallitzin**) (1770-1840) of Md. and Pa., Roman Catholic clergyman, colony founder, and writer, d. unm.

22, 23. Fedor, Prince Golitzin (Gallitzin) (brother of the second Alexei) = Anna Izmalov

23, 24. Nicolas, Prince Golitzin (Gallitzin) = Praskovya Shuvalov

24, 25. Fedor, Prince Golitzin (Gallitzin) = Varvara Shapov

25, 26. Michael, Prince Golitzin (Gallitzin) = Marie Louise Julia, Countess Baranov

26, 27. Vladimir, Prince Golitzin (Gallitzin) = Sophia Delianov

27, 28. Michael, Prince Golitzin (Gallitzin) = Anna Lopuchin

28, 29. Sergei, Prince Golitzin (Gallitzin) = Claudia Bazykin

29, 30. George, Prince Golitzin (Gallitzin) = Ludmila Lisitski

30, 31. **Anna, Princess Golitsyn** (Gallitzin) of Mass. = **Sergei Kravchenko**, b. 1960, physicist.

20. Ivan, Prince Golitsyn (brother of the first Alexei) = Xenia Morosov

21. Maria, Princess Golitsyn = Gregori, Prince Dolgoruki

22. Alexei, Prince Dolgoruki = Praskovya, Princess Khilkov, daughter of Youri, Prince Khilkov (and Domma, Princess Kassimowsky), son of Jakov (Jacob), Prince Khilkov (and Anna Lopuchin), son of Vassili, Prince Khilkov (and Irina, Princess Volkonsky), son of Ivan, Prince Khilkov (and ——), son of 18. Vassili, Prince Khilkov, above, and ——

23. Nikolai, Prince Dolgoruki = Anna Bredichin

24. Praskovya, Princess Dolgoruki = Dimitri Naryshkin

25. Anna Naryshkin = Paul (Pavel) Naryshkin, a cousin

26. Konstantin Naryshkin = Sophia Ushakov

27. Maria Naryshkin = Platon, Prince Obolensky-Neledinsky-Meletzky

28. **Serge(i), Prince Obolensky** (-Neledinsky-Meletzky) (1890-1978), sometime of N.Y. and Mich. = (1) Katharina, Princess Yourievsky, widow of Alexander, Prince Bariatinski, and daughter of Alexander II, Czar of Russia, d. 1881, and his morganatic wife Catherine, Princess Dolgoruki; (2) (Ava) Alice Muriel Astor, daughter of capitalist and inventor John Jacob Astor (IV) (and Ava Lowle Willing), son of financier William (Backhouse) Astor, Jr. and society leader Caroline Webster Schermerhorn, SETH; and (3) Mrs. Marylin Fraser-Wall. Alice Muriel, sister of financier and philanthropist (William) Vincent Astor, married (2) Raymond von Hoffmannsthal, son of the dramatist Hugo

The Royal Descents of 900 Immigrants

von Hoffmannsthal; (3) Philip John Ryves Harding; (4) David Pleydell-Bouverie. Ivan, Prince Obolensky (-Neledinsky-Meletzky), son of Serge and Alice, is an investment banker and publisher (who married Claire McGinnis and Mary Elizabeth Morris).

Sources: *ES* 2: 23: 17, 14, 3, 1 (Golitsyn, Galitsine, Michael to Demetrius Augustus) and *DAB* (D.A., Prince Golitzin/Gallitzin); *ES* 2: 3: 1: 168 (Patrikeev), 2: 2: 124 (Gedymin, Lithuania), 2: 2: 144-45 (Grand Princes of Moscow), 2: 2: 147 (Suzdal), 2: 2: 141-42 (Rostov), 2: 2: 131 ([Ts]Chernigo[w]/v, Grand Princes of Kiev), 2: 2: 120, 122 (Poland), 2: 3: 5: 832 (Riapolovsky, Khilkov/Chilkov); *ES* 2: 23: 14-15 (Golitsyn, to Mrs. Kravchenko/Krawtschenko) and *WWA* 2012 (2011), p. 2476; *ES* 2: 23: 1 (Golitsin), 2: 3: 5: 836-37 (Dolgoruki), 2: 3: 5: 832-33 (Khilkov), 2: 24: 11, 10A (Narys[c]hkin), 2: 3: 5: 905 (Obolensky), *GH des A*, vol. 90, *Fürstliche Häuser*, vol. 13 (1987), pp. 492-93 (Obolensky), *WWA* 2015, p. 3201 (Ivan Obolensky) and *BP*, 107[th] ed., 2003, p. 171 (Astor). For the alleged descent from Genghis Khan, see *The Plantagenet Connection* 9 (2001): 140-53, a discussion from soc.genealogy.medieval. Note the common Romanov and Golitsyn/Galitsine descent from Ivan, Prince Vsevoloje at generation 13 of the Romanov chart. Ivan probably lived in the early or mid-fifteenth century; his son-in-law, Ivan Boulgar Patrikeev above, died in 1498 (*ES* 2: 3: 1: 168).

Tatiana, Princess Golitzin (Gallitzyn), daughter of 26, 27. Vladimir, Prince Golitzin (Gallitzyn) and Sophia Delianov, married Peter Lopuchin (brother of Anna Lopuchin, wife of 27, 28. Michael, Prince Golitzin/Gallitzyn) and was the mother of Tatiana Lopuchin, who married Dimitri, Prince Golitzin (Gallitzyn, not however, of patrilineal Golitzin/Gallitzyn descent) who died in New York. Piotr, Prince Galitzine (Gallitzyn), b. 1955, a son of these last, is a Chicago businessman, head since 2008 of the American operations of TMK IPSCO (Interprovincial Steel and Pipe Corp.), who married Maria Anna (Charlotte Zita Elisabeth Regina Thérèse), Archduchess of Austria, daughter of Rudolf (Syringus Peter Karl Franz Joseph Robert Otto Antonius Maria Pius Benedikt Ignatius Laurentius Justiniani Markus d'Aviano), Archduke of Austria (and Xenia, Countess Czernichew-Besobrazow), son of Karl (Charles) I, Emperor of Austria, d. 1922, and Zita of Bourbon-Parma. The three eldest daughters of Prince Peter (Piotr) and Archduchess Maria Anna were born in New Jersey and California. See *ES* 2: 23: 131 (Lopuchin), 2: 23: 14

The Royal Descents of 900 Immigrants

(Galitzin) and *Almanach de Gotha*, 189th ed., vol. 2 (2013), pp. 332-33 (Galitzine) and vol. 1 (2012), pp. 47, 50-51. This line was brought to my attention by Anthony Glenn Hoskins of Santa Rosa, Calif.

The Royal Descents of 900 Immigrants

1. Boleslaw III, King of Poland, d. 1158 (son of Wladislaw I, King of Poland, d. 1102, and Judith of Bohemia, his first wife) = (2) Salome of Berg-Schelklingen

2. Casimir II, Prince of Sandomir and Krakow, Kujamien and Mazovia = Helena of Znaim

3. —— of Poland = Vsevolod III, Grand Prince of Kiev

4. (St.) Michael, Prince of Chernigov, Grand Prince of Kiev = Maria of Halicz

5. Mstislav, Prince Karachev = ——

6. Tite, Prince Karachev and Kozelak = ——

7. Fedor, Prince Kozelak = ——

8. Tite, Prince Kozelak = ——

9. Vladimir, Prince Kozelak = ——

10. Ivan "Puzynina," Prince Kozelak = ——

11. Ivan, Prince Kozelak-Puzyna = ——

12. Timofei, Prince Kozelak-Puzyna = ——

13. Peter, Prince Kozelak-Puzyna = ——

14. Bogdan, Prince Kozelak-Puzyna = ——

15. David, Prince Kozelak-Puzyna = ——

16. Ivan, Prince Kozelak-Puzyna = Christina Oziebłowska

17. Mikhail Nikita, Prince Kozelak-Puzyna = Sophia Szczuczanka

18. Sophia, Princess Kozelak-Puzyna = Samuel Węsławski

19. Sophia Węsławski = Emmanuel Władisław (Ladislaus), Count Tyszkiewicz

20. Theodore (Fedor), Count Tyszkiewicz = Helena Bykowska

21. Stanislaw Anthony, Count Tyszkiewicz = Evanor Anna Biłłozorowna

22. Eleanor, Countess Tyszkiewicz = Michael Guilgud

23. John Gielgud (to England) = Cunegonda Szemiotowna

24. Adam Gielgud = Aniela Leontina Aszpergerowa

25. Frank Henry Gielgud = Kate Terry Lewis, daughter of Arthur Lewis and actress Kate Terry, sister of Dame Ellen Terry, Marion and Fred Terry, also actors/actresses

26. **(Sir) (Arthur) John Gielgud** (1904-2000), the actor, sometime of N.Y. and Calif., d. unm. Films include *Becket, The Charge of the Light Brigade, The Elephant Man, Chariots of Fire, Arthur*, and *Gandhi*.

Sources: Various biographies, autobiographies or memoirs by Sir John, his brother Val Henry Gielgud, or their mother Kate Terry Gielgud, plus English census, death and other records for generations 23-26; *GH des A*, vol. 23, *Gräfliche Häuser* B, vol. 2 (1960), pp. 453-54 (generations 18-22) (Tyszkiewicz); Nicolas Ikonnikov, *La Noblesse de Russie*, 1st ed., at least 11 vols. (1935-40) and 2nd ed., 26 vols. (1957-66) (Kozelak-Puzyna); *ES* 2: 2: 120, 122 (Poland), 131 ([Ts]Chernigo[w]/v) and Nikolas Ikonnikov, *La Noblesse de Russie*, 2nd ed., vol. A1, *La Descendance de Rurik* [1937], #s 45, 61, 83, 106, 127, 158, 188 [generations 3-9]). This line was first dictated to me by telephone by the late William Addams Reitwiesner.

The Royal Descents of 900 Immigrants

1. Louis VI, King of France, d. 1137 = Adela of Savoy
2. Robert I, Count of Dreux = Agnes de Baudemont
3. Alix of Dreux = Raoul I, Sire de Coucy
4. Agnes de Coucy = Gilles de Beaumez, Châtelain de Bapaulme
5. Gilles de Beaumez, Châtelain de Bapaulme = (Jeanne?) de Bailleul
6. ⸺ de Beaumez (daughter) = Jean I de Sombreffe
7. Jean II de Mareau, Sire de Sombreffe = ⸺
8. Johann III, Sire de Sombreffe = Jutta von Wevelinghoven
9. Wilhelm I von Sombreffe = Margarethe von Kerpen
10. (illegitimate by ⸺) Maria von Sombreffe = Heinrich Typoets
11. Thonis Typoets = Beater van Beele
12. Maria Typoets = Jan Pijpelinckx
13. Hendrik Pijpe alias Pijpelinckx = Clara de Thovion
14. Maria Pijpelinckx = Jan Rubens
15. Peter Paul Rubens (1577-1640), the Baroque painter = (1) Isabelle Brant; (2) Hélène Fourment
16. (by 1) Nicolas Rubens, Seigneur of Rameyen = Constance Helman
17. Hélène Rubens = Jean-Baptiste Lunden
18. Jeanne-Catherine Lunden = Jean-Jacques du Mont dit de Brialmont
19. Hélène-Françoise du Mont dit de Brialmont = Jean-Baptiste de la Bistrate, Seigneur of Laer and Neerwinde
20. Isabelle-Hélène de la Bistrate = Albert-Jean Stier
21. **Henri-Joseph Stier**, Seigneur of Aertselaer, of Md. = Marie-Louise Peeters. Their daughter, Rosalie Eugenia Stier, married George Calvert, son of Benedict "Swingate" Calvert and Elizabeth Calvert, SETH, and was the mother of George Henry Calvert, poet, and Charles Benedict Calvert, congressman and

agriculturalist, who married Elizabeth Stewart and Charlotte Augusta Morris respectively.

Sources: *TG* 9 (1988): 45-73, Hervé Douxchamps, *Rubens et ses Descendants,* vol. 4 (1985), *passim,* and Robert Winder Johnson, *The Ancestry of Rosalie Morris Johnson,* vol. 1 (1905), chart at beginning and pp. 196-211 (P.P. Rubens to H.J. Stier); *Archiv für Sippenforschung* 43 (1977):263-66 (generations 8-15); *ES* 2: 11: 14 (Sombreffe), 2: 27: 32 (Coucy), 2: 3: 1: 63 (Dreux); H.M. West Winter, *The Descendants of Charlemagne (800-1400), Part I, "Brandenburg Updated," Generations I-XIV* (1987) and *Part II, The Continental Descendants, Generations XV-XVI* (1991), generations 12-87, 13-147, 14-250, 14-835, 15-1180, and 16-1589 (generations 1-6), plus *D de la N,* vol. 2, p. 663 (Beaumez).

The Royal Descents of 900 Immigrants

1. Henry I, King of England, d. 1135 = Matilda of Scotland
2. (illegitimate by ——) Robert of Caen, 1st Earl of Gloucester = Mabel FitzHamon
3. Maud of Gloucester = Ranulph de Gernon, 2nd Earl of Chester
4. Hugh Kevelioc, 3rd Earl of Chester = Bertrade de Montfort
5. Agnes de Meschines = William de Ferrers, 4th Earl of Derby
6. Bertha de Ferrers = Sir Ralph Bigod, son of Hugh Bigod, 3rd Earl of Norfolk, Magna Carta surety, and Maud Marshall, SETH
7. Sir John Bigod = Isabel ——
8. Sir Roger Bigod = Joan ——
9. Joan Bigod = Sir William Chauncey
10. John Chauncey = Margaret Giffard
11. John Chauncey = Anne Leventhorp
12. John Chauncey = Alice Boyce
13. John Chauncey = Elizabeth Proffit
14. Henry Chauncey = Lucy ——
15. George Chauncey = Anne Welsh
16. **Rev. Charles Chauncey** (1592-1671/2) of Mass., nonconformist clergyman, 2nd president of Harvard College = Catherine Eyre.

13. William Chauncey (son of John and Alice Boyce) = —— Garland
14. Henry Chauncey = Joan Tenderyng
15. Elizabeth Chauncey = Richard Huberd
16. Edward Huberd = Jane Southall
17. Margaret Huberd = Richard Harlakenden
18. **Mabel Harlakenden** of Mass. = (1) John **Haynes** (c. 1594-1653/4), colonial governor of Mass. and Conn.; (2) Samuel

Eaton. Roger Harlakenden, a brother of Mabel, also came to Mass. and married (1) Emlin —— and (2) Elizabeth Bosvile (of Mass., ARD, SETH, who later married Herbert Pelham of Mass., first treasurer of Harvard College, also ARD, SETH) but left no NDPTS.

Sources: *RA* 2: 129-33 (Chauncey), 1: 164-66 (Bigod), 2: 560-61 (Ferrers), 2: 148-54 (Chester), 3: 86-88 (Gloucester), 3: 223-25 (Harlakenden), *AR8*, lines 69A, 69, 124, 125, 127, *MCS5*, line 3, *Baker*, vol. 1, p. 123 (Ferrers to Sir John and Sir Ralph Bigod); W.C. Fowler, *Memorials of the Chaunceys* (1858), first chart opposite p. 54 esp., *Clutterbuck*, vol. 2, pp. 400-1 and *NEHGR* 148 (1994): 161-66 (Chauncey); *Yorkshire Archaeological Journal* 32 (1934-36): 172-82, 187-89, 201 (Bigod); *NEHGR* 15 (1861): 327-29, 120 (1966): 243-47, reprinted in *EO* 2: 2: 210-12, 215-19 (Harlakenden).

Note that all immigrant descendants of Henry I, King of England, charted herein are through his illegitimate son Robert of Caen, 1st Earl of Gloucester, via the latter's son, William FitzRobert, 2nd Earl of Gloucester, or daughter Maud, Countess of Chester, and through either William's illegitimate daughter Mabel, wife of Gruffudd ab Ifor Bach, or Maud's son, Hugh Kevelioc, 3rd Earl of Chester.

The Royal Descents of 900 Immigrants

1. Henry I, King of England, d. 1135 = Matilda of Scotland
2. (illegitimate by ——) Robert of Caen, 1st Earl of Gloucester = Mabel FitzHamon
3. William FitzRobert, 2nd Earl of Gloucester = Hawise de Beaumont
4. (illegitimate by ——) Mabel of Gloucester = Gruffudd ab Ifor Bach
5. Mawd ferch Gruffudd = Hywel ap Madog
6. Cynwrig ap Hywel of Radur = Angharad ferch Lewys
7. Hywel ap Cynwrig of Radur = (1) —— Maelog; (2) —— ferch Ieuan
8. (maternity uncertain) Meurig ap Hywel of Radur = Crisli ferch Adam Fychan
9. Dafydd ap Meurig of Radur = Ela ferch Hopkin
10. Gwladys ferch Dafydd = Ieuan ap Rhys
11. Mawd ferch Ieuan = Llywelyn ap Hywel Fychan
12. Sir Dafydd Gam = Gwenllian ferch Gwilym ap Hywel Grach. Their daughter Gwladys married Sir William ap Thomas and was the mother of William Herbert, 1st Earl of Pembroke, father illegitimately, by Mawd ferch Adam Turberville, of Richard Herbert of Ewyas, father by Margaret Cradock of William Herbert, 1st Earl of Pembroke of the second creation, and Thomas Herbert of Abergavenny. Alice Herbert, an illegitimate daughter of Thomas Herbert of Abergavenny, married William Jenkin and was the mother of Elizabeth Jenkin, wife of Jenkin Dawkin, SETH, and maternal grandmother of Mrs. Margaret Fleming Bowen of Mass., SETH.
13. Thomas ap Dafydd Gam = —— (*Bartrum 1*, p. 104 gives him only a son, Sir Dafydd Gam, d.s.p., no daughters)
14. Gwenhwyfar ferch Thomas = Ieuan Goch ab Ieuan Ddu
15. Rhys ab Ieuan Goch = ——
16. Tudur ap Rhys = ——

17. Rhys Goch ap Tudur = ——
18. Ieuan ap Rhys Goch = ——
19. Huw ab Ieuan = ——
20. Thomas ap Huw = —— (a son, Cadwalader Thomas, married Ellen Owen, SETH, and was the father of John Cadwalader of Pa., SETH)
21. John Thomas = (1) Anne Lloyd; (2) Katherine Robert of Pa.
22. (by 2) **Robert Jones** of Pa. = Ellen Jones.
22. (by 1) Elizabeth Jones = Rees Evan
23. **Sidney Rees** of Pa. = Robert **Roberts**, son of John Roberts of (Pencoyd) Pa., ARD, SETH, and Mrs. Gainor Pugh Roberts, ARD, SETH.

Members of this family who also immigrated to Pa. but left no NDTPS include:

1. Thomas Jones, son of John Thomas and Anne Lloyd and husband of Anne Griffith
2-3. Cadwalader Jones and Katherine Jones, wife of Robert Roberts (son of Hugh Roberts of Pa., ARD, SETH, and Mrs. Jane Owen Roberts, ARD, SETH), son and daughter of John Thomas and Katherine Robert
4-5. Evan Rees and David Rees, brothers of Mrs. Sidney Rees Roberts
6-7. Elizabeth and Mably Owen, sisters, wives respectively of Thomas Andrews (no issue) and Edward Price, and daughters of Owen ap Huw (and ——), brother of 20. Thomas ap Huw above.

Sources: *WFP* 1, pedigrees I and II, pp. 7-23, 36-39 esp.; *Merion*, pp. 252-60, 294-303; *NGSQ* 67 (1979): 165 esp. (plus citations to *Bartrum 1* and *2* as given on p. 166). Further research should be undertaken to confirm the above line from Thomas ap Dafydd Gam to Thomas ap Huw.

The Royal Descents of 900 Immigrants

1. Henry I, King of England, d. 1135 = Matilda of Scotland
2. (illegitimate by ——) Robert of Caen, 1st Earl of Gloucester = Mabel FitzHamon
3. William FitzRobert, 2nd Earl of Gloucester = Hawise de Beaumont
4. (illegitimate by ——) Mabel of Gloucester = Gruffudd ab Ifor Bach
5. Hywel Felyn ap Gruffudd = Sara le Sore
6. Nest ferch Hywel Felyn = Llywelyn ab Ifor
7. Ifor ap Llywelyn = Tangwystl ferch Rhys ap Hywel Sais
8. Llywelyn ab Ifor = Angharad ferch Morgan ap Maredudd
9. Ifor Hael ap Llywelyn = Nest ferch Rhun ap Gronwy Fychan
10. Rhys ab Ifor Hael = ——
11. Efa ferch Rhys = Morgan ap Dafydd
12. Elen ferch Morgan = Owain ap Gruffudd
13. Maredudd ab Owain = Ellyw ferch Rhys Ddu
14. Gwenllian ferch Maredudd = Dafydd Lloyd ap Dafydd
15. Rhys ap David Lloyd = Margaret ferch Ieuan ab Owain
16. Sir Thomas Pryce = Florence Clunn, daughter of Howell Clunn ap Meyrick and Lleucu, daughter of Henriffri ap Llywelyn and ——, daughter of Dafydd Las ap Hywel Fychan and ——, daughter of Ieuan ap Rhys and Gwladys ferch Dafydd, SETH
17. John Pryce = Gwenllian ferch Llywelyn ap Morus
18. John Price = Joan ——
19. **Joan(na) Price** of Me. = George **Cleeve**, dep. president of Lygonia (Me.), founder of Portland (then Falmouth), Me.

Sources: *George Cleeve Association Newsletter* 13, issue #2 (Spring 1999): 3-6 (generations 11-19), 9-12 and charts following (generations 8-19), 15, issue #1 (Fall 2000): 1-4 (John M. Plummer); *Bartrum 1*:209, 200, 202, 299, 497, 398, 514, 796, 600; *Bartrum 2*: 715 (Pryce), 692 (Clunn).

The Royal Descents of 900 Immigrants

1. Henry I, King of England, d. 1135 = Matilda of Scotland
2. (illegitimate by ——) Robert of Caen, 1st Earl of Gloucester = Mabel FitzHamon
3. William FitzRobert, 2nd Earl of Gloucester = Hawise de Beaumont
4. (illegitimate by ——) Mabel of Gloucester = Gruffudd ab Ifor Bach
5. Hywel Felyn ap Gruffudd = Sara le Sore
6. Madog ap Hywel Felyn = Iwerydd ferch Lewys ap Rhys
7. Joan ferch Madog = Dafydd ab Owain Fychan
8. Goleuddydd ferch Dafydd = Rhys Llwyd, son of Adam (and Elen ferch Llywelyn o'r Cwmwd ap Hywel Hen), son of Rhys ab Einion Sais and Gwladys, daughter of Llywelyn (and ——), son of Hywel Felyn ap Gruffudd, 5. above, and Sara le Sore
9. Gwilym ap Rhys Llwyd = Margred ferch John ap Jenkin
10. Gwenllian ferch Gwilym = Jenkin Gunter
11. Margred Gunter = Roger ap John
12. John ap Roger = Mawd Aubrey
13. Alice ferch John = Owain ap Jenkin
14. Gruffudd Bowen = Anne Berry
15. Philip Bowen = Elsbeth Vaughan
16. Francis Bowen = Ellen Franklyn
17. **Griffith Bowen** of Mass. = Margaret Fleming of Mass, ARD, SETH.
18. Henry Bowen = Elizabeth Johnson
19. John Bowen = Hannah Brewer
20. Abigail Bowen = Caleb Kendrick
21. Benjamin Kendrick = Sarah Harris
22. Anna Kendrick = Benjamin Pierce, Jr.

23. Franklin Pierce (1804-1869), 14th U.S. President = Jane Means Appleton

Sources (for this and ten [possibly twenty-one] other lines from Gruffudd ab Ifor Bach to either Griffith Bowen or his wife Margaret Fleming, SETH): *AR8*, lines 179, 124, *NGSQ* 67 (1979): 163-66, *CN* 19 (1986-87): 335-41, 588-96, and *Lineage Book, Descendants of the Illegitimate Sons and Daughters of the Kings of Britain*, no. 156; AT of Griffith Bowen and Margaret Fleming compiled by the late William Addams Reitwiesner, based largely on *Bartrum 1* (pp. 209, 210, 248, 107-9), *Bartrum 2* (pp. 1650, 248, 649, to generation 14) and correspondence among Bartrum, William C. Rogers and the late General Herman Nickerson, Jr.

The Royal Descents of 900 Immigrants

1. Henry I, King of England, d. 1135 = Matilda of Scotland
2. (illegitimate by ——) Robert of Caen, 1st Earl of Gloucester = Mabel FitzHamon
3. Maud of Gloucester = Ranulph de Gernon, 2nd Earl of Chester
4. Hugh Kevelioc, 3rd Earl of Chester = Bertrade de Montfort
5. Mabel of Chester = William d'Aubigny, 3rd Earl of Arundel
6. Nicole d'Aubigny = Roger de Somery
7. Joan de Somery = John le Strange (IV) of Knokyn
8. John le Strange (V), 1st Baron Strange of Knokyn = Maud de Wauton
9. Elizabeth le Strange = Gruffudd o'r Rhuddallt ap Madog Fychan ap Madog Crupl
10. Gruffudd Fychan ap Gruffudd o'r Rhuddallt = Elen ferch Thomas, great-aunt of Owen Tudor, founder of the Tudor dynasty and husband of Katherine of France, widow of Henry V, King of England. Elen was not, according to Bartrum, a descendant of Llywelyn Fawr ab Iorwerth, Prince of North Wales, and Joan Plantagenet.
11. Lowri ferch Gruffudd Fychan (sister of Owen Glendower, the Welsh rebel hero) = Robert Puleston
12. Angharad Puleston = Edwart (Iorwerth) Trevor ap Dafydd ab Ednyfed Gam
13. Rose Trevor = Sir Otewell Worsley
14. Margaret Worsley = Adrian Whetehill
15. Sir Richard Whetehill = Elizabeth Muston
16. Margery Whetehill = Edward Isaac
17. Mary Isaac = Thomas Appleton
18. **Samuel Appleton** of Mass. = Judith Everard of Mass., ARD, SETH.
19. John Appleton = Priscilla Glover

20. Priscilla Appleton = Joseph Capen
21. Mary Capen = Thomas Baker, Jr.
22. Priscilla Baker = Tarrant Putnam, Jr.
23. Priscilla Putnam = Adam Brown, Jr.
24. Israel Putnam Brown = Sally Briggs
25. Sally Brown = Israel C. Brewer
26. Sarah Almeda Brewer = Calvin Galusha Coolidge
27. John Calvin Coolidge = Victoria Josephine Moor
28. (John) Calvin Coolidge (Jr.) (1872-1933), 30th U.S. President = Grace Anna Goodhue

Sources: *AR8*, lines 249, 124-26, *RA* 5: 61-63 (Gruffudd Fychan, generation 10, le Strange), 4: 674-76 (Somery), 2: 252-54 (d'Aubigny), 2: 148-54 (Chester), 3: 86-88 (Gloucester), and sources cited therein, esp. *Mary Isaac* (Appleton, Isaac, Whetehill, Worsley, Trevor, Rose Trevor).

The Royal Descents of 900 Immigrants

1. Henry I, King of England, d. 1135 = Matilda of Scotland

2. (illegitimate by ——) Robert of Caen, 1st Earl of Gloucester = Mabel FitzHamon

3. Maud of Gloucester = Ranulph de Gernon, 2nd Earl of Chester

4. Hugh Kevelioc, 3rd Earl of Chester = Bertrade de Montfort

5. (illegitimate by ——) Amicia de Meschines = Ralph de Mainwaring

6. Bertrade de Mainwaring = Henry de Audley

7. Emma de Audley = Gruffudd ap Madog, Prince of Powys Fadog, d. 1270, son of Madog ap Gruffud Maelawr, Prince of Powys Fadog, d. 1236, and Ysota, daughter of Ithel, King of Gwent. This Madog was a son of Gruffudd Maelawr (and Angharad, daughter of Owain Gwynedd, King of North Wales), son of Madog (and Susanna, daughter of Gruffudd ap Cynan ab Iago, King of Gwynedd), son of Maredudd (and Hunydd ferch Eunydd ap Gwernwy), son of Bleddyn (and Haer ferch Cynillon ab Y Blaidd Rhûdd), son of Cynfyn ap Gwerystan, lord of Powys, and Angharad, Queen of Powys and South Wales, SETH.

8. (alleged daughter or granddaughter of Gruffudd ap Madog according to Bartrum, probably by Emma; daughter according to Ormerod and older sources) Margred ferch Gruffudd = Sir John Arderne

9. Sir John Arderne = Ellen de Wastenays

10. Matilda Arderne = Robert Legh

11. (probably) Agnes Legh = Roger Hulton

12. Adam Hulton = ——

13. Roger Hulton = Elena Hulton, a cousin

14. Emma Hulton = Richard Parr

15. Richard Parr = Elizabeth Travers

16. Hugh Parr = (1) Constance Tildesley; (2) Isabel Dychefield

17. (maternity uncertain) Dorothy Parr = William Gregory

18. Hugh Gregory = Mary ——

19. William (or Thomas) Gregory = Dorothy Beeston

20. John Gregory = Alice ——

21. **Henry Gregory** of Conn. = ——.

Sources: *TAG* 38 (1962): 171-74 (Gregory, Parr) and *PCF Lancashire* (Hulton pedigree, which, like other sources, including *Baines*, vol. 3: chart between pp. 40 and 41, and *Croston*, vol. 3, pp. 139-40) almost certainly in error, add two more Roger Hultons between generations 13 and 14, a mistake brought to my attention by David Ebel of Boston; *Ormerod*, vol. 3, p. 661 (Legh of Adlington, which pedigree does not include the above Agnes), vol. 2, pp. 85, 79-81 (Arderne, Powys Fadog); *Bartrum 1*, pp. [47], 28, 30-31 (where Margredd, wife of Sir John Arderne, is included as noted above); J.Y.W. Lloyd, *The History of the Princes, the Lords Marcher, and the Ancient Nobility of Powys Fadog*, vol. 1 (1881), pp. 67-68, 71-72, 87-88, 100-9, 111-20, 149-54, 158-72; *Delafield*, vol. 2, pp. 589-97 (Powys Fadog, Audley, Mainwaring); and *RA* 4: 282 (which does not include Margred, wife of Sir John Arderne), 1: 199-200 (Audley, Mainwaring), 2: 148-54 (Chester), 3: 86-88 (Gloucester). The Hulton pedigree identifies the wife of Roger, #11, as Agnes, daughter of Robert Legh of Adlington, and chronology best places Agnes as a daughter of Robert Legh and Matilda Arderne. Documentation for generations 7-8, 10-11 and 13-14 is eagerly sought. Other royal descents are likely via Dorothy Beeston at generation 19, said to be a daughter of "George Beeston of co. Cheshire" (but also identified as "Dorothy came from Beeston" without a surname, in Frank A. Barnes, *Priory Demesne to University Campus: A Topographic History of Nottingham University* [1993], pp. 110-11, a source brought to my attention by John C. Brandon of Columbia, S.C.).

The Royal Descents of 900 Immigrants

1. Henry I, King of England, d. 1135 = Matilda of Scotland
2. (illegitimate by ——) Robert of Caen, 1st Earl of Gloucester = Mabel FitzHamon
3. Maud of Gloucester = Ranulph de Gernon, 2nd Earl of Chester
4. Hugh Kevelioc, 3rd Earl of Chester = Bertrade de Montfort
5. (illegitimate by ——) Amicia de Meschines = Ralph de Mainwaring
6. Sir Roger de Mainwaring = ——
7. Sir William de Mainwaring = ——
8. William de Mainwaring = ——
9. Roger de Mainwaring = Christian de Birtles
10. William de Mainwaring = Mary Davenport
11. William de Mainwaring = Elizabeth Leycester
12. Randall Mainwaring = Margery Venables
13. Sir John Mainwaring = Margaret Delves
14. (said to be) Mary Mainwaring = Hugh Hassall
15. Margaret Hassall = Thomas Bressey
16. Ralph Bressey = Margaret Massey
17. Richard Bressey = Elizabeth Bulkeley (daughter of Randall Bulkeley of Haughton, whom I cannot trace from printed sources)
18. Thomas Bressey = Amy Booth (daughter of Thomas Booth of Cholmondeley, whom I cannot trace from printed sources)
19. Thomas Brassey = ——
20. **Thomas Brassey** of Pa. = (prob.) Margaret Steen.

Sources: Unpublished mss. by Anthony Glenn Hoskins of Santa Rosa, California, a descendant of Thomas Brassey, which cites parish registers of Nantwich, Cheshire (also extracted on the IGI), James Hall, *A History of the Town and Parish of Nantwich* (1883), pp. 414-15 and Sir G.J.

Armytage, Bt. and J.P. Rylands, *Visitations of Cheshire, 1613* (*HSPVS*, vol. 59, 1909), pp. 41-42 (Brassey/Bressie), plus *NEHGR* 112 (1958): 27-34, 43 (reprinted in *EO* 2: 1: 286-93, 303) (generations 13-19— Brassey/Bressie, Hassall, Mainwaring), *Ormerod* 3: 296 (Hassall), 1: 478-81 (Mainwaring of Over Peover), 3: 229 (Mainwaring of Warmincham), *TG* 7-8 (1986-87): 61-62, 115-16 (generations 1-6) and *AR8*, lines 124, 125. *RA* 1: 199-200 (Mainwaring), 2: 148-54 (Chester), 3: 86-88 (Chester) covers only generations 1-6.

The Royal Descents of 900 Immigrants

1. Henry I, King of England, d. 1135 = Matilda of Scotland
2. (illegitimate by ——) Robert of Caen, 1st Earl of Gloucester = Mabel FitzHamon
3. Maud of Gloucester = Ranulph de Gernon, 2nd Earl of Chester
4. Hugh Kevelioc, 3rd Earl of Chester = Bertrade de Montfort
5. Mabel of Chester = William d'Aubigny, 3rd Earl of Arundel
6. Nicole d'Aubigny = Roger de Somery
7. Margaret de Somery = Ralph Basset
8. Ralph Basset, 1st Baron Basset of Drayton = Hawise ——
9. Margaret Basset = Edmund Stafford, 1st Baron Stafford
10. Ralph Stafford, 1st Earl of Stafford = Katherine Hastang [he = (2) Margaret de Audley, SETH]
11. Margaret Stafford = Sir John Stafford, a cousin
12. Joan Stafford = John Draycote
13. John Draycote = Agnes Gascoigne
14. Roger Draycote = ——
15. Jane Draycote = Thomas Noel
16. Robert Noel = Matilda Brereton
17. James Noel = Elizabeth ——
18. Dorothy Noel = William Swinfen
19. Arthur Swinfen = Alice Ragdale
20. Elizabeth Swinfen = John Dugdale
21. Mary Dugdale, sister of Sir William Dugdale, the antiquarian and genealogist = Richard Sewall, brother of Henry Sewall of Mass.
22. **Henry Sewall**, Secretary of Md., = Jane Lowe of Md., ARD, SETH, who married (2) Charles Calvert, 3rd Baron Baltimore (1637-1715), colonial governor of Md., ARD, SETH.

The Royal Descents of 900 Immigrants

Sources: Research of Brice McAdoo Clagett for *Seven Centuries: Ancestors for Twenty Generations of John Brice de Treville Clagett and Ann Calvert Brooke Clagett* (mss. sent to various scholars during Brice's lifetime) and based in part on *MG* 2: 318-20 (Sewall), John Burke, *A Genealogical and Heraldic History of the Commoners of Great Britain and Ireland*, vol. 1 (1834, rep. 1977), p. 488 and W.H. Hamper, *The Life, Diary and Correspondence of Sir William Dugdale* (1827); *Shaw*, vol. 2, pp. 28*-29* (Swinfen); *Salt*, 1914, pp. 66-67 (Noel), 1925, pp. 113-15 (Draycote; Clagett also cites *Calendar of Fine Rolls* 9: 339 and *Calendar of Patent Rolls, 1452-1461,* pp. 111, 559, 677), *Wiltshire Notes and Queries* 3 (1899-1901): 193-94 (which lists no daughters of Sir John and Margaret Stafford, however; Joan's parentage is based largely, no doubt, on chronology, her father's possession of Sandon, and a visitation of Derbyshire); *RA* 4: 678-79 (Stafford, again listing no daughters for Sir John and Margaret Stafford), 5: 5-11 (Stafford, Basset), 4: 674-76 (Chester), 3: 86-88 (Gloucester), and *AR8*, lines 55, 124-26 (generations 1-11).

The Royal Descents of 900 Immigrants

1. Henry I, King of England, d. 1135 = Matilda of Scotland
2. (illegitimate by ——) Robert of Caen, 1st Earl of Gloucester = Mabel FitzHamon
3. Maud of Gloucester = Ranulph de Gernon, 2nd Earl of Chester
4. Hugh Kevelioc, 3rd Earl of Chester = Bertrade de Montfort
5. Agnes de Meschines = William de Ferrers, 4th Earl of Derby
6. Bertha de Ferrers = Sir Ralph Bigod, son of Hugh Bigod, 3rd Earl of Norfolk, Magna Carta surety, and Maud Marshall, SETH
7. Sir John Bigod = Isabel ——
8. Sir Roger Bigod = Joan ——
9. Sir John Bigod = Amy ——
10. Joan Bigod = Sir Walter Calverley
11. Walter Calverley = Elizabeth Markenfield
12. Joan Calverley = John Wentworth
13. Thomas Wentworth = Jane Mirfield
14. Roger Wentworth = Elizabeth Wentworth, a cousin
15. Thomas Wentworth = Elizabeth Flintell/Flinthill
16. Thomas Wentworth = Ursula Swinnoe
17. William Wentworth = Margery Hales
18. Richard Wentworth = Anne Holgate
19. **Thomas Wentworth** of Va. = (1) Sarah Joiner; (2) Elizabeth Hodgson.

Sources: *PCF Yorkshire* (Wentworth pedigree) and J.W. Clay, ed., *Dugdale's Visitation of Yorkshire*, vol. 3 (1917), pp. 364-65; *RA* 1: 441-42 (Calverley to 13. Thomas Wentworth), 1: 164-66 (Ferrers-Bigod to Calverley), 2: 560-61 (Ferrers), 2: 148-54 (Chester), 3: 86-88 (Gloucester). See also *BRMF1*, pp. 460-61 (Wentworth).

The Royal Descents of 900 Immigrants

1. Henry I, King of England, d. 1135 = Matilda of Scotland
2. (illegitimate by ——) Robert of Caen, 1st Earl of Gloucester = Mabel FitzHamon
3. Maud of Gloucester = Ranulph de Gernon, Earl of Chester
4. Hugh Kevelioc, 3rd Earl of Chester = Bertrade de Montfort
5. (illegitimate by ——) Amicia de Meschines = Ralph de Mainwaring
6. Bertrade de Mainwaring = Henry de Audley
7. Emma de Audley = Gruffudd ap Madog, Prince of Powys Fadog
8. Margred ferch Gruffudd = Sir John Arderne
9. Agnes Arderne = Sir John Whetenhall
10. Margaret Whetenhall = Adam Bostock
11. Adam Bostock = Janet Bradshaw
12. Sir Ralph Bostock = Isabel Lawton
13. Sir Adam Bostock = Elizabeth Venables
14. Nicholas Bostock = Catherine Mobberly
15. Hugh Bostock = Joan Del Heath
16. William (Richard?) Bostock = Margery Higginson
17. Elizabeth Bostock = Richard Branch
18. William Branch = Catherine Jennings
19. Lionel Branch = Valentia Sparkes
20. **Christopher Branch** of Va. = Mary Addie.
21. Christopher Branch, Jr. = ——
22. Mary Branch = Thomas Jefferson
23. Thomas Jefferson, Jr. = Mary Field
24. Peter Jefferson = Jane Randolph

The Royal Descents of 900 Immigrants

25. Thomas Jefferson (1743-1826), 3rd U.S. President = Mrs. Martha Wayles Skelton

25. Mary Jefferson (sister of Thomas) = John Bolling (III), a great-great-great-grandson of Pocahontas and John Rolfe

26. Archibald Bolling = Catherine Payne

27. Archibald Bolling, Jr. = Anne E. Wigginton

28. William Holcombe Bolling = Sallie Spiers White

29. Edith Bolling = (1) Norman Galt; (2) (Thomas) Woodrow Wilson (1856-1924), 28th U.S. President

Sources: *GVFVM* 1:208-32 (Branch), plus a forthcoming Branch-Bostock article by John Anderson Brayton (based in part on the wills of Richard and Elizabeth [Bostock] Branch); W. H. Rylands, ed., *Four Visitations of Berkshire, 1532, 1566, 1623 and 1665-6*, vol. 2 (*HSPVS*, vol. 57, 1908), pp. 76-78 (Bostock); *Ormerod*, vol. 3, p. 259 (Bostock), vol. 2, pp. 195 (Whetenhall), 85, 77 (Arderne, Powys Fadog); *Delafield*, vol. 2, pp. 589-97 (Powys Fadog, Audley and Mainwaring); *AR8*, lines 125, 124. *RA* 4: 282 does not include a daughter Margaret for Gruffudd ap Madog, Prince of Powys Fadog and Emma de Audley.

The Royal Descents of 900 Immigrants

1. Henry I, King of England, d. 1135 = Matilda of Scotland
2. (illegitimate by ——) Robert of Caen, 1st Earl of Gloucester = Mabel FitzHamon
3. Maud of Gloucester = Ranulph de Gernon, 2nd Earl of Chester
4. Hugh Kevelioc, 3rd Earl of Chester = Bertrade de Montfort
5. Mabel of Chester = William d'Aubigny, 3rd Earl of Arundel
6. Nicole d'Aubigny = Roger de Somery
7. Joan de Somery = John le Strange (IV) of Knokyn
8. John le Strange (V), 1st Baron Strange of Knokyn = Maud de Wauton
9. Elizabeth le Strange = Gruffudd o'r Rhuddallt ap Madog Fychan ap Madog Crupl
10. Gruffudd Fychan ap Gruffudd o'r Rhuddallt = Elen ferch Thomas, great-aunt of Owen Tudor, founder of the Tudor dynasty and husband of Katherine of France, widow of Henry V, King of England (Elen was not, according to Bartrum, a descendant of Llywelyn Fawr ab Iorwerth, Prince of North Wales, and Joan Plantagenet)
11. Owen Glendower (Owain ap Gruffudd Fychan), the Welsh rebel hero = Margaret Hanmer
12. Janet ferch Owain = Sir John de Croft
13. William de Croft = Margaret Walwyn
14. Richard Croft the younger = Anne Fox
15. Anne Croft = Sir John Rodney, son of Thomas Rodney (and Isabel ——), son of Sir Walter Rodney and Margaret Hungerford, son of Walter Hungerford, 1st Baron Hungerford, and Catherine Peverell, daughter of Sir Thomas Peverell and Margaret Courtenay, daughter of Sir Thomas Courtenay (and Muriel de Moels), son of Hugh Courtenay, 1st Earl of Devon (and Agnes St. John), son of Sir Hugh Courtenay and Eleanor le Despencer, SETH
16. George Rodney = Elizabeth Kirton

17. Agatha Rodney = Thomas Hodges

18. George Hodges = Eleanor Rosse

19. George Hodges = Anne Mansell

20. Jane Hodges = John Strachey, son of William Strachey (and Elizabeth Cross) son of William Strachey, historian and 1st secretary of the Virginia Colony, ARD, SETH, and Frances Forster

21. John Strachey = Elizabeth Elletson. Their son, Henry Strachey, married Helen Clark and was the father of Sir Henry Strachey, 1st Bt., great-grandfather of the writer (Giles) Lytton Strachey, for whose ancestry and noted near kinsmen see *NEHGS NEXUS* 16 (1999): 30-31.

22. **John Strachey** of Va. = (1) Elizabeth Vernon; (2) Mary ——.

Sources: *AP&P*, 4: 3: 251-55, 257, *Strachey*, pp. 41-62, 296-97 esp. (and footnote 4, pp. 43-44 for Hodges) and Barbara Strachey, *The Strachey Line: An English Family in America, in India, and at Home, 1570 to 1902* (1985), esp. the charts on pp. 20, 36, 42, 80, 122, 142 and front and back endpapers; *WC*, pp. 444-46 (Rodney); O.G.S. Croft, *The House of Croft of Croft Castle* (1949), pp. 28-39, 148-53, and G.D. Squibb, ed., *Wiltshire Visitation Pedigrees, 1623* (*HSPVS*, vol. 105-6, 1954), p. 90 (Hungerford); *RA* 5: 61-63 (le Strange, to Elizabeth and Gruffudd), 4: 674-76 (Somery), 2: 252-54 (d'Aubigny), 2: 148-54 (Chester), 3: 86-88 (Gloucester), *AR8*, lines 251, 124-26.

The Royal Descents of 900 Immigrants

1. Henry I, King of England, d. 1135 = Matilda of Scotland
2. (illegitimate by ——) Robert of Caen, 1st Earl of Gloucester = Mabel FitzHamon
3. Maud of Gloucester = Ranulph de Gernon, 2nd Earl of Chester
4. Hugh Kevelioc, 3rd Earl of Chester = Bertrade de Montfort
5. Mabel of Chester = William d'Aubigny, 3rd Earl of Arundel
6. Nicole d'Aubigny = Roger de Somery
7. Joan de Somery = John le Strange (IV) of Knokyn
8. John le Strange (V), 1st Baron Strange of Knokyn = Eleanor de Montz, a first wife
9. Sir Hamon le Strange = Margaret Vernon
10. Hamon le Strange = Katherine Camoys
11. Sir John le Strange = Eleanor Walkfare
12. John le Strange = Alice Bemain (Beaumont?)
13. Roger le Strange = Jane Bebe (Beke?)
14. Henry le Strange = Katherine Drury, sister of the Sir Robert Drury, Speaker of the House of Commons, who married Anne Calthorpe, SETH
15. John le Strange = Margaret le Strange, not an agnate near cousin
16. Barbara le Strange = Robert Mordaunt
17. Anne Mordaunt = Thomas Crochrode
18. Anne Crochrode = John Alston
19. William Alston = Mary Greene
20. Solomon Alston = Mary ——
21. **John Alston** of N.C. = Mary ——.

Sources: *South Carolina Magazine of Ancestral Research* 34 (2006): 63-68 (David L. Kent, with various citations to Lionel Cresswell, *Stemmata Alstoniana* [1905], plus parish registers, wills and court proceedings, covering generations 16-21); Walter C. Metcalfe, ed., *Visitations of Essex, 1552, 1558, 1570, 1612 and 1634*, vol. 1 (*HSPVS*, vol. 13, 1878), pp. 335 (Alston), 184-85 (Crochrode), 253-54 (Mordaunt); Brig. Gen. Sir Edward Earle Gascoyne Bulwer, ed., *Visitation of Norfolk, 1563*, vol. 1 (1878), pp. 62-64 (Strange), Hamon le Strange, *Le Strange Records* (1916), pp. 154-271, esp. 159, 184 and C. L'Estrange Ewen, *Observations on the le Stranges* (1946), esp. chart opposite p. 1. From the work of Messrs. Kent and Cresswell, the two John Alstons of N.C. and S.C. respectively were third cousins (the John Alston who married Dorothy Temple was a nephew of the John Alston who married Anne Crochrode).

The Royal Descents of 900 Immigrants

1. Donald III Bane, King of Scotland, d. 1099 (uncle of Duncan II, King of Scotland, who d. 1094) = ——
2. Bethoc of Scotland = Uchtred of Tynedale
3. Hextilda of Tynedale = Richard Comyn
4. William Comyn, 1st Earl of Buchan = Sarah FitzHugh (see *CP* 11:143)
5. Jean Comyn = William Ross, 2nd Earl of Ross
6. William Ross, 3rd Earl of Ross = Eupheme ——
7. Hugh Ross, 4th Earl of Ross = Margaret Graham
8. Hugh Ross of Balnagown = Margaret de Barclay
9. William Ross of Balnagown = Christian (Livingston?)
10. Walter Ross of Balnagown = Katherine McTyre
11. Hugh Ross of Balnagown = ——
12. William Ross of Little Allan = Grizel McDonald
13. Walter Ross of Shandwick = Janet Tulloch
14. Hugh Ross of Balmachy = ——
15. Donald Ross of Balmachy = Margaret Innes
16. Walter Ross of Balmachy = Jean Douglas
17. Hugh Ross of Balmachy = Katherine Macleod
18. George Ross of Balmachy = Margaret McCulloch
19. Andrew Ross of Balbair = ——
20. David Ross of Balbair = Margaret Stronach
21. **Rev. George Ross** of Del. = (1) Joanna Williams; (2) Catherine Van Gezel (father by 2 of George Ross, Jr., 1730-1779, signer of the Declaration of Independence, Pennsylvania patriot and jurist, and of Gertrude Ross, wife of Isaac Till and George Read, 1733-1798, also a signer of the Declaration of Independence, Federalist statesman and U.S. senator).

The Royal Descents of 900 Immigrants

Sources: Harmon Pumpelly Read, *Rossiana: Ross, Read and Related Families* (1908), pp. 2-6, 8-10, 31, 40-45 (a revision of Francis Neville Reid, *The Earls of Ross and Their Descendants* [1894], pp. 2-5, 8-9, 26-27, 35-36); *CP* and *SP* (Ross), *SP* 1:504-5 (Comyn); *AR8*, line 121A.

The Royal Descents of 900 Immigrants

1. William I, the Conqueror, King of England, d. 1087 = Matilda of Flanders
2. Adela of England = Stephen II, Count of Blois
3. William of Champagne, Seigneur de Sully (elder brother of Stephen, King of England) = Agnes de Sully
4. Margaret of Champagne = Henry, Count of Eu
5. John, Count of Eu = Alice d'Aubigny, daughter of William d'Aubigny, 1st Earl of Arundel, and Adeliza of Louvain, widow of Henry I, King of England
6. Ida of Eu = William Hastings
7. Thomas Hastings = ——
8. Hugh Hastings = Helen Alveston
9. Thomas Hastings = Amicia ——
10. Sir Nicholas Hastings = Emeline Heron
11. Sir Hugh Hastings = Beatrix ——
12. Sir Nicholas Hastings = Agnes ——
13. Sir Ralph Hastings = Margaret Herle
14. Sir Ralph Hastings = Isabel Sadington
15. Margaret Hastings = Sir Roger Heron
16. Isabel Heron = Thomas Hesilrig
17. Thomas Hesilrig = Elizabeth Brocket
18. William Hesilrig = Elizabeth Staunton
19. Thomas Hesilrig = Lucy Entwisle
20. Anne Hesilrig = Edward Catesby
21. Michael Catesby = Anne Odim
22. Kenelm Catesby = Alice Rudkin
23. Mark Catesby = (poss.) Lucretia ——
24. John Catesby = Elizabeth Jekyll

25. **Mark Catesby** (c. 1679-1749), naturalist, traveler to and writer on the South (Va., S.C., Ga., and Fla.) = (1) ——; (2) Mrs. Elizabeth —— Rowland.

25. **Elizabeth Catesby** of Va. = (1) William **Cocke**, Secretary of Va.; (2) John Holloway, treasurer of Va., Speaker of the House of Burgesses.

Sources: *Oxford DNB*, *DAB* (Mark Catesby), Sir A.R. Wagner, *English Genealogy*, 3rd ed. (1983), p. 226, and L.H. Jones, *Captain Roger Jones of London and Virginia* (1891), pp. 117-23 (Catesby and Cocke); G.A. Armytage, ed., *Visitation of Rutland, 1618-19* (*HSPVS*, vol. 3, 1870), p. 33 (Catesby); John Fetherston, ed., *Visitations of Leicestershire, 1619* (*HSPVS*, vol. 2, 1870), p. 15 (Hesilrig); George F. Farnham, *Leicestershire Medieval Pedigrees* (1925), chart opp. p. 57 (Hesilrig, Heron, Hastings); *Collins*, vol. 6, pp. 643-48 (Hastings); *MGH*, 4th ser., 3 (1908-9): 18-19 (Counts of Eu), *RA* 2: 519-20 (Eu), 1: 389-91 (Blois) and *AR8*, lines 139, 169. A new monograph on this Hastings line would be welcome.

The Royal Descents of 900 Immigrants

1. Bela I, King of Hungary, d. 1063 = Richeza of Poland
2. Sophie of Hungary = Magnus, Duke of Saxony
3. Wulfhilde of Saxony = Henry IX, Duke of Bavaria
4. Wulfhilde of Bavaria = Rudolf, Count of Bregenz
5. Elizabeth of Bregenz = Hugh II, Count Palatine of Tübingen
6. Hugh I, Count of Bregenz, Count of Montfort = Mechtild (Matilda) von Wangen
7. Elizabeth of Montfort = Manegold I, Count of Nellenburg
8. Eberhard III, Count of Nellenburg = ——
9. Manegold II, Count of Nellenburg = Agnes von Eschenburg
10. Margareta of Nellenburg = Manegold von Brandis
11. Thüring II von Brandis = Katharina von Weissenburg
12. Ursula von Brandis = Rudolf II von Arburg
13. Rudolf III von Arburg = Anfelisa von Grünenburg
14. Anfelisa von Arburg = Henman (Hans) II von Rüssegg (ancestors Q42387-88 of Prince Charles, Prince of Wales—see *Paget*, p. 373)
15. Jakob von Rüssegg, Baron zu Roggenbach = Barbara, Baroness von Wineck
16. Apollonia von Rüssegg = Rudolf Herport
17. Peter Herport = Anna Keller von Schleitheim
18. Ursula Herport = Lucas von Treuffen genannt Loewensprung
19. Marie von Treuffen genannt Loewensprung = Anton von Graffenried
20. Abraham von Graffenried = Ursula von Diesbach
21. Christoph von Graffenried = Anna von Muhlinen (Mülinen)
22. Anton von Graffenried = Catherine Jenna (Jenner)
23. **Christoph(er), Baron von Graffenried** (1661-1743), Landgrave of North Carolina, founder of New Bern = Regina

von Tscharner. Outlined below, even though her husband's descent from 11 *RD* immigrants is outlined elsewhere herein, is the de Graffenried descent of First Lady Laura Lane (Welch) Bush.

24. **Christopher de Graffenried** of Va. = Barbara Needham.

25. Tscharner de Graffenried = Mary Baker

26. Baker de Graffenried = Sarah Vass

27. Mary Baker de Graffenried = Gideon Johnson, Jr.

28. Jane (Jincey) Johnson = David Chadwell

29. Mary Chadwell = James T. Aldridge

30. Nancy Jane Aldridge = William Franklin Welch

31. Mark Anthony Welch = Marie Lula (or Lula Marie) Lane

32. Harold Bruce Welch = Jenna Louise Hawkins

33. Laura Lane Welch = George Walker Bush (b. 1946), 43rd U.S. President, SETH

Sources: A 24-generation AT of Christopher de Graffenried of Va., prepared by Robert Battle of Tacoma, Washington, and the late William Addams Reitwiesner of Washingon, D.C., placed on one of the latter's websites (http://homepages.rootsweb.com/~addams/presidential/graffenried. html - for an ancestor table of Laura Bush simply substitute *welch* for *graffenried*). Cited sources, at NEHGS and/or the Library of Congress, include Thomas P. de Graffenried, *History of the de Graffenried Family from 1191 A.D. to 1925* (1925), pp. 27-28, 56-73, 141-47 (and 149-55, plus Katherine Reynolds, *Descendants of Baker and Sarah Vass de Graffenried – Virginia and North Carolina,* vol. 1 [1962], esp. pp. 76, 234) (for generations 23-28); le Vicomte de Ghellinck Vaernewyck, *La Généalogie de la Maison de Diesbach* (1921), esp. pp. 265, 267 (generations 17-20); Eduard Rubel, *Ahnentafel Rübel-Blass, Tafelband* (1939), pp. 134, 219, 216, 295-96, 262 (generations 1-17), 264 (Richeza of Poland to Otto II, Holy Roman Emperor, d. 983). Generations 1-16 are also covered in *ES,* 1: 1: 11, 18 and 2: 2: 154, 12: 25, 47, 50, 86, 120, 107, 123. For generations 29-30 see F.R. Aldridge and Rosalie C. Batson, *Aldridge Records,* vol. 2 (1975), p. 76. Generations 30-33 were documented, largely by Mr. Battle, from census records, etc. of Fannin and Tarrant Cos., Texas, and

Pontotoc Co., Oklahoma, plus Texas VRs at the Dept. of Vital Statistics, Austin, and the Texas birth and death indexes. Mark Lane Welch, an uncle of Mrs. Bush, appears in *Who's Who in the South and Southwest,* 16th ed. (1978-79), p. 777.

The Royal Descents of 900 Immigrants

1. Henry I, King of France, d. 1060 = Anne of Kiev
2. Hugh Magnus, Duke of France and Burgundy = Adelaide of Vermandois
3. Isabel of Vermandois = Robert de Beaumont, 1st Earl of Leicester
4. Maud de Beaumont = William de Lovel
5. William de Lovel = Isabel ——
6. John de Lovel = Katherine Basset
7. John de Lovel = Maud Sydenham
8. Maud de Lovel = Sir Ralph de Gorges
9. Sir Ralph de Gorges = Eleanor (Ferre?)
10. Eleanor de Gorges = Sir Theobald Russell
11. Sir Theobald Gorges alias Russell = Agnes Wyke
12. Thomas Gorges = Agnes Beauchamp
13. Sir Theobald Gorges = Jane Hankford
14. Elizabeth Gorges = Thomas Grenville
15. Sir Thomas Grenville = Isabella Gilbert
16. Sir Roger Grenville = Margaret Whitleigh
17. Jane Grenville = Edmund Specott
18. Jane Specott = William Snelling
19. Thomas Snelling = Joan Elford
20. **William Snelling** of Mass. = Margery (or Margaret) Stagg.

16. Jane Grenville (sister of Sir Roger) = Sir John Chamond
17. Richard Chamond = Margaret Trevener
18. Gertrude Chamond = Walter Porter
19. Mary Porter = Richard Penhallow

20. Chamond Penhallow = Anne Tamlyn

21. **Samuel Penhallow** (1665-1726) of N.H., merchant, jurist, historian and public official = (1) Mary Cutts; (2) Mrs. Abigail Atkinson Winslow Osborn.

16. Philippa Grenville (sister of Sir Roger and Jane) = Francis Harris

17. William Harris = Catherine Esse

18. Jane Harris = John Harris, a cousin

19. Frances Harris = Thomas Kestell

20. Frances Kestell = Nicholas Morton

21. **Charles Morton** (c. 1627-1698) of Mass., Puritan clergyman and schoolmaster = Joan ———.

Sources: *NEHGR* 52 (1898): 342-46, reprinted in *EO2*: 3: 274-78 (Snelling), *VD*, pp. 694 (Snelling), 706 (Specott); *MCS5*, line 23 and sources cited therein, esp. *VC*, pp. 360-61 (Penhallow), 383 (Porter), 84 (Chamond), 190-91 (Grenville) (for virtual disproof of the Courtenay line, and lack of proof for the Bonville alternative [*MCS5*, lines 22, 90A, 90, 144, 142] see Charles Fitch-Northen, "A Revision of the Grenville Pedigree" in *Devon and Cornwall Notes and Queries* 34 [1978-81]: 154-61); *Gorges*, pp. 13-40 and chart at end, *RA* 3: 624-26 (Lovel), 5: 268-74 (Beaumont, Vermandois) (generations 1-7), *AR8*, lines 215, 50, 53; *DAB* (Penhallow and Morton) and *VC*, pp. 264 (Kestell), 206, 209 (Harris). Note: John Drake of Windsor, Conn. (see *MCS5*, line 22, and *AR8*, line 234) has now been proved not to be the son of William Drake and Philippa Dennis; Douglas Richardson of Salt Lake City plans an article on this immigrant's immediate pre-American history.

The Royal Descents of 900 Immigrants

1. Henry I, King of France, d. 1060 = Anne of Kiev
2. Hugh Magnus, Duke of France and Burgundy = Adelaide of Vermandois
3. Isabel of Vermandois = Robert de Beaumont, 1st Earl of Leicester
4. Isabel de Beaumont = Gilbert de Clare, 1st Earl of Pembroke
5. Richard de Clare ("Strongbow"), 2nd Earl of Pembroke = Eve of Leinster, daughter of Dermot MacMurrough (Diarmait MacMurchada), King of Leinster, d. 1171, and Mor Ua Tuathail
6. Isabel de Clare = William Marshall, 1st Earl of Pembroke
7. Eve Marshall = Sir William de Braose
8. Eve de Braose = Sir William de Cantilupe
9. Milicent de Cantilupe = Eudo la Zouche
10. Elizabeth la Zouche = Sir Nicholas Poyntz
11. Nicholas Poyntz = ——
12. Pontius Poyntz = Eleanor Baldwin
13. Sir John Poyntz = ——
14. John Poyntz = Matilda Perth
15. William Poyntz = Elizabeth Shaw
16. Thomas Poyntz = Anne Calva
17. Susanna Poyntz = Sir Richard Saltonstall, uncle of the Sir Richard Saltonstall who married Grace Kaye, SETH
18. Elizabeth Saltonstall = Richard Wyche
19. Henry Wyche = Ellen Quinnell
20. **Henry Wyche** of Va. = ——.

18. Judith Saltonstall (sister of Elizabeth) = Edward Rich
19. Edward Rich = Susan Percy
20. Sir Peter Rich = Anne Evans

21. Edward Rich = ——
22. **Anne Rich** of Va. = Francis **Willis**.

16. Margaret Poyntz (sister of Thomas) = John Barley
17. John Barley = Philippa Bradbury, aunt of the William Bradbury who married Anne Eden, SETH
18. Margaret Barley = Edward Bell
19. **Anne Bell** = Sir Ferdinando **Gorges** (c. 1565-1647), founder and lord proprietor of Maine, ARD, SETH.

Sources: *RA* 5: 413-15 (Wyche, Saltonstall, Poyntz), 4: 288-89 (Poyntz), 2: 82-86 (la Zouche, Cantilupe/Cantelowe), 1: 557 (Braose/Brewes), 4: 40-47 (Marshall), 4: 336-40 (de Clare), 5: 268-74 (Beaumont, Vermandois), *MCS5*, lines 60-60A, *AR8*, lines 253, 66, 50, 53, 175 and sources cited therein, esp. *GVFWM* 5:596-600 (Wyche), *Saltonstall*, pp. 6-7, 12, Sir John MacLean, *Historical and Genealogical Memoir of the Family of Poyntz* (1886, rep. 1983), pp. 18-21, 29-38, 47-48, this last a chart that differs somewhat from *MCS5*; *TAG* 21 (1944-45): 237-38 (Mrs. Willis), 52 (1976): 176-77, 247 (Lady A.B. Gorges). See also Scott C. Steward, *The Descendants of Dr. Nathaniel Saltonstall of Haverhill, Massachusetts* (2013), pp. 6-12 and John Brooks Threlfall, *The Ancestry of Thomas Bradbury (1611-1695) and His Wife Mary (Perkins) Bradbury (1615-1700) of Salisbury, Massachusetts*, 3rd ed. (2006), pp. 9-10, 17-20, 37-40.

The Royal Descents of 900 Immigrants

1. Henry I, King of France, d. 1060 = Anne of Kiev
2. Hugh Magnus, Duke of France and Burgundy = Adelaide of Vermandois
3. Isabel of Vermandois = Robert de Beaumont, 1st Earl of Leicester
4. Isabel de Beaumont = Gilbert de Clare, 1st Earl of Pembroke
5. Richard de Clare ("Strongbow"), 2nd Earl of Pembroke = Eve of Leinster, daughter of Dermot MacMurrough (Diarmait MacMurchada), King of Leinster, d. 1171, and Mor Ua Tuathail
6. Isabel de Clare = William Marshall, 1st Earl of Pembroke
7. Eve Marshall = Sir William de Braose
8. Eve de Braose = Sir William de Cantilupe
9. Milicent de Cantilupe = Sir Eudo la Zouche
10. Elizabeth la Zouche = Sir Nicholas Poyntz
11. Nicholas Poyntz = ——
12. Edward Poyntz = ——
13. Maud Poyntz = Thomas Barrett
14. Robert Barrett = Margery Knolles
15. John Barrett = Philippa Harpersfield
16. Cecily Barrett = William Colepepper (Culpeper), SETH
17. John Colepepper (Culpeper) = Elizabeth Sidley
18. John Colepepper (Culpeper) = Ursula Woodcock. Their son John Colepepper (Culpeper) was probably the immigrant to Northumberland Co., Va., who married Mary —— but left no NDTPS.
19. **Thomas Colepepper** (Culpeper) of Va. = Katherine St. Leger of Va., ARD, SETH. Their daughter, Frances Colepepper (Culpepper), Virginia political figure, married (1) Samuel Stephens, colonial governor of Ga.; (2) Sir William Berkeley (1608-1677), colonial governor of Va., ARD, SETH; and (3) Philip Ludwell (d. 1717), planter, Virginia councilor, colonial governor of N.C. and S.C., ARD, SETH. A son, John

Colepepper (Culpeper) of N.C., participated in the 1677 Culpeper Rebellion (named after him) against Act. Gov. Thomas Miller (of Albemarle).

18. Thomas Colepepper (Culpeper) (brother of John II) = Anne Slaney

19. John Colepepper (Culpeper), 1st Baron Colepepper (Culpeper) = Judith Colepepper (Culpeper), his second cousin, see below

20. **Thomas Colepepper** (Culpeper), **2nd Baron Colepepper** (Culpeper) (1635-1689), colonial governor of Va., returned to England = Margaret van Hesse (parents of Catherine Colepepper [Culpeper], wife of Thomas Fairfax, 5th Baron Fairfax, ARD, SETH, and mother of Thomas Fairfax, 6th Baron Fairfax, of Va., proprietor of the Northern Neck of Virginia, ARD, SETH).

17. Francis Colepepper (Culpeper) (brother of John I) = Joan Pordage

18. Sir Thomas Colepepper (Culpeper) = Elizabeth Cheney

19. Judith Colepepper (Culpeper) = John Colepepper (Culpeper), 1st Baron Colepepper (Culpeper), her second cousin, see above.

Sources: *RA* 2: 368-72 (Colepepper/Culpeper), 5: 413 (Poyntz), 4: 288-89 (Poyntz), 2: 82-86 (la Zouche, Cantilupe/Cantelowe), 1: 557 (Braose, Brewes), 4: 40-47 (Marshall), 4: 336-40 (de Clare), 5: 268-74 (Beaumont, Vermandois) and *MCS5*, line 16D, *GVFVM2*: 400, 408-87, 493-509, 520-48, and *Sussex Archaeological Collections* 47 (1904): 57-74 (and charts opp. pp. 56 and 72 esp.) (Colepepper/Culpeper); Walter C. Metcalfe, ed., *Visitations of Essex, 1552, 1558, 1570, 1612, 1634* (*HSPVS*, vol. 13, 1878), pp. 145-46, 268 (Barrett, Poyntz) and *MGH*, 5th series, 6 (1926-28): 81-87, esp. 83-84 (Margery Knolles).

The Royal Descents of 900 Immigrants

1. Henry I, King of France, d. 1060 = Anne of Kiev
2. Hugh Magnus, Duke of France and Burgundy = Adelaide of Vermandois
3. Isabel of Vermandois = (2) William de Warren, 2nd Earl of Surrey
4. William de Warren, 3rd Earl of Surrey = Ela of Ponthieu, mother by her second husband, Patrick, Earl of Salisbury, of Ela, Countess of Salisbury, wife of William Longespee, Earl of Salisbury, SETH
5. Isabel de Warren = Hamelin Plantagenet, Earl of Surrey, illegitimate son of Geoffrey Plantagenet, Count of Anjou, and half-brother of Henry II, King of England
6. Ela de Warren = William FitzWilliam
7. Ellen FitzWilliam = Sir John de Lungviliers
8. Sir John de Lungviliers = ——
9. Margaret de Lungviliers = Sir Geoffrey de Neville
10. Robert de Neville = Isabel de Byron
11. Sir Robert de Neville = Joan de Atherton
12. Sir Robert de Neville = Margaret de la Pole
13. Margaret de Neville = Sir William Harington
14. Margaret Harington = Richard Braddyll
15. John Braddyll = Emote Pollard
16. Edward Braddyll = Jennett Crombock
17. John Braddyll = Jennett Foster
18. Edward Braddyll = Anne Ashton
19. Dorothy Braddyll = John Talbot
20. John Talbot = Mabel Carleton
21. George Talbot = Anne Ryley
22. **George Talbot**, Jr., known as **Peter Talbot**, of Mass. = (1) Mrs. Mary Gold Wodell; (2) Mrs. Hannah Clarke Frizzell.

The Royal Descents of 900 Immigrants

Sources: Joseph Gardner Bartlett, *The English Ancestry of Peter Talbot of Dorchester, Massachusetts* (1917), pp. 35-85 esp. (Talbot, Braddyll); James Croston, *County Families of Lancashire and Cheshire* (1887), pp. 253-55 esp. (Harrington of Farleton); F.L. Weis, *500 Ancestors of John Prescott of Lancaster and of James Prescott of Hampton* (1960, a work that does not, however, prove the parentage of the immigrants it treats), charts covering the ancestry of Sir William Harington of Farleton and Hornby and Margaret de Neville (#s28 and 30 esp.); *RA* 3: 315-21 (Harington, Neville, Lungviliers, but does not list a daughter Margaret for Sir William Harington and Margaret de Neville), 2: 671-72 (FitzWilliam), 5: 304-8 (Warren), 5: 268-74 (Vermandois) and *AR8*, line 247 and *TG* 4 (1983): 184, note 25. Bartlett's research should probably be reviewed (his patrilineal descent for Thomas Newberry of Mass. has been disproved).

The Royal Descents of 900 Immigrants

1. Henry I, King of France, d. 1060 = Anne of Kiev
2. Hugh Magnus, Duke of France and Burgundy = Adelaide of Vermandois
3. Isabel of Vermandois = Robert de Beaumont, 1st Earl of Leicester
4. Robert de Beaumont, 2nd Earl of Leicester = Amicia de Gael
5. Robert de Beaumont, 3rd Earl of Leicester = Petronilla de Grandmesnil
6. Margaret de Beaumont = Saire de Quincy, 1st Earl of Winchester, Magna Carta surety
7. Roger de Quincy, 2nd Earl of Winchester = Helen of Galloway, a descendant of Ethelred II "the Unready," King of England, d. 1016; see *AR8*, lines 38, 34
8. Elizabeth de Quincy = Alexander Comyn, 2nd Earl of Buchan
9. Elizabeth Comyn = Gilbert de Umfreville, 1st Earl of Angus
10. Robert de Umfreville, 2nd Earl of Angus = Eleanor (de Montfichet?)
11. Thomas de Umfreville = Joan de Roddam
12. Sir Robert de Umfreville = Isabel ——
13. (said to be) (illegitimate by ——) William Umfreville = ——
14. William Umfreville = ——
15. Andrew Umfreville = ——
16. Roger Umfreville = —— Luddington
17. Gervase/Jarvis Umfreville = Katherine Digby
18. John Umfreville = ——
19. **John Umfreville/Humphreville** of Conn. = ——.

Sources: *TAG* 72 (1997): 15-19; *Surtees*, vol. 2, pp. 325, 395, citing an Umfreville pedigree compiled about 1710 by Simon Segar, plus one in "Philpot's Collections in the College of Arms"; *TG* 26 (1910): 193-97, 202-3, 208-10 and *NF* 1:211-15 (de Umphreville); *RA* 4: 13-17 (Umfreville,

The Royal Descents of 900 Immigrants

to generation 12), 2: 3-6 (Comyn), 4: 437-49 (Quincy), 3: 558-62 (Beaumont of Leicester), 5: 268-74 (Vermandois) and *AR8*, lines 224, 53. The Segar and Philpot pedigrees, perhaps as reported by Surtees, were probably the major source for the Umfreville article in John Burke, *A Genealogical and Heraldic History of the Commoners of Great Britain and Ireland,* 4 vols. (1834-38, rep. 1977), 2:191-95, but a thorough monograph on the progeny, in Farnham Royal, Bucks, and Ewell, Surrey of Sir Robert de Umfreville, Knight of the Garter, d. 1436, #12 above, is much needed.

The Royal Descents of 900 Immigrants

1. Henry I, King of France, d. 1060 = Anne of Kiev
2. Hugh Magnus, Duke of France and Burgundy = Adelaide of Vermandois
3. Isabel of Vermandois = Robert de Beaumont, 1st Earl of Leicester
4. Robert de Beaumont, 2nd Earl of Leicester = Amicia de Gael
5. Margaret Beaumont = Sir Ralph de Toeni
6. Ida de Toeni, mistress of Henry II, King of England, and mother of William Longespee, Earl of Salisbury = Roger Bigod, 2nd Earl of Norfolk, Magna Carta surety, son of Roger Bigod, 1st Earl of Norfolk and Juliana de Vere, daughter of Aubrey de Vere and Alice de Clare, daughter of Gilbert de Clare and Adeliza of Clermont, SETH
7. Hugh Bigod, 3rd Earl of Norfolk, Magna Carta surety = Maud Marshall, daughter of William Marshall, 1st Earl of Pembroke, and Isabel de Clare, SETH
8. Sir Hugh Bigod = Joan de Stuteville
9. Roger Bigod, 5th Earl of Norfolk = Aveline Bassett
10. (almost certainly illegitimate, but just possibly a daughter of Roger Bigod, 4th Earl of Norfolk [= Isabel of Scotland], elder brother of Sir Hugh Bigod at generation 8) Christian Bigod = Sir John Jermy
11. Sir William Jermy = Ellen Lampett
12. Sir John Jermy = Joan Halys
13. Sir Thomas Jermy = Isabel St. Aubin
14. Sir William Jermy = Elizabeth Hunhall
15. John Jermy = Margaret Multney
16. Sir John Jermy = Elizabeth Wroth, sister of the John Wroth who married Elizabeth Lewknor, SETH
17. Elizabeth Jermy = Henry Repps
18. Henry Repps = Elizabeth Grimstone

19. Anne Repps = Sir William Woodhouse

20. Henry Woodhouse = Anne Bacon, daughter of Sir Nicholas Bacon, Lord Keeper, by Jane Ferneley, and half-sister of Francis Bacon, 1st Viscount St. Albans, the Lord Keeper, Lord Chancellor, philosopher and scientist

21. Henry Woodhouse, governor of Bermuda = Mrs. Judith (Manby?) Haen

22. **Henry Woodhouse** of Va. = (1) Mary (Sothren?); (2) Mary ——.

Sources: *LDBR* 1, pp. 92-93 and *AP&P* 4: 3: 678-80; G.H. Dashwood, ed., *Visitation of Norfolk 1563*, vol. 1 (1878), pp. 195-96 (Repps), 107 (Jermy); Walter Rye, ed., *Visitations of Norfolk, 1563, 1589 and 1613* (*HSPVS*, vol. 32, 1891), pp. 321 (Woodhouse), 230-31 (Repps), 172-73 (Jermy); *RA* 1: 362-69 (where, however, no illegitimate children are listed for the 3rd, 4th, or 5th Bigod earls of Norfolk, therein considered the 5th, 6th, and 7th Earls), 5: 171-72 (Toeni), 3: 558-59 (Beaumont), 5: 268-74 (Vermandois), *MCS5*, lines 153-5 and *AR8*, lines 246, 151, 106. See also *Parliament, 1509-1558*, vol. 3, pp. 653-65, and *Parliament, 1558-1603*, vol. 3, pp. 646-47 (Sir William and Henry Woodhouse, father and son). A Jermy monograph, definitely identifying Christian Bigod and Isabel St. Aubyn, is much needed. The above probable identification of Christian Bigod is based largely on chronology and acceptance of the Jermy pedigree as given by Dashwood.

The Royal Descents of 900 Immigrants

1. Henry I, King of France, d. 1060 = Anne of Kiev
2. Hugh Magnus, Duke of France and Burgundy = Adelaide of Vermandois
3. Isabel of Vermandois = Robert de Beaumont, 1st Earl of Leicester
4. Isabel de Beaumont = Gilbert de Clare, 1st Earl of Pembroke
5. Richard de Clare ("Strongbow"), 2nd Earl of Pembroke = Eve of Leinster, daughter of Dermot MacMurrough (Diarmait MacMurchada), King of Leinster, d. 1171, and Mor Ua Tuathail
6. Isabel de Clare = William Marshall, 1st Earl of Pembroke
7. Eve Marshall = Sir William de Braose
8. Eve de Braose = Sir William de Cantilupe
9. Milicent de Cantilupe = Sir Eudo la Zouche
10. Roger la Zouche = ——
11. —— la Zouche = Sir Anketil Malory
12. Sir Anketil Malory = Alice de Driby, daughter of John de Driby and Amy de Gaveston, daughter of Piers de Gaveston, 1st Earl of Cornwall, but probably not by Margaret de Clare, SETH, who married secondly Hugh de Audley, 1st Earl of Gloucester
13. Sir William Malory = Margaret ——
14. (Sir) Thomas Malory, whose knighthood is disputed, claimed by some to be the author of *Le Morte d'Arthur* = Elizabeth Kinsman
15. Anthony Malory = Alice Farington
16. William Mallory = Joan Chamber
17. William Mallory = Elizabeth Gregory
18. Horatio Mallory of Bermuda = Dorothy Forster
19. **Elizabeth Mallory** of S.C. = William **Rivers.**

Sources: Research of Brice McAdoo Clagett for *Seven Centuries: Ancestors for Twenty Generations of John Brice de Treville Clagett and*

Ann Calvert Brooke Clagett, mss. sent to various scholars in Brice's lifetime, which cites, among other Mallory sources, Julia E. Mercer, *Bermuda Settlers of the 17th Century* (1982), pp. 59, 123, 134, 163, the 1611 will of William Mallory of Southwark, Surrey (#17 above) naming son Horatio, correspondence with Sheila V. Mallory Smith, author of *A History of the Mallory Family* (1985) (see charts on pp. 139, 147-49, esp.), *TAG* 35 (1959): 101-4, plus *Wilson*, pp. 33-34 (Rivers), *NGSQ* 88 (2000): 32-49 (Amy de Gaveston), and Rivers, Mallory, Zouche and Driby notes in the bibliography to Mr. Clagett's work; *GM* 13 (1959-61): 172 (also cited by Mr. Clagett), *Nichols*, vol. 4, p. 38, and John Bridges and Rev. Peter Whalley, *The History and Antiquities of Northamptonshire*, vol. 2 (1791), p. 254 (la Zouche); *RA* 2: 82-86 (la Zouche [but not including Roger or his daughter ——, wife of Sir Anketil Malory], Cantilupe/Cantelowe), 1: 557 (Braose/Brewes), 4: 40-47 (Marshall), 4: 336-40 (de Clare), 5: 268-74 (Beaumont, Vermandois) and *AR8*, lines 66, 53. Mr. Clagett was dubious of the Driby-Tattershall-d'Aubigny descent suggested in *TAG* 37 (1961): 47-51, 40 (1964): 95-99.

The Royal Descents of 900 Immigrants

1. Mieszko II Lambert, King of Poland, d. 1034 = Richeza of Lorraine, daughter of Ezzo, Count Palatine of Lorraine and Matilda of Saxony, daughter of Otto II, Holy Roman Emperor, d. 983, and Theophano Skleros
2. Gertrude of Poland = Isjaslaw, Grand Prince of Kiev
3. Jaropolk, Prince of Vladimir and Turow = Kunigunde of Orlamünde
4. Anastasia of Turow = Gleb, Prince of Minsk
5. Vsevolod, Prince of Strezew = ──
6. Wlazko, Prince of Kukenois = ──
7. Sophia of Kukenois = Theodoricus von Kokenhusen
8. Sophia von Kokenhusen = Johannes de Tisenhusen
9. Johannes de Tisenhusen = ──
10. Bartholomeus von Tisenhusen = Elsebe Warendorp
11. Peter von Tisenhusen = Katherine ──
12. Fromhold von Tisenhusen = ──
13. Fromhold von Tisenhusen = Gertrude von Rosen
14. Fabian von Tisenhusen = Madlena von Kruse
15. Madlena (Magdalena) von Tisenhusen = Johann von Uexküll
16. Johann von Uexküll = Anna von Rosen
17. Jürgen (Georg) von Uexküll = Magdalene von Bremen
18. Hans Jürgen (Georg) von Uexküll = Maria von Plater
19. Jürgen (Georg) Detlov von Uexküll = Anna Maria von Uexküll, a cousin
20. Berend Johann von Uexküll = Renata Helene von Budberg
21. Anna Elisabeth von Uexküll = Karl Friedrich Hoyningen-Huene
22. Berend Johann von Hoyningen-Huene = Anna von Stackelberg
23. Eduard Friedrich Eberhard von Hoyningen-Huene = Emilie Versmann

24. (Friedrich Alexander) Emil, Baron Hoyningen-Huene = Marie von Weymarn

25. Emil Bernhard, Baron Hoyningen-Huene = Lilli, Baroness von Engelhardt

26. Eduard Rudolf Max, Baron von Hoyningen-Huene = Marion Hagen

27. **Armin Hagen, Baron Hoyningen-Huene** of Calif., known as **Peter Berlin** (b. 1942), leading gay icon of the 1970s (*Nights in Black Leather, That Boy*), photographer and model, unm.

Sources: *ES* 2: 2: 120 (Poland), 128 (Rurikids), 130 (Wladimir and Turow), 127 (Polock/Polozk) (together generations 1-7); *GH des A*, vol. 27, *Freiherrliche Häuser A*, vol. 4 (1962), pp. 383-84, 459, 465-67 (Tiesenhausen); *Gothaisches Genealogisches Taschenbuch der Freiherrlichen Häuser 1942*, p. 537 (Uexküll), *GH des A*, vol. 16, *Freiherrlicher Häuser B*, vol. 2 (1957), pp. 176-77, 179, 183, 185-87 (Hoyningen-Huene, generations 20-27), vol. 150, *Freiherrliche Häuser*, vol. 25 (2011), pp. 162, 169 (generations 25-27). This line was developed and brought to my attention by Anthony Glenn Hoskins of Santa Rosa, California (who compiled a 30-generation ancestor table for Peter Berlin), aided by the Hoyningen-Huene family.

The Royal Descents of 900 Immigrants

1. Robert II, King of France, d. 1031 = Constance of Provence
2. Adela of France = Baldwin V, Count of Flanders
3. Baldwin VI, Count of Flanders (and I, Count of Hainault, brother of Matilda of Flanders, wife of William I the Conqueror, King of England, d. 1087) = Richilde ——
4. Baldwin II, Count of Hainault = Ida of Louvain
5. Baldwin III, Count of Hainault = Yolande of Guelders
6. Ida of Hainault = Roger III de Toeni
7. Godeheut de Toeni = William de Mohun
8. Yolande de Mohun = Ralph FitzWilliam
9. —— (daughter) = ——
10. Isabel —— (granddaughter and co-heiress of Ralph FitzWilliam) = Nicholas Martin
11. Avice Martin = Sir Nicholas Carew
12. Nicholas Carew = Lucy Willoughby
13. Sir Nicholas Carew = Isabel, daughter of Alice de la Mare
14. Elizabeth Carew = Sir Roger Lewknor, son of Sir Thomas Lewknor (and Joan D'Oyly), son of Sir Roger Lewknor (and Katherine Bardolf), son of Sir Thomas Lewknor (and Sybil ——), son of Sir Roger Lewknor and Joan de Keynes, daughter of Richard de Keynes (and Alice de Mankesy), son of Richard de Keynes and Sarah de Huntingfield, daughter of Sir William de Huntingfield, Magna Carta surety (and Isabel FitzWilliam), son of Roger de Huntingfield and Alice de Senlis (St. Liz), daughter of Saire de Quincy and Matilda de St. Liz, SETH, who married firstly Robert de Clare
15. Sir Thomas Lewknor = (1) Philippa Dalyngridge; (2) Elizabeth Echyngham
16. (by 1) Jane (or Joan) Lewknor = Thomas Goodere
17. John Goodere = Alice Brent
18. John Goodere = Alice Frowick
19. Henry Goodere = Jane Greene

20. Anne Goodere = Henry Cooke
21. Edmund Cooke = Elizabeth Nichols
22. Theodora Cooke = Sir Thomas Josselyn
23. **John Josselyn** (c. 1608-post 1675), traveler (to New England), author and naturalist, d. unm. His brother Henry Josselyn (= Mrs. Margaret —— Cammock) was dep. gov. of Maine but is not known to have left any children.

21. Mary Cooke (sister of Edmund) = William Strachey
22. **William Strachey** (c. 1572-post 1618), first secretary of the Virginia Colony = Frances Forster.
23. William Strachey = Eleanor Read
24. **William Strachey** of Va. = (1) Mary Miller; (2) Martha ——. John Strachey, his half-brother (son of Elizabeth Cross) married Jane Hodges, ARD, SETH, and was the paternal grandfather of John Strachey of Va., ARD, SETH.

Sources: *AR8*, lines 211 (generations 42-43 only), 187, 148, 163, 128 and *NEHGR* 71 (1917): 248-50, repr. in *EO* 1: 1: 488-90 (Josselyn); Robert Hovenden, ed., *Visitation of Kent, 1619-21* (*HSPVS*, vol. 42, 1898), pp. 117-18 (Cooke); Sir G.J. Armytage, Bt., ed., *Middlesex Pedigrees as Collected by Richard Mundy* (*HSPVS*, vol. 65, 1914), pp. 23-24 (Goodere); *Lewes*, pp. 148-50, 158-59 (Lewknor); *Berry's Surrey*, pp. 3-4, *Parliament, 1386-1421*, vol. 1, pp. 482-85 (Nicholas Carew, husband of Isabel), *VC*, p. 68 (Carew); *Proceedings of the Somersetshire Archaeological and Natural History Society* 65 (1920, for the year 1919): 15-21 (FitzMartin) and *CP* (Martin); *TG* 9 (1988): 4-5, 26 (Mohun); *RA* 3: 568-72 (Lewknor, Keynes), 3: 373-77 (Huntingfield), 2: 644-45 (Quincy), 1: 277-80 (St. Liz, Northumberland), 4: 99 (FitzWilliam, Mohun), 5: 170-71 (Toeni); *ES*, charts for Hainault, Flanders and France. The Mohun-FitzWilliam-Martin-Carew descent was developed by Douglas Richardson; see also *Sussex Archaeological Collections* 63 (1922): 181-202 (Keynes), and George Bellew, "The Family of de Quincy and Quincy" (ms. at NEHGS, 1934), esp. vol. 1, pp. 2, 4-6; *AP&P* 4: 3: 250-57 and *Strachey*, pp. 10-27, 29. Identification of the parents of Isabel (gen. 10), granddaughter of Ralph FitzWilliam, would be welcome, as would definitive monographs on the Goodere family and the several Sir Roger and Sir Thomas Lewknor(s).

The Royal Descents of 900 Immigrants

1. Robert II, King of France, d. 1031 = Constance of Provence
2. Robert I, Duke of Burgundy = Hélie of Semur-en-Auxois
3. Henry I, Duke of Burgundy = Sybil of Barcelona
4. Eudes I, Duke of Burgundy = Matilda of Burgundy
5. Alice of Burgundy = William III Talvas, Count of Alençon and Ponthieu
6. Guy II, Count of Ponthieu = Ida ――――
7. John I, Count of Ponthieu = Laure de St.-Valery
8. Hélène of Ponthieu = William de Stoteville (Guillaume d'Estouteville, Seigneur d'Estoutemont) of Stratfield, Hampshire
9. Alice of Stratfield = Robert de Say
10. Sir William de Say = Sybil ――――
11. Robert de Say = Emma ――――
12. Sir Thomas de Say = Isabel ――――
13. Sybil de Say = ――――
14. Elizabeth ―――― (only daughter and heir) = Sir Nicholas Dabridgecourt, possible son of Sir Sanchet Dabridgecourt (Dabrichecourt), Knight of the Garter
15. Sir John Dabridgecourt = Joan Lynde
16. John Dabridgecourt = Agnes Bekingham
17. Thomas Dabridgecourt = Beatrice ――――
18. (probably) Elizabeth Dabridgecourt = Ralph Staverton
19. Elizabeth Staverton = Thomas Burgoyne
20. Christopher Burgoyne = Thomasine Freville
21. Thomasine Burgoyne = Robert Shute
22. Anne Shute = John Leete

23. **William Leete** (c. 1613-1683), colonial governor of Conn. = (1) Anna Payne; (2) Sarah Rutherford; (3) Mrs. Mary Newman Street.

Sources: *MCS5,* line 128 (generations 20-23), plus Joseph Leete and J.C. Anderson, *The Family of Leete*, 2nd ed. (1906), esp. pp. 128 (and pedigree facing), 138-39, 162 (and pedigree facing), plus E.A. Stratton, *Applied Genealogy* (1988), pp. 70-72, 74, 165, 170 (disproof of the Peyton descent and of the identification of Rose Peyton as the wife of Robert Freville and mother of Thomasine [Freville] Burgoyne) and *NEXUS* 13 (1996): 129 (disproof of any Haselden descent); J.W. Clay, ed., *Visitations of Cambridge, 1575 and 1619* (*HSPVS*, vol. 41, 1897), p. 25 (Burgoyne); W.H. Rylands, ed., *The Four Visitations of Berkshire*, vol. 1 (*HSPVS*, vol. 56, 1907), pp. 130-31, W.H. Rylands, ed., *Visitations of Hampshire, 1530, 1575, and 1622-34* (*HSPVS*, vol. 64, 1913), p. 69 and Charles Kerry, *The History and Antiquities of the Hundred of Bray in the County of Berks* (1861), p. 62 (William Staverton, son of Ralph and Elizabeth, living 1509-55) (all Staverton, with discrepancies); *The Topographer and Genealogist* 1 (1846): 197-98, 200-3, 207, William Page, ed., *The Victoria History of Hampshire and the Isle of Wight*, vol. 4 (1911), pp. 57-59 and *Parliament, 1386-1421,* vol. 2, pp. 731-33 (Dabridgecourt, Say); *ES* 2: 13: 103 (Estouteville of Stratfield) and 2: 3: 3: 635 (Ponthieu); *AR8,* lines 108, 109. The forename of Elizabeth Dabridgecourt and her place in the Dabridgecourt pedigree require further proof; the above affiliation is based largely on chronology, but Say-Estouteville descent seems almost certain. The Ponthieu ancestry of the Dabridgecourts, as well as disproof of Haselden descent, was brought to my attention by Mrs. Gerald (Sarah) Polkinghorne of Minneapolis. A further monograph on generations 14-19 would be welcome.

The Royal Descents of 900 Immigrants

1. Robert II, King of France, d. 1031 = Constance of Provence
2. Robert I, Duke of Burgundy = Hélie of Semur-en-Auxois
3. Henry I, Duke of Burgundy = Sybil of Barcelona
4. Eudes I, Duke of Burgundy = Matilda of Burgundy
5. Alice of Burgundy = William III Talvas, Count of Alençon and Ponthieu
6. Ela Talvas = Patrick, Earl of Salisbury
7. (prob.) Isabel FitzPatrick = Walter Waleran
8. Isabel Waleran = William de Neville
9. Joan de Neville = Jordan St. Martin
10. Sir William St. Martin = Christiana ——
11. Sir Reynold/Reginald St. Martin = Eva ——
12. Sir Lawrence St. Martin = Sybil Lorti
13. Joan St. Martin = Robert Calston
14. Lawrence Calston = Felicity Combe
15. Thomas Calston = Joan Childrey
16. Elizabeth Calston = William Darrell. Their son, Sir George Darrell, married Margaret Stourton and was the father of Elizabeth Darrell, wife of John Seymour, SETH, and mother of Sir John Seymour, husband of Margery Wentworth, SETH. The last were parents of Queen Jane Seymour, third wife of Henry VIII, King of England, and mother of Edward VI, King of England.
17. Constantine Darrell = Joan Collingborne
18. Anne Darrell = John Erneley
19. John Erneley = Lucy Cooke
20. Jane Erneley = Thomas Byfleet
21. Jane Byfleet = Philip Cottington
22. James Cottington = Grace Popley

23. Jane Cottington = Thomas Ludwell. Their sons Thomas, d. unm., and John Ludwell (= Mrs. Judith Morseley Stevens) also immigrated to Va., but left no NDTPS.
24. **Philip Ludwell** (d. 1717) of Va., planter, Virginia councilor, colonial governor of N.C. and S.C. = (1) Mrs. Lucy Higginson Burwell Bernard, SETH; (2) Lady Frances Colepepper (Culpeper) Stephens Berkeley, ARD, SETH.

Sources: *GVFWM* 3: 460-75, *VGE*, pp. 318, 666-68, *GGE*, pp. 718-19, *NEHGR* 33 (1879): 220-21, Parish Register Society, vols. 60, 68, *The Registers of Bruton, co. Somerset*, vol. 1, *1554-1681*, vol. 2, *1681-1812* (1907, 1911), IPM of Philip Cottington (27 May 1617) (The National Archives [TNA], ref. C142/361/104) and Chancery Proceedings, Charles I, Bills and Answers, L, 55 Bundle; Ludwell vs. Worsley (documents dated 3 May 1632 and 22 June 1633 [TNA, C21/L7/14]) (Ludwell, Cottington); *CP* (Cottington), *Notes and Queries for Somerset and Dorset* 10 (1907): 102-4 (Dyer, Byfleet); G.D. Squibb, ed., *Wiltshire Visitation Pedigrees, 1623* (*HSPVS*, vols. 105-6 [1953-54]), pp. 55-56 (Erneley); 1507 will of Constantine Darell (PCC, 34 Adams), *Wiltshire Archaeological and Natural History Magazine* 4 (1858): 226-27 and chart between esp. (Darell), 81 (1987): 63-67 (Thomas Calston, with mention of his descent via St. Martin from Ela, Countess of Salisbury), and J.J. Watney, *The Wallop Family and Their Ancestry* (1928), pp. 255, 167, 680, 811 (Dar[r]ell, Calston, St. Martin, Neville, Waleran); *Parliament, 1386-1421*, vol. 2, pp. 465-66 (Thomas Calston); Sir R.C. Hoare, 2[nd] Bt., *The Modern History of South Wiltshire*, vol. 5 (1837), pt. 1, p. 21 (Waleran, de Neville, St. Martin, Calston), and Rev. C. Moor, ed., *Knights of Edward I, Volume 4* (*HSPVS*, vol. 83, 1931), pp. 185-86 (Sir William, Sir Reginald, and Sir Lawrence de St. Martin); H.G.D. Liveing, *Romsey Abbey: An Account of the Benedictine House of Nuns* (1906), pp. 63-87, esp. chart opposite p. 74 (with some mistakes, as noted by J.A. Brayton) and *CP* 11: 375-77 (Salisbury); *AR8*, line 108. This line was developed and contributed by John Anderson Brayton of Memphis, Tenn.

The Royal Descents of 900 Immigrants

1. Ethelred II "the Unready," King of England, d. 1016 = (1) Ælfflæd
2. Elgiva of England = Uchtred, Earl (Ealdorman) of Northumbria
3. Edith of Northumbria = Maldred, lord of Carlisle and Allendale
4. Gospatrick I, Earl of Northumbria and Dunbar = ——, sister of Edmund
5. Gospatrick II, 2nd Earl of Dunbar = Sybil Morel
6. Juliana of Dunbar = Ralph de Merlay
7. Roger de Merlay = Alice de Stuteville
8. Agnes de Merlay = Richard Gobion
9. Hugh Gobion = Matilda ——
10. Joan Gobion = John de Morteyn
11. Sir John de Morteyn = Joan de Rothwell
12. Lucy de Morteyn = Sir John Giffard
13. Sir Thomas Giffard = Elizabeth de Missenden
14. Roger Giffard = Isabel Stretle
15. Thomas Giffard = Eleanor Vaux
16. John Giffard = Agnes Winslow, daughter of Thomas Winslow and Agnes Throckmorton, daughter of Sir John Throckmorton and Eleanor Spinney, SETH
17. Roger Giffard = Mary Nanseglos
18. Nicholas Giffard = Agnes Master
19. Margaret Giffard = Hugh Sargent
20. Roger Sargent = Ellen Makerness
21. **Rev. William Sargent** of Mass. = (1) Hannah ——; (2) Mary ——; (3) Mrs. Sarah —— Minshall.

17. Thomas Giffard (brother of Roger) = Joan Langston
18. Amy Giffard = Richard Samwell

The Royal Descents of 900 Immigrants

19. Susanna Samwell = Peter Edwards
20. Edward Edwards = Ursula Coles
21. Margaret Edwards = Henry Freeman
22. **Alice Freeman** of Mass. and (presumably) Conn. = (1) John **Thompson**; (2) Robert **Parke**.
23. Mary Thompson = Joseph Wise
24. Sarah Wise = Stephen Williams

25. Joseph Williams = Abigail Davis	25. Stephen Williams, Jr. = Mary Capen
26. Joseph Williams, Jr. = Martha Howell	26. Mary Williams = Benjamin May
27. Joseph Williams (III) =	27. Susanna May

28. Benjamin Williams = Sarah Copeland Morton
29. Susan May Williams = **Jérôme-Napoléon Bonaparte**, a native of Camberwell, Surrey, England, later a resident of Baltimore, son of Jérôme Bonaparte, King of Westphalia (1807-1813), Prince of Montfort, sometime of Baltimore, d. 1860 (youngest brother of Napoléon I, Emperor of the French) and his first wife, Elizabeth Patterson of Baltimore. The younger son of Susan and Jerome was Charles Joseph Bonaparte (1851-1921), U.S. Attorney-General and Secretary of the Navy (under Theodore Roosevelt), civil service reformer, who was of Napoleonic imperial descent through his father but of earlier royal ancestry only as outlined above.

23. Dorothy Thompson (sister of Mary) = Thomas Parke, son of the above Robert Parke and Martha Chaplin, his first wife
24. Dorothy Parke = Joseph Morgan (ancestors of the late Diana, Princess of Wales and her sons, H.R.H. Prince William of Wales, Duke of Cambridge, and H.R.H. Prince Henry of Wales, SETH. See G.B. Roberts and W.A. Reitwiesner, *American Ancestors and Cousins of The Princess of Wales* [1984], pp. 21-32, 143-44, *TG* 4 [1983]: 176-82, 184-86, and Richard K. Evans, *The Ancestry of Diana, Princess of Wales, for Twelve*

The Royal Descents of 900 Immigrants

Generations [2007], pp. 1-9, 13, 19, 28, 41, 60, 93, 146, 217, 331, 387, 415, 458).

25. Joseph Morgan, Jr. = Sarah Emmons
26. Dorothy Morgan = Henry Van Kirk
27. Henry Van Kirk, Jr. = ——
28. William Van Kirk = Deborah Watters
29. Charity Malvina Van Kirk = Isaac Haines Dickerson
30. Phoebe Elizabeth Dickerson = George Tryon Harding
31. Warren Gamaliel Harding (1865-1923), 29th U.S. President = Mrs. Florence Mabel Kling DeWolfe

17. William Giffard (brother of Roger and Thomas) = —— Vachell
18. Anne Giffard = Richard Curson
19. Catherine Curson = Edmund Towneley
20. Francis Towneley = Catherine Forster. Their son, Edmund Towneley, is said to have immigrated to Md. and may have left descendants.
21. Francis Towneley = Anne Elborough
22. Francis Towneley = ——
23. Jeremiah Towneley = Frances Andrews
24. **Margaret Frances Towneley** of Md. = Richard **Chase.**

Sources: *AR8*, lines 41-43, 34, 29A and sources cited therein, esp. *NEHGR* 74 (1920): 231-37, 267-83, 75 (1921): 57-63, 129-42, 79 (1925): 358-78 (reprinted in *EO* 1: 1: 595-638 and *EO* 2: 2: 18-38), plus *Moriarty* (Sargent); *MCS5*, line 63, *TAG* 13 (1936-37): 1-8, 14 (1937-38): 145-46, 29 (1953): 215-18, *Blackman,* pp. 55-134, 138-58 (an ancestor table of Mrs. Parke for 32 generations, with an extensive bibliography), *Hawes, Freeman and James,* and *NEHGR* 141 (1987): 105. F.A. Hill, *The Mystery Solved: Facts Relating to the "Lawrence-Towneley," "Chase-Towneley" Marriages and Estate Question* (1888), chart in packet esp. (Mrs. Chase), W.H. Turner, ed., *Visitations of Oxfordshire, 1566, 1574, and 1634* (*HSPVS*, vol. 5, 1871), p. 131 (Curson). For Edmund Towneley, see *BRMF1*: 428 and Sir G.J. Armytage, ed., *Middlesex Pedigrees as Collected by Richard Mundy* (*HSPVS*, vol. 65, 1914), pp. 170-71. For the line from Mrs. Parke to the Bonapartes see *TAG* 56 (1980): 80-82, F.L. Weis, "Robert Williams of Roxbury, Massachusetts, and Some of His Descendants" (typescript, 1945), pp. 21-23, 52-54, 127-39, 320-21, Christopher Johnston, ed., *Society of Colonial Wars in the State of Maryland* (1905), p. 125 (pedigree of John Savage Williams), and G.N. Mackenzie, *Colonial Families of the United States of America* (rep. 1966), vols. 1 (1907), pp. 598-603 (Williams), 5 (1915), pp. 68-71 (Bonaparte). For the Parke descent of Harding, see *New England Ancestors* 3 (2002), 5-6: 34-35, and *AAP2009, 2012*, pp. 98-100, 102, 253-54, 348-49, 636.

The Royal Descents of 900 Immigrants

1. Ethelred II "the Unready", King of England, d. 1016 = (1) Ælfflæd

2. Elgiva of England = Uchtred, Earl (Ealdorman) of Northumbria

3. Edith of Northumbria = Maldred, lord of Carlisle and Allendale

4. Gospatrick I, Earl of Northumbria and Dunbar = ——, sister of Edmund

5. Gospatrick, 2nd Earl of Dunbar = Sybil Morel

6. Juliana of Dunbar = Ralph de Merlay

7. Roger de Merlay = Alice de Stuteville

8. Agnes de Merlay = Richard Gobion

9. Hugh Gobion = Matilda ——

10. Joan Gobion = John de Morteyn

11. Sir John de Morteyn = Joan de Rothwell

12. Lucy de Morteyn = Sir John Giffard, whose patrilineal descent from Osbern de Bolebec and Avelina, sister of Gunnora, wife of Richard I, Duke of Normandy (and great-grandmother of William I, the Conqueror, King of England and his full or half-sister, Judith of Normandy, both SETH) is treated in *EO* 2: 1: 622-28

13. Alice Giffard = Sir John Anne (Alice's maternity is uncertain— she was possibly a daughter of Sir John's second wife, Alice de Montfort, a likely illegitimate daughter, by Lora de Ullenhall, of Peter [or Piers] de Montfort, 3rd Baron Montfort, son of John de Montfort, 1st Baron Montfort [and Alice de la Plaunche, a kinswoman of Eleanor of Castile, wife of Edward I, King of England—see J.C. Parsons, *The Court and Household of Eleanor of Castile in 1290* (1977), pp. 48-50], son of Sir Peter de Montfort (and Maud de la Mare), son of Sir Peter de Montfort and Alice de Audley, daughter of Henry de Audley and Bertrade de Mainwaring, SETH.)

14. Alice Anne = William Raynsford

15. Elizabeth Raynsford = Stephen Agard, son of George Agard and Elizabeth Middlemore, daughter of Richard Middlemore and Margery Throckmorton, SETH

16. Katherine Agard = Harold Kinnesman

17. Elizabeth Kinnesman = Thomas Dexter

18. Stephen Dexter = Anne Turland

19. Gregory Dexter = Isabel ——

20. **Rev. Gregory Dexter** of R.I. = Abigail Fuller.

Sources: *Rhode Island History* 20 (1961): 125-26 ("A Note on Gregory Dexter" by Bradford F. Swan, author of *Gregory Dexter of London and New England, 1610-1700* [1949]), Jane Fletcher Fiske for Roberta Stokes Smith, *Thomas Clemence of Providence, Rhode Island and His Descendants to the Year 2007* (2007), pp. 1-3; L.F. Salzman, ed., *The Victoria County History of the County of Northampton*, vol. 4 (1937), p. 202 (Thomas, Elizabeth, Stephen and the elder Gregory Dexter), 159 (Agard), and *The Victoria History of the County of Warwick*, vol. 5 (1949), p. 155 (Agard), Walter C. Metcalfe, *Visitations of Northamptonshire, 1564, 1618-19* (1887), p. 103 (Kinsman), and *NEHGR* 139 (1985): 229-30 (Raynsford, but where the second husband of Elizabeth Raynsford is mistakenly given as George Agard, not Stephen); J.W. Walker, *Yorkshire Pedigrees, A-F* (*HSPVS*, vol. 94, 1942), pp. 13, 17-18 (Anne); *Moriarty* 4: 268 (noting the kinship between Catholic chantry priest Alexander Ann and his "well beloved cosyn Roger Giffard"); *Publications of the Bedfordshire Historical Record Society* 14 (1931): 68-70 and *Berks, Bucks & Oxon Archaeological Journal*, new ser., 5 (1899-1900): 21, 44 (on Alice de Montfort and her four husbands); *AR8*, lines 42, 41, 34 and sources cited therein (generations 1-12 above), and *RA* 4: 132-38 (Montfort), 1: 199-200 (Audley, Mainwaring), 2: 148-54 (Chester), 3: 86-88 (Gloucester). W.P.W. Phillimore and W.F. Carter, *Some Account of the Family of Middlemore* (1901), pp. 29-43, omits Elizabeth Raynsford, wife of George Agard, but her parentage is proved by Chancery IPM (ser. 2), XXV, 10, cited in *VCH Warwick* 5: 155, note 74. The Throckmorton descent was developed, with further sources, by Shawn H. Potter of Woodbridge, Virginia, and posted on soc.gen.medieval; further material

The Royal Descents of 900 Immigrants

was contributed by Robert O'Connor of Christchurch, New Zealand. The wife of the elder Gregory Dexter is given as Isabel in the 1623 baptism of her daughter, a younger Isabel, in Old, Northamptonshire. A monograph on Alice (Giffard) Anne is much needed.

The Royal Descents of 900 Immigrants

1. Ethelred II "the Unready", King of England, d. 1016 = (1) Ælfflæd
2. Elgiva of England = Uchtred, Earl of Northumbria
3. Edith of Northumbria = Maldred, lord of Carlisle and Allendale
4. Gospatrick I, Earl of Northumbria and Dunbar = ——, sister of Edmund
5. Gospatrick II, 2nd Earl of Dunbar = Sybil Morel
6. Edgar of Dunbar = Alice de Greystoke
7. Agnes of Dunbar = Anselm le Fleming
8. Eleanor le Fleming = Ralph d'Eyncourt
9. Sir Ralph d'Eyncourt = Alice ——
10. Elizabeth d'Eyncourt = Sir William de Strickland
11. Joan de Strickland = Robert Washington
12. Robert Washington = Agnes le Gentyl
13. John Washington = Joan de Croft
14. John Washington = ——
15. Robert Washington = Margaret ——
16. Robert Washington = Elizabeth Westfield
17. John Washington = Margaret Kitson
18. Lawrence Washington = Amy Pargiter (their son Robert Washington married Elizabeth Light and was the father of Lawrence Washington, husband of Margaret Butler, SETH)
19. Magdalen Washington = Anthony Humphrey
20. Alice Humphrey = Thomas Watts
21. John Watts = Elizabeth ——
22. Anthony Watts = Joanna Bennett
23. Elizabeth Watts = Henry Addington
24. Anthony Addington = Mary Hiley

The Royal Descents of 900 Immigrants

25. Henry Addington, 1st Viscount Sidmouth, British Prime Minister = Ursula Mary Hammond

26. Frances Addington = George Pellew

27. **Henry Edward Pellew, 6th Viscount Exmouth** (title never assumed) (1828-1923) of N.Y. (and Washington, D.C.), philanthropist, treated in the *DAB* = (1) Eliza Jay; (2) Augusta Jay (sisters).

Sources: *BP* and *CP* (Sidmouth, Exmouth); Eversley M.G. Belfield, *The Annals of the Addington Family* (1959), pp. 18-26 and chart at end esp.; George Horace Sydney Lee Washington, *The Earliest Washingtons and Their Anglo-Saxon Connections* (1964), chart opp. p. 24, part II esp.; *AR8*, lines 41, 34, and *TG* 4 (1983): 184, note 25. See also *Burke's Presidential Families of the U.S.A.*, 2nd ed. (1981), pp. 14-15 (Washington) and Charles Mosley, ed., *American Presidential Families* (1993), pp. 46-49.

The Royal Descents of 900 Immigrants

1. Hugh Capet, King of France, d. 996 = Adelaide of Poitou
2. Edith of France = Rainier IV, Count of Hainault
3. Beatrix of Hainault = Ebles I, Count of Roucy
4. Alice of Roucy = Hildouin IV, Count of Montdidier
5. Margaret of Montdidier = Hugh I, Count of Clermont
6. Adeliza of Clermont = Gilbert de Clare
7. Richard de Clare = Adeliza de Meschines
8. Roger de Clare, 2nd Earl of Hertford = Maud de St. Hilaire
9. Aveline de Clare = Geoffrey FitzPiers, Earl of Essex
10. Hawise FitzGeoffrey = Sir Reynold de Mohun
11. Alice de Mohun = Robert de Beauchamp
12. Sir Humphrey de Beauchamp = Sybil Oliver
13. Sir John Beauchamp = Joan de Nonant
14. Sir John Beauchamp = Margaret Whalesburgh
15. Elizabeth Beauchamp = William Fortescue
16. William Fortescue = Matilda Falwell
17. John Fortescue = Joan Prutteston
18. Joan Fortescue = Thomas Hext
19. Thomas Hext = Wilmot Poyntz
20. Margery Hext = John Collamore
21. Peter Collamore = Edith ——
22. Thomas Collamore = Agnes Adams. Their son, Peter Collamore, was almost certainly the immigrant of that name to Mass., who married Mary —— and died without surviving issue; his chief heir was his nephew ("cousin") Anthony, below. In addition, a daughter, Joan Collamore, is said to have married —— Blackmer and to have been the mother of William Blackmer/Blackmore of Mass., husband of Mrs. Elizabeth Curtis Bankes.

The Royal Descents of 900 Immigrants

23. John Collamore = Mary Nicholl
24. (very probably) **Anthony Collamore** of Mass. = Sarah Chittenden.
25. Elizabeth Collamore = Timothy Symmes
26. Timothy Symmes, Jr. = Mary Cleves
27. John Cleves Symmes = Anna Tuthill
28. Anna Tuthill Symmes = William Henry Harrison (1773-1841), 9th U.S. President
29. John Scott Harrison = Elizabeth Ramsey Irwin
30. Benjamin Harrison (1833-1901), 23rd U.S. President = (1) Caroline Lavinia Scott; (2) Mrs. Mary Scott Lord Dimmick

21. Henry Collamore (brother of Peter) = Margaret Blight
22. Elizabeth Collamore = Bartholomew Harris
23. **Agnes Harris** of Conn. = (1) William **Spencer**; (2) William **Edwards**.
24. (by 1) Sarah Spencer = John Case
25. Mary Case = William Alderman
26. Sarah Alderman = Thomas Moses
27. Amy Moses = William Halladay
28. James Halladay = Rebecca Copley
29. James Halladay, Jr. = ——   29. Calvin Halladay = Esther Fisher
30. Thompson Halladay   =   30. Rachel Halladay
31. Anna Maria Halladay = Jacob Robert Neahr
32. Henry Clay Neahr = Anna Serepta Wells
33. Hortense Neahr = William Stephenson Bloomer
34. Elizabeth Ann Bloomer, known as Betty Ford (1918-2011), promoter of alcohol and drug rehabilitation, founder of the

The Royal Descents of 900 Immigrants

Betty Ford Center in Rancho Mirage, Calif., author
= (1) William G. Warren; (2) Gerald Rudolph Ford, Jr. (1913-2006), 38th U.S. President, Congressman, SETH

19. Agnes Hext (sister of Thomas) = Sir Lewis Pollard

20. Philippa Pollard = Sir Hugh Paulet

21. George Paulet = Ysabel Perrin

22. Rachel Paulet = Sir Philip de Carteret

23. Rachel de Carteret = Benjamin La Cloche

24. Rachel La Cloche = Helier de Carteret, atty. gen. of the Isle of Jersey

25. **Philip de Carteret** (1639-1682), first colonial governor of N.J. = Mrs. Elizabeth Smith Lawrence, widow of William Lawrence of L.I. She married (3) Richard Towneley of N.J. Both of her other husbands are ARD, SETH.

25. **Peter de Carteret**, colonial governor of N.C. = ——.

Sources: *RA* 3: 233-35 (Harris, Collamore, Hext), 1: 111-12 (Fortescue), 4: 511-13 (Beauchamp), 4: 100-1 (Mohun), 2: 512-16 (FitzPiers), 2: 172-80 (FitzGeoffrey, FitzPiers, de Clare), 2: 233-34 (Clermont) and *AR8*, lines 106, 151, 246, 246B, 246E, *TAG* 63 (1988): 33-45, *TG* 9 (1988): 6-9, 27-30 esp., and for Anthony Collamore, unpublished research of Douglas Richardson of Salt Lake City, based partly on *VD*, pp. 216-17, Charles Hatch, *Genealogy of the Descendants of Anthony Collamore of Scituate, Massachusetts* (1915), pp. 9-25, and the Northam, Devon, parish register; (*Journal of*) *North Carolina Genealogy* 16 (1970): 2537-52 and *BLG* (1952), pp. 638, 1685-86 (de Carteret), Colin G. Winn, *The Pouletts of Hinton St. George* (1976), p. 23 and tabular pedigree opposite p. 120, and *VD,* pp. 598 (Pollard), 484 (Hext). For William Blackmer/Blackmore of Mass., whose parentage lacks proof, see M.L. Holman, *The Scott Genealogy* (1919), pp. 265-66.

Note that the immigrant descendants charted herein of Hugh Capet, King of France, are all through a great-granddaughter, Alice of Roucy, wife of Hildouin IV, Count of Montdidier, and all except Jean-François Gignilliat, via Alice's granddaughter, Adeliza of Clermont, wife of the English Gilbert de Clare. The most recent common ancestor of Adeliza's immigrant descendants charted on these several (above and next) pages was Sir Humphrey de Beauchamp, d. 1316/17, a twelfth-generation descendant of this king.

The Royal Descents of 900 Immigrants

1. Hugh Capet, King of France, d. 996 = Adelaide of Poitou
2. Edith of France = Rainier IV, Count of Hainault
3. Beatrix of Hainault = Ebles I, Count of Roucy
4. Alice of Roucy = Hildouin IV, Count of Montdidier
5. Margaret of Montdidier = Hugh I, Count of Clermont
6. Adeliza of Clermont = Gilbert de Clare
7. Richard de Clare = Adeliza de Meschines
8. Roger de Clare, 2nd Earl of Hertford = Maud de St. Hilaire
9. Aveline de Clare = Geoffrey FitzPiers, Earl of Essex
10. Hawise FitzGeoffrey = Sir Reynold de Mohun
11. Alice de Mohun = Robert de Beauchamp
12. Sir Humphrey de Beauchamp = Sybil Oliver
13. Eleanor Beauchamp = John Bampfield
14. John Bampfield = Isabel Cobham
15. John Bampfield = Joan Gilbert
16. Thomas Bampfield = Agnes Coplestone
17. Agnes Bampfield = John Prowse
18. Richard Prowse = Margaret Norton
19. John Prowse = Joan Orchard
20. Robert Prowse = ——
21. John Prowse = Alice White
22. John Prowse = Elizabeth Collack alias Colwyck
23. Agnes Prowse = John Trowbridge
24. **Thomas Trowbridge** of Conn. = Elizabeth Marshall.
25. Thomas Trowbridge, Jr. = Sarah Rutherford
26. Thomas Trowbridge (III) = Mary Winston
27. Sarah Trowbridge = John Russell

28. Rebecca Russell = Ezekiel Hayes

29. Rutherford Hayes = Chloe Smith

30. Rutherford Hayes, Jr. = Sophia Birchard

31. Rutherford Birchard Hayes (1822-1893), 19th U.S. President = Lucy Ware Webb

Sources: *AR8*, lines 246G, 246B, 246, 151, 106 and *TG* 9 (1988): 3-39 (Charles Fitch-Northen), based largely on *TAG* 18 (1941-42): 129-37, 57 (1981): 31-33, record sources cited in both, and printed sources cited in *NEHGR* 141 (1987): 99. For the first twelve generations see, as with the chart immediately preceding, *RA* 4: 511-12 (Beauchamp), 4: 100-1 (Mohun), 2: 510-16 (FitzPiers), 2: 172-80 (FitzGeoffrey, FitzPiers, de Clare), 2: 233-34 (Clermont).

The Royal Descents of 900 Immigrants

1. Hugh Capet, King of France, d. 996 = Adelaide of Poitou
2. Edith of France = Rainier IV, Count of Hainault
3. Beatrix of Hainault = Ebles I, Count of Roucy
4. Alice of Roucy = Hildouin IV, Count of Montdidier
5. Adélaïde of Montdidier = Fulk de Grandson
6. Ebles de Grandson = Adelaide ──
7. Barthélemy de Grandson, Seigneur de la Sarraz and Belmont = ──
8. Jordan de Grandson, Seigneur de Belmont = Petronelle ──
9. Columba de Grandson = Rodolphe, Count of Gruyères
10. Beatrix de Gruyères = Aymon de Blonay, Seigneur de St. Paul
11. Jeannette de Blonay = Guillaume de Langin
12. Rodolphe de Langin = Isabelle de Pontverre
13. (of uncertain maternity) Marguerite de Langin = Henri d'Allinges, Seigneur de Coudrée
14. Nicolette d'Allinges = François de Greysier
15. Marguerite de Greysier = Jean de Rovorée, Seigneur du Crest and La Roche d'Ollon
16. Jean de Rovorée, Seigneur de Bonneveaux = Isabelle de Dompierre
17. Jean de Rovorée, co-Seigneur de Saint-Triphon and des Ormonts = Marie de Confignon
18. Guigues de Rovorée, Seigneur de Saint-Triphon and des Ormonts = (perhaps) Guillauma de Montvuagnard
19. Pierre de Rovorée, Seigneur de Granges (in Valais) = two or three times
20. (of uncertain maternity) Guigues de Rovéréaz = twice
21. (of uncertain maternity) Claudia Antonia de Rovéréaz = Georges de Ville

22. Marie de Ville = Abraham Gignilliat

23. **Jean-François Gignilliat** of S.C. = (1) ——; (2) Suzanne Le Serrurier.

Sources: *TAG* 53 (1977): 129-31 (Henry Bainbridge Hoff) and sources cited therein, esp. Comte E. Amédée de Foras, *Armorial et Nobiliaire de l'Ancien Duché de Savoie* (1863-1938); *ES* 2: 11: 153 (Grandson), 2: 15: 3 (Gruyères), 2: 15: 22 (Blonay) and *AR8*, lines 151, 106. See also *Bulletin de la Société de l'Histoire du Protestantisme Français* 134 (1988): 59-60, 66, on the immigrant's unknown first wife.

The Royal Descents of 900 Immigrants

1. Louis IV, King of France, d. 954 (probable grandson maternally of Edward the Elder, King of England, d. 924) = Gerberga, daughter of Henry I the Fowler, German Emperor, d. 936

2. Charles, Duke of Lower Lorraine = Adelaide ——

3. Adelaide of Lower Lorraine = Albert I, Count of Namur

4. Albert II, Count of Namur = Regelinde of Lower Lorraine

5. Albert III, Count of Namur = Ida of Saxony

6. Godfrey, Count of Namur = Sybil of Château-Porcien

7. Elizabeth of Namur = Gervais, Count of Rethel

8. Milicent of Rethel = (2) Richard de Camville

9. William de Camville = Auberée de Marmion

10. William de Camville = Iseuda ——

11. Thomas de Camville = Agnes ——

12. Felicia de Camville = Philip Durvassal

13. Thomas Durvassal = Margery ——

14. Margery Durvassal = William de la Spine

15. William de la Spine = Alice de Bruley

16. Sir Guy de la Spine/Spinney = Katherine ——

17. Eleanor Spinney = Sir John Throckmorton

18. Sir Thomas Throckmorton = Margaret Olney

19. Sir Robert Throckmorton = Catherine Marrow

20. Richard Throckmorton = Jane Beaufoe

21. Goditha Throckmorton = Thomas Neale

22. John Neale = Grace Butler, daughter of John Butler (and Anne Travers), son of John Butler and Elizabeth Elliot, daughter of John ap Jenkin Elliot (and Sined [Jenet] Perrot), son of Jenkin Elliot and Sined (Jenet) Barrett, daughter of William Barrett (and Margred ferch Hugh Howel), son of Henry Barrett allegedly by Eleanor l'Archdekne (see *RD500*, 1993, p. 374,

but see Barrett note in the bibliography for *Seven Centuries* below). Brice McAdoo Clagett also indicates that, via Perrot(t) and Howel, plus Turberville and Wogan, Grace Butler was descended from various Welsh kings and rulers, as can be traced in *Bartrum 1* and *2*.

23. Raphael Neale = Jane Baker
24. **James Neale** of Md. = Anna Maria Gill, daughter of Benjamin Gill of Md. by Mary Mainwaring, probably also of Md., ARD, SETH.

19. Margery Throckmorton (sister of Sir Robert) = Richard Middlemore
20. Thomas Middlemore = Anne Littleton
21. Margaret Middlemore = Edward Underhill
22. John Underhill = Margery Wylmer
23. Humphrey Underhill = Jane Thrift
24. Humphrey Underhill = —— Hall
25. **Humphrey Underhill** of N.Y. = Mrs. Sarah —— Smith.
25. **Mary Underhill** of N.Y. = (1) Thomas **Naylor**; (2) Richard **Stites**.

Sources: *Maryland Genealogical Society Bulletin* 31 (1989-1990): 136-53 (Brice McAdoo Clagett on James Neale, with an ancestor table for 9 generations, plus Neale, Butler, Throckmorton and de la Spine/Spinney, Elliot, Barrett, and l'Archdeacon sources cited therein), later corrected in part in Brice McAdoo Clagett, *Seven Centuries: Ancestors for Twenty Generations of John Brice de Treville Clagett and Ann Calvert Brooke Clagett*, mss. sent to various scholars in Brice's lifetime, *MG* 2:248-52 (Neale), *Throckmorton*, pp. 43-51, 65-67 and chart opposite p. 68 (de la Spine/Spinney, Durvassal, de Camville) and *Blackman*, pp. 81-82, 84, 86, 88, 90, 94, 97 (generations 9-17, with 10 omitted); V.J. Watney, *The Wallop Family and Their Ancestry,* vol. 1 (1928), p. 200, taken in part, no doubt, from Sir William Dugdale, *The Antiquities of Warwickshire,* 2nd ed., vol. 2 (1730), p. 847 and *Nichols,* vol. 3, part 1, p. 350, but corrected in *TAG* 21 (1944-45): 95-96 and *Moriarty,* vol. 6, pp. 472-73, vol. 8, pp. 357-58 (de Camville, Counts of Rethel); *TAG* 20 (1943-44): 255-56 (Milicent of Rethel) and *AR8*, lines 246A, 148-49; W.P.W. Phillimore and W.F. Carter, *Some Account of the Family of Middlemore* (1901), pp. 29-46, plus further Middlemore and other research by Robert O'Connor of Christchurch, New Zealand, and Edwin R. Deats and Harry Macy, Jr., *Underhill Genealogy*, vol. 6 (1980), pp. 1067-74, based in part on J.H. Morrison, *The Underhills of Warwickshire* (1932).

The Royal Descents of 900 Immigrants

1. Louis IV, King of France, d. 954 (probable grandson maternally of Edward the Elder, King of England, d. 924) = Gerberga, daughter of Henry I the Fowler, German Emperor, d. 936
2. Charles, Duke of Lower Lorraine = Adelaide ——
3. Adelaide of Lower Lorraine = Albert I, Count of Namur
4. Albert II, Count of Namur = Regelinde of Lower Lorraine
5. Albert III, Count of Namur = Ida of Saxony
6. Godfrey, Count of Namur = Sybil of Château-Porcien
7. Elizabeth of Namur = Gervais, Count of Rethel
8. Milicent of Rethel = (1) Robert Marmion
9. Robert Marmion = ——
10. William Marmion = ——
11. Geoffrey Marmion = Rosamond ——
12. William Marmion = Matilda (le Justice?)
13. John Marmion = Margery de Nottingham
14. Thomas Marmion = Agnes ——
15. Alice Marmion = William Harlyngrugge
16. Cecilia Harlyngrugge = John Rede
17. Joan Rede = Walter Cotton
18. William Cotton = Alice Abbot
19. Edmund Cotton = Alice Conyers
20. George Cotton = Jane Goldingham
21. Elizabeth Cotton = Francis Bacon
22. Elizabeth Bacon = Sir James Bacon, a cousin, son (by Margaret Rawlings) of James Bacon, brother of Sir Nicholas Bacon, Lord Keeper and Lord Chancellor, husband of Jane Cooke, SETH)
23. James Bacon = (1) —— ——; (2) Martha Woodward

The Royal Descents of 900 Immigrants

24. (by 1) **Nathaniel Bacon** (1620-1692), Acting Gov. of Va. = (1) Mrs. Anne Bassett Smith; (2) Mrs. Elizabeth Kingsmill Tayloe.

24. (by 2) Martha Bacon (half-sister of Act. Gov. Nathaniel) = Anthony Smith

25. **Abigail Smith** of Va. = Lewis **Burwell**, Jr.

26. Elizabeth Burwell = Benjamin Harrison (III)

27. Benjamin Harrison (IV) = Anne Carter

28. Benjamin Harrison (V), signer of the Declaration of Independence = 28. Elizabeth Bassett, daughter of 27. William Bassett (IV) (and Elizabeth Churchill), son of William Bassett (III) and 26. Joanna Burwell, sister of Elizabeth (Burwell) Harrison above

29. William Henry Harrison (1773-1841), 9th U.S. President = Anna Tuthill Symmes

30. John Scott Harrison = Elizabeth Ramsey Irwin

31. Benjamin Harrison (1833-1901), 23rd U.S. President = (1) Caroline Lavinia Scott; (2) Mrs. Mary Scott Lord Dimmick

Sources: Unpublished research by John Anderson Brayton, based in part on *WV*, pp. 363-64, 372 (and chart following)-80, 383-86 (Burwell, Smith, Bacon), John W. Clay, ed., *Visitations of Cambridge, 1575 and 1619* (*HSPVS*, vol. 41, 1897), p. 21, 23, John Brooks Threlfall, *The Ancestry of Thomas Bradbury (1611-1695) and His Wife Mary (Perkins) Bradbury (1615-1700) of Salisbury, Massachusetts*, 3rd ed. (2006), esp. pp. 135-50, 179-203, plus the wills of George Cotton (d. 1554), generation #20 above, and George's sister Audrey, listed in M.A. Farrow and Percy Millican, *Index to Wills Proved in the Consistory Court of Norwich, 1550-1603* (*The Index Library*, vol. 73, 1950), p. 46. Criticism of the linkage between generations 9 and 10 was published in *TG* (1988): 80-87 and answered by a note at the end of *AR8*, line 246A. Note also *The New Hampshire Genealogical Record* 16 (1999): 145-48.

The Royal Descents of 900 Immigrants

1. Robert I, King of France, d. 923 = (1) Aelis ──

2. ──── of France = Herbert II, Count of Vermandois, son of Herbert I, Count of Vermandois (and ────), son of Pepin, Lord of Peronne and St. Quentin, Count near Paris (and ────), son of Bernhard, King of Italy (d. 818) (and Cunigunde of Parma), son of Pepin, King of Italy (and ────), son of the Emperor Charlemagne (d. 814) and Hildegardis of Kraichgau

3. Robert, Count of Meaux and Troyes = Adelaide of Burgundy

4. Adela of Vermandois = Geoffrey I, Count of Anjou

5. Ermengarde of Anjou = Conan I, Duke of Brittany

6. Judith of Brittany = Richard II, Duke of Normandy

7. Robert I, Duke of Normandy

8. (possibly by Herlève of Falaise) Adelaide of Normandy, full or half-sister of William I, the Conqueror, King of England = (1) Enguerrand II, Count of Ponthieu, son of Hugh III, Count of Ponthieu (and Bertha of Aumale), son of Enguerrand I, Count of Ponthieu (and Adela, possibly of Westfriesland), son of Hugh I, Count of Ponthieu and (almost certainly) Gisela, daughter of Hugh Capet, King of France, SETH, and Adelaide of Poitou; (2) Lambert, Count of Lens, son of Eustace I, Count of Boulogne, and Maud, daughter of Lambert, Count of Louvain and Gerberga of Lower Lorraine, daughter of Charles, Duke of Lower Lorraine (and Adelaide ────), SETH, son of Louis IV, King of France, SETH, and Gerberga of Germany; (3) Eudes II, Count of Troyes and Aumale

9. (by 1, according to Catherine Morton and Hope Muntz, eds., *The Carmen de Hastingae Proelio of Guy, Bishop of Amiens* (1972), p. 127, or by 2, according to older sources and Douglas Richardson in *RA*) Judith of Ponthieu or Lens = Waltheof II, Earl of Huntingdon, Northampton and Northumberland

10. Matilda of Northumberland = (1) Simon de St. Liz, Earl of Huntingdon and Northampton; (2) David I, King of Scotland, d. 1153, SETH

11. (by 1) Matilda de St. Liz = Robert de Clare

12. Walter FitzRobert = Maud de Lucy

The Royal Descents of 900 Immigrants

13. Alice FitzWalter (sister of Robert FitzWalter, leader of the Magna Carta barons) = Gilbert Pecche
14. Hamon Pecche = Eve ——
15. Gilbert Pecche = Joan de Creye
16. Gilbert Pecche, 1st Baron Pecche = Iseult ——

The immigrants treated below are not as nearly related as those on most "combined immigrant" charts in this volume, but are covered in this single long chart to avoid duplication of the above first 16 generations.

17. Gilbert Pecche, 2nd Baron Pecche = Joan ——
18. Katherine Pecche = Sir Thomas Notbeam
19. Margaret Notbeam = John Hinkley
20. Cecily Hinkley = Henry Caldebeck
21. Thomasine Caldebeck = Thomas Underhill
22. Anne Underhill = Thomas Knighton
23. Joan Knighton = Charles Bull
24. Richard Bull = Alice Hunt
25. Elizabeth Bull = John Lawrence
26. Thomas Lawrence = Joan Antrobus of Mass., who m. (2) John Tuttle
27. **Jane Lawrence** of Mass. = George **Giddings**.
28. Joseph Giddings = Susanna Rindge
29. Joseph Giddings, Jr. = Grace Wardwell
30. Susanna Giddings = William Torrey
31. Joseph Torrey = Deborah Holbrook
32. William Torrey = Anna Davenport
33. Samuel Davenport Torrey = Susan Holman Waters

34. Louisa Maria Torrey = Alphonso Taft, diplomat, U.S. Secretary of War and Attorney General
35. William Howard Taft (1857-1930), 27th U.S. President = Helen Herron

27. **John Lawrence** of Flushing, Long Island, N.Y. = Susanna ——.
27. **Thomas Lawrence** of Newtown, Long Island, N.Y. = (1) Mary ——; (2) Mary Ferguson.
28. (by 1) Mary Lawrence (very probably, see *TAG* 17 [1940-41]: 74-78) = Thomas Walton
29. William Walton = Mary Santvoort
30. Jacob Walton = Maria Beekman
31. Abraham Walton = Grace Williams
32. Maria Eliza Walton = James Roosevelt
33. Isaac Roosevelt = Mary Rebecca Aspinwall
34. James Roosevelt = Sara Delano
35. Franklin Delano Roosevelt (1882-1945), 32nd U.S. President = (Anna) Eleanor Roosevelt

27. **William Lawrence** of Flushing, Long Island, N.Y. = (1) Elizabeth ——; (2) Elizabeth Smith (She = [2] Philip de Carteret, first colonial governor of N.J., and [3] Richard Towneley of N.J. Both of her later husbands were ARD, SETH.).
27. **Mary Lawrence** of Mass. = Thomas **Burnham**.

17. Sir Simon Pecche (brother of the 2nd Baron Pecche) = Agnes Holme
18. Margaret Pecche = John Hunt
19. Iodena Hunt = Thomas Cornish
20. John Cornish = ——
21. John Cornish = Agnes Walden

The Royal Descents of 900 Immigrants

22. Mary Cornish = Thomas Everard
23. Henry Everard = ——
24. Thomas Everard = Margaret Wiseman
25. John Everard = Judith Bourne
26. **Judith Everard** of Mass. = Samuel **Appleton** of Mass., ARD, SETH.
27. John Appleton = Priscilla Glover
28. Priscilla Appleton = Joseph Capen
29. Mary Capen = Thomas Baker, Jr.
30. Priscilla Baker = Tarrant Putnam, Jr.
31. Priscilla Putnam = Adam Brown, Jr.
32. Israel Putnam Brown = Sally Briggs
33. Sally Brown = Israel C. Brewer
34. Sarah Almeda Brewer = Calvin Galusha Coolidge
35. John Calvin Coolidge = Victoria Josephine Moor
36. (John) Calvin Coolidge (Jr.) (1872-1933), 30th U.S. President = Grace Anna Goodhue

21. Margaret Cornish (sister of the second John) = Thomas Mildmay
22. Walter Mildmay = Mary Everard (sister of Thomas Everard who married Mary Cornish)
23. Thomas Mildmay = Anne Reade
24. John Mildmay = Frances Rainbow
25. Thomas Mildmay = Olive Nuttal
25. Thomasine Mildmay = John Boddie
26. Mary Mildmay = 23. Thomas Boddie
27. John Boddie = Mary ——
28. **William Boddie** of Va. = (1) Anna ——; (2) Elizabeth ——; (3) Mrs. Mary (——) Griffin.

The Royal Descents of 900 Immigrants

24. Thomasine Mildmay (sister of John) = Anthony Bourchier
25. Thomas Bourchier = ──
26. Anne Bourchier = Thomas Rich
27. Susan Rich = Edward Bathurst
28. **Lancelot Bathurst** of Va. = ──.

16. Margery Pecche (sister of the 1st Baron Pecche) = Sir Nicholas de Criol
17. Sir Nicholas de Criol = Rohesia ──
18. Sir John de Criol = Lettice ──
19. Ida de Criol = Sir John Brockhull
20. William Brockhull = Margaret ──
21. Nicholas Brockhull = Katherine Wood
22. William Brockhull = ──
23. John Brockhull = ──
24. Edward Brockhull = Mildred Ellis
25. Marion Brockhull = Thomas Harfleet
26. Henry Harfleet = Mary Slaughter
27. Martha Harfleet = John Halsnode
28. John Halsnode = Margaret Ladd
29. **Margaret Halsnode** of N.J. = John **Denn(e)**.

Lawrence Sources: *RA* 3: 548-52 (Lawrence, Bull, Knighton, Underhill, Caldebeck, Hinkley), 4: 329-34 (Pecche), 2: 644-46 (FitzWalter, FitzRobert), 1: 277-80 (St. Liz, Northumberland) and following the Lens solution, 1: 208-11 (Lens, Normandy), 1: 464 (Boulogne), 5: 483-89 (generations 1-8) and *AR8*, line 148; *TG* 10 (1989, published 1994): 3-30 (David L. Greene) and sources cited therein, esp. the Pecche article in *CP* (vol. 10, pp. 333-38), Joan Corder, ed., *Visitation of Suffolk, 1561, Part I* (*HSPVS*, new ser., vol. 2, 1981), pp. 78, 86, 88 esp. (Pecche to

Knighton) and Walter C. Metcalfe, ed., *Visitation of Hertfordshire, 1634* (*HSPVS*, vol. 22, 1896), p. 34 (Bull). See also Consuelo Furman, "St. Albans Origin of John Lawrence of New Amsterdam, Thomas Lawrence of Newtown, L.I., William Lawrence of Flushing, L.I." (typescript, revised 1955), pp. 2-4 (but ignore her identification of John Lawrence's wife, paternal grandmother of the immigrants), 9-41.

Everard, Boddie and **Bathurst** Sources: *TAG* 27 (1951): 208-10, *NEHGR* 160 (2006): 109-11, *FNE*, pp. 315, 391-410, *VHG*, pp. 230-33, *HSF* 1:338, Pecche article in *CP*, esp. vol. 10, p. 337, note 1) and *TG* 10 (1989, published 1994): 3-5, 23-24, and sources for generations 1-16 as above; (Mrs. Appleton and Boddie); *HSF* 8: 135-37 (Bathurst); T.F. Fenwick and W.C. Metcalfe, eds., *Visitation of Gloucester, 1682-3* (1884), pp. 142-43 (Rich), 20 (Bourchier); W.C. Metcalfe, ed., *Visitations of Essex, 1552, 1558, 1570, 1612 and 1634*, vol. 1 (*HSPVS*, vol. 13, 1878), pp. 250-51, 452 (Mildmay). A thorough monograph on the immediate ancestry of William Boddie of Va. would be welcome, since J.B. Boddie gives few details. See also J.T. and J.B. Boddie, *Boddie and Allied Families* (1918), introductory data and charts. *RA* 4: 333-34 gives a Simon Pecche as a brother but not a second son of the 1st Baron. *VHG*, *HSF* 1 and Rev. Charles Moor, *Knights of Edward I, Volume 4* (*HSPVS*, vol. 83, 1932), p. 24 (messuage at Holyngborn, held jointly by the 1st Baron, his wife Iseult and their son Simon), all cover or mention a second son of the 1st Baron and the chronology seems likely.

Halsnode Sources: *TAG* 68 (1993): 193-204 (generations 15-29 by Col. Charles M. Hansen), *TG* 10 (1989, published 1994): 3-5, 23-24 (generations 1-15 by Neil D. Thompson). See also Arthur Adams, *Richard Hancock and The Founding of Bridgeton, New Jersey* (1936, reprinted from *Proceedings of the New Jersey Historical Society* 54 [1936]: 209-17); James Robinson Planché, *A Corner of Kent, or Some Account of the Parish of Ash-Next-Sandwich* (1864), pp. 339-40, 347 (Harfleet); *Berry's Kent*, p. 106 (Brockhull); *MGH*, 5th ser., 6 (1926-28): 255-56 and *Publications of the Bedfordshire Historical Record Society* 14 (1931): chart opp. p. 133 esp. (Criol); *CP* (Pecche); *RA* 4: 329-33 (de Criol/Kyriel, Pecche) and sources for generations 1-15 as above. Material on the immediate family of Mrs. Margaret Halsnode Denn(e) was also collected by the late Mary Ann Nicholson.

The Royal Descents of 900 Immigrants

1. Turlough Oge O'Conor Don, King of Connaught, d. 1406 = Evaine O'Kelly
2. Felim Geancach O'Conor Don = Edwina O'Conor Sligo
3. Owen Caech O'Conor Don = Devorgilla O'Conor Roe
4. Carbery O'Conor Don = ——
5. Dermot O'Conor Don = Dorothy O'Conor Roe
6. Sir Hugh O'Conor Don = Mary O'Rourke of Breffney
7. Cathal O'Conor = Anne O'Molloy of Aughtertire
8. Charles Oge O'Conor = Cecilia O'Flynn of Ballinlough
9. Denis O'Conor = Mary O'Rourke of Breffney, a cousin
10. Charles O'Conor, antiquary = Catharine O'Fagan
11. Charles O'Conor, said to have died in America = —— Dillon. Their son, Denis O'Con(n)or and daughter Catherine O'Connor, also immigrated to N.Y. but to my knowledge left no NDTPS.
12. **Thomas O'Con(n)or** of N.Y. = Margaret O'Connor. Their son, Charles O'Conor (1804-84) was a noted lawyer, 1872 presidential candidate (the first nominated Catholic), and leader of the Friends of Ireland, who married Mrs. Cornelia Livingston McCracken.

Sources: *BIFR*, pp. 901-2 and *DAB* (Charles O'Conor). I first noticed the likely gentry origin of this immigrant while perusing Henry L.P. Beckwith, ed., *A Roll of Arms* (of) *the Committee on Heraldry of the New England Historic Genealogical Society* (2013), at pp. 271-72. John Blythe Dobson of Winnipeg, Manitoba, brings to my attention a volume on Google Books: Figgis Hodges, *The O'Conors of Connaught: An Historical Memoir* (1891). Chapter 25, pp. 292-307, covers the antiquary and his American descendants.

The Royal Descents of 900 Immigrants

1. Cynfyn ap Gwerystan, lord of Powys = Angharad, Queen of Powys and South Wales
2. Rhywallon, Prince of Powys, d. 1070 = ——
3. Sionet of Powys = Ednyfed ap Llywarch Gam
4. Rhys Sais ab Ednyfed = Efa ferch Gruffudd Hir
5. Elidir ap Rhys Sais = Nest ferch Lles
6. Sandde ab Elidir = ——
7. Hwfa ap Sandde = ——
8. Hwfa Gryg ap Hwfa = ——
9. Hwfa Fychan ap Hwfa Gryg = ——
10. Iorwerth ap Hwfa Fychan = ——
11. Madog Foel ab Iorwerth = ——
12. (possibly illegitimate) Rheinallt ap Madog Foel = ——
13. Owain ap Rheinallt = ——
14. Robert ab Owain = ——
15. William Coetmor = ——
16. Ieuan Coetmor = ——
17. Lewys ab Ieuan = Anne Wilson
18. Andrew Lewis = Mary Herring
19. **Thomas Lewis** of Maine = Elizabeth Marshall of Maine, ARD, SETH.
20. Judith Lewis = James Gibbins
21. Hannah Gibbins = —— Hibbert
22. Mary Hibbert = Joseph Jewett
23. Nathan Jewett = Deborah Lord
24. David Jewett = Sarah Selden
25. Elizabeth Jewett = Anselm Comstock

26. Betsey Comstock = Daniel Butler
27. George Selden Butler = Elizabeth Ely Gridley
28. Amy Gridley Butler = George Manney Ayer
29. Adele Augusta Ayer = Levi Addison Gardner
30. Dorothy Ayer Gardner = (1) Leslie Lynch King, m. (2) Gerald Rudolf Ford
31. Leslie Lynch King, Jr., whose name was changed to Gerald Rudolph Ford, Jr. (1913-2006), 38th U.S. President = Mrs. Elizabeth Ann (Betty) Bloomer Warren, known as Betty Ford (1918-2011), promoter of alcohol and drug rehabilitation, founder of the Betty Ford Center in Rancho Mirage, Calif., author, SETH

Sources: *NEHGR* 101 (1947): 3-23, reprinted in *EO* 2: 2: 627-48; *Davis* 2: 445-65 (Lewis); *Bartrum 1*, pp. 47, 870, 887, 889, 890 and *Bartrum 2*, p. 1699 (generations 1-17).

The Royal Descents of 900 Immigrants

Immigrants Whose Royal Descents
or Improved Royal Descents
Were Received or Developed
After Much of this Volume had been Indexed

The Royal Descents of 900 Immigrants

1. Eric XIV, King of Sweden, d. 1577, son of Gustav (I) Vasa, King of Sweden, and Katherine of Saxe-Lauenburg, SETH = Katherine Månsdotter

2. (illegitimate by Agda Persdotter) = Virginia Eriksdotter = Håken Hand

3. Catherina Hand = Johann Rytter

4. Sofia Rytter = Axel, Baron Spens

5. Virginia, Baroness Spens = Henning Adolf, Baron Kruuse

6. Sofia Charlotta Kruuse = Sven, Baron Duwall, a descendant of Gustav I Vasa, King of Sweden

7. Axel, Baron Duwall = Anna Vendela Prytz

8. Axel Vilhelm, Baron Duwall = Sara Catherina Broman

9. Axel Jakob, Baron Duwall = Louisa Katharina, Countess Wachtmeister

10. Margaretha Louisa Charlotta, Baroness Duwall = Nils, Baron Gyllenstierna

11. Axel, Baron Gyllenstierna = Hedvig, Baroness Snoilsky. The spouses of 9., 10., and 11. above were all descendants of John III, King of Sweden, son of Gustav I Vasa, King of Sweden.

12. Hedvig Christina, Baroness Gyllenstierna = Carl Gustaf Moritz Ture, Count Lewenhaupt, son of Carl-Johan, Count Lewenhaupt (and Julia Regina Turinna, Baroness Uggla), son of Charles Emil, Count Lewenhaupt (and Aurora Vilhelmina, Baroness Alströmer), son of Mauritz Casimir, Count Lewenhaupt, SETH, and his first wife, Ulrica Charlotta, Countess Lewenhaupt, a cousin, daughter of Charles Emil, Count Lewenhaupt (and Berta Cronhielm), son of Carl Gustav, Count Lewenhaupt, and Anna Wilhelmine, Countess von Königsmarck, daughter of Conrad Christopher, Count von Königsmarck, and Maria Christina, Baroness Wrangel, daughter of Swedish Field Marshal Herman Wrangel and Amalia Magdalena of Nassau-Siegen, daughter of John III, Count of Nassau-Siegen and Margaret of Schleswig-Holstein-Sonderburg, daughter of John II, Duke of Schleswig-Holstein-Sonderburg (and Elizabeth of Brunswick), son of Christian III, King of Denmark, d. 1559, and Dorothea of Saxe-Lauenburg, SETH. Of the spouses in this line,

Carl Gustav and Mauritz Casimir, Counts Lewenhaupt, were descendants of John III, King of Sweden, son of Gustav I Vasa, King of Sweden.

13. **Hedvig Margaretha, Countess Lewenhaupt**, of Calif. = Jan-Casimir (Eric Emil, Count) **Lewenhaupt**, b. 1916, SETH, San Francisco retailer and longtime board member (director) of the Hastings College of the Law at the University of California, ARD, SETH.

Sources: Extensive research by Thomas F. Gede of Davis, Calif., also in *Elgenstierna*, vol. 4, pp. 612-16, 605-6 (Lewenhaupt), vol. 3, pp. 365-66 (Gyllenstierna), vol. 2, p. 361-62 (Duwall), vol. 4, p. 316 (Kruuse), vol. 7, p. 429 (Spens), vol. 6, p. 242 (Reuter/Rytter), vol. 3, p. 481-872 (Hand), vol. 9, pp. 33-34, 20 (Wrangel); *ES*, charts for Königsmarck (2: 20: 15) and Nassau-Siegen, Schleswig-Holstein-Sonderburg and Denmark.

The Royal Descents of 900 Immigrants

1. Ferdinand I, Holy Roman Emperor, d. 1564 = Anne of Bohemia, SETH

2. Maria of Austria = William III, Duke of Cleves, Juliers and Berg

3. Marie Eleanor of Cleves = Albert Frederick, Duke of Prussia

4. Magdalen Sybilla of Prussia = John George I, Elector of Saxony, son of Christian I, Elector of Saxony (and Sophia of Brandenburg), son of Augustus, Elector of Saxony and Anne of Denmark, daughter of Christian III, King of Denmark, and Dorothea of Saxe-Lauenburg, SETH.

5. Augustus, Duke of Saxe-Weissenfels = Anna Maria of Mecklenburg-Schwerin

6. Magdalen Sybil of Saxe-Weissenfels = Frederick II, Duke of Saxe-Gotha

7. Anna Sophia of Saxe-Gotha = Louis Frederick I, Prince of Schwarzburg-Rudolstadt

8. William Henry, Prince of Schwarzburg-Rudolstadt = (morganatic) Henriette-Caroline Gebsuer, Baroness von Brockenburg

9. Louise Henrietta, Baroness von Brockenburg = Christoph Ferdinand Anton, Count von Rantzow

10. Julius Friedrich Ludwig, Count von Rantzow, of St. Croix = Elizabeth de Windt

11. Juliette Marie Elizabeth, Countess von Rantzow = William Stephen Jacobs

12. Marie Louise Rantzow Jacobs = Benton Danielsen

13. **Josephine Alma Danielsen** of N.Y. = Carl Conrad **Berg**. A daughter, Agnes Marie Louise Berg, married Louis Joseph Barta and was the mother of Frank Kenneth Barta, churchman and Virgin Islands genealogist (co-author with Henry Bainbridge Hoff of a de Windt monograph in *TG* 3, 4, 6, 10, 24 [1982, 1983, 1985, 1989, 2010]), d. unm.

The Royal Descents of 900 Immigrants

Sources: *PSECD* 3, pp. 667-70 (submitted by F.K. Barta) (line from Ferdinand, but undocumented), plus *TG* 4 (1983): 27-28, 53; *ES2*, charts for Schwarzburg-Rudolstadt, Saxe-Gotha, Saxe-Weissenfels, Saxony, Prussia, Cleves, Austria and Denmark. Louis Frederick I, Prince of Schwarzburg-Rudolstadt and Anna Sophia of Saxe-Gotha, at generation 7 above, are ancestors I 63-64, p. 11, in *Prince Charles*, and the lines above continue at J 127-28, p. 18, I 557-58, p. 13, J 715-16, p. 22, K 1429-30, p. 35, K 73-74, p. 28, L 139-40, 145-48, p. 43, M 279-80, 289-90, p. 66, N 559-60, 579-80, p. 100, M 1-2, p. 62.

The Royal Descents of 900 Immigrants

1. Christian III, King of Denmark, d. 1559 = Dorothea of Saxe-Lauenburg

2. Dorothea of Denmark = William, Duke of Brunswick-Lüneburg

3. Dorothea of Brunswick-Lüneburg = Charles I, Count Palatine of Zweibrücken-Birkenfeld

4. Sophie of Zweibrücken-Birkenfeld = Kraft, Count of Hohenlohe-Neuenstein

5. Charlotte Susanna Maria of Hohenlohe-Neuenstein = Ludvig Wierich, Count Lewenhaupt

6. Carl Julius, Count Lewenhaupt = Christina Gustaviana, Baroness Horn, a descendant of John III, King of Sweden, son of Gustav I Vasa, King of Sweden

7. Mauritz Casimir, Count Lewenhaupt = (2) Anna, Baroness Palbitski, daughter of Ulric Adolf, Baron Palbitski, and Hon. Anna Sunderland, daughter of Kenneth Sutherland, 3rd Baron Duffus (and Charlotte Christina, Baroness Sjöbard), son of James Sutherland, 2nd Baron Duffus (and Margaret Mackenzie), son of Alexander Sutherland, 1st Baron Duffus, and Margaret Stewart, daughter of James Stewart, 4th Earl of Moray and Margaret Home, SETH. The 4th Earl of Moray was a great-great-grandson of James V, King of Scotland, d. 1542 (and Margaret Erskine).

8. Ludvig Wierich, Count Lewenhaupt = Ebba Margaretha, Baroness Palbitski, a first cousin, daughter of Adam, Baron Palbitski (and Magdalena Dorothea Moréen), son of Ulric Adolf, Baron Palbitski, and Anna Sutherland above.

9. Fabian Mathias Emil, Count Lewenhaupt = Justina Margaretha Travenfert

10. Ludvig Fabian Mathias Emil, Count Lewenhaupt = Ida Felicia Louise Gosling, a descendant of John III, King of Sweden, mentioned above

11. **Eric Emil Audley, Count Lewenhaupt**, of Calif. = Azalea Caroline Keyes. Their son, Jan-Casimir (Eric) Emil, Count Lewenhaupt, b. 1916, San Francisco retailer and longtime board member (director) of the Hastings College of the Law at the

The Royal Descents of 900 Immigrants

University of California, who married Hedvig Margaretha, Countess Lewenhaupt, also of Calif., a cousin, ARD, SETH.

Sources: extensive research by Thomas F. Gede of Davis, Calif., also in *Elgenstierna*, vol. 4, pp. 610-13, 625, 627 (Lewenhaupt, to Jan-Casimir [Eric Emil]); vol. 5, pp. 622 (Palbitski), *ES*, charts for Hohenlohe-Neuenstein (2: 17: 6), Zweibrücken-Birkenfeld, Brunswick-Lüneburg and Denmark, *SP*, vol. 3, pp. 207-13 (Duffus, including the Palbitski marriage), *SP*, *CP* and *BP* (Moray).

The Royal Descents of 900 Immigrants

1. Sigismund I, King of Poland, d. 1548 (son of Casimir IV, King of Poland, and Elizabeth of Austria, SETH) = (1) Barbara Zápolya, (2) Bona Sforza
2. (illegitimate by Katarzyna Telniczanka) Katarzyna of Poland = George II, Count of Montfort-Pfannberg
3. James, Count of Montfort-Pfannberg = Katharina Fugger von Kirchberg
4. Katharina of Montfort = Adam von Neuhaus
5. Lucia Ottilia von Neuhaus = Wilhelm Slawata
6. Joachim Ulrich Slawata of Chlumu and Kosumberka = Franziska von Meggau
7. Johann Georg Joachim Slawata, Baron Slawata = Maria Margareta Trautson
8. Maria Magdalena Slawata = Norbert Leopold Kolowrat-Liebsteinsky
9. Norbert Vincent Kolowrat-Liebsteinsky = Maria Anna von Althann
10. Eleonora Kolowrat-Liebsteinsky = Franz Ferdinand von Schrattenbach
11. Maria Johanna Josefa Franziska Klara Serafina von Schrattenbach = Joseph Karl von Zierotin
12. Antonia von Zierotin, Duchess von Lilgenau = Johann Nepomuk, Count Mittrowsky von Mitrowitz
13. Wilhelm, Count Mittrowsky von Mitrowitz = Marie Josephine, Baroness Schröfl von Mannsperg
14. Wladimir, Graf Mittrowsky von Mitrowitz = Julie von Salis-Zizers
15. Josepha Juliane, Countess Mittrowsky von Mitrowitz = Hubert Karl Sigismund Joseph Franz, Count de la Fontaine and d'Harnoncourt-Unverzagt, a descendant of Albert II, Holy Roman Emperor, King of Hungary and Bohemia, d. 1439, for whom see pp. 221-22.

16. **René Vladimir Hubert Maria, Count de la Fontaine and d'Harnoncourt-Unverzagt**, known as **René d'Harnoncourt** (1901-68), director of the Museum of Modern Art in New York City, expert on Native American art = Sara Carr. Their daughter, Anne Julie d'Harnoncourt (1943-2008), wife of Joseph Rishel, was director and CEO of the Philadelphia Museum of Art, 1982-2008.

Sources: *GH des A*, vol. 23, *Gräfliche Häuser B*, vol. 2 (1960), p. 117, 119 (de la Fontaine and d'Harnoncourt-Unverzagt); *Gothaisches Genealogisches Taschenbuch der Deutschen Gräflichen Häuser* 50 (1857): 512-13 (Mittrowsky von Nemýssl); Ignaz von Schönfeld, *Adelsschematismus des Österreichen Kaiserstaates*, vol. 1 (1824), 1: 200 (ancestor table of a sister of Antonia von Zierotin, at generation 12); *Böhmens Burgen, Festen und Bergschlösser*, vol. 6 (1848), pp. 5-117, at pp. 8, 12, 13, 14, 85 (Neuhaus); *Sitzungberichte der Kaiserlichen Academie der Wissenschaften, Philosophisch-Historische Classe* 9 (1853): 791-856b, at 831-32, and *ES2*: 12: 53-54 (Montfort-Pfannberg). This improved line was brought to my attention by John Blythe Dobson of Winnipeg, Manitoba, Canada.

The Royal Descents of 900 Immigrants

1. James V, King of Scotland, d. 1542 = (1) Madeleine of France; (2) Mary of Guise

2. (illegitimate by Eupheme Elphinstone) Robert Stewart, 1st Earl of Orkney = Janet Kennedy, daughter of Gilbert Kennedy, 3rd Earl of Cassillis, and Margaret Kennedy, SETH

3. Jean Stewart = Patrick Leslie, 1st Baron Lindores

4. Elizabeth Leslie = Sir James Sinclair, 1st Bt.

5. Anne Sinclair = George Mackenzie, 1st Earl of Cromarty

6. Sir James Mackenzie, 1st Bt. = Elizabeth Mackenzie   6. Jean Mackenzie = Sir Thomas Stewart, 1st Bt.

7. Elizabeth Mackenzie   =   7. Sir John Stewart, 3rd Bt.

8. Sir John Stewart, 4th Bt. = Clementina Stewart of Ballechin

9. Sir George Stewart, 5th Bt. = Catherine Drummond of Logie Almond

10. **Sir William (George) Drummond-Stewart, 7th Bt.** (1795-1871), sometime of Missouri and points west, traveler in the American West (especially the Rocky Mountains), collector of American Indian/Native American artifacts, novelist, patron of Western artist Alfred Jacob Miller (see *ANB*) = Christian Mary Stewart.

Sources: *WWWA, Historical Volume, 1607-1896, Revised Edition* (1963), p. 579 (Sir William Drummond Stewart), Odessa Davenport, *Scotsman in Buckskin* (1963), *passim*, esp. pp. 4-5, 17-19 (parentage and marriage), *CB* (Stewart, later Drummond-Stewart of Grandtully), *CP* or *BP* (Cromarty, Caithness [Sinclair], Lindores, Orkney).

The Royal Descents of 900 Immigrants

1. James I, King of Scotland, d. 1437 = Joan Beaufort, daughter of John Beaufort, Marquess of Somerset and Dorset, and Margaret Holand, SETH

2. Joan Stewart, "the dumb lady" = James Douglas, 1st Earl of Morton

3. John Douglas, 2nd Earl of Morton = Janet Crichton

4. Elizabeth Douglas = Robert, Lord Keith

5. Jean Keith = John Lyon, 6th Baron Glamis

6. Margaret Lyon = Gilbert Kennedy, 4th Earl of Cassillis, son of Gilbert Kennedy, 3rd Earl of Cassillis and Margaret Kennedy, SETH

7. Hon. Hew Kennedy = Katharine M'Dowell

8. Gilbert Kennedy = ——

9. Gilbert Kennedy = —— Montgomery

10. **Catherine Kennedy** of Pa. = William **Tennent** (1673-1746), Presbyterian clergyman, founder of the "Log College." Their sons include Presbyterian clergyman Gilbert Tennent, a leader in the Great Awakening (= [1] ——, [2] Mrs. Cornelia De Peyster Clarkson; [3] Mrs. Sarah [——] Spofford) and William Tennent, Jr., also a noted Presbyterian clergyman, and like his brother Gilbert, a supporter of The College of New Jersey (= Mrs. Catherine Van Brugh Noble). This last was the father of William Tennent (III), noted Congregationalist minister in S.C., who married Suzanne Vergereau.

Sources: *DAB*, *ANB* and *Oxford DNB* on the several noted Tennents, and esp. James McGuire and James Quinn, *Dictionary of Irish Biography*, vol. 5 (2009), pp. 110-11 (for Gilbert Kennedy, also a Presbyterian clergyman, brother of Catherine Kennedy Tennent, which names his sister and parents and states the kinship to the Earls of Cassillis, plus the other *DIB* Tennent entries as well); *GM* 7 (1935-37): 593 (in a series of "Fasti of the Irish Presbyterian Church" by Rev. James and Rev. S.G. McConnell), covering Thomas Kennedy, "eld. s. of Gilbert Kennedy [b. 1625], Ardmillan, Ayrshire, and neph. of John, 6th Earl of Cassilis; bro. of Rev. Gilbert Kennedy, Dundonald"; Hew Scott, ed., *Fasti Ecclesiae Scoticanae*, vol. 2, part 1 (1868), p. 117, for Rev. Gilbert Kennedy of Girvan at generation 9 above; *SP* and *CP* (Cassillis [to Gilbert at generation 8], Glamis, Marischal and Morton); *RA* 1: 656-59 (first four generations). The probability of royal descent for Mrs. Tennent was brought to my attention by Henry Bainbridge Hoff.

The Royal Descents of 900 Immigrants

1. Edward III, King of England, d. 1377 = Philippa of Hainault
2. John of Gaunt, Duke of Lancaster = Catherine Roët
3. Henry Beaufort, Cardinal Beaufort
4. (illegitimate, allegedly, but probably not, by Alice FitzAlan, who = John Cherleton, 4th Baron Cherleton of Powis) Jane Beaufort = Sir Edward Stradling
5. Sir Henry Stradling = Elizabeth Herbert
6. Thomas Stradling = Janet Mathew
7. Jane Stradling = Sir William Griffith
8. Edward Griffith = Jane Puleston
9. Eleanor Griffith = Sir Nicholas Bagenall
10. Frances Bagenall = Oliver Plunkett, 4th Baron Louth
11. Matthew Plunkett, 5th Baron Louth = Mary FitzWilliam
12. Margaret Plunkett = Sir Christopher Aylmer, 1st Bt., see p. 487. A grandson was Sir Peter Warren of N.Y., naval officer in the American colonies; a great-grandson was Sir William Johnson, 1st Bt., of N.Y., Mohawk Valley pioneer and superintendent of Indian affairs in the American colonies; great-great-grandchildren were Guy Johnson of N.Y., northern superintendent of Indian affairs 1774-1782, and a loyalist, his wife and first cousin Mary Johnson (daughter of Sir William, 1st Bt.) and loyalist John Dease of N.Y., Detroit and Montréal, also an official in the Indian Department; and great-great-great-grandchildren were Mrs. Matilda Cecilia Dowdall Shedden of N.J. and Peter Warren Dease, the Canadian Arctic explorer.

Sources: *CB* (Aylmer), *CP* (Louth) and Bagenall, Griffith, Stradling and Beaufort sources per p. 382—*BIFR*, p. 45 (Bagenall), *PACF*, pp. 56-57 (Griffith) and *RA* 2: 345-46 (Griffith, which unfortunately omits the above Edward Griffith at generation 8), 5: 52-57 (Stradling, Beaufort). This improved descent was brought to my attention by John Blythe Dobson of Winnipeg, Manitoba, Canada.

The Royal Descents of 900 Immigrants

1. Edward III, King of England, d. 1377 = Philippa of Hainault
2. Lionel of Antwerp, Duke of Clarence = Elizabeth de Burgh
3. Philippa Plantagenet = Edmund Mortimer, 3rd Earl of March
4. Elizabeth Mortimer = Sir Henry "Hotspur" Percy
5. Henry Percy, 2nd Earl of Northumberland = Eleanor Neville
6. Catherine Percy = Edmund Grey, 1st Earl of Kent
7. George Grey, 2nd Earl of Kent = Catherine Herbert
8. Hon. Anthony Grey = —— Holland
9. George Grey = Margery Salvain
10. Anthony Grey, 9th Earl of Kent = Magdalen Purefoy
11. Henry Grey, 10th Earl of Kent = Amabel Benn
12. Elizabeth Grey = Banastre Maynard, 3rd Baron Maynard
13. Dorothy Maynard = Sir Robert Hesilrige, 6th Bt., son of Sir Robert Hesilrige (and Bridget Rolle), son of Sir Arthur Hesilrige, 2nd Bt., the Puritan leader, and Dorothy Grevile, SETH
14. Sir Arthur Hesilrige, 7th Bt. = Hannah Sturges
15. **Sir Robert Hesilrige, 8th Bt.**, sometime of Mass. = Sarah Walter.

Sources: *TAG* 88 (2016): 257-69 (John C. Brandon; the immigrant, his wife and descendants. Charles Fairfax Henley, Sir Robert's great-grandson [p. 269] and Kittie Jones, his wife, left a daughter, Norma Lavinia Henley, who married Sidney Gordon Gilbreath, Tennessee educator; see *NCAB, Current Volume A* [1930]: 177); *Nichols*, vol. 4, pt. 1, p. 245 (Grey), *CB* (Hesilrige) and *CP* (Kent, Northumberland, March). Note also *RA* 3: 131-34 (Grey, to Hon. Anthony), 4: 355-59 (Percy).

The Royal Descents of 900 Immigrants

1. Edward III, King of England, d. 1377 = Philippa of Hainault
2. John of Gaunt, Duke of Lancaster = Catherine Roët
3. Joan Beaufort = Ralph Neville, 1st Earl of Westmoreland
4. Richard Neville, 1st Earl of Salisbury = Alice Montagu
5. Eleanor Neville = Thomas Stanley, 1st Earl of Derby
6. George Stanley, Baron Strange = Joan Strange, daughter of John Strange, 8th Baron Strange of Knokyn, and Jacquetta Woodville, sister of Elizabeth Woodville, Queen of Edward IV, King of England
7. Sir James Stanley = Anne Hart
8. Eleanor Stanley = Gilbert Langtree
9. Edward Langtree = Isabella Anderton
10. Catherine Langtree = William Thornborough, son of Rowland Thornborough (and Jane Dalton), son of William Thornborough (and Ethelred Carus), son of Sir William Thornborough and Thomasine Bellingham, SETH
11. Charles Thornborough = Elizabeth Leybourne, daughter of Thomas Leybourne and Dorothy Lascelles, daughter of William Lascelles and Elizabeth Tunstall, daughter of Francis Tunstall and Anne Bold, daughter of Richard Bold (and Elizabeth Gerard, daughter of Sir Thomas Gerard and Margaret Trafford, SETH), son of Sir Richard Bold (and Margaret Boteler, daughter of Sir Thomas Boteler and Margaret Delves, SETH), son of Sir Henry Bold and Dulcia Savage, SETH
12. Robert Thornborough/Thornburg = Sarah Jackson. Two younger sons, Thomas and Walter Thornborough ("Thornburg") immigrated to Va., married (Mary —— and Margaret —— respectively) and left descendants but no NDTPS.
12. **Edward Thornborough/Thornburg** of Pa. = —— ——.

Sources: Charles C. Thornburgh III, *A Discourse on the Thornburg Family* [*of England, Ireland and America*] (1979, hastily assembled and repetitive, brought to my attention by Randall R. M. Redman of

Sicklerville, N.J., who also found that a Thomas Langtree was among the four Quakers of the Ulster Province Meeting assigned to determine the suitability of the 1686 marriage of Robert Thornborough and Sarah Jackson of co. Cavan; an earlier Thomas Langtree was the son and heir of Edward and Isabella of generation 9), pp. 79-80, 82-86, esp. 85-86, which cites Dwight H. Thornburg, *Short Family History* (1954, not yet seen) and *BRMF2*, pp. 219-23, which lists various sources on pp. 214-15; *Baines 2*, vol. 4, p. 226 and Leonard Smethby and Randle Holme, "Letters of the Claims of the College of Arms in Lancashire in the Time of James the First," p. 5 (#3 of Rev. F.R. Raines, *Chetham Miscellanea*, vol. 5, *Chetham Society Publications* [*CSP*] 46 [1875] [Langtree]) and *CSP* 88 (1873): 288 (Stanley); *RA* 5: 28-31 (Stanley), 4: 124-26 (Neville), *TCWAAS* 10 (1889), chart opp. p. 124 (Layborn, Leyburne), *Foster's V of Yorkshire*, p. 61 (Lascelles), *Baines 1*, vol. 4, p. 616 (Tunstall), *Baines 2*, vol. 5 p. 25 (Bold), *PCF2* (Gerard), *RA* 1: 446-48 (Boteler), 3: 83 (Gerard).

The Royal Descents of 900 Immigrants

1. Edward III, King of England, d. 1377 = Philippa of Hainault
2. Lionel of Antwerp, Duke of Clarence = Elizabeth de Burgh
3. Philippa Plantagenet = Edmund Mortimer, 3rd Earl of March
4. Elizabeth Mortimer = Sir Henry "Hotspur" Percy
5. Henry Percy, 2nd Earl of Northumberland = Eleanor Neville
6. Anne Percy = Sir Thomas Hungerford
7. Mary Hungerford = Edward Hastings, 2nd Baron Hastings
8. Anne Hastings = Thomas Stanley, 2nd Earl of Derby
9. Edward Stanley, 3rd Earl of Derby = Dorothy Howard, daughter of Thomas Howard, 2nd Duke of Norfolk and Agnes Tilney, SETH
10. Henry Stanley, 4th Earl of Derby = Margaret Clifford, SETH
11. (illegitimate by ——) Dorothy Stanley = Sir Cuthbert Halsall
12. Anne Halsall = Thomas Clifton
13. **James Clifton** of Md. = Anne **Brent** of Md., ARD, SETH.

Sources: *Baines 2*, vol. 5, p. 385 (Clifton, Halsall), *CP* (Derby, Hastings, Northumberland) and *RA* 5: 32 (Stanley), 3: 370-71 (Hastings), 3: 363-64 (Hungerford), 4: 355-59 (Percy), 4: 174-76 (Mortimer).

The Royal Descents of 900 Immigrants

1. Edward III, King of England, d. 1377 = Philippa of Hainault
2. Lionel of Antwerp, Duke of Clarence = Elizabeth de Burgh
3. Philippa Plantagenet = Edmund Mortimer, 3rd Earl of March
4. Elizabeth Mortimer = Sir Henry "Hotspur" Percy
5. Henry Percy, 2nd Earl of Northumberland = Eleanor Neville
6. Anne Percy = Sir Thomas Hungerford
7. Mary Hungerford = Edward Hastings, 2nd Baron Hastings
8. Anne Hastings = Thomas Stanley, 2nd Earl of Derby
9. Margaret Stanley = Robert Radcliffe, 1st Earl of Sussex
10. Jane Radcliffe = Anthony Browne, 1st Viscount Montagu
11. Hon. Anthony Browne = Mary Dormer
12. Anthony Maria Browne, 2nd Viscount Montagu = Jane Sackville
13. Mary Browne = Hon. William Arundell, son of Thomas Arundell, 1st Baron Arundell of Wardour, SETH (he = [2] Anne Philipson) and Mary Wriothesley, daughter of Henry Wriothesley, 2nd Earl of Southampton, and Mary Browne, daughter of Anthony Browne, 1st Viscount Montagu, and Jane Radcliffe above
14. Mary Arundell = Sir Henry Tichborne, 3rd Bt., son of Sir Richard Tichborne, 2nd Bt., SETH, and Susan Waller, a second wife, daughter of William Waller (and —— Somester), son of Sir Richard Waller and Margery Paulet, daughter of William Paulet, 1st Marquess of Winchester (and Elizabeth Willoughby), son of Sir John Paulet and Alice Paulet, SETH.
15. Letitia Tichborne = Henry Whetenhall. Two sons, (Father) Henry and John Whetenhall, also immigrated to Md., the former to the Maryland Jesuit Mission, 1724-ca. 1736-37; the latter apparently died unmarried.
16. **Elizabeth Whetenhall** of Md. = Notley **Rozer/Rozier**.

Sources: Research of Nathan W. Murphy of Salt Lake City, posted on soc.genealogy.medieval and based on the 1727 and 1732 wills of Notley and Mrs. Elizabeth Whetenhall Rozier (the former witnessed by [Father] Henry and John Whetenhall and the latter by [Father] Henry Whetenhall only) and Henry Foley, *Records of the English Province of the Society of Jesus*, vol. 7, pt. 2 (1883), p. 831 (biography of Father Henry Whetenhall, naming his parents and indicating residence in Maryland as above); *EB* and *CB* (Tichborne), W. Harry Rylands et al., *Visitations of Hampshire, 1530, 1575, 1622* (*HSPVS*, vol. 64, 1913), p. 140 (Waller) and *BP* (Winchester), *RA* 2: 170 (Arundell of Wardour) and *EP* (Browne, Viscounts Montagu); *RA* 5: 136-38 (Browne), 2: 43-44 (Radcliffe), 5: 32 (Stanley), 3: 370-71 (Hastings), 3: 363-64 (Hungerford), 4: 355-59 (Percy), 4: 174-76 (Mortimer). This line was brought to my attention by Douglas Richardson and the Internet posting by John C. Brandon.

The Royal Descents of 900 Immigrants

1. Louis IV (of Bavaria), Holy Roman Emperor, d. 1347 = (1) Beatrix of Glogau; (2) Margaret of Holland

2. (by 2) William, Count of Holland = Matilda Plantagenet of Lancaster

3. (illegitimate by Catharina Gerrit Busendochter) Elisabeth van Beieren = Brustijn van Herwijnen, Heer van Stavenisse

4. Adelise van Herwijnen = Otto, Heer van Haeften

5. Walraven, Heer van Haeften = Hendrika van Varick

6. Beatrix van Haeften = Johan, Heer van Rossem

7. Meralda van Rossem = Willem van Gendt, Heer van Oyen en [and] Dieden

8. Walraven van Gendt, Heer van Oyen en Dieden = Elisabeth von Raesfeld

9. Johan Gerard van Gendt, Heer van Oyen en Dieden = Wilhelmina von Wachtendonk (ancestors of Juliana, Queen of The Netherlands)

10. (illegitimate by ——) Moralla Jans van Gendt = Hendrik Copes van Vorden

11. Otto Copes = Josina Schade van Westrum

12. Moralla Catharina Copes = Johan Louis van Cattenburch

13. Willem Hendrik van Cattenburch, Heer van Grijpskerke en [and] Poppendamme = Jeanne des Tombe

14. Dirk Lodewijk van Cattenburch = Wilhelmina Antonia Erbervelt

15. Cornelia Margaretha Wilhelmina van Cattenburch = Isaac Nicolaas Johan van Mierop

16. Johan Hendrik Daniel Schenkenberg van Mierop = Johanna Elisabeth Beelaerts

17. Lodewijk Hendrik Schenkenberg van Mierop = Jannetje Gijsbertje Pijnacker Hordijk

18. Lodewijk Hendrik Schenkenberg van Mierop = Marie Constance Legrand

19. Lodewijk Hendrik Schenkenberg van Mierop = Johanna Louisa Thies

20. Robert Lodewijk Schenkenberg van Mierop = Marianne Yvonne Wientjes

21. **Marcus Lodewijk Schenkenberg van Mierop**, known as **Marcus Schenkenberg**, sometime of Calif., b. 1968, model and actor, unm.

Sources: A well-documented ancestor table for Marcus Schenkenberg, at www.genealogics.org/ahnentafel.php?personID=100491635&tree=LEO&parentset=0&generations=12 [and connecting pages], covering this entire line, plus Wikipedia article on the model; Ian Fettes and Leo van de Pas, *Plantagenet Cousins* (2007), pp. 18-20 (Wilhelm/William V of Bavaria to Marcus Schenkenberg); *Nederland's Patriciaat* (1960), pp. 256, 262-63, 265-67, (1972), p. 29 ([Schenckenberg] van Mierop), (1971), p. 89, 87 (van Cattenburch, Copes), W. Wynaendts van Resandt, *Genealogie van Hasselt* (1934), p. 363 (Copes), *Kwartierstatenboek* VI (1985), VII 166 47, *Ancestors of Queen Juliana*, #2868, #5736-37, *ES* 2: 8: 85 (van Gen[d]t, von Raesfeld), *Kwartierstatenboek VI* (1985), VII 186 (van Rossem), VII 191 7 (van Haeften), Rob Dix and Zeno Deurvorst, *Afstammingsreeksen van de Hertogen van Brabant* (2006), p. 151 (van Herwijnen). This descent was brought to my attention by John Blythe Dobson of Winnipeg, Manitoba, Canada, and Leo van de Pas wrote that the possibility of medieval ancestry for Marcus Schenkenberg was first suggested by Anthony Glenn Hoskins of Santa Rosa, California.

The Royal Descents of 900 Immigrants

1. Alphonso IX, King of León, d. 1230 = Berengaria, Queen of Castile, d. 1246, daughter of Alphonso VIII, King of Castile, and Eleanor Plantagenet, daughter of Henry II, King of England, d. 1189, and Eleanor of Aquitaine

2. Berengaria of León and Castile = John de Brienne, King of Jerusalem and Emperor of Constantinople, d. 1237

3. Jean de Brienne = Jeanne de Châteaudun

4. Blanche de Brienne = Sir William de Fienes

5. Margaret de Fienes = Edmund Mortimer, 1st Baron Mortimer

6. Maud Mortimer = Theobald de Verdun, 2nd Baron Verdun

7. Margery de Verdun = Sir John Crophull

8. Thomas Crophull = Sybil Delabere

9. Agnes Crophull = (1) Sir Walter Devereux, SETH; (2) Sir John Parr

10. (by 2) Sir Thomas Parr = Agnes Tunstall

11. Elizabeth Parr = Sir Christopher Moresby

12. Anne Moresby = Sir James Pickering

13. Anne Pickering = Sir Robert Bellingham

14. Thomasine Bellingham = Sir William Thornborough

15. Nicholas Thornborough = Isabella Salkeld

16. **Thomas Thornborough/Thornburg** of Va. = Alice Lane.

Sources: Charles C. Thornburgh III, *A Discourse on the Thornburg Family [of England, Ireland, and America]* (1979, hastily assembled and repetitive, brought to my attention by Randall R. M. Redman of Sicklerville, N.J.), pp. 35, 59, 96, 114, etc., which cites Dwight H. Thornburg, *Short Family History* (1954, not yet seen); Joseph Foster, ed., *Visitations of Cumberland and Westmorland, 1615, 1666* (n.d.), p. 4 (Bellingham); Joseph Nicolson and Richard Burn, *The History and Antiquities of the Counties of Westmorland and Cumberland*, vol. 1 (1777), p. 263 (Pickering); *Prince Charles*, vol. 2, #s P 57213-14 (p. 259),

Q 114427-28 (p. 428) (Pickering, Moresby, Parr); *RA* 4: 305 (Parr), 5: 245-50 (Crophull/Crophill, Verdun), 4: 168-70 (Mortimer), 1: 473-75 (Fiennes), 1: 536-40 (Brienne, León). The entire known ancestry of Sir James Pickering and Anne Moresby, for many generations, is charted in Ernest Flagg Henderson III, *Ancient, Medieval and More Recent Ancestors of Ernest Flagg Henderson IV and Roberta Campbell Henderson*, 4 vols. (2013), beginning on chart *BMM*, p. 85, and continuing, on this line, on charts *BMMR*, p. 256, and *BMBWH*, p. 544.

The Royal Descents of 900 Immigrants

1. William the Conqueror, King of England, d. 1087 = Matilda of Flanders
2. Adela of England = Stephen II, Count of Blois
3. Theobald II, Count of Champagne (elder brother of Stephen, King of England) = Matilda of Carinthia
4. Marie of Champagne = Odo, Duke of Burgundy
5. Matilda of Burgundy = Robert IV, Count of Auvergne
6. Marie of Auvergne = Albert, Baron de La Tour du Pin
7. Sibylle de La Tour du Pin = Siboud III de Beauvoir
8. Marguerite de Beauvoir = Guigues I Alleman, Seigneur de Champs and de Valbonnais
9. Odon II Alleman, Seigneur de Champs and de Valbonnais = Catherine Bérenger
10. Philippine Alleman = Amédée II, Seigneur de Chevron-Villette
11. Humbert IV de Chevron-Villette, Seigneur de Chevron and de Villette = Philippine ——
12. Humbert V de Chevron-Villette, Seigneur de Chevron and de Villette = Amphélise d'Aigle
13. Philippine de Chevron-Villette = Aymon d'Oron, Seigneur de Bossonens and d'Attalens
14. Catherine d'Oron = Jean de Blonay, Seigneur de St. Paul
15. Catherine de Blonay = Antoine de Belletruche, Seigneur d'Annuys
16. Pierre de Belletruche, Seigneur d'Annuys = Marie Bonivard, daughter of Pierre Bonivard, Seigneur de Saint-Michel des Déserts, and Marguerite de Grolée, daughter of Guy de Grolée, Seigneur de Saint-André-de-Briord (and Bonne de Chalant), son of Guy de Grolée, Seigneur de Passins (and Catherine de Varey), son of Guy de Grolée, Seigneur de Neyrieu, and Catherine de Tullins, daughter of Guy II, Seigneur de Tullins, and Béatrix de Montluel, daughter of Guy de Montluel, Seigneur de Châtillon, and Marguerite Alleman, daughter of the above Odon II

Alleman, Seigneur de Champs and de Valbonnais, and Catherine Bérenger

17. Mye de Belletruche = François de Poypon, Seigneur de Chanay
18. Jeanne de Poypon = Jean Favre
19. Antoine Favre = Philiberte ─────
20. Marie Favre = Jean de La Maisonneuve
21. Élisabeth de La Maisonneuve = Marin Gallatin
22. Marin Gallatin = Sarah de Tudert
23. Françoise Gallatin = Jean Gallatin, her first cousin once removed, son of Louis Gallatin (and Victoria Carcassola), son of Aimé Gallatin (and Madeleine Humbert), son of Marin Gallatin and Élisabeth de La Maisonneuve (see generation 21 above)
24. Jean Gallatin = Barbe Gervais
25. Abraham Gallatin = Louise-Susanne Vaudenet
26. Jean Gallatin = Sophie-Albertine Rolaz du Rosey
27. **(Abraham-Alphonse) Albert Gallatin** (1761-1849) of N.Y., U.S. Secretary of the Treasury under Jefferson, diplomat, a founder of New York University = (1) Sophie D'Allègre; (2) Hannah Nicholson.

Sources: "The Gallatin Genealogy," in Henry Adams, ed., *The Writings of Albert Gallatin*, vol. 3 (1879), pp. 593-615, William Plumb Bacon, *Ancestry of Albert Gallatin...and of Hannah Nicholson* (1914), esp. the Gallatin charts on pp. 6-8 (generations 21-27); Jacques-Augustin Galiffe, *Notices Généalogiques sur les Familles Genevoises*, 1st ed., vol. 1 (1829), pp. 366-80 (Gallatin), 385-94 (La Maisonneuve), 115-25 (Favre); E. Amédée de Foras, *Armorial et Nobiliaire d'Ancien Duchée de Savoie*, vol. 5 (1910), pp. 15-19 (Poypon), vol. 1 (1863), pp. 171-74 (Belletruche), 211-32 (Blonay), 247-52 (Bonivard), vol. 2 (1878), pp. 5-31 (Chevron-Villette); André de Moura, *40,000 Ancêtres du Comte de Paris (1908-1999)*, vol. 2, *Générations #26 à 65* (2007) (generations 1-9, esp. pp. 444, 518 for generations 8-9, plus Montluel and Tullins), which cites Michel Rieuford, *Les Allemans de Dauphiné et de Faucigny* (1988); and *D de la N* 9: 887-88, 894-95, 909-10 (Grolée). This line was developed and brought to my attention by John Blythe Dobson of Winnipeg, Manitoba, Canada.

The Royal Descents of 900 Immigrants

An Addition to the Duncanson Chart on p. 248

10. Katherine/Catalin Duncanson = Sander Leendertze (Alexander) Glen

11. Johannes Sanderse (John Alexander) Glen = Anna Peeck

12. Jacob Sanderse (Alexander) Glen (N.Y. to Md.) = Anne Hanson

13. Jacob Glen (Jr.) = Rebecca Miller

14. Martha Glen = Thomas Maslin (III)

15. Michael Miller Maslin = Eliza Sarah Mohler

16. Caroline Maslin = Robert Ewing

17. Caroline Maslin Ewing = John Vernou Bouvier

18. John Vernou Bouvier, Jr. = Maude Frances Sergeant

19. John Vernou Bouvier (III) = Janet Norton Lee. Their daughter, (Caroline) Lee Bouvier, known as Lee Radziwill, b. 1933, socialite, = (1) Michael Temple Canfield; (2) Stanislaus Albert, Prince Radziwill, sometime of N.Y., SETH; (3) Herbert David Ross, film and Broadway producer/director. Her only son was noted television producer Anthony (Stanislaus Albert, Prince) Radziwill (1959-1999), who married Carole Di Falco, the television actress known as Carole Radziwill.

20. Jacqueline Lee Bouvier, known as Jackie Kennedy or Jackie Onassis (1929-1994), society and fashion leader, editor, = (1) John Fitzgerald Kennedy (1917-1963), senator, 35th U.S. president, SETH, son of Joseph Patrick Kennedy, the financier and diplomat; brother of Robert Francis Kennedy, U.S. Senator and Attorney General, of Edward Moore Kennedy, U.S. Senator, of Mrs. (Robert) Sargent Shriver, Jr. (Eunice Mary Kennedy), wife of the Democratic vice-presidential nominee, of Mrs. Jean Ann Kennedy Smith, diplomat, and of Mrs. Peter (Sidney Ernest Aylen, later) Lawford (Patricia Helen Kennedy), wife of the actor, SETH; uncle of Congressman Joseph Patrick Kennedy (III) and Patrick Joseph Kennedy, and of Maria (Owings) Shriver, television newscaster and wife of Arnold (Alois) Schwarzenegger, bodybuilder, actor, and governor of

California; and great-uncle of Congressman Joseph Patrick Kennedy (IV). Mrs. Kennedy married (2) Aristotle Socrates Onassis (1906-1975), Greek shipping magnate. The President and Jacqueline's daughter, Caroline Bouvier Kennedy (b. 1957, wife of Edwin Arthur Schlossberg), is a diplomat.

Sources: Alexander Bannerman, ed., *Executive Papers* 13 (2016): 9-18 (plus a specially printed extended monograph issued in early 2017; more will appear in #14): 9-18 (a full AT of Mrs. Onassis, the former First Lady), plus John Sanders, [*Centennial Address Relating to the*] *Early History of Schenectady and Its First Settlers* (1879), pp. 29-38, with some coverage of the Baltimore Glens and mention (p. 38) of a visit of the book's author and a brother to their cousins, Judge Elias Glen (a grandson of Jacob Sanderse [Alexander] Glen and Anne Hanson at generation 12 above) and the Judge's son John (later also a judge) in Baltimore in 1825.

The Royal Descents of 900 Immigrants

**Two Speculative
Descents for Six Further
Immigrants to New England,
Including Israel Stoughton
and the Wife of Plymouth Colony Gov. John Carver**

The tentative lines that follow are offered as possibilities of keen interest that merit, and I hope will receive from well known scholars and readers, further attention. Articles on Bellingham and Lewknor daughters would be major contributions eagerly received. The descents below might be confirmed, disproved, or changed substantially, or alternative descents might be found for hitherto untraced spouses.

The Royal Descents of 900 Immigrants

1. John "Lackland," King of England, d. 1216 = Isabel of Angoulême
2. (illegitimate by —— de Warenne) Richard FitzRoy = Rohese of Dover
3. Lorette de Dover = Sir William Marmion
4. John Marmion, 1st Baron Marmion = Isabel ——
5. John Marmion, 2nd Baron Marmion = Maud Furnival
6. Avice Marmion = John Grey, 1st Baron Grey of Rotherfield
7. Sir Robert Grey, later Marmion = Lora St. Quintin
8. Elizabeth Marmion = Henry FitzHugh, 3rd Baron FitzHugh
9. Eleanor FitzHugh = Sir Thomas Tunstall
10. Elizabeth Tunstall = Sir Robert Bellingham
11. —— (daughter) Bellingham = said to marry Augustine Porter
12. Augustine Porter = Ellen Smith
13. Katherine Porter = William Smith, not a known kinsman
14. Eleanor Smith = Alexander White
15. **Catherine White** of Mass. = (1) (George?) **Leggett**; (2) John **Carver** (c. 1576-1621), first Governor of the Plymouth Colony (no descendants).
15. Bridget White = Rev. John Robinson (c. 1576-1624/5), minister of the Pilgrims in Leyden
16. **Isaac Robinson** of Mass. = (1) Margaret Hanford, niece of Timothy Hatherly, founder of Scituate, Mass.; (2) Mary ——.

Sources: *TAG* 17 (1940-41): 210-15, 18 (1941-42): 45-47 (Robinson, by Mary Lovering Holman); *MD* 43 (1993): 183-86 (Alexander White and his family, by R.S. Wakefield); *Lincolnshire Pedigrees*, pp. 899 (Smith of Honington and the Close of Lincoln [William and Eleanor]), 791 (Porter of Belton and Syston)—but note C.B. Norcliffe, ed., *Visitation of Yorkshire, 1563-64* (*HSPVS*, vol. 16, 1881), pp. 22-23, which lists five daughters of [Sir] Robert Bellingham and Elizabeth Tunstall, with their husbands, but none married to an Augustine Porter; Edmund Miller, *George Herbert's Kinships: An Ahnentafel with Annotations* (1993), p. 33, 49, 85-86 (generations 8-10) and *RA* 4: 274-76 (Grey), 4: 31-33 (Marmion), 1: 184-85 (Dover). This intriguing possible descent, which requires further documentation for generations 9-11, was developed and brought to my attention by Richard E. Brenneman of Boston, Mass. Descendants of Isaac Robinson are covered in *TAG* 18 (1941-42): 45-55, 56 (1980): 147 and Robinson Genealogical Society, *Robinson Genealogy*, vol. 1, *Descendants of the Rev. John Robinson, Pastor of the Pilgrims* (1926).

The Royal Descents of 900 Immigrants

1. Robert I, King of France, d. 923 = (1) Aelis ——

2. ____ of France = Herbert II, Count of Vermandois, son of Herbert I, Count of Vermandois (and ——), son of Pepin, Lord of Peronne and St. Quentin, Count near Paris (and ——), son of Bernhard, King of Italy (d. 818) (and Cunigunde of Parma), son of Pepin, King of Italy (and ——), son of the Emperor Charlemagne (d. 814) and Hildegardis of Kraichgau

3. Robert, Count of Meaux and Troyes = Adelaide of Burgundy

4. Adela of Vermandois = Geoffrey I, Count of Anjou

5. Ermengarde of Anjou = Conan I, Duke of Brittany

6. Judith of Brittany = Richard II, Duke of Normandy

7. Robert I, Duke of Normandy

8. (possibly by Herlève of Falaise) Adelaide of Normandy, full or half-sister of William I, the Conqueror, King of England = (1) Enguerrand II, Count of Ponthieu, son of Hugh III, Count of Ponthieu (and Bertha of Aumale), son of Enguerrand I, Count of Ponthieu (and Adela, possibly of Westfriesland), son of Hugh I, count of Ponthieu and (almost certainly) Gisela, daughter of Hugh Capet, King of France, SETH, and Adelaide of Poitou; (2) Lambert, Count of Lens, son of Eustace I, Count of Boulogne, and Maud, daughter of Lambert, Count of Louvain and Gerberga of Lower Lorraine, daughter of Charles, Duke of Lower Lorraine (and Adelaide ——), SETH, son of Louis IV, King of France, SETH, and Gerberga of Germany; (3) Eudes II, Count of Troyes and Aumale

9. (by 1, according to Catherine Morton and Hope Muntz, eds., *The Carmen de Hastingae Proelio of Guy, Bishop of Amiens* [1972], p. 127, or by 2, according to older sources and Douglas Richardson in *RA*) Judith of Ponthieu or Lens = Waltheof II, Earl of Huntingdon, Northampton and Northumberland

10. Matilda of Northumberland = (1) Simon de St. Liz, Earl of Huntingdon and Northumberland; (2) David I, King of Scotland, d. 1153, SETH

The Royal Descents of 900 Immigrants

11. Matilda de St. Liz = (1) Robert de Clare, SETH; (2) Saire de Quincy

12. (by 2) Alice de Senlis (St. Liz), who took her mother's surname) = Roger de Huntingfield

13. Sir William de Huntingfield, Magna Carta surety = Isabel FitzWilliam

14. Sarah de Huntingfield = Richard de Keynes

15. Richard de Keynes = Alice de Mankesey

16. Joan de Keynes = Sir Roger Lewknor

17. Sir Thomas Lewknor = Sybil ———

18. Sir Roger Lewknor = Katherine Bardolf

19. (possibly) Beatrix Lewknor = (1) Thomas Kemp (by whom she was the mother of John Kemp, Archbishop of York and Canterbury); (2) Ralph Roper

20. (possibly) Edmund Roper = ———

21. Agnes Roper = Walter Colepepper (Culpeper)

22. Sir John Colepepper (Culpeper) = Agnes Gainsford

23. Isabel Colepepper (Culpeper) = Walter Roberts

24. (very probably) Joan Roberts = Richard Exhurst

25. Mary Exhurst = Edward Stoughton

26. Francis Stoughton = Agnes ———

27. Thomas Stoughton = Katherine ———

28. **Thomas Stoughton** of Conn. = (1) Elizabeth Thomson; (2) Mrs. Margaret Barret Huntington.

28. **Israel Stoughton** of Mass. (1602/3-1644), founder of Dorchester, Mass., commander against the Pequot Indians, 1637, lt.-col. in English Parliamentary army = Elizabeth Knight, sister of Ursula Knight, wife of David Yale of Conn., ARD, SETH. Israel and Elizabeth were the parents of William Stoughton, Lt. Gov. and Acting Gov. of Mass., and Chief Justice of "Oyer and Terminer" during the Salem witchcraft

trials (d. unm.), and Rebecca Stoughton, wife of William Tailer and mother of Elizabeth Tailer, wife of John Nelson (c. 1654-1734) of Mass., merchant, proponent of French expulsion from North America, and public official, ARD, SETH. See under the above John Nelson for a second Stoughton descent to 32nd U.S. President Franklin Delano Roosevelt.

28. **Judith Stoughton** of Mass. = (1) **John Denman**; (2) —— **Smead**.
28. **Elizabeth Stoughton** of Mass. = (1) John **Scudder**; (2) Rev. Robert **Chamberlain** (and was the mother of Joanna Chamberlain, wife of Richard Betts of L.I.).
29. (by 1) Elizabeth Scudder = Samuel Lathrop
30. Abigail Lathrop = John Huntington
31. Martha Huntington = Noah Grant
32. Noah Grant, Jr. = Susanna Delano
33. Noah Grant (III) = Rachel Kelley
34. Jesse Root Grant = Hannah Simpson
35. Ulysses Simpson Grant (1822-1885), 18th U.S. President = Julia Boggs Dent

30. Samuel Lathrop, Jr. (brother of Abigail) = Hannah Adgate
31. Hannah Lathrop = Jabez Perkins
32. Hannah Perkins = Joshua Huntington
33. Lydia Huntington = Ephraim Bill
34. Lydia Bill = Joseph Howland
35. Susan Howland = John Aspinwall, Jr.
36. Mary Rebecca Aspinwall = Isaac Roosevelt
37. James Roosevelt = Sara Delano
38. Franklin Delano Roosevelt (1882-1945), 32nd U.S. President = (Anna) Eleanor Roosevelt

The Royal Descents of 900 Immigrants

Sources: *TAG* 33 (1957): 105-12, 29 (1953): 193-204 (Stoughton), 72 (1997): 295-97 (Scudder, Chamberlain) and Ethel Stokes, F.A. Stoughton, E. McL. Turner and P.B. Turner, *The English Ancestry of Thomas Stoughton, 1588-1684, of Windsor, Conn.* (1958); *Foundations* 1 (2003-5): 46-50 (Exhurst) and *NEHGR* 165 (2011): 245-60, 166 (2012): 46-70 (Exhurst, Roberts, Colepepper [Culpeper], Roper, by Adrian Benjamin Moreira da Silva-Burke, John Blythe Dobson, and Janet [Paulette Chevalley] Wolfe); *RA* 3: 568-70, 3: 373-77, 2: 644-45, 1: 277-80, 1: 208-11, 5: 483-91 (generations 1-19) and George Bellen, "The Family of de Quincy and Quincy" (mss. at NEHGS, 1934), esp. vol. 1, pp. 2, 4-6. Generations 20-22 are based on chronology and various facts and probabilities noted in the *NEHGR* articles and elsewhere. I suggest that Beatrix Lewknor, b. say 1352 (the older of her two brothers was born 1347), likely daughter of Sir *Roger* Lewknor and (=1340) Katherine Bardolf, may have married twice: (1) in say 1374 Thomas Kemp, and (2) say 1382 Ralph Roper (living 1401, d. by 1429), who = (2) an Alice ——. Beatrix and Thomas left at least two sons, Sir Thomas Kemp (say 1375-say 1420), who married another Alice ——, b. say 1382; and (2) John Kemp, b. 1380/81, Archbishop of York and Canterbury. Beatrix and Ralph Roper possibly had a son, Edmund Roper (say 1383-1433), who married (1) ——, an unknown wife; (2) the second Alice above, widow of Edmund's half-brother, Sir Thomas Kemp. Edmund Roper and his unknown first wife left a daughter, Agnes Roper, b. say 1404, wife of John Bedgebury, d. 1424, and by 1429 of Walter Colepepper (Culpeper). Edmund Roper and Alice (——) Kemp left at least two sons, a younger Edmund Roper and John Roper, both b. in the 1420s. Sir Thomas Kemp and Alice —— (later Roper) also left two sons (older half-brothers of the younger Edmund and John Roper)—Sir William Kemp, the Archbishop's heir, and Thomas Kemp, Bishop of London, whose career was sponsored by his archbishop uncle. Further documents to confirm, disprove, or alter this proposed Lewknor-Roper-Colepepper (Culpeper)-Roberts descent are eagerly awaited. For notable Stoughton descendants see the author's "Royal Descents, Notable Kin and Printed Sources" columns on the NEHGS website at www.americanancestors.org, #s 22, 23, and 56.

The Royal Descents of 900 Immigrants

PRESIDENTIAL ADDENDUM

Since this book was first published, as *RD500* in 1993, two of our four U.S. presidents (G.W. Bush and Obama) and First Lady Laura Welch Bush have been descendants of immigrants herein. The descents are outlined, as are RDs of earlier presidents (and First Ladies whose husbands had no RD immigrant ancestor) on the pertinent previous charts. I have found no certain RD immigrant ancestors for the defeated 1996, 2000, and 2016 presidential candidates (Robert [Joseph] Dole, Albert [Arnold] Gore, Jr., and Hillary [Diane] Rodham Clinton) but the two major candidates for the 2004 Democratic nomination and the defeated Republican candidates of 2008 and 2012 have at least one immigrant ancestor herein and on average five. In the format of "Notable Kin" books and columns, these descents for John Forbes Kerry (from 14 RD immigrants), Howard (Brush) Dean (III) (3), John Sidney McCain (III) (1) and (Willard) Mitt Romney (4) are as follows. As discussed in the introduction to this work, such descents are shared by millions of Americans.

1. **John Forbes Kerry**, b. 1943, U.S. senator and Secretary of State; Richard John Kerry & Rosemary Isabel Forbes; James Grant Forbes & Margaret Tyndal Winthrop; Francis Blackwell Forbes & Isabel Clarke, Robert Charles Winthrop, Jr. and Elizabeth Mason; John Murray Forbes and Anne Howell, Robert Charles Winthrop, orator, speaker of the U.S. House of Representatives, and U.S. senator, & Elizabeth Cabot Blanchard, Robert Means Mason & Sarah Ellen Francis; James Grant Forbes & Frances Elizabeth Blackwell, Thomas Lindall Winthrop & Elizabeth Bowdoin Temple, Francis Blanchard & Mary Anne Cabot, Jeremiah Mason (III) & Mary Means, Ebenezer Francis, Jr. & Elizabeth Thorndike; *Rev. John Forbes* & Dorothy Murray, John Still Winthrop & Jane Borland, Sir John Temple, 8th Bt., & Elizabeth Bowdoin, Samuel Blanchard & Elizabeth Gardner, Francis Cabot & Anna (Nancy) Clarke, Jeremiah Mason, Jr. & Elizabeth Fitch, Israel Thorndike, sailor and merchant, & Mercy Trask; *James Murray & Barbara Bennet*, John Winthrop & Anne Dudley, Francis Borland & Jane Lindall, Robert Temple & Mehitable Nelson, James Bowdoin, Jr., Revolutionary statesman and governor of Mass., & Elizabeth Erving, John Gardner & Elizabeth Pickering, John Clarke & Sarah Pickering, Jeremiah Mason & Mary Clark, Andrew Thorndike & Anna Morgan; Joseph Dudley, governor of Mass., & Rebecca Tyng, Timothy Lindall & Jane Poole, *John Nelson*

The Royal Descents of 900 Immigrants

& Elizabeth Tailer, James Bowdoin & Hannah Pordage, Timothy Pickering & Mary Wingate (parents of Elizabeth and Sarah, and of U.S. Secretary of War and State Timothy Pickering, Jr.), Daniel Mason, Jr. & Dorothy Hobart, Paul Thorndike, Jr. & Mary Bachelder; *Gov. Thomas Dudley* of Mass. & *Mrs. Katherine Deighton Hackburne,* John Poole & Elizabeth Brenton, *George Pordage* & Elizabeth Lynde, Joshua Wingate & Mary Lunt, Jeremiah Hobart & Elizabeth Whiting, Paul Thorndike & Mary Patch; *William Poole & Jane Greene, Simon Lynde* & Hannah Newgate, Henry Lunt, Jr. & Jane Browne, Rev. Samuel Whiting & *Elizabeth St. John,* John Thorndike & *Elizabeth Stratton*; Abraham Browne & Jane Skepper/Skipper, John Stratton & *Anne Derehaugh*; *Rev. William Skepper/Skipper* & Jane ⸺.

2. **Howard (Brush) Dean (III)**, b. 1948, governor of Vermont, 1991-2003; Howard Brush Dean, Jr. & Andrea Belden Maitland; James William Maitland & Sylvia Wigglesworth; Thomas A. Maitland & Helen Abbie Van Voorhis, Henry Wigglesworth & Olive Gertrude Belden; Bartow White Van Voorhis & Helen Tappen, Mead Belden & Gertrude Woolson; *James William Maitland* & Agnes Jane O'Reilly, Peter Crannel Tappen & Sarah Lorania Trowbridge, Royal Denison Belden & Olive Cadwell; Joseph Trowbridge, Jr. & Olive Clark, John Cadwell (III) & Annar Atwell; Joseph Trowbridge & Trial Morehouse, Joseph Atwell, Jr. & Miriam Case; Isaac Trowbridge & Ruth Perry, Nathaniel Case & Miriam Burr; James Trowbridge & Hester How, Samuel Case & Mary Westover; William Trowbridge & Elizabeth Lamberton, John Case & Sarah Spencer; *Thomas Trowbridge* & Elizabeth Marshall, William Spencer & *Agnes Harris*.

3. **John Sidney McCain (III)**, b. 1936; John Sidney McCain, Jr. & Rebecca Wright; John Sidney McCain & Catherine Daisy Davey Vaulx, James Junius Vaulx & Margaret Garside; James Vaulx & Eliza Geddy Fenner; Richard Fenner, Jr. & Ann McKinney Geddy; Richard Fenner & *Anne Coddington.*

4. **(Willard) Mitt Romney**, b. 1947; George Wilcken Romney, president of American Motors, governor of Michigan and Cabinet official, & Lenore Emily LaFaunt; Gaskell Romney & Anne Amelia Pratt, Harold Arundle LaFaunt & Alma Luella Robison; Helemon Pratt & Anna Joanna Dorothea Wilcken, Charles Edward Robison &

The Royal Descents of 900 Immigrants

Rosetta Mary Berry; Parley Parker Pratt, Mormon leader, & Mary Woods, Lewis Robison & Clarissa Minerva Duzette, Robert Berry, Jr. & Elnora Lucretia Warner; Jared Pratt & Charity Dickinson, Philemon Duzette, Jr. & Elizabeth Jane King, Robert Berry & Nancy Russell, Luther Warner & Permelia Stanton; Samuel Dickinson & Huldah Griffith, Joel King & Lucy Pierce, Oliver Russell & Nancy Newton, David C. Warner & Mary Russell; Christopher Dickinson & Mary Cole, William Pierce & Sarah Richardson, Ellis Russell & Jane Catherine Wolcott (parents of Oliver and Mary); Samuel Dickinson & Mary Cole, Jonathan Richardson & Elizabeth Bates, Thomas Wolcott & Catherine Loomis; Charles Dickinson & (only poss.) Philip(pa) Greene; William Cole & Anne Pinder, John Bates & Mary Farwell, Henry Wolcott & Jane Allyn; (only poss.) John Greene, Jr. & Anne Almy, John Cole & Susanna Hutchinson, Henry Farwell & *Olive Welby*; (only poss.) William Almy & *Audrey Barlow*, William Hutchinson & *Anne Marbury*, Thomas Allyn & Abigail Warham; Matthew Allyn & *Margaret Wyatt*.

Sources:

1. **Kerry:** *New England Ancestors* 1 (2000), 2: 40-41 and sources cited therein (for Dudley and Deighton lines); *Forbes* pp. 384-85 and *MGH*, 4th ser. vol. 2 (1906-7): 166 (Murray, Bennet); Josephine C. Frost, *Ancestors of Henry Rogers Winthrop and his Wife Alice Woodward Babcock* (1927), pp. 56-58, 323-24, 389-91 (Borland, Lindall, Poole); Temple Prime, *Some Account of the Temple Family*, 4th ed. (1899), pp. 54-60, *Descent of John Nelson and of His Children*, 2nd ed. (1894), esp. pp. 4-7, 11-13, and *Some Account of the Bowdoin Family, with Notes on the Families of Pordage, Lynde, Newgate, Erving*, 2nd ed. (1894), esp. pp. 4-7, 11-21, 30-34, plus Danny D. Smith, *Preliminary Study of the Descendants of Governor James Bowdoin II, 1726-1790* (1996), pp. 4-7, 11-12, 18-19, 26-27, 34, 39, 43; Harrison Ellery and C.P. Bowditch, *The Pickering Genealogy*, 3 vols. (1897), pp. 81-86, 111-12, 121-23, 233-34, 249-50, 295-96, 408-9, 427, 672-75, 955-56; Joseph Dow, *History of the Town of Hampton, New Hampshire*, vol. 2 (1893, repr. 1988), pp. 1044-45 (Wingate); *Davis* 2, pp. 533-39 (Lunt) and *TAG* 20 (1942-43): 77-85 (Lunt, Browne, Skepper/Skipper), M.H. Stafford, S.C. Steward and J.B. Arthaud, *A Thorndike Family History* (2000), pp. 17-36, 42-45, 75-77, 108-18, and *NEHGR* 15 (1861): 217, 224, 319-20

(Mason), partly corrected by John T. Fitch, *Descendants of the Reverend James Fitch, 1622-1702*, vol. 1 (1997), pp. 53-54, 138-40.
2. **Dean:** current *Who's Who in America* (H.B. Dean III), *Who Was Who in America*, vol. 8, *1982-1985* (1985), p. 258 (J.W. Maitland II, 1890-1968) and various New York *Social Registers*, including the first (1887); E.W. Van Voorhis, *A Genealogy of the Van Voorhees Family in America* (1888), pp. 227-28, Rev. F. W. Chapman, *The Trowbridge Family* (1872), p. 151 (Tappan) and F.B. Trowbridge, *The Trowbridge Genealogy* (1908), pp. 48, 123-24, 126-27, 129, 134, 154-55; Jessie P. Van Z. Belden, *Concerning Some of the Ancestors and Descendants of Royal Denyson Belden and Olive Cadwell Belden* (1898), pp. 178-80, 225-27 (Wigglesworth, Belden, Cadwell), *NEHGR* 71 (1971); 82, 273 (1775 baptisms of sisters Olive and Anner Atwell, aged about 15 and 13 years), Ruth Cost Duncan, *John Case and His Descendants* (1991), pp. 1-2, 4-5, 12, and *TAG* 27 (1951):162, 63(1988):33-45 (Spencer, Harris).
3. **McCain:** McCain and Vaulx research by the late William Addams Reitwiesner, aided by George Larson, Robert Battle, and Nicholas Dixie Coddington (esp. the 1900 census of Washington Co., Ark., for James J. Vaulx, and Vaulx and Fenner census data from Madison Co., Tenn.); FindAGrave Internet data and tombstone photographs for John Sidney McCain, Jr., Katherine Davey Vaulx McCain, Rev. James Junius Vaulx and James and Eliza Geddy Vaulx; *Lineage Book, National Society of the Daughters of the American Revolution*, vols. 119 (1931), p. 167, 124 (1932), p. 150 (Mrs. Mary Vaulx Rose and Huetha Snowden Vaulx, daughters of James Junius Vaulx and Margaret Garside, both to Richard Fenner, Jr.; Walter S. Powell, ed., *Dictionary of North Carolina Biography*, vol. 2 (1986), pp. 186-87 (Richard Fenner, Sr. and Jr.), which cites the July 1972 issue of *Family Findings* (journal of the Mid-West Tenn. Genealogical Society).
4. **Romney:** *NK* 2, pp. 212, 214, *ANB* (G.W. Romney), A.D. Pratt, *Pratt Pioneers of Utah* (1967), pp. xvi-xvii, xxii, 2-3, 59-62, 104-5, 109, 112 (entire Anne [Marbury] Hutchinson line), Marston Watson, *Royal Families: Americans of Royal Descent*, vol. 2, *Reverend Francis Marbury and Five Generations of his Descendants through Anne (Marbury) Hutchinson and Katherine (Marbury) Scott* (2004), pp. 1-5, 11, 27-28, 67-68 (but ignore the claimed John Howland descent), 211 (to Samuel Dickinson and

Huldah Griffith), *TAG* 42 (1966): 188-90 (Charles Dickinson), 89 (2017): 145-54 (on which Paul M. Gifford suggests that Samuel Dickinson, b. "say 1704", was probably a son of Charles Dickinson not by Philip(pa) Greene [d. "probably by about 1704"] but by a fourth wife, Sarah ———, whom Charles married "probably by about 1704"), G.S. Greene and L.B. Clarke, *The Greenes of Rhode Island* (1903), pp. 59-62, 75-77 and *GM* 1, pp. 43-47 (Almy); Veldron Robison Matheson (a first cousin of Mrs. G.W. Romney), *The Illustrious Robisons*, 2 vols. (1976), *passim*, esp. charts on pp. 36, 737, 835 (entire Farwell and Allyn descents), largely confirmed by American Heraldic Society, *A Genealogy of the King Family* (1930), p. 33 (plus Duzette and Robison family group sheets at the Family History Library in Salt Lake City), F.C. Pierce, *Pierce Genealogy, Being the Record of the Posterity of Thomas Pierce* (1882), pp. 54-55, J.D. Farwell, J.H. Abbott and L.M. Wilson, *The Farwell Family* (1929), pp. 25-37, 45, 64 (to Mrs. Pierce), *Portrait and Biographical Album of Hillsdale County, Mich.* (1888), pp. 583-84 (Robert Berry), G.E. Russell, *Descendants of William Russell of Salem, Mass., 1674* (1989), pp. 37-40, 76-78 (to Nancy [Russell] Berry), L.C. Warner and Mrs. J.G. Nichols, *The Descendants of Andrew Warner* (1919), pp. 200-1, 702-4 (to Elnora [Warner] Berry), J.B. Wolcott and C.V. Ward, *Wolcott Immigrants and Their Early Descendants* (2002), pp. 17, 46-47, 139-40, 366-67 (to Luther Warner and Nancy [Russell] Berry) and *FNE* (1926, repr. 1973), pp. 221-22, 267-68 (Allyn).

The Royal Descents of 900 Immigrants

Appendix

From Kings via the American Colonies to Recent Sovereigns:
Lines from Royally Descended Immigrants to
the Present British Royal Family,
Princes of Monaco, and the late Queen Geraldine of the Albanians

14.	Richard Bernard of Va. (see p. 495) = (2) 20. Anna Cordray of Va. (see p. 737)	17. Mary Towneley of Va. (see p. 700) = Augustine Warner	12. Col. George Reade of Va. (see p. 310) Elizabeth Martiau
15,21.	Anne Bernard = John Smith	18. Augustine Warner, Jr.	= 13. Mildred Reade
16,22.	John Smith, Jr.=	14,19. Mary Warner	

15,17,20,23. Mildred Smith = Robert Porteus

16,18,21,24. Robert Porteus, native of Va. who returned to England (with his father), 1730 graduate of Peterhouse College, Cambridge, rector of Cockayne Hatley, Bedfordshire = Judith Cockayne

17,19,22,25. Mildred Porteus = Robert Hodgson

18,20,23,26. Robert Hodgson, Dean of Carlisle = Mary Tucker

19,21,24,27. Henrietta Mildred Hodgson = Oswald Smith

20,22,25,28. Frances Dora Smith = Claude Bowes-Lyon, 13th Earl of Strathmore and Kinghorne

21,23,26,29. Claude George Bowes-Lyon, 14th Earl of Strathmore and Kinghorne = Nina Cecilia Cavendish-Bentinck

22,24,27,30. Lady Elizabeth Angela Marguerite Bowes-Lyon, H.M. Queen Elizabeth The Queen Mother (1900-2002) = H.M. George VI (1895-1952), King of Great Britain, 1936-1952

23,25,28,31. H.M. Queen Elizabeth II (b. 1926), Queen of Great Britain since 1952 = H.R.H. Prince Philip of Greece and Denmark, Duke of Edinburgh (b. 1921)

24,26,29,32. H.R.H. Prince Charles Philip Arthur George of Great Britain, Prince of Wales (b. 1948) = (1) Lady Diana Frances Spencer, later H.R.H. The Princess of Wales and then Diana, Princess of Wales (1961-1997), see following page; (2) Mrs. Camilla (Rosemary Shand) Parker Bowles, now H.R.H. The Duchess of Cornwall, SETH

The Royal Descents of 900 Immigrants

25,27,30,33. (by 1) H.R.H. Prince William Arthur Philip Louis of Wales, Duke of Cambridge, b. 1982, = 2011 Catherine Elizabeth Middleton, now H.R.H. The Duchess of Cambridge, b. 1982, SETH

26, 28, 31, 34. H.R.H. Prince George Alexander Louis of Cambridge, b. 2013

26, 28, 31, 34. H.R.H. Princess Charlotte Elizabeth Diana of Cambridge, b. 2015

25,27,30,33. (by 1) H.R.H. Prince Henry Charles Albert David of Wales, b. 1984

Sources: *NK* 1: 1-8 and sources cited therein, plus *GM* 23 (1989-91): 263-64, 338.

The Royal Descents of 900 Immigrants

22. Alice Freeman of Mass. and (presumably) Conn. (see p. 858) = (1) John Thompson; (2) Robert Parke
23. (by 1) Dorothy Thompson = Thomas Parke, her step-brother
24. Dorothy Parke = Joseph Morgan
25. Margaret Morgan = Ebenezer Hibbard
26. Keziah Hibbard = Caleb Bishop
27. Lucy Bishop = Benajah Strong
28. Dr. Joseph Strong = Rebecca Young
29. Eleanor Strong = John Wood
30. Ellen Wood = Frank(lin H.) Work
31. Frances Eleanor (Ellen) Work = James Boothby Burke Roche, 3rd Baron Fermoy (see elsewhere herein for their daughter, Hon. Mrs. Cynthia Burke Roche Burden Cary of Newport, R.I.)
32. Edmund Maurice Burke Roche, 4th Baron Fermoy = Ruth Sylvia Gill
33. Hon. Frances Ruth Burke Roche = Edward John Spencer, 8th Earl Spencer
34. Lady Diana Frances Spencer, later H.R.H. The Princess of Wales, and Diana, Princess of Wales (1961-1997) = H.R.H. Prince Charles Philip Arthur George of Great Britain, Prince of Wales (b. 1948), see preceding page
35. H.R.H. Prince William Arthur Philip Louis of Wales, b. 1982, = 2011 Catherine Elizabeth Middleton, now H.R.H. The Duchess of Cambridge, b. 1982, SETH
36. H.R.H. Prince George Alexander Louis of Cambridge, b. 2013
36. H.R.H. Princess Charlotte Elizabeth Diana of Cambridge, b. 2015
35. H.R.H. Prince Henry Charles Albert David of Wales, b. 1984

Sources: *AACPW,* pp. 21-32, 92-97, 143-44 esp., and Richard K. Evans, *The Ancestry of Diana, Princess of Wales, for Twelve Generations* (2007), esp. pp. 1-9, 13, 19, 28-29, 41, 60, 93, 146, 217, 331, etc.

The Royal Descents of 900 Immigrants

10,11. Rev. John Oxenbridge (1608/9-1674) of Mass., Puritan clergyman (see p. 324) = (1) Jane Butler

11,12. Bathshua Oxenbridge = Richard Scott of Jamaica

12,13. Bathshua Scott = 12,13. Julines Hering of Jamaica, son of 11,12. Nathaniel Hering and Elizabeth Cockcroft, see p. 324

13,14. Bathshua Hering = Peter Beckford, Speaker of the House of Assembly of Jamaica

14,15. William Beckford, alderman and Lord Mayor of London = Maria Hamilton

15,16. William Beckford, art collector and man of letters, author of *Vathek* = Margaret Gordon, daughter of Charles Gordon, 4th Earl of Aboyne (and Margaret Stewart, sister-in-law of John Murray, 4th Earl of Dunmore, colonial governor of N.Y. and Va., and daughter of Alexander Stewart, 6th Earl of Galloway, and Catherine Cochrane, SETH), son of John Gordon, 3rd Earl of Aboyne (son of Charles Gordon, 2nd Earl of Aboyne, and Elizabeth Lyon, SETH), and Grace Lockhart, daughter of George Lockhart of Carnwath and Euphemia Montgomery, SETH

16,17. Susan Euphemia Beckford = Alexander Hamilton, 10th Duke of Hamilton, 7th Duke of Brandon, son of Archibald Hamilton, 9th Duke of Hamilton, 6th Duke of Brandon, and Harriet Stewart, also a daughter of Alexander Stewart, 6th Earl of Galloway, and Catherine Cochrane, SETH

17,18. William Alexander Anthony Archibald Hamilton, 11th Duke of Hamilton, 8th Duke of Brandon = Princess Marie Amelie Elizabeth Caroline of Baden

18,19. Lady Mary Victoria Douglas-Hamilton = (1) Albert I (-Honoré-Charles Grimaldi), sovereign Prince of Monaco (1848-1922)

19,20. Louis II (-Honoré-Charles-Antoine Grimaldi), sovereign Prince of Monaco (1870-1949) = Ghislaine-Marie-Françoise Dommanget

20,21. (by Marie-Juliette Louvet) Charlotte (-Louise-Juliette Grimaldi), hereditary Princess of Monaco, Duchess of Valentinois = Count Pierre (-Marie-Xavier-Raphaël-Antoine-Melchior) de Polignac, SETH

21,22. Rainer III (-Louis-Henry-Maxence-Bertrand), sovereign Prince of Monaco (1923-2005) = Grace (Patricia) Kelly, the American actress

22,23. Albert II (-Alexandre-Louis-Pierre), sovereign Prince of Monaco b. 1958, = Charlene Lynette Wittstock, b. 1978

23, 24. Jacques-Honoré-Rainier, Prince of Monaco, Marquis des Baux, b. 2014, twin of Gabriella below

23, 24. Gabriella-Thérèse-Marie, Countess des Carladès, Princess of Monaco, b. 2014, twin of Jacques above

22, 23. Caroline-Louise-Marguerite, Princess of Monaco, b. 1957 (sister of Albert II) = (1) Philippe Junot; (2) Stefano Casiraghi; (3) Ernest Augustus, Prince of Hanover, b. 1954

22, 23. Stéphanie-Marie-Élisabeth, Princess of Monaco, b. 1965 (sister of Albert II and Caroline) = (1) Daniel Ducruet; (2) Adans Lopez Peres

Sources: *TAG* 31 (1955): 60-62, reprinted in *JIC*, pp. 133-36; John Britton, *Graphical and Literary Illustrations of Fonthill Abbey, Wiltshire, with Heraldical and Genealogical Notices of the Beckford Family* (1823), esp. Table I, p. 42, Table VI, p. 56, and pp. 64-67; *CP* (Aboyne, Galloway, Hamilton); *BRFW 1*: 408-9, 198, and Jacques Arnold, *The Royal Houses of Europe: The Sovereign Principalities of Liechtenstein and Monaco* (2011), charts B3A, B4A, B5A, B6A, B7B.

24. Thomas Trowbridge of Conn. (see p.551) = Elizabeth Marshall
25. James Trowbridge = Margaret Atherton
26. Elizabeth Trowbridge = John Merrick, Jr.
27. Sarah Merrick = Jonathan Fuller
28. Sarah Fuller = Edward Learned
29. Edward Learned, Jr. = Sarah Pratt
30. Mary Learned = Seth Harding
31. Edward Learned Harding = Lucy Booker Ramsay
32. Mary Virginia Ramsay Harding = John Henry Steuart
33. Gladys Virginia Steuart = (1) Julius, Count Apponyi de Nagy-Apponyi
34. Géraldine (Margit Virginia Olga Mária), Countess Apponyi de Nagy-Apponyi, Queen of the Albanians (1915-2002) = 1938 Zog I, King of the Albanians (formerly Ahmed Bey Zogu) (1895-1961, king 1928-39)
35. Leka I, styled King of the Albanians *post* 1961 (1939-2011) = Susan Barbara Cullen-Ward (1941-2004)
36. Leka II (Anwar Zog Reza Baudouin Msiziwe Zogu), styled King of the Albanians since 2011 (b. 1982) = Elia Zaharia (b. 1983)

Sources: *TAG* 53 (1977): 18-20 and *BRFW 1*: 8 (generations 30-35); W.L. Learned, *The Learned Family* (1898), pp. 52-54, 86-87 and E.L. James, *The Learned Family in America, 1630-1967* (1967), pp. 16-17, 34-35; W.H. Fuller, *Genealogy of Some Descendants of Captain Matthew Fuller, John Fuller of Newton...* (1914), p. 129; G.B. Merrick, *Genealogy of the Merrick-Mirick-Myrick Family of Massachusetts, 1636-1902* (1902), pp. 101-2; F.B. Trowbridge, *The Trowbridge Genealogy* (1908), pp. 39-48, 503-6.

The Royal Descents of 900 Immigrants

French-Canadian Immigrants of Royal Descent, both France to Québec or Acadia, and Québec to the United States: A Compilation of Such Lines in Print, in French or English, as Researched and Generally Accepted by Contemporary Scholars

The Royal Descents of 900 Immigrants

The Royal Descents of 900 Immigrants

Since about 1980 the royal descent literature for immigrants from France to French Canada (Québec) has enjoyed a major flowering. Denis Beauregard has acted as a kind of clearinghouse or collector of such lines in his CD *Genealogy of the French in North America*; his bibliography, alphabetical by immigrant, Québec Royal Descents, is at www.francogene.com/gfna/998/qrd30.htm. (This bibliography includes some figures who left no descendants and are important to Canadian history only.) On this CD Denis also traced the royal descents of the last four of the immigrants treated in this section.

The RD of Léon Levrault, Sieur de Langis, was developed by René Jetté in *La Traité de Généalogie* (1991; some other RDs therein have been altered or rejected), who also compiled an AT for Michel d'Amours, Sieur de Chauffours, and the latter's sister Élisabeth, wife of Louis-Théandre Chartier, Sieur de Lotbinière, in *Dictionnaire Généalogique des Familles du Québec des Origines à 1730* (1983). Jetté co-authored, with Roland-Yves Gagné (see below), J.P. DuLong, Gail F. Moreau and J.A. Dubé, *Table d'Ascendance de Catherine Baillon* (2001), which covered not only Catherine but Pierre and Marie-Louise-Élisabeth Bazin, great-grandchildren of Catherine's half-sister. The RD of (1) Jacques Guéret dit Dumont was traced by Paul Cassady in both *Connecticut Maple Leaf* (vol. 16, 2013-14) and a monograph at the French Canadian Genealogical Society of Connecticut Library; that of (2) Jeanne-Marie de Motin, wife of two Acadian governors, by M.W. Talbot (based largely on research by Abbé A. Couillard Despres with the John Bradstreet addition by Stephen A. White); and that of (3) Anne-Élisabeth de Tarragon by Roland de Tarragon and Jean-Claude Dolivet, in two 2016-17 issues of *Michigan's Habitant Heritage* (and later "improved" by John Blythe Dobson). The possible patrilineal descent of Julien-Charles Sévigné dit la Fleur, now doubted by Beauregard, was proposed by Marcel Fournier in *Les Bretons en Amérique Française, 1504-2004*, and again "improved" by Dobson. The remainder of the RDs that follow were published in *Mémoires*, the premier (and I think superb) journal in French Canadian genealogy. Roland-Yves Gagné, the leading published scholar on French Canadian royal descents, wrote or co-authored all but three of these articles (on d'Amours, Bazin, and Josette de Saint-Paul). I much admire Gagné's achievement; he and Beauregard are obvious candidates to undertake a compendium of all proved—and perhaps proposed but rejected—French Canadian descents from Capetians, Plantagenets, and Hohenstaufens. I hope this preliminary assemblage aids or even inspires such a work.

The Royal Descents of 900 Immigrants

1. Robert III of Scotland, d. 1406 = Annabella Drummond
2. Mary Stewart = George Douglas, 1st Earl of Angus
3. William Douglas, 2nd Earl of Angus = Margaret Hay
4. Helen Douglas = William Graham, 2nd Baron Graham
5. William Graham, 1st Earl of Montrose = Annabella Drummond, sister of Margaret Drummond, mistress of James IV, King of Scotland
6. Nicole Graham = John Murray of Abercairney
7. Marion Murray = Malcolm Robertson of Carwhin
8. —— Robertson = Donald Mente(i)th of Carwhin
9. Jean de Menteith/Jehan de Monteth, Seigneur d'Argentenay = Suzanne Hotman
10. Dorothée de Menteith = Nicolas d'Ailleboust, Seigneur de Coulôgnes-la-Madeleine
11. **Charles-Joseph d'Ailleboust, Seigneur des Musseaux** (d. 1700), soldier, jurist, businessman, acting governor of Montréal = Catherine le Gardeur.
11. Suzanne d'Ailleboust = Abraham Martin
12. **Marie Martin** of Québec = Christophe **Février**.

Sources: *Mémoires* 51 (2000): 71-85 (Roland-Yves Gagné; entire line) and sources cited therein, plus *DCB* 1: 49. The late Andrew B. W. MacEwen of Stockton Springs, Maine, however, doubted that two avowed Scottish cousins in France—John Gordon, SETH, husband of Geneviève Petau, and the above Jean de Menteith/Jehan de Monteith, Seigneur d'Argentenay—were kinsmen via common descent from William Graham, 1st Earl of Montrose. For the ancestry of John Gordon (illegitimate son by Barbara Logie of Alexander Gordon, Bishop of the Isles and of Galloway) see Ernest Flagg Henderson III, *Ancient, Medieval and More Recent Ancestors of Ernest Flagg Henderson IV and Roberta Campbell Henderson*, 4 vols. (2013), pp. 36, 92, 94, 282-91, 299-315, etc.

The Royal Descents of 900 Immigrants

1. Philip III, King of France, d. 1285 = (1) Isabella of Aragón; (2) Marie of Brabant
2. (by 1) Charles of France, Count of Valois = Maud de Châtillon of St.-Pol
3. Isabel of Valois = Peter I, Duke of Bourbon
4. Catherine de Bourbon = Jean VI, Count d'Harcourt and d'Aumale
5. Marguerite de Harcourt = Jean II, Sire d'Estouteville
6. Louis, Sire d'Estouteville = Jeanne Paynel
7. Michel, Sire d'Estouteville = Marie de la Roche-Guyon
8. Catherine d'Estouteville = Henri, Seigneur d'Espinay
9. Jeanne d'Espinay = Jacques de Beauvau, Seigneur de Tigny and de Ternay
10. Jacques de Beauvau, Seigneur de Tigny and de Ternay = Marguerite Bigot
11. Jacqueline de Beauvau = François Menard, Seigneur de Toucheprès
12. David Menard, Seigneur de Toucheprès = Renée Petit
13. Antoine Menard, Seigneur de Toucheprès = Anne le Roux
14. Marie Menard = Charles Levrault, Seigneur de Naintré
15. Pierre Levrault, Seigneur de La Maisonneuve = Anne Aignon
16. **Léon Levrault, Sieur de Langis**, of Québec = (1) Marguerite Trottier; (2) Catherine-Gabrielle Jarret.

Sources: Réné Jetté, *La Traité de Généalogie* (1991), pp. 158-59; *ES* 2: 2: 12, 22 (France, Orléans), 2: 3: 72 (Bourbon), 2: 10: 124, 125 (Harcourt), 2: 13: 106, 107 (Estouteville), 2: 13: 51 (Beauvau, with the parents of Jeanne d'Espinay) (generations 1-11), *D de la N*, vol. 13, pp. 760-63 (Mesnard de Toucheprès, where, however, Marie Mesnard [generation 14] is said to marry "Charles de Mons, Seigneur de Beaulieu and de Richemont," not treated in the Mons or Monts section of *D de la N* or in *Anselme*); Réné Jetté, *Dictionnaire Généalogique des Familles du Québec des Origines à 1730* (1983), p. 734 (the immigrant, wives, and parents).

The Royal Descents of 900 Immigrants

1. Henry III, King of England, d. 1272 = Eleanor of Provence
2. Beatrix Plantagenet = John II, Duke of Brittany
3. Marie of Brittany = Guy III de Châtillon, Count of St. Pol
4. Beatrix de Châtillon = John of Flanders, Vicomte de Châteaudun
5. Marie of Flanders = Ingelger, Seigneur d'Amboise
6. Marguerite d'Amboise = Pierre II de Sainte-Maure Montgaugier, Vicomte de Bridiers
7. Jean de Sainte-Maure Nevele, Count of Benaon = Jeanne des Roches
8. Charlotte de Sainte-Maure = Guy II de Laval, Seigneur de Loué
9. Pierre de Laval, Seigneur de Loué = Philippe de Beaumont
10. Marquise de Laval = René du Bellay, Seigneur de La Lande
11. Jacques du Bellay, Count of Tonnerre = Antoinette de La Palu
12. Eustache du Bellay, Seigneur de Commequiers = Guyonne d'Orange
13. Charles du Bellay, Seigneur de La Feuillée = Radégonde des Rotours
14. Gabrielle du Bellay = 15. Renaud de Sevigné, Sieur de Montmoron, see below
15, 16. (said to be, perhaps doubtful) Gilles de Sevigné = Gillette de Foy
16, 17. **Julien-Charles Sévigny dit la Fleur**, of Québec = Marguerite Roignon dit La Roche.

Sources: Marcel Fournier, *Les Bretons en Amérique Française, 1504-2004* (2005), pp. 382-85 (Sévigné, generations 14-16); Louis Morire, *Le Grand Dictionnaire Historique*, new ed. (1759), vol. 2, pp. 318-19 (du Bellay); *ES*1: 3: 126, 128 (Laval, under Montmorency); and André de Moura, *40,000 Ancêtres du Comte de Paris (1908-1999)*, rev. ed., 2 vols. (2007), generations 17-374, 18-416, 21-277, 22-394, 24-318, 26-343, 28-6, 29-272 (Henry III to Charlotte de Sainte-Maure). Denis Beauregard, "despite the speculations" of Marcel Fournier, now doubts this line, or would at least like to see stronger proof that Sévigné's father married both Marie de Keraldanet and Gillette de Foy. The husband of Gillette might be another Gilles. If Gillette's husband was not the son of Gabrielle du Bellay, this line fails. If Julien-Charles's father was an illegitimate son of the Renaud at generation 15, the following royal descent, developed by John Blythe Dobson, would hold.

3. Henry II, Count of Champagne, King of Jerusalem (1181-92), d. 1197 (son of Henry I, Count of Champagne, d. 1180, and his first wife, Marie of France, daughter of Louis VII, King of France, d. 1180, and Eleanor of Aquitaine) = Isabella of Anjou, Queen of Jerusalem, d. 1206

4. Philippa of Champagne = Érard de Brienne, Seigneur de Rameru

5. Jeanne de Brienne = Matthew III, Seigneur de Montmorency

6. Matthew IV, Seigneur de Montmorency, Admiral and Grand Chamberlain of France = Jeanne de Lévis

7. Jean I, Seigneur de Montmorency = Jeanne de Calletort

8. Mathieu de Montmorency, Seigneur d'Auvraymesnil = Aiglantine de Vendôme

9. Mathieu II de Montmorency, Seigneur d'Auvraymesnil = Jeanne Bracque

10. Charles de Montmorency, Count de Richemont, Constable of France = Jeanne Rataut

11. Jacqueline de Montmorency = Guillaume VI, Seigneur de Sévigné

12. François de Sévigné, Sieur du Plexis-Olivet = Catherine de La Charonière

13. Bertrand de Sévigné, Sieur des Tresmes = Marguerite de Champaigné

14. Gilles de Sévigné, Sieur de Saint-Didier = Charlotte de Montmoron

15. Renaud de Sévigné, Sieur de Montmoron = Gabrielle du Bellay, see above

The Royal Descents of 900 Immigrants

1. Henry III, King of England, d. 1272 = Eleanor of Provence
2. Beatrix Plantagenet = John II, Duke of Brittany
3. Blanche of Brittany = Philip I, Count of Artois
3. Marie of Brittany = Guy III de Châtillon, Count of St. Pol
4. Marie of Artois = John of Flanders, Count of Namur
4. Catherine of Artois = John II, Count of Aumale
4. Isabel de Châtillon, = Guillaume, Seigneur de Coucy
5. Marie of Namur = Thibaut de Bar, Seigneur de Pierrepont
5. Blanche of Aumale = John V, Count of Harcourt
6. Yolande de Bar = Eudes VII, Seigneur de Grancey
6. Jeanne de Harcourt = 5. Raoul de Coucy, Seigneur de Montmirel
7. Jeanne de Grancey = Jean IV, Seigneur de Châteauvillain
6, 7. Blanche de Coucy = Hugh II, Count of Roucy and Braine
8. Marie de Châteauvillain = Aimé de Sarrebruche, Seigneur de Commercy
7, 8. Jean VI, Count of Roucy and Braine = Isabel de Montagu
9. Robert de Sarrebruche, Seigneur de Commercy = 8, 9. Jeanne, Countess of Roucy and Braine
9, 10. Jeanne de Sarrebruche = Christophe de Brabançon, Seigneur de Cany-sur-Matz
10, 11. François de Brabançon, Seigneur de La Ferté = Françoise de Villers
11, 12. Marguerite de Brabançon = Robert de Joyeuse, Count of Grandpré
12, 13. François de Joyeuse, Seigneur de Champigneulle = Nicole-Françoise de Beauvais
13, 14. Jean de Joyeuse, Seigneur de Champigneulle = Nicole des Ancherins
14, 15. Louise de Joyeuse = Charles de Longueval, Sieur des Ormes

The Royal Descents of 900 Immigrants

15, 16. Antoinette de Longueval = Guillaume Couvent

16, 17. **Anne Couvent** of Québec = (1) Philippe **Amiot**; (2) Jacques **Maheu**.

16, 17. Charlotte Couvent = Louis le Dran [Ledran]

17, 18. **Toussaint le Dran [Ledran]** of Québec = Louise Menacier.

Sources: *Mémoires* 58 (2007): 17-58 (R.-Y. Gagné and Laurent Kokanosky), esp. 18-20, 49 and sources cited therein, plus *PA* 2: 1: 42-48 (Henry III of England), 106 (Artois), 3: 533-35 (Brittany, Châtillon de St. Pol) (together the first four generations), *Anselme*, vol. 6, p. 106 (Châtillon de St. Pol), 8, p. 544 (Coucy), 534-36 (Sarrebruche) and *ES* 2: 3: 4: 680. Roucy Crusader ancestry (to John de Brienne, King of Jerusalem and Emperor of Constantinople, d. 1237, SETH) can be traced via de Châteauville, Nevers, Dampierre (Flanders) and Brienne; see *Connecticut Maple Leaf* 14 (2009-11): 195-99.

Note: For the line from Henry III, King of England, and Eleanor of Provence to Mrs. Rose Stoughton Otis of N.H. and her French-Canadian grandchildren see pp. 623-24.

The Royal Descents of 900 Immigrants

1. Henry III, King of England, d. 1272 = Eleanor of Provence
2. Beatrix Plantagenet = John II, Duke of Brittany
3. Arthur II, Duke of Brittany = Yolande of Dreux
4. Alix of Brittany = Bouchard VI, Count of Vendôme
5. Bouchard de Vendôme, Seigneur de Feuillet and de Segré = Marguerite de Brienne, see note below
6. Pierre de Vendôme, Seigneur de Segré and de Nesle = Jeanne de Chazé
7. Alix de Vendôme = Robert IV, Seigneur d'O
8. Isabelle d'O = Philip I de La Haye, Seigneur de La Haye-Hue
9. Jean de La Haye, Seigneur du Bouillon = Jeanne de Grosparmy
10. Robert de La Haye, Seigneur du Bouillon = Robine du Bois
11. Marguerite de La Haye = Guillaume I de Méhérenc, Seigneur des Londes
12. Guillaume II de Méhérenc, Seigneur des Londes = Isabeau de Malherbe
13. Denis de Méhérenc, Seigneur des Londes = Anne de Grosparmy
14. Guillaume III de Méhérenc, Seigneur de Laubel = Françoise de Maugny
15. Guillaume IV de Méhérenc, Seigneur de La Conseillère = Marguerite de Sandret
16. Adrien de Méhérenc, Seigneur de Montmirel and La Conseillère = Jeanne du Pont
17. Jean de Méhérenc, Seigneur de Montmirel and de La Conseillère = Jeanne du Mesnil
18. Françoise de Méhérenc = Jean Guéret
19. René Guéret = Madeleine Vigoureux
20. **Jacques Guéret dit Dumont** of Québec = Anne Tardif.

The Royal Descents of 900 Immigrants

Sources: *Connecticut Maple Leaf* 16 (2013-14): 19-22 (Paul Cassady) and sources cited therein, esp. Paul le Portier, "Familles Médiévales Normandes," assembled by Mr. Cassady as "Ancestry of Jacques Guéret dit Dumont" at the French-Canadian Genealogical Society of Connecticut (FCGSC) Library (Tolland, Conn.); *ES*, tables for Brittany and England. This descent was also posted on soc.genealogy.medieval by Jean Bunot.

Marguerite de Brienne at generation 5 above was a daughter of Jean II de Brienne, Vicomte de Beaumont (and Marguerite de Poitiers), son of Robert de Brienne, Vicomte de Beaumont (and Marie de Craon), son of Jean I de Brienne, Vicomte de Beaumont, and Jeanne de La Guerche, SETH, on the next chart. For Brienne see *Anselme* 6: 132-34, 136-38, *ES* 2: 3: 4: 683, 684, *RA* 1: 536-40, 303-7, and *BP* (recent) (Beaumont).

The Royal Descents of 900 Immigrants

1. Alphonso IX, King of León, d 1230 = Berengaria, Queen of Castile, d. 1246, daughter of Alphonso VIII, King of Castile, and Eleanor Plantagenet, daughter of Henry II, King of England, d. 1189, and Eleanor of Aquitaine

2. Berengaria of León and Castile = John de Brienne, King of Jerusalem and Emperor of Constantinople, d. 1237

3. Louis de Brienne, Vicomte de Beaumont = Agnès de Beaumont

4. Jean I de Brienne, Vicomte de Beaumont = Jeanne de La Guerche

5. Anne de Brienne = Payen de Chourses, Seigneur de Malicorne

6. Patri/Patry de Chourses, Seigneur de Rabestan = Denise de Bauçay

7. Patri/Patry (II) de Chourses, Seigneur de Saint-Aubin = Jeanne Pegaze

8. Jeanne de Chourses = Patrice d'Argenson, Seigneur d'Avesnes

9. Perrine d'Argenson = Jean Cholet, Seigneur de Dangeaul

10. Marie Cholet = Florentin Girard, Seigneur de Barenton

11. Jeanne Girard = Christophe de Mésenge (Mazange), Seigneur de Saint-Paul-le-Gautier

12. Renée de Mésenge (Mazange) = Gilles de Prunelé, Seigneur de La Porte

13. Jacques de Prunelé, Baron de Saint-Germain-le-Désirée = Jacqueline de Graffart

14. Jacqueline de Prunelé = Michel de Hallot

15. Jacqueline de Hallot = Isaac de Varenne(s), Seigneur de Villegruau

16. Élisabeth/Isabelle de Varennes = Pierre de Merlin, Seigneur de La Carrée

17. Élisabeth/Isabelle de Merlin = Loup de Tarragon, Seigneur de Juvainville

18. **Anne-Élisabeth de Tarragon** of Québec = Gilles **Couturier dit la Bonté**.

The Royal Descents of 900 Immigrants

Sources: *MHH* 37 (2016): 188-96, 38 (2017): 12-18 (Roland de Tarragon and Jean-Claude Dolivet, as reported by Kathryn Conway) (generations 16-18, plus an RD for Pierre de Merlin, Seigneur de la Carrée, from Louis VI, Kings of France, from Counts of Dreux, Châtillon, Vieuxpont, d'Illiers, Fromentières, Savary, and Chapuiset); *D de la N*, 10: 219 (Hallot), 16: 466-67 (Prunelé); C. Bernois, "Recherches sur Autry et les Seigneuries qui Dépendaient," part 1, *Annales de la Société Historique & Archéologique du Gâtinais* 10 (1892): 60-63 (Mazange, where, however, Jeanne Girard is mistakenly said to be Florentin Girard's daughter by Catherine d'Avaugour, who was Florentin's mother); *Anselme*, vol. 8 (pp. 159-60) (Cholet); *Cartulaire de l'Abbaye Cistercienne de Perseigne, précédé d'une notice historique* (1880), p. 226 (d'Argenson, under Le Vasseur); Amb. Ledru, "Le Maine sous le Règne de Jean le Bon, 1350-1364," part 5, *La Province de Maine* 7 (1899): 287 (where Denise de Bauçay and her son, Patrice de Chaourses, Seigneur de Saint-Aubin, were granted permission to conduct masses in a certain chapel); André de Moura, *40000 Ancêtres du Comte de Paris (1908-1999)*, rev. ed., 2 vols. (2007), vol. 1, entries 22-891, 23-985, 28-64, 29-73, 30-121, 32-171 (generations 1-6). This "improved" descent through Élisabeth/Isabel de Varennes was developed and brought to my attention by John Blythe Dobson of Winnipeg, Manitoba, Canada.

The Royal Descents of 900 Immigrants

1. Philip II Augustus, King of France, d. 1223 = Agnès of Meran
2. Marie of France = Henry I, Duke of Brabant
3. Elizabeth of Brabant = Dietrich, Count of Cleves
4. Matilda of Cleves = Gerard of Luxembourg, Seigneur de Durbay
5. Marguerite of Luxembourg = Jean III, Seigneur de Ghistelles
6. Jean IV, Seigneur de Ghistelles = Marie de Haverskerke
7. Roger de Ghistelles, Seigneur de Dudzeele and Staaten = Marguerite de Dudzeele
8. Isabelle de Ghistelles = Arnould VI de Gavre, Baron d'Escornaix
9. Catherine de Gavre = Guy I le Bouteillier, Seigneur de La Boutillerie and La Roche-Guyon
10. Guy II le Bouteillier, Seigneur de La Bouteillerie and de La Roche-Guyon = Isabeau Morhier
11. Jean le Bouteillier, Seigneur de La Bouteillerie and de La Roche-Guyon = ——
12. Bénigne le Bouteillier = Jacques Maillard, Seigneur de Champaigne
13. Miles Maillard, Seigneur du Breuil and de La Boissière = Marie Morant
14. Renée Maillard = Adam Baillon, Seigneur de Valence
15. Alphonse Baillon, Seigneur de La Mascotterie = (1) Claude Depuy; (2) Louise de Marle, a cousin of Suzanne Hotman, wife of Jean de Menteith/Jehan de Monteth, Seigneur d'Argentenay
16. (by 2) **Catherine Baillon** of Québec = Jacques **Miville**.
16. (by 1) Élisabeth Baillon = Paul Hanot
17. Élisabeth Hanot = Pierre Philippes
18. Élisabeth Philippes = Pierre Bazin
19. **Pierre Bazin** of Québec = Thérèse Fortier.

19. **Marie-Louise-Élisabeth Bazin** of Québec = (1) Jean-Baptiste **Amiot** (1717-1769), merchant; (2) Gabriel Elzéar Taschereau.

Sources: René Jetté, John P. DuLong, Roland-Yves Gagné, Gail F. Moreau, and Joseph Dubé, "Alternative Royal Gateway from Catherine de Baillon to Charlemagne," posted at http://habitant.org/baillon/table1.htm, plus (by the same five authors), *Table d'Ascendance de Catherine Baillon (12 Generations)* (2001), based in part on *Mémoires* 48 (1997): 190-216 (esp. 195-96, by the first four authors of the above article and book), 53 (2002): 13-39 (esp. chart on p. 37 for the Bazins, by Jean-René Côté and Anita Seni), with some additions, etc., in 57 (2006): 225-27 (Gagné). Pages 177-79 of the 2001 book disprove the line proposed in René Jetté, *La Traité de Généalogie* (1991), pp. 113-14. For the de Roye ancestry of Catherine Baillon, which includes the parents of Joan of Dammartin, Countess of Ponthieu, second wife of Ferdinand III, King of Castile, d. 1252, SETH, see *MHH* 30 (2009): 5-18 (DuLong and Jean Bunot); note also *MHH* 32 (2011): 116-21, 156-66 (DuLong). For the kinship of Louise de Marle and Suzanne Hotman see *La Traité de Généalogie* above, p. 157. J.B. Amiot is treated in *DCB* 3: 13.

The Royal Descents of 900 Immigrants

1. Frederick I Barbarossa, Holy Roman Emperor, d. 1190
   = (2) Beatrix of Burgundy

2. Otto, Count Palatine of Burgundy = Margaret of Blois, daughter of Theobald V, Count of Blois and Alix of France, daughter of Louis VII, King of France, and Eleanor of Aquitaine, SETH

3. Beatrix of Burgundy = Otto I, Duke of Meran, Count Palatine of Burgundy

4. Adelaide of Burgundy = Hugh de Châlon, Count Palatine of Burgundy

5. Guye (Gillette) of Burgundy = Thomas III, Count of Savoy-Piemont

6. Philip of Savoy-Piemont, Prince of Achaya = Catherine de la Tour du Pin

7. Jeanne of Savoy-Piemont = Amé de Poitiers, Seigneur de St.-Vallier

8. Marguerite de Poitiers = Geoffrey, Seigneur de Bressieux

9. Alix de Bressieux = Guillaume de Grolée, Seigneur de Neyrieu

10. Marguerite de Grolée = Aymar de Beauvoir, Seigneur de Villette

11. Isabelle de Beauvoir = Petremand de Chevron, Seigneur de Villette

12. André de Chevron, Seigneur de Villette = Marguerite de Chalant

13. Urbain de Chevron, Seigneur de Villette = Philiberte Villette

14. Louise de Chevron = Irené de Moyria, Seigneur Mailla

15. Claude de Moyria = Claude de Seyturier, Seigneur Cornod

16. Antoinette de Seyturier = Claude de Salins, Seigneur Charmée and Vincelles

17. Claude de Salins, Seigneur Vincelles = Anne de Chantepinot

18. Marie de Salins = Louis de Motin, Seigneur de Roeux-Corcelles, a descendant of Philip de Courtenay, King of Constantinople, d. *ante* 1218, via de Motin, d'Urfé, de Montagny, d'Albon, d'Oingt, de Roussillon, de Forez, and Courtenay

19. **Jeanne-Marie de Motin** of Québec = (1) Charles **de Menou**, Seigneur d'Aulnay-Charnizay (ca. 1604-1650), Governor of

The Royal Descents of 900 Immigrants

Acadia; (2) Charles-Amador **Turgis de Saint-Étienne**, Sieur de La Tour (1593-1666), Governor of Acadia.[1]

20. Jacques de Saint-Étienne de La Tour = Anne Melanson

21. Marie-Agathe de Saint-Étienne de La Tour = Edmund Bradstreet, British lieutenant in Nova Scotia

22. **John Bradstreet** (1714-1774) of N.Y., British army officer during the French and Indian Wars, landowner = Mrs. Mary Aldridge Bradstreet.

Sources: M.W. Talbot, *Royal Ancestry of Jeanne Motin, First Lady of Acadia* (1998), esp. pp. 1-4, 6, 8, 10, 13, 16, 19, 24, 29, 35, 43 (from PDF at https://www.yumpu.com/en/document/view/5343813/jeanne-motin-lagenealogy.net), based largely on Abbé A. Couillard Despres, *Charles Latour et son Temps* (1930), and confirmed, for generations 1-10, by *ES* 2: 1: 1: 866 (Andechs of Meran), 2: 2: 60 (Burgundy-Ivrea), 2: 2: 190-91 (Savoy-Piemont), *Anselme* 4: 81 (Poitiers) and *D de la N* 9: 890-91 (Grolée). For husbands of Jeanne-Marie de Motin, see *DCB* 1: 502-6, 592-93. For the Bradstreet line, brought to my attention by John C. Brandon, see Stephen A. White, *Dictionnaire Généalogique des Familles Acadiennes* (1999), pp. 1433-37 (Turgis de Saint-Étienne de La Tour) and *ANB*.

---

[1] Charles-Amador Turgis de Saint-Étienne, Sieur de La Tour, was a son of Claude Turgis de Saint-Étienne, Sieur de La Tour, and Marie de Salazar, daughter of Hector de Salazar (and Antoinette de Courselles). Hector is thought to belong to the noble family of this name and *could* chronologically be a grandson of Hector de Salazar, Baron de Saint-Just (and Hélène de Chastellux), son of Jean de Salazar(t), Seigneur de Saint-Just, Marcilly and Montagu, and Marie de La Trémouille, illegitimate daughter of George de La Trémouille, Count of Guînes, SETH). Such a line is proposed in *Mémoires* 38 (1987): 269-88, 48 (1997): 331-33, 49 (1998): 265-68, esp. chart on p. 266 (Michel Turquois, Philippe Prince, and Janko Pavsic), and René Jetté, *La Traité de Généalogie* (1991), pp. 601-15. Note also *D de la N*, vol. 18, p. 215 (Salazar), and *Anselme*, vol. 4, pp. 164-66 (La Trémouille). Given the lack of an every-generation Salazar descent, I treat this likely line only as an addendum to the descent for Turgis's third wife, Jeanne-Marie de Motin, mother of five of his eight children (two of the remaining three were daughters in religious orders). SETH above indicates that the royal descent of George de La Trémouille, Count of Guînes, appears elsewhere in this volume.

The Royal Descents of 900 Immigrants

1. Louis VI, King of France, d. 1137 = Adela of Savoy
2. Robert I, Count of Dreux = Hawise d'Evreux
3. Alix of Dreux = Raoul III de Nesle, Count of Soissons
4. Eleanor de Nesle = Étienne II de Sancerre, Seigneur de Châtillon-sur-Loing
5. Comtesse de Sancerre = Adam III, Vicomte de Melun
6. Adam IV, Vicomte de Melun = Jeanne de Sully, daughter of Henri II, Sire de Sully, and Pernelle de Joigny, daughter of Gaucher II de Joigny, Seigneur de Château-Renard and Amicie de Montfort, daughter of Simon III de Montfort, Earl of Leicester, and Alix de Montmorency, SETH
7. Charles de Melun = Agnès d'Issy
8. Yolande de Melun = Guillaume de Vaudétar
9. Jean I de Vaudétar, Seigneur de Pouilly-le-Fort = Pernelle des Landes
10. Pierre I de Vaudétar, Seigneur de Pouilly-le-Fort = Marguerite de Chanteprime
11. Jean II de Vaudétar, Seigneur de Pouilly-le-Fort = Marguerite de Claustre
12. Pierre II de Vaudétar, Seigneur de Pouilly-le-Fort = Antoinette Baillet
13. Jeanne-Catherine de Vaudétar = Jean Le Clerc, Seigneur d'Armenonville
14. Anne Le Clerc = Jean IV Le Prévost, Seigneur de Malassise-lès-Étampes
15. Jeanne Le Prévost = Pierre d'Amours, Seigneur du Serrin
16. Louis d'Amours, Sieur du Plessis
17. (illegitimate by Élisabeth Tessier) **Mathieu d'Amours, Sieur de Chauffours** (1618-1695), town-major of Québec, shipowner, member of the Conseil Souverin = Marie Marsolet.

17. (illegitimate by Élisabeth Tessier) **Élisabeth d'Amours**, of Québec = Louis-Théandre **Chartier**, Sieur de Lotbinière (1612-post 1695), jurist, "father of the Canadian legislature."

Sources: *Mémoires* 32 (1981): 94-96 (Aimé Trottier) and sources cited therein, plus *DCN* 1: 201-3 (Chartier), 245 (Damours); René Jetté, *Dictionnaire Généalogique des Familles du Québec des Origines à 1730* (1983), pp. 300-1 (AT of the sibling immigrants, covering only generations 8-17 in this line); *Anselme*, vol. 5, pp. 224-25 (Melun), vol. 2, pp. 847-48 (Sancerre), vol. 2, pp. 500-2 (Nesle, Count of Soissons); *RA* 2: 467-69 (Dreux); *ES* 2: 7: 14 (Joigny).

The Royal Descents of 900 Immigrants

1. Louis VI, King of France, d. 1137 = Adela of Savoy
2. Robert I, Count of Dreux = Agnes de Baudemont
3. Robert II, Count of Dreux = Yolande de Coucy
4. Robert III, Count of Dreux = Eleanor de St.-Valéry
5. Robert I de Dreux, Count of Squilacce-Calabria = Isabelle de Villebéon
6. Robert II de Dreux, Seigneur de Beu = Yolande de Vendôme
7. Jean I de Dreux, Seigneur de Châteauneuf-en-Thymerais and Beaussart = Marguerite de la Roche
8. Étienne dit Gauvin de Dieux, Vicomte de Dreux = Philippine de Maussigny
9. Gauvin II de Dreux, Baron d'Esneval = Jeanne d'Esneval, a descendant of various Crusader rulers and Eastern Roman [Byzantine] emperors (including John I Comnenus, d. 1143), via Montfort and d'Ibelin)
10. Robert de Dreux, Baron d'Esneval = Guillemette de Ségrie
11. Jacques de Dreux, Vicomte de Beaussart = Agnes de Mareuil
12. Blanche de Dreux = Guillaume de Villiers, Seigneur de Villiers-sur-Port and des Deux-Jumeaux
13. Charles de Villiers, Seigneur de Villiers-sur-Port = Jeanne d'Ouessey
14. Catherine de Villiers = Olivier d'Aigneaux, Seigneur de Douville and de La Chesnée
15. Charles d'Aigneaux de l'Isle = Renée Davy
16. Robert d'Aigneaux de Douville = Jacqueline Mayne
17. **Michel d'Aigneaux d'Ouville** of Québec = Marie Lamy.

Sources: *Mémoires* 52 (2001): 95-104 (R.-Y. Gagné and Paul Leportier), esp. 95-97 and sources cited therein. Note also *ES* 2: 31: 63-66 (Dreux, through generation 12).

The Royal Descents of 900 Immigrants

1. Henry I, King of England, d. 1135 = Matilda of Scotland
2. (illegitimate by Sybil Corbet) Reginald FitzRoy or de Mortain, Earl of Cornwall = Mabel FitzWilliam
3. Maud Fitz Reginald = Robert de Beaumont, Count of Meulan, great-grandson of Henry I, King of France, and Anne of Kiev (see *AR8*, lines 52, 50)
4. Waleran, Count of Meulan = Marguerite de Fougères
5. Raoul I de Meulan, Seigneur du Courseulles-sur-Mer = Jeanne Painel
6. Raoul II de Meulan, Seigneur de Courseulles de Bernières = Agnès de Hibouville
7. Raoul III de Meulan, Seigneur de Courseulles de Bernières = ——
8. Jeanne de Meulan = Guillaume de Bricqueville
9. Nicolas de Bricqueville, Seigneur de La Haye = Jeanne de Juvigny
10. Jeanne de Bricqueville = Vigor de Clinchamp, Seigneur de Mézerets
11. Olivier de Clinchamp, Seigneur de Mézerets = Jeanne de Caudecoste
12. Anne de Clinchamp = Mathieu de Bailleul, Seigneur de Piencourt and Canthelou
13. Catherine de Bailleul = François du Bose, Seigneur d'Hermival
14. Christine du Bose = Guillaume de Nollent
15. Michel de Nollent = Marie Lhermitte
16. Jean de Nollent = Blanche Varin
17. Françoise de Nollent = Beuzeville (Eure) Jacques Leblond
18. **Nicolas Leblond** of Québec = Marguerite Leclerc.

The Royal Descents of 900 Immigrants

Sources: *Mémoires* 63 (2012): 33-51 (R.-Y. Gagné), esp. 49 (largely generations 8-18), plus *ES* 2: 3: 4: 700, 702 (Beaumont and Meulan, generations 3-8) and *RA* 5: 276-77, 1: 8-18 (first three generations).

The Royal Descents of 900 Immigrants

1. Henry I, King of England, d. 1135 = Matilda of Scotland
2. (illegitimate by ——) Aline/Alix (of England) = Mathieu de Montmorency, Constable of France
3. Bouchard IV, Seigneur de Montmorency = Laurette of Hainault
4. Alix de Montmorency = Simon III de Montfort, Earl of Leicester, a descendant of Henry I, King of France, SETH
5. Guy de Montfort, Count of Bigorre = Pétronille de Comminges
6. Pétronille de Montfort = Raoul V Tesson, Seigneur de la Roche-Tesson
7. Jean I Tesson, Seigneur de Subligny = ——
8. Jean II Tesson, Seigneur de Subligny = Thomasse ——
9. Isabelle Tesson = Roland III de Vassy, Seigneur de La Forêt-Auvray
10. Jeanne de Vassy = Raoul Rousée, Seigneur de La Nocherie
11. Perlette Rousée = Jean de La Poterie
12. Almaric de La Poterie, Seigneur de La Nocherie = Philipotte de Lignon
13. Jean de La Poterie, Seigneur de La Nocherie = Perrette de Roussel
14. Jeanne de La Poterie = (Jean?) de Saint-Germain
15. Olivier de Saint-Germain, Sieur du Post = Jeanne de Rouellé
16. François de Saint-Germain, Sieur du Post = Hélène de Corday
17. Olivier de Saint-Germain, Sieur du Post = Françoise de Breul
18. Stévenotte de Saint-Germain = Gervais Le Marchand, Sieur de La Bellonière
19. **Jeanne Le Marchand** of Québec = Mathieu **Le Neuf**, Sieur du Hérisson.

Sources: *Mémoires* 51 (2000): 209-26 (René Jetté, R.-Y. Gagné, J.P. DuLong, and Paul Leportier), esp. 223-25, 53 (2002): 143-44 (Jetté), and sources cited therein. For carlier Le Neuf generations see *Mémoires* 63 (2012): 174-98, 64 (2013): 9-27, 199-216 (Gagné). Note 36, pp. 221-22, of the 2000 article covers the possibility of Jeanne's descent from Guillaume de Corday and Isabel d'Esneval, the latter a descendant of Crusader rulers and Eastern Roman [Byzantine] emperors via d'Esneval, as was Québec immigrant Michel d'Aigneaux d'Ouville, SETH (see p. 956 herein and *Mémoires* 52: 96-97, esp. note 5). For the identification of a great-great-granddaughter of Jeanne and Mathieu, Josette de Saint-Paul, wife of Antoine Petit dit St.-Michel, see *Mémoires* 58 (2007): 58-75 (Danielle Côté).

The Royal Descents of 900 Immigrants

The four charts outlined below were taken from the website (now on CD-ROM and DVD) of Denis Beauregard of Sainte-Julie, Québec, with references covering the entire lines of J.V. l'Abbadie, Baron de Saint-Castin and L. J. de Gannes de Falaise, the first eleven generations in the line of L. J. Legouès, seigneur de Grais, and the first 15 generations in the line of Pierre de Saint-Ours, Seigneur de Saint-Ours and Deschaillons. Monographs on each of these lines, in *Mémoires* or elsewhere, perhaps already planned, are eagerly awaited.

1. Philip III, King of France, d. 1285 = (1) Isabella of Aragon; (2) Marie of Brabant

2. (by 1) Charles of France, Count of Valois = Catherine de Courtenay, daughter of Philip de Courtenay, Emperor of Constantinople, d. 1283, and Beatrix of Naples

3. Jeanne of Valois = Robert III, Count of Artois, son of Philip of Artois, Seigneur de Conches, and Blanche of Brittany, SETH.

4. Catherine of Artois = John II, Count of Aumale

5. Blanche of Aumale = John V, Count of Harcourt

6. Philippe de Harcourt, Seigneur de Bonnestable = Jeanne de Tilly

7. Gerard de Harcourt, Baron de Bonnestable = Marie Malet de Graville

8. Jacques de Harcourt, Baron de Beuvron = Marie de Ferrières

9. Blanche de Harcourt = Guillaume IV, Seigneur de Bétheville

10. Jacques, Seigneur de Bétheville = Marguerite le Veneur

11. Jeanne de Bétheville = Guillaume, Seigneur de Saint-Gilles

12. Jacques, Seigneur de Saint-Gilles = Marguerite de Pierrepont

13. Jean, Seigneur de Saint-Gilles = Joachine de Thère

14. Bonaventure, Seigneur de Saint-Gilles = Jacqueline de Montaigu

15. Jacques, Seigneur de Saint-Gilles = Françoise Bouhier

16. Catherine-Bonne de Saint-Gilles = Charles le Gouez, Seigneur de Grais and de Merville

17. **Louis-Joseph Legouès, Seigneur de Grais**, of Québec = Marguerite Legardeur de Tilly, who m. (2) Pierre de Saint-Ours, Seigneur de Saint-Ours and Deschaillons, of Québec, ARD, SETH; (3) Charles Lemoine de Longeuil. Marguerite's sister Louise Legardeur de Tilly m. Louis-Joseph de Gannes de Falaise, ARD, SETH.

Sources: *D de la N* 3: 81 (de Betheville); *ES* 2: 10: 124, 126, 132 or *Anselme* 5: 132, 139-40, 146-47 (Harcourt); *ES* 2: 3: 1: 124B (Aumale), 2: 2: 63 (Castile and Aumale), 2: 3: 1: 70 (Artois); *RA* 1: 145-47, 1: 549-50, 5: 231-32, 3: 30-32 (France), 5: 539 (Courtenay) (first three generations).

The Royal Descents of 900 Immigrants

1. Henry III, King of England, d. 1272 = Eleanor of Provence
2. Beatrix Plantagenet = John II, Duke of Brittany
3. Blanche of Brittany = Philip of Artois, Seigneur de Conches
4. Jeanne of Artois = Gaston I, Count de Foix and Bigorre
5. Roger Bernard I de Foix, Vicomte de Castelbon = Constance de Luna
6. Roger Bertrand II de Foix, Vicomte de Castelbon = Girarde de Navailles
7. Isabel de Foix = Archibaud de Grailly, Vicomte de Castelbon
8. Jean III, Count de Foix and de Bigorre = (1) Jeanne of Navarre; (2) Jeanne d'Albret; (3) Jeanne of Aragón
9. (illegitimate by ──) Bernard de Béarn, Seigneur de Genderest = Catherine de Viella
10. Jean de Béarn, Seigneur de Gerderest = Marguerite de Gramont
11. (illegitimate, possibly by Marie de Bordenave) Bertrand de Béarn-Bonasse, Seigneur de La Bastide-Villefranche = Marie de Bescat
12. (probably) François de Béarn-Bonasse = Marie de Sacaze
13. Henri de Béarn-Bonasse = Jeanne de Belsunce
14. Jacques de Béarn-Bonasse = Madeleine de Làas
15. Isabeau de Béarn-Bonasse = Jean-Jacques l'Abbadie, Baron de Saint-Castin
16. **Jean-Vincent l'Abbadie, Baron de Saint-Castin** (1652-1707), French soldier and Abenaki chief = (1) Marie Pidiwamiskwa; (2) Mechtilde de Niousqué.

Sources: *ANB*, *DCB* 2: 4-7, A. de Dufau de Maluquer, "Notice généalogique sur la maison d'Abbadie de Maslacq," *Proc. and Trans. of the Royal Society of Canada*, ser. 1, vol. 2 (1895): 86-87 (generations 14-16, brought to my attention by John Blythe Dobson); Robert LeBlant, *Une Figure Légendaire de l'Histoire Acadienne: Le Baron de Saint-Castin* (1934), esp. pp. 23-39 (Béarn-Bonasse) (generations 7-16), plus *Anselme*, vol. 3, pp. 348, 350, 370-73, 392 (Foix, generations 4-10); *RA* 1: 145-46, 1: 549-50 (first three generations) (together the entire line).

The Royal Descents of 900 Immigrants

1. Alphonso IX, King of León, d. 1230 = Berengaria, Queen of Castile, d. 1246, daughter of Alphonso VIII, King of Castile, and Eleanor of England, daughter of Henry II, King of England, and Eleanor of Aquitaine
2. Berengaria of León and Castile = John de Brienne, King of Jerusalem, Emperor of Constantinople, d. 1237
3. Louis de Brienne, Vicomte de Beaumont = Agnès de Beaumont
4. Jeanne de Brienne = Guy VII de Montmorency, Sire de Laval
5. Philippa de Montmorency = Guillaume de Voyer, Seigneur de Mousé
6. Renaud de Voyer, Seigneur de Paulmy (Paumiz, Paumis) = Nicole de Pressigny
7. Philippon de Voyer, Seigneur de Paulmy = Jeanne de Vernæuil
8. Jean de Voyer, Seigneur de Paulmy = Alix de Cluys
9. Pierre de Voyer, Seigneur de Paulmy = Marguerite de Bez
10. Jeanne de Voyer = Mathurin de Gannes, Seigneur de Mondidier
11. Louis de Gannes = Marie de Terves
12. Louis de Gannes = Bertheleonne de Monnins
13. François de Gannes, Sieur de Mondidier = Jeanne de Besdon
14. René de Gannes, Sieur de Mondidier = Renée de Ferrou
15. Louis de Gannes de Falaise de Rosne = Françoise Lebloy
16. **Louis-Joseph de Gannes de Falaise** of Québec (1658-1714), soldier = (1) Barbe Denis; (2) Louise Legardeur de Tilly, sister of Marguerite (Legardeur de Tilly) (Legouès) (Saint-Ours) Lemoine, SETH, pp. 962, 965; (3) Marguerite le Neuf de la Vallière.

Sources: Stephen A. White, *Dictionnaire Généalogique des Familles Acadiennes* (1999), pp. 651-57, 660-64 (Gannes, generations 10-16), *Anselme*, vol. 6, pp. 593-95 (Voyer de Paulmy, generations 5-10, without wives for 5 and 6), vol. 3, p. 627, *ES* 1: 3 (1976): 115 (Montmorency-Laval); *RA* 1: 8-18, *ES* 2: 3: 682-83 (Brienne), *ES* 2: 2: 62-63 (Castile and Leon); *RA* 1: 303-7 (Beaumont), 1: 536-39 (Brienne), 2: 114-16 (Castile) (first three generations) (together the entire line minus Nicole de Pressigny).

The Royal Descents of 900 Immigrants

1. Louis VI, King of France, d. 1137 = Adela of Savoy
2. Peter of France, Seigneur de Courtenay = Elizabeth de Courtenay
3. Peter I, King of Constantinople, d. 1218 = Yolande of Hainault
4. Eleanor de Courtenay = Philip I de Montfort, Seigneur de la Ferté-Alais
5. Philip II de Montfort, Seigneur de la Ferté-Alais = Jeanne de Lévis
6. Jeanne de Montfort-l'Amaury = Louis I of Savoy, Baron de Vaud, son of Thomas II, Count of Savoy (and Beatrix Fieschi), brother of Beatrix of Savoy, wife of Raymond Berenger V, Count of Provence, and mother of Margaret, Eleanor, Sancha and Beatrix of Provence, wives respectively of Louis IX, King of France, Henry III, King of England, Richard of England, Duke of Cornwall and King of the Romans (all three SETH), and Charles I, King of Naples and Sicily
7. Beatrix of Savoy-Vaud = Geoffrey I, Seigneur de Clermont
8. Aynard II, Vicomte de Clermont = Agatha de Poitiers
9. Sybil de Clermont = Bertrand, Seigneur de Chateauneuf
10. Anne de Chateauneuf = Guigues Alleman, Seigneur d'Uriage
11. Aymonette Alleman = Aynard de Beaumont, Seigneur des Adrets
12. Aynard de Beaumont, Seigneur des Adrets = Françoise de Laire
13. Antoine de Beaumont, Seigneur de la Tour = Claude Marc
14. Ennemond de Beaumont de Saint-Quentin = Louise Ravier
15. Roland de Beaumont, Seigneur de Saint-Quentin = Jeanne Ferland-Teste
16. Diane de Beaumont de Saint-Quentin = Antoine de Calignon
17. Jeanne de Calignon = Henri de Saint-Ours
18. **Pierre de Saint-Ours, Seigneur de Saint-Ours and Deschaillons** (1640-1724) of Québec, soldier = (1) Marie Mullois; (2) Marguerite Legardeur de Tilly, previously wife of Louis-Joseph Legouès, Seigneur de Grais, of Québec, ARD, SETH (she m. [3] Charles Lemoine de Longueil). Marguerite's sister Louise Legardeur de Tilly m. Louis-Joseph de Gannes de Falaise, ARD, SETH.

Sources: *DCB* 2: 592-93 (Saint-Ours); Henri Jougla de Morenas, *Grand Armorial de France*, vol. 2 (1938), pp. 36-37 (Beaumont de Saint-Quentin, generations 11-15); *D de la N* 2: 678-81 (Beaumont des Adrets and Saint-Quentin, generations 10-13), 1: 349-50 (Allemand) (Savoy), *ES* 2: 28: 22 (Clermont), *ES* 2: 2: 190, 193 (Savoy), *ES* 2: 3: 4: 643 (Montfort), *ES* 2: 2: 17 (Courtenay), *ES* 2: 2: 11 (France), *ES* 2: 2: 70 (Provence) (together generations 1-15). For generations 17-18 Denis Beauregard cites *Armorial de Dauphine*.

The Royal Descents of 900 Immigrants

Introduction to Section Two

The following charts outline the descents to (1) Pierre Trudeau (F.D. Roosevelt, Sir Winston [L. Spencer-] Churchill, and Trudeau, all SETH, are in my opinion the greatest twentieth-century political leaders of the three major English-speaking countries in the Western world); and (2) various French-Canadian immigrants to the U.S. The latter immigrants, or one or more descendants, have been major figures in U.S. history or contemporary culture.[2] The first dozen or so immigrants, various of whose notable descendants are charted, are themselves descended from either Anne Couvent, wife firstly of Philippe Amiot, or Catherine Baillon, wife of Jacques Miville. The Couvent and Baillon progenies, perhaps the largest RD such in French Canada, seem also to be the most studied. Included thereafter, as compiled by John Blythe Dobson, are at least one immigrant descendant each of five other RD French pioneers to Québec, charts intended as an initial sample of such notables. Comparable groups of distinguished descendants for each of the remaining French immigrants (including the Rose and Hotesse [Otis] kinsmen) may well exist and, if published, appear in a future addendum to this volume. The scholars listed in 1-3 below developed (and those in 4-5 confirmed) the Baillon and Couvent lines, except for those of Ryan Gosling and Anna Paquin, largely from marriage registers indexed by the Institut Généalogique Drouin or Father Antonin Loiselle:

> (1) Diane Wolford Sheppard, whose ATs for Angelina Jolie and Madonna and article on Archbishop A.H. Vigneron, all in *Michigan's Habitant Heritage*, are cited, but who also compiled ATs for Jean Chrétien, Jack Kerouac, "Mike" Gravel, Robert Goulet, Edward Brisbois (great-grandfather of the Wahlbergs), Céline Dion, Alanis Morrisette, Mario Lemieux, and Eric Gagné);

> (2) the late René Jetté (the Catherine Baillon volume, with a chart to Jean Chrétien and Céline Dion);

> (3) Baillon volume co-author Roland-Yves Gagné (especially the cited charts in vol. 29 of *Michigan's Habitant Heritage*);

---

[2] The two exceptions are François Chrétien of N.H., and Olivine Laforme, his wife, also of N.H., grandparents of Canadian Prime Minister Jean Chrétien.

(4) John P. Hickey, Jr., who reviewed a preliminary draft of the Baillon and Couvent descendant charts and undertook some further research (he did not, however, cover the Gravel, Wahlberg, Eric Gagné, Gosling, or Paquin descents).

(5) Thomas Allaire of Mendon, Mass., who has long worked on the ancestry of Pierre Trudeau and, at my request, meticulously checked all of the Baillon and Couvent descendant charts (except for Gosling and Paquin), confirming each line (for one generation in the Gravel descent a source was not found).

Paul-Émile Racan-Bastien has published ancestor tables, cited on the respective charts, for Pierre Trudeau, Jean Chrétien, Céline Dion, and Madonna. Massachusetts vital records research, largely for Donnie and Mark Wahlberg, was undertaken mostly by Christopher Challender Child of NEHGS, through whom I also received much of Diane Sheppard's work. Final entries in this section include a line from Rev. William Sargent of Mass., to A.H. Vigneron, Archbishop of Detroit; the descent from Nicolas Leblond to musician Justin (Drew) Bieber,[3] the youngest immigrant in this book; and the five descents mentioned above, brought to my attention (as were the Racan-Bastien volumes) by J.B. Dobson (for Gosling, Michael Sarrazin, and forebears of Paul Theroux, Chloë Sevigny, and Beyoncé). Additions, especially for the RD immigrants other than Baillon and Couvent, are welcome but should also be sent to the several scholars mentioned above who trace the French-Canadian ancestry of noted American figures. I encourage French-Canadian genealogical scholars to publish *in book form* not only a compendium of RD descents to French Canada, but also a volume of such royal descents from French Canada to the United States. The obvious candidate for the latter project is certainly Diane Wolford Sheppard.

---

[3] Bieber's Nicolas Leblond descent was found by Julie Helen Otto on the Internet; I immediately recognized Leblond as an RD immigrant to early Québec, and Julie and I then documented Bieber's Canadian line, as shown on p. 984 (Leblond's descent had been developed largely by Roland-Yves Gagné in *Mémoires* 63 [2012]).

The Royal Descents of 900 Immigrants

16, 17. **Anne Couvent** of Québec = Philippe **Amiot**; (2) Jacques **Maheu**

17, 18. (by 1) Mathieu Amiot, Seigneur de Villeneuve = Marie Miville

18, 19. Jeanne-Anne-Marie Amiot = Paul Tessier

19, 20. Anne-Marie Tessier = Louis-Étienne Gagné dit Belavance

20, 21. Pierre Gagné de Belavance = Marie-Catherine Langtin dit Jereme

21, 22. René-Amable Gagné dit Belavance = Marie-Renée Hamelin dit Lacave

22, 23. Marguerite Gagné dit Belavance = Louis Trudeau

23, 24. Louis Trudeau = Louise Dupuis

24, 25. Joseph Trudeau = Malvina Cardinal

25, 26. Charles-Émile Trudeau = Grace Elliot

26, 27. **Pierre Elliot Trudeau** (1919-2000), Prime Minister of Canada, 1968-79, 1980-84 = Margaret Joan Sinclair

27, 28. **Justin Pierre James Trudeau** (b. 1971), 23rd Prime Minister of Canada, 2015- = Sophie Grégoire

Sources: Paul-Émile Racan-Bastien, *Généalogie Ascendante de Pierre Elliott Trudeau, Premier Ministre du Canada, Originaire du Québec* (2001) and *MHH* 29 (2008): 14-15 (Tessier to P.E. Trudeau) (chart by Roland-Yves Gagné showing Trudeau's kinship, via Tessier, to Eric Gagné and via earlier Gagnés to Senator Hillary Rodham Clinton, Madonna [Ciccone] and Québec premiers Sir Lomer Gouin, Daniel Johnson, Jr., Pierre-Marc Johnson and Robert Bourassa); Diane's Database (Diane Wolford Sheppard) and confirming research by Thomas Allaire and John P. Hickey, Jr., per the introduction to this section on French Canadian immigrants.

The Royal Descents of 900 Immigrants

16. **Catherine Baillon** of Québec = Jacques **Miville**

17. Jean Miville = Marie-Madeleine Dubé

18. Marie-Madeleine Miville = Nicolas Lizot

19. Marie-Josèphe Lizot = Joseph Ouellet

20. Brigitte-Josèphe Ouellet = Michel Saint Pierre dit Dessaint

21. Marie-Josèphe Dessaint, dit Saint Pierre = Joseph Blais

22. Joseph Blais = Marie Boisvert

23. Élisabeth Blais = François Chrétien

24. **François Chrétien**, sometime of N.H. (where he) = 28. **Olivine Laforme**, sometime of N.H., see below.

25. Willie Chrétien = 25. Marie Boisvert, a fourth cousin, see below

26. (**Joseph-Jacques**) **Jean Chrétien**, b. 1934, 20th Prime Minister of Canada, 1993-2003 = Aline Chaîné

Sources: *Catherine Baillon* (2001), p. 15, and Paul-Émile Racan-Bastien, *Généalogie Ascendante de Jean Chrétien* (2002). John Blythe Dobson notes a second Catherine Baillon descent, via the Prime Minister's mother, from http://www.nosorigines.qc.ca, verified in the Drouin Collection; 25. Marie (Boisvert) Chrétien; 24. Philippe Boisvert (and Agnès Gélinas); Pierre Boisvert and 23. Philomène Bourassa; Frédéric Bourassa and 22. Julie Saint-Pierre; 21. Michel Saint-Pierre (and Hannah a.k.a. Anne England [not McLean]); 20 above. In addition, Olivine (Laforme) Chrétien at generation 24 was descended from 21. Antoine Desrosiers dit du Tremble and Anne du Hérisson, SETH, also as follows: 28. (in the le Neuf descent) Olivine (Laforme) Chrétien; Godfroi Laforme and 27. Aurélie Garceau; 26. François Garceau and Charlotte Boisvert; Charles Garceau and 25. Thérèse Desrosiers; 24. Jean-Baptiste Desrosiers dit du Tremble and Angélique Bourré; 23. Louis Desrosiers dit du Tremble and Thérèse Fafard (covered thus far by Racan-Bastien); 22. Jean Desrosiers dit du Tremble and Marie-Françoise Dandonneau; 21. Antoine Desrosiers dit du Tremble and 21. Anne du Hérisson, SETH, granddaughter of Mathieu le Neuf, Sieur du Hérisson, and 19. Jeanne Le Marchand of Québec, SETH.

16. **Catherine Baillon** of Québec = Jacques **Miville**
17. Jean Miville = Marie-Madeleine Dubé
18. Marie-Angélique Miville = Mathurin Bérubé
19. Marie-Josèphe Bérubé = Jean-Baptiste Lévesque
20. Pierre Lévesque = Marie-Josèphe Dionne
21. Marie-Josèphe Lévesque = Guillaume Malenfant
22. Jean-Baptiste Malenfant = Marie-Anathalie Destroismaisons
23. Séverine Malenfant = Édouard Kerouac
24. Jean-Baptiste Kerouac = Clementine Bernier of N.H.
25. **Leon Alcide Kerouac** of N.H. and Mass. = Gabrielle Lévesque, see below.
26. **Jean-Louis LeBris "Jack" Kerouac** (1922-69), novelist and "Beat" poet, author of *On the Road* = (1) Edie Parker; (2) Joan Harvey; (3) Stella Sampas

18. Jean-Bernard Miville (brother of Marie-Angélique) = Marie-Françoise Soucy
19. Marie-Françoise Miville = François-Germain Ouellet
20. Marie-Théodiste Ouellet = Augustin Dionne dit Sansoucy
21. Felicité Dionne = Pierre-François Jean
22. **François-Xavier Jean** of N.H. = Marie-Louise Mignot.
23. Marie-Joséphine Jean = Louis Lévesque, a first cousin once removed of René Lévesque, premier of Québec
25. Gabrielle Lévesque = Leo Alcide Kerouac, see above.

Sources: *MHH* 29 (2008): 182 (Séverine Malenfant to Jack Kerouac); *Connecticut Maple Leaf* 8 (1997-98): 30-33 and *Mémoires* 32 (1981): 89-90 (on the Kerouac patrilineal descent, by agnate cousins of the novelist/poet). Line confirmed by Thomas Allaire and John P. Hickey, Jr. For Kerouac's kinship to René Lévesque see René Jetté, *La Traité de Généalogie* (1991), p. 190.

16, 17. **Anne Couvent** of Québec = (1) Philippe **Amiot**
17, 18. Mathieu Amiot, Seigneur de Villeneuve = Marie Miville
18, 19. Anne-Marie Amiot = Jean Huard
19, 20. Jeanne Huard = Joseph-Ange Couture
20, 21. Marie-Louise Couture = Pierre Bourassa
21, 22. Ignace Bourassa = Marguerite Brault
22, 23. Ignace Bourassa = Marie-Antoinette Leboeuf
23, 24. Antoine Bourassa = Josèphe/Josephte Plouf
24, 25. Louis-Cléophas Bourassa = Elmire Allard
25, 26. Frédéric Bourassa = Caroline Baril
26, 27. **Marie Bourassa** of Mass. = Alphonse **Gravel**.
27, 28. **Maurice Robert "Mike" Gravel**, b. 1930, U.S. Senator from Alaska = Rita Jeannette Martin

Source: Diane's Database (Diane Wolford Sheppard) and Mass. VRs. Line confirmed except for one generation (not disproved, but no source was found) by Thomas Allaire.

16, 17. **Anne Couvent** of Québec = (1) Philippe **Amiot**

17, 18. Mathieu Amiot, Seigneur de Villeneuve = Marie Miville

18, 19. Anne-Marie Amiot = Jean Huard

19, 20. Marie-Anne Huard = Charles Couture

20, 21. Geneviève Couture = Guillaume Roy

21, 22. Marie-Louise Roy = Louis Labrecque

22, 23. Louis Labrecque = Marie-Louise Mercier

23, 24. Françoise Labrecque = André-Louis Goulet

24, 25. Thomas Goulet = Marceline Fortin

25, 26. Joseph Goulet = Marie Lamontagne dit Bacquet

26, 27. **Joseph-Georges-André Goulet** of Mass. = Jeannette Gauthier.

27, 28. **Robert (-Gerard) Goulet** (1933-2007), singer, stage, film and television actor = (1) Louise Longmore; (2) Carol Lawrence (Carol Maria Leraia), b. 1932, singer, stage and television actress; (3) Vera Chochroska Novak

Sources: *MHH* 29 (2008): 183 (last three generations only); Diane's Database (Diane Wolford Sheppard), line confirmed by Thomas Allaire and John P. Hickey, Jr.

16. **Catherine Baillon** of Québec = Jacques **Miville**

17. Jean Miville = Marie-Madeleine Dubé

18. Marie-Madeleine Miville = Nicolas Lizot

19. Nicolas Lizot = Marie-Ursule Mignault dit Labrie

20. Marie-Anne Lizot = François Bertrand

21. Joseph-Marie Bertrand = Marie-Judith Chaput

22. Jean-Baptiste Bertrand = Marie-Marguerite Jetté

23. Léon Bertrand = Marie-Anne Perrault

24. **Louis J. Bertrand** of Ill. = Marie-Virginie-Adelphine Maillet.

25. George Bertrand = Marie-Louise Angéline Leduc

26. Rolland F. Bertrand = Lois June Gowens

27. Marcia Lynne Bertrand, actress as Marguerite Bertrand (1950-2007) = Jon Voight, b. 1938, actor

28. **Angelina Jolie Voight**, actress as **Angelina Jolie**, b. 1975 = (1) Jonny Lee **Miller**, British actor; (2) William Robert **Thornton**, actor, as Billy Bob Thornton, b. 1955; (3) [William] Brad[ley] **Pitt**, b. 1963, actor, previously married to actress Jennifer [Joanna] Aniston, SETH

Sources: *MHH* 29 (2008): 71-74, 113-14, 116, 171 (generations 17-28) (Diane Wolford Sheppard).

16, 17. **Anne Couvent** of Québec = (1) Philippe **Amiot**

17, 18. Mathieu Amiot, Seigneur de Villeneuve = Marie Miville

18, 19. Jeanne-Anne-Marie Amiot = Paul Tessier

19, 20. Marie-Catherine Tessier = Jean-Baptiste Dupuis

20, 21. Louis-Albert Dupuis = Felicité Gibault

21, 22. Marie-Josèphe Dupuis = Eustache Demers (III)

22, 23. Eustache Demers (IV) = Marie-Louise Martin

23, 24. Eustache Demers (V) = Zoe Vézina

24, 25. **Eustache Demers (VI)** of Mich. = Louise Massé.

25, 26. Marie-Louise Demers = Guillaume-Henri Fortin, see p. 988

26, 27. Élise Fortin = Willard Fortin, a cousin, see p. 988

27, 28. Madonna Louise Fortin = Silvio Anthony Ciccone

28, 29. **Madonna Louise Veronica Ciccone**, rock star and actress, as **Madonna**, b. 1958 = (1) Sean **Penn**, actor; (2) Guy Stuart **Ritchie**, b. 1958, filmmaker, sometime of N.Y. or Calif., ARD, SETH.

Sources: Paul-Émile Racan-Bastien, *Généalogie Ascendante Lignée Canadienne de Madonna (Madonna Louise Veronica Ciccone)* (2015); *MHH* 15 (1994): 39-41, 45-51, 53, 55, 57-58, 76, 78, 86, 88, 132 (Diane Wolford Sheppard). Note also *MHH* 29 (2008): 14-17, 181. René Jetté, *Dictionnaire Généalogique des Familles du Québec des Origines à 1730* (1983) covers the first several generations of descendants for each of Madonna's three RD immigrant ancestors—Anne (Couvent) Amiot, Nicolas Leblond, and Jeanne (Le Marchand) Le Neuf (see p. 988).

16, 17. **Anne Couvent** = (1) Philippe **Amiot**

17, 18. Mathieu Amiot, Seigneur de Villeneuve = Marie Miville

18, 19. Marie-Françoise Amiot = Charles Gingras

19, 20. Jean Gingras = Marie-Madeleine Lefebvre

20, 21. Marie-Charlotte Gingras = Louis Doré

21, 22. Étienne Doré = Marie-Louise Coron

22, 23. Marie-Archange Doré = Jean-Baptiste Grignon

23, 24. Marie-Archange Grignon = Joseph Sigouin

24, 25. Julienne Sigouin = Benjamin Brisebois

25, 26. Roger Brisebois = Jane Delamater

26, 27. **Edward Brisbois** of (Boston) Mass. = Ellen Floyd McKittrick.

27, 28. Leone B. Brisbois = Arthur Ambrose Donnelly

28, 29. Alma Louise Donnelly = Donald Edward Wahlberg

29, 30. **(Donald Edmond) "Donnie" Wahlberg (Jr.)**, b. 1969, singer ("New Kids on the Block") and actor = (1) Kimberly Fey; (2) Jenny McCarthy, actress

29, 30. **Mark (Robert Michael) Wahlberg**, b. 1971, singer ("Marky Mark and the Funky Bunch"), actor and producer = Rhea Durham

Sources: Mass. VRs research by Christopher Challender Child (with Julie Helen Otto and G.B. Roberts); Diane's Database (Diane Wolford Sheppard) (to Edward Brisbois), line confirmed for Canadian generations by Thomas Allaire. An ancestor table of Mark Wahlberg by the late W.A. Reitwiesner covers generations 21/22 to 29/30, with citations to Mass. VRs.

16. **Catherine Baillon** of Québec = Jacques **Miville**

17. Jean Miville = Marie-Madeleine Dubé

18. Marie-Geneviève Miville = Joseph Lavoie

19. Joseph Lavoie = Marie-Madeleine Michaud

20. Marie-Josèphe Lavoie = Pierre-Bernard Lévesque

21. Geneviève Lévesque = Claude Letourneau

22. Claude Letourneau = Delima Paradis Michaud

23. Marceline Letourneau = Joseph-Adélard Dion

24. Adélard Dion = 24. Esther Lévesque, see below

16, 17. **Anne Couvent** of Québec = (1) Philippe **Amiot**

17, 18. Mathieu Amiot, Sieur de Villeneuve = Marie Miville

18, 19. Anne-Marie Amiot = Jean Huard

19, 20. Mathieu Huard = Marie-Jeanne Jourdain

20, 21. Marie-Josèphe Huard = Pierre Drapeau

21, 22. Pierre Drapeau = Marie-Josèphe Maranda

22, 23. Marie-Josèphe Drapeau = Olivier Barriault

23, 24. Olivier Barriault = Sophie Tardif

24, 25. Joseph-Norbert Barriault = Alma Pelletier, see p. 989

25. Joseph-Charles-Adélard Dion = 25, 26. Marie-Ernestine Barriault

26. Adhémar Dion = 26, 27. Marie-Thérèse Tanguay

27, 28. **Céline (-Marie-Claudette) Dion**, b. 1968, singer, of Nevada when performing in Las Vegas = René **Angelil**.

Sources: *Catherine Baillon* (2001), p. 17, Paul-Émile Racan-Bastien, *Généalogie Ascendante de Céline Dion* (2014) and *MHH* 29 (2008): 181 (23-27/28); Diane's Database (Diane Wolford Sheppard), confirmed by Thomas Allaire and John P. Hickey, Jr. Esther (Lévesque) Dion, 24 above, was the daughter of 23. Jean Lévesque (and Marguerite Valles), son of 22. Georges Lévesque (and Monique Lachaume), son of 21. Joseph-Marie Lévesque (and Esther Rioux), son of Pierre-Bernard Lévesque and Marie-Josèphe Lavoie, 20. above.

16, 17. **Anne Couvent** of Québec = (1) Philippe **Amiot**

17, 18. Mathieu Amiot, Seigneur de Villeneuve = Marie Miville

18, 19. Anne-Marie Amiot = Jean Huard

19, 20. Jean-Baptiste Huard = Angélique Jourdain

20, 21. Geneviève Huard = Louis Pellerin

21, 22. Marie-Anne Pellerin = Jean-Baptiste Gagné

22, 23. Jean-Baptiste Gagné = Thérèse Roy

23, 24. Vital Gagné = Marguerite Chamberland

24, 25. Hermine Gagné = Nazaire Mercier

25, 26. Marie Mercier = Joseph Morrisette

26, 27. Joseph-Hillaire Morrisette = Noelia Gertrude McConnell

27, 28. Alan-Joseph Morrisette = Lucille Hunault

28, 29. Alan Morrisette = Georgia Mary Anne Feuerstein

29, 30. **Alanis (Nadine) Morrisette**, b. 1974, singer, sometime of Calif. = Mario **Treadway**.

Sources: *MHH* 29 (2008): 181 (generations 25/26 to 29/30); Diane's Database (Diane Wolford Sheppard), line confirmed by Thomas Allaire and John P. Hickey, Jr.

16, 17. **Anne Couvent** of Québec = (1) Philippe **Amiot**

17, 18. Mathieu Amiot, Sieur de Villeneuve = Marie Miville

18, 19. Marie-Françoise Amiot = Charles Gingras

19, 20. Marie-Charlotte Gingras = François Rochon

20, 21. Augustin Rochon = Marguerite Beauchamp

21, 22. Jean-Baptiste Rochon = Marie-Françoise Papineau

22, 23. Nicolas Rochon = Marie Lavergne LeBuis

23, 24. (Marie-) Louise Rochon = Olivier "Levi" Bélaire

24, 25. Julien-Olivier Bélaire = Mathilda Seguin

25, 26. Mary-Ann Bélaire = Joseph Brown

26, 27. Marie-Yvette Brown = George Gosling

27, 28. Thomas Ray Gosling = Donna Wilson

28, 29. **Ryan [Thomas] Gosling**, b. 1980, actor, of California, who has two children with Eva [de la Caridad] Mendez, known as Eva Mendes, actress.

Sources: This line was brought to my attention by John Blythe Dobson of Winnipeg, Manitoba, and developed on http://www.perche-quebec.com/files/ryan-gosling/indivus/ryan-gosling-en.htm; the items cited for generations 16/17 through Nicolas Rochon were taken from the Drouin Collection and the Programme de Recherche en Démographie Historique [PRDH] database of the Université de Montréal (http://www.genealogie.umontreal.ca), as examined by Jean-François Loiseau. Sources for later generations include more items from the Drouin Collection plus marriage registers and "Lee Johnson's Family Tree" on http://gw2.geneanet.org/leej49.

16, 17. **Anne Couvent** of Québec = (1) Philippe **Amiot**

17, 18. Mathieu Amiot, Sieur de Villeneuve = Marie Miville

18, 19. Anne-Marie Amiot = Jean Huard

19, 20. Marie-Anne Huard = Charles Couture

20, 21. Joseph Couture = Angélique Roy

21, 22. Angélique Couture = Louis Gosselin

22, 23. Angélique Gosselin = Thomas Larue

23, 24. Thérèse Larue = Paul Paquin

24, 25. **Paul-Jean Paquin**, sometime of Mass. = Marcelline Phaneuf, sometime of Mass.

25, 26. Adélard Paquin = Marie Allaire

26, 27. Albert-Joseph Paquin = Agnes Jansen

27, 28. Brian Paquin = Mary Brophy

28, 29. **Anna (-Hélène) Paquin**, b. 1982, actress (second-youngest Academy Award winner, 1993) = Stephen Moyer, actor

Sources: "Pascoe/Zintel/Worms/Nau/Naud/Nault/Neault…," database at http://worldconnect.rootsweb.ancestry.com/cbi-bin/igm.cgi?db=2708896 (generations 22/23-28/29, based on personal knowledge); "Généalogie du Québec et d'Amérique Française" at http://nosorigines.qc.ca/ (generations 16/17-22/23), with selected documentary sources. This line was brought to my attention by John Blythe Dobson of Winnipeg, Manitoba, Canada.

The Royal Descents of 900 Immigrants

16, 17. **Anne Couvent** of Québec = (1) Philippe **Amiot**

17, 18. Mathieu Amiot, Seigneur de Villeneuve = Marie Miville

18, 19. Jeanne-Anne-Marie Amiot = Paul Tessier

19, 20. Anne-Marie Tessier = Louis-Étienne Gagné dit Belavance

20, 21. Paul Gagné dit Belavance = Marie-Michelle Brault

21, 22. Paul Gagné = Marie-Catherine Hubert dit Lacroix

22, 23. Joseph Gagné = Angélique Pitre

23, 24. Claire Gagné = Michel Mallet

24, 25. Michel Mallet = Caroline Faubert

25, 26. Marguerite Mallet = Joseph Briere

26, 27. Marie-Jeanne Briere = Armand Lemieux

27, 28. Jean-Guy Lemieux = Pierrette Leroux

28, 29. **Mario Lemieux**, b. 1965, of Pa., professional hockey player and later co-owner and CEO of the Pittsburgh Penguins = Natalie Asselin.

Sources: *MHH* 29 (2008): 183 (last two generations only); Diane's Database (Diane Wolford Sheppard), line confirmed by Thomas Allaire and John P. Hickey, Jr.

The Royal Descents of 900 Immigrants

16, 17. **Anne Couvent** of Québec = (1) Philippe **Amiot**

17, 18. Mathieu Amiot, Seigneur de Villeneuve = Marie Miville

18, 19. Jeanne-Anne-Marie Amiot = Paul Tessier

18, 19. Catherine Ursule Amiot = Jean-Baptiste Duquet dit Desrochers

19, 20. Anne-Marie Tessier = Louis-Étienne Gagné dit Belavance

19, 20. Charles Duquet = Catherine Mallet

20, 21. Paul Gagné dit Belavance = Marie-Michelle Brault

20, 21. Marie-Madeleine Duquet = Claude Duranceau dit Brindamour

21, 22. Vital Gagné = Louise Lepage

21, 22. Marie-Madeleine Duranceau dit Brindamour = Michel Lefebvre

22, 23. Paul Gagné = 22, 23. Catherine Lefebvre

23, 24. Louis Gagné = Domithilde Leduc

24, 25. Charles Gagné = Marguerite Beaudry

25, 26. Arthur Gagné = Valentine Durocher

26, 27. Gérard Gagné = Dolores Millette

27, 28. Richard Gagné = Carole Roux

28, 29. **Eric Gagné**, b. 1976, of Mass., professional baseball player, World Series pitcher for the Boston Red Sox = Valerie Hervieux.

Sources: *MHH* 29 (2008): 14-15 (Tessier to Eric Gagné and P.E. Trudeau, as noted under the chart outlining the latter's descent from Anne Couvent), 183; Diane's Database, line confirmed by Thomas Allaire.

21. **Rev. William Sargent** of Mass. (see p. 857) = (3) Mrs. Sarah ——— Minshull

22. John Sargent = (3) Lydia Chipman, daughter of John Chipman and Hope Howland, daughter of Mayflower passengers John Howland and Elizabeth Tilley

23. William Sargent = Mary Lewis

24. Zathiah Sargent = Robert Livingston/Leventon

25. John Livingston = Mary Todd

26. Polly Livingston = Joseph Burt, Jr.

27. Mary Burt of Montreal, Québec = Étienne (Stephen) Rose

28. **Joseph Rose** of Mich. = Catherine Thomas   28. **Rose-Hermine Rose** of Mich. = Joseph **Mercereau**

29. Jean-Baptiste Rose =   29. Marie-Louise Mercereau

30. Eva Marie Rose = Henry Joseph Vigneron

31. Elwin Vigneron = Bernardine Kott

32. **Allen Henry Vigneron**, b. 1948, Archbishop of Detroit since 2009, unm.

Sources: *MHH* 30 (2009): 90-93 (entire line); Elizabeth Pearson White, *John Howland of the Mayflower, Volume 3, The First Five Generations: Documented Descendants through His Third Child, Hope^2 Howland, Wife of John Chipman* (2008), pp. 17-35, 42-44, 93-95, 336-37 (to John Livingston); E.C. Cogswell, *History of New Boston, New Hampshire* (1864), pp. 439-40 and Westmoreland History Committee, *History of Westmoreland (Great Meadow), New Hampshire, 1741-1970 and Genealogical Data* (1976), pp. 490, 360-61 (Livingston, Burt, to Mary/Polly, b. 1795); *Who's Who in America, 2012* (2011), p. 4596. This line was developed by Diane Wolford Sheppard.

The Royal Descents of 900 Immigrants

18. **Nicolas Leblond** of Québec = Marguerite Leclerc

19. Marie-Madeleine Leblond = Nicolas Roy

20. François-Nicolas Roy = Marie-Thérèse Allard

21. Marie-Françoise Roy = Jean-Baptiste Eli dit Breton

22. Jean-Baptiste Eli dit Breton = Marie-Louise Labrecque

23. Charles Eli dit Breton = Olive Goulet

24. Gilbert Breton = Adelina Trahan

25. Joseph-François-Amedée Breton = Antoinette Audet

26. Marie-Alphonsine-Germaine Breton = Joseph-Roland Gameau Germain

27. Estelle Germain = Venant-Eugène Henry

28. Diane M. Henry = (1) Michael Mallette; (2) Bruce Dale

29. (by 1) Patricia "Patty" Mallette; whose son, with Jeremy Bieber, is

30. **Justin [Drew] Bieber**, b. 1994, sometime of Calif., musician, unm.

Sources: www.famouskin.com/family-tree.php?name=21972+justin+bieber, which cites various records from the Drouin Collection, 1621-1968, for [Eli dit] Breton; Cyprien Tanguay, *Dictionnaire Généalogique des Familles Canadiennes, Septième Volume* (1890), section 1, pp. 69, 79-80 for Roy, and René Jetté, *Dictionnaire Généalogique des Familles du Québec, des Origines à 1730* (1983), p. 1019, col. 2 (plus *Université de Montréal, Programme de recherché en démographie historique* database [PRDH]) for Leblond. Generations 10-13 are treated on various websites (e.g. www.ethnicelebs.com/justin-bieber) and Wikipedia. A full ancestor table, but without dates, places, or references (just names) appears on https://famouskin.com/ahnentafel.php?name=21972+justin+bieber, compiled by Rich Hall.

The Royal Descents of 900 Immigrants

The following four immigrants and figures, plus a le Neuf descent for Céline Dion, were traced by John Blythe Dobson of Winnipeg, Manitoba, a major contributor to this volume, and were developed largely from the Internet sources cited below. These lines—plus those for Gosling and Paquin (both also traced by Dobson) and Justin Bieber—were not checked by Thomas Allaire or John P. Hickey, Jr. I hope various French-Canadian scholars will find in notarial or parish records, marriage registers, censuses, etc., further documentation for these descents.

21. **Anne-Élisabeth de Tarragon** of Québec = Gilles **Couturier dit La Bonté**
22. Pierre Couturier dit La Bonté = Gertrude Maugras
23. Joseph Couturier dit La Bonté = Marie-Louise Allard
24. Michel Couturier dit La Bonté = Marguerite Caron
25. Marguerite Couturier dit La Bonté = Antoine Badayac dit Laplante
26. Geneviève Badayac = Jean-Baptiste Théroux
27. Pierre Théroux = (Marie-) Eugénie Loiseau dit Cardin
28. **(Joseph-Louis-) Eugène Théroux** of Mass. = Eva Brousseau.
29. Albert-Eugène Theroux = Anne Francesca Dittami
30. **Paul Edward Theroux**, b. 1941, American travel writer and novelist = (1) Anne Castle; (2) Sheila Donnelly. An older brother, Alexander Louis Theroux, b. 1939, is an American poet and novelist married to artist Sarah Son; a younger brother, Peter Christopher Sebastian Theroux, b. 1956, is an American writer and translator. The two sons of Paul Edward and Anne (Castle) Theroux are Marcel Raymond Theroux, b. 1968, British novelist and broadcaster, and Louis Sebastian Theroux, b. 1970, British documentary filmmaker and broadcaster, who married (1) Susanna Kleeman; (2) Nancy Strang, television director.
30. Eugène-Albert Theroux = Phyllis Grissim
31. **Justin Paul Theroux**, b. 1971, screenwriter and actor = Jennifer [Joanna] Aniston, b. 1969, the actress and former wife of [William] Brad[ley] Pitt, b. 1963, actor, SETH

The Royal Descents of 900 Immigrants

Sources: The entire line can be found in the database "Généalogie du Québec et d'Amérique Française" at http://www.nosorigines.qc.ca/, which cites documentary sources. FindAGrave entries cover generations 27-30; Wikipedia treats Paul, Alexander, Peter, Louis, Marcel, and Justin Theroux, plus Jennifer Aniston and Brad Pitt.

12. **Marie Martin** of Québec = Christophe **Février**
13. Marie-Anne Février = Louis Menard
14. Jean-Baptiste Menard = Marie-Françoise Lebeau
15. Marie-Anne Menard = Charles Robert dit Lafontaine
16. Marie-Josèphe Robert dite Lafontaine = Marc-Antoine Huot
17. Marguerite Huot = François Hebert
18. Adrien-André Hebert = Felicité Richard
19. Gilbert Hebert = Françoise Chasles
20. Cordélie Hebert = William Logan
21. Laby Logan = Alphonse Sarrazin, see below
22. Bernard-Alphonse Sarrazin = Mary Maud Enid Scott
23. **Jacques-Michel-André Sarrazin**, known as **Michael Sarrazin** (1940-2011), sometime of Calif., film and television actor, d. unm.

A second line for Michael Sarrazin is from Nicolas Leblond, as follows:

18. **Nicolas Leblond** of Québec = Marguerite Leclerc
19. Catherine Leblond = Jean Rioux, Seigneur de Trois-Pistoles
20. Nicolas Rioux, Seigneur de Trois-Pistoles = Louise Asselin
21. Catherine Rioux = Paul Lepage
22. Antoine Lepage dit Molais = Marie-Josephte Côté
23. Marie-Élisabeth Lepage = François Maisonneuve
24. Thérèse Maisonneuve = François Corbeil
25. Olive Corbeil = Louis Marineau dit Hostin
26. Léocadie Marineau dite Hostin = Joseph Sarrazin
27. Alphonse Sarrazin = Laby Logan, see above

The Royal Descents of 900 Immigrants

Sources: Both lines above appear on the database "Généalogie du Québec et d'Amérique Française" at http://www.nosorigines.qc.ca/, which cites documentary sources. The actor is treated on Wikipedia.

The above Catherine Leblond and Jean Rioux, Seigneur de Trois-Pistoles, at generation 19, and Anne Desrosiers and Jacques Turcot at generation 22 on p. 989, are also ancestors, per sources listed on p. 975, of Madonna (via two more immigrants to Michigan), as follows:

23. Madeleine-Jacquette Turcot (sister of Marie-Madeleine) = Jean-Baptiste Toupin

24. Marie-Madeleine Toupin = Louis-Joseph Delisle

25. Louis-Joseph Delisle = Marie-Gertrude Lemieux

20. Vincent Rioux (brother of Nicolas) = Marie-Catherine Côté

26. Marie-Louise Delisle = Joseph-Romain Fortin

21. Vincent Rioux = Julienne Drouin

27. Joseph-Romain Fortin = Geneviève Fortin, a cousin

22. Vincent Rioux = Marie-Josèphe Sirois

28. François Fortin = Victoire Blier

23. Felicité Rioux = Narcisse Fortin

29. **Nazaire ("Henry") Fortin**, of Mich. = Émilie Daniel

24. **Narcisse ("Nelson") Fortin**, of Mich. = Rose Lajoie

30. Guillaume-Henri Fortin = Marie-Louise Demers, see p. 975

25. Willard Fortin   =   31. Élise ("Elsie") Fortin

26, 32. Madonna Louise Fortin = Silvio Anthony Ciccone

27, 33. **Madonna Louise Veronica Ciccone**, rock star and actress, as **Madonna,** b. 1958 = (1) Sean **Penn**, actor; (2) Guy Stuart **Ritchie**, b. 1958, filmmaker, sometime of N.Y. or Calif., ARD, SETH.

19. **Jeanne Le Marchand** of Québec = Mathieu **Le Neuf**, Sieur du Hérisson

20. Michel Le Neuf, acting governor of Trois-Rivières, royal judge = ⎯⎯

21. (probably illegitimate) Anne du Hérisson = Antoine Desrosiers

22. Anne Desrosiers = (1) Jacques Turcot; (2) Jean Debidabé

23. (by 1) Marie-Madeleine Turcot = François Rivard dit Lavigne

24. Marie-Josephte Rivard = Jean-Nicolas Vézina

25. Clothilde Vézina = Charles Brisson dit Tilly

26. Jean-Baptiste Brisson dit Tilly = Marie-Josephte Boutin

27. **Godefroi Brisson dit Tilly** of Mass. = Marie-Rose Arsenault.

28. Marie-Louise Brisson = Charles-Eusèbe Sevigny

29. Wilfred Sevigny = Rose Marois

30. Harold Sweet Sevigny = (Mary?) Ernestine Stevens

31. (Harold) David Sevigny = Janine Malinowski

32. **Chloë [Stevens] Sevigny**, b. 1974, actress, unm.

Sources: The entire line is given in the database "Généalogie du Québec et d'Amérique Française," at http://nosorigines.qc.ca/, which cites documentary sources. The actress is treated on Wikipedia.

The singer Céline (-Marie-Claudette) Dion, see p. 977, is also a descendant of 21. Anne du Hérisson and Antoine Desrosiers, as follows: 28. Alma (Pelletier) Barriault; 27. Amable Pelletier (and Célina Beaulieu); François Pelletier and 26. Marguerite Desrosiers; 25. Joseph-Marie-Jean Desrosiers dit du Tremble (and Josephte Dubé); 24. Louis Desrosiers dit du Tremble (and Marie-Judith Després); 23. Michel Desrosiers dit du Tremble (and Marie-Jeanne Moreau); 22. Jean Desrosiers dit du Tremble (and Marie-Françoise Dandonneau), SETH, under Jean Chrétien; 21 above. For sources, see p. 977.

16. **Jean-Vincent l'Abbadie, Baron de Saint-Castin** (1652-1707), French soldier and Abenaki chief = (1) Marie Pidiwamiskwa; (2) Mechtilde de Niousqué

17. (by 2) Ursule d'Abbadie de Saint-Castin = Louis d'Amours de Chaffours, son of Louis d'Amours, Sieur de Chaffours (and Marguerite Guyon), son of **Mathieu d'Amours, Sieur de Chaffours** of Québec, and Marie Marsolet, SETH

18. **Jean-Baptiste d'Amours de Louvières** of Louisiana = Geneviève Bergeron.

19. Anastasie d'Amours de Louvières = Pierre-René Leblanc

20. Constance Leblanc = Joseph-René Broussard

21. Joséphine-Adelania Broussard = Rosemond Broussard, a cousin

22. Eloy-René Broussard = Josephine Lesser

23. Odilia Broussard = Eugène-Gustave DeRouen

24. Agnès DeRouen = Lumis Albert Beyincé

25. Célestina "Tina" Anne Beyincé = Mathew Knowles

26. **Beyoncé Giselle Knowles**, known as **Beyoncé**, b. 1981, singer = Shawn [Corey] Carter, rapper (as "Jay Z"), b. 1969.

27. **Solange Knowles**, actress, singer, b. 1986 = (1) Alan Ferguson; (2) Daniel Smith.

Sources: Jacques Noël, "Beyoncé...avec un accent aigu," http://www.magazineprestige.com/Beyonce-avec-un-accent-aigu, citing his book *La Diaspora Québécoise* (2016) (generations 21-26); Vita B. and John R. Reaux, "Jean-François Broussard and Catherine Richard," *Attakapas Gazette* 6 (1971): 4-8 (generations 19-22); Yves Drolet, *Dictionnaire Généalogique de la Noblesse de la Nouvelle-France* (2017) (entries for Abbadie de Saint-Castin and Amours de Chaffours).

The Royal Descents of 900 Immigrants

An Hispanic Royal Descent, Probably One of Hundreds

Included on the following several pages is perhaps the most extraordinary royal descent I have yet encountered—from James I, King of Aragón, d. 1265, with an illegitimate line from Eleanor of Aquitaine, Queen of France and England, through the Ponce de León family to which the explorer may belong, Guzmáns of Argentina, *Californios* (Hispanic residents of California between 1769 and 1848, before statehood), with Irish Lynch ancestry, to Ana Isabel Lynch Ortíz (b. 1861). Ana married Roberto Guevara Castro, a first cousin twice removed of the general for whom the Castro district of San Francisco was named; her son, Ernest Rafael Guevara Lynch, was the father of Ernesto "Che" Guevara, the Argentine-born Cuban and Bolivian revolutionary leader, Cuban cabinet official and diplomat, and author of *The Motorcycle Diaries*. This descent, first found on the Internet by Christopher Challender Child (whose interest in his wife's Dominican ancestry may expand into a broader Hispanic expertise), was later meticulously documented, at my request, by the already mentioned (and charted) Thomas Frederick Gede. Mr. Gede's sources, listed below, include various websites and Google Books, the latter often not at NEHGS and referenced, with footnotes, not simply a list of sources, almost exactly as provided by Mr. Gede. Another extraordinary set of royal descents appears in Ramon Darío Suarez, *Genealogía del Libertador*, 2nd ed. (1983), for Simón Bolivar.

I know virtually nothing about Caribbean, Mexican, or Central or South American genealogy. The published ancestor table of Charles F.H. Evans (see Steven Edwards, ed., *The Complete Works of Charles Evans: Genealogy and Related Topics* [2003], pp. 209-45 [originally in *TG* 4 (1983): 230-65, 6 (1985): 191-92]) and such tables, compiled by the late William Addams Reitwiesner on the Brazilian ancestry of Queen Silvia of Sweden, the Cuban ancestry of María Teresa, Grand Duchess of Luxembourg, and the Argentine ancestry of Queen Maxima of The Netherlands, plus even the most cursory perusal of the great *Enciclopedia Heráldica y Genealógica Hispano-Americana*, 88 vols. (1919-63) by Alberto and Arturo García Caraffa (and that set's 15 later successor volumes) will convince anyone that Latin American sources, both printed and documentary, are vast. I thus hope that another scholar, or team of scholars—perhaps not, however, in my lifetime—will produce a compendium of Conquistador and later Latin American royal descents, probably mostly from kings of Castile, Aragón, or León. As with my

The Royal Descents of 900 Immigrants

almost lifetime work on British and Continental royal descents covered herein—and as with the now-flourishing work on such French Canadian lines—an Hispanic study would certainly produce startling results. These descents might also suggest much of the genealogical evolution of the Caribbean, Mexico, and Central and South America.

The Royal Descents of 900 Immigrants

1. James (Jaime) I, King of Aragón, d. 1276 = (3) Teresa Gil de Vidaure[1]

2. Jaime Fernández de Aragón, Barón de Xérica (or Ejérica), b. 1238[2] = Elfa de Azagra,[3] b. ca. 1250, daughter of Álvaro Pérez de Azagra, Señor de Albarra, and Marguerite of Navarre, illegitimate daughter of Theobald I, King of Navarre, d. 1253, son of Theobald III, Count of Champagne (and Sancha of Navarre), son of Henry I, Count of Champagne, and Marie of France, daughter of Louis VII, King of France, d. 1180, and Eleanor of Aquitaine

3. Jaime II, Señor de Xérica[4] = Beatríz de Lauria[5]

4. Beatríz de Xérica[6] = Pedro Ponce de León,[7] II. Señor de Marchena, d. 1352[8]

---

[1] Carmen Orcástegui Gros, *Crónica de San Juan de la Peña* (Versión aragonesa), *Edición Critica*, Zaragoza: Diputación Provincial, Institución "Fernando el Católico," 1985, p. 88 (Lat. pp. 148-49) (Univ. of Calif. Los Angeles [UCLA] Library Call No. DP124.8.P343 1985).

[2] Jerónimo Zurita, *Anales de la Corona de Aragón*, Tomo Primero (1st ed.) (Zaragoza, 1562), p. 227 (Bibliothèque nationale et universitaire Strasbourg-B.N.U.S., Call No. D.12.241), also on Google Books; Juan F. Rivarola y Pineda, *Monarquía Española, Blason de su Nobleza*, parte primera, imprenta de Alfonso de Mora 1736, p. 69 (Newberry Library, Chicago, Call No. Case folio CR115.S7 R58 1736), also on Google Books.

[3] F.W. Hodcroft, "Elpha: nombre enigmático de Cantar del Mío Cid" (1984), monograph, pp. 44-45, (http://ifc.dpz.es/recursos/publicaciones/09/23/04hodcroft.pdf).

[4] *Anales, supra*, p. 227; *Blason de su Nobleza, supra*, p. 69; Francisco de Moxó y de Montoliu, *La Casa de Luna*, Münster, Westfalen: Aschedorffsche Verlagsbuchhandlung (1990), pp. 169, 216.

[5] *Anales, supra*, p. 423; *Blason de su Nobleza, supra*, p. 69.

[6] Sometimes called Beatríz de Lauria, not to be confused with her mother; Luis de Salazar y Castro, *Índice de las Glorias de la Casa Farnese*, 1st ed. (Madrid 1716, imprenta de Francisco del Hierro), p. 584 (UCLA Library "No call number" SRLF Non-Circ Request at UCLA YRL Special Collections), also on Google Books; *Nobiliario del Conde de Barcelos Don Pedro*, Alonso de Paredes, 1646, Madrid, Tit. XXI, Ponços, 9, p. 132, also on Google Books (Newberry Library Call No. folio Greenlee 4536.P37 1646); Francisco Ruano, *Casa de Cabrera en Córdoba*,

5. Pedro Ponce de León, IV. Señor de Marchena,[9] d. ca. 1374, m. 1363[10] = Sancha de Haro[11]

6. Pedro Ponce de León, V. Señor de Marchena, Conde de Arcos,[12] d. 1418 = María de Ayala[13] (daughter of Pedro López, Señor de Ayala y Salvatierra (and Leonor de Guzmán), and granddaughter of Fernán Pérez, Señor de Ayala, and Elvira Álvarez de Ceballos, these last the maternal grandparents of Sancha de Ayala, wife of Sir Walter Blount, SETH)[14]

7. Juan Ponce de León, Conde de Arcos, d. 1469[15] = (prob. a mistress) Catalina González de Oviedo.[16] He is thought by Hugh Thomas to be probably the paternal grandfather of Juan Ponce de León, d. 1521, who conquered Puerto Rico and discovered Florida, both in 1508. The intervening generation is uncertain, and the descent would probably run through two illegitimacies.

8. Eutropio Ponce de León[17] = (prob. 2) Catalina de Vera Zurita[18]

---

en la oficina de D. Juan Rodríguez (1779), p. 46 (University of Wisconsin, Madison Library Special Collections, Call No. CS959 C3), also on Google Books.
[7] Salazar, *Índice, supra*, p. 584; *Casas de Cabrera, supra*, pp. 45-46.
[8] Salazar, *Índice, supra*, p. 584. See also *ES* 2: 2: 70, *ES* 2: 3: 129B (first four generations, plus charts for Navarre, Champagne, and France).
[9] *Ibid*; *Casa de Cabrera, supra*, pp. 47-48.
[10] Salazar gives d. 1387; however, testament was ordered (*otorgado*), 7 Dec. 1374, see Rafael Sánchez Saus, *Caballería y linaje en la Sevilla medieval: estudio genealógico y social* (1st ed.) (San Fernando, 1989), p. 349.
[11] *Casa de Cabrera, supra*, p. 48; also Salazar, *Índice, supra*, p. 584.
[12] Salazar, *Índice*, p. 584; *Casa de Cabrera, supra*, pp. 49-50.
[13] *Ibid*.
[14] A postulated descent from Henry II of England via Juana García Carrillo, great-grandmother of María and Sancha, cannot be proved; see *NEHGR* 152 (1998): 36-48, esp. 42-44 (Todd A. Farmerie and Nathaniel L. Taylor on Sancha de Ayala).
[15] *Casa de Cabrera, supra*, pp. 51-58; Rivarola y Pineda, *Blasón de su Nobleza, supra*, p. 71.
[16] *Casa de Cabrera, supra*, p. 56; Hugh Thomas (later Hugh Swynnerton Thomas, Baron Thomas of Swynnerton), *Rivers of Gold: The Rise of the Spanish Empire, from Columbus to Magellan* (2003), p. 543.
[17] *Ibid*; also *Índice de la Colección de don Luís de Salazar y Castro, Tomo X*, 18.832 #4, "Descendencia de don Estropo [Eutropio] Ponce de León, hijo del II

9. Violante Ponce de León[19] = Ruy Díaz de Guzmán y Riquelme[20]

10. Alonso Riquelme de Guzmán of Asunción, Paraguay[21] = Ursula de Irala[22]

11. Catalina de Guzmán of Buenos Aires, Argentina[23] = Jerónimo López de Alanis[24]

12. Rodrigo [Ponce de León] López de Alanis[25] = Isabel Naharro de Humanes[26]

13. María Ponce de León y Navarro[27] = Agustín de Labayen[28]

14. Juana de Labayen[29] = Gaspar de Avellaneda[30]

Conde de Arcos [de la Frontera]," Manuscrito anónimo en 4 folios, B-24, folio 100-103.
[18] Flavio Rivera Montealegre, *Genealogía de la familia MONTEALEGRE: Sus Antepasados en Europa y sus Descendientes en América* (Trafford Publishing, 2011), p. 347 (not deposited in libraries, with a limited view on Google Books).
[19] *Ibid.*
[20] *Ibid.*, at p. 348; Ruy Díaz de Guzmán, *Argentina: Historia del Descubrimiento, Conquista y Población del Rio de la Plata*, C. Casavalle (1882), p. 12 (UC Berkeley Library Call No. F2841. D5 1962), also on Google Books.
[21] Ruy Díaz de Guzmán, *Argentina*, *supra*, at 12; Montealegre, *Genealogía*, pp. 348-49.
[22] *Ibid.*
[23] *Boletín*, vol. 10, Universidad de Buenos Aires, Instituto de Investigaciones Históricas (Buenos Aires: El Instituto, 1930), p. 65 (University of Virginia Library Call No. F2801.B965); Montealegre, *Genealogía*, p. 349.
[24] *Ibid.*
[25] Montealegre, *Genealogía*, pp. 349-51; *Boletín*, vol. 10, Instituto de Investigaciones, *supra*, p. 65.
[26] *Ibid.*
[27] Montealegre, *Genealogía*, p. 351 (as María Ponce de León y Navarro); *Boletín*, *supra*, p. 65 (as María Ponce de León, according to "Genealogía de Che Guevara: Raíces Sinaloenses y Californias de Che Guevara," https://genealogiadelcheguevara.blogspot.com/2009/10/raices-sinaloenses-y-californias-del.html).
[28] Montealegre, *Genealogía*, p. 352; *Boletín*, *supra*, p. 65.

15. María Rosa de Avellaneda[31] = Juan de San Martín[32]

16. Francisca Javiera de San Martín[33] = Marcos José de Riglos[34]

17. María Jacinta de Riglos y San Martín[35] = Mariano José de Zavaleta Aramburu (1762-1837)[36]

18. María Isabel Zavaleta Riglos[37] (1795-1883) = Patricio Julián José Lynch Roo[38] (1789-1881)[39]

19. **Francisco de Paula Eustaquio Lynch Zavaleta**, sometime of San Francisco, Calif. (1817-1886)[40] = Mrs. Eloïsa Ortíz Alfaro Eldridge (1834-1913).[41]

---

[29] *Ibid.*; also Guillermo Lohmann Villena, *Los Americanos en las Órdenes Nobiliarias* (Editorial CSIC Press, 1993), p. 350 (genealogy of Miguel Fermín de Riglos y San Martín) (UC Berkeley Library [Bancroft] Call No. CS95.L6).
[30] *Ibid.*
[31] Montealegre, *Genealogía*, p. 353; Lohmann Villena, *supra*, p. 350.
[32] Montealegre, *Genealogía*, p. 354; Lohmann Villena, *supra*, p. 350.
[33] Lohmann Villena, *supra*, p. 350.
[34] *Ibid.*
[35] Carlos F. Ibarguren, "Mariano Francisco J. Zavaleta Aramburu, Biografía Histórica," monograph, digested from *Los Antepasados, a lo largo y más allá de la Historia Argentina* (1983), p. 3 (http://studylib.es/doc/291421/zavaleta-aramburu-mariano-francisco-joseph) (Author Ibarguren is a kinsman of the Lynch family.)
[36] *Ibid.*, pp. 1, 30.
[37] *Ibid.*, p. 12; Montealegre, *Genealogía*, pp. 359-60.
[38] *Ibid.*
[39] Montealegre erroneously gives Patricio's death date as 20 May 1869; it should be 1881. See "Boletín del Instituto Argentino de Ciencias Genealógicas," issue 162 (1989), p. 190.
[40] Eduardo A. Coghlan, "Los Irlandeses en Argentina: Su Actuación y Descendencia," Part 2 (1987), p. 627, with no evidence that Francisco was born in California; Coghlan gives Buenos Aires as his birthplace. He was born there 29 March 1817 and baptized at Nuestra Señora de la Merced, Buenos Aires, the next day ("Argentina, Capital Federal, Catholic Church Records, 1737-1977," online image at www.familysearch.org). Exiled after the Battle of Quebracho Herrado (east Córdoba Province, Argentina, 28 Nov. 1840, an episode of the Argentine Civil Wars of 1814-1880), Francisco became consul in San Francisco in the 1840s, where he married 1 Aug. 1854 Eloïsa Ortíz, a Chilean and widow of Carlos [Charles] Eldridge;

20. Ana Isabel Lynch Ortíz,[42] b. San Francisco, Calif. 1861, d. by 1948 = Roberto Guevara Castro,[43] b. Calif. 1855, son of Juan Antonio Guevara Calderón, b. Argentina ca. 1820, settled in Calif., and María Concepción Dolores Castro Peralta, daughter of Guillermo Castro García, *Californio*, b. Monterey 1809, first cousin of *Comandante* General José Antonio Castro Amador (acting governor of Alta California, 1835-1836, for whom San Francisco's Castro district is named) and María Luisa Bárbara Guadelupe Peralta, daughter of Luís María Peralta, a settler with Juan Bautista de Anza in 1776, *comisionado* of Pueblo San José and recipient of one of the largest Spanish land grants, Rancho San Antonio (most of the present-day East Bay region of Calif.), and his wife María Josefa Alviso, sister of Ignacio Alviso, for whom Alviso, California (now part of Silicon Valley) is named

21. Ernesto Rafael Guevara Lynch,[44] b. 1900 = Celia de la Serna Llosa[45]

22. **Ernesto "Che" Guevara de la Serna** (1928-1967), Argentine-born Cuban and Bolivian revolutionary leader, Cuban cabinet official and diplomat, and author of *The Motorcycle Diaries* = (1) Hilda Gadea Acosta; (2) Aleida March Torres

---

also Daniel James, *Che Guevara: A Biography* (2001), pp. 26-30. At San Francisco in the 1852 state census, "Buenos Ayres"-born F. Lynch, clerk, 35, gave his most recent previous residence as "Guaquil," possibly Guayaquil, Ecuador. "Frank E. Lynch" was at San Juan, Monterey County, Calif., in 1860 with his Chilean-born wife and Calif.-born older children (1860 U.S. Census, Monterey Co., Calif., San Juan twp., Series M653, Roll 60, pp. 984-985). The family had returned to Buenos Aires by 13 Oct. 1871, when son Guillermo Rufino Lynch Ortíz was baptized at Santiago Apostól, Baradero, Buenos Aires ("Argentina, Buenos Aires, Catholic Church Records, 1635-1981," online image database at www.familysearch.com).
[41] *Ibid.*
[42] *Ibid.*; also Montealegre, *Genealogía*, p. 366. Ana Isabel's national origin is given as "N[orte] Americana" [i.e., U.S.] in "Argentina, National Census, 1895," online image database at www.familysearch.org.
[43] *Ibid.* The Frank E. Lynch and Juan A. Guevara families at San Juan, Calif. are separated by only four households in the 1860 census cited above.
[44] James, *Che Guevara, supra*, pp. 26-30; Montealegre, *Genealogía*, p. 370.
[45] *Ibid.*

The Royal Descents of 900 Immigrants

The Royal Descents of 900 Immigrants

55 Remarkable Descents, Kinships, or Near Kin-to-Near Kin Genealogical Connections Outlined and Charted in This Volume

In the list below, "to" indicates descent (from ancestor A to descendant B, various generations later); "and" indicates kinship between the two or more listed figures; and "on chart with" indicates kinship to someone nearly related to the other notable(s).

1. Philip II, King of Spain, to Brooke Shields, p. 18 herein

2. Prince Carl of Solms-Braunfels, sometime of Texas, as a first cousin of German Emperor William I, and a second cousin of Queen Victoria, p. 40

3. Kings of Denmark and Gustav I Vasa, King of Sweden, to Mrs. Kofi Annan, p. 60

4. James Boswell, on chart with Henry Robinson Luce, pp. 90-91

5. Lady Elizabeth Foster, Duchess of Devonshire, to Anna Wintour, p. 117

6. Wives of Sir Henry Morton Stanley (Dorothy Tennant) and Ezra Pound (Dorothy Shakespear), p. 130-31

7. "Rob Roy" MacGregor and Mrs. Karl Marx (Johanna [Jenny] Bertha Julie von Westphalen), pp. 146-47

8. Gordon Marquesses of Huntly to Stanislaus Poniatowski, King of Poland, and Queen Mathilde of The Netherlands, pp. 154-55, 163-64

9. Lord Byron on chart with James Monroe and Theodore Roosevelt, p.

10. James IV, King of Scotland, to President Harry S Truman, pp. 171-72

The Royal Descents of 900 Immigrants

11. William the Silent and Baron von Steuben, p. 181

12. Queen Victoria and "Ben" Bradlee of the *Washington Post*, pp. 182-83

13. Pope Paul III Farnese and a sister-in-law of Lucretia Borgia to the von Trapp singers, pp. 186-87

14. Hernán Cortés, on chart with Andrew and Paul Mellon, pp. 189-93

15. Queen Victoria and the Moravian Zinzendorfs, pp. 196-97

16. Agnès Sorel and Diane de Poitiers to the Marquis de La Fayette and Philippe I, King of the Belgians, pp. 200-4

17. Kings of France and Gustav I Vasa, King of Sweden to the husband of Gladys Moore Vanderbilt of "The Breakers" (Ladislaus [László], Count Széchényi), pp. 208-9

18. John Napier (of logarithms) to Alexander Hamilton, p. 214

19. William Penn on chart with the Marquis de Sade, pp. 226-27

20. Cesare Borgia to Alexis de Tocqueville, pp. 293-94

21. Lord Byron, Jane Austen, and the Leveson-Gower progeny to Warren Buffett and Gary Boyd Roberts, this work's author, pp. xii-xiv, 295-99

22. American descendants of Mary Boleyn and possibly King Henry VIII, pp. 300-4

23. Richard More of the *Mayflower*, Anthony Trollope, Peter and Zara Phillips (children of Princess Anne) and Julie Helen Otto, the author's collaborator on this work, pp. 319-21

24. The Woodvilles of late medieval England to Francis Scott Key, p. 334

25. Elizabeth Plantagenet of York, Queen of Henry VII, and William Byrd II, p. 342

The Royal Descents of 900 Immigrants

26. Fletcher Christian on chart with George Washington, p. 363

27. Gov. Thomas Dudley to wives of Lord Beaverbrook (Gladys Henderson Drury) and Norman Mailer (Lady Jeanne Louise Campbell), pp. 370-71

28. Harriet Martineau, the Duchess of Cambridge, Prince George, and Princess Charlotte, pp. 379-80

29. Saltonstalls of Mass. (via cross-references) and W.H. Auden, pp. 403-4

30. John I de Lusignan, titular King of Cyprus, Jerusalem, and Armenia, d. 1432, to the Empress Joséphine, p. 442

31. Parliamentary leader John Hampden and U.S. Senator John McCain, pp. 466-67, 469

32. The poet Shelley and the presidents Bush, p. 474

33. Edmund Spenser, Samuel Pepys, the Guinnesses of Ireland, and Anne Hutchinson, pp. 478-81

34. The fourth and last wife of Gov. John Winthrop (Margaret Tyndal) and Salem witchcraft victim Rev. George Burroughs, pp. 483-84

35. James Madison on chart with Barack Obama (with kinship to Robert E. Lee mentioned in the introduction), pp. 497-98

36. Wellington and The Queen Mother on chart with Eisenhower aide Kay Summersby, pp. 546-47

37. Courtenays, Earls of Devon (and of Powderham Castle) to Lowells of Mass., p. 569

38. Anne Boleyn and Mamie Eisenhower, p. 588

39. James Oglethorpe's sister Eleanor to the Kings of Italy, pp. 613-14

40. Rudolf I, Holy Roman Emperor, founder of the Habsburgs, to Vladimir Nabokov, pp. 617-18

The Royal Descents of 900 Immigrants

41. Jean-Luc Godard and the Masaryks of Czechoslovakia, pp. 634-35

42. The wife of Fritz Lang (Thea Harbou) and Claus von Bülow, p. 645

43. Thoreau and the Duchess of Cornwall, p. 655

44. Charles VII Bonde, King of Sweden, to Jake and Maggie Gyllenhaal, pp. 662-63

45. Romanovs of Russia to Tolstoy and Mme. Blavatsky, pp. 791-96

46. Genghis Khan (only an alleged ancestor) and Byzantine emperors on chart with John Jacob and Vincent Astor, pp. 797-800

47. Peter Paul Rubens and Calverts of Maryland, pp. 804-5

48. Stracheys and "Signer" Caesar Rodney, pp. 824-25

49. De Graffenrieds of N.C. to First Lady Laura Welch Bush of Texas, pp. 832-33

50. Queen Jane Seymour, Edward VI, and Ludwells of Virginia, pp. 855-56

51. Napoléon I Bonaparte, Diana, Princess of Wales, and Warren G. Harding, pp. 858-59

52. Scottish Livingstons to Jackie Kennedy Onassis (pp. 914-15)

53. Robert Goulet and Anna Paquin, pp. 973, 980, who share four generations of French-Canadian ancestry

54. Madonna and Chloë Sevigny, pp. 988-89, who share four generations of French-Canadian ancestry

55. Sancha de Ayala, her American descendants and Che Guevara, pp. 993-97, *passim*

The Royal Descents of 900 Immigrants

LIST OF ABBREVIATED SOURCES

AACPW	Gary Boyd Roberts and William Addams Reitwiesner, *American Ancestors and Cousins of The Princess of Wales* (1984)
AAP2009, 2012	Gary Boyd Roberts, *Ancestors of American Presidents 2009 Edition* (2012 reprint, with changes)
AL3, 4	Carl Boyer 3rd, *Ancestral Lines,* 3rd ed. (1998), 4th ed. (2015)
ANB	*American National Biography,* 24 vols. (1999)
Anselme	Père Anselme de Sainte-Marie, *Histoire Généalogique et Chronologique de la Maison Royale de France, des Pairs, Grands Officiers de la Couronne et de la Maison du Roy, et des Anciens Barons du Royaume* (3rd ed., 8 vols., 1726-33, reissued in 9 vols. 1879-82, partial revision by Pol Potier de Courcy [of vols. 4 & 9])
AP&P	Virginia M. Meyer and John Frederick Dorman, *Adventurers of Purse & Person, Virginia 1607-1624/5,* 3rd ed. (1987)
AP&P4	John Frederick Dorman, *Adventurers of Purse and Person, Virginia, 1607-1624/5,* 4th ed., 3 vols. (2004, 2005, 2007)
AR7	F.L. Weis, W.L. Sheppard, Jr., and David Faris, *Ancestral Roots of Certain American Colonists Who Came to America Before 1700,* 7th ed. (1992)
ARD	<u>A</u>lso of <u>R</u>oyal <u>D</u>escent
Ardingly, Horsham, Lewes	John Comber, *Sussex Genealogies* (*Ardingly Centre,* 1932; *Horsham Centre,* 1931; *Lewes Centre,* 1933)
AT	ancestor table

The Royal Descents of 900 Immigrants

Baillie	J.G.B. Bulloch, *Genealogical and Historical Records of The Baillies of Inverness, Scotland, and Some of their Descendants in the United States of America* (1923)
Catherine Baillon	René Jetté, John Philip Dulong, Roland-Ives Gagné, Gail F. Moreau, and Joseph A. Dubé, *Table d'Ascendance de Catherine Baillon: 12 Générations* (2001)
Baines1	Edward Baines, *History of the County Palatine and Duchy of Lancaster*, 4 vols. (1836)
Baines2	Edward Baines and James Croston, *The History of the County Palatine and Duchy of Lancaster*, rev. ed., 5 vols. (1888-93)
Baker	George Baker, *The History and Antiquities of the County of Northampton*, 2 vols. (1822-41)
Bartrum 1,2	P.C. Bartrum, *Welsh Genealogies, A.D. 300-1400*, 8 vols. (1974) and *Welsh Genealogies, A.D. 1400-1500*, 18 vols. (1983)
Bernards of Abington	Mrs. Napier Higgins, *The Bernards of Abington and Nether Winchendon, A Family History*, 4 vols. (1903-4)
Berry's Bucks	William Berry, *Pedigrees of Buckinghamshire Families* (1837)
Berry's Hants	William Berry, *Pedigrees of the Families in the County of Hants* (1833)
Berry's Kent	William Berry, *Pedigrees of the Families in the County of Kent* (1830)
Berry's Surrey	William Berry, *Pedigrees of Surrey Families* (1837)
BDSCHR	W.B. Edgar and N.L. Bailey, eds., *Biographical Directory of the South Carolina House of Representatives*, 4 vols. (1974-84)
BIFR	*Burke's Irish Family Records* (1976)

The Royal Descents of 900 Immigrants

Blackman	H.J. Young, *The Blackmans of Knight's Creek: Ancestors and Descendants of George and Maria (Smith) Blackman*, rev. ed. (1980)
BLG	*Burke's Landed Gentry (Burke's Genealogical and Heraldic History of the Landed Gentry [of Great Britain])* (often further identified by publication year, edition, and/or page)
BLGI	*Burke's Genealogical and Heraldic History of the Landed Gentry of Ireland* (4 editions — 1899, 1904, 1912 and 1958)
Blomefield	Francis Blomefield and Rev. Charles Parkin, *An Essay Towards a Topographical History of the County of Norfolk*, 2nd ed., 11 vols. (1805-10)
Blore	Thomas Blore, *The History and Antiquities of the County of Rutland* (1811)
BP	*Burke's Peerage (Burke's Genealogical and Heraldic History of the Peerage, Baronetage, and Knightage)*, various editions
BRB	Marquis of Ruvigny and Raineval, *The Blood Royal of Britain, Being a Roll of the Living Descendants of Edward IV and Henry VII, Kings of England, and James III, King of Scotland* (1903, rep. 1994)
BRFW	*Burke's Royal Families of the World, Volume 1, Europe and Latin America* (1977)
BRMF 1,2	Robert W. Barnes, *British Roots of Maryland Families,* 2 vols. (1999, 2002)
BSIC	J.G.B. Bulloch, *A History and Genealogy of the Families of Bulloch and Stobo and of Irvine of Cults* (1911)
Stephen Bull	Henry DeSaussure Bull, *The Family of Stephen Bull of Kinghurst Hall, County Warwick, England and Ashley Hall, South Carolina, 1600-1960* (1961)

The Royal Descents of 900 Immigrants

Bulkeley	D.L. Jacobus, *The Bulkeley Genealogy* (1933)
Burnett of Leys	George Burnett, *The Family of Burnett of Leys* (1901)
Catherine Baillon	See under Baillon
CB	G.E. Cokayne, *Complete Baronetage*, 5 vols. (1900-6)
Charles II	Col. Charles M. Hansen and Neil D. Thompson, *The Ancestry of Charles II, King of England: A Medieval Heritage* [12 Generations] (2012, 2014)
Chester of Chicheley	R.E.C. Waters, *Genealogical Memoirs of the Extinct Family of Chester of Chicheley, Their Ancestors and Descendants*, 2 vols. (1878)
Clarence	Marquis of Ruvigny and Raineval, *The Plantagenet Roll of The Blood Royal: The Clarence Volume, Containing the Descendants of George, Duke of Clarence* (1905, rep. 1994)
Jeremy Clarke	A.R. Justice, *Ancestry of Jeremy Clarke of Rhode Island and Dungan Genealogy* (1922)
William Clopton	Lucy L. Erwin, *The Ancestry of William Clopton of York County, Virginia, with Records of Some of his Descendants* (1939)
Clutterbuck	Robert Clutterbuck, *The History and Antiquities of the County of Hertford*, 3 vols. (1815-27)
CN	*The Connecticut Nutmegger*
Collins	Sir Egerton Brydges, ed., *Collins' Peerage of England,* 9 vols. (1812)
Cornewall	C.G. Savile Foljambe, 4th Earl of Liverpool, and Compton Reade, *The House of Cornewall* (1908)
Courcelles	M. le Chevalier de Courcelles, *Histoire Généalogique et Héraldique des Pairs de France*, 12 vols. (1822-33)

The Royal Descents of 900 Immigrants

CP	Vicary Gibbs, etc., *The [New] Complete Peerage,* 13 vols. (1910-59)
CRFP	J.W. Jordan, ed., *Colonial and Revolutionary Families of Pennsylvania,* 3 vols. (1911, rep. 1978)
CRLA	American Historical Company, Inc., *Colonial and Revolutionary Lineages of America,* 25 vols. (1939-68)
CVR	Clarence V. Roberts, *Ancestry of Clarence V. Roberts and Frances A. (Walton) Roberts* (1940)
DAB	*Dictionary of American Biography*, 20 vols. plus index (1928-37), and eight supplements (to deaths through 1970) and *Comprehensive Index* (1944-90)
DCB	*Dictionary of Canadian Biography*, vols. 1-14, covering persons dying through 1920, plus *Index* (covering persons dying through 1900 only (1966-91)
Davis 1-3	W.G. Davis, *Massachusetts and Maine Families in the Ancestry of Walter Goodwin Davis (1885-1966): A Reprinting in Alphabetical Order by Surname of the Sixteen Multi-Ancestor Compendia (plus Thomas Haley of Winter Harbor and His Descendants) Compiled by Maine's Foremost Genealogist, 1916-1963* (with introduction by Gary Boyd Roberts) (3 vols., 1996)
D de la N	Francois Alexandre Aubert de la Chenaye-Desbois et Badier, *Dictionnaire de la Noblesse,* 19 vols., 1863-76 (a reprint of the last 18th cent. [3rd] ed.)
Delafield	J.R. Delafield, *Delafield: The Family History,* 2 vols. (1945)
DGA	Heinrich Banniza von Bazan and Richard Müller, *Deutsche Geschichte in Ahnentafeln,* 2 vols. (1939-42)

The Royal Descents of 900 Immigrants

Diana 12G	Richard K. Evans, *The Ancestry of Diana, Princess of Wales, for Twelve Generations* (2007)
Diane's Database	"wolfordsheppard," a large RootsWeb WorldConnect Project database which includes full French-Canadian ancestor tables to the early seventeenth century for many notables with French-Canadian forebears: http://wc.rootsweb.ancestry.com/cgi-bin/igm.cgi?db=wolfordsheppard
[Oxford] DNB	*Oxford Dictionary of National* [British] *Biography*, 60 vols. (2004), with *Oxford Dictionary of National Biography, 2001-2004* (2009), plus *Index of Contributors* (2004), which massively expands the late nineteenth-century edition and its various supplements, with no subject deletions)
Douglas	Sir Robert Douglas of Glenbervie, 6th Bt., *The Baronage of Scotland* (1798)
DP	*Debrett's Peerage and Baronetage* or *Debrett's Peerage, Baronetage, Knightage and Companionage*, various editions
Drummond	Henry Drummond, *History of Noble British Families*, 2 vols., 1846 (vol. 1: Ashburnham, Arden, Compton, Cecil, Harley, Bruce; vol. 2: Perceval, Dunbar, Hume, Dundas, Drummond, Neville)
Duncumb	John Duncumb and W.H. Cooke, *Collections Toward the History and Antiquities of the County of Hereford,* 5 vols. (1804-97)

The Royal Descents of 900 Immigrants

Dunster	Sir H.C. Maxwell Lyte, *A History of Dunster and of the Families of Mohun & Luttrell*, 2 vols. (1909)
DVY	J.W. Clay, ed., *Dugdale's Visitation of Yorkshire with Additions*, 3 vols. (1899, 1907, 1917)
Earwaker	*East Cheshire: Past and Present; or a History of the Hundred of Macclesfield in the County Palatine of Chester*, 2 vols. (1877-80)
EB	John Burke and John Bernard Burke, *A Genealogical and Heraldic History of the Extinct and Dormant Baronetcies of England, Ireland and Scotland*, 2nd ed. (1841, repr. 1985)
Edmond Hawes	See under Hawes
Elgenstierna	Gustaf Elgenstierna, *Den Introducerade Svenska Adelns Ättartavlor Med Tillägg Och Rättelser,* 9 vols. (1925-36)
EO 1,2	*English Origins of New England Families From The New England Historical and Genealogical Register*, 1st ser. (3 vols., 1984), 2nd ser. (3 vols., 1985)
EP	Sir Bernard Burke, *A Genealogical History of the Dormant, Abeyant, Forfeited, and Extinct Peerages of the British Empire*, new ed., 1883 (repr. 1962, 1969)
ES	Wilhelm Karl, Prinz von Isenburg, Frank, Baron Freytag von Loringhoven, and Detlev Schwennicke, *Europäische Stammtafeln: Stammtafeln zur Geschichte der Europäischen Staaten*, old ser., 5 vols. (1936, 1937, 1956, 1957, 1978), new ser., vols. 1-21 (vol. 3 in 4 parts) (1978-2002)
Essex	Marquis of Ruvigny and Raineval, *The Plantagenet Roll of The Blood Royal: The Isabel of Essex Volume, Containing the Descendants of Isabel (Plantagenet), Countess of Essex and Eu* (1908, repr. 1994)

The Royal Descents of 900 Immigrants

Charles Evans	Lindsay L. Brook, ed., *Studies in Genealogy and Family History in Tribute to Charles Evans on the Occasion of His Eightieth Birthday* (Association for the Promotion of Scholarship in Genealogy, Ltd., Occasional Publication No. Two, 1989)
Exeter	Marquis of Ruvigny and Raineval, *The Plantagenet Roll of the Blood Royal: The Anne of Exeter Volume, Containing the Descendants of Anne (Plantagenet), Duchess of Exeter* (1907, rep. 1994)
FMG	John W. Clay, ed., *Familiae Minorum Gentium Diligentiā Joseph Hunter, Sheffieldiensis, S.A.S.*, 4 vols. (Publications of the Harleian Society, Visitation Series, vols. 37-40, 1894-96)
FNE	Ernest Flagg, *Genealogical Notes on the Founding of New England* (1926, rep. 1973)
Forbes	Alistair and Henrietta Tayler, *The House of Forbes* (1937)
Foster's V of Yorkshire	Joseph Foster, ed., *Visitations of Yorkshire, 1584-5 and 1612* (1875)
G A de F	Henri Jougla de Morenas, *Grand Armorial de France*, 6 vols. (1934-49)
GDMNH	C.T. Libby, Sybil Noyes, and W.G. Davis, *Genealogical Dictionary of Maine and New Hampshire* (1928-1939, rep. 1972)
GF	Hubert Cuny and Nicole Dreneau, *Le Gotha Français: État Présent des Familles Ducales et Princières (depuis 1940)* (1989)
GGE	H. F. Waters, *Genealogical Gleanings in England*, 2 vols. (1901-1907, reprint 1969)
G H des A	*Genealogisches Handbuch des Adels*, 1951- (125+ vols. to date)

Glover	Stephen Glover and Thomas Noble, *The History and Gazetteer of the County of Derby*, 2 vols. (1829-33)
GM	*Genealogists' Magazine*
GM 1-7	Robert Charles Anderson, *The Great Migration: Immigrants to New England, 1634-1635*, 7 vols. (1999-2011) (vols. 1 and 2 with George F. Sanborn Jr. and Melinde Lutz Sanborn)
GMB 1-3	Robert Charles Anderson, *The Great Migration Begins: Immigrants to New England, 1620-1633*, 3 vols. (1995)
Gordon	J.M. Bulloch, ed., *The House of Gordon*, 3 vols. (1903-12)
Gorges	Raymond Gorges, *The Story of a Family Through Eleven Centuries, Being a History of the Gorges Family* (1944)
GPFPGM	*Genealogies of Pennsylvania Families From The Pennsylvania Genealogical Magazine*, 3 vols. (1982)
GPFPM	*Genealogies of Pennsylvania Families From The Pennsylvania Magazine of History and Biography*, 1 vol. (1981)
Gresleys of Drakelowe	Falconer Madan, *The Gresleys of Drakelowe* (1899)
GVFT	*Genealogies of Virginia Families From Tyler's Quarterly Historical and Genealogical Magazine*, 4 vols. (1981)
GVFVM	*Genealogies of Virginia Families From The Virginia Magazine of History and Biography*, 5 vols. (1981)
GVFWM	*Genealogies of Virginia Families From the William and Mary College Quarterly Magazine*, 5 vols. (1982)

The Royal Descents of 900 Immigrants

The Habsburg Dynasty	Jacques Arnold, *The Royal Houses of Europe: The Habsburg Dynasty of Austria-Hungary: Descendants of Maria Theresa and Franz, Duke of Lorraine* (2007)
Hamilton	George Hamilton, *A History of the House of Hamilton* (1933)
Edmond Hawes	J.W. Hawes, *Edmond Hawes of Yarmouth, Massachusetts, an Emigrant to America in 1635, His Ancestors, Including the Allied Families of Brome, Colles, Greswold, Porter, Rody, Shirley, and Whitfield, and Some of His Descendants* (1914)
Hawes, Freeman and James	H.J. Young, *The Carolingian Ancestry of Edmond Hawes, Alice Freeman, and Thomas James* (1983) and *Some Ancestral Lines of Edmond Hawes, Alice Freeman, and Thomas James* (1984)
The Hohenzollern Dynasty	Jacques Arnold, *The Royal Families of Europe: The Hohenzollern Dynasty of Prussia: The Descendants of King Friedrich Wilhelm I*, 2 vols. (2011)
HSF	J.B. Boddie, *Historical Southern Families*, 23 vols. (1957-80)
HSPVS	*Harleian Society Publications, Visitations Series* (ongoing)
HVG	Rev. H.E. Hayden, *Virginia Genealogies* (1891, rep. 1959)
Mary Isaac	W.G. Davis, *The Ancestry of Mary Isaac* (1955)
Isham	H.W. Brainerd, *A Survey of the Ishams in England and America* (1938)
Jeremy Clarke	See under Clarke
JIC	N.D. Thompson and R.C. Anderson, *A Tribute*

	to John Insley Coddington on the Occasion of the Fortieth Anniversary of the American Society of Genealogists (Association for the Promotion of Scholarship in Genealogy, Ltd., Occasional Publication No. One, 1981)
Keeler-Wood	Josephine C. Frost, *Ancestors of Evelyn Wood Keeler, Wife of Willard Underhill Taylor* (1939)
Kempe	Frederick Hitchin-Kemp, *A General History of the Kemp and Kempe Families of Great Britain and Her Colonies* (1902)
Kimber	Edward Kimber and Richard Johnson, *The Baronetage of England,* 3 vols. (1771)
LDBR 1,2,3,4,5	H.H. d'Angerville, *Living Descendants of Blood Royal,* 5 vols. (1959-73)
Ligon	W.D. Ligon and E.L. Whittington, *The Ligon Family and Connections,* 3 vols. (1947, rep. 1988; 1957; 1973)
Lincolnshire Pedigrees	Rev. Canon A.R. Maddison, *Lincolnshire Pedigrees,* 4 vols. (Publications of the Harleian Society, Visitations Series, vols. 50-52, 55, 1902-4, 1906)
Lipscomb	George Lipscomb, *The History and Antiquities of the County of Buckingham,* 4 vols. (1847)
Lives of the Berkeleys	John Smyth of Nibley, *The Lives of the Berkeleys, Lords of the Honour, Castle, and Manor of Berkeley in the County of Gloucester from 1066 to 1618,* Sir John MacLean, ed., 3 vols. (1883-85)
Lodge	John Lodge and Mervyn Archdall, *The Peerage of Ireland,* 7 vols. (1789)
Roger Ludlow	H.F. Seversmith, *The Ancestry of Roger Ludlow* (1964) (vol. 5 of *Colonial Families of Long Island, New York, and Connecticut*)

The Royal Descents of 900 Immigrants

Manning and Bray	Rev. Owen Manning and William Bray, *The History and Antiquities of the County of Surrey*, 3 vols. (1795-1814)
Marbury	M.B. Colket, Jr., *The English Ancestry of Anne Marbury Hutchinson and Katherine Marbury Scott* (1936)
Mary Isaac	See under Isaac
MCS4, 5	F.L. Weis, W.L. Sheppard, Jr., and David Faris, *The Magna Charta Sureties, 1215*, 4th ed. (1991), 5th ed. (with William R. Beall, 1999)
Mémoires	*Mémoires de la Societé Généalogique Canadienne Française*
Merion	T.A. Glenn, *Merion in the Welsh Tract* (1896, rep. 1970)
M&G	G.T. Clark, *Limbus Patrum Morganiae et Glamorganiae* (1886)
MG	*Maryland Genealogies: A Consolidation of Articles from the Maryland Historical Magazine*, 2 vols. (1980)
MGH	*Miscellanea Genealogica et Heraldica*
MHH	*Michigan's Habitant Heritage*
Montgomery	T.H. Montgomery, *A Genealogical History of the Family of Montgomery, Including the Montgomery Pedigree* (1863)
Morant	Philip Morant, *The History and Antiquities of the County of Essex*, 2nd ed., 2 vols. (1768)
MP	Marquis of Ruvigny and Raineval, *The Plantagenet Roll of the Blood Royal: The Mortimer-Percy Volume, Containing the Descendants of Lady Elizabeth Percy, née Mortimer* (1911, rep. 1994)
NAW	*Notable American Women, 1607-1950, A Biographical Dictionary*, 3 vols. (1971); *The*

The Royal Descents of 900 Immigrants

	Modern Period [1951-75] (1980); and *Completing the Twentieth Century* (2004)
NDTPS	Notable Descendants Treated in Printed Sources
NEHGR	*The New England Historical and Genealogical Register*
NEXUS	*NEHGS NEXUS* (1983-1999)
NF 1,2	W.P. Hedley, *Northumberland Families*, 2 vols. (1968-70)
NGSQ	*National Genealogical Society Quarterly*
NHN	*A* [New] *History of Northumberland*, 15 vols. (1893-1940)
Nichols	John Nichols, *The History and Antiquities of the County of Leicester*, 4 vols. in 8 (1795-1815)
NYGBR	*The New York Genealogical and Biographical Record*
NK 1,2	G.B. Roberts, *Notable Kin, Volume One* and *Volume Two* (1998, 1999)
Ormerod	George Ormerod and Thomas Helsby, *The History of the County Palatine and City of Chester*, 2nd ed., 3 vols. (1882)
Oxford DNB	See *DNB*
PACF	J.E. Griffith, *Pedigrees of Anglesey and Carnarvonshire Families* (1914)
Parliament 1386-1421	J.S. Roskell, Linda Clark and Carol Rawcliffe, *The History of Parliament, The House of Commons, 1386-1421*, 4 vols. (1992)
Parliament 1509-1558	S.T. Bindoff, *The History of Parliament, The House of Commons, 1509-1558*, 3 vols. (1982)
Parliament 1558-1603	P.W. Hasler, *The History of Parliament, The House of Commons, 1558-1603*, 3 vols. (1981)

The Royal Descents of 900 Immigrants

Parliament 1660-1690	Basil Duke Henning, *The History of Parliament, The House of Commons, 1660-1690*, 3 vols. (1983)
Parliament 1715-1754	Romney Sedgwick, ed., *The History of Parliament, The House of Commons, 1715-1754*, 2 vols. (1970)
PCF Lancashire	Joseph Foster, *Pedigrees of the County Families of England, Vol. 1 - Lancashire* (1873)
PCF Yorkshire	Joseph Foster, *Pedigrees of the County Families of Yorkshire*, 2 vols. (1874)
PMHB	*The Pennsylvania Magazine of History and Biography*
Prince Charles (elsewhere *Paget*)	Gerald Paget, *The Lineage and Ancestry of Prince Charles, Prince of Wales*, vol. 2 (1977)
PSECD 2,3	J.O. Buck, A.E. Langston, and T.F. Beard, eds., *Pedigrees of Some of the Emperor Charlemagne's Descendants*, vols. 2-3 (1974-78). Undocumented, cited as seldom as possible, and always with at least one other source.
RA	Douglas Richardson, *Royal Ancestry: A Study in Colonial and Medieval Ancestry*, 5 vols. (2013)
RD	Royal descent
RHS	A.C. Addington, *The Royal House of Stuart: The Descendants of King James VI of Scotland, James I of England*, 3 vols. (1969-76)
RLNGF	Joseph Foster, *The Royal Lineage of Our Noble and Gentle Families*, vol. 1 (1883), vol. 2 (1884)
Roger Ludlow	See under Ludlow
Rutherford	W.K. and A.C.Z. Rutherford, *Genealogical History of the Rutherford Family*, 2 vols. (1969), rev. ed., 2 vols. (1979), 2nd rev. ed., 2 vols. (1986)

The Royal Descents of 900 Immigrants

Saint Allais	M. de Saint Allais, *Nobiliaire Universel de France, ou Recueil Général des Généalogies Historiques des Maisons Nobles de ce Royaume*, 21 vols. (rep. 1872-77)
Salt	William Salt Archaeological Society, *Collections for a History of Staffordshire* (ongoing journal)
Saltonstall	Leverett Saltonstall, *Ancestry and Descendants of Sir Richard Saltonstall, First Associate of the Massachusetts Bay Colony and Patentee of Connecticut* (1897)
SCG	*South Carolina Genealogies: Articles from the South Carolina Historical (and Genealogical) Magazine*, 5 vols. (1983)
Scott of Scots Hall	J.R. Scott, *Memorials of the Family of Scott of Scots Hall in the County of Kent* (1876)
SETH	See Elsewhere in This Volume
Shaw	Rev. Stebbing Shaw, *History and Antiquities of Staffordshire*, 2 vols. (1798-1801)
Shirleiana	E.P. Shirley, *Stemmata Shirleiana* (1873)
SMF 1,2,3	J.J. Muskett, *Suffolk Manorial Families*, 3 vols. (1900-10)
SP	Sir J.B. Paul, *The Scots Peerage*, 9 vols. (1904-14)
Stephen Bull	See under *Bull*
Strachey	C.R. Sanders, *The Strachey Family, 1588-1932, Their Writings and Literary Associations* (1953)
Surtees	Robert Surtees, *The History and Antiquities of the County Palatine of Durham*, 4 vols. (1816-40)
TAG	*The American Genealogist*
TCWAAS	*Transactions of the Cumberland & Westmorland Antiquarian & Archaeological Society*

The Royal Descents of 900 Immigrants

TG	*The Genealogist* (London, 1877-1922; New York, Salt Lake City, and Sausalito, Calif., 1980-present)
Thoroton	John Throsby, *Thoroton's History of Nottinghamshire*, 3 vols. (1797)
Throckmorton	C.W. Throckmorton, *A Genealogical and Historical Account of the Throckmorton Family in England and the United States with Brief Notes on Some of the Allied Families* (1930)
Tixall	Sir Thomas Clifford, 1st Bt., and Arthur Clifford, *A Topographical and Historical Description of the Parish of Tixall in the County of Stafford* (1817)
TM	*Tyler's Quarterly Historical and Genealogical Magazine*
TSA	*The Scottish Antiquary*
TVG	*The Virginia Genealogist*
UGHM	*The Utah Genealogical and Historical Magazine*
VC	J.L. Vivian, *The Visitations of Cornwall, Comprising the Heralds' Visitations of 1520, 1573, and 1620, with Additions* (1887)
VD	J.L. Vivian, *The Visitations of the County of Devon* (1895)
VGE	Lothrop Withington, *Virginia Gleanings in England: A Consolidation of Articles from The Virginia Magazine of History and Biography* (1980)
VHG	J.B. Boddie, *Virginia Historical Genealogies* (1954, rep. 1965)
VM	*The Virginia Magazine of History and Biography*
WC	G.E. McCracken, *The Welcome Claimants: Proved, Disproved and Doubtful, With an Account of Some of Their Descendants* (1970,

The Royal Descents of 900 Immigrants

	Publications of the Welcome Society of Pennsylvania, Number 2)
Wentworth	John Wentworth, *The Wentworth Genealogy, English and American*, 2nd ed., 3 vols., (1878)
WFP 1,2	T.A. Glenn, *Welsh Founders of Pennsylvania*, 2 vols. (1911-13, rep. 1970)
Whitney	Henry Melville, *The Ancestry of John Whitney* (1896)
William Clopton	See under Clopton
Wilson	Y.L. Wilson, *A Carolina-Virginia Genealogy* [Wilson Family] (1962)
WV	Clayton Torrence, *Winston of Virginia and Allied Families* (1927)
WWA	*Who's Who in America*
WWAW	*Who's Who in American Women*
WWWA	*Who Was Who in America*

The Royal Descents of 900 Immigrants

Index

by Julie Helen Otto,
edited by Gary Boyd Roberts, and
proofread by Margaret Foye Mill

Introduction
to the Index

Numbers below refer to pages, and the same name can refer to several persons on various charts. Men are listed under their surnames and each title noted herein; women are listed under maiden surname, husband's surname, and any title they bear in their own right, but not under titles they bear through their husbands. Kings, queens, princes, princesses, archdukes, grand dukes, margraves, landgraves, counts, and other members of sovereign or some mediatized houses are listed by first names (those by which they are known) and sovereignty or place (kingdom, duchy, county, etc.), and many females or non-sovereigns are designated simply as "of". Princes, dukes, marquesses, counts, or barons with surnames (Radziwill, Polignac, La Fayette, Tolstoy) are indexed by surname only. The prefixes *de, d', de la, la, le, l'*, and *von* are usually ignored (except when the prefix is capitalized) in the alphabetization itself; surnames beginning with *del, des, du, von der, van, van de*, and *van der* are usually alphabetized *with* the prefix. *Alias, dit* and *genannt* can have various meanings and derivations, but sometimes mean simply "called". Hyphenated surnames, listed separately, usually immediately follow the first of the two or three surnames hyphenated, and multiple first names usually appear under the first name, or sometimes the first name by which the person was known.

Welsh names before the use of surnames (Gruffudd ap Llywelyn, Elen ferch Ieuan) are listed under first names only, but for later Welsh women who married Englishmen, often also under the surnames of husbands. Scottish lairds (but not, generally, peers, baronets, or clergymen) are designated as, for example, "of Blairhall," and indexed under surname but not place. "Lord" or "Hon." for younger sons of dukes and marquesses, or earls, viscounts, and barons, is sometimes retained on both charts and index, but knighthood ("Sir") supersedes "Hon." and "Lady" is used only for immigrants who are either the wives of knights or the daughters of earls, marquesses, or dukes. European princesses or members of mediatized houses are, except *usually* for immigrants, not indexed under their husbands' surnames; other European (i.e. Continental) wives of equal or higher rank than their husbands are *usually* indexed under each married surname. Cross-references denote *some* common surname variations. Usually, however, I have followed my sources and some related surnames are not generally combined.

Note: In April 2016 Douglas Richardson, author of *Royal Ancestry*, visited me in Boston and reviewed this volume as compiled through that date. As noted on p. xli of the introduction, my use of *de* (and sometimes *d', de la, la, le, l', von*, etc.) is somewhat arbitrary. Douglas usually deletes *de* from Botetourte, Greystock, Marmion, Ros, Tibetot, and Welles. He adds *de* to, probably among other surnames, Arundel, Badlesmere, Bal(l)iol, Beauchamp, Beaumont, Beke, Berkeley, Chaworth, Courtenay, Crophill (Crophull), Ferrers, Furnival, Grey, Hastings, Montagu, Mortimer, Pateshulle (not Patshull), Roët (I instead followed Judy Perry's article in *Foundations* 1 [2003-5]: 164-174, and dropped the *de*), Stafford, Strathbogie, Swinnerton, and Vaux (Douglas also adds *de la* to Roche, and *le* to Bigod). He usually uses English (or Scottish) forenames taken from documents (what individuals were called, or called themselves, at the time, usually to about 1400 or later), omitting Latin and often French, German or Spanish versions: Adele (not Adela), Alice (or Alix for French queens or noblewomen) (not Adeliza or Adelaide), Aline (not Aveline), Amice (not Amicia), Anne (not Anna), Aubrey (not Auberée), Benet (not Benedicta), Cecily (not Cecilia), Ellen (not Elena), Eudes (not Eudo), Euphame (not Euphemia), Fulk (not Fulke), Hilary (not Hilaria), and de St.-Hilary (not de St.-Hilaire) as a surname, Idoine (not Idonea), Isabel (not Isabella), Isolde (not Isoult or Iseula), Jacquette (not Jacquetta), Joan, later Jane, the Scottish Jean or the French Jeanne (for Scottish or French queens and noblewomen) (not Joanna), Katherine (not Catherine), Marine or Mary (not Marina), Marion (not Mariot or Mariota), Maud (not Matilda, even for Matilda of Flanders, queen of William I "the Conqueror", King of England), Maurice (not Morris), Nichole or Colette (not Nichola), Orabel (not Orabella) (Fitz) Otes (not [Fitz] Otho), Perin or Perina (not Pernel or Petronilla), Reynold (not Reginald), Rohese (not Rohesia), Sanche (not Sancha), and Saher (not Saire). Douglas uses Andrew, 1st Baron Windsor (not Andrews) and Sir Thebaud (or Tebaud), not Sir *Theobald* Vernon.

Douglas uses Arundel as the surname of every FitzAlan post Edmund FitzAlan, 8th Earl of Arundel, and Alice de Warren (Douglas has Warrenne) and refers to Margaret, Duchess of Norfolk, as Margaret Marshal, not Margaret Plantagenet. His preferred medieval surnames, doubtless also among others, include d'Aubeney or Daubeney (not

1024

d'Aubigny), Avenel (not Avenal), Basinges (not Basynges/Basing), Bernake (not Bernacke), Bourgchier (not Bourchier), Brewes (not Braose), de Brus (not Bruce), Cantelow (not Cantilupe), Champernoun (not Champernowne), Culpeper only (not Colepepper), Dalyngrigge (not Dalyngridge), Darell (not Dayrell), Deincourt (not Deyncourt), Fiennes (not de Fienes), FitzWarin (not Fitzwarin), Isaac only (not Ysac), Leek (not Leke), Marshal (not Marshall), Pateshulle (not Patshull), of Ross (not Ross) for earls of Ross, Sulney (not Solney), Tailboys (not Talboys), Tendring (not Tenderyng), Tiptoft (separate from Tibetot), Tony (not Toeni), Warenne (not Warren), and la Zouche Mortimer (not la Zouche de Mortimer). Among medieval titles Douglas prefers Beauchamp of Powick (not Powyck), Neville, Barons Latimer (not Latymer), and Ormond (not Ormonde) (and Thomas Ormond, not Butler, for the 7th Earl). Douglas refers to Maud, Countess of Essex, as Maud de Mandeville (not Maud FitzGeoffrey), and to Alan FitzRoland, Lord of Galloway (not Alan, Lord of Galloway). Robert of Caen, 1st Earl of Gloucester, Mabel FitzHamon his wife, and Hawise de Beaumont, their daughter-in-law, are called Robert FitzRoy, 1st Earl of Gloucester, Maud FitzRobert, and Hawise of Gloucester. Hamelin, son of Geoffrey Plantagenet, Count of Anjou, is not called Plantagenet (a surname admittedly used only by later historians). Robert de Beaumont, first husband of Isabel of Vermandois, called himself (and is sometimes considered by peerage law—see *CP* 7: 927) Earl of Leicester; Douglas refers to him by only his French title, Count of Meulan, and his agnate descendants are "of Meulan," not de Beaumont. In descents from Hugh Capet, King of France, Adeliza des Meschines is called Adeliza of Chester, and Geoffrey FitzPiers is Geoffrey FitzPeter.

Douglas agreed with the caveats I mention for Act. Gov. Nathaniel Bacon and Mrs. Abigail Smith Burwell; Christopher Branch; Mark Catesby and Mrs. Elizabeth Catesby Cocke; Mrs. Elizabeth Bullock Clement(s); the patrilineal descent of Gov. Thomas Dudley; Gov. William Leete; James Neale, Humphrey Underhill, and Mrs. Mary Underhill Naylor Stites; Anthony Savage; Constant and Thomas Southworth; William Strother; Thomas Wingfield; and Henry Woodhouse. Douglas queries, or would like to see monographs on, the Harcourt-Crispe link in the ancestry of Thomas Warren and Gov. Robert, Thomas, and John Gibbes of S.C., the Grey-Disney link in the line of Richard Wright, the la Zouche descent of Sir Anketil Malory in the ancestry of Mrs. Elizabeth Mallory Rivers, the FitzPatrick-Waleran link in the ancestry of Philip Ludwell, and the Cornish descent of Mrs. Judith

Everard Appleton. All of these queries concern kinships from in the High Middle Ages; the Gibbes and Malory lines were developed by the late Brice McAdoo Clagett, the Wright descent by the late Timothy Field Beard, the Ludwell line by John Anderson Brayton, and the Warren and Everard lines by the late Lundie W. Barlow, all major twentieth-century genealogical scholars (and all except Barlow cited for other lines herein). If any of these links/lines are disproved, alternate royal descents are probable and can be outlined in future editions of this work or supplements to it.

Names in the acknowledgments and appendices I and V-X are indexed; the unindexed appendices II-IV are a list of the 970 immigrants themselves, including the 45 French Canadians; 610 major notable figures who appear anywhere on the charts except in the first generation; and the 84 monarchs (mostly kings) at the top of the charts from whom these 970 descend. Also unindexed is the list of "50 Remarkable Descents, Kinships and Near Kin-to-Near Kin Genealogical Connections Outlined and Charted in This Volume" that immediately precedes the list of abbrevations, again since all persons named in these kinships already appear in the index. In this "Introduction to the Index," only entries in this volume, not any alternates, are indexed.

References at the end of each chart are indexed selectively; authors of books are omitted, but names in book titles and authors of journal articles (when specified) are indexed. Names at the end of source sections, and names cited in documents or explanations of evidence are also included. As is shown by the above discussion of Douglas Richardson's work, cross-referencing all versions of noble surnames (much less forenames), both medieval and modern, would be impossible. Indexing rules can vary somewhat, so for these several reasons some patience and experience may be necessary to find all the names you seek. I suggest browsing—both text and index—and finding surprises.

Every effort has been made to review this index for typographical errors, surnames or first names that might be combined, and names initially omitted or later discarded. Errors and omissions, however, are inevitable and corrections are welcome.

INDEX

ABBADIE (L')
  Isabeau (de Béarn-Bonasse) 963
  Jean-Jacques, Baron de Saint-Castin 963
  Jean-Vincent, Baron de Saint-Castin 961, 963, 990
  Marie (Pidiwamiskwa) 963, 990
  Mechtilde (de Niousqué) 963, 990
ABBADIE DE SAINT-CASTIN (L')
  Ursule 990
ABBOT(T)
  Alice 579, 877
  Anne (Mauleverer) xli, lvi, 374
  family xxiv
  John 374
  Susanna (Parris) 324
ABEL(L)
  Caleb 500
  Elizabeth (Humphrey) 511
  Experience 500
  family xxiv, xlviii
  Frances (Cotton) 500
  George 500
  Joanna (____) 500
  Margaret (Post) 500
  Robert x, xix, xlviii, lxviii, clx, 500
  Thomas 511
ABERCORN
  James Hamilton, 1st Duke of 25, 28
  James Hamilton, 1st Earl of 157
  James Hamilton, 6th Earl of 157
  Louisa Jane (Russell), Duchess of 28
ABERCROMBY
  Alexander, of Glassaugh 273
  Elspeth 285
  Helen (Meldrum) 273
  James (Gen.) clxxi, 273
  John, of Glassaugh 273
  Katherine 163
  Katherine (Dunbar) 273
  Katherine (Gordon) 273
  Mary (Duff) 273
ABERDEEN
  William Gordon, 2nd Earl of 67
ABERGAVENNY
  Edward Neville, 1st Baron xxv, 314, 324, 357, 387, 405, 417, 429
  Edward Neville, 5th Baron 405
  Edward Neville, 6th Baron 405
  George Neville, 2nd Baron 118, 324, 347, 357, 405, 417, 429
  George Neville, 3rd Baron 122, 347
  Henry Neville, 4th Baron 122
  Henry Neville, 7th Baron 405
  William Beauchamp, Baron xxv, 417, 500, 551, 574, 588, 596
ABERNETHY
  Alexander, 4th Baron Saltoun of Abernethy 273
  Barbara 210
  Beatrix 273
  family 7
  James, 3rd Baron Saltoun of Abernethy 273
  Laurence, 1st Baron Saltoun of Abernethy 273
  Margaret (____) 273

1027

Margaret (Borthwick) 273
Maria (Cheremeteff) (Grove), Countess cliv, 7
Robert G. cliv, 7
William (Sir) 273
William, of Saltoun 273
____ (Stewart) 273
____ [Mary?] (Stewart) 273

ABINGTON/ HABINGTON
Joyce (Shirley) 653
Mary 653
Richard 653

ABNEY
Bathshua (____) 677
Dannett 677
Edmund 677
Ellen (Wolseley) 677
family lxi, 677
George 677
Katherine (Ludlam) 677
Mary (Brooksby) 677
Mary (Lee) (Abney) 677
Paul 677

ABOYNE
Charles Gordon, 1st Earl of 154
Charles Gordon, 2nd Earl of 155, 933
Charles Gordon, 4th Earl of 933
John Gordon, 3rd Earl of 933

ABRAHALL
Alice 425

ACCARON
Antoinette-Rosalie 616

ACHAYA
Philip of Savoy-Piemont, Prince of 952

ACHESON
Alice Caroline (Stanley) xviii, 364, 434
Dean Gooderham xviii, 364, 434
Isabella 216
Margaret 165

ACHEY (D')
Marguerite-Étiennette 293

ACHIMS
Mary (Fulford) 295, 392, 522
Thomas 392

ACHS
Naomi Foner 663

ACLAND
Elizabeth 76
Margaret Sarah 563

ACRE
Joan Plantagenet of, Princess of England xxxix, 466, 483, 489, 491, 495, 505, 508, 514, 528, 536, 547, 565, 567, 575, 577, 584, 587, 590, 592, 594, 606, 607, 615

ACTON
Eleanor 425
Isabel 530
Joan 490

ACWORTH
Joan 483

ADAIR
Anne 462

ADAM
ap Rhys ab Einion Sais ap Hywel Felyn ap Gruffudd 811
Mary (Robertson) 219
Robert 219
William 219

ADAMS
Abigail (Smith) xlii, 375, 393
Agnes 866
Amy 337
Anne 138
Arthur xlv, lvi
Elizabeth (Noyes) 654
Elizabeth (Watts) 424
Jane clviii, 424, 567
John 424
John, Jr., 2nd U.S. President xlii, 375, 393

John Quincy, 6th
U.S. President
375, 393
Louisa Catherine
(Johnson) 375,
393
Marie Dupuy 13
Mary (Staines) 424
Poyntz 424
Robert 424
Sarah 138, 654
Sarah (Foxton) 424
William 654
ADDIE
Mary 822
ADDINGTON
Anthony 864
Arthur Charles xxi,
xxix, xlv
Elizabeth (Watts)
864
Frances 865
Henry 864
Henry, 1st Viscount
Sidmouth, Prime
Minister 865
Mary (Hiley) 864
Ursula Mary
(Hammond) 865
ADELA
of Normandy,
Princess of
England 642,
830, 911
Princess of France
851
of Savoy, Queen of
France 804, 954,
956, 965

ADELAIDE
Archduchess of
Austria, Queen of
Sardinia, Queen of
Italy 614
of Burgundy 735,
879, 919, 952
of Poitou, Queen of
France 866, 870,
872, 879, 919
Princess of Saxe-
Meiningen, Queen
of Great Britain 9
ADELIZA
of Louvain, Queen of
England, wife of
William d'Aubigny,
1st Earl of Arundel
830
ADGATE
Hannah 921
ADHÉMAR
Constance (de
Poitiers) 735
Dauphine (de
Glandevez) 735
Douce (Gaucelme)
735
Hugh III, Seigneur
de la Garde 735
Hugh IV, Seigneur
de la Garde 735
Lambert III,
co-Seigneur de
Monteil 735
Louis, co-Seigneur
de Monteil 735
Mabile (du Puy) 735
Marguerite 735

ADOLF I
of Nassau-Wies-
baden, Holy Roman
Emperor 617
ADOLPH
Anthony 381
AEHRENTHAL
Princes von 198
ÆLFLÆD
wife of Ethelred II
"the Unready,"
King of England
857, 861, 864
AELIS
Queen of France
879, 919
AERDES
Jan 248
Janet/Jannette
(Duncanson) 248
AERTSDR.
Neelken Geerlof
776
AERTSELAER
Henri-Joseph Stier,
Seigneur of vii,
liv, lxviii, 804, 805
AESWIJN (VAN)
Elisabeth (van
Haeften) 447
Henrica 447
Willem 447
AFFETON (DE)
Katherine 743
AGARD
Elizabeth (Middle-
more) 862
Elizabeth
(Raynsford) 862

George 862
Katherine 369, 862
Stephen 369, 862
Susan (Burnaby) 369
AGASSI
Andre 18
AGLIONBY
Anne (Musgrave) 361
Henry 361
Mary 361
AGMONDESHAM
Helen 710
AGNELLI
Clara Jeanne 20
Edoardo 20
Giovanni 20
Virginia (Bourbon del Monte Santa Maria) 20
AGNES
of Barby 184
of Burgundy 440
of Meran, Queen of France 950
Philip ap Maredudd 582
AGNEW
Andrew (Sir), 5th Bt. 144
Catherine (Blennerhasset) 144, 325
Eleanor (Agnew) 144
Elizabeth 144, 145
Elizabeth (Saunders) 144

Elizabeth (Wilkinson) 144
family, of Lucknow 145
James (Sir), 4th Bt. 144
James, of Howlish 144
Margaret 144, 145, 325
Maria Anne 249
Mary 144, 145
Mary (Montgomery) 144
Robert 144, 325
AGUESSAU (D')
Henriette-Anne-Louise 288
AGUILAR
Carlos de Arellano, Count of 191
AHERNE
Brian de Lacey 463
Joan de Beauvoir (de Havilland) [Joan Fontaine] xvii, 463
AIGLE (DE L')
Amphélise 911
Henri-Louis-Espérance de Laërce des Acres, Count 206
AIGNEAUX (D') (DE DOUVILLE/ D'OUVILLE)
Catherine (de Villiers) 956

Jacqueline (Mayne) 956
Marie (Lamy) 956
Michel 956
Olivier, Seigneur, Seigneur de la Chesnée 956
Robert 956
AIGNEAUX (D') (DE L'ISLE)
Charles 956
Renée (Davy) 956
AIGNON
Anne 941
AIKENHEAD
Jean 159, 160
AILESBURY
Charles Brudenell-Bruce, 1st Marquess of 80
Ernest Augustus Charles Brudenell-Bruce, 3rd Marquess of 80
Thomas Bruce, 3rd Earl of Elgin, 2nd Earl of 80, 81
Thomas Brudenell-Bruce, 1st Earl of 80
AILLEBOUST (D')
Catherine (le Gardeur) 940
Charles-Joseph, Seigneur des Musseaux 940
Dorothée (de Menteith) 940

Nicolas, Seigneur
  d'Argentenay 940
  Suzanne 940
AILLY (D')
  Jean de Picquigny,
    Seigneur 733
AINSLEY
  Jacqui 63
AINSLIE
  Barbara 241
  Frances Anne 30
  John 92
  Mary (Mackenzie)
    (Clarke) (Drayton),
    Lady 92
AIRLIE
  David Graham
    Drummond Ogilvy,
    7th Earl of 22
  John Ogilvy, 2nd
    Baron of 256
AIRMINE
  Elizabeth 389
  Elizabeth (Hicks)
    389
  Martha (Eure) 389
  William (Sir) 389
  William (Sir), 1st
    Bt. 389
AISLABY
  Anne 343
AITCHISON
  Caroline Emma
    Nepean 93
AITKEN
  Gladys Henderson
    (Drury) 371
  Janet Gladys 69,
    371

William Maxwell,
  1st Baron Beaver-
  brook 69, 371
ALAGONIA (D')
  Claire 615
ALBA
  Fadrique Álvarez de
    Toledo, 2nd Duke
    of 191
  Fernando Álvarez
    de Toledo, 3rd
    Duke of, gov. of
    the Spanish
    Netherlands 191
**ALBANIA (THE
  ALBANIANS)**
  Elia (Zaharia),
    Queen of 935
  Géraldine Margit
    Virginia Olga
    Mária, Countess
    Apponyi de Nagy-
    Apponyi, Queen of
    xl, 929, 935
  Leka I, King of xl,
    935
  Leka II, King of xl,
    935
  Susan Barbara
    (Cullen-Ward),
    Queen of 935
  Zog I [Ahmed Bey
    Zogu], King of 935
ALBANY
  Murdoch Stewart,
    2nd Duke of 264
  Robert Stewart, 1st
    Duke of 264, 269,
    272, 273, 280, 283

ALBARRA (DE)
  Álvaro Pérez, Señor
    993
ALBEMARLE
  Christopher Monck,
    2nd Duke of 103,
    104
  George Monck, 1st
    Duke of 103, 104
  William Anne
    Keppel, 2nd Earl
    of 25
  William Coutts
    Keppel, 7th Earl of
    655
ALBERT
  Count of Nassau-
    Weilberg 184
  Prince of Prussia 8
  Prince of Saxe-Co-
    burg-Gotha, Prince
    Consort of Great
    Britain 2, 45, 290
ALBERT I
  Duke of Bavaria,
    Count of 451
  Holy Roman
    Emperor 449, 451
**ALBERT I HONORÉ-
  CHARLES**
  Grimaldi, Sovereign
    Prince of Monaco
    20, 933
ALBERT II
  Holy Roman
    Emperor, King of
    Hungary and
    Bohemia 187,
    220, 895

King of the Belgians 142, 201, 204
ALBERT II
ALEXANDRE-LOUIS-PIERRE
Grimaldi, Sovereign Prince of Monaco xl, 934
ALBERT III
Duke of Saxony 451
ALBERT VII
Count of Schwarzburg-Rudolstadt 182, 196
ALBERT FREDERICK
of Brandenburg-Schwedt 56
Duke of Prussia 47, 54, 56, 891
ALBERTINE
of Brandenburg-Schwedt 56
ALBERTINE JOHANETTE
of Nassau-Hadamar 38
ALBERTINE LEOPOLDINE WILHELMINE JULIA MARIA
Princess of Montenuovo 11
ALBIS (D')
Clarisse (Bontoux) 635
François 635
Hippolyte (Adrien-Henri-François-Hippolyte) 635
Pauline (Auguste-Pauline) 635
Pauline-Victoire (Liquier) 635
ALBON (D')
Beatrix 642
family 952
ALBRET (D')
Alain, Count of Gavre 287, 293
Catherine (de Rohan) 287, 293
Charlotte 287, 293
Françoise (de Châtillon-Blois) 287, 293
Isabelle 287
Jean, King of Navarre 287, 293
Jean, Vicomte de Tartas 287, 293, 459
Jeanne 963
Jeanne-Baptiste 18
ALBUQUERQUE
Sancho of Castile, Count of 191
ALCOCK
Joanna 571
John 571
Sarah (Palgrave) 571
ALDEBOROUGH
Eleanor 374
ALDENBURG (VON)
Anthony II, Count 54

Charlotte Sophie 54
ALDERMAN
Mary (Case) 867
Sarah 867
William 867
ALDERSON
Georgiana Caroline xxxviii
ALDRIDGE
James T. 833
Mary 953
Mary (Chadwell) 833
Nancy Jane 833
ALENÇON
William III Talvas, Count of, Count of Ponthieu 737, 853, 855
ALES
ferch Ieuan ap Madog Gwenwys 650
ALEXANDER
Catherine 165, 211
Grand Duke of Russia 5
Margaret (Stirling) (Forbes) vi, lxiii, lxvii, clxvii, 174, 175
Prince of Hesse 41
Rose 522, 523
ALEXANDER I
King of Yugoslavia 3
ALEXANDER II
Czar of Russia 2, 3, 5, 799

1032

ALEXANDER III
  Czar of Russia 5
ALEXANDER VI
  Pope [Rodrigo
    Borgia] 287, 293
**ALEXANDER
  NEVSKY**
  Grand Prince of
    Kiev and Vladimir
    791, 797
ALEXANDRA
  Mother [Ileana,
    Princess of Rou-
    mania] xviii, xlv,
    3
  Princess of Greece
    and Denmark 3
  of Saxe-Altenburg 7
ALEXANDRINE
  Princess of Prussia
    8
ALEXEI
  Grand Duke of
    Russia 5
ALFONSO V
  King of Naples
    186, 189
ALICE
  (Montagu-Douglas-
    Scott), Princess of
    Great Britain,
    Duchess of
    Gloucester 25, 28
  ferch John 811
  Princess of Batten-
    berg, Princess of
    Greece and
    Denmark 3, 41

ALINGE (D')
  Clotilde Constance
    645
ALINGTON
  Dorothy (Cecil)
    345
  Elizabeth 76
  Elizabeth
    (Tollemache)
    431, 432
  Giles (Sir) 345
  Juliana 431
  Juliana (Noel) 431
  Katherine 345
  Susan 345
  William Alington,
    1st Baron 431
  William Alington,
    2nd Baron 431
ALIX
  Princess of France
    735, 952
ALLAIRE
  Marie 980
  Thomas xii, 968,
    969, 971, 972, 973,
    976, 977, 978, 981,
    982
ALLAN
  Sue xx, 525
ALLARD
  Elmire 972
  Marie-Louise 985
  Marie-Thérèse 984
ALLÈGRE (D')
  Sophie 912
ALLEMAN
  Anne (de
    Châteauneuf) 965

  Aymonette 965
  Catherine (Bérenger)
    911, 912
  Guigues, Seigneur
    d'Uriage 965
  Guigues I, Seigneur
    de Champs and de
    Valbonnais 911
  Marguerite 911
  Marguerite (de
    Beauvoir) 911
  Odon II, Seigneur
    de Champs and de
    Valbonnais 911,
    912
  Philippine 911
ALLEN
  Anne (Brazier) 655
  Anne (Laugharne)
    116
  David 116
  Elizabeth 116
  Elizabeth
    (Hensleigh) 116
  Elizabeth Eleanor
    Mabel 254
  Hope 13
  Jane xix, xxxv,
    lviii, lix, clx, 702,
    730, 746
  Joan (Bartlett) 116
  John 116
  John Bartlett 116
  Joseph 655
  Letitia Dorothea
    76
  Lydia (Brewer) 655
  Mary 127, 318,
    654, 655, 656

1033

Mary (Faircloth) 702
Nathaniel 655
Rebecca (Ward) lviii, lx, cxlviii, cli, clx, clxxix, 655, 656
Sarah Cantey Whitaker xlv
Thomas 702
Walter 655
ALLENDALE
Maldred, lord of Carlisle and 857, 861, 864
ALLINGES (D')
Henri, Seigneur de Coudrée 872
Marguerite (de Langin) 872
Nicolette 872
ALLYE
Mary 320
ALLYN
Abigail 672
Abigail (Warham) 672, 925
Jane 925
John (Rev.) 297
Katherine (Deighton) (Hackburne) (Dudley) xxiv, clx, clxxii, 297
Margaret (Wyatt) xix, liv, lv, lxiv, clxii, clxxv, 672, 674, 925
Mary 673
Matthew 672, 925

Thomas 672, 673, 925
ALMAZOV
Maria (Golitzin) 794
Peter 794
Varvara 794
ALMOTT
Bridget (Naunton) 680
Catherine 680
Thomas 680
ALMQUIST
Agnes Maria Caroline 51
ALMY
Anne 763, 925
Audrey (Barlow) xi, xix, xlviii, lx, cxlii, clxiii, clxxxii, 763, 765, 925
Christopher 764
Elizabeth 764
Elizabeth (Cornell) 764
William 763, 765, 925
ALPHONSO III King of Portugal 619
ALPHONSO VIII King of Castile 647, 909, 948, 964
ALPHONSO IX King of León 647, 709, 909, 948, 964
ALSOP
Cleere 589

Corinne Douglas (Robinson) 164
Dorothy (Bentley) 588
Elizabeth lxii, lxvi, clxii, clxxv, 588, 589
Elizabeth (Heires) 588
George 588
John 588, 589
Joseph Wright (IV) 164
Joseph Wright (V) 164
Stewart Johonnot Oliver 164
Temperance (Gilbert) 588, 589
Timothy 588
ALSTON
Anne (Crochrode) 826, 827
Dorothy (Temple) 356, 827
Elizabeth (Turgis) (Harris) 356
Elizabeth Mary 380
family xxiv, li
John li, lvii, lix, cxlii, clxviii, 356, 826, 827
Mary (___) 826
Mary (Greene) 826
Solomon 826
Thomasine (Brooke) 356
William 356, 826

ALSTRÖMER
Aurora Vilhelmina, Baroness 889
ALSWN
Fechan ferch Hywel 770
ALTHANN (VON)
Anna Maria, Countess 35
Maria Anna 895
ALVA
James Erskine, Lord 175
ÁLVAREZ DE TOLEDO
Beatrix (Pimentel y Pacheco) 191
Fadrique, 2nd Duke of Alba 191
Fernando, 3rd Duke of Alba, gov. of the Spanish Netherlands 191
García, Marquess of Coria 191
Isabel (de Zuñiga y Pimentel) 191
Leonor, Grand Duchess of Tuscany 191, 192
María Osorio (Pimentel), Marquesa de Villafranca del Bierzo 191
Pedro, Marquess of Villafranca del Bierzo 191
ALVES
Anne 93

ALVESTON
Helen 830
ALVISO
Ignacio 997
María Josefa 997
ALVITO E ORIOLA
Diogo Lopes Lobo, Senhor 619
ALWEY
Dorothy 495
AMADEUS I
of Savoy, Prince of Carignan 18
AMADEUS IV
Count of Savoy, ruler of Milan 642
AMADEUS VIII
Duke of Savoy 442
AMADOR PINEDA
Perla 521
AMBERLEY
John Russell, Viscount 22
AMBOISE (D')
Ingelger, Seigneur 942
Marguerite 634, 942
AMCOTTS
Alexander 528
Frances 528
Jane (Fulnetby) 604
Martha 604
Richard (Sir) 604
Susan (Disney) 528
AMELIA
Princess of Hesse-Darmstadt 41

AMELIA AUGUSTA
Princess of Saxe-Meiningen 43
AMELIA HENRIETTE CHARLOTTE
Countess of Solms-Baruth 141
AMHERST
Elizabeth (Cary) 390, 755
Elizabeth (Kerrill) 755
Jane (Dalison) 390, 755
Jeffrey 755
Jeffrey (Gen., Gov.), 1st Baron Amherst of Holmesdale and Montréal xlviii, cxlii, clxxvii, 390, 755, 756
Mary Rothes Margaret Tyssen, Baroness Amherst of Hackney 73
AMIENS
Guy, Bishop of 879, 919
AMIOT
Anne (Couvent) 945, 967, 969, 972, 973, 975, 976, 977, 978, 979, 980, 981, 982
Anne-Marie 972, 973, 977, 978, 980
Catherine-Ursule 982

Jean-Baptiste 950, 951
Jeanne-Anne-Marie 969, 975, 981, 982
Marie (Miville) 969, 972, 973, 975, 976, 977, 978, 979, 980, 981, 982
Marie-Françoise 976, 979
Marie-Louise-Élisabeth (Bazin) 939, 950
Mathieu, Seigneur de Villeneuve 969, 972, 973, 975, 976, 977, 978, 979, 980, 981, 982
Philippe 945, 967, 969, 972, 973, 975, 976, 977, 978, 979, 980, 981, 982
AMORY. *see* **DAMERIE/AMORY**
AMOURS (D')
Élisabeth 939
Jeanne (Le Prévost) 954
Louis, Sieur de Chauffours 990
Louis, Sieur du Plessis 954
Marguerite (Guyon) 990
Marie (Marsolet) 954, 990
Mathieu, Sieur de Chaffours 990

Michel, Sieur de Chauffours 939
Pierre, Seigneur du Serrin 954
AMOURS (D') DE CHAUFFOURS
Louis 990
Ursule (l'Abbadie de Saint-Castin) 990
AMOURS (D') DE LOUVIÈRES
Anastasie 990
Geneviève (Bergeron) 990
Jean-Baptiste 990
AMSTEL (VAN)
Catharina 776
AMSTEL VAN IJSSELSTEIN
Arnoud, knight 776
AMUSCO
Pedro Manrique de Lara y Mendoza, Lord of Treviño and 191
AMY
Katherine 742
AMYROLD
Catherine 383
ANASTASIA
Princess Mscislawska 621
Princess of Moscow 621
Romanov, Czarina (Empress) of Russia 14, 792

ANCASTER
Robert Bertie, 1st Duke of 117
ANDERSON
Alison 255
Daniel 159
Elizabeth xiii, 670
family 160
Janet 285
Jerome E. vii, viii, xlv, l, lxi, 309, 704
Katherine 560
Katherine (Hopton) 670
Lucretia 670
Margaret 266
Margaret (Tytler) 159, 160
Mary 375, 393
Robert Charles viii, xxix, xlv, xlix, lix, lxiv, lxix
Thomas 670, 671
Worth S. viii, xlv, lviii, 344
ANDERTON
Alice (Standish) 611
Dorothy 611
Eleanor 561
Hugh 611
Isabel 701
Isabella 902, 903
ANDREA
(Colonna), Prince of Stigliano 189
ANDREW
Anne 533
Grand Duke of Russia 5

Grand Duke of Russia
[Andrew Romanoff]
clvii, 5
Prince of Greece and
Denmark 3, 41
ANDREWS
Andrew xiv
Anne 608
Cicely Isabel
(Fairfield)
[Rebecca West]
406
Elizabeth 503
Elizabeth (Owen)
809
Elizabeth (Stratton)
503, 608
Esther (Royce) xiv
Eunice xiv
Frances 859
Henry Maxwell 406
John 503, 608
Mary 90
Philippa 126
Thomas 809
**ANDREWS-
READING**
Michael 399
ANDRIA
dukes of 190
ANDRIES
Claude 438
**ANDRONICUS II
PALAEOLOGUS**
Emperor of
Byzantium 797
ANDROS
Edmund (Gov. Sir)
537

ANGELIL
Céline-Marie-
Claudette (Dion)
[Céline Dion]
967, 977, 989
René 977
**ANGELINA
CATERINA**
d'Este, of Modena
18
ANGELL
Mary 554
Rebecca (Mellish)
358
ANGELOS
Isaac II, Emperor of
Byzantium 640,
733
ANGHARAD
ferch Dafydd 692,
770
ferch Elise ap
Gruffudd 694
ferch Lewys 808
ferch Morgan ap
Maredudd 810
ferch Owain
Gwynedd 815
ferch Thomas ap
Gwion 650, 659,
686, 694
Queen of Powys and
South Wales 815,
886
ANGLESEY
James Annesley, 3rd
Earl of 22
ANGOULÊME
Isabel of, Queen of

England 372, 650,
653, 657, 659, 661,
665, 667, 670, 672,
676, 678, 680, 682,
684, 686, 687, 689,
691, 692, 693, 694,
695, 697, 785, 917
ANGUS
Archibald Douglas,
5th Earl of 250,
251, 252
David Douglas, 7th
Earl of 90, 96,
210
George Douglas, 1st
Earl of 240, 241,
248, 250, 251, 252,
254, 255, 257, 258,
261, 266, 268, 940
George Douglas, 4th
Earl of 250, 251,
252
Gilbert de
Umfreville, 1st
Earl of 843
Maud of 697
Robert de
Umfreville, 2nd
Earl of 730, 843
William Douglas,
2nd Earl of 240,
248, 250, 251, 252,
254, 257, 258, 940
William Douglas, 9th
Earl of 250, 251
**ANHALT-
BERNBERG**
Charles Frederick,
Prince of 56

1037

Charlotte, Princess
  of 56
Christiane, Princess
  of 56
Victor Amadeus,
  Prince of 56
Victor Frederick,
  Prince of 56
ANHALT-ZERBST
Joachim Ernest,
  Prince of 184
John II, Prince of
  181, 182, 184
Maria of 181, 182
Sophie, Princess of
  [Catherine II "the
  Great," Empress of
  Russia] 14, 615,
  792
Sybil of 184
ANHEUSER
family xviii
ANHOLT (VAN)
Dirk van Bronck-
  horst- Batenburg,
  Heer 445
ANISTON
Jennifer Joanna
  [Jennifer Aniston]
  974, 985, 986
ANJOU (D')
Antoinette (de
  Chabannes) 205
Charles, Duke of
  Maine 205
Charles II, Prince of,
  Prince of France,
  King of Naples and
  Sicily 459

Eleanor, Princess of,
  Princess and Queen
  of Sicily 451
Ermengarde of
  879, 919
Françoise 205
Geoffrey I, Count of
  879, 919
Geoffrey
  Plantagenet, Count
  of 841, 1025
Isabella, Queen of
  Jerusalem,
  Countess of
  Champagne 943
Margaret of 459
Marie of, Queen of
  France 202, 208
René, 2nd Baron de
  Mézières 205
ANKETILL
Christopher 493
Elizabeth (Francis)
  493
Margaret 493
ANLEZY (D')
Charlotte (de
  Chastellux) 440
Claude, Seigneur de
  Menetou-Couture
  440
Renée (du Bus)
  440
Robert, Seigneur de
  Menetou-Couture
  440
**ANLEZY (D') alias
DE MENETOU**
Françoise 440

ANNA
Archduchess of
  Austria 220, 449,
  451
of Brunswick-
  Grubenhagen 451
of Mazovia 621
of Nassau-
  Dillenburg 184
Princess of Great
  Britain, wife of
  William IV of
  Orange, Stadholder
  of The Netherlands
  8
ANNA ELEANOR
of Hesse-Darmstadt
  58, 432
of Nassau-Weilburg
  184
ANNA JULIANE
Princess of Nassau-
  Saarbrücken 56
ANNA KATHARINA
Princess of Branden-
  burg, Queen of
  Denmark 35, 37
ANNA MARIA
of Simmern, Queen
  of Sweden 40, 43
ANNA SOPHIA
Princess of
  Brunswick-
  Wolfenbüttel 43,
  44
ANNABELLA
(Drummond), Queen
  of Scotland 239,
  241, 243, 245, 248,

249, 250, 251, 252,
253, 254, 255, 256,
257, 258, 260, 261,
263, 264, 266, 267,
268, 940
(Stewart), Princess
of Scotland viii,
176, 223
ANNAN
Kofi Atta lxiv, 60
Nina Maria (Nane)
(Lagergren)
(Cronstedt) viii,
lxiv, cxlii, 60
Noel xxxvii
ANNANDALE
Robert Bruce, lord
of 787, 789
ANNE
(Boleyn), Queen of
England 300,
428, 539, 551, 588,
596
(de Foix), Queen of
Bohemia and
Hungary xxv,
287, 615
(Hyde), Duchess of
York 22, 24, 122,
678, 679, 727, 780,
781, 782
(Neville), Queen of
England 118
Alexander 862
Alice 861
Alice (de Montfort)
861
Alice (Giffard)
861, 863

ferch Rhys Vaughan
229
John (Sir) 861
of Kiev, Queen of
France 739, 778,
780, 783, 785, 787,
789, 835, 837, 839,
841, 843, 845, 847,
957
Princess of Bohemia,
Holy Roman
Empress 40, 43,
54, 56, 192, 287,
290, 615, 891
Princess of Bohemia,
Queen of England
714
Princess of Denmark
891
Princess of Denmark,
Queen of England
and Scotland 35,
38, 47, 49, 52, 785
Queen of Great
Britain 71, 122,
615, 678, 679, 781
**ANNE ELIZABETH
ALICE LOUISE**
Princess of Great
Britain, The
Princess Royal
321
ANNE-MARIE
Princess of Orléans,
Queen of Sardinia
18
ANNES
ferch Dafydd 657,
689, 692, 693

ferch Gwyn ap
Madog 650, 659,
686, 694
ferch John ap
Maredudd 657
ANNESLEY
Catherine 22
James, 3rd Earl of
Anglesey 22
ANNUYS (D')
Antoine de
Belletruche,
Seigneur 911
Pierre de
Belletruche,
Seigneur 911
ANSELME
Père xxvii
ANSLEY
Abel 764
Ann 764, 773
Lydia (Morris) 764
Mary 764
ANSON
family 28
Harriet Georgiana
Louisa (Hamilton)
28
Louisa Goddard
(Van Wagenen)
28
Thomas George,
2nd Earl of
Lichfield 28
William (Hon.) clii
William, Hon. 28
ANSTRUTHER
Agnes 276
Christian 155

ANSTRUTHER-GOUGH-CALTHORPE
  Gabriella Zanna Vanessa [Gabriella Wilde] 75
  John Austen 75
  Vanessa Mary Teresa (Hubbard) 75
ANTHONY ULRICH
  Duke of Saxe-Meiningen 43, 46
ANTHORNE
  Jane 665
ANTOINETTE AMALIA
  Princess of Brunswick-Wolfenbüttel 44
ANTOING (D')
  François de Melun, Baron 287
  Hugh I de Melun, Seigneur, Seigneur d'Épinoy 733
ANTON MARIA FRANZ LEOPOLD BLANKA KARL JOSEPH IGNAZ RAPHAEL MICHAEL MARGARETA NICETAS
  Archduke of Austria, Prince of Tuscany 2, 6
ANTROBUS
  Joan 880

ANTWERP
  Lionel Plantagenet of, Prince of England, Duke of Clarence xxxix, 107, 114, 119, 126, 133, 134, 305, 310, 317, 319, 327, 333, 342, 347, 349, 351, 355, 359, 361, 363, 374, 379, 384, 385, 389, 399, 401, 414, 418, 425, 431, 901, 904, 905
ANZA (DE)
  Juan Bautista (Gen.) 997
APPLETON
  Agnes (Clarke) 607
  Alice 607
  Anne (Sulyard) 607, 608
  family lii, lxii
  Frances (Gerard) (Speake) (Peyton) 515
  Henry 607
  Jane Means xliii, 582, 812
  John 371, 813, 882
  Joyce (Tyrrell) 607
  Judith (Everard) xix, xxxvii, xlvii, lii, lv, lxi, clx, 371, 813, 882, 884, 1026
  Margaret (Roper) 607
  Mary (Isaac) 661, 813

  Priscilla 814, 882
  Priscilla (Glover) 371, 813, 882
  Roger 607, 608
  Samuel xix, xxxvii, lii, lv, lvi, clx, 371, 813, 882
  Sarah 371
  Thomas 607, 661, 813
  William Sumner 585
APPONYI DE NAGY-APPONYI
  Géraldine Margit Virginia Olga Mária, Countess, Queen of the Albanians xl, 929, 935
  Gladys Virginia (Steuart) 935
  Julius, Count 935
APSLEY
  Alice 328, 662
  Edward (Sir) 662
  Elizabeth (Elmes) 662
APTHORPE
  East (Rev.) 475
  Elizabeth (Hutchinson) 475
  Harriet 475
AQUITAINE
  Eleanor, Duchess of, Queen of France, Queen of England 647, 735, 737, 742, 746, 749, 752, 754,

757, 760, 761, 763, 766, 768, 770, 772, 774, 776, 909, 943, 948, 952, 964, 991, 993

ARAGÓN (DE)
Alonzo, Archbishop of Zaragoza 140
Ana de 140
Constance, Princess of Sicily, Queen of 642
Elizabeth, Princess of, Princess of Sicily 51, 451
Ferdinand II, King of, V of Castile, I of Spain 46, 140, 186, 189, 615, 717
Frederick II, King of Sicily, Prince of 451
Isabella, Princess of, Queen of France 459, 941
James (Jaime) I, King of 991, 993
Jeanne, Princess of 963
Joanna, Princess of, Queen of Naples 186, 189
Louis II, King of Naples, Sicily, Jerusalem, and 205
Marie of Châtillon-Blois, Queen of Naples, Sicily, Jerusalem, and 205
monarchs of xv
Peter II, King of 51
Peter III, King of 642

ARBURG (VON)
Anfelisa 832
Anfelisa (von Grünenburg) 832
Rudolf II 832
Rudolf III 832
Ursula (von Brandis) 832

ARBUTHNOT(T)
Anne (Alves) 93
Caroline Emma Nepean (Aitchison) 93
Eliza (Fraser) 93
George 93
Isabel 278
James of Arbuthnott 278
Jean 159
Jean (Stewart) 278
John Alves 93
John Bernard 93
Mary (Arbuthnot) 93
Mary (Urquhart) 93
Olive (Blake) 93
Patricia Evangeline Anne 93
Robert, of Haddo 93
William (Sir), 1st Bt. 93

ARCHBOLD
Felicia 592
ARCHER
Anne 475, 539
ARCHERA
Laura 436
ARCO-ZINNEBERG (VON)
Helena, Countess 15
Leopoldine, (von Waldburg-Zeil), Countess 15
Louis Joseph, Count 15
Maximilian Joseph, Count 15
ARCOS (DE)
Juan Ponce de León, Conde 994
Pedro Ponce de León, V Señor de Marchena, Conde 994
ARDEN
Catherine 138
_____ 719
ARDERNE
Agnes 763, 768, 770, 822
Ellen (de Wastenays) 815
John (Sir) 815, 816, 822
Margred (ferch Gruffudd) 815, 816, 822
Matilda 815, 816
ARELLANO (DE)
Ana 191

Carlos, Count of
Aguilar 191
ARÉVALO
Álvaro de Zuñiga,
Duke of Plasencia,
Bejar and 191
ARGALL
Elizabeth 514
Mary (Scott) 514
Richard 514
Samuel (Gov.) (Sir)
514
ARGENSON (D')
Jeanne (de
Chourses) 948
Patrice, Seigneur
d'Avesnes 948
Perrine 948
ARGENTEAU (D')
Charlotte-Jacqueline,
Countess of Esneux,
Baroness of
Melsbroeck 81
ARGENTENAY (D')
Jean/Jehan de
Menteith/Monteith,
Seigneur 940, 950
ARGIES (D')
Jeanne 733
ARGYLL
Archibald
Campbell, 2nd Earl
of 280, 283
Archibald
Campbell, 4th Earl
of 154, 249
Archibald
Campbell, 7th Earl
of 154

Archibald
Campbell, 9th Earl
of 93
Colin Campbell, 1st
Earl of 269, 280,
283
Colin Campbell, 3rd
Earl of 249
Colin Campbell, 6th
Earl of 154
George Douglas
Campbell, 8th
Duke of 69, 75
Ian Douglas
Campbell, 11th
Duke of 69, 371
John Campbell, 4th
Duke of 93
John Douglas Suth-
erland Campbell,
9th Duke of 75
ARIZONA
John Joseph
Meakins (Rt.
Rev.), Bishop of
567
ARKEL
John V, Lord of
459
Maria of, heiress of
Guelders 459
ARMAGH
John Bramhall, Arch-
bishop of 467
Michael Boyle,
Archbishop of
340
Richard Robinson,
1st Baron Rokeby,

Archbishop of
390, 391
Ulysses Burgh,
Bishop of 480
ARMAGNAC
Jeanne of 205, 440
ARMENIA
John I, titular King
of, titular King of
Cyprus and
Jerusalem 442
**ARMENONVILLE
(D')**
Jean Le Clerc,
Seigneur 954
ARMINE
Anne 335
ARMISTEAD
Elizabeth 730
John 730
Judith (Hone) 730
ARMOUR
Alexandra
(Galitzine)
(Romanoff),
Princess xii, clii,
793, 796
Gabriella (Clark)
498
Harry Ellington
498
Lester xii, 5, 793,
796
Malvina Belle
(Ogden) 794
Mary Elizabeth
(Lester) 794
Philip Danforth
794

Philip Danforth, Jr. 793, 794
Ruth Lucille 498, 726
ARMSTRONG
Anne 430
ARNOLD
Alice 557
Alicia xxiv, liii, lxi, lxviii, clxvi, 333
Anne (Knipe) 333
Elizabeth 715
family xxxvii
Jacques xxi, xxix, xlv
Jane 436
Julia (Sorell) 436
Julia Frances 436
Mary (Penrose) 436
Mary Augusta [Mrs. Humphrey Ward] 436
Matthew 436
Michael 333
Thomas 436
ARNOUX
Simone-Louise 47
ARPAJON (D')
Anne (de Bourbon) 200
Anne-Charlotte (le Bas de Montargis) 200
Anne-Claudine-Louise 200, 288
Charles, Baron 200
Charlotte 201

Charlotte (de Castelpers) 200
Charlotte (de Vernou de la Rivière-Bonneuil) 200
Françoise (de Montal) 200
Gloriande (de Lauzières) 200
Jacques, Vicomte d'Hauterive 200
Jaquette (de Castelnau-Clermont-Lodeve) 200
Jean II, Baron 200
Jean V, Baron 200
Jean-Louis, Marquis de Severac 200
Jeanne 200, 203
Louis d'Arpajon, Duc 200
Louis d'Arpajon, Marquis 200
ARQUES (D')
Elizabeth (Elliot[t]) (Butler) 311
ARRAN
James Hamilton, 1st Earl of 154, 157, 167, 168, 179, 210, 213, 214, 216, 218
James Hamilton, 2nd Earl of, Duke of Châtellerault 154, 157, 167, 168, 177, 179
James Stewart, 1st Earl of 88

ARRIZA
Joachim-Antoine Ximeniz de Palafox, 6th Marquis of 292
ARSCOTT
Mary 103
ARSENAULT
Marie-Rose 989
ARSOLI
Camillo VIII Massimiliano Massimo, Prince of 20
Camillo Vittorio Emanuele Massimo, Prince of 20, 21
ARTHUR
Alice (Berkeley) 557
John 557
Margaret 557
Margaret (Butler) 557
Richard 557
ARTHUR II
Duke of Brittany 442, 946
ARTOIS
Blanche of xxvi, 623, 625, 628, 630, 632
Bona of, Duchess of Burgundy 438, 445
Catherine of 944, 961
Jeanne of 963
Marie of 944

Philip I, Count of 944
Philip of, Seigneur de Conches 961, 963
Robert III, Count of 961

ARUNDEL(L) (DE) (OF)
Alice 642
Anne 349, 588
Anne (Hon.) xvii, xxxv, clxv, 339, 739
Anne (Philipson) 109, 339, 905
Blanche (Somerset) 110
Cecily (Compton) 110
Edmund FitzAlan, 8th Earl of 642, 1024
Eleanor 345, 491
Elizabeth 110, 337, 466
Elizabeth (Grey) 339
Elizabeth (Morley) 588
Elizabeth (Panton) 110
Frances 125
Henry, 3rd Baron Arundell of Wardour 110
Henry, 5th Baron Arundell of Wardour 110
Joan (Moyns) 491
John (Sir) 339, 588, 761
John FitzAlan, 1st Baron 632
John FitzAlan, 2nd Baron 491
Juliane (Grenville?) 642
Katherine (Chidiock) 761
Margaret 110, 761
Margaret (Howard) 339, 605
Margaret (Spencer) 110
Margaret (Willoughby) 339
Mary 109, 905
Mary (Browne) 905
Mary (Wriothesley) 110, 905
Matthew (Sir) 339
Ralph 642, 643
Richard FitzAlan, 7th Earl of 642
Richard FitzAlan, 9th Earl of 508, 514, 547, 584, 594, 607, 632, 642
Richard FitzAlan, 10th Earl of 497, 500, 510, 514, 517, 524, 532, 551, 554, 558, 560, 563, 565, 571, 574, 588, 596, 611, 613
Thomas (Sir) 339, 491, 605
Thomas, 1st Baron Arundell of Wardour 109, 339, 905
Thomas, 2nd Baron Arundell of Wardour 110
Thomas, 4th Baron Arundell of Wardour 110
William (Hon.) 905
William d'Aubigny, 1st Earl of 830
William d'Aubigny, 3rd Earl of 813, 819, 824, 826

ASBECK (VAN)
Elbrig Willemine Henriette, Baroness 446

ASCHEBERG (VON)
Eleanora Elisabeth, Countess 216

ASFORDBY
Alice (Wolley) 343
Eleanor (Newcomen) 343
John 343
Martha (Burton) 343
William lii, clxxii, 343

ASHBURNHAM
Anne 430
Elizabeth (Beaumont), Baroness of Chamond 430
Elizabeth (Dudley) 691
Helen 691

Isabel (Sackville) 429
John 429
John (Sir) 430
Lora (Berkeley) 429
Mary (Fane) 429
Thomas 691
ASHBY
Constantia (Broughton) 471
Elizabeth (Bennet) 471
Elizabeth (Thorowgood) 471
George 471
John lxvii, cxlii, clxxiii, 471, 472
Mary (Gedney) 471
ASHCOMBE
Ronald Calvert Cubitt, 3rd Baron 655
ASHCROFT
Peggy, Dame 10
ASHE
Henry 400
John 468
John Baptista 468
Loveday (Moyle) 400
Mary (Batt) viii, xlix, cxlii, clxix, clxxv, 468
Prudence 400
ASHER
Elizabeth (Duster) 64

Jane 64
Margaret Augusta (Eliot) 64
Peter [of "Peter and Gordon"] xviii, clii, 64
Richard Alan John 64
Victoria Jane 64
Wendy (Worth) 64
ASHFIELD
Florence 543
ASHLEY
Craig Stanley viii, xlv, 360
Edwina Cynthia Annette (Hon.) (Dame) 299
ASHLEY COOPER
Anthony, 7th Earl of Shaftesbury 299
ASHMOLE
Myrtle Jane (Goodacre) lxiii, clii, 323
Philip (Nelson Philip) (Prof.) 323
ASHTON
Anne 841
Dorothy Violet 74
Mary 524, 525
___ 370
ASHWELL
Beatrice Hamilton 246
ASKE
Anne (Sutton) 328

Eleanor (Markenfield) 328
Eleanor (Ryther) 328
Elizabeth 328, 329
Elizabeth (Clifford) 328
Elizabeth (Dawney) 329
Elizabeth (Lacy) 329
Helen 329
Jane 329
John 328
Robert 328, 329
Robert (Sir) 328
ASPALL/ASPALE (DE)
John (Sir) 682
Katherine (Pecche) 682
Mirabel 682
Mirabel (Wake) 682
Thomas (Sir) 682
ASPEREN
Philip Jacob van den Boetzelaer, Lord of 460
Rutger van den Boetzelaer, Lord of, Lord of Langerak, Merweden and Carnisse 460
Wessel van den Boetzelaer, Lord of Langerak and 459

Wessel van den
  Boetzelaer, Lord of
  Merwede and   460
ASPINWALL
  John   355, 375, 394
  John, Jr.   355, 376,
    394, 524, 921
  Mary Rebecca   356,
    376, 394, 524, 881,
    921
  Rebecca (Smith)
    355, 375, 394
  Susan (Howland)
    355, 376, 394, 524,
    921
  William   xxix
ASPRIÈRES (D')
  François de
    Morlhon, Seigneur
    634
ASQUITH
  family   xxxviii
  Helen Kelsall
    (Melland)   306
  Helen Violet,
    Baroness Asquith
    of Yarnbury   306
  Herbert Henry
    Asquith, 1st Earl of
    Oxford and
    Asquith   306
ASSCHENFELDT
  Christiane   clv, 37,
    45
  Edith-Marie
    (Lehmann-von
    Schreiber)   37
  Friedrich Gustav
    Kuno   37

Herbert Christian
  (Dr.)   37
Siga (Rosenberger)
  37
ASSELIN
  Louise   987
  Natalie   981
ASTAIRE
  Adele [Marie
    Austerlit]   xvii,
    clii, 23, 26
  Fred [Fred Austerlit]
    26
ASTLEY
  Alice   570, 672,
    674
  Anne   434, 682
  Elizabeth   233, 395
  Frances   548
  Joan   749
  Mary (Denny)   395,
    548
  Thomas   395, 548
ASTON
  Edward (Sir)   368,
    728
  Elizabeth   368
  Elizabeth (Barton)
    728
  Elizabeth (Delves)
    728
  Elizabeth (Leveson)
    368
  Frances   561, 574
  Hannah (Jordan)
    506, 728
  Immyn   525
  Isabella (Brereton)
    728

Joan (Bowles)   368,
  728
Joan (Lyttleton)   728
John   728
John (Sir)   728
Joyce (Freville)
  728
Joyce (Nason)   728
Leonard   728
Mary   728
Robert (Sir)   728
Roger (Sir)   728
Susan   506
Walter   728
Walter (Col.)
  xxxv, xlvi, xlvii,
  lxii, lxiv, clxvi,
  clxxvi, 506, 728,
  729
Walter (Sir)   368
ASTOR
  (Ava) Alice Muriel
    799, 800
  Ava Lowle
    (Willing)   799
  Caroline Webster
    (Schermerhorn)
    44, 799
  Charlotte Augusta
    44
  Ellen Tuck (French)
    63
  family   xxxvi,
    xxxviii, 66
  Gertrude (Gartsch)
    66
  John Jacob, IV   799
  John Jacob, VI   63,
    66

1046

Mary Jacqueline
[Jacqueline Astor]
66
Roberta Brooke
(Roswell) (Kuser)
(Marshall) [Brooke
Astor] 86
William Backhouse,
Jr. 44, 799
William Vincent
[Vincent Astor]
66, 799
ASTRID
JOSEPHINE
CHARLOTTE
FABRIZIA
ELISABETH
PAOLA MARIA
Princess of the
Belgians,
Archduchess of
Austria 201
ASZPERGEROWA
Aniela Leontina
803
AT SEE
Elizabeth 343
Elizabeth
(Wentworth) 342
Joan/Jane 342, 343
Martin (Sir) 342
ATHERTON (DE)
Joan 841
Margaret 520, 935
ATHOLL
David Strathbogie,
2nd Earl of 528
David Strathbogie,
8th Earl of 697

David Strathbogie,
10th Earl of 697
earls of 284
John Murray, 1st
Duke of 66, 67
John Murray, 1st
Marquess of 62,
637
John Murray, 3rd
Duke of 66
John Murray, 4th
Duke of 66
John Stewart, 1st
Earl of 219, 249,
256, 261, 278, 283
John Stewart, 2nd
Earl of 151, 170,
261, 266, 283
John Stewart, 3rd
Earl of 261, 266
John Stewart, 4th
Earl of 88, 146,
176
John Strathbogie,
9th Earl of 697
ATHOLL (DE)
Aymer (Sir) 697
Isabel 697
Mary (___) 697
ATKINS
Anne (Mackenzie),
Lady 92
Edmund 92
ATKINSON
Abigail 836
Anne 434
Caroline Stewart
434
Frances 434

ATSEA
Mary 778
ATTALENS (D')
Aymon d'Oron,
Seigneur de
Bossonens and
911
ATWATER
Anna Maria (Drury)
clii, 371, 372
Henry Green 371
Margaret 371
ATWELL
"Annar" 924, 926
Joseph, Jr. 924
Miriam (Case) 924
Olive 926
AUBAIS (D')
Louis de Baschi,
Baron 735
AUBERJONOIS
Augusta (Madeleine-
Augusta) (Grenier)
635
Fernand liii, clii,
83, 635, 636
Gustave 635
Judith Helen
(Mahalyi) 83, 635
Laure-Louise-Napo-
léone- Eugénie-
Caroline (Murat)
(Frank), Princess
clii, 83, 635
Pauline (Auguste-
Pauline) (d'Albis)
635
René (Victor-René)
635, 636

René Murat 83,
635, 636
AUBIGNÉ (D')
Françoise, Marquise
de Maintenon
[Mme. de
Maintenon] 288
Françoise-Charlotte-
Amable, Marquise
de Maintenon
[Mme. de
Maintenon] 288
AUBIGNY
John Stewart, lord
of 215
AUBIGNY (D')
Alice 830
family 1024
Isabel 653, 705,
710, 713, 715, 719,
727, 728
Nicole 813, 819,
824, 826
William, 1st Earl of
Arundel 830
William, 3rd Earl of
Arundel 813, 819,
824, 826
AUBREY
Barbara 338, 410
Elizabeth (Thomas)
338
Jane (Mathew) 338
Mawd 811
William 338
AUCHER
Affra (Cornwallis)
509
Anne 469

Anthony (Sir) 509
Edward 509
Elizabeth 509
Elizabeth (Guilford)
469
Henry 469
Mabel (Wroth) 509
AUCHINLECK
Alexander Boswell,
Lord 150
Elizabeth 250, 251,
252
AUCKLAND
William Eden, 1st
Baron 102
AUDELEY
Elizabeth 592
AUDEN
Constance Rosalie
(Bicknell) 403
Erika Julia Hedwig
Gründgens (Mann)
404
George Augustus
403
Wystan Hugh (W.H.)
xi, xvii, xlviii, clii,
404
AUDET
Antoinette 984
AUDLEY (DE)
Alice 761, 861
Bertrade (de
Mainwaring) 815,
822, 861
Ela (Longespee)
761
Elizabeth 423

Elizabeth (Court-
enay) (Luttrell)
423, 569
Emma 815, 822,
823
George Thicknesse-
Touchet, 19th
Baron 111
George Touchet, 9th
Baron 427
Henry 815, 822,
861
Henry Touchet, 10th
Baron 427
Hugh, 1st Earl of
Gloucester 495,
505, 575, 577, 590,
615, 847
Hugh de Audley, 1st
Baron 761
Humphrey (Sir)
423, 569
Isolde (Mortimer)
761
James 761
James Touchet, 2nd
Baron 377, 410,
411, 423
James Touchet, 7th
Baron 427
John Touchet, 8th
Baron 427
Margaret 334, 495,
505, 575, 577, 590,
615, 819
Margaret (de Clare)
(de Gaveston)
495, 505, 575, 577,
590, 615, 847

1048

**AUDLEY or
TOUCHET**. *see also*
TOUCHET or
AUDLEY
AUERSPERG (VON)
Alfred Eduard
Friedrich Vincenz
Martin Maria,
Prince 646
Martha Sharp
"Sunny"
(Crawford) 646
AUFFEMORDT
Evelyn 98
AUFRERE
Anthony 144
Louisa Anna/Louise
Anne 144
Mariana Matilda
(Lockhart-Wishart)
144
AUGUST
Prince of Prussia
16
AUGUSTA
(von Harrach),
Princess of
Liegnitz, Countess
of Hohenzollern 8
Countess of
Waldeck 57
Princess of
Brunswick, Queen
of Württemberg
12
Princess of Denmark
35, 47, 49
Princess of Great
Britain 12
Princess of Prussia
13
Princess of Saxe-
Gotha, Princess of
Wales 12, 27
Princess of
Schwarzburg-
Sondershausen 56
**AUGUSTA AMALIA
LUDOVICA
GEORGIA**
of Bavaria 442
AUGUSTA MARIE
Princess of
Holstein-Gottorp
43, 46
AUGUSTA SOPHIE
Princess of Sulzbach
35
AUGUSTUS
Count Palatine of
Sulzbach 35, 49
Duke of Saxe-
Weissenfels 891
Elector of Saxony
891
AUGUSTUS I
Prince of Schwarz-
burg-Sondershausen
56
**AULNAY (D')-
CHARNIZAY**
Charles de Menou
(Gov.), Seigneur
952, 953
AUMALE
Bertha of 879, 919
Blanche of 944,
961
Eudes II, Count of
Troyes and 879,
919
Jean VI, Count of,
Count of Harcourt
and 941
John II, Count of
944, 961
AUNOY (D')
family 294
AUSTEN
Cassandra (Leigh)
299
George (Rev.) 299
Jane xxiv, 299
  358
AUSTERLIT
Fred [Fred Astaire]
26
Marie [Adele
Astaire] xvii, clii,
23, 26
AUSTIN
Drusilla 702
AUSTRIA 201
Adelaide, Arch-
duchess of, Queen
of Sardinia, Queen
of Italy 614
Anna, Archduchess
of 220, 449, 451
Anton Maria Franz
Leopold Blanka
Karl Joseph Ignaz
Raphael Michael
Margareta Nicetas,
Archduke of,
Prince of Tuscany
2, 6

Astrid Josephine Charlotte Fabrizia Elisabeth Paola Maria, Princess of the Belgians, Archduchess of   201

Carlota (Marie-Charlotte-Amélie-Auguste-Victoire-Clémentine-Léopoldine), Princess of the Belgians, Archduchess of, Empress of México   288

Caroline Augusta, Princess of Bavaria, Empress of   11

Catherine, Archduchess of   291

Elizabeth, Archduchess of, Queen of Poland   194, 195, 196, 198, 895

Elizabeth, Princess of Savoy, Archduchess of   614

Elizabeth, Princess of Württemburg, Empress of   11

emperors of   615

Ferdinand, Archduke of, Duke of Modena   15

Francis I, Emperor of, Holy Roman Emperor   11

Karl (Charles) I, Emperor of   201, 800

Karl Pius Maria Adelgonde Blanka Leopold Ignaz Raphael Michael Salvator Kyrill Angelus Barbara, Archduke of, Prince of Tuscany   6

Karl Salvator, Archduke of, Prince of Tuscany   6

Lorenz Otto Carl Amadeus Thadeus Maria Pius Andreas Marcus d'Aviano, Archduke of   201

Margaret, Archduchess of   451

Margaret of, Queen of Bohemia   621

Maria, Archduchess of   40, 43, 54, 56, 891

Maria Anna Charlotte Zita Elisabeth Regina Thérèse, Archduchess of   xii, cliv, 800

Maria Antonia (Marie-Antoinette), Archduchess of, Queen of France   267

Maria Josepha, Archduchess of, Electress of Saxony, Queen of Poland   20

Maria Ludovika, Archduchess and Empress of, Princess of Modena   11

Maria Teresa of Tuscany, Archduchess of, Queen of Sardinia   614

Maria Theresa, Archduchess of, Queen of the Two Sicilies   6

Maria Theresa, Empress of   xxi, lxx, 15

Maria Theresa, Princess of the Two Sicilies, Empress of   11

Marie Louise, Archduchess of, Empress of the French   11

Marie Ludovika, Archduchess and Empress of, Princess of Modena   11

Matilda, Archduchess of   617

Maximilian, Archduke of, Emperor of Mexico   30, 38, 288

monarchs of 45
Rainier, Archduke
    of 614
Rudolf Franz Karl
    Joseph, Crown
    Prince of 288
Rudolf Syringus
    Peter Karl Franz
    Joseph Robert Otto
    Antonius Maria
    Pius Benedikt
    Ignatius Laurentinus Justiniani
    Markus d'Aviano,
    Archduke of 800
Stefan [Stefan Habsburg-Lothringen],
    Archduke of, Prince
    of Tuscany 2, 6
Stéphanie-Clotilde-
    Louise-Hermine-
    Maria-Charlotte,
    Princess of the
    Belgians, Crown
    Princess of 288
Zita of Bourbon-
    Parma, Empress of
    800
AUVERGNE
    Bertrand VI de la
        Tour, Count of,
        Count of Boulogne
        637
    Jean I de la Tour,
        Count of, Count of
        Boulogne 637
    Marie of 911
    Robert IV, Count of
        911

AUVRAYMESNIL (D')
    Mathieu de
        Montmorency,
        Seigneur 943
AUWERGHEM (DE L')
    Nicolas Triest,
        Seigneur 438
AUZET (D')
    Louis de Baschi,
        Seigneur 735
AVAGOUR (D')
    Catherine 949
AVALOS (D')
    Alfonso II Felice,
        Prince of
        Francavilla and
        Montesarchio
        186, 189
    Caterina 186
    Ferdinando
        Francesco II,
        Prince of
        Francavilla and
        Montesarchio
        186, 189
    Francesca 189
    Íñigo, Prince of
        Francavilla 189
    Ippolita 189
    Isabella (Gonzaga)
        186, 189
    Isabella, Princess of
        Francavilla 189
    Lavinia Feltrina
        (della Rovere)
        186, 189

Nicolo, Prince of
    Montesarchio and
    Troia 189
AVANT
    David A., Jr. xlvi,
        lxi
AVELLANEDA (DE)
    Gaspar 995
    Juana (de Labayen)
        995
    María Rosa 996
AVELLINO
    Francesco Marino
        Caracciolo, Prince
        of 189, 192
    Marino II Caracciolo,
        Prince of 189
AVENAL
    family 1025
    Richard 700, 705,
        708, 710, 713, 715,
        719, 721, 723, 725,
        727, 728, 730
    ___ 700, 705,
        708, 710, 713, 715,
        719, 721, 723, 725,
        727, 728, 730
AVERITT
    Amy (Spooner) xiii
    Benjamin xiii
    Fereby xiii
AVERY
    Elizabeth 95
    family xxiv
    Joseph 95
    Margaret
        (Mackenzie) xlvi,
        cxlviii, 95

Susanna (Palmes) xxiv, 304
AVESNES (D')
Bouchard 774, 776
Guy of, Bishop of Utrecht 774, 776
Maria of 776
Patrice d'Argenson, Seigneur 948
AVILES (D')
Emilie 227
AVON
Anthony [Robert Anthony] Eden (Prime Minister), 1st Earl of 585, 648
AXSON
Ellen Louise xlii, 463, 465, 508, 673, 726
Isaac Stockton Keith 463, 508, 726
Margaret Jane (Hoyt) 463, 508, 672, 726
Rebecca Longstreet (FitzRandolph) 463, 508, 726
Samuel Edward 463, 508, 672, 726
Sarah Anne (Palmer) 463
AXTELL
Rebecca 742
AYALA (DE)
María 994
Sancha xiii, xiv, lv, lxv, lxviii, 676, 709, 717, 994

AYER
Adele Augusta 630, 654, 887
Amy Gridley (Butler) 630, 654, 887
Daniel 654
Elida Vanderburgh (Manney) 654
George Manney 630, 654, 887
John Varnum 654
Polly (Chase) 654
Samuel 654
Sarah (Adams) 654
AYERS
Augustine H. xlvi, lxvii, 472
AYLEN [later LAWFORD]
May Somerville (Bunny) (Cooper) 563
Peter Sydney Ernest [Peter Lawford] xvii, clxxiv, 26, 564, 914
AYLESBURY
Anne (Denman) 780
Eleanor 506, 532, 575, 763
Frances 626, 678, 780
Isabel 706
Katherine (Pabenham) (Cheyne/Cheney) 705, 763
Thomas (Sir) 705, 763

Thomas (Sir), 1st Bt. 780
AYLMER
Alison (Fitzgerald) 487
Anne 486, 487
Bartholomew 486, 487
Catherine 487
Christopher 487
Christopher (Sir), 1st Bt. 487, 900
Elizabeth 296
Ellen (Warren) 487
Gerald 487
Gerald (Sir) 487
Judith 730, 731
Margaret (Chevers) 486
Margaret (Plunkett) 487, 900
AYRAULT
family 155
AYRE/EYRE
John 674
Margery 674
Mary (Pollard) 674
AYSCOUGH
Anne 115
Edward (Sir) 114
Frances (Clifford) 114
Jane 528
AYTON
Margaret 222
AZAGRA (DE)
Álvaro Pérez, Señor de Albarra 993
Elfa 993

BABCOCK
  Alice Woodward 925
BABINGTON
  Adrian 628
  Catherine 628
  Catherine (Kendall) 628
  Catherine (Vermuyden) 628
  Eleanor (Beaumont) 628
  Eleanor (Humphrey) 628
  Elizabeth 413, 628, 717, 754
  family xxxvii
  Humphrey 628
  Margaret (Cave) 628
  Thomas 628
BABTHORPE
  Barbara (Constable) 127, 131
  Margaret 127
  William (Sir) 127
BACHELDER
  Mary 924
BACHELIN (VON)
  Inez [Inez Storer] 5
BACHMETEV
  Elisabeth 793
BACKHOUSE
  Agnes (Curzon) 575
  Elizabeth cxlii, 528, 575, 576
  Elizabeth (Borlase) 575

  Nicholas 575
  Samuel 575
BACKWELL
  Mary 320
BACON
  Anne 846
  Anne (Bassett) (Smith) 878
  Anne (le Gros) 494
  Edmund (Sir), 4th Bt. 345
  Elizabeth 353, 403
  Elizabeth (Bacon) 877
  Elizabeth (Brooke) 494
  Elizabeth (Cotton) 877
  Elizabeth (Crane) 345
  Elizabeth (Duke) 494, 561
  Elizabeth (Kingsmill) (Tayloe) 878
  Frances 345
  Francis 877
  Francis, 1st Viscount St. Albans [Sir Francis Bacon] 684, 846
  James 877
  James (Sir) 877
  Jane (Cooke) 684, 877
  Jane (Ferneley) 846
  Letitia 335
  Margaret (Rawlings) 877

  Martha 878
  Martha (Woodward) 877
  Mary 584, 586
  Nathaniel 494
  Nathaniel (Act. Gov.) cl, clxxxi, 878, 1025
  Nathaniel (Gov.) (rebel) 494, 561
  Nicholas (Sir) 684, 846, 877
  Thomas 494
BACQUEHEM (DE)
  Marie-Bonne 438
BADAYAC (dit LAPLANTE)
  Antoine 985
  Geneviève 985
  Marguerite (Couturier dit La Bonté) 985
BADDELEY. *see* CLINTON-BADDELEY
  Hermione [Hermione Youlanda Ruby Clinton-Baddeley Tennant Willis] xvii, lxiii, clii, 78, 109, 113
BADEN
  Beatrix of 291
  Cäcilie Auguste of 5
  Catherine of 291
  Charles I, Margrave of 291

1053

Charles Louis,
  Prince of 41
James I, Margrave
  of 291
Marie Amelie
  Elizabeth Caroline,
  Princess of 933
Wilhelmine of 41
BADEN-BADEN
Bernhard III,
  Margrave of 208
Edward Fortunatus,
  Margrave of 208,
  209
Maria Anna,
  Princess of 49
BADEN-DURLACH
Anna of 195
Catherine, Princess
  of 43
Charles Gustav,
  Margrave of 43,
  44
Christine Juliane,
  Princess of 43
Ernest, Margrave of
  195, 198
Frederick VI,
  Margrave of 40,
  43
Frederick VII,
  Margrave of 43,
  46
Joanna, Princess of
  40
**BADEN-
  RODEMACHERN**
Christopher II,
  Margrave of 208

Hermann
  Fortunatus,
  Margrave of 208
Maria Sidonia of
  208
BADLESMERE
Elizabeth 497, 500,
  510, 517, 524, 532,
  551, 554, 558, 560,
  563, 565, 571, 574,
  588, 596, 611, 613
family xli
Margaret 710, 719
Margery 713, 715,
  727, 728
BAGENALL
Anne 382
Eleanor (Griffith)
  382, 900
Frances 900
Nicholas (Sir) 382,
  900
BAGNARA
Francesco Ruffo,
  Duke of, Prince of
  Motta San
  Giovanni 189
BAGOT
Harriet (Villiers)
  72
Mary 517
Richard, Bishop of
  Bath and Wells 72
Sidney Leveson
  Lane 72
**BAGRATION-
  MUKHRANSKY**
Constantine, Prince
  7

Ekaterina
  (Ratchitch) 7
Irina (Czernichew-
  Besobrasow),
  Countess 7
Teymuraz, Prince
  clii, 7
BAIKIE
Anna 85, 88
Barbara 88
James 88
Marjorie 85
Sibella (Halcro) 88
BAILEY
Donald A. 616
BAILLET
Antoinette 954
family 294
BAILLEUL (DE)
Agnes 460
Anne (de
  Clinchamp) 957
Catherine 957
Mathieu, Seigneur
  de Piencourt and
  Canthelou 957
____ 804
BAILLIE
Alexander, of
  Dunain 239, 255,
  283
Anne Elizabeth
  225, 283
Elizabeth (Forbes)
  255
Elizabeth (Mackay)
  283
Euphemia (Bertram)
  152

George, of
  Hardington 152
Jean (Baillie) 283
Jean (Mackenzie)
  239, 255, 283
John, of Balrobert
  283, 284
Kenneth (Col.)
  xxxv, l, clxviii,
  clxxii, clxxix,
  clxxxviii, 283
Margaret 151
Mary 239, 255
Mary Ann
  (Mackintosh) 152
Robert xlvii, lxiv,
  cxlii, 152
William, of Dunain
  255

BAILLON
Adam, Seigneur de
  Valence 950
Alphonse, Seigneur
  de La Mascotterie
  950
Catherine 939,
  950, 951, 967, 970,
  971, 974, 977
Claude (Depuy)
  950
Élisabeth 950
family 967, 968
Louise (de Marle)
  950, 951
Renée (Maillard)
  950

BAINBRIDGE
Harriet 580
Phebe 249

BAINTON
Anne lxix, clx,
  468, 678
Ferdinando 468
Joan (Weare alias
  Browne) 468

BAIRNSFATHER
Mary 268

BAKER
Alice (Eilken) 5
Dorothy 553
Eleanor "Nonie"
  Trego 117
Elizabeth 312, 313
Florence Evelyn 465
George (Sir), 3rd Bt.
  120
Hannah 553
Jane 875
Jim 362
Mary 833
Mary (Capen) 814,
  882
Mary Isabella
  (Sutton) 120
Natalie Bayard
  (Howard)
  (Gordon) 127
Priscilla 814, 882
Thomas, Jr. 814,
  882
William Thompson,
  Jr. 127

BAKER WILBRAHAM
George Barrington
  (Sir), 5th Bt. 120
Joyce Christabel
  (Kennaway) 120

Katherine Frances
  (Wilbraham) 120
Mary Frances 120
Philip Wilbraham
  (Sir), 6th Bt. 120

BALDWIN
Catherine
  (Mackworth) 727
Eleanor 383, 753,
  837
Elizabeth (Alsop)
  lxii, lxvi, clxii,
  clxxv, 588, 589
family clxxxii, 727
Frances xi, xlix,
  liii, liv, cxlvii,
  clxviii, clxxxii, 727
Francis 727
Gertrude 138
Henry 727
James 727
Joan (___)
  (Spendly) 727
John 727
Mary (Beakbaine)
  230
Oliver 727
Richard 588, 589
Sarah 589
Stewart viii, xlvi,
  cxc, cxci, 652, 660
Sylvanus 588
William 727

BALDWIN I
Count of Hainault,
  VI of Flanders 851

BALDWIN II
Count of Hainault
  851

1055

BALDWIN III
  Count of Hainault
    851
BALDWIN V
  Count of Flanders
    851
BALDWIN VI. *see*
  BALDWIN I
BALDWIN IX
  Count of Flanders,
    Emperor of
    Constantinople
    774, 776
BALFOUR
  Anna 98
  Barbara 85, 89
  Barbara (Moodie)
    85
  Cecilia
    (Elphinstone) 270
  Elizabeth
    (Karadjorjevic)
    (Oxenberg),
    Princess of
    Yugoslavia 3
  George, of Pharay
    85
  Georgiana Elizabeth
    70
  Georgiana Isabella
    (Campbell) 70
  Henrietta Scott
    (Smith) 270, 549
  Isabel 222
  James (Prof.), of
    Pilrig 270
  James, of Pilrig
    270
  Jean (Whytt) 270

John 70
John, of Pilrig 270
Lewis 270, 549
Louisa 270, 549
Louisa (Hamilton)
  270
Margaret Isabella
  270
Marion 549
Marjorie (Baikie)
  85
Neil Roxburgh 3
Patrick, of Pharay
  85
BALIOL
  Cecily 780
  family xli
  John 780
  John, King of
    Scotland 780
BALL
  Alfred L. 131
  Armine (von
    Tempski) 131,
    132
  Elias 349
  Elizabeth 584, 647
  Elizabeth
    (Harleston) lxiv,
    lxviii, 349
  Frances
    (Ravenscroft)
    xlviii, cxlviii, 518
  Joseph 518
  Lebbeus 584, 647
  Mary 310, 515,
    518, 700
  Thankful (Stowe)
    584, 647

BALLENTINE
  John 463, 465
  Mary (Tucker)
    463, 465
BALLINGER
  Elizabeth
    (Elkington) 768
  Elizabeth (Groff)
    769
  Joshua 769
  Samuel 769
  Sarah 769
  Sarah (Jones) 769
  Thomas 768
BALSAC (DE)
  Catherine 154, 215
BALSTON
  James Peter Henry
    128
  Penelope Eleanor
    (Elphinstone-
    Dalrymple) cxlv,
    128
BALTIMORE
  Anne (Arundell)
    Calvert (Hon.),
    Baroness xli, clxv
  barons (lords)
    xxiv, lxii, 605
  Benedict Leonard
    Calvert, 4th Baron
    29, 340
  Cecil Calvert, 2nd
    Baron xvii, xxxv,
    clxv, clxxvi, 339,
    676, 739
  Charles Calvert
    (Gov.), 3rd Baron
    339, 512, 819

Charles Calvert
(Gov.), 5th Baron
clxxxix, 29, 312
Charlotte (Lee)
Calvert, Baroness
lxiv, lxv
George Calvert, 1st
Baron Baltimore
739
BAMFIELD
Ursula 392
BAMPFIELD
Agnes 870
Agnes (Coplestone)
870
Eleanor
(Beauchamp) 870
Isabel (Cobham)
870
Joan (Gilbert) 870
John 870
Thomas 870
BAÑARES
Pedro de Zuñiga y
Manrique, Count
of 191
BANDRÉ-DU
PLESSIS (DE)
Henriette-Adolfina
792
BANÉR
Anna 452
BANGOR
Nicholas Robinson,
Bishop of 563
BANGS
Jeremy Dupertuis
clxxxiv

BANKES
Elizabeth (Curtis)
866
BANKS
Charles Edward
(Dr.) xxix
Katherine 387, 710
Margaret (Domville)
(Hatton) xix, lvi,
lxii, lxiv, cxlix, cli,
clxvi, 560
Mary 339
Richard 560
BANNER
Erik 644
Karen (Gøye) 644
Kirsten 644
BANNERMAN
Alexander xliii,
xlvi, 344
Margaret 223
BAN(N)ISTER
Frances (Walker)
lxviii, cxlviii, 399
Mary 353
Thomas 399
BAPAULME
Gilles de Beaumez,
Châtelain of 804
BAR (DE)
Thibaut, Seigneur de
Pierrepont 944
Yolande 944
BAR (DU)
Annibal, Count
615
Claude de Grasse,
Count 615

Claude de Grasse,
Seigneur 615
BARANOV
Marie Louise Julia,
Countess 798
BARANTYNE
John 353
Margaret 353
Mary (Reade) 353
Mary (Stonor) 353
William 353
BARBANÇON (DE)
Yolande 287
BARBARA
(Zápolya), Queen of
Poland 895
of Brandenburg-
Anspach 194
BARBER
Charles 662
family 662, 664
Mary 235
Mary (Duckenfield)
662
William 662
BARBERIN DE
REIGNAC
Julie-Célestine 203
BARBY
Agnes of 184
BARBY-
MÜHLINGEN
Albert V, Count of
181, 182
Maria of 181, 182
BARCELONA
Sybil of 853, 855
BARCLAY
Ann (Ford) 148

Christian (Mollison) 148, 256
David 148
David, of Urie 148
Elizabeth Lucy 148
family xxxvii, lv
family, of Bury Hill, formerly of Mathers and Urie 149
family, of Leyden 149
George 144
Jean 148
John lxv, 148, 149
Katherine (Gordon) 148
Katherine (Rescarrick?) 148
Louisa Anna/Louise Anne (Aufrere) 144
Margaret 828
Matilda Antonia 144
Priscilla (Freame) 148
Robert 148, 256
Robert ("Gov.") 148, 256
Susanna (Willet) 148
____ 282

BARCROFT
Charles 772, 773
Elizabeth (Wood) xlix, cxlii, 772, 773
Jane 772, 773

BARDOLF
Agnes (Poynings) 483, 489, 536, 587, 606
Cecily 483, 489, 536, 587, 606
Elizabeth (Damory) 483, 489, 536, 587, 606
John Bardolf, 3rd Baron 483, 489, 536, 587, 606
Katherine 851, 920, 922
William Bardolf, 4th Baron 483, 489, 536, 587, 606

BARENTON (DE)
Florentin Girard, Seigneur 948, 949

BARFOOT
Henrietta Elizabeth Digby 308

BARGENY
John Hamilton, 1st Baron 155

BARHAM
Charles 514
Elizabeth (Ridley) 514
Eve 108
Katherine (Filmer) 514
Robert 514

BARIATINSKI
Katharina (Yourievsky) 799

BARIL
Caroline 972

BARING
Claire Leonora 33
Ethel (Stanley Errington) 123
Evelyn, 1st Earl of Cromer 123

BARING-GOULD
Ceil (Moody) 136
Diana Amelia (Sabine) 136
Edward Sabine 136
Grace (Taylor) 136
Harriet R. (Stuart) 136, 138
Judith A. 136
Marian Darragh (Linton) 136
Sabine 136
William 136
William Drake cxlii, 136, 139
William Stuart 136

BARKER
Anne (Steventon) 411
Barbara (Dungan) 488
Deliverance 578
Elizabeth (Peters) 578
family 578
Frances 475
George 411, 412, 578
Margaret 411, 412
Robert/Thomas 578
Sarah 76
Theodosia 578

1058

BARKHAM
Edward (Sir), 1st Bt. 607
Frances (Berney) 607
Margaret 127, 607
BARLEY
John 838
Margaret 838
Margaret (Poyntz) 838
Philippa (Bradbury) 838
BARLOW
Arabella 666
Arabella (Trevanion) 666
Audrey xi, xix, xlviii, lx, cxlii, clxiii, clxxxii, 763, 765, 925
Elizabeth (Hardwick) ["Bess of Hardwick"] 468, 512, 706
Ellen (Stafford) 763
family 763, 765
Lundy W. 1026
Stafford 763, 765
Thomas 763
William 666
BARNABY
Mary (Abington/ Habington) 653
Richard 653
Winifred 653
BARNARD
Christopher, 1st Baron Barnard 34

Gilbert Vane, 2nd Baron 34
W. Charles 397
BARNARDISTON
Anne (Polstead) 567
Frances (Harris) 567
Jane (Adams) 567
John 567
Joseph 567
Mary 567
Mary (Knightley) 567
Miriam (Saunders) 567
Samuel 567
Thomas 567
BARNE
Anne 509
Anne (Sandys) 509
William (Sir) 509
BARNES
Aimee Maxine 146
Charles xlv, cxlii, 359, 360
Dorothy (Drury) 359, 360
Edward 359, 360
Elizabeth 743
family 360
Mary (Hand) 359
Robert xxix, xlvi
Thomasine (Shepherd) 359
William 359, 360
BARNEWALL
Anne 486, 488, 545, 546

BARNEY
Margaret 680
BARNS
Elizabeth 390
BARR
Millicent 702
BARRAS (DE/DI)
Jeanne 735
BARRE (DE LA)
Alice (Talbot) 530, 553, 555, 603
Elizabeth 530, 553, 555, 603
Thomas (Sir) 530, 553, 555, 556, 603
BARRET(T)
Agnes (ferch Philip ap Maredudd) 582
Anne 711
Cecily 467, 783, 839
Edward 711
Eleanor (l'Archdekne) 874
Elen (ferch Owain ap Gruffudd) 582
Elizabeth xxiv, 355
Elizabeth (Lytton) 711
family 875
Henry 582, 874
Isham 711
John 839
Lettice 300
Margaret 582, 920
Margaret (ferch Hugh Howell) 874

1059

Margery (Knolles) 839, 840
Maud (Poyntz) 839
Philippa (Harpesfield) 839
Robert 839
Sined/Jenet 874
Thomas 839
William 582, 874
BARRIAULT
Alma (Pelletier) 977, 989
Joseph-Norbert 977
Marie-Ernestine 977
Marie-Josèphe (Drapeau) 977
Olivier 977
Sophie (Tardif) 977
BARRINGTON
Francis (Sir), 1st Bt. 114
Joan 114
Joan (Cromwell) 114
John Parker, 1st Baron 121
Thomas (Sir) 114
Winifred (Pole) 114
BARROW
Geoffrey B. xxviii
BARRY
Jane Mallory (Birkin) xviii, clii, 28

John [Jonathan Barry Prendergast] xviii, clii, 27, 28
BARTA
Agnes Marie Louise (Berg) 891
Frank Kenneth (Rev.) 891, 892
Louis Joseph 891
BARTLETT
Joan 116
Joseph Gardner xlvi, clxxxiv, clxxxv, 842
BARTON
Elizabeth 728
Grace 129
BARTRUM
Peter C. xxvii, xxix, xlvi, lvi, lxii, lxiv, lxv, 660, 692, 812, 813, 815, 824
BARWICK
Frances 129
BAS DE MONTARGIS (LE)
Anne-Charlotte 200
BASCHI (DE/DI)
Anne (de Rochemore) 735
Balthazard, Seigneur de Saint-Estève 735
Berthold, Seigneur en parti di Vitozzo 735
Jeanne (de Barras) 735

Louis, Baron d'Aubais 735
Louis, Seigneur d'Auzet 735
Louis, Seigneur de Saint-Estève 735
Louise 735
Louise (de Varas) 735
Marguerite (du Faur) 735
Marguerite Adhémar 735
Melchionne (de Matheron) 735
Thadée, Seigneur de Saint-Estève 735
BASIL II
Grand Prince of Moscow 621, 797
BASIL III
Grand Prince of Moscow 797
BASKERVILLE
Catherine 109
James (Sir) 505
Jane 295, 296, 647
John lxiv, cxlii, 235, 412
Magdalen (Hope) 235
Mary (Barber) 235
Sybil 505
Sybil (Devereux) 505
BASS
Annie 458
BASSET
Hawise (___) 819

Katherine 835
Margaret 819
Margaret (de
  Somery) 819
Ralph 819
Ralph, 1st Baron
  Basset of Drayton
  819
BASSETT
  Arthur (Sir) 103
  Aveline 845
  Catherine 614
  Catrin 410
  Edward 297
  Eleanor (Chichester)
  103
  Elizabeth 496, 503,
  730, 878
  Elizabeth (Churchill)
  730, 878
  Elizabeth (Lygon)
  297
  Frances (Planta-
  genet) 103
  Jane 297
  Joan 653
  Joanna (Burwell)
  878
  John 103
  Margaret 103
  Mary 429, 430,
  614
  Mary (Evans) 410
  Thomas 410
  William (III) 878
  William (IV) 730,
  878
BASYNGES/BASING
  Alice 727

Elizabeth (la
  Zouche) 727
family 1025
John (Sir) 727
BATCHCROFT
  Elizabeth 587
BATE
  Kerry William
  clxxxv
BATES
  Elizabeth 925
  John 925
  Mary (Farwell)
  925
  Rachel 688
BATH
  John Bourchier, 1st
  Earl of 392, 436
  Josiah Thomas
  (Ven.), Arch-
  deacon of 320
  Thomas Thynne, 1st
  Marquess of 70
  Thomas Thynne,
  2nd Marquess of
  70, 73
BATH and WELLS
  Richard Bagot,
  Bishop of 72
BATHURST
  Edward 883
  Lancelot xlvii,
  clxvi, 883
  Susan (Rich) 883
BATISFORD
  Elizabeth 783
BATT
  Alice (St. Barbe)
  678

Anne (Bainton)
  lxix, clx, 468, 678
Christopher xlviii,
  lii, lv, clx, clxxv,
  468, 678
Dorothy 678
family lii
Joan (Byley) 678
Mary viii, xlix,
  cxlii, clxix, clxxv,
  468
Mary (___) 468
Samuel (Rev.) 468
Thomas 678
BATTE
  Amy (___) (Butler)
  505
  Elizabeth (Horton)
  506
  Elizabeth (Parry)
  505
  family xi, xlvii,
  507
  Henry xlix, lxiv,
  clxvi, clxxiv,
  clxxxii, 506
  John 505
  Martha (Mallory)
  505
  Mary (___) 505
  Mary (Lounds)
  506
  Robert 505
  Susan (Aston)
  (Major) 506
  Thomas xlix, lxiv,
  clxvi, clxxiv,
  clxxxii, 505, 506
  William 506

BATTENBERG
Alexander, Prince of, Prince of Bulgaria, Count von Hartenau 41
Alice, Princess of [Princess Andrew of Greece] 3, 41
Louis, Prince of, 1st Marquess of Milford Haven 41
BATTHYÁNY NÉMET-UJVÁR
Juliana, Countess, Princess Montenuovo 11
BATTLE
Robert viii, xlvi, xlviii, lxiv, lxvi, lxvii, 78, 94, 95, 336, 663, 833, 926
BATTY
Elizabeth Frances 380
BAUÇAY (DE)
Denise 948, 949
BAUD
Wilhelmina Vincentia Maria 460
BAUDEMONT (DE)
Agnès 804, 956
BAUDOUIN
King of the Belgians 142
BAUDRENGHIEN (DE)
Charlotte 438

BAUER
Catharina Elisabeth 450
Ida May 120
BAUGH
Anne 331
Eleanor (Copley) 642
Elizabeth (___) (Sharp) (Parker/Packer) 642
family 642, 643
John 642
Margery (Crocker) 642, 643
Mary (Wakeman) 642
Rowland 642
Thomas 642
William liii, lxi, cxlviii, 642, 643
BAUX (DE)
Cecilia 642
marquesses 190
BAVARIA
Agnes, Princess of 617
Albert I, Duke of, Count of Holland 451
Amalia of 237
Augusta Amalia Ludovica Georgia of 442
Caroline Augusta of, Empress of Austria 11
Catherine of 451
Elizabeth of 451

Henry IX, Duke of 832
Isabella, Princess of, Queen of France 226
Jacqueline, Princess of 229, 231, 233, 235
Louis II, Duke of 617
Louis IV of, Holy Roman Emperor 51, 52, 447, 449, 451, 617, 907
Margaret of 438
Matilda of 449, 451
Otto of, Count Palatine of Mosbach 237
William/Wilhelm V, Count of Holland 908
Wulfhilde of 832
BAVARIA-LANDSHUT
Elizabeth, Princess of 52
Frederick, Duke of 51
Joanna of 237
Stephen II, Duke of 451
Stephen III, Duke of 51
BAVARIA-MUNICH
Albert III, Duke of 451
Ernest, Duke of 451
John, Duke of 451

BAVEY (VAN)
  Lodewijk van
    Marlot, Heer 460
BAXTER
  Agnes 87
  Dorothy 353
  Elizabeth 269
BAYER/BEYER
  Hanne Karin Blarke
    [Anna Karina]
    635
BAYFIELD
  St. Clair [John St.
    Clair Roberts]
    clii, 364, 365
BAYLEY
  Charlotte Elizabeth
    155
  Elizabeth Ann
    [Mother, later St.,
    Elizabeth Ann
    Seton] 222
  Margaret
    (Sherburne) 700
  Mary 722
  Richard 700
**BAYLEY alias
  SHERBURNE**
  Agnes (Harington)
    700, 703
  Richard 700, 703
BAYLY
  Sarah 421, 533
BAYNARD
  Anne (Blake) 743
  Anne (Hobbes) 743
  Barbara 406, 522
  Elizabeth (Barnes)
    743

Elizabeth
  (Blackwell) 743
Henry 743
Jane 508
Joan (Stukeley)
  743
John lxiv, 743
Martha (Prickman)
  743
Mary (Bennett)
  743
Philip 743
Robert 743
Thomas 743
BAYNE
  Anne 266
BAYNHAM
  Anne 295
  Margaret 721
BAYNTON/BAINTON
  Anne (Cavendish)
    468
  Edward (Sir) 468
  family 632
  Ferdinando 468
  Henry 468, 632
  Isabel (Leigh) 468
  Joan 632
  Joan (Echyngham?)
    632
  Joan (Weare alias
    Browne) 468
  John (Sir) 632
BAZIN
  Élisabeth (Philippes)
    950
  Marie-Louise- Élisa-
    beth 939, 950
  Pierre 939, 950

Thérèse (Fortier)
  950
BAZYKIN
  Claudia 799
BEACH
  Mary 218
BEADON
  Charlotte 306
BEALL
  William R. xix
BEALS
  Rixford A. 303
BEARD
  Annette Knowles
    (Huddleston) 79
  Cornelius Collins 79
  Gertrude Field
    (Finley) 79
  Maximillian 79
  Natalie Sudler
    (Turner) 79
  Philadelphia
    (Stuart-Menteth)
    79
  Stuart-Menteth 79
  Timothy Field xx,
    xlvi, xlix, lvii, lxvi,
    79, 275, 1026
BEARDSELL
  Eileen Pamela 622
BÉARN (DE)
  Bernard, Seigneur
    de Gerderest 963
  Catherine (de
    Viella) 963
  Jean, Seigneur de
    Gerderest 963
  Marguerite (de
    Gramont) 963

BÉARN-BONASSE (DE)
  Bertrand, Seigneur de La Bastide-Villefranche 963
  François 963
  Henri 963
  Isabeau 963
  Jacques 963
  Jeanne (de Belsunce) 963
  Madeleine (de Làas) 963
  Marie (de Bescat) 963
  Marie (de Sacaze) 963

BEATI JACOBI
  Charlotte Wilhelmine 620

BEATON
  Janet 154, 157, 167, 168, 179, 210, 213, 214, 216, 218, 257

BEATRICE
  of Portugal 400
  of York, Princess of Great Britain 25

BEATRIX
  of Burgundy (wife of Frederick I Barbarossa, Holy Roman Emperor) 640, 733, 735, 952
  of Burgundy and Bourbon 634, 638
  of Castile, Queen of Portugal 619
  of Glogau (wife of Louis IV, Holy Roman Emperor) 51, 447, 449, 451, 907
  Plantagenet, Princess of England 442, 633, 942, 946, 963
  Princess of Bohemia 640
  Princess of Naples, Empress of Constantinople 72, 961
  Princess of Provence, Queen of Naples and Sicily 965
  of Savoy, Queen of Sicily 642

BEATTIE
  Betty 96

BEATTY
  Christiana (Clinton) xlvii, 351
  John 351
  Joseph M., Jr. xlvii

BEAUCHAMP (DE)
  Agnes 835
  Alice (de Mohun) 866, 870
  Alice (de Toeni) 547, 783
  Anne 118, 295, 419, 492, 532, 575, 576
  Beatrice 737, 763, 766, 768, 770
  Cecily 740
  Edith (Stourton) 547
  Edward Seymour, Baron 69, 76, 80
  Eleanor 300, 345, 396, 407, 427, 870
  Elizabeth xxv, 324, 331, 332, 357, 405, 417, 421, 429, 743, 866
  Elizabeth (Stafford) 332, 506, 532, 575
  family clxxxvi
  Guy, 10th Earl of Warwick 783
  Henry Seymour, Baron 80
  Humphrey (Sir) 869, 870
  Ida (Longespee) 737, 741, 763, 766, 768, 770
  Isabel (le Despencer) xxv, 357, 417, 429
  Joan 500, 551, 574, 588, 596
  Joan (de Nonant) 674, 866
  Joan (FitzAlan) xxv, 417, 500, 551, 574, 588, 596
  John (Sir) 547, 674, 866
  John, 1st Baron Beauchamp of Powyck 506, 575
  John, 2nd Baron Beauchamp of Hatch 740

Margaret 506, 547, 590
Margaret (Ferrers) 506, 575
Margaret (St. John) 740
Margaret (Whalesburgh) 866
Marguerite 979
Mary 676
Mary (___) 547
Maud 783
Philippa 495, 577, 590, 615
Richard, 1st Earl of Worcester xxv, 357, 405, 417, 429
Richard, 2nd Baron Beauchamp of Powyck 332, 506, 532, 575
Robert 866, 870
Roger 547
Roger (Sir) 547
Roger, 1st Baron Beauchamp of Bletsoe 547
Susanna 213
Sybil (Oliver) 870
Sybil (Patshull) 547
Walter (Sir) 547
William 737, 763, 766, 768, 770
William, Baron Abergavenny xxv, 417, 500, 551, 574, 588, 596

___ (___), wife of Sir Roger (*not* Joan Clopton) 547
BEAUCLERK
Charles, 1st Duke of St. Albans 33
Charles George 33
Diana (de Vere) 33
Diana (Spencer) 33
Emily Charlotte (Ogilvie) 33
Jane Elizabeth 33
Mary (Norris) 33
Sidney, Lord 33
Topham 33
BEAUDRY
Marguerite 982
BEAUFOE
Jane 719, 874
BEAUFORT
Anne 407
Edmund, 1st Duke of Somerset 300, 345, 396, 407, 427
Eleanor 300, 418
Eleanor (Beauchamp) 300, 345, 396, 407, 427
family xxxii, lxv
Henry, 2nd Duke of Somerset 345, 396
Henry Beaufort, Cardinal xii, xxv, lxix, clxxii, 295, 298, 337, 375, 382, 900
Henry Charles Somerset, 6th Duke of 64

Jane 295, 337, 375, 382, 900
Joan xxxiv, 107, 114, 119, 126, 133, 314, 324, 331, 339, 357, 366, 368, 370, 387, 393, 395, 397, 398, 403, 405, 413, 417, 418, 419, 426, 429, 433, 434, 902
Joan, Queen of Scotland xxv, 152, 160, 173, 176, 219, 222, 223, 225, 241, 249, 256, 261, 273, 278, 280, 283, 898
John, 1st Duke of Somerset 547
John, Marquess of Somerset and Dorset xxv, 222, 300, 345, 396, 407, 427, 547, 898
Margaret 427, 547
Margaret (Beauchamp) (St. John) 547
Margaret (Holand) xxv, 222, 300, 345, 396, 407, 427, 547, 898
BEAUFORT (DE)
Wilhelmina Cornelia 446
BEAUHARNAIS (DE)
Alexandre-Marie, Vicomte 292, 442

1065

Eugène-Rose, 1st
Duke of Leuchtenberg, Viceroy of
Italy 442, 443,
444
Joséphine (Marie-Josèphe-Rose)
(Tascher de la
Pagerie) [Joséphine,
Empress of the
French] 292, 442,
443, 444
BEAULIEU (DE)
Célina 989
Charles de Mons,
Seigneur, Seigneur
de Richemont 941
Henrietta [Henrietta
Johnston] v, lxvii,
cxliv, 430
BEAUMEZ (DE)
Agnes (de Coucy)
804
Gilles, Châtelain of
Bapaulme 804
___ 804
BEAUMONT (DE)
Agnès 948, 956,
964
Alice (Stukeley)
744
Amicia (de Gael)
843, 845
Anne (Armstrong)
430
Anne (Saunders)
429
Anthony 430

Antoine, Seigneur
de La Tour 965
Aymonette
(Alleman) 965
Aynard, Seigneur
des Adrets 965
Catherine 503,
569, 608
Catherine (Farnham)
429
Claude (Marc) 965
Colette (Clarke)
429
Constance 630
Eleanor 628
Eleanor
(Plantagenet)
625, 628, 630
Eleanor (Sutton)
407, 628, 630, 676
Elizabeth 625
Elizabeth (Mitton)
628
Elizabeth
(Willoughby)
628, 630
Elizabeth, Baroness
of Chamond 430
Ennemond,
Seigneur de Saint-Quentin 965
Ermengarde, Queen
of Scotland 700,
705, 708, 710, 713,
715, 719, 721, 723,
725, 727, 728, 730,
732
Françoise (de Laire)
965

George 429
Hawise 808, 810,
811, 1025
Henry (Sir) 628,
630, 676
Henry Beaumont,
3rd Baron 625,
628, 630
Henry Beaumont,
5th Baron 628
Hugh 744
Isabel lxix, 837,
839, 847
Jean I de Brienne,
Vicomte 947, 948
Jean II de Brienne,
Vicomte 947
Jeanne (Ferland-Teste) 965
Joan 560
Joan (Darcy) 429
Joan (Heronville)
628, 630
Joan (Pauncefoot)
429
John 429
John (Sir) 628
John Beaumont, 2nd
Baron 625, 628,
630
John Beaumont, 4th
Baron 625, 628,
630
Katherine
(Everingham)
625, 628, 630
Louis de Brienne,
Vicomte 948, 964
Louise (Ravier) 965

Margaret 680, 681, 682, 744, 843, 845
Margaret (de Vere) 625, 628, 630
Marguerite (de Fougères) 957
Mary 111
Mary (Basset) 429, 430
Mary (Bassett) 614
Mary, Countess of Buckingham 430
Maud 550, 739, 835
Maud (FitzReginald) 739, 957
Mona Josephine Stapleton, Baroness 72
Nicholas 429
Petronilla (de Grandmesnil) 843
Philippe 942
Richard 429
Robert, 1st Earl of Leicester, Count of Meulan 739, 835, 837, 839, 843, 845, 847, 957, 1025
Robert, 2nd Earl of Leicester 843, 845
Robert, 3rd Earl of Leicester 843
Robert de Brienne, Vicomte 947
Roland, Seigneur de Saint-Quentin 965
Thomas (Sir) 429, 744

Thomasine (Wise) 744
William 429, 430, 614
BEAUMONT DE SAINT-QUENTIN (DE)
Diane 965
BEAUPRÉ (DE)
Isabel 687, 695
Isabel (FitzWilliam) 687, 695
Margaret (de Furneaux) 687, 695
Ralph (Sir) 687, 695
Stephen (Sir) 687, 695
BEAUREGARD
Denis xii, 939, 942, 961, 966
BEAUSSART (DE)
Jacques de Dreux, Vicomte 956
BEAUVAIS (DE)
Nicole-Françoise 944
BEAUVAU (DE)
Françoise 202
Isabeau (de Clermont) 202
Jacqueline 941
Jacques, Seigneur de Rivau 202
Jacques, Seigneur de Tigny and de Ternay 941
Jeanne (de Terney) 941

Marguerite (Bigot) 941
BEAUVOIR (DE)
Aymar, Seigneur de Villette 952
Isabelle 952
Marguerite 911
Marguerite (de Grolée) 952
Siboud III 911
Sibylle (de La Tour du Pin) 911
BEAUVOIS (DE)
Sophia (van Lodensteyn) lvii
BEAVERBROOK family xxxviii
William Maxwell Aitken, 1st Baron 69, 371
BEBE [BEKE?]
Jane 826
BECK
Catharina 620
BECKENSHAW
Alice 297
BECKER
Elizabeth 222, 377
BECKFORD
Bathshua (Hering) 933
Margaret (Gordon) 933
Maria (Hamilton) 933
Peter 933
Susan Euphemia 933
William 933

1067

William "Vathek" 933
BECKWITH
Arthur 127
Elizabeth (Brockenbrough) (Dickenson) 127
Elizabeth (Jennings) 127
Henry Lyman Parsons xlvii, cxci
Marmaduke (Sir), 3rd Bt. lix, 127
Mary (Wyvill) 127
Roger (Sir), 1st Bt. 127
BEDDAM
Muriel Marie 194
BEDELL
Alice 720
BEDFORD
John Russell, 4th Duke of 25, 62, 75
John Russell, 6th Duke of 25, 28
BEDGEBURY
Agnes (Roper) 920, 922
John 922
BEDINGFIELD
Judith 403
BEDWELL
James R. 698
BEECHER
Alice 302
BEECHING
Susanna 348

BEEKMAN
Cornelia 243
Maria 881
BEELAERTS
Johanna Elisabeth 907
BEELE (VAN)
Beater 804
BEERSE
August Leopold van Pallandt, Heer, Heer van Eerde and Oosterveen 445
BEESTON
Dorothy 816
George 816
BÉGON
Marie-Claire-Thérèse 455
BEHRA
Robert xlvii, l, liv, lvi, 400, 559
BEHREND
Eleonore Melitta 224
BEHRS
Sophia A. 794
BEIEREN (VAN)
Elisabeth 447, 907
BEIGHTON
Margaret 757
BEINROTH
Anna Charlotte Elisabeth 37
BEJAR
Álvaro de Zuñiga, Duke of Plasencia, Arévalo and 191

BEKE
Elizabeth 752, 760, 772
Margaret 778
BEKINGHAM
Agnes 853
BELA I
King of Hungary 832
BELA IV
King of Hungary 621
BÉLAIRE
Julien-Olivier 979
Marie-Louise (Rochon) 979
Mary-Ann 979
Mathilda (Seguin) 979
Olivier "Levi" 979
BELASYSE
Arabella 129
Barbara 130
Barbara (Cholmley) 129
Grace (Barton) 129
Henry (Hon.) 129, 130
Thomas, 1st Viscount Fauconberg 129
BELAUNEY (DE)
Joan 682
BELDEN
Gertrude (Woolson) 924
Mead 924
Olive (Cadwell) 924, 926

Olive Gertrude 924
Royal Denison
924, 926
**BELEVSKY-
ZHUKOVSKY**
Alexis, Count 5
Elizabeth, Countess
clvi, 5
BELFIELD
Eversley M. G.
xlvii
**BELGIUM (THE
BELGIANS)**
Albert II, King of
142, 201, 204
Astrid Josephine
Charlotte Fabrizia
Elisabeth Paola
Maria, Princess of,
Archduchess of
Austria 201
Baudouin, King of
142
Carlota (Marie-
Charlotte-Amélie-
Auguste-Victoire-
Clémentine-Léopol-
dine), Princess of,
Archduchess of
Austria, Empress
of México 288
Claire (Coombs),
Princess of 201
Éleanore, Princess
of 204
Élisabeth, Princess
of 204
Emmanuel Leopold,
Prince of 204

Gabriel Baudouin,
Prince of 204
Laurent Benoit
Baudouin Marie,
Prince of 201
Leopold I, King of
45, 182, 196, 237,
290
Mathilde-Marie-
Christiane-Ghislaine
(d'Udekem d'Acoz),
Queen of [Mathilde,
Queen of the
Belgians] 154,
155, 201, 203, 204
monarchs of 45,
81, 141, 288, 444,
615
Paola [Paola
Margherita
Giuseppina
Consiglia Ruffo di
Calabria], Queen
of xl, 201, 204
Philippe I, King of
xl, 201, 204
Stéphanie-Clotilde-
Louise-Hermine-M
aria- Charlotte,
Princess of, Crown
Princess of Austria
288
BELGRAVE
Dorothy 757
Margaret/Margery
(Cotton) 757
Richard 757
BELKNAP
Elizabeth 505

BELL
Anne xlv, 295,
296, 522, 838
Bertha Etelka
(Surtees) 100
Edward 100, 838
Evangeline 100
Frances 429
Jane 131
John C. (Col.) xlvii
Margaret (Barley)
838
Mary Eleanor
(Fulford) 696
Sarah Eleanor 696
William Henry 696
BELLAY (DU)
Antoinette (de La
Palu) 942
Charles, Seigneur de
La Feuillée 942
Eustache, Seigneur
de Commequiers
942
Gabrielle 943
Guyonne (d'Orange)
942
Jacques, Count of
Tonnerre 942
Marquise (de Laval)
942
Radégonde (des
Rotours) 942
René, Seigneur de
La Lande 942
BELLENDEN
Mary 93
BELLERS
Marina 512

BELLETRUCHE (DE)
Antoine, Seigneur d'Annuys 911
Catherine (de Blonay) 911
Marie (Bonivard) 911
Mye 912
Pierre, Seigneur d'Annuys 911

BELLEW
Henry Edward, 6th Viscount Bellew xlvii

BELLINGHAM
Alice 389
Alice (Luddington) 528
Anne (Pickering) 909
Elizabeth (Backhouse) cxlii, 528, 575, 576
Elizabeth (Tunstall) 917, 918
family xxiv, 528, 529, 916, 918
Frances (Amcotts) 528
Jane (Eure/Evers) 528, 529
John 528
Penelope (Pelham) 301, 528, 576
Richard 528
Richard (Gov.) xlviii, clxxiv, 301, 528, 575, 576

Robert (Sir) 909, 917, 918
Thomasine 902, 909
William 528
_____ 917

BELLOMONT
Richard Coote (Gov.), 1st Earl of 107

BELMONT
Alva Erskine (Smith) (Vanderbilt) 26, 174, 175
August 174
Barthélemy de Grandson, Seigneur de la Sarraz and 872
Jordan de Grandson, Seigneur (de) 872
Oliver Hazard Perry 174
Sara (Whiting) 144

BELOW (VON)
Eleonore Melitta (Behrend) 224
Friederike Caroline Alexandrine Emma (von Keyserlingk), Countess 224
Friedrich Karl Bogislav 224
Georg [Anton Georg Hugo] 224
Gustav Friedrich Eugen 224
Karl Emil Gustav 224

Marie Eleonore Dorothea 58, 224
Marie Karoline Elizabeth (von der Goltz) 224

BELSUNCE (DE)
Jeanne 963

BELVEZER (DE)
Anne 203
Guyon, Baron de Jalavoux and d'Oradeur, Seigneur de Joncheres 200
Jeanne (d'Arpajon) 200

BEMAIN [BEAUMONT?]
Alice 826

BENAON
Jean de Sainte-Maure Nevele, Count of 942

BENAUGES
Gaston II de Foix, Count of 287, 615

BENAVENTE
Fadrique of Castile, Duke of 190

BENAVIDES (DE)
Teresa 140

BENCE-JONES
Caroline (Dickinson) 334
Philippa Frances 335
William 334

BENN
Amabel 901

1070

BENNET(T)
  Andrew, of Chesters 210
  Anne 210, 348
  Archibald, of Chesters 210
  Barbara xxxiii, xxxv, clxviii, 210, 211, 790, 923
  Barbara (Rutherford) 210, 211
  Dorothy (Collingwood) 210
  Elizabeth 471
  family xxxiv
  Henrietta Maria (Neale) 512
  Isabella 33
  Jack Franklin 217
  Jane 504
  Joanna 864
  Mary 743
  Richard, Jr. 512
  Shirley Elizabeth (Goodwin) viii, xlvii, lv, lxiv, lxviii, 153, 213, 217, 490, 708
  Susannah Maria 512
BENTINCK
  Charlotte Sophie (von Aldenburg) 54
  Christian Frederick Anthony Bentinck, Count 54
  Hans William, 1st Earl of Portland 54
  Jane Martha (Temple) 54
  Mary 121
  Mary Catherine (van Tuyll van Serooskerken) 54
  Sarah Margaret (Gerdes) 54
  Wilhelm Friedrich (William Frederick) Bentinck, Count clii, 54
  Wilhelmina Sara (Gerdes) 54
  Wilhelmine Auguste Friederike 54
  William Bentinck, 1st Count 54
  William Frederick (Wilhelm Friedrich) Bentinck, 1st Count 54
  William Frederick (Wilhelm Friedrich) Bentinck, Count li, cliii
  William Gustavus Frederick Bentinck, 2nd Count 54
BENTINCK-SMITH
  Marion (Jordan) 54
  Phebe (Keyes) 54
  William 54
  William Frederick 54
BENTLEY
  Dorothy 588
BERCHTOLD
  Esther Elizabeth (Prazmova de Bilkova) 220
  Franz Anthony, Count 220
  Franz Carl, Count 220
  Leopold, Count 220
  Ludmilla Gizella Theresa, Countess 220
  Ludmilla Maria Theresa Wratislavová (Mitrowitz and Schönfeld), Countess 220
  Marie Esther Elisabeth (von Sinzendorf) 220
  Marie Johanna (von Magnis) 220
  Marie Teresa Eleanora (Petrvaldská de Petrvaldu) 220
  Matthias Ernest, Count 220
  Prosper Anthony, Count 220
  Sigismund Andreas Corsinus, Count 220

1071

Susanna Polyxena Catharina (of Mansfeld-Vorderort), Countess 220
BERENDRECHT (VAN)
Clara 774
BERENGARIA
Princess and Queen of Castile, Queen of León 647, 709, 909, 948, 964
Princess of León and Castile, Queen of Jerusalem, Empress of Constantinople 909, 948, 964
Princess of Portugal, Queen of Denmark 644
BÉRENGER
Catherine 911, 912
BERESFORD
Cornelius 474
Dorothy xxxv, lxiv, cxlii, 474, 477
Dorothy (Cromer) (Seyliard) 477
Dorothy (Mellish) cxlviii, 311
Elizabeth (Seyliard) 474
Emilia Katherine 179
Richard 311
Sarah (Blakeway) (Logan) 311

BERG
Agnes Marie Louise 891
Albert A. 618
Carl Conrad 891
Gerhard VI of Juliers, Count of 459
Henry W. 618
Josephine Alma (Danielsen) xii, lvii, clii, 891
William III, Duke of Cleves, Juliers and 40, 43, 54, 56, 891
BERG (VON)
Anna Maria 45
BERG-SCHELKLINGEN
Salome of, Queen of Poland 791, 797, 802
BERGER
Debra 21
BERGERON
Geneviève 990
BERGGREN
Malvina Sofia Ulrika 457
BERGKVARA
Arvid Trolle, Lord of, Lord of Bo 452
BERKELEY
Alice 357, 358, 557
Anne 295, 338, 357, 429
Anne (Savage) 336

Catherine 298
Catherine (Heywood) 541
Catherine (Howard) 333, 334
Dorothy 541
Eleanor (Constable) 336, 598
Elizabeth 296, 297, 532, 676, 691
Elizabeth (Betteshorne) 676, 691
Elizabeth (Bluet) 541
Elizabeth (Burghill) 541
Elizabeth (Jermy) 297
Elizabeth (Killigrew) 296
Elizabeth (le Despencer) 541
Elizabeth (Neville) 357, 429
Elizabeth (Norborne) (Devereux) 345, 346
Elizabeth (Reade) 297, 298
Eve (la Zouche) 676, 691
family xxiv, lx
Frances (Colepepper/Culpeper) (Stephens) 296, 347, 839, 856
Henry (Sir) 296
Henry, Baron Berkeley 333, 336

1072

Isabel 295
Isabel (de Dover/de Chilham) 676, 691
Isabel (Dennis) 296
Isabel (Mead) 295, 598
Isabel (Mowbray) 295, 541, 557, 598
James (Sir) 541
James Berkeley, 6th Baron 295, 541, 557, 598
Jane 541
Joan 423, 598
Joan (Ferrers) 676, 691
Joan (Strangeways) (Willoughby) 372
John (Sir) 296, 676, 691
John, 1st Baron Berkeley of Stratton 296
John Symmes 345
Katherine (de Clivedon) 541, 676, 691
Lora 429
Margaret (Chettle) 541
Margaret (Dyer) 541
Margaret (Guy) 541
Margaret (Lygon) 296
Margaret (Mortimer) 541

Mary 77, 136, 232, 297, 333
Maurice 295, 598
Maurice (Sir) 296, 676, 691
Maurice Berkeley, 2nd Baron 676, 691
Maurice Berkeley, 4th Baron 541
Norborne (Gov.), 1st Baron Botetourt 345
Richard 541
Richard (Sir) 297, 298
Rowland 541
Thomas 357, 429, 541
Thomas, Baron Berkeley 336
Thomas Berkeley, 1st Baron 676, 691
Thomas Berkeley, 3rd Baron 541, 676, 691
Thomas Berkeley, 8th Baron 598
William 541
William (Sir) (Gov.) clxxii, 296, 347, 839
William Berkeley, 1st Marquess of 372
BERKSHIRE
Thomas Howard, 1st Earl of 482

BERLIN
Peter [Armin Hagen, Baron Hoyningen-Huene] xii, lviii, clii, clv, 850
BERNACKE
family 1025
Joan (Marmion) 684
John (Sir) 684
Maud 684
BERNADOTTE
Désirée [Desideria] (Clary), Queen of Sweden 83
Jean-Baptiste [Charles XIV John], King of Sweden 83
BERNARD
Alice (Haselwood) 495
Amelia (Offley) xlviii, lvii, clxxiv, 495, 531, 684
Anna (Cordray) xl, lxiv, clxvi, clxxvi, 495, 737, 741, 930
Anne 930
Beheathland 565
Cecily (Muscote) 495
Dorothy (Alwey) 495
Elizabeth 496
Elizabeth (Woolhouse) 495
family lvii
Francis 495, 496

Francis (Sir), 1st Bt. (Gov.) lvii, clxxiii, 495, 531, 684
John   495
Lucy (Higginson) (Burwell)   495
Margaret (Daundelyn)   495
Margaret (Scrope)   495
Margery (Winslowe)   495
Mary (Woolhouse)   495
Richard   xl, clxvi, clxxiii, 495, 496, 737, 930
Sarah (___)   495
Thomas   495, 496
William (Col.) xxxiv, liii, clxvi, clxxiii, 495
BERNARD de SASSENAY (DE)
Marie-Anne-Claude   184
BERNERS
Abigail   494
John Bourchier, Baron   331, 353, 420, 421, 428
Margery   331, 353, 420, 421, 428
BERNERS-LEE
Cecil Burford   520
Conway   520
Helen Lane Campbell (Gray)   520

Mary Lee (Woods)   520
Timothy John "Tim" (Sir)   xviii, liii, lxiv, lxxi, clii, 520
BERNEY
Alice (Appleton)   607
Frances   607
Henry   607
John   607
Juliana (Gawdy)   607
Margaret (Read)   607
Margery (Wentworth)   607
Thomas (Sir)   607
BERNHARD
King of Italy   879, 919
BERNHARD III Margrave of Baden-Baden   208
BERNHARD CASIMIR FREDERICK GUSTAV HENRY WILHELM EDWARD Prince of Lippe   47
BERNHARD LEOPOLD FRIEDRICH EBERHARD JULIUS KURT KARL GOTTFRIED PETER Prince of Lippe-Biesterfeld, Prince

Consort of The Netherlands   1, 47
BERNIER
Clementine   971
BERNSTORFF (VON)
Andreas Hans August   37
Auguste Friederike   37
Clara Eleonore (von Bülow)   37
Eleonore Katharina (von Bülow)   37
family   37
BERRINGTON
Alice   584
BERRY
Anne   811
dukes of   186
Elizabeth   421
Elnora Lucretia (Warner)   925, 927
John, Duke of   440
John I, Duke of   205, 440
Laura   362
Marie of   205, 440
Nancy (Russell)   925, 927
Robert   925
Robert, Jr.   925
Rosetta Mary   925
BERRYMAN
Elizabeth   563
BERTELSON
Miriam Elliott   viii, xlvii, cxc, 660

BERTHIER
  Louis-Alexandre, Prince of Neuchâtel and Wagram, Napoleonic Marshal 83
  Malcy-Louise-Caroline-Frédérique 83
  Marie-Françoise (Lhutilier de la Serre) 83
  Napoléon, Prince and Duke de Wagram 83
  Zénaïde (Clary) 83
BERTIE
  Albinia 117
  Albinia (Farringdon) 117
  Anne (Casey) 117
  Gwendoline Theresa Mary 585, 648
  Robert, 1st Duke of Ancaster 117
  Vere (Lord) 117
BERTRAM
  Alexander, of Nisbet 152
  Cecilia (Kennedy) 152
  Euphemia 152
  Helen (Murray) 152
  William, of Nisbet 152
BERTRAND
  François 974
  George 974
  Jean-Baptiste 974
  Joseph-Marie 974
  Léon 974
  Lois June (Gowens) 974
  Louis J. 974
  Marcia Lynne [Marguerite Bertrand] 974
  Marie-Anne (Lizot) 974
  Marie-Anne (Perrault) 974
  Marie-Judith (Chaput) 974
  Marie-Louise-Angéline (Leduc) 974
  Marie-Marguerite (Jetté) 974
  Marie-Virginie-Adelphine (Maillet) 974
  Rolland F. 974
BÉRUBÉ
  Marie-Angélique (Miville) 971
  Marie-Josèphe 971
  Mathurin 971
BERWICK
  Anna 738
  James FitzJames, 1st Duke of 24
BESCAT (DE)
  Marie 963
BESDON (DE)
  Jeanne 964
BESSE (DE)
  Gabrielle (de Celle) 440
  Gilbert, Seigneur de la Richardie 440
  Marguerite 440
BESSILES
  Alice (Harcourt) 372
  Elizabeth 372
  William 372
BEST
  Caroline (Scott) 136
  Charles 116
  Dorothy 136
  Frances (Shelley) 136
  George 136
  James 136
  Mary Ellen 116
  Mary Norcliffe (Dalton) 116
BETANELI/ BETANELLY
  Helena Petrovna (Hahn) (Blavatsky) [Mme. Blavatsky] clxxvii, 792, 795
  Mikheil C. 792
BETENSON
  Albinia (Wray) 117
  Richard 117
  Theodosia 117
BETHEVILLE (DE)
  Blanche (de Harcourt) 961
  Guillaume IV, Seigneur 961
  Jacques, Seigneur 961
  Jeanne 961
  Marguerite (le Veneur) 961

BÉTHISY (DE)
Catherine-Éléonore-
Eugénie 613
Eleanor (Ogle-
thorpe) xl, 613
Eugène-Marie,
Marquis de
Mézières 613
BETHLEN VON BETHLEN
Cornelia, Countess 57
BETHOC
of Scotland 828
BETHUNE
Agnes (Anstruther) 276
Christian (Stewart) 276, 277
John, of Balfour 276, 277
Margaret 276
BETTESHORNE
Elizabeth 676, 691
BETTS
Joanna (Chamber-
lain) 921
Richard 921
BEU (DE)
Robert II de Dreux, Seigneur 956
BEUTHEN-KOSEL
Eliska of 713
BEUVRON (DE)
Jacques de Harcourt, Baron 961
BEVAN
Barbara (Aubrey) 338, 410

Joely (Richardson) 247
John liv, 338, 410
Rosie 723
Timothy 247
BEVEREN (VAN)
Anthony de
Bourgogne, Count
de La Roche, Heer 438, 445
BEVILLE
Amy (___) (Butler) 420
Essex lx, 420
John 420
Mary (Clement) 420
Mary (Saunders) 420
Robert 420
BEVYLE
Rose 687, 695
BEWICKE
Dorothy 100
BEY
Ali Kemal, Interior
Minister of Turkey 12
BEYINCÉ
Agnès (DeRouen) 990
Célestina "Tina"
Anne 990
Lumis Albert 990
BEYNE (DE)
Jacques d'Estoute-
ville, Seigneur,
Baron d'Ivry 208
BEZ (DE)
Marguerite 964

BIANCHI
Angela 190
BICKLEY
Francis (Sir), 3rd Bt. 534
Joseph xlvii, liii, lxiv, clxxiv, 534
Mary (Winch) 534
Sarah (Shelton)
(Gissage) 534
BICKNELL
Constance Rosalie 403
Richard Henry 403
Selina Acton (Birch) 403
BIDDLE
family xxiv
BIDDULPH
Anne (Joliffe) 138
Augusta (Roberts) 138
John 138
Mary Anne 138
Michael 138
Penelope
(Dandridge) 138
Robert 138
BIEBER
Jeremy 984
Justin Drew lxiii, 968, 984
BIELKE
Axel 452
Barbro 452
Brigitta, Queen of
Sweden 663
Carin 663
Elsa (Posse) 452

BIGGER
Elizabeth 695
BIGOD
Amy (___) 821
Aveline (Bassett) 845
Bertha (de Ferrers) 806, 821
Christian 845, 846
family clxxxii, 725, 846
Hugh (Sir) 730, 845
Hugh, 3rd Earl of Norfolk 806, 821, 845, 846
Ida (de Toeni) 737, 741, 742, 746, 749, 752, 754, 757, 760, 761, 763, 766, 768, 770, 772, 845
Isabel (___) 806, 821
Joan 730, 806, 821
Joan (___) 806, 821
Joan (de Stuteville) 730, 845
John (Sir) 806, 807, 821
Juliana (de Vere) 845
Maud (Marshall) 806, 821, 845
Ralph (Sir) 806, 807, 821
Roger (Sir) 806, 821
Roger, 2nd Earl of Norfolk 737, 742, 746, 749, 752, 754, 757, 760, 761, 763, 766, 768, 770, 772, 845
Roger, 4th Earl of Norfolk 845, 846
Roger, 5th Earl of Norfolk 845, 846
BIGOD alias FELBRIGG
Elizabeth (Scales) 713
Roger (Sir) 713
BIGORRE (DE)
Gaston I de Foix, Count de Foix and 963
Guy de Montfort, Count 959
Jean III, Count de Foix and 963
BIGOT
Marguerite 941
BILL
Ephraim 921
Lydia 524, 921
Lydia (Huntington) 921
BILLE
Anne 644
Beate 646
Bent 644
Claus 646
Else 644
Gyde (Galen) 644
Inger (Galen) 644
Jakob (knight) 644
Lisbet (Ulfstand) 646

Maeritslef 644
Margrethe (Brahe) 644
Margrethe (Rønnow) 646
Peder 644
Regitze 644
Sidsel (Lunge) 644, 646
Steen Basse 646
Torbern (knight) 644, 646
BILLINGTON
Elizabeth 467
BILLOZOROWNA
Evanor Anna 802
BINET DE MARCOGNET
Marie-Louise 227
BINFIELD
Caroline Charlotte 98
BIRCH
Henry William Rous 403
John Brereton 403
Louisa Judith (Rous) 403
Lydia (Mildred) 403
Mary 379
Selina Acton 403
BIRCHARD
Drusilla (Austin) 702
Elias 702
Sarah (Jacob) 702
Sophia 656, 702, 871

BIRD
   Margaret (___) 347
   Mary 344
BIRKBECK
   Elizabeth Lucy (Barclay) 148
   Emma 148
   family, of Westacre 149
   Henry 148
BIRKIN
   Andrew Timothy 27
   David Leslie 27
   Henry Laurence 27
   Jane Mallory xviii, clii, 27, 28
   Judy Mary (Gamble) [Judy Campbell] 27
   Olive Isobel (Russell) 27
BIRTLES (DE)
   Christian 817
BIRTWISTLE
   Susan Elizabeth 383
BISBY
   Phebe 670
BISCHOFFSHEIM
   Marie-Laure- Henriette- Anne 227
   Marie-Thérèse-Anne-Josèphe-Germaine (de Chévigné) 227
   Maurice-Jonathan 227
BISCOE
   Mary 750

BISHOP
   Anne 65
   Caleb 932
   Jane 736
   Keziah (Hibbard) 932
   Lucy 932
BISTRATE (DE LA)
   Hélène-Françoise (du Mont dit de Brialmont) 804
   Isabelle-Hélène 804
   Jean-Baptiste, Seigneur of Laer and Neerwinde 804
BJÖRNRAM
   Carin 267
BLACK
   Catherine 245
   Harrison 496
   Harrison (Dr.) xlvii
BLACKADDER
   Janet 456
BLACKMAN
   Jean 321
BLACKMER/ BLAKEMORE
   Elizabeth (Curtis) (Bankes) 866
   Joan (Collamore) 866
   William 866, 868
   ___ 866
BLACKWELL
   Elizabeth 743
   Frances Elizabeth 923

BLACKWOOD
   Caroline [Lady Caroline Maureen Hamilton-Temple-Blackwood Freud Citkowitz Lowell] xviii, 31
BLADEN
   Anne 327, 752
   Anne (Van Swearingen) 312, 327, 753
   Barbara 313
   Barbara (Janssen) cxlviii, cl, 312, 313
   Elizabeth 327
   family xxiv
   Harriot 313
   Isabella (Fairfax) 327
   Martin 104
   Mary (Gibbs) 104
   Nathaniel 327
   Thomas (Gov.) 312, 313
   William lix, clxv, 104, 312, 327, 752, 753
BLAENEY
   Lucy 689
BLAIR
   Christian 260
   David, of Adamton 150
   David, of Giffordland 150
   Eric Arthur [George Orwell] 122
   John (Gov.) 260

Margaret (Blair) 150
Margaret (Boswell) 150
Mary (Munro) 260
Sarah lxiii, 150
Sarah (___) (Lawson) 150
William, of Giffordland 150
BLAIR-SMITH
   Trevania Barlow (Dallas) 666
   Victoria Anne (Meeks) 666
BLAIS
   Élisabeth 970
   Joseph 970
   Marie (Boisvert) 970
   Marie-Josèphe (Dessaint dit Saint-Pierre) 970
BLAKE
   Anne 743
   Dorothy 602
   Mary 93
   Olive 93
   Susan 472
BLAKENEY
   Bridget 465
BLAKENHAM
   John Hugh Hare, 1st Viscount 80
BLAKEWAY
   Jacob 319
   Sarah 311
BLAKISTON
   Anne (Bowes) 101

Barbara (Lawson) 317
Elizabeth 101
Elizabeth (Bowes) 317
Elizabeth (Gerard) 317
family xxxiv, lix
Francis (Sir), 3rd Bt. 101
George 317
Jane (Lambton) 101
John 317
Margaret 317, 335
Margaret (Fenwick) 101
Margaret (James) 317
Marmaduke 317
Nathaniel (Gov.) 205, 317
Nehemiah 317
Phebe (Johnston) 317
Ralph (Sir), 1st Bt. 101
Susan (Chambers) 317
William (Sir) 101
BLANCA
   Princess of Spain 6
BLANCHARD
   Elizabeth (Gardner) 923
   Elizabeth Cabot 923
   Francis 923
   Mary Anne (Cabot) 923

Samuel 923
Susannah 519
BLANCHE
   of Artois 623, 625, 628, 630, 632
BLAND
   Anne (Bennett) 348
   Dorothy (Mrs. Jordan), mistress of William IV, King of Great Britain 9
   Frances 464
   Margaret 781
BLAQUIERE (DE)
   Eliza (Roper) 109
   Louisa Emily 109
   Peter Boyle 109
BLATCHFORD
   Anne 350
BLAVATSKY
   Helena Petrovna (Hahn) [Mme. Blavatsky] xvii, xxvi, clxxvii, 792, 795
   Nikifor Vassilievitch 792
BLAW
   Janet 86
   Mary (Traill) 85
   William 85
BLAYNEY
   Margaret (___) 300
BLECHYNDEN
   Alice 778
   John 778

Margaret (Crispe)
(Crayford)   778
BLEDDYN
  ap Cynfyn ab
    Gwerystan   815
BLEECKER
  Gertrude   548
BLEIDT
  Ann Elizabeth   150
BLENCOWE
  Anne (Mallison)   322
  Anthony   321
  Apollonia (Tolson)   321
  Elizabeth   322
  Grace (Sandford)   322
  Henry (Sir)   322
  John   322
  Richard   321
  Winifred (Dudley)   321
BLENNERHASSET
  Agnes   405
  Avice (Conway)   325
  Catherine   144, 325
  Conway   144, 325
  Elizabeth   508
  Elizabeth (Cornwallis)   508
  Elizabeth (Cross)   325
  Elizabeth (Denny)   405
  Elizabeth (Harman)   325
  Elizabeth (Lacy)   144, 325

family   xxxiv, lv
Harman   144, 325
Jane (Denny)   405
John   325, 405, 508
Margaret (Agnew)   144, 145, 325
Margaret (Crosbie)   405
Martha (Lynne)   325, 405
Mary   405
Robert   325
Ruth (Blennerhasset)   405
Thomas   405
BLEW-JONES
  Sophie   97
BLEWETT
  Edith   595
  family   595
  Joan (Fitzjames)   595
  Joan (St. Maure)   595
  Margaret   715
  Nicholas   595
  Walter   595
BLIER
  Victoire   988
BLIGH
  Elizabeth   464
  Elizabeth (Gorges) (Courtenay)   295, 296, 522
  Susan Rachel   23
  William   522
BLIGHT
  Margaret   867

BLISS
  Abigail (Williams)   672
  Alexander   672
  Margaret   672
BLOIS
  Margaret of   735, 952
  Stephen II, Count of   642, 830, 911
  Theobald V, Count of   735, 952
BLONAY (DE)
  Aymon, Seigneur de St. Paul   872
  Catherine   911
  Catherine (d'Oron)   911
  Jean, Seigneur de St. Paul   911
  Jeannette   872
BLOOD
  James H.   138
  Victoria (Claflin) (Woodhull) [Victoria C. Woodhull]   138
BLOOMER
  Elizabeth Ann "Betty" [Betty Ford]   xlii, xliii, 631, 655, 867, 868, 887
  Hortense (Neahr)   867
  William Stephenson   867
BLOSSOM
  Elizabeth   725

1080

BLOUNT
  Anna (Willix)
    (Riscoe) 359, 530
  Anne 110, 780
  Anne (Croft) 530,
    553
  Anne (Fisher) 530
  Bridget (Broome)
    531
  Charles 531
  Constance 676, 677
  Dorothy 340
  Dorothy (Grey)
    340
  Elizabeth 324, 405,
    417, 462, 501, 503
  Elizabeth (___)
    530
  Elizabeth
    (Columbell) 530
  Elizabeth "Bessy"
    530
  Frances 530
  Frances (___)
    530, 531
  Frances (Blount)
    530
  George 530, 531
  Isabel (Acton) 530
  James lxviii, lxix,
    cxlii, clxviii, clxxiv,
    359, 530, 531
  John (Sir) 530
  Joyce 553
  Katherine (Peshall)
    530
  Margaret (Gresley)
    716
  Robert 530

  Rosamond
    (Freschville) 530
  Sancha (de Ayala)
    xiii, xiv, lv, lxv,
    lxviii, 676, 709,
    717, 994
  Sencha/Sanche 716
  Thomas 530, 531
  Thomas (Sir) 530,
    553, 716
  Walter 530
  Walter (Sir) xiv,
    676, 709, 994
  William, 4th Baron
    Mountjoy 340
BLOXAM
  Adelaide Caroline
    362
BLOYOU
  Amicia 665
BLOYS/BLOSSE
  Martha 682
BLUET
  Anne 340
  Arthur 340
  Dorothy (Blount)
    340
  Elizabeth 541
  Elizabeth (Portman)
    340
  Joan (Lancaster) 340
  John 340
  Mary (Chichester)
    340
  Richard 340
BLUNDELL
  Alice Mary,
    Baroness Lovat
    23

BLUNSTON
  Hannah (Levis)
    384
  Michael 384
BLUNT
  Mary (Flood) 516
  Mary Fanny 78
BLUX
  Katherine 748
BLYTHE
  Margaret 676
BO
  Arvid Trolle, Lord
    of Bergkvara and
    452
BOAL
  Jeanne-Marie-
    Bernarde (de
    Menthon) liii, clii,
    206, 443
  Margaret Mathilde
    206, 443
  Mathilde Dolores
    (Denis de Lagarde)
    lx, clii, 443
  Pierre de Lagarde
    206, 443
  Pierre Denis-
    Lagarde 443
  Theodore Davis 443
**BOBRINSKI/
  BOBRINSKOY**
  Alexandra
    (Pizarjewa) 14
  Alexis, Count 14
  Anna Dorothea (von
    Ungern-Sternberg),
    Baroness 14
  family 14

Gregori, Count
[Prof. George
Vladimir Bobrin-
skoy] clii, 14
Julia (Junosha-
Belinslava) [Jun-
òsza-Biélinska] 14
Maria (Nikonowa) 14
Paul, Count 14
Theodora (Platt) 14
Vladimir, Count 14
**BOBRKU
LIGEZIANKA (Z)**
Konstance 621
BODDEN
Margarethe Agnes
"Grete" 232
BODDIE
Anna (___) 882
Elizabeth (___)
882
family 884
John 882
John Bennett, II
xlvii, xlix, lii, lv,
lx, lxi, lxii, lxiv,
lxv, lxviii, lxix,
lxx, lxxi, 884
Mary (___) 882
Mary (___)
(Griffin) 882
Mary (Mildmay) 882
Thomas 882
Thomasine
(Mildmay) 882
William xlvii,
clxxxi, 882, 884
BODE
Louise Mary 464

BODINE
Ronny O. viii,
xlviii, lxvii
BODMAN
Michael P. xlviii,
234, 312
BODRERO
Lydia 20
BOELENDOCHTER
Clementia Gerrit
774
**BOETZELAER
(VAN DEN)**
Agnes (de Bailleul)
460
Amélie (van
Marnix) 460
Anna Florentina 460
Anne (van der Noot)
460
Françoise/Francina
(van Praet) 459
Philip Jacob, Lord
of Asperen 460
Rutger, Lord of
Langerak, Merwede,
Asperen and
Carnisse 460
Wessel, Lord of
Asperen and
Merwede 460
Wessel, Lord of
Langerak and
Asperen 459
BOGESUND
Eric Stenbock,
Count of 452
BOGGE
Isabel Allen 197

BOHEMIA
Albert II, Holy
Roman Emperor,
King of Hungary
and 187, 220, 895
Anne (de Foix),
Queen of, Queen
of Hungary xxv,
287, 615
Anne, Princess of,
Holy Roman
Empress 40, 43,
54, 56, 192, 287,
290, 615, 891
Anne, Princess of,
Queen of England
714
Beatrix, Princess of
640
Bona, Princess of,
Queen of France
205, 287, 293, 438,
440, 442, 445
Cunigunde, Princess
of Germany, Queen
of 640
Dagmar, Princess of,
Queen of Denmark
644
Elizabeth, Princess of
England and Scot-
land, Queen of 38
Elizabeth of (wife of
Albert II, Holy
Roman Emperor,
King of Hungary
and Bohemia)
187, 220

Frederick V, Elector Palatine of the Rhine, I of Bohemia (the "Winter King") 38, 56
Judith of, Queen of Poland 791, 797, 802
Kunigunde of Halicz, Queen of 621
Ladislaus V, King of, King of Hungary 287, 615
Margaret of Austria, Queen of 621
Przemysl Ottokar II, King of 621
Wenceslaus I, King of 640
BOHLEN (VON)
Carl Christian Ferdinand 620
Charlotte Wilhelmine (Beati Jacobi) 620
Friederike Konstantine Henriette (Sandreczky von Sandraschütz), Countess 619
Philipp Christian 619
Wilhelmine Philippine Luise 620
BOHUN (DE)
Alice 547, 783
Audrey (Coke) 353
Baxter 353

Dorothy (Baxter) 353
Edmund 353
Edmund (Chief Justice) 353
Eleanor xxv, 331, 353, 392, 393, 409, 420, 421, 428, 436, 478, 512, 530, 553, 555, 582, 601, 603
Elizabeth 497, 500, 510, 517, 524, 532, 551, 554, 558, 560, 563, 565, 571, 574, 588, 596, 611, 613
Elizabeth (Badlesmere) 497, 500, 510, 517, 524, 532, 551, 554, 558, 560, 563, 565, 571, 574, 588, 596, 611, 613
Elizabeth (Knevet) 353
Elizabeth (Plantagenet), Princess of England 478, 497, 500, 503, 510, 512, 517, 524, 530, 532, 543, 551, 553, 554, 555, 558, 560, 563, 565, 569, 571, 573, 574, 582, 588, 595, 596, 601, 603, 608, 611, 613
family lxix, 561
Francis 353
Henry, 1st Earl of Hereford 783

Humphrey, 2nd Earl of Hereford 783
Humphrey, 4th Earl of Hereford and Essex 478, 497, 500, 503, 510, 512, 517, 524, 530, 532, 543, 551, 553, 554, 555, 558, 560, 563, 565, 569, 571, 573, 574, 582, 588, 595, 596, 601, 603, 608, 611, 613
Humphrey IV 783
Margaret 503, 543, 547, 569, 573, 595, 608
Margaret (Lawrence) 353
Mary xxv, 229, 231, 233, 235, 378, 412, 603
Mary (Brampton) 353
Maud (de Lusignan), of Eu 783
Maud (FitzGeoffrey), Countess of Essex 783
Nicholas 353
William, 1st Earl of Northampton xxxix, 497, 500, 510, 517, 524, 532, 551, 554, 558, 560, 563, 565, 571, 574, 588, 596, 611, 613
BOIJE
Margareta 267

BOISSEVAIN
  Charles-Hercule
    clii, 41
  Marie-Thérèse-Vera-
    Zwetana (von
    Hartenau), Countess
    von Hartenau clii,
    41
BOISVERT
  Agnès (Gélinas) 970
  Charlotte 970
  Marie 970
  Philippe 970
  Philomène
    (Bourassa) 970
  Pierre 970
BOLD
  Anne 902
  Dulcia/Dulce
    (Savage) 497, 498,
    902
  Elizabeth (Gerard)
    902
  Henry (Sir) 497, 902
  Margaret (Boteler)
    902
  Maud 497
  Richard 902
  Richard (Sir) 902
BOLEBEC (DE)
  Isabel 680
  Osbern 861
BOLESŁAW
  Duke of Kosul 640
BOLESŁAW III
  Duke of Mazovia
    621
  King of Poland
    791, 797, 802

BOLESŁAW IV
  Duke of Mazovia
    621
BOLEYN
  Alice 588
  Anne (Tempest)
    539, 540
  Anne, Queen of
    England 300, 428,
    539, 551, 588, 596
  Edward (Sir) 539,
    540
  Elizabeth 539
  Elizabeth (Howard)
    300, 588
  family xxxii
  Jane 596
  Margaret 429, 551
  Margaret (Butler)
    300, 539, 551, 588,
    596
  Mary xii, lviii,
    300, 303
  Thomas, 1st Earl of
    Wiltshire, Earl of
    Ormonde 300, 588
  William (Sir) 300,
    539, 551, 588, 596
BOLIVAR
  Simón 991
BOLKO I
  of Schliesen-Lieg-
    nitz, Duke of
    Schweidnitz 640
BOLKO II
  of Schliesen-Lieg-
    nitz, Duke of
    Fürstenburg and
    Münsterberg 640

BOLLE
  Anne (Tyrwhit)
    720
  ____ 720
BOLLES
  Anne 471
  Anne (Goodrick)
    471
  Benjamin 471
  Elizabeth (Perkins)
    471
  Joseph xlvi, lxvii,
    clxii, 471, 472
  Mary (Howell?) 471
  Mary (Witham),
    Baronetess of
    Nova Scotia 471
  Thomas 471
BOLLING
  Anne (Cocke) 728
  Anne E.
    (Wigginton) 278,
    301, 387, 711, 823
  Archibald 278,
    301, 387, 711, 823
  Archibald, Jr. 278,
    301, 387, 711, 823
  Catherine (Payne)
    278, 301, 387, 711,
    823
  Edith xlii, 278,
    301, 387, 711, 823
  Elizabeth 729
  John xiv
  John (III) 387, 711,
    823
  Mary (Jefferson)
    387, 711, 823
  Mary (Kennon) xiv

1084

Robert, Jr. 728
Sallie Spiers
 (White) 278, 301,
 387, 711, 823
William Holcombe
 278, 301, 387, 711,
 823
BOLTON
Elizabeth 480
Mary H. (Lynch)
 222
BOMARZO
Francesco Borghese,
 3rd Duke of 24
Francesco Marco
 Luigi Costanzo
 Borghese, 6th
 Duke of cliii, 24
Marco Borghese,
 4th Duke of 24
Paolo Borghese, 5th
 Duke of 24
BOMBELLES
Charles-René,
 Count 11
BONA
(Sforza), Queen of
 Poland 895
of Artois 438, 445
Princess of
 Bohemia, Queen of
 France 205, 287,
 293, 438, 440, 442,
 445
BONAPARTE
Caroline (Marie-
 Annonciade-
 Caroline), Queen
 of Naples 82

Charles Joseph
 xviii, 858
Elizabeth (Patterson)
 858
Eugénie de Montijo
 (Eugenia María
 Ignace Augustine de
 Portocarrero de
 Guzmán y Kirkpat-
 rick), Empress of the
 French 291, 292
 family 860
Jérôme, King of
 Westphalia, Prince
 of Montfort xl,
 858
Jérôme-Napoléon
 xviii, xl, 858
Joseph, King of
 Spain 83
Joséphine (Marie-
 Josèphe- Rose) (de
 Tascher de la
 Pagerie) (de Beau-
 harnais), Empress
 of the French
 292, 442, 443
Julie (Marie-Julie)
 (Clary), Queen of
 Spain 83
Napoléon I,
 Emperor of the
 French 11, 82,
 157, 292, 442, 858
Napoléon III (Louis
 Napoléon),
 Emperor of the
 French 49, 291,
 292

Susan May
 (Williams) xl,
 858
BONCAMPAGNI
family 193
BOND
James [fictional
 character] 27
Mary 426
Sarah 138
BONDE
Brigitta (Bielke),
 Queen of Sweden
 663
Charles VIII, King
 of Sweden 457,
 663, 664
Christina 663
Filip, Lord of
 Bordsjoe and
 Seckestad 457
Karin (Snakenborg)
 457
Katarina (Ulfsdotter)
 452
Mårta 457
Marta Tordsdotter
 452, 454
Tord, Lord of
 Bordsjoe 452
BONHAM
family xxxviii
BONHAM CARTER
Helen Violet
 (Asquith),
 Baroness Asquith
 of Yarnbury 306
Helena xi, xvii,
 xlviii, cliii, 306, 309

Henry 306
Maurice (Sir) 306
Raymond Henry 306
Sibella Charlotte (Norman) 306
BONIVARD
Marguerite (de Grolée) 911
Marie 911
Pierre, Seigneur de Saint-Michel des Déserts 911
BONNER
Anthony 533
Bridget (Savage) 533
Mary 533
BONNESON (DE)
Judith Elizabeth 244
BONNESTABLE (DE)
Gérard de Harcourt, Baron 961
Philippe de Harcourt, Seigneur 961
BONNET DE LA CHABANNE (DE)
Anne 440
BONNEVEAUX (DE)
Jean de Rovorée, Seigneur 872
BONTOUX
Clarisse 635
BONVILLE
Agnes 595
Alice (Dennis) 742
Catherine (Neville) 339
Cecily 743
Cecily, Baroness Harington and Bonville 339, 370
Edith (Blewett) 595
Edmund 595
Elizabeth 547, 594
Elizabeth (Courtenay) 742
Elizabeth (FitzRoger) 742
family 595
Humphrey 595
Isabella 742, 743
Jane (Tregion) 595
Joanna (Wynslade) 595
John 595, 742
Margaret (Grey) 742
William Bonville, 1st Baron 742, 743
William Bonville, Baron Harington and 339, 370
BOONE
Charles 743
Mary (Garth) 743, 744
Sarah Anne (Tatnall) (Peronneau) 743
Thomas (Gov.) xlviii, cxlii, 743, 745
BOOTH
Alice 561, 757, 758
Amy 817
Anne 483
Anne (Owen) 560, 561
Anne (Thimbleby) 715
Audrey 710
Catherine (Mumford) 464
Dorothy (St. John) 560
Elizabeth 715
Elizabeth (Boteler) 561
Elizabeth (Trafford) 561
Elizabeth (Warburton) 560, 561
Ellen (Montgomery) 687
George (Sir) 561, 687
George (Sir), 1st Bt. 560
Jane 561, 687
John 715
John (Sir) 560
Katherine (Anderson) 560
Katherine (Montfort) 687
Margaret (Hopton) 710
Mary (Cooke) 560
Maud (Dutton) 687

1086

Philip (Sir) 710
St. John 560, 561
Thomas liv, 560, 817
William 464
William (Sir) 560, 561, 687
BOOTH-TUCKER
Emma Moss (Booth) [Emma Moss Booth-Tucker] 464
family lxix
Frederick St. George de Lautour 464, 465
Louise Mary (Bode) 464
Mary (Reid) 464
BOOTHBY
Anne (Brownell) 377
Benjamin 377
Charlotte (Cunningham) 377
Eleanor (Curzon) 377
Elizabeth Caroline 378
Grisel (Halford) 377
James Brownell 377
Martha (Hobson) 377
Richard 377
Susanna (___) 377

Thomas 377
William 377
BOOTHE
Ross, Jr. xlviii, lv
BORBERG
Claus Cecil [Claus von Bülow] liii, cliii, 645
Eleanora (Ibsen) 645
Jonna (von Bülow) 645
Svend 645
BORCHGRAVE D'ALTENA
Alexandra D. (Villard) 112
Arnaud-Charles-Paul-Marie-Philippe, Count [Arnaud de Borchgrave] xviii, 112
Audrey Dorothy Louise (Townshend) 112
Baudouin, Count 112
Dorothy (Solon) 112
Eileen (Ritschel) 112
BORDEN
Alice Louisa 53
Frederick Wilson 53
Susan Wilhelmina (Swain) 53

BORDSJOE
Filip Bonde, Lord of, Lord of Seckestad 457
Tord Bonde, Lord of 452
BORGHESE
Amanda (Leigh) 24
Anna (dei Conti Scheibler) 24
Arabella (FitzJames) 24
family xi, xlviii
Francesca (Salviati) 24
Francesco, 3rd Duke of Bomarzo 24
Francesco Marco Luigi Costanzo, 6th Duke of Bomarzo cliii, 24
Isabel Fanny Louise (Porgès) 24
Lorenzo, Prince 24
Marcella (Fazi) (Mauritzi) [Princess Marcella Borghese] 24
Marco, 4th Duke of Bomarzo 24
Paolo, 5th Duke of Bomarzo 24
Scipione, Duca Salviati 24
BORGIA [BORJA]
Cesare, Duc de Valentinois, tyrant of Italy 287, 293

1087

Charlotte (d'Albret)
287, 293
family 192
Louisa, Princess 293
Lucretia, Duchess of
Modena and
Ferrara 287, 293
Rodrigo [Pope
Alexander VI]
287, 293
BORIS
Prince of Rostov
791
BORLAND
Francis 923
Jane 923
Jane (Lindall) 923
BORLASE
Anne 710
Anne (Lytton) 557,
575, 710, 711
Elizabeth 575
John (Sir) 557,
575, 710
Joyce 557
BOROVSK
Maria of 797
BORREGARD
Jon Havtoreson,
Lord of, Lord of
Huseby 452, 457
BORTHWICK
Agnes 253
Catherine 219
Margaret 273
BOSANQUET
Bernard 335
Esther (Cleveland)
335

Frederick Albert
(Sir) 335
Philippa Frances
(Bence-Jones) 335
Philippa Ruth
[Philippa Foot]
cliv, 335
William Sidney
Bence 335
BOSCAWEN
Alice 407
BOSSONENS (DE)
Aymon d'Oron,
Seigneur, Seigneur
d'Attalens 911
BOSTOCK
Adam 822
Adam (Sir) 822
Anne 336, 396
Catherine
(Mobberly) 822
Elizabeth 822, 823
Elizabeth
(Venables) 822
family 823
Hugh 822
Isabel (Lawton)
822
Janet (Bradshaw)
822
Joan (Del Heath)
822
Margaret 468
Margaret
(Whetenhall) 822
Margery
(Higginson) 822
Nicholas 822
Ralph (Sir) 822

William (Richard?)
822
BOSTWICK
Mary 244
BOSVILE
Elizabeth 291, 301,
339, 807
family 344
Godfrey 339
Isabel (Hastings)
343
Julia Louisa 27
Margaret 343
Margaret (Grevile)
339
Thomas 343
BOSWELL
Alexander (Sir), 1st
Bt. 90
Alexander, Lord
Auchinleck 150
Anne (Cramond)
150
Anne (Hamilton)
150
David, of
Auchinleck 128,
150
Elizabeth (Bruce)
150
Euphemia (Erskine)
150
Griselle/Graca
(Cumming) 90
Isabel (Wallace)
128, 150
James 150
James, of Auchinleck 90, 150

Jane 464
John (Dr.) 150
Margaret 150
Margaret (Cunning-
 ham) 150
Margaret
 (Montgomerie)
 90, 150
Marion 128
Marion (Crawford)
 150
Robert, of St.
 Boswells 150
Sibella 150
Sibella (Sandeman)
 150
Stephen Ralph 424
Theresa 90
BOTELER (LE)
(sometimes
BUTLER)
Alice 702, 754,
 757
Alice (Apsley)
 328, 662
Alice (Plumpton)
 (Sherburne) 700
Ankaret 749
Anne 302, 600
Anne (Spencer)
 302
Catherine (Knollys)
 302
Catherine (Waller)
 536
Constance (Vane)
 716
Cresset (St. John)
 754

Dorothy 730
Ela (de Herdeburgh)
 749, 754, 757
Elizabeth xlvii, liii,
 clxvi, clxxvii, 561,
 716, 754, 755
Elizabeth (Cokayne)
 716
Elizabeth (Drury)
 536, 730
Elizabeth
 (Langham) 302
Elizabeth (Villiers)
 536
family 537
Grizel (Roche) 536
Helen 536
Henry (Sir) 536
Isabel 564
Isabel (Willoughby)
 716
Jane (Elliott) 754
Joan (Christopher)
 (Mountstephen)
 754
John 716, 754
John (Sir) 302,
 524, 536, 537, 662,
 700
John, 1st Baron
 Boteler of
 Bramfield 536
Margaret 574, 902
Margaret (Delves)
 524, 561, 564, 902
Margaret (Stanley)
 524
Margery 524, 525
Mary 536

Philip 716
Philip (Sir) 302,
 536, 537, 716, 730
Thomas xlvii, clxv,
 clxxvii, 754, 755
Thomas (Sir) 524,
 561, 564, 902
William (Sir) 702
William, 1st Baron
 Boteler of Wem
 749, 754, 757
BOTETOURT
Norborne Berkeley
 (Gov.), 1st Baron
 345
BOTETOURTE (DE)
Ada 763, 768, 770
Elizabeth 737
Joan 766
Joan (de Somery)
 715, 728
Joan (Gernon) 766
John (Sir) 766
John de Botetourte,
 1st Baron 715,
 728, 737, 763, 766,
 768, 770
John de Botetourte,
 2nd Baron 715,
 728
Joyce 506, 715, 728
Joyce (la Zouche de
 Mortimer) 715,
 728
Margaret (__) 766
Maud/Matilda
 (FitzThomas)
 715, 728, 737, 763,
 766, 768, 770

1089

Thomas 715, 728
BOTHWELL
  Agnes Stewart, Countess of 128, 143, 146, 150, 151, 152, 159, 161, 163, 165, 166, 170, 177
  Francis Stewart, 1st Earl of 90, 96
  James Hepburn, 4th Earl of 90
  Patrick Hepburn, 1st Earl of 173, 222, 225
BOTILLER (LE)
  Clemence 650, 652, 657, 659, 680, 682, 686, 689, 692, 693, 694
BOTREAUX
  Elizabeth (Beaumont) 625
  Margaret clxxxiv, 625
  William Botreaux, 3rd Baron 625
BOTTLENBERG (VAN) genaamd VON SCHIRP
  Ida Margaretha 445
BOUCHER
  Frances 305
BOUHIER
  Françoise 961
BOUILLON (DE)
  Robert de la Marck, Duc 202

BOULAINVILLIERS (DE)
  Antoine, Count of Courtenay 205
  Françoise (d'Anjou) 205
  Jeanne (de Briçon) 205
  Jeanne-Catherine (de Vieuxpont) 205
  Philippe, Count of Courtenay 205
  Philippe, Count of Fauquemburghe 205
  Renée 205, 206
BOULOGNE
  Bertrand VI de la Tour, Count of Auvergne and 637
  Eustace I, Count of 879, 919
  Godfrey, Count of clxxxv
  Jean I de la Tour, Count of Auvergne and 637
  Matilda of, Queen of England 774, 776
BOURASSA
  Antoine 972
  Caroline (Baril) 972
  Elmire (Allard) 972
  Frédéric 970, 972
  Ignace 972
  Josèphe/Josephte (Plouf) 972
  Julie (Saint-Pierre) 970
  Louis-Cléophas 972
  Marguerite (Brault) 972
  Marie 972
  Marie-Antoinette (Leboeuf) 972
  Marie-Louise (Couture) 972
  Philomène 970
  Pierre 972
  Robert, Premier of Québec 969
BOURBON (DE) (OF)
  Anne 200, 293
  Catherine 941
  Cesare, Count of Busset 293
  Charles I, Duke of 205, 293, 440
  Claude 205
  Claude, Count of Busset 293
  Isabelle 438, 445
  James I, Count of la Marche 638
  Jean I, Seigneur de Carency 638
  Jeanne (de Châtillon-St. Pol) 638
  Jeanne (de Vendômois) 638

Jeanne-Catherine 638
John I, Count of La Marche and Vendôme 638
John I, Duke of 205, 440
Louis, Bishop of Liège 293
Louis, Count of Roussillon 200, 205
Louis-Alexandre, Count of Toulouse 287
Louis I, Duke of 634, 638
Louis-Jean-Marie, Duke of Penthièvre 287
Louis-Philippe-Joseph "Égalité," Duke of Orléans 287, 288
Louisa (Borgia), Princess 293
Louise (de Montmorillon) 293
Margaret 442, 634
Marguerite (de La Rochefoucauld) 293
Marie-Victoire-Sophie (de Noailles) 287
Peter, Baron de Busset 293
Peter I, Duke of 941

Philip, Baron de Busset 293
Philippote (de Plaines) 638
Pierre, Seigneur de Carency 638
Sidoine alias Edmée 440
Suzanne 205
BOURBON DEL MONTE SANTA MARIA
Carlo, Prince of San Faustino 20
Géneviève B. (Lyman) (Casey) 20
Jane Allen (Campbell) 20
Kay Linn (Sage) cliii
Lydia (Bodrero) 20
Maria Francesca (Massimo) 20
Ranieri, Prince of San Faustino cliii, 20
Virginia 20
BOURBON-MONTPENSIER
Charlotte of 62
Gabrielle of 636
BOURBON- PARMA
Zita of, Empress of Austria 800
BOURBON-PENTHIÈVRE (DE)
Louise-Marie-Adélaïde 287

BOURBON-SOISSONS (DE)
Marie 18
BOURBON-VENDÔME
Charlotte of 442
Jeanne of 637
BOURCHIER
Anne 403, 428, 883
Anne (Plantagenet) (Stafford) 331, 353, 392, 393, 403, 409, 420, 421, 428, 436
Anne (Woodville) 134
Anthony 883
Catherine (Howard) 353
Cecily 134
Cecily (Daubeny) 392, 436
Dorothy 392
Elizabeth 409, 436
Elizabeth (Dinham) 392, 409, 436
Elizabeth (Hall) 354
Elizabeth (Tilney) 300, 333, 353, 420, 428, 605, 705
Elizabeth (Verney) 354
family 1025
Fulk, Baron Fitzwarin 392, 409, 436
Henry, Count of Eu, 1st Earl of Essex xl, 134

Humphrey (Sir)
300, 353, 420, 428,
705
Isabel (Plantagenet)
134
James (Sir) 353
Joan clxxxiii, 331,
353, 421
John (Sir) 354
John, 1st Earl of
Bath 392, 436
John, Baron Berners
331, 353, 420, 421,
428
Margaret 420
Margery (Berners)
331, 353, 420, 421,
428
Mary 354, 701
Mary (Banister)
353
Ralph (Sir) 354
Thomas 883
Thomasine
(Hankford) 392,
409, 436
Thomasine
(Mildmay) 883
William, Baron
Fitzwarin 392,
409, 436
William, Count of
Eu 134, 331, 353,
392, 393, 403, 409,
420, 421, 428, 436
William Bourchier,
Viscount 134
BOURDIN
Louise Rosalie 108

**BOUREAU
(BOURREAU) de la
CHEVALERIE**
Marie-Françoise
442
BOURG (DU)
Catherine 202
BOURGOGNE (DE)
Anne 438
Anthony, Count de
La Roche, Heer van
Beveren 438, 445
Antoine, Seigneur
de Capelle 438
Claude (Andries)
438
Jeanne 445
Marie (de La
Viéville) 438, 445
BOURNE
Anne 492, 648
Dorothy (Lygon)
492
John 492
Judith 882
Margaret 311
**BOURNONVILLE
(DE)**
Alexander de
Bournonville, Duc
287, 291
Ambrose-François
de Bournonville,
Duc 287
Anne (de Melun)
287, 291
Lucrèce-Françoise
(de La Vieuville)
287

Marie-Françoise
287
Oudard, Count of
Hennin-Lietard
291
BOURRÉ
Angélique 970
BOUTIN
Marie-Josephte
989
BOUVIER
Caroline Lee [Lee
Radziwill] xviii,
xlv, 16, 17, 74, 914
Jacqueline Lee
[Jackie Kennedy
Onassis] xl, xlii,
xliii, xlvi, 16, 74,
914, 915
Janet Norton (Lee)
914
John Vernou 914
John Vernou, Jr.
914
John Vernou (III)
914
Maude Frances
(Sergeant) 914
BOVENHOLT
Adolf Werner I van
Pallandt, Heer von,
Heer von
Griethuysen 445
BOVILLE
Eleanor 680
BOWDOIN
Elizabeth 923
Elizabeth (Erving)
923

1092

Hannah (Pordage) 924
James 924
James, Jr. (Gov.) 923, 925
BOWEN
Abigail 582, 811
Anne (Berry) 811
Elizabeth (Johnson) 582, 811
Ellen (Franklyn) 811
Elsbeth (Vaughan) 811
Ethel Kate 117
Francis 811
Griffith xix, xlvi, lxii, clx, 582, 583, 811, 812
Gruffudd 811
Hannah (Brewer) 582, 811
Henry 582, 811
John 582, 811
Margaret (Fleming) xix, xlvi, lxii, clx, clxxv, 582, 583, 808, 811, 812
Philip 811
Richard LeBaron xlviii, li
BOWERS
Anne 497
BOWES
Agnes 421
Anne 101
Charity 691
Cordelia xx

Cordelia (Bowes) xx
Elizabeth 317
Elizabeth (Blakiston) 101
Elizabeth (Clifford) 317
George 101
George (Sir) 317
Margery 100, 317, 389, 399, 414, 416
Mary (Gilbert) 101
Mary Eleanor 101
Muriel (Eure) 317
Ralph (Sir) 317
William (Sir) 101
BOWES-LYON
Charlotte (Grinstead) 101
Claude, 13th Earl of Strathmore and Kinghorne 101, 930
Claude George, 14th Earl of Strathmore and Kinghorne 930
Elizabeth Angela Marguerite, Queen of Great Britain [HM Queen Elizabeth The Queen Mother] xl, xlii, liv, 101, 121, 419, 545, 930
Frances Dora (Smith) 101, 930
John, 9th Earl of Strathmore 101

Mary Eleanor (Bowes) 101
Mary Elizabeth Louisa Rodney (Carpenter) 101
Nina Cecilia (Cavendish-Bentinck) 930
Thomas, 11th Earl of Strathmore 101
Thomas, Lord Glamis 101
BOWKER
Elizabeth 111
BOWLES
Joan 368, 728
Margaret 598
Sydney 22
BOWMAN
Elizabeth 311
BOWYER
Alice 543
Anne 628
Anne (Salter) 543
Elizabeth 592
Henry (Sir) 543
Margaret (Weld) 543
Susanna (Woolston) 348
William (Sir), 1st Bt. 543
BOXHOLM
Lindorm Ribbing, Lord of 457
BOYCE
Alice 806
BOYD
Agnes (Livingston) 131

Christian (Hamilton)
165, 174
Elinor   127
Elizabeth   251, 252
Euphemia (Ross)
   131
Fannie Kate (Root)
   xiii, xiv
George Wesley   xiii
Hugh Blair   xiii
Isabel   165
James Boyd, 9th
   Baron   131
Jean (Cuninghame)
   131
Jean (Ker)   174
John   xiii
Katherine (Creyke)
   131
Lettice (Boyd)   131
Margaret   154, 157,
   167, 168, 179
Margaret
   (Campbell)   157,
   174
Marion   157, 174
Mary Elizabeth
   "Betty"   xiii
Mary Elizabeth
   (Bressie)   xiii
Mary Stovall
   (Puryear)   xiii
Robert (Hon.)   174
Robert Boyd, 7th
   Baron   165, 174
Thomas Boyd, 6th
   Baron   157, 174
William, 1st Earl of
   Kilmarnock   131

William, 2nd Earl of
   Kilmarnock   131
William, 3rd Earl of
   Kilmarnock   131
William, 4th Earl of
   Kilmarnock   131
BOYD (later HAY)
Isabel (Carr)   131
James, 15th Earl of
   Erroll   131
BOYER
Carl, 3rd   viii, x, xlii,
   xliii, xlviii, lxviii,
   501, 570, 690
BOYLE
Charles, 4th Earl of
   Orrery   73
Eleanor   340
Elizabeth   478
Elizabeth (Cecil)   73
Jane   382
Joan (Cope)   478
John, 5th Earl of Cork
   and Orrery   73
Kay   xviii, xlv, cliv,
   15
Lucy   73
Margaret (Hamilton)
   73
Mary (O'Brien)   340
Michael,
   Archbishop of
   Armagh   340
Stephen   478
BOYLES
Mary   211
BOYNE
Gustavus Hamilton,
   1st Baron   167

BOYNTON
Elizabeth   425
BOYS (DE)
Alice   653, 661
Margaret   521
BRAAM (VAN)
Ambrosia Wilhelm-
   ina (van Rijck)   460
Geertruida Helena
   460
Jacob Andreas   460
Jacob Pieter   460
Ursula Matha
   (Feith)   460
BRABANÇON (DE)
Christophe, Seig-
   neur de Cany-sur-
   Matz   944
François, Seigneur
   de La Ferté   944
Françoise (de
   Villers)   944
Jeanne (de
   Sarrebruche)   944
Marguerite   944
BRABANT
Elizabeth of   950
Henry I, Duke of
   950
Henry II, Duke of
   733
Marie of, Queen of
   France   941, 961
Matilda of   733
BRABAZON
Chambré, 5th Earl
   of Meath   120
Juliana (Chaworth)
   120

Mary 120
BRACCIANO
  Paolo Giordano
    Orsini, Duke of
    192
BRACHET
  Marie-Madeleine
    455
BRACKLEY
  Thomas Egerton, 1st
    Viscount 518
BRACQUE
  Jeanne 943
BRADBURY
  Anne (Eden) 579,
    838
  Elizabeth (Whitgift)
    579
  family vii
  Mary (Perkins)
    579, 838, 878
  Philippa 838
  Sarah (Pike) 476
  Thomas xlv, lviii,
    lix, lxix, clx,
    clxxiv, 579, 838,
    878
  William 579, 838
  Wymond 579
BRADDYLL
  Anne (Ashton) 841
  Dorothy 841
  Edward 841
  Emote (Pollard)
    841
  Jennett (Crombock)
    841
  Jennett (Foster)
    841

John 841
Margaret (Harington)
  841, 842
Richard 841
BRADFORD
  Alice (Carpenter)
    (Southworth) 524
  Dorothy (May) xx,
    lix
  Elizabeth
    (Southworth) 525
  family xx
  Gertrude Eldred
    371
  Kevin viii, xlviii,
    407, 408
  Robert 525
  William (Gov.) xx,
    524, 525
BRADING
  Elizabeth 491
BRADLEE
  Benjamin
    Crowninshield
    "Ben" 183
  Frederick Josiah, Jr.
    183
  Josephine (de
    Gersdorff) 183
BRADLEY
  Harold Wheeler
    "Hal" xlvi, xlviii,
    lxvi, lxvii, 706
  Mabel Bayard 198
BRADSHAW
  Alice 318, 547
  Janet 822
  Sarah (Levis) 384
  Thomas 384

**BRADSHAW-
ISHERWOOD**
  Christopher William
    [Christopher
    Isherwood] xvii,
    liv, clxxiv, 549
  Francis Edward 548
  Kathleen Machell
    (Smith) 548
BRADSTREET
  Anne (Dudley)
    [Anne Bradstreet]
    370, 371
  Anne (Wood) 370
  Dudley 370
  Edmund 953
  John xlviii, cxlviii,
    939, 953
  Margaret 370
  Marie-Agathe (de
    Saint-Étienne de la
    Tour) 953
  Mary (Aldridge)
    (Bradstreet) 953
  Simon (Gov.) 370
BRADY
  James Cox xviii,
    116
  Victoria May (Pery),
    Lady 116
BRADYLL
  John 841
BRAEM (DE)
  Marie 438
BRAGA
  Pamela 66
BRAGANZA
  Catherine of, Princess
    of Portugal, Queen

of England and
   Scotland 22, 25,
   29, 30, 31, 33, 34
Teodosio
   (Theodore) II,
   Duke of 140
BRAGG
John 316
Mary (Scott) 316
BRAHE
Beata Margareta,
   Countess 452,
   453
Beate (Bille) 646
Ebba, Countess
   267, 453
Eric, Count of
   Visingsborg 452
Kirsten Barbara
   (Jørgensdatter)
   646
Margrethe 644
Otto 646
Tyge (Tycho) 646
BRAINE
Hugh II, Count of
   Roucy and 944
Jean VI, Count of
   Roucy and 944
Jeanne, Countess of
   Roucy and 944
BRAINERD
Homer Worthington
   xlviii
BRAITHWAITE
Anna (Lloyd)
   clxxi, 231
Anna Lloyd 231,
   232, 378

Anna Mary 231
Charles Lloyd 231
family 232
Isaac 231
Joseph Bevan 231
Martha (Gillett)
   231
Susanna (Wilson)
   231
BRÅKENHIELM
Christina
   Margaretha 53
Eva Sofia
   (Silfverswård) 53
Per 53
BRAMHALL
John, Archbishop of
   Armagh 467
___ 467
BRAMPTON
Mary 353
BRAMSHOT
Elizabeth 691
BRANCAS (DE)
Jeanne 615
BRANCH
Catherine (Jennings)
   822
Christopher viii,
   xi, xlix, liii, lxix,
   clxvi, clxxvii,
   clxxx, 822, 1025
Christopher, Jr.
   822
Elizabeth (Bostock)
   822, 823
family 823
Lionel 822
Mary 822

Mary (Addie) 822
Richard 822, 823
Valentia (Sparkes)
   822
William 822
BRANDENBURG
Anna Katharina,
   Princess of, Queen
   of Denmark 35, 37
Beatrix of 640
Dorothea of 52
Frederick I, Elector
   of 52
Frederick II, Elector
   of 52
George William,
   Elector of 54
Herman V,
   Margrave of 449,
   451
Joachim I, Elector
   of 181, 182, 184
John Cicero, Elector
   of 220
John Sigismund,
   Elector of 54
Judith of 449, 451
Louise Charlotte,
   Princess of 54, 56
Margaret of 181,
   182, 184
Otto III, Margrave
   of 640
Otto V, Margrave of
   640
Sophia of 891
Ursula, Princess of
   220

**BRANDENBURG-
ANSPACH**
  Barbara of 194
  Caroline, Princess
    of, Queen of Great
    Britain 8, 12, 27
  Dorothea Frederica
    of 40
  Elizabeth of 195,
    198
  Frederick, Margrave
    of 194, 196, 198
  John Frederick,
    Margrave of 40
  Sophie of 196
**BRANDENBURG-
SCHWEDT**
  Albert Frederick of
    56
  Albertine of 56
  Dorothea, Princess
    of 49
  Frederick William,
    Margrave of 16
  Louise of 16
BRANDIS (VON)
  Katharina (von
    Weissenburg)
    832
  Manegold 832
  Thüring 832
  Ursula 832
BRANDLING
  ___ 106
BRANDON
  Alexander Hamilton,
    10th Duke of
    Hamilton, 7th Duke
    of 933

  Anne clxxxviii,
    517
  Archibald Hamilton,
    9th Duke of
    Hamilton, 6th
    Duke of 933
  Catherine clxxxviii
  Charles, 1st Duke of
    Suffolk clxxxiii,
    62, 69, 76, 79, 80
  Eleanor clxxxviii,
    62, 69, 70, 79, 361,
    571
  Elizabeth clxxxviii
  Elizabeth (Wingfield)
    clxxxiii, 517, 571
  family clxxxviii
  Frances 62, 69, 76,
    80
  Henry, 2nd Duke of
    Suffolk clxxxviii
  John C. viii, xi,
    xlv, xlvi, xlviii, lii,
    lv, lix, lx, lxi, lxiv,
    lxvii, lxviii, lxix,
    lxxi, 24, 28, 86, 87,
    89, 94, 113, 125,
    132, 153, 160, 234,
    247, 272, 298, 303,
    309, 313, 316, 338,
    346, 358, 365, 391,
    404, 412, 469, 490,
    492, 501, 504, 507,
    518, 529, 531, 537,
    540, 544, 552, 577,
    612, 666, 669, 678,
    681, 741, 745, 756,
    759, 765, 901, 906,
    953

  Margaret clxxxviii
  Margaret, the younger
    clxxxiii, clxxxviii
  William (Sir)
    clxxxiii, clxxxviii,
    517, 571
  William Alexander
    Anthony Archibald
    Hamilton, 11th
    Duke of Hamilton,
    8th Duke of 933
    ___ clxxxiii
BRANDOW
  James C. xlix
BRANFORD
  Mary 382
BRANT
  Isabelle 804
BRANTISLAND
  James Wemyss, 1st
    Baron 98
**BRAOSE (DE)
[BREWES]**
  Agnes (de Clifford)
    653
  Beatrix 653
  Eve 837, 839, 847
  Eve (Marshall)
    680, 837, 839, 847
  family li, lxviii,
    1025
  Isabel 650, 657,
    659, 686, 689, 692,
    693, 694
  Joan (Howard) 653
  Mary (de Ros) 653
  Maud 680
  Peter (Sir) 653

William (Sir) 653, 680, 837, 839, 847
BRASHER
Jenny 308
BRASSEY
Margaret (Steen) 817
Thomas xii, lviii, cxlii, 817
BRASSIEUR (LE)
Anne 311
Anne (Mellish) (Splatt) 311
Francis 311, 312
BRAULT
Marguerite 972
Marie-Michelle 981, 982
BRAUN (VON)
Emmy Melitta Cécile (von Quistorp) xviii, 224
Magnus Alexander Maximilian, Freiherr 224
Maria Irmengard Emmy Luise Gisela (von Quistorp), Baroness liii, clxx, 59, 224
Wernher Magnus Maximilian, Freiherr xviii, 59, 224
BRAY
Anne 315
Mary clxxxv

BRAYBROOKE
Joan 543, 595
Joan (de la Pole), Baroness Cobham 543, 595
Reginald (Sir) 543, 595
Richard Aldworth Neville, 2nd Baron 77
BRAYNE
Anne Butler 278
BRAYTON
John Anderson viii, xi, xliii, xlvi, xlvii, xlix, l, liv, lvii, lxiv, lxvi, lxviii, lxix, clxxxii, clxxxiv, clxxxvii, cxc, 313, 323, 358, 360, 386, 469, 490, 506, 579, 606, 610, 664, 707, 727, 731, 773, 788, 823, 856, 878, 1026
BRAZIER
Anne 655
BRECK
Abigail 479, 716
BREDICHIN
Anna 799
BREDOW (VON)
Friederike Frances Adelheid 39
Gottliebe 617
BREGENZ
Elizabeth of 832
Hugh I, Count of, Count of Montfort 832

Rudolf, Count of 832
BREITHOLTZ
Catharina Mariana 51
Claes Didrik 51
Eleanora (Koskull), Baroness 51
BREMEN (VON)
Magdalene 849
BRENNEMAN
Richard E. xliii, l, 553, 918
BRENT
Alice 851
Anne cxlviii, 332, 904
Anne (Baugh) 331
Anne (Berkeley) 357, 429
Anne (Calvert) (Brooke) 331
Chester Horton 1
Elizabeth 750
Elizabeth (Greene) 332
Elizabeth (Reed) 331
family xxxiv, 1
Frances (Whitgreaves) (Harrison) 331
Fulke 331
George clxix, 331, 332
Giles (Dep. Gov.) 331, 332
Giles, Jr. 332
Henry 331
John 357, 429

1098

Kittamaquund
  (___) 331, 332
  Margaret 331, 357, 429
  Mariana (Peyton) 331
  Mary 331
  Mary (Brent) 332
  Mary (Sewall)
    (Chandler) 332
  Richard 331
  Robert 331
  Winifred Lee 433
BRENTON
  Elizabeth 924
BRERETON
  Alice (Ipstones) 760, 772
  Alicia (___) 760
  Catherine (Wylde) 772
  Cuthbert 760
  Dorothy 772, 773
  Edward 772
  Eleanor 497
  Eleanor (Brereton) 562
  Eleanor (Dutton) 562, 760
  Elizabeth 500, 752, 753, 773
  Elizabeth (Green) 760
  Elizabeth (Roydon) 772
  Elizabeth (Salisbury) 772
  Emma (Carrington) 687, 760

Isabel (Boteler) 564
Isabella 728
Jane 235, 563
Janet 773
Joan (___) 687
Joan (House/Howes) 760
John 760, 772, 773
Katherine
  (Bulkeley) 760
Margaret (Gwyn)
  (Kempton) 773
Margaret (Savage) 122
Margaret (Wynn) 772
Margery 687
Mary 122, 560, 562
Mary (Griffith) 563
Matilda 819
Owen 772, 773
Ralph 687
Randall 687, 760
Randall (Sir) 563, 564, 760, 772
William 760
William (Sir) 562, 772, 773
William Brereton, 1st Baron 122
BRERETON/ BRIERTON
  John (Rev.) 760
  Margaret (___) 760
BRESSEY
  Amy (Booth) 817

Elizabeth (Bulkeley) 817
Margaret (Hassall) 817
Margaret (Massey) 817
Ralph 817
Richard 817
Thomas 817
BRESSIE
  Constance
    (Shepherd) 670
  Edmund 670
  Elizabeth (Ligon) xiii
  Hannah (Hart) 670
  John xiii, 670
  Joseph Addison xiii
  Lucretia (Anderson) 670
  Martha Ann (Edens) xiii
  Mary Elizabeth xiii
  Phebe (Bisby) 670
  Thomas lii, lxv, lxviii, clxii, clxxv, 670
BRESSIEUX (DE)
  Alix 952
  Geoffrey, Seigneur 952
  Marguerite (de Poitiers) 952
BRESTAU (DE)
  Urbain de Menon, Seigneur de Turbilly, Count 455
BRET (LE)
  Lucia 672

BRETON
Adelina (Trahan) 984
Antoinette (Audet) 984
Gilbert 984
Joseph-François-Amedée 984
Marie-Alphonsine-Germaine 984
BRETT
Anne (Gerard) (Broadhurst) 515
Dorothy (Best) 136
Dorothy Eugénie (Hon.) 137
Eleanor Frances Weston (Van de Weyer) 137
Eugénie (Mayer) 136
Joseph George 136
Mary 710
Reginald Baliol, 2nd Viscount Esher 137
Sylvia Leonora (Hon.) [H.H. The Ranee of Sarawak] 137
William Baliol, 1st Viscount Esher 136
BREUL (DE)
Françoise 959
BREULH (DU)
Marie-Anne 205

BREUNNER-ENKEVOIRTH
Agathe Johanna Maria Gobertina, Countess 187
August Ferdinand Paul Ludwig, Count 187
August Johann Evangelist Karl Borromäus Josef, Count 187
Franz Anton, Reichsgraf 186
Josef Ludwig Nepomuk Franz de Paula Kajetan Xavier, Count 187
Karl Borromäus Ignaz Josef, Count 187
Maria Agatha Franziska Ludovica Stephanie (Széchényi), Countess 187
Maria Anna Josefa Franziska Walpurgis (von Pergen), Countess 187
Maria Franziska Emanuela (von Rottal) 186
Maria Josepha Franziska Anna Judith Walpurga Magdalena (von Khevenhüller zu Frankenburg), Countess 187
Maria Teresia (Esterházy de Galántha), Countess 187

BREWER
Hannah 582, 811
Israel C. 342, 814, 882
Lydia 655
Sally (Brown) 342, 814, 882
Sarah Almeda 342, 526, 814, 882

BREWSTER
Abigail viii, lvii, cxlii, clxxxii, 539
Catherine (Offley) 349
Elizabeth (___) (Watkins) 349
Isabel 328
John 539
Mirabel (Poley) 349
Nathaniel (Rev.) 503, 539
Sarah clxiv, 539
Sarah (Ludlow) 503, 539
Thomas (alias Seckford) 349
William 349
___ (Reymes) 539

BREYER
Joanna Freda (Hare) (Hon.) lxv, cxlii, 81

Stephen Gerald
  lxv, 81
BRÉZÉ (DE)
  Diane (de Poitiers),
    Duchess de
    Valentinois 202
  Françoise 202
  Jacques, Count de
    Maulévrier 202
BRIBY
  Bengt Königsmarck,
    Lord of 452, 454
BRIÇON (DE)
  Jeanne 205
BRICQUEVILLE (DE)
  Guillaume 957
  Jeanne 957
  Jeanne (de Juvigny) 957
  Jeanne (de Meulan) 957
  Nicolas, Seigneur de
    la Haye 957
BRIDGER
  Clyde A. 688
  Elizabeth 463
  family xi
BRIDGES. *see also*
  BRUGES/BRYDGES
  and BRYDGES
  Amy 337
  Joan 526
  Margaretta 548
  Mary (Woodcock)
    xlviii, cxlii,
    clxxxiv, 506, 507
  Robert 506, 507
  Ursula 423

BRIDGWATER
  John Egerton, 1st
    Earl of 70
  John Egerton, 2nd
    Earl of 70, 73
  John Egerton, 3rd
    Earl of 70
  Scroope Egerton, 1st
    Duke of 70
BRIDIERS (DE)
  Pierre II de
    Sainte-Maure
    Montgaugier,
    Vicomte 942
BRIEG
  Margaret of 451
BRIEN
  Jean 305
BRIENNE (DE)
  Agnès (de
    Beaumont) 948, 964
  Anne 948
  Blanche 647, 909
  Charles of
    Luxembourg,
    Count of 208
  Érard, Seigneur de
    Rameru 943
  family 945
  Jean 647, 909
  Jean I, Vicomte de
    Beaumont 947, 948
  Jean II, Vicomte de
    Beaumont 947
  Jeanne 943, 964
  Jeanne (de Château-
    dun) 647, 909

  Jeanne (de La
    Guerche) 947, 948
  John, King of
    Jerusalem, Emperor
    of Constantinople
    647, 909, 945, 948, 964
  Louis, Vicomte de
    Beaumont 948, 964
  Marguerite 946, 947
  Marguerite (de
    Poitiers) 947
  Marie (de Craon) 947
  Robert, Vicomte de
    Beaumont 947
BRIERE
  Joseph 981
  Marguerite (Mallet) 981
  Marie-Jeanne 981
BRIGGS
  Sally 342, 814, 882
BRIGHAM
  Abigail 702, 747
  Margaret 719
BRIGITTA
  (Bielke), Queen of
    Sweden 663
BRIONNE
  Charles-Louis of
    Lorraine, Prince of
    Lambesc, Count of 613
BRIS(E)BOIS
  Benjamin 976
  Edward 967, 976

Ellen Floyd
 (McKittrick) 976
Jane (Delamater)
 976
Julienne (Sigouin)
 976
Leone B. 976
Roger 976
BRISSON
 Marie-Louise 989
BRISSON dit TILLY
 Charles 989
 Clothilde (Vezina)
  989
 Godefroi 989
 Jean-Baptiste 989
 Marie-Josephte
  (Boutin) 989
 Marie-Rose
  (Arsenault) 989
BRISTOL
 Edward Chetwynd,
  Dean of 323
 Frederick Augustus
  Hervey, 4th Earl of
  117, 334
BRISTOW
 Caroline 315
BRITT
 Joan 471
BRITTANY 226
 Alix of 946
 Arthur II, Duke of
  442, 946
 Blanche of 944,
  961, 963
 Conan I, Duke of
  879, 919
 Isabel of 226

Joanna, Princess of
 Navarre, Duchess
 of, Queen of
 England 226,
 229, 231, 233, 235,
 287, 293
John II, Duke of
 442, 633, 942, 946,
 963
John V, Duke of
 226, 287, 293
John VI, Duke of
 226
Judith of 879, 919
Margaret of 287,
 293
Marie of 633, 942,
 944
BRITTON
 Alice 508
 John 934
BROADHURST
 Anne (Gerard) 515
 Mary Anne 321
BROCAS
 Eleanor (Eltonhead)
  498
 William 498
BROCKBURY
 Margaret 740
BROCKENBROUGH
 Elizabeth 127
**BROCKENBURG
(VON)**
 Henriette Caroline
  Gebsuer, Baroness
  891
 Louise Henrietta,
  Baroness 891

BROCKET
 Elizabeth 830
BROCKHULL
 Edward 883
 Ida (de Criol) 883
 John 883
 John (Sir) 883
 Katherine (Wood)
  883
 Margaret (___)
  883
 Marion 357, 883
 Mildred (Ellis) 883
 Nicholas 883
 William 883
BROCKMAN
 Maria Elisabet 457
BRODIE
 Janet 97
BRODNAX
 Anne 474, 729
 Anne (___) 474
 Dorothy (Beresford)
  xxxv, lxiv, cxlii,
  474, 477
 Edward 474
 John 474, 477
 Mary (Brown) 474
 Mary (Skerme)
  474
 Rebecca
  (Champion)
  (Travis) 474
 Robert 474
 William 474
BRODRICK
 Anne 341
 Anne (Hill) 341
 John (Sir) 341

BROMAN
Sara Catherina 889
BROME
Beatrix (Shirley) 654
Constance 466, 567
Elizabeth 654, 670
Elizabeth (Arundel) 466
Isabel 654
John 654
Katherine 405
Katherine (Lampeck) 466, 654
Nicholas 466, 654
BROMFIELD
Edward clx, 491
Elizabeth (Brading) 491
Frances (Kempe) 491
Henry 491
Mary (Danforth) 491
BROMFLETE
Margaret 317, 328, 363, 384
BROMILOW
Anne 63
BROMLEY
Elizabeth 534
Elizabeth (Fortescue) 534
George 534
Jane (Lacon) 534
Thomas (Sir), Lord Chancellor 534

BROMWICH
Elizabeth 352, 647
family clxxxvi
BRONCKHORST-BATENBURG (VAN)
Dirk, Heer van Anholt 445
Elisabeth 445
Elisabeth (de Noyelles) 445
BRONFMAN
Carolyn Elizabeth Ann (Townshend) (Capellini), Lady xlv, 9
Edgar Miles xviii, 9
BROOKE
Alice (Tyrrell) 543, 544
Anne 126, 427, 543, 628
Anne (Bray) 315
Anne (Calvert) 331
Anne (Carew) 543
Anne (Everton) 543
Anne (Touchet) 427
Catharine/Catherine 261, 327
Charles Vyner (Sir), H.H. Rajah of Sarawak 137
Dorothy (Heydon) 314
Dorothy (Neale) 676
Edward 543

Elizabeth 137, 167, 314, 315, 336, 494, 595
Florence (Ashfield) 543
Frances (Newton) 315
George 543
George, 9th Baron Cobham 315
Joan (Braybrooke) 543, 595
John, 7th Baron Cobham 314
Katherine (Neville) 427
Margaret 315
Margaret (Neville) 314
Mary 722
Mary (Wolseley) lxi, clxxv, 676, 699
Rachel 120
Reginald 543
Richard (Sir) 427
Robert (Act. Gov.) li, clxxxix
Roger 676
Sylvia Leonora (Brett) (Hon.), H.H. Ranee of Sarawak 137
Thomas 427
Thomas (Sir) 543, 595
Thomas, 8th Baron Cobham 314
Thomasine 356

William, 10th Baron
  Cobham 315
BROOKSBY
  Mary 677
BROOME
  Bridget 531
BROPHY
  Mary 980
BROSSE (DE)
  Claudia 442
  Isabel 226
  Jean III, Count of
    Penthièvre 226
  Louise (de Laval)
    226
BROTHERTON
  Thomas Plantagenet
    of, Prince of
    England, Earl of
    Norfolk 462, 470,
    473, 486, 493, 519,
    522, 526, 534, 539,
    541, 545, 557, 564,
    579, 580, 598, 599,
    604, 605, 609
BROUGHAM
  Henry Peter, 1st
    Baron Brougham
    and Vaux 102
  Mary Anne (Eden)
    102
BROUGHTON
  Anne (Dixwell)
    676, 750
  Constantia 471
  Edward 676, 750
  Ellen 333, 676
  Helen (Pell) 750

Mary (Biscoe) 750
Thomas clxxvii, 750
BROUSSARD
  Catherine (Richard)
    990
  Constance (Leblanc)
    990
  Eloy-René 990
  Jean-François 990
  Josephine (Lesser)
    990
  Joséphine-Adelania
    (Broussard) 990
  Joseph-René 990
  Odilia 990
  Rosemond 990
BROUSSEAU
  Eva 985
BROWN(E)
  Abraham 344, 924
  Adam 342
  Adam, Jr. 342,
    814, 882
  Alice (___) 730
  Alice (Gage) 339,
    340
  Anne 306
  Anne (___) 491
  Anne (Rich) 653
  Anne, Lady 465
  Anthony 730, 731
  Anthony (Hon.)
    355, 402, 905
  Anthony (Sir) 339,
    340, 345
  Anthony, 1st
    Viscount Montagu
    355, 414, 905

Anthony Maria, 2nd
  Viscount Montagu
  109, 905
Bryan 33
Catherine 492
Christopher 730
David T. 1, 104
Dorothy 355
Dorothy (Boteler)
  730
Eleanor 491
Eleanor (Arundel)
  345, 491
Eleanor (Shirley)
  653
Eleanor (Watts) 653
Elizabeth 109, 345,
  414
Elizabeth (Paston)
  491
Elizabeth (Somerset)
  109
Elizabeth (Warrener)
  730
Esther (Parkman)
  342
Frances 515
Francis 730, 731
Frideswide
  (Guilford) 469,
  477, 492, 552
George (Sir) 491
Grace (Pinchbeck)
  730, 731
Henrietta 22
Israel Putnam 342,
  814, 882
Jane 121, 146, 484,
  924

Jane (Radcliffe) 355, 905
Jane (Sackville) 109, 905
Jane (Skepper/ Skipper) 344, 924
Joseph 979
Joyce 730, 731
Katharine (Dickson) lii
Lucy (Neville) 340, 345
Mabel 340
Margaret 486
Margaret (Dacre) 414
Margaret (Mathew) 730
Marie-Yvette 979
Mary 114, 339, 396, 474, 905
Mary (Dormer) 355, 402, 905
Mary (Savage) 653
Mary-Ann (Bélaire) 979
Matthew (Sir) 469, 492, 552
Nathaniel lii, lvi, lviii, lxviii, clxxv, 653, 656
Nicholas 653
Percy 653
Priscilla (Putnam) 342, 814, 882
Rachel Claire (Ward) xvii, 33
Rebecca 534
Robert 491, 730, 731

Sally 342, 814, 882
Sally (Briggs) 342, 814, 882
Sarah 772
Sarah Caroline 334
Thomas (Sir) 345, 491
Thomas, 3rd Viscount Montagu 109
William (Sir) 653

BROWNELL
Anne 377

BROWNING
Anne 498
Charles Henry xxviii
Daniel 303
Elizabeth (Barrett) xxiv, 355
James 498
Jane (Davis) 302
Robert 355
Susannah (Hickman) 498

BROWNLOW
Elizabeth 73

BRUCE
Ailsa Nora (Mellon) 100, 190
Alexander, of Cultmalundie 152
Alison (Reid) 456
Angelica Mary (Selby) 145
Anne Colquhoun (Fairlie) 144
Charlotte Isabella (O'Grady) 145

Charlotte-Jacqueline (D'Argenteau), Countess of Esneux, Baroness of Melsbroeck 81
Christian 163
Constantia Pamela Alice 67
David (Sir), of Clackmannan 456
David Kirkpatrick Este xviii, 100, 190
Edward (Sir), of Blairhall 456
Elizabeth 65, 80, 150
Elizabeth (de Burgh), Queen of Scotland 456
Elizabeth (Seymour) 80, 81
Elizabeth (Stewart) 456
Eupheme 732
Euphemia (Montgomery) 243
Evangeline (Bell) 100
family 1025
family, of Stenhouse 145
George (Sir), of Carnock 456
Helen 152
Isabel (de Clare) 787, 789
Jane Catherine (Clark) 144

Janet 243
Janet (Blackadder) 456
Janet Turing 563
Jean (Fleming) 163
Jean (Oliphant) 152
Jean (Stewart) 456
John (Sir), of Airth 163
John, of Clackmannan 456
Margaret 456, 787, 788
Margaret (Elphinstone) 163
Margaret (Primrose) 456
Mariot (Herries) 456
Mary 128, 789
Mary (Agnew) 144
Matilda 456
Maud 789
Michael (Sir), 6th Bt. 144
Robert (Sir), of Airth 243
Robert, Earl of Carrick 787, 789
Robert, lord of Annandale 787, 789
Robert I, King of Scotland 456, 787, 789
Thomas, 3rd Earl of Elgin, 2nd Earl of Ailesbury 80, 81

Violet Pauline (Shelton) [Violet Campbell] 145
William (Sir), 7th Bt. 144
William, of Airth 163
William Cunningham 144
William Cunningham (Sir), 9th Bt. 145
William Nigel Ernle [Nigel Bruce] cliii, 145
William Waller (Sir), 10th Bt. 145
BRUDENELL
Anne 25, 31
Anne (Bishop) 65
Elizabeth 537
Elizabeth (Bruce) 65, 80
George, 3rd Earl of Cardigan 65, 80
Harriet Georgiana 65
Penelope Anne (Cooke) 65
Robert (Hon.) 65
Robert, 6th Earl of Cardigan 65
BRUDENELL-BRUCE
Charles, 1st Marquess of Ailesbury 80
Ernest Augustus Charles, 3rd

Marquess of Ailesbury 80
Ernestine Mary 80
Henrietta Maria (Hill) 80
Louisa Elizabeth (Horsley-Beresford) 80
Susanna (Hoare) 80
Thomas, 1st Earl of Ailesbury 80
BRUEN
Anne (Fox) 688
Dorothy (Holford) 687
Esther (Lawrence) 688
John 687, 688
Obadiah xxxv, lviii, clxii, clxxv, 688
Sarah 688
Sarah (Seeley) 688
BRUERE
Frances 130, 464
BRUGES/BRYDGES.
see BRIDGES
BRÛLART
Edmée-Nicole-Pulchérie 206
BRULEY (DE)
Alice 874
BRUN
Winifred, wife of Ali Kemal Bey 12
BRUNDAGE
Avery 8
Marianne Charlotte Katharina Stefanie

(Reuss-Köstritz),
Princess xlv, 8
BRUNSWICK
Augusta, Princess
of, Queen of
Württemberg 12
Charles II William
Ferdinand, Duke of
12
Elizabeth of 889
**BRUNSWICK-
BEVERN**
Ferdinand Albert I,
Duke of 44
**BRUNSWICK-
GÖTTINGEN**
Elizabeth of 451
Otto II, Duke of 451
**BRUNSWICK-
GRUBENHAGEN**
Anna of 451
Eric, Duke of 451
**BRUNSWICK-
KALENBURG**
George, Duke of
58
**BRUNSWICK-
LÜNEBURG**
Dorothea of 60,
893
Elizabeth of 452
Henry, Duke of
451, 454
Katherine of 52,
449, 451
Otto I, Duke of
451
Otto II, Duke of
452

Wilhelmine Amalie,
Princess of 20
William, Duke of
58, 60, 432, 893
**BRUNSWICK-
LÜNEBURG-CELLE**
Ernest, Duke of
220
Margaret of 220
**BRUNSWICK-
WOLFENBÜTTEL**
Anna Sophia,
Princess of 43, 44
Antoinette Amalia,
Princess of 44
Elizabeth Christina,
Princess of, Queen
of Prussia 13
Ferdinand Albert II,
Duke of 44
Katharine, Princess
of 52
Sophia Antoinette,
Princess of 44
BRUS (DE)
Margaret 708
BRUSYARD
Margery 680
BRYAN
Elizabeth 395, 420
Margaret (Bourchier)
420
Thomas (Sir) 420
BRYDGES. *see also*
BRIDGES, BRUGES/
BRYDGES
James, 1st Duke of
Chandos 299
Mary 299

BRYNNER
Jacqueline (Thion
de la Chaume)
(Wiener de
Croisset) 227
Yul 227
BUCCLEUCH
Walter Scott, 1st
Earl of 210
William Henry
Montagu Douglas
Scott, 6th Duke of
28
BUCHAN
Alexander Comyn,
2nd Earl of 843
James Stewart, 1st
Earl of 241, 273,
285
William Comyn, 1st
Earl of 828
BUCHANAN
Alexander Carlisle
245
Andrew clxxxvi, 245
Annabel 264
Catherine (Black)
245
Elizabeth (Clarke)
245
Elizabeth (Curzon)
245
Elizabeth (Leckie)
245
Elizabeth (Mayne)
clxxxvi, 245
Elizabeth (Spear)
245
family lxiii, 245, 247

family, of Ramelton xlii
George clxxxvi, 245
George, of Blairlusk 245
George, of Gartincaber 245
George, of that Ilk 245
James 245
James, 15th U.S. President xlii, clxxxvi, 245, 247
James, of Ramelton 245
James, Sr. xlii, clxxxvi
Jane 245
Jane (Nixon) 245
Jane (Russell) 245
Janet (___) clxxxvi, 245
Janet (Buchanan) 245
John clxxxvi, 245
John, of Blairlusk 245
John, of Donaghanie 245
John, of Gartincaber 245
John, of Omagh 245
John, of Ramelton 245
Margaret (Edmonstone) 245
Robert clxxxvi, 245
Robert Stewart 245
Sarah (Sproule) 245
Thomas, of Carbeth 245
Thomas, of Ramelton 245
Walter clxxxvi, 245
William clxxxvi, 245

BUCHNER
Anna Elisabeth 645

BUCK
Ellen (Neville) clxxxiii
Howard M. xlvii, l, liv, lvi, 559
J. O. xx
Kenelm clxxxiii

BUCKINGHAM
Edward Stafford, 3rd Duke of 333, 347, 431
George Villiers, 1st Duke of 430, 536
Henry Stafford, 2nd Duke of 333, 347, 431
Henry Stafford, 3rd Duke of 431
Humphrey Stafford, 1st Duke of 393, 403
Mary Beaumont, Countess of 430

BUCKINGHAM-SHIRE
George Hobart, 3rd Earl of 117

BUDBERG (VON)
Renata Helene 849

BUDLONG
Adela R. 76

BUFFUM
Robert 761
Thomasine (Ward) (Thompson) vii, lii, lxxi, clx, clxxvii, clxxx, clxxxviii, 741, 761, 762

BUFKIN
Anne (Garrett) 473
Anne (Guilford) 473, 474, 475
Anne (Walthall) 473
Henry 473
Leven/Levin lxiv, cxlviii, 473
Mary (Newby) 473
Sarah (Flood) 473

BULGARIA (THE BULGARIANS)
Alexander, Prince of Battenberg, Prince of, Count von Hartenau 41
monarchs of 45, 288, 614

BULKELEY
Anne 24
Catherine (Griffith) 396
Dorcas 748
Dorothy (Brereton) 773
Edward 519, 702, 746
Elizabeth clxi, clxxvi, 747, 817

1108

Elizabeth (Brereton) 773
Elizabeth (Grosvenor) 746
family xxiv, xxxiv, l, lviii, lxxi
Frances 519
Grace (Chetwode) lix, clx, 574, 746
Jane (Allen) xix, xxxv, lix, clx, 702, 746
Katherine 396, 760
Lucian (___) 702, 746
Margaret (Savage) 396
Martha clxi, clxxvi, 747
Mary (Burgh) 396
Olive (Irby) 519, 746
Peter 702, 746
Peter (Rev.) xix, xxxv, clx, clxxvi, 574, 702, 746
Randall 817
Rebecca 702, 746
Rebecca (Wheeler) 702, 746
Richard (Sir) 396
Sarah 747
Thomas 746, 773
BULL
Alice (Hunt) 880
Burnaby 369
Charles 880
Elizabeth 880

Henry DeSaussure xlv, l
Joan (Knighton) 880
John 382
Josias 369
Katherine (Agard) 369
Mary 369, 382
Mary (Branford) 382
Richard 880
Sarah (Nowell) 369
Stephen l, clxviii, 369, 382
William 369
BULLARD
Edward 463, 465
Sarah (Tucker) (Harris) cxlviii, 463, 465
BULLER
Alice (Hayward) 550
Audrey Divett xlv, lxi, cxlv, 305
Caroline (Buller) 305
Catherine 550
Charles George 305
Elizabeth (Gould) 305
Elizabeth Caroline (Hunter) 305
Frances (Boucher) 305
Francis 550

Frank 305
Husey (Gould) 305
James 305
Jean (Brien) 305
John 305
John Francis 305
Margaret (Tretherff) 550
Rebecca (Trelawny) 305
Richard 550
Richard (Sir) 550
Thomasine (Williams) 550
William 305
BULLOCH
Anne (Irvine) 225, 283
James 225, 283
James Stephens 225, 283, 471
Joseph Gaston Baillie (Dr.) l
Martha 225, 283, 471
Martha (Stewart) 225, 283, 471
BULLOCK
Alice (Berrington) 584
Alice (Kingsmill) 584
Edward 584, 585, 586
Elizabeth xxxv, lxi, cxliii, clx, clxxv, clxxix, 86, 584, 586, 1025
Gilbert 584

Margaret (Norris/
 Norreys) 584
Mary (Bacon) 584,
 586
Richard 584
Thomas 584
William 584, 586
___ (___)
 (Johnson), wife of
 Edward 584
BULMER
 Elizabeth 135
BÜLOW (VON)
 Armgard Agnes
  (von Pentz),
  Countess 37
 Barthold Dietrich 37
 Clara Eleonore 37
 Claus [Claus Cecil
  Borberg] xxii, liii,
  cliii, 645
 Eleonore Katharina
  37
 Emil Faye 645
 Fanny Frederikke
  Augusta (Poulson)
  645
 Frits Toxwerdt 645
 Hartwig Dietrich 37
 Jonna 645
 Marie Gabrielle
  (Toxwerdt) 645
 Martha Sharp
  "Sunny" (Crawford)
  (von Auersperg)
  646
 Sibilla Sophie
  Hedwig (von
  Bülow) 37

BUNBURY
 Henry (Sir), 3rd Bt.
  235
 Isabella 235
 Susan (Hanmer)
  235
BUNCOMBE
 Anne (___) 609
 Edward xlix, cxlii,
  609
 Elizabeth Dawson
  (Taylor) 609
 Hester (___) 609
 John 609
 Mary (Paulet) 609
 Thomas 609
BUND
 Anne (Wilmot)
  541
 Anne Susanna Kent
  541
 Mary (Parsons)
  541
 Susanna (Johnson)
  541
 Susanna (Vernon)
  541
 Thomas 541
 Thomas Henry 541
 William 541
BUNDY
 McGeorge 86
BUNNY
 Marriot Margaret
  380
 May Somerville
  563
BUNOT
 Jean 947, 952

BUNSEN (VON)
 Berta xviii, lvii,
  148, 149
 Emma (Birkbeck)
  148
 Georg Friedrich
  148
BUÑUEL
 Luís 227
BURBANK
 Lilia 90
BURD
 Edward, of
  Ormiston 275
 James lxiii, lxvi,
  275
 Jean (Haliburton)
  275
 Sarah (Shippen)
  275
BURDEN
 Arthur Scott 378
 Cynthia (Burke
  Roche), (Hon.)
  Mrs. cxliii, 27,
  378, 932
 Eileen 377
 Sarah (___) 314
BURDET
 Elizabeth 763
BURDG
 Almira Park 764
 Jacob 764
 Jacob, Jr. 764
 Jane M. (Heming-
  way) 764
 Joseph 764
 Judith (Smith) 764

Miriam (Matthews) 764
Oliver 764
Sarah (Morris) 764
BÜREN
Frederick of Egmont, Count of 459
BURGAT (DE)
Bonne 442
BURGESS
John 702
Martha 702
Mary (Worden) 702
BURGH (DE)
Agnes (Tyrwhit) 403
Anne (Cobham), *de jure* Baroness Cobham 403
Catherine 403
Catherine (Clinton) 403
Cecily (Baliol) 780
Dorothea 480
Edmund Burgh, 2nd Baron 403
Elizabeth 107, 114, 119, 126, 133, 134, 305, 310, 317, 319, 327, 333, 342, 347, 349, 351, 355, 359, 361, 363, 374, 379, 384, 385, 389, 399, 401, 414, 418, 425, 431, 901, 904, 905

Elizabeth, Queen of Scotland 456
Frances (Vaughan) 403
Hawise 780
John (Sir) 780
Mary 302, 396
Mary (Kingsmill) 480
Thomas Burgh, 3rd Baron 403
Thomas Burgh, 5th Baron 403
Ulysses, Bishop of Armagh 480
William Burgh, 4th Baron 403
BURGHERSH
Elizabeth 491, 505, 575
BURGHILL
Elizabeth 541
BURGHLEY
William Cecil, 1st Baron 68, 315, 345, 470, 554, 684
BURGOS
Guy 27
Sarah Consuelo (Spencer-Churchill) (Russell) clvii, 27
BURGOYNE
Christopher 853
Elizabeth (Staverton) 853
Ellen clxxxvi
family clxxxvi
Judith 534

Thomas 853
Thomasine 684, 853
Thomasine (Freville) 853, 854
BURGUNDY
Adelaide of 735, 879, 919, 952
Agnes of 293, 440
Alice of 737, 853, 855
Beatrix of (wife of Frederick I Barbarossa, Holy Roman Emperor) 640, 733, 735, 952
Charles "the Bold," Duke of 438, 445
Eudes I, Duke of 853, 855
Eudes II, Duke of 642
Guye (Gillette) of 952
Henry I, Duke of 853, 855
Hugh de Châlon, Count Palatine of 735, 952
Hugh III, Duke of 642
Hugh Magnus, Duke of France and 835, 837, 839, 841, 843, 845, 847
Hypolite of 735
John, Duke of 438
Margaret of 642

Margaret of, Queen
of France 455
Marie of 442
Mary of 438, 445
Matilda of 853,
855, 911
Odo, Duke of 911
Otto I, Duke of
Meran, Count
Palatine of 735,
952
Otto of
Hohenstaufen,
Count Palatine of
735, 952
Philip II, Duke of
438, 442, 445
Philip III, Duke of
438, 445
Robert I, Duke of
853, 855
**BURGUNDY and
BOURBON**
Beatrix of 634, 638
BURKE. *see also*
MOREIRA DA
SILVA-BURKE
Adrian Benjamin
Moreira Da Silva
248, 922
John xxiv, 844
John Bernard xxiv
Margaret 308
Margaret (O'Brien)
601
Mary 601
Richard, 2nd Earl of
Clanricarde 601

BURKE ROCHE
Cynthia (Hon.)
cxliii, 27, 378, 932
Edmund, 1st Baron
Fermoy 378
Edmund Maurice,
4th Baron Fermoy
378, 932
Elizabeth Caroline
(Boothby) 378
Frances Eleanor
"Ellen" (Work)
378, 932
Frances Ruth 932
James Boothby, 3rd
Baron Fermoy
378, 932
Ruth Sylvia (Gill)
378, 932
BURLEY
family 729
BURMAN (DE)
Jeanne 205
BURNABY
Anne (Woodhull)
368
Elizabeth (Sapcotts)
368
Richard 368
Susan 369
Thomas 368
BURNET/BURNETT
Alexander, of Leys
159, 250, 273
Anna Maria (Van
Horne) 273
Catherine 250
Gilbert, Bishop of
Salisbury 273

Isabel clxiv, clxxi,
250, 269, 789
Jean 159
Jean (Arbuthnot)
159
Katherine (Gordon)
250, 273
Margaret (Douglas)
159, 250
Maria (Stanhope)
273
Mary (Scott) 273
Rachel (Johnston)
273
Robert 250, 269,
273
Thomas (Sir), 1st
Bt. 159, 250
William (Gov.)
clxxi, 273
____ (Forbes) 250,
269
BURNHAM
Alice (Eltonhead)
xix, xxxiv, clxvi,
clxxiii, 329, 498,
607, 697
Mary (Lawrence)
clx, 881
Rowland 498
Thomas 881
BURR
Aaron (Vice Pres.)
144, 325
Abigail (Brewster)
viii, lvii, cxlii,
clxxxii, 539
Daniel 539
Miriam 924

BURRADON/
BOROUGHDON
(DE)
  Eleanor 730
  Elizabeth (de
    Umfreville) 730
  Gilbert (Sir) 730
BURRINGTON
  George (Gov.) 104
BURROUGH(S)
  Bridget (Higham)
    484
  family lxii
  Frances (Sparrow)
    484
  George 484
  George (Rev.) 484
  Hannah (Fisher) 484
  Mary (___) 484
  Nathaniel lvi, lxii,
    lxvi, clx, 484
  Rebecca (Style) 484
  Sarah (Ruck)
    (Hathorne) 484
  Thomas 484
  William Seward, II
    49
BURROW
  Dionis 761
BURT
  Abigail 524
  Joseph, Jr. 983
  Mary 983
  Polly (Livingston)
    983
BURTON
  Beatrice Maud
    Boswell (Eliott)
    liv, cxlii, 90

  Elizabeth Rosemond
    (Taylor) (Hilton)
    (Wilding) (Todd)
    (Fisher) [Elizabeth
    Taylor] 21, 190
  Frank Vincent, Jr. 90
  Leila Eliott 90
  Martha 343
  Mary 530
  Timothy William
    "Tim" 306
BURWELL
  Abigail (Smith) xi,
    xlix, liii, lxix, cxlii,
    clxvi, clxxxi, 878,
    1025
  Elizabeth 496, 878
  Joanna 878
  Lewis, Jr. 878
  Lucy (Higginson)
    495, 856
BUS (DU)
  René, Seigneur de
    Tizon 440
  Renée 440
  Sidoine alias Edmée
    (de Bourbon) 440
BUSCH
  Adolphus 57, 136
  Augustus Anheuser,
    Jr. "Gussie" 57,
    136
  family xviii
BUSENDOCHTER
  Catharina Gerrit
    447, 907
BUSH
  Barbara (Pierce)
    xlii, xliii, 243, 474,

    479, 572, 585, 632,
    688, 703, 716, 729,
    747, 769
  Dorothy (Walker)
    243, 474, 479, 572,
    585, 703, 716, 729,
    747
  Flora (Sheldon)
    243, 474, 479, 572,
    585, 703, 716, 729,
    747
  George Herbert
    Walker, 41st U.S.
    President 243,
    474, 479, 572, 585,
    632, 688, 703, 716,
    729, 747, 769
  George Walker,
    43rd U.S. President
    xxxv, 243, 244,
    474, 479, 572, 585,
    632, 688, 703, 716,
    729, 747, 769, 833,
    923
  Harriet Eleanor
    (Fay) 474, 479,
    572, 585, 703, 716,
    729, 747
  James Smith 474,
    479, 572, 585, 703,
    716, 729, 747
  Laura Lane (Welch)
    xxxv, xlii, xliii,
    243, 474, 479, 572,
    585, 632, 688, 703,
    716, 729, 747, 769,
    833, 834
  Prescott Sheldon
    (Sen.) 243, 474,

479, 572, 585, 703, 716, 729, 747
Robin 569
Samuel Prescott 243, 474, 479, 572, 585, 703, 716, 729, 747
BUSSCHE-LOHE (VON DEM)
Friederike Charlotte Sabine Wilhelmine 58
BUSSET (DE)
Cesare of Bourbon, Count 293
Claude of Bourbon, Count 293
Peter of Bourbon, Baron 293
Philip of Bourbon, Baron 293
BUTE
John Stuart, 3rd Earl of 299
BUTLER. *see also* BOTELER (LE) (sometimes BUTLER)
Almeric Amory 674
Amory (Rev.) 674
Amy (___) 420, 505
Amy Gridley 630, 654, 887
Anne 582, 583
Anne (Colclough) 382
Anne (de Welles) 500, 582, 583, 601

Anne (Hankford) 392, 551, 588, 596
Anne (Travers) 874
Betsey (Comstock) 630, 887
Catherine (O'Reilly) 601
Courtland Philip Livingston 243
Daniel 630, 887
Dorothea 334
Edmund (Sir) 382, 601
Edmund (Sir), 2nd Bt. 382
Eleanor 382, 601
Eleanor (de Bohun) 478, 512, 530, 553, 555, 582, 601, 603
Eleanor (Eustace) 382
Eleanor (Loftus) 382
Elizabeth 500, 574
Elizabeth (Darcy) 582, 601
Elizabeth (Elliot[t]) 311, 874
Elizabeth Ely (Gridley) 630, 887
Elizabeth Slade (Pierce) 243
Ellen 601, 602
family lxix, 602, 674
Fanny (Worsley) 475

Frances Anne "Fanny" (Kemble) 382
George Selden 630, 887
Grace 478, 874, 875
Harriet (Apthorpe) 475
Henrietta (FitzJames) (Waldegrave) clxxxix
Henrietta (Percy) 382
James 382
James (Sir) 601
James, 1st Earl of Ormonde 478, 512, 530, 553, 555, 582, 601, 602, 603
James, 2nd Earl of Ormonde 582, 601
James, 3rd Earl of Ormonde 500, 582, 583, 601
James, 4th Earl of Ormonde 500, 502, 551, 553, 555, 574, 588, 596, 601
James, 9th Earl of Ormonde 382
Jane 324, 933
Jane (Boyle) 382
Joan 601, 602
Joan (Beauchamp) 500, 551, 574, 588, 596

1114

Joan (Damerie/
　Amory)　674
Joan (FitzGerald)
　382
John　515, 674, 874
Judith (Livingston)
　243
Juliana (Hyde)　382
Margaret　300, 515,
　539, 551, 557, 588,
　596, 864
Margaret
　(FitzGerald)　382,
　601
Margaret (Greeke)
　515
Margaret (Sutton)
　515
Margaret Coats　385
Mary　liv, clxxv,
　clxxx, 157, 674
Mary (Middleton)
　382
Mary Elizabeth
　243
Petronilla　478,
　512, 530, 553, 555,
　603
Pierce　clxix,
　clxxiii, 382
Pierce [Pierce Butler
　Mease]　382
Piers, 3rd Viscount
　Galmoye　clxxxix
Piers, 8th Earl of
　Ormonde　382,
　601
Richard (Sir)　601,
　602

Richard (Sir), 5th
　Bt.　382
Sabina
　MacMorough
　(Kavanagh)　601
Samuel　475, 476,
　674
Samuel, Bishop of
　Lichfield and
　Coventry　475,
　476
Samuel Herrick
　243
Sarah　382, 590
Shile (O'Carroll)
　601
Thomas　475
Thomas (Sir), 1st
　Bt.　382
Thomas (Sir), 3rd
　Bt.　382
Thomas, 7th Earl of
　Ormonde　392,
　551, 588, 596,
　1025
William　515
William (Rev.)　674
BUTSHEAD
　Winifred　522
BUTTERFIELD
　Anne　463
BYAM
　Amelia Jane　302,
　303
　Anne (Gunthorpe)
　302
　Dorothy (Knollys)
　302
　Edward　302

Edward Samuel
　302
Eleanor (Prior)　302
Lydia (Thomas)
　302
Mary (Burgh)　302
William　302
BYE
　Arthur Edward
　clxxxix
　Margaret (Davis)
　clxxxix
　Thomas　clxxxix
BYERLEY
　Elizabeth　753
BYFIELD
　Elizabeth　239
BYFLEET
　Jane　855
　Jane (Erneley)　855
　Thomas　855
BYKOWSKA
　Helena　802
BYLEY
　Joan　678
BYNG
　George, 4th
　Viscount
　Torrington　73
　Georgiana Elizabeth
　25
　Isabella Elizabeth
　70, 73
　Lucy (Boyle)　73
　Sarah　346
BYRD
　Dorothy　411
　Lucy (Parke)　348
　Maria (Taylor)　348

1115

Mary (Horsmanden)
(Filmer) 348
William (I) 348
William (II) 348
BYRNE
John 177
Tilda (Katherine
Matilda) (Swinton)
clviii, 177
BYRON
Catherine (Gordon),
of Gight 163
George Gordon
(later Noël) Byron,
6th Baron xxiv,
163, 296, 298
Isabel 841
John 163
Margaret 670
BYRTH
Anne Stuart 753
BYSSHE
Helen 474
BYZANTIUM
Andronicus II
Palaeologus,
Emperor of 797
emperors of xv
Irene "of the East,"
Princess of lxiii,
lxvii, 640, 733
Isaac II Angelos,
Emperor of 640,
733
John I Comnenus,
Emperor of 956
Maria Lascaris,
Princess of, Queen
of Hungary 621

**CABEZA DE VACA
Y GUEVARA**
Branca (de Sousa)
619
Luíz 619
CABOT
Anna "Nancy"
(Clarke) 923
Anne 97
family xxxvi
Mary Anne 923
CÄCILIE AUGUSTE
of Baden 5
CADOGAN
Alexandra Mary 27
Sarah 31
CADWALADER
Jane (John) 651,
652, 694
John clxiv, 651,
652, 809
Martha (Jones) 651
Robert 651, 694
CADWALADR
ap Maredudd 650
ap Robert 650, 694
CADWELL
"Annar" (Atwell)
924, 926
John (III) 924
Mehitable 673
Olive 924, 926
CAEN
Robert of, 1st Earl of
Gloucester 806,
807, 808, 810, 811,
813, 815, 817, 819,
821, 822, 824, 826,
1025

CAESAR
Alice 307
CAGE
Catherine (Stewart)
264, 265
Hugh 264
CAHILL
Jeanne Maud
(Martineau) (Grew-
cock) cliii, 380
John Thomas 380
CAIMOT
Martha 659
CAIRNCROSS
Elizabeth 211
Isabella 275
CAIRNS
——— 159
CAITHNESS
William Sinclair,
3rd Earl of Orkney,
1st Earl of 278
CALDEBECK
Cecily (Hinkley)
880
Henry 880
Thomasine 880
CALDWELL
Hannah (Stillman)
213
CALIGNON (DE)
Antoine 965
Diane (de Beaumont
de Saint-Quentin)
965
Jeanne 965
CALL
Michel L. x

CALLENDAR
  Alexander
    Livingston, 3rd
    Earl of 161
CALLETORT (DE)
  Jeanne 943
CALLOWHILL
  Hannah 226
CALSTON
  Elizabeth 855
  Felicity (Combe)
    855
  Joan (Childrey)
    855
  Joan (St. Martin)
    855
  Lawrence 855
  Robert 855
  Thomas 855, 856
CALTHORPE
  Anne 359, 483,
    489, 536, 537, 826
  Anne (___) 606
  Anne (Cromer) 606
  Anne (Hastings) 577
  Christopher xlix,
    liii, cxliii, 606
  Dionysia 577
  Edmund 577
  Edward 606
  Elizabeth 596
  Elizabeth
    (Stapleton) 483,
    489, 536, 606
  Elizabeth
    (Wentworth) 596
  family viii
  Jane (Boleyn) 596
  John 596
  Mary (Leveson)
    577
  Mary (Say) 596
  Maud (Thurton)
    606
  Philip (Sir) 596
  Prudence 606
  Richard 577
  Thomasine (Gavell)
    606
  William (Sir) 483,
    489, 536, 606
CALVA
  Anne 837
CALVELEY
  Eleanor 561
CALVERLEY
  Elizabeth (Marken-
    field) 821
  Frances 710
  Joan 821
  Joan (Bigod) 821
  Walter 821
  Walter (Sir) 821
CALVERT
  Alice 700
  Anne 331
  Anne (Arundell)
    (Hon.) xvii, xxxv,
    clxv, 339, 739
  Anne (Mynne) 739
  Anne (Wolseley)
    lxi, lxii, 676, 699
  Benedict Leonard,
    4th Baron
    Baltimore 29, 340
  Benedict "Swingate"
    clxxxix, 29, 804
  Caroline (Hon.)
    29, 100, 312, 313
  Cecil, 2nd Baron
    Baltimore xxxv,
    clxv, clxxvi, 339,
    676, 739
  Charles (Gov.), 3rd
    Baron Baltimore
    339, 512, 819
  Charles (Gov.), 5th
    Baron Baltimore
    clxxxix, 29, 312
  Charles (Gov.) 29
  Charles Benedict
    804
  Charlotte (Lee), Lady
    xvii, xxxv, lxiv, lxv,
    clxv, 29, 340
  Charlotte Augusta
    (Morris) 805
  Eleanor 29, 363
  Elizabeth (Calvert)
    29, 804
  Elizabeth (Stewart)
    805
  family liii, lxii,
    lxx, clxv
  George 804
  George, 1st Baron
    Baltimore 739
  George Henry 804
  Grace (Hon.) 739
  Helen/Ellen (Hon.)
    739
  Jane (Lowe) (Sewall)
    xxxv, clxv, clxxiv,
    332, 339, 512, 819
  Leonard (Hon.)
    (Gov.) xli, lxii,

1117

clxix, clxxvi, 676, 739
Margaret (Charleton) 339
Mary (Banks) (Thorpe) 339
Mary (Darnall) 339
Mary (Janssen) cxlviii, 29, 312
Mary (Wolseley) clxxv
Philip (Hon.) (Gov.) 676
Rebecca (Gerard) 29
Rosalie Eugenia (Stier) 804

CALVERT alias LAZENBY alias BUTLER
Charles clxxxix

CAMBRIDGE
Catherine Elizabeth (Middleton), Duchess of xvii, xlii, l, lxiv, lxvii, lxxi, 101, 380, 381, 931, 932
Charlotte Elizabeth Diana of, Princess of Great Britain xlii, 25, 380, 931, 932
George Alexander Louis of, Prince of Great Britain xlii, 25, 380, 931, 932
Richard Plantagenet, Earl of 107, 114, 119, 126, 133, 134

William Arthur Philip Louis of Wales, Prince of Great Britain, Duke of xlii, 25, 380, 858, 931, 932

CAMERON
Allan Gordon 85
David William, Prime Minister xxiv, 10
Edith Agnes (Levita) 10
Evelyn Jephson (Flower) [Evelyn Cameron] cliii, 85
Ewen Donald 10
Ewen Somerled vi, lxiii, cliii, 85
Ian Donald 10
Julia (Wheelock) 85
Mary Colebrooke (Traill) 85, 86
Mary Fleur (Mount) 10
Samantha Gwendoline (Sheffield) 10

CAMMOCK
Margaret (___) 852

CAMOYS
Eleanor 623, 738
Elizabeth (le Latimer) 737
Elizabeth (Louches) 737
Elizabeth (Mortimer) (Percy) 737

Francis Robert Stonor, 4th Baron 66
Joan (Poynings) 737, 740
John (Sir) 737
Katherine 826
Margaret 737, 738
Ralph Francis Julian Stonor, 5th Baron 66
Richard (Sir) 737, 740
Thomas, 1st Baron Camoys 737
Thomas Stonor, 3rd Baron 66

CAMPBELL
Adelaide Constance 31
Agnes (Douglas) 154
Agnes (Lamont), of that Ilk 263
Agnes (Shaw) 271
Aimee Marie Suzanne (Lawrence) 69
Anna (M'Cowle) 263
Annabel/Agnes (Keith) 154
Anne 154, 156
Anne (Campbell), of Kinochtree 147
Anne, of Orchard 147
Archibald (Hon.) 269, 280, 283

1118

Archibald, 2nd Earl
 of Argyll 280, 283
Archibald, 4th Earl
 of Argyll 154,
 249
Archibald, 7th Earl
 of Argyll 154
Archibald, 9th Earl
 of Argyll 93
Archibald, of
 Auchinbreck and
 Kilmichael 263
Archibald, of Auch-
 indarroch 263
Archibald, of
 Glenlyon 146
Barbara 289
Beatrix 179
Camilla Elizabeth
 390, 391
Caroline (Howard)
 71
Colin (Sir), of
 Glenorchy 264
Colin, 1st Earl of
 Argyll 269, 280,
 283
Colin, 3rd Earl of
 Argyll 249
Colin, 6th Earl of
 Argyll 154
Donald, Abbot of
 Coupar Angus 280
Donald, of Kilmory
 263
Douglas Walter 69
Dugald, of
 Auchinbreck and
 Kilmichael 263
Duncan (Lieut. Col.)
 390, 391
Duncan (Sir), 1st Bt.
 146
Duncan, of
 Kilmichael 263
Duncan Campbell,
 1st Baron 263,
 264, 269, 280, 283
Elizabeth
 (Elphinstone) 93
Elizabeth (Freind)
 390, 391
Elizabeth
 (Somerville) 269,
 280, 283
Elizabeth (Stewart)
 280, 283
Elizabeth (Thynne)
 70, 71
Elizabeth Georgiana
 (Sutherland-
 Leveson-Gower)
 69, 75
family 570
Florence (Lamont),
 of Silvercraigs 263
George, of Cesnock
 271
George, of Glasnock
 and Cesnock 271
George Douglas, 8th
 Duke of Argyll
 69, 75
Georgiana Isabella
 70
Grizel xlviii, cxlix,
 240, 263, 570
Grizel/Elizabeth
 (Stewart), of
 Kildon[n]an 263
Hay (Sir), 1st Bt.
 177
Helen 269, 270, 271
Helen (Woddrop)
 263
Henrietta (Stewart)
 93
Hugh (Sir), of
 Cawdor 93
Hugh, 3rd Earl of
 Loudoun 143
Hugh, of
 Middlewellwood
 270
Ian Douglas, 11th
 Duke of Argyll
 69, 371
Isabel 248, 253,
 275, 285
Isabel (Drummond)
 157, 174
Isabel (Mackintosh)
 146
Isabel (Stewart)
 269, 280, 283
Isabella (Campbell)
 147
James (Sir), of
 Ardkinglas 147
James, 2nd Earl of
 Loudoun 143
Jane Allen 20
Janet 213, 249,
 261, 266, 283
Janet (Campbell), of
 Loudoun 271

Janet (Montgomery) 271
Janet Gladys (Aitken) 69, 371
Jean 93, 168
Jean (Campbell) 146, 147
Jean (Campbell), of Ardentinny 147
Jean (Gordon) 249
Jean (MacLachlan) 263
Jean (Stewart) 146
Jeanne Louise, Lady 70, 371
John 270
John (Hon.) 93
John, 4th Duke of Argyll 93
John, 4th Earl of Loudoun 143
John, of Cesnock 271
John, of Fernoch 263
John, of Orchard 147
John Campbell, 1st Baron Cawdor 71
John Douglas Sutherland, 9th Duke of Argyll 75
John Frederick, 1st Earl Cawdor 70, 71
Judy [Judy Mary Gamble] 27
Katherine (Drummond) 280

Katherine (Napier) 170
Lilias 170
Madeline Caroline Frances Eden 78
Margaret 146, 157, 174
Margaret (Campbell) 271
Margaret (Campbell), of Ardkinglas 263
Margaret (Dalrymple) 143
Margaret (Graham) 154, 249
Margaret (Montgomery) 143
Margaret (Stewart) 263, 264
Margaret (Stirling) 264
Margaret, of Keithick 280
Margaret, of Lochnell 216
Marian 216
Mariot 264
Marjory (Stewart) 269, 280, 283
Mary (Bellenden) 93
Matthew (Sir), of Loudoun 157, 174
Nicholas, Dean of Lismore Cathedral 280

Olivia Rowlandson (Milns) 69
Patrick (Mrs.) [Beatrice Stella (Tanner) Cornwallis-West] 585, 648
Patrick, of Stuck 263
Rachel (Farquhar) 270
Robert (Sir), 3rd Bt. 146
Robert, of Orchard 147
Robert, of Woodside 170
Sarah (Izard) 93
Susan 177
Susan Mary (Murray) 177
Susanna, of Scamadall 249
Thomas, of Middlewellwood 270
Walter, Lord 69
William (Lord) (Gov.) 93
William, of Middlewellwood 270
CAMPE
Anna 774
Meta of 451
CAMVILLE (DE)
Agnes (___) 874
Auberée (de Marmion) clxxxi, 874
family lxii

Felicia 874
Idoine 761
Iseuda (___) 874
Richard clxxxi, 874
Thomas 874
William clxxxi, 874
CANADA
  Allan Napier MacNab (Sir), 1st Bt., Premier of 655
CANALI
  Anna Teresa 18
CANFIELD
  Caroline Lee (Bouvier) [Lee Radziwill] xviii, xlv, 16, 17, 74, 914
  Michael Temple 914
CANIFF
  Phebe 589
CANNON
  Margaret Jane 166
CANTERBURY
  Archibald Campbell Tait, Archbishop of 177
  John Kemp, Archbishop of York and 920, 922
  John Moore, Archbishop of 100
  John Whitgift, Archbishop of 579

William Freind, Dean of 390, 391
CANTHELOU (DE)
  Mathieu de Bailleul, Seigneur de Piencourt and 957
CANTILUPE (DE)/ CANTELOW
  Catherine 474, 783
  Eve (de Braose) 837, 839, 847
  family 1025
  Joan 780, 785
  Milicent 676, 691, 837, 839, 847
  William (Sir) 837, 839, 847
CANY-SUR-METZ (DE)
  Christophe de Brabançon, Seigneur 944
CAPELL
  Algernon, 2nd Earl of Essex 121
  Anne cl, 121, 484
  Arthur (Sir) 121
  Arthur, 1st Earl of Essex 121, 122
  Arthur Capell, 1st Baron 121
  Charlotte 121
  Elizabeth (Morrison) 121
  Elizabeth (Percy) 121
  Gamaliel (Sir) 121
  Giles (Sir) 761

Harriot (Bladen) 313
Henry (Sir) 121
Isabel (Newton) 761
Jane (Browne) 121
Jane (Hyde) 121
Katherine (Manners) 121, 122, 123
Margaret 761
Margaret (Arundell) 761
Margaret (Grey) 121
Mary 80
Mary (Bentinck) 121
Theodosia 122
Theodosia (Montagu) 121
William (Sir) 761
William, 3rd Earl of Essex 121
William Anne, 4th Earl of Essex 313
CAPELLE (DE)
  Antoine de Bourgogne, Seigneur 438
CAPELLINI
  Antonio 9
  Carolyn Elizabeth Ann (Townshend), Lady xlv, 9
CAPEN
  Joseph 814, 882
  Mary 814, 858, 882
  Priscilla (Appleton) 814, 882

CAPET
  family 939
  Hugh, King of
    France 725, 866,
    868, 870, 872, 879,
    919, 1025
CARACCIOLO
  Francesca
    (d'Avalos) 189
  Francesco Marino,
    Prince of Avellino
    189, 192
  Geronima
    (Pignatelli) 189
  Giovanna 189
  Marino II, Prince of
    Avellino 189
CARCASSOLA
  Victoria 912
CARDIGAN
  George Brudenell,
    3rd Earl of 65, 80
  Robert Brudenell,
    6th Earl of 65
CARDINAL
  Malvina 969
CARENCY (DE)
  Catherine 733
  Jean I de Bourbon,
    Seigneur 638
  Pierre de Bourbon,
    Seigneur 638
CAREW
  Anne 543
  Avice (Martin) 851
  Dorothy 338
  Edmund (Sir) 547
  Eleanor (Hoo) 462
  Elizabeth 594, 851
  Elizabeth (Bonville)
    547, 594
  Elizabeth (Bryan)
    395, 420
  Elizabeth (FitzAlan)
    547, 594
  Isabel 420
  Isabel (___) 851,
    852
  James 462
  Jessica (Jessie)
  Philippa 66
  Joan (Carminow)
    547
  Joan (Courtenay)
    547
  Katherine 547
  Katherine (Huddersfield) 547
  Leonard (Sir) 547,
    594
  Lucy (Willoughby)
    851
  Malyn (Oxenbridge)
    420, 462
  Margaret 462, 465
  Margaret (Dinham)
    547
  Mary 395
  Nicholas 851
  Nicholas (Sir) 395,
    420, 547, 851, 852
  Richard (Sir) 420,
    462
  Thomas 547
  Thomas (Sir) 547,
    594
CAREY. *see also*
  CARY/CAREY
CARIGNAN
  Amadeus I of Savoy,
    Prince of 18
  Charles-Emanuel of
    Savoy, Prince of
    613
  Emanuel Philibert of
    Savoy, Prince of 18
  Louis Victor of
    Savoy, Prince of
    18
  Thomas of Savoy,
    Prince of 18
  Victor Amadeus I of
    Savoy, Prince of 18
  Victor Amadeus II
    of Savoy, Prince of
    613
CARINTHIA
  Mathilde von
    Sponheim,
    Duchess of 911
  Matilda of 911
  Maud of 642
CARL [FREDERICK WILLIAM CHARLES LOUIS GEORGE ALFRED ALEXANDER]
  Prince of Solms-
    Braunfels clxx
CARLADÈS
  Gabriella-Thérèse-
    Marie Grimaldi,
    Princess of
    Monaco, Countess
    of 934
CARLE
  Anne 108

CARLETON
Edward lviii, lxi, lxvii, clx, 398, 667, 668
Ellen (Newton) lviii, lxi, lxvii, clx, 398, 667, 668
Ellen (Strickland) 398
family lxi, lxvii
Jane (Gibbon) 398
John 398
Mabel 841
Mary 434
Walter 398

CARLINE
Mary 629

CARLINO
Giraldona 186, 189

CARLISLE
Edmund Law, Bishop of 363
Frederick Howard, 5th Earl of 71
George Howard, 6th Earl of 25, 69, 71
Maldred, lord of, lord of Allendale 857, 861, 864
Robert Hodgson, Dean of 930

CARLSON
Elivera Mathilda 589

CARLYLE
Adam 787, 788
Adam, of Lymekilns 787
Alexander, of Bridekirk 787

Barbara (Johnston) 787
Catherine 787
Elizabeth (Kirkpatrick) 787
Ellen (Carruthers) 787, 788
Herbert, of Bridekirk 787
John (Sir) 787, 788
Lancelot 787
Margaret (Bruce) 787, 788
Margaret (Cunningham) 787
Mary 787
William 787
William (Sir) 787
William, of Torthorwald 787

CARMICHAEL
Catherine 143
Elizabeth 90, 96

CARMINOW
Joan 547
Joanna 665
Margaret 550

CARNARVON
Henry George Herbert, 2nd Earl of 76, 77
Henry Herbert, 1st Earl of 76
Henry John George Herbert, 3rd Earl of 76

CARNAZET (DE)
Jacqueline 442

CARNEGIE
Agnes 256, 257
James George Alexander Bannerman, 3rd Duke of Fife 9
Magdalen 161

CARNISSE
Rutger van den Boetzelaer, Lord of Langerak, Merweden, Asperen and 460

CAROLATH-BEUTHEN
Charles Erdmann, Prince of 43
Henry, Prince of 43
Lucie, Princess of 44

CAROLINE
Princess of Brandenburg-Anspach, Queen of Great Britain 12, 27

CAROLINE (MARIE-ANNONCIADE CAROLINE)
(Bonaparte) Murat, Queen of Naples 82

CAROLINE AUGUSTA
Princess of Bavaria, Empress of Austria 11

CAROLINE CHRISTINE
Princess of Saxe-Eisenach 43

CAROLINE HENRIETTA CHRISTINE
Countess Palatine of Zweibrücken-Birkenfeld 41
CAROLINE-LOUISE-MARGUERITE
Grimaldi, Princess of Monaco 934
CARON
Marguerite 985
Marie-Anne (Perthius) 623
CARONDELET (DE)
Alexandre, Baron de Noyelle, Vicomte de La Hestre 438
Antoine, Baron de Noyelle, Vicomte de La Hestre 438
family lx
François-Louis-Hector (Gov.), Baron de Noyelle, Vicomte de la Hestre and du Langue liii, clxxiii, 438
Jean-Louis, Baron de Noyelle, Vicomte de la Hestre and du Langue 438
Jeanne-Louise (de Lannoy), Countess 438
María (Castaños Aragorri Uriarte Olivide) 438
Marie-Angélique-Bernard (de Rasoir) 438
Marie-Bonne (de Bacquehem) 438
CAROW
Edith Kermit xliii, 225, 283, 471
CARPENTER
Alice 524
Alicia Maria 76, 78
Almeria, Lady 27
Mary Elizabeth Louisa Rodney 101
CARPENTIER (DE)
Isabella (de Villers) 633
Jan 633
Josina (van Hecke) 633
Maria lxvi, 633
Roelant 633
Sophia (van Culenburg/Culemburg) 633
CARR
Caleb 763
Caleb, Jr. 763
Elizabeth 343
Isabel 131
Joanna (Slocum) 763
Patience 764
Philip(pa) (Greene) 763
Sara 221, 896
CARRE
Elizabeth 275

CARRÉE (DE LA)
Pierre de Merlin, Seigneur 948, 949
CARRICK
Marjorie of 787, 789
Robert Bruce, Earl of 787, 789
CARRINGTON
Anne (Mayo) 557
Elizabeth Hannah xlix, clxxix, 557
Ellen (Warburton) 560
Emma 687, 760
family xxiv
George xlix, clxvi, clxxix, 557
Henningham (Codrington) 557
Jane (Mellowes?) 557
John (Sir) 560
Margaret 560
Paul 557
CARRITHERS
Ashley 190
Catherine Conover (Mellon) (Warner) 190
CARROLL
Anne (Plater) 602
Charles (Dr.) 1, 602
Charles (III), of Carrollton 121
Dorothy (Blake) 602
family 415
family, of Carrollton xxiv

Lewis [Charles Lutwidge Dodgson] xxiv, 107
Mary (Darnall) 120, 121
CARRUTHERS
Catherine (Carlyle) 787
Ellen 787, 788
Simon 787
CARSTAIRS
Bethia 276
CARTER
Ann (Ansley) 764, 773
Anne 470, 496, 503, 878
Arabella (Williamson) 470
Beyoncé Giselle (Knowles) 968, 990
Daniel 470
Donna Dean 793
Eleanor 366
Eleanor (Duckworth) 772
Eleanor (Eltonhead) (Brocas) 498
Elizabeth (Landon) 503
Elizabeth (Pannill) 470
Harriet 108
Isaac 772
James 772
James Earl 422, 764, 773

James Earl, Jr. ("Jimmy"), 39th U.S. President 422, 696, 765, 773
Jane (___) 772
John 498, 503
Katherine (Dale) 470
Kindred 772
Lillian (Bessie Lillian) (Gordy) 422, 764, 773
Littleberry Walker 764, 773
Magdalene (Moore) 772, 773
Mary (___) 470
Mary Ann Diligent (Seals) 764, 773
Moore 772
Nina (Pratt) 422, 764, 773
Robert "King" 503
Rosalynn (Eleanor Rosalynn) (Smith) xlii, xliii, 422, 696, 765, 773
Sarah (Browne) 772
Sarah (Ludlow) xix, xxxiv, clxvi, 498, 503
Shawn Corey "Jay Z" 990
Susanna 708
Thomas 470
Thomas, Jr. 470
Thomas (III) 772, 773
Wiley 764, 773

William Archibald 422, 764, 773
CARTERET (DE)
Anne (Dowse) 527
Anne (Seale) 527
Elizabeth (Smith) (Lawrence) 552, 868, 881
Frances 527
Frances (Worsley) 69
Francis 527
Georgiana Caroline 69, 70
Helier 868
John, 1st Earl Granville, Prime Minister 69, 226
Louisa 70
Peter (Gov.) liv, lix, clxxviii, 868
Philip (Gov.) liv, lix, clxxviii, 552, 868, 881
Philip (Sir) 527, 868
Rachel 868
Rachel (La Cloche) 868
Rachel (Paulet) 868
Sophia 226
Sophia (Fermor) 226
CARTHEW
Anne (Denny) 540
Elizabeth (Mitchell) 540
Laura 540
Mary (Colby) 539

Thomas 539, 540
CARTLEDGE
Edmund 384
Mary (Need) 384
CARTWRIGHT
Anne 128
CARUS
Ethelred 902
CARVER
Catherine (White)
 (Leggett) xl, l, cli,
 916, 917
John (Gov.) xl, cli,
 916, 917
CARY/CAREY
Catherine 134,
 300, 303
Cynthia 27
Cynthia (Burke
 Roche) (Burden),
 (Hon.) Mrs.
 cxliii, 27, 378, 932
Elizabeth 390, 755
George 390
Guy Fairfax 27, 378
Henry, 1st Baron
 Hunsdon 300
Isabella (Ingram)
 390
Jay A. 726
Joan Mildred Elton
 542
John 504
Kathryn Teresa
 Marguerite 734
Lettice (Barrett) 300
Lucius Charles, 6th
 Viscount Falkland
 390

Margaret (Spencer)
 300
Martha 504
Mary (Boleyn) xii,
 lviii, 300, 303
Philadelphia 431
Thomas 300
William xii, 300
CARYL
Patience/Anne
 531, 684
CARYLL
John (Sir) 414
Mary 414, 416
Mary (Dormer) 414
CASA DE SOUSA (DA)
María Pais Ribeira,
 15th Senhora 619
CASADO DE ACEVEDO Y DEL MAZO
Isidro, 1st Marquess
 of Monteleón 140
María Francisca (de
 Velasco) 140
CASADO DE ACEVEDO Y ROSALES
María Teresa
 (Martínez del Mazo
 y Velázquez) 140
Pedro 140
CASADO DE ACEVEDO Y VELASCO
Antonio, 3rd
 Marquess of
 Monteleón 140

Margareta
 (Huguetan),
 Countess of
 Gyldensteen 140
CASADO Y HUGUETAN (DE)
Enriqueta (Henrietta)
 Juana Francisca
 Susanna 141, 142
CASE
John 867, 924, 926
Mary 867
Mary (Westover)
 924
Miriam 924
Miriam (Burr) 924
Nathaniel 924
Samuel 924
Sarah (Spencer)
 867, 924
CASEY
Anne 115, 117
Géneviève B.
 (Lyman) 20
CASIMIR
Count of Lippe-
 Brake 194
CASIMIR II
Prince of Sandomir
 and Krakow, Kuja-
 mien and Mazovia
 791, 797, 802
CASIMIR IV
King of Poland 194,
 195, 196, 198, 895
CASIRAGHI
Caroline-Louise-
 Marguerite
 (Grimaldi) (Junot),

Princess of
 Monaco 934
 Stefano 934
CASSADY
 Paul 939, 947
CASSIDY
 Clara L. (McGrew) 545
 Hugh Gilbert 545
 Juanita (Newton) (Harris) 545
 Lewis Cochran 545
 Mary Dorothea (Fagan) 545
CASSILLIS
 Archibald Kennedy, 11th Earl of 253
 David Kennedy, 1st Earl of 253
 Gilbert Kennedy, 2nd Earl of 253
 Gilbert Kennedy, 3rd Earl of 82, 253, 897, 898
 Gilbert Kennedy, 4th Earl of 898
CASTAÑOS ARAGORRI URIARTE OLIVIDE
 María 438
CASTELBON (DE)
 Archibaud de Grailly, Vicomte 963
 Roger Bernard I de Foix, Vicomte 963
 Roger Bernard II de Foix, Vicomte 963

CASTELL-CASTELL
 Adelaide Clotilde Augusta of 47
 Clotilde, Countess of 8
 Frederick Louis Henry, Count of 47
CASTELL-REMLINGEN
 Sophia Theodora of 182
 Wolfgang Dietrich, Count of 182, 237
 Wolfgang George, Count of 182
CASTELNAU-CLERMONT-LODEVE (DE)
 Jacquette 200
CASTELPERS (DE)
 Charlotte 200
CASTILE
 Alphonso VIII, King of 647, 909, 948, 964
 Beatrix of, Queen of Portugal 619
 Berengaria, Princess and Queen of, Queen of León 647, 709, 908, 909, 948, 964
 Eleanor, Princess of England, Queen of 647, 909, 948, 964
 Eleanor, Princess of, Queen of England xxvi, 466, 478, 483, 489, 491, 495, 497,

500, 503, 505, 508, 510, 512, 514, 517, 524, 528, 530, 532, 536, 543, 547, 551, 553, 554, 555, 558, 560, 563, 565, 567, 569, 571, 573, 574, 575, 577, 582, 584, 587, 588, 590, 592, 594, 595, 596, 601, 603, 606, 607, 608, 611, 613, 615, 861
 Ferdinand II, King of Aragón, V of, I of Spain 46, 140, 186, 189, 615, 717
 Ferdinand III, King of 951
 Henry II, King of 190, 191
 Isabel, Princess of, Duchess of York 107, 114, 119, 126, 133, 134, 377, 410, 411, 412, 423
 Isabella I, Queen of, I of Spain 46, 140
 Joan of Dammartin, Countess of Ponthieu, Queen of 951
 Leonor Sánchez of 190, 191
 monarchs of xv
CASTILLION
 Barbara 590
 Elizabeth (St. John) 590
 Francis (Sir) 590

CASTLE
Anne 985
CASTLEHAVEN
James Touchet, 6th
Earl of 110
CASTLEMAINE
Roger Palmer, 1st
Earl of 109
CASTRO
María Luisa Bárbara
Guadalupe (Peralta
Alviso) 948, 997
CASTRO AMADOR
José Antonio (Gov.),
Comandante
General 991, 997
CASTRO GARCÍA
Guillermo 997
CASTRO PERALTA
María Concepción
Dolores 997
CATANEO
Jane 117
CATELYN/CATLIN
Hester 490
Mary 738
CATES
Larry W. xlix, l,
330
CATESBY
Alice (Rudkin) 830
Anne (Hesilrig) 830
Anne (Odim) 830
Edward 830
Elizabeth clxvi,
clxxx, 831, 1025
Elizabeth (___)
(Rowland) 831

Elizabeth (Jekyll)
830
Isabel (Tresham)
403
John 830
Kenelm 830
Lucretia (___) 830
Margaret 403
Mark lxix, clxxx,
830, 831, 1025
Michael 830
Thomas 403
CATHCART
Alan Cathcart, 6th
Baron 128
Alan Cathcart, 7th
Baron 128
Elizabeth
(Dalrymple) 128
Margaret 128
Marion (Boswell)
128
CATHERINE
Archduchess of
Austria 291
of Bavaria 451
of Braganza,
Princess of
Portugal, Queen of
England and
Scotland 22, 25,
29, 30, 31, 33
de' Medici, Queen
of France 637
of Mecklenburg-
Schwerin 196
Princess Dolguruki
(Princess Youri-
evsky) (second wife

of Alexander II,
Czar of Russia) 5
Princess of Baden-
Durlach 43
Princess of Spain 18
Princess of Sweden
40, 43
**CATHERINE II
"THE GREAT"**
Empress of Russia
[Sophie, Princess
of Anhalt-Zerbst]
14, 615, 792
CATLETT
Rebecca 497, 532
CATLIN/CATELYN.
see CATELYN/
CATLIN
CATRIN
ferch Dafydd ap
Gethin 659
ferch Edward ap
Gruffudd 692
ferch Elisha ap
Dafydd 229
ferch Hywel ap
Jenkin 660
ferch Jenkin ap
Havard 410
ferch Robert ap
Gruffudd 658
ferch Trahaearn ap
Morgan 582
ferch William
Dafydd 658
**CATTENBURCH
(VAN)**
Cornelia Margaretha
Wilhelmina 907

Dirk Lodewijk 907
Jeanne (des Tombe) 907
Johan Louis 907
Moralla Catharina (Copes) 907
Wilhelmina Antonia (Erbervelt) 907
Willem Hendrik, Heer van Grijpskerke en Poppendamme 907

CAUDECOSTE (DE)
Jeanne 957

CAULFIELD
Anne (Rothe) 308
Charles 308
Hans 308
Hans James 308
Jenny (Brasher) 308
Lilian May clvii, 308
Margaret (Wood) 308
Mary Anne (Ellis) 308

CAUNTON
Anna 684

CAVANAGH
Harrison Dwight 1

CAVANIGLIA
Anna Giuseppa 189, 192
Carlo Onero, Duke of San Giovanni 192
Cecilia (de Ponte Carafa Tovar) 192
Eleanora (Sforza) 192
Troiano, Marquess of San Marco 192

CAVE
Anne 466, 467, 717
Anthony 467, 717
Bridget 387, 717
Elizabeth 629
Elizabeth (Danvers) 717
Elizabeth (Lovett) 467, 717
Margaret 470, 628
Margaret (Cecil) 470, 717
Martha 717
Mary 467, 717
Roger 470, 717
Thomas (Sir) 717

CAVENDISH
Adele (Astaire) [Marie Austerlit] xvii, clii, 26
Andrew Robert Buxton, 11th Duke of Devonshire 26
Anne 73, 333, 468, 512
Blanche Georgiana (Howard) 25
Charles Arthur Francis, Lord 26
Deborah Vivien (Freeman-Mitford) [Deborah Mitford] 22, 23, 26
Dorothy Evelyn 26
Edward, Lord 25
Edward William Spencer, 10th Duke of Devonshire 26
Elizabeth 70
Elizabeth (Hardwick) (Barlow) ["Bess of Hardwick"] 468, 512, 706
Elizabeth (Hervey) (Foster) [Lady Elizabeth Foster] 117
Emma (Lascelles) 25
Evelyn (Petty-Fitzmaurice) 25
Georgiana (Spencer) 69, 75
Georgiana Dorothy 25, 69, 71
Grace (Talbot) 512
Henry 512
Kathleen (Kennedy) 26
Margaret (Bostock) 468
Mary Alice (Gascoyne-Cecil) 26
Victor Christian William, 9th Duke of Devonshire 25
William (Sir) 468, 512
William, 5th Duke of Devonshire 69, 117
William, 7th Duke of Devonshire 25

William John
   Robert, Marquess
   of Hartington   26
**CAVENDISH-
BENTINCK**
   Elizabeth   70
   Nina Cecilia   930
CAWDOR
   John Campbell, 1st
     Baron   71
   John Frederick
     Campbell, 1st Earl
     70, 71
CAY (DE)
   Malyne   353
CAZENOVE
   Margareta Helena
     (van Jever)   635
   Marie   635
   Marie (de Rapin)
     635
   Théophile   xii,
     xxxii, liii, cliii,
     635, 636
CECIL
   Albinia   115
   Algernon (Hon.)
     334
   Anna   68
   Anne (Cavendish)   73
   Brownlow, 2nd
     Marquess of Exeter
     73, 74
   Brownlow, 8th Earl
     of Exeter   73
   Catherine (Howard)
     334
   Charlotte (Garnier)
     73

Cornelia Stuyvesant
     (Vanderbilt)   73, 74
   David, 3rd Earl of
     Exeter   73
   Diana   334
   Dorothy   345
   Dorothy (Neville)
     334, 345, 346, 482
   Edith Stuyvesant
     (Dresser)   73, 74
   Elizabeth   73, 482,
     554
   Elizabeth (Brooke)
     315, 336
   Elizabeth (Brown-
     low)   73
   Elizabeth (Drury)
     482
   Elizabeth (Egerton)
     73
   family   liv
   Frances (Manners)
     73
   George Henry
     Vanderbilt   74
   Georgina Sophia
     (Pakenham)   73
   Hannah Sophia
     (Chambers)   73
   Henry, 1st Marquess
     of Exeter   73
   Isabella (Poyntz)   73
   John, 4th Earl of
     Exeter   73
   John, 5th Earl of
     Exeter   73
   John, 6th Earl of
     Exeter   73

John Francis
     Amherst (Hon.)
     cliii, 73, 74
   Margaret   470, 717
   Mary Lee (Ryan)   74
   Mary Rothes
     Margaret Tyssen
     (Amherst),
     Baroness Amherst
     of Hackney   73
   Mildred (Cooke)
     68, 315, 684
   Nancy (Owen)   74
   Robert, 1st Earl of
     Salisbury, Lord
     Treasurer   315,
     336
   Sarah (Hoggins)   73
   Sophia   74
   Thomas, 1st Earl of
     Exeter   345, 482
   Thomas Chambers
     (Hon.)   73
   William, 1st Baron
     Burghley   68, 315,
     345, 470, 554, 684
   William, 2nd Earl of
     Exeter   482
   William, 2nd Earl of
     Salisbury   334, 336
   William, Lord   73
   William Alleyne,
     3rd Marquess of
     Exeter   73
   William Amherst
     Vanderbilt   74
CECILY
   Princess of Sweden
     208

CELLE (DE)
François, Seigneur du Puy 440
Françoise (d'Anlezy alias de Menetou) 440
Gabrielle 440
CELLES (DE)
Antoine-Philippe-(Fiacre)-Ghislain de Vischer, Baron 206
CERVETERI
Alessandro Ruspoli, Prince of 21
Francesco Maria Quinto Ruspoli, Prince of 21
Francesco Maria Ruspoli, Prince of 21
Giovanni Ruspoli, Prince of 21
CESI
Olympia 192
CEVA (DI)
Luisa 642
CHABANNES (DE)
Antoinette 205
Catherine 202
Jean, Count of Dammartin 205
CHABRIÈRES (DE)
Marie-Anne 638
CHADWELL
David 833
Jane "Jincey" (Johnson) 833
Mary 833

CHAFFANJON
Arnaud 1
CHAFIN
Amphillis 626
Amphillis (Hyde) 626
Thomas 626
CHAHANNAI (DE)
Marie 455
CHAÎNÉ
Aline 970
CHALANT (DE)
Bonne 911
Marguerite 952
CHALENCON (DE)
Louis-Melchior-(Armand) de Polignac, Marquis 289
CHÂLON (DE)
Hugh, Count Palatine of Burgundy 735, 952
CHALONER
Anne (Bowes) 101
Caroline 101
Edward 101
Emma (Harvey) 101
Frances 327
Mary (Finney) 101
Nicola Sophia 179
William 101
CHAMBERLAIN alias SPICER
Amphyllis 670
CHAMBERLAIN(E)/ CHAMBERLAYNE
Anna 780
Anne 478

Constance 551
Dorothy lxx, clxxix, 133
Edmund 133
Eleanor (Colles) 133
Elizabeth (Stoughton) (Scudder) xiv, cli, 921
Elizabeth (Stratton) 133
Grace (Strangways) 133
Joan 847
Joanna 921
Mary 409
Mary (Wood) 133
Robert (Rev.) xiv, 921
Thomas lxx, 133
CHAMBERLAND
Marguerite 978
CHAMBERS
Charles xlviii, lxi, cxlviii, cli, clx, 86, 501
Elizabeth (Palmes) 501
family xi
Hannah Sophia 73
Joan 847
Lillie Boyce 629
Rebecca (Patefield) 501
Robert 501
Susan 317
CHAMIER
family 362
Georgina Grace 361

CHAMOND
  Elizabeth Beaumont, Baroness of 430
  Gertrude 835
  Jane (Grenville) 835, 836
  John (Sir) 835
  Margaret 665
  Margaret (Trevener) 835
  Richard 835
CHAMPAGNE
  Henry I, Count of 774, 776, 943, 993
  Henry II, Count of, King of Jerusalem 943
  Margaret of 830
  Marie of 642, 911
  Marie of, Empress of Constantinople 776
  Philippa of 943
  Theobald II, Count of 911
  Theobald III, Count of 993
  Theobald IV, Count of 642
  William of, Seigneur de Sully 830
CHAMPAIGNE (DE)
  Jacques Maillard, Seigneur 950
CHAMPAIGNÉ (DE)
  Marguerite 943

CHAMPERNOWNE (DE)
  Alice (Astley) 570, 672, 674
  Eleanor (de Rohant) 672
  Elizabeth 305, 672
  Elizabeth (Reynell) 672
  Elizabeth (Valletort) 672
  family 1025
  Jane 547, 548
  Joan 548, 569, 570, 573, 674, 675
  Joan (of Cornwall) 672
  John 672
  John (Sir) 547
  Katherine (Carew) 547
  Katherine (Daubeny) 672, 674
  Margaret (Courtenay) 547
  Margaret (Hamley) 672
  Philip (Sir) 547
  Richard 672
  Richard (Sir) 570, 672, 674
  Thomas (Sir) 672
CHAMPIGNEULLE (DE)
  François de Joyeuse, Seigneur 944
  Jean de Joyeuse, Seigneur 944

CHAMPION
  Rachel 231
  Rebecca 474
CHAMPION DE CRESPIGNY
  Mary Charmian Sara 453
CHAMPS (DE)
  Guigues I Alleman, Seigneur, Seigneur de Valbonnais 911
  Odon II Alleman, Seigneur, Seigneur de Valbonnais 911, 912
CHANAY (DE)
  François de Poypon, Seigneur 912
CHANDLER
  Abigail 656
  Abigail (Hale) 656
  Isaac 656
  Mary (Sewall) 332
CHANDOS
  James Brydges, 1st Duke of 299
CHANLER
  Amélie Louise (Rives) 194
CHANTEPINOT (DE)
  Anne 952
CHANTEPRIME (DE)
  Marguerite 954
CHAPLIN
  Diana 119
  Martha 858
CHAPMAN
  Louisa (Vansittart) 102

William 102
**CHAPMAN
[LAWRENCE]**
Thomas Robert
Tighe (Sir), 7th Bt.
102
CHAPUISET (DE)
counts 949
CHAPUT
Marie-Judith 974
CHARDIN
Julia 361
CHARE/CHAIRE
Anne 720
CHARLEMAGNE
Holy Roman
Emperor vi, xx,
xxii, xxvii, lxx,
626, 805, 879, 919
CHARLES
Duke of Lower
Lorraine 874,
877, 879, 919
Prince of France,
Count of Valois
459, 941, 961
"the Bold," Duke of
Burgundy 438,
445
CHARLES I
of Anjou, Prince of
France, King of
Naples and Sicily
965
Count Palatine of
Zweibrücken-
Birkenfeld 60
Duke of Bourbon
205, 293, 440

Duke of Lorraine
291
Emperor of Austria
201, 800
King of England and
Scotland 241,
430, 467
Landgrave of Hesse-
Philippsthal 43
Margrave of Baden
291
CHARLES II
Duke of Lorraine
637
Grand Duke of
Mecklenburg-
Strelitz 40
King of England and
Scotland xii, xxv,
lvii, lxviii, 22, 25,
29, 30, 31, 33, 34,
103, 109, 615, 627
King of Navarre
287, 290, 293
Prince of Anjou and
France, King of
Naples and Sicily
459
CHARLES VI
King of France 226
CHARLES VII
King of France
202, 203, 208, 209
CHARLES VIII
(Bonde), King of
Sweden 457, 663,
664
CHARLES IX
King of France 637

King of Sweden
40, 43
CHARLES XIII
King of Sweden 615
**CHARLES XIV
JOHN**
King of Sweden
[Jean-Baptiste
Bernadotte] 83
CHARLES ALBERT
King of Sardinia
18, 614
**CHARLES
ALEXANDER**
Duke of Württem-
berg-Stuttgart 49
**CHARLES
EMANUEL**
of Savoy, Prince of
Carignan 613
**CHARLES
EMANUEL I**
Duke of Savoy 18
**CHARLES
FREDERICK**
Prince of Anhalt-
Bernberg 56
CHARLES GUSTAV
Margrave of Baden-
Durlach 43, 44
**CHARLES II
WILLIAM
FERDINAND**
Duke of Brunswick
12
CHARLES LOUIS
of Lorraine, Prince
of Lambesc, Count
of Brionne 613

Prince of Baden 41
CHARLES PHILIP ARTHUR GEORGE
Prince of Great Britain, Prince of Wales lxiii, 209, 380, 655, 832, 930, 932
CHARLETON
Margaret 339
CHARLOTTE
of Nassau-Dillenburg 62, 637
Princess of Anhalt-Bernberg 56
Princess of Mecklenburg-Schwerin 8
Princess of Savoy, Queen of France 200, 205
Princess of Saxe-Hildeburghausen 12
Princess Royal of Great Britain, Queen of Württemberg 12
CHARLOTTE (CARLOTA) (MARIE-CHARLOTTE-AMÉLIE-AUGUSTE-VICTOIRE-CLÉMENTINE-LÉOPOLDINE)
Princess of the Belgians, Archduchess of Austria, Empress of México 288
CHARLOTTE (SOPHIE CHARLOTTE)
Princess of Mecklenburg-Strelitz, Queen of Great Britain 40
CHARLOTTE AMELIA CAROLINE
Princess of Hesse-Philippsthal 43, 46
CHARLOTTE ELIZABETH DIANA
of Cambridge, Princess of Great Britain xlii, 25, 380, 931, 932
CHARLOTTE LOUISE
Princess of Prussia, Empress of Russia 5, 7
CHARLOTTE-LOUISE-JULIETTE
Grimaldi, Hereditary Princess of Monaco, Duchess of Valentinois 289, 933
CHARLTON (DE)
Alan 746
Alicia (Horde) 697
Anne 746
Anne (Mainwaring) 697, 746
Catherine 325
Cecily 697
Elena (la Zouche) 746
Emma (Harby) 325
Margery (FitzAker) 746
Mary (Corbet) 746
Richard 697, 746
Robert 325, 746
Thomas 746
William 697
CHARMÉE AND VINCELLES (DE)
Claude de Salins, Seigneur 952
CHARNELLS (DE)
Matilda 768, 770
CHARONIÈRE (DE LA)
Catherine 943
CHARTERIS
Janet 98
CHARTERIS-WEMYSS
Katherine 80
CHARTIER
Élisabeth (d'Amours) 939, 955
Louis-Théandre, Sieur de Lotbinière 939, 955
CHASE
Betsy Miller 53
Margaret Frances (Towneley) clxxviii, 859, 860

Polly 654
Richard 859
CHASLES
Françoise 987
CHASTELLUX (DE)
Charlotte 440
Hélène 953
CHÂTEAU-DU-LOIR
François de Rohan, Seigneur de Gié, Baron 455
CHÂTEAU-PORCIEN
Sybil of 874, 877
CHÂTEAU-RENARD (DE)
Gaucher II de Joigny, Seigneur 954
CHÂTEAUDUN (DE)
Jeanne 647, 909
John of Flanders, Vicomte 942
CHÂTEAUNEUF (DE)
Anne 965
Bertrand, Seigneur 965
Jean de Rieux, Seigneur 226
Sybil (de Clermont) 965
CHÂTEAUNEUF-EN-THYMERAIS (DE)
Jean I de Dreux, Seigneur 956
CHÂTEAUROUX (DE)
François de Maillé de la Tour-Landry,

Baron de la Tour-Landry, Count 455
CHÂTEAUVILLAIN (DE)
Jean IV, Seigneur 944
Jeanne (de Grancey) 944
Marie 944
CHÂTEAUVILLE (DE)
family 945
CHÂTELLERAULT
James Hamilton, 2nd Earl of Arran, Duke of 154, 157, 167, 168, 177, 179
CHÂTILLON (DE)
Beatrix 942
Catherine 733
Catherine (de Carency) 733
counts 949
Guy de Montiuel, Seigneur 911
Guy II, Count of St.-Pol 733
Guy III, Count of St.-Pol 633, 942, 944
Hugh, Seigneur de Leuze 733
Isabel 633, 944
Jacques, Seigneur de Leuze 733
Jeanne (d'Argies) 733
Jeanne, of St.-Pol 638

Maud, of St.-Pol 941
CHÂTILLON-BLOIS (DE)
Françoise 287, 293
Marie of, Queen of Naples, Sicily, Jerusalem, and Aragón 205
CHÂTILLON-SUR-LOING (DE)
Étienne II de Sancerre, Seigneur 954
CHAUFFOURS (DE)
Louis d'Amours, Sieur 990
Mathieu d'Amours, Sieur 990
Michel d'Amours, Sieur 939
CHAUNCEY
Alice (Boyce) 806
Anne (Leventhorp) 806
Anne (Welsh) 806
Bertha 100
Catherine (Eyre) 806
Charles (Rev.) clx, clxxvii, 806
Elizabeth 806
Elizabeth (Proffit) 806
George 806
Henry 806
Joan (Bigod) 806
Joan (Tenderyng) 806
John 806
Lucy (____) 806

Margaret (Giffard) 806
William 806
William (Sir) 806
___ (Garland) 806
CHAUVIGNY
family 442
CHAVANIAC (DE)
Marie-Catharine 201
CHAVCHAVADZE
David, Prince 4
Eugenie (de Smitt) 4
family 4
Helen (Husted) 4
Judith (Clippinger) 4
Nina (Romanoff), Grand Duchess of Russia cliii, 4
Paul, Prince 4
CHAWORTH
Catherine 706
family xli
Grace (Manners) 120
Isabel (Aylesbury) 706
Juliana 120
Maud 623, 625, 628, 630, 632
Patrick Chaworth, 3rd Viscount Chaworth 120
Thomas (Sir) 706
CHAZÉ (DE)
Jeanne 946
CHEDWORTH
Margaret 353
CHEIREL
Micheline 98

CHENECEY (DE)
Thomas de Pillot, Seigneur, Marquis de Coligny 184
CHENEY/CHEYNE/ CHEYNEY
Anne xlix, lxi, cli, 136, 667, 668
Anne (Holme) 667
Catherine 491
Elizabeth 705, 721, 840
Elizabeth (___) 667
Elizabeth (Cokayne) 667, 705
Elizabeth (Rempston) 667
family 669
Frances (Cheney) 667
Jane 668
John 667, 668
John (Sir) 667
Katherine (Pabenham) 705, 763
Laurence 667, 705
William 667
William (Sir) 705
CHENOWETH
Hannah 725
CHEREMETEV/ CHEREMETEFF
Alexandra, Countess 7
Anna (Cheremetev), Countess 794
Catherine cliii
Catherine (Wiazemsky), Princess 794

Catherine, Countess 794, 796
Daria (Tatistchev) 794
Dimitri, Count 794, 795
Irina (Vorontzov-Dachkov), Countess 794, 795
Maria, Countess 7
Nikita, Count 7
Sergei, Count 7, 794
Varvara (Almazov) 794
Vassili, Count 794
CHERLETON
Alice (FitzAlan) xxv, 295, 337, 375, 382, 515, 600, 900
Edward, 5th Baron Cherleton of Powis xxv, 515, 600
Eleanor (Holand) xxv, 515, 600
John, 4th Baron Cherleton of Powis xxv, 295, 337, 375, 382, 515, 600, 900
Joyce 515, 600
CHERNIGOV
Maria of 791, 797
Michael (St.), Prince of, Grand Prince of Kiev 791, 797, 802
CHESELDINE/ CHESELDYNE
Bridget (Faulkner) 478
Grace (Dryden) 478

Kenelm lxviii,
    cxliii, 478
Mary (Gerard) 478
CHESTER
  Bridget (Sharpe)
    757
  Dorcas 747, 758
  Dorothy (Hooker)
    757
  family 758
  George Lloyd,
    Bishop of 686
  Hugh Kevelioc, 3rd
    Earl of 778, 780,
    785, 787, 789, 806,
    807, 813, 815, 817,
    819, 821, 822, 824,
    826
  Hugh Lupus, Earl of
    xx
  John 757
  Leonard xi, xix,
    xlviii, lxi, cxlviii,
    cli, clxiii, 757, 759
  Mabel of 813, 819,
    824, 826
  Mary (Wade) 757
  Ranulph de Gernon,
    2nd Earl of 806,
    813, 815, 817, 819,
    821, 822, 824, 826
  Thomas Mallory,
    Dean of 505, 668
CHESTERFIELD
  Philip Dormer
    Stanhope, 4th Earl
    of 107
  Philip Stanhope, 1st
    Earl of 107, 109

CHESTOV
  Xenia 792
CHETHAM
  Elizabeth 111
  Margaret 382
  Mary (Drake)
    clxxxvi
CHETTLE
  Margaret 541
CHETWODE
  Dorothy (Needham)
    574
  Grace lix, clx, 574,
    746
  Richard (Sir) 574
CHETWYND
  Edward 323
  Elizabeth 320, 323
  Elizabeth (Ferrers)
    592
  Helena (Harington)
    323
  Jane (Salter) 323,
    592
  John 323
  Margerie (Middle-
    more) 323
  Mary 592
  Thomas 323, 592
  William (Sir) 592
**CHETWYND-
    TALBOT**
  Charles Alexander
    Price 137
  Gerard 137
  Margaret (Mackay)
    137
  Matilda Charlotte
    Palgrave clvii, 137

  Maud (Fleming) 137
CHEVERS
  Eleanor (de Welles)
    486
  Margaret 486
  Walter 486
CHÉVIGNÉ (DE)
  Adhéaume-Marie-
    Mériadec 227
  Laure-Marie-
    Charlotte (de Sade)
    227, 228
  Marie-Thérèse-Anne-
    Josèphe-Germaine
    227
CHEVRON (DE)
  André, Seigneur de
    Villette 952
  Isabelle (de
    Beauvoir) 952
  Louise 952
  Marguerite (de
    Chalant) 952
  Petremand, Seigneur
    de Villette 952
  Philiberte (Villette)
    952
  Urbain, Seigneur de
    Villette 952
**CHEVRON-
    VILLETTE (DE)**
  Amédée II, Seigneur
    911
  Amphélise (d'Aigle)
    911
  Humbert IV, Seigneur
    de Chevron and de
    Villette 911

1137

Humbert V, Seigneur
 de Chevron et de
 Villette 911
Philippine 911
Philippine (__) 911
Philippine (Alleman)
 911
CHEYNE/CHENEY.
 See also CHENEY/
 CHEYNE/CHEYNEY
 Elizabeth 309
CHICHELE
 Agatha (Eltonhead)
 (Kellaway) (Worm-
 eley) clxvi, clxxiii,
 484, 491, 498, 551
 Anne (Bourne) 492
 Dorothy (Kempe)
 491, 492
 Henry (Sir) (Dep.
 Gov.) 491, 498
 Thomas 492
 Thomas (Sir) 491,
 492
CHICHESTER
 Amyas 672
 Edward 436
 Eleanor 103
 Elizabeth 436, 744
 Elizabeth (Bourchier)
 436
 Frances 672
 Gertrude (Courtenay)
 436
 Jane (Giffard) 672
 John 744
 John (Sir) 436
 Margaret (Beaumont)
 744

Mary 340
CHIDIOCK
 John (Sir) 761
 Katherine 761
 Katherine (Lumley)
 761
CHIFFINCH
 Amphillis (Chaffin)
 626
 Dorothy (Tannet) 626
 Elizabeth 626
 family 627
 Thomas 626, 627
 William 627
CHIGI-ALBANI
 Sigismundo, Prince,
 6th Prince of
 Farnese 18
 Teresa 18
CHILD
 Amy 279
 Arlene (Ovalle) 991
 Christopher
 Challender vi,
 xlii, l, lv, lxi, lxiii,
 lxiv, lxvii, lxxi,
 131, 521, 556, 570,
 632, 968, 976, 991
 Hannah 572
 Isabella 548
CHILDREY
 Joan 855
CHILDS
 Virginia Lowrie 662
**CHILHAM (DE)/
 DOVER (DE)**
 Isabel 676, 691
CHILTON
 Mary clxxxiii

CHIPMAN
 Hope (Howland) 983
 John 983
 Lydia 983
CHIRNSIDE
 Joan 402
CHISHOLM
 Ann 214
 James (Sir), of
 Cromlix 168
 James, Bishop of
 Dunblane 258
 Jean 168, 258, 283
 Jean (Drummond)
 168
CHITTENDEN
 Sarah 867
CHOATE
 Caroline 183
CHOISEUL
 family 442
CHOLET
 Jean, Seigneur de
 Dangeaul 948
 Marie 948
 Perrine (d'Argenson)
 948
CHOLMLEY
 Barbara 129
 Henry (Sir) 127
 Margaret 127
 Margaret (Babthorpe)
 127
 Mary 129
 Richard (Sir) 127,
 129
 Susanna (Legard)
 127

CHOLMONDELEY
  Betty Cecile
    (Sassoon) 65
  George Henry Hugh
    Cholmondeley, 4th
    Marquess of 65
  George Horatio
    Charles Cholmond-
    eley, 5th Marquess
    of 65
  George Hugh
    Cholmondeley, 6th
    Marquess of 65
  Lavina Margaret
    (Leslie) 65
  Margaret Lavinia 65
  Winifred Agnes
    (Kingscote) 65
CHONKHOV
  Ekaterina 793
CHOURSES (DE)
  Anne (de Brienne)
    948
  Denise (de Bauçay)
    948, 949
  Jeanne 948
  Jeanne (Pegaze)
    948
  Patri/Patry (II),
    Seigneur de Saint-
    Aubin 948, 949
  Patri/Patry, Seigneur
    de Rabestan 948
  Payen, Seigneur de
    Malicorne 948
CHRÉTIEN
  Aline (Chaîné) 970
  Élisabeth (Blais)
    970

  François 967, 970
  Joseph-Jacques-Jean
    (Canadian Prime
    Minister) 967,
    970, 989
  Marie (Boisvert) 970
  Olivine (Laforme)
    967, 970
  Willie 970
CHRISTIAN
  Anne (Dixon) 363
  Bridget (Senhouse)
    363
  Charles 363
  Count of Waldeck-
    Wildungen 141,
    181
  Fletcher 363, 365
  John 363
  Mary 363
CHRISTIAN I
  Elector of Saxony
    891
CHRISTIAN III
  King of Denmark
    52, 58, 60, 432,
    889, 891, 893
CHRISTIAN IV
  King of Denmark
    35, 37, 52
CHRISTIAN V
  King of Denmark
    615
CHRISTIAN IX
  King of Denmark
    453
CHRISTIANE
  Princess of Anhalt-
    Bernberg 56

CHRISTINA
  Queen of Sweden
    615
CHRISTINE
  Princess of Hesse-
    Eschewege 44
  Princess of
    Mecklenburg-
    Güstrow 47
  Princess of Saxony,
    Queen of Denmark
    181, 182, 184
CHRISTINE
HENRIETTA
  of Hesse-Rheinfels-
    Rotenburg 18
CHRISTINE
JULIANE
  Princess of Baden-
    Durlach 43
CHRISTINE
MAGDALEN
  Princess of
    Zweibrücken-
    Kleeberg 40, 43
CHRISTOPHER
  Joan 754
  Prince of Greece
    and Denmark 3, 4
CHRISTOPHER I
  Margrave of Baden
    291
CHRISTOPHER II
  Margrave of Baden-
    Rodemachern
    208
CHRISTOU
  Christos, Jr. viii, l,
    lv, 556

CHUDLEIGH
Dorothy 436, 437
Elizabeth (Fortescue) 436
family 675
George (Sir), 2nd Bt. 436
James 674
James (Sir) 674, 675
Joan (Champer-nowne) 674, 675
John 674
Margaret (___) 674
Margaret (or Mary) (Stourton) 674
Margaret (Tremayne) 674
Petronell 674, 675
Radigond (FitzWalter) 674
CHURCH
Caleb 571
Deborah 571
Deborah (Perry) 571
Joseph 571
Katherine 406
Mary xiii
Mercy (Pope) 571
CHURCHILL. see also SPENCER-CHURCHILL
Anne 75
Arabella clxxxix, 24, 536
Charles 536, 537
Elizabeth 70, 730, 878
Elizabeth (Armistead) 730

Elizabeth (Drake) 536
Harriet xlvi, lii, 536, 537
John, 1st Duke of Marlborough 24, 62, 70, 71, 75, 536
Mary (Gould) 536
Sarah (Jennings) 71, 75
William 730
Winston (Sir) 536
CHUTE
___ 405
CIBÒ
family 192
CIBON (DE)
Christine 616
CICCONE
Madonna Louise (Fortin) 975, 988
Madonna Louise Veronica [Madonna] xvii, cxlvi, 63, 380, 967, 969, 975, 988
Silvio Anthony 975, 988
CITKOWITZ
Caroline Maureen (Hamilton-Temple-Blackwood) (Freud), Lady [Caroline Blackwood] xviii, 31
Israel 31
CIVITELLA-CESI
Marino Torlonia, 4th Prince of 18

CLAFLIN
Victoria [Victoria C. Woodhull] xvii, 138
CLAGETT
Ann Calvert Brooke vii, li, clxxxix, 499, 513, 559, 602, 604, 779, 820, 848, 875
Brice McAdoo vii, viii, xlvii, l, liv, lvi, lviii, lix, lx, lxiv, lxviii, lxix, lxxi, clxxxix, 139, 151, 280, 303, 312, 476, 498, 499, 513, 533, 559, 602, 604, 639, 723, 779, 820, 847, 848, 875, 1026
Elizabeth (Wiseman) 302
John Brice de Treville vii, li, clxxxix, 499, 513, 559, 602, 604, 779, 820, 847, 875
Lettice (Mitchell) 302
Margaret Marie 639
Martha (Clifton) 302
Mary (Allen) 127
Richard 302
Wiseman l, 302, 303, 304
CLAIBORNE
Elizabeth (Boteler/Butler) xlvii, liii, clxvi, clxxvii, 754, 755
William 754

1140

CLANRICARDE
  Richard Burke, 2nd
    Earl of 601
CLAPHAM
  Christopher (Sir) 321
  George 321
  Margaret 321
  Margaret (Oldfield)
    321
  Martha (Heber) 321
CLARE (DE)
  Adeliza (de
    Meschines) 866,
    870
  Alice 680, 845
  Aveline 866, 870
  Eleanor 491, 505,
    508, 514, 547, 575,
    584, 594, 607
  Elizabeth 466, 483,
    489, 528, 536, 567,
    587, 592, 606
  family xxxix, 725
  Gilbert 845, 866,
    869, 870
  Gilbert, 1st Earl of
    Pembroke 837,
    839, 847
  Gilbert, 3rd Earl of
    Gloucester, 7th
    Earl of Hertford
    466, 483, 489, 491,
    495, 505, 508, 514,
    528, 536, 547, 567,
    575, 577, 584, 587,
    590, 592, 594, 606,
    607, 615
  Isabel 787, 789,
    837, 839, 845, 847

  Isabel (de Beaumont)
    lxix, 837, 839, 847
  Joan (Plantagenet)
    of Acre, Princess
    of England xxxix,
    466, 483, 489, 491,
    495, 505, 508, 514,
    528, 536, 547, 565,
    567, 575, 577, 584,
    587, 590, 592, 594,
    606, 607, 615
  Margaret 495, 505,
    575, 577, 590, 615,
    847
  Matilda (de St. Liz)
    851, 879, 920
  Maud (de St.
    Hilaire) 866, 870
  Richard 866, 870
  Richard ("Strong-
    bow"), 2nd Earl of
    Pembroke 837,
    839, 847
  Robert 851, 879,
    920
  Roger, 2nd Earl of
    Hertford 866, 870
CLARELL
  Anne 515
  Elizabeth 528, 721
  Elizabeth (Reygate)
    721
  Elizabeth (Scrope)
    528
  family 722
  Isabel (Comyn) 721
  Maud (Montgomery)
    721

  Thomas 528, 721
  Thomas (Sir) 721
  William 721
CLARENCE
  George Plantagenet,
    1st Duke of xl,
    lxvi, 107, 114
  Lionel Plantagenet of
    Antwerp, Prince of
    England, Duke of
    xxxix, 107, 114,
    119, 126, 133, 134,
    305, 310, 317, 319,
    327, 333, 342, 347,
    349, 351, 355, 359,
    361, 363, 374, 379,
    384, 385, 389, 399,
    401, 414, 418, 425,
    431, 901, 904, 905
CLARENDON
  Edward Hyde, 1st Earl
    of 626, 678, 780
  Edward Hyde
    (Gov.), 3rd Earl of
    122, 679
  George William
    Villiers, 4th Earl of
    121
  Henry Hyde, 2nd
    Earl of 122
  Thomas Villiers, 1st
    Earl of 121
CLARK(E). *see also*
    CLERKE (CLARKE)
  Abigail (Maverick)
    632
  Agnes 607
  Anna "Nancy" 923

1141

Annabel Lucy 247
Anne 211, 535
Anne (Hyde) 427
Barbara (Murray)
   clxix, 211
Christopher
   Columbus 498
Colette 429
Deborah 129
Dinah 266
Ebenezer (III) 673
Elizabeth 245, 479,
   493, 715
Eunice (Pomeroy)
   673
Frances (Latham)
   (Dungan) xiii,
   241, 468, 488
Gabriella 498
George (Lieut. Gov.)
   427
Helen 825
Isabel 923
Jane Catherine 144
Jean 275
Jeremiah (Act. Gov.)
   xii, xiii, xiv, lix,
   clxiii, 241, 468, 488
Jerusha 673
John 923
John (Ivan John)
   246
John A. viii, 219
Lettice 783
Lucy Catherine
   Louisa 383
Lynn Rachel
   (Redgrave) xi,
   xvii, xlii, clvii, 246

Mary xiii, 241,
   468, 632, 923
Mary (Mackenzie),
   Lady 92
Matthew 632
Olive 924
Puma [Kelly] 247
Ralph 530
Rebecca 377, 670
Renata 223
Robert 92
Sarah 106, 589
Sarah (Pickering)
   923, 924
Susan Catherine
   (Overall) 498
Thomas 211
Ursula 530
CLARKSON
Cornelia (De
   Peyster) 898
David 750
Elizabeth (Kenrick)
   750
Katherine (Van
   Schaick) 750
Matthew lvi, clxiv,
   clxxvii, 750
CLARY
Désirée [Desideria],
   Queen of Sweden
   83, 198
Julie (Marie-Julie),
   Queen of Spain 83
Zénaïde 83
**CLARY AND ALD-
   RINGEN (VON)**
Francis Wenceslaus,
   Prince 208

Leontine, Countess
   16
Maria Josepha,
   Countess 208
CLAUDIA
Princess of Nassau-
   Hadamar 35
CLAUDIA (CLAUDE)
Princess of France
   637
CLAUSTRE (DE)
Marguerite 954
CLAXTON
Felicia 425
CLAYPOOLE
Adam 554
Dorothy (Wingfield)
   554
Edward 554
Elizabeth (___) 554
Elizabeth (Cecil)
   554
Elizabeth (Cromwell)
   554
family xxiv, l, 554
Helen (Mercer) 554
James lvi, lxv,
   lxvii, clxiv, 554
John 554
Mary (Angell) 554
Norton l, lvi, lxv,
   lxvii, cxlviii, 554
Rachel (___) 554
CLAYTON
Alice (Bowyer) 543
Charlotte xlix, liii,
   cli, 543, 781
Elizabeth (Whiting)
   543

John   xlviii, liii, cl,
    543
John (Sir)   543
Lucy (___)   543
Roger   cxci
CLAYTOR
Elizabeth   384
CLEEVE
George   810
Joan(na) (Price)
    lxiii, cxliii, clxii, 810
CLEMENT(S)
Augustine   584, 585
Elizabeth   555, 584
Elizabeth (Bullock)
    xxxv, lxi, cxliii,
    clx, clxxv, clxxix,
    86, 584, 586, 1025
Gloria (Hallward)
    [Gloria Grahame]
    xviii, 362
Mary   420
Stanley   362
**CLEMM VON
HOHENBERG**
Anna Christa Stefanie
    8
CLENCH
Catherine (Almott)
    680
Joan (Webbe)   680
John   680
Robert   680
Thomasine   xlviii,
    lxvii, cxlix, clxxx,
    680, 681
CLERE
Alice (Boleyn)   588
Anne   588

Anne (Tyrrell)   588
Edward (Sir)   588
family   589
Frances (Fulmerston)
    588
John (Sir)   588
Robert (Sir)   588
Susan   385
CLEREL (DE)
Bernard-Bonaventure,
    Count de Tocque-
    ville   293
Catherine-Antoinette
    (Damas)   293
Hervé-Louis-
    François, Count de
    Tocqueville   293
Louise-Madeleine
    (le Peltier)   293
**CLEREL DE
TOCQUEVILLE
(DE)**
Alexis-Henry
    [Alexis de
    Tocqueville]   xvii,
    294
Mary (Mottley)   294
CLERKE (CLARKE)
Elizabeth (Ferrers)
    467
Elizabeth (Wilsford)
    467
George   467
James   467
Jane   467
Mary (Saxby)   467
Mary (Weston)   467
William   467

**CLERMONT (DE)
(OF)**
Adeliza   845, 866,
    868, 869, 870
Agatha (de Poitiers)
    965
Aynard II, Vicomte
    965
Catherine-Marie
    (d'Escoubleau de
    Sourdis)   202
Charles-Henri,
    Count, Count de
    Tonnerre   202
counts   725
Geoffrey I, Seigneur
    965
Henri, Count de
    Tonnerre   202
Hugh I, Count   866,
    870
Isabeau   202
Isabella   186, 189
Isabella, Queen of
    Naples   186, 189
Robert, Prince of
    France, Count
    634, 638
Sybil   965
CLEVELAND
Aaron (IV)   500
Abiah (Hyde)   500
Anne (Neal)   500
Barbara (Villiers)
    Palmer, Duchess of
    22, 29, 33, 34, 109
Charles Fitzroy, 2nd
    Duke of, 1st Duke
    of Southampton   34

1143

Esther 335
Frances (Folsom)
  335, 500
Grover (Stephen
  Grover), 22nd and
  24th U.S. President
  335, 500
Margaret (Falley)
  500
Richard Falley 500
William 500
CLEVES
Adolf of, Count of
  Mark 459
Dietrich, Count of
  950
Engelberta of Mark
  and 459
Magdalena, Princess
  of 40, 43, 56
Marie Eleanor,
  Princess of 47,
  54, 56, 891
Mary 867
Matilda of 950
William III, Duke of,
  Duke of Juliers and
  Berg 40, 43, 54,
  56, 891
CLICK
Shannan 65
CLIFFORD
Agnes 653
Anne 384
Anne (Dacre) 361
Anne (St. John)
  317, 361, 384, 431
Anne Frances May 9

Catherine 401, 431
Dorothy 363
Eleanor (Brandon)
  62, 70, 79, 361
Elizabeth 317, 328,
  359, 413
Elizabeth (de Ros)
  469
Elizabeth (Percy)
  305, 317, 319, 328,
  342, 349, 359, 363,
  384, 385, 469
Florence (Pudsey)
  363
Frances 114, 361,
  362
Frances (Drury) 114
Francis, 4th Earl of
  Cumberland 362
Grisold (Hughes)
  362
Henry, 1st Earl of
  Cumberland 75,
  361, 401, 431
Henry, 2nd Earl of
  Cumberland 62,
  70, 75, 79, 361
Henry Clifford, 10th
  Baron 317, 361,
  363, 384, 431
Joan (Dacre) 317,
  318, 319, 328, 359,
  363, 384
John Clifford, 7th
  Baron 305, 317,
  319, 328, 342, 349,
  359, 363, 384, 385,
  469

John Clifford, 9th
  Baron 317, 328,
  363, 384
Margaret 62, 70,
  79, 904
Margaret (Brom-
  flete) 317, 328,
  363, 384
Margaret (Percy)
  75, 361, 401, 431
Mary 305, 342,
  349, 385
Matilda 319
Nicholas (Sir) 114
Philippa 466, 469,
  567, 592
Thomas Clifford,
  6th Baron 469
Thomas Clifford,
  8th Baron 317,
  319, 328, 359, 363,
  384
CLIFTON
Anne (Brent)
  cxlviii, 332, 904
Anne (Halsall) 904
Catherine 362
Catherine O'Brien,
  Baroness 122
Catherine Stuart,
  Baroness 122
Clifford (Sir) 362
Frances (Clifford)
  362
Frances (Finch) 362
Gervase (Sir), 1st
  Bt. 362
James xlviii,
  cxlviii, 332, 904

1144

Martha 302
Thomas 904
CLINCHAMP (DE)
  Anne 957
  Jeanne (de
    Bricqueville) 957
  Jeanne (de
    Caudecoste) 957
  Olivier, Seigneur de
    Mézerets 957
  Vigor, Seigneur de
    Mézerets 957
CLINKSCALES
  Elizabeth Ann 422
CLINTON
  Anne (Carle) 108
  Arbella, Lady 108
  Augusta 108
  Catherine 403
  Charles xlvii, 351
  Christiana xlvii, 351
  DeWitt (Gov.) 351
  Edmund (Adm.), 1st
    Earl of Lincoln 530
  Edward (Sir) 108
  Elizabeth
    (Denniston) 351
  Elizabeth (Kennedy)
    351
  Elizabeth (Knevet)
    108
  Elizabeth (Morrison)
    351
  Elizabeth (Smith)
    351
  Elizabeth "Bessy"
    (Blount) (Talboys)
    530
  family xxxvii

Francis 108
Francis, 6th Earl of
  Lincoln 108
George (Gov., Vice
  Pres.) 351
George (Hon.)
  (Gov.) 108
Harriet (Carter) 108
Henry (Sir) 108,
  113
Henry, 2nd Earl of
  Lincoln 107, 351
Hillary Diane
  (Rodham) (Sen.),
  U.S. Secretary of
  State 923, 969
Ida (de Odingselles)
  (de Herdeburgh)
  687, 749, 754, 757
Idonea (de Say)
  687
James 351
James (Gen.) 351
Joan 677
John de Clinton, 1st
  Baron 687, 749,
  754, 757
John de Clinton, 2nd
  Baron 687
John de Clinton, 3rd
  Baron 687
Katherine (Hastings)
  107, 109, 111
Margaret 687
Margery (Corbet)
  687
Mary (Deighton)
  108
Mary (DeWitt) 351

Priscilla (Hill) 108
Susan (Penniston)
  108
Susan, Lady 108,
  301
Thomas, 3rd Earl of
  Lincoln 107, 108
William 351
CLINTON alias
FYNES
  Elizabeth (Hickman)
    351
  Henry (Sir) 351
CLINTON-
BADDELEY. *see*
  also BADDELEY
  Constance Louisa
    (Dyer) 108
  Elizabeth 113
  family 113
  Frederick 113
  Frederick Henry 108
  Harriet 113
  Henry 113
  Henry Salkeld 108
  Hermione Youlanda
    Ruby [Hermione
    Baddeley] xvii,
    lxiii, clii, 78, 109,
    113
  Louise Rosalie
    (Bourdin) 108
  Madeleine Angela
    [Angela Baddeley]
    108
  Mary (O'Callaghan)
    108
  Paul Frederick Henry
    113

1145

Susan (le Mesurier)
  108
William 113
William Herman
  108
CLIPPINGER
Judith 4
CLIVEDON (DE)
Katherine 541,
  676, 691
CLOPTON
Anne (Booth)
  (Dennett) 483
Elizabeth (Sutcliffe)
  483
family lxii
Joan 547
Margaret (Maidstone)
  483
Margery
  (Waldegrave) 483
Thomasine liv,
  483, 714
Walter 483
William liv, clxvi,
  483
CLUNN
Florence 810
CLUYS (DE)
Alix 964
CLYDE
Elizabeth
  (Wellesley) 74
Jeremy (Michael
Jeremy Thomas)
  xviii, cliii, 74
Thomas 74
Vanessa (Field) 74

COATS
Audrey Evelyn
  (James) 68
Muir Dudley 68
COBB
Catherine 462
COBHAM
Anne Cobham, *de
  jure* Baroness 403
Eleanor 229, 231,
  233, 235
George Brooke, 9th
  Baron 315
Isabel 870
Joan 543, 595
Joan (de la Pole)
  Braybrooke,
  Baroness 543, 595
John Brooke, 7th
  Baron 314
John Cobham, 3rd
  Baron 543, 595
Margaret (Courtenay)
  543, 595
Thomas Brooke, 8th
  Baron 314
Thomas Cobham
  (Sir), *de jure* 5th
  Baron 403
William Brooke,
  10th Baron 315
COBLEIGH
Jane (Fortescue)
  672
John 672
Margaret 672
COCHRANE
Alexander lxx, 251
Anne (Murray) 62

Bethiah (Douglas)
  251
Catherine 62, 933
Elizabeth 128, 270
Hannah (de Witt/
  Worth) 128
Helen 98
Hugh, of
  Glanderston 251
Isabella (Ramsay)
  251
Jane (Stuart) 128
John 128
John (Sir) 128
John, 4th Earl of
  Dundonald 62
John, of Glanderston
  251
Lucy Douglas 63
Margaret 143
Margaret (Rae) 251
Margaret
  (Strickland) 128
Mary (Bruce) 128
Susannah 128
Thomas, 8th Earl of
  Dundonald 128
William 128
COCKAYNE
Judith 930
COCKBURN
Alexander (Sir), 4th
  Bt. 165
Alice 241
Andrew Myles
  xviii, xlvi, xlviii,
  cliii, 94
Claud (Francis
  Claud) 93

Eliza 34
Helen 165
Helen (Elphinstone) 165
Leslie Corkill (Redlich) 94
Margaret (Acheson) 165
Marion (Sinclair) 165
Olivia Jane [Olivia Wilde] xi, xviii, xlv, xlvi, xlviii, cliii, 21, 94
Patricia Evangeline Anne (Arbuthnot) 93
William (Sir), 1st Bt. 165
William (Sir), 2nd Bt. 165

COCKCROFT
Caleb 324
Elizabeth 324, 933
Elizabeth (Oxenbridge) 324, 326

COCKE
Anne 728
Anne (Goodere) 323
Elizabeth 170
Elizabeth (Catesby) clxvi, clxxx, 831, 1025
Elizabeth (Littleberry?) 728
Frances 320, 323
John 323
Katherine 170

Mary (Aston) 728
Richard 728
Richard, the younger 728
William 831

COCKWORTHY
Thomasine 632, 743

COCTEAU
Jean 227

CODD
Anne (Bennett) (Bland) 348
Anne (Hynson) (Randall) (Wickes) 348
Anne (Mottrom) (Wright) (Fox) 348
Mary (St. Leger) liii, 348
St. Leger liii, 348
William 348

CODDINGTON
Anne viii, li, lxiv, cxliii, 467, 469, 924
Dixie 467
Elizabeth 120, 433
Hannah 467
Hannah (Waller) 467
John Insley viii, xxviii, li, lii, liv, lvii, lxv, lxvi, 54, 83, 367, 726
Mary 480
Nicholas Dixie li, 469, 926

CODE
Anna/Anne (Whetenhall) 358
John 358

CODRINGTON
Elizabeth (___) 557
Giles 557
Henningham 557
Henningham (Drury) 557
Isabel (Porter) 557
Joyce (Borlase) 557
Richard 557
Robert 557

COËTIVY (DE)
Gillette 208
Louise 636
Olivier, Seigneur de Taillebourg 208

COETMOR
Ieuan 886
William 886

COFFIN
Elizabeth (___) 295, 522

COGAN
Frances clxxxv
Mary 361, 503, 539

COGHLAN
Eduardo A. 996

COKAYNE
Bridget 368
Elizabeth 667, 705, 716
George Edward ["G.E.C."] xxiv, li, 679

Ida (Grey) 705, 716
John 705, 716
COKE
Anne 628
Audrey 353
Catherine (Charlton) 325
Elizabeth (Robie) 325
family xxxiv, lv
John 325
Richard 325
Sarah (Hoge) 325
COKER
Elizabeth 741
COLAHAN
Mary Dorothea 545
COLBERT (DE)
Jean-Baptiste, Marquis of Seignelay 202
Marie-Henriette 202
COLBY
Anne (Archer) 539
John 539
Mary 539
Mary (Hobart) 539
Thomas 539
COLCLOUGH
Anne 382
COLDHAM
Peter Wilson xxix, li, 591
COLE
Anne (Mansfield) (Keayne) 318
Anne (Pinder) 925

Elizabeth 522
John 925
Margery 603
Martha 524
Mary 137, 925
Mary (Dering) 603
Mary (Waller) 603
Samuel 318
Solomon 603
Susanna (Hutchinson) 925
Thomas 603
William 925
COLE-HAMILTON
Arthur (Hon.) 179
Arthur Willoughby 179
Claud William 179
Emilia Katherine (Beresford) 179
Letitia (Hamilton) 179
Letitia Grace 179
Nicola Sophia (Chaloner) 179
COLEBROOK
Mary 85
COLEPEPPER/ CULPEPER
Agnes (Gainsford) 469, 551, 920
Agnes (Roper) (Bedgebury) 920, 922
Alexander 551
Anne (Aucher) 469
Anne (Slaney) 840
Catherine 129, 840

Cecily (Barrett) 467, 783, 839
Constance 551
Constance (Chamberlaine) 551
Elizabeth 157, 467, 469
Elizabeth (Cheney/Cheyne) 840
Elizabeth (Ferrers) 468
Elizabeth (Hawte) 551
Elizabeth (Sidley) 839
family lvii, 839, 1025
Frances 296, 347, 839, 856
Francis 840
Isabel 920
Isabel (Worsley) 468
Joan (Pordage) 840
John 347, 359, 839, 840
John (Sir) 469, 551, 920
John Colepepper/Culpeper, 1st Baron 840
Joyce 468, 476, 605
Judith (___) 347
Judith (Colepepper/Culpeper) 840
Katherine (St. Leger) liii, 296, 347, 839
Lettice (Clarke) 783

Margaret (___)
  (Bird) 347
Margaret (van Hesse)
  129, 840
Martin 783
Mary (___) 839
Mercy 396, 783
Richard 468
Samuel (Sir) 396
Sarah (Mayo) 347
Thomas lxiv,
  clxxvii, 296, 347,
  551, 839, 840
Thomas (Sir) 840
Thomas Colepepper/
  Culpeper (Gov.),
  2nd Baron clxxvii,
  129, 840
Ursula (Woodcock)
  839
Walter 469, 783,
  920, 922
William 467, 469,
  839
William (Sir) 468
COLES
  Mary Emma 146
  Ursula 858
COLIGNY (DE/OF)
  Anna Elizabeth de
    Sandersleben,
    Countess 184
  Anne 184
  Charles-François-
    Emanuel-Edwige
    de Pillot, Marquis
    184
  Charles-Ignace de
    Pillot, Marquis 184

Karl Leopold, Baron
  von l'Esperance
  and Sandersleben,
  Count 184
Thomas de Pillot,
  Seigneur de Chen-
  ecey, Marquis 184
COLKET
  Meredith Bright, Jr.
    xlviii, li, lviii, lxvi
**COLLACK alias
COLWYCK**
  Elizabeth 870
COLLAMORE
  Agnes (Adams)
    866
  Anthony lxiv,
    clxxx, clxxxviii,
    866, 867, 868
  Edith (___) 866
  Elizabeth 867
  Henry 867
  Joan 866
  John 866, 867
  Margaret (Blight)
    867
  Margery (Hext)
    866
  Mary (___) 866
  Mary (Nicholl)
    867
  Peter 866, 867
  Sarah (Chittenden)
    867
  Thomas 866
COLLES
  Anne (Thynne)
    385
  Eleanor 133

Elizabeth 385
Elizabeth (Darcy)
  385
family 386
Humphrey 385
John 385
Ursula 654
___ 385
COLLETON
  Anne 742, 743
  Anne (Kendall) 742
  Elizabeth 743
  James (Gov.) lxiii,
    742, 743
  John (Sir), 1st Bt.
    742
  Katherine (Amy)
    742
  Peter 742
  Thomas, Landgrave
    of South Carolina
    743
  Ursula (Hull) 742
  ___ (Mead) 743
COLLEY
  Elizabeth Isabella
    (Wingfield) 158
  Frances (Trench)
    157
  George Francis
    Pomeroy 157
  Gertrude Theodosia
    158
  Henry 157
  Henry FitzGeorge
    158
  Mary 157
  Mary (Hamilton)
    157

1149

COLLIER
Elizabeth 524
Gertrude Barbara Rich 130
Harriet (Nicholas) 130
Henry Theodosius Browne (Adm.) 130
Katherine Delano Price [Katherine Delano Price Collier St. George] 465
COLLINGBORNE
Joan 855
COLLINGRIDGE
Alice 642
Alice (Arundel) 642
Bartholomew 642
Sarah (___) 642
William 642
COLLINGWOOD
Dorothy 210
COLLINS
William xxvii
COLLOREDO-MANSFELD
Ferdinand, Count of 198
Ferdinand Johannes Hieronymus Maria, Count of 198
Ferdinand Peter Ernst, Count of 198
Franz de Paula Ferdinand Gundaccar, Count of 198
Franz Ferdinand Romanus, Count of liii, cliii, 198
Franz Gundaccar, Prince of 198
Joseph, Prince of 198
COLONNA
Andrea, Prince of Stigliano 189
Cecilia (Ruffo) 189
Clelia 190
COLQUHOUN
John (Sir), 1st Bt. 151, 170
John (Sir), 2nd Bt. 151
Lilias 151, 170
Lilias (Graham) 151, 170
Margaret (Baillie) 151
COLT
family 155
COLUMBELL
Elizabeth 530
COLUMBERS (DE)
Alice (Peneshurst) 695
Egeline (Courtenay) 672, 674, 695
Joan 695
John 695
Philip 672, 695
___ 672
COLVILLE
Margaret 282
COLVIN
___ 264

COMBE
Felicity 855
COMBERFORD
Dorothy (Fitz-Herbert) 757, 758
Henry 758
Mary 757
Thomas 757, 758
COMBES
Elizabeth (Roe) 512
COMBOURCIER (DE)
Claude 202
COMIN/COMING.
see CUMING/CUMMING/CUMMINGS
COMMEQUIERS (DE)
Eustache du Bellay, Seigneur 942
COMMERCY (DE)
Aimé de Sarrebruche, Seigneur 944
Robert de Sarrebruche, Seigneur 944
COMMINGES (DE)
Pétronille 959
COMNENUS
John I, Emperor of Byzantium 956
COMPTON
Cecily 110
Charlotte, Baroness Ferrers of Chartley 112
Elizabeth 614

Elizabeth (Shirley),
 Baroness Ferrers of
 Chartley 112
Elizabeth (Spencer)
 111
Frances (Hastings)
 111
George, 4th Earl of
 Northampton 112
Henry Compton, 1st
 Baron 111
James, 3rd Earl of
 Northampton 112
James, 5th Earl of
 Northampton 112
Jane (Fox) 112
Mary 105
Mary (Beaumont)
 111
Mary (Noel) 112
Spencer, 1st Earl of
 Wilmington 112
Spencer, 2nd Earl of
 Northampton 111
William, 1st Earl of
 Northampton 111
COMSTOCK
 Anselm 630, 886
 Betsey 630, 887
 Elizabeth (Jewett)
  630, 886
COMYN
 Alexander (Sir), of
  Altyre 281
 Alexander, 2nd Earl
  of Buchan 843
 Alice (de Ros) 721
 Elizabeth 843

Elizabeth (de
 Quincy) 843
Euphemia (Dunbar)
 281
Hextilda (of Tyne-
 dale) 828
Isabel 721
Jean 281, 828
Joan 697
John (Sir) 721
Margaret (Gordon),
 of Haddo 281
Marjory 732
Maud (___) 721
Richard 828
Sarah (FitzHugh) 828
Thomas (Sir), of
 Altyre 281
William, 1st Earl of
 Buchan 828
CONAN I
 Duke of Brittany
  879, 919
CONCHES (DE)
 Philip of Artois,
  Seigneur 961, 963
CONFIGNON (DE)
 Marie 872
CONGDON
 Pauline Ellen Laing
  101, 102
CONINCK (DE)
 Frederic 634
 Jean 634
 Louise-Philippine
  634
 Marie (de Joncourt)
  634
 Marie-Henriette 635

Susanne-Esther (de
 Rapin) 634
CONINGSBY
 Amphyllis 713
 Barbara (Gorges)
  405, 406
 Cecily (Neville)
  405
 FitzWilliam 405
 Humphrey 405
 Letitia 405
 Lettice (Loftus) 405
 Thomas Coningsby,
  1st Earl of 405
CONNAUGHT
 Geoffrey
  Osbaldeston, Chief
  Justice of 433
 kings of xl
 Turlough Oge
  O'Conor Don,
  King of 885
CONRAD III
 Duke of Mazovia
  621
CONSTABLE
 Agnes (Wentworth)
  719
 Anne 123, 403, 719
 Anne (Roper) 123
 Anne (Sherborne)
  123
 Barbara 127, 131
 Catherine 123, 401
 Catherine (Holme)
  343
 Eleanor 336, 598
 Elizabeth (Stokes)
  344

1151

Everilda 131
Frances 343
Frances (Metham) 123
Francis 719
Henry (Sir) 401
Isabel 667, 668
Jane (Conyers) 123, 126
Joan 668
Joan (Fulthorpe) 344, 719
Joan (Neville) 402
John (Sir) 401, 402, 667
Katherine 126
Katherine (Manners) 126
Lora (FitzHugh) 667
Margaret (Brigham) 719
Margaret (Dormer) 401, 402
Margaret (Radcliffe) 123
Margaret (Scrope) 401
Margaret (Tyrwhit) 123
Margery 725
Margery/Mariora 667, 668
Marmaduke 343, 344
Marmaduke (Sir) 123, 126, 127, 131
Marmaduke (Sir), 2nd Bt. 123
Philip (Sir) 123

Philip (Sir), 1st Bt. 123
Philip (Sir), 3rd Bt. 123
Robert 719
Robert (Sir) 126, 719
Sarah 532
William (Sir) 344, 719
___ 719
___ (Arden) 719

CONSTABLE-MAXWELL
Angela Mary 72
Angela Mary Charlotte (Fitzalan-Howard) 72
Anne Mary Teresa 72
Marmaduke Francis, 11th Baron Herries 72

CONSTANCE
Princess of Hungary, Queen of Galicia 621
Princess of Sicily, Queen of Aragón 51, 642
of Provence, Queen of France 851, 853, 855

CONSTANTINE
Grand Duke of Russia 7
Prince Bagration-Mukhransky 7

CONSTANTINE II
Prince of Rostov and Uglich 791, 797

CONSTANTINE III
Prince of Rostov 791, 797

CONSTANTINOPLE
Baldwin IX, Count of Flanders, Emperor of 774, 776
Beatrix, Princess of Naples, Empress of 961
Berengaria, Princess of León and Castile, Queen of Jerusalem, Empress of 909, 948, 964
John de Brienne, King of Jerusalem, Emperor of 647, 909, 945, 948, 964
Marie of Champagne, Countess of Flanders, Empress of 774, 776
Peter I, King of 965
Philip de Courtenay, Emperor of 952, 961, 965
Yolande of Hainault, Empress of 965

CONTI SCHEIBLER (DEI)
Anna 24

CONWAY
Avice 325
Edwin 497

Edwin, Jr. 497, 532
Eleanor Rose 497, 532
Elizabeth (Thornton) 497, 532
Eltonhead 497
family xxiv
Frances 497
Francis 532
Kathryn 949
Martha (Eltonhead) clxvi, clxxiii, 497
Rebecca (Catlett) 497, 532
CONWY
Jonet 686
CONY
Susan 613
CONYERS
Agnes 419
Agnes (Bowes) 421
Alice 877
Alice (Neville) 419
Anne 105
Anne (Dawney) 421
Christopher 419
Christopher (Sir) 725
Eleanor 421
Ellen (Rolleston) 725
family 381
George (Sir) 421
Jane xlii, 123, 126
Joan 725
John (Sir) 421, 725

Margaret 697
Margaret (St. Quintin) 725
COOK(E)
Andrew 628
Andrew (Sir) 628
Anna (Caunton) 684
Anne 628
Anne (Bowyer) 628
Anne (Brooke) 628
Anne (FitzWilliam) 684
Anne (Goodere) 852
Anthony (Sir) 684
Ebenezer 628
Edmund 852
Edward 628
Elizabeth 665
Elizabeth (Babington) 628
Elizabeth (Haynes) lxiv, cxliii, 587
Elizabeth (Nichols) 852
family 628
Henry 852
Jane 684, 877
Joan 548
John Hutchinson vi
Joseph 587
Lucy 855
Mary 486, 560, 852
Matilda 579
Mildred 68, 315, 684
Penelope Anne 65

Philippa 684
Raeola Ford 585
Richard (Sir) 684
Stephena Verdel 5, 793
Theodora 852
Thomas 628
COOKSON
Elizabeth 100
COOLEY
Carey (Shands) 458
Elizabeth Armistead 458
Hollis Welbourn 458
COOLIDGE
Calvin 526
Calvin Galusha 342, 526, 814, 882
Grace Anna (Goodhue) 342, 526, 748, 758, 814, 882
Hannah (Priest) 526
John 526
John Calvin 342, 526, 747, 758, 814, 882
John Calvin, Jr., 30th U.S. President 342, 526, 748, 758, 814, 882
Josiah 526
Mary (Jones) 526
Obadiah, Jr. 526
Rachel (Goddard) 526
Sarah (Thompson) 526

1153

Sarah Almeda
  (Brewer) 342,
  526, 814, 882
Victoria Josephine
  (Moor) 342, 526,
  747, 758, 814, 882
COOMBS
Claire 201
COOPER
Agnes Cecil
  Emmeline (Duff)
  9, 10
Alfred (Sir) 9, 10
Anne (Spencer),
  Lady 299
Anne Frances May
  (Clifford) 9
Anthony Ashley, 7th
  Earl of Shaftesbury
  299
Cropley Ashley, 6th
  Earl of 299
Diana Olivia
  Winifred Maud
  (Manners) [Lady
  Diana Cooper] 9
Duff (Alfred Duff),
  1st Viscount
  Norwich 9
Ellen Emily 433
John Julius, 2nd
  Viscount Norwich
  9
Mary (Makins)
  (Hon.) 9
May Somerville
  (Bunny) 563
Stephanie Agnes 10
Sybil Mary 10

COOTE
Catherine (Nanfan)
  107, 462
Letitia 462
Mary (St. George)
  462
Richard, 1st Baron
  Coote of Coloony
  462
Richard, 1st Earl of
  Bellomont (Gov.)
  107, 462
COPE
Bridget (Raleigh)
  478, 480
Elizabeth 123, 423,
  478, 481
Elizabeth (Fane) 122
Isabel 135
Joan 478
John (Sir) 478
Oliver cxc
William 122
COPES
Josina (Schade van
  Westrum) 907
Moralla Catharina
  907
Otto 907
COPES VAN
VORDEN
Hendrik 907
Moralla Jans (van
  Gendt) 907
COPLESTONE
Agnes 870
COPLEY
Anne (Boteler)
  302, 600

Anne (Cressy) 600
Anne (Hoo) 473,
  580
Catherine (Luttrell)
  493
Eleanor 426, 477,
  603, 642
Frisalina (Warde)
  600
Lionel 600
Lionel (Gov.) 302,
  600
Magdalen (Prideaux)
  493
Margaret 580
Mary 331
Rebecca 867
Roger (Sir) 473, 580
Thomas 494
Thomas (Rev.) 493
Thomas (Sir) 493
William 493, 600
CORBEIL
François 987
Olive 987
Thérèse (Maison-
  neuve) 987
CORBET(T)
Anna 412
Anne 233
Anne (Barrett) 711
Anne (Windsor) 501
Catherine 534, 711
Dorothy 500, 501
Elizabeth 349
Elizabeth (Devereux)
  500, 534
Elizabeth (Hopton)
  233, 319, 534

Elizabeth (Vernon)
  319, 412, 500
Jane 319
Margaret 501, 506
Margaret (___)
  534, 746
Margery 687
Mary 233, 534, 746
Richard (Sir) 500,
  534
Robert 534, 746
Robert (Sir) 319,
  412, 500
Roger (Sir) 233,
  319, 501, 534
Sybil 739, 957
Thomas 711
CORBIN
Alice 329
Alice (Eltonhead)
  (Burnham) xix,
  xxxiv, clxvi,
  clxxiii, 329, 498,
  607, 697
family xxiv
Frances 607
Henry xix, xxxiv, lx,
  clxvi, clxxv, 329,
  498, 607, 697, 699
Thomas 697
Winifred
  (Grosvenor) 697
CORDAY (DE)
Hélène 959
**CORDIER DE
LAUNAY DE
MONTREUIL**
Renée-Pélagie 227

CORDOVA
family 190
CORDRAY
Anna xl, lxiv,
  clxvi, clxxvi, 495,
  737, 741, 930
Bridget 738
Bridget (Goddard)
  737, 740
Eleanor 737
family 737, 741
Jane (Morris) 740
Jane (Seymour) 740
John 737
Samuel 737
Sarah (___) 737
Thomas 740
William 737, 740
CORE
Mary (Humphries)
  768
CORIA
García Alvarez de
  Toledo, Marquess
  of 191
**CORK and
ORRERY**
John Boyle, 5th Earl
  of 73
CORNELL
Elizabeth 764
CORNISH
Agnes (Walden)
  881
Iodena (Hunt) 881
John 881
Margaret 882
Mary 882
Thomas 881

CORNOD
Claude de Seyturier,
  Seigneur 952
CORNWALEYS. *see
also* CORNWALLIS/
CORNWALEYS
**CORNWALL alias
BIRCHARD**
Drusilla (Austin)
  702
Roger 702
**CORNWALL/
CORNEWALL**
Anne (Corbet) 233
Edmund 530, 553,
  555, 603
Eleanor 233, 553,
  555, 603
Elizabeth (Barre)
  530, 553, 555, 603
Elizabeth
  (Devereux) 233
H.R.H. The Duchess
  of [Camilla
  Rosemary Shand
  Parker Bowles]
  655, 656, 930
Joan 653, 661
Joan (___) 653,
  661
Joan of 672
Piers de Gaveston,
  1st Earl of 698,
  847
Reginald FitzRoy or
  de Mortain, Earl of
  739, 957
Richard (Sir) 653,
  661

Richard Plantagenet, Earl of, King of the Romans xxxix, 652, 653, 661, 672, 965
Thomas (Sir) 233
___ 702
CORNWALLIS
Affra 509
Anne (Fincham) 494, 596
Anne (Jernegan) 596
Charles (Sir) 494, 596
Charles Cornwallis (Gen.), 2nd Marquess 64, 597
Elizabeth clxxxvii, 426, 494, 508
Elizabeth (Parker) 596
Elizabeth (Stanford) clxxxvii, 508
family clxxxvii, 597
Jemima 64
John (Sir) 508, 596
Mary (Sulyard) 508, 596
Penelope (Wiseman) 596
Philippa (Tyrrell) 508
Thomas 508
Thomas (Sir) 596
William clxxxvii, 508
William (Sir) 596

CORNWALLIS/ CORNWALEYS
Thomas lx, cli, 508, 596, 597
CORNWALLIS-WEST
Beatrice Stella (Tanner) [Mrs. Patrick Campbell] 585, 648
George Frederick Myddleton 585, 648
Jennie (Jerome) (Spencer-Churchill) 584, 585, 648
CORON
Marie-Louise 976
CORREALE
Clelia (Colonna) 190
Francesco Maria, Count of Terranova 190
Matilda 190
CORTÉS
Hernán, 1st Marquess del Valle de Oaxaca 191
Juana (de Zuñiga y Arellano) 191
Juana Estefanía, Marquesa del Valle de Oaxaca 191, 192
CORTÉS (DE MONROY)
Ana (de Arellano) 191

Martín, 2nd Marquess del Valle de Oaxaca 191
CORTÉS Y ARELLANO
Juana 192
CORWIN
Matthew cxc
COSBY
Alexander 307
Anne (Loftus) 307
Dorcas (Sidney) 307
Elizabeth 33
Elizabeth (L'Estrange) 307
Elizabeth (Pigott) 307
Francis 307
Grace (Montagu) 33, 115, 307
Mary (Seymour) 307
Richard 307
William (Gov.) 33, 115, 307
COSIMO I
de' Medici, Grand Duke of Tuscany 191, 192
COSSÉ (DE)
Catherine-Françoise-Charlotte 288
COSSINS
Elizabeth Susanna (Thicknesse-Touchet) 111
John 111

Sarah Beresford 111
CÖSTER
  Maria Louisa Cecilia
    Vilhelmina 51
CÔTÉ
  Danielle 960
  Jean-René 951
  Marie-Catherine 988
  Marie-Josephte 987
COTTINGTON
  Grace (Popley) 855
  James 855
  Jane 856
  Jane (Byfleet) 855
  Philip 855, 856
COTTON
  Alice (Abbot) 579, 877
  Alice (Conyers) 877
  Audrey 574, 878
  Bridget 426
  Bridget (Hoar) 297
  Catherine 579
  Clement clxxxiv
  Constance (Leventhorpe) clxxxiv
  Edmund 877
  Elizabeth 877
  family vii
  Frances 500
  George 877, 878
  Hannah (Freese) 297, 298
  Jane (Goldingham) 877
  Joan (FitzHerbert) 757, 758
  Joan (Rede) clxxxiv, 877
  John 757, 758
  John (Rev.) lx, clxxxiv, 579
  Leonard cxliii, clxxii, 297, 298
  Lucy 335
  Margaret (Howard) 335
  Margaret/Margery 757
  Mary (Mainwaring) 500
  Maud 697
  Richard 500
  Thomas (Rev.) 297
  Thomas (Sir), 2nd Bt. 335
  Walter clxxxiv, 877
  William 579, 877
  Winifred 603
COUCY (DE)
  Agnes 804
  Aubert, Seigneur de Dronai 633
  Blanche 944
  Guillaume, Seigneur 633, 944
  Isabel (de Châtillon) 633, 944
  Jeanne (de Harcourt) 944
  Jeanne (de Ville-Savoir) 633
  Marie 633
  Raoul, Seigneur de Montmirel 944
  Raoul I, Sire 804
  Yolande 956
COUDENHOVE (DE)
  Charlotte (de Baudrenghien) 438
  Jacqueline (Triest) 438
  Jean, Seigneur de Gendtbrugghe 438
  Jeanne 438
  Nicolas de Coudenhove, Seigneur 438
COUDRÉE (DE)
  Henri d'Allinges, Seigneur 872
COULOGNE (DE)
  Nicolas d'Aillebouet, Seigneur 940
COUPAR ANGUS
  Donald Campbell, Abbot of 280
COUPET
  Cecile 109
COURCELLES (DE)
  Jean-Baptiste-Pierre-Julien xxvii
COURLAND
  Frederick Casimir, Duke of 56
  James, Duke of 54, 56
  Louise Elizabeth of 54, 55
  Marie Dorothea, Princess of 56
  William, Duke of 54, 56

COURSELLES (DE)
  Antoinette 953
COURSEULLES DE BERNIÈRES (DE)
  Raoul II de Meulan, Seigneur 957
  Raoul III de Meulan, Seigneur 957
COURSEULLES-SUR-MER (DE)
  Raoul de Meulan, Seigneur 957
COURSEY
  Elizabeth 281
COURSOLLES
  Charlotte 655
COURTENAY (DE)
  Agnes (St. John) 824
  Anne (Wake) 569, 573
  Antoine de Boulainvilliers, Count of 205
  Catherine 961
  Edward 522
  Edward (Sir) 547
  Egeline 672, 674, 695, 713
  Eleanor 965
  Eleanor (le Despencer) 713, 739, 824
  Elizabeth 423, 503, 550, 569, 573, 608, 742, 965
  Elizabeth (___) 547, 573
  Elizabeth (Gorges) 295, 296, 522
  Elizabeth (Hungerford) 569, 570, 573
  Emeline (Daunay) 547
  family xli, 952
  Gertrude 436
  Hugh (Sir) 547, 550, 713, 739, 824
  Hugh, 1st Earl of Devon 824
  Hugh, 2nd Earl of Devon 503, 543, 547, 569, 573, 595, 608
  Isabel 739
  Isabel (de Vere) 739
  Jane (Fowell) 573
  Joan 547
  Joan (Champernowne) 569, 570, 573
  John (Sir) 569, 573, 739
  Margaret 543, 547, 595, 824
  Margaret (Carminow) 550
  Margaret (de Bohun) 503, 543, 547, 569, 573, 595, 608
  Mary (de Vernon) 672, 695, 739
  Maud (Beaumont) 550
  Muriel (de Moels) 824
  Peter, Prince of France, Seigneur 965
  Philip 573
  Philip (Sir) 547, 569, 573
  Philip, Emperor of Constantinople 952, 961, 965
  Philippa (l'Archdekne) 547, 550
  Philippe de Boulainvilliers, Count of 205
  Robert (Sir) 672, 695, 739
  Thomas (Sir) 824
COURTHOPE
  Frances 605
COUTIER
  Marie-Anne 293
COUTURE
  Angélique 980
  Angélique (Roy) 980
  Charles 973, 980
  Geneviève 973
  Jeanne (Huard) 972
  Joseph 980
  Joseph-Ange 972
  Marie-Anne (Huard) 973, 980
  Marie-Louise 972
COUTURIER dit LA BONTÉ
  Anne-Élisabeth (de Tarragon) 948, 985

Gertrude (Maugras) 985
Gilles 948, 985
Joseph 985
Marguerite 985
Marguerite (Caron) 985
Marie-Louise (Allard) 985
Michel 985
Pierre 985
COUVENT
Anne 945, 967, 969, 972, 973, 975, 976, 977, 978, 979, 980, 981, 982
Antoinette (de Longueval) 945
Charlotte 945
family 967, 968
Guillaume 945
COVENTRY
Mary 779
Samuel Butler, Bishop of Lichfield and 475, 476
COVERT
Anne (Covert) 691
Anne (Hendley) 691
Charity (Bowes) 691
Elizabeth clxxv, 366, 691
John 691
Richard 691
Walter (Sir) 691
COWAN
Sophronia C. 422
COWARD
Alice (Britton) 508

Arthur Sabin 242
Deliverance 508, 726
Hugh 508
John 508
Noël Pierce xvii, lvii, lxxix, cxliii, clxxi, 240, 242
Patience (Throckmorton) 508
Violet Agnes (Veitch) 242
COWDRAY
Weetman Harold Miller Pearson, 2nd Viscount 80
COX
Anne 314, 721
Frances 268
Mary 167
COXE
Elizabeth 648
COYTMORE
Alice 376
Elizabeth xxxv, li, 375
Jane (Williams) 375
Katherine (Myles) (Gray) 375, 701
Martha (Rainsborough) 375
Rowland 375, 376, 701
Thomas 375
William 375
CRABBE
Madeleine Augusta 100

CRACROFT/ CRAYCROFT
Anne (___) 604
John vii, viii, l, clxxv, clxxix, 604
Martha (Amcotts) 604
Robert 604
CRADOCK
Charlotte 368
Damaris 580
Hannah 111
Margaret 808
CRAIG
Carol Mary (Williams) 362
Daniel Wroughton xii, liii, cliii, 362
family 362
Fiona (Loudon) 362
Francis Northrop xlviii, li, lv, lix, lxviii
Rachel (Weisz) 362
Rosalinde Maud (Jones) 362
Timothy John Wroughton 362
William John Gartland 362
CRAIGHEAD (CRAGHEAD)
Agnes (Heart/Hart) 87
Alexander 87
Catherine cxlix, cli, clxi, 87

family xlviii, lxx
Margaret (Wallace) 87
Robert (Rev.) 87
Thomas (Rev.) cxlviii, 87
CRAIGIE
Catherine 90
CRALL
Leander Howard lii
CRAM
Jeanne Louise (Campbell) (Mailer), Lady 70, 371
John Sergeant 70
CRAMM (VON)
Armgard Cunigunde Alharda Agnes Oda 47
Barbara Woolworth (Hutton) (Mdivani) (Haugwitz- Hardenberg-Reventlow) (Grant) (Troubetzkoy) (Rubirosa) xviii, 44, 46, 63
CRAMOND
Anne 150
CRANAGE
Dorothy 319
CRANDALL
Ralph James v, vi
CRANE
Elizabeth 345
Frances Anita 635
Robert (Sir), 1st Bt. 345

Susan (Alington) 345
CRANSTON
Christian (Stewart) 241
Elizabeth (Stewart) 90
Isabella 90
James (Hon.) 90
James (Rev.) 241
John (Gov.) lxix, clxiii, clxxi, clxxix, clxxxviii, 240, 241, 242, 468
John, of Bold 241
Mary (Clarke) 241, 468
CRAON (DE)
Isabel 634
Marie 947
CRASTER
Alice (Mitford) 328
Edmund 328
Eleanor (Forster) 328
George 328
Isabel 328
CRATHORNE
Everilda (Constable) 131
Katherine 131
Thomas 131
CRAUFORD. see CRAWFORD
CRAVEN
Christopher (Gov.) 321
Elizabeth (Staples) 321

Margaret (Clapham) 321
William (Sir) 321
CRAWFORD/ CRAUFORD
Alexander Lindsay, 2nd Earl of 282
Anna 253
Annabella 144
Anne (Lamont) 173
Barbara 173
David, of Kerse 150
David Lindsay, 1st Earl of 275, 276, 282, 285
David Lindsay, 3rd Earl of 282
David Lindsay, 9th Earl of 282
Elizabeth 214, 307
Elizabeth (Cunyngham) 214
James, of Crosbie 214
Jane (Crawford) 214
Joan (Fleming) 150
Marion 150
Martha Sharp "Sunny" 646
Mary Ann 764
Patrick, of Auchenames 214
William, of Auchenames 173

1160

CRAYCROFT. *see*
CRACROFT/
CRAYCROFT
CRAYFORD
 Anne 778
 Anne (Norton) 778
 Edward 778
 John 778
 Margaret (Crispe)
  778
 Mary (Atsea) 778
 William (Sir) 778
CRAZE
 Mary 744
CREEK/CREYKE
 Alice (Eltonhead)
  (Burnham)
  (Corbin) xix,
  xxxiv, clxvi,
  clxxiii, 329, 498,
  607, 697
 Henry 498
CREIGHTON
 Jennie 44
CRERAR
 Ann 82, 83
CRESSET
 Jane (Corbet) 319
 Joan (Wrottesley)
  319
 Margaret 319
 Richard 319
 Thomas 319
CRESSWELL
 Catherine clxxxv
 Elizabeth (Lumley?)
  clxxxv
 Lionel 826, 827
 Robert clxxxv

CRESSY
 Anne 600
 Eleanor (Evering-
  ham) 600
 Gervase 600
 Susanna 116
CRESWICK
 Elizabeth 340
CREWE
 Charlotte (Lee)
  (Calvert), Lady,
  Baroness
  Baltimore clxv,
  29, 340
 Christopher 29
CREYE (DE)
 Joan 880
CREYKE
 Katherine 131
 Katherine
  (Crathorne) 131
 Margaret (Thorn-
  borough) 131
 Ralph 131
CRICHTON
 Catherine
  (Borthwick) 219
 Catherine
  (Carmichael) 143
 Christian 275, 276,
  285
 Elizabeth 143, 176,
  241
 Elizabeth (Fleming)
  143
 Elizabeth (Seton)
  143
 Elizabeth (Swift) 143
 Emily Florence 179

 Henry George Louis
  (Hon.) (Sir) 179
 James (Sir) 219
 James Crichton, 2nd
  Baron 219
 Janet 160, 223, 898
 Janet (Dunbar) 219
 Letitia Grace (Cole-
  Hamilton) 179
 Margaret 219
 Margaret (Stewart)
  219
 Marion (Livingston)
  219
 William 143
 William, 1st Earl of
  Dumphries 143
 William, 2nd Earl of
  Dumphries 143
 William Crichton,
  3rd Baron 219
 William Crichton,
  5th Baron 143
**CRIECHINGEN
 (VON)**
 Antoinette Elisabeth
  208
CRIOL (DE)
 Ida 883
 John (Sir) 883
 Lettice (___) 883
 Margery (Pecche)
  883
 Nicholas (Sir) 883
 Rohesia (___) 883
CRIPPS
 Evelyn Florence 321
 Mary (Splatt) 311
 William 311

CRISLI
  ferch Adam Fychan 808
CRISP
  Frederick Arthur xxi, clxxxvii
CRISPE
  Agnes (Queke) 778
  Anne (Phillips or Fettiplace) 778
  Avice (Denne) 778
  Elizabeth 419
  family 1025
  Henry 778
  Joan (Dyer) 778
  Joan (Sevenoaks) 778
  John 778
  Margaret 778
  Matilda (Harcourt) 778
CROCHRODE
  Anne 826, 827
  Anne (Mordaunt) 826
  Thomas 826
CROCKER/CROKER
  Agnes (Bonville) 595
  Alice (Dormer) 642
  Anstice (Tripp) 595
  Beula Benton (Edmondson) 480
  Elizabeth (Frazier) 480
  Eyre Coote clxxiii, 480
  family 643
  Frances (Welstead) 480
  Francis 595
  George 595
  Harriet (Dillon) 480
  Henry xviii, 480
  Hugh 595
  Isabel (Skinner) 642
  John 480, 642
  Margery 642, 643
  Mary (Pennefather) 480
  Richard 595
  Richard Welstead xviii, 480
  Tabitha 595
  Thomas 642
  ___ (Pascoe) 595
CROFT
  Anne 530, 553, 614, 824
  Anne (Fox) 824
  Edward 555
  Eleanor (Cornwall) (Mortimer) 530, 553, 555, 603
  Elizabeth 505
  Janet (ferch Owain) 824
  Joan 864
  John (Sir) 824
  Joyce (Skull) 555
  Margaret clxxxiv, 555
  Margaret (Walwyn) 824
  Richard (Sir) 530, 553, 555, 603
  Richard, the younger 824
  William 824
CROFTON
  Charlotte (Stewart) 63
  Edward (Sir), 3rd Bt. 63
  Frederica 63
CROISSET (DE). *see* WIENER DE CROISSET
CROMARTY
  George Mackenzie, 1st Earl of 92, 897
  George Mackenzie, 3rd Earl of 92
  John Mackenzie, 2nd Earl of 92
CROMBOCK
  Jennett 841
CROMER
  Alice (Hawte) 474, 552
  Anne 357, 466, 606, 721, 783
  Anne (Wotton) 474
  Barbara 474
  Catherine (Cantilupe/Cantelow) 474, 783
  Dorothy 474, 477
  Elizabeth (Fiennes) 783
  Elizabeth (Guilford) 474, 475
  Evelyn Baring, 1st Earl of 123

James 474
James (Sir) 474, 783
William 474, 783
William (Sir) 474, 552
CROMWELL
Anne 307
Dorothy 476
Edward Cromwell, 3rd Baron 307
Elizabeth 349, 466, 534, 554
Elizabeth (Bromley) 534
Elizabeth (Seymour) 307
family 709
Frances 307, 308, 781
Frances (Rugge) 307
Gregory Cromwell, 1st Baron 307
Henry Cromwell, 2nd Baron 307, 308, 349
Joan 114
Mary (Paulet) 307, 349
Maud 684
Maud (Bernacke) 684
Oliver (Sir) 534
Oliver, Lord Protector 114, 130, 466, 476, 534, 554, 781
Ralph Cromwell, 2nd Baron 684

CRONHIELM
Beata 889
CRONSTEDT
Claes 60
Nina Maria (Nane) (Lagergren) viii, lxiv, cxlii, 60
CROPHILL/ CROPHULL
Agnes 647, 909
John (Sir) 647, 909
Margery (de Verdun) 647, 909
Sybil (Delabere) 647, 909
Thomas 647, 909
CROSBIE
Anne 434
Margaret 405
CROSBY
Frances Coffin 144
CROSHAW
Unity 300
CROSLEY
Mary 505
CROSS
Elizabeth 325, 825, 852
Jacomine (___) xx
John xx
Mary 130
Thomasine xx
CROWLEY
Mary 231
CROWNE
Agnes (Mackworth) (Watts) 319
William 319

CROWNINSHIELD
family xxxvi
Helen Suzette 183
CROWTHER
G. Rodney lii
CROY
Alfred, Prince of, 10th Duke of 38
Berthe-Rosine-Ferdinande of 38
Charles-Alexander, Duke of 292
Marie-Anna-Charlotte-Joséphine 292
Marie-Claire of 292
CROY-HAVRE
Ferdinand-Joseph-François, Duke of 292
Jean-Baptiste-François-Joseph, Duke of 292
Philip-Antoine-José de Palafox y 292
Philip-Francis, Duke of 292
CROZIER
Helen 96
William Armstrong xxix
CRUMPTON
Jane (___) 319
CRUZ (DE)
Antoine-Louis Damas, Count 293
Étienne Damas, Count 293
François Damas, Count 293

Louis-Alexander
　Damas, Count
　293
CRYMES
　Alice (Lovell)　426
　Christiana (___)
　　426
　George (Sir), 1st Bt.
　　426
　Margaret (More)
　　426
　Mary (Bond)　426
　Thomas (Sir)　426
　Thomas (Sir), 2nd
　　Bt.　426
　William　lxiv
　William (Dr.)
　　cxlviii, 426
CUBITT
　Ronald Calvert, 3rd
　　Baron Ashcombe
　　655
　Rosalind Maud
　　(Hon.)　655
　Sonia Rosemary
　　(Keppel)　655
CUDWORTH
　Damaris　580
　Damaris (Cradock?)
　　580
　family　581
　James　lxiv, clx,
　　clxxv, 580
　Jane　581
　Mary (Machell)
　　580, 581
　Mary (Parker)　580
　Ralph　580

CULCHETH
　Anne　366
CULEMBORG (VAN)
　Aleid　459
　Jasper, Heer van
　　Werth　445
　Jeanne (de
　　Bourgogne)　445
　Magdalena　445
　Sophia　633
CULLEN-WARD
　Susan Barbara,
　　Queen of the
　　Albanians　935
CULLICK
　Elizabeth (Fenwick)
　　330
CULVERWELL
　___　701
CUMBERBATCH
　Abraham Perry　101
　Benedict Timothy
　　Carlton　xi, xvii,
　　xlviii, cliii, 101,
　　179
　Caroline (Chaloner)
　　101
　Helene Gertrude
　　(Rees)　101
　Henry Alfred　101
　Henry Carlton　101,
　　102
　Louisa (Hanson)
　　101
　Pauline Ellen Laing
　　(Congdon)　101,
　　102
　Robert Cecil　102
　Robert William　101

　Sophie Irene
　　(Hunter)　xlviii,
　　cliii, 101, 179
　Timothy Carlton
　　[Timothy Carlton]
　　101
　Wanda (Ventham)
　　101
CUMBERLAND
　Francis Clifford, 4th
　　Earl of　362
　Henry Clifford, 1st
　　Earl of　75, 361,
　　401, 431
　Henry Clifford, 2nd
　　Earl of　62, 70, 75,
　　79, 361
**CUMMINGS/CUM-
MING/ COMING(S)/
COMINS**
　Abigail (Wesson)
　　272
　Affra (Harleston)
　　349
　Alexander　281
　Alexander (Sir), 2nd
　　Bt.　272
　Amy (Whitehall)
　　272
　Anna (Tulloch)　281
　Anne　261, 262
　David　281
　Elizabeth (Coursey)
　　281
　Grace Dunlop　129
　Griselle/Graca　90
　Helen (Cuming)
　　xlviii, cxlviii, 272
　Isabella　272

Jean (Rose)   281
John   349
John (Dr.)   272
Margaret (Leslie), of Aikenway   281
Robert   272
William   lix, cxlviii, 281
William, Jr.   281
William, of Presley   281

CUNIGUNDE. *see also* **KUNIGUNDE**
of Parma, Queen of Italy   879, 919
Princess of Germany, Queen of Bohemia   640

CUNNINGHAM/ CUNYNGHAM/ CUNINGHAM(E)
Alexander, 5th Earl of Glencairn   213, 214, 216, 218
Alexander, of Craigends   214, 218
Charlotte   377
Elizabeth   214, 241, 269
Elizabeth (Cunyngham) (Crawford)   214, 218
Elizabeth (Heriot)   244
Elizabeth (Livingston)   244
Elizabeth (Napier)   214

Elizabeth (Stewart)   214, 218
Gabriel, of Craigends   244
James, of Achenyeard   244
Janet (Cunyngham)   214
Janet (Gordon)   213, 214, 216, 218
Jean   131, 218
Jean (Hamilton)   213, 214, 216, 218
Judith Elizabeth (de Bonneson)   244
Margaret   150, 213, 216, 787
Margaret (Fleming)   244
Mary   244
Mary (Stewart) (Douglas) (Kennedy), Princess of Scotland   239, 240, 241, 243, 245, 248, 250, 251, 252, 253, 254, 255, 257, 258, 260, 261, 266, 267, 268, 940
Rebecca   214
Rebecca (Muirhead)   244
Richard, of Glengarnock   244
Robert   244
William   244
William, 6th Earl of Glencairn   213, 214, 216, 218

William, of Craigends   214, 218

CUPPER
Audrey (Peyto)   722
Dorothy   563, 722
John   722

CURE
Rachel (FitzWilliam) (Huddleston) (Hall) (Reppes)   394
Richard   394

CURFMAN
Robert Joseph   viii, lii, lxix, 658

CURIE
Henrietta Hedwige, Baroness von l'Esperance   184

CURRER-BRIGGS
Noel   xxix, xlvii, lii

CURTIS
Alison E. (MacCarthy-Willis-Bund)   cliii, 542
Anne (Revell)   lxx, cxlviii, 757, 758
Dorothy (Tennant) (Stanley)   130
Eleanor Colson   460
Henry   130
Jeanet Ellinwood (Sullivan)   542
John   757, 758
Lewis Perry (Prof.)   542

Lewis Perry, Jr.
 (Prof.) 542
Thomas 758
CURWAYN
John cxc
CURWAYN alias SYBERTOFT
family cxc
CURWEN
George cxc
Henry (Sir) 327, 330
Mabel 327, 329
Mary (Fairfax) 327, 330
CURWEN/CORWIN
family cxc
CURZON/CURSON
Agnes 575
Anna Maria 222
Anne (Giffard) 859
Catherine 754, 780, 859
Eleanor 377
Eleanor (Vernon) 377
Elizabeth 245
Elizabeth (Becker) 222, 377
Elizabeth (Lygon) 575
Elizabeth (Stevens) 377
Emily Mary 65
family 576
Francis 377
George 377, 576
Isabel (Symonds) 377
John 377

Millicent (Sacheverell) 377
Rebecca 222
Rebecca (Clark) 377
Richard lxiii, 222, 377, 859
Richard William Penn, 1st Earl Howe 65
Samuel 377
Susanna (___) 377
Thomas 575
CUSER (DE)
Ida (van Oosterwijk) 774
Willem/William 774, 775
CUSER VAN OOSTERWIJK
Clementia Gerrit (Boelendochter) 774
Coenraad 774
Ida 774
CUSHIN
Edmund 587
Elizabeth 587
Frances (Richers) 587
CUSTIS
Daniel Parke 29
Eleanor (Calvert) 29, 363
Elizabeth Parke 363, 365
George Washington Parke 29

John Parke 29, 363
Martha (Dandridge) 29, 170, 301, 310, 515, 700
Martha Parke 170
Mary Anne Randolph xxxiv, 29
Mary Lee (FitzHugh) 29
CUTHBERT
George, of Castle Hill 176
James 1, 176
Jean (Hay) 176
John, of Castle Hill 176
Magdalen (Fraser) 176
Mary (Hazzard) (Wigg) 176
Patience (Stobo) (Hamilton) 176
CUTTING
John 654
Mary 654
Mary (Ward) lviii, lx, cxlviii, cli, clx, clxxix, 654, 655, 656
CUTTS
Mary 836
CYNFYN
ap Gwerystan, lord of Powys 815, 886
CYNILLON
ab Y Blaidd Rhûdd 815

CYNWRIG
 ap Hywel of Radur
  808
 ap Llywelyn 650,
  659, 686, 694
CYPRUS
 Anne de Lusignan,
  Princess of 442
 John I, titular King
  of, titular King of
  Jerusalem and
  Armenia 442
CZARTORYSKI
 Adam Louis, Prince
  290
 Elizabeth Bianca
  Maria Constance,
  Princess 290
 Maria Louisa
  (Krasinski),
  Countess 290
 princes 155
 Wladyslaw, Prince
  290
**CZERNICHEW-
 BESOBRASOW**
 Irina, Countess 7
 Xenia, Countess 800
CZERNIN
 Anna, Countess 198
DABNEY
 Susannah 421, 533
D'ABO
 Dorothy Primrose
  (Harbord) 135
 Edward 135
 Margaret Evelyn
  (Lyndon) 135

Michael David
 ("Mike") 135
Olivia Jane cliii, 135
**DABRIDGECOURT/
DABRICHECOURT**
 Agnes (Bekingham)
  853
 Beatrice (___) 853
 Elizabeth 853, 854
 Elizabeth (___) 853
 family clxxxvi, 854
 Joan (Lynde) 853
 John 853
 John (Sir) 853
 Nicholas (Sir) 853
 Sanchet (Sir) 853
 Thomas 853
DACRE
 Anne 361
 Anne Lennard,
  Baroness 109
 Elizabeth 335
 Elizabeth
  (Greystock) 414
 Elizabeth (Talbot)
  414
 Joan 317, 318,
  319, 328, 359, 363,
  384
 Mabel 402
 Margaret 414
 Philippa (Neville)
  318
 Thomas, 6th Baron
  Dacre, of Gilsland
  318
 Thomas Dacre, 3rd
  Baron, of Gilsland
  414

Thomas Fiennes, 8th
 Baron 428
William Dacre, 4th
 Baron, of Gilsland
 414
DADE
 Beheathland
  (Bernard) 565
 family xxiv
 Francis liii, lxii,
  clxvi, 565
 Mary (Wingfield)
  565
 William 565
DAFYDD. *see also*
 DAVID
 ab Elise 689
 ap Madog 693
 ap Meurig of Radur
  808
 ab Owain Fychan
  811
 ap Rhys ab Ieuan
  692
DAFYDD FYCHAN
 ap Dafydd 693
DAFYDD GOCH
 ap Trahaearn Goch
 ap Madog 650,
  659, 686, 694
DAFYDD LAS
 ap Hywel Fychan
  810
DAFYDD LLOYD
 ap Dafydd 810
DAFYDD LLWYD
 ab Elise 657
 ap Cynwrig 650,
  659, 686, 694

ap Gruffudd 686
DAFYDD O'R BALA
ap Maredudd 659
DAGMAR
  Princess of Bohemia,
  Queen of Denmark
  644
DAGMAR (MARIE SOPHIE FREDERIKE DAGMAR) (MARIA FEODOROVNA)
  Princess of Denmark, Empress of Russia 5
DAGWORTHY
  Anne Phoebe Penn 333
DALE
  Bruce 984
  Diana (Skipwith) xxxv, lviii, clxvi, 470
  Diane M. (Henry) (Mallette) 984
  Edward 470
  Elizabeth (Throckmorton) 297
  family xxiv
  Katherine 470
  Thomas (Sir) (Gov.) 297
DALÌ
  Salvador 227
DALISON
  Elizabeth (Dighton) 755
  Elizabeth (Oxenden) 755
  Frances (Stanley) 389, 755
  Jane 390, 747, 755
  Jane (Etherington) 390
  Mary 755
  Mary (Spencer) 755
  Maximilian 389, 755
  Maximilian (Sir) 755
  Silvester (Deane) 755
  Susan (Style) 389
  Thomas 389, 390
  William 755
  William (Sir) 755
DALLAS
  Alexander James 666
  Arabella Maria (Smith) clxv, clxxv, 666
  George Mifflin 666
  Trevania Barlow 666
DALLETT
  Francis James viii, lii, 11
DALMAHOY
  Jean 90
DALRYMPLE
  Agnes 173
  Elizabeth 128, 215
  Margaret 143
DALSTON
  Anne (Bolles) 471
  Catherine 472
  Catherine (Tamworth) cxci
  Charles (Sir), 3rd Bt. 472
  Elizabeth (Kirkbride) cxci
  family clxxxix, cxci
  George (Sir) cxci
  John cxci
  John (Sir), 2nd Bt. 472
  John (Sir), of Dalston cxci
  Magdalen cxci
  Margaret (Ramsden) 472
  Susan (Blake) 472
  William (Sir), 1st Bt. 471
DALTON
  Isabella (Wray) 116
  Jane 902
  John 116
  Mary Norcliffe 116
DALTON (later NORCLIFFE)
  Anne (Wilson) 116
  Thomas Norcliffe 116
DALYELL
  James (Sir), 3rd Bt. 171
  Katherine (Drummond) 258
  Magdalen viii, lxi, lxx, cxliii, 171, 258, 259

Tam (Mrs.) 259
Thomas (Sir), 1st
  Bt. 258
Thomas [Tam] (Sir),
  11th Bt. 171, 258
**DALYNGRIGGE/
DALYNGRIDGE**
  family 1025
  Philippa 738, 851
DAMAS
  Antoine-Louis, Count
    de Cruz 293
  Catherine-Antoinette
    293
  Étienne, Count de
    Cruz 293
  François, Count de
    Cruz 293
  Louis-Alexander,
    Count de Cruz 293
  Louise (de
    Pracomtal) 293
  Marguerite-
    Étiennette
    (d'Achey) 293
  Marie-Anne
    (Coutier) 293
  Marie-Louise 293
DAMERIE/AMORY
  Emmot (Thomas)
    674
  George 674
  Joan 674
  John 674
  Margery
    (Ayre/Eyre) 674
DAMMARTIN
  Jean de Chabannes,
    Count of 205

Jean III, Seigneur de
  Rambures, Count of
  Guines and 205
Joan of, Countess of
  Ponthieu, Queen of
  Castile 951
Matilda of, Queen
  of Portugal 619
DAMORY
  Elizabeth 483, 489,
    536, 587, 606
  Elizabeth (de Clare)
    483, 489, 536, 587,
    606
  Roger Damory, 1st
    Baron 483, 489,
    536, 587, 606
**DAMPIERRE
(FLANDERS)**
  family 945
DANA
  Anne (Fitzhugh)
    155
  Anne Frisbie 155
  Charlotte Elizabeth
    (Bayley) 155
  Edmund 155
  Francis 155
  Helen (Kinnaird)
    155
  Richard Henry 155
  Richard Henry, Jr.
    155
  Sophia Willard
    155
  William Pulteney
    cliii, 155
DANBY
  Mary 374

DANCER
  Anchoretta (Rogers)
    383
  Catherine
    (Amyrold) 383
  Charity 383
  Loftus (Sir), 3rd Bt.
    383
  Sarah (Loftus) 383
  Thomas (Sir), 1st
    Bt. 383
  Thomas (Sir), 4th
    Bt. 383
DANDONNEAU
  Marie-Françoise
    970, 989
DANDRIDGE
  Dorothea
    (Spotswood) 278,
    301
  Dorothea
    Spotswood 219
  Martha 29, 170,
    278, 301, 310, 515,
    700
  Nathaniel West
    278, 301
  Penelope 138
  Unity (West) 301
  William 301
DANFORTH
  Mary 491
DANGEAUL (DE)
  Jean Cholet,
    Seigneur 948
D'ANGERVILLE
  H. H. xx, lii
DANIEL
  Émilie 988

Prince of Perejaslavl
  791, 797
DANIELL
  Dorothy
    (Chamberlayne)
    lxx, clxxix, 133
  Robert 133
DANIELS
  Arthur Noyes 185
  Dolorès (Dedons de
    Pierrefeu) 185
DANIELSEN
  Benton 891
  Josephine Alma
    xii, lvii, clii, 891
  Marie Louise
    Rantzow (Jacobs)
    891
DANVERS
  Agnes 295
  Anna 716
  Anna (Stradling)
    716
  Anne (Coke) 628
  Anne (Manser)
    629
  Dorothy 346
  Eleanor 346
  Elizabeth 717
  Elizabeth
    (Babington) 628
  Elizabeth (Cave)
    629
  Elizabeth (Neville)
    346
  Elizabeth (Truxton)
    629
  Ellen (Lacy) 629
  family 629

Henry 628
John 629
John (Sir) 346, 716
Mary (Carline) 629
Mary (Moore) 629
Mary Emma 629
Richard 629
Thomas lviii,
  cxliii, 629
William 628, 629
D'ANVERS
  Alice Cahen 112
DARCY
  Arthur (Sir) 395
  Dowsabel (Tempest)
    395
  Edward (Sir) 395
  Eleanor (Scrope)
    395
  Elizabeth 385, 390,
    582, 601
  Elizabeth (Astley)
    395
  Elizabeth
    (Wentworth) 385
  Eupheme (Langton)
    395
  Frances 315
  Isabella 395
  Joan 429
  Joan (de Greystock)
    395, 429
  John 395, 429
  Katherine 482
  Mary (Carew) 395
  Richard 395
  Roger 385
  Thomas Darcy, 1st
    Baron of 395

Ursula 126
William (Sir) 395
DARDEL
  Augusta Charlotta
    (Silfverschiöld) 60
  Fredrik Elias August
    60
  Fritz August 60
  Fritz Ludvig 60
  Georg Alexander 60
  Hedwig Sophie
    Charlotta Amalia
    (Lewenhaupt),
    Countess 60
  Maria Sofia
    (Wising)
    (Wallenberg) 60
  Nina Viveka Maria
    60
  Sofia Matilda
    (Norlin) 60
DARLEY
  Elizabeth Jane 481
  John 481
  Susanna (Guinness)
    481
DARLINGTON
  Henry Vane, 1st
    Earl of 34
  Sophia Charlotte,
    Countess von
    Platen and Haller-
    mund, Countess of
    Leinster, Countess
    of 58, 432
DARNALL
  Anne (Talbot) lxix,
    cxlviii, cli, clxv,
    120, 124, 125, 339

family xxiv, 124
Henry 120, 125, 339
Henry, Jr. 125
Mary 120, 121, 125, 339
Rachel (Brooke) 120
Susannah Maria (Bennett) 512
DARNLEY
Catherine 22
Henry Stewart, Lord xii
DARRELL
Anne 855
Constantine 855, 856
Elizabeth 741, 855
Elizabeth (Calston) 855
Elizabeth (Cheney/Cheyne) 721
Elizabeth (Horne) 721
Frances 721
George (Sir) 855
Henry 721
Joan (Collingborne) 855
Margaret (Stourton) 855
Mary (Roydon) 721
Thomas 721
Thomasine (Gresley) 721
William 855

DARTE
Joan 744
DARWIN
Caroline Sarah 117
Charles Robert xxiv, 116, 117
Emma (Wedgwood) 116
family xxxvii, xxxviii
Robert Waring 116
Susanna (Wedgwood) 116
DASHWOOD
Anne 62, 63, 80
G. H. 846
DAUBENY
Cecily 392, 436
Katherine 672, 674
DAUNAY
Emeline 547
DAUNDELYN
Margaret 495
DAVENPORT
Anna 880
Barbara (Ivory) 130
Elizabeth (___) 654
Elizabeth (Fitton) 752
Henry 130, 653
John (Rev.) li, lii, lxv, lxviii, clxiii, clxxv, 654, 656
Katherine 752
Katherine (Radcliffe) 752
Margery (Mainwaring) 752

Martha (Talbot) 130
Mary 130, 592, 817
Parnell 407
Thomas 752
William 130
Winifred (Barnaby) 653
DAVERS
Elizabeth 117, 334
DAVID
Ellis 658
Hannah (Price) (Jones) 651, 658
Prince of Scotland, Earl of Huntingdon 768, 778, 779, 780, 785, 787, 789
DAVID [DAFYDD]
ap Llywelyn Fawr, Prince of North Wales xxxii, 650, 652, 657, 659, 686, 689, 692, 693, 694
DAVID I
King of Scotland xxvi, 778, 779, 780, 783, 785, 787, 789, 879, 919
DAVID LLOYD
ap John Griffith 657
DAVID LLWYD
ab Elise 658
DAVID/DAVIS
Mary 423
DAVIE
Humphrey 308

John (Sir), 1st Bt. 308
Juliana (Strode) 308
Mary (White) 308
Sarah (Gibbon) (Richards) 308
DAVIES
Edward J. lii
Elizabeth (Seymour) 27
Isabella Clara 27
Lucy 79
Mary 30
William Griffith 27
DAVIS. *see also* DAVID/DAVIS
Abigail 858
Edith (Luckett) (Robbins) 673
Eleanor 166
family lii
Harriet Albina 379
Jane 302
Jefferson 421, 533
Loyal Edward (Dr.) 673
Lydia (Harwood) 747, 758
Margaret clxxxix
Mary 747, 758
Nancy (Anne Francis [Robbins] Reagan) xlii, xliii, 673
Nathaniel 747, 758
Nathaniel, Jr. 747, 758
Rachel 526
Sarah (Farmer) 501

Sarah Knox (Taylor) 421, 533
Susanna (Lane) 747, 758
Walter Goodwin, Jr. xxviii, xlvii, xlviii, lii, lv, lvi, lxi, lxii, lxv, lxxi, 671, 762 366, 779
DAVISON
Catherine (Cheremetev) cliii, 794, 796
Daniel Pomeroy cliii, 794
Mary 100, 102
DAVY
Renée 956
DAVYE
Jane 300
DAWKIN
Alice 582
Elizabeth (Jenkin) 582, 808
Jenkin 582, 808
Margaret (Barrett) 582
William 582
DAWKINS
Alice Clara (Tufnell) 108
Augusta (Clinton) 108
Clinton George Augustus 108
Clinton George Evelyn 108
Clinton John 108
Eve (Barham) 108

Frances Enid (Smythies) 108
Francis Henry 108
Henry 108
Jean Mary Vyvyan (Ladner) 108
Marianne Jane (Robarts) 108
Marion Ellina (Stamp) 108
Richard (Clinton Richard) (Prof.) xviii, lxiii, 108, 113
Sarah (Ward) (Hon.) [Lalla Ward] 108, 113
DAWNAY/DAWNEY
Anne 421
Dorothy (Neville) 421
Elizabeth 329
John (Sir) 421
Lewis Payan (Hon.) 72
Marion Vere 72
Mary 414
Sidney Leveson Lane (Bagot) 72
Victoria (Grey) 72
William Henry, 8th Viscount Downe 72
DAWSON
Susannah 722
DAY
Elizabeth (Story) 710
Helen (Wentworth) 710

1172

Laraine [Laraine
  (Johnson)
  (Hendricks)
  (Durocher)
  Grilikhes] 424
Wentworth liv,
  710, 712
William 710
DAYRELL
  family 1025
  Margaret 427
  Margaret (Beaufort)
    427
  Mary 463
  Richard (Sir) 427
**DAYRELL-
  BROWNING**
  Vivien Muriel 549
DAYTON
  Phebe 643
DE HAVILLAND.
  see also HAVILAND
  Charles Richard 462
  Joan de Beauvoir
    [Joan Fontaine]
    463
  Lilian Augusta
    (Ruse) 462
  Margaret Letitia
    (Molesworth) 462
  Olivia Mary xvii,
    462
  Walter Augustus
    462
DE LANCEY
  Anne Charlotte 128
  Susannah 487
DE PEYSTER
  Cornelia 898

DE SALIS
  Harriet (Bainbridge)
    580
DE WITT/WORTH
  Hannah 128
DEAN
  Andrea Belden
    (Maitland) 161,
    924
  Howard Brush, Jr.
    161, 924
  Howard Brush (III)
    (Gov.) xli, 161,
    162, 923, 924, 926
  Judith (Steinberg)
    162
DEANE
  Eleanor 335
  Silvester 755
DEARBORN
  David Curtis viii,
    xliii, lii, 232, 671
DEASE
  Anne (Johnson) 487
  family xl, liii
  John 487, 900
  Peter Warren 488,
    900
  Richard 487
**DEBEVOISE/
  DE BEAUVOIS**
  Carel 775
  Sophia (van
    Lodensteyn)
    xxxii, 775
DEBIDABÉ
  Anne (Desrosiers)
    (Turcot) 989
  Jean 989

DEBNAM
  Ann 701
  Mary 701
DeBUTTS
  Katherine Mary
    McCrea 592
  Marianne (Welby)
    115
  Samuel 115
DEDONS
  Alain, Count de
    Pierrefeu 185
  Aline-Anne (de
    Quérangel) 184
  Catherine 184
  Elsa (Tudor) 185
  Louis-Dolorès-
    Emmanuel-
    Alphonse, Count
    de Pierrefeu 184
  Louis-Joseph-Léonce,
    Marquis de Pierre-
    feu 184
  Marie-Simone-
    Léopoldine (de
    Pillot) 184
**DEDONS de
  PIERREFEU**
  Dolorès 185
  Katharine 185
DEICWS DDU
  ap Madog Goch 650
DEIGHTON
  family lviii, lx,
    lxviii, 297
  Frances clxii,
    clxxii, 297
  Jane lxviii, clxi,
    clxxii, 297

1173

Jane (Bassett) 297
John (Dr.) 297
Katherine xxiv,
  clx, clxxii, 297,
  370, 373, 924
Mary 108
DEL HEATH
Joan 822
DEL VALLE DE OAXACA
Hernán Cortés, 1st
  Marquess 191
Juana Estefanía
  Cortés, Marquesa
  del Valle de
  Oaxaca 192
Martín Cortés de
  Monroy, 2nd
  Marquess 191
DELABERE
Sybil 647, 909
DELAFIELD
family ix, lxi
DELAMATER
Jane 976
DELANO
Catherine Robbins
  (Lyman) 211,
  479, 571, 716
Deborah (Church)
  571
Sara 211, 356, 376,
  394, 479, 524, 571,
  716, 881, 921
Susanna 921
Warren 571
Warren, Jr. 211,
  479, 571, 716

DELANY
Mary (Granville)
  clxxxix
DELAVAL
Elizabeth 111
DELAWARE (DE LA WARR). *see* LA
WARR(E) (DE) (DELAWARE)
DELIANOV
Sophia 799, 800
DELISLE
Louis-Joseph 988
Marie-Gertrude
  (Lemieux) 988
Marie-Louise 988
Marie-Madeleine
  (Toupin) 988
DELL
Hannah 401
DELLA PORTA RODIANI
Giacinta 20
DELLA ROVERE
Eleanor (Gonzaga)
  of Mantua 186,
  189
family 192
Francesco Maria I,
  Duke of Urbino
  186, 189
Giuliano [Pope
  Julius II] 192
Guidobaldo II, Duke
  of Urbino 186, 189
Lavinia Feltrina, of
  Urbino 186, 189
Vittoria (Farnese)
  186, 189

DELLA SCALA
Beatrice, of Verona
  640
DELMÉ
Anne 27
DELVES
Elizabeth 728
Joan 721, 723
Margaret 524, 561,
  564, 817, 902
DELVIN
Christopher Nugent,
  3rd Baron 340
DEMERS
Eustache (III) 975
Eustache (IV) 975
Eustache (V) 975
Eustache (VI) 975
Louise (Massé)
  975
Marie-Josèphe
  (Dupuis) 975
Marie-Louise 975,
  988
Marie-Louise
  (Martin) 975
Zoë (Vezina) 975
DEMIDOV
Olga 793
DEN HERTOG
Bert 775
DENBIGH
Rudoph William
  Basil Feilding, 8th
  Earl of 77
William Feilding, 1st
  Earl of 368
William Feilding,
  3rd Earl of, 2nd

Earl of Desmond 64
William Basil Percy Feilding, 7th Earl of 77
DENIS
Barbe 964
DENIS DE KERENDERN
Anna María Teresa (Massa de Leunda y Aristiguieta) 443
François-Marie, Baron de Trobriand 443
DENIS DE KERENDERN DE TROBRIAND
Louise-Jeanne-Arnolde-Nicolasse-Marie ("Fanny") 443
DENIS DE LAGARDE
Louis-Pierre-Marie-Auguste 443
Ludovic-Eugène 443
Marie-Victoire-Desirée (d'Haussy) 443
Mathilde Dolores lx, clii, 443
Matilde-Ignacia de la Caridad (Montalvo y Rodríguez) 443
DENISON
Daniel 371

Elizabeth 371
Ida Emily Augusta 177
Patience (Dudley) 371
DENMAN
Anne 780
Anne (Blount) 780
Anne (Hercy) 780
Francis 780
John 921
Judith (Stoughton) cli, 921
DENMARK
Anna Katharina, Princess of Brandenburg, Queen of 35, 37
Anne, Princess of 891
Anne, Princess of, Queen of England and Scotland 35, 38, 47, 49, 52, 785
Augusta, Princess of 35, 47, 49
Berengaria, Princess of Portugal, Queen of 644
Christian III, King of 52, 58, 60, 432, 889, 891, 893
Christian IV, King of 35, 37, 52
Christian V, King of 615
Christian IX, King of 453

Christine, Princess of Saxony, Queen of 181, 182, 184
Dagmar, Princess of Bohemia, Queen of 644
Dorothea, Princess of 58, 60, 432, 893
Dorothea, Princess of Saxe-Lauenburg, Queen of 58, 60, 432, 889, 891, 893
Elizabeth, Princess of 181, 182, 184
Frederick II, King of 47, 49, 52, 645
Frederick VI, King of 645
John I, King of 141, 181, 182, 184
Margaret, Princess of Saxony, Queen of 141
Marie Sophie Frederikke Dagmar (Maria Feodorovna), Princess of, Empress of Russia 5
monarchs of xv, 45, 444, 453, 615
Sophie, Princess of Mecklenburg-Güstrow, Queen of 47, 49, 52
Waldemar II, King of 644
DENN(E)
Anne 739
Avice 778

1175

John 883
Margaret (Halsnode) xlv, lvi, 883, 884
DENNEHY
Josephine 793
DENNETT
Anne (Booth) 483
DENNIS/DENYS
Agnes (Danvers) 295
Alice 742
Anne 338, 392
Anne (Berkeley) 295, 338
Eleanor 295, 296, 532
family 298
Fortune (Norton) 295
Frances 295
Gilbert 298
Gilbert (Sir) 298
Hugh 295
Isabel 296
John 295
Katherine (or Joan) (Stradling) 295, 298
Katherine (Trye) 295
Morris 295, 298
Philippa 836
Sarah 726
Walter (Sir) 295
William (Sir) 295, 338
DENNISTON
Elizabeth 351

DENNY
Abigail (Berners) 494
Agnes (Blennerhasset) 405
Anne 540
Anne (Hill) 493
Anthony (Sir) 548
Barry 405
Barry (Sir), 1st Bt. 405
Edward 405
Edward (Sir) 493
Elizabeth 405
Henry 493
Henry Lyttelton Lyster (Rev.) lii
Hill 494
Jane 405
Jane (O'Connor) 405
Joan (Champernowne) 548
Letitia 405
Letitia (Coningsby) 405
Margaret (Edgcumbe) 493
Mary 395, 548
Mary (Fitch) 493
Mary (Hill) 494
Peter 493
Thomas (Sir) 405
William (Lt. Gov., Gov.) 494
DENT
Elizabeth (Fowke) 722

Ellen Bray (Wrenshall) 722
Frederick Fayette 722
George 722
Julia Boggs xlii, 722, 921
Mary (Brooke) 722
Mary Eleanor (___) 722
Peter 722
Peter, Jr. 722
Susannah (Dawson) 722
William 722
DENTON
Diana Elizabeth 361
Isabel 654
Isabel (Brome) 654
Jane (Webb) 654
John 654
Thomas 654
DENWOOD
Elizabeth 787
DEPUY
Claude 950
DERBY
Edward Stanley, 3rd Earl of 75, 355, 904
Ferdinando Stanley, 5th Earl of 70, 79
Henry Stanley, 4th Earl of 62, 70, 75, 79, 904
James Stanley, 7th Earl of 62, 637
Thomas Stanley, 1st Earl of 355, 397, 433, 902

Thomas Stanley, 2nd Earl of 355, 904, 905
William de Ferrers, 4th Earl of 806, 821
William Stanley, 6th Earl of 62
DEREHAUGH
 Anne xlvi, cxlvi, clxii, 661, 706, 924
 Mary (Wright) 661
 William 661
DERING
 Anne (Ashburnham) 430
 Anthony (Sir) 429
 Benetta 357
 Edward (Sir) 430
 Edward (Sir), 2nd Bt. 430
 Elizabeth (Owen) 603
 Frances (Bell) 429
 Henrietta (de Beaulieu) [Henrietta Johnston] v, lxvii, cxliv, 430
 John 357, 429
 Margaret (Brent) 357, 429
 Margaret (Twisden) 357, 358, 429
 Mary 603
 Mary (Harvey) 430
 Nicholas 603
 Richard 357, 429
 Robert lxvii, 430
 Thomas 603
 Winifred (Cotton) 603
DERMOT/ DIARMAIT
 MacMurrough/Mac Murchada, King of Leinster 837, 839, 847
DERNFORD
 Joan 594
DeROUEN
 Agnès 990
 Eugène-Gustave 990
 Odilia (Broussard) 990
DERVIEU DE VILLARS
 Barthélémy, Comte 443
 Louise-Jeanne-Arnolde-Nicolasse-Marie ("Fanny") (Denis de Kerendern de Trobriand) 443
DERWENTWATER
 Edward Radcliffe, 2nd Earl of 30
 James Radcliffe, 3rd Earl of 30
DES ACRES
 Henri-Louis-Espérance de Laërce, Count de l'Aigle 206
 Marie-Louise-Geneviève 206
 Pulchérie-Félicité-Cyrette (de Vischer) 206
DES ADRETS
 Aynard de Beaumont, Seigneur 965
DES ANCHERINS
 Nicole 944
DES BAUX
 Jacques-Honoré Grimaldi, Prince of Monaco, Marquis 934
DES DEUX-JUMEAUX
 Guillaume de Villiers, Seigneur de Villiers-sur-Port and 956
DES GRANGES (IN VALAIS)
 Pierre de Rovorée, Seigneur 872
DES LANDES
 Pernelle 954
DES LONDES
 Denis de Méhérenc, Seigneur 946
 Guillaume I de Méhérenc, Seigneur 946
 Guillaume II de Méhérenc, Seigneur 946
DES MUSSEAUX
 Charles-Joseph d'Ailleboust, Seigneur 940

DES ORMES
  Charles de Longue-
    val, Sieur 944
DES ORMONTS
  Guigues de Rovorée,
    co-Seigneur of
    Saint-Triphon and
    872
  Jean de Rovorée,
    co-Seigneur of
    Saint-Triphon and
    872
DES ROCHES
  Jeanne 942
DES ROTOURS
  Radégonde 942
DES TRESMES
  Bertrand de
    Sévigne, Sieur
    943
DESCHAILLONS (DE)
  Pierre de Saint-
    Ours, Seigneur de
    Saint-Ours and
    962, 965
DESHA
  Phoebe Ann 174
DESMOND
  George Feilding, 1st
    Earl of 368
  Gerald FitzGerald,
    3rd Earl of 601
  James FitzGerald,
    6th Earl of 601
  William Feilding,
    3rd Earl of
    Denbigh, 2nd Earl
    of 64

DESPAIN
  Bruce xlviii, lii, 316
DESPENCER (LE)
  Anne 505
  Anne (Ferrers)
    491, 505, 575
  Constance
    (Plantagenet)
    377, 410, 417, 423
  Edward (Sir) 491,
    505, 575
  Edward Despencer,
    3rd Baron 491,
    505, 575
  Eleanor 713, 739,
    824
  Eleanor (de Clare)
    491, 505, 508, 514,
    547, 575, 584, 594,
    607
  Elizabeth 491, 541
  Elizabeth (Burghersh)
    491, 505, 575
  Elizabeth (de
    Tibetot) 710, 719
  Hugh le Despencer,
    1st Baron 491,
    505, 508, 514, 547,
    575, 584, 594, 607
  Isabel xxv, 357,
    405, 417, 429, 508,
    514, 547, 584, 594,
    607, 642
  Margaret 478, 505,
    575
  Margery 309, 596,
    661, 710, 719
  Mary Neville,
    Baroness 122

  Philip (Sir) 710, 719
  Thomas, 1st Earl of
    Gloucester 377,
    410, 417, 423
DESPRÉS
  A. Couillard (Abbé)
    939
  Marie-Judith 989
DESROSIERS
  Anne 988, 989
  Marguerite 989
  Thérèse 970
DESROSIERS dit du TREMBLE
  Angélique (Bourré)
    970
  Anne (du Hérisson)
    970, 989
  Antoine 970, 989
  Jean 970, 989
  Jean-Baptiste 970
  Joseph-Marie-Jean
    989
  Josephte (Dubé) 989
  Louis 970, 989
  Marie-Françoise
    (Dandonneau)
    970, 989
  Marie-Jeanne
    (Moreau) 989
  Marie-Judith
    (Després) 989
  Michel 989
  Thérèse (Fafard)
    970
DESSAINT dit SAINT-PIERRE.
  see SAINT-PIERRE
    dit DESSAINT

D'ESTOUTEVILLE.
see ESTOUTEVILLE
(D')/TOUTEVILLE/
DE STUTEVILLE
DESTROISMAISONS
  Marie-Anathalie 971
DETHICK
  Anne 723, 724
DETROIT
  Allen Henry
    Vigneron,
    Archbishop of
    967, 968, 983
**DEUX-JUMEAUX
(DES).** see DES
DEUX-JUMEAUX
DEVEREUX
  Agnes (Crophill/
    Crophull) 647
  Anne 138, 346,
    352
  Anne (Ferrers)
    505, 534
  Barbara 111
  Catherine (Arden)
    138
  Cecily (Bourchier)
    134
  Dorothy 134, 136
  Dorothy (Hastings)
    134
  Edward (Sir), 1st Bt.
    138
  Edward, 8th Viscount
    Hereford 346
  Elizabeth 137, 233,
    500, 534, 647
  Elizabeth (Bromwich)
    352, 647

Elizabeth (Merbury)
    352
  Elizabeth (Norborne)
    345, 346
  Frances 69, 75, 80
  Frances (Walsing-
    ham) 75, 134
  Jane (Scudamore)
    111, 137
  John, 2nd Baron
    Ferrers of Chartley
    134
  Lettice (Knollys)
    134
  Margaret 137
  Margaret (Garneys)
    134
  Mary (Grey) 134
  Penelope 135, 136
  Richard (Sir) 134,
    137, 138
  Robert, 2nd Earl of
    Essex 75, 134,
    135, 136
  Sybil 505
  Walter 352, 647
  Walter (Sir) 352,
    647, 909
  Walter, 1st Baron
    Ferrers of Chartley
    505, 534
  Walter, 1st Earl of
    Essex 134, 137
  Walter, 1st Viscount
    Hereford lxvi, 134
  William (Sir) 111,
    137, 138
DEVIOCK
  John 687

Margaret 687
  Margaret (Longland)
    687
DEVON
  Hugh Courtenay, 1st
    Earl of 824
  Hugh Courtenay,
    2nd Earl of 503,
    543, 547, 569, 573,
    595, 608
  William de Vernon,
    5th Earl of 739
DEVONSHIRE
  Andrew Robert
    Buxton Cavendish,
    11th Duke of 23,
    25, 26
  Edward William
    Spencer Cavendish,
    10th Duke of 26
  Ruth 358
  Victor Christian
    William
    Cavendish, 9th
    Duke of 25
  William Cavendish,
    5th Duke of 69,
    117
  William Cavendish,
    7th Duke of 25
DeWITT
  Mary 351
DeWOLFE
  Florence Mabel
    (Kling) 764, 859
DEXTER
  Abigail (Fuller) 862
  Anne (Turland)
    862

1179

Elizabeth (Kinnesman) 862
Gregory 862, 863
Gregory (Rev.) lxiii, cxlviii, cli, clxxx, 862
Isabel 863
Isabel (___) 862, 863
Stephen 862
Thomas 862

DEYNCOURT/ DEINCOURT
Alice 754
family 1025
Margaret 710, 719, 730

DEYNSELL
Elizabeth 743

DI FALCO
Carole [Carole Radziwill] 17, 914

DIANA
Princess of Wales [Diana Frances Spencer] viii, xviii, xl, xlii, xliii, liv, 25, 32, 101, 306, 377, 380, 416, 417, 432, 482, 492, 543, 552, 576, 755, 858, 859, 930, 932

DICK
Elizabeth Tatham 440, 626

DICKENSON
Elizabeth (Brockenbrough) 127

DICKERSON
Charity Malvina (Van Kirk) 859
Isaac Haines 859
Phoebe Elizabeth 764, 859

DICKINSON
Caroline 334
Charity 925
Charles 925, 927
Christopher 925
Huldah (Griffith) 925, 927
Mary (Cole) 925
Philip(pa) (Greene) 925
Samuel 925, 926
Sophia (Smith) 334
William 334

DICKSON
Euphan 90
Jane (Nevin) 308
Katharine lii

DIEBOLD
R. Bruce xxii, liii, 646

DIÉGUEZ
María Dolores 158

DIESBACH (VON)
Ursula 832

DIETRICHSTEIN (VON)-PROSKAU-LESLIE
Theresia Rosa, Countess 45

DIETRICHSTEIN-HOLLENBURG
Anna Amelia of 182, 237

DIETZ
Howard 124, 481
Tanis Eva Bulkeley (Guinness) (Montagu) 124, 481

DIGBY
Anne (Grey) 749
Catherine (Griffin) 749
Constantia Pamela Alice (Bruce) 67
Edward Henry Trafalgar Digby, 10th Baron 67
Edward Kenelm Digby, 11th Baron 67
Edward St. Vincent Digby, 9th Baron 66
Elizabeth 706, 727, 749, 780
Elizabeth (Slater) 706
Emily Beryl Sissy (Hood) 67
Everard 749
Jane 312
Jane Elizabeth 363
John 706
John (Sir) 749, 780
Katherine 843
Katherine (Stockbridge) 749
Pamela Beryl (Hon.) 67
Rose (Prestwiche/ Perwyche) 749
Simon 749

Theresa Anne Maria
 (Fox-Strangways)
 66
William 749
DIGGES
 Anne (St. Leger)
  347, 467
 Bridget (Wilsford)
  467
 Dudley (Sir) 347
 Edward (Gov.) liii,
  clxvi, 347
 Elizabeth (Page) 347
 Leonard 467
 Mary (Kempe) 347
 Thomas 347, 467
DIGGS
 Anne 168
DIGHTON
 Elizabeth 755
 Joyce (St. Paul) 755
 Robert 755
DILLON
 Charles Dillon-Lee,
  12th Viscount 22,
  23
 Charlotte (Lee) 22
 Frances 23
 Harriet 480
 Henry Augustus
  Dillon-Lee, 13th
  Viscount 22
 Henry Dillon, 11th
  Viscount 22
 Jane (Moore) 601
 Lucas (Sir) 601
 Mary 601
 ___ 885

DILLON-LEE
 Charles, 12th
  Viscount Dillon
  22, 23
 Henrietta (Browne)
  22
 Henrietta Maria 22
 Henry Augustus, 13th
  Viscount Dillon 22
DIMITRI
 Grand Duke of
  Russia 3
DIMITRI IV
 Grand Prince of
  Moscow 621, 797
 Prince of Suzdal and
  Vladimir 791, 797
DIMMICK
 Mary Scott (Lord)
  496, 503, 731, 867,
  878
DIMOND
 James L. 624
 Loretta-Marie 624
DINHAM
 Elizabeth 392, 409,
  436
 Margaret 547
DION
 Adélard 977
 Adhémar 977
 Céline-Marie-
  Claudette [Céline
  Dion] 967, 977,
  989
 Esther (Lévesque)
  977
 Joseph-Adélard
  977

 Joseph-Charles-
  Adélard 977
 Marie-Ernestine
  (Barriault) 977
 Marie-Thérèse
  (Tanguay) 977
DIONNE
 Felicité 971
 Marie-Josèphe 971
**DIONNE dit
 SANSOUCY**
 Augustin 971
 Marie-Théodiste
  (Ouellet) 971
DISNEY
 Emeline 785
 family 1025
 Jane (Ayscough) 528
 Jane (Middleton)
  785
 John 785
 Katherine (Leake)
  785
 Lucy (Felton) 785
 Mary 334
 Mary (de Grey) 785
 Nele (Hussey) 528
 Richard 528, 785
 Susan 528
 William (Sir) 785
DITTAMI
 Anne Francesca 985
DIXON
 Anne 363
DIXWELL
 Abigail (Herdson)
  750
 Anne 676, 750

Bathsheba (Howe) 750
Charles 750
Elizabeth 750
Elizabeth (Brent) 750
Elizabeth (Knight) 750
Ellen (Lowe) 750
Humphrey 750
Joanna (____) (Ling) 750
John clxxvii, 750
Mary (Grey) 750
William 750

DOAN
Barbara Woolworth (Hutton) (Mdivani) (Haugwitz-Hardenberg-Reventlow) (Grant) (Troubetzkoy) (Rubirosa) (von Cramm) xviii, 44, 46, 63

DOBKIN
family 6
John Howard 6
Maria Immaculata Pia (von Habsburg), Countess cxliii, 6

DOBSON
David xxix
John Blythe xii, l, liii, lxiv, lxx, lxxi, clxx, 21, 50, 59, 141, 183, 188, 197, 199, 203, 206, 228, 238, 291, 362, 439, 447, 448, 454, 461, 520, 616, 618, 734, 896, 900, 908, 913, 922, 963, 967, 968, 979, 980
Susannah 753

DOBYNS
Daniel xlix, cxliii, 466, 467
Edmund 466
Elizabeth (Billington) 467
Elizabeth (Dudding) 467
Elizabeth (Godson?) (Smith) 467
family viii
Ursula (Waller) 466, 467

DOD
Margaret 518

DODDINGTON
John 493
Margaret (Anketill) 493
Mary 493

DODGE
Jane (Evans) xlviii, cxliii, 690
John 690
Winifred Lovering (Holman) lviii, lx, lxi, lxx

DODGSON
Charles Lutwidge [Lewis Carroll] xxiv, 107

DOHERTY
Sara B. viii, liii, 704

DOHNA-CARMIN-DEN (VON)
Anna (Oxenstierna), Countess 452
Christopher Delphicus, Burggraf 452
family 453

DOILLON
Jacques 28

DOLE
Robert Joseph (Sen.) 923

DOLGORUKI/ DOLGURUKI/ DOLGOROUKOV/ DOLGURUKOV
Alexei, Prince 799
Anastasia (Ladyjensky) 792
Anna (Bredichin) 799
Catherine, Princess, Princess Yourievsky [second wife of Alexander II, Czar of Russia] 5
Elena, Princess 792
Gregori, Prince 799
Henriette-Adolfina (de Bandré-du Plessis) 792
Katharine, Princess 799
Maria (Golitsyn) 799
Natalie, Princess 794
Nikolai, Prince 799
Paul, Prince 792
Praskovya (Khilkov) 799

Praskovya, Princess 799
Vassili, Prince 792
DOLIVET
Jean-Claude 939, 949
DOMMANGET
Ghislaine-Marie-Françoise, Princess of Monaco 933
DOMPIERRE (DE)
Isabelle 872
DOMVILLE
Edward 560
Eleanor (Leycester) 560
family 561, 562
Gilbert 560
Margaret xix, lxii, lxiv, cxlix, cli, clxvi, 560
Margaret (Carrington) 560
Margaret (Sneyde) 560
Peter 560
DONAHUE
Nancy Custer (Lawson) 53
Richard King 53
DONALD III BANE
King of Scotland 828
DONGAN. *see also* DUNGAN
Jane (Rochfort) 486
John 486, 487, 488
John (Sir), 2nd Bt. 486

Margaret (Browne) 486
Margaret (Foster) 486, 488
Mary (Cooke) 486
Mary (Talbot) 486
Michael 486
Ruth (Floyd) 487
Sarah (Towneley) 487
Thomas 486, 487
Thomas (Gov.), 2nd Earl of Limerick lii, liii, clxxiii, 486, 488
Thomas T. lii, liii
Walter 486, 487
Walter (Sir), 1st Bt. 486
____ (Talbot) 486
DÖNHOFF (VON)
Emilie Alexandrine, Countess 223
DONIPHAN
Anderson 171, 258
Elizabeth 171, 258
Magdalen (Monteith) 171, 258
DONNE
Anne (More) 426
John 426
DONNELLY
Alma Louise 976
Arthur Ambrose 976
Leone B. (Brisbois) 976
Sheila 985

DONOVAN
Patricia 125
DORCHESTER
Catherine Sidley, Countess of 22
DORÉ
Étienne 976
Louis 976
Marie-Archange 976
Marie-Charlotte (Gingras) 976
Marie-Louise (Coron) 976
DORIA-PAMFILI-LANDI
Giovanni Andrea, Prince, 2nd Prince of Torriglia 18
Leopoldina 18
Luigi, Prince of Valmontore, 3rd Prince of Torriglia 18
Teresa (Orsini) 18
DORMAN
John Frederick x, xlix, liii, clxxxvi
DORMER
Alice 642
Alice (Collingridge) 642
Elizabeth (Browne) 414
Geoffrey 642
Margaret 401, 402
Mary 355, 402, 414, 905
Robert Dormer, 1st Baron 414

DÖRNBERG (VON)
Hyme Friederike
  Georgine Elisabeth
  Pauline Johanna
  Magdalena (zu
  Innhausen und
  Knyphausen),
  Countess 58
Luise Marie Emilie
  Pauline, Baroness
  58
Philipp Friedrich
  Ernst, Baron 58
DOROTHEA
  of Brandenburg 52
  of Brunswick-
    Lüneburg 60
  Princess of Brand-
    enburg-Schwedt 49
  Princess of
    Denmark 60, 432
  Princess of Saxe-
    Lauenburg, Queen
    of Denmark 52,
    58, 60, 432, 889,
    891, 893
**DOROTHEA
  FREDERICA**
  Princess of Branden-
    burg-Anspach 40
DORSET
  John Beaufort,
    Marquess of
    Somerset and xxv,
    222, 300, 345, 396,
    407, 427, 547, 898
  Thomas Grey, 1st
    Marquess of 339,
    340, 370

Thomas Grey, 2nd
    Marquess of 339,
    340
DORTH (VAN)
  Dirck, Heer 447
  Henrica (van
    Aeswijn) 447
  Joanna (van
    Rossem) 447
  Josina 447
  Maria Dorothea
    (Droste zu Senden)
    447
  Seyno, Heer 447
DOTTI
  Andrea 446
  Edda Kathleen (van
    Heemstra) (Hep-
    burn-Ruston)
    (Ferrer) [Audrey
    Hepburn] viii, xvii,
    lxix, cxliv, 446
DOUD
  Eli 589
  Elivera Mathilda
    (Carlson) 589
  John Sheldon 589
  Mamie Geneva
    xlii, 589
  Maria (Riggs) 589
  Mary Cornelia
    (Sheldon) 589
  Royal Houghton
    589
DOUGLAS
  Agnes 154, 160
  Agnes (Horn) 225
  Agnes (Keith) 250,
    252, 256

Anne 98
Annie (Johnson) 166
Archibald (Sir), of
  Dornock 166
Archibald (Sir), of
  Glenbervie 250,
  251, 252, 256, 257
Archibald, 5th Earl
  of Angus 250,
  251, 252
Archibald Douglas,
  4th Earl of 249,
  256
Archibald Douglas,
  5th Earl of 249,
  256
Barbara (Farquhar-
  son) 251
Bethiah 251
Catherine (Stewart)
  154, 157, 167, 168,
  179
Claire Alison 166
David, 7th Earl of
  Angus 90, 96, 210
Eleanor 789
Eleanor (Davis) 166
Elizabeth 223, 252,
  255, 256, 257, 261,
  266, 267, 268, 898
Elizabeth (Auchin-
  leck) 250, 251,
  252
Elizabeth (Boyd)
  250, 251, 252
Elizabeth (Irvine)
  251
Elizabeth (Ochter-
  loney) 251

Eupheme (Grant) 249, 256
Euphemia 225
Francis, of Aberdeen and Paisley 251
George, 1st Earl of Angus 240, 241, 248, 250, 251, 252, 254, 255, 257, 258, 261, 266, 268, 940
George, 4th Earl of Angus 250, 251, 252
Giles/Egidia 278
Giles/Egidia (Graham) 250
Giles/Egidia (Stewart), Princess of Scotland 275, 278
Grizel (Forbes) 225
Helen 248, 254, 256, 257, 258, 940
Isabel 161
Isabel (Ker) 166
Isabel (Sibbald) 250, 251, 252
Isabella (Moncreiffe) 166
James (Sir) 166
James, 1st Earl of Morton 173, 222, 223, 225, 898
James, 3rd Earl of Morton 154, 157, 167, 168, 179
James, of Jamaica 166
Janet 173, 222, 225, 275, 276, 285
Janet (Crichton) 160, 223, 898
Jean (Stewart) 166
Joan (Stewart), "the dumb lady," Princess of Scotland 173, 222, 223, 225, 898
John 251
John, 2nd Earl of Morton 160, 223, 898
John, of Inchmarlo 225
John, of Leith 251
John, of Tilquhillie 225
Lucy 155
Margaret 90, 96, 154, 157, 159, 167, 168, 177, 179, 210, 249, 250, 256
Margaret (Hamilton) 90, 96, 156, 210
Margaret (Hay) 248, 250, 251, 252, 254, 257, 258, 940
Margaret (Stewart), Princess of Scotland 249, 256
Margaret Jane (Cannon) 166
Mary 163, 241
Mary (Fleming) 166
Mary (Gordon) 155, 156
Mary (Henchman) 166
Mary (Stewart), Princess of Scotland 239, 240, 241, 243, 245, 248, 250, 251, 252, 253, 254, 255, 257, 258, 260, 261, 266, 267, 268, 940
Robert 166
Robert (Sir), 6th Bt., of Glenbervie xxvii
Robert (Sir), of Glenbervie 250
Robert, of Blackmiln 251
Robert Langton clxxix, 166
Samuel 166
Samuel, of Jamaica 166
Thomas, of Jamaica 166
William (Rev.), of Aboyne 251
William (Rev.), of Midmar 251
William (Sir), of Glenbervie 250, 251, 252
William (Sir), of Nithsdale 278
William, 1st Earl of Queensberry 166
William, 2nd Earl of Angus 240, 248, 250, 251, 252, 254, 257, 258, 940

William, 9th Earl of
Angus 250, 251
William Douglas,
1st Marquess of
155, 156
William Sholto, 1st
Baron Douglas of
Kirtleside, British
air marshal 166
___ (James) 166
___ (Watson) 166
**DOUGLAS-
HAMILTON**
Mary Victoria 20,
933
DOUGLAS-HOME
Alexander Frederick
("Sir Alec"), 14th
Earl of Home,
Prime Minister
xxiv, 25
**DOUGLAS-
STEWART**
William George (Sir),
7th Bt. clviii
DOUGLASS
Adele (Astaire)
(Cavendish)
[Marie Austerlit]
26
Kingman 26
**DOUHET DE
MARLAT (DE)**
Anne (de Belvezer)
200, 203
Antoine, Seigneur
de Védrine 200,
203
Françoise 200, 203

DOURNEFF
Helen 5
DOUXCHAMPS
Hervé liv
DOVER (DE)
Isabel 697
Lorette 372, 667,
670, 678, 684, 917
Richard 697
Rohese of 372,
667, 670, 676, 678,
684, 691, 697, 917
**DOVER (DE)/
CHILHAM (DE)**
Isabel 676, 691
DOW
Mary 254
DOWDALL
Anne (Johnson)
488
Eleanor 545
Matilda Cecilia xl,
liii, clxxiii, 488,
900
Walter 488
DOWNE
William Henry
Dawney, 8th
Viscount 72
DOWNES
___ 757
DOWNSHIRE
Arthur Wills
Blundell Trumbull
Sandys Roden Hill,
5th Marquess of
70
Arthur Wills John
Wellington

Trumbull Blundell
Hill, 6th Marquess
of 70
DOWNTON
Joan 551
DOWRISH
Anne (Farringdon)
632
Grace 632
Thomas 632
DOWSE
Anne 527
Elizabeth (Paulet)
527
Francis (Sir) 527
DOYLE
Tim clxxxv
D'OYLEY/D'OYLY
Christiana 736
Joan 851
Margaret 680
Priscilla 526
DOZIER
Joan de Beauvoir
(de Havilland)
(Aherne) [Joan
Fontaine] xvii,
463
William 463
DRAKE
Abraham 344
Elizabeth 419, 536
Helen (Boteler)
536
Henry 419
Jane (Lunt) 344
Joan (Gawton) 419
John 836
John (Sir) 536

Martha 344
Martha (Eaton) 344
Mary clxxxvi
Mary (Lee) 419
Nathaniel 344
Philippa (Dennis) 836
Robert xi, xlvi, xlix, lxiv, lxvi, clxvii, clxxiii, 419
William 836
DRAPEAU
Marie-Josèphe 977
Marie-Josèphe (Huard) 977
Marie-Josèphe (Maranda) 977
Pierre 977
DRAYCOTE
Agnes (Gascoigne) 819
Jane 819
Joan (Stafford) 819, 820
John 819
Roger 819
DRAYTON
Charlotte Augusta (Astor) 44
Helen Fargo (Squiers) 44
James Coleman 44
Margaret Astor 44
Mary (Mackenzie) (Clarke), Lady 92
Thomas 92
William Backhouse Astor 44

DREFELD
Gjord 644
Ingeborg 644
Kirsten (Banner) 644
DRESSER
Edith Stuyvesant 73, 74
DREUX (DE) (OF)
Agnes (de Baudemont) 804, 956
Agnès (de Mareuil) 956
Alain d'Albret, Count 287
Alix 804, 954
Blanche 956
counts 949
Eleanor (de St.-Valéry) 956
Étienne dit Gauvin de Dieux, Vicomte 956
Gauvin II, Baron d'Esneval 956
Guillemette (de Ségrie) 956
Hawise (d'Evreux) 954
Isabelle (de Villebéon) 956
Jacques, Vicomte de Beaussart 956
Jean I, Seigneur de Châteauneuf-en-Thymerais 956
Jeanne (d'Esneval) 956

Marguerite (de La Roche) 956
Philippine (de Maussigny) 956
Robert, Baron d'Esneval 956
Robert I, Count of 804, 954, 956
Robert I, Count of Squilacce-Calabria 956
Robert II, Count of 956
Robert II, Seigneur de Beu 956
Robert III, Count of 956
Yolande (de Coucy) 956
Yolande (de Vendôme) 956
Yolande of 442, 946
DREW
Ada 321
DREXEL
Jacqueline (Mary Jacqueline) (Astor) 66
John Nicholas 66
John R., III 66
Noreen (Mildred Sophia Noreen) (Stonor) (Hon.) [Hon. Mrs. Drexel] cliii, 66
Pamela (Braga) 66
DRIBY (DE)
Alice 746, 847

Amy (de Gaveston) 847, 848
family 373, 697, 746
John 847
DROGHEDA
Henry Moore, 1st Earl of 137
Henry Moore, 3rd Earl of 137
DROMORE
James Mahon, Dean of 465
DRONAI (DE)
Aubert de Coucy, Seigneur 633
DROSTE ZU SENDEN
Maria Dorothea 447
DROUIN
Juliette 988
DRUMMOND
Agnes 143, 171, 173, 285
Angela Mary (Constable-Maxwell) 72
Annabella, Queen of Scotland 239, 241, 243, 245, 248, 249, 250, 251, 252, 253, 254, 255, 256, 257, 258, 260, 261, 263, 264, 266, 267, 268, 940
Anne 168
Anne (Hay), of Keillor 168
Catherine (Hamilton) 168

Catherine, of Logie Almond 897
Catherine Elizabeth 65
Charlotte Theresa 66
David, of Bourland 171
David Drummond, 2nd Baron 151, 258
Dorothy (Lower) 136
Elizabeth (Drummond) 171
Elizabeth (Graham) 258
Helen (Menteith) 171
Henrietta Maria 136
Henry Roger 65, 66
Isabel 157, 174
James (Sir), of Machany 168
James, 1st Baron Maderty 168
James Eric, 16th Earl of Perth [Sir Eric Drummond] 72
Jean 151, 152, 161, 168, 170
Jean (Chisholm) 168
Jean (Stirling) 258, 259
John (Sir), of Innerpeffry 143, 157, 159, 163, 165, 168, 171, 173, 174

Katherine 258, 280
Lilias (Ruthven) 151, 170, 258
Magdalen (Dalyell) 258, 259
Malcolm, of Bourland 171
Margaret 143, 148, 154, 157, 159, 163, 165, 168, 171, 173, 174, 176, 940
Margaret (Murray) 65
Margaret (Scott) 285
Margaret (Stewart) 143, 157, 159, 163, 165, 168, 171, 173, 174
Margaret, of Drummonderinoch 264
Margaret Gwendolyn Mary, Lady 72
Marjorie (Elphinstone) 285
Mary 258
Maurice (Sir) 136
Patrick, of Carnock 285
Robert 65
Robert (Sir), of Carnock 285
Susannah (Wells) 65
Sybilla 257
Walter 258
William (Sir), of Riccarton 258, 259

William, 4th
 Viscount
 Strathallan 65
William, of
 Riccarton 258
Winifred
 (Thompson) 65
**DRUMMOND-
STEWART**
 Christian Mary
  (Stewart) 897
 William George
  (Sir), 7th Bt. 897
DRURY
 Anna Maria clii,
  371, 372
 Anne 483, 537
 Anne (Calthorpe)
  359, 483, 489, 536,
  537, 826
 Audrey (Rich) 359
 Bridget 359, 489,
  596
 Charles Vallancy
  371
 Charles William 371
 Charlotte Augusta
  (Hayne) 371
 Dorothy 359, 360
 Elizabeth 482, 536,
  730
 Elizabeth (Brudenell)
  537
 Elizabeth (Sotehill)
  359
 Elizabeth (Stafford)
  114, 482
 Elizabeth Sophia
  (Poyntz) 371

family lxii
Frances 114
Frances Amelia
 (Hazen) 371
Gladys Henderson
 371
Henningham 557
Katherine 826
LeBaron 371
Mary Louise
 (Henderson) 371
Robert 359
Robert (II) (Sir) 537
Robert (Sir) 359,
 483, 489, 536, 537,
 826
Ward Chipman
 371
William (Sir) 114,
 359, 482
DRUSE
 Joseph L. xxi
DRYDEN
 Bridget 478, 708
 Elizabeth 481, 482
 Elizabeth (Cope)
  423, 478, 481
 Elizabeth (Howard)
  482
 Ellen (Neale) 478
 Erasmus 481
 Erasmus (Sir), 1st
  Bt. 481, 482
 family lvi, 482
 Frances (Wilkes)
  481, 482
 Grace 478
 John 423, 478,
  481, 482

Mary 423
Mary (Emyley)
 481
Mary (Pickering)
 481
Nicholas 481
Stephen 478
DU BOIS
 Robine 946
DU BOSE
 Catherine (de
  Bailleul) 957
 Christine 957
 François, Seigneur
  d'Hermival 957
DU BOUILLON
 Jean de La Haye,
  Seigneur 946
 Robert de La Haye,
  Seigneur 946
DU BREUIL
 Miles Maillard,
  Seigneur, Seigneur
  de La Boissière
  950
DU BREULH
 Marie-Anne 205
DU CREST
 Jean de Rovorée,
  Seigneur, Seigneur
  de La Roche
  d'Ollon 872
DU FAUR
 Marguerite 735
DU HÉRISSON
 Anne 970, 989
 Mathieu Le Neuf,
  Sieur 959, 970,
  989

1189

DU LANGUE
François-Louis-Hector de Carondelet (Gov.), Vicomte de la Hestre and, Baron de Noyelle liii, clxxiii, 438

DU MESNIL
Jeanne 946

DU MONT dit DE BRIALMONT
Hélène-Françoise 804
Jean-Jacques 804
Jeanne-Catherine (Lunden) 804

DU PLESSIS
Louis d'Amours, Sieur 954

DU PLEXIS-OLIVET
François de Sévigné, Sieur 943

DU PONT
Jeanne 946

DU POST
François de Saint-Germain, Sieur 959
Olivier de Saint-Germain, Sieur 959

DU PUY
François de Celle, Seigneur 440
Mabile 735
Marie-Anne 226

DU SERRIN
Pierre d'Amours, Seigneur 954

DUANY
Andres M. 11
Elizabeth [Elzbieta] Maria (Plater-Zyberk) 11

DUBÉ
Joseph A. 939, 951
Josephte 989
Marie-Madeleine 970, 971, 974, 977

DUBLIN
Arthur Smyth, Archbishop of 480

DUCASSE
Jane 433

DUCIE
Thomas Reynolds Moreton, 1st Earl of 77

DUCKENFIELD
family 664
Martha (Fleetwood) 662
Mary 662
Robert 662
Susanna (Garraway) (Hartley) 662
William 662

DUCKWORTH
Eleanor 772

DUCRUET
Daniel 934
Stéphanie-Marie-Élisabeth (Grimaldi), Princess of Monaco 934

DUDDING
Elizabeth 467

DUDLEY. see also SUTTON; SUTTON alias DUDLEY
Anne 923
Anne [Anne Bradstreet] 370, 371
Catherine (Hutton) 321
Dorothy (Sanford) 321
Dorothy (Yorke) 370, 373
Edmund 321, 477, 691
Edward Sutton alias Dudley, 2nd Baron 370, 426
Elizabeth 691
Elizabeth (Bramshot) 691
Elizabeth (Grey) 477
family vii, x, xxiv, lv, clxxxii, 372
Grace (Threlkeld) 321
Guilford, Lord 477
Henry 370
Jane (Grey), Queen of England [Lady Jane Grey] xxiv, 69, 80, 477
Jane (Guilford) 477
John 691

John, 1st Duke of
  Northumberland
  477
John Sutton, 1st
  Baron 676, 691
John Sutton alias
  Dudley, 3rd Baron
  370
Joseph (Gov.) 537,
  923
Katherine (Deighton)
  (Hackburne) xxiv,
  clx, clxxii, 297, 370,
  373, 924
Lettice (Knollys)
  477
Mary 321, 477
Patience 371
Rebecca (Tyng)
  923
Richard 321
Robert, 1st Earl of
  Leicester 134,
  477
Roger (Capt.) 370,
  372, 373
Susanna (Thorne)
  370, 372, 373
Thomas 321
Thomas (Gov.) xi,
  xix, xxiv, xxxvii, li,
  lv, lix, clx, clxxii,
  clxxxii, 297, 370,
  372, 373, 924, 1025
William Humble
  Eric Ward, 3rd
  Earl of 33
Winifred 321
___ (Ashton) 370

DUDZEELE (DE)
Marguerite 950
Roger de Ghistelles,
  Seigneur, Seigneur
  of Staaten 950

DUFF
Agnes Cecil
  Emmeline 9, 10
Alexander George,
  1st Duke of Fife 9
Anne (Innes) 163
Anne Elizabeth
  Clementina 9
James, 5th Earl of
  Fife 9
Jean 163
Margaret 163
Mary 273
Patrick, of Craigston
  163

DUFFELL
Judith 781

**DUFFERIN AND
AVA**
Basil Sheridan
  Hamilton-Temple-
  Blackwood, 4th
  Marquess of 31, 32
Frederick Temple-
  Blackwood, 1st
  Marquess of,
  Governor-General
  of Canada, Viceroy
  of India 32

DUFFUS
Alexander Sunder-
  land, 1st Baron 893
James Sunderland,
  2nd Baron 893

Kenneth Sunder-
  land, 3rd Baron
  893

DUGDALE
Elizabeth (Swinfen)
  819
John 819
Mary 819
William (Sir)
  xxvii, lv, 589, 819,
  820

DUKE
Doris 103
Edward (Sir), 1st Bt.
  561
Elinor (Panton)
  561
Elizabeth 494, 561
James Buchanan
  103
Margaret (Basset)
  103
Mary (Hampton?)
  103
Richard 103
Thomas lx, cxlviii,
  103
Washington 103

DULANY
Margaret 270

DuLONG
John P. 939, 951,
  959

DUMARESQ
Elias 527
Frances (de
  Carteret) 527
Philip clxxiv, 527
Susan (Ferry) 527

1191

DUMPHRIES
William Crichton,
  1st Earl of 143
William Crichton,
  2nd Earl of 143
DUNBAR
Agnes (Mure) 732
Agnes of 864
Alexander (Sir) 732
Alexander (Sir), of
  Cumnock 260
Alexander, of
  Conzie and
  Kilbuyack 266
Alexander, of
  Machermore 732
Anna 255
Anne (Bayne) 266
Antonie, of
  Machermore 732
Archibald (Sir), of
  Newton and
  Thunderton, *de
  jure* 4th Bt. of
  Northfield 266
Archibald, of
  Newton and
  Thunderton 266
Asa 655
Cecily (FitzJohn) 732
Cuthbert, of
  Blantyre and
  Enterkine 732
Cynthia 655
David (Sir), of
  Cumnock and
  Blantyre 732
Dinah (Clark) 266
Edgar of 864
Elizabeth (Forbes) 266
Elizabeth (Hacket) 266
Eupheme (Bruce) 732
Euphemia 281
George Dunbar, 9th
  Earl of 732
Gospatrick I, Earl of
  Northumbria and
  857, 861, 864
Gospatrick II, 2nd
  Earl of 857, 861, 864
Isabel (Randolph) 281, 732
James, of Newton 266
Janet 219
Jean 252, 732
Jean (Falconer) 260
Jean (Murdoch) 732
John, 1st Earl of
  Moray 219, 281
John, of Blantyre
  and Enterkine 732
John, of Hempriggs 266
John, of
  Machermore 732
Juliana of 857, 861
Katherine 273
Margaret 260
Margaret
  (Anderson) 266
Margaret
  (Mackenzie) 266
Margaret (Seton?) 219
Mariot 252, 256
Marjorie (Stewart),
  Princess of
  Scotland 219
Marjorie, of Conzie
  and Kilbuick 281
Marjory 272
Marjory (Comyn) 732
Mary (Jones) 655
Mary (Montgomery) 732
Patrick (Sir) 281, 732
Patrick (Sir), of
  Cumnock and
  Mochrum 732
Patrick Dunbar, 4th
  Earl of 732
Patrick Dunbar, 5th
  Earl of 732
Patrick Dunbar, 6th
  Earl of 732
Patrick Dunbar, 7th
  Earl of 732
Priscilla 156
Robert, of Newton
  and Thunderton 266
Thomas, 2nd Earl of
  Moray 219
William lxv, 240, 266
William, of
  Hempriggs 266

____ (Stewart) 732
DUNBLANE
　James Chisholm,
　　Bishop of 258
DUNCAN II
　King of Scotland
　　828
DUNCANSON
　Ann/Annette 248
　family xl, xlvi, l,
　　lxiv, 914
　Helen (Livingston)
　　248
　James (Rev.),
　　minister of Alloa
　　248
　Janet/Jannette 248
　Katherine/Catalin
　　cxlix, cli, clxiv,
　　248, 914
　Margaret/Margret
　　cl, cli, clxviii, 248
　Maria 248
DUNCH
　Deborah (Pilking-
　　ton) 738
　Deborah [Lady
　　Deborah Moody]
　　clxxvi, 738, 740
　Harriet 135
　Walter 738
DUNCOMBE
　Katherine 538
DUNDAS
　Anne (Murray) 151
　Bethia 279
　Christian 174
　Elizabeth (Moore)
　　151

　family viii, l
　Isabel (Maule) 278
　James clxx, 151
　James (Sir), of
　　Arniston 174
　James, of
　　Doddington 278
　John, of Manour 151
　Marion (Boyd) 174
　Thomas clxx, 151
DUNDONALD
　John Cochrane, 4th
　　Earl of 62
　Thomas Cochrane,
　　8th Earl of 128
DUNGAN. *see also*
　DONGAN
　Barbara 488
　family 488
　Frances 488
　Frances (Latham)
　　xiii, 241, 468, 488
　Richard 488
　Thomas 488
　William 488
DUNGANNON
　Arthur Hill, 1st
　　Baron 340
DUNHAM
　Catherine (Good-
　　night) 726
　Hannah (Cheno-
　　weth) 725
　Jacob 726
　Jacob Mackey 726
　Jacob William 726
　Jonathan 725
　Louise Eliza (Stroup)
　　726

　Madelyn Lee
　　(Payne) 498, 726
　Mary (Smith) 725
　Mary Ann
　　(Kearney) 726
　Ralph Waldo
　　Emerson 498,
　　726
　Ruth Lucille
　　(Armour) 498,
　　726
　Samuel 725
　Stanley Ann 498,
　　726
　Stanley Armour
　　498, 726
DUNLOP
　Archibald lxvi,
　　cxliii, 218
　Bessie (____) 218
　Elizabeth (Roberton)
　　170, 218
　James, of Dunlop
　　218
　James, of Garnkirk
　　170, 218
　Jean 170
　Jean (Somerville)
　　218
　Lilias (Campbell)
　　170
　Mary (Beach) 218
DUNMORE
　Charles Murray, 1st
　　Earl of 62, 66, 67
　John Murray (Gov.),
　　4th Earl of 62, 933
　William Murray, 3rd
　　Earl of 62

1193

DUNNE/O'DOYNE
Clare 602
DUNSCOMB
Caroline Birch
(Durnford) 626
Caroline Durnford
vi, lxx, clvi, 440,
626
family 441, 626
John William 626
DUNTZFELT
Cecile Olivia 635
Christian Wilhelm
635
Marie-Henriette (de
Coninck) 635
DUPIRE
Jean 187
Martina (von Trapp)
clviii, 187
DUPUIS
Félicité (Gibault)
975
Jean-Baptiste 975
Louis-Albert 975
Louise 969
Marie-Catherine
(Tessier) 975
Marie-Josèphe 975
DUQUET
Catherine (Mallet)
982
Charles 982
Marie-Madeleine
982
DUQUET dit
DESROCHERS
Catherine-Ursule
(Amiot) 982

Jean-Baptiste 982
DURANCEAU dit
BRINDAMOUR
Claude 982
Marie-Madeleine
982
Marie-Madeleine
(Duquet) 982
DURBAY (DE)
Gerard of Luxem-
bourg, Seigneur
950
DURHAM
George Frederick
D'Arcy, 2nd Earl
of 28
James Pilkington,
Bishop of 738
Rhea 976
DURNFORD
Caroline Birch 626
Elias Walker 626
family 441, 626
Jane Sophia (Man)
626
DUROCHER
Laraine (Johnson)
(Hendricks)
[Laraine Day]
424
Leo 424
Valentine 982
DURVASSAL
Felicia (de
Camville) 874
Margery 874
Margery (___) 874
Philip 874
Thomas 874

DUSSEN (VAN DER)
Machteld 774
DUSTER
Elizabeth 64
DUTTON
Anne 611
Eleanor 561, 562,
760
Eleanor (Anderton)
561
Eleanor (Calveley)
561
Eleanor (Legh) 561
Frances 137, 362
Hugh 561
Jane (Booth) 561
John 561
John (Sir) 687
Margaret (Savage)
687
Maud 687
Piers (Sir) 561
Thomas 561
DUVALL
Jeffery A. xlix, liv,
727
Louisiana 498
Susanna 256
DUWALL
Anna Vendela
(Prytz) 889
Axel, Baron 889
Axel Jakob, Baron
889
Axel Vilhelm,
Baron 889
Louisa Katherina
(Wachtmeister),
Countess 889

Margaretha Louisa
  Charlotta 889
Sara Catherina
  (Broman) 889
Sofia Charlotta
  (Kruuse) 889
Sven, Baron 889
DUYCKINCK
Maria 88
DUZETTE
Clarissa Minerva
  925
Elizabeth Jane
  (King) 925
Philemon, Jr. 925
DWIGHT
Lydia 672
DWNN
Catherine (Wogan)
  582
Harry 582
Janet/Sioned 582
Margaret (Wogan)
  582
Owain 582
DYCHEFIELD
Isabel 815
**DYCKWOOD alias
  PETERS**
Martha (Treffry)
  665
Thomas 665
DYDDGU
ferch Dafydd Llwyd
  686
DYER
Constance Louisa
  108
Joan 778

Margaret 541
DYKE
Constance 737
DYMOKE
Alice 343, 470,
  471
Anne 311, 471
Anne (Talboys)
  310, 311, 389, 399,
  414
Bridget (Fiennes)
  311
Edward (Sir) 310,
  311, 389, 399, 414
Frances 310
Jane 579, 604
Joanna (Griffith)
  470
Lionel (Sir) 470
Margaret 389, 399,
  414, 471
Margaret (de
  Welles) 470, 471,
  579, 604
Robert (Sir) 311
Thomas (Sir) 470,
  471, 579, 604
DYN(E)WELL
Anne 579
Katherine
  (Fulnetby) 579
William 579
EASLEY
Julia 150
EATON
Anne (Lloyd) (Yale)
  xix, xxxvii, xlvi,
  lvii, clxiii, 252,
  657, 686

family vii
Hannah 252
Mabel
  (Harlakenden)
  (Haynes) xix,
  lxix, clxiii, clxxvii,
  587, 806, 807
Martha 344
Samuel 587, 806,
  807
Theophilus (Gov.)
  252, 686
EBEL
David li, liv, 816
EBNER (VON)
Clara 641
EBSWORTH
Elizabeth 177
ECHYNGHAM
Elizabeth 738, 851
family clxxxii, 632
Joan 632
Joan (FitzAlan)
  632
William (Sir) 632
EDDOWES
Catherine (Moulson)
  367
Eleanor (Carter)
  366
Elizabeth (Nevet)
  366, 367
family li
John 367
Ralph 366, 367,
  376
Roger 366, 367
Sarah (Kenrick)
  367, 376

EDEN
Anne 579, 838
Anne Clarissa
  (Spencer- Churchill)
  585, 648
Anthony [Robert
  Anthony], 1st Earl
  of Avon (Prime
  Minister) 585,
  648
Caroline (Calvert)
  (Hon.) 29, 100,
  102, 312, 313
Catherine (Shafto)
  100
Eleanor (Elliott) 102
Elizabeth (Heigham)
  579
Henry 579
John (Sir), 2nd Bt.
  100
Margaret (Lambton)
  100
Marianna (Jones)
  102
Mary 100
Mary (Davison)
  100, 102
Mary Anne 102
Robert (Sir), 1st Bt.
  100
Robert (Sir), 1st Bt.
  (Gov.), of Md.
  29, 100, 102, 312
Robert (Sir), 3rd Bt.
  100
Thomas 102
William, 1st Baron
  Auckland 102

EDENS
Ezekiel xiii
Fereby (Averitt) xiii
James xiii
Martha Ann xiii
Mary (Gammill)
  xiii
**EDGCOMBE/
EDGCUMBE/
EDGECOMB**
Anne 665
Joan 594
Joan (Dernford) 594
Joan (Tremayne)
  594
Katherine Elizabeth
  (Hamilton) 28
Margaret 493
Margaret (Luttrell)
  493
Peter 493
Piers (Sir) 594
Richard (Sir) 594
William Henry, 4th
  Earl of Mount
  Edgcumbe 28
EDGEWORTH
Anna Maria (Elers)
  312, 313
Elizabeth (___) 312
family 313
Maria 312
Richard xlix, cxliii,
  312
Richard Lovell 312
EDINBURGH
Alfred, Prince of
  Great Britain,
  Duke of 2

Marie of, Princess
  of Great Britain,
  Queen of
  Roumania 2
Philip, Prince of
  Greece and
  Denmark, Prince of
  Great Britain, Duke
  of 3, 41, 930
EDITH
Princess of France
  866, 870, 872
EDMONDS
Susanna 592
EDMONDSON
Beula Benton 480
EDMONSTONE
Alice Frederica
  [Mrs. Alice
  Keppel] 655
Archibald (Sir) 245
Janet (Shaw) 245
Margaret 245
Mary (Stewart)
  (Douglas) (Ken-
  nedy) (Cunning-
  ham) (Graham),
  Princess of Scotland
  239, 240, 241, 243,
  245, 248, 250, 251,
  252, 253, 254, 255,
  257, 258, 260, 261,
  266, 267, 268, 940
Matilda (Stewart)
  245
William (Sir) 245
William (Sir), of
  Culloden 240,
  245

1196

EDMUND
  Plantagenet, Prince
    of England, 1st
    Earl of Lancaster
    xxvi, 623, 625,
    628, 630, 632
  Plantagenet of Langley, Prince of
    England, 1st Duke
    of York   xxxix,
    107, 114, 119, 126,
    133, 134, 377, 410,
    411, 423
  Plantagenet of Woodstock, Prince of
    England, 1st Earl of
    Kent   515, 600
EDNYFED
  ap Llywarch Gam
    886
EDWARD
  ap John Wyn   660
  ap Watkyn   660
  Griffith   652
  Gwyn ap Hywel   555
  Jane   651, 652
  Lowry (Evans)   652
  Margaret   652
  Plantagenet, "the
    Black Prince,"
    Prince of England,
    Prince of Wales
    600
  Prince of Great
    Britain, Duke of
    Kent   45
EDWARD I
  King of England   ix,
    xxiv, xxvi, xxxi,
xxxix, lxvii, clxxii,
clxxiii, 462, 466,
470, 473, 478, 483,
486, 489, 491, 493,
495, 497, 500, 503,
505, 508, 510, 512,
514, 515, 517, 519,
522, 524, 526, 528,
530, 532, 534, 536,
539, 541, 543, 545,
547, 551, 553, 554,
555, 557, 558, 560,
563, 565, 567, 569,
571, 573, 574, 575,
577, 579, 580, 582,
584, 587, 588, 590,
592, 594, 595, 596,
598, 599, 600, 601,
603, 604, 605, 606,
607, 608, 609, 611,
613, 615, 737, 763,
766, 768, 770, 861
  King of Portugal
    190
EDWARD III
  King of England
    ix, xii, xxiv, xxv,
    xxvii, xxxi, xxxiv,
    xxxix, xli, clxxii,
    clxxiii, 107, 114,
    119, 126, 133, 134,
    295, 300, 305, 310,
    314, 317, 319, 324,
    327, 331, 333, 337,
    339, 342, 345, 347,
    349, 351, 353, 355,
    357, 359, 361, 363,
    366, 368, 370, 374,
    375, 377, 379, 382,
384, 385, 387, 389,
392, 393, 395, 396,
397, 398, 399, 400,
401, 403, 405, 407,
408, 409, 410, 411,
413, 414, 417, 418,
419, 420, 421, 423,
425, 426, 427, 428,
429, 431, 433, 434,
436, 459, 774, 775,
776, 900, 901, 902,
904, 905
EDWARD IV
  King of England
    xxxix, xl, clxxxvi,
    100, 103, 105, 106,
    107, 114, 119, 126,
    133, 134, 208, 323,
    333, 339, 346, 347,
    370, 397, 412, 431,
    433, 514, 902
EDWARD VI
  King of England
    305, 705, 741, 855
EDWARD VII
  King of Great
    Britain   9, 137,
    655
EDWARD THE ELDER
  King of England
    874, 877
EDWARD FORTUNATUS
  Margrave of
    Baden-Baden
    208, 209
EDWARDS
  Agnes   660

1197

Agnes (Harris)
  (Spencer) xix, lxiv,
  clxiii, 867, 924
Alexander 652
Annabella 115
Catherine (Griffith)
  (Morris) 652, 693
Edward 858
Elizabeth 149
John lvi
John [John ap
  Edward] 660
Margaret 858
Peter 858
Sarah (___) 730
Susanna (Samwell)
  858
Ursula (Coles) 858
William lvi, 867
William [William ap
  Edward/Bedward]
  cxc, 660
**EDWART
(IORWERTH)
TREVOR**
  ap Dafydd ab
  Ednyfed Gam
  813
EERDE (VAN)
  August Leopold van
  Pallandt, Heer, Heer
  van Beerse and
  Oosterveen 445
EFA
  ferch Einion ap
  Celynin 650, 659,
  686, 694
  ferch Gruffudd Hir
  886

ferch Madog 657,
  692
ferch Rhys 810
EFFERN (VON)
  Charlotte Dorothea,
  Countess 181
  Gerhard Ludwig,
  Baron 181
EGAN-BAKER
  Maryan lviii, 629
EGEDE (VAN)
  Adolf Werner II van
  Pallandt, Heer van
  Zuthem and 445
EGERTON
  Ann Elizabeth
  (Bleidt) 150
  Anna 713
  Anne 72
  Elizabeth 73
  Elizabeth
  (Cavendish) 70
  Elizabeth
  (Churchill) 70
  Elizabeth
  (Ravenscroft) 518
  Frances (Stanley)
  70
  Graham 150
  Jane (Powlett) 70
  John, 1st Earl of
  Bridgewater 70
  John, 2nd Earl of
  Bridgewater 70,
  73
  John, 3rd Earl of
  Bridgewater 70
  John Walden 150
  Julia (Easley) 150

Louisa 71, 72
Mary 517, 518
Mary (Marjori-
  banks) 150
Philip Henry 150
Rachel (Russell)
  71, 75
Rebecca Crenshaw
  (White) 150
Scroope, 1st Duke
  of Bridgewater 70
Sibella (Boswell)
  150
Thomas, 1st
  Viscount Brackley
  518
William 150
William Graham
  150
EGGENBERG (VON)
  Maria Franziska,
  Princess 198
EGGERTSEN
  Virginia 402
EGIDIA. see
  GILES/EGIDIA
EGLINTON
  Alexander
  Montgomery, 6th
  Earl of 143
  Alexander
  Montgomery, 8th
  Earl of 143
  Alexander
  Montgomery, 9th
  Earl of 143, 144
  Hugh Montgomery,
  1st Earl of 243,
  269, 270, 271

Hugh Montgomery,
2nd Earl of 173
Hugh Montgomery,
3rd Earl of 143,
173
Hugh Montgomery,
7th Earl of 143
**EGLOFFSTEIN
(AUF/ VON/VON
AND ZU)**
Albrecht Christoph
640
Amalie (de Montperny), Marquise de
Montperny 641
Anna Maria
(Schertel von
Burtenbach) 640
Clara (von Ebner)
641
Conrad Wilhelm
Siegmund 641
Ernst Friedrich 641
family 141, 641
Friedrich Ernst
Sigismund Kamill,
Baron [Frederick W.
von Egloffstein]
lxiii, cliv, 141, 641
Hedwig (von
Schlieben) 640
Hedwig Florentine
Louisa Friederike
(von Reltzenstein)
641
Hieronymus 640
Irmgard (von
Kiesenwetter) liii,
cliv, 141, 641

Louise Magdalena
(von Lassberg),
Baroness 641
Ludwig Friedrich
Heinrich 641
Maria Dorothea
(von Wildenstein)
640
Sigmund 640
Wilhelm Georg
Friedrich Christian
Heinrich 641
EGMOND (VAN)
Catharina 459
EGMONT
Frederick of, Count
of Büren 459
John I, Count of
291, 459
John II, Count of
291
John II, Lord of
459
John Percival, 1st
Earl of 430
Lamoral, Count of,
Prince of Gavre
290, 291, 459
Marie Christine of
291
William, Count of
459
EGREMONT
Charles Wyndham,
1st Earl of 76, 77,
78
George O'Brien
Wyndham, 2nd
Earl of 78

EGYPT
pharaohs of xv
EILERS
Marlene viii, liv
EILKEN
Alice 5
EINION
ab Ithel 689
ap Deicws Ddu
650
ap Gruffudd 657,
692
EINSIEDEL (VON)
Christiane
Wilhelmine,
Countess 142
EISENHOWER
Dwight David
(Gen.), 34th U.S.
President xviii,
xlii, 546, 589
Mamie Geneva
(Doud) xlii, 589
ELA
ferch Hopkin 808
ELBOROUGH
Anne 859
ELCHINGEN (D')
Michel Ney,
Napoleonic
Marshal, Duke,
Prince of Moscow
83
ELDER
Faye Valeta 620
ELDRIDGE
Bridget 311
Carlos [Charles]
996

Eliza Jane (___)
  656
Eloïsa (Ortíz Alfaro)
  996, 997
  George 656
ELEANOR
  Duchess of
    Aquitaine, Queen
    of France, Queen
    of England 647,
    735, 737, 742, 746,
    749, 752, 754, 757,
    760, 761, 763, 766,
    768, 770, 772, 774,
    776, 909, 943, 948,
    952, 964, 991, 993
  ferch Richard ap
    Howell 518
  of Naples 186, 189
  Plantagenet, Princess
    of England, Queen
    of Castile 647, 909,
    948, 964
  Princess of Castile,
    Queen of England
    xxvi, 466, 478,
    483, 489, 491, 495,
    497, 500, 503, 505,
    508, 510, 512, 514,
    524, 528, 530, 532,
    536, 543, 547, 551,
    553, 554, 555, 558,
    560, 563, 565, 567,
    569, 571, 573, 574,
    575, 577, 582, 584,
    587, 588, 590, 592,
    594, 595, 596, 601,
    603, 606, 607, 608,
    611, 613, 615, 861

Princess of
  Provence, Queen
  of England 623,
  625, 628, 630, 632,
  633, 942, 944, 945,
  946, 963, 965
Princess of Sicily
  and Anjou, Queen
  of Sicily 51, 451
Princess of the
  Belgians 204
ELEANOR
CATHERINE
  Princess of
    Zweibrücken-
    Kleeberg 44
ELEN
  ferch Cadwaladr ap
    Robert 650
  ferch Gruffudd ap
    Hywel 230
  ferch Hywel ap
    Gruffudd 229,
    230
  ferch John 659, 689
  ferch John Wynne
    229
  ferch Llywelyn o'r
    Cwmwd ap Hywel
    Hen 811
  ferch Morgan 810
  ferch Owain ap
    Gruffudd 582
  ferch Thomas 657,
    813, 824
  Llwyd 689
ELEN LLWYD
  ferch Robert ap
    Morgan 229

ELERS
  Anna Maria 312,
    313
  Edward Hungerford
    313
  Mary (Hungerford)
    312, 313
  Paul 312, 313
ELFORD
  Joan 573, 835
ELGENSTIERNA
  Gustaf xxvii
ELGIN
  Grace 421
  Thomas Bruce, 3rd
    Earl of, 2nd Earl of
    Ailesbury 80, 81
ELI dit BRETON
  Charles 984
  Jean-Baptiste 984
  Marie-Françoise
    (Roy) 984
  Marie-Louise
    (Labrecque) 984
  Olive (Goulet) 984
ELIA
  (Zaharia), Queen of
    the Albanians 935
ELIDIR
  ap Rhys Sais 886
ELIOT/ELIOTT/
ELLIOT/ELLIOTT
  Alexander Boswell
    90
  Andrew lxvi, cliv,
    96
  Arthur Augustus
    Boswell (Sir), 9th
    Bt. 90

Beatrice Maud
  Boswell liv, cxlii,
  90
Catherine (Craigie)
  90
Charles George
  Cornwallis 64
Clare Louisa
  (Phelips) 64
Constance Rhiannon
  (Guest) 64
Edward Granville 64
Edward Granville,
  3rd Earl of St.
  Germans 64
Eleanor 102, 165,
  211
Eleanor (Eliott) 90
Elizabeth 311
Euphan (Dickson)
  90
family, of Lodgewill
  96
Frances Anna Maria
  22
Francis (Sir), 5th Bt.
  90
Georgiana Augusta
  (Leveson-Gower)
  64
Gertrude (Mary
  Gertrude) 268
Gilbert (Sir), 1st Bt.
  90
Gilbert (Sir), 2nd Bt.
  165
Gilbert (Sir), 3rd Bt.
  90
Grace 969

Helen (Crozier) 96
Helen (Steuart) 165
Henry, of Dinfee 96
Isabella (Cranston)
  90
James, of Larriston
  96
Jane 754
Janet 96
Janet (Scott) 96
Janet/Jean (Eliot) 96
Jean 210
Jean (Stewart) 96
Jemima
  (Cornwallis) 64
John (Sir), 4th Bt. 90
Lilia (Burbank) 90
Margaret (Eliot) 96
Margaret (Murray)
  90
Margaret (Schuman)
  96
Margaret Augusta 64
Mary (Andrews) 90
Mary (Butler) 366
Mary (Russell) 90
Mary (Scott) 210
Maxine 268
Robert, of Redhaugh
  96
Robert, of
  Whitthaugh 96
Sined/Jenet (Barrett)
  874
Theresa (Boswell) 90
Walter, of
  Hermitage 96
William viii, liv,
  lxv, 96, 240

William (Sir), 2nd
  Bt. 90
William (Sir), 6th
  Bt. 90
William, 2nd Earl of
  St. Germans 64
William, of Lariston
  210
William Francis
  (Sir), 7th Bt. 90
ELISE
  ap Gruffudd 657
  ab Iorwerth ab
  Owain Brogyntyn
  657, 689, 692, 693
ELIZABETH
  (de Burgh), Queen
    of Scotland 456
  (Woodville) (Grey),
    Queen of England
    100, 103, 105, 106,
    134, 208, 323, 333,
    339, 346, 347, 370,
    397, 412, 431, 433,
    514, 902
  Archduchess of
    Austria, Queen of
    Poland 194, 195,
    196, 198, 895
  of Bavaria 451
  of Bohemia (wife of
    Albert II, Holy
    Roman Emperor,
    King of Hungary
    and Bohemia) 187,
    220
  of Brandenburg-
    Anspach 195, 198

1201

of Brunswick-
  Göttingen 451
of Brunswick-
  Lüneburg 452
ferch Humphrey ap
  Thomas 690
ferch Morgan ap
  William clxxxv
of Hesse-Darmstadt
  184
Karadjorjevic,
  Princess of
  Yugoslavia 3
of the Kumans,
  Queen of Hungary
  459
of Leuchtenberg 194
of Nassau-Siegen
  141, 181
of Nassau-
  Wiesbaden 617
of Nürnberg (wife of
  Rupert III, Holy
  Roman Emperor)
  237, 291
Plantagenet (of York),
  Queen of England
  62, 69, 76, 79, 80,
  347, 348
Plantagenet, Princess
  of England xxxix,
  478, 497, 500, 503,
  510, 512, 517, 524,
  530, 532, 543, 551,
  553, 554, 555, 558,
  560, 563, 565, 569,
  571, 573, 574, 582,
  588, 595, 596, 601,
  603, 608, 611, 613

Princess of Bavaria-
  Landshut 52
Princess of
  Denmark 181,
  182, 184
Princess of England
  and Scotland,
  Queen of Bohemia
  38
Princess of France,
  Queen of Spain
  637
Princess of Savoy
  614
Princess of Sicily
  and Aragón 51,
  451
Princess of the
  Belgians 204
Princess of Würt-
  temberg, Empress
  of Austria 11
Princess of
  Zweibrücken 56
of Saxe-Altenburg 7
of Tirol (wife of
  Albert I, Holy
  Roman Emperor)
  449, 451
ELIZABETH I
Queen of England
  xxiv, xxxix, 75,
  134, 300, 345, 470,
  539, 554, 588, 596,
  684, 705
ELIZABETH II
Queen of Great
  Britain xl, 3, 41,
  321, 323, 930

**ELIZABETH
ANGELA
MARGUERITE**
(Bowes-Lyon),
  Queen of Great
  Britain [HM Queen
  Elizabeth The
  Queen Mother]
  xl, xlii, liv, 101,
  121, 419, 545, 930
**ELIZABETH
CHARLOTTE**
Princess of the
  Palatinate 54
**ELIZABETH
CHRISTINA**
Princess of
  Brunswick-
  Wolfenbüttel,
  Queen of Prussia
  13
ELKINGTON
Alice (Wodhull) 768
Ann (___) 768
Elizabeth 768
George xxxv, xlv,
  lvi, lxiv, lxviii,
  clxiv, clxxvii, 768
Joseph 768
Mary (Humphries)
  (Core) 768
William 768
ELLAND
___ 667
ELLEN
of Wales 682, 683
ELLENBOROUGH
Edward Law, 1st
  Baron 363

Edward Law, 1st Earl
 of, Governor- Gen.
 of India 363
ELLETSON
 Elizabeth 825
ELLICOTT
 Andrew 595
 Mary (Fox) liv,
  clxv, clxxix, 595
 William M. liv
ELLIMAN
 Ludlow cxci
ELLIOT(T). *see*
 ELIOT/ELIOTT/
 ELLIOT/ELLIOTT
ELLIOTT/ELLIS
 Eleanor 497
ELLIS
 ap Huw 693
 ap Rees [Ellis Price]
  229, 511
 Elen 230
 Ellis 510
 Lydia (Humphrey)
  510
 Margaret (ferch
  Ellis Morris) 229
 Margaret (Roberts)
  229, 230
 Mary Anne 308
 Mildred 883
 Rowland 229, 230,
  511
 William 693
ELLIS WILLIAM
 ap Huw 659
ELLYW
 ferch Edward ap
  Ieuan 650

ferch Rhys Ddu
 810
ELMEDEN (DE)
 Elizabeth (de
  Umfreville)
  clxxxix
 family clxxxix
 William (Sir)
  clxxxix
ELMES
 Alice (St. John)
  662
 Edmund 662
 Elizabeth 662
 Margaret 311
ELPHINSTONE
 Alexander
  Elphinstone, 2nd
  Baron 285
 Alexander
  Elphinstone, 4th
  Baron 159, 163,
  165
 Catherine (Erskine)
  285
 Cecilia 270
 Elizabeth 93
 Eupheme 82, 85,
  87, 92, 98, 897
 Helen 165
 Jean 159
 Jean (Livingston)
  159, 163, 165
 Margaret 163
 Margaret (Drum-
  mond) 159, 163,
  165
 Marjorie 285

Robert Elphinstone,
  3rd Baron 159,
  163, 165
**ELPHINSTONE-
 DALRYMPLE**
 Edith Ethel
  (LeBreton) 128
 Flora Loudoun
  (MacLeod) 128
 Francis Napier (Sir),
  7th Bt. 128
 Helenora Catherine
  (Heron-Maxwell)
  128
 Hew Drummond
  128
 Penelope Eleanor
  cxlv, 128
 Robert Graeme
  (Sir), 5th Bt. 128
ELSBETH
 ferch Dafydd Llwyd
  229
 ferch Maredudd ap
  Hywel 231
 ferch Owain 689
 ferch Robert ap
  Morgan 770
ELTONHEAD
 Agatha clxvi,
  clxxiii, 484, 491,
  498, 551
 Alice xix, xxxiv,
  clxvi, clxxiii, 329,
  498, 607, 697
 Anne (Bowers)
  497
 Anne (Sutton) 497
 Eleanor 498

family viii, l
Jane clxxiii, 498, 599
Jane (___) 498
Jennet (Gerard) 497
Katherine 498
Martha clxvi, clxxiii, 497
Richard 497
William 497, 498

ELWES
Cary (Ivan Simon Cary) xvii, xlvi, cxliii, 77, 78
Dominick (Bebe Evelyn Dominick) 77
Gervase Henry 77
Gloria Ellinor (Rodd) 77
Simon Edmund Vincent Paul 77
Tessa Georgina (Kennedy) 77
Winefride Mary Elizabeth (Feilding) 77

ELY
Elizabeth (Fenwick) (Cullick) 330

EMANUEL PHILIBERT
Prince of Savoy, Prince of Carignan 18

EMERY
[Anna] Audrey 3
Elizabeth 673

EMES
Anne 648

EMMANUEL LEOPOLD
Prince of the Belgians 204

EMMET
Alexandra Temple 406
Elizabeth (Mason) 325
family xxxiv
Jane (Patten) 325
John Patten 325, 464
Lily Dulany 406
Mary Byrd Farley (Tucker) 325, 464, 465
Robert 325
Thomas Addis xvii, clxiv, 325

EMMISON
Frederick George (F. G.) xxix

EMMONS
Sarah 859

EMPSON
Joan 359

EMYLEY
Mary 481

ENDICOTT
family xxxvi

ENGAINE
Anice (de Fauconberge) 705
Elizabeth 705
Joan (Peveral) 705
John Engaine, 2nd Baron 705

Nicholas (Sir) 705

ENGELBERTA
of Mark and Cleves 459

ENGELHARDT (VON)
Lilli, Baroness 850

ENGLAND 605
Adela of Normandy, Princess of 642, 911
Adeliza of Louvain, Queen of, wife of William d'Aubigny, 1st Earl of Arundel 830
Ælflæd, wife of Ethelred II, King of 857, 861, 864
Aline/Alix of 959
Anne (Boleyn), Queen of 300, 428, 539, 551, 588, 596
Anne (Neville), Queen of 118
Anne, Princess of Bohemia, Queen of 714
Anne, Princess of Denmark, Queen of Scotland and 35, 38, 47, 49, 52, 785
baronets in xv
Beatrix Plantagenet, Princess of 442, 633, 942, 946, 963
Catherine of Braganza, Princess of Portugal, Queen

of, Queen of
Scotland 22, 25,
29, 30, 31, 33, 34
Charles I, King of,
King of Scotland
430, 467
Charles II, King of,
King of Scotland
xii, xxv, lvii, lxviii,
22, 25, 29, 30, 31,
33, 34, 103, 109,
615, 627
Edmund Plantagenet
of Langley, Prince
of, 1st Duke of York
xxxix, 107, 114,
119, 126, 133, 134,
377, 410, 411, 423
Edmund Plantagenet
of Woodstock,
Prince of, 1st Earl
of Kent 515, 600
Edmund Planta-
genet, Prince of, 1st
Earl of Lancaster
xxvi, 623, 625, 628,
630, 632
Edward I, King of
ix, xxiv, xxvi, xxxi,
xxxix, lxvii, clxxii,
clxxiii, 462, 466,
470, 473, 478, 483,
486, 489, 491, 493,
495, 497, 500, 503,
505, 508, 510, 512,
514, 515, 517, 519,
522, 524, 526, 528,
530, 532, 534, 536,
539, 541, 543, 545,
547, 551, 553, 554,
555, 557, 558, 560,
563, 565, 567, 569,
571, 573, 574, 575,
577, 579, 580, 582,
584, 587, 588, 590,
592, 594, 595, 596,
598, 599, 600, 601,
603, 604, 605, 606,
607, 608, 609, 611,
613, 615, 737, 763,
766, 768, 770, 861
Edward III, King of
ix, xii, xxiv, xxv,
xxvii, xxxi, xxxiv,
xxxix, xli, clxxii,
clxxiii, 107, 114,
119, 126, 133, 134,
295, 300, 305, 310,
314, 317, 319, 324,
327, 331, 333, 337,
339, 342, 345, 347,
349, 351, 353, 355,
357, 359, 361, 363,
366, 368, 370, 374,
375, 377, 379, 382,
384, 385, 387, 389,
392, 393, 395, 396,
397, 398, 399, 400,
401, 403, 405, 407,
408, 409, 410, 411,
413, 414, 417, 418,
419, 420, 421, 423,
425, 426, 427, 428,
429, 431, 433, 434,
436, 459, 774, 775,
776, 900, 901, 902,
904, 905
Edward IV, King of
xxxix, xl, clxxxvi,
100, 103, 105, 106,
107, 114, 119, 126,
133, 134, 208, 323,
333, 339, 346, 347,
370, 397, 412, 431,
433, 514, 902
Edward VI, King of
305, 705, 741, 855
Edward "the Black
Prince," Prince of,
Prince of Wales
600
Edward the Elder,
King of 874, 877
Eleanor, Duchess of
Aquitaine, Queen
of France, Queen
of 647, 735, 737,
742, 746, 749, 752,
754, 757, 760, 761,
763, 766, 768, 770,
772, 774, 776, 909,
943, 948, 952, 964,
991, 993
Eleanor, Princess of
Castile, Queen of
xxvi, 466, 478, 483,
489, 491, 495, 497,
500, 503, 505, 508,
510, 512, 514, 524,
528, 530, 532, 536,
543, 547, 551, 553,
554, 555, 558, 560,
563, 565, 567, 569,
571, 573, 574, 575,
577, 582, 584, 587,
588, 590, 592, 594,

595, 596, 601, 603,
606, 607, 608, 611,
613, 615, 861
Eleanor, Princess of
Provence, Queen of
623, 625, 628, 630,
632, 633, 942, 944,
945, 946, 963, 965
Eleanor, Princess of,
Queen of Castile
647, 909, 948, 964
Elgiva of 857, 861,
864
Elizabeth I, Queen
of xxiv, xxxix,
75, 134, 300, 345,
470, 539, 554, 588,
596, 684, 705
Elizabeth (Planta-
genet) of York,
Queen of 62, 69,
76, 79, 80, 347, 348
Elizabeth (Woodville)
(Grey), Queen of
100, 103, 105, 106,
134, 208, 323, 333,
339, 346, 347, 370,
397, 412, 431, 433,
514, 902
Elizabeth, Princess
of Scotland and,
Queen of Bohemia
38
Elizabeth Planta-
genet of Lancaster,
Princess of 400
Elizabeth Planta-
genet, Princess of
xxxix, 478, 497,

500, 503, 510, 512,
517, 524, 530, 532,
543, 551, 553, 554,
555, 558, 560, 563,
565, 569, 571, 573,
574, 582, 588, 595,
596, 601, 603, 608,
611, 613
Ethelred II "the
Unready," King of
xxvi, 843, 857,
861, 864
Hannah 970
Henry I, King of
xxvi, xxxix, 652,
658, 739, 741, 806,
807, 808, 810, 811,
813, 815, 817, 819,
821, 822, 824, 826,
830, 957, 959
Henry II, King of
vii, x, xxvi, xxxii,
xxxix, 507, 647,
652, 658, 735, 737,
741, 742, 746, 749,
752, 754, 757, 760,
761, 763, 766, 768,
770, 772, 774, 776,
841, 845, 909, 948,
964, 994
Henry III, King of
ix, xxxix, 623, 625,
628, 630, 632, 633,
683, 942, 944, 945,
946, 963, 965
Henry IV, King of
xxv, 229, 231, 233,
235, 287, 293, 378,
412

Henry V, King of
226, 603, 813, 824
Henry VII, King of
xxxix, lxvi, 62, 69,
76, 79, 80, 226,
347, 348, 361, 477,
547, 605, 691
Henry VIII, King of
xii, xl, lviii, 136,
139, 232, 300, 303,
305, 530, 539, 551,
596, 605, 741, 855
Isabel of Angoulême,
Queen of 372, 650,
653, 657, 659, 661,
665, 667, 670, 672,
676, 678, 680, 682,
684, 686, 687, 689,
691, 692, 693, 694,
695, 697, 785, 917
James I, King of, VI
of Scotland xxv,
xlv, 35, 38, 47, 49,
52, 69, 76, 80, 430,
536, 785
James II, King of,
VII of Scotland
clxxxix, 22, 24,
122, 536, 615, 627,
678, 727, 781
Jane (Grey) Dudley,
Queen of [Lady Jane
Grey] 69, 80, 477
Jane (Seymour),
Queen of 305,
705, 741, 855
Joan Plantagenet of
Acre, Princess of
xxxix, 466, 483,

489, 491, 495, 505,
508, 514, 528, 536,
547, 565, 567, 575,
577, 584, 587, 590,
592, 594, 606, 607,
615
Joanna, Princess of
Navarre, Duchess
of Brittany, Queen
of 226, 229, 231,
233, 235, 287, 293
John "Lackland,"
King of vii, x,
xxvi, xxxii, xxxix,
372, 650, 652, 653,
657, 659, 661, 665,
667, 670, 672, 674,
676, 678, 680, 682,
684, 686, 687, 689,
691, 692, 693, 694,
695, 696, 697, 699,
709, 785, 917
John of Gaunt,
Prince of, Duke of
Lancaster xxxix,
295, 300, 314, 324,
331, 337, 339, 345,
357, 366, 368, 370,
375, 382, 387, 393,
395, 396, 397, 398,
400, 403, 405, 407,
413, 417, 419, 421,
426, 427, 429, 433,
434, 900, 902
Katherine (Howard),
Queen of 339, 468,
605
Katherine de Valois,
Princess of France,

Queen of, wife of
Owen Tudor 226,
603, 813, 824
Lionel Plantagenet
of Antwerp, Prince
of, Duke of
Clarence xxxix,
107, 114, 119, 126,
133, 134, 305, 310,
317, 319, 327, 333,
342, 347, 349, 351,
355, 359, 361, 363,
374, 379, 384, 385,
389, 399, 401, 414,
418, 425, 431, 901,
904, 905
Margaret (Tudor),
Princess of, Queen
of Scotland 143,
146, 148, 150, 151,
152, 154, 157, 159,
161, 163, 165, 166,
167, 168, 170, 171,
173, 174, 176, 177,
179
Margaret, Princess
of France, Queen
of xxvi, 462, 470,
473, 486, 493, 515,
519, 522, 526, 534,
539, 541, 545, 557,
579, 580, 598, 599,
600, 604, 605 609
Mary (Tudor),
Princess of, Queen
of France, Duchess
of Suffolk xxxix,
clxxxiii, clxxxviii,
62, 69, 76, 79, 80

Mary Beatrice,
Princess of
Modena, Queen of
Scotland and 22,
24
Mary II, Queen of,
Queen of Scotland
122, 615, 678, 679,
781
Matilda, Princess of
Scotland, Queen of
739, 806, 808, 810,
811, 813, 815, 817,
819, 821, 822, 824,
826, 957, 959
Matilda of Boulogne,
Queen of 774, 776
Matilda of Flanders,
Duchess of
Normandy, Queen
of 642, 830, 851,
911, 1024
monarchs of xv
Philippa of Hainault,
Queen of 107, 114,
119, 126, 133, 134,
295, 300, 305, 310,
314, 317, 319, 324,
327, 331, 333, 337,
339, 342, 345, 347,
349, 351, 353, 355,
357, 359, 361, 363,
366, 368, 370, 374,
375, 377, 379, 382,
384, 385, 387, 389,
392, 393, 395, 396,
397, 398, 399, 400,
401, 403, 405, 407,
409, 410, 411, 413,

1207

414, 417, 418, 419, 420, 421, 423, 425, 426, 427, 428, 429, 431, 433, 434, 436, 459, 774, 775, 776, 900, 901, 902, 904, 905
Richard II, King of xxiv, xxv, 714
Richard III, King of cxxvi, 107, 114, 118, 119, 126, 133
Stephen, King of 642, 774, 776, 830, 911
Thomas Plantagenet of Brotherton, Prince of, Earl of Norfolk xxxix, 462, 470, 473, 486, 493, 519, 522, 526, 534, 539, 541, 545, 557, 564, 579, 580, 598, 599, 604, 605, 609
Thomas Plantagenet of Woodstock, Prince of, 1st Duke of Gloucester xxv, xxxix, 331, 353, 392, 393, 409, 420, 421, 428, 436
William I "the Conqueror," Duke of Normandy, King of xx, 642, 830, 851, 861, 879, 911, 919, 1024
William III, Prince of Orange, King of, King of Scotland 615

ENGLEFIELD
Elizabeth 625, 626
ENGLISH
Isabel 700
ENKEVOIRTH
Johann Ferdinand Franz Leopold, Count of 186
Maria Antonia Cäcilia, Countess 186, 187
ENTWISTLE
Lucy 830
ENXARA (DE)
María Peres 619
ENZESFELD (VON)
Luís de Tovar/Ludwig von Tovar, Baron 619
EPES
Anne (Isham) 711
Francis 357
Francis (III) 711
Francis (IV) 711
John 357
Martha 711
Peter 357
Sarah (___) 711
Thomasine (Fisher) 357
William 357
ÉPINOY (D')
Hugh de Melun, Prince 287
Hugh I de Melun, Seigneur d'Antoing and 733

Pierre de Melun, Prince 287, 292
EPPLEY
Constance Rivington (Russell) (Winant) 165
Ethelberta Pyne (Russell) 165
Marion 166
ERBACH
Dorothea of 182
George III, Count of 182
ERBACH-SCHÖNBERG
Caroline Ernestine of 182
ERBERVELT
Wilhelmina Antonia 907
ERDESWICK
Elizabeth (Dixwell) 750
Sampson 750
ERGADIA (DE)
Isabel 456
Joanna (Isaac/Ysac) 456
John, of Lorne 456
ERIC
Duke of Brunswick-Grubenhagen 451
ERIC XIV
King of Sweden 51, 53, 889
ERICK
Mary 482

ERICSSON
  Amelia Jane (Byam) 302, 303
  John xvii, 302
ERIK
  Skarsholmslaegten, Duke of Sønder-Halland 644
ERIKSDOTTER
  Constantia 51
  Virginia 53, 889
ERLANDSSON
  Elin (Ulfsdotter), of Ervalla 457
  Henrik, Lord of Fyllingarum 457
ERMENGARDE
  (de Beaumont), Queen of Scotland 700, 705, 708, 710, 713, 715, 719, 721, 723, 725, 727, 728, 730, 732
ERNELEY
  Anne (Darrell) 855
  Jane 855
  John 855
  Lucy (Cooke) 855
ERNEST
  Duke of Brunswick-Lüneburg-Celle 220
  Elector of Saxony 451
  Margrave of Baden-Durlach 195, 198
ERNEST I
  Duke of Saxe-Coburg-Gotha 45

ERNEST ASCHWIN GEORG CAROL HEINRICH IGNATZ
  Prince of Lippe-Biesterfeld clvi, 47
ERNEST AUGUSTUS
  Elector of Hanover 58, 432
  King of Hanover 40
  Prince of Hanover 934
ERNEST CASIMIR FREDERICK CHARLES EBERHARD
  Count of Lippe-Biesterfeld 47
ERNEST FREDERICK II
  Duke of Saxe-Coburg-Saalfeld 44
ERNST
  Max 15
ERRINGTON
  Abraham lx, clxxxv
  Catherine (Cresswell) clxxxv
  family vii
  Roger clxxxv
ERROLL
  Andrew Hay, 8th Earl of 145
  George Hay, 7th Earl of 145, 152, 223

  James Boyd (Hay), 15th Earl of 131
  William George, 18th Earl of 9
  William Hay, 3rd Earl of 223
  William Hay, 6th Earl of 145
  William Hay, 17th Earl of 131
ERSKINE
  Alexander, of Shielfield 275
  Alexander Erskine, 3rd Baron 275, 276, 285
  Catherine 285
  Charles (Sir) 174, 215
  Charles (Sir), 1st Bt. 174
  Christian 243, 276
  Christian (Crichton) 275, 276, 285
  Christian (Dundas) 174
  Christian (Stirling) 275
  Elizabeth 248, 252, 256, 260
  Elizabeth (___) 275
  Elizabeth (Carre) 275
  Elizabeth (Haliburton) 275
  Elizabeth (Lindsay) 243, 275, 276, 285
  Euphemia 150

Evelyn Hilda Stuart 23
Henry, of Chirnside 275
Isabel (Campbell) 248, 275, 285
Isabella (Cairncross) 275
James, Lord Alva 175
James, of Little Sauchie and Balgownie 275
James, of Shielfield 275
Janet (Douglas) 275, 276, 285
Janet (Wilson) 275
Jean 174
Jean (Stirling) (Stirling) 175
John, 2nd Earl of Mar 215
John, of Dun 260
John, of Shielfield 275
Katherine (Monypenny) 260
Margaret 93, 95, 97, 254, 893
Margaret (Halcro) 275
Margaret (Haliburton) 275
Margaret (Simpson) 275
Marjory/Elizabeth (Graham) 260
Mary 174, 215

Mary (Hope) 174, 215
Mary (Stewart) 215
Ralph, of Dunfermline 275
Ralph, of Shielfield 275
Robert 275
Robert Erskine, 1st Baron 243, 275, 276, 285
Robert Erskine, 4th Baron 248, 275, 285
Thomas Erskine, 2nd Baron 275, 276, 285
___ 275, 282

ERVALLA
Elin Ulfsdotter of 457
Peder Ulfsson, Lord of, Lord of Huseby 457
Ulf Pedersson, knight, lord of 457
Ulv Jonson, Lord of, Lord of Faanoe, Vreta, Saeby and Huseby 452, 457

ERVING
Elizabeth 923

ERWIN
Lucy L. liv, lxii
Thomas S. viii, liv, 425, 712

ESCHENBURG (VON)
Agnes 832

ESCORNAIX (D')
Arnould VI de Gavre, Baron 950

ESCOUBLEAU (D') DE SOURDIS
Catherine-Marie 202

ESHELMAN
Lillian 120

ESHER
Reginald Baliol Brett, 2nd Viscount 137
William Baliol Brett, 1st Viscount 136

ESNEUX (D')
Charlotte-Jacqueline d'Argenteau, Countess of, Baroness of Melsbroeck 81

ESNEVAL (D')
family 960
Gauvin II de Dreux, Baron 956
Jeanne 956
Robert de Dreux, Baron 956

ESPERANCE (VON L')
Henrietta Hedwige Curie, Baroness 184

ESPERANCE and SANDERSLEBEN (VON L')
Karl Leopold, Baron, Count of Coligny 184

ESPINAY (D')
　Catherine (d'Estouteville) 941
　Henri, Seigneur 941
　Jeanne 941
ESSE
　Catherine 836
ESSEN (VON)
　Gertrude Ida Eugenia, Baroness 453
ESSEX
　Algernon Capell, 2nd Earl of 121
　Arthur Capell, 1st Earl of 121, 122
　Geoffrey FitzPiers, Earl of 866, 870, 1025
　Henry Bourchier, Count of Eu, 1st Earl of xl, 134
　Humphrey de Bohun, 4th Earl of Hereford and 478, 497, 500, 503, 510, 512, 517, 524, 530, 532, 543, 551, 553, 554, 555, 558, 560, 563, 565, 569, 571, 573, 574, 582, 588, 595, 596, 601, 603, 608, 611, 613
　Jane 475
　Maud FitzGeoffrey, Countess of 783, 1025
　Robert Devereux, 2nd Earl of 75, 134, 135, 136
　Walter Devereux, 1st Earl of 134, 137
　William Anne Capell, 4th Earl of 313
　William Capell, 3rd Earl of 121
ESSEX (DE)
　Agnes 680
ESTAING (D'). *see also* GISCARD d'ESTAING
　Catherine (de Chabannes) 202
　Catherine (du Bourg) 202
　Charles-François, Marquis de Saillans 202
　Charlotte (d'Arpajon) 201
　Claude (de Combourcier) 202
　François, Vicomte 202
　Gabriel, Vicomte 201
　Gaspard, Baron de Saillans 202
　Gilberte (de la Rochefoucauld) 202
　Jacques, Baron de Plauzet 202
　Jean, Baron de Saillans 202
　Jean III, Vicomte 202
　Jean-Baptiste-Charles-Henri-Hector, Comte xvi, cliv, 202
　Marie-Henriette (de Colbert) 202
　Marie-Sophie (Rousselet de Châteaurenault) 202
　Philiberte (de la Tour de Saint-Vidal) 202
ESTAMPES (D')
　Jean, Seigneur de La Ferté-Nabert 634
　Madeleine (de Husson) 634
　Marguerite 634
ESTAPLES (D')
　Marie 733
ESTE (D')
　Angelina Caterina, of Modena 18
　Isabella, of Modena 186, 189
　Maria Beatrice, Princess of Modena 15
　Maria Theresa Felicitas, of Modena 287
ESTELL
　Emily Rogers 545
ESTERHÁZY DE GALÁNTHA
　Anna Maria, Countess 15
　Maria Teresia, Countess 187

ESTONIA
Knud Skarsholm-slaegten, Duke of 644
ESTOUTEMONT (D')
William/Guillaume d'Estouteville/ Touteville/ de Stuteville, Seigneur 853
ESTOUTEVILLE (D')/TOUTEVILLE/ DE STUTEVILLE
Alice 857, 861
Anne (Robertson) 393, 394
Catherine 941
Charles 393
Charlotte 208
family 854
Jacques, Seigneur de Beyne, Baron d'Ivry 208
Jean II, Sire 941
Jeanne (Payer) 941
Joan 730, 845
Louis, Sire 941
Margaret xxxv, lxv, cxlvi, clxi, 393
Marguerite (de Harcourt) 941
Marie (de la Roche-Guyon) 941
Michel, Sire 941
William/Guillaume, Seigneur d'Estoutemont 853
ESTUMY
Maud 740

ETHELRED II "THE UNREADY"
King of England xxvi, 843, 857, 861, 864
ETHERINGTON
Jane 390
ETHERSTONE
Elizabeth clxxxix
ETWELL
Joan 768
EU
Henry, Count of 830
Henry Bourchier, Count of, 1st Earl of Essex xl, 134
Ida of 830
John, Count of 830
Maud de Lusignan, of 783
William Bourchier, Count of 134, 331, 353, 392, 393, 403, 409, 420, 421, 428, 436
EUDES I
Duke of Burgundy 853, 855
EUDES II
Duke of Burgundy 642
EUDOXIA
of Suzdal 621
EUGÈNE
Prince of Savoy 289
EUGÈNE-ROSE
de Beauharnais, 1st Duke of Leuchtenberg, Viceroy of Italy 442, 443, 444
EUGÉNIE
de Montijo (Eugenia Maria Ignace Augustine de Portocarrero de Guzmán y Kirkpatrick), Empress of the French 291, 292
EUGENIE
of York, Princess of Great Britain 25
EULENBURG (VON)
Barbara 617
EUPHEMIA
of Mazovia, Queen of Galicia 621
of Ross, Queen of Scotland 275, 276, 278, 282, 285
of Rügen, Queen of Norway 452, 457
EURE
Anne 317, 389
Barbara 415
Elizabeth 414
Elizabeth (Lennard) 399
Elizabeth (Willoughby) 317
Frances 100, 399
Francis (Sir) 399
Isabel (de Atholl) 697
Isabel (Reresby) 528
Lucy (Noel) 414, 416

Margaret 697
Margaret (Dymoke)
  389, 399, 414
Margery (Bowes)
  100, 317, 389, 399,
  414, 416
Martha 389
Mary (Dawney)
  414
Muriel 317
Muriel (Hastings)
  317
Ralph (Sir) 100,
  317, 389, 399, 414,
  416, 697
Ralph Eure, 3rd
  Baron 414
Robert 528
William Eure, 1st
  Baron 317
William Eure, 2nd
  Baron 389, 399,
  414
William Eure, 4th
  Baron 414, 416
EURE/EVERS
Jane 528, 529
EUSTACE
Alison 340, 601
Eleanor 382
EVAN
Elizabeth (Jones)
  809
Evan Lloyd 651,
  652
Rees 809
EVANS
Anne 539, 837
Anne (___) 651

Cadwalader 651,
  652, 660
Catherine
  (Oxenberg) xvii,
  xlv, liv, 3
Catrin (Vaughan)
  410
Charles Frederick
  Holt xxix, liv,
  lvii, lx, lxii, 679,
  714, 991
David 410, 651
Delilah (___) 555
Dorothea 658
Edward 555
Eleanor 690
Ellen 652
Ellen (Morris) 651,
  660
Ellen/Ellinor (Jones)
  690
Ellinor 690
family 651
Gwen 651, 652
Hannah (Price)
  (Jones) (David)
  651, 658
Jane xlviii, cxliii,
  690
John, of Merion and
  Radnor lvi, cxc,
  660
John, of Radnor l,
  liv, cxliii, clxxiv,
  555, 556
Lowry 652
Margaret 652, 692
Margaret (John)
  651

Mary 410, 690,
  693
Richard K. viii, liv,
  lix, 75, 492, 576
Robert 652
Robert J. [Robert J.
  Shapera] 3
Sarah 652
Thomas clxix, 651,
  652, 658
Titus 690
EVANS alias JONES
family 555
EVE
Hannah (___) 311
of Leinster 837,
  839, 847
EVERARD
Anne 580, 738
Dorothy 337
Elizabeth (Gibbs)
  114
family 1026
Henry 882
Hugh (Sir), 3rd Bt.
  114
Joan (Barrington)
  114
John 882
Judith xix, xxxvii,
  xlvii, lii, lv, lxi,
  clx, 371, 813, 882,
  884, 1026
Judith (Bourne)
  882
Margaret (Wiseman)
  882
Mary 882
Mary (Brown) 114

1213

Mary (Cornish) 882
Richard (Sir), 1st Bt. 114
Richard (Sir), 2nd Bt. 114
Richard (Sir), 4th Bt. clxviii, 114
Susan (Kidder) 114
Thomas 882
EVERETT
  Anthony Michael 34
  Rupert Hector xvii, cxliii, 34
  Sara (MacLean) 34
EVERINGHAM
  Anne (Fairfax) 600
  Eleanor 600
  Henry (Sir) 600
  Katherine 625, 628, 630
  Kimball G. x
EVERSFIELD
  Bridget 474
EVERTON
  Anne 543
EVREUX (D')
  Hawise 954
EWING
  Caroline (Maslin) 914
  Caroline Maslin 914
  Robert 914
EXETER
  Brownlow Cecil, 2nd Marquess of 73, 74
  Brownlow Cecil, 8th Earl of 73

David Cecil, 3rd Earl of 73
Henry Cecil, 1st Marquess of 73
John Cecil, 4th Earl of 73
John Cecil, 5th Earl of 73
John Cecil, 6th Earl of 73
John Holand, 1st Duke of 352, 400
John Holand, 2nd Duke of 400
Robert Holand, Bastard of 400
Thomas Cecil, 1st Earl of 345, 482
William Alleyne, 3rd Marquess of 73
William Cecil, 2nd Earl of 482
EXHURST
  Joan (Roberts) 920
  Mary 920
  Richard 920
EXMOUTH
  Henry Edward Bellew, 6th Viscount xlvii, 865
EYCHEN (VON)
  Maria 208, 209
EYNCOURT (D')
  Alice (___) 864
  Eleanor (le Fleming) 864
  Elizabeth 864

Ralph 864
Ralph (Sir) 864
EYRE
  Anchoretta (Eyre) 383
  Anne 306, 309, 528
  Anne (Markham) 413
  Anthony 413
  Catherine 806
  Charity (Dancer) 383
  Edward 413, 528
  Eleanor (Baldwin) 383
  Elizabeth (Babington) 413
  Elizabeth (Pole) 413
  Elizabeth (Reresby) 413, 528
  Gervase 413
  Gervase (Sir) 413
  Hastings Elles John 383
  Jane (Purefoy) 383
  Joan (White) 383
  John 383
  Lucy Catherine
  Louisa (Clarke) 383
  Mary 413
  Mary (Neville) 413
  Minna Mary Jessica (Royds) 383
  Philip Homan 383
  Richard 383
  Richard Charles Hastings (Sir) cliv, 383

Richard Galfridus
 Hastings Giles 383
Samuel 383
Susan Elizabeth
 (Birtwistle) 383
EZZO
 Count Palatine of
 Lorraine 849
FAALLNES
 Johan Gädda, Lord
 of 452
FAANOE
 Erik Trolle, Lord of,
 Lord of Lagnoe
 452
 Ulv Jonson, Lord of
 Ervalla, Vreta,
 Saeby, Huseby and
 452, 457
FACKNALLT
 Janet (Brereton) 773
 John 773
FADEEV
 Andrei 792
 Ekaterina 792
 Elena (Dolgoroukov),
 Princess 792
 Elena ["Zinaïde
 R___sky"] 792
FADRIQUE
 of Castile, Duke of
 Benavente 190
FAFARD
 Thérèse 970
FAGAN
 Alice (Segrave) 545
 Amy (Nangle) 545
 Beale (Knowles)
 545

Cecily (Holmes)
 545
Christiana
 (FitzMaurice)
 545
Christopher 545
Christopher
 Alexander 545
Eliza 546
Emily Rogers
 (Estell) 545
Helena (Trant) 546
John 545
John Francis 545
Louis Estell 545
Mary (Nagle) 545
Mary Dorothea
 545
Mary Dorothea
 (Colahan) 545
Mary Seton (Walsh)
 545
Nicholas 546
Nicholas
 FitzMaurice cliv,
 545
Patrick 545
Richard 545
Stephen 546
Thomas 545
FAIG
 Ken, Jr. cxci
FAIRCLOTH
 Elizabeth (___)
 702
 Grace (Standish)
 702
 Lawrence 702
 Mary 702

Millicent (Barr)
 702
Ralph 702
Thomas 702
FAIRFAX
 Agnes (Gascoigne)
 327, 328, 379
 Anne 600
 Anne (Harrison)
 129
 Benjamin 379, 381
 Bridget (Springer)
 379, 381
 Catherine (Cole-
 pepper/Culpeper)
 129, 840
 Catherine
 (Constable) 401
 Deborah (Clarke)
 (Gedney) 129
 Dorothy 401
 Elizabeth (Aske)
 328, 329
 Elizabeth (Manners)
 600
 family xlii, l
 Ferdinando Fairfax
 (Gen.), 2nd Baron
 329
 Frances 100, 329
 Frances (Barwick)
 129
 Frances (Chaloner)
 327
 Frances (Sheffield)
 327, 329
 Gabriel 328
 Helen (Aske) 329
 Henry (Hon.) 129

1215

Henry Fairfax, 4th
  Baron 129
Isabel (Thwaites)
  600
Isabella 327
Jane (Palmes) 327,
  401, 501
Jane (Stapleton)
  401
John 379, 381
Mabel (Curwen)
  327, 329
Mary 327, 330
Mary (Birch) 379
Mary (Cholmley)
  129
Mary (Sheffield)
  329
Nathaniel 381
Nicholas (Sir) 327,
  401, 501
Philip (Sir) 327
Sarah 379, 381
Sarah (Galliard)
  379
Sarah (Walker)
  129
Thomas (Sir) 327,
  379
Thomas Fairfax, 1st
  Baron 329
Thomas Fairfax, 1st
  Viscount 401
Thomas Fairfax, 5th
  Baron 129, 840
Thomas Fairfax, 6th
  Baron 129, 840
William clxvii, 379
William (Gov.) 129

William (Sir) 327,
  329, 401, 600
William (Sir) (Gen.)
  327
FAIRFIELD
Abigail 342
Arabella (Rowan)
  97, 405, 406
Arthur 97
Charles 405
Charles George 97,
  405, 406
Cicely Isabel
  [Rebecca West]
  406
Dorothy 97
Esther (Gott) 342
Isabella Campbell
  (Mackenzie) 405
Sarah (Skepper/
  Skipper) 342
Sophie (Blew-Jones)
  97
Walter 342
William 342
FAIRLIE
Anne Colquhoun
  144
FALAISE
Herlève of 879,
  919
FALCONER
Agnes (Carnegie)
  256, 257
Agnes (Spens) 252
Alexander lxiii,
  cxliii, clxxi, 256
Alexander (Sir), of
  Halkerton 256, 257

Alexander, of
  Halkerton 252, 256
Anna (Quare) 256
Archibald, of
  Coltfield 252
Catherine 257
David 256
David (Sir), of
  Glenfarquhar 257
David (Sir), of
  Newton 257
David, of Halkerton
  252, 256
Elizabeth (Douglas)
  252, 256
Elizabeth (Erskine)
  252, 256, 260
family lvi, 256,
  257, 262
George, of
  Halkerton 252,
  256, 260
Gilbert 256
Hannah (Hardiman)
  256
Hannah (Jones)
  252
Isabel (Gray) 256
Jane 256
Jean 260
Jean (Dunbar) 252
John 256
John (Sir), Master of
  the Mint of
  Scotland 256
John, of Tulloch and
  Phesdo 252
Margaret (Hepburn)
  257

Margaret (Mollison) 256
Mariot (Dunbar) 252, 256
Mary (Norvell) 257
Patrick cxliii, 252
Susanna (Duvall) 256
Sybilla (Ogilvy) 256, 257

FALKENBERG/ FALKENBURG (VON) (DE)
Anna 640
Beatrix 653, 661, 672
Hedwig Eleonora (Wachtmeister), Baroness 453
Magdalena Sophia, Countess 453
Melker, Count 453

FALKENHAYN (VON)
Eugene Georg Nikolaus 58
Luise Marie Emilie Pauline (von Dörnberg), Baroness 58
Theda Elisabeth Klementine Franziska 58, 224

FALKENSTEIN
Gertrude, Princess von Hanau und zu Horowitz, Countess von Schaumburg 13

FALKLAND
Lucius Charles Cary, 2nd Viscount 390

FALLEY
Margaret 500
Margaret Dickson liv, 594

FALWELL
Matilda 866

FANE
Elizabeth 122
Francis, 1st Earl of Westmoreland 122
Mary 429
Mary (Mildmay) 122
Mary (Neville), Baroness le Despencer 122
Thomas (Sir) 122
Thomas, 8th Earl of Westmoreland 122

FARINGTON
Alice 847

FARIS
David vii, ix, x, xi, xix, xxvii, xlvii, liv, lxii, lxvii, 549

FARMER
Alice Augusta 109
Arthur Augustus 109
Louisa Emily (de Blaquiere) 109
Mary 231
Sarah 501

FARMERIE
Todd A. viii, xlvii, l, li, liv, lv, lvi, lxv, lxviii, lxxi, 674, 675

FARNESE
Alessandro [Pope Paul III] 186, 188, 189, 192
family 193
Sigismundo V, Prince Chigi-Albani, 6th Prince of 18
Vittoria 186, 189

FARNHAM
Catherine 429

FARQUHAR
Rachel 270

FARQUHARSON
Barbara 251
Margaret 790

FARRAND
Rebecca 508

FARRAR
Cecily (____) (Jordan) 343
Cecily (Kelke) 343
family 344
John 343
Margaret (Lacy) 343
William xlv, liii, lviii, clxxii, 343

FARRINGDON
Albinia 117
Anne 632
Charles 632
Margery (Stukeley) 632

1217

Theodosia
  (Betenson) 117
Thomas 117
FARWELL
  Anne 306
  Anne (Browne) 306
  George 306
  George (Sir) 306
  Hannah 520
  Hannah (Learned) 519
  Henry 519, 520, 925
  Jonathan 519
  Joseph 519
  Mary 925
  Mary (Seymour) 306
  Olive (Welby) lix, clx, clxxiv, 519, 925
  Rachel 519
  Susannah (Blanchard) 519
  Susannah (Richardson) 519
FAUBERT
  Caroline 981
FAUCETTE
  Rachel 214
FAUCONBERGE (DE)
  Anice 705
  Isabel (de Ros) 705
  Walter de Fauconberge, 2nd Baron 705

FAULKNER
  Bridget 478
  Claude W. xlviii, lv
FAUNT
  family 697
  Mabel 111
FAUQUEMBURGHE
  Philippe de Boulainvilliers, Count of 205
FAUQUIER
  Catherine (Dalston) 472
  Francis (Lt. Gov.) 472
FAVRE
  Antoine 912
  Jean 912
  Jeanne (de Poypon) 912
  Marie 912
  Philiberte (___) 912
FAWCETT
  Charlotte 12
FAWKENER
  Everard (Sir) 536, 537
  Harriet (Churchill) xlvi, lii, 536, 537
FAY
  Elizabeth (Wellington) 571
  Hannah (Child) 572
  Harriet (Howard) 479, 572, 585, 702, 716, 747

  Harriet Eleanor 474, 479, 572, 585, 703, 716, 729, 747
  Joanna (Phillips) 572
  John, Jr. 571
  John (III) 572
  Jonathan 572
  Jonathan, Jr. 572, 702, 747
  Lucy (Prescott) 572, 702, 747
  Samuel Howard 474, 479, 572, 585, 703, 716, 729, 747
  Samuel Prescott Phillips 479, 572, 585, 702, 716, 747
  Susan (Shellman) 474, 479, 572, 585, 703, 716, 729, 747
FAY (DE)
  Adrienne-Jenny-Florimonde 201
  Anastasie-Louise-Pauline (Motier) 201
  Just-Charles-César, Count de la Tour-Maubourg 201
FAY (DE LA)
  Bertrand de Sallmard, Seigneur de Ressiz and 638
  Claude I de Sallmard, Seigneur de Ressiz and 638
  Claude II de Sallmard, Seigneur de Ressiz and 638

1218

Geoffrey I de
  Sallmard, Seigneur
  de Ressiz, Mont-
  fort, and 638
Geoffrey II de
  Sallmard, Seigneur
  de Ressiz and 638
FAZI
  Marcella [Princess
  Marcella Borghese]
  24
FEA
  Isabell 85
**FEATHERSTONE-
  HALGH/FEATHER-
  STONEHAUGH**
  Jane cxci
  Mary 698, 699
FEHN
  family xxii
FEILDING. *see also*
  FIELDING
  Basil 368
  Bridget (Stanhope)
    368
  Dorothy (Lane) 368
  Elizabeth (Aston)
    368
  George, 1st Earl of
    Desmond 368
  Mary 64
  Mary (Berkeley) 77
  Mary (King) 64
  Mary Elizabeth
    Kitty (Moreton)
    77
  Rudolph William
    Basil, 8th Earl of
    Denbigh 77
  Susan (Villiers) 368
  William (Sir) 368
  William, 1st Earl of
    Denbigh 368
  William, 3rd Earl of
    Denbigh, 2nd Earl
    of Desmond 64
  William Basil Percy,
    7th Earl of
    Denbigh 77
  Winefride Mary
    Elizabeth 77
FEITH
  Anna (van
    Scherpenberg)
    460
  Anna Charlotte (van
    Hardenbroek) 460
  Arnold Hendrik
    460
  Gijsbert Jan 460
  Ursula Matha 460
FELBRIGG (DE)
  Alana 713
  Margaret (of
    Teschen?) 713,
    714
  Simon (Sir) 713,
    714
FELD (DE LA)
  Arturo, Count 190
  Giuseppe Uberto,
    Count 190
  Margherita
    (Maresca
    Donnorso
    Correale) 190
  Maria Luisa,
    Countess 190
FELDMANN
  Friedrich Karl 8
  Marianne Charlotte
    Katharina Stefanie
    (Reuss-Köstritz)
    (Brundage),
    Princess 8
FELICE GWYN
  ferch John ap Llwyd
    Kemeys 338
**FELIX
  CONSTANTIN
  ALEXANDER
  JOHANN
  NEPOMUK**
  Prince of Salm-Salm
    38
FELT
  Philippa (Andrews)
    126
FELTON
  Cecily 705
  Cecily (Seckford)
    705
  Elizabeth 334
  Elizabeth (Howard)
    334
  Henry (Sir), 2nd Bt.
    350
  Lucy 785
  Margery (Sampson)
    705
  Robert 705
  Susan 350, 605
  Susan (Tollemache)
    350
  Thomas 705
  Thomas (Sir), 4th
    Bt. 334

FENNE
  Margaret 118, 324, 347, 357, 405, 417, 429
FENNER
  Ann McKinney (Geddy) 924
  Anne (Coddington) viii, li, lxiv, cxliii, 467, 469, 924
  Eliza Geddy 924, 926
  Richard 467, 924, 926
  Richard, Jr. 924, 926
FENWICK
  Agnes (Harbottle) 599
  Alice (Apsley) (Boteler) 328, 662
  Anne (Culcheth) 366
  Anthony 599
  Barbara (Mitford) 599
  Barbara (Ogle) 366
  Catherine (Haselrige) 328, 331
  Cuthbert lxii, clxxv, clxxix, clxxxviii, 498, 599
  Dorothy 366
  Dorothy (Forster) 328
  Edward 366
  Elizabeth 328, 330

  Elizabeth (Covert) clxxv, 366, 691
  Elizabeth (Gargrave) 366
  Elizabeth (Gibbes) 366
  Elizabeth (Haggerston) 599
  family xxiv, xxxiv, 367
  George 328, 331, 599, 662, 719
  Isabel (Selby) 599
  Jane (Eltonhead) (Moryson) clxxiii, 498, 599
  John li, lxvi, 366, 367, 691
  Magdalen (Hunt) 719
  Margaret 101
  Margaret (___) 719
  Margaret (Mills) 366
  Margery (Mitford) 366, 599
  Mary (___) 719
  Mary (Grey) 366
  Mary (Marten) 366
  Mary (Savill) (Porter) (Lawson) 719
  Priscilla 366, 367
  Ralph 366, 599
  Richard 366
  Robert 366
  Roger (Sir) 599
  Sarah (Neville) 366

  Sarah (Patey) 366
  Stephen 599
  Thomas lxvi, 719
  Walter 719
  William 366
  ___ (Constable) 719
FERDINAND
  Archduke of Austria, Duke of Modena 15
FERDINAND I
  Holy Roman Emperor 40, 43, 54, 56, 192, 287, 290, 615, 619, 891, 892
  King of Naples 186, 189
  King of Roumania 2
  King of Spain, II of Aragón, V of Castile 46, 140, 186, 189, 615, 717
FERDINAND II. *see also* **FERDINAND I [SPAIN]**
  King of Portugal 290
  King of the Two Sicilies 6
FERDINAND III
  King of Castile 951
FERDINAND V. *see* **FERDINAND I**
FERDINAND ALBERT I
  Duke of Brunswick-Bevern 44

FERDINAND ALBERT II
Duke of Brunswick-Wolfenbüttel 44
FERGUSON
Alan 990
Christina 111
Elizabeth (Graeme) 168
Grizel 276
Henry Hugh 168
Mary 881
Sarah Margaret, Duchess of York 25
Solange (Knowles) 990
FERLAND-TESTE
Jeanne 965
FERMOR
Agnes 475
Anne 713
Henrietta Louisa (Jeffreys) 226
Juliana xvii, 226
Mary 335, 567
Sophia 226
Thomas, 1st Earl of Pomfret 226
FERMOY
Edmund Burke Roche, 1st Baron 378
Edmund Maurice Burke Roche, 4th Baron 378, 932
James Boothby Burke Roche, 3rd Baron 378, 932

FERNÁNDEZ DE ARAGÓN
Jaime, Baron de Xérica/Ejérica 993
FERNÁNDEZ DE CÓRDOVA Y ARAGÓN
Juana 140
FERNÁNDEZ DE VELASCO
Bernardino, 6th Duke of Frias 140
Iñigo, 4th Duke of Frias 140
Iñigo Melchior, 8th Duke of Frias 140
Juan, 5th Duke of Frias 140
FERNE
Elizabeth 334
FERNELEY
Jane 846
FERRAND
Eleanor 321
Mary (Dudley) 321
Thomas 321
FERRARA
Hercules I, Duke of, Duke of Modena 186, 189
Lucretia (Borgia), Duchess of, Duchess of Modena 287, 293
FERRE
Eleanor 835
FERRER
Edda Kathleen (van Heemstra)

(Hepburn-Ruston) [Audrey Hepburn] viii, xvii, lxix, cxliv, 446
Mel (Melchor Gastón) 446
Sean Hepburn 446
FERRERS (DE)
Agnes (de Meschines) 806, 821
Anne 491, 505, 534, 567, 575
Anne (Hastings) 592
Bertha 806, 821
Charlotte (Compton), Baroness, of Chartley 112
Constance (Brome) 466, 567
Edmund (Sir) 505, 575
Edward (Sir) 466, 467, 567
Elizabeth 366, 395, 429, 466, 467, 468, 528, 592
Elizabeth (Belknap) 505
Elizabeth (Freville) 466, 567, 592
Elizabeth (Shirley), Baroness, of Chartley 112
Elizabeth (Stafford) 505, 575
Ellen (Roche) 505, 575
family, of Groby xli
Henry (Sir) 466, 567

Henry, 2nd Baron
  Ferrers of Groby
  466, 528, 567, 592
Henry, 4th Baron
  Ferrers of Groby
  466, 567, 592
Isabel (de Verdun)
  466, 528, 567, 592
Joan 676, 691
Joan (Beaufort)
  xxxiv, 107, 114, 119,
  126, 314, 324, 331,
  339, 357, 366, 368,
  370, 387, 393, 395,
  397, 398, 403, 405,
  413, 417, 418, 419,
  426, 429, 433, 434,
  902
Joan (Poynings)
  466, 567, 592
John (Sir) 592
John, 4th Baron
  Ferrers of Chartley
  505, 575
John Devereux, 2nd
  Baron, of Chartley
  134
Margaret 506, 575
Margaret (Despencer)
  478, 505, 575
Margaret (Heckstall)
  466, 567
Margaret (Ufford)
  466, 567, 592
Mary 398, 413
Maud (Stanley) 592
Philippa 478, 512
Philippa (Clifford)
  466, 469, 567, 592
Robert (Sir) 366,
  395, 398, 413, 429
Robert, 5th Baron
  Ferrers of Chartley
  478, 505, 575
Robert Shirley, 1st
  Earl 134
Thomas (Sir) 466,
  468, 567, 592
Walter, 4th Earl of
  Derby 806, 821
Walter Devereux,
  1st Baron, of
  Chartley 505, 534
William (Sir) 505,
  506
William, 3rd Baron
  Ferrers of Groby
  466, 567, 592
William, 4th Earl of
  Derby 806, 821
William, 5th Baron
  Ferrers of Groby
  466, 567, 592
**FERRERS of
CHARTLEY, of
GROBY.** *see*
FERRERS (DE)
FERRIÈRES (DE)
  Marie 961
  Vincent-Sylvestre
   de Timbrune de
   Valence, Marquis
   206
FERROU (DE)
  Renée 964
FERRY
  Susan 527

FERSEN (VON)
  Frederick Axel,
   Count 267
  Hans Axel, Count
   xvii, xxvi, lxviii,
   240, 267
  Hedwig Catharina
   (de la Gardie),
   Countess 267
**FESTETICS VON
TOLNA**
  Maria Matilda
   Georgina, Countess
   20, 142
  Mary Victoria
   (Douglas-Hamilton),
   Princess of Monaco,
   Princess 20, 933
  Tassilo, Prince 20
FETTES
  Ian 290, 447
FETTIPLACE
  Anne 373, 778
  Elizabeth 648
  Elizabeth (Bessiles)
   372
  Mary 647
  Richard 372
FEUERSTEIN
  Georgia Mary Anne
   978
FEUILLET (DE)
  Bouchard de
   Vendôme, Seigneur
   de Segré and 946
FÉVRIER
  Christophe 940, 987
  Marie (Martin)
   940, 987

Marie-Anne 987
FEY
  Kimberly 976
FIALLOS
  Lucia (Navarro
    Richardson) 521
  Salvadora (Somoza
    Urcuyo) 521
FIALLOS GIL
  Francisco 521
FIALLOS NAVARRO
  Francisco 521
FIELD
  Audrey Evelyn
    (James) (Coats)
    68
  Jane (Cheney) 668
  Marshall 68
  Marshall, III xviii, 68
  Mary 822
  Mary (___) 738
  Vanessa 74
FIELDER/FEILDER
  Anne l, lxii, cxlix, cli, clxviii, 603
  family 603
  Margery (Cole) 603
  William 603
FIELDING. *see also* FEILDING
  Anne 678, 749
  Bridget (Cokayne) 368
  Charlotte (Craddock) 368
  Edmund 368

Henrietta clxxii, 368
Henry 368
John 368
Sarah (Gould) 368
FIEN(N)ES (DE)
  Alexandra ("Alex")
  Elizabeth
    (Kingston) 158
  Anne (Bourchier) 428
  Blanche (de Brienne) 647, 909
  Bridget 311
  Elizabeth 783
  Elizabeth
    (Batisford) 783
  family 1025
  James, 1st Baron
    Saye and Sele 783
  Jennifer Anne Mary
    Alleyne (Lash) 158
  Joan (___) 783
  Joan (de Say) 783
  Joseph Alberic
    xvii, cxliii, 158
  Magnus Hubert 158
  Margaret 647, 909
  María Dolores
    (Diéguez) 158
  Mark 158
  Martha Maria 158
  Mary 428
  Ralph Nathaniel
    xvii, cxliii, 158
  Sophia Victoria 158

Thomas, 8th Baron
    Dacre 428
  William (Sir) 647, 783, 909
FIESCHI
  Beatrix 965
FIFE
  Alexander George
    Duff, 1st Duke of 9
  James Duff, 5th Earl
    of 9
  James George
    Alexander
    Bannerman
    Carnegie, 3rd
    Duke of 9
FILLIOL
  Catherine 305
FILMER
  Edward (Sir) 514
  Elizabeth (___) 514
  Elizabeth (Argall) 514
  Henry clxvii, 514
  Katherine 514
  Mary (Horsmanden) 348
  Robert (Sir) 514
  Samuel 348
FINCH
  Frances 69, 362
  Heneage, 3rd Earl of
    Winchilsea 69
  Jane 314
  Mary (Seymour) 69
  Selina 134
FINCHAM
  Anne 494, 596

FINCK (VON)
  Catharina (Beck) 620
  Victor Ernst Hermann xxii, lv, cliv, 620
  Wilhelm Ernst 620
  Wilhelmine Philippine Luise (von Bohlen) 620
FINCK VON FINCKELSTEIN
  Amelia Louisa 194
FINGULA
  of the Isles 269, 270, 280, 283, 284
FINK
  Clara 620
FINLAY
  Sylvia Joan 158
FINLEY
  Gertrude Field 79
FINN
  Faryl 148
  ___ O'Kennedy 601
FINNEY
  Mary 101
FIRCKS (VON)
  Benigna (von der Osten-Sacken) 617
  Christoph 617
  Maria Elisabeth 617
FISH
  Elizabeth 109
FISHER
  Agnes 662

Anne 530
Benetta (Dering) 357
Elizabeth (___) 357
Elizabeth Rosemond (Taylor) (Hilton) (Wilding) (Todd) [Elizabeth Taylor] 21, 190
Esther 867
Hannah 484
John xlix, liii, 357
Margery (Maude) cxc
Sarah 342
Thomasine 357, 761
FITCH
  Elizabeth 923
  James (Rev.) 926
  Mary 493
FITCH-NORTHEN
  Charles viii, lv, lix, 871
FITTON
  Elizabeth 752
FITZAKER
  Margery 746
FITZALAN
  Alice xxv, 295, 337, 375, 382, 515, 600, 900
  Alice (de Warren) 642, 1024
  Alicia (of Saluzzo) 642
  Edmund (Sir) 508, 514, 547, 584, 594, 607

Edmund, 8th Earl of Arundel 642, 1024
Eleanor (Maltravers) 632
Eleanor (Plantagenet) 632, 642
Elizabeth xxiii, xxiv, xxv, xxvi, xxxi, 473, 493, 497, 510, 517, 522, 524, 532, 541, 547, 554, 557, 558, 560, 563, 565, 571, 574, 594, 598, 605, 611, 613
Elizabeth (de Bohun) 497, 500, 510, 517, 524, 532, 551, 554, 558, 560, 563, 565, 571, 574, 588, 596, 611, 613
Elizabeth (Despencer) 491
family xxvi, xxxi, xxxii, xxxiv, 561
Isabel (le Despencer) 508, 514, 547, 584, 594, 607, 642
Joan xxv, 417, 500, 551, 574, 588, 596, 632
John, 1st Baron Arundel 632
John, 2nd Baron Arundel 491
Philippa 508, 514, 584, 607
Richard, 7th Earl of Arundel 642

1224

Richard, 9th Earl of
  Arundel 508, 514,
  547, 584, 594, 607,
  632, 642
Richard, 10th Earl of
  Arundel 497, 500,
  510, 517, 524, 532,
  551, 554, 558, 560,
  563, 565, 571, 574,
  588, 596, 611, 613
Sybil (Montagu)
  508, 514, 547, 584,
  594, 607
**FITZALAN-
  HOWARD**
  Angela Mary
    Charlotte 72
  Anne Mary Teresa
    (Constable-
    Maxwell) 72
  Augusta (Talbot) 72
  Augusta Mary
    Minna Catherine
    (Lyons) 71
  Bernard Edward,
    3rd Baron Howard
    of Glossop 72
  Carina Mary
    Gabriel, Lady
    cliv, 72
  Charlotte Sophia
    (Sutherland-
    Leveson-Gower)
    71
  Clara Louise
    (Greenwood) 72
  Edward George, 1st
    Baron Howard of
    Glossop 72

Francis Edward, 2nd
  Baron Howard of
  Glossop 72
Henry Charles, 13th
  Duke of Norfolk
  71
Henry Granville,
  14th Duke of
  Norfolk 71, 72
Miles Francis, 17th
  Duke of Norfolk
  72, 75
Mona Josephine
  (Stapleton),
  Baroness
  Beaumont 72
Victoria
  Alexandrina 71
FITZCLARENCE
  Elizabeth 9
  family 10
FITZGEOFFREY
  Hawise 866, 870
  Maud, Countess of
    Essex 783, 1025
FITZGERALD
  Alison 487
  Alison (Eustace)
    340, 601
  Charles Lionel 334
  Desmond 334
  Dorothea (Butler)
    334
  Edward Thomas
    334
  Eleanor (Butler)
    601
  Elizabeth (Grey)
    340

Elizabeth Parker
  Clark (Salisbury)
  334
Ellen 340
Emma (Green) 334
George 334
Gerald, 3rd Earl of
  Desmond 601
Gerald, 8th Earl of
  Kildare 340, 601
Gerald, 9th Earl of
  Kildare 340
Gerald, 11th Earl of
  Kildare 340
James, 6th Earl of
  Desmond 601
Joan 382
Joan (FitzGerald)
  601
Lionel Charles
  Henry William
  334
Mabel (Browne)
  340
Margaret 382, 601
Mary (Burke) 601
Mary (Hervey) 334
Sarah Caroline
  (Brown) 334
Thomas (Sir) 480
Thomas, 7th Earl of
  Kildare 601
FITZGIBBON
  Arabella 341
FITZHAMON
  Mabel 806, 808,
    810, 811, 813, 815,
    817, 819, 821, 822,
    824, 826, 1025

FITZHERBERT
Alice (Booth) 757, 758
Alice (Longford) 757
Dorothy 757, 758
Elizabeth (Marshall) 757, 758
Henry 757
Joan 757, 758
Mary Anne (Smythe) (Weld) [Mrs. Maria FitzHerbert] 123
Nicholas 757, 758
Ralph 757, 758
William 757
___ (Downes) 757

FITZHUGH
Alice (Neville) 324, 368, 434
Anne 155, 261
Anne Frisbie (Dana) 155
Daniel Holker 155
Eleanor 398, 917
Elizabeth 324, 366, 368, 369, 407, 434
Elizabeth (Marmion) 667, 917
Eustache 700, 725
family 155
Henry FitzHugh, 3rd Baron 667, 917
Henry FitzHugh, 5th Baron 324, 368, 369, 434
Lora 667
Margery (Willoughby) 369, 667
Mary Lee 29
Sarah 828
William FitzHugh, 4th Baron 369, 667

FitzIVES
Isabel 665
Isabel (FitzRoy) 665, 687, 695, 696
Richard (Sir) 665, 687, 695

FITZJAMES
Anne (Bulkeley) 24
Arabella 24
Charles, 2nd Duke of FitzJames 24
Édouard, 4th Duke of FitzJames 24
Élisabeth-Alexandrine (le Vassor) 24
Henrietta (FitzJames) clxxxix
Jacques-Charles, 3rd Duke of FitzJames 24
Jacques-Marie-Emanuel, 5th Duke of FitzJames 24
James, 1st Duke of Berwick 24
Joan 595
Marguerite (de Marnier) 24
Marie-Claudine-Silvie (de Thiard) 24
Victoire-Louise-Josèphe (Gouyon) 24

FITZJOHN
Cecily 732

FITZLEWIS
Elizabeth 566, 613

FITZMAURICE
Christiana 545

FitzOTHO/FitzOTES
Beatrice (de Beauchamp) 737, 763, 766, 768, 770
Thomas (Sir) 737, 763, 766, 768, 770

FITZPATRICK
Eleanor (de Vitré) 737
Evelyn (Leveson-Gower), Lady 299
family 1025
Isabel 855
John, 1st Earl of Upper Ossory 299
Louise, Lady 299
William, Earl of Salisbury 737

FITZPATRICK/ MacGILLAPATRICK
Sadbh ní Giolla Phadraig 601

FITZPAYN
Isabel 737

FITZPIERS
Aveline (de Clare) 870
Geoffrey, Earl of Essex 866, 870, 1025

Lucy 700, 705, 710, 713, 715, 719, 721, 725, 727, 728, 730
FITZRANDALL/ FITZRANULPH/ FITZRALPH
family 725
FITZRANDOLPH
Benjamin 726
Christopher 725
Deliverance (Coward) 508, 726
Edward xi, li, lxix, clxiv, clxxvi, clxxxii, 725
Eleanor (Hunter) 508, 726
Elizabeth (Blossom) 725
family 726
Frances (Howis) 725
Isaac 508, 726
James 508, 726
Jane (Langton) 725
Joan (Conyers) 725
John 725
Mary (Holley) 725
Mary (Jones) 725
Nathaniel 725, 726
Prudence 725
Rebecca (Seabrook) 726
Rebecca Longstreet 463, 508, 726
Samuel 725
Sarah (Dennis) 726

FITZREGINALD
Maud 739, 957
FITZRICHARD
Rose (Bevyle) 687, 695
William (Sir) 687, 695
FITZROBERT
Ela 687, 749, 754, 757
Hawise (de Beaumont) 808, 810, 811
Ida (Longespee) 687, 741, 749, 754, 757
Maud (de Lucy) 879
Maud, Countess of Chester 807
Walter 879
Walter (Sir) 687, 749, 754, 757
William, 2nd Earl of Gloucester xxxii, 807, 808, 810, 811
FITZROGER
Alice (___) 742
Elizabeth 742
Elizabeth (Holand) 742
Henry (Sir) 742
John 742
FITZROY
Anne (Pulteney) 34
Augustus, Lord 33
Augustus Henry, 3rd Duke of Grafton 33

Blanche Adeliza 33
Caroline (Pigot) 33
Charles, 2nd Duke of Cleveland, 1st Duke of Southampton 34
Charles, 2nd Duke of Grafton 27, 33
Charlotte 22, 29
Elizabeth (Cosby) 33
Elizabeth (Wrottesley) 33
Grace 34
Henrietta (Somerset) 27, 33
Henry 33
Henry, 1st Duke of Grafton 33
Henry, Lord 33
Isabel 665, 687, 695, 696
Isabella 27
Isabella (Bennet) 33
Jane Elizabeth (Beauclerk) 33
Richard 372, 667, 670, 676, 678, 684, 691, 697, 917
FITZROY (DE MORTAIN)
Mabel (FitzWilliam) 739, 957
Reginald, Earl of Cornwall 739, 957
FITZSIMON
Jane 710

1227

FITZTHOMAS
Maud/Matilda   715, 728, 737, 763, 766, 768, 770
FITZWALTER
Alice   880
Radigond   674
Robert   880
FITZWARIN
family   1025
Fulk Bourchier, Baron   392, 409, 436
William Bourchier, Baron   392, 409, 436
FITZWILLIAM
Anne   684
Anne (Hawes)   393, 684
Ela (de Warren)   841
Eleanor (Greene)   684
Elizabeth (Clarell)   528
Elizabeth (Knevet)   393, 394
Ellen   841
family   xlv, 529, 709
Frances   471
George   471
Helen (Villiers)   684
Isabel   687, 695, 851, 920
Joan (Britt)   471
Joan (Gunby)   471
John   471, 684

John (Sir)   684
Mabel   739, 957
Margaret   393, 528
Margaret (Dymoke)   471
Margaret (Wygersley)   471
Mary   900
Mary (Skipwith)   471
Maud (Cromwell)   684
Rachel   394
Ralph   851, 852
Richard   393, 394
Richard (Sir)   528
Thomas   471
William   841
William (Sir)   393, 684
Yolande (de Mohun)   851
FITZWILLIAM or FITZRALPH
___   851
FLAGG
Ernest   xlvii, lii, liv, lv, lvi, lxi, lxii
FLAGLER
Anne Louise (Lamont)   306
Elizabeth Lamont   305
Harry Harkness   305, 306
Henry Morrison   306
Mary (Harkness)   306

FLANDERS
Baldwin IX, Count of, Emperor of Constantinople   774, 776
Baldwin V, Count of   851
Baldwin VI, Count of, I of Hainault   851
John of, Vicomte de Châteaudun   942
Margaret of   438, 442, 445, 774, 776
Marie of   942
Matilda of, Duchess of Normandy, Queen of England   642, 830, 851, 911, 1024
FLATSBURY
Jane   120
FLAVIN
Barbara   521
FLEETE
Deborah (Scott)   314
Edward   314
Henry   liii, 314
John   314
Reginald   314
Sarah (___) (Burden)   314
William   314
FLEETWOOD
Anna (Uggla)   662
Anne (Luke)   662
Brita (Gyllenstierna)   662, 663

Eleonora Margareta,
  Baroness 662
George (Gen.),
  Baron 662, 663
Gustaf Adolf, Baron
  662
Gustaf Miles, Baron
  662
Märta (Stake) 662
Martha 662
Mary 136
Miles (Sir) 662
FLEMING
  Agnes 143, 159,
    161, 163, 165
  Alice (Dawkin)
    582
  Alice (Kirkby) 611
  Barbara 611
  Barbara (Fletcher)
    611
  Barbara (Hamilton)
    177
  Daniel (Sir) 611,
    612
  Dorothy (Cromwell)
    476
  Eleanor 363
  Elizabeth 143
  Elizabeth (Ross)
    152, 163, 166
  Helen (Bruce) 152
  Henry 582
  James Fleming, 4th
    Baron 177
  Janet 243
  Jean 152, 163, 177
  Joan 150
  Joan (Stewart) 143,
    146, 150, 151, 152,
    159, 161, 163, 165,
    166, 170, 177
  John, 1st Earl of
    Wigtown 152
  John Fleming, 2nd
    Baron 218
  John Fleming, 5th
    Baron 152, 163,
    166
  Joyce (Jones)
    (Hoskins) 515
  Lilias (Graham)
    152
  Malcolm, of
    Gilmerton 152
  Malcolm Fleming,
    3rd Baron 143,
    146, 150, 151, 152,
    159, 161, 163, 165,
    166, 170, 177
  Margaret xix, xlvi,
    lxii, clx, clxxv, 88,
    146, 151, 152, 161,
    170, 218, 244, 582,
    583, 808, 811, 812
  Margaret (Stewart)
    218
  Martha 662
  Mary 166, 476
  Maud 137
  Thomas (Sir) 476
  William 611
FLEMING (LE)
  Eleanor 864
FLETCHER
  Barbara 611
  Elizabeth (__) 475
  Mary 364
FLICKINGER
  Jacob Marion 769
  Lula Dell 769
  Sarah (Haines) 769
**FLINTELL/
FLINTHILL**
  Elizabeth 821
FLITNER
  Stanwood E. 666
FLOOD
  Mary 516
  Sarah 473
**FLOTTE-D'AGOULT
(DE)**
  Marguerite 615
FLOWER
  Anne 374
  Evelyn Jephson
    [Evelyn Cameron]
    cliii, 85
FLOWERDEW
  Temperance 300
FLOYD
  Julia 66, 67
  Ruth 487
FLUDD
  Katherine 551
FOGELBERG
  Caroline
    Wilhelmina 53
FOIX (DE)
  Anne (de
    Villeneuve) 615
  Anne, Queen of
    Bohemia and
    Hungary xxv,
    287, 615
  Catherine (de Foix)
    287, 615

Constance (de Luna) 963
family 291
Gaston I de Foix, Count, Count de Bigorre 963
Gaston II, Count of Benauges 287, 615
Germaine (Germana), Queen of Aragón 140
Girarde (de Navailles) 963
Isabel 963
Isabelle (d'Albret) 287
Jean, Vicomte de Meille 615
Jean III, Count, Count de Bigorre 963
Jeanne (d'Albret) 963
Jeanne-Françoise 442
John, 1st Earl of Kendal xiv, xxv, 287, 615
Louise 287
Margaret (Kerdeston) xiv, xxv, lvii, lxviii, 287, 289, 615, 616
Marthe 615
Roger Bernard I, Vicomte de Castelbon 963
Roger Bernard II, Vicomte de Castelbon 963

FOLEY
David M. lv
FOLLIOTT (FOLIOT)
Anne (Strode) 308
Edward (Rev.) clxvii, clxxii, 296
Elizabeth (Aylmer) 296
Elizabeth (Moore) 296
family lx
Frances 64, 308
Henry Folliott (Foliot), 1st Baron 299, 308
John 296
John (Sir) 296
Katherine (Lygon) 296, 308
Thomas 296, 308
FOLSOM
Frances 335, 500
FONTAINE
Joan [Joan de Beauvoir (de Havilland) (Aherne) (Dozier) (Young) Wright] xvii, 463
FONTAINE (DE LA)
Hubert Heinrich, Count, Count d'Harnoncourt-Unverzagt 220
Hubert Karl Sigismund Joseph Franz, Count, Count d'Harnoncourt-Unverzagt 220

René Vladimir Hubert Maria, Count, Count d'Harnoncourt-Unverzagt [René d'Harnoncourt] liii
FONTANAFREDDA
Rosa Teresa Vercellana, Countess di Mirafiori and 614
FONTENILLES (DE)
François de La Roche, 1st Marquis 205
FOOT
Michael Richard Daniel 335
Philippa Ruth (Bosanquet) [Philippa Foot] cliv, 335
FORBES
Agnes (Fraser) 789
Agnes (Lumsden) 790
Alexander 268
Alexander (Sir), of Pitsligo 789
Alexander, of Aquorthies and London 148
Alexander, of Ballogie 250
Alexander, of Newe 789, 790
Alexander, of Pitsligo 273

Alexander, of Tolquhon 255
Alexander Forbes, 1st Baron 255, 256, 261, 266, 267, 268
Alison (Anderson) 255
Anna (Dunbar) 255
Anna (Lunan) 268
Annabel 256
Anne (Howell) 923
Archibald, of Deskrie 790
Arthur Forbes, 10th Baron 159
Arvid (Forbes), Baron Forbus 267
Beatrix (Abernethy) 273
Carin (Björnram) 267
Catherine (Stewart) 261
Charles John (Sir), 4th Bt. 68
Christian 149
Christian (Gordon) 261, 266
Christian (Lundin) 261, 266
Christian (Mercer) 255, 267, 268
David 174
Delia Stirling 174
Dorothy (Murray) 790, 923
Duncan, of Corsindae 255, 267, 268
Duncan, of Culloden 255
Elizabeth 255, 261, 266
Elizabeth (Douglas) 255, 256, 257, 261, 266, 267, 268
Elizabeth (Forbes), of Brux 789
Elizabeth (Gordon) 255, 268
Elizabeth (Graham) 255
Elizabeth (Keith) 255
Elizabeth (Wishart) 250
Elizabeth/Elspeth 159
Ernald 267
Evelyn Elizabeth 68
family lxviii
Frances Elizabeth (Blackwell) 923
Francis Blackwell 923
Giles/Egidia (Keith) 255, 261, 266, 267, 268
Grizel 225
Helen (Forbes), of Culquhonny 790
Helen (Lundie) 267
Helen (Moncreiffe) 68
Isabel (Burnett) 789
Isabel (Clarke) 923
Isabel (Gordon) 790
James (Jacob), of Sweden 267
James, of Corsindae 255, 268
James, of Inverurie 268
James Forbes, 2nd Baron 255, 261, 266, 267, 268
James Grant 923
Janet (Forbes) 255
Janet (Forbes), of Tolquhon 255
Janet (Gordon) 255, 268
Janet (Ogilvy) 225
Janet (Robertson) 790
Jean (Barclay) 148
Jean (Elphinstone) 159
Jean (Erskine) 174
Jean (Forbes) 250
Jean (Forbes), in Mills of Drum 268
Jean (Lumsden) 789
Jean (Ramsay) 225
John (Rev.) lxviii, clxix, 790, 923
John, of Bandley 255
John, of Culloden lxviii, 255
John, of Deskrie 790
John, of Fort Duquesne 240, 255

1231

John, of Newe 789
John, of Pitnacardell 268
John, of Pittencrieff 255
John, of Tombeg 268
John Forbes, 6th Baron 261, 266
John Murray 923
Katherine (Mortimer) 255
Malcolm, of Tolquhon 255
Margaret 268
Margaret (Douglas) 250
Margaret (Farquharson) 790
Margaret (Forbes) 255
Margaret (Gordon) 789
Margaret (Lumsden) 255, 268
Margaret (Stirling) vi, lxiii, lxvii, clxvii, 174, 175
Margaret Tyndal (Winthrop) 923
Margareta (Boije) 267
Margareta (Penters) 267
Maria (Hay) 789
Marion 273
Mariota (Ogilvy) 789
Mary (Bairnsfather) 268
Mary, of Monymusk 93
Mattias (Matthew) 267
Robert, of Barnes 250
Rosemary Isabel 923
Thomas, of Waterton 225
William (Sir), 1st Bt. 250
William (Sir), of Pitsligo 174, 789
William, of Corsindae 255, 268
William, of Culquhonny 790
William, of Daach 789
William, of Monymusk 250
William, of Newe 789, 790
William, of Pitsligo 789
William, of Tolquhon 225, 255, 268
William, of Tombeg 268
William Forbes, 3rd Baron 261, 266
____ 250, 269
____ (Hay), of Burnthill 268
____ (Leith) 255

FORBES-ROBERTSON
Frances (Cox) 268
Frank 268
Honoria Helen (McDermott) 268
John 268
Johnston (Sir) 268
Louise (Wilson) 268
Mary Gertrude (Elliott) 268
Muriel Elsa Florence [Muriel Forbes] clvii, 268
Norman 268
Sydney (Thornton) 268

FORBUS
Arvid (Forbes), Baron 267
Sofia Juliana, Baroness 267, 453

FORD
Ann 148
Charles 436
Dorothy (Chudleigh) 436, 437
Dorothy Ayer (Gardner) (King) 630, 655, 887
Elizabeth 436
Elizabeth Ann "Betty" (Bloomer) (Warren) [Betty Ford] xlii, xliii, 631, 655, 867, 868, 887

Gerald Rudolf 630, 655, 887
Gerald Rudolph, Jr. "Jerry," 38th U.S. President [Leslie Lynch King, Jr.] 631, 655, 868, 887
Grace (Kitchell) 688
Mary (Flood) (Blunt) 516
Phebe 688
Samuel, Jr. 688
FOREEST (VAN)
Catryn 774
Ida (Cuser van Oosterwijk) 774
Jan Herpertsz. 774
FOREZ (DE)
family 952
FORREST
Isabel 325
Robert clxxxv
FORRESTER
Agnes (Graham) 248, 258
Barbara 243
Elizabeth (Erskine) 248
"Frank" [Henry William Herbert] 76
James (Sir) 248
Margaret 248, 258
Walter (Sir), of Torwood and Garden 248, 258
FORSTER
Catherine 552, 859

Dorothy 328, 847
Dorothy (Ogle) 328
Edward Morgan (E.M.) 107
Eleanor 328
Florence (Wharton) 328
Frances 852
Isabel (Brewster) 328
Jane (Arnold) 436
John 328
Mary 625
Phyllis (Forster) 328
Thomas 328
Thomas (Sir) 328
William Edward 436
FORTENSKY
Elizabeth Rosemond (Taylor) (Hilton) (Wilding) (Todd) (Fisher) (Burton) (Warner) [Elizabeth Taylor] 21, 190
FORTESCUE
Bartholomew 743
Catherine 77
Eleanor (Norris) 743
Elizabeth 436, 534, 743
Elizabeth (Beauchamp) 743, 866
Elizabeth (Champernowne) 672
Elizabeth (Chichester) 436

Elizabeth (Deynsell) 743
Ellen (Moore) 743
Frances 110
Frances (Stanley) 110
Francis (Sir) 110, 120
Grace (Manners) 110, 120
Hester (Grenville) 77
Hugh 436
Hugh Fortescue, 1st Earl 77
Isabella (Jamys) 743
Jacquetta (St. Leger) 743
Jane 672
Joan 866
Joan (Prutteston) 672, 866
John 436, 672, 743, 866
John (Sir) 110, 743
John (Sir), 2nd Bt. 110
Margaret 349
Margaret (Arundell) 110
Martin 743
Mary 120
Mary (Rolle) 436
Mary (Speccot) 436
Matilda (Falwell) 866
William 672, 743, 866

FORTH
　Mary 501
FORTIER
　Thérèse 950
FORTIN
　Élise "Elsie"
　　(Fortin) 975, 988
　Émilie (Daniel)
　　988
　Felicité (Rioux)
　　988
　François 988
　Geneviève (Fortin)
　　988
　Guillaume-Henri
　　975, 988
　Joseph-Romain
　　988
　Madonna Louise
　　975, 988
　Marceline 973
　Marie-Louise
　　(Delisle) 988
　Marie-Louise
　　(Demers) 975,
　　988
　Narcisse 988
　Narcisse ("Nelson")
　　988
　Nazaire ("Henry")
　　Fortin 988
　Rose (Lajoie) 988
　Victoire (Blier)
　　988
　Willard 975, 988
FOSTER
　Albinia Jane
　　(Hobart-Hampden)
　　117

　Alice Jane Blanche
　　117
　Augustus John (Sir),
　　1st Bt. 117
　Caroline Emily
　　(Marsh) 117
　Cavendish Hervey
　　(Sir), 3rd Bt. 117
　Elizabeth 512
　Elizabeth
　　(Etherstone)
　　clxxxix
　Elizabeth (Hervey),
　　Lady [Lady
　　Elizabeth Foster]
　　117
　Florence (Narcissa
　　Florence) 364
　Isabella (Todd)
　　117
　Jennett 841
　John Frederick 117
　John Thomas 117
　Joseph lv
　Lydia 479, 715
　Margaret 486, 488
　Margaret (White)
　　486
　Thomas clxxxix
　Walter 486
　＿＿ 359
FOTHERINGHAM
　Katherine 282
FOUACE
　Sarah 123
FOUDRAS (DE)
　Madeleine 638
FOUGÈRES (DE)
　Marguerite 957

FOULD-SPRINGER
　Thérèse Carmen
　　May (Poppy),
　　Baroness 73
FOULIS
　Elizabeth 223
　John (Sir), 1st Bt.
　　223
　Margaret (Primrose)
　　223
　Robert Munro, 14th
　　Baron of 260
FOULKE
　ap Thomas 658
　Edward lxv, 651,
　　658, 660
　Ellen (Hughes)
　　651, 652, 658, 660
　Gwen (Evans) 651,
　　652
　Thomas 651
FOURMENT
　Hélène 804
FOURNIER
　Marcel 942
FOWELL
　Jane 573
FOWKE
　Anne
　　(Thoroughgood)
　　722
　Dorothy (Cupper)
　　563, 722
　Elizabeth 722
　Gerard (Col.) liii,
　　lxvi, clxvii, clxxvi,
　　722
　John 563, 722
　Joyce 697

Margaret 563
Margery (Morton) 697
Mary (Bayley) 722
Roger 697, 722
Susanna (___) 722
Thomas 722
FOWLER
  Elizabeth (Alsop) (Baldwin) lxii, lxvi, clxii, clxxv, 588, 589
  Frances Leveson 79
  Hannah 548
  William 589
FOX
  Anne 688, 824
  Anne (Mottrom) (Wright) 348
  Charles James (Hon.) 31
  Edward 246
  Francis 595
  Georgiana Caroline (Lennox) 31
  Henry, 1st Baron Holland 31
  James 246
  Jane 112
  Margaret 706
  Mary liv, clxv, clxxix, 595
  Natasha (Richardson) xi, xvii, xlii, clvii, 246
  Robert Michael John 246

Tabitha (Croker) 595
FOX-STRANGWAYS
  Caroline Leonora (Murray) 66
  Henry Stephen, 3rd Earl of Ilchester 66
  Theresa Anne Maria 66
FOXALL
  Elizabeth (Garway) 670, 671
  Mary 670, 671
  Thomas 670, 671
FOXLEY
  Francis 423
  Mary 357
  Mary (Dryden) 423
  Sarah 423
FOXTON
  Sarah 424
FOY (DE)
  Gillette 942, 943
FRADD
  Brandon viii, xlviii, li, lii, lv, lviii, lix, lx, clxxxiii, 372, 569, 678
FRAISWELL
  Elizabeth 590
FRAME
  Ida M. 146
FRANCAVILLA
  Alfonso II Felice d'Avalos, Prince of, Prince of Montesarchio 186, 189

Ferdinando Francesco II d'Avalos, Prince of, Prince of Montesarchio 186, 189
  Íñigo d'Avalos, Prince of 189
  Isabella d'Avalos, Princess of 189
  princes of 190
FRANCE (THE FRENCH)
  Adela, Princess of 851
  Adela of Savoy, Queen of 804, 954, 956, 965
  Adelaide of Poitou, Queen of 866, 870, 872, 879, 919
  Aelis (___), Queen of 879, 919
  Agnes of Meran, Queen of 950
  Alix, Princess of 735, 952
  Anne of Kiev, Queen of 739, 778, 780, 783, 785, 787, 789, 835, 837, 839, 841, 843, 845, 847, 957
  Catherine (de'Medici), Queen of 637
  Charles, Prince of, Count of Valois 459, 941, 961

Charles II, Prince of Anjou and, King of Naples and Sicily 459
Charles VI, King of 226
Charles VII, King of 202, 203, 208, 209
Charles IX, King of 637
Charlotte, Princess of Savoy, Queen of 200, 205
Claudia (Claud), Princess of 637
Constance of Provence, Queen of 851, 853, 855
Edith, Princess of 866, 870, 872
Eleanor, Duchess of Aquitaine, Queen of, Queen of England 647, 735, 737, 742, 746, 749, 752, 754, 757, 760, 761, 763, 766, 768, 770, 772, 774, 776, 909, 943, 948, 952, 964, 991, 993
Eleanor, Princess of, Queen of Sicily 51
Elizabeth, Princess of, Queen of Spain 637
Eugénie (Eugenia María Ignace Augustine de Portocarrero de Guzmán y Kirkpatrick), Empress of 291, 292
Francis II, King of 637
Gerberga of Germany, Queen of 874, 877, 879, 919
Gisela, Princess of 879, 919
Henry I, King of 681, 739, 778, 780, 783, 785, 787, 789, 835, 837, 839, 841, 843, 845, 847, 957, 959
Henry II, King of 202, 637, 735
Henry III, King of 637
Henry IV, King of, King of Navarre 62, 192, 293, 615, 637, 638
Hugh Capet, King of xxvi, 725, 866, 868, 870, 872, 879, 919, 1025
Hugh Magnus, Duke of, Duke of Burgundy 835, 837, 839, 841, 843, 845, 847
Isabella, Princess of Aragón, Queen of 459, 941, 961
Isabella, Princess of Bavaria, Queen of 226
Joanna, Princess of 226
Joanna, Princess of, Queen of Navarre 287, 293, 455
John II, King of 186, 189, 205, 287, 293, 438, 440, 442, 445
Joséphine (Marie-Josèphe-Rose) (de Tascher de la Pagerie) (de Beauharnais) Bonaparte, Empress of 292, 442, 443, 444
Katherine de Valois, Princess of, Queen of England, wife of Owen Tudor 226, 603, 813, 824
kings of 615
Louis IV, King of xxvi, 720, 874, 877, 879, 919
Louis VI, King of 804, 949, 954, 956, 965
Louis VII, King of 735, 774, 776, 943, 952, 993
Louis IX (St.), King of 634, 638, 965
Louis X, King of 455
Louis XI, King of 200, 203, 205
Louis XIII, King of xxi, lxx, 289

Louis XIV, King of 287, 288, 289
Louis XVI, King of 294
Louis-Philippe, King of 288, 290, 291, 294
Madeleine, Princess of, Queen of Scotland 82, 85, 87, 88, 90, 92, 93, 95, 96, 97, 98, 897
Margaret, Princess of Provence, Queen of 634, 638, 965
Margaret, Princess of, Queen of England xxvi, 462, 470, 473, 486, 493, 515, 519, 522, 526, 534, 539, 541, 545, 557, 579, 580, 598, 599, 600, 604, 605, 609
Margaret, Princess of, Queen of, Queen of Navarre 637
Margaret, Princess of Scotland, Queen of 200, 205
Margaret of Burgundy, Queen of 455
Maria Amelia Theresa, Princess of the Two Sicilies, Queen of 288, 290
Marie, Princess of 774, 776, 943, 950, 993

Marie de' Medici, Queen of 192
Marie Louise, Archduchess of Austria, Empress of 11
Marie of Anjou, Queen of 202, 208
Marie of Brabant, Queen of 941, 961
Marie-Antoinette (Maria Antonia), Archduchess of Austria, Queen of 267
Mary (Tudor), Princess of England, Queen of, Duchess of Suffolk xxxix, clxxxiii, clxxxviii, 62, 69, 76, 79, 80
Mathieu de Montmorency, Constable of 959
Michelle, Princess of 438, 445
monarchs of xv
Napoléon I (Bonaparte), Emperor of 11, 82, 157, 292, 442, 858
Napoléon III (Louis Napoléon Bonaparte), Emperor of 49, 291, 292
Peter, Prince of, Seigneur de Courtenay 965

Philip II Augustus, King of 950
Philip III, King of 459, 941, 961
Philip VI, King of 459
Robert, Prince of, Count of Clermont 634, 638
Robert I, King of 879, 919
Robert II, King of xxvi, 851, 853, 855
seigneurs in xv
___, Princess of 879, 919
FRANCESCO MARIA I (della Rovere), Duke of Urbino 186, 189
de' Medici, Grand Duke of Tuscany 192
FRANCEYS
Jane 372, 670, 678
FRANCHESE
Egle 21
FRANCHI
Anne Eleanora 49
FRANCIS
Anne Ayers 673
Duke of Saxe-Coburg-Saalfeld 45, 46, 182
Ebenezer, Jr. 923
Elizabeth 493, 746
Elizabeth (Thorndike) 923

Elizabeth Robbins
(Root) 673
Frederick Augustus 673
Hannah 340
Jessie Anne
(Stevens) 673
John 493
Luke 673
Manning 673
Margaret
(Wyndham) 493
Maud 565
Mehitable (Sackett) 673
Sarah Ellen 923
FRANCIS I
(of Lorraine), Holy Roman Emperor 15
FRANCIS II
(Gonzaga),
Marquess of
Mantua 186, 189
Holy Roman
Emperor, I of
Austria 11
King of France 637
FRANCKENSTEIN (VON AND ZU)
Anna Maria
(Esterházy de Galántha),
Countess 15
family 15
Heinrich, Baron 15
Helena (von
Arco-Zinneberg),
Countess 15

Joseph, Baron cliv, 15
Kay (Boyle) (Vail) xviii, xlv, cliv, 15
Konrad, Baron 15
FRANÇOISE
of Luxembourg,
Countess of Gavre 291, 459
FRANÇOISE-ISABELLE
of Guise 3
FRANCZISKA
Princess of
Montenuovo 11
FRANK
Jean-Paul 83
Laure-Louise-Napoléone-Eugénie-Caroline (Murat),
Princess clii, 83, 635
FRANKELIN
Constantia
(Eriksdotter) 51
Henrik 51
Maria Catharina 51
FRANKLAND
Agnes (Surriage) 130
Arabella (Belasyse) 129
Charles Henry (Sir), 4th Bt. 130
Charlotte 130
Elizabeth (Russell) 121, 130
Henry (Gov.) 130
Mary 121

Mary (Cross) 130
Sarah (Rhett) 130
Thomas (Sir), 2nd Bt. 121, 130
Thomas (Sir), 5th Bt. (Adm.) 130
William (Sir), 1st Bt. 129
FRANKLIN
Abigail 747, 758
Benjamin (Hon.) 87
Mary 87
FRANKLYN
Ellen 811
FRANQUEMENT (VON)
Eleanore von
Württemberg,
Baroness 49
FRASER
Agnes 789
Alexander (Sir), of
Philorth 789
Alexander, of
Errogie 82
Alice Mary
(Blundell) 23
Amelia (Murray) 67
Andrew, of Torosay 216
Angus, of Errogie 82
Anna Isabella
(MacLean),
Baroness MacLean 216
Anne (Mackay) 82
Anne Laughton
(Smith) 82

Antonia Margaret Caroline (Pakenham) [Lady Antonia Fraser] xxxviii, 73, 122, 299
Beatrix (Wemyss) 176
Caroline Georgina 82
Catherine 67
Charlotte Georgiana (Jerningham) 23
Eleanor (Douglas) 789
Eliza 93
Elizabeth 216
Elizabeth (Stewart) 176
family clxxxii
Hugh, 5th Baron Lovat 176
Hugh, 9th Baron Lovat 67
James (Sir), of Brae 176
Jean (Fraser) 82
Jean (Stewart) 176
Joanna (Ross) 789
John, of Inverlochy and Pictou 216
Magdalen 176
Margaret (Moray) 789
Margaret Mary 23
Marjory 152, 239
Mary (Bruce) 789
Mary (Stewart) 216
Simon 82

Simon, 6th Baron Lovat 176
Simon, 13th Baron Lovat 23
Thomas cxlix, clxxxii, 82
Thomas, 12th Baron Lovat 23
William (Sir), of Philorth 789, 790
FRASER-WALL
Marylin (___) 799
FRAUENBERG (VON)
Leonard II, Count of Haag 237
Maximiliana 237
FRAY
Katherine 331, 763
FRAZIER
Elizabeth 480
FREAKE
Elizabeth (Clarke) 493
John lxi, cxlix, 493, 494
Mary (Doddington) 493
Thomas 493
FREAME
Priscilla 148
FREDERICA
Princess of Hesse-Darmstadt 40
Princess of Hesse-Darmstadt, Queen of Prussia 13
Princess of Mecklenburg-

Strelitz, Queen of Hanover 40
FREDERICK
Count of Waldeck 57
Count Palatine of Zweibrücken 56
Jean 66
Landgrave of Hesse-Eschewege 44
Margrave of Brandenburg-Anspach 194, 196, 198
FREDERICK I
Elector of Brandenburg 52
Elector of Saxony 52, 449, 451
King of Bohemia (the "Winter King") [Frederick V, Elector Palatine of the Rhine] 38, 56
King of Prussia 56, 58, 432
King of Württemberg 12
FREDERICK I BARBAROSSA
Holy Roman Emperor 640, 733, 735, 952
FREDERICK II
(Gonzaga), Duke of Mantua, Marquess of Montferrat 186, 189

1239

Duke of Liegnitz 196
Duke of Saxe-Gotha 891
Elector of Brandenburg 52
Elector of Saxony 451
King of Denmark 47, 49, 52
King of Sicily, Prince of Aragón 51
Landgrave of Hesse-Homburg 54, 55
Margrave of Meissen, Landgrave of Thuringia 449, 451

FREDERICK III
Duke of Holstein-Gottorp 47
Duke of Liegnitz 196
Holy Roman Emperor 291
Margrave of Meissen 449, 451

FREDERICK IV
Landgrave of Leuchtenberg 237
Prince of Waldeck-Pyrmont 56

FREDERICK V. *see* FREDERICK I [BOHEMIA]

FREDERICK VI
King of Denmark 645
Margrave of Baden-Durlach 40, 43

FREDERICK VII
Margrave of Baden-Durlach 43, 46

FREDERICK AUGUSTUS II
Elector of Saxony, King of Poland 20

FREDERICK CASIMIR
Duke of Courland 56

FREDERICK EUGENE
Duke of Württemberg 49

FREDERICK LOUIS
Prince of Great Britain, Prince of Wales 12, 27

FREDERICK WILLIAM
Elector of Hesse 13
Margrave of Brandenburg-Schwedt 16

FREDERICK WILLIAM I
King of Prussia 16

FREDERICK WILLIAM II
King of Prussia 8, 13

FREDERICK WILLIAM III
King of Prussia 8, 40

FREDERICK WILLIAM CHARLES LOUIS GEORGE ALFRED ALEXANDER
Prince of Solms-Braunfels [Prince Carl of Solms-Braunfels] 40, 41

FREEBODY
Cecily 407

FREEMAN
Alice xix, xxxvii, xl, lvi, lxi, lxviii, lxix, lxxi, clxiii, clxxviii, 858, 859, 932
Henry 858
Margaret (Edwards) 858

FREEMAN-MITFORD. *see also* MITFORD
Algernon Bertram, 1st Baron Redesdale 22
Clementina Gertrude Helen (Ogilvy) 22
David Bertram Ogilvy, 2nd Baron Redesdale 22
Deborah Vivien, Duchess of Devonshire [Deborah Mitford] 22, 23, 26

Diana (Hon.) [Diana
 Mitford] 23
family xxiv,
 xxxviii
Jessica Lucy (Hon.)
 [Jessica Mitford]
 xvii, 23, 26
Nancy (Hon.)
 [Nancy Mitford]
 22, 26
Sydney (Bowles)
 22
Unity Valkyrie
 (Hon.) [Unity
 Mitford] 22
FREESE
Hannah 297, 298
FREIND
Elizabeth 390, 391
Grace (Robinson)
 390
William, Dean of
 Canterbury 390,
 391
FREMANTLE
Agnes (Lyon) 341
Albinia Frances
 (Jefferyes) 341
Delvin David 341
Emma (Isaacs) 341
John 341
Leila Hope
 (Fremantle) 341
Margery Hilda
 clvi, 341
Sidney Robert (Sir)
 341
Stephen Francis
 William 341

FRENCH
Ellen Tuck 63
Robert L. 525
FRESCHVILLE
Rosamond 530
FREUD
Caroline Maureen
 (Hamilton-Temple-
 Blackwood), Lady
 [Caroline Black-
 wood] xviii, 31
Lucian Michael
 xviii, 31
Sigmund, Dr. 31
FREVILLE
Baldwin (Sir) 466,
 506, 715, 728
Elizabeth 466, 567,
 592
Joyce 728
Joyce (de
 Botetourte) 506,
 715, 728
Margaret 100, 653,
 715
Maud (le Scrope)
 466, 715, 728
Robert 854
Thomasine 853,
 854
FRIAS
Bernardino
 Francisco
 Fernández de
 Velasco, 6th Duke
 of 140
Iñigo Fernández de
 Velasco, 4th Duke
 of 140

Iñigo Melchior
 Fernández de
 Velasco, 8th Duke
 of 140
Juan Fernández de
 Velasco, 5th Duke
 of 140
FRICKE
Barbara cxc
FRITCHER
Judith 645
FRITCHLEY
Mary 528
FRIZZELL
Hannah (Clarke)
 841
FROHNE
Adelaide 37
**FROMENTIÈRES
 (DE)**
counts 949
FRONSAC (DE)
Charles de Rohan,
 Seigneur de Gié,
 Vicomte 455
FROST
Carina Mary Gabriel
 (Fitzalan-Howard),
 Lady cliv, 72
David Paradine
 xviii, cliv, 72
Edmund 680
Thomasine (Clench)
 xlviii, lxvii, cxlix,
 clxxx, 680, 681
FROWICK
Alice 552, 851
Isabel 552

1241

FUGGER von KIRCHBERG
  Katharina 895
FULFORD
  Anne (Dennis) 392
  Dorothy (Bourchier) 392
  James 695
  John (Sir) 392
  Martha Ellen (Halley) 695
  Mary cxci, 295, 392, 522
  Mary Eleanor 696
  Thomas 392
  Ursula (Bamfield) 392
FULLER
  Abigail 862
  Elizabeth 670
  John 935
  Jonathan 935
  Matthew 935
  Sarah 935
  Sarah (Merrick) 935
FULMERSTON
  Frances 588
FULNETBY
  Elizabeth (Goodrick) 604
  Godfrey 604
  Jane 604
  Jane (Dymoke) 579, 604
  Jane (Herenden) 604
  John 579, 604
  Katherine 579
  Margaret (Grantham) 604
  Vincent (Sir) 604
FULTHORPE
  Joan 344, 719
FULTON
  Harriet (Livingston) 616
  Robert 616
FUNCK
  Kristina Beata Wilhelmina, Baroness 453
FURMAN
  Consuelo 884
FURNEAUX (DE)
  Margaret 687, 695
FURNESS
  Joanna 363
FURNIVAL
  Maud 372, 667, 670, 678, 684, 917
FÜRSTENBERG (VON, ZU)
  Bolko II of Schliesen-Liegnitz, Duke of, Duke of Münsterberg 640
  Clara Jeanne (Agnelli) 20
  Diane (Halfin) [Diane von Fürstenberg] xlv, 20
  Egon (Eduard Egon Peter Paul Giovanni), Prince xlv, 20
  Karl Emil Anton Maximilian Leo Wratislaw, Prince 20
  Katharina Eleanora, Princess 186
  Lynn (Marshall) 20
  Maria Matilda Georgina (Festetics von Tolna), Countess 20
  Maximilian Egon II, Prince 20
  Tassilo Egon Maria Karl Georg Leo, Prince 20
  Wratislaus I, Prince 186
FURSTER
  Heinrich 449
  Margaretha (von Hessen) 449
  ____ 449
FUSTE
  Joan 474
FYLLINGARUM
  Henrik Erlandsson, Lord of 457
  Ulf Henriksson, Lord of 457
GABRIEL BAUDOUIN
  Prince of the Belgians 204
GABRIELLA
  Princess of Savoy-Carignan 18

GABRIELLA-THÉRÈSE-MARIE
Grimaldi, Princess of Monaco, Countess of Carladès 934
GÄDDA
Johan, Lord of Faallnes 452
Karin (Königsmarck) 452
Kristina 452
GADEA ACOSTA
Hilda 997
GAEL (DE)
Amicia 843, 845
GAGARIN
Andrei, Prince 793
Daria, Princess 798
Donna Dean (Carter) 793
Ekaterina (Chonkhov) 793
Jamie (Porter) 793
Maria (Obolensky), Princess 793
Michael, Prince 793, 796
Sergei, Prince cliv, 793, 796
GAGE
Alice 339, 340
Benedicta Maria Theresa (Hall) 110
Hedwig Maria Gertrud Eva (van Chappuis) 5

John (Sir), 4th Bt. 136
Margaret (Kemble) 110
Mary 136
Mary (Middlemore) 136
Thomas (Hon.) (Gov.) cxliii, 110
Thomas Gage, 1st Viscount 110
GAGNÉ
Angélique (Pitre) 981
Arthur 982
Carole (Roux) 982
Catherine (Lefebvre) 982
Charles 982
Claire 981
Dolores (Millette) 982
Domithilde (Leduc) 982
Eric 967, 968, 969, 982
family 969
Gérard 982
Hermine 978
Jean-Baptiste 978
Joseph 981
Louis 982
Louise (Lepage) 982
Marguerite (Beaudry) 982
Marguerite (Chamberland) 978

Marie-Anne (Pellerin) 978
Marie-Catherine (Hubert dit Lacroix) 981
Marie-Françoise 623
Paul 981, 982
Richard 982
Roland-Yves xii, 939, 940, 945, 951, 956, 958, 959, 967, 969
Thérèse (Roy) 978
Valentine (Durocher) 982
Valerie (Hervieux) 982
Vital 978, 982
GAGNÉ dit BELAVANCE
Anne-Marie (Tessier) 969, 981, 982
Louis-Étienne 969, 981, 982
Marguerite 969
Marie-Catherine (Langtin dit Jereme) 969
Marie-Michelle (Brault) 981, 982
Marie-Renée (Hamelin dit Lacave) 969
Paul 981, 982
Pierre 969
René-Amable 969

GAIN(E)SFORD
Agnes 469, 551, 920
Margaret 625, 626
Sarah 744
GAINSBOURG
Serge 28
GAKERLIN
Mary 241
GALANTE
Olivia Mary (de Havilland) (Goodrich) 462
Pierre Paul 462
GALE
Bridget (Walrond) 745
Elizabeth (Denwood) 787
family 788
George xlix, cxliii, 787, 788
John 787
Katherine 745
Mary 85
Mary (Carlyle) 787
Mildred (Warner) (Washington) 787
Theophilus (Rev.) 745
Ursula 668
GALEN
Christine (Skarsholmslaegten) 644
Gyde 644
Inger 644
Torbern (knight) 644

GALICIA
Constance, Princess of Hungary, Queen of 621
Euphemia of Mazovia, Queen of 621
Leo (Lew), King of 621
Maria, Princess of 621
Youri I, King of 621
GALITZINE/ GOLITSYN
Adelaide Amalia (von Schmettau), Countess 798
Alexandra (Mestchersky), Princess 793
Alexandra, Princess xii, clii, 5, 793, 796
Alexei, Prince 792, 798
Anastasia (Prozorovsky), Princess 798
Anastasia, Princess 792
Andrei, Prince 798
Anna clv, 800
Anna (___) 798
Anna (Izmalov) 798
Anna (Lopuchin) 799, 800
Anna (Soukine) 792

Anna, Princess clv, 799
Boris, Prince 792, 794
Claudia (Bazykin) 799
Daria (Gagarin), Princess 798
Demetrius Augustine, Prince cliv, clxxvii, 798
Dimitri, Prince 798, 800
Ekaterina (Troubetskoy), Princess 793
Elizabeth, Princess 195
Eudoxia (___) 798
Euphemia (Piliemanov-Sabourov) 798
family xxii, 800
Fedor, Prince 798
George, Prince 799
Irina (Khilkov), Princess 792, 798
Ivan, Prince 798, 799
Josephine (Dennehy) 793
Ludmila (Lisitski) 799
Maria (Khvorostinine), Princess 792, 794
Maria (Miloslavsky) 794
Maria, Princess 792, 794, 799

1244

Marie Louise Julia
  (Baranov),
  Countess 798
Michael, Prince
  798, 799, 800
Natalie (Dolgurokov),
  Princess 794
Nic(h)olas, Prince
  cliv, 793, 796, 798
Paul, Prince 793
Peter, Prince xii,
  cliv, 800
Praskovya
  (Shuvalov) 798
Sergei, Prince 794,
  799
Sophia (Delianov)
  799, 800
Tatiana (Lopuchin)
  800
Tatiana, Princess
  800
Varvara (Shapov)
  798
Vladimir, Prince
  799, 800
Xenia (____) 798
Xenia (Morosov)
  799
Youri, Prince 798
GALLATIN
Abraham 912
Abraham-Alphonse-
  Albert, U.S.
  Treasury Sec. xii,
  xvii, liii, cliv, 912
Aimé 912
Barbe (Gervais)
  912

Élisabeth (de La
  Maisonneuve)
  912
Françoise (Gallatin)
  912
Hannah (Nicholson)
  912
Jean 912
Louis 912
Louise-Susanne
  (Vaudenet) 912
Madeleine
  (Humbert) 912
Marin 912
Sarah (de Tudert)
  912
Sophie (D'Allègre)
  912
Sophie-Albertine
  (Rolaz du Rosey)
  912
Victoria
  (Carcassola) 912
GALLIARD
Sarah 379
GALLOP
Phillis 171, 258
GALLOWAY
Alan, lord of 780,
  1025
Alexander Gordon,
  Bishop of the Isles
  and 148, 940
Alexander Stewart,
  6th Earl of 62,
  933
Devorguilla of 780
George Stewart, 8th
  Earl of 63

Helen of 843
John Stewart, 7th
  Earl of 62, 63, 64,
  80
GALMOYE
Piers Butler, 3rd
  Viscount clxxxix
GALT
Axel 644
Birgette 645
Edith (Bolling)
  xlii, 278, 301, 387,
  711, 823
Gjord 644
Ingeborg (Drefeld)
  644
Mette (Rantzau) 644
Norman 278, 301,
  387, 711, 823
Peder 644
Regitze (Rosen-
  krantz) 644
GALTON
family xxxvii
GALVINGTON
Alice 609
GALWAY
John Monckton, 1st
  Viscount 119
GAM
Dafydd (Sir) 808
Gwladys 337, 352,
  808
GAMAGE
Eleanor/Margaret
  548
Jane (Champer-
  nowne) 547, 548
Margaret 605

Margaret (St. John) 547
Robert 547
Thomas (Sir) 547
GAMBLE
French Addison 77
Judy Mary [Judy Campbell] 27
GAMMILL
Mary xiii
GANNES (DE)
Bertheleonne (de Monnins) 964
François, Sieur de Mondidier 964
Jeanne (de Besdon) 964
Jeanne (de Voyer) 964
Louis 964
Marie (de Terves) 964
Mathurin, Seigneur de Mondidier 964
René, Sieur de Mondidier 964
Renée (de Ferrou) 964
GANNES DE FALAISE (DE)
Barbe (Denis) 964
Louise (Legardeur de Tilly) 962, 964, 965
Louis-Joseph 961, 962, 964, 965
Marguerite (le Neuf de la Vallière) 964

GANNES DE FALAISE DE ROSNE (DE)
Françoise (Lebloy) 964
Louis 964
GANNOCK
Jane (Huddleston) 394
William 394
GANTT
Anne (Fielder) 1, lxii, cxlix, cli, clxviii, 603
Thomas 603
GARCEAU
Aurélie 970
Charles 970
Charlotte (Boisvert) 970
François 970
Thérèse (Desrosiers) 970
GARCÍA CARAFFA
Alberto 991
Arturo 991
GARCÍA CARRILLO
Juana 994
GARDE (DE LA)
Hugh III Adhémar, Seigneur 735
Hugh IV Adhémar, Seigneur 735
GARDEUR (LE)
Catherine 940
GARDINER
Abraham 643
Abraham, Jr. 643

David 643
Julia xlii, 643
Juliana (MacLachlan) 643
Mary (Smith) 643
Patience 231
Phebe (Dayton) 643
GARDNER
Adele Augusta (Ayer) 630, 654, 887
Dorothy Ayer 630, 655, 887
Elizabeth 923
Elizabeth (Pickering) 923, 924
Evelyn Florence Margaret Winifred 401
John 923
Levi Addison 630, 654, 887
GARFIELD
James Abram, 20th U.S. President xlii, 480
Lucretia (Rudolph) xlii, 480
GARGRAVE
Elizabeth 366
GARLAND
____ 806
GARNEYS
Margaret 134
Mirabel 682
GARNIER
Charlotte 73

GARONZIK
  Joseph vi
GARRAWAY
  Susanna 662
GARRETT
  Anne 473
GARRIGUE
  Cecile Olivia
    (Duntzfelt) 635
  Charlotte 635
  Charlotte Lydia
    (Whiting) 635
  family 636
  Jacques-Louis 635
  Rudolph Pierre xviii,
    xxvi, lxvii, 635
GARSIDE
  Margaret 924, 926
GARTH
  Charles 744, 745
  Elizabeth (Colleton)
    743
  John 744
  Mary 743, 744
  Thomas 743
GARTSCH
  Gertrude 66
GARWAY
  Elizabeth 670, 671
  Elizabeth
    (Anderson) 670
  William (Sir) 670,
    671
GASCOIGNE
  Agnes 327, 328,
    379, 413, 819
  Anna (Hobbes)
    (Mompeson)
    clxxxvii

Anne 317
Dorothy 374
Elizabeth 310, 389,
  399, 414, 725
Elizabeth (Singleton)
  clxxxvii
Francis clxxxvii
Henry clxxxvi,
  clxxxvii
Isabel 126
Jane (Neville) 398,
  413
Margaret 328, 398
Margaret (Percy)
  310, 327, 374, 379,
  389, 399, 414
Thomas clxxxvi,
  clxxxvii
William (Sir) 310,
  327, 374, 379, 389,
  398, 399, 413, 414
GASCOIGNE/
GASKINS
  family clxxxvii
  Thomas clxxxvi
GASCOYNE-CECIL
  Georgiana Caroline
    (Alderson)
    xxxviii
  Mary Alice 26
  Robert Arthur
    Talbot, 3rd
    Marquess of
    Salisbury, Prime
    Minister xxxviii
GASKELL
  Christiana Gulielma
    (Penn) 149
  Peter 149

GASTELIN
  Juliana 695
GATES
  Elizabeth (Emery)
    673
  George Porterfield
    673
  George Williams
    673
  Jerusha (Clark)
    673
  Margaret "Madge"
    673
  Samuel, Jr. 673
  Sarah D. (Todd)
    673
GAUCELME
  Douce 735
GAUNT [GHENT]
  John of, Prince of
    England, Duke of
    Lancaster xxxix,
    295, 300, 314, 324,
    331, 337, 339, 345,
    357, 366, 368, 370,
    375, 382, 387, 393,
    395, 396, 397, 398,
    400, 403, 405, 407,
    413, 417, 419, 421,
    426, 427, 429, 433,
    434, 900, 902
GAVELL
  Thomasine 606
GAVESTON (DE)
  Amy 373, 387,
    697, 847, 848
  family 746
  Margaret (de Clare)
    847

1247

Piers, 1st Earl of
Cornwall 698,
847
GAVRE (DE)
Alain d'Albret,
Count of 293
Arnould VI, Baron
d'Escornaix 950
Catherine 950
Françoise of
Luxembourg,
Countess of 291
Isabelle (de
Ghistelles) 950
Lamoral, Count of
Egmont, Prince of
290, 291, 459
GAWDY
Juliana 607
GAWTON
Joan 419
GAYER
Agnes 254
GAYLORD
Joanna xiv
**GAZELLI DI
ROSSANA**
Augusto Filippo
Stanislas 201
Luisa Albertina
Cristina Giovanni
201
Maria Cristina
Giovanna Luigia
(Rignon) 201
GEBSUER
Henriette Caroline,
Baroness von
Brockenburg 891

GEDDING
Anne (Astley) 682
Constance 682
Margery (Watkins)
682
Mirabel
(Aspall/Aspale)
682
Thomas 682
William 682
GEDDY
Ann McKinney
924
GEDE
Clara (Fink) 620
Dorothy Eleanor
620
Faye Valeta (Elder)
620
Henry Frederick
620
Henry Godfrey 620
Jacqueline Frances
Strange (Weske)
620
Robert Henry 620
Thomas Frederick
viii, xxii, xlvii, lv,
lxiii, 213, 221,
620, 890, 894, 991
GEDGE
Mary 548
GEDNEY
Andrew 471
Deborah (Clarke)
129
Dorothy (Skipwith)
471
Mary 471

GEDYMIN
Grand Duke of
Lithuania 797
GEERS
Elizabeth 123
Elizabeth (Cope)
123
Thomas 123
GÉLINAS
Agnès 970
GENDEREST (DE)
Jean de Béarn,
Seigneur 963
GENDT (VAN)
Elisabeth (von
Raesfeld) 907
Johan Gerard, Heer
van Oyen en Dieden
907
Meralda (van
Rossem) 907
Moralla Jans 907
Walraven, Heer van
Oyen en Dieden
907
Wilhelmina (von
Wachtendonk) 907
Willem, Heer van
Oyen en Dieden
907
**GENDTBRUGGHE
(DE)**
Jean de Coudenhove,
Seigneur 438
GENGHIS KHAN
Khan of the Golden
Horde 797, 800
GENTYL (LE)
Agnes 864

GEORGE
Count of Nassau-
  Dillenburg 194
David 652
Duke of Brunswick-
  Kalenburg 58
Duke of Brunswick-
  Lüneburg 432
Duke of
  Württemberg-
  Mömpelgard 184
Grand Duke of
  Russia 4
Margaret (Edward)
  652
Margrave of
  Leuchtenberg 194
Prince of Waldeck-
  Pyrmont 56
GEORGE I
Elector of Hanover,
  King of Great
  Britain xxi, lxx,
  58, 432
King of Greece 3
GEORGE II
King of Great
  Britain 8, 12, 27,
  28
GEORGE III
King of Great
  Britain 10, 40,
  299, 615
GEORGE IV
King of Great
  Britain 123
GEORGE V
King of Great
  Britain 453

GEORGE VI
King of Great
  Britain 930
GEORGE
ALEXANDER
LOUIS
  of Cambridge,
  Prince of Great
  Britain xlii, 25,
  380, 931, 932
GEORGE WILLIAM
Elector of
  Brandenburg 54
Landgrave of Hesse-
  Darmstadt 40
GEORGIA
Bagration princes of
  7
Constantine
  Bagration-
  Mukhransky, Prince,
  a prince of 7
Teymuraz Bagration-
  Mukhransky
  (Prince), a prince of
  clii, 7
GÉRALDINE
(Apponyi de Nagy-
  Apponyi), Queen
  of the Albanians
  [Géraldine Margit
  Virginia Olga
  Mária, Countess
  Apponyi de
  Nagy-Apponyi]
  xl, 929, 935
GERARD
Alice 561
Alice (Boteler) 702

Anne 515
Bridget 558
Catherine 558
Constance clxxxiv,
  702
Constance (Rowson)
  558
Eleanor (Dutton) 561
Elizabeth 317, 902
Elizabeth (___) 29
Elizabeth Sumner
  111
family xxiv, 558
Frances 515
Gilbert, 2nd Baron
  Gerard of Gerard's
  Bromley 561
Grace (___) 558
Isabel (___) 558
Jane (Legh) 558
Jennet 497
John 29, 558, 702
Margery (Trafford)
  558, 902
Marmaduke 558
Mary 478
Maud (Bold) 497
Rebecca 29
Rose (___)
  (Tucker) 558
Susannah (Snow)
  29, 317, 478, 515,
  558
Thomas xxxv, lv,
  clxv, 29, 317, 478,
  497, 515, 558, 559
Thomas (Sir) 558,
  902
William 558

1249

Winifred 558
GERBERGA
  of Germany, Queen
    of France 874,
    877, 879, 919
GERDEREST (DE)
  Bernard de Béarn,
    Seigneur 963
  Jean de Béarn,
    Seigneur 963
GERDES
  Sarah Margaret 54
  Wilhelmina Sara 54
GERGEN
  Anne Elizabeth
    (Wilson) cliv,
    232, 378
  David Richmond
    xviii, 232
GERHARD VI
  Count of Berg 459
GERLACH
  Anna Dorothea
    Eleonore Christine
    449
GERLACH I
  Count of Nassau-
    Wiesbaden 617
GERMAIN
  Estelle 984
  Joseph-Roland
    Gameau 984
  Marie-Alphonsine-
    Germaine (Breton)
    984
**GERMAINE
(GERMANA)**
  (de Foix), Queen of
    Aragón 140

GERMANY
  Cunigunde, Princess
    of, Queen of
    Bohemia 640
  emperors of 615
  Gerberga of, Queen
    of France 874,
    877, 879, 919
  Henry I "the
    Fowler," Emperor
    of 874, 877
  monarchs of 45
  nobility in xv
  William I, Emperor
    of 41
  William II, Emperor
    of 20
GERNON (DE)
  Joan 766
  Ranulph, 2nd Earl
    of Chester 806,
    813, 815, 817, 819,
    821, 822, 824, 826
**GERSDORFF
(DE/VON)**
  Carl August 183
  Carlotta Justina 237
  Caroline (Choate)
    183
  Ernst Bruno liii,
    clxx, 183
  family xl
  Helen Suzette
    (Crowninshield)
    183
  Josephine 183
GERTRUDE
  of Hohenberg (wife
    of Rudolf I, Holy

    Roman Emperor)
    449, 451, 617
GERVAIS
  Barbe 912
GERWITZ
  Isaac (Dr.) 618
GETTY
  Aileen 21
  J. (John) Paul 645
**GHIKA-
PEREVOSTCHIKOV**
  Elisabeth (Belevsky-
    Zhukovsky) clvi, 5
  Peter 5
GHISTELLES (DE)
  Isabelle 950
  Jean III, Seigneur
    950
  Jean IV, Seigneur
    950
  Marguerite (de
    Dudzeele) 950
  Marie (de
    Haverskerke) 950
  Roger, Seigneur de
    Dudzeele and
    Staaten 950
GIBAULT
  Felicité 975
GIBBES
  Ann (Murrey) 779
  Basil 779
  Elizabeth 366
  Elizabeth (____)
    779
  family vii, l, lxviii,
    1026
  Jane (Tournay)
    778

John clxxx, 779, 1025
Mary (Coventry) 779
Robert 779
Robert (Gov.) clxviii, 366, 779, 1025
Stephen 778
Thomas 779, 1025
___ (Davis) 366, 779
GIBBINS
Hannah 630, 886
James 630, 886
Judith (Lewis) 630, 886
GIBBON
Jane 398
Sarah 308
GIBBS
Anne 103, 104
Elizabeth 114
Elizabeth (Pride) l, cl, 103, 104
Elizabeth (Sheafe) 738
Elizabeth (Temple) 738
Gertrude (Wroughton) 738
Henry (Sir) 738
John (Gov.) 103
Love 463
Mary 104
Ralph (Sir) 738
Rebecca 766
Robert lxx, clx, clxxvi, 738

Vicary xxiv, li
GIBSON
Alexander, of Durie 223
Elizabeth (Foulis) 223
Helen 223
Renata (Clark) 223
GIBSON (VON)
Archibald Gibson, Baron 223
GIDDINGS
George 682, 880
Grace (Wardwell) 880
Jane (Lawrence) clx, 682, 880
Joseph 880
Joseph, Jr. 880
Mary 682
Susanna 880
Susanna (Rindge) 880
GIÉ (DE)
Charles de Rohan, Seigneur, Vicomte de Fronsac 455
François de Rohan, Seigneur, Baron de Château-du-Loir 455
Pierre de Rohan, Seigneur, Count de Marle 455
GIEDDE
Margrethe 645
GIELGUD. *see also* GUILGUD
Adam 803

Aniela Leontina (Aszpergerowa) 803
Arthur John (Sir) viii, xvii, lxiv, cliv, 803
Cunegonda (Szemiotowna) 802
Frank Henry 803
John 802
Kate Terry (Lewis) 803
Val Henry 803
GIESSEN (VAN)
Christina 776
Geertken 776
GIFFARD
Agnes (Master) 857
Agnes (Winslow) 857
Alice 861, 863
Amy 857
Anne 859
Cassandra 676
Eleanor (Vaux) 857
Elizabeth (de Missenden) 857
Isabel (Stretle) 857
Jane 672
Joan (Langston) 857
John 857
John (Sir) 857, 861
Lucy (de Morteyn) 857, 861
Margaret 806, 857

1251

Margaret (Cobleigh) 672
Mary (Nanseglos) 857
Nicholas 857
Roger 857, 859, 862
Roger (Sir) 672
Thomas 857, 859
Thomas (Sir) 857
William 859
____ (Vachell) 859
GIFFORD
Anne 526
Catherine 462
Eleanor (Paulet) 526
family 564
Joan (Bruges/ Brydges) 526
John 526
Paul McKee lvi, lvii, lix, lxii, lxiii, 257
William (Sir) 526
GIGNILLIAT
Abraham 873
family vii
Jean-François lvii, 868, 873
Marie (de Ville) 873
Suzanne (Le Serrurier) 873
GIL DE VIDAURE
Teresa 993
GILBERT
Anne (Clere) 588
Cleer 589
family 589
Horace Durham 185
Isabella 835

Joan 870
Katharine (Dedons de Pierrefeu) 185
Mary 101
Temperance 588, 589
William xxix, 588, 589
GILBREATH
Norma Lavinia (Henley) 901
Sidney Gordon 901
GILBY
Ellen 708
GILDREDGE
Jane 112
GILES/EGIDIA
Stewart, Princess of Scotland 275, 278
GILL
Anna Maria 512, 558, 559, 676, 875
Benjamin 558, 559, 875
family 559
Mary (Mainwaring) xlvii, l, lvi, clxv, clxxxii, 400, 558, 559, 875
Raymond clxxxvii
Ruth Sylvia 378, 932
GILLESPIE
Elspeth 276
GILLETT
Martha 231
GILLOIS
Yvonne-Noele-Marie 83

GILLON
Alexander 311
Mary (Splatt) (Cripps) 311
GINGRAS
Charles 976, 979
Jean 976
Marie-Charlotte 976, 979
Marie-Françoise (Amiot) 976, 979
Marie-Madeleine (Lefebvre) 976
GIRARD
Catherine (d'Avagour) 949
Florentin, Seigneur de Barenton 948, 949
Jeanne 948
Marie (Cholet) 948
GIRLINGTON
Isabel 327, 343
Katherine (Hildyard) 343
William 343
GIRÓN DE GUZMÁN (DE)
María 140
GISCARD d'ESTAING
Anne-Aymone (Sauvage de Brantes) 185
Frédéric 185
May 185
Sophie 185
Valéry (Pres.) 185

GISELA
Princess of France
879, 919
GISSAGE
Sarah (Shelton)
534
GLADSTONE
Catherine (Glynne)
77
William Ewart,
Prime Minister 77
GLAMIS
John Lyon, 6th
Baron 898
Thomas Bowes-
Lyon, Lord 101
GLANDEVEZ (DE)
Dauphine 735
GLASSBOROW
Valerie 379
GLASSBROOK
Mary (Paulet)
(Buncombe) 609,
610
GLEASON
Abigail 656
GLEB
Prince of Minsk
849
GLEMHAM
Anne 571
Eleanor (Brandon)
571
John 571
GLEN
Anna (Peeck) 914
Anne (Hanson)
914, 915
Elias 915

Elizabeth (Wilson)
xlviii, cli, 112, 113
family xl, xlvi, 915
Jacob, Jr. 914
Jacob Sanderse
[Alexander] 914,
915
James (Gov.) 112,
113
Johannes Sanderse
[John Alexander]
914
John 915
Katherine/Catalin
(Duncanson) cxlix,
cli, clxiv, 248, 914
Martha 914
Rebecca (Miller)
914
Sander [Alexander]
Leendertsz. 248,
914
GLENCAIRN
Alexander
Cunyngham, 5th
Earl of 213, 214,
216, 218
William
Cunyngham, 6th
Earl of 213, 214,
216, 218
GLENCONNER
Edward Priaulx
Tennant, 1st Baron
78
GLENDOWER
Owen [Owain ap
Gruffudd Fychan]
657, 813, 824

GLENN
Thomas Allen viii,
xlvi, lvi, lxv
GLENTWORTH
Henry Hartstonge
Pery, Viscount 115
William Cecil Pery,
1st Baron 115
GLOGAU
Beatrix of (wife of
Louis IV, Holy
Roman Emperor)
51, 447, 449, 451,
907
Przemysl I Nosak,
Duke of Teschen
and 713
GLOUCESTER
Alice (Montagu-
Douglas-Scott),
Princess of Great
Britain, Duchess of
25, 28
Gilbert de Clare, 3rd
Earl of, 7th Earl of
Hertford 466, 483,
489, 491, 495, 505,
508, 514, 528, 536,
547, 567, 575, 577,
584, 587, 590, 592,
594, 606, 607, 615
Hugh de Audley, 1st
Earl of 495, 505,
575, 577, 590, 615,
847
Humphrey
Plantagenet, Duke
of 229, 231, 233,
235

Mabel of 808, 810, 811
Maud of 806, 813, 815, 817, 819, 821, 822, 824, 826
Richard, Prince of Great Britain, 2nd Duke of 25
Robert of Caen, 1st Earl of 806, 807, 808, 810, 811, 813, 815, 817, 819, 821, 822, 824, 826, 1025
Thomas le Despencer, 1st Earl of 377, 410, 417, 423
Thomas Plantagenet of Woodstock, Prince of England, 1st Duke of xxv, xxxix, 331, 353, 392, 393, 409, 420, 421, 428, 436
William FitzRobert, 2nd Earl of xxxii, 807, 808, 810, 811
William Henry, Prince of Great Britain, Duke of 27

GLOVER
Priscilla 371, 813, 882
William Stanard lxxi

GLYNNE
Catherine 77
Mary (Neville) 77
Stephen Richard (Sir), 8th Bt. 77

GOBION
Agnes (de Merlay) 857, 861
Hugh 857, 861
Joan 857, 861
Matilda (___) 857, 861
Richard 857, 861

GODARD
Anna (Karina) [Hanne Karin Blarke Bayer/Beyer] 635
Anne-Françoise-Sophie (Wiazemsky) 635, 795
Jean-Luc 635, 636, 795
Odile (Monod) 634
Paul 634

GODDARD
Anne (Gifford) 526
Bridget 737, 740
Edward 526, 527, 737
Elizabeth (Miles) 526
Elizabeth (Walrond) 526
family 564
Josiah 526
Martha 563, 564
Mary (Kingsmill) 737
Priscilla (D'Oyley) 526
Rachel 526

Rachel (Davis) 526
Richard 526
Thomas 526
William lviii, lxiv, clx, clxxiv, 526, 563

GODFREY
Arabella (Churchill) 536
Charles 536

GODMAN
Elizabeth 475

GODSON
Elizabeth 467

GODWIN
Mary Wollstonecraft [Mary Shelley] 474

GOES (VAN DER). see VAN DER GOES

GOFFE
Abigail (Richardson) 585
Frances (Whalley) 781
Hannah (Sumner) 585
John 585
Martha 585
William 585, 781

GOFORTH
Anne (Skipwith) lviii, cxlix, cli, 409
William 409

GOLD
Mary 841

GOLDEN HORDE (THE)
Genghis Khan, Khan of 797, 800

Maria of 797
Toktai, Khan of 797
GOLDING
Arthur 766
Elizabeth (Towe) 766
Elizabeth (Worthy) 766
Ephraim lvii, cxliv, 766, 767
family 767
Gideon 766
John 766, 767
Margery 68, 766
Percival 766
Rebecca (Gibbs) 766
Thomas 766
Ursula (Marston) 766
Ursula (Roydon) 766
William 767
GOLDINGHAM
Jane 877
GOLDSMITH
Carole Elizabeth 379
GOLDWELL
Catherine clxxxvii
GOLEUDDYDD
ferch Dafydd 582, 811
GOLIGHTLY
Culcheth xlviii, cxlix, 366, 367
Dorothy (Fenwick) 366

Mary (Butler) (Elliott) 366
Robert 366
GOLITSYN. *see* GALITZINE/ GOLITSYN
GOLOVINE
Anastasia 791
Anna (Kholmsky), Princess 791
Ivan 791
Maria (Odoevsky), Princess 791
Peter 791
GOLTZ (VON DER)
Marie Karoline Elizabeth 224
GONNES (DE)
Adolf, Herr van Vuylcoop 733, 734
Louise (van Alendorp) 733
Maria 733
Paschina (Ruysch) 733
Philippe 733, 734
GONTARD (VON)
Adalbert 57
family xviii
Susanna (Schilling von Canstatt), Baroness cliv, 57
GONZAGA
Anna, of Nevers and Mantua 38
Camillo, Count of Novellara 186
Caterina (d'Avalos) 186

Eleanor 186, 189
Ferdinando Francesco II, Prince of Francavilla and Montesarchio 186
Francis II, Marquess of Mantua 186, 189
Frederick II, Duke of Mantua, Marquess of Montferrat 186, 189
Isabella 186, 189
Isabella (d'Este) 186, 189
Lavinia Teresa 186
Margaret (Palaeologina), of Montferrat 186, 189
GONZAGA-MYSZKOWSKI
Zygmunt, Count Wielopolski, Marquis 11
GONZÁLEZ DE OVIEDO (DE)
Catalina 994
GOOD
William lvi, 562
GOODACRE
Hugh John Mackenzie 323
John Duncan 323
Myrtle Jane lxiii, clii, 323
Nancy Jacqueline (Parsons) 323

GOODALE
Elizabeth   126
GOODE
John   lxiv, cxc
GOODERE
Alice (Brent)   851
Alice (Frowick)   552, 851
Anne   323, 852
family   852
Henry   851
Jane (Greene)   851
Jane (Hawte)   323, 552, 738
Jane/Joan (Lewknor)   851
John   552, 851
Thomas   323, 851, 852
GOODFELLOW
Anne   518
GOODHALL
Jane   111
GOODHUE
Grace Anna   342, 526, 748, 758, 814, 882
GOODMAN
Glenn H.   xlvii, l, li, liv, lvi, 400, 559
GOODNIGHT
Catherine   726
GOODRICH
Marcus Aurelius   462
Olivia Mary (de Havilland)   462
GOODRICK
Anne   471

Anne (Dymoke)   471
Elizabeth   604
John   471
Lionel   471
Winifred (Sapcott)   471
GOODWIN
Anne (Spencer)   596
Catherine   596
Edna Beatrix (Maguire)   217
Harold   217
John (Sir)   596
Margaret (Mayne)   412
Shirley Elizabeth   viii, xlvii, lv, lxiv, lxviii, 153, 213, 217, 490, 708
Stephen   412
GOODWYN
French Addison (Gamble)   77
GOOKIN
Catherine   778
Daniel   778
GOOR (VAN)
Balthasar   776, 777
Catharina (van Amstel)   776
Christina (van Giessen)   776
Daniel, knight   776
Elisabeth (van Rijswick)   776
Geertken (van Giessen)   776

Jan   776
Johan   776
Margriet (van Goor)   776
Willemke   776, 777
William   776
___ (van Hameland?)   776
GORBATY-SHUISKY
Alexander, Prince   791
Anastasia (Golovine)   791
Boris, Prince   791
Ivan, Prince   791, 795
Vassili, Prince   795
GORDON
Alexander (Sir), of Lochinvar   239
Alexander, 1st Earl of Huntly   176, 281
Alexander, 3rd Earl of Huntly   176, 249
Alexander, 12th Earl of Sutherland   82, 148
Alexander, Bishop of the Isles and of Galloway   148, 940
Alexander, of Gight   163
Alexander, of Lesmoir   273
Alexander Gordon, 4th Duke of   25, 28, 31, 64, 67

1256

Annabella (Stewart), Princess of Scotland 176, 223
Anne 93, 97
Anne (Campbell) 154, 156
Anne (Hamilton) 154
Catherine (Burnet) 250
Catherine (Gordon) 67
Catherine, Lady 154
Catherine, of Gight [Mrs. John Byron] 163
Charles, 1st Earl of Aboyne 154
Charles, 2nd Earl of Aboyne 155, 933
Charles, 4th Earl of Aboyne 933
Charlotte 31, 32
Christian 261, 266
Cosmo George Gordon, 3rd Duke of 67
Elizabeth 161, 163, 176, 255, 268
Elizabeth (Keith) 148, 154, 176
Elizabeth (Lyon) 155, 933
Elizabeth, Countess of Sutherland 71
Geneviève (Petau) 148, 940
George, 1st Marquess of Huntly 93, 97, 154, 161
George, 2nd Earl of Huntly 176, 223
George, 2nd Marquess of Huntly 154, 155, 156
George, 4th Earl of Huntly 148, 154, 176
George, 5th Earl of Huntly 154
George, 15th Earl of Sutherland 98
George, of Gight 163
Georgiana 25, 28
Grace (Lockhart) 933
Helen 155, 239
Helen (Cochrane) 98
Helen (Riddell) 250
Helen (Stewart) 88, 148
Helen (Urquhart) 273
Henrietta (Stewart) 93, 97, 154, 161
Isabel 92, 223, 276, 790
James (Sir), 1st Bt. 273
James (Sir), of Lesmoir 273
Jane (Maxwell) 25, 31, 64, 67
Janet 213, 214, 216, 218, 239, 255, 268
Janet (Kennedy) 239
Janet (Mudie) 250
Janet (Stewart) 176, 249
Jean 82, 249
Jean (Gordon) 82, 148
Jean (Wemyss) 98
Joanna, of Cairston 88
John 148, 940
John, 3rd Earl of Aboyne 933
John, 11th Earl of Sutherland 88, 148
John, 16th Earl of Sutherland 98
John Gordon, Lord 148, 154, 176
John Steele 481
Katherine 148, 250, 273
Katherine (Innes) 163
Louisa 64
Louisa (Lucy) (Gordon) 148
Margaret 281, 789, 933
Margaret (Duff) 163
Margaret (Stewart) 148, 154, 176, 933
Margaret, of Haddo 281
Marion (Forbes) 273

1257

Mary 155, 156
Natalie Bayard
  (Howard) 127
Peter Alan 127
Rebecca (Keith)
  273
Robert (Sir), 1st Bt.
  148
Robert, of Pitlurg
  250
Susan 67
Susan (Murray) 67
Thomas lxv, clxxi,
  250
William, 2nd Earl of
  Aberdeen 67
GORDON
  [SUTHERLAND]
  Katherine (Morison)
    98
  William, Lord
    Strathnaver 98
GORDY
  (Bessie) Lillian
    422, 764, 773
GORE
  Albert Arnold, Jr.
    923
  Barbara 590
  Eleanor 308
  Frances 308
  Rhea 65
  Sidney 307
GORGES
  Agnes (Beauchamp)
    835
  Alexander 523
  Anne (Bell) xlv,
    295, 296, 522, 838

Anne (Howard)
  522, 523
Anne (Walsh) 522
Anne (Webb) 522
Barbara 405, 406
Barbara (Baynard)
  406, 522
Bridget 457
Cecily (Lygon)
  295, 296, 522
Dorothy (Speke)
  296
Edmund (Sir) 522
Edward 295, 522
Edward (Sir) 296,
  522
Eleanor 835
Eleanor (Ferre?)
  835
Elizabeth 296, 522,
  835
Elizabeth (___)
  (Coffin) 295, 522
Elizabeth (Cole)
  522
Elizabeth (Gorges)
  (Courtenay)
  (Bligh) 295, 296
Elizabeth (Gorges)
  (Smith) liii,
  clxxiii, 296, 457,
  522
family xvii, xxiv,
  lvi, 458
Ferdinando 406
Ferdinando (Sir),
  Lord Proprietor of
  Maine xvii, liii,
  lvi, lx, clxxii,

clxxiii, 295, 392,
  406, 457, 522, 838
Helena Bååt
  (Snakenborg)
  457, 458, 522
Henry 406, 522
Jane (Hankford)
  835
Mary (___)
  (Vaulx) 523
Mary (Fulford)
  (Achims) 295,
  392, 522
Mary (Poyntz) 522
Mary (Sanford)
  522
Maud (de Lovel)
  835
Meliana (Hilliard)
  406
Ralph (Sir) 835
Raymond lvi, lx
Robert 522
Robert, gov.-gen. of
  New England 296
Rose (Alexander)
  (Mallock) 522,
  523
Theobald (Sir) 835
Thomas 835
Thomas (Dep. Gov.)
  522, 523
Thomas (Sir) 457,
  522
Tristram 522
William (Sir) 522
William, gov. of
  New Somerset-
  shire, Maine 296

Winifred (Butshead) 522
GORGES alias RUSSELL
Agnes (Wyke) 835
Theobald (Sir) 835
GORHAM
Desire 654
Desire (Howland) 654
John 654
Mary 405
GORING
Constance 310, 480, 584, 737
Constance (Dyke) 737
family 741
Joan (Hewster) 737
John 737
Margaret (Radmylde) 737, 738
GORSUCH
Anne (Lovelace) xxxiv, liii, lxix, clxvi, 509
family lv
John (Rev.) 509
GÖRZ
Katharina of 451
GOSLING
Donna (Wilson) 979
George 979
Ida Felicia Louise 893
Marie-Yvette (Brown) 979

Ryan Thomas 967, 968, 979
Thomas Ray 979
GOSSE
Anne 401
GOSSELIN
Angélique 980
Angélique (Couture) 980
Louis 980
GOSTLETT
Anne (Hungerford) 320
Benjamin 320, 322
Charles 320
Elizabeth (Chetwynd) 320, 323
Helena 320
Marie (___) (Short) 320
William 320
GOSTWICK
Anne (Wentworth) 306
Edmund (Sir), 2nd Bt. 306
Mary 306
GOTHERSON
Daniel (Maj.) 314, 316
Dorothea (Scott) xlviii, lii, cxliv, 314, 316
GOTT
Esther 342
GOUEZ (LE)
Catherine-Bonne (de Saint-Gilles) 962

Charles, Seigneur de Grais and de Merville 962
GOUIN
Lomer (Sir), Premier of Québec 969
GOULD
Deborah 564
Elizabeth 305
Husey 305
Mary 103, 534, 536
Sarah 368
Vera Chochroska (Novak) 973
GOULDWELL
Frances 605
GOULET
André-Louis 973
Carol Maria (Leraia) [Carol Lawrence] 973
Françoise (Labrecque) 973
Joseph 973
Louise (Longmore) 973
Marceline (Fortin) 973
Marie (Lamontagne dit Bacquet) 973
Olive 984
Robert-Gérard 967, 973
Thomas 973
GOUSHILL
Elizabeth 517, 554, 565, 571, 613

Elizabeth (FitzAlan)
(Mowbray) xxiii,
xxiv, xxv, xxvi,
xxxi, xxxii, 473,
493, 497, 510, 517,
522, 524, 532, 541,
554, 557, 558, 560,
563, 565, 571, 574,
598, 605, 611, 613
family xxiv, 561,
564
Joan 397, 497, 510,
517, 524, 532, 558,
560, 563, 574, 611
Robert (Sir) xxiv,
xxxi, 497, 510,
517, 524, 532, 554,
558, 560, 563, 565,
571, 574, 611, 613
GOUYON
Victoire-Louise-
Josèphe 24
GOVE
Mary (Shard) 318
GOW
Anna Katherine 179
Jane Emily (Scott)
179
Michael (James
Michael) (Sir) 179
GOWENS
Lois June 974
GOWER
Eleanor 553
Francis 553
John Leveson-
Gower, 1st Earl
xxiv, 33, 62, 64,
299

Joyce (Blount) 553
Lowys 514
Margaret (Hunt)
553
Richard 553
GOWRIE
William Ruthven,
1st Earl of 151,
170
GØYE
Anne (Bille) 644
Karen 644
Steen 644
GRACE
ferch Cadwaladr ap
Robert 660
GRACE PATRICIA
(Kelly), Princess of
Monaco 934
GRAEME
Anne (Diggs) 168
Anne (Drummond)
168
Elizabeth 168
Thomas (Dr.)
cxlix, 168
Thomas, of
Balgowan 168
GRAFFART (DE)
Jacqueline 948
**GRAFFENRIED
(VON) (DE)**
Abraham 832
Anna (von Muhlinen/
Mülinen) 832
Anton 832
Baker 833
Barbara (Needham)
833

Catherine (Jenna/
Jenner) 832
Christoph 832
Christopher 833
Christoph(er), Baron
viii, xxvi, xxxv, xlvi,
lxiv, cxliv, 832, 833
family 833
Marie (von Treuffen
genannt Loewen-
sprung) 832
Mary (Baker) 833
Mary Baker 833
Mercedes 67
Regina (von
Tscharner) 832,
833
Sarah (Vass) 833
Tscharner 833
Ursula (von
Diesbach) 832
GRAFTON
Augustus Henry
Fitzroy, 3rd Duke
of 33
Charles Fitzroy, 2nd
Duke of 27, 33
Henry Fitzroy, 1st
Duke of 33
GRAHAM
Agnes 248, 258
Annabella (Drum-
mond) 258, 940
Anne 161
Barbara (Stewart) 85
Charity 480
Christian 254
Christian (Erskine)
243

Elizabeth   161, 243, 255, 258
Giles/Egidia   250
Gillian Mary Millicent   25
Helen (Douglas)   248, 254, 256, 257, 258, 940
Isabel (Douglas)   161
James, 1st Marquess of Montrose   161
James, 2nd Marquess of Montrose   161
James, of Airth   161
Janet (Lovell)   260
Jean   256, 258
Jean (Drummond)   151, 152, 161, 170
John, 3rd Earl of Montrose   151, 152, 161, 170
John, 4th Earl of Montrose   151, 161
John, of Breckness   85
Katherine   328
Lilias   151, 152, 170
Louise   112
Magdalen (Carnegie)   161
Margaret   154, 249, 789, 828
Margaret (Fleming)   151, 152, 161, 170
Margaret (Ruthven)   151, 161, 170
Margaret, Countess of Menteith   264, 269, 272, 273, 280, 283
Marjory/Elizabeth   260
Mary   85, 89, 732
Mary (Livingston)   161
Mary (Stewart) (Douglas) (Kennedy) (Cunningham), Princess of Scotland   239, 240, 241, 243, 245, 248, 250, 251, 252, 253, 254, 255, 257, 258, 260, 261, 266, 267, 268, 940
Matilda (___)   260
Nicole   940
Patrick Graham, 1st Baron   243
Robert   151, 152, 161, 170
Robert (Sir), of Fintry   260
William (Sir), of Kincardine   240, 260
William, 1st Earl of Montrose   258, 940
William Graham, 2nd Baron   248, 254, 256, 258, 940

GRAHAME
Gloria [Gloria (Hallward) (Clements) (Ray) (Howard) Ray]   xviii, 362
Jean (Jeannie [McDougall] Hallward)   362

GRAILLY (DE)
Archibaud, Vicomte de Castelbon   963
Isabel (de Foix)   963

GRAIS (DE)
Charles le Gouez, Seigneur, Seigneur de Merville   962
Louis-Joseph Legouès, Seigneur   961, 962, 965

GRAMMONT (DE)
Just-Madeleine   638

GRAMONT (DE)
Anna-Quintana-Albertine- Ida (Grimaud), Comtesse d'Orsay   49
Antoine-Alfred-Agénor de Gramont, 10th Duke   49
Antoine-Alfred-Agénor de Gramont, 11th Duke   49
Antoine-Héraclius-Geneviève-Agénor de Gramont, 9th Duke   49

Antoine-Louis-Marie
de Gramont, 8th
Duke 49
Emma Mary
(McKinnon) 49
family 291
Gabriel-Antoine-
Armand, Count 49
Louise-Gabrielle-
Renée-Aglaë (de
Polignac) 49
Marguerite 963
Maria (Ruspoli) 49
Marie (Negroponte)
49
**GRAMONT (DE)
[MORGAN]**
Margaret (Kinnicutt)
49
Nancy (Ryan) 49
Sanche-Armand-
Gabriel [Ted
Morgan] vi, xviii,
liii, clxx, 49
GRANBY
John Manners,
Marquess of 119
GRANCEY (DE)
Eudes VII, Seigneur
944
Jeanne 944
Yolande (de Bar)
944
**GRANDMESNIL
(DE)**
Petronilla 843
GRANDPRÉ
Robert de Joyeuse,
Count of 944

GRANDSON (DE)
Adelaide (___) 872
Barthélemy, Seigneur
de la Sarraz and
Belmont 872
Columba 872
Ebles 872
Fulk 872
Jordan, Seigneur de
Belmont 872
Petronelle (___) 872
**GRANGE (DE LA)
DE BART DU
BOU[S]CHET**
François de Pons,
Seigneur 200
GRANGER
Eve 247
GRANT
Alexander 88
Anne Charlotte 66
Barbara 266, 283
Barbara (Baikie) 88
Barbara Woolworth
(Hutton) (Mdivani)
(Haugwitz-
Hardenberg-
Reventlow) xviii,
44, 46, 63
Cary [Archibald
Alec Leach] 44
Elizabeth 163
Elizabeth (Forbes)
261
Elizabeth (Innes) 261
Eupheme 249, 256
family 261, 262, 266
Fynvola Susan
(Maclean) 65

Grizel (Grant) 261
Hannah (Simpson)
921
Helen (Ogilvy) 261
Hugh John Mungo
xvii, lxix, cxliv,
66, 364
James, of Freuchie
97, 261
James Murray 65
Janet 97
Janet (Brodie) 97
Jean 266
Jesse Root 921
John, of Ballindalloch
261, 262
John, of Freuchie
261, 266
Julia Boggs (Dent)
xlii, 722, 921
Lillias (Murray) 266
Lodovick, of Freuchie
and Grant 97
Margaret 249, 261,
262
Margaret (Stewart)
261, 266
Martha (Huntington)
921
Mary (Stewart) 97
Nelly 261
Noah 921
Noah (III) 921
Noah, Jr. 921
Patrick, of
Ballindalloch 261
Patrick, of Whytree
261, 262
Rachel (Kelley) 921

Sibella 88
Susanna (Delano) 921
Ulysses Simpson (Gen.), 18th U.S. President xlii, 722, 921
GRANTHAM
Margaret 604
Thomas Robinson, 1st Baron 121
GRANVILLE
John Carteret, 1st Earl, Prime Minister 69, 226
Mary clxxxix
GRASSE (DE)
Angélique (de Rouxel) 616
Annibal, Count du Bar 615
Antoinette-Rosalie (Accaron) 616
Catherine (de Pien) 616
Christine (de Cibon) 616
Claire (d'Alagonia) 615
Claude, Count du Bar 615
family vii
François [de Grasse-Rouville], Seigneur de Valette 616
François-Joseph-Paul de Grasse, Count, Marquis de Tilly xvi, xxvi, lvii, 616

Honoré, Seigneur de Valette 615
Jean-Pierre-Charles, Seigneur de Valette 616
Jeanne (de Brancas) 615
Marguerite (de Flotte-d'Agoult) 615
Marthe (de Foix) 615
Sylvie 616
Véronique (de Villeneuve-Trans) 616
GRASSE DE PAU (DE)
Caroline 616
GRAUN
Antoinette Theodora 618
GRAVEL
Alphonse 972
Marie (Bourassa) 972
Maurice Robert "Mike" (Sen.) 967, 968, 972
Rita Jeannette (Martin) 972
GRAVES
Priscilla 656
GRAY
Adelaide (Lane) 520
Agnes 248
Andrew Gray, 2nd Baron 256
Annabel (Forbes) 256

Barbara (Ruthven) 99
Caroline Maria 115
Elizabeth 661
Elizabeth (Stewart) 256
Emilie Caroline (Pery) 115
Gilbert 256
Giles/Egidia (Mercer) 256
Helen Lane Campbell 520
Henry 115
Isabel 256
Jean 98
John S. 520
Katherine (Myles) 375, 701
Marion (Ogilvy) 99, 256
Mary (Stewart) 98
Parnell 701
Patrick 256
Patrick Gray, 4th Baron 99, 256
Patrick Gray, 5th Baron 99
Patrick Gray, 6th Baron 98, 99
Thomas 701
___ 105
GRAYSON
Susannah Monroe 173
GREAT BRITAIN
Adelaide, Princess of Saxe-Meiningen, Queen of 9

1263

Albert, Prince of
Saxe-Coburg-Gotha,
Prince Consort of
2, 45, 290
Alfred, Prince of,
Duke of Edinburgh
2
Alice (Montagu-
Douglas-Scott),
Princess of, Duchess
of Gloucester 25,
28
Anna, Princess of
(wife of William IV
of Orange,
Stadholder of The
Netherlands) 8
Anne, Queen of
71, 122, 615, 678,
679, 781
Anne Elizabeth
Alice Louise,
Princess of, The
Princess Royal
321
Augusta, Princess of
12
Beatrice of York,
Princess of 25
Caroline, Princess of
Brandenburg-Ansp
ach, Queen of 8,
12, 27
Catherine Elizabeth
(Middleton),
Princess of,
Duchess of
Cambridge 101,
380, 381, 931, 932

Charles Philip Arthur
George, Prince of,
Prince of Wales
lxiii, 209, 380, 655,
832, 930, 932
Charlotte (Sophie
Charlotte), Princess
of Mecklenburg-
Strelitz, Queen of
40
Charlotte, Princess
Royal of, Queen of
Württemberg 12
Charlotte Elizabeth
Diana of
Cambridge, Princess
of xlii, 25, 380,
931, 932
Diana Frances
(Spencer), Princess
of, Princess of
Wales 25, 32,
101, 306, 377, 380,
416, 417, 432, 482,
492, 543, 552, 576,
755, 858, 859, 930,
932
Edward, Prince of,
Duke of Kent 45
Edward VII, King of
9, 137, 655
Elizabeth II, Queen
of xl, 3, 41, 321,
323, 930
Elizabeth Angela
Marguerite
(Bowes-Lyon),
Queen of [HM
Queen Elizabeth

The Queen Mother]
xl, xlii, liv, 101, 121,
419, 545, 930
Eugenie of York,
Princess of 25
Frederick Louis,
Prince of, Prince of
Wales 12, 27
George I, Elector of
Hanover, King of
xxi, lxx, 58, 432
George II, King of
8, 12, 27, 28
George III, King of
10, 40, 299, 615
George IV [George
Augustus Frederick],
King of 123
George V, King of
453
George VI, King of
930
George Alexander
Louis of Cambridge,
Prince of xlii, 25,
380, 931, 932
Henry (Harry)
Charles Albert
David of Wales,
Prince of xlii, 25,
344, 858, 931, 932
Louise Caroline
Alberta, Princess
of 75
Marie of Edinburgh,
Princess of, Queen
of Roumania 2
monarchs of 45,
615

Philip, Prince of
  Greece and
  Denmark, Prince
  of, Duke of
  Edinburgh 3, 41,
  930
Richard, Prince of,
  2nd Duke of
  Gloucester 25
royal family of 929
Sophie Charlotte,
  Princess of
  Hanover and,
  Queen of Prussia
  58, 432
Sophie Dorothea,
  Princess of, Queen
  of Prussia 16
Sophie Helen
  (Rhys-Jones),
  Princess of,
  Countess of
  Wessex 465
Victoria, Queen of
  xl, liv, 2, 10, 41,
  45, 75, 182, 196,
  237, 290
William IV, King of
  9
William Arthur
  Philip Louis of
  Wales, Prince of,
  Duke of
  Cambridge xlii,
  25, 380, 858, 931,
  932
William Henry,
  Prince of, Duke of
  Gloucester 27

GREECE
George I, King of 3
monarchs of 45,
  453, 615
Olga, Grand Duchess
  of Russia, Queen of
  3
GREECE and
DENMARK
Alexandra, Princess
  of 3
Andrew, Prince of
  3, 4, 41
Christopher, Prince
  of 3, 4
Marie, Princess of 4
Michael, Prince of 3
Nicholas, Prince of
  3, 4
Olga, Princess of 3
Philip, Prince of,
  Prince of Great
  Britain, Duke of
  Edinburgh 3, 41,
  930
GREEKE
Margaret 515
GREEN
Elizabeth 760
GREENE
Abby 548
Agnes 713
Anne 512, 513,
  731, 749
Anne (Almy) 763,
  925
Anne (Cox) 721
Azubah (Ward)
  479

Carleton 549
Cecily (Walrond)
  743, 745
Charles Henry 549
David L. (Prof.)
  viii, lii, lvi, lviii,
  lxi, lxii, lxvi, lxix,
  lxxi, 883
Edward 548, 549
Eleanor 684
Elizabeth 332, 478
Elizabeth (Taylor)
  479
Emily (Smythies)
  548, 549
Emily Smythies
  548
Emma 334
family 721
Frances (Darrell)
  721
Graham [Henry
  Graham] 549
Jane xi, xlix, lxv,
  cxlvi, clxi, 337,
  647, 743, 745, 851,
  924
Jane Whytt
  Elizabeth Ann
  (Wilson) 549
John 479, 549, 743
John, Jr. 763, 925
Lucretia 480
Margaret (Webb?)
  721
Margaretta
  (Smythies) 549
Marina (Bellers)
  512

1265

Marion Raymond
  (Greene) 549
Mary 826
Mary (Talbot) 512
Nathaniel, Jr. 479
Philip(pa) 763, 925
Philippa (Ferrers)
  478
Robert 721
Thomas (Gov.)
  xix, cxliv, clxxvi,
  721, 779
Thomas (Sir)
  lxviii, 478, 512,
  721
Vivien Muriel
  (Dayrell-
  Browning) 549
Winifred (Seyborne)
  (Harvey) 721
GREENGLASS
Marian [Mary-Ann]
  717
GREENHOW
Elizabeth
  (Martineau) 379
Frances Elizabeth
  [Frances Lupton]
  379
Thomas Michael
  379
GREENSTREET
Margaret 518
GREENWOOD
Clara Louise 72
GRÉGOIRE
Sophie 969
GREGOR
Elmer Russell 146

Ida M. (Frame) 146
GREGOR [later McGREGOR]
Charles Russell
  146
Hester Ann
  (Gregory) 146
GREGORY
Alice (___) 816
Dorothy (Beeston)
  816
Dorothy (Parr) 815
Elizabeth 123, 847
Elizabeth (Geers)
  123
Henry li, liv, cxlix,
  cli, clxiii, clxxx,
  clxxxviii, 816
Hester Ann 146
Hugh 816
John 816
Mary (___) 816
William 123, 815
William (or
  Thomas) 816
GRELLE (DE)
Hawise (de Burgh)
  780
Joan 780
Robert (Sir) 780
GRENIER
Augusta (Madeleine-
  Augusta) 635
GRENVILLE
Catherine 77
Elizabeth (Gorges)
  835
Elizabeth
  (Wyndham) 77

family lv
George (Hon.) 77
Hester 77
Isabella (Gilbert)
  835
Jane 835, 836
Juliane 642
Margaret
  (Whitleigh) 835
Philippa 836
Roger (Sir) 835,
  836
Thomas 835
Thomas (Sir) 835
GRESHAM
Elizabeth 417
GRESLEY
Anne (Stanley)
  697, 721
Cecilia (Leeson)
  320
Charles 320
Elizabeth 697
Elizabeth (Clarell)
  721
family 722
Francis 320
Henry 320
Joan (___) 320
Joan (More) 320
John 320
John (Sir) 697, 721
Katherine 721
Katherine
  (Walsingham) 320
Margaret 716
Mary 320
Mary (Allye) 320
Thomas (Sir) 320

Thomasine 721
GREVILE/
GREVILLE
 Blanche (Whitney) 331
 Doddington 135
 Dorothy 331, 901
 Edward (Sir) 339
 Elizabeth (Grey) 339
 Elizabeth (Willoughby) 331, 339
 family clxxxiii
 Frances 302
 Fulke 331
 Fulke (Sir) 331, 339
 Katherine 331
 Margaret 295, 339, 532
 Mary (Copley) 331
 Robert 331
GREWCOCK
 Derek 380
 Jeanne Maud (Martineau) cliii, 380
GREY. *see also* VAUGHAN or GREY
GREY (DE)
 Agnes 750
 Alice 425
 Alice (Neville) 425
 Amabel (Benn) 901
 Anne 323, 339, 351, 414, 749
 Anne (Fielding) 678, 749
 Anne (Grey) 351

Anthony (Hon.) 901
Anthony, 9th Earl of Kent 901
Antigone (Plantagenet) 229, 231, 233, 235, 377, 411
Avice (Marmion) 372, 667, 670, 678, 917
Beatrice (___) 749
Bennett (Launcelyn) 749
Catherine 352
Catherine (Herbert) 351, 352, 414, 901
Catherine (Percy) 351, 414, 901
Cecily 370
Cecily (Bonville), Baroness Harington and Bonville 339, 370
Charles Grey, 2nd Earl 72
Constance (Holand) 352
Dorothy 340
Edmund, 1st Earl of Kent 351, 352, 414, 901
Edward (Sir) 749, 750
Eleanor (le Strange) 705, 749
Eleanor (Lowe) 749
Elizabeth 132, 229, 231, 233, 235, 339, 340, 378, 414, 477, 901

Elizabeth (___) 366, 749
Elizabeth (Hastings) 785, 786
Elizabeth (Isaac) 749
Elizabeth (Woodville), later Queen of England 100, 103, 105, 106, 134, 208, 323, 333, 339, 346, 347, 370, 397, 412, 431, 433, 514, 902
Elizabeth, Baroness Lisle 103
family 1025
family, of Codnor xli
family, of Powis xli
family, of Rotherfield xli
family, of Wilton xli
George 901
George, 2nd Earl of Kent 351, 414, 901
Henry, 1st Duke of Suffolk 69, 76, 80
Henry, 2nd Earl of Tankerville 229, 231, 233, 235, 377, 411
Henry, 10th Earl of Kent 901
Humphrey 678, 749
Ida 705, 716
Jane, Queen of England [Lady Jane Grey] xxiv, 69, 80, 477
Joan 373

1267

Joan (Astley) 749
Joan/Genet
  (Mowbray) xxv,
  425, 519, 599
John 749
John (Sir) 323,
  339, 352, 370
John, 1st Baron Grey
  of Rotherfield 372,
  667, 670, 678, 917
John, 8th Baron
  Grey of Wilton
  351
John, Lord 339
Joyce (Hoord) 749
Katherine 69, 76, 80
Magdalen (Purefoy)
  901
Margaret 121, 742
Margaret (Touchet or
  Audley) (Vaughan)
  377, 411
Margaret (Wotton)
  339
Margery 678
Margery (de
  Greystock) 366
Margery (Salvain)
  901
Mary 134, 366,
  750, 785, 786
Mary (Browne)
  339
Maud 372, 519,
  599, 670, 678
Ralph (Sir) 366
Reginald, 2nd Baron
  Grey of Ruthyn
  705, 749

Reginald, 3rd Baron
  Grey of Ruthyn
  749, 785
Reginald/Reynold
  749
Richard, Baron Grey
  of Powis 377,
  378, 411, 412
Robert 749
Roger, 1st Baron
  Grey of Ruthyn
  785, 786
Tacy 351
Thomas 749
Thomas (Sir) xxv,
  366, 425, 519, 599
Thomas, 1st
  Marquess of
  Dorset 339, 340,
  370
Thomas, 2nd
  Marquess of
  Dorset 339
Victoria 72
___ (Holland) 901
GREY [MARMION]
  Lora (St. Quintin)
  667, 917
  Robert (Sir) 667,
  917
GREY of POWIS. *see*
  GREY (DE)
GREY of
  ROTHERFIELD.
  see GREY (DE)
GREY of RUTHYN.
  see GREY (DE)
GREY of WILTON.
  see GREY (DE)

GREY or
  VAUGHAN
  Elizabeth 377, 411
GREYSIER (DE)
  François 872
  Marguerite 872
  Nicolette (d'Allinges)
  872
GREYSTOCK/
  GREYSTOKE (DE)
  Alice 864
  Elizabeth 407, 414
  Elizabeth (Ferrers)
  366, 395, 429
  Elizabeth (FitzHugh)
  366, 369, 407
  Elizabeth (Grey)
  132, 414
  Joan 395, 429
  John de Greystock,
  4th Baron 366,
  395, 429
  Margery 366
  Maud 462, 470,
  473, 486, 539, 545,
  579, 580, 604
  Ralph de Greystock,
  5th Baron 366,
  369, 407
  Robert (Sir) 132, 414
GRICE
  Margaret 702
GRIDLEY
  Elizabeth Ely 630,
  887
GRIETHUYSEN
  Adolf Werner I van
  Pallandt, Heer von
  Bovenholt and 445

GRIFFIN
Anna (Chamberlain) 780
Catherine 749, 780
Catherine (Curzon) 754, 780
Christian (Stuart), Lady li, 155
Cyrus 155
Elizabeth (le Latimer) 780
family lv
Isabel 754
Margaret (Pilkington) 780
Mary 427
Mary (___) 882
Nicholas 754, 780
Richard 780
Thomas (Sir) 780
GRIFFITH
ab Evan 651
Anne 809
Catherine 396, 652, 693
Dorothy 375, 411, 412
Edward 382, 651, 900
Eleanor 382, 900
Elizabeth 412
Hugh 652
Huldah 925, 927
Jane (Puleston) 382, 510, 563, 900
Jane (Stradling) 375, 382, 396, 510, 563, 900

Joan (Troutbeck) 510, 563
Joanna 470
John 657
Margaret (Barker) 411, 412
Mary 563
Mary (___) 652
Richard 411, 412
Robert 652
Sybil 510
William (Sir) 375, 382, 396, 510, 563, 900
GRIGNON
Jean-Baptiste 976
Marie-Archange 976
Marie-Archange (Doré) 976
GRIJPSKERKE en POPPENDAMME (VAN)
Willem Hendrik van Cattenburch, Heer 907
GRILIKHES
Laraine (Johnson) (Hendricks) (Durocher) [Laraine Day] 424
Michel 424
GRILL
Ebba Frederica Regina 453
GRIMALDI
Albert I Honoré-Charles, Sovereign

Prince of Monaco 20, 933
Albert II Alexandre-Louis-Pierre, Sovereign Prince of Monaco xl, 934
Caroline-Louise-Marguerite, Princess of Monaco 934
Charlene Lynette (Wittstock) [Princess Charlene of Monaco] 934
Charlotte-Louise-Juliette, Hereditary Princess of Monaco, Duchess of Valentinois 289, 933
family 291
Gabriella-Thérèse-Marie, Princess of Monaco, Countess of Carladès 934
Ghislaine-Marie-Françoise (Dommanget) [Ghislaine, Princess of Monaco] 933
Grace Patricia (Kelly) [Princess Grace of Monaco] 934
Jacques-Honoré-Rainier, Prince of Monaco, Marquis des Baux 934
Louis II Honoré-Charles-Antoine, Sovereign Prince

1269

of Monaco xl, 20, 933
Mary Victoria (Douglas-Hamilton), Princess of Monaco, Princess Festetics von Tolna 20, 933
Onorato II, Prince of Monaco 190
Rainier III Louis-Henry-Maxence-Bertrand, Sovereign Prince of Monaco xl, 289, 290, 934
Stéphanie-Marie-Élisabeth, Princess of Monaco 934

GRIMAUD
Anna-Quintana-Albertine-Ida, Comtesse d'Orsay 49
Eleanore (von Württemberg), Baroness von Franquement 49
Jean-François-Louis-Marie-Albert-Gaspard, Count d'Orsay 49

GRIMES/GRYMES. *see also* CRYMES

GRIMOD
Françoise-Thérèse 294

GRIMSBY
family 697

GRIMSTON
Catherine 121
Margaret 667

GRIMSTONE
Elizabeth 845

GRINSTEAD
Charlotte 101

GRIP
Marina 663

GRISSIM
Phyllis 985

GRISSOM
Joyce L. 330

GRIZOLS (DE)
Jean-Baptiste de Saignes, Seigneur 440

GROENEWOUDE and HINDERSTEIN (VAN)
Gijsbert Johan van Hardenbroek, Heer 460

GROFF
Elizabeth 769

GROLÉE (DE)
Alix (de Bressieux) 952
Bonne (de Chalant) 911
Catherine (de Tullins) 911
Catherine (de Varey) 911
Guillaume, Seigneur de Neyrieu 952
Guy, Seigneur de Neyrieu 911
Guy, Seigneur de Saint-André-de-Brior 911
Marguerite 911, 952

GRONWY
ap Hywel y Gadair 693

GRONWY LLWYD
ab Y Penwyn 693

GROOT WEEDE
Johan van Weede, Heer van 734

GROS (LE)
Anne 494
Elizabeth 426
Elizabeth (Cornwallis) 426, 494
Frances (Paston) 494
Thomas 494
Thomas (Sir) 426, 494

GROSPARMY (DE)
Anne 946
Jeanne 946

GROSVENOR
Alice 497
Anne (Charlton) 746
Dorothy (Pudsey) 697
Eleanor 750
Elizabeth 746
Elizabeth (Mitton) 750
Gawen 697
Joyce (Fowke) 697
Katherine 518
Margaret (Mainwaring) 746

Nicholas 750
Randall 746
Walter 697
Winifred 697
GROTZ
 Elizabeth 88
GROUT
 John, Jr. 370
 Phoebe 370
 Phoebe (Spofford) 370
GROVE
 Brandon Hambright, Jr. cliv, 7
 family 7
 Maria (Cheremeteff), Countess cliv, 7
GRUBBE
 Anne Elisabeth (Vind) 645
 Christiane Charlotte 645
 Didrik 645, 646
 family 646
 Gjertrud 644
GRUFFUDD
 ab Einion 657, 689
 ab Ifor Bach 807, 808, 810, 811, 812
 ap Cynan ab Iago, King of Gwynedd 815
 ap Cynwrig ap Bleddyn Llwyd 686
 ap Dafydd 689
 ap Hywel 650
 ap Hywel ap Madog 692
 ap Llywelyn ap Cynwrig 657, 692
 ap Madog, Prince of Powys Fadog 815, 822, 823
 ap Nicholas 582
 ap Rhys 658
GRUFFUDD FYCHAN
 ap Gruffudd o'r Rhuddalt 657, 813, 824
GRUFFUDD MAELAWR
 ap Madog 815
GRUFFUDD NANNAU
 ap Hywel 229
GRUFFUDD O'R RHUDDALLT
 ap Madog Fychan ap Madog Crupl 813, 824, 825
GRUNDY
 Alice clxxxvi
GRÜNENBURG (VON)
 Anfelisa 832
GRUNWELL
 June E. 580
GRUSINSKI
 Daria, Princess 793
GRUYÈRES (DE/OF)
 Beatrix 872
 Columba (de Grandson) 872
 Rodolphe, Count of 872
GUBBERTZ
 Anna 216
GUEFFEN
 Diana (Rigg) [Diana Rigg] 23
 Menachem 23
GUELDERS
 Maria of 459
 Maria of Arkel, heiress of 459
 Mary of, Queen of Scotland 148, 154, 157, 167, 168, 174, 179, 210, 213, 214, 215, 216, 218, 219, 459
 Yolande of 851
GUÉMENÉ (DE)
 Charles de Rohan, Seigneur 455
 Louis I de Rohan, Seigneur 455
GUÉRET
 Françoise (de Méhérenc) 946
 Jean 946
 Madeleine (Vigoureux) 946
 René 946
GUÉRET dit DUMONT
 Anne (Tardif) 946
 Jacques 939, 946, 947
GUESCLIN (DE)
 Catherine 455
GUEST
 Amy (Phipps) 63

1271

Caroline-Cécile-
  Alexandrine-Jeanne
  (Murat), Princess
  cliv, 63, 83
Constance Rhiannon
  64
Cornelia Henrietta
  Maria (Spencer-
  Churchill) 63
Elizabeth Sturgis
  (Polk) 63
Ellen Tuck (French)
  (Astor) 63
Frederick Edward
  (Hon.) 63
Helena Woolworth
  (McCann) 63
Ivor Bertie, 1st
  Baron Wimborne
  63, 64
Lucy Douglas
  (Cochrane) 63
Raymond Richard
  63, 83
Winston Frederick
  Churchill 63
GUEVARA
  Aleida (March
  Torres) 997
  Ana Isabel (Lynch
  Ortíz) 991, 997
  Celia (de la Serna
  Llosa) 997
  Cisco 9
  Hilda (Gadea
  Acosta) 997
  María Concepción
  Dolores (Castro
  Peralta) 997

**GUEVARA
CALDERÓN**
  Juan Antonio 997
**GUEVARA
CASTRO**
  Roberto 991, 997
**GUEVARA DE LA
SERNA**
  Ernesto "Che" xxii,
  lv, lxiii, 991, 995,
  997
GUEVARA LYNCH
  Ernesto Rafael
  991, 997
GUGAJEW
  Nina 195
GUGGENHEIM
  Marguerite "Peggy"
  15
GUIBERT
  Elizabeth (Gerard)
  (Blakiston) (Rymer)
  317
  Joshua 317
GUIDO
  Michael Anne
  xlvii, lvi, lxiv,
  lxviii, 470, 708
GUIDOBALDO II
  (della Rovere),
  Duke of Urbino
  186, 189
GUIL(D)FORD
  Anne 473, 474,
  475
  Anne (Pympe)
  469, 477
  Barbara (West)
  473, 475

Dorothy 320, 475
Edward (Sir) 469,
  477, 492
Eleanor (West)
  469, 477, 492
Elizabeth 469, 474,
  475
Elizabeth (Mortimer)
  426, 469, 473, 477,
  492, 552
Frideswide 469,
  477, 492, 552
George 426, 469,
  473, 477, 492, 552
Jane 477
John (Sir) 473
Mary 426, 552
Richard 477
Richard (Sir) 469,
  477
GUILFORD
  Joan S. clxxxiii
GUILGUD
  Eleanor
  (Tyszkiewicz),
  Countess 802
  Michael 802
GUILLENS (DE)
  Eléonore 638
GUILLERMO
  Bernardo Frederico
  cliv, 1
  Eva (Prinz-Valdes)
  1
  Jorge Pérez 1
  Maria Cristina (of
  The Netherlands) 1
GUILLET (DE)
  Françoise 638

GUÎNES (DE) (OF)
George de La
  Trémouille, Seigneur
  de La Trémouille,
  Count 634, 953
Jean III, Seigneur,
  Count of Dam-
  martin and 205
GUINNESS
Adelaide Maria
  (Guinness) 23, 31
Anne (Lee) 481
Arthur 481
Arthur Ernest (Hon.)
  31
Benjamin Lee 308
Benjamin Lee (Sir),
  1st Bt. 31, 308, 481
Benjamin Seymour
  clv, 124, 481
Bridget Henrietta
  Frances (Williams-
  Bulkeley) clv,
  124, 481
Bryan Walter, 2nd
  Baron Moyne 23
Daphne Suzannah
Diana Joan (Hon.)
  clv, 23
Diana (Freeman-
  Mitford) (Hon.)
  [Diana Mitford]
  23
Edward Cecil, 1st Earl
  of Iveagh 23, 31
Elizabeth (Guinness)
  31, 308, 481
Elizabeth Jane
  (Darley) 481
Evelyn Hilda Stuart
  (Erskine) 23
family xviii
Henrietta Eliza (St.
  Lawrence) 308
Jane (Nevin)
  (Dickson) 308
Jonathan Bryan, 3rd
  Baron Moyne 23
Josephine
  (Strangman) 308
Kenelm Edward Lee
  "Bill" 308
Kenelm Ernest Lee
  "Tim" (Sir), 4th
  Bt. clv, 308
Marie Clotilde
  (Russell) 31
Maureen Constance
  31
Richard Seymour
  481
Susanna 481
Suzanne (Lisney) 23
Tanis Eva Bulkeley
  124, 481
Walter Edward, 1st
  Baron Moyne 23
GUISE
Elizabeth 351
Joan (Pauncefort)
  351
John 351
Mary (Rotsy) 351
Mary of, Queen of
  Scotland 82, 85,
  87, 88, 90, 92, 93,
  95, 96, 97, 98, 897
Tacy (Grey) 351
William 351
GUISE (ORLÉANS-FRANCE)
Françoise-Isabelle
  of 3
GUN
William Townsend
  Jackson (W.T.J.)
  xxix, lvi
GUNBY
Joan 471
GUNTER
Gwenllian (ferch
  Rhys Llwyd) 811
Jenkin 811
Margred 811
GUNTHORPE
Anne 302
GUNTON
Alice 571
GURDON
Brampton 353, 661
Elizabeth 661
family lxii
Muriel xlvi, lxii, lxxi,
  clxi, 291, 353, 374
Muriel (Sedley)
  353, 661
GURNEY
family xxxvii
GURREA (DE)
Ana 140
GUSTAV I (VASA)
King of Sweden 40,
  43, 51, 52, 53, 198,
  208, 267, 453, 889,
  890, 893
GUSTAV VI ADOLF
King of Sweden 41

GUSTAV ADOLF
Duke of Mecklen-
burg-Güstrow 47
GUTHRIE
Bethia 278
Clara 67
GUTTORMSDATTER
Helene 644
GUY
Margaret 541
GUYON
Marguerite 990
GUZMÁN (DE)
Ana (de Silva y
Mendoza) 140
Catalina 995
Eleanor (de Zuñiga
y Sotomayor) 140
family 991
Gaspar Philip, Count-
Duke of Olivares
191
Isabel 140
Juan Carlos, Count
of Niebla 140
Juana (de Sándoval
y Rojas) 140
Leonor (de Zuñiga y
Guzmán) 191
Luisa Francisca,
Queen of Portugal
140, 142
Teresa 191
Violante (Ponce de
León) 995
**GUZMÁN Y
ARAGÓN (DE)**
Ana 140

**GUZMÁN Y
RIBERA (DE)**
Juan Alonso, 3rd
Duke of Medina
Sidonia 191
**GUZMÁN Y
RIQUELME (DE)**
Ruy Díaz 995
**GUZMÁN Y SILVA
(DE)**
Juan Manuel
Domingo, 8th
Duke of Medina-
Sidonia 140
**GUZMÁN Y SOTO-
MAYOR (DE)**
Alfonso Pérez (Adm.),
7th Duke of Medina-
Sidonia 140, 142
**GVÖRY VON
RADVÁNY**
Maria, Countess 35
GWEN
ferch Gruffudd 693
ferch Gruffudd Goch
ab Ieuan 686
ferch Ieuan Dew ap
Meurig 650
GWENHWYFAR
ferch Gronwy ab
Ieuan 657, 659,
689, 694
ferch Richard Llwyd
657
ferch Robin 689
ferch Thomas 808
GWENLLIAN
ferch Einion ap
Ieuan Llwyd 650

ferch Gwilym 811
ferch Gwilym ap
Hywel Grach 808
ferch Llywelyn ap
Morus 810
ferch Maredudd
810
ferch Rhys Llwyd
811
ferch William ap
Gruffudd 659
GWENT
Ithel, King of 815
GWERFUL
ferch Ieuan ab
Einion 693
ferch Llywelyn ap
Dafydd 650
GWILYM
ap Rhys Llwyd 811
GWINNETT
Anne (Bourne) 648
Anne (Emes) 648
Button 648, 649
Elizabeth (Coxe)
648
Elizabeth (Laurence)
648
Elizabeth (Randle)
648
George 648
Samuel 648
GWYLADYS
ferch Dafydd 808,
810
GWYLADYS DDU
of Wales 680
GWYN
Hugh 510

1274

Jane (Owen) 510
Margaret 773
Sybil 510
GWYNEDD
  Gruffudd ap Cynan
    ab Iago, King of
    815
GWYNN
  Eleanor "Nell" 33
GWYNNE
  Alice Claypoole
    35, 209
GYE
  Grace (Dowrish)
    632
  John 632
  Mary xix, xxxv,
    lviii, clxi, clxxv,
    clxxxii, 632
  Mary (Prowse) 632
  Robert 632
GYLDENSTEEN
  Margareta
    Huguetan,
    Countess of 140
GYLDENSTIERNE
  Knud 644
  Margrethe 644
  Peder 644
  Regitze (Bille) 644
  Sidsel (Ulfstand)
    644
GYLLENHAAL
  Anders Leonard
    lxiv, lxv, cxliv,
    662, 663
  Anna (Hård af
    Torestorp) 662
  Charles Edward 664

Christina Lovisa
  (Westling) 662
family 663
Frederik Leonard
  662
Hugh Anders 662
Jacob Benjamin
  "Jake" 663
Leonard 662
Leonard Efraim
  662, 664
Maggie Ruth 663
Naomi Foner (Achs)
  663
Selma Amanda
  (Nelson) 662
Stephen Roark
  662, 663
Virginia Lowrie
  (Childs) 662
Virginia Philo
  (Pendleton) 662,
  664
GYLLENHIELM
  Sophia 267, 453
GYLLENSTIERNA
  Anna (Ribbing)
    663
  Anna (Vistorp) 663
  Axel, Baron 889
  Brita 662, 663
  Carin (Bielke) 663
  Carl 663
  Christina (Bonde)
    663
  Erik 663
  family 664
  Hedvig (Snoilsky),
    Baroness 889

Hedvig Christina,
  Baroness 889
Karin 452
Margaretha Louisa
  Charlotta (Duwall),
  Baroness 889
Marina (Grip) 663
Nils, Baron 889
GYLLENSVÄRD
  Anna Maria 51
HAAG
  Leonard II von
    Frauenberg, Count
    of 237
HAAKON V
  King of Norway
    452, 457
HAAKONSDOTTER
  Agnes, of Norway
    452, 457, 458
**HABINGTON/
ABINGTON**
  Joyce (Shirley)
    653
  Mary 653
  Richard 653
HABSBURG (VON)
  family xiv, 327,
    329, 349, 353, 438,
    445, 717
  Maria Immaculata
    Pia, Countess
    cxliii, 6
**HABSBURG-
LOTHRINGEN
(VON)**
  family 2
  Mary Jerrine
    (Soper) 2

Stefan [Stefan, Archduke of Austria, Prince of Tuscany] 2
HACKBURNE
　Katherine (Deighton) xxiv, clx, clxxii, 297, 370, 373, 924
　Samuel 297
HACKET
　Elizabeth 266
HACKSHAW
　Mary 324
HADLEY
　Arthur Twining, II 90
　Leila Eliott (Burton) 90
HADNALL
　Mary 301, 501, 502
HAEFTEN (VAN)
　Adelise (van Herwijnen) 447, 907
　Beatrix 907
　Elisabeth 447
　Hendrika (van Varick) 447, 448, 907
　Otto, Herr 447, 907
　Walraven, Heer 447, 448, 907
HAEN
　Judith (Manby?) 846
HAER
　ferch Cynillon ab Y Blaidd Rhûdd 815

HAERSOLTE (VAN)
　Anna Elisabeth 445
HAES (DE)
　Margaret 447
HAGEN
　Marion 850
HAGGERSTON
　Anne (Constable) 123
　Carnaby (Sir), 3rd Bt. 123
　Carnaby (Sir), 5th Bt. 123
　Elizabeth 599
　Elizabeth (Middleton) 123
　Frances (Smythe) 123
　Mary 123
　Mary (Silvertop) 123
　Thomas (Sir), 4th Bt. 123
　William 123
HAHN
　Helena Petrovna [Mme. Blavatsky] xvii, xxvi, clxxvii, 792, 795
HAHN VON ROTHERHAHN
　Elena (Fadeev) ["Zinaïde R___sky"] 792
　Peter 792
HAIG
　Andrew, of Bemersyde 285

　Barbara (Spotswood) 285
　Christina (Jameson) 285
　Elizabeth (McDougall) 285
　Elspeth (Abercromby) 285
　family 285
　George, of Newbigging 285
　Gertrude Marguerite (Hoppin) 285
　Hattie (Leamon) 285
　Isabel (Home) 285
　Isabel (Ramsey) 285
　James 285
　James, of Alloa 285
　James, of Bemersyde 285
　Janet (Anderson) 285
　John, of Bonnington 285
　John, of Orchard Farm 285
　John, of the Garthlands 285
　Margaret (Kerr) 285
　Margaret (Stein) 285
　Marie (de St. Paule) 285
　Mary (Mackenzie) 285
　Mary Caroline (Murray) 285
　Robert clv, 285
　Robert, of Bemersyde 285

Robert, of St. Ninians 285
Robert Murray 285
William, of Bemersyde 285
HAINAULT
Baldwin I, Count of, VI of Flanders 851
Baldwin II, Count of 851
Baldwin III, Count of 851
Beatrix of 866, 870, 872
counts of 725
Ida of 851
Joanna of 459
John I, Count of 774, 775, 776
John II, Count of 459
Laurette of 959
Marie of 634, 638
Philippa of, Queen of England 107, 114, 119, 126, 133, 134, 295, 300, 305, 310, 314, 317, 319, 324, 327, 331, 333, 337, 339, 342, 345, 347, 349, 351, 353, 355, 357, 359, 361, 363, 366, 368, 370, 374, 375, 377, 379, 382, 384, 385, 387, 389, 392, 393, 395, 396, 397, 398, 399, 400, 401, 403, 405, 407, 409, 410, 411, 413, 414, 417, 418, 419, 420, 421, 423, 425, 426, 427, 428, 429, 431, 433, 434, 436, 459, 774, 775, 776, 900, 901, 902, 904, 905
Rainier IV, Count of 866, 870, 872
William III, Count of Holland and 459
Yolande of, Empress of Constantinople 965
HAINES
Allen 769
Jonathan 769
Mary Jane (Sprague) 769
Sarah 769
Sarah (Ballinger) 769
HAK
Helle 644
HALCRO
Barbara (Stewart) 88
Esther (Thomson) 88
Henry 88
Hugh 88
Jean (Stewart) 88
Margaret 275
Sibella 88
HALDANE
Christian (Graham) 254
Elizabeth (Lundin) 254
Euphemia (Shaw) 254
James (Sir), of Gleneagles 254
James, of Myreton 254
Janet (Higgins) 254
Jean 254
John (Sir), of Gleneagles 254
John, of Gleneagles 254
John, of Myreton 254
Joseph, of Myreton 254
Margaret (Erskine) 254
Marjorie (Lawson) 254
HALE
Abigail 656
Abigail (Gleason) 656
John 656
Priscilla (Markham) 656
Thomas, Jr. 656
HALES (DE)
Alice lxix, 462, 470, 473, 486, 493, 519, 522, 526, 534, 539, 541, 545, 557, 579, 580, 598, 599, 604, 605, 609
Frances 22
Margery 821
HALFIN
Diane, Princess zu Fürstenberg [Diane von Fürstenberg] xlv, 20

1277

**HALFORD/
HOLFORD**
  Elizabeth (Mallory)
    668
  Grisel 377
  Richard 668
  Thomas 668
**HALIBURTON/
HALLIBURTON**
  Elizabeth 275
  family 275
  George, Lord
    Provost of
    Edinburgh 275
  Jean 275
  Jean (Clark) 275
  Margaret 275
  Patrick, of Muir-
    houselaw 275
  ___ (Erskine) 275
HALICZ
  Kunigunde of,
    Queen of Bohemia
    621
  Maria of 791, 797,
    802
HALIFAX
  George Montagu,
    1st Earl of 105
HALL
  Alice 311, 613
  Anne 311
  Anne (Willoughby)
    311
  Anne (Winter) 110
  Benedict 110
  Benedicta Maria
    Theresa 110
  Clarissa 584, 648

  Edward 311
  Elizabeth 311, 354,
    532, 768
  Elizabeth
    (Wingfield) 311,
    354, 470, 613
  Frances (Fortescue)
    110
  Francis 311, 354,
    470, 613
  Henry 311
  Henry Benedict
    110
  Jane 409, 470
  Jane (___) 110
  Jane (Neale) 311
  Margaret 100, 379
  Margaret (Elmes)
    311
  Mary 110
  Rachel 311
  Rachel (FitzWilliam)
    (Huddleston) 394
  Rich 984
  Ursula (Sherington)
    354, 470
  ___ 394, 875
HALLADAY
  Amy (Moses) 867
  Anna Maria 867
  Calvin 867
  Esther (Fisher) 867
  James 867
  James, Jr. 867
  Rachel (Halladay)
    867
  Rebecca (Copley)
    867
  Thompson 867

  William 867
HALLEY
  Martha Eleanor
    (Jacob) 695, 696
  Martha Ellen 695
  Nathaniel Thomas
    695
HALLOT (DE)
  Jacqueline 948
  Jacqueline (de
    Prunelé) 948
  Michel 948
HALLWARD
  Adelaide Caroline
    (Bloxam) 362
  Charles Berners
    362
  Elizabeth Anne
    (Morgan) 362
  Emily Jane (Leslie)
    362
  Gloria [Gloria
    Grahame] xviii,
    362
  Jeannie (McDougall)
    [Jean Grahame]
    362
  John 362
  Mary (Lambarde)
    362
  Reginald Francis 362
  Reginald Michael
    Bloxam xviii, lix,
    362
HALLWIN (DE)
  Marie-Josephine-
    Barbara 292
HALSALL
  Anne 904

Cuthbert (Sir) 904
Dorothy (Stanley) 904
Maud 433
HALSEY
Elizabeth 643
HALSNODE
John 883
Margaret xlv, lvi, 883, 884
Margaret (Ladd) 883
Martha (Harfleet) 883
HALSTEAD
Jennet 700
HALTON
Frances 471
HALYS
Joan 845
HAMBY
Catherine xxxv, lxx, clxi, clxxvi, 478, 715
Edward 715
Elizabeth (Arnold) 715
Elizabeth (Booth) 715
Margaret (Blewett) 715
Robert 715
William 715
HAMDEN
Barbara 526
HAMELAND (VAN)
____ 776
HAMELIN dit LACAVE
Marie-Renée 969

HAMERTON
Agnes 398
Grace 697
Matilda 700
HAMILTON
Albertha Frances
Anne 26, 28
Alexander (Dr.) lvi, 270
Alexander (Hon.) lvi, clxiv, 214
Alexander, of Grange 214
Alexander Hamilton, 10th Duke of, 7th Duke of Brandon 933
Anne 150, 154, 156
Archibald 376
Archibald Hamilton, 9th Duke of, 6th Duke of Brandon 933
Barbara 177
Beatrice Frances 28
Beatrix (Campbell) 179
Beatrix (Hamilton) 269
Catherine 31, 66, 168
Christian 165, 174
Claud (Sir), of Shawfield 179
Claud, 1st Baron Paisley 156, 167, 179
Claud, of Beltrim 179

Claud, of Montalony and Fahy 179
Claud, of Strabane 179
David, of Broomhill 269
Elizabeth 148, 215, 218
Elizabeth (Brooke) 167
Elizabeth (Cochrane) 270
Elizabeth (Cole-pepper) 157
Elizabeth (Home) 210
Elizabeth (Pollok) 214
Elizabeth (Reading) 157
Elizabeth (Schuyler) 214
family lvi
Frederick (Sir) 167
Gavin, of Airdrie 269
George lvi
George (Sir), 1st Bt. 157
Georgiana Susan 28
Gustavus, 1st Baron Boyne 167
Harriet (Stewart) 933
Harriet Georgiana Louisa 28
Isabel 173, 269
Isabella (____) 179

1279

Isabella (Wingfield) 179
James 157, 214
James, 1st Duke of Abercorn 25, 28
James, 1st Earl of Abercorn 157
James, 1st Earl of Arran 154, 157, 167, 168, 179, 210, 213, 214, 216, 218
James, 2nd Earl of Arran, Duke of Châtellerault 154, 157, 167, 168, 177, 179
James, 6th Earl of Abercorn 157
James, of Torrence 269
James Hamilton, 1st Baron 148, 154, 157, 167, 168, 179, 210, 213, 215, 216, 218
Jane (Montgomery) 269
Janet (Beaton) 154, 157, 167, 168, 179, 210, 213, 214, 216, 218
Janet (Hamilton) 269
Janet (Hamilton), of Leckprevick 179
Janet (Home) 210
Jean 213, 214, 216, 218
Jean (Campbell) 168

John (Sir), of Lettrick 168
John (Sir), of Samuelston 210
John, 1st Baron Bargeny 156
John, of Airdrie 269
John, of Grange 214
John Hamilton, 1st Marquess of 168
Joshua 167
Katherine 215
Katherine (Hamilton) 269
Katherine Elizabeth 28
Letitia 179
Letitia (Hamilton) 179
Louisa 270
Louisa Jane 28
Louisa Jane (Russell) 25, 28
Margaret 73, 90, 96, 156, 210
Margaret (Douglas) 154, 157, 167, 168, 177, 179
Margaret (Dulany) 270
Margaret (Lyon) 168
Margaret (Semphill) 269
Margaret (Seton) 156, 157, 167, 179
Maria 933

Marion (Boyd) 157
Mary 157
Mary (___) 179
Mary (Butler) 157
Mary (Cox) 167
Mary (Erskine) 215
Mary (Robertson) 270
Mary (Stewart), Princess of Scotland 148, 154, 157, 167, 168, 179, 210, 213, 214, 215, 216, 218
Maud Evelyn 25, 26, 28
Patience (Stobo) 176
Rebecca (Cunyngham) 214
Robert (Sir), 3rd Bt., of Airdrie 270
Robert, of Torrence 269
Sarah 376
Sarah (Wynne) 376
Sidney (Vaughan) 167
Susan Euphemia (Beckford) 933
William (Rev. Dr., Prof.) 270
William (Sir), of Manor Elieston 179
William, of Beltrim 179
William, of Wishaw 215
William Alexander Anthony Archibald Hamilton, 11th

Duke of, 8th Duke
of Brandon 933
HAMILTON-COX
Henry cxliii, 167
Letitia Eleanor
(Hutcheson) 167
HAMILTON-HILL
Deirdre 246, 247
**HAMILTON-
TEMPLE-
BLACKWOOD**
Basil Sheridan, 4th
Marquess of
Dufferin and Ava
31, 32
Caroline Maureen,
Lady [Caroline
Blackwood] xviii,
31
Maureen Constance
(Guinness) 31
HAMLEY
Margaret 672
HAMMARSKJÖLD
Agnes Maria Caroline
(Almquist) 51
Carl Ake 51
Carl Gustaf 51
Catharina Mariana
(Breitholtz) 51
Charlotta Eleonora
(Rääf i Smaland)
51
Dag Hjalmar Agne
Carl xviii, xxvi, 51
Knut Hjalmar
Leonard 51
Knut Vilhelm 51

Maria Louisa
Cecilia Vilhelmina
(Cöster) 51
HAMMERSLEY
Francis 332
Mary (Brent)
(Brent) 332
HAMMETT
Mary 744
HAMMOND
Ursula Mary 865
HAMPDEN
Anne 466, 467
Anne (Cave) 466,
467, 717
Dorothy 467
Elizabeth
(Cromwell) 466
Elizabeth (Ferrers)
466
Griffith 466, 467,
717
John 300, 466
Lettice (Knollys)
300
William 466
HAMPTON
Mary 103
**HANAU UND ZU
HOROWITZ
(VON)**
Augusta Maria
Gertrude, Princess,
Countess von
Schaumburg 13
Gertrude (Falken-
stein), Princess,
Countess von
Schaumburg 13

**HANAU-
LICHTENBERG**
Charlotte Christine
of 40
John Reinhold III,
Count of 40
HANBURY
Barbara 537
HANCHETT
Deliverance
(Barker) 578
Justinian 578
HANCOCK
Richard 884
HAND
Catherina 53, 889
Håken 53, 889
Mary 359
Virginia (Eriksdotter)
889
HANFORD
Margaret 917
HANKEY
Mariora Beatrice
Evelyn Rochfort
177
HANKFORD
Anne 392, 551,
588, 596
Jane 835
Thomasine 392,
409, 436
HANMER
Catherine (Mostyn)
235
Catherine (Salter)
235
Dorothy (Trevor)
235

Ermin 235
Jane (Brereton) 235
Jane (Salusbury) 235
John 235
John (Sir), 1st Bt. 235
Margaret 824
Margaret (Kynaston) 235
Peregrine (North) 235
Richard 235
Sarah 504
Susan 235
Susan (Hervey) 235
Thomas (Sir) 235
Thomas (Sir), 2nd Bt. 235
William 235
HANNUNTYTÄR
Catherine 267
HANOT
Élisabeth 950
Élisabeth (Baillon) 950
Paul 950
HANOVER
Ernest Augustus, Elector of 58, 432
Ernest Augustus, King of 40
Ernest Augustus, Prince of 934
Frederica, Princess of Mecklenburg-Strelitz, Queen of 40

George I, Elector of, King of Great Britain lxx, 58, 432
Sophie Charlotte, Princess of, Princess of Great Britain, Queen of Prussia 58, 432
HANSDOTTER
Catherine 453
HANSEN
Charles M. (Col.) viii, xii, xxv, xlv, lii, liv, lv, lvi, lxi, lxii, lxv, lxvii, lxviii, cxc, 374, 616, 714, 769, 771, 884
Hannah 111
James L. lvii
HANSON
Anne 914, 915
Louisa 101
HARALDSEN
Sonia, Queen of Norway xxii
HARBERTON
Arthur Pomeroy, 1st Viscount 157
John Pomeroy, 4th Viscount 157
HARBORD
Anne Elizabeth (Riley-Smith) 135
Dorothy Primrose 135
Edward, 2nd Baron Suffield 135

Edward Ralph 135
Elizabeth Pole (Schenley) 135
Emily Harriet (Shirley) 135
Philip 350
Ralph 135
Susan (Felton) 350, 605
HARBORNE
Anne (Radcliffe) 399
Frances (Eure) 399
John 399
Katherine 399
HARBOTTLE
Agnes 599
Bertram 418, 599
Eleanor 389, 418
Guischard (Sir) 418
Joan (Lumley) 418, 599
Joan (Willoughby) 418
Margaret (___) 418
Margaret (Ogle) 599
Ralph (Sir) 418
Robert (Sir) 599
HARBOU (VON)
Andreas (Maj. Gen.) 645
Andreas Paul Adolph 645
Ane Marie (Praetorius) 645
Anna Elisabeth (Buchner) 645
Birgette (Galt) 645

Christian 645
Christiane Charlotte
  (Grubbe) 645
Clotilde Constance
  (d'Alinge) 645
Else (Thermo) 645
Fredrik Hans Walter
  645
Friderica (Walter)
  645
Fritz xxii, liii,
  cxliv, 645
Judith (Fritcher) 645
Marie Elisabeth
  Wilhelmine
  "Mimi" 645
Matilde (Hensen)
  645
Niels 645
Paul Mathias 645
Thea xxii, clvi, 645
Theodor Carl
  Nicolaus 645
HARBY
Emma 325
Katherine 324
Katherine
  (Throckmorton)
  324, 325
Thomas 324
HARCOURT
Agnes 353, 403
Alice 372
Anne (Norris) 670
Edith (St. Clair)
  372
Ellen (la Zouche)
  373, 778
family 1025

Hilaria (Hastings)
  778
Isabella 319
Jane 678
Jane (Franceys)
  372, 670, 678
Joan (Grey) 373
John 670
John (Sir) 353,
  373, 778, 779
Lettice clxxxiii,
  670, 671
Margaret
  (Barantyne) 353
Margaret (Beke)
  778
Margaret (Byron)
  670
Matilda 778
Maud (Grey) 372,
  670, 678
Richard (Sir) 372,
  778
Robert (Sir) 670,
  671
Thomas (Sir) 372,
  373, 670, 678
William (Sir) 373,
  778
HARCOURT (DE)
Blanche 961
Gérard, Baron de
  Bonnestable 961
Jacques, Baron de
  Beuvron 961
Jean IV, Sire de
  Rieux and de
  Rochefort, Count
  of 226

Jean VI, Count of,
  Count of Aumale
  941
Jeanne 944
Jeanne (de Tilly)
  961
John V, Count of
  944, 961
Marguerite 941
Marie (de Ferrières)
  961
Marie (Malet de
  Graville) 961
Philippe, Seigneur
  de Bonnestable
  961
**HÅRD AF
TORESTORP**
Anna 662
Eleonora Margareta
  (Fleetwood),
  Baroness 662
Ulrik Gustaf 662
HARDEN
Sybil 740
**HARDENBROEK
(VAN)**
Anna Charlotte
  460
Anna Maria (van
  Marlot) 460
Gijsbert Johan, Heer
  van Groenewoude
  and Hinderstein
  460
**HARDENBURG-
REVENTLOW
(VON)**
Lucie, Countess 43

HARDIMAN
　Hannah 256
HARDING
　Alice Muriel (Astor) (Obolensky-Neledinsky-Meletzky) (von Hoffmansthal) 799, 800
　Amos 764
　Catherine 534
　Charles Alexander 764
　Edward Learned 935
　Elizabeth (Madison) 764
　Florence Mabel (Kling) (DeWolfe) 764, 859
　George Tryon 764, 859
　Lucy Booker (Ramsay) 935
　Mary (Learned) 935
　Mary Ann (Crawford) 764
　Mary Virginia Ramsay 935
　Philip John Ryves 800
　Phoebe (Tripp) 764
　Phoebe Elizabeth (Dickerson) 764, 859
　Seth 935
　Warren Gamaliel, 29th U.S. President 764, 859, 860

HARDWICK
　Elizabeth (Leke) 512, 565, 706
　Elizabeth (Pinchbeck) 513
　Elizabeth ["Bess of Hardwick"] 468, 512, 706
　John 512, 565, 706
　Mary 565, 706
HARDY
　Charles (Adm., Sir), the younger cxliv, 346
　Elizabeth (Tate) xlviii, cxliv, 346
　Jane (Conyers) xlii
HARE
　Beryl Nancy (Pearson) 80
　Ernestine Mary (Brudenell-Bruce) 80
　Freda (Johnstone) 80
　Joanna Freda (Hon.) lxv, cxlii, 81
　John Hugh, 1st Viscount Blakenham 80
　Kathleen Mary 70
　Richard Granville, 4th Earl of Listowel 80
　William, 3rd Earl of Listowel 80
HARFLEET
　Henry 883
　Marion (Brockhull) 357, 883

　Martha 883
　Mary (Slaughter) 883
　Thomas 357, 883
HARGROVE
　Ellen Blanch 231
HARINGTON
　Ada (Drew) 321
　Ada Constance Helen 321
　Agnes 700, 703
　Anne 497
　Edward Musgrove 320
　Edward Templer 321
　Elizabeth 517
　Esther (Lens) 320
　Frances 517
　Helena 323
　Helena (Gostlett) 320
　Henry 320
　Henry (Sir) 517
　Isabel (English) 700
　James (Sir) 416, 517
　Jane Ann (Thomas) 320
　John 320
　Lucy (Sidney) 416, 517
　Mabel 416
　Margaret 841, 842
　Margaret (de Neville) 841, 842
　Martha (Musgrove) 320
　Mary (Backwell) 320

Nicholas (Sir) 700
Ruth (Pilkington)
  517
Sarah 79, 107
Susanna Isabella
  320
William (Sir) 841,
  842
**HARINGTON and
BONVILLE**
Cecily Bonville,
  Baroness 339, 370
William Bonville,
  Baron 339, 370
HARKNESS
Mary 306
HARLAKENDEN
Elizabeth (Bosvile)
  291, 301, 339, 807
Emlin (___) 807
Mabel xix, lxix,
  clxiii, clxxvii, 587,
  806, 807
Margaret (Huberd)
  806
Richard 806
Roger 339, 807
HARLESTON
Affra 349
Elizabeth lxiv,
  lxviii, 349
Elizabeth (___) 349
Elizabeth (Willis)
  349
Jane (Wentworth)
  349
John lxiv, lxviii,
  349

HARLYNGRUGGE
Alice (Marmion) 877
Cecilia 877
William 877
HARMAN
Eleanor 697
Elizabeth 325
Sarah 590
HARMANSON
Gertrude (Littleton)
  310
Henry 310
Sophia 310
HARMAR
Anne (South[e]y)
  233, 311
**HARNONCOURT
(D')**
Anne Julie 221,
  896
family xl
**HARNONCOURT
(D')- UNVERZAGT**
Hubert Heinrich,
  Count de la
  Fontaine and 220
Hubert Karl
  Sigismund Joseph
  Franz, Count de la
  Fontaine and 220,
  895
Josepha Juliane
  (Mittrowsky von
  Mitrowicz),
  Countess 220
Ludmilla Gizella
  Theresa (Berchtold),
  Countess 220

René Vladimir
  Hubert Maria, Count
  de la Fontaine and
  [René d'Harnon-
  court] liii, lv, clv,
  220, 896
Sara (Carr) 221, 896
HARO (DE)
Sancha 994
HARPESFIELD
family 1025
John 630
Joyce (Mitton) 630
Philippa 839
**HARPESFIELD alias
MITTON**
Anna (Skrimshire)
  630
Edward 630
**HARRACH (VON)
(OF)**
Augusta, Princess of
  Liegnitz, Countess
  of Hohenzollern
  (morganatic wife
  of Frederick
  William III, King
  of Prussia) 8
Carl, Count 198
Leonhard V, Count
  198
Leonhard VII Karl,
  Count 198
Maria Anna
  Elisabeth,
  Countess 198
HARRIMAN
(William) Averell
  xviii, 67

Pamela Beryl (Digby)
 (Spencer-Churchill)
 (Hayward) (Hon.)
 67
HARRINGTON
 Abigail 520
HARRIS
 Adria/Audrey
  (Hoare) 538
 Agnes xix, lxiv,
  clxiii, 867, 924
 Anna 632
 Anne (Ruther) 548
 Arthur 483, 548
 Audrey Jane
  Penelope (Parsons)
  305, 306
 Bartholomew 867
 Catherine (Esse)
  836
 Christopher 548
 Dorothy 483
 Dorothy (Waldegrave)
  483, 484, 548
 Elizabeth
  (Collamore) 867
 Elizabeth (Turgis)
  356
 Elizabeth Harkness
  lxi, 306
 Elizabeth Lamont
  (Flagler) 305
 family xi
 Frances 548, 567,
  836
 Frances (Astley) 548
 Francis 836
 Henry Flagler 305,
  306

Jane (Harris) 836
Joan (Cooke) 548
John 836
John Andrews (III)
 305
Juanita (Newton)
 545
Louisa Ellen 320
Mary xiii, 295, 538
Mary (Gedge) 548
Philippa (Grenville)
 836
Sarah 582, 811
Sarah (Tucker)
 cxlviii, 463, 465
Thomas 538
Tucker 465
William 463, 548,
 836
William (Sir) 548
HARRISON
 Anna 412
 Anna Tuthill
  (Symmes) xlii,
  496, 503, 731, 867,
  878
 Anne 129, 411
 Anne (Carter) 496,
  503, 878
 Benjamin xlvii,
  cxliv, clxvii, 496
 Benjamin, Jr. 496
 Benjamin (III) 496,
  878
 Benjamin (IV)
  496, 503, 878
 Benjamin (V) 496,
  503, 730, 878

Benjamin, 23rd U.S.
 President 496,
 503, 731, 867, 878
Blanche (Mayne)
 411, 412
Caroline Lavinia
 (Scott) 496, 503,
 731, 867, 878
Charles 411
Elizabeth (Bassett)
 496, 503, 730, 878
Elizabeth (Bernard)
 496
Elizabeth (Burwell)
 496, 878
Elizabeth Ramsey
 (Irwin) 496, 503,
 731, 867, 878
Fairfax lvii
family 496
Frances
 (Whitgreaves) 331
Francis Burton 496
Hannah (___) 496
John 412
John Scott 496,
 503, 731, 867, 878
Jonathan 496
Joseph 496
Learner Blackman
 496
Margaret 241
Mary (___) 496
Mary Scott (Lord)
 (Dimmick) 496,
 503, 731, 867, 878
Richard 496
Thomas 496
William 496

William Henry, 9th
U.S. President
496, 503, 731, 867,
878
HARROWDEN
Nicholas Vaux, 1st
Baron Vaux of
324, 434
HARRY
Daniel lxviii, cxc
family lvi
Hugh lxviii, cxc
HART
Anne 397, 902
Catherine clxxxvii
Hannah 670
HART-DAVIS
Richard Vaughan 10
Rupert Charles (Sir)
10
Sybil Mary (Cooper)
10
HARTE
Ada Elinor clvi, 567
Alice Eleanor
(Taylor) 567
Charles Edward
clv, 567
Eliza Howes
(Meakins) 567
family lxx
John 567
John Joseph, Bishop
of Arizona 567
Ruth Elizabeth
(Weisenstein) 567
HARTENAU (VON)
Alexander, Prince of
Battenberg, Prince

of Bulgaria, Count
41
Johanna Maria
(Loisinger) 41
Marie-Thérèse-Vera-
Zwetana, Countess
clii, 41
HARTINGTON
William John
Robert Cavendish,
Marquess of 26
HARTLEY
Margaret 700
Susanna (Garraway)
662
HARTOPP
Agnes (Lister) 475
Dorothy 475
William (Sir) 475
HARTSHORN
Christian 607
HARTSTONGE
Alice 364
HARTUNG
Catharina 449
HARVEY
Emma 101
Joan 971
Lucy Maria 535
Mary 430
Winifred (Seyborne)
721
HARWOOD
Lydia 747, 758
HASELDEN
family 854
HASELRIGE/
HESILRIG(E)
Anne 830

Arthur (Sir), 2nd Bt.
331, 901
Arthur (Sir), 7th Bt.
901
Bridget (Rolle)
901
Catherine 328, 331
Dorothy (Grevile)
331, 901
Dorothy (Maynard)
901
Elizabeth (Brocket)
830
Elizabeth (Staunton)
830
Hannah (Sturges)
901
Isabel (Heron) 830
Lucy (Entwistle)
830
Robert (Sir) 901
Robert (Sir), 6th Bt.
901
Robert (Sir), 8th Bt.
xlviii, cxlix, 901
Sarah (Walter) 901
Thomas 830
William 830
HASELWOOD
Alice 495
HASSALL
Hugh 817
Margaret 817
Mary (Mainwaring)
817
HASTANG
John 763
Katherine 819
Maud 763

Maud (Trussell) 763
HASTINGS
Agnes (___) 830
Amicia (___) 830
Anne 355, 577, 592, 904, 905
Anne (Gascoigne) 317
Anne (Morley) xxv, 317, 342, 343, 577
Barbara (Devereux) 111
Beatrix (___) 830
Catherine 107
Catherine Maria 79
Dorothy 134
Dorothy (Port) 107
Edmund (Sir) 577
Edward (Sir) 111
Edward Hastings, 2nd Baron 355, 904, 905
Elizabeth 109, 111, 342, 343, 785, 786
Elizabeth (Stanley) 79
Emeline (Heron) 830
family xli, 344, 831
Ferdinando, 6th Earl of Huntingdon 79
Frances 111
Frances Leveson (Fowler) 79
Francis, 2nd Earl of Huntingdon 107

Francis Hastings, Lord 79, 107
George (Sir) 107
George, 4th Earl of Huntingdon 107, 109, 111
Hannah (Cradock) 111
Helen (Alveston) 830
Henry 111
Henry (Sir) 111, 778, 780, 785
Henry, 5th Earl of Huntingdon 79
Hilaria 778
Hugh 830
Hugh (Sir) 317, 830
Isabel 343
Isabel (de Valence) 785
Isabel (Sadington) 830
Jane 111
Jane (Goodhall) 111
Joan (de Cantilupe) 780, 785
John Hastings, 1st Baron 785
John Hastings, (*de jure*) Baron xxv, 317, 342, 343, 577
Katherine 107, 109, 111
Katherine (Pole) 107
Lora 780
Lucy (Davies) 79

Mabel (Faunt) 111
Margaret 830
Margaret (Herle) 830
Mary (Hungerford) 355, 904, 905
Mary (Wodehouse) 577
Muriel 317
Nicholas (Sir) 830
Ralph (Sir) 830
Sarah (Harington) 79, 107
Seymour (Prynne) 107
Theophilus, 7th Earl of Huntingdon 79
Thomas 830
Walter 111
William 830
HASWELL
Mary 368, 464
HATCH
Elizabeth (Fortescue) 743
Jane 743
Lewis 743
HATCHER
Patricia Law xlix, lvii, 731
HATFIELD
Alice (Hercy) 781
Anne 464
Antonia (Norcliffe) 401
Dorothy 401
Elizabeth 781
Henry 781
John 401

1288

HATHAWAY
  Gertrude Bradbury
    (Withington) 649
  Richard C. 649
HATHERLY
  Timothy 917
HATHORNE
  Sarah (Ruck) 484
HATLEY
  Anne (Porter) 467
  Dorothy (Hampden)
    467
  Esther (Whitaker)
    467
  Henry 467
  Jane 467
  John 467
  Robert 467
HATTON
  family xxiv, 561,
    562
  Frances 135
  Margaret (Domville)
    xix, lvi, lxii, lxiv,
    cxlix, cli, clxvi,
    560
  Martha 433
  Richard 560
HAUCKE (VON)
  Julia, Countess 41
HAUGH
  Atherton 747
  Elizabeth (Bulkeley)
    (Whittingham)
    clxi, clxxvi, 747
HAUGWITZ (VON)
  Juliane Elisabeth 619
  Nicholas Heinrich
    619

Sophie Elisabeth
  (Zahradecky von
  Zahradek),
  Baroness 619
HAUGWITZ-
HARDENBURG-
REVENTLOW
  Barbara Woolworth
    (Hutton) (Mdivani)
    xviii, 44, 46, 63
  Cheryl (Holdridge)
    44
  Curt Henry Eberhard
    Erdmann George,
    Count cxliv, 44, 46
  Curt Ulrich Henry,
    Count 44
  Gabrielle (Schneider)
    44
  George Erdmann
    Charles Ferdinand,
    Count 44
  Jill (Oppenheim)
    [Jill St. John] 44
  Lance George
    William Detlev,
    Count 44
  Margaret Astor
    (Drayton) 44
HAUSSY (D')
  Marie-Victoire-
    Desirée 443
HAUTERIVE (D')
  Jacques d'Arpajon,
    Vicomte 200
HAUTPONT (DE)
  Jean-Baptiste de
    Lannoy, Seigneur
    438

HAVELAAR
  Johanna Maria
    Christina 733
HAVERSKERKE (DE)
  Marie 950
HAVILAND. *see also*
  DE HAVILLAND
  Elizabeth (Guise)
    351
  Jane clxii, 351
  Robert 351
HAVTORESON
  Jon, Lord of
    Borregard and
    Huseby 452, 457
HAWES
  Anne 393, 684
  Constance 670
  Desire (Gorham) 654
  Edmond lvii, lxv,
    lxviii, lxxi, clxi,
    clxxv, 654, 656
  Elizabeth (Brome)
    654, 670
  family lii, 656
  James William lii,
    lvii, lxv, lxxi
  Jane (Porter) 654
  John 654
  Thomas 654, 670
  Ursula (Colles) 654
  William 654
HAWKE
  Catherine (Brooke)
    327
  Edward 327
  Edward Hawke
    (Adm.), 1st Baron
    327

1289

Elizabeth (Bladen) 327
HAWKINS
Hannah 479, 715
Jenna Louise 833
Lois 589
Mary Eliza 592
HAWTAYNE
family 441
HAWTE
Alice 474, 552
Elizabeth 551
family 552
Isabel (Frowick) 552
Jane 314, 323, 551, 552, 738
Mary (Guilford) 552
Thomas (Sir) 552
William (Sir) 552
HAWTEN
Edward 643
Margaret 643
Margery (Crocker) 643
HAY
Agnes Georgiana Elizabeth 9
Andrew, 8th Earl of Erroll 145
Anne, of Keillor 168
Christian 241
David (Sir), of Yester 241
Dulcibella Jane 131
Eleanor 143, 145, 161
Elizabeth 222, 223, 225

Elizabeth (Crichton) 241
Elizabeth (Cunningham) 241
Elizabeth (FitzClarence) 9
Emily 67
George, 7th Earl of Erroll 145, 152, 223
George, 8th Marquess of Tweeddale 67
Georgiana Barbara 111
Helen (Stewart) 145
Isabel (Gordon) 223
Jane (Bell) 131
Jean 176, 177
Jean (Hay) 145
John (Sir), 7th Bt. 111
John, 2nd Marquess of Tweeddale 177
John Hay, 1st Baron, of Yester 241
John Hay, 2nd Baron, of Yester 241
Louisa 68
Margaret 152, 248, 250, 251, 252, 254, 257, 258, 940
Margaret (Hay) 177
Margaret (Logie) 223
Margaret (Robertson) 145, 152, 223

Maria 789
Mary 210
Mary (Douglas) 241
Mary (Maitland) 177
Sarah Beresford (Cossins) 111
Susan (Montagu) 67
Thomas 223
William, 3rd Earl of Erroll 223
William, 6th Earl of Erroll 145
William, 17th Earl of Erroll 131
William, Lord 177
William George, 18th Earl of Erroll 9
____, of Burnthill 268
HAY-MACKENZIE
Anne 33
HAYDEN
Horace Edwin 498
HAYES
Anne 254
Chloe (Smith) 656, 871
Ezekiel 871
Lucy Ware (Webb) 656, 702, 871
Rebecca (Russell) 871
Rutherford 656, 871
Rutherford, Jr. 656, 702, 871
Rutherford Birchard, 19th U.S. President 656, 702, 871

Sophia (Birchard) 656, 702, 871
HAYNE
Charlotte Augusta 371
HAYNES
Elizabeth lxiv, cxliii, 587
John (Gov.) 587, 806
Mabel (Harlakenden) xix, lxix, clxiii, clxxvii, 587, 806, 807
Mary (Thornton) 587
HAYNIN (DE)
Antoinette (de Tenremonde) 733
François de Haynin, Seigneur 733
Jacques de Haynin, Seigneur, Seigneur de Louvegnies 733
Jean 733
Marguerite 733
Marie (de Roison) 733
Marie (d'Estaples) 733
HAYWARD
Alice 550
Elizabeth 318
Leland 67
Martha (Washington) 515
Pamela Beryl (Digby) (Spencer-Churchill) (Hon.) 67

Samuel 515
HAZEN
Frances Amelia 371
Sarah (LeBaron) 371
William 371
HAZZARD
Mary 176
HEART/HART
Agnes 87
Agnes (Baxter) 87
David 87
Jean (Mowat) 87
John 87
HEATH
Mary (Drake) (Chetham) clxxxvi
HEATLEY
Margaret 266
HEBER
Eleanor (Ferrand) 321
Martha 321
Thomas 321
HEBERT
Adrien-André 987
Cordélie 987
Felicité (Richard) 987
François 987
Françoise (Chasles) 987
Gilbert 987
Marguerite (Huot) 987
HECKSTALL
Margaret 466, 567

HEDWIG
Princess of Holstein-Gottorp 49
HEDWIGER (VON)
Anna Sabina, Countess von Sponeck 184
HEEMSTRA (VAN)
Arnoud Jan Anne Aleid, Baron 446
Edda Kathleen [Audrey Kathleen Ruston] [Audrey Hepburn] viii, xvii, xxvi, lxix, cxliv, 446
Elbrig Willemine Henriette (van Asbeck), Baroness 446
Ella, Baroness 446
Frans Julius Johan, Baron 445
Henrietta Philippina Jacoba (van Pallandt), Baroness 445
Wilhelmina Cornelia (de Beaufort) 446
Willem Hendrik Johan, Baron 446
HEIDECK (ZU)
Anna 617
John III, Herr 617
Ottilia (Schenk[in] von Limburg-Gaildorf) 617
HEIGHAM
Anne (Munnings) 579

Catherine (Cotton) 579
Clement 579
Elizabeth 579
Jane 302
Matilda (Cooke) 579
Thomas 579
HEIN
Margaret Edith 16
HEIRES
Elizabeth 588
HELE
Elizabeth (Strode) 573
Frances 573
Rebecca 305
Walter 573
HELEN
Grand Duchess of Russia 3
HELENA
of Liegnitz 196
HELIGAN
Belyn (Sir) 665
Isabel 665
Isabel (FitzIves) 665
Margaret (Prideaux) 665
Richard 665
HELION
Alice (Swinborne) 766, 767
Elizabeth 766, 767
Isabel 607
John 766, 767
HELMAN
Constance 804
HELY-HUTCHINSON
Louisa Lucy 177

HEMINGWAY
Jane M. 764
HENCHMAN
Daniel 647
family 648
Hannah 584, 647
Mary 166
Mary (Poole) 647
Sarah (Woodward) lviii, lxi, lxx, cxliv, clxi, 647, 649
HENCKEL VON DONNERSMARCK
Anna Maria (von Berg) 45
Annalise (von Zitzewitz) 45
Christiane (Asschenfeldt) 45
counts 46
Edwin Hugo, Count 45
Elias Andreas, Count 195
Florian Maria Georg Christian, Count clv, 37, 45
Friedrich Carl, Count 45
Helena Constantia, Countess 195
Leo Ferdinand, Count 45
Wilhelmine (von Wchinitz und Tettau), Baroness 45
HENDERSON
Berta (von Bunsen) xviii, lvii, 148, 149

Christian 97
Ernest Flagg 148
Ernest Flagg, Jr. xviii, 148, 149
Ernest Flagg (III) ix, lvii, lxiv, 149, 348, 775, 940
Ernest Flagg (IV) ix, lvii, 149, 910, 940
Faryl (Finn) 148
Marcia 726
Margaret 82
Mary Gill Caldwell (Stephens) 148, 149
Mary Louise 371
Roberta Campbell ix, lvii, 149, 348, 775, 910, 940
Sam 726
HENDLEY
Anne 691
Helen (Ashburnham) 691
Walter (Sir) 691
HENDRICKS
James Ray 424
Laraine (Johnson) [Laraine Day] 424
HENEAGE
Agnes Elizabeth Winona Leclerq (Joy) (Salm-Salm) [Princess Salm-Salm] 30, 38
Catherine (Petre) 30
Charles 30, 38

Frances (Tasburgh) 30
Frances Anne (Ainslie) 30
George Fieschi 30
George Robert 30
HENLEY
  Catherine (Hungerford) 312
  Charles Fairfax 901
  Kittie (Jones) 901
  Norma Lavinia 901
  Robert (Sir) 312
  Williamsa 312
HENNEBERG
  Henry VI, Count of 449, 451
  Jutta of 640
  Katherine of 449, 451
HENNEBERG-SCHLEUSSINGEN
  Anna of 617
HENNIN-LIETARD
  Oudard de Bournonville, Count of 291
HENRIFFI
  ap Llywelyn 810
HENRIKSSON
  Agneta (Lillie) 457
  Ulf, Lord of Fyllingarum 457
HENRY
  Alexander 219
  Diane M. 984
  Dorothea Spotswood (Dandridge) 219
  Duke of Brunswick-Lüneburg 451, 454
  Duke of Mecklenburg, Prince Consort of The Netherlands 8
  Estelle (Germain) 984
  family lvi
  Jean (Robertson) 219
  John lvi, clxvii, 219
  Lou 371
  Patrick 219
  Prince of Carolath-Beuthen 43
  Prince of Scotland, Earl of Huntingdon 774, 776, 778, 779, 780, 783, 785, 787, 789
  Sarah (Shelton) 219
  Sarah (Winston) (Syme) 219
  Venant-Eugène 984
HENRY I
  Duke of Brabant 950
  Duke of Burgundy 853, 855
  King of England xxvi, xxxix, 652, 658, 739, 741, 806, 807, 808, 810, 811, 813, 815, 817, 819, 821, 822, 824, 826, 830, 957, 959
  King of France 681, 739, 778, 780, 783, 785, 787, 789, 835, 837, 839, 841, 843, 845, 847, 957, 959
HENRY I "THE FOWLER"
  German Emperor 874, 877
HENRY II
  Count of Champagne, King of Jerusalem 943
  Duke of Brabant 733
  King of Castile 190, 191
  King of England vii, x, xxvi, xxxii, xxxix, 507, 647, 652, 658, 735, 737, 741, 742, 746, 749, 752, 754, 757, 760, 761, 763, 766, 768, 770, 772, 774, 776, 841, 845, 909, 948, 964, 994
  King of France 202, 637, 735
HENRY III
  King of England ix, xxxix, 623, 625, 628, 630, 632, 633, 683, 942, 944, 945, 946, 963, 965
  King of France 637
HENRY IV
  King of England xxv, 229, 231, 233, 235, 287, 293, 378, 412
  King of France and Navarre 62, 192, 293, 615, 637, 638

HENRY V
Duke of Mecklen-
burg-Schwerin 220
King of England
226, 603, 813, 824
HENRY VII
King of England
xxxix, lxvi, 62, 69,
76, 79, 80, 226, 347,
348, 361, 477, 547,
691
HENRY VIII
King of England xii,
xl, lviii, 136, 139,
232, 300, 303, 305,
530, 539, 551, 596,
605, 741, 855
HENRY IX
Duke of Bavaria 832
**HENRY (HARRY)
CHARLES
ALBERT DAVID**
of Wales, Prince of
Great Britain xlii,
25, 344, 858, 931,
932
HENRY (JUNIOR)
Landgrave of Hesse
617
HENSEN
Matilde 645
HENSHAW
Elizabeth (Sumner)
397
family vii
Joshua lxxi, clxi,
clxxix, 397
Katherine
(Houghton) 397

William 397
HENSLEIGH
Elizabeth 116
HEPBURN. *see also*
HEPBURN-RUSTON
James, 4th Earl of
Bothwell 90
Janet 173, 222, 225
Janet (Douglas)
173, 222, 225
Jean 90, 96, 272
Margaret 257
Patrick, 1st Earl of
Bothwell 173,
222, 225
HEPBURN-RUSTON
Edda Kathleen van
Heemstra [Audrey
Hepburn] viii, xvii,
xxvi, lxix, cxliv, 446
Ella (van Heemstra),
Baroness 446
Joseph Victor
Anthony 446
HERBERT
Adela R. (Budlong)
76
Agnes 725
Alice 808
Anne 229
Anne (___) 711
Anne (Devereux)
346, 352
Catherine 351,
352, 414, 901
Charlotte 226
Elizabeth 337, 345,
346, 375, 382, 396,
689, 900

Elizabeth (Acland)
76
Elizabeth Alicia Mary
(Wyndham) 76
Eveline Alicia
Juliana 76, 77
Frances 77
George 918
Henrietta Anna
(Howard) 76
Henriette-Mauricette
(de Penancoët de
Kéroualle) 226
Henry, 1st Earl of
Carnarvon 76
Henry George, 2nd
Earl of Carnarvon
76, 77
Henry John George,
3rd Earl of
Carnarvon 76
Henry William
["Frank Forrester"]
76
Laura Letitia
Gwendolyn Evelyn
401
Letitia Dorothea
(Allen) 76
Margaret (Cradock)
808
Mary (Woodville)
346
Maud 333, 347, 361,
389, 401, 418, 431
Philip, 7th Earl of
Pembroke 226
Richard, of Ewyas
808

1294

Sarah (Barker) 76
Thomas, of
   Abergavenny 808
William (Hon.) 76,
   77
William, 1st Earl of
   Pembroke (1st crea-
   tion) 346, 352, 808
HERCULES I
Duke of Modena and
   Ferrara 186, 189
HERCY
Alice 781
Anne 780
Barbara 781
Elizabeth (Digby)
   727, 780
Ellen 727
Humphrey 727, 780
HERDEBURGH (DE)
Ela 749, 754, 757
Ida (de Odingselles)
   687, 749, 754, 757
Roger (Sir) 749,
   754, 757
HERDEG
John 430
HERDSON
Abigail 750
HEREFORD
Edward Devereux,
   8th Viscount 346
Henry de Bohun, 1st
   Earl of 783
Humphrey de Bohun,
   2nd Earl of 783
Humphrey de Bohun,
   4th Earl of, Earl of
   Essex 478, 497,

500, 503, 510, 512,
517, 524, 530, 532,
543, 551, 553, 554,
555, 558, 560, 563,
565, 569, 571, 573,
574, 582, 588, 595,
596, 601, 603, 608,
611, 613
Walter Devereux, 1st
   Viscount lxvi, 134
HERENDEN
Jane 604
HERING
Anna Maria
   (Morris) 324
Bathshua 933
Bathshua (Scott)
   933
Elizabeth (Cock-
   croft) 324, 933
Elizabeth (Hughes)
   324
Julines 324, 933
Mary (Inglis) 324
Mary Helen 324
Nathaniel 324, 933
Oliver 324
HERIOT(T)
Elizabeth 244
Mary 506
HERLE
Margaret 830
HERMAN V
Margrave of Brand-
   enburg 449, 451
HERMANN
FORTUNATUS
Margrave of Baden-
   Rodemachern 208

HERMIVAL (DE)
François du Bose,
   Seigneur 957
HERNDON
John Goodwin lvii
Mary (Waller?)
   cxci, cxcii
HERON
Andrew, of Bargaly
   732
Andrew, of
   Kirrouchtrie 732
Ann (Vining) 732
Anne (Ogle) 519
Benjamin clxxvi,
   clxxx, 732
Elizabeth 310, 519
Elizabeth (Cochrane)
   128
Elizabeth (Heron)
   519
Emeline 830
Isabel 830
Jean (Dunbar) 732
John (Sir) 519
Margaret (Hastings)
   830
Mary 128
Mary (Graham) 732
Mary (Howe) 732
Patrick 128, 732
Roger (Sir) 830
William (Sir) 519
HERON-MAXWELL
Helenora Catherine
   128
John Shaw (Sir), 4th
   Bt. 128
Mary (Heron) 128

HERONVILLE
Joan 628, 630
HERPORT
Anna (Keller von Schleitheim) 832
Apollonia (von Rüssegg) 832
Peter 832
Rudolf 832
Ursula 832
HERRIES
Mariot 456
Marmaduke Francis Constable-Maxwell, 11th Baron 72
HERRING
Mary 886
HERRON
Helen xliii, 318, 881
HERTFORD
Edward Seymour, 1st Earl of 69, 76, 80
Francis Seymour, 1st Marquess of 27
Gilbert de Clare, 3rd Earl of Gloucester, 7th Earl of 466, 483, 489, 491, 495, 505, 508, 514, 528, 536, 547, 567, 575, 577, 584, 587, 590, 592, 594, 606, 607, 615
Roger de Clare, 2nd Earl of 866, 870
HERTZEL
Thomas Benjamin lvii

HERVEY
Elizabeth (Davers) 117, 334
Elizabeth (Felton) 334
Elizabeth (Lady) [Lady Elizabeth Foster] 117
Frances Selina 65
Frederick Augustus, 4th Earl of Bristol 117, 334
John, 1st Baron Hervey of Ickworth 23, 117, 334
John, 1st Earl of Bristol 334
Lepell 22, 23
Louisa Theodosia 334
Mary 334
Mary (Lepell) 23, 117, 334
Susan 235
HERVIEUX
Valerie 982
HERWIJNEN (VAN)
Adelise 447, 907
Brustijn, Heer van Stavenisse 447, 907
Elisabeth (van Beieren) 447, 907
HESELTINE
Rose 320
HESILRIG/ HESELRIGE. *see* HASELRIGE/ HESILRIG(E)

HESKETH
Helen 700
HESS
Barbara Gay 371
Carl Barton clv, 11
Ludmilla Maria (of Schwarzenburg), Princess clv, 11
HESSE
Agnes of 617
Alexander, Prince of 41
Frederick William, Elector of 13
Henry (junior), Landgrave of 617
Louis I, Grand Duke of 41
Louis I, Landgrave of 449
Louis II, Grand Duke of 41
Louis II, Landgrave of 449, 450
Marie of, Empress of Russia 2, 3, 5
Victoria, Princess of 41
William II, Elector of 13
HESSE (VAN)
Margaret 129, 840
HESSE-DARMSTADT
Amelia of 41
Anna Eleanor of 58, 432
Elizabeth of 184

1296

Frederica, Princess of,
  Queen of Prussia
  13
Frederica of 40
George William,
  Landgrave of 40
Louis IX, Landgrave
  of 41
Louis VIII,
  Landgrave of 40
Louise Henriette of
  41
HESSE-ESCHEWEGE
Christine, Princess
  of 44
Frederick, Landgrave
  of 44
HESSE-HOMBURG
Frederick II, Land-
  grave of 54, 55
Wilhelmina Marie
  of 54
HESSE-
  PHILIPPSTAL
Charles I,
  Landgrave of 43
Charlotte Amelia
  Caroline, Princess
  of 43, 46
HESSE-RHEINFELS-
  ROTENBURG
Christine Henrietta
  of 18
Joseph, Landgrave
  of 38
Marie Louise of 38
HESSELL
Jane 126

HESSEN (VON)
Margaretha 449
HESTRE (DE LA)
Alexandre de
  Carondelet, Baron
  de Noyelle, Vicomte
  438
Antoine de
  Carondelet, Baron
  de Noyelle,
  Vicomte 438
François-Louis-
  Hector de Carondelet
  (Gov.), Vicomte,
  Vicomte du Langue,
  Baron de Noyelle
  liii, clxxiii, 438
Jean-Louis de
  Carondelet, Baron
  de Noyelle,
  Vicomte, Vicomte
  du Langue 438
HETLEY
Judith 720
HETT
family clxxxvi
HEUBEL
Caroline 147
HEUGEL UND
  POLLOGWITZ
  (VON)
Eleanor Charlotte
  619
HEVYN
Anne 653
HEWSTER
Joan 737
HEXT
Agnes 868

Joan (Fortescue)
  866
Margery 866
Thomas 866, 868
Wilmot (Poyntz)
  866
HEYDON
Christian 744
Dorothy 314
HEYWARD
Mary 347
HEYWOOD
Catherine 541
Grace 528
HIBBARD
Ebenezer 932
Keziah 932
Margaret (Morgan)
  932
HIBBERT
Hannah (Gibbins)
  630, 886
Mary 630, 886
____ 630, 886
HIBOUVILLE (DE)
Agnès 957
HICKEY
John P., Jr. xii,
  968, 969, 971, 973,
  977, 978, 981
HICKLING
Douglas ix, lvi,
  lvii, lix, lxii, 260,
  280, 703
HICKMAN
Edwin 497
Eleanor (Elliott/
  Ellis) 497
Elizabeth 351

Hannah (Lewis) 498
James 498
Martha (Thacker) 497
Susannah 498
Thomas, Jr. 497
HICKS
Elizabeth 389
HIDEN
Martha Woodruff liii
HIERTA
Bengt 53
Catharina 53
Christina (Stierna) 53
HIETT
family clxxxvi
HIGGINS
Ellinor (Evans) 690
James Ward 690
Janet 254
John lxix, clxxxviii, 124, 125, 745
Napier (Mrs.) lvii
HIGGINSON
family xxxvi
Lucy 495, 856
Margery 822
HIGHAM
Bridget 484
Phyllis (Waldegrave) 484
Thomas 484
HILDEGARDIS
of Kreichgau (wife of Charlemagne, Holy Roman Emperor) 879, 919
HILDYARD
Elizabeth (Hastings) 342, 343
Isabel 342
Joan/Jane (at See) 342, 343
Katherine 342, 343
Piers (Sir) 342
Robert (Sir) 342, 343
HILEY
Mary 864
HILL
Anne 340, 341, 493
Anne (Stafford) 340
Anne (Trevor) 340
Arthur, 1st Baron Dungannon 340
Arthur Wills Blundell Trumbull Sandys Roden, 5th Marquess of Downshire 70
Arthur Wills John Wellington Trumbull Blundell, 6th Marquess of Downshire 70
Dorothy 126
Eleanor (Boyle) 340
Georgiana Elizabeth (Balfour) 70
Henrietta Maria 80
Joan 345, 396
Kathleen Mary (Hare) 70
Kathleen Nina 70
Lawrence clxxxiv
Margaret 493, 569
Mary 494, 508
Michael 340
Priscilla 108
William 340
HILLIARD
Meliana 406
HILTON
Anne (Yorke) 106
Elizabeth 715
Elizabeth (Kitchen) 106
Elizabeth Rosemond (Taylor) [Elizabeth Taylor] 21, 190
Godfrey, Baron Luttrell 715
Hannah (___) (Moore) 106
Henry 106
Isabel (Selby) 106
John 106
Margaret (Metcalfe) 106
Margery (Willoughby) 715, 716
Mehitabel (Lawrence) 106
Ralph lxii, 106
Robert 106
Sarah (Clarke) 106
Sibyl (Lumley) 106
William 106
William (Sir) 106
___ (Brandling) 106

HINDERSTEIN (VAN)
Gijsbert Johan van Hardenbroek, Heer van Groenewoude and 460
HINKLEY
Cecily 880
John 880
Margaret (Notbeam) 880
HINOJOSA (DE)
Abraham 447
Alexander xii, xxxii, liii, clv, 447
Margaret (de Haes) 447
Maria (Tengnagell) 447
HINTON
John xlix, cxc
HOAR/HOARE
Adria/Audrey 538
Bridget 297
Bridget (Lisle) clxxii, 297, 298
Julian (Tripplett) 538
Leonard 297
Philip lvii
Susanna 80
Thomas 538
HOBART
Albinia (Bertie) 117
Anne (Reymes) 539
Dorothy 924
Elizabeth (Whiting) 924

George, 3rd Earl of Buckinghamshire 117
George Vere 117
Jane (Cataneo) 117
Jeremiah 924
Mary 539
Thomas 539
HOBART-HAMPDEN
Albinia Jane 117
HOBBES
Anna clxxxvii
Anne 743
HOBSON
Martha 377
HODGES
Agatha (Rodney) 825
Anne (Mansell) 825
Eleanor (Rosse) 825
George 825
Jane 825, 852
Thomas 825
HODGSON
Elizabeth 821
Henrietta Mildred 121, 930
Mary (Tucker) 930
Mildred (Porteous) 930
Robert 930
Robert, Dean of Carlisle 930
HODSDON
Vesta 520
HOFF
Henry Bainbridge vii, viii, xii, xlvi, li, lvii, 325, 408, 447,

540, 591, 616, 767, 776, 873, 891, 899
HOFFMAN
Anna Josina (van der Pot) 733
Catharina Frederica Cornelia (van Hangest d'Ivoy) 733
family lvii, 734
Jan Jacob 734
Johan Frederic 733
Johanna Maria Christina (Havelaar) 733
Kathryn Teresa Marguerite (Cary) 734
Mathilda Petronella Hermanna (Schadee) 734
Willem Johan [William J.] liii, lvii, clv, 447, 733, 734
HOFFMANSTHAL (VON)
Alice Muriel (Astor) (Obolensky-Neledinsky-Meletzky) 799, 800
Hugo 799, 800
Raymond 799
HOGBEN
Dorothea (Scott) (Gotherson) xlviii, lii, cxliv, 314, 316
Joseph 314

HOGE
Sarah 325
HOGGINS
Sarah 73
HOHENBERG
Gertrude of (wife of Rudolf I, Holy Roman Emperor) 449, 451, 617
HOHENEMS
Francis William, Count of 186
Katharina Eleanora (zu Fürstenberg), Princess 186
Maria Franziska, Countess of 186
HOHENLOHE-LANGENBURG
Charles Louis, Prince of 47, 141
Christian Albert Louis, Prince of 47
Frederica Christine Emilie, Princess of 47
HOHENLOHE-NEUENSTEIN
Charlotte Susanna Maria of 60, 893
Kraft, Count of 60, 893
HOHENLOHE-SPECKFELD (VON)
Elizabeth 617
Godfrey, Herr 617
HOHENLOHE-UFFENHEIM (VON)
Louis, Herr 617

HOHENLOHE-WALDENBURG-PFEDELBACH
Louis Eberhard, Count of 182
Sophie Juliana of 182
HOHENSTAUFEN
family 939
Otto of, Count Palatine of Burgundy 735, 952
HOHENZOLLERN
Anna Ursula of 195
Augusta von Harrach, Princess of Liegnitz, Countess of (morganatic wife of Frederick William III, King of Prussia) 8
Charles I, Count of 195, 198
Joachim I, Count of 195
John George, Count of 195
Marie Jacoba of 198
HOHENZOLLERN-HECHINGEN
Hermann Friedrich, Count of 208
Maria Josepha of 208
Philip, Count of 208
HOLAND
Alice (FitzAlan) xxv, 515, 600

Anne (Montagu) 400
Anne (Plantagenet) xl, 119, 126, 133
Anne (Stafford) 400
Constance 352
Edmund, 4th Earl of Kent xxv, 377, 410, 423
Eleanor xxv, 107, 114, 119, 126, 133, 134, 377, 410, 411, 423, 515, 600
Elizabeth 742
Elizabeth (Plantagenet) 352, 400
family vii, xli
Jane 400
Joan (Plantagenet), "The Fair Maid of Kent," Princess Dowager of Wales 107, 400, 515, 600
John, 1st Duke of Exeter 352, 400
John, 2nd Duke of Exeter 400
Margaret xxv, 222, 300, 345, 396, 407, 427, 547, 898
Margaret (___) 400
Maud 752, 760, 772
Maud (la Zouche) 742, 752, 760, 772
Robert, "Bastard of Exeter" 400
Robert Holand, 1st Baron 742, 752, 760, 772

Thomas, 1st Earl of
  Kent 107, 400,
  515, 600
Thomas, 2nd Earl of
  Kent xxv, 515,
  600
HOLBROOK
  Chloe 632
  Deborah 880
HOLDEN
  Frances (Dungan)
  488
HOLDRIDGE
  Cheryl 44
HOLFORD
  Dorothy 687
  Jane (Booth)
   (Dutton) 561, 687
  John (Sir) 687
  Margery (Brereton)
  687
  Thomas 561
  Thomas (Sir) 687
HOLGANSKI
  Anne of 621
HOLGATE
  Anne 821
HOLLAND
  Adelaide of 774,
  775, 776
  Albert I, Duke of
   Bavaria, Count of
   451
  Georgiana Caroline
   (Lennox), Baroness
   31
  Henry Rich, 1st Earl
   of 135
  Lucy 668

Margaret of (wife of
  Louis IV, Holy
  Roman Emperor)
  51, 447, 449, 451,
  907
William V of
  Bavaria, Count of
  447, 907, 908
William III, Count
  of, Count of
  Hainault 459
  ___ 901
HOLLES
  Elizabeth 34
HOLLEY
  Mary 725
HOLLICK
  Martin Edward ix,
   xxviii, lviii, lix,
   409, 579, 624
HOLLINGSWORTH
  Harry lviii
HOLLOWAY
  Elizabeth (Catesby)
   (Cocke) clxvi, 831
  John 831
HOLLYMAN
  Mary 307
HOLMAN
  Mary Campbell
   (Lovering) 917
  Winifred Lovering
   lviii, lx, lxi, lxx
HOLME
  Agnes 881
  Anne 667
  Anne (Aislaby) 343
  Catherine 111, 343
  Edward 111

Elizabeth (Bowker)
  111
Elizabeth (Chetham)
  111
Jane (Hastings) 111
John 111, 343, 667
Katherine (Hildyard)
  342
Margery/Mariora
  (Constable) 667,
  668
Robert 667
William 111, 342
  ___ (Elland) 667
HOLMES
  Alvahn xlv, lviii
  Cecily 545
  Martha (Pomeroy)
   594
  Mary Jane 171, 258
  Sherlock 136
  William 594
HOLMSTEAD
  Margaret 661
**HOLSTEIN-
GOTTORP**
  Augusta Marie,
   Princess of 43, 46
  Frederick III, Duke
   of 47
  Hedwig of 35, 49
  John Adolf, Duke of
   35, 47, 49
  Magdalena Sybil,
   Princess of 47
**HOLY ROMAN
EMPEROR**
  Adolf I of Nassau-
   Wiesbaden 617

Albert I 449, 451
Albert II, King of
  Hungary and
  Bohemia 187,
  220, 895
Charlemagne vi,
  xx, xxii, xxvii, lxx,
  626, 805, 879, 919
emperors 615
Ferdinand I 40, 43,
  54, 56, 192, 287,
  290, 615, 619, 891,
  892
Francis I (of Lorraine)
  15
Francis II 11
Frederick I
  Barbarossa 640,
  733, 735, 952
Frederick III 291
Henry I "the
  Fowler" 874, 877
Joseph I 20
Leopold II 614
Louis IV, of Bavaria
  51, 52, 447, 449,
  451, 617, 907
Maria Theresa, Holy
  Roman Empress
  (Empress of
  Austria) 15
Maximilian I 438,
  445
Otto II 849
Rudolf I 449, 451,
  617
Rupert III of
  Wittelsbach 237,
  291

HOLYNSKA
  Zénaïde 227, 622
HOME. *see also*
  HUME
  Alexander Frederick
    ("Sir Alec")
    Douglas-Home,
    14th Earl of, Prime
    Minister xxiv, 25
  Anne 177
  Elizabeth 210, 334
  Elizabeth (Proctor)
    90
  Elizabeth (Stewart)
    285
  family lv
  George lviii, 90
  George (Sir), 3rd Bt.
    90
  Isabel 285
  Janet 210
  Jean (Dalmahoy) 90
  John (Sir), of
    Renton 90
  Margaret 90, 93,
    272, 893
  Margaret (Home) 90
  Margaret (Stewart)
    90
  Marion 272
  Mungo 285
  Patrick (Sir), 1st Bt.
    90
HOMES
  Catherine (Craighead)
    cxlix, cli, clxi, 87
  Mary (Franklin) 87
  Robert 87
  William (Rev.) 87

HOMMEL
  Sylvia 13
HONDFORD
  John (Sir) 407
  Katherine 407, 500
  Margaret (Savage)
    407
HONE
  Dorothy 731
  Elizabeth (Parsons)
    730
  Jane (Allen) 730
  Joyce (Browne)
    730, 731
  Judith 730
  Judith (Aylmer)
    730, 731
  Sarah (___) (Edwards)
    (Richardson) 730
  Theophilus xi, xix,
    xxxiv, xlix, lvii,
    cxlix, cli, clxvii,
    clxxx, 730, 731
  Thomas 730, 731
  William 730
HONORAT II
  of Savoy, Count of
    Tenbe and
    Sommerive 442
HONSTEIN
  Agnes, Countess of
    195
HONYMAN
  Hannah 634
HOO
  Anne 473, 580
  Eleanor 462
  Eleanor (de Welles)
    462, 473, 580

Thomas Hoo, 1st
  Baron 462, 473,
  580
HOOD
  Emily Beryl Sissy
    67
HOOGSTRAETEN
  Maximilian Friedrich, Prince of
    Salm-Salm, Duke
    of 38
**HOOGSTRATEN
(VAN)**
  Alida Hendrika Maria
    (Wigman) 460
  David Jan 460
  Eleanor Colson
    (Curtis) 460
  François 460
  Jan Samuel François
    liii, clix, 460
  Louise Dorothea
    Adrienne (van
    Son) 460
  Nicholas Frans 460
HOOKE
  Jane (Whalley)
    xlviii, 781
  William (Rev.) 781
HOOKER
  Dorothy 757
  Sarah 318
  Thomas (Rev.) 757
HOOPER
  Anne (Clarke) 211
  William 211
HOORD
  Joyce 749

HOOVER
  Herbert Clark, 31st
    U.S. President 371
  Hulda Randall
    (Minthorn) 371
  Jesse Clark 371
  Lou (Henry) 371
HOPE
  Charles 34
  Eliza (Cockburn)
    34
  Elizabeth (Knight)
    235
  Frederick 34
  George 235
  Gwendoline
    Katherine Leonora
    34
  John 235
  Josephine Mary 71
  Leonora Louisa
    Isabella (Orde) 34
  Magdalen 235
  Margaret (Puleston)
    235
  Mary 174, 215
  Maud (Ravenscroft)
    235
  Susan Anne
    (Sawyer) 34
  William 235
HOPE-SCOTT
  James Robert 71
  Victoria
    Alexandrina
    (Fitzalan-Howard)
    71
HOPE-VERE
  Anne (Vane) 34

  Charles 34
HOPKINS
  Anne (Yale) 658
  Dorothy E. ix,
    lviii, lxiv, 527
  Edward 658
  Temperance (Gilbert)
    (Alsop) 588
  William 588
HOPPIN
  Gertrude Marguerite
    285
HOPTON
  Arthur (Sir) 311
  Edward 670, 671
  Eleanor (Lucy)
    534
  Elizabeth 233, 319,
    534, 560
  Elizabeth (Wolrich)
    670
  Frances 312
  Jane (Kemeys) 311
  Katherine 670
  Margaret 710
  Margaret
    (Wentworth) 710
  Mary 311
  Rachel (Hall) 311
  Robert 311, 312
  Thomas (Sir) 534
  William (Sir) 710
HORDE
  Alicia 697
HORDIJK
  Jannetje Gijsbertje
    Pijnacker 907
HORE
  Edith 697

HORN
 Agnes 225
 Christina Gustaviana, Baroness 60, 893
HORNE
 Elizabeth 721
HORNER
 Amy 337
 Jane (Popham) 337
 Thomas 337
HORSLEY-BERESFORD
 Louisa Elizabeth 80
HORSMANDEN
 Anne (Jevon) 348
 Daniel 348
 Daniel (Rev.) 348
 Daniel, Jr. (Chief Justice) 348
 Mary 348
 Mary (Reade) (Vesey) 348
 Susanna (Beeching) 348
 Susanna (Woolston) (Bowyer) 348
 Ursula (St. Leger) liii, 348
 Warham clxvii, 348
HORTON
 Elizabeth 506
HOSKINS
 Anthony Glenn ix, xii, li, lviii, lxix, 298, 300, 303, 622, 801, 817, 908

 Joyce (Jones) 515
HOTESSE. *see* OTIS/HOTESSE
HOTMAN
 Suzanne 940, 950, 951
HOTZ
 Lila 91
HOUGH
 Ephraim xiv
 Ephraim, Jr. xiv
 Eunice (Andrews) xiv
 Hannah (Royce) xiv
 Sarah xiv
HOUGHTON
 Alice 497
 Anne 534
 Ellen (Parker) 397
 Evan 397
 Katherine 397
 Margaret (Stanley) 397
 Richard 397
 Richard (Sir), 3rd Bt. 107
 Sarah (Stanhope) 107
HOUSE/HOWES
 Joan 760
HOUSTON
 Anne (Hamilton) 156
 Isabel (Johnstone) 156
 Patrick 156
 Patrick (Sir), 1st Bt. 156

 Patrick (Sir), 5th Bt. lix, 156
 Priscilla (Dunbar) 156
HOUSTOUN
 family lv
HOVIOUS
 Matthew lviii, lx, 656
HOW
 Hester 924
HOWARD
 Agnes (Tilney) 355, 605, 904
 Alice (de Boys) 653, 661
 Alice (Tendring) 661
 Alice Augusta (Farmer) 109
 Anna (Lillie) 479, 585, 716
 Anne 522, 523
 Anne (Witham) 127
 Barbara (Villiers) 334
 Blanche Georgiana 25
 Caroline 71
 Caroline Georgiana 25
 Catherine 314, 333, 334, 335, 353, 387
 Catherine (Knevet) 334, 482
 Catherine Mary (Neave) 127
 Cecil de Blaquiere clv, 109

1304

Cecile (Coupet) 109
Cecilia Dowdall (Riggs) 127
Charles (Sir) 605
Charles, 1st Earl of Nottingham 605
Cy 362
Dorothy 75, 355, 904
Ebenezer 585
Edmund, Lord 468, 605
Elizabeth 300, 334, 482, 565, 584, 588, 607, 661, 710
Elizabeth (Cecil) 482
Elizabeth (Dacre) 335
Elizabeth (Home) 334
Elizabeth (Stafford) 333, 431
Elizabeth (Tilney) (Bourchier) 300, 333, 353, 420, 428, 605, 705
family xxiv, xxxii
Frances (Courthope) 605
Frances (Gouldwell) 605
Frances (Vere) 62, 333, 431
Francis (Gov.), 5th Baron Howard of Effingham 315, 350, 605
Francis (Sir) 605
Frederick, 5th Earl of Carlisle 71
George clv, 127
George, 6th Earl of Carlisle 25, 69, 71
George Henry 109
Georgiana Dorothy (Cavendish) 25, 69, 71
Gertrude (Lyte) 335
Gloria (Hallward) (Clements) (Ray) [Gloria Grahame] xviii, 362
Harriet 479, 572, 585, 702, 716, 747
Harriet Elizabeth Georgiana 33, 69, 71
Henrietta Anna 76
Henry 127, 661
Henry (Sir) 127
Henry, Earl of Surrey 333, 335, 431
Henry Francis (Sir) 127
Henry Howard, Earl of 62
Isabel 473, 477
James, 3rd Earl of Suffolk 334
Jane 123
Jane (Monson) 605
Joan 653
Joan (de Cornwall) 653, 661
Joan (Walton) 661
John (Sir) 653, 661
John, 1st Duke of Norfolk 353, 473, 493, 522, 605, 661
Joyce (Colepepper/ Culepeper) (Leigh) 468, 476, 605
Katherine (Moleyns) 473, 493, 522, 605
Katherine, Queen of England 339, 468, 605
Margaret 335, 339, 431, 493, 605
Margaret (Audley) 334
Margaret (Chedworth) 353
Margaret (Gamage) 605
Margaret (Mowbray) 314, 473, 493, 522, 605, 661
Margaret Caroline (Leveson-Gower) 71
Margery (Scales) 661
Marie Ernestine (von der Schulenberg) 127
Martha (Goffe) 585
Mary (Allen) (Clagett) (Perrin) 127
Mary (Hussey) 661
Miriam 75

1305

Natalie Bayard   127
Natalie Bayard
  (Merrill)   127
Philadelphia
  (Pelham)   315,
  605
Philip   127
Robert (Sir)   314,
  473, 493, 522, 605,
  661
Samuel   479, 585,
  716
Susan (Felton)
  (Harbord)   350, 605
Sylvia   318
Theophilus, 2nd Earl
  of Suffolk   334
Thomas, 1st Earl of
  Berkshire   482
Thomas, 1st Earl of
  Suffolk   334, 335,
  482
Thomas, 1st
  Viscount Howard
  of Bindon   335
Thomas, 2nd Duke
  of Norfolk   300,
  333, 353, 355, 605,
  705, 904
Thomas, 3rd Duke of
  Norfolk   333, 431
Thomas, 4th Duke
  of Norfolk   334
William (Sir)   605
William, 1st Baron
  Howard of
  Effingham   605
William, Lord   335

HOWARD of
GLOSSOP
Bernard Edward
  Fitzalan-Howard,
  3rd Baron   72
Edward George
  Fitzalan-Howard,
  1st Baron   72
Francis Edward
  Fitzalan-Howard,
  2nd Baron   72

HOWE
Annabella (Scrope)
  431
Bathsheba   750
Emanuel Scrope
  Howe, 2nd
  Viscount   432
George Augustus
  Howe (Gen.), 3rd
  Viscount   432
John Grubham   431
Julia (Alington)   431
Mary   732
Richard William
  Penn Curzon, 1st
  Earl   65
Scrope Howe, 1st
  Viscount   431
Sophie Charlotte
  Maria (von
  Kielmansegge)
  432

HOWEL
family   875

HOWELL
Anne   923
Edward   liv, lxiv,
  cxlix, cli, clxiv, 643

Eleanor (___)   643
Elizabeth (Halsey)
  643
Frances (Paxton)
  643
Henry   643
Josiah   643
Margaret (Hawten)
  643
Martha   858
Mary   471
Mary (Johnes)   643
Phebe   643
Richard   643

HOWELL CLUNN
ap Meyrick   810

HOWES
Elizabeth   567
Mary (Barnardiston)
  567
Samuel   567

HOWIS
Frances   725

HOWLAND
Abigail (Burt)   524
Desire   654
Elizabeth
  (Southworth)   524
Elizabeth (Tilley)
  654, 983
Hope   983
John   654, 926, 983
Joseph   524, 921
Lydia (Bill)   524, 921
Martha (Cole)   524
Nathaniel   524
Nathaniel, Jr.   524
Susan   355, 376,
  394, 524, 921

HOWTH
　Nicholas St. Lawrence, 16th Baron 486
　Thomas St. Lawrence, 1st Earl of 308
　Thomas St. Lawrence, 3rd Earl of 308
　William St. Lawrence, 2nd Earl of 308
HOYLE
　Ann (Debnam) 701
　Edward 701
　Mary (Towneley) 701
　Samuel 701
HOYNINGEN-HUENE (VON)
　Anna (von Stackelberg) 849
　Anna Elisabeth (von Uexküll) 849
　Armin Hagen ["Peter Berlin"], Baron xii, lviii, clii, clv, 850
　Berend Johann 849
　Eduard Friedrich Eberhard 849
　Eduard Rudolf Max, Baron 850
　Emil Bernhard, Baron 850
　Emilie (Versmann) 849
　family 850
　Friedrich Alexander Emil, Baron 856
　Karl Friedrich 849
　Lilli (von Engelhardt) 850
　Marie (von Weymarn), Baroness 850
　Marion (Hagen) 850
HOYT
　Margaret (Bliss) 672
　Margaret Jane 463, 508, 672, 726
　Nathan 672
HOZIER
　Clementine Ogilvy 67, 585, 648
HUARD
　Angélique (Jourdain) 978
　Anne-Marie (Amiot) 972, 973, 977, 978, 980
　Geneviève 978
　Jean 972, 973, 977, 978, 980
　Jean-Baptiste 978
　Jeanne 972
　Marie-Anne 973, 980
　Marie-Jeanne (Jourdain) 977
　Marie-Josèphe 977
　Mathieu 977
HUBBARD (HUBERT)
　Elizabeth [Marie-Élisabeth Wabert] 623
　Jane 463
　Judith (Knapp) xix, lxi, lxiv, lxv, cxliv, clxi, clxxv, 682
　Louise [Louise-Arel Wabert/Ouabard] 623
　Mary (Giddings) (Pearce) 682
　Mary (Rogers?) 682
　Miriam (Howard) 75
　Theodore Bernard Peregrine 75
　Vanessa Mary Teresa 75
　William 682
　William, Jr. (Rev.) 682
HUBERD
　Edward 806
　Elizabeth (Chauncey) 806
　Jane (Southall) 806
　Margaret 806
　Richard 806
HUBERT dit LACROIX
　Marie-Catherine 981
HUDDERSFIELD
　Katherine 547
HUDDLESTON
　Alice 426
　Annette Knowles 79
　Bridget (Cotton) 426
　Elizabeth (Sutton) 426
　Isabel (Neville) 426
　Jane 394

1307

John (Sir) 426
Rachel
  (FitzWilliam) 394
Richard 394
William 426
HUDSON
Anne 551
HUGFORD
Elizabeth
  (Fettiplace) 648
Elizabeth (Rudhall)
  648
John 648
Margaret 648
Margaret (Hugford)
  648
William 648
HUGH
ap Cadwaladr ap
  Rhys 659
ap Gruffudd [Hugh
  Nannau] 229
Capet, King of
  France xxvi, 725,
  866, 868, 870, 872,
  879, 919, 1025
HUGH III
Duke of Burgundy
  642
HUGH MAGNUS
Duke of France and
  Burgundy 835,
  837, 839, 841, 843,
  845, 847
HUGHES
Anne 467
Elizabeth 324
Ellen 651, 652,
  658, 660

family xxxiv
Grisold 362
John 660
**HUGHES/PUGH/
HUGH**
John xlvii, cxliv,
  659
Martha (Caimot)
  659
HUGUETAN
Margareta, Countess
  of Gyldensteen
  140
HULL
Henry 742
Mary xiii
Ursula 742
Ursula (Larder)
  742
William 742
HULTON
Adam 815
Agnes (Legh) 815,
  816
Elena (Hulton) 815
Emma 815
Roger 815, 816
HUMBERT
Madeleine 912
HUME. *see also*
HOME
Bethia (Dundas) 279
Catherine (Falconer)
  257
David 257
Edgar Erskine lviii
Isabel 279
James 279
Joseph 257

HUMPHREY
ap Hugh 510
ap Hywel 229
Plantagenet, Duke
  of Gloucester
  229, 231, 233, 235
HUMPHREY(S)
Alice 864
Anne clxi, 229,
  301, 501, 511
Anthony 864
Benjamin 510
Daniel clxix,
  clxxiv, 510
Eleanor 628
Elizabeth 301, 511
Elizabeth (Medford)
  510
Elizabeth (Pelham)
  108, 301
Elizabeth (Rees)
  510
Elizabeth (Thomas)
  510
Goditha 511
Gwen (Jones)
  (____) 652
Hannah (Wynne)
  510
Jane (Humphrey)
  511
John 511, 652
John (Dep. Gov.)
  108, 301
John, Jr. 301
Joseph 510
Lydia 510
Magdalen
  (Washington) 864

1308

Margaret (Evans) 652
Margaret (Vaughan) 510
Mary (Llewelyn) 510
Owen 510, 511
Robert 652
Samuel 510, 511
Susan (Clinton), Lady 108
HUMPHREY(S)/ OWEN
Rebecca xxiv, clxv, clxxiv, clxxxii, 510, 651
HUMPHRIES
Mary 768
HUNAULT
Lucille 978
HUNGARY
Albert II, Holy Roman Emperor, King of, King of Bohemia 187, 220, 895
Anne (de Foix), Queen of Bohemia and xxv, 287, 615
Anne, Princess of Bohemia and, Holy Roman Empress 40, 43, 54, 56, 192, 287, 290, 615, 891
Bela I, King of 832
Bela IV, King of 621
Constance, Princess of, Queen of Galicia 621

Elizabeth of the Kumans, Queen of 459
Ladislaus V, King of Bohemia and 287, 615
Maria Lascaris, Princess of Byzantium, Queen of 621
Marie, Princess of, Queen of Naples and Sicily 459
Richeza of Poland, Queen of 832, 833
Sophie, Princess of 832
Stephen V, King of 459
HUNGERFORD
Anne 320
Anne (Grey) 323
Anne (Percy) 355, 904, 905
Anthony 312
Bridget 297
Catherine 312
Catherine (Peverell) 570, 824
Edward (Sir) 312, 323
Edward Digby Gerard 312, 313
Eleanor 625
Elizabeth 569, 570, 573
Elizabeth (Baker) 312, 313

Frances (Cocke) 320, 323
Jane (Digby) 312
John (Sir) 297
Katherine clxxxiv
Lucy 396
Margaret 824
Margaret (Botreaux) clxxxiv, 625
Margery (Long) 320
Mary 312, 313, 355, 904, 905
Mary (Berkeley) 297
Mary (Yorke) 323
Rachel (Jones) 312
Robert 320, 323
Robert Hungerford, 2nd Baron clxxxiv, 625
Thomas (Sir) 355, 904, 905
Walter 320
Walter Hungerford, 1st Baron 570, 824
HUNHALL
Elizabeth 845
HUNSDON
Henry Cary, 1st Baron 300
HUNT
Alice 880
Elizabeth 571
Ephraim, Jr. 571
Frances (Paget) 135
Iodena 881
Jane (Ward) 135
Joanna (Alcock) 571

1309

John 881
John Griffiths l, lv, lviii, lix, lx, lxi, lxvii, lxix, lxxi, 398, 507, 720
Magdalen 719
Margaret 553
Margaret (Pecche) 881
Mary 590
Rowland 135
Sarah 136
Sarah (Witts) 135
Thomas 135
Virginia Lloyd 117
HUNTER
Anna Katherine (Gow) 179
Charles 179
Christian 319
Eleanor 508, 726
Elizabeth (Crawford) 214
Elizabeth (Orby) 214
Elizabeth Caroline 305
James 214
Margaret (Spalding) 214
Robert (Gov.) 214
Robert, of Hunterston 214
Sophie Irene xlviii, cliii, 101, 179
HUNTINGDON
David, Prince of Scotland, Earl of 768, 778, 779, 780, 785, 787, 789

Ferdinando Hastings, 6th Earl of 79
Francis Hastings, 2nd Earl of 107
George Hastings, 4th Earl of 107, 109, 111
Henry, Prince of Scotland, Earl of 774, 776, 778, 779, 780, 783, 785, 787, 789
Henry Hastings, 5th Earl of 79
Simon de St. Liz, Earl of, Earl of Northampton 778, 779, 780, 783, 785, 787, 789, 879, 919
Theophilus Hastings, 7th Earl of 79
Waltheof II, Earl of, Earl of Northampton and Northumberland 779, 789, 879, 919
William Herbert, 2nd Earl of Pembroke (1st creation), Earl of 346
HUNTINGFIELD (DE)
Alice (de Senlis/St. Liz) 851, 920
Isabel (FitzWilliam) 851, 920
Roger 851, 920

Sarah 851, 920
William (Sir) 851, 920
HUNTINGTON
Abigail (Lathrop) 921
Hannah (Perkins) 921
Jayne (Sarah Jayne) (Simpson) ix, lviii, 629
John 921
Joshua 921
Lydia 921
Margaret (Barrett) 920
Martha 921
Park William, Jr. 629
HUNTLEY
Melinda 519, 520
HUNTLY
Alexander Gordon, 1st Earl of 176, 281
Alexander Gordon, 3rd Earl of 176, 249
George Gordon, 1st Marquess of 93, 97, 154, 161
George Gordon, 2nd Earl of 176, 223
George Gordon, 2nd Marquess of 154, 155, 156
George Gordon, 4th Earl of 148, 154, 176

George Gordon, 5th
  Earl of 154
HUNYDD
  ferch Eunydd ap
    Gwernwy 815
HUOT
  Marc-Antoine 987
  Marguerite 987
  Marie-Josèphe
    (Robert dite
    Lafontaine) 987
HUSEBY
  Jon Havtoreson,
    Lord of Borregard
    and 452, 457
  Peder Ulfsson, Lord
    of Ervalla and
    457
  Ulv Jonson, Lord of
    Ervalla, Faanoe,
    Vreta, Saeby and
    452, 457
HUSSEY
  Anne (Denne) 739
  Anne (Grey) 351,
    414
  Bridget 351
  Elizabeth xlix, lxi, cl,
    414, 416, 739, 741
  Joanna (___) 739
  John 739
  John (Rev.) 741
  John Hussey, 1st
    Baron 351, 414
  Mary 661
  Mary (Catlin/
    Catelyn) 739
  Mary (Wroth) 739,
    741

Nathaniel 739, 741
Nele 528
Susanna 623
Thomas xlix, lxi,
  cxlix, 739, 741
HUSSON (DE)
  Antoinette (de La
    Trémouille) 634,
    636
  Charles, Count de
    Tonnerre 634
  Madeleine 634
HUSTED
  Helen 4
HUSTON
  Allegra clv, 9
  Anjelica 65
  Enrica "Ricki"
    (Soma) 9, 65
  Jack Alexander
    xvii, clv, 65
  John 9, 65
  Margaret Lavina
    (Cholmondeley)
    65
  Rhea (Gore) 65
  Walter 65
  Walter Anthony 65
HUTCHESON
  Letitia Eleanor 167
HUTCHINSON
  Anne (Marbury)
    xix, xxxv, xlviii,
    clxiii, clxxiii, 478,
    480, 925, 926
  Bridget 480
  Catherine (Hamby)
    xxxv, lxx, clxi,
    clxxvi, 478, 715

Edward 478, 479,
  715
Eliakim 475
Elisha 479, 715
Elizabeth 475, 479,
  715
Elizabeth (Clarke)
  479, 715
Elizabeth (Shirley)
  475
family x
Hannah 479, 716
Hannah (Hawkins)
  479, 715
J. R. xxix
Jack T. ix, lviii, 529
Lydia (Foster) 479,
  715
Susanna 925
Vera 546
William 478, 480,
  925
HUTTOFT
  Elizabeth 476
HUTTON
  Anne (Lascelles)
    698, 699
  Barbara Woolworth
    xviii, 44, 46, 63
  Beatrice 374
  Catherine 321
  Edna (Woolworth)
    44
  Edward 698, 699
  Edward Francis 44
  Franklyn Laws 44
  Juliana 361
  Margaret 698, 699

1311

Marjorie
  Merriweather
  (Post) 44
Nedenia [Dina
  Merrill] 44
HUW
  ab Ieuan 809
  ap Dafydd Fychan
  693
  ap Thomas 659
HUXLEY
  Aldous Leonard
  xvii, lxv, cxliv, 436
  Julia Frances
  (Arnold) 436
  Julian Sorell (Sir)
  436
  Laura (Archera)
  436
  Leonard 436
  Maria (Nys) 436
HUYBERT (DE)
  Anthony Hermansz.
  xxxii, 774
  Cornelia (van der
  Meer van
  Berendrecht) 774
  Helena (van Zyll)
  774
  Herman Anthonisz.
  774
  Lucretia (Rooden-
  burgh) 774
HWFA
  ap Sandde 886
HWFA FYCHAN
  ap Hwfa Gryg 886
HWFA GRYG
  ap Hwfa 886

HYDE
  Abiah 500
  Amphillis 626
  Amphillis
  (Tichborne) 626
  Anne 427
  Anne (Brooke) 427
  Anne, Duchess of
  York 22, 24, 122,
  678, 679, 727, 780,
  781, 782
  Catherine (O'Brien),
  Baroness Clifton
  122
  Edward 427
  Edward (Gov.)
  cxliv, 427
  Edward (Gov.), 3rd
  Earl of Clarendon
  122, 679
  Edward, 1st Earl of
  Clarendon 626,
  678, 780
  Experience (Abell)
  500
  Frances (Aylesbury)
  626, 678, 780
  Henry 678
  Henry, 2nd Earl of
  Clarendon 122
  James 500
  Jane 121
  John 500
  Juliana 382
  Katherine (Rigby)
  427
  Laurence 626
  Mary (Langford) 678
  Phillis (Sneyd) 427

Robert 427
Sarah (Marshall) 500
Theodosia (Capell)
  122
HYLTON
  Mary 717
HYNSON
  Anne 348
HYRNE
  Edward 471
  Elizabeth (Massing-
  berd) 471
HYWEL
  ab Einion 650
  ap Cadwaladr (Hywel
  Fychan) 694
  ap Cynwrig of
  Radur 808
  ap Jenkin 229
  ap Madog 808
  ap Rhys 689
HYWEL FELYN
  ap Gruffudd 810,
  811
HYWEL FYCHAN
  ap Hywel ap
  Gruffudd 659
HYWEL LLWYD
  ap Dafydd o'r Bala
  659
HYWEL VAUGHAN
  ap Gruffudd ap
  Hywel 229
HYWEL Y GADAIR
  ap Madog 693
IBARGUREN
  Carlos F. 996
IBELIN (D')
  family 956

IBRACKAN
 Henry O'Brien,
  Lord 122
IBSEN
 Eleanora 645
 Henrik 645
IDA
 Countess lxiv
IEUAN
 ab Einion 692
 ap Hywel 689
 ap John 410
 ap Maredudd 659, 694
 ap Rhys 808, 810
 ap Rhys Goch 809
 ap Thomas 658
 Gwyn ap James ap Rhys 555
IEUAN GOCH
 ab Ieuan Ddu 808
 ap Dafydd Goch 650, 659, 686, 694
IFOR
 ap Llywelyn 810
IFOR HAEL
 ap Llywelyn 810
IKONNIKOV
 Nicolas xxii, xxvii
ILCHESTER
 Henry Stephen Fox-Strangways, 3rd Earl of 66
ILEANA
 Princess of Roumania (Mother Abbess Alexandra) xviii, xlv, 2, 6

ILIVE/ILIFFE
 Elizabeth 78
ILLIERS (D')
 counts 949
ILPENDAM (VAN)
 Geertruy [Gertrude] Jansdr. 775
ILYINSKI
 Angela Philippa (Kaufman) 4
 Mary Evelyn (Prince) 4
 Paul R. [Paul, Prince Romanovsky-Ilyinski] clvii, 4
IMOGINA
 of Isenburg-Limburg (wife of Adolf I, Holy Roman Emperor) 617
INCHIQUIN
 Dermod O'Brien, 5th Baron 340
 Murrough O'Brien, 4th Baron 340
INGLEBY
 Anne (Neville) 123
 David 123
 Margaret 100
 Mary 123
INGLIS
 Mary 324
 Mary Jane 97
 Sarah 276
INGOLDSBY
 Anthony 748
 Barbara 535
 Dorcas (Bulkeley) 748

 Elizabeth (Cromwell) 534
 George (Sir) 534
 Mary (Gould) 534
 Olive 748
 Richard (Sir) 534
INGOLDSTHORPE
 Isabel 345, 426
INGRAM
 Arthur 389, 390
 Arthur (Sir) 389
 Eleanor (Slingsby) 389, 390
 Elizabeth (Barns) 390
 Isabella 390
 Jane (Mallory) 389
INNES
 Alexander, of Rosieburn 163
 Anne 163
 Christian (Bruce) 163
 Elizabeth 163, 239, 261
 Elizabeth (Gordon) 163
 Elizabeth (Grant) 163
 Grizel (Stewart) 95
 Helen (Strachen) 163
 Jean 95
 Jean (Duff) 163
 Jean (Ross) 95
 John, of Edingight 163
 Katherine 163
 Katherine (Abercromby) 163

Margaret 828
Robert (Sir), 1st Bt. 95
Robert (Sir), 2nd Bt. 95
___, wife of David Robertson of Muirton 219
INNHAUSEN UND KNYPHAUSEN (ZU)
Carl Wilhelm eorg, Count 58
Hyme Friederike Georgine Elisabeth Pauline Johanna Magdalena, Countess 58
Louise Charlotte Sophia Friederike (von Kielmansegge), Countess 58
IORWERTH
ap Hwfa Fychan 886
IPSTONES
Alice 760, 772
Maud (Swinnerton) 760, 772
William (Sir) 760, 772
IRALA (DE)
Ursula 995
IRBY
Anthony (Sir) 115
Elizabeth 115
Frances (Wray) 115
Olive 519, 746
IRELAND
Barbara (Eure) 415
Charles 415

Elizabeth 415
Elizabeth (Eure) 414
Francis 415
Francis (Sir) 414
Isabel (Jessop) 415
James 415
John cxlix, 415
kings of clxxxiii
Margaret 476
Mariana (Webb) 415
Mariana/Marina 415
Mary 415
Ralph 415
Sarah (___) 415
William 415
William de Welles (Sir), Lord Deputy of 486, 488, 545, 546
Winifred 415
IRENE "OF THE EAST"
Princess of Byzantium lxiii, lxvii, 640, 733
IRONMONGER
Bridget (Cordray) 738
Cordray 738
Elizabeth (___) 738
Elizabeth (Jones) 738
family lxiv
Francis clxxvi, 738, 740
Martha 738
Mary (___) (Field) 738
Samuel 738

William clxvii, clxxvi, 738, 740
IRVINE
Anne 225, 283
Anne Elizabeth (Baillie) 225, 283
Charles, of Over Boddam 225
Elizabeth 251
Euphemia (Douglas) 225
John, of Georgia xxxv, l, clxviii, 225, 283
IRWIN
Elizabeth Ramsey 496, 503, 731, 867, 878
May Imelda Josephine 116
ISAAC
Edward 813
Elizabeth 749
Margery (Whetehill) 813
Mary 661, 813
ISAAC II ANGELOS
Emperor of Byzantium 640, 733
ISAAC/YSAC
family 1025
Joanna 456
Matilda (Bruce) 456
Thomas 456
ISAACS
Emma 341

1314

ISABEL/ISABELLA
(de Joigny), Queen
of Norway 452,
457
of Angoulême,
Queen of England
372, 650, 653, 657,
659, 661, 665, 667,
670, 672, 676, 678,
680, 682, 684, 686,
687, 689, 691, 692,
693, 694, 695, 697,
785, 917
of Bourbon 438, 445
of Clermont, Queen
of Naples 186,
189
Countess of Lennox
264
D'Este, of Modena and
Ferrara 186, 189
ferch Rhys Llwyd
582
Princess of Aragón,
Queen of France
459, 941, 961
Princess of Bavaria,
Queen of France
226
Princess of Castile,
Duchess of York
107, 114, 119, 126,
133, 134, 377, 410,
411, 412, 423
Princess of Portugal
438, 445
Princess of Scotland
845

ISABELLA I
Queen of Castile,
Queen of Spain
46, 140
ISDELL
Anne Isabella 433
ISELIN
Eleanor [Nora] 198
ISENBURG-
BUDINGEN
Augusta Marie
Gertrude (von
Hanau und zu
Horowitz), Princess,
Countess von
Schaumburg 13
Ferdinand
Maximilian, Prince
of 13
Gertrude Philippina
Alexandra Marie
Augustine Louise,
Princess of 13
ISENBURG-
LIMBURG
Imogina of (wife of
Adolf I, Holy
Roman Emperor)
617
ISHAM
Anne 711
Anne (Borlase)
710
Euseby (Sir) 710
Henry xix, xxxiv,
xxxvii, xlviii,
clxvii, 387, 710
Katherine (Banks)
(Royall) 387, 710

Mary 387, 710
Mary (Brett) 710
William 710
ISHERWOOD
Christopher
[Christopher
William Bradshaw-
Isherwood] xvii,
liv, clxxiv, 549
ISJASLAW
Grand Prince of
Kiev 849
ISLE (D')-
BOUCHARD
Catherine 634

ISLE OF MAN
Charlotte Murray,
Baroness Strange,
Lady of the 66
ISLES (THE)
Alexander Gordon,
Bishop of, Bishop
of Galloway 148,
940
Fingula of 269,
270, 280, 283, 284
Mary of 789
ISSARESCU
Stefan Virgil 2
ISSY (D')
Agnès 954
ITALY
Adelaide, Arch-
duchess of Austria,
Queen of Sardinia,
Queen of 614
Bernhard, King of
879, 919

1315

Cesare Borgia, Duc de Valentinois, tyrant of 287, 293
Cunigunde of Parma, Queen of 879, 919
Eugène-Rose de Beauharnais, 1st Duke of Leuchtenberg, Viceroy of 442, 443, 444
monarchs of xl, 45, 614, 615
Pepin, King of 879, 919
Victor Emanuel II, King of Sardinia, King of 18, 614

ITHEL
ap Gwrgeneu Fychan 689
King of Gwent 815

IVAN I
Czar of Russia xxii
Grand Prince of Moscow 791, 797

IVAN II
Grand Prince of Moscow 797

IVAN III
"first" Czar of Russia 797

IVAN IV "the TERRIBLE"
Czar of Russia 792

IVAN VI
Czar of Russia 615

IVE
Rose 623

IVEAGH
Edward Cecil Guinness, 1st Earl of 23, 31

IVORY
Anne (Talbot) 130
Barbara 130
John (Sir) 130

IVRY (D') 208
Jacques d'Estouteville, Seigneur de Beyne, Baron 208

IVYE
Elizabeth (Malet) 695
Judith 695, 696
Thomas 695

IWARDBY
Jane 590

IWERYDD
ferch Lewys ap Rhys 811

IZARD. see also SHILLINGFORD alias ISODE/IZARD
Benjamin 717
Dorothy (___) (Smith) 717
Edward 717
Elizabeth (___) 717
Elizabeth (Prior/Pryor) 717
George 717
Grizel (Newdigate) 717
Marian [Mary-Ann] (Greenglass) 717
Mary (___) (Smith) (Middleton) 93, 717
Mary (Blake) 93
Mary (Turgis) 93
Ralph xiv, xlix, cxlix, cli, clxviii, 93, 717
Sarah 93
Walter 93
William 717

IZMALOV
Anna 798

JACKSON
Sarah 902, 903

JACOB
Benjamin 695
Eleanor (Odell) 695
Joseph, Jr. 702
Martha Eleanor 695, 696
Mary (Storrs) 702
Sarah 702

JACOBS
Barbara Annis 402
Juliette Marie Elizabeth (von Rantzow) 891
Marie Louise Rantzow 891
William Stephen 891

JACOBUS
Donald Lines xxvii, xxviii, l, lii, lv, lvi, lviii, lxix, lxxi, 46

JACQUELINE
Princess of Bavaria 229, 231, 233, 235

**JACQUES-
  HONORÉ**
  Grimaldi, Prince of
    Monaco, Marquis
    des Baux   934
JACQUET
  Jean (Jan) Paul   633
  Maria (de Carpentier)
    633
JAGOW (VON)
  Maria Justina
    Dorothea   181
JALAVOUX (DE)
  Guyon de Belvezer,
    Baron, Baron
    d'Oradeur,
    Seigneur de
    Jonchères   200
JAMES
  ab Ieuan Gwyn
    (James ap Rhys)
    555
  Anne   407
  Audrey Evelyn   68
  Bridget (Littleton)
    407
  Duke of Courland
    54, 56
  Elizabeth   708
  Evelyn Elizabeth
    (Forbes)   68
  family   407
  Henry   407
  Katherine (Blux)
    748
  Margaret   317
  Olive (Ingoldsby)
    748
  Ruth (Jones)   748

  Thomas (Rev.)
    lviii, lix, lxix, lxxi,
    clxiv, clxxvi, 748
  William Dodge   68
  ____   166
JAMES (JAIME) I
  King of Aragón
    991, 993
JAMES I
  King of Scotland
    viii, 145, 152, 160,
    173, 176, 222, 223,
    225, 898
  Margrave of Baden
    291
JAMES I and VI
  King of England, VI
    of Scotland   xxv,
    xlv, 35, 38, 47, 49,
    52, 69, 76, 80, 430,
    536, 785
JAMES II
  King of Scotland
    xxv, 145, 148, 154,
    157, 167, 168, 174,
    179, 210, 213, 214,
    215, 216, 218, 219,
    459
JAMES II and VII
  King of England,
    VII of Scotland
    clxxxix, 22, 24,
    122, 536, 615, 627,
    678, 727, 781
JAMES IV
  King of Scotland
    xxv, xxxix, xl, 128,
    143, 146, 148, 150,
    151, 152, 154, 157,

    159, 161, 163, 165,
    166, 167, 168, 170,
    171, 173, 174, 176,
    177, 179, 940
JAMES V
  King of Scotland
    xxv, xxxix, xl, 82,
    85, 87, 88, 90, 92,
    93, 95, 96, 97, 98,
    893, 897
**JAMESON/
  JAMIESON**
  Christina   285
  Margaret   161
JAMYS
  Isabella   743
JANE
  (Grey) Dudley,
    Queen of England
    [Lady Jane Grey]
    xxiv, 69, 80, 477
  (Seymour), Queen
    of England   305,
    705, 741, 855
  ferch Cadwaladr ap
    Maredudd   650,
    651
  ferch Humphrey ap
    Hywel   229
  ferch Maredudd
    694
  ferch Maredudd ab
    Ieuan   650, 660
  ferch Rhys ap
    Gruffudd   687,
    723
  ferch Richard
    Thomas   770

1317

JANET
  ferch Hywel 689
  ferch Owain 824
JANSEN
  Agnes 980
JANSSEN
  Barbara cxlviii, cl, 312, 313
  Mary, Baroness cxlviii, 29
  Theodore (Sir), 1st Bt. 312
  Williamsa (Henley) 312
JAQUET
  Jean (Jan) Paul 633
  Maria (de Carpentier) lxvi, 633
JAROPOLK
  Prince of Vladimir and Turow 849
JARRET
  Catherine-Gabrielle 941
JARVIS
  Elizabeth (Duke) (Bacon) 561
JASON
  Elizabeth 343
JAY
  Augusta 865
  Eliza 865
  family 247
  James 246
  Julia Madeleine 246
  Sarah Jane (Robinson) 246
JEAMES
  family clxxxvi

JEAN
  D'Albret, King of Navarre 287, 293
  Felicité (Dionne) 971
  François-Xavier 971
  Marie-Joséphine 971
  Marie-Louise (Mignot) 971
  Pierre-François 971
JEANES
  Martha 431
JEANNE
  (de Valois), Princess of France 459
  Princess of Navarre 963
JEFFERSON
  Jane (Randolph) 387, 711, 822
  Martha (Wayles) (Skelton) xliii, 387, 711, 823
  Mary 387, 711, 823
  Mary (Branch) 822
  Mary (Field) 822
  Peter 387, 711, 822
  Thomas 822
  Thomas, 3rd U.S. President 387, 711, 823, 912
  Thomas, Jr. 822
JEFFERYES
  Albinia Frances 341
  Anne (Brodrick) 341
  Arabella (Fitzgibbon) 341

  James 341
  James St. John 341
JEFFREYS
  Charlotte (Herbert) 226
  Edward Miller lix
  Henrietta Louisa 226
  Herbert (Gov.) (Sir) lix, 541
  Jane (Berkeley) 541
  John Jeffreys, 2nd Baron 226
  Susanna (___) 541
  William 541
JEKYLL
  Elizabeth 830
JELIHORVAKY
  Vera 111
JELOWICKA
  Marie 622
JENKIN
  Alice (Herbert) 808
  Elizabeth 582, 808
  William 808
JENKINS
  (Narcissa) Florence (Foster) 364
JENKINSON
  Louisa Theodosia (Hervey) 334
  Robert Banks, 2nd Earl of Liverpool (Prime Minister) 334
JENNA/JENNER
  Catherine 832

JENNEY
  Anne (Reade) 489
  Arthur 489
  Arthur (Sir) 489
  Ela (Jernegan) 489
  Francis 489
  Helen (Stonard) 489
  Isabel 489, 711
  Margaret clxxxvii, 588
JENNINGS
  Catherine 822
  Edmund (Act. Gov.) xxxiv, xlvii, liii, clxvii, 127, 607
  Edmund (Sir) 127, 607
  Elizabeth 127
  family xi
  Frances (Corbin) 607
  Margaret (Barkham) 127, 607
  Sarah 71, 75
JEPHSON
  Elizabeth (Norris/Norreys) 428
  John (Sir) 428
  Mary cxliv, 428, 466
JERMY
  Christian (Bigod) 845, 846
  Elizabeth 297, 845
  Elizabeth (Hunhall) 845
  Elizabeth (Wroth) 845
  Ellen (Lampett) 845
  family 846

  Isabel (St. Aubin) 845, 846
  Joan (Halys) 845
  John 845
  John (Sir) 845
  Margaret (Multney) 845
  Thomas (Sir) 845
  William (Sir) 845
JERMYN
  Jane 350
  John 350
  Mary (Tollemache) 350
  Sarah (Stephens) 350
  Susan 349
  Thomas 350
JERNEGAN
  Anne 596
  Anne (Tassell) 490
  Bridget 490
  Bridget (Drury) 489, 596
  Ela 489
  Ela (Spelman) 489
  Elinor (__) [Wentworth?] 489
  Elizabeth (Thompson) 489
  family xlvii
  George 489, 490
  John (Sir) 489, 490, 596
  Penelope 489
  Thomas xlix, lxviii, cxliv, 489, 490

JERNINGHAM
  Anne (Blount) 110
  Catherine (__) 110
  Charlotte Georgiana 23
  Frances (Dillon) 23
  Frances Henrietta (Sulyarde) 23
  Francis (Sir), 3rd Bt. 110
  George William, 2nd Baron Stafford 23
  Henry xlvi, cxliv, 110
  Henry (Sir), 2nd Bt. 110
  Mary (Hall) 110
  Mary (l'Espine) 110
  William (Sir), 6th Bt., 1st Baron Stafford 23
JÉRÔME
  Bonaparte, King of Westphalia, Prince of Montfort xl, 858
JEROME
  Aaron 584, 647
  Aurora (Murray) 584, 647
  Clarissa (Hall) 584, 648
  Elizabeth (Ball) 584, 647
  Isaac 584, 648
  Jennie 63, 584, 585, 648
  Leonard Walter 584, 648

JERSEY
  George Bussy
    Villiers, 4th Earl of
    72
  William Villiers, 3rd
    Earl of 72
JERUSALEM
  Berengaria, Princess
    of León and Castile,
    Queen of, Empress
    of Constantinople
    647, 909, 948, 964
  Henry II, Count of
    Champagne, King
    of 943
  Isabella of Anjou,
    Queen of, Countess
    of Champagne 943
  John de Brienne,
    King of, Emperor of
    Constantinople
    647, 909, 945, 948,
    964
  John I, titular King
    of, titular King of
    Cyprus and
    Armenia 442
  Louis II, King of
    Naples, Sicily,
    Aragón, and 205
  Marie of Châtillon-
    Blois, Queen of
    Naples, Sicily,
    Aragón, and 205
JESSOP
  Isabel 415
JESTER
  Annie Lash liii

JETTÉ
  Marie-Marguerite
    974
  René xii, 939, 941,
    951, 953, 959, 967
JEVON
  Anne 348
JEWETT
  David 630, 886
  Deborah (Lord)
    630, 886
  Elizabeth 630, 886
  Joseph 630, 886
  Mary (Hibbert)
    630, 886
  Nathan 630, 886
  Sarah 126
  Sarah (Selden)
    630, 886
JOACHIM I
  Elector of
    Brandenburg 181,
    182, 184
JOACHIM ERNEST
  Prince of Anhalt-
    Zerbst 184
JOAN
  (Beaufort), Queen of
    Scotland xxv, 152,
    160, 173, 176, 219,
    222, 223, 225, 241,
    249, 256, 261, 273,
    278, 280, 283, 898
  (Stewart), Princess
    of Scotland, "the
    dumb lady" 173,
    222, 223, 225, 898
  of Dammartin,
    Countess of

    Ponthieu, Queen of
    Castile 951
  ferch Evan Lloyd
    Fychan 233
  ferch Ieuan ap
    Gwilym Fychan
    410
  ferch Madog 811
  Plantagenet, "The
    Fair Maid of
    Kent," Princess
    Dowager of Wales
    107, 400, 515, 600
  Plantagenet of Acre,
    Princess of England
    xxxix, 466, 483, 489,
    491, 495, 505, 508,
    514, 528, 536, 547,
    565, 567, 575, 577,
    584, 587, 590, 592,
    594, 606, 607, 615
JOANNA
  of Aragón, Queen of
    Naples 186
  Archduchess of
    Austria, Grand
    Duchess of
    Tuscany 192
  of Hainault 459
  of Juliers 459
  Princess of Aragón,
    Queen of Naples
    189
  Princess of Baden-
    Durlach 40
  Princess of France,
    Queen of Navarre
    287, 293, 455

Princess of Navarre 455
Princess of Navarre, Duchess of Brittany, Queen of England 186, 226, 229, 231, 233, 235, 287, 293
JOHN
  ab Edward cxc
  ab Edward [John Edwards] 660
  ab Evan 651, 652
  ab Ieuan ab Owain 231
  ap Gruffudd [John Nannau] 229
  ap Jenkin Elliot 874
  ap Maredudd 657, 659, 689, 694
  ap Maredudd Llwyd 686
  ap Roger 811
  de Brienne, King of Jerusalem, Emperor of Constantinople 647, 909, 945, 948, 964
  Duke of Bavaria-Munich 451
  Duke of Burgundy 438
  Gainor 651
  of Gaunt, Prince of England, Duke of Lancaster xxxix, 295, 300, 314, 324, 331, 337, 339, 345, 357, 366, 368, 370, 375, 382, 387, 393, 395, 396, 397, 398, 400, 403, 405, 407, 413, 417, 419, 421, 426, 427, 429, 433, 434, 900, 902
  Hugh clxxxiii, clxxxviii
  Jane 651, 652, 694
  Jane (Pugh or Hughes) 652, 660
  Margaret 651, 652, 659
  William 652, 660
JOHN "LACKLAND"
  King of England vii, x, xxvi, xxxii, xxxix, 372, 650, 652, 653, 657, 659, 661, 665, 667, 670, 672, 674, 676, 678, 680, 682, 684, 686, 687, 689, 691, 692, 693, 694, 695, 696, 697, 699, 709, 785, 917
JOHN I
  (de Lusignan), titular King of Cyprus, Jerusalem, and Armenia 442
  Count of Egmont 291, 459
  Count of Nassau-Dillenburg 194
  Count Palatine of Zweibrücken 43, 56
  Duke of Berry 205, 440
  Duke of Bourbon 205, 440
  Duke of Mazovia 621
  King of Denmark 141, 181, 182, 184
JOHN I COMNENUS
  Emperor of Byzantium 956
JOHN II
  Count of Egmont 291
  Count of Hainault 459
  Count Palatine of Simmern 291
  Count Palatine of Zweibrücken 56
  Duke of Brittany 442, 633, 942, 946, 963
  Duke of Schleswig-Holstein-Sonderburg 889
  King of France 186, 189, 205, 287, 293, 438, 440, 442, 445
  Lord of Egmont 459
  Prince of Anhalt-Zerbst 181, 182, 184
JOHN III
  King of Sweden 267, 453, 889, 890, 893
JOHN IV
  King of Portugal 140

JOHN V
  Duke of Brittany
    226, 293
  Duke of Saxe-
    Lauenburg 52
JOHN VI
  Duke of Brittany
    226
JOHN ADOLF
  Duke of Holstein-
    Gottorp 47, 49
JOHN CASIMIR
  Count of Nassau-
    Weilberg 184
  Count Palatine of
    Zweibrücken-Klee-
    berg 43
JOHN CICERO
  Elector of
    Brandenburg 220
JOHN FREDERICK
  Margrave of
    Brandenburg-
    Anspach 40
JOHN GEORGE I
  Elector of Saxony
    47, 891
JOHN SIGISMUND
  Elector of
    Brandenburg 54
JOHN WILLIAM
  Duke of Saxe-
    Eisenach 43
JOHNES
  Mary 643
JOHN/JONES
  Robert 652
JOHNSON
  Ada May (Rich) 424

Allegra G. A.
  (Mostyn-Owen)
  12
Anne 487, 488
Anne (___) 488
Anne (Warren) 487
Annie 166
Arbella (Clinton),
  Lady 108
Boris (Alexander
  Boris de Pfeffel) 12
Caleb xx
Catherine (Nangle)
  488
Catherine
  (Weissenburg)
  487
Charles Robert 488
Charlotte (Fawcett)
  12
Christopher 487
Clarence Irwin 424
Daniel, Jr., Premier
  of Québec 969
Edward (Capt.)
  639
Elizabeth 582, 811
family xl, liii, lxiv
Gideon, Jr. 833
Guy clxxiii, 487,
  488, 900
Hannah 589
Irene (Williams)
  12
Isaac 108
Jane "Jincey" 833
John 488
Laraine [Laraine
  Day] 424

Lee 979
Louisa Catherine
  375, 393
Maria 130
Marina Claire
  (Wheeler) 12
Mary (Johnson)
  487, 488, 900
Mary Baker (de
  Graffenried) 833
Mary Louisa 639
Pierre-Marc, Premier
  of Québec 969
Rosalie Morris 805
Samuel (Dr.) 90, 150
Stanley Patrick clv,
  12
Susanna 541
Wilfred [Osman Ali
  Wilfred Kemal] 12
Will xlix, lix, 125,
  247
William (Sir), 1st
  Bt. clxxiii, 487,
  488, 900
William Perry liv,
  lix
JOHNSTON
  Barbara 787
  Charles clv, 111
  Christopher lix
  Edith Duncan lix
  Georgiana Barbara
    (Hay) 111
  Gideon (Rev.) 430
  Henrietta (de
    Beaulieu) (Dering)
    [Henrietta Johnston]
    v, lxvii, cxliv, 430

Phebe 317
Rachel 273
Vera (Jelihorvaky) 111
William 111
JOHNSTONE
Barbara 155
Euphan (Scott) clxiv, clxxix, 276
Freda 80
Isabel 156
John 276
JOIGNY (DE)
Amicie (de Montfort) 954
Gaucher II, Seigneur de Château-Renard 954
Isabel, Queen of Norway 452, 457
Pernelle 954
JOINER
Sarah 821
JOLIE
Angelina [Angelina Jolie Voight Miller Thornton Pitt] 967, 974
JOLIFFE
Anne 138
Benjamin 138
Margaret (Skinner) 137
Mary (Joliffe) 138
Thomas 137
JONCHÈRES (DE)
Béatrix 226
Guyon de Belvezer, Baron de Jalavoux

and d'Oradeur, Seigneur 200
JONCOURT (DE)
Marie 634
JONES
Anne (Bluet) 340
Cadwal(l)ader 340, 652, 727, 809
Charlotte (Coursolles) 655
Dorothy (Walker) xi, xlix, cxliv, clxvii, clxxvi, 706
Eleanor (Evans) 690
Elisha 655
Elizabeth 738, 809
Elizabeth (Creswick) 340
Elizabeth (ferch Humphrey ap Thomas) 690
Ellen (Jones) 809
Ellen/Ellinor 690
Ephraim 655
family 362
Frances 105
Frances (Baldwin) (Townshend) xi, xlix, liii, liv, cxlvii, clxviii, clxxxii, 727
Frances (Hopton) 312
Gainor (Lloyd) 652
Gainor (Penrhyn) 233
Gilbert 233
Gwen 652
Hannah 252
Hannah (Eaton) 252

Hannah (Francis) 340
Hannah (Price) 651, 658
Howard Edward 361
Hugh lvi, cxc, 660
Humphrey 233
Jane (Edward) 651, 652
Jerry E. 330
Joan (Moore) 233
John 340, 651, 690
Joyce 515
Katherine 809
Kittie 901
Marianna 102
Martha 651
Martha (Ironmonger) 738
Martha (Smith) 340
Mary liv, lx, cxlix, cli, clxv, clxxi, 149, 231, 233, 515, 526, 655, 725
Mary (Allen) 655
Mary (Clarke) (Cranston) 468
Mary (Littleton) 233
Penelope 264
Philip 468
Rachel 312
Rees 651, 658
Rice 312
Richard 727
Robert lvi, clxv, clxxx, 652, 738, 809
Roger (Capt.) 706, 707, 831

1323

Rosalinde Maud 362
Rosa(linde) Zeiman
  (Smith) 361, 362
Ruth 748
Sarah 307, 555, 769
Sophia 655
Thomas 690, 809
William 340
William (Dep. Gov.)
  252
JONET
  ferch Gwilym ap
  Llywelyn Llwyd
  686
JONET ANWYL
  ferch Thomas ap
  Morus 692
JONSON
  Agnes (Haakons-
  dotter) 452, 457,
  458
  Havtore 452, 457,
  458
  Ulv, Lord of
  Ervalla, Faanoe,
  Vreta, Saeby and
  Huseby 452, 457
JOPLIN(G)
  Arthur 698, 699
  Janis Lyn 698
  Margaret (Hutton)
  698, 699
  Mary (Featherstone-
  halgh) 698, 699
  Ralph cxlix, 698,
  699
  Robert 698, 699
JORDAN
  Cecily (____) 343

Hannah 506, 728
Marion 54
Mrs. (Dorothy
  Bland) (mistress of
  William IV, King
  of Great Britain) 9
JØRGENSDATTER
  Kirsten Barbara 646
JOSEPH
  Bonaparte, King of
  Spain 83
JOSEPH I
  Holy Roman
  Emperor 20
JOSÉPHINE
  (Marie-Josèphe-Rose)
  (de Tascher de la
  Pagerie) (de Beau-
  harnais) Bonaparte,
  Empress of the
  French 292, 442,
  443, 444
JOSIAS
  Count of Walbeck
  181
JOSLIN
  Alice (Woods) 520
  Esther 520
  Peter 520
JOSSELYN
  Henry (Dep. Gov.)
  852
  Jane 710
  John clxxvii, clxxx,
  852
  Margaret (____)
  (Cammock) 852
  Theodora (Cooke)
  852

Thomas (Sir) 852
JOURDAIN
  Angélique 978
  Marie-Jeanne 977
JOY
  Agnes Elizabeth
  Winona Leclerq
  [Princess Salm-
  Salm] xlv, 30, 38
JOYEUSE (DE)
  François, Seigneur
  de Champigneulle
  944
  Jean, Seigneur de
  Champigneulle
  944
  Louise 944
  Marguerite (de
  Brabançon) 944
  Nicole (des
  Ancherins) 944
  Nicole-Françoise
  (de Beauvais) 944
  Robert, Count of
  Grandpré 944
JUDITH
  of Bohemia, Queen of
  Poland 791, 797,
  802
  of Brandenburg
  449, 451
JULIANA
  of Nassau-Dillenburg
  182, 196
  Queen of The
  Netherlands 1, 47
JULIERS
  Joanna of 459
  Margaret of 451, 459

William III, Duke of 451
William III, Duke of, Duke of Cleves and Berg 40, 43, 54, 56, 891
William V, Duke of 459
William VI, Duke of 459

JULIUS II
Pope [Giuliano della Rovere] 192

JULIUS PETER HERMANN AUGUST
Count of Lippe-Biesterfeld 47

JUNNER
Sarah 102

JUNOSHA-BELIN-SLAVA (JUNÒSZA-BIELINSKA)
Julia 14

JUNOT
Caroline-Louise-Marguerite (Grimaldi), Princess of Monaco 934
Philippe 934

JUSTICE
Alfred Rudolph lix

JUSTICE (LE)
Matilda 877

JUVAINVILLE (DE)
Loup de Terragon, Seigneur 948

JUVIGNY (DE)
Jeanne 957

KANN
Lilli 57

KARACHEV
Mstislav, Prince 802

KARACHEV AND KOZELAK
Tite, Prince 802

KARADJORJEVIC
Elizabeth, Princess of Yugoslavia 3
Paul, Prince Regent of Yugoslavia 3

KARELLA
Marina 3

KARINA
Anna [Hanne Karin Blarke Bayer/Beyer] 635

KARL (CHARLES) I
Emperor of Austria 201, 800

KARL PIUS MARIA ADELGONDE BLANKA LEOPOLD IGNAZ RAPHAEL MICHAEL SALVATOR KYRILL ANGELUS BARBARA
Archduke of Austria, Prince of Tuscany 6

KARL SALVATOR
Archduke of Austria, Prince of Tuscany 6

KASSIMOWSKY
Domma, Princess 799

KATHARINA/ KATHARINE/ KATHERINE
(Howard), Queen of England 339, 605
de Valois, Princess of France, Queen of England, wife of Owen Tudor 226, 603, 813, 824
of Görz 451
Princess of Brunswick-Lüneburg 52, 449, 451
Princess of Brunswick-Wolfenbüttel 52
Princess of Saxe-Lauenburg, Queen of Sweden 51, 52, 53, 889
Princess of Saxony 52

KATHERINE/JEAN/ ELIZABETH
Princess of Scotland 275, 276, 282, 285

KATZENELNBOGEN
Ottilie of 291

KAUFHOLZ
Anna Justina (Kuehle) 449
C. Frederick (Charles Frederick), Jr. xxii, lix, 450

Catharina Elisabeth
 (Bauer) 450
Charles Frederick
 450
Elizabeth
 (Trautman) 450
Ernst Philipp
 Wilhelm 449
family lix, 449
Frederick Gottlieb
 450
Friedrich Georg
 clv, 450
Grace Maud (Worst)
 450
Mary (Roth) 450
KAUFMAN
Angela Philippa 4
KAVANAGH
Sabina
 MacMorough 601
___ MacMorough
 601
KAY
Elizabeth 701
Elizabeth (Strother)
 421
Elizabeth Ann
 (Clinkscales) 422
Grace (Elgin) 421
James 421
James, Jr. 422
Mary 422
Robert 421
KAYE
Anna (Tyrwhit) 719
Anne (Flower) 374
Dorothy
 (Mauleverer) 374
Edward 719, 720
family 720
Grace 374, 837
John 374
Lucy 481, 719, 720
Robert 374
KEARNEY
Mary Ann 726
KEATE
Anne cxci
KEAYNE
Anne (Mansfield)
 318
Robert 318
**KEGLEVICH VON
BUZIN**
August, Count 35
Augusta, Countess
 35
KEITH
Agnes 93, 95, 97,
 250, 252, 256
Alexander (Sir), 2nd
 Bt. 223
Annabel/Agnes
 154
Anne (Newbury)
 223
Elizabeth 148, 154,
 176, 223, 255
Elizabeth (Douglas)
 223, 898
Elizabeth (Hay) 223
George, 4th Earl
 Marischal 223
Giles/Egidia 255,
 261, 266, 267, 268
James (Sir), of
 Benholm 223
Jean 898
Jean (Smith) 223
Margaret (Banner-
 man) 223
Margaret (Keith) 93,
 95, 97, 154, 223
Margaret (Lindsay)
 223
Margaret (Ogilvy)
 223
Rebecca 273
Robert, Lord 223,
 898
William (Sir), 1st
 Bt. 223
William (Sir), 3rd
 Bt. 223
William (Sir), 4th
 Bt. (Gov.) 223
William (Sir), of
 Ludquhairn 223
William, 3rd Earl
 Marischal 93, 95,
 97, 154, 223
William, Lord 223
KELKE
Anne 343
Cecily 343
Christopher 327,
 343
Elizabeth (at See) 343
Elizabeth (Carr) 343
Isabel (Girlington)
 327, 343
Jane (St. Paul) 343
Roger 343
Thomasine (Skerne)
 343
William 343

KELLAWAY
  Agatha (Eltonhead)
    clxvi, clxxiii, 484,
    491, 498, 551
  William 498
KELLER VON
SCHLEITHEIM
  Anna 832
KELLEY
  David Humiston ix,
    li, lv, lix, clxxxiii,
    clxxxv, 372
  Rachel 921
KELLY
  Grace Patricia
    [Princess Grace of
    Monaco] 934
KEMAL
  Osman Ali Wilfred
    [Wilfred Johnson]
    12
KEMBLE
  Frances Anne
    "Fanny" 382
  Margaret 110
  Richard 643
KEMEYS
  Abby (Greene) 548
  Alice (Thomas) 548
  Edward 548, 549
  Elizabeth (Thornton)
    548
  Elizabeth Thornton
    548
  Gertrude (Bleecker)
    548
  Hannah (Fowler)
    548
  Jane 311

  Joan (Lewis) 548
  Laura Sparkes
    (Swing) 548
  Lewis 548
  Margaret (Morgan)
    548
  Mary (____) 548
  Mary (Witty) 548
  Nicholas 548
  William clxxiv, 548
KEMP(E)
  Alice (____) 922
  Amy 470
  Amy (Moyle) 491
  Anne 475, 491
  Beatrix (Lewknor)
    920, 922
  Bridget (____) 484
  Catherine (Cheney)
    491
  Dorothy 491, 492
  Dorothy (Harris) 483
  Dorothy (Thompson)
    347, 470, 491
  Edmund 484
  Edward 484, 491
  Eleanor (Browne)
    491
  Elizabeth (Wilmot)
    491
  Elizabeth (Wormeley)
    483, 551
  family liv, lxii
  Frances 491
  Jane (Browne) 484
  John 484
  John, Archbishop of
    York and Canter-
    bury 920, 922

  Mary 347
  Mary (Oglander) 491
  Matthew 484
  Richard (Act. Gov.)
    xlvii, 483, 484, 551
  Robert 483
  Robert (Sir), 1st Bt.
    484
  Thomas 491, 920
  Thomas (Sir) 347,
    470, 491, 922
  Thomas, Bishop of
    London 922
  William (Sir) 491,
    922
KEMPSON
  Beatrice Hamilton
    (Ashwell) 246
  Eric William
    Edward 246
  family 247
  Frederick Robertson
    246
  Julia Madeleine (Jay)
    246
  Rachel 246
KEMPTON
  Margaret (Gwyn)
    773
KENDAL
  John de Foix, 1st
    Earl of xiv, xxv,
    287, 615
KENDALL
  Anne 742
  Catherine 628
  Jane (Holand) 400
  Jane (Rous) 400
  John 400

1327

Katherine (Munday) 400
Lawrence 400
Mary 400
Walter 400
KENDRICK
Abigail (Bowen) 582, 811
Anna 582, 811
Benjamin 582, 811
Caleb 582, 811
Sarah (Harris) 582, 811
KENNAWAY
Joyce Christabel 120
KENNEDY
Agnes (Borthwick) 253
Agnes (Kennedy) 253
Alexander (Sir), of Culzean 253
Alexander, of Craigoch and Kilhenzie 253
Anna (Crawford) 253
Archibald cxc, 240, 253
Archibald, 11th Earl of Cassillis 253
Caroline Bouvier 915
Catherine xii, lvii, cl, 243, 898
Cecilia 152
David, 1st Earl of Cassillis 253

David, of Kirkmichael 128
Edward Moore (Sen.) 26, 564, 914
Elizabeth 351
Elizabeth (Makgill) 253
Elizabeth (Montgomery) 239, 253
Eunice Mary 26, 564, 914
family lx, cxci
Gilbert 898
Gilbert (Rev.), of Girvan 898, 899
Gilbert, 2nd Earl of Cassillis 253
Gilbert, 3rd Earl of Cassillis 82, 253, 897, 898
Gilbert, 4th Earl of Cassillis 898
Gilbert Kennedy, 1st Baron 239, 240, 243, 253
Helen (Smith) cxci
Henrietta (Whiteford) 128
Hew (Hon.) 898
Iain cxc
Isabel (Campbell) 253
Jacqueline Lee (Bouvier) [Jackie Kennedy Onassis] xl, xlii, xliii, xlvi, 16, 74, 914, 915

James (Sir), of Dunure 239, 240, 243, 253
Janet 82, 84, 85, 87, 92, 98, 151, 170, 239, 897
Jean Ann 26, 564, 914
John Fitzgerald, 35th U.S. President xlii, 16, 26, 53, 564, 914, 915
John Kennedy, 2nd Baron 239, 253
Joseph Patrick 26, 564, 914
Joseph Patrick (III) 26, 564, 914
Joseph Patrick (IV) 26, 564, 915
Katharine (M'Dowell) 898
Katherine (Maxwell) 239, 243, 253
Kathleen 26
Margaret (Kennedy) 82, 253, 897, 898
Margaret (Lyon) 898
Mary (Stewart) (Douglas), Princess of Scotland 239, 240, 241, 243, 245, 248, 250, 251, 252, 253, 254, 255, 257, 258, 260, 261, 266, 267, 268, 940
Mary (Walter) (Schuyler) 253

Mary Primrose 128
Patricia Helen 26,
 564, 914
Patrick Joseph 26,
 564, 914
Robert Francis (Sen.),
 U.S. Attorney- Gen.
 26, 564, 914
Tessa Georgina 77
Thomas (Rev.) 898
Thomas (Sir), of
 Culzean 253
William lx, cxliv,
 cxc
___ (Montgomery)
 898
___ (Mussam) 253
KENNON
Elizabeth (Worsham)
 xiv
Mary xiv
Richard xiv
KENRICK
Edward 376
Elizabeth 750
Elizabeth (Lodge)
 750
family 376
John 376, 750
Mary (Quarrell) 376
Matthew 750
Rebecca (Percival)
 750
Samuel Savage 376
Sarah 367, 376
Sarah (Hamilton)
 376
Sarah (Savage) 376

KENT
Anthony Grey, 9th
 Earl of 901
David L. li, lix, 826
Edmund Grey, 1st
 Earl of 351, 352,
 414, 901
Edmund Holand, 4th
 Earl of xxv, 377,
 410, 423
Edmund Plantagenet
 of Woodstock,
 Prince of England,
 1st Earl of 515,
 600
Edward, Prince of
 Great Britain,
 Duke of 45
George Grey, 2nd
 Earl of 351, 414,
 901
Henry Grey, 10th
 Earl of 901
Joan Plantagenet,
 "The Fair Maid
 of," Dowager
 Princess of Wales
 107, 400, 515, 600
Thomas Holand, 1st
 Earl of 107, 400,
 515, 600
Thomas Holand,
 2nd Earl of xxv,
 515, 600
KENYON
Edward Ranulph
 592
Frances Margaret
 592

John Robert 592
Katherine Mary
 McCrea (DeButts)
 592
Louise Charlotte
 (Lloyd) 592
Mary Eliza
 (Hawkins) 592
Thomas 592
KEPPEL
Alice Frederica
 (Edmonstone)
 [Mrs. Alice
 Keppel] 655
Anne (Lennox) 25
Elizabeth 25
George (Hon.) 655
Sonia Rosemary
 655
William Anne, 2nd
 Earl of Albemarle
 25
William Coutts, 7th
 Earl of Albemarle
 655
KER
Frances Catherine
 465
Isabel 166
Jean 174
KERALDANET (DE)
Marie 943
KERDESTON
Elizabeth (de la
 Pole) 615
family 291
Margaret xiv, xxv,
 lvii, lxviii, 287,
 289, 615, 616

Thomas (Sir) 615
KERMAN (DE)
 Donatien de Maillé,
  Marquis 227
 Henri de Maillé,
  Marquis 226
KEROUAC
 Clementine (Bernier)
  971
 Edie (Parker) 971
 Édouard 971
 Gabrielle (Lévesque)
  971
 Jean Louis LeBris
  "Jack" 967, 971
 Jean-Baptiste 971
 Joan (Harvey) 971
 Leon-Alcide 971
 Séverine (Malenfant)
  971
 Stella (Sampas) 971
KÉROUALLE (DE)
 Guillaume de
  Penancoët,
  Seigneur 226
KERPEN (VON)
 Margarethe 804
KERR
 Katherine 241
 Louisa 31
 Margaret 210, 285
KERRILL
 Elizabeth 755
 Mary (Dalison) 755
 Thomas 755
KERRY
 John Forbes (Sen.),
  Secretary of State
  xli, 923

Richard John 923
 Rosemary Isabel
  (Forbes) 923
  ___ 565
KESSEL (VON)
 Catharina 459
KESTELL
 Frances 836
 Frances (Harris)
  836
 Thomas 836
KEVELIOC
 Hugh, 3rd Earl of
  Chester 778, 780,
  785, 787, 789, 806,
  807, 813, 815, 817,
  819, 821, 822, 824,
  826
KEVERELL
 family clxxxvi
KEY
 Anne Arnold (Ross)
  333
 Anne Phoebe
  Charlton 333
 Anne Phoebe Penn
  (Dagworthy) 333
 family xxiv
 Francis 333
 Francis Scott 333
 John Ross 333
KEYES
 Azalea Caroline 893
 Phebe 54
KEYNES (DE)
 Alice (de Mankesy)
  851, 920
 Joan 851, 920
 Richard 851, 920

Sarah (de Hunting-
  field) 851, 920
KEYSERLINGK
(VON)
 Emilie Alexandrine
  (von Dönhoff),
  Countess 223
 Friederike Caroline
  Alexandrine Emma,
  Countess 224
 Helen (Gibson) 223
 Otto Alexander
  Heinrich Dietrich,
  Count 223
 Otto Ernst, Count
  223
KHEVENHÜLLER
ZU FRANKEN-
BURG (VON)
 Maria Josepha
  Franziska Anna
  Judith Walpurga
  Magdalena,
  Countess 187
KHILKOV
 Andrei, Prince 798
 Anna (Lopuchin)
  799
 Dimitri, Prince 798
 Domma (Kassimow-
  sky), Princess 799
 Fedor, Prince 798
 Irina (Volkonsky),
  Princess 799
 Irina, Princess 792,
  798
 Ivan, Prince 799
 Jakov (Jacob),
  Prince 799

Praskovya, Princess 799
Vassili, Prince 798, 799
Youri, Prince 799
KHOLMSKY
Anna, Princess 791
Daniel, Prince 791
Vassilissa (Vsevo-lodje), Princess 791
KHOVRINE
Eudoxia 797
KHVOROSTININE
Anastasia, Princess 794
Elena (Lykov-Obolensky), Princess 792, 795
Fedor, Prince 792
Maria, Princess 792, 794
KIDD
Charles ix, xxix, lix
KIDDER
Susan 114
KIELMANSEGGE (VON)
Charlotte Wilhelmine Hedwig (von Spörcken), Baroness 58
Friederike Charlotte Sabine Wilhelmine (von dem Bussche-Lohe) 58
Friedrich, Count 58
Friedrich Otto Gott-hardt, Count 58

George Ludwig, Baron 58
Johann Adolf, Baron 58, 432
Louise Charlotte Sophia Friederike, Countess 58
Melusina Agnes (von Spörcken), Baroness 58
Sophie Charlotte (von Platen and Haller-mund), Countess of Leinster and Darlington 58, 432
Sophie Charlotte Marie 432
KIESENWETTER (VON)
Ernestine Adelaide (Reuss-Köstritz), Countess 141
Ernst Philip 141
Irmgard liii, cliv, 141, 641
KIESLER
Hedwig Eva Maria [Hedy Lamarr] xvii, clvi, 98
KIEV
Alexander Nevsky, Grand Prince of, Grand Prince of Vladimir 791, 797
Alexander Olelko, Prince of 621
Anne of, Queen of France 739, 778, 780, 783, 785, 787,

789, 835, 837, 839, 841, 843, 845, 847, 957
Isjaslaw, Grand Prince of 849
Michael (St.), Prince of Chernigov, Grand Prince of 791, 797, 802
Rurik, Lord of 795
Vsevelod III, Grand Prince of 791, 797, 802
KILDARE
Gerald FitzGerald, 8th Earl of 340, 601
Gerald FitzGerald, 9th Earl of 340
Gerald FitzGerald, 11th Earl of 340
Thomas FitzGerald, 7th Earl of 601
KILLEEN
Christopher Plunkett, 2nd Baron 486
KILLEN
Judith Balfour 177
KILLIGREW
Anne 417, 427
Dorothy 305
Elizabeth 296, 665
Jane (Petit) (Trevanion) 665
John 665
KILLKENY
Christiana 433
KILMARNOCK
William Boyd, 1st Earl of 131

1331

William Boyd, 2nd
  Earl of   131
William Boyd, 3rd
  Earl of   131
William Boyd, 4th
  Earl of   131
KILMOREY
Robert Needham,
  1st Viscount   561
KING
Ann Robinson   lix,
  281
Anne   115
Anne (Ayscough)
  115
Anne (Roberts)   563
Bridget (Neville)   115
Caroline Maria   144
Dorothy Ayer (Gardner)   630, 655, 887
Edward   115
Elizabeth   563, 714
Elizabeth Jane   925
Frances   308
Frances (Folliott)
  64, 308
Frances (Gore)   308
George Harrison Sanford   lvi, lvii, lix, lxii
Henry (Sir), 3rd Bt.
  308
Isabella   308
Isabella (Wingfield)
  308
Joel   925
Leslie Lynch   630,
  655, 887
Leslie Lynch, Jr.
  [Pres. Gerald

Rudolph Ford, Jr.]
  631, 655, 868, 887
Lucy (Pierce)   925
Martha (Goddard)
  563, 564
Mary   64
Mary (Middlemore)
  115
Neville   115
Richard   563
Robert (Sir)   64, 308
Robert (Sir). 1st Bt.
  308
Thomas   563
KINGHORNE
Claude Bowes-Lyon,
  13th Earl of Strathmore and   101, 930
Claude George
  Bowes-Lyon, 14th
  Earl of Strathmore
  and   930
KINGSCOTE
Emily Mary
  (Curzon)   65
Isabella Frances Anne
  (Somerset)   64
Robert Nigel Fitzharding (Sir)   65
Thomas Henry   64
Winifred Agnes   65
KINGSMILL
Alice   584, 738
Anne   310
Anne (Warcop)   310
Bridget   428
Bridget (Raleigh)
  428, 480

Constance (Goring)
  310, 480, 584, 737
Dorothea   480
Dorothy (St. Leger)
  480
family   741
Frances (Reade)   310
Francis (Sir)   480
John   310
John (Sir)   310,
  480, 584, 737
Levina   480
Margaret (Pistor)   310
Mary   480, 737
Thomas   310
William   310, 480
William (Sir)   428,
  480
____ (Clifford)   480
KINGSTON
Alexandra ("Alex")
  Elizabeth   158
Eleanor   343, 409
KINGSTON-UPON-HULL
Evelyn Pierrepont,
  1st Duke of   64
KINLOCH
Francis (Sir), 2nd
  Bt.   92
James   92
Marie Esther (Page)
  92
Mary (Leslie)   92
Susannah (____)
  (Strode)   92
KINNAIRD
Barbara (Johnstone)
  155

1332

Charles Kinnaird,
  6th Baron 155
George 155
Helen 155
Helen (Gordon) 155
KINNESMAN
  Elizabeth 862
  Harold 862
  Katherine (Agard)
    862
KINNICUTT
  Margaret 49
**KINSKY VON
WCHINITZ UND
TETTAU**
  Franziska, Countess
    11
  Friedrich Karl, Count
    45
  Sophie (Mensdorff-
    Pouilly), Countess
    45
  Wilhelmina, Countess
    45
KINSMAN
  Elizabeth 847
KIRBY
  Katherine 100
KIRK
  Marshall Kenneth
    vii, viii, xlv, li, lv,
    lviii, lix, lx, lxix,
    clxxxiii, clxxxiv,
    clxxxv, 298, 372,
    579
KIRKBRIDE
  Bernard cxci
  Elizabeth cxci
  family clxxxix

Jane (Featherstone-
  haugh) cxci
Joseph clxxxix, cxci
Magdalen (Dalston)
  cxci
Matthew cxci
KIRKBY
  Agnes (Lowther)
    363, 364
  Alice 611
  Eleanor 363
  Isabella 742
  Jane (Rigby) 611
  Joanna (Furness)
    363
  Roger 363, 611
  William 363
KIRKPATRICK
  Elizabeth 787
  Kenneth W. [Marshall
    Kenneth Kirk] lix
  María Manuela, of
    Closeburn 292
KIRTON
  Elizabeth 307, 824
  John 625
  Margaret (Offley)
    625
  Margaret (White)
    625
  Mary 625
  Mary (Sadler) 625
  Stephen 625
  Thomas 625
KITCHELL
  Abraham 688
  Grace 688
  Joseph 688
  Rachel (Bates) 688

Sarah (Bruen) 688
KITCHEN
  Elizabeth 106
KITSON
  Margaret 864
KLAMBAUER
  Erika 187
KLEEMAN
  Susanna 985
KLEIN-ROGGE
  Rudolf 645
  Thea (von Harbou)
    xxii, clvi, 645
KLING
  Florence Mabel
    764, 859
KLINGSPOR
  Margareta Maria 53
KNAPP
  John 682
  Judith xix, lxi,
    lxiv, lxv, cxliv,
    clxi, clxxv, 682
  Margaret (Poley)
    682
  Martha (Bloys/
    Blosse) 682
  Mary 315
  Robert 682
KNATCHBULL
  Mary 314, 316
KNEVET
  Abigail 353
  Agnes (Harcourt)
    353, 403
  Anne (Lacy) 393
  Catherine 334, 482
  Catherine (Burgh)
    403

Charles   393
Edmund (Sir)   353
Elizabeth   108, 353, 393, 394, 403
Elizabeth (Bacon)   403
Joan (Bourchier)   353
Joan (Stafford)   393
John   353, 403
Muriel (Parry)   403
Thomas   403
Thomas (Sir)   403
William (Sir)   393
KNIGHT
Elizabeth   235, 708, 750, 920
Margaret Elizabeth   289
Ursula   657, 920
KNIGHTLEY (DE)
Anna (de Charlton)   746
Anne (Ferrers)   567
Eleanor (Throckmorton)   755
Joan (Skenard)   755
Mary   567
Mary (Fermor)   567
Richard (Sir)   567, 755
Susan   596, 755
Valentine (Sir)   567
William   746
KNIGHTLEY DE CHARLTON (DE)
Elizabeth (Francis)   746
Thomas   746

KNIGHTON
Anne (Underhill)   880
Joan   880
Thomas   880
KNIPE
Anne   333
Anne (Wolseley)   333
Thomas   333
KNIVETON
Anne (Dethick)   723, 724
Barbara   723, 724
John   723, 724
Margaret (Montgomery)   723
KNOCHE
Anna Margaretha (von Sothen)   449
Christine Elizabeth   449
family   449
Sebastian   449
KNOLLES
Margery   839, 840
KNOLLYS
Alice (Beecher)   302
Anne   300, 302
Anne (Cheney)   xlix, lxi, cli, 667, 668
Catherine   302
Catherine (Cary)   134, 300, 303
Dorothy   302
family   669
Francis   302
Francis (Sir)   134, 300, 303

Hanserd (Rev.)   667, 668
Jane (Heigham)   302
Lettice   134, 300, 302, 477
Ottilia (de Merode)   302
Richard   302, 303
Robert   303
Thomas (Sir)   302
KNOWLES
Anne   757
Beale   545
Beyoncé Giselle   968, 990
Célestina "Tina" Anne (Beyincé)   990
Mathew   990
Solange   990
KOEHLER
Catharine Elisabeth   440
KOENIG
Marlene (Eilers)   viii, liv
KOKANOSKY
Laurent   945
KOKENHUSEN (VON)
Sophia   849
Theodoricus   849
KOLIN
Grace   16
KOLOWRAT-LIEBSTEINSKY
Eleonora   895

Maria Anna (von
  Althann) 895
Maria Magdalena
  (Slawata) 895
Norbert Leopold
  895
Norbert Vincent
  895
**KÖNIGSMARCK
(VON)**
  Anna Wilhelmine,
    Countess 889
  Bengt, Lord of
    Briby 452, 454
  Conrad Christopher,
    Count 889
  Karin 452
  Maria Christina
    (Wrangel),
    Baroness 889
  Marta Tordsdotter
    (Bonde) 452, 454
KORFF (VON)
  Antoinette Theodora
    (Graun) 618
  Eleanore
    Margarethe (von
    der Osten-Sacken)
    618
  family 618
  Ferdinand Nicholas
    Victor, Baron 618
  Katherina 617
  Maria, Baroness 618
  Nicolas, Baron 618
  Nina (Shishkov)
    618
  Wilhelm Carl,
    Baron 618

KOSKULL
  Anders 51
  Anders, Baron 51
  Anna Catharina
    (Stromberg) 51
  Anna Maria
    (Gyllensvärd) 51
  Eleonora, Baroness
    51
  Erik 51
  Maria Catharina
    (Frankelin) 51
KOSTCZANKA
  Anna 621
KOSTKA
  Jan 621
  Sophia (Odrowazna)
    621
KOSUL
  Boleslaw, Duke of
    640
  Euphemia of 640
  Wratislaw, Duke of
    Schliesen-Beuthen
    and 640
KOTT
  Bernardine 983
KOZELAK
  Fedor, Prince 802
  Ivan "Puzynina,"
    Prince 802
  Tite, Prince 802
  Vladimir, Prince
    802
KOZELAK-PUZYNA
  Bogdan, Prince
    802
  Christina
    (Ozieblowska) 802

  David, Prince 802
  Ivan, Prince 802
  Mikhail Nikita,
    Prince 802
  Peter, Prince 802
  Sophia (Szczuczanka)
    802
  Sophia, Princess
    802
  Timofei, Prince 802
KRAICHGAU
  Hildegardis of (wife
    of Charlemagne,
    Holy Roman
    Emperor) 879, 919
KRAKOW
  Casimir II, Prince of,
    Prince of Sandomir,
    Kujamien and
    Mazovia 791, 797,
    802
KRASINSKI
  Maria Louisa,
    Countess 270,
    290
KRAVCHENKO
  Anna (Golitzin/
    Gallitzine),
    Princess clv, 190,
    799, 800
  Sergei clv, 799
KROMIN
  Maria 793
KRONOBÄCK
  Gustaf Stenbock,
    Baron of, Baron of
    Oresten 452, 453
KRUSE (VON)
  Madlena 849

KRUUSE
Henning Adolf, Baron 889
Sofia Charlotta 889
Virginia (Spens), Baroness 889
KUEHLE
Anna Dorothea Eleonore Christine (Gerlach) 449
Anna Justina 449
Christine Elizabeth (Knoche) 449
family 449
Georg Valentin 449
Johann Heinrich 449, 450
KÜHL
Eddy 521
KUJAMIEN
Casimir II, Prince of, Prince of Sandomir, Krakow and Mazovia 791, 797, 802
KUKENOIS
Sophia of 849
Wlazko, Prince of 849
KUMANS (THE)
Elizabeth of, Queen of Hungary 459
KUNIGUNDE
of Halicz, Queen of Bohemia 621
KÜNZIG
Sophie 98
KURAKIN
Ekaterina, Princess 795

KURIE
Dorothy Eleanor (Gede) 620
Franz Newell Devereux 620
KURTWICH
Anne 105
KURZ
Charles G. (Dr.) li, lx, 280
KURZBACH (VON)
Sigismund VI, Herr 196
Sophia 195, 196
KUSER
Roberta Brooke (Roswell) [Brooke Astor] 86
KUTSCHERA
Maria Augusta 187
KYME (DE)
Joan (Bigod) 730
Lucy 730
Lucy (de Ros) 730
Philip de Kyme, 1st Baron 730
William (Sir) 730
KYNASTON 231
Elizabeth (Grey) 229, 231, 233, 235
Elsbeth (ferch Maredudd ap Hywel) 231
Humphrey 231
Jane 233
Margaret 231, 235
Mary 229, 660
Roger (Sir) 229, 231, 233, 235

KYNNYNMOND
Cecilia 222
KYRLE
Anne (Waller) 466, 467
James 466
Mary (Jephson) cxliv, 428, 462
Richard (Sir) (Gov.) cxliv, 428, 466
LA BARRE (DE) D'ERQUELINNES
Marie José, Countess 122
LA BASTIDE-VILLE-FRANCHE (DE)
Bertrand de Béarn-Bonasse, Seigneur 963
LA BELLONIÈRE (DE)
Gervais Le Marchand, Sieur 959
LA BOISSIÈRE (DE)
Miles Maillard, Seigneur, Seigneur du Breul and 950
LA BOURDONNAYE (DE)
Marie-Thérèse-Anne-Luglienne 206
LA BOUTEILLERIE (DE)
Guy I le Bouteillier, Seigneur, Seigneur de La Roche-Guyon 950

Guy II le Bouteillier, Seigneur, Seigneur de La Roche-Guyon 950
Jean le Bouteillier, Seigneur, Seigneur de La Roche-Guyon 950
LA BOUVERIE (DE)
Bertrand 733
Isabel (de Melun) 733
LA BOUVERIE (DE) dit DE VIANE
Catherine 733
LA CHESNÉE (DE)
Olivier d'Aigneaux, Seigneur de Douville and 956
LA CLOCHE
Benjamin 868
Rachel 868
Rachel (de Carteret) 868
LA CONSEILLÈRE (DE)
Adrien de Méhérenc, Seigneur de Montmirel and 946
Guillaume IV de Méhérenc, Seigneur 946
Jean de Méhérenc, Seigneur de Montmirel and 946
LA FAYETTE (DE). *see also* MOTIER, MOTIER DE LA FAYETTE

Marie-Joseph-Paul-Yves-Roch-Gilbert Motier, Marquis xvi, xxvi, xl, l, liii, clxx, 201, 203, 288, 291
Michel-Louis-Christophe-Roch-Gilbert Motier, Marquis 201, 203
LA FERTÉ (DE)
François de Brabançon, Seigneur 944
LA FERTÉ-ALAIS (DE)
Philip I de Montfort, Seigneur 965
Philip II de Montfort, Seigneur 965
LA FERTÉ-NABERT (DE)
Jean d'Estampes, Seigneur 634
LA FEUILLÉE (DE)
Charles du Bellay, Seigneur 942
LA FONTAINE (DE)
Hubert Heinrich, Count, Count d'Harnoncourt-Unverzagt 220
Hubert Karl Sigismund Joseph Franz, Count, Count d'Harnoncourt-Unverzagt 895
René Vladimir Hubert Maria,

Count, Count d'Harnoncourt-Unverzagt [René d'Harnoncourt] lv, clv, 220, 896
LA FORÊT-AUVRAY (DE)
Roland III de Vassy, Seigneur 959
LA GARDIE (DE)
Axel Julius, Count 267, 453
Christina Katarina, Countess 453
Ebba (Brahe), Countess 267, 453
Hedwig Catharina, Countess 267
Hedwig Catharina (Lillie), Countess 267
Jacob, Count 267, 453
Magnus Julius, Count 267
Pontus, Baron 267, 453
Sofia Juliana (Forbus), Baroness 453
Sophia (Gyllenhielm) 267, 453
LA GUERCHE (DE)
Jeanne 947, 948
LA HAYE (DE)
Isabelle (d'O) 946
Jean, Seigneur du Bouillon 946
Jeanne (de Grosparmy) 946

1337

Marguerite 946
Nicolas de
 Bricqueville,
 Seigneur 957
Philip I, Seigneur de
 La Haye-Hue 946
Philip I, Seigneur
 d'O 946
Robert, Seigneur du
 Bouillon 946
Robine (du Bois)
 946
LA LANDE (DE)
René du Bellay,
 Seigneur 942
**LA MAISONNEUVE
(DE)**
Élisabeth 912
Jean 912
Marie (Favre) 912
Pierre Levrault,
 Seigneur 941
**LA MASCOTTERIE
(DE)**
Alphonse Baillon,
 Seigneur 950
LA NOCHERIE (DE)
Almaric de La
 Poterie, Seigneur
 959
Jean de La Poterie,
 Seigneur 959
Raoul Rousée,
 Seigneur 959
LA PALU (DE)
Antoinette 942
LA PORTE (DE)
Gilles de Prunelé,
 Seigneur 948

LA POTERIE (DE)
Almaric, Seigneur de
 La Nocherie 959
Jean 959
Jean, Seigneur de
 La Nocherie 959
Jeanne 959
Perlette (Rousée)
 959
Perrette (de
 Roussel) 959
Philipotte (de
 Lignon) 959
LA RIVIÈRE (DE)
Charles-Yves-Jacques
 de La Rivière,
 Count, Marquis de
 Paulmy 203
Charles-Yves-
 Thibault de La
 Rivière, Marquis
 203
Joseph-Yves-
 Thibault-Hyacinthe
 de La Rivière,
 Marquis 203
Julie-Célestine
 (Barberin de
 Reignac) 203
Julie-Louise-Céleste
 (de La Rivière) 203
Marie-Françoise-
 Céleste (de Voyer)
 203
Marie-Louise-Julie
 201, 203
LA ROCHE (DE)
Anthony de
 Bourgogne, Count,

Heer van Beveren
 438, 445
Charlotte (de
 Rambures) 205
François, 1st Marquis
 de Fontenilles 205
Marguerite 956
Renée-Charlotte 205
**LA ROCHE
D'OLLON (DE)**
Jean de Rovorée,
 Seigneur du Crest
 and 872
**LA ROCHE-GUYON
(DE)**
Guy I le Bouteillier,
 Seigneur de La
 Bouteillerie and
 950
Guy II le Bouteillier,
 Seigneur de La
 Bouteillerie and
 950
Jean le Bouteillier,
 Seigneur de La
 Bouteillerie and
 950
Marie 941
**LA ROCHE-TESSON
(DE)**
Raoul V Tesson,
 Seigneur 959
**LA ROCHE-
FOUCAULD (DE)**
Gilberte 202
Marguerite 293
**LA SPINE (DE)/
SPINNEY.** *see also*
SPINNEY

**LA TOUR
D'AUVERGNE
(DE)**
  Madeleine 637
**LA TRÉMOUILLE
(DE)**
  Anne 205
  Anne (de Laval)
    636
  Antoinette 634,
    636
  Catherine (d'Isle-
    Bouchard) 634
  Charles, Count de
    Taillebourg 636
  Charlotte 62, 637
  Charlotte (of Nassau-
    Dillenburg) 62, 637
  Claude, Duc de
    Thouars 62, 637
  family 637
  François, Vicomte
    de Thouars 636
  Gabrielle (of
    Bourbon-
    Montpensier) 636
  George de La
    Trémouille,
    Seigneur, Count of
    Guînes 634, 953
  Guy V, Sire 634
  Jeanne (de Mont-
    morency) 637
  Louis I, Vicomte de
    Thouars 634, 637
  Louis II, Vicomte de
    Thouars 636
  Louis III, Duc de
    Thouars 637
  Louise 637
  Louise (de Coëtivy)
    636
  Madeleine (of
    Savoy) 637
  Marguerite
    (d'Amboise) 634
  Marie 953
  Marie (de Sully) 634
**LA WARR(E) (DE)
(DELAWARE)**
  Catherine 780
  Eleanor (Mowbray)
    623
  family xxiv, xxxiv,
    li, liii, 576
  Joan 623
  Joan (de Grelle) 780
  John de la Warre,
    2nd Baron 780
  Reynold West, 6th
    Baron 623
  Roger de La Warre,
    3rd Baron La
    Warre 623
  Thomas West, 2nd
    Baron 300, 301,
    302
  Thomas West, 8th
    Baron 426, 473,
    477, 603
  Thomas West
    (Gov.), 3rd Baron
    300, 301, 491
  William West, 10th
    Baron 475, 476
LA ZOUCHE (DE).
  see also ZOUCHE
  Agnes (Greene) 713
  Alan, 1st Baron
    Zouche of Ashby
    742, 746, 752, 760,
    772
  Ela (Longespee) 742,
    746, 752, 760, 772
  Eleanor (de
    Segrave) 742,
    746, 752, 760, 772
  Elena 746
  Elizabeth 727, 837,
    839
  Elizabeth (de Ros)
    713, 727
  Ellen 373, 778
  Eudo 676, 691,
    837, 839, 847
  Eve 676, 691, 847
  family 1025
  Katherine 713, 714
  Maud 742, 752,
    760, 772
  Milicent (de
    Cantilupe) 676,
    691, 837, 839, 847
  Roger 847, 848
  Roger (Sir) 742,
    746, 752, 760, 772
  William, 2nd Baron
    Zouche of Haryng-
    worth 713, 727
  William, 3rd Baron
    Zouche of
    Haryngworth 713
    847, 848
**LA ZOUCHE DE
MORTIMER (DE)**
  family 1025
  Joyce 715, 728

LÀAS (DE)
Madeleine 963
LABAYEN (DE)
Agustín 995
Juana 995
María (Ponce de
León y Navarro)
995
LABRECQUE
Françoise 973
Louis 973
Marie-Louise 984
Marie-Louise
(Mercier) 973
Marie-Louise (Roy)
973
LACE
Christian clxxxiv
LACHAUME
Monique 977
LaCOAST
Louisa Maria 27
LACON
Jane 534
Mary (Corbet) 534
Thomas (Sir) 534
LACY
Agnes (Savile) 343
Alice (Symmes)
343
Anne 393
Elizabeth 144, 325,
329
Ellen 629
family 344
Gerard 343
Hugh 343
Joan 561
Margaret 343

LADD
Margaret 883
LADISLAUS V
King of Bohemia and
Hungary 287, 615
LADNER
Jean Mary Vyvyan
108
LADYJENSKY
Anastasia 792
Anna 792
Ekaterina (Romo-
danovsky), Princess
792
Ivan 792
LAER
Jean-Baptiste de la
Bistrate, Seigneur
of, Seigneur of
Neerwinde 804
LaFAUNT
Alma Luella
(Robison) 924
Harold Arundle 924
Lenore Emily 924,
927
LAFORME
Aurélie (Garceau)
970
Godfroi 970
Olivine 967, 970
LAGERFELT
Adolf Israel Gustav,
Baron Lagerfelt
453
Caroline Eugénie,
Baroness liii, clv,
453

Ebba Frederica
Regina (Grill)
453
Gertrude Ida
Eugenia (von
Essen), Baroness
453
Gustav Adolf, Baron
453
Israel, Baron 453
Israel Karl Gustav
Eugène, Baron
453
Kristina Beata
Wilhelmina
(Funck) 453
Magdalena Sophia
(Falkenberg),
Countess 453
Mary Charmian
Sara (Champion de
Crespigny) 453
LAGERGREN
Gunnar Karl
Andreas 60
Nina Maria (Nane)
viii, lxiv, cxlii, 60
Nina Viveka Maria
(Dardel) 60
LAGNOE
Erik Trolle, Lord of
Faanoe and 452
LAGOMARSINO
Alba Julia 98
LAING
Anne (Palmes) 304
LAIRE (DE)
Françoise 965

LAIZER (DE)
Jérôme, Seigneur de Siougeat 440
Louise 440
Marguerite (de Besse) 440
LAJOIE
Henriette 187
Rose 988
LAKE
Anne (Stratton) 706
Elizabeth 565
William 706
LAMARR
Hedy [Hedwig Eva Maria Kiesler] xvii, clvi, 98
LAMBARDE
Grace (Parsons) 362
Mary 362
Thomas 362
LAMBART
Charles 137
Frances (Dutton) 137
Frances Thomasine 137
Gustavus 137
Thomasina (Rochfort) 137
LAMBERT
Anne 126
David Allen vi
LAMBERTON
Elizabeth 924
LAMBESC
Charles-Louis of Lorraine, Prince of, Count of Brionne 613

LAMBTON
Agnes (Lumley) 100
Beatrice Frances (Hamilton) 28
Catherine (Widdrington) 100
Dorothy 100
Dorothy (Bewicke) 100
Eleanor (Tempest) 100
Frances (Eure) 100
Freville 100
George Frederick D'Arcy, 2nd Earl of Durham 28
Jane 101
John 100, 101
Katherine (Kirby) 100
Margaret 100
Margaret (Freville) 100
Margaret (Hall) 100
Ralph 100, 101
Robert 100
Thomas 100
Thomas (Sir) 100
Thomasine (Milwood) 100
William 100
LAMMER
Auguste Caroline 188
LAMOIGNON (DE)
Chrétien-Guillaume (Christian William), Baron des Malesherbes 294

Françoise Thérèse (Grimod) 294
Marie-Thérèse 293, 294
LAMONT
Agnes, of that Ilk 263
Anne 173
Anne Louise 306
Barbara (Semphill) 173
Colin (Sir), of Ineryne 173
Florence, of Silvercraigs 263
LAMONTAGNE dit BACQUET
Marie 973
LAMORAL
1st Prince of Ligne 292
Count of Egmont, Prince of Gavre 290, 291, 459
LAMPECK
Katherine 466, 654
LAMPETT
Ellen 845
LAMY
Marie 956
LANCASTER
Blanche Plantagenet, Duchess of 400
Edmund Plantagenet, Prince of England, 1st Earl of xxvi, 623, 625, 628, 630, 632

Elizabeth Plantagenet of, Princess of England 400
Henry Plantagenet, 3rd Earl of 623, 625, 628, 630, 632
Joan 340
John of Gaunt, Prince of England, Duke of xxxix, 295, 300, 314, 324, 331, 337, 339, 345, 357, 366, 368, 370, 375, 382, 387, 393, 395, 396, 397, 398, 400, 403, 405, 407, 413, 417, 419, 421, 426, 427, 429, 433, 434, 900, 902
Matilda Plantagenet of 907

LANDI
family 190

LANDON
Elizabeth 503

LANDSBURG-VELEN (VON)
Emma, Baroness 39
Ignaz, Baron 38

LANE
Adelaide 520
Alice 909
Charles 520
Dorothy 368, 387
Elizabeth (Vincent) 387
John, Jr. 747, 758
Katherine (Whiting) 747, 758

Lucinda (Taplin) 520
Marie Lula/Lula Marie 833
Maud (Parr) 368
Ralph (Sir) 368
Richard 387
Susanna 747, 758

LANG
Fritz xvii, clvi, 645
Thea (von Harbou) (Klein-Rogge) xxii, clvi, 645

LANGDALE
Elizabeth 123

LANGENBERGER
Marie Adolfine 289

LANGERAK
Rutger van den Boetzelaer, Lord of, Lord of Merweden, Asperen and Carnisse 460
Wessel van den Boetzelaer, Lord of, Lord of Asperen 459

LANGFORD
Alice 716
Edward 678, 716
Mary 678
Mary (St. Barbe) 678
Sencha/Sanche (Blount) 716

LANGHAM
Elizabeth 302

LANGIN (DE)
Guillaume 872

Isabelle (de Pontverre) 872
Jeannette (de Blonay) 872
Marguerite 872
Rodolphe 872

LANGIS (DE)
Léon Levrault, Sieur 939, 941

LANGLE (DE)
Philippe de Noyelles, Vicomte 633

LANGLEY
Edmund Plantagenet of, Prince of England, 1st Duke of York xxxix, 107, 114, 119, 126, 133, 134, 377, 410, 411, 423

LANGSTON
Joan 857
A. L. xx

LANGTIN dit JEREME
Marie-Catherine 969

LANGTON
Anne 409
Eupheme 395
Jane 725

LANGTREE
Catherine 902
Edward 902, 903
Eleanor (Stanley) 902
Gilbert 902
Isabella (Anderton) 902, 903
Thomas 903

LANGUE (DU)
François-Louis-Hector de Carondelet (Gov.), Baron de Noyelle, Vicomte de la Hestre and 438
Jean-Louis de Carondelet, Baron de Noyelle, Vicomte de la Hestre and 438

LANNES DE MONTEBELLO
André-Roger 227
Edith Bradford (Myles) 227
Emilie (d'Aviles) 227
George-Ernest-Casimir 227
Germaine (Wiener de Croisset) 227
Marie (Lubomirska), Princess 227
Philippe (Guy Philippe) xxvi, liii, clxxi, 227
René 227

LANNOY (DE)
Jean-Baptiste, Seigneur de Hautpont 438
Jeanne (de Coudenhove) 438
Jeanne-Louise, Countess 438

LANS
Herta 97

LANSDOWNE
Henry Charles Keith Petty-Fitzmaurice, 5th Marquess of 25, 28
William Petty, 1st Marquess of, 2nd Earl of Shelburne, Prime Minister 226, 299

LANTE DELLA ROVERE
Marie-Anna-Césarine 292

LARA Y MENDOZA (DE)
Pedro Manrique, lord of Amusco and Treviño 191

L'ARCHDEKNE
Eleanor 325, 534, 874
Philippa 547, 550

LARDER
Edmund 742
Isabella (Bonville) 742, 743
Ursula 742

LARSON
George xlviii, xlix, lxxi, 94, 132, 926

LARUE
Angélique (Gosselin) 980
Thérèse 980
Thomas 980

LASCARIS
Anna 442
Maria, Princess of Byzantium, Queen of Hungary 621

LASCELLES
Anne 698, 699
Anne (Thwaites) 698
Caroline Georgiana (Howard) 25
Dorothy 902
Elizabeth 343
Elizabeth (Tunstall) 902
Emma 25
Francis 698
Susan (Wandesford) 698
Thomas (Sir) 698
William 698, 902
William Saunders Sebright (Hon.) 25

LASH
Jennifer Anne Mary Alleyne 158

LASSBERG (VON)
Louise Magdalena, Baroness 641

LATHAM
Frances 241, 468, 488

LATHROP
Abigail 921
Elizabeth xiv
Elizabeth (Scudder) xiv, 921
Hannah 921
Hannah (Adgate) 921
Samuel xiv, 921
Samuel, Jr. 921

LATIMER (LE)
  Catherine (de La
    Warre) 780
  Elizabeth 737, 780
  Elizabeth (de
    Botetourte) 737
  Lora (Hastings) 780
  Thomas, 1st Baron
    Latimer of
    Braybrooke 780
  Warin, 2nd Baron
    Latimer of
    Braybrooke 780
  William, 3rd Baron
    Latimer 737
LATOUR
  Charles 953
LATROBE
  Benjamin Henry 590
  Lydia (Sellon) 590
  Lydia M. viii, lvii,
    cxlvi, 590
LATYMER
  barons (lords) 1025
  George Neville, 1st
    Baron 331, 421
  John Neville, 4th
    Baron 345, 418
  Richard Neville, 2nd
    Baron 331, 421
LAUBEL (DE)
  Guillaume III de
    Méhérenc,
    Seigneur 946
LAUDER
  Katherine 272
LAUDERDALE
  John Maitland, 1st
    Duke of 177

John Maitland, 1st
  Earl of 177
LAUGHARNE
  Anne 116
  Rowland (Sir) 116
  Theodosia (Wray)
    116, 117
LAUNCE
  Isabella (Darcy) 395
  John 395
  Mary xxiv, lix,
    clxii, 395
LAUNCELYN
  Bennett 749
LAURENCE
  Elizabeth 648
  Margaret (Hugford)
    648
  William 648
**LAURENT-BENOIT-
  BAUDOUIN-MARIE**
  Prince of the
    Belgians 201
LAURIA (DE)
  Beatríz 993
LAUSITZ (VON DER)
  Clara Spinucci,
    Countess 20
  Maria Christina
    Sabina, Princess of
    Saxony, Countess
    20
LAUTOUR (DE)
  Wilhelmina Douglas
    464
LAUZIÈRES (DE)
  Gloriande 200
LAVAL (DE)
  Anne 636

Charlotte (de Sainte-
  Maure) 942
Guy II, Seigneur de
  Loué 942
Guy VII de
  Montmorency, Sire
  964
Guy XIV, Count 226
Jeanne (de Brienne)
  964
Louise 226
Marquise 942
Philippe (de
  Beaumont) 942
Pierre, Seigneur de
  Loué 942
LAVERGNE
LEBUIS
  Marie 979
LAVOIE
  Joseph 977
  Marie-Geneviève
    (Miville) 977
  Marie-Josèphe 977
  Marie-Madeleine
    (Michaud) 977
LAW
  Anne (Towry) 363
  Edmund, Bishop of
    Carlisle 363
  Edward, 1st Baron
    Ellenborough 363
  Edward, 1st Earl of
    Ellenborough,
    Governor-General
    of India 363
  Elizabeth Parke
    (Custis) 363, 365
  family 365

1344

Ida Catherine
  Villiers 363
Jane Elizabeth
  (Digby) 363
Mary (Christian) 363
Octavia Catherine
  (Stewart) 363
Thomas xlix, cxliv,
  363, 365
LAWFORD
  Anne (Wright) 563
  Deborah (Gould)
    564
  Janet Turing (Bruce)
    563
  Margaret Sarah
    (Acland) 563
  Mary Anne (Rowan)
    564
  May Somerville
    (Bunny) (Cooper)
    (Aylen) 563
  Patricia (Seaton) 564
  Patricia Helen
    (Kennedy) 26,
    564, 914
  Peter Sydney Ernest
    [Peter Lawford]
    xvii, clxxiv, 26,
    564, 914
  Samuel 563
  Sydney Turing
    Barlow (Sir) 563,
    564
  Thomas Acland
    563
LAWRENCE
  Aimee Marie
    Suzanne 69

Carol [Carol Maria
  Leraia] 973
David Herbert
  Richards (D. H.)
  137
Elizabeth (___)
  881
Elizabeth (Bull)
  880
Elizabeth (Smith)
  552, 868, 881
Emma 719
Esther 688
family xxxiv, lvi,
  lxviii
Jane clx, 682, 880
Joan (Antrobus)
  880
John clxiv, 880,
  881, 884
Margaret 353
Mary clx, 881
Mary (___) 881
Mary (Ferguson)
  881
Mehitabel 106
Susanna (___)
  881
Suzanna 199
Thomas xxxv,
  clxiv, 880, 881,
  884
Thomas Edward,
  "Lawrence of
  Arabia" [aka T. E.
  Shaw] xxiv, 101,
  102
William clxiv, 868,
  881, 884

LAWSON
  Alice Louisa
    (Borden) 53
  Anne 127
  Anne (Wentworth)
    708
  Anthony Borden 53
  Barbara 317, 425
  Christopher xlviii,
    lvi, lxiv, lxviii,
    clxxvi, 708
  Elizabeth (James)
    708
  John 708
  Kurt Anthony 53
  Marjorie 254
  Mary (Savill)
    (Porter) 719
  Nancy Custer 53
  Raymond Carl 53
  Sarah (___) 150
  Susan (Ritchie) 53
LAWTON
  Isabel 822
LE BOUTEILLIER
  Bénigne 950
  Catherine (de Gavre)
    950
  Guy I, Seigneur de
    La Bouteillerie and
    La Roche-Guyon
    950
  Guy II, Seigneur de
    La Bouteillerie and
    La Roche-Guyon
    950
  Isabeau (Morhier)
    950

1345

Jean, Seigneur de La Bouteillerie and La Roche-Guyon 950
LE BRASSIEUR
 Anne (Mellish) (Spratt) cxlviii
LE BRET. *see* BRET (LE)
LE CLERC
 Anne 954
 Jean, Seigneur d'Armenonville 954
 Jeanne-Catherine (de Vaudétar) 954
LE DRAN/LEDRAN
 Charlotte (Couvent) 945
 Louis 945
 Louise (Menacier) 945
 Toussaint 945
LE GENTYL. *see* GENTYL (LE)
LE GOUEZ. *see* GOUEZ (LE)
LE GROS. *see* GROS (LE)
LE HUNTE
 Alice (Ryves) 364
 Anne 364
 Thomas 364
LE MARCHAND
 Gervais, Sieur de la Bellonière 959
 Jeanne 959, 970, 975, 989
 Stévenotte (de Saint-Germain) 959

LE NEUF
 Jeanne (Le Marchand) 959, 970, 975, 989
 Mathieu, Sieur du Hérisson 959, 970, 989
 Michel (Act. Gov.) 989
LE PRÉVOST
 Anne (Le Clerc) 954
 Jean IV, Seigneur de Malassis-lès-Étampes 954
 Jeanne 954
LE SERRURIER
 Suzanne 873
LE STRANGE/ L'ESTRANGE. *see also* STRANGE
 Alice (Bemain) [Beaumont?] 826
 Ankaret 478, 512, 530, 553, 555, 603
 Ankaret (le Boteler) 749
 Anne (Astley) 434
 Anne (Atkinson) 434
 Anne (Crosbie) 434
 Anne (Vaux) 434
 Barbara 826
 Caroline Stewart (Atkinson) 434
 Dorothy (Moore) 434
 Edmund 434
 Eleanor 705, 749

 Eleanor (de Montz) 826
 Eleanor (Walkfare) 826
 Elizabeth 307, 813, 824, 825
 Elizabeth (___) 434
 Elizabeth (Malone) 434
 Elizabeth (Sandes) 434
 Frances (Atkinson) 434
 George 434
 Hamon 434, 826
 Hamon (Sir) 826
 Henrietta Maria (L'Estrange) 434
 Henry 434, 826
 Henry Peisley 434
 Jane (Bebe) [Beke?] 826
 Joan (de Somery) 813, 824, 826
 John 826
 John (IV), of Knokyn 813, 824, 826
 John (Sir) 826
 John (V), 1st Baron Strange of Knokyn 813, 824, 826
 John, 2nd Baron Strange of Blackmere 749
 Katherine (Camoys) 826
 Katherine (Drury) 826

Margaret (le
 Strange) 826
Margaret (Vernon)
 826
Mary (Carleton)
 434
Maud (de Wauton)
 813, 824
Richard 434
Roger 826
Sarah 364, 434
Thomas 434
Thomas (Sir) 434
William 434
LEA
 J. Henry xxix
 Lydia 335
LEACH
 Archibald Alec
 [Cary Grant] 44
LEAKE
 Katherine 785
LEAMON
 Hattie 285
LEARNED
 Edward 935
 Edward, Jr. 935
 Hannah 519
 Mary 935
 Sarah (Fuller) 935
 Sarah (Pratt) 935
LEATHERBEE
 Frances Anita
 (Crane) 635
LeBARON
 Joseph 371
 Sarah 371
 Sarah (Leonard) 371

LEBEAU
 Marie-Françoise
 987
LEBLANC
 Anastasie (d'Amours
 de Louvières) 990
 Constance 990
 Pierre-René 990
LEBLOND
 Beuzeville (Eure)
 Jacques 957
 Catherine 987, 988
 Françoise (Nollent)
 957
 Marguerite (Leclerc)
 957, 984, 987
 Marie-Madeleine
 984
 Nicolas 957, 968,
 975, 984, 987
LEBLOY
 Françoise 964
LEBOEUF
 Marie-Antoinette
 972
LeBRETON
 Edith Ethel 128
**LEBZELTERN
 (VON)**
 Theresia 198
LECHFORD
 Thomas xxix
LECHMERE
 Anne (Winthrop)
 396
 Edmund 396
 Lucy (Hungerford)
 396
 Nicholas 396

Penelope (Sandys)
 396
Thomas lxviii,
 cxlv, 396
LECKIE
 Elizabeth 245
LECLERC
 Marguerite 957,
 984, 987
LECONFIELD
 George Wyndham,
 1st Baron 78
**LEDEBUR ZU
 WICHELN (VON)**
 Caspar Benedikt
 Anthon Johann
 Nepomuk, Baron
 208
 Maria Josepha,
 Baroness 208
 Maria Josepha (von
 Clary and
 Aldringen),
 Countess 208
LEDIG-ROWOHLT
 Heinrich Maria
 618
LEDOUX
 Louise Amalia 197
LEDUC
 Domithilde 982
 Marie-Louise-Angél
 ine 974
LEE
 Agnes (Conyers)
 419
 Alice Hathaway
 xliii, 225, 283, 471
 Anne 481

Benjamin 481
Charles (Gen.)
 235, 236, 412
Charlotte 22
Charlotte, Lady,
 Baroness Baltimore
 xvii, xxxv, lxiv, lxv,
 clxv, 29, 340
Christopher Carter,
 K.M. lx, cxc, 103,
 443, 597, 722
Dorothy 319, 355
Dorothy (Browne)
 355
Edmund 355
Edward, Archbishop
 of York 419
Edward Henry, 1st
 Earl of Lichfield
 22, 29
Eleanor (Wrottesley)
 319
Elizabeth (Crispe)
 419
family xxxv
Frances (Hales) 22
Francis Preston
 Blair, III (Gov.)
 206, 443
Geoffrey 419
George Henry, 2nd
 Earl of Lichfield
 22
Isabella (Bunbury)
 235
Jane (Corbet) 319
Janet Norton 914
John 235
Joyce (Worsley) 419

Margaret Mathilde
 (Boal) 206
Mary 419, 667, 677
Mary Anne
 Randolph (Custis)
 xxxiv, 29
Richard 319, 419
Robert Edward
 (Gen.) xxxiv, 29
Susanna (Smyth)
 481
Thomas (Sir) 319
LEECH/LECHE
Elizabeth (Leke)
 (Hardwick) 706
Margaret 706
Ralph 706, 707
LEESON
Cecilia 320
Francis G. 358
LEET
Irene Haines lx
LEETE
Alice (Grundy)
 clxxxvi
Anna (Payne) 854
Anne (Shute) 853
Ellen (Burgoyne)
 clxxxvi
family clxxxvi
John clxxxvi, 853
Mary (Newman)
 (Street) 854
Phebe clxxxvi
Robert clxxxvi
Sarah (Rutherford)
 854
William (Gov.) xix,
 lxiii, lxviii, clxiii,

clxxviii, clxxx,
 clxxxvi, clxxxviii,
 854, 1025
LEEUW (DE)
Antonia Louise
 733
Cornelia Henriette
 (van Weede) 733
Daniel 733
LEFEBVRE
Catherine 982
Marie-Madeleine
 976
Marie-Madeleine
 (Duranceau dit
 Brindamour) 982
Michel 982
LEGARD
Isabel (Hildyard)
 342
Joan 342
Ralph 342
Susanna 127
**LEGARDEUR DE
TILLY**
Louise 962, 964,
 965
Marguerite 962,
 964, 965
LEGGE
Mary 361
LEGGETT
Catherine (White)
 xl, l, cli, 916, 917
George 917
LEGH
Agnes 815, 816
Catherine (Savage)
 561

Eleanor 561
Ellen (Savage) 558
Jane 558
Margaret
  (Tyldesley) 558
Matilda (Arderne)
  815, 816
Peter 558
Peter (Sir) 558
Robert 815, 816
Thomas 561
LEGOUÈS
  Louis-Joseph,
    Seigneur de Grais
    961, 962, 965
  Marguerite (Legardeur
    de Tilly) 962, 964,
    965
LEGRAND
  Marie Constance
    908
**LEHMANN-VON
  SCHREIBER**
  Edith-Marie 37
LEICESTER
  Robert de Beaumont,
    1st Earl of, Count of
    Meulan 835, 837,
    839, 843, 845, 847,
    1025
  Robert de Beaumont,
    2nd Earl of 843,
    845
  Robert de
    Beaumont, 3rd
    Earl of 843
  Robert Dudley, 1st
    Earl of 134, 477

Simon III de
  Montfort, Earl of
  954, 959
LEIGH
  Amanda 24
  Anne 476
  Cassandra 299
  Catherine (Berkeley)
    298
  Elizabeth (West) 476
  Elizabeth
    (Whorwood) 299
  Frances (Harington)
    517
  Francis (Sir) 517,
    518
  Isabel 468
  Jane (Walker) 299
  Joanna (Pury) 299
  John 476
  John (Sir) 476
  Joyce (Colepepper/
    Culpeper) 468,
    476, 605
  Juliana 517
  Margaret (Ireland)
    476
  Margery (Saunders)
    476
  Mary (Brydges) 299
  Mary (Egerton)
    517, 518
  Mary (Fleming)
    476
  Ralph 468, 476,
    605
  Rowland 298
  Theophilus 299

Thomas 299, 476
William 299
William (Sir) 299,
    517
LEIGHTON
  Abigail 138
  Abigail (Stephens)
    138
  Anne (Devereux)
    138
  Edward 138
  Gertrude (Baldwin)
    138
  Robert 138
LEIJONHUFVUD
  Margareta, Queen of
    Sweden 40, 43,
    198, 208, 267, 453
**LEININGEN-
  HARTENBURG**
  Anna Marie Louise
    of 43
  John Frederick,
    Count of 43
**LEININGEN-
  HILDESHEIM**
  Louise of 40
**LEININGEN-
  WESTERBURG**
  Joanna Elizabeth of
    142
  Sophia Magdalena
    of 142
**LEININGEN-
  WESTERBURG-
  SCHAUMBURG**
  George William,
    Count 142

LEINSTER
  Dermot MacMurr-
   ough/ Diarmait
   Mac-Murchada,
   King of 837, 839,
   847
  Eve of lxviii, 837,
   839, 847
  Sophia Charlotte,
   Countess von Platen
   and Hallermund,
   Countess of,
   Countess of
   Darlington 58, 432
LEKA I
  King of the
   Albanians xl, 935
LEKA II
  [Leka Anwar Zog
   Reza Baudouin
   Msiziwe Zogu],
   King of the
   Albanians xl, 935
LEKE
  Catherine (Chaworth)
   706
  Elizabeth 512, 706
  family 1025
  Margaret (Fox) 706
  Thomas 706
  William 706
LEMIEUX
  Armand 981
  Jean-Guy 981
  Marie-Gertrude 988
  Marie-Jeanne
   (Briere) 981
  Mario 967, 981

  Natalie (Asselin)
   981
  Pierrette (Leroux)
   981
LEMING
  Anne 343
  Anne (Kelke) 343
  Roger 343
**LEMOINE de
  LONGUEIL**
  Charles 962, 965
  Marguerite (Legardeur
   de Tilly) (Legouès)
   (Saint-Ours) 962,
   964, 965
LENNARD
  Anne (Palmer) 109
  Anne, Baroness
   Dacre 109
  Elizabeth 399
  Rachel 405
  Thomas, 1st Earl of
   Sussex 109
LENNOX
  Adelaide Constance
   (Campbell) 31
  Anne 25
  Arthur, Lord 31
  Charles Lennox, 1st
   Duke of Richmond
   and 25, 31
  Charles Lennox, 2nd
   Duke of Richmond
   and 31
  Charles Lennox, 4th
   Duke of Richmond
   and 31
  Charlotte (Gordon)
   31

  Constance Charlotte
   Elisa 31
  Esmé Stewart, 1st
   Duke of 47, 154,
   215
  George Henry, Lord
   31
  Georgiana Caroline
   31
  Isabella, Countess of
   264
  John Stewart, 3rd
   Earl of 145, 148,
   215
  Louisa (Kerr) 31
  Matthew Stewart,
   2nd Earl of 148,
   215, 218
  Sarah (Cadogan)
   31
LENS
  Esther 320
  Judith of Ponthieu
   or 879, 919
  Lambert, Count of
   879, 919
LENT (VAN)
  Geertruit Jansdr.
   776
LEO (LEW)
  King of Galicia
   621
LEÓN
  Alphonso IX, King
   of 647, 709, 909,
   948, 964
  Berengaria, Princess
   of, Princess of
   Castile, Queen of

Jerusalem, Empress
 of Constantinople
 647, 909, 948, 964
Berengaria, Queen
 of Castile, Queen
 of 647, 709, 909,
 948, 964
LEONARD
Nathaniel 371
Olivia Jane (d'Abo)
 cliii, 135
Patrick Raymond
 135
Priscilla (Rogers)
 371
Sarah 371
LEONOR
 (Alvarez de Toledo),
 Grand Duchess of
 Tuscany 191, 192
**LEONORA
 CHRISTINA**
Countess of
 Schleswig-Holstein
 35
LEOPOLD I
King of the Belgians
 45, 182, 196, 237,
 290
LEOPOLD II
Holy Roman
 Emperor 614
**LEOPOLD
 EBERHARD**
Duke of
 Württemberg-
 Mömpelgard 184,
 185

LEPAGE
Catherine (Rioux)
 987
Louise 982
Marie-Élisabeth 987
Paul 987
LEPAGE dit MOLAIS
Antoine 987
Marie-Josephte
 (Côté) 987
LEPELL
Mary 23, 117, 334
LEPORTIER
Paul 956, 959
LERAIA
Carol Maria [Carol
 Lawrence] 973
LEROUX
Pierrette 981
LESLIE
David, 1st Baron
 Newark 92
Elizabeth 92, 897
Emily Jane 362
Jean (Stewart) 92,
 897
Joan (Yorke) 92
Lavina Margaret 65
Margaret, of
 Aikenway 281
Mary 92, 143
Patrick, 1st Baron
 Lindores 92, 897
L'ESPINE
Mary 110
LESSEPS (DE)
Ferdinand-Marie 292
LESSER
Josephine 990

LESTER
Mary Elizabeth
 794
LETOURNEAU
Claude 977
Delima Paradis
 (Michaud) 977
Geneviève
 (Lévesque) 977
Marceline 977
LEUCHTENBERG
Agnes of 640
Amalia of 237
Elizabeth of 181, 194
Eugène-Rose de
 Beauharnais, 1st
 Duke of, Viceroy
 of Italy 442, 443,
 444
Frederick IV,
 Landgrave of 237
George, Landgrave
 of 194
LEUZE (DE)
Hugo de Châtillon,
 Seigneur 733
Jacques de
 Châtillon, Seigneur
 733
LEVENTHORP(E)
Anne 806
Constance clxxxiv
Katherine (Hunger-
 ford) clxxxiv
Katherine (Sampson)
 clxxxiv
Nicholas clxxxiv
LEVERSAGE
Eleanor 752

Eleanor (Sheffield) 752
Katherine (Davenport) 752
William 752
LEVESEY
Emma 525
LEVESON
Christian 315
Elizabeth 368
Frances (Sondes) 315
John (Sir) 315
Mary 577
LEVESON-GOWER
Anne (Hay-Mackenzie) 33
Charlotte Sophia 64, 71
Cromartie, 4th Duke of Sutherland 33
Elizabeth (Gordon), Countess of Sutherland 71
Evelyn (Pierrepont) 33, 62, 64, 299
family 298, 299
George Granville, 1st Duke of Sutherland 71
George Granville William, 3rd Duke of Sutherland 33
Georgiana Augusta 64
Gertrude 25, 62, 75
Granville, 1st Marquess of Stafford 64, 71, 75
John, 1st Earl Gower xxiv, 33, 62, 64, 299
Louisa (Egerton) 71, 72
Margaret Caroline 71
Mary 33
Millicent Fanny (St. Clair-Erskine) 33
Rosemary Millicent 33
LÉVESQUE
Esther 977
Esther (Rioux) 977
Gabrielle 971
Geneviève 977
Georges 977
Jean 977
Jean-Baptiste 971
Joseph-Marie 977
Louis 971
Marguerite (Valles) 977
Marie-Josèphe 971
Marie-Josèphe (Bérubé) 971
Marie-Josèphe (Dionne) 971
Marie-Josèphe (Lavoie) 977
Marie-Joséphine (Jean) 971
Monique (Lachaume) 977
Pierre 971
Pierre-Bernard 977
René, Premier of Québec 971
LEVINE
Rachel (Faucette) 214
LEVIS
Christopher 384
Elizabeth (Claytor) 384
Hannah 384
Mary (Need) 384
Samuel lxi, cxlv, 384
Sarah 384
LÉVIS (DE)
Jeanne 943, 965
LEVITA
Arthur Francis 10
Edith Agnes 10
Stephanie Agnes (Cooper) 10
LEVRAULT
Anne (Aignon) 941
Catherine-Gabrielle (Jarret) 941
Charles, Seigneur de Naintré 941
Léon, Sieur de Langis 939, 941
Marguerite (Trottier) 941
Marie (Menard) 941
Pierre, Seigneur de La Maisonneuve 941
LEWENHAUPT
Adolf Fredrik, Count 60
Anna (Palbitski), Baroness 893
Anna Wilhelmine (von Königsmarck), Countess 889
Aurora Vilhelmina (Alströmer), Baroness 889

1352

Azalea Caroline
 (Keyes) 893
Beata (Cronhielm)
 889
Carl Gustaf, Count
 889
Carl Gustaf Moritz
 Ture, Count 889
Carl-Johan, Count
 889
Carl Julius, Count
 60, 893
Charles Emil, Count
 889
Christina
 Gustaviana (Horn),
 Baroness 60, 893
Ebba Margaretha
 (Palbitski),
 Baroness 893
Eric Emil Audley,
 Count clvi, 893
Fabian Mathias
 Emil, Count 893
family xxii, lv
Hedvig Amalia,
 Countess 60
Hedvig Christina
 (Gyllenstierna),
 Baroness 889
Hedvig Margaretha
 (Lewenhaupt),
 Countess xxii, lv,
 clvi, 890, 894
Hedvig Sophie
 Charlotta Amalia,
 Countess 60
Ida Felicia Louise
 (Gosling) 893

Jan-Casimir Eric
 Emil, Count 890,
 893, 894
Julia Regina
 Turinna (Uggla),
 Baroness 889
Justina Margaretha
 (Travenfert) 893
Ludvig Fabian
 Mathias Emil,
 Count 893
Ludvig Wierich,
 Count 60, 893
Mauritz Casimir,
 Count 60, 889, 893
Ulrika Charlotta
 (Lewenhaupt),
 Countess 60, 889
LEWIS
Andrew 886
ap John (Sir) 565
ap Robert 229
Arthur 803
Eleanor/Margaret
 (Gamage) 548
Elizabeth (Marshall)
 xl, lii, lv, clxii, 630,
 886
Elizabeth (Newlin)
 230
Ellis 230
Evan 555
Evan Robert xxxiv,
 650, 651, 652
family lii, 652
Hannah 498
Joan 338, 548
Judith 630, 886
Kate (Terry) 803

Kate Terry 803
Mary 338, 983
Mary (___) 229
Mary (Beakbaine)
 (Baldwin) 230
Mary (Herring) 886
Morgan 555
Robert 650
Susanna 243
Thomas xl, clxii,
 630, 886
William 548
LEWKNOR
Anne (___) 623
Anne (Everard)
 580, 738
Barbara 551
Beatrix 920, 922
Dorothy (Wroth)
 580
Edmund 623, 624
Edward 580, 738
Eleanor 738
Eleanor (Camoys)
 623, 738
Elizabeth 623, 624,
 738, 845
Elizabeth (Carew)
 851
Elizabeth (Echyng-
 ham) 738, 851
Elizabeth
 (Radmylde) 738
family 624, 852,
 916, 922
Jane (Tirrell) 623
Jane/Joan 851
Joan (de Keynes)
 851, 920

Joan (D'Oyly) 851
Katherine (Bardolf)
851, 920, 922
Margaret (___)
580, 738
Margaret (Copley) 580
Mary 580
Mary (West) 623
Nicholas 738
Philippa (Dalyng-
ridge) 738, 851
Roger 623, 624
Roger (Sir) 623,
624, 738, 851, 852,
920, 922
Sybil (___) 851, 920
Thomas (Sir) 738,
851, 852, 920

LEWYS
ab Ieuan 886
ap Gruffudd 650
ap John Gruffudd
229, 230
Ellis 230

LEXA VON AEHRENTHAL
Maria, Baroness 198

LEYBOURNE
Dorothy (Lascelles) 902
Elizabeth 902
Thomas 902

LEYCESTER
Eleanor 560
Elizabeth 817

LHERMITTE
Marie 957

LHUTILIER DE LA SERRE
Marie-Françoise 83

LICHFIELD
Edward Henry Lee,
1st Earl of 22, 29
George Henry Lee,
2nd Earl of 22
Laurence Nowell,
Dean of 369, 701
Samuel Butler,
Bishop of, Bishop
of Coventry 475, 476
Thomas George
Anson, 2nd Earl of 28

LICHLITER
Asselia Strobhar lx

LIECHTENSTEIN
Marie, Princess of 19
Sovereign Princes of 154, 198

LIECHTENSTEIN-FELDSBERG
Hartman II of 237
Judith of 237

LIÈGE
Louis of Bourbon,
Bishop of 293

LIEGNITZ
Frederick II, Duke of 196
Frederick III, Duke of 196
Helena of 196

LIGHT
Elizabeth 864

LIGHTFOOT
Alice (Corbin) 329
Elizabeth (Phillips) 329
Elizabeth (Tailer/Taylor) 329
family xlix, l, lxv, 330
Jane (Aske) 329
John cxlix, cli, 329
Philip cxlix, 329
Richard 329

LIGNE
Lamoral, 1st Prince of 292
Yolande of 292

LIGNON (DE)
Philipotte 959

LIGON. *see also* LYGON
Ann (___) xiii
Elizabeth xiii
Elizabeth (Anderson) xiii
family vii, xiii, xxiv,
xxxiv, xxxvii, lx,
lxv, 298, 299
Joseph xiii
Mary xiii
Mary (Church) xiii
Mary (Harris) xiii, 295, 538
Mary (Worsham) xiii, xiv
Matthew xiii
Richard xiii
Thomas xiii
Thomas (Col.) xii, xiii, xxvii, xlvii, liii,

lx, lxv, lxviii, lxxi,
clxvii, clxxii, 295,
538
William Daniel
xlvii, li, lviii, lx,
lxv, lxviii, lxxi
LILGENAU (VON)
Antonia von Zierotin,
Duchess 895, 896
LILLIE
Abigail (Breck)
479, 716
Agneta 457
Anna 479, 585, 716
Beatrice Gladys "Bea"
xvii, cxlv, 67
Hannah (Ruck)
479, 716
Hedwig Catharina,
Countess 267
John 479, 716
Theophilus 479, 716
LILLINGTON
Mary (Batt) (Ashe)
xlix, cxlii, clxix,
clxxv
LIMBREY
John 369
Mary (Bull) (Webb)
369
LIMERICK
Edmund Henry Pery,
1st Earl of 115
Thomas Dongan
(Gov.), 2nd Earl of
lii, liii, clxxiii, 486,
488
Thomas Smyth,
Bishop of 480

William Hale John
Charles Pery, 3rd
Earl of 115
William Henry
Edmond de Vere
Sheaffe Pery, 4th
Earl of 116
William Henry
Tennison Pery, 2nd
Earl of 115
LINCOLN
Edmund Clinton
(Adm.), 1st Earl of
530
Francis Clinton, 6th
Earl of 108
Henry Clinton, 2nd
Earl of 107, 351
Thomas Clinton, 3rd
Earl of 107, 108
LINDALL
Jane 923
Jane (Poole) 923
Timothy 923
LINDEMANS
Leo 438
LINDORES
Patrick Leslie, 1st
Baron 92, 897
LINDSAY
Alexander, 2nd Earl
of Crawford 282
Alexander, of
Haltoun 282
David (Rev.) clxix,
282
David (Sir), of
Beaufort and
Edzell 282

David, 1st Earl of
Crawford 275,
276, 282, 285
David, 3rd Earl of
Crawford 282
David, 9th Earl of
Crawford 282
David, Bishop of
Ross 278, 282
Elizabeth 243, 275,
276, 285
Isabel 256
Isabel (Livingston)
282
Janet (Ramsay)
278, 282
Jerome (Sir), of
Annatland and the
Mount 282
Katherine (Fother-
ingham) 282
Katherine/Jean/
Elizabeth (Stewart),
Princess of Scotland
275, 276, 282, 285
Margaret 223
Margaret (Colville)
282
Marjory (___) 282
Marjory (Ogilvy)
282
Rachel 278
Susanna (___) 282
Walter (Sir), of
Beaufort and
Edzell 282
___ (Barclay) 282
___ (Erskine) 282

1355

LINDSAY (DE)
family 768
LING
Joanna (___) 750
LINLEY
Isabel 501
LINLITHGOW
Alexander Livingston, 1st Earl of 143, 161
Alexander Livingston, 2nd Earl of 161
George Livingston, 3rd Earl of 161
LINTON
Emily (Wade) 540
Laura (Wade) 540
Margaret Wade clvi, 540
Marian Darragh 136
William James xlix, 540
LIONEL
of Antwerp, Prince of England, Duke of Clarence xxxix, 107, 114, 119, 126, 133, 134, 305, 310, 317, 319, 327, 333, 342, 347, 349, 351, 355, 359, 361, 363, 374, 379, 384, 385, 389, 399, 401, 414, 418, 425, 431, 901, 904, 905
LIPPE-BIESTERFELD
Bernhard Casimir Frederick Gustav Henry Wilhelm Edward, Prince of 47
Bernhard Leopold Friedrich Eberhard Julius Kurt Karl Gottfried Peter, Prince of, Prince Consort of The Netherlands 1, 47
Ernest Aschwin Georg Carol Heinrich Ignatz, Prince of clvi, 47
Ernest Casimir Frederick Charles Eberhard, Count of 47
Julius Peter Hermann August, Count of 47
LIPPE-BRAKE
Casimir, Count of 194
Otto, Count of 194
Sophia Hedwig of 194
LIPPE-DETMOLD
Simon VII, Count of 141
Sophie Elizabeth of 142
LIQUIER
Antoine 635, 636
Marie (Cazenove) 635
Pauline-Victoire 635
LISITSKI
Ludmila 799

LISLE
Alice (Beckenshaw) 297
Arthur Plantagenet, 1st Viscount 103
Bridget clxxii, 297, 298
Bridget (Hungerford) 297
Elizabeth Grey, Baroness 103
John 297
William (Sir) 297
LISNEY
Suzanne 23
LISTER. *see also* **LYSTER**
Agnes 475
Martin (Sir) 475
Mary (Wenman) 475
Rosamond 524
LISTOWEL
Richard Granville Hare, 4th Earl of 80
William Hare, 3rd Earl of 80
LITHUANIA
Anna of 621
Gedymin, Grand Duke of 797
Sophie of 621, 797
LITTA
Pompeo, Count xxvii
LITTLEBERRY
Elizabeth 728
LITTLEHALE
Hannah 632

1356

LITTLEHALES
  Sarah 590, 591
**LITTLETON/
LYTTELTON/
LYTTLETON**
  Alice (Thornes)
    233
  Anne 875
  Anne (South[e]y)
    (Harmar) 233, 311
  Bridget 407
  Caroline (Bristow)
    315
  Christian (Temple)
    315
  Edward (Sir) 137,
    233
  Elizabeth (Bowman)
    311
  Elizabeth (Stanley)
    407
  Elizabeth (Talbot)
    407
  Gertrude 310
  Joan 728
  John 233, 407
  Margaret 137
  Margaret (Devereux)
    137
  Mary 233
  Mary (Macartney)
    315
  Mary (Walter) 233
  Nathaniel xlviii,
    liii, 233, 310
  Roger 407
  Southey 310, 311
  Thomas (Sir), 4th
    Bt. 315
  William Henry
    Lyttelton, 1st
    Baron (Gov.) 315
LIVANOS
  Eugenia 23
LIVERPOOL
  Robert Banks
    Jenkinson, 2nd
    Earl of 334
LIVINGSTON
  Agnes 131
  Agnes (Douglas)
    160
  Agnes (Fleming)
    143, 159, 161, 163,
    165
  Agnes (Gray) 248
  Agnes (Livingston)
    243
  Alexander (Rev.),
    minister of
    Monyabroch 243
  Alexander, 1st Earl
    of Linlithgow
    143, 161
  Alexander, 2nd Earl
    of Linlithgow 161
  Alexander, 3rd Earl
    of Callendar 161
  Alexander, of Over
    and Nether Inches
    243
  Alexander
    Livingston, 5th
    Baron 160
  Alida (Schuyler)
    (Van Rensselaer)
    243
  Anne 143
  Anne (Graham) 161
  Barbara (Forrester)
    243
  Barbara (Livingston)
    243
  Caroline (de Grasse
    de Pau) 616
  Christian 828
  Cornelia 885
  Cornelia (Beekman)
    243
  Eleanor (Hay) 143,
    145, 161
  Elizabeth 244
  Elizabeth (Gordon)
    161
  Elizabeth (Graham)
    243
  Elizabeth (Maule)
    161
  family xxxii, xxxv
  George, 3rd Earl of
    Linlithgow 161
  Gilbert 243
  Gilbert James 243
  Harriet 616
  Helen 248
  Henry (Rev.),
    minister of St.
    Ninians 248
  Henry, of Falkirk
    248
  Henry Walter, Jr.
    616
  Isabel 282
  James 243, 244
  Janet (Bruce) 243
  Janet (Fleming) 243
  Jean 159, 163, 165

John 983
John (Rev.), minister of Ancrum 243
Judith 243
Judith (Newcomb) 243
Margaret (Forrester) 248
Margareta (Schuyler) 244
Marion 219
Mary 161
Mary (Batt) (Ashe) 468
Mary (Todd) 983
Polly 983
Robert 244
Robert, the elder, of Livingston Manor xix, xxxv, liv, clxiv, clxxi, 240, 243, 244
Robert, the younger xxxv, liv, clxiv, clxxi, 240, 244
Susanna (Lewis) 243
William (Rev.) 468
William (Rev.), minister of Monyabroch 243
William, of Kilsyth 243
William Livingston, 6th Baron 143, 159, 160, 161, 163, 165

LIVINGSTON/ LEVENTON
Robert 983

Zathiah (Sargent) 983

LIZOT
Marie-Anne 974
Marie-Josèphe 970
Marie-Madeleine (Dubé) 974
Marie-Madeleine (Miville) 970, 974
Marie-Ursule (Mignault dit Labrie) 974
Nicolas 970, 974

LLEUCU
ferch Henriffi ap Llywelyn 810
ferch Hywel ap Meurig Fychan 659, 694
ferch Madog 693
ferch Maredudd 686

LLEWELYN
Mary 510

LLOYD
Agnes 657
Anna clxxi, 231
Anne xix, xxxvii, xlvi, lvii, clxiii, 252, 657, 686, 809
Anne (Wilkinson) 686
Catrin (Wynn) 231, 232
Charles 231
Elizabeth (Lort) 231
Elizabeth (Pigott) 657
Elizabeth (Sneyd) 592

Elizabeth (Stanley) 231
family vii, xxiv, xxxvii, lv
Frances 657
Gainor 652
George, Bishop of Chester 686
Henry 355
John 231, 657
John Robert 592
Louise Charlotte 592
Margaret 355, 375, 394
Martha (Shakespear) 592
Mary (Crowley) 231
Mary (Farmer) 231
Mary (Jones) liv, lx, cxlix, cli, clxv, clxxi, 231, 233
Patience (Gardiner) (Story) 231
Rachel (Champion) 231
Rebecca (Nelson) 355
Robert lvi, cxci
Sampson 231
Thomas (Dep. Gov.) liv, lx, clxxi, clxv, 231, 232, 233, 378
William 592

LLYWELYN
ab Ifor 810
ap Dafydd, Constable of Rhuddlau 650, 659, 686, 694

ap Gruffudd Llwyd
  ap Robin 686
ap Hywel Fychan
  808
LLYWELYN FAWR
  ap Iorwerth, Prince
  of North Wales
  650, 657, 659, 680,
  682, 686, 689, 692,
  693, 694, 813, 824
**LOBANOV-
  ROSTOVSKY**
  Alexandra
    (Saltykov) 795
  Anastasia
    (Ourrossov),
    Princess 795, 796
  Ekaterina (Kurakin),
    Princess 795
  Ivan, Prince 795
  Jakov (Jacob),
    Prince 795
  Marie, Princess 795
LOBKOWICZ
  Amelia Franziska,
    Princess 11
  Anna Maria (von
    Althann) 35
  family 19
  Ferdinand August,
    Prince of 35, 49
  Ferdinand Joseph,
    Prince of 19
  Ferdinand Philip
    Joseph, Prince of
    18
  Ferdinand Zdenko
    Maria, Prince of
    19

Franz Joseph
  Maximilian, Prince
  of 18
Leopold Willibald,
  Prince 11
Maria Elisabeth,
  Princess of 35
Maria Ludovica,
  Princess of 49
Maximilian Erwin
  Maria Joseph
  Antonius von
  Padua Heinrich
  Thomas, Prince of
  clvi, 19, 142
Moritz Aloyse
  Joseph Marcellin,
  Prince of 19
Philip Hyacinth,
  Prince of 35
Wenceslaus
  Eusebius, Prince of
  35, 49
LOCKE
  John 580
  Mary (Evans)
    (Williams) 690
  William 690
LOCKHART
  Euphemia
    (Montgomery)
    143, 933
  Fergusia (Wishart)
    144
  George, of Carnwath
    143, 144, 933
  Grace 933
  Mary 239

**LOCKHART-
  WISHART**
  Annabella
    (Crawford) 144
  James (Sir), 1st Count
    of Lockhart 144
  Mariana Matilda 144
**LODENSTEYN
  (VAN)**
  Cornelis 774
  Geertruy [Gertrude]
    Jansdr. (van
    Ilpendam) 775
  Jan 775
  Sophia xxxii, lvii,
    775
  Sophia (van der
    Meer van
    Berendrecht) 774
LODER. *see also*
  LOWE
  Alba Julia
    (Lagomarsino) 98
  Ann E. 111
  Evelyn (Auffemordt)
    98
  Hedwig Eva Maria
    (Kiesler) [Hedy
    Lamarr] xvii, clvi,
    98
  John [William John
    Muir Lowe] clvi,
    98
  Micheline (Cheirel)
    98
  Sophie (Künzig) 98
LODGE
  Eleanor (Grosvenor)
    750

1359

Elizabeth 750
Jasper 750
John xxvii
LOFTUS
Adam (Sir) 383
Anne 307
Anne (Bagenall) 382
Dudley (Sir) 382
Eleanor 382
Eleanor (Butler) 382
Jane (Vaughan) 383
Lettice 405
Margaret (Chetham) 382
Nicholas 382, 383
Nicholas (Sir) 382
Sarah 383
LOGAN
Amy (Child) 279
Cordélie (Hebert) 987
Isabel (Hume) 279
James clxv, clxxii, 279
Laby 987
Patrick 279
Sarah (Blakeway) 311
Sarah (Read) 279
William 987
LOGIE
Barbara 148, 940
Margaret 223
LOISEAU
Jean-François 979
LOISEAU dit CARDIN
Marie-Eugénie 985
LOISELLE
Antonin (Fr.) 967
LOISINGER
Johanna Maria 41
LOLLE
Amee 653
LOMAX
Edward Lloyd (E. L.) lx
LONDON
Thomas Kemp, Bishop of 922
LONG
Catherine Maria 346
Eleanor (Wrottesley) 320
Henry (Sir) 320
Margery 320
Mary (Tate) 346
Samuel 346
LONG/LANG
Anne 249
LONGESPEE
Ela 742, 746, 752, 760, 761, 772
Emmeline (de Riddleford) 742, 746, 752, 760, 772
Ida 687, 737, 741, 749, 754, 757, 763, 766, 768, 770
Idoine (de Camville) 761
Stephen 741, 742, 746, 752, 760, 772
William (Sir) 761
William, 1st Earl of Salisbury vii, 658, 687, 737, 741, 742, 746, 749, 752, 754, 757, 760, 761, 763, 766, 768, 770, 772, 841, 845
LONGFORD
Alice 754, 757
Alice (Deincourt) 754
Alice (le Boteler) 754, 757
Elizabeth 561
Margery/Margaret (Solney) 754
Nicholas (Sir) 754, 757
William Lygon Pakenham, 4th Earl of 73
LONGLAND (DE)
Isabel (de Beaupré) 687, 695
Joan 695
John 687, 695
Margaret 687
LONGMORE
Louise 973
LONGUEVAL (DE)
Antoinette 945
Charles, Seigneur des Ormes 944
Louise (de Joyeuse) 944
LONGVILLIERS
family 442
LOOCKERMANS
Maria (Duncanson) (MacFasse) 248
Pieter 248

1360

LOOMIS
Catherine 925
Mary 213
LOPES LOBO
Diogo, Senhor de
  Alvito e Oriola 619
Isabel (de Sousa)
  619
LOPES PACHECO
Violante 619
LÓPEZ COLLADA
María Luisa 521
LÓPEZ de ALANIS
Catalina (de Guzmán)
  995
Isabel (Naharro de
  Humanes) 995
Jerónimo 995
Rodrigo Ponce de
  León 995
LOPEZ PERES
Adans 934
Stéphanie-Marie-
  Élisabeth (Grimaldi)
  (Ducruet), Princess
  of Monaco 934
LOPUCHIN
Anna 799, 800
Peter 800
Sophia 194
Tatiana 800
Tatiana (Golitzin/
  Gallitzine),
  Princess 800
LORD
Charles M. lx
Deborah 630, 886
Mary Scott 496,
  503, 731, 867, 878

LORENZ OTTO
CARL AMADEUS
THADEUS MARIA
PIUS ANDREAS
MARCUS
D'AVIANO
Archduke of Austria
  201
LORENZO II
de' Medici, Duke of
  Urbino 637
LORNE
John Stewart, 2nd
  Baron 269, 270,
  280, 283, 284
Robert Stewart, 1st
  Baron 269, 280,
  283
LORRAINE
Catherine of 291
Charles I, Duke of
  291
Charles II, Duke of
  637
Charles-Louis of,
  Prince of Lambesc,
  Count of Brionne
  613
Ezzo, Count
  Palatine of 849
Francis I of, Holy
  Roman Emperor
  15
Richeza of, Queen
  of Poland 849
LORRAINE-
BRIONNE
Marie-Thérèse-
  Josèphe of 613

LORSIGNOL (DE)
Marie de Mailly,
  Dame 633
LORT
Elizabeth 231
LORTI
Sybil 855
LOSSE (DE)
Marie-Louise 206
LOTBINIÈRE (DE)
Louis-Théandre
  Chartier, Sieur
  939, 955
LOUCHES
Elizabeth 737
LOUDON
Fiona 362
LOUDOUN
Hugh Campbell, 3rd
  Earl of 143
James Campbell,
  2nd Earl of 143
John Campbell, 4th
  Earl of 143
LOUÉ (DE)
Guy II de Laval,
  Seigneur 942
Pierre de Laval,
  Seigneur 942
LOUGHNAN
Ludivina 79
LOUIS
Prince of Battenberg,
  1st Marquess of
  Milford Haven 41
LOUIS I
Duke of Bourbon
  638
Duke of Savoy 442

Grand Duke of
Hesse 41
Landgrave of Hesse
449
LOUIS II
Duke of Bavaria
617
Grand Duke of
Hesse 41
King of Naples,
Sicily, Jerusalem
and Aragón 205
Landgrave of Hesse
449, 450
**LOUIS II HONORÉ-
CHARLES-
ANTOINE**
Grimaldi, Sovereign
Prince of Monaco
xl, 20, 933
LOUIS IV
of Bavaria, Holy
Roman Emperor
51, 52, 447, 449,
451, 617, 907
King of France
xxvi, 720, 874,
877, 879, 919
LOUIS VI
King of France
804, 949, 954, 956,
965
LOUIS VII
King of France
735, 774, 776, 943,
952, 993
LOUIS VIII
Landgrave of Hesse-
Darmstadt 40

LOUIS IX
Landgrave of Hesse-
Darmstadt 41
LOUIS IX (ST.)
King of France
634, 638, 965
LOUIS X
King of France 455
LOUIS XI
King of France
200, 203, 205
LOUIS XIII
King of France
xxi, lxx, 289
LOUIS XIV
King of France
287, 288, 289
LOUIS XVI
King of France 294
LOUIS FREDERICK
Duke of
Württemberg-
Mömpelgard 184
LOUIS FREDERICK I
Prince of Schwarz-
burg- Rudolstadt
891, 892
LOUIS-PHILIPPE
King of the French
288, 290, 291, 294
**LOUIS-PHILIPPE-
JOSEPH
"ÉGALITÉ"**
de Bourbon, Duke
of Orléans 287,
288
LOUIS VICTOR
of Savoy, Prince of
Carignan 18

LOUISE
Princess of
Battenberg, Queen
of Sweden 41
Princess of
Mecklenburg-
Strelitz, Queen of
Prussia 8, 40
Princess of Nassau-
Saarbrücken 47
**LOUISE
(FREDERICA
DOROTHEA
LOUISE
PHILIPPINE)**
Princess of Prussia
16
**LOUISE CAROLINE
ALBERTA**
Princess of Great
Britain 75
**LOUISE
CHARLOTTE**
Princess of Branden-
burg 54, 56
**LOUISE
DOROTHEA**
Princess of Saxe-
Gotha 45
**LOUISE
ELIZABETH**
of Courland 54, 55
**LOUISE
HENRIETTE**
Princess of Hesse-
Darmstadt 41
LOUISE JULIANE
Princess of Pfalz
56

1362

LOUISE SYBIL
of Waldeck-
Wildungen 181
LOUNDS
Mary 506
LOURIE
Arthur Vincent 5
Elisabeth (Belevsky-
Zhukovsky) (Ghika-
Perevostchikov),
Countess clvi, 5
LOUTH
Matthew Plunkett,
5th Baron 900
Oliver Plunkett, 4th
Baron 900
LOUVAIN
Adeliza of, Queen of
England (wife of
William d'Aubigny,
1st Earl of Arundel)
830
Ida of 851
Lambert, Count of
879, 919
Maud of 879, 919
LOUVEGNIES (DE)
Jacques de Haynin,
Seigneur de
Haynin and 733
LOUVET
Marie-Juliette 933
LOVAT
Hugh Fraser, 5th
Baron 176
Hugh Fraser, 9th
Baron 67
Simon Fraser, 6th
Baron 176

Simon Fraser, 13th
Baron 23
Thomas Fraser, 12th
Baron 23
LOVECRAFT
Mary (Fulford)
cxci
LOVEL (DE)
Isabel (___) 835
John 835
Katherine (Basset)
835
Maud 835
Maud (de
Beaumont) 835
Maud (Sydenham)
835
William 835
LOVELACE
Anne xxxiv, liii,
lxix, clxvi, 509
Anne (Barne) 509
Charlotte (Clayton)
xlix, liii, cli, 543,
781
Dudley 509
Elizabeth (Aucher)
509
family 509
Francis (Gov.) liii,
lxix, 509
John Lovelace
(Gov.), 4th Baron
clxxvii, 543, 781
Mary (___) 509
Mary (Neville) 781
Richard 509
Thomas 509
William 781

William (Sir) 509
LOVELL
Alice 426, 596
Alice (Huddleston)
426
Charles 426
Eleanor (Morley)
596
Elizabeth (le Gros)
426
Janet 260
Julia 361
Penelope Eleanor
(Elphinstone-
Dalrymple)
(Balston) cxlv, 128
Russell Alexander,
Jr. 128
Thomas (Sir) 426
William 596
LOVERING
Mary Campbell 917
LOVETT
Anna (Danvers) 716
Elizabeth 467, 717
Elizabeth (Boteler)
716
Thomas 716
LOVEWELL
Catherine 519, 520
Nehemiah 519
Rachel (Farwell)
519
LOWE. *see also*
LODER
Anne (Cavendish)
333, 512
Caroline Charlotte
(Muir) 98

1363

Catherine
(Pilkington) 512
Eleanor 749
Elizabeth (Foster)
512
Elizabeth (Roe)
(Combes) 512
Ellen 750
family li, lii, 512
Frances Bruster (de
Salvo) 98
Henry liii, clxxiv,
512
Isabel 333
Jane xxxv, clxv,
clxxiv, 332, 339,
512, 819
John 512
Nicholas clxxiv,
512
Susannah Maria
(Bennett) (Darnall)
512
Vincent 333, 512
William Henry 98
William Henry Muir
98
William John Muir
[John Loder] clvi,
98
LOWELL. *see also*
LOWLE
Caroline Maureen
(Hamilton-Temple-
Blackwood) (Freud)
(Citkowitz), Lady
[Caroline Black-
wood] xviii, 31
Charles 86

Elizabeth 126
Elizabeth (Goodale)
126
family xxxvi, 569,
570
Harriet Brackett
(Spence) 86
James Russell 86
John 126
John (Judge) 570
Percival xix, xlviii,
lv, lxv, cxlv, clxi,
86, 126, 569, 570
Rebecca (___)
126, 569
Robert Traill
Spence, IV xviii,
31, 86
**LÖWENSTEIN-
WERTHEIM-
ROCHEFORT**
Victoria Felicitas of
38
**LÖWENSTEIN-
WERTHEIM-
ROSENBERG**
Marie Josephine
Sophie, Princess of
40
LOWER
Dorothy 136
Penelope (Perrott)
136
William (Sir) 136
LOWER LORRAINE
Adelaide of 874,
877
Charles, Duke of
874, 877, 879, 919

Gerberga of 879,
919
Regelinde of 874,
877
LOWIN
Elizabeth 358
LOWLE. *see also*
LOWELL
Ava 412
Christian (Percival)
569
family 412
Richard 569
LOWNDES
Alice (___) 752
Anne Stuart (Byrth)
753
Charles clxix, 752,
753
Christopher lix,
752, 753
Eleanor (Baldwin)
753
Elizabeth (Byerley)
753
Elizabeth (Tasker)
752
Jane (Weld) 752
John 752
Margaret (Poole)
752
Mary Elizabeth
clvi, 753
Richard 752, 753
Ruth (Rawlins)
752
Sarah (___) 752
Susannah (Dobson)
753

William 753
LOWRI
  ferch Dafydd 692
  ferch Dafydd ab
    Ieuan 659
  ferch Edward ap
    Dafydd 658
  ferch Elise 658
  ferch Gruffudd
    Fychan 770, 813
  ferch Hywel Llwyd
    660
  ferch Tudur ap
    Gruffudd Fychan
    657, 689
LOWTHER
  Agnes 363, 364
  Christopher (Sir)
    363
  Dorothy (Clifford)
    363
  Eleanor 364
  Eleanor (Fleming)
    363
  Eleanor (Musgrave)
    363
  Frances (Middleton)
    363
  Hugh (Sir) 363
  John 109
  John (Sir) 363
  John (Sir), 1st Bt.
    364
  Maria Jo(h)anna
    (Somerset) xlvi,
    cxlvi, 109
  Mary (Fletcher)
    364
  Richard (Sir) 363

LUBOMIRSKI
  Adam Johann
    Kasimir Stanislaus,
    Prince 622
  Alexander Michael,
    Prince 621
  Alexi(s) Jean, Prince
    xii, clvi, 622
  Aniela Teresa
    (Michowska) 622
  Anna, Princess 16
  Casimir, Prince
    227, 622
  Eileen Pamela
    (Beardsell) 622
  Françoise (Zaluska),
    Countess 622
  George (Jerzy)
    Sebastian, Prince
    621
  George Alexander,
    Prince 622
  Giada (Torri) 622
  Jeanne-Marie (de
    Villiers-Terrage)
    622
  Joanna (von
    Starzhausen) 622
  Josef, Prince 622
  Katherine Anne
    (Sapieha), Princess
    621
  Konstance (z
    Bobrku
    Ligezianka) 621
  Ladislaus Jean
    Adam, Prince 622
  Louisa (Sosnowska)
    622

Louisa Honorata
    (Pociejowna) 622
Marie (Jelowicka)
    622
Marie, Princess 227
Martin Stanislaus,
    Prince 622
princes 155
Sophia (Ostrogska),
    Princess 621
Stanislaus, Prince
    621, 622
Stanislaus Michael
    Heinrich, Prince
    622
Wanda Marie Helena
    (Lubomirska),
    Princess 622
Zénaïde (Holynska)
    227, 622
LUBY
  Elizabeth Pamela
    Audrey 9
LUCE
  Henry Robinson, Jr.
    91
  Henry Robinson, III
    90, 91
  Leila Eliott (Burton)
    (Hadley) (Smitter)
    (Musham) 90
  Lila (Hotz) 91
LUCKETT
  Edith 673
LUCRETIA
  (Borgia), Duchess of
    Modena and
    Ferrara 293

LUCY (DE)
Eleanor 534
Eleanor
 (l'Archdekne)
 326, 534
Elizabeth (Wayte)
 clxxxvi, 100, 103,
 105, 106
Margaret
 (Mowbray) xxv,
 534
Maud 326, 879
Reginald (Sir) xxv,
 534
Walter (Sir) 326,
 534
LUDDINGTON
Alice 528
____ 843
LUDLAM
Katherine 677
LUDLOW
Anne 377, 411
Benedicta 723
Edith (Windsor)
 503
Elizabeth (Grey)
 378
Elizabeth (Vaughan
 or Grey) 377,
 378, 411, 412
family li, lxvi
Francis 503
Gabriel xxxv, clxiv,
 clxxiv, 503, 504
George 503, 504
Jane (Bennett) 504
Jane (Pyle) 503
John 503

John (Sir) 377,
 378, 411
Margery clxxxv,
 768, 770
Martha (Cary) 504
Mary (Cogan) 503,
 539
Phyllis (____) 503
Roger (Dep. Gov.)
 clxiii, 503, 504,
 539
Sarah xix, xxxiv,
 clxvi, 498, 503,
 539
Sarah (Hanmer) 504
Thomas 503, 504
LUDWELL
family 856, 1026
Frances (Colepepper/
 Culpeper)
 (Stephens)
 (Berkeley) 347,
 839, 856
Jane (Cottington)
 856
John 856
Judith (Morseley)
 (Stevens) 856
Lucy (Higginson)
 (Burwell) 856
Philip (Gov.) xi,
 xxxv, xlix, cxlv,
 clxvii, 347, 839,
 856, 1026
Thomas 856
LUGG
Jane (Deighton)
 lxviii, clxi, clxxii,
 297

John 297
LUISA FRANCISCA
 (de Guzmán), Queen
 of Portugal 140,
 142
LUKE
Anne 662
Margaret (St. John)
 662
Nicholas (Sir) 662,
 663
LUKYN/LUCKEN
Judith 654
Thomasine (Walter)
 654
William 654
LUMLEY
Agnes 100
Anne (Conyers) 105
Anne (Kurtwich)
 105
Anthony (Hon.)
 105
Eleanor (Neville)
 761
Frances (Jones) 105
Frances (Shelley)
 105
Isabel (Radcliffe)
 100
Joan 418, 599
John (Hon.) 105
Katherine 761
Margaret (not
 Elizabeth)
 (Plantagenet)
 clxxxv, clxxxvi,
 100, 105, 106
Mary 105

1366

Mary (Compton) 105
Ralph Lumley, 1st Baron 761
Richard, 1st Earl of Scarbrough 105
Richard Lumley, 1st Viscount 105
Richard Lumley, 5th Baron 105
Roger 100, 105
Sibyl 106
Thomas clxxxv, 100, 105, 106
___ (Gray) 105
LUMSDEN
Agnes 790
Jean 789
Margaret 255, 268
LUNA (DE)
Constance 963
LUNAN
Anna 268
LUNDEN
Hélène (Rubens) 804
Jean-Baptiste 804
Jeanne-Catherine 804
LUNDIE
Helen 267
LUNDIN
Christian 261, 266
Elizabeth 254
LUNGE
Sidsel 644, 646
LUNGVILIERS (DE)
Ellen (FitzWilliam) 841

John (Sir) 841
Margaret 841
LUNSFORD
Anne (Hudson) 551
Barbara (Lewknor) 551
Elizabeth (Wormeley) (Kempe) 483, 551
family lv
John 551
John (Sir) 551
Katherine (Fludd) 551
Katherine (Neville) cxlv, 417, 551, 552
Mary (Sackville) 551
Thomas 551
Thomas (Sir) lx, 417, 483, 551, 552
LUNT
Henry, Jr. 344, 924
Jane 344
Jane (Browne) 344, 924
Mary 924
Mary (___) 126
LUPÉ (DE)
Jean, Seigneur de Maravat 634
Marguerite (de Morlhon) 634
Percide 634
LUPTON
Frances Elizabeth (Greenhow) [Frances Lupton] 379

Francis 379
Francis Martineau 379
Harriet Albina (Davis) 379
Olive Christiana 379
LUSIGNAN (DE)
Anne, Princess of Cyprus 442
Hugh X, Count of la Marche 785
John I, titular King of Cyprus, Jerusalem, and Armenia 442
Maud, of Eu 783
LUTTRELL
Andrew (Sir) 493, 503, 569, 608
Anne (Aylmer) 486, 487
Catherine 493
Catherine (Beaumont) 503, 569, 608
Eleanor 569
Elizabeth 503, 608
Elizabeth (Courtenay) 423, 503, 569, 608
Godfrey Hilton, Baron 715
Hugh (Sir) 493, 503, 569, 608
James (Sir) 569
John (Sir) 493, 569
Margaret 486, 493
Margaret (Hill) 493, 569
Margaret (Touchet) 569

Margaret (Wyndham) 493, 494
Mary (Ryce) 493
Thomas (Sir) 486
LUXEMBOURG
  Charles of, Count of Brienne 208
  Françoise of 208
  Françoise of, Countess of Gavre 291, 459
  Gerard of, Seigneur de Durbay 950
  Grand Dukes of 45, 141, 288, 444
  Jacqueline of 208
  Marguerite of 950
  María Teresa (Mestre y Batista), Grand Duchess of 991
  Philippa of 459
LYFFE
  Amice 695
  Margery (Stawell) 695
  Richard 695
LYGON. *see also* LIGON
  Anne 532
  Anne (Beauchamp) 295, 492, 532, 575, 576
  Cecily 295, 296, 522
  Dorothy 492
  Eleanor (Dennis) 295, 296, 532
  Elizabeth 296, 297, 575, 576

Elizabeth (Berkeley) 296, 297, 532
Elizabeth (Pratt) 295
family 123, 576
Frances (Dennis) 295
George (Rev.) 576
Henry 296, 532
Katherine 296, 308
Margaret 296
Margaret (Grevile) 295, 532
Richard 295, 492, 532, 575, 576
Richard (Sir) 295, 532
Thomas 295, 296
William 295, 296, 532
LYKOV-OBOLENSKY
  Anastasia (Romanov) 792
  Boris, Prince 792
  Elena, Princess 792, 795
  Feodosia, Princess 795
  Maria, Princess 794
LYLE
  Jean 269
LYMAN
  Abigail (Moseley) 673
  Anne Jean (Robbins) 210, 479, 716
  Catherine Robbins 211, 479, 571, 716

Géneviève B. 20
John (III) 673
Joseph (III) 210, 479, 716
Mindwell 673
LYNCH
  Eloïsa (Ortíz Alfaro) (Eldridge) 996, 997
  family 991, 997
  María Isabel (Zavaleta Riglos) 996
  Mary H. 222
LYNCH ORTÍZ
  Ana Isabel 991, 997
  Guillermo Rufino 997
LYNCH ROO
  Patricio Julián José 996
LYNCH ZAVALETA
  Francisco de Paula Eustaquio ("Frank E.") lv, lxiii, clvi, 996, 997
LYNDE
  Elizabeth 357, 924
  Elizabeth (Digby) 749
  Enoch 749
  Hannah (Newgate) 357, 749, 924
  Joan 853
  Simon lxv, clxi, clxxvi, 357, 749, 924
LYNDON
  Margaret Evelyn 135

LYNES
  Anne (Seymour)
    (Powell) 598
  Philip 598
LYNNE
  George 325
  Isabel (Forrest) 325
  Martha 325, 405
  Martha (Throck-
    morton) 325
LYON
  Agnes 341
  Elizabeth 155, 933
  Jean (Keith) 898
  John, 6th Baron
    Glamis 898
  Margaret 168, 898
LYONS
  Augusta Mary Minna
  Catherine 71
LYSTER. *see also*
  LISTER
  Anne Isabella
    (Isdell) 433
  Anthony 433
  Armstrong 433
  Christiana
    (Killkeny) 433
  Deborah (Osbald-
    eston) 433
  Elizabeth 120
  Elizabeth
    (Coddington)
    120, 433
  Ellen Emily
    (Cooper) 433
  Henry Francis
    LeHunte (Dr.)
    433

Jane (Ducasse) 433
John 120, 433
Martha (Hatton)
  433
Mary (Tisdall) 120
Thomas 433
Walter 433
William 120
William John 433
William Narcissus
  (Rev.) lii, 433
Winifred Lee
  (Brent) 433
___ (O'Kelly)
  433
LYTE
  Elizabeth 598
  Gertrude 335
LYTE-HOWARD
  Charles 335
  Rebecca (Webb)
    335
LYTTELTON/
  LYTTLETON. *see*
  LITTLETON/
  LYTTELTON/
  LYTTLETON
LYTTON
  Anne 557, 575,
    710, 711
  Audrey (Booth)
    710
  Elizabeth 711
  Frances (Calverley)
    710
  Robert (Sir) 710
  William (Sir) 710
MABERLY
  Mary 121

MABLI
  ferch Maredudd ap
    Henry Dwnn 582
MACARTNEY
  Mary 315
MacCARTHY/
  McCARTHY
  Alexander 546
  Eliza (Fagan) 546
  Eugene Joseph
    (Sen.) 108
  Helen 546
  Jenny 976
  John Leader 542
  Mary Susanna
    (Willis-Bund) 542
MacCARTHY-
  MORROGH
  Anne (Stubbman)
    546
  Donal Florence 546
  James 546
  Kathleen Helen
    [Kay Summersby]
    xviii, cxlvi, 546
  Vera (Hutchinson)
    546
MacCARTHY-
  WILLIS-BUND
  Alison E. cliii, 542
  family 542
  Francis Leader 542
  Joan Mildred Elton
    (Carey) 542
MacDONALD, later
  BOSVILLE
  Alexander William
    Robert, Sir, *de jure*
    12th Baronet 27

Matilda Eliza
(Moffat) 27
**MacDONALD/
McDONALD**
Doug (Prof.) lx,
lxv, 261, 262
Florence, of Morrer
213, 249
Godfrey Bosville
Macdonald, 3rd
Baron 27
Grizel 828
Julia 123
Louisa Maria
(LaCoast) 27
Marian, of
Clanranald 213
____ (mistress of Sir
James Stewart of
Baldoran) 264
**MacDOWALL/
McDOWALL**
Elizabeth (Graham)
161
Isabella Graham 161
James 161
Margaret (Jamieson)
161
William, of
Garthland 161
MacEWEN. *see also*
McEWEN
Aimee Maxine
(Barnes) 146
Andrew Brian
Wendover viii, xi,
lxi, lxx, 147, 218,
242, 247, 257, 259,
263, 266, 281, 940

Maynard Leslie 146
MacFASSE
Jan 248
Maria (Duncanson)
248
**MacGILLAPATRICK/
FITZPATRICK**
Sadhbh ní Giolla
Phadraig 601
MacGREGOR
Daniel ix, lx, lxi
MACHELL
Jane (Woodruff)
580
John 580, 581
Mary 580, 581
Mary (Lewknor) 580
Matthew 580
**MACKAY/MacKAY/
McKAY**
Agnes (Sinclair) 82
Angus, of Bighouse
82
Ann (____) [Mrs.
Ann (____)
Stephens?] 82
Ann (Crerar) 82, 83
Anne 82
Barbara (Murray),
of Pennyland 82
Christina
(McMillan) 217
Elizabeth 283
Elizabeth (Sinclair),
of Brims 82
Elizabeth Florence
217
Elizabeth McLachlan
(MacLean) 216

George lxiii, cxlv,
82, 83, 216
George Alexander
xlvii, cxlv, 217
Helen 68
Hugh (Huistern
Dhu), of Farr 82
Hugh, of Strathy 82
James, of Ga. 82, 83
Jane 695
Jane (Mackay), of
Reay 82
Jane (Sinclair), of
Ulbster 82
Jean (Gordon) 82
Jean (Mackay) 82
John 82
John, of Dirlot and
Strathy 82
John, of Strathy 82
Margaret 137
Margaret (Henderson)
82
Sarah (More) 82
Sinclair 82
William, of Bighouse
82
MACKENZIE
Agnes 239
Agnes, of Kintail 146
Alexander (Sir), 2nd
Bt., of Gairloch 97
Alexander (Sir), 3rd
Bt., of Gairloch 97
Alexander, of Coul
283
Alexander, of
Davochmaluag 95

Anne (Sinclair) 92, 897
Anne, Lady 92
Barbara (Grant) 266, 283
Christian (Henderson) 97
Christian (Munro) 283
Colin, of Kintail 266, 283
Colin, of Pluscardine 266
Elizabeth 897
Elizabeth (Mackenzie) 897
Elizabeth (Rose) 95
Elizabeth (Stewart) 239, 283
family 266
George, 1st Earl of Cromarty 92, 897
George, 3rd Earl of Cromarty 92
George Norbury 422
Hector (Sir), 4th Bt., of Gairloch 97
Isabel (Gordon) 92
Isabel (Ogilvie) 266
Isabella Campbell 405
James (Sir), 1st Bt. 897
Janet (Grant) 97
Janet (Mackenzie) 97
Jean 239, 255, 283, 897
Jean (Chisolm) 283
Jean (Grant) 266
John, 2nd Earl of Cromarty 92
John, of Eileanach 97
Kenneth (Sir), 1st Bt. 283
Kenneth (Sir), of Kintail 239, 283
Kenneth Mackenzie, 1st Baron, of Kintail 266
Kythé Caroline 97
Margaret xlvi, cxlviii, 95, 266, 893
Margaret (Heatley) 266
Margaret (Mackenzie), of Redcastle 97
Mary 283, 285
Mary (Murray) 92
Mary, Lady 92
Mary Jane (Inglis) 97
Roderick (Sir), 2nd Bt., of Scatwell 97
Thomas, of Pluscardine 266
MACKINTOSH/ McINTOSH
Agnes (Mackenzie), of Kintail 146, 239
Elizabeth (Byfield) 239
Elizabeth (Innes) 239
Elizabeth (Mackintosh/ McIntosh) 239
family liv, lxv, 240
Helen (Gordon) 239
Henry clxiii
Henry (Col.) clxxi, 239
Isabel 146
Janet (Gordon) 239
John Mohr clxxi, 152, 239
Lachlan clxiii, clxxi, 239
Lachlan, of Borlum 239
Lachlan, of Knocknagel 239
Lachlan, of Mackintosh 146, 239
Margaret (Ogilvie), of Deskford 239
Marjory (Fraser) 152, 239
Mary (Baillie) 239, 255
Mary (Lockhart) 239
Mary (Reade) 239
Mary Ann 152
William, of Borlum 239, 255
William, of Mackintosh 239
MACKWORTH
Agnes 319
Alice (Basynges/ Basing) 727

Anne (Hall) 311
Anne (Sherard) 727
Beatrix (___) 727
Catherine 727
Dorothy (Cranage) 319
Dorothy (Lee) 319
Elizabeth (Hall) 311
Ellen (Hercy) 727
Francis 727
George 311, 727
Henry 727
Henry (Sir), 2nd Bt. 311
John 727
Margaret 311, 475
Mary (Hopton) 311
Richard 319
Thomas 319, 727
Thomas (Sir), 1st Bt. 311
MacLACHLAN. *see* McLACHLAN
MACLEAN/ MacLEAN/McLEAN/ MACLAINE
Allan, of Conn. clxxi, 213
Allan, of Grisiboll 213
Anna (Gubbertz) 216
Anna Isabella MacLean, Baroness 216
Anne (Long/Lang) 249

Anne (MacLean), of Kilmore in Mull 213
Archibald 249
Beathag (MacLean) 216
Catherine (MacLean) 213
Charles, of Borreray 249
David MacLean, Baron (Friherre) 216
Donald Charles Hugh 34
Eleonora Elisabeth (von Ascheberg), Countess 216
Elizabeth (Fraser) 216
Elizabeth (McLachlan), of McLachlan 216
Elizabeth McLachlan 216
family xlvii, lv, 213, 217, 249
Florence (MacDonald), of Morrer 213, 249
Florence (MacLean) 249
Florence (MacLeod), of MacLeod 249
Fynvola Susan 65
Gwendoline Katherine Leonora (Hope) 34

Hannah (Stillman) (Caldwell) 213
Hector, of Duart 213, 216, 249
Hector, of Kingairloch and Pictou, N.S. 216
Hector, of Lochbuie 216
Hector, of Torloisk 216
Hector Charles Donald (Sir) 34
Hector Roy, of Coll 249
Hugh (Ewen), of Balliphetrish 213
Hugh, of Kingairloch 216
Isabella (Acheson) 216
Janet (Campbell) 213, 249
Janet (MacLean) 216
John (Prof.) clxxi, 240, 249
John (Sir), 1st Bt., 1st Adlad Macklier (Sweden) 216
John Cassilis 65
John Garbh, of Drimnin 213
Lachlan (Sir), of Duart 213, 216
Lachlan, of Coll 249
Lachlan, of Kingairloch 216
Lachlan, of Lochbuie 216

Lachlan, of Torloisk 213, 216
Margaret 216, 249
Margaret (Campbell), of Lochnell 216
Margaret (Cunyngham) 213, 216
Margaret (MacLean) 216
Margaret Isobel (Randolph) 65
Marian (Campbell) 216
Marian (MacDonald), of Clanranald 213
Marion (MacLean) 249
Mary 144, 216
Mary (Loomis) 213
Mary (Maclaine) 216
Mary (MacLean) 213
Neil, of Conn. clxx, 213
Neil, of Drimnacross 213, 249
Opre (Vyvyan) 34
Phebe (Bainbridge) 249
Sara 34
Susanna (Beauchamp) 213
Susanna (Campbell), of Scamadall 249

MacLEOD/McLEOD
Alexander (Rev.) clxxi, 249
Flora Loudoun 128
Florence, of MacLeod 249
Katherine 828
Margaret (MacLean) 249
Maria Anne (Agnew) 249
Neil 249

MACMILLAN
Dorothy Evelyn (Cavendish) 26
Harold [Maurice Harold], 1st Earl of Stockton, Prime Minister 26

MacNAB
Allan Napier (Sir), 1st Bt., Premier of the Canadas 655
Mary (Stuart) 655
Sophia Mary 655

MACY
Harry, Jr. lx

MADDISON
Arthur Roland (A.R.) (Rev.) lx

MADDOX
Mary 152

MADELEINE
Princess of France, Queen of Scotland 82, 85, 87, 88, 90, 92, 93, 95, 96, 97, 98, 897

MADERTY
James Drummond, 1st Baron 168

MADISON
Dorothea "Dolly" (Payne) (Todd) 497, 532
Eleanor Rose (Conway) 497, 532
Elizabeth 764
James 497, 532
James, Jr., 4th U.S. President 497, 532

MADOG
ab Elise 657, 689, 692, 693
ab Ieuan 693
ap Gruffudd Maelawr, Prince of Powys Fadog 815
ap Hywel Felyn 811
ap Maredudd 815

MADOG FOEL
ab Iorwerth 886

MADOG GOCH
ab Ieuan Goch 650

MADONNA
Ciccone [Madonna Louise Veronica Ciccone] 63, 380, 967, 969, 975, 988

MADUELL
Charles R., Jr. lx

MAFRA E ERICEIRA (DE)
Alvaro Dias de Sousa, Senhor 619
Diogo Afonso de Sousa, Senhor 619
Lope Dias de Sousa, Senhor 619

1373

MAGAN
 Anne Catherine
  (Richards) 120
 Ida May (Bauer)
  120
 Lillian (Eshelman)
  120
 Percy Tilson 120
 Percy Tilson, Jr.
  clvi, 120, 124
MAGDALEN SYBIL
 Princess of Holstein-
  Gottorp 47
MAGDALEN SYBILLA
 Princess of Prussia
  47, 891
MAGDALENA
 Princess of Cleves
  40, 43
 of Schwarzburg-
  Rudolstadt 182,
  196
 of Waldeck 181
MAGILL
 family 441, 626
MAGNIS (VON)
 Marie Johanna 220
MAGNUS
 Duke of Saxony
  832
MAGNUS II
 Duke of
  Saxe-Lauenburg
  52
MAGRUDER/ McGRUDER
 Alexander li, lx,
  clxvi, 270, 280

Elizabeth (___) 280
 family 280
 Margaret (Campbell),
  of Keithick 280
 Sarah (___) 280
 Thomas Garland, Jr.
  280
MAGUIRE
 Edna Beatrix 217
 Elizabeth Florence
  (McKay) 217
 Osborne 217
MAHALYI
 Judith Helen 83, 635
MAHEU
 Anne (Couvent)
  (Amiot) 945, 967,
  969, 972, 973, 975,
  976, 977, 978, 979,
  980, 981, 982
 Jacques 945, 969
MAHLER
 Leslie ix, xlvii,
  xlviii, xlix, lii, lviii,
  lx, lxx, cxc, 358,
  384, 492, 494, 501,
  586, 649, 656, 669,
  683, 741, 759, 765
MAHON
 Anne (Browne),
  Lady 465
 Anne (Symes) 364
 family xviii, lxvi,
  434
 Frances Catherine
  (Ker) 465
 George Charles
  clxxii, 364, 434
 Henry 364

 James, Dean of
  Dromore 465
 Jane Caroline 364,
  434
 Ross 465
 Sarah (L'Estrange)
  364, 434
 Sophia Madelina
  Olivia 465
MAIDMAN
 Sarah 350
MAIDSTONE
 Margaret 483
MAILER
 Jeanne Louise
  (Campbell), Lady
  70, 371
 Norman xviii, 70,
  371
MAILLA
 Irené de Moyria,
  Seigneur 952
MAILLARD
 Bénigne (le
  Bouteillier) 950
 Jacques, Seigneur de
  Champaigne 950
 Marie (Morant) 950
 Miles, Seigneur du
  Breuil and de La
  Boissière 950
 Renée 950
MAILLÉ (DE)
 Donatien, Marquis
  de Kerman 227
 Henri, Marquis de
  Kerman 226
 Marie-Anne (du
  Puy) 226

Marie-Eléonore 227
Marie-Louise (Binet de Marcognet) 227
Mauricette (de Ploëuc) 226
MAILLÉ DE LA TOUR-LANDRY (DE)
  François, Baron de la Tour-Landry, Count de Châteauroux 455
  Françoise (called Diane) (de Rohan) 455
  Madeleine 455
MAILLET
  Marie-Virginie-Adelphine 974
MAILLY (DE)
  Antoinette 633
  Catherine (de Mamez) 633
  Colart (Nicholas) de Mailly, Baron 633
  Gilles VI de Mailly, Baron 633
  Jean II de Mailly, Baron 633
  Marie (de Coucy) 633
  Marie (de Mailly), Dame de Lorsignol 633
MAINE
  Charles, Count of 205
  Charles d'Anjou, Duke of 205

Ferdinando Gorges (Sir), Lord Proprietor of xvii, liii, lvi, lx, clxxii, clxxiii, 295, 392, 406, 457, 522, 838
MAINTENON (DE)
  Françoise-Charlotte (-Amable) (d'Aubigné), Marquise [Mme. de Maintenon] 288
MAINWARING (DE)
  Agnes (Arderne) 763, 768, 770
  Amicia (de Meschines) 815, 817, 822
  Anna Maria 859
  Anne 559, 697, 746
  Arthur (Sir) 500
  Bertrade 815, 822, 861
  Christian (de Birtles) 817
  Dorothy (Corbet) 500, 501
  Elizabeth (Brereton) 500
  Elizabeth (Leycester) 817
  family xxiv, 559
  Hannah (Raymond) 400
  John (Sir) 407, 500, 817
  Katherine 407
  Katherine (Hondford) 407, 500

Margaret 746
Margaret (Delves) 817
Margaret (Mainwaring) 500
Margaret (Savage) 746, 752, 753
Margaret (Torbock) 400, 558
Margery 752
Margery (Venables) 817
Mary xlvii, l, lvi, clxv, clxxxii, 400, 500, 558, 559, 817, 875
Mary (___) 400
Mary (Davenport) 817
Matilda 763, 768, 770
Oliver xlvii, l, liv, lvi, clxiii, clxxiii, 400, 558, 559
Prudence (Ashe) 400
Ralph 815, 817, 822
Randall 746, 752, 753, 817
Randall (Sir) 500
Richard 400
Richard (Sir) 500
Roger 763, 768, 770, 817
Roger (Sir) 817
Thomas (Sir) 763, 768, 770
Warin 763, 768, 770
William 817
William (Sir) 817

MAISONNEUVE
François 987
Marie-Élisabeth
  (Lepage) 987
Thérèse 987
MAITLAND
Agnes Jane
  (O'Reilly) 161,
  924
Andrea Belden
  161, 924
Anne (Home) 177
Helen Abbie (Van
  Voorhis) 161,
  924
Isabel (Seton) 177
Isabella Graham
  (Macdowall) 161
James William
  cxlv, 161, 162, 924
James William II
  161, 924, 926
Jean (Fleming) 177
John, 1st Baron
  Thirlestane 177
John, 1st Duke of
  Lauderdale 177
John, 1st Earl of
  Lauderdale 177
Mary 177
Sylvia (Wigglesworth) 161, 924
Thomas, of
  Dundrennan 161
Thomas A. 161,
  924
MAIVERS (DE)
Pierre II de Rapin,
  Baron 634

MAJOR
Deborah (St.
  Nicholas) 358
Jerman 358
Susan (Aston) 506
MAKERNESS
Ellen 857
MAKGILL
Elizabeth 253
MAKINS
Mary (Hon.) 9
MALASSIS-LÈS-ÉTAMPES (DE)
Jean IV Le Prévost,
  Seigneur 954
MALCOLM IV
King of Scotland
  778, 780, 785, 787,
  789
MALEFAUNT
Alison 582
MALENFANT
Guillaume 971
Jean-Baptiste 971
Marie-Anathalie
  (Destroismaisons)
  971
Marie-Josèphe
  (Lévesque) 971
Séverine 971
MALESHERBES (DE)
Chrétien-Guillaume
  (Christian William)
  de Lamoignon,
  Baron 294
MALET
Alice (Young) 695
Amice (Lyffe) 695

Baldwin 695
Elizabeth 695
Hugh 695
Isabel (Michell)
  695
Joan (Roynon) 695
Joan (Wadham)
  695
Thomas 695
William 695
MALET de GRAVILLE
Marie 961
MALHERBE (DE)
Isabeau 946
MALI
ferch Gruffudd 693
ferch Ieuan 692
ferch Tudur 693
MALI LLWYD
ferch Llywelyn ab
  Ieuan 650
MALICORNE (DE)
Payen de Chourses,
  Seigneur 948
MALINOWSKI
Janine 989
MALL
Frances 307
MALLET
Caroline (Faubert)
  981
Catherine 982
Claire (Gagné) 981
Marguerite 981
Michel 981
MALLETTE
Diane M. (Henry)
  984

Michael 984
Patricia "Patty" 984
MALLISON
Anne 322
MALLOCK
Rose (Alexander) 522, 523
MALLORY/MALORY
Alice (Bellingham) 389
Alice (de Driby) 746, 847
Alice (Farington) 847
Anketil (Sir) 746, 847, 848, 1025
Anne (Eure) 389
Anthony 847
Dorothy (Forster) 847
Elizabeth viii, li, cxlvi, 668, 847, 1025
Elizabeth (Gregory) 847
Elizabeth (Kinsman) 847
Elizabeth (Vaughan) 505, 668, 669
family clxxxii, 373, 697, 746, 1026
Frances (___) 668
Horatio 847, 848
Jane 389
Jane (___) 668
Jane (Norton) 132, 668
Joan (Chamber) 847

Joan (Constable) 668
John (Sir) 389, 668
Lucy (Holland) 668
Margaret (___) 847
Margaret (___) (Corbet) 746
Margaret (Thwaites) 668
Martha 505
Mary (Moseley) 389
Mary (Oldfield) 668
Philip (Rev.) 668
Richard 668
Roger xi, xlvii, xlix, clxvii, clxxxii, 668
Thomas 668
Thomas (Rev.), Dean of Chester 505, 668
Thomas (Sir) 847
Ursula (Gale) 668
William 389, 847, 848
William (Sir) 132, 668, 746, 847
___ (la Zouche) 847, 848
MALLT
ferch Gruffudd 582
ferch Gruffudd ap Cadwgon 582
ferch Hywel Fychan ap Hywel 659

ferch Maredudd Ddu 689
MALONE
Elizabeth 434
MALORY. *see* MALLORY/MALORY
MALTRAVERS
Eleanor 632
MALTZAN (VON)
Barbara Helena, Baroness 195
Johann Bernard II, Baron of Wartenburg and Penzlin 195
MAMEZ (DE)
Catherine 633
MAN
Elizabeth (St. Lo) 626
Elizabeth (Wiseman) 626
George St. Lo 626
Jane Sophia 626
William 626
MANBY
Judith 846
MANCHESTER
Charles Montagu, 1st Duke of 135
Edward Montagu, 2nd Earl of 135
Robert Montagu, 3rd Duke of 135
Robert Montagu, 3rd Earl of 135
William Montagu, 5th Duke of 67

1377

**MANCINI-
MAZARINI**
  Diane-Adélaïde-
    Zéphirine 289
  family 291
  Jacques-Hippolyte,
    Marquis de
    Mancini 289
MANDERSCHEID
  Walpurga of 459
MANFIELD
  Eleanor 721
MANFRED
  King of Sicily 642
MANFRED III
  Marquess of
    Saluzzo 642
MANKESY (DE)
  Alice 851, 920
MANN
  Erika Julia Hedwig
    Gründgens 404
  Thomas 404
MANNERS
  Anne 120, 123
  Anne (St. Leger)
    lxvi, 119, 121, 123,
    126, 133
  Bridget (Sutton)
    119
  Catherine (Noel) 119
  Catherine (Russell)
    119
  Diana Olivia
    Winifred Maud
    [Lady Diana
    Cooper] 9
  Dorothy (Vernon)
    110, 119
  Eleanor (de Ros)
    119, 600
  Eleanor (Paston)
    119
  Elizabeth 119, 122,
    123, 431, 600
  Frances 73, 122,
    123
  Frances (Montagu)
    119
  Frances (Seymour)
    119
  George (Sir) 119,
    120
  George, Baron Ros
    119, 121, 123, 126,
    133
  Grace 110, 120
  Grace (Pierpont)
    119
  John (Sir) 110,
    119, 121, 122, 123
  John, 1st Duke of
    Rutland 119, 120
  John, 2nd Duke of
    Rutland 119
  John, 3rd Duke of
    Rutland 119
  John, 8th Earl of
    Rutland 119
  John, Marquess of
    Granby 119
  Katherine 121,
    122, 123, 126
  Margaret 133
  Robert (Sir) 119,
    600
  Thomas, 1st Earl of
    Rutland 119
MANNERS-SUTTON
  Anne (Manners)
    120
  Diana (Chaplin) 119
  George (Lord) 119
  John 120
  Mary Georgiana
    120
MANNEY
  Elida Vanderburgh
    654
MANNING
  family clxxxviii
  Hugh clxxxiii,
    clxxxviii
  John clxxxiii
  Margaret (Brandon)
    clxxxiii
  ____ (Brandon)
    clxxxiii
MANNOCK
  Bridget 385
MANRIQUE
  Leonor 191
**MANRIQUE DE
ZUÑIGA**
  Juana 191
MÅNSDOTTER
  Katherine 51, 53,
    889
MANSEL(L)
  Anne 825
  Mary 130
MANSER
  Anne 629
**MANSFELD-
HINTERORT**
  John, Count of 220
  Maria of 220

1378

**MANSFELD-
VORTERORT**
Anna (Czernin),
 Countess 198
Carl Franz, Count of
 198
Franz Maximilian,
 Count of 198
Heinrich Franz,
 Count of 198
Maria Anna Elisa-
 beth (von Harrach),
 Countess 198
Maria Eleanore of
 198
Maria Isabella,
 Countess of 198
Philip V, Count of
 220
Susanna Polyxena
 Catharina,
 Countess of 220
MANSFIELD
Anne 318
Anne (Eure) 317
Elizabeth cxlvii,
 clxii, 318
Elizabeth (___) 318
family xxxiv, xlv,
 xlix, lxiv
John 318
John, M.P. 318
Lancelot 317
Mary (Shard)
 (Gove) 318
MANTUA
Francis II Gonzaga,
 Marquess of 186,
 189
Frederick II
 Gonzaga, Duke of,
 Marquess of
 Montferrat 186,
 189
Isabella Gonzaga of
 186, 189
Margaret (Palaeolo-
 gina) of Montferrat,
 Duchess of 186,
 189
MAPLETHORPE
Anne 717
MAR
John Erskine, 2nd
 Earl of 215
Marjory of 697
MARANDA
Marie-Josèphe 977
MARAVAT (DE)
Jean de Lupé,
 Seigneur 634
MARBURY
Anne [Anne
 Hutchinson] xix,
 xxxv, xlviii, clxiii,
 clxxiii, 478, 480,
 925, 926
Bridget (Dryden)
 478, 708
family x, xxxiv,
 xlviii, li, lvi, lxviii
Francis (Rev.) 478,
 708, 926
Katherine xlviii,
 clxiii, clxxiii, 478,
 708, 926
MARC
Claude 965
MARCH
Edmund Mortimer,
 3rd Earl of 107,
 114, 119, 126, 133,
 134, 305, 310, 317,
 319, 327, 333, 342,
 347, 349, 351, 355,
 359, 361, 363, 374,
 379, 384, 385, 389,
 399, 401, 414, 418,
 425, 431, 901, 904,
 905
Roger Mortimer, 4th
 Earl of 107, 114,
 119, 126, 133, 134
MARCH TORRES
Aleida 997
MARCHANT
Alexander, Sieur de
 St. Michel 480
Dorothea
 (Kingsmill) 480
Elizabeth 480
MARCHE (DE LA)
Hugh X de Lusignan,
 Count 785
James I, of Bourbon,
 Count 638
John I, Count, Count
 of Vendôme 638
MARCHENA (DE)
Pedro Ponce de
 León, II Señor
 190, 993
Pedro Ponce de León,
 IV Señor 994
Pedro Ponce de León,
 V Señor, Conde de
 Arcos 994

MARCILLY
  Jean de Salazar(t),
    Seigneur, Seigneur
    of Saint-Just and
    Montagu 953
MARCK (DE LA)
  Diane 202
  Françoise (de Brezé)
    202
  Robert, Duc de
    Bouillon 202
MARE (DE LA)
  Alice 851
  Maud 861
MAREAU (DE)
  Jean II, Sire de
    Sombreffe 804
MAREDUDD
  ab Ieuan 650, 659,
    689, 694
  ab Ieuan ap Robert
    694
  ab Ieuan Goch 686
  ab Owain 810
  ap Bleddyn 815
  ap Henry Dwnn 582
  ap Hywel ap Tudur
    659, 694
MAREDUDD
LLWYD
  ap John 686
  ap Llywelyn 686
MARESCA
DONNORSO
  Giovanni Antonio,
    Count of Tronco
    190
  Maria Margherita (di
    Sangro) 190

Matilda (Correale)
  190
Nicola, 3rd Duke of
  Serracapriola 190
MARESCA
DONNORSO
CORREALE
  Margherita 190
MAREUIL (DE)
  Agnès 956
MARGARET
  (Palaeologina) of
    Montferrat,
    Duchess of Mantua
    186, 189
  (Stewart), Princess
    of Scotland 219,
    249, 256
  (Tudor), Princess of
    England, Queen of
    Scotland 143,
    146, 148, 150, 151,
    152, 154, 157, 159,
    161, 163, 165, 166,
    167, 168, 170, 171,
    173, 174, 176, 177,
    179
  Archduchess of
    Austria 451
  of Austria, Queen of
    Bohemia 621
  of Bourbon 442,
    634
  of Brieg 451
  of Brittany 287, 293
  of Burgundy, Queen
    of France 455
  ferch Ellis Morris
    229

  ferch Ieuan ab
    Owain 810
  ferch James ab Ieuan
    Gwyn (Margred
    ferch James ap
    Rhys) 555
  ferch John ap Lewys
    229
  ferch Richard ab
    Ieuan ap David ab
    Ithel Fychan 772
  of Flanders 438,
    442, 445, 774, 776
  of Holland (wife of
    Louis IV, Holy
    Roman Emperor)
    51, 447, 449, 451,
    907
  of Juliers 451, 459
  of Nassau-Dillenburg
    194
  Princess of Branden-
    burg 181, 182, 184
  Princess of France,
    Queen of England
    xxvi, 462, 470,
    473, 486, 493, 515,
    519, 522, 526, 534,
    539, 541, 545, 557,
    579, 580, 598, 599,
    600, 604, 605, 609
  Princess of France,
    Queen of France
    and Navarre 637
  Princess of Provence,
    Queen of France
    634, 638, 965
  Princess of Saxony
    220, 451, 454

Princess of Saxony,
Queen of Denmark
141
Princess of Scotland,
Queen of France
200, 205
of Schwarzburg-
Leutenberg 452
of Scotland 780, 783
MARGRED
ferch Einion 689
ferch Einion ab Ithel
659, 694
ferch Gronwy
Llwyd 693
ferch Gruffudd 692,
815, 816, 822, 823
ferch Hugh Howel
874
ferch James ap Rhys
555
ferch Jenkin ab
Ieuan 657
ferch John ap Jenkin
811
ferch John ap Robert
657
ferch Madog 689
ferch Morus 694
ferch Morus Gethin
ap Rhys 686
ferch Thomas
Gethin 659
ferch Tudur 689
MARIA
Archduchess of
Austria 40, 43,
54, 56, 891
of Arkel, heiress of
Guelders 459
Grand Duchess of
Russia 7
of Guelders 459
of Halicz 791, 797,
802
Princess of Galicia
621
**MARIA AMELIA
THERESA**
Princess of the Two
Sicilies, Queen of the
French 288, 290
MARIA ANNA
Princess of Baden-
Baden 49
**MARIA ANNA
CHARLOTTE
ZITA ELISABETH
REGINA
THÉRÈSE**
Archduchess of
Austria xii, cliv,
800
MARIA BEATRICE
d'Este, of Modena
15
**MARIA CHRISTINA
SABINA**
Princess of Saxony,
Countess von der
Lausitz 20
MARIA CRISTINA
Princess of Sardinia,
Queen of the Two
Sicilies 6
Princess of The
Netherlands 1
**MARIA
FEODOROVNA
(MARIE SOPHIE
FREDERIKKE
DAGMAR)**
Princess of Denmark,
Empress of Russia
5
**MARIA
IMMACULATA**
Princess of the Two
Sicilies 6
MARIA JOSEPHA
Archduchess of
Austria, Electress
of Saxony, Queen
of Poland 20
**MARIA
LEOPOLDINA**
Princess of Modena,
Archduchess of
Austria 15
MARIA LUDOVIKA
Archduchess and
Empress of Austria,
Princess of Modena
11
**MARIA
MAGDALENA**
of Waldeck-
Wildungen 141
MARIA TERESA
(Mestre y Batista),
Grand Duchess of
Luxembourg 991
of Tuscany,
Archduchess of
Austria, Queen of
Sardinia 614

1381

MARIA THERESA
Archduchess of
Austria, Queen of
the Two Sicilies 6
Empress of Austria
xxi, lxx, 15
Princess of the Two
Sicilies 11
**MARIA THERESA
FELICITAS**
d'Este of Modena
287
MARIANNE
Princess of The
Netherlands 8
MARIE
of Anjou, Queen of
France 202, 208
of Brabant, Queen of
France 941, 961
of Burgundy 442
of Champagne,
Empress of
Constantinople
774, 776
of Châtillon-Blois,
Queen of Naples,
Sicily, Jerusalem,
and Aragón 205
of Edinburgh,
Princess of Great
Britain, Queen of
Roumania 2
Grand Duchess of
Russia 2
of Hainault 634
of Hesse, Empress
of Russia 2, 5

Princess of France
774, 776, 943, 950,
993
Princess of Greece
and Denmark 4
Princess of
Hungary, Queen of
Naples and Sicily
459
Princess of
Liechtenstein 19
Princess of Saxony
613
**MARIE AMELIE
ELIZABETH
CAROLINE**
Princess of Baden
933
**MARIE-
ANTOINETTE
(MARIA ANTONIA)**
Archduchess of
Austria, Queen of
France 267
**MARIE
DOROTHEA**
Princess of
Courland 56
MARIE ELEANOR
Princess of Cleves
47, 54, 56, 891
**MARIE
ELIZABETH**
Princess of Saxony
47
MARIE LOUISE
Archduchess of
Austria, Empress
of the French 11

**MARIE-THÉRÈSE-
JOSÈPHE**
of Lorraine-Brionne
613
**MARINEAU dit
HOSTIN**
Léocadie 987
Louis 987
Olive (Corbeil) 987
MARJORIBANKS
Mary 150
MARJORIE
of Carrick 787, 789
(Stewart), Princess of
Scotland 219, 281
MARK
Adolf of Cleves,
Count of 459
MARK and CLEVES
Engelberta of 459
MARKENFIELD
Alice 374
Dorothy (Gascoigne)
374
Eleanor 328
Elizabeth 821
Ninian (Sir) 374
MARKHAM
Anne 413
Elizabeth (Webster)
656
Kika 246
Lydia (Ward) 656
Margaret 744
Mary (Widdrington)
329
Priscilla 656
Priscilla (Graves)
656

Robert (Sir), 3rd Bt.
  329
Ursula 328, 329
William lviii, lx,
  cxlix, cli, clxi,
  clxxix, 656
MARKLE
  Doria Loyce
    (Ragland) 344
  Doris May
    (Sanders) 344
  Gordon Arnold
    344
  Meghan (Rachel
    Meghan) 344
  Thomas Wayne 344
MARLBOROUGH
  Charles Richard
    John Spencer-
    Churchill, 9th
    Duke of 26
  George Charles
    Spencer-Churchill,
    8th Duke of 26, 28
  George Spencer, 4th
    Duke of 62, 299
  George Spencer-
    Churchill, 5th Duke
    of 62, 80, 299
  George Spencer-
    Churchill, 6th
    Duke of 63
  John Churchill, 1st
    Duke of 24, 62,
    70, 71, 75, 536
  John Robert Edward
    Spencer-Churchill,
    10th Duke of 27

John Winston
  Spencer-Churchill,
  7th Duke of 26, 63
MARLE (DE)
  Louise 950, 951
  Pierre de Rohan,
    Seigneur de Gié,
    Count 455
MARLOT (VAN)
  Anna Florentina (van
    den Boetzelaer) 460
  Anna Maria 460
  Lodewijk, Heer van
    Bavey 460
MARMIER (DE)
  Marguerite 24
MARMION (DE)
  Agnes (___) 877
  Alice 877
  Auberée clxxxi, 874
  Avice 372, 667,
    670, 678, 917
  Elizabeth 667, 917
  family vii
  Geoffrey 877
  Isabel (___) 372,
    667, 670, 678, 684,
    917
  Joan 684
  John 877
  John Marmion, 1st
    Baron 372, 667,
    670, 678, 684, 917
  John Marmion, 2nd
    Baron 372, 667,
    670, 678, 684, 917
  Lorette (de Dover)
    372, 667, 670, 678,
    684, 917

Margery (de
  Nottingham) 877
Matilda (le Justice?)
  877
Maud (Furnival)
  372, 667, 670, 678,
  684, 917
Robert clxxxi, 877
Rosamond (___) 877
Thomas 877
William 877
William (Sir) 372,
  667, 670, 678, 684,
  917
___ (___), wife of
  Robert clxxxi
MARNEY
  Elizabeth
    (Sergeaux) 607
  Emma 607
  William (Sir) 607
MARNIER (DE)
  Marguerite 24
MARNIX (VAN)
  Amélie 460
MAROIS
  Rose 989
MARROW
  Catherine 874
MARSDEN
  Elizabeth 611
MARSH
  Caroline Emily 117
  Catherine 380
  William Birnie "Bill"
    (Dr.) vi, viii
MARSHALL
  Elizabeth xl, lii, lv,
    clxii, 520, 630,

1383

757, 758, 870, 886, 924, 935
Elizabeth (Howes) 567
Eve 680, 837, 839, 847
family 1025
George W. xxviii
Isabel 653, 661, 672
Isabel (de Clare) 837, 839, 845, 847
John Joseph 567
Katherine (Mitton) 630
Lynn 20
Mary Anne 567
Maud 806, 821, 845
Roberta Brooke (Roswell) (Kuser) [Brooke Astor] 86
Roger 630
Sarah 500
William, 1st Earl of Pembroke 837, 839, 845, 847
MARSOLET
Marie 954, 990
MARSTON
Ursula 766
MARTEN
Henry (Sir), the younger 366
Mary 366
MARTIAU
Elizabeth 310, 930
MARTIN
Abraham 940
Austin 144
Avice 851
Elizabeth (Agnew) 144, 145
Frances Coffin (Crosby) 144
Henry Austin (Dr.) 144
Henry James 144
Isabel (___) 851, 852
John Biddulph 138
Marie 940, 987
Marie-Louise 975
Mary (McLean) 144
Mary Anne (Biddulph) 138
Nicholas 851
Rita Jeannette 972
Robert 138
Suzanne (d'Ailleboust) 940
Victoria (Claflin) (Woodhull) (Blood) [Victoria C. Woodhull] xvii, 138
MARTINEAU
Alice Margaret (Vaughan Williams) 380
Catherine (Marsh) 380
David 379
Edith Jane 63, 380
Edward 380
Eleanor (Rogers) 380
Elizabeth 379
Elizabeth (Rankin) 379
Elizabeth Frances (Batty) 380
Elizabeth Mary (Alston) 380
family xlii
Harriet xvii, l, lxiv, lxvii, lxxi, clvi, 379
Henry Austin (Dr.) clvi
Hubert 380
Hubert Melville 380
Jeanne Maud cliii, 380
John 380
Margaretta Sarah (Mason) 380
Marriot Margaret (Bunny) 380
Maud (Morris) (Schwab) 380
Peter Finch 380
Philip 380
Philip Hubert (Sir) 380
Sarah (Meadows) 379
Thomas 379, 380
William 380
MARTÍNEZ DEL MAZO
Juan Bautista 140
MARTÍNEZ DEL MAZO Y VELÁZQUEZ
María Teresa 140
MARVIN
Jerome Place 688
Julia Anne (Place) 688

Mabel   632, 688
Martha Anne
   (Stokes)   688
Phebe (Ford)   688
Robert   688
Samuel Ross   688
MARX
Johanna (Jenny)
   Bertha Julie (von
   Westphalen)   147
Karl   147
MARY
(Stewart), Princess of
   Scotland   148, 154,
   157, 167, 168, 179,
   210, 213, 214, 215,
   216, 218, 239, 240,
   241, 243, 245, 248,
   250, 251, 252, 253,
   254, 255, 257, 258,
   260, 261, 266, 267,
   268, 940
(Tudor), Princess of
   England, Queen of
   France, Duchess of
   Suffolk   xxxix,
   clxxxiii, clxxxviii,
   62, 69, 76, 79, 80
of Burgundy (wife of
   Maximilian I, Holy
   Roman Emperor)
   438, 445
ferch Rheinallt   658
ferch Thomas ap
   Robert   658
ferch Tudur Vaughn
   229
of Guelders, Queen of
   Scotland   148, 154,
   157, 167, 168, 174,
   179, 210, 213, 214,
   215, 216, 218, 219,
   459
of Guise, Queen of
   Scotland   82, 85,
   87, 88, 90, 92, 93,
   95, 96, 97, 98, 897
Queen of Scots   xii,
   xl, 90
MARY II
Queen of England
   and Scotland   122,
   615, 678, 679, 781
MARY BEATRICE
Princess of Modena,
   Queen of England
   and Scotland   22, 24
MARY VICTORIA
(Douglas-Hamilton),
   Princess of Monaco,
   Princess Festetics
   von Tolna   20, 933
MASARYK
Charlotte (Garrigue)
   635
family   xxvi
Frances Anita (Crane)
   (Leatherbee)   635
Jan Garrigue   635
Tomas Jan (Tomas
   Garrigue), President
   of Czechoslovakia
   xviii, 635
MASHAM
Damaris (Cudworth)
   580
Francis (Sir), 3rd Bt.
   580
MASLIN
Caroline   914
Eliza Sarah (Mohler)
   914
Martha (Glen)   914
Michael Miller   914
Thomas (III)   914
MASON
Anne   537
Anne (Sanford)   480
Arabella   480
Avice (McLaughlin)
   325
Catherine (Power)
   325
Daniel, Jr.   924
Dorothy (Hobart)
   924
Elijah   480
Elizabeth   325, 923
Elizabeth (Fitch)   923
George   323
James   325
Jeremiah   923
Jeremiah (III)   923
Jeremiah, Jr.   923
John   325, 480, 537
Lucretia (Greene)
   480
Margaretta Sarah
   380
Mary (Clark)   923
Mary (Means)   923
Mary (Stanton)
   480
Peleg Sanford   480
Robert Means   923
Sarah Ellen
   (Francis)   923

MASSA DE LEUNDA Y ARISTIGUIETA
Anna María Teresa 443
MASSÉ
Louise 975
MASSEY
Annette Fanny 131
Margaret 817
Margery Hilda (Fremantle) clvi, 341
Raymond Hart xvii, clvi, 341
MASSIMO
Barbara 21
Camillo VIII Massimiliano, Prince of Arsoli 20
Camillo Vittorio Emanuele, Prince of Arsoli 20, 21
Giacinta (della Porta Rodiani) 20
Maria Francesca 20
MASSINGBERD
Anne (Mildmay) 471
Dra(y)ner (Sir) 471
Elizabeth 471
Frances (FitzWilliam) 471
Frances (Halton) 471
Thomas 471
MASTER
Agnes 857

MATARAZZO
Claudia 21
MATHER
Cotton (Rev.) 579
Margaret 540
Margaret Wade (Linton) clvi, 540
Thomas William 540
MATHERON (DE)
Melchionne 735
MATHESON
Veldron Robison 927
MATHEW
Alice (Raglan) 338
Humphrey 338
Jane 338
Janet 337, 375, 382, 900
Katherine (Mathew) 338
Margaret 730
Mary (Lewis) 338
Miles 338
William 338
MATHEWS
Frances 613
MATHILDE-MARIE-CHRISTIANE-GHISLAINE
(d'Udekem d'Acoz), Queen of the Belgians 154, 155, 201, 203, 204
MATILDA
Archduchess of Austria 617
of Bavaria 449, 451

of Boulogne, Queen of England 774, 776
of Dammartin, Queen of Portugal 619
of Flanders, Duchess of Normandy, Queen of England 642, 830, 851, 911, 1024
of Northumberland, Queen of Scotland 778, 780, 783, 785, 787, 789, 879, 919
Princess of Scotland, Queen of England 739, 806, 808, 810, 811, 813, 815, 817, 819, 821, 822, 824, 826, 957, 959
of Saxony 849
MATTHEWS
Miriam 764
MAUD
ferch Ieuan 689
MAUDE
Alice (Hartstonge) 364
Anne 364
Anthony 364
Frances (Wandesford) 364
Margery cxc
Robert 364
MAUDIT/MAUDUIT
Eleanor 564
Eleanor (Robinson alias Norris) 563
Elizabeth 563, 564

Elizabeth
  (Berryman) 563
Elizabeth (King)
  563
family lx
Isaac 563
Jasper 563
John 563
Mercy (___) 563
William lx, cxlix,
  563
MAUGHAM
  Somerset 49
MAUGNY (DE)
  Françoise 946
MAUGRAS
  Gertrude 985
MAULE
  Bethia (Guthrie)
    278
  Eleanor 278
  Elizabeth 161
  Isabel 278
  Isabel (Arbuthnott)
    278
  Robert, of Panmure
    278
  William 278
MAULEVERER
  Agnes 708
  Alice (Markenfield)
    374
  Anne xli, lvi, 374
  Anne (Pearson) 374
  Beatrice (Hutton)
    374
  Dorothy 374
  Edmund 374
  Edmund (Sir) 374

Eleanor
  (Aldeborough)
    374
James 374
Mary (Danby) 374
Robert 374
William 374
MAULÉVRIER (DE)
  Jacques de Brezé,
    Count 202
MAUNDER
  ___ 665
MAURIAC
  François 795
  Marie-Thérèse 795
MAURICE (OWEN)
  Richard 689
MAURITZI
  Marcella (Fazi)
    [Princess Marcella
    Borghese] 24
MAUROY (DE)
  Radegonde 202
MAUSSIGNY (DE)
  Philippine 956
MAUSSION (DE)
  Charlotte-Germaine
    227
MAVERICK
  Abigail 632
  Anna (Harris) 632
  Elias 632
  John (Rev.) 632
  Mary (Gye) xix,
    xxxv, lviii, clxi,
    clxxv, clxxxii, 632
MAWD
  ferch Adam
    Turberville 808

ferch Dafydd Llwyd
  650, 652, 659, 686,
  694
ferch Gruffudd 808
ferch Ienaf ab Abba
  657
ferch Ieuan 808
ferch Oliver ap
  Thomas Pryce
  231
MAXIMA
  (Zorriguieta y
  Cerruti), Queen of
  The Netherlands
  991
MAXIMILIAN
  Archduke of
  Austria, Emperor
  of México 30, 38,
  288
MAXIMILIAN I
  Holy Roman
  Emperor 438, 445
MAXWELL
  Jane 25, 31, 64, 67
  Katherine 239, 243,
    253
  Lucy (Douglas) 155
  Mary 155
  Robert, 4th Earl of
    Nithsdale 155
MAY
  Benjamin 858
  Cordelia (Bowes)
    xx
  Dorothy xx, lix
  Henry xx
  John xx
  Katherine (___) xx

1387

Mary (Williams) 858
Susanna 858
Thomasine (Cross)
 xx
MAYER
Eugénie 136
MAYNARD
Banastre Maynard,
 3rd Baron 901
Dorothy 901
Eileen (Burden) 378
Elizabeth (Grey) 901
Sheila 378
Walter 378
MAYNE
Anne 412
Blanche 411, 412
Dorothy 411, 412
Dorothy (Griffith)
 411, 412
Elizabeth clxxxvi,
 245
Jacqueline 956
James 412
John 411
Margaret 411, 412
Symon 412
MAYO
Anne 557
Sarah
 347**MAZANGE**
(DE). *see also*
 MÉSENGE (DE)
MAZARIN(I)
Jules (Giulio),
 Cardinal 289
MAZOVIA
Anna of 621
Bołeslaw III, Duke
 of 621
Bołeslaw IV, Duke
 of 621
Casimir II, Prince
 of, Prince of
 Sandomir, Krakow
 and Kujamien
 791, 797, 802
Conrad III, Duke of
 621
Euphemia of, Queen
 of Galicia 621
John I, Duke of 621
Trojden, Duke of
 621
Ziemowit III, Duke
 of 621
McADAM
Anne Charlotte
 (Delancey) 128
Gloriana Margaret
 (Nicoll) 128
James 128
John Loudon clvi,
 128
Susannah
 (Cochrane) 128
Wilhelmina Hannah
 128
McCAIN
Catherine/Katherine
 Daisy Davey
 (Vaulx) 924, 926
family 926
John Sidney 924
John Sidney, Jr.
 924, 926
John Sidney (III)
 (Sen.) xli, 923, 924
Rebecca (Wright)
 924
McCANN
Helena Woolworth
 63
McCARTHY. *see*
 MacCARTHY/
 McCARTHY
McCARTNEY
(James) Paul (Sir)
 64
McCLENACHAN
Martha 211
McCONNELL
James (Rev.) 898
Noelia Gertrude 978
S. G. (Rev.) 898
McCRACKEN
Cornelia (Livingston)
 885
George Englert
 (Prof.) lvi, lxi, cxcii
McCULLOCH
Margaret 828
McCURDY
Mary Burton Derrick-
 son xlvi, lxi
McDERMOTT
Honoria Helen 268
McDONALD. *see*
 MacDONALD/
 McDONALD
McDOUGALL
Elizabeth 285
Janet 264
Jeannie 362
McDOWALL. *see*
 MacDOWALL/
 McDOWALL

McEWEN. *see also*
  MacEWEN
  Benjamin 146
  Benjamin, Jr. 146
  Benjamin Beecher 146
  John William lxi, cxlv, 146
  Mary Ann (Robinson) 146
  Mary Emma (Coles) 146
  Matilda Sarah (Robinson) 146
McGINNIS
  Claire 800
McGOWAN
  Bertha Eleanor 116
McGREGOR
  Donald Glas, of Glengyle 146
  James 146
  Jane (Brown) 146
  John 146, 147
  Margaret 146
  Margaret (Campbell) 146
  Margaret (McGregor) 146, 147
McGREGOR [later GREGOR]
  Charles Russell lxi, cliv, 146
  Hester Ann (Gregory) 146
McGREGOR or CAMPBELL
  Mary (McGregor), of Comermore 146

Robert ("Rob Roy"), of Inversnaid 146
McGREGOR or CAMPBELL [later DRUMMOND]
  Annabella (McNicoll) 146
  James, of Innervonchell 146
McGREW
  Clara L. 545
McKAY. *see* MACKAY/MacKAY/McKAY
McKELLAR
  Jessie Victoria 112
McKINNON
  Emma Mary 49
McKITTRICK
  Ellen Floyd 976
McLACHLAN/ MacLACHLAN
  Elizabeth, of McLachlan 216
  Jean 263
  Juliana 643
McLAUGHLIN
  Anne (Bromilow) 63
  Avice 325
  Catherine (Blenner-hasset) 325
  Doris Margaretta 63
  Edith Jane (Martineau) 63, 380
  Edward 63
  Frederica (Crofton) 63

George Harry (Dr.) lx, 68
Hubert 63
Richard 325
Vivian Guy Ouseley 63, 380
McLEAN. *see* MacLEAN
McLEOD. *see* MacLEOD/McLEOD
McMILLAN
  Christina 217
McNEILL
  family 570
  Grizel (Campbell) xlviii, cxlix, 240, 263, 570
  Neill Dubh ["Black Neill"] 263, 570
M'COWLE
  Alan 263
  Anna 263
  Iain [John] 263
McTYRE
  Katherine 828
MDIVANI
  Barbara Woolworth (Hutton) xviii, 44, 46, 63
M'DOWELL
  Katharine 898
MEABURNE
  Catherine 127
MEAD
  Isabel 295, 598
  ____ 743
MEADE
  George 385

George Gordon
(Gen.) 385
Henrietta Constantia
(Worsam) xi,
xlix, cxlv, clxv,
385, 386
Margaret Coats
(Butler) 385
Margaretta
(Sergeant) 385
Richard Worsam
385
MEADOWS
John 379, 381
Margaret (Hall) 379
Philip 379
Sarah 379
Sarah (Fairfax)
379, 381
MEAKINS
Charles William
567
Eliza Howes 567
Mary Anne
(Marshall) 567
MEANS
Mary 923
MEASE
James 382
Pierce Butler [Pierce
Butler] 382
Sarah (Butler) 382
MEASE/MEARS
Katherine
(Eltonhead) 498
Thomas 498
MEATH
Chambré Brabazon,
5th Earl of 120

MEAUTYS
Frances 684
Hercules 684
Philippa (Cooke) 684
MEAUX
Robert, Count of,
Count of Troyes
879, 919
MECKLENBURG
Henry, Duke of,
Prince Consort of
The Netherlands 8
William, Duke of 8
**MECKLENBURG-
GÜSTROW**
Christine of 47
Gustav Adolf, Duke
of 47
Sophie, Princess of,
Queen of Denmark
47, 49, 52
**MECKLENBURG-
SCHWERIN**
Anna Maria of 891
Catherine of 196
Charlotte, Princess
of 8
Henry V, Duke of
220
Paul Frederick,
Grand Duke of 8
Sophia of 220
**MECKLENBURG-
STRELITZ**
(Sophie) Charlotte,
Princess of, Queen
of Great Britain 40
Charles II, Grand
Duke of 40

Frederica, Princess of,
Queen of Hanover
40
Louise, Princess of,
Queen of Prussia
8, 40
MEDE
Catherine (Corbett)
711
Jane 711
John (Sir) 711
**MEDEHEM/
MEDEM (VON)**
Anna 449
Hermann 449
____ (Furster) 449
MEDFORD
Elizabeth 510
MEDICI. *see also*
DE' MEDICI
MEDICI (DE')
Catherine, Queen of
France 637
Cosimo I, Grand
Duke of Tuscany
191, 192
Francesco Maria I,
Grand Duke of
Tuscany 192
Isabella 192
Leonor (Álvarez de
Toledo) 191, 192
Lorenzo II, Duke of
Urbino 637
Madeleine (de la
Tour d'Auvergne)
637
Marie, Queen of
France 192

1390

MEDINA-SIDONIA
  Alfonso Pérez de
    Guzmán y
    Sotomayor (Adm.),
    7th Duke of 140,
    142, 191
  dukes of 142
  Juan Alonso de
    Guzmán y Ribera,
    3rd Duke of 191
  Juan Alonso Pérez
    de Guzmán y
    Zuñiga, 6th Duke
    of 140
  Juan Manuel
    Domingo de
    Guzmán y Silva,
    8th Duke of 140
MEEKS
  Victoria Anne 666
MEGGAU (VON)
  Franziska 895
MÉHÉRENC (DE)
  Adrien, Seigneur de
    Montmirel and La
    Conseillère 946
  Anne (de Grosparmy)
    946
  Denis, Seigneur des
    Londes 946
  Françoise 946
  Françoise (de
    Maugny) 946
  Guillaume I,
    Seigneur des
    Londes 946
  Guillaume II,
    Seigneur des
    Londes 946

  Guillaume III,
    Seigneur de Laubel
    946
  Guillaume IV,
    Seigneur de La
    Conseillère 946
  Isabeau (de
    Malherbe) 946
  Jean, Seigneur de
    Montmirel and de
    La Conseillère
    946
  Jeanne (du Mesnil)
    946
  Jeanne (du Pont)
    946
  Marguerite (de La
    Haye) 946
  Marguerite (de
    Sandret) 946
MEILLE (DE)
  Jean de Foix,
    Vicomte 615
MEISSEN
  Frederick II,
    Margrave of,
    Landgrave of
    Thuringia 449,
    451
  Frederick III,
    Margrave of 449,
    451
MELANSON
  Anne 953
MELDRUM
  Helen 273
MELFORD
  Anne (Clifford)
    384

  Dionise (___) 384
  Mary 384
  Ralph 384
  Thomas 384
MELLAND
  Helen Kelsall 306
MELLISH
  Anne cxlviii, 311,
    357, 358
  Anne (Metham)
    311
  Bridget (Eldridge)
    311
  Dorothy cxlviii,
    311
  Edward 311
  Henry 358
  Reason 311
  Rebecca 358
MELLON
  Ailsa Nora 100, 190
  Andrew William 190
  Catherine Conover
    190
  Elizabeth Harkness
    (Harris) lxi, 306
  family ix, lxi
  Henry Coxe Stokes
    lxi, 306
  James Ross (II)
    "Jay" ix, xlv, lx,
    lxi, 190, 309
  Paul 190
  Thomas (Judge) 190
  Vivian (Rüesch)
    lx, lxi, cxlv, clxx,
    190
MELLOWES
  Abraham 747

Jane 557
Martha (Bulkeley) clxi, clxxvi, 747
MELSBROECK
 Charlotte-Jacqueline d'Argenteau, Countess of Esneux, Baroness of 81
MELUN (DE)
 Adam III, Vicomte 954
 Adam IV, Vicomte 954
 Agnès (d'Issy) 954
 Anne 287, 291
 Anne-Marie 292
 Charles 954
 François, Baron d'Antoing 287
 Hippolite (de Montmorency) 287
 Hugh, Prince d'Épinoy 287
 Hugh I, Seigneur d'Antoing and d'Épinoy 733
 Isabel 733
 Jeanne (de Sully) 954
 Louise (de Foix) 287
 Marguerite (de Picquigny) 733
 Marie-Anne 987
 Pierre, Prince d'Épinoy 287, 292
 Yolande 954

 Yolande (de Barbançon) 287
MENACIER
 Louise 945
MENARD
 Anne (le Roux) 941
 Antoine, Seigneur de Toucheprès 941
 David, Seigneur de Toucheprès 941
 François, Seigneur de Toucheprès 941
 Jacqueline (de Beauvau) 941
 Jean-Baptiste 987
 Louis 987
 Marie 941
 Marie-Anne 987
 Marie-Anne (Février) 987
 Marie-Françoise (Lebeau) 987
 Renée (Petit) 941
MENDES
 Eva [Eva de la Caridad Mendez] 979
MENDOZA CARRILLO DE ALBORNOZ (DE)
 Pedro, Count of Priego 191
MENETOU-COUTURE (DE)
 Claude d'Anlezy, Seigneur 440
 Robert d'Anlezy, Seigneur 440

MENON (DE)
 Elizabeth 455
 François, Seigneur de Turbilly 455
 Madeleine (de Maillé de la Tour-Landry) 455
 Marie (de Chahannai) 455
 Urbain, Seigneur de Turbilly, Count de Brestau 455
MENOU (DE)
 Charles (Gov.), Seigneur d'Aulnay-Charnizay 952, 953
 Jeanne-Marie (de Motin) 939, 952, 953
 Marie-Louise 293
MENSDORFF-POUILLY (VON)
 Alfonso Frederick, Count 45
 Emanuel, 1st Count 45
 Sophie, Countess 45
 Theresia Rosa (von Dietrichstein-Proskau-Leslie), Countess 45
MENTEITH/ MONTEITH [later DALYELL]
 James (Sir), 3rd Bt. 171, 258, 259
 Magdalen 171, 258

1392

Magdalen (Dalyell) viii, lxi, lxx, 171, 258, 259
Phillis (Gallop) 171, 258
Thomas cxlix, 171, 258, 259

MENTEITH/ MONTEITH/ MENTETH (DE). *see also* MENTEITH/ MONTEITH [later DALYELL]
Agnes (Drummond) 171
Christian (Mylne) 171
Donald 940
Dorothée 940
family, of Auldcathie 171
Helen 85
Helen, of Maner 171
James, of Auldcathie 171, 258, 259
Jean/Jehan, Seigneur d'Argentenay 940, 950
Margaret (Sandilands) 171
Margaret Graham, Countess of 264, 269, 272, 273, 280, 283
Suzanne (Hotman) 940, 950, 951
Thomas 171
____ (Robertson) 940

MENTHON (DE)
Bernard-Auguste-Marie-Ghislaine, Count 206
Bernard-Auguste-René, Count 206
Jeanne-Marie-Bernarde liii, clii, 206, 443
Marie-Louise-Geneviève (des Acres) 206
Marie-Thérèse-Anne-Luglienne (de La Bourdonnaye) 206

MENZIE
Elizabeth 264

MERAN
Agnes of, Queen of France 950
Otto I, Duke of, Count Palatine of Burgundy 735, 952

MERBURY
Elizabeth 352

MERCER
Anne (Munro) 276
Christian 255, 267, 268
family lv
Giles/Egidia 256
Helen 554
Hugh (Dr.) clxxix, 276
Isabel (Gordon) 276
Isabel (Smith) 276
John (Rev.) 276

Lilias (Row) 276
Thomas, of Todlaw 276
William (Rev.) 276

MERCEREAU
Joseph 983
Marie-Louise 983
Rose-Hermine (Rose) 983

MERCIER
Hermine (Gagné) 978
Marie 978
Marie-Louise 973
Nazaire 978

MERE
Margaret 407

MERLAY (DE)
Agnes 857, 861
Alice (de Stuteville) 857, 861
Isabel 723
Isabel (de Ros) 723
Ralph 857, 861
Roger 857, 861
Roger (Sir) 723

MERLIN (DE)
Élisabeth/Isabelle 948
Élisabeth/Isabelle (de Varennes) 948
Pierre, Seigneur de La Carrée 948, 949

MERODE (DE)
Ottilia 302

MERRIAM
Abigail Fiske 111

MERRICK
Abigail (Harrington) 520

Elizabeth (Trowbridge) 520, 935
John, Jr. 520, 935
John (III) 520
John (IV) 520
Keziah (Stratton) 520
Lucy 520
Sarah 935
MERRILL
Dina [Nedenia (Hutton) (Rumbrough) Robertson] 44
George David 344
Gertrude May 344
Jacob Lee 344
Mary (Bird) 344
Mary (Smith) 344
Natalie Bayard 127
MERRIMAN
Margaret (Mather) 540
Margaret Mather 540
Thaddeus 540
MERRITON/ MERITON/ MERYTON
Anne 785
George, Dean of York 785
Mary (Randes) 785
MERTON
Eleanor 695
MERVILLE (DE)
Charles le Gouez, Seigneur de Grais and 962

MERWEDE
Rutger van den Boetzelaer, Lord of, Lord of Langerak, Asperen and Carnisse 460
MERZELIKIN
Olga 195
MESCHINES (DE)
Adeliza 866, 870, 1025
Agnes 806, 821
Amicia 815, 817, 822
Maud 778, 779, 780, 785, 787, 789
MÉSENGE/ MAZANGE (DE)
Christophe, Seigneur de Saint-Paul-le-Gautier 948
Jeanne (Girard) 948, 949
Renée 948
MESNARD DE TOUCHEPRÈS
family 941
MESSEY-BEAUPRÉ (DE)
Charlotte-Victorine-Clémentine-Angélique 184
MESTCHERSKY
Alexandra, Princess 793
MESTRE Y BATISTA
María Teresa, Grand Duchess of Luxembourg 991

MESURIER (LE)
Susan 108
META
of Campe 451
METCALFE
Margaret 106
METHAM
Alice (Hall) 311
Anne 311
Anne (Dymoke) 311
Charles 311
Frances 123
Robert 311
METHVEN
Henry Stewart, 1st Baron 151, 170
MEULAN (DE)
Jeanne 957
Raoul I, Seigneur de Courseulles-sur-Mer 957
Raoul II, Seigneur de Courseulles de Bernières 957
Raoul III, Seigneur de Courseulles de Bernières 957
Robert de Beaumont, 1st Earl of Leicester, Count of 837, 839, 843, 845, 847, 1025
Robert de Beaumont, Count 739, 957
Waleran, Count of 957
MEURIG
ap Hywel of Radur 808

MÉXICO
Carlota (Marie-Charlotte-Amélie-Auguste-Victoire-Clémentine-Léopoldine), Princess of the Belgians, Archduchess of Austria, Empress of 288
Maximilian, Archduke of Austria, Emperor of 30, 38, 288
monarchs of 45

MEYER
Gerhard lxi
Virginia M. liii

MEYSENBURG (VON)
Klara Elisabeth 58, 432

MEYSZTOWICZ
Maria 11

MÉZERETS (DE)
Olivier de Clinchamp, Seigneur 957
Vigor de Clinchamp, Seigneur 957

MÉZIÈRES (DE)
Eugène-Marie de Béthisy, Marquis 613
Louis d'Anjou, 1st Baron 205
René d'Anjou, 2nd Baron 205

MICHAEL
(St.), Prince of Chernigov, Grand Prince of Kiev 791, 797, 802
Grand Duke of Russia 5
Prince of Greece and Denmark 3

MICHAEL I
King of Roumania (later Prime Minister) 288

MICHAEL III
Czar of Russia 792

MICHAUD
Delima Paradis 977
Marie-Madeleine 977

MICHELL
Catherine 474
Isabel 695
Mary Catherine 474

MICHELLE
Princess of France 438, 445

MICHOWSKA
Aniela Teresa 622

MIDDLEMORE
Anne (Littleton) 875
Elizabeth 862
Henrietta Maria (Drummond) 136
Margaret 875
Margery 323
Margery (Throckmorton) 862, 875
Mary 115, 136
Richard 862, 875
Robert 136
Thomas 875

MIDDLETON
Carole Elizabeth (Goldsmith) 379
Catherine (Constable) 123
Catherine Elizabeth, Duchess of Cambridge xvii, xlii, l, lxiv, lxvii, lxxi, 101, 380, 381, 931, 932
Elizabeth 123, 359
Elizabeth (Langdale) 123
Frances 363
Henry 92
Henry (Gov.) 324
Henry Willoughby, 8th Baron 27
Jane 785
Mary 382, 781
Mary (___) (Smith) 93, 717
Mary (Bull) 382
Mary (Ingleby) 123
Mary (Mackenzie) (Clarke) (Drayton) (Ainslie), Lady 92
Mary Helen (Hering) 324
Michael Francis 379
Olive Christiana (Lupton) 379
Peter 123
Peter (Sir) 123
Peter Francis 379
Richard Noel 379
Thomas 382

Valerie (Glassborow) 379
William 123
MIEROP (VAN)
Cornelia Margaretha Wilhelmina (van Cattenburch) 907
Isaac Nicolaas Johan 907
MIESZKO II LAMBERT
King of Poland 849
MIGNAULT dit LABRIE
Marie-Ursule 974
MIGNOT
Marie-Louise 971
MILAN
Amadeus IV, Count of Savoy, ruler of 642
MILBORNE
Anne 506, 647
Eleanor 296
Elizabeth 295
Elizabeth (Devereux) 647
Jane (Baskerville) 295, 296, 647
John 647
Simon 295, 296, 647
MILDMAY
Anne 471
Anne (Reade) 882
family lxii
Frances (Rainbow) 882
John 882, 883

Margaret (Cornish) 882
Mary 122, 882
Mary (Everard) 882
Olive (Nuttal) 882
Thomas 882
Thomasine 882, 883
Walter 882
MILDRED
Daniel 403
Lydia 403
MILES
Ada Elinor (Harte) clvi, 567
Alice 484
Elizabeth 526
Ella Frances 567
Francis Frederick 567
MILFORD HAVEN
Louis, Prince of Battenberg, 1st Marquess of 41
MILGRAM
Heather 129
MILHOUS
Almira Park (Burdg) 764
Franklin 764
Hannah 764
MILL
Margaret Foye "Meg" vi
MILLER
Angelina Jolie (Voight) [Angelina Jolie] 967, 974
John 654
Jonny Lee 974

Lydia 584, 647
Margaret Hardwick xiii
Mary 852
Mary (Ward) (Cutting) lviii, lx, cxlviii, cli, clx, clxxix, 654, 655, 656
Rebecca 914
Thomas (Act. Gov.) 840
MILLETTE
Dolores 982
MILLIGAN
Jane 244
MILLS
Margaret 366
MILNS
Olivia Rowlandson 69
MILOSLAVSKY
Maria 794
MILTON
Frances xvii, clviii, 320, 322
Mary (Gresley) 320
William 320
MILWOOD
Thomasine 100
MINSHALL
Sarah (___) 857, 983
MINSK
Gleb, Prince of 849
MINTHORN
Hulda Randall 371
John 370
Lucinda (Sherwood) 370

Mary (Wasley) 370
Theodore 370
MIRAFIORI (DI)
　Rosa Teresa
　　Vercellana,
　　Countess, Countess
　　of Fontanafredda
　　614
MIRFIELD
　Jane 821
MIRZAYANTZ
　Alexandra (of Greece
　　and Denmark),
　　Princess clvi, 3
　family 3
　Nicolas clvi, 3
MISSENDEN (DE)
　Elizabeth 857
MITCHELL
　Elizabeth lxi, 540,
　　643
　Lettice 302
　Margaret 219
MITFORD. *see also*
　FREEMAN-
　　MITFORD
　Alice 328
　Alice (Abrahall?)
　　425
　Barbara liv, cxlvii,
　　clxxxii, 314, 425,
　　599
　Barbara (Lawson)
　　425
　family 425
　Henry 425
　John 425
　Margery 366, 425,
　　599

Mary (Widdrington)
　425
Philip 425
MITROWICZ AND
　SCHÖNFELD
　Ludmilla Maria
　　Theresa
　　Wratislavová,
　　Countess 220
MITTON
　Agnes (Grey) 750
　Constance
　　(Beaumont) 630
　Elizabeth 628, 750
　Joan 506, 507
　John 630
　Joyce 630
　Katherine 630
　Margaret (Corbet)
　　506
　Margaret (Peshall)
　　506
　Richard 750
　Richard (Sir) 506
　William 506
MITTROWSKY
　VON MITROWICZ
　Antonia (von
　　Zierotin), Duchess
　　von Lilgenau 895,
　　896
　Johann Nepomuk,
　　Count 895
　Josepha Juliane,
　　Countess 220, 895
　Julie (von Salis-
　　Zizers) 895
　Marie Josephine
　　(Schröfl von

　　Mannsperg),
　　　Baroness 895
　Wilhelm, Count 895
　Wladimir, Count 895
MIVILLE
　Catherine (Baillon)
　　939, 950, 951, 967,
　　970, 971, 974, 977
　Jacques 950, 967,
　　970, 971, 974, 977
　Jean 970, 971, 974,
　　977
　Jean-Bernard 971
　Marie 969, 972, 973,
　　975, 976, 977, 978,
　　979, 980, 981, 982
　Marie-Angélique
　　971
　Marie-Françoise 971
　Marie-Françoise
　　(Soucy) 971
　Marie-Geneviève
　　977
　Marie-Madeleine
　　970, 974
　Marie-Madeleine
　　(Dubé) 970, 971,
　　974, 977
MOBBERLY
　Catherine 822
MODENA
　Angelina Caterina
　　d'Este of 18
　Ferdinand, Arch-
　　duke of Austria,
　　Duke of 15
　Hercules I, Duke of,
　　Duke of Ferrara
　　186, 189

Lucretia (Borgia),
  Duchess of,
  Duchess of Ferrara
  287, 293
Maria Beatrice
  d'Este, of 15
Maria Leopoldina,
  Princess of,
  Archduchess of
  Austria 15
Maria Ludovika,
  Archduchess and
  Empress of
  Austria, Princess
  of 11
Maria Theresa Felicitas d'Este of 287
Mary Beatrice,
  Princess of, Queen
  of England and
  Scotland 22, 24
MOELS (DE)
Muriel 824
MOERKERKE (VAN)
Lodewijk van Praet,
  Heer 459
MOFFAT
Matilda Eliza 27
MOHLER
Eliza Sarah 914
MOHUN (DE)
Alice 866, 870
Godeheut (de Toeni) 851
Hawise (Fitz-Geoffrey) 866, 870
Reynold (Sir) 866, 870
William 851

Yolande 851
MOLE
Edward 561
Elizabeth (Duke)
  (Bacon) (Jarvis) 561
MOLESWORTH
Anne (Adair) 462
Catherine (Cobb) 462
family 465
John 462
Letitia (Coote) 462
Louise (Tomkyns) 462
Margaret Letitia 462
Richard 462
Robert Molesworth,
  1st Viscount 462
William (Hon.) 462
MOLEYNS
Katherine 473, 493, 522, 605
MOLLENBURG (AUF) (ZU)
Georg Ehrenreich
  von Rogendorf,
  Baron 619
Wilhelm von Rogendorf, Baron 619
MOLLER (VON)
Elizabeth 793
MOLLISON
Christian 148, 256
Margaret 256
MOLTKE (VON)
Georgine Marie
  Elizabeth Eugenie,
  Countess 16

MOLYNEUX
Anne 611
Anne (Dutton) 611
Elizabeth (Stanley) 611
Jane (Rugge) 611
Richard (Sir) 611
Thomas (Sir) 611
William (Sir) 611
MOMPESON
Anna (Hobbes) clxxxvii
MONACO
Albert I Honoré-Charles Grimaldi,
  Sovereign Prince
  of 20, 933
Caroline-Louise-Marguerite
  Grimaldi, Princess
  of 934
Charlotte-Louise-Juliette Grimaldi,
  Hereditary Princess
  of, Duchess of
  Valentinois 289, 933
Gabriella-Thérèse-Marie Grimaldi,
  Princess of,
  Countess of
  Carladès 934
Jacques-Honoré
  Grimaldi, Prince
  of, Marquis des
  Baux 934
Louis II Honoré-Charles-Antoine
  Grimaldi, Sovereign

Prince of xl, 20, 933
Mary Victoria
  (Douglas-Hamilton),
  Lady, Princess of,
  Princess Festetics
  von Tolna 20, 933
Onorato II Grimaldi,
  Prince of 190
Rainier III Louis-
  Henry-Maxence-
  Bertrand Grimaldi,
  Sovereign Prince
  of 289, 290, 934
Sovereign Princes of
  291, 929
Stéphanie-Marie-
  Élisabeth Grimaldi,
  Princess of 934
MONCELET
  Charles-Annet des
    Rosiers, Seigneur
    440
  François des Rosiers,
    Seigneur 440
**MONCELET alias
  MOSLÉ (DE)**
  Catharine Elisabeth
    (Koehler) 440
  Jean-Charles 440
MONCK
  Anthony 103
  Christopher, 2nd
    Duke of Albemarle
    103, 104
  Elizabeth 103
  Elizabeth (Smythe)
    103
  Frances (Plantagenet)
    (Basset) 103

George, 1st Duke of
  Albemarle 103, 104
John 104
Mary (Arscott) 103
Mary (Gould) 103
Thomas 103
Thomas (Sir) 103
MONCKTON
  Elizabeth (Manners)
    119
  John, 1st Viscount
    Galway 119
  Robert (Hon.)
    (Gov.) 119
MONCREIFFE
  Catherine (Murray)
    67
  Clara (Guthrie) 67
  David (Sir), 6th Bt.
    68
  Elizabeth (Ramsay)
    67
  Helen 68
  Helen (Mackay) 68
  Isabella 166
  Louisa (Hay) 68
  Thomas (Sir), 3rd
    Bt. 67
  Thomas (Sir), 5th
    Bt. 67
  Thomas (Sir), 7th
    Bt. 68
  William (Sir), 4th
    Bt. 67
MONDEFORD
  Mary 713
MONDIDIER (DE)
  François de Gannes,
    Sieur 964

Mathurin de Gannes,
  Seigneur 964
René de Gannes,
  Sieur 964
MONINGTON
  Elizabeth (Milborne)
    295
  Sybil 295
  Thomas 295
MONLÉON (DE)
  Rose 16
MONNINS (DE)
  Bertheleonne 964
MONOD
  Adolphe-Louis-
    Frédéric-Théodore
    634
  Cécile (Naville) 634
  Hannah (Honyman)
    634
  Jean 634
  Julien 634
  Louise-Philippine
    (de Coninck) 634
  Marie (Vallette) 634
  Odile 634
  William 634
MONROE. *see also*
  MUNRO/MUNROE
  Fanny 163
  James, 5th U.S.
    President 163, 260
MONS (DE)
  Charles, Seigneur de
    Beaulieu and de
    Richemont 941
MONS/MONTS (DE)
  family 941

MONSON
Jane 605
MONTAGNY (DE)
family 952
MONTAGU (DE)
Alice 324, 339, 345, 368, 370, 397, 419, 426, 433, 434, 902
Anne 400, 565
Anne (Rich) 135
Anne (Yelverton) 135
Anthony Browne, 1st Viscount 355, 414, 905
Anthony Maria Browne, 2nd Viscount 109, 905
Charles, 1st Duke of Manchester 135
Charles Greville, Lord (Gov.) 135
Doddington (Greville) 135
Edward 105, 115
Edward, 2nd Earl of Manchester 135
Elizabeth (Bulmer) 135
Elizabeth (Irby) 115
Elizabeth (Pelham) 105, 115
Frances 119
George 115
George, 1st Earl of Halifax 105
Grace 33, 115, 307
Harriet (Dunch) 135

Henry Pole, 1st Baron 107, 114
Isabel 944
Jane (Sackville) 109, 905
Jean de Salazar(t), Seigneur of Saint-Just, Marcilly and 953
Joan (Neville) 107
John, 1st Earl of Salisbury 565
John Montagu, 3rd Baron 565
John Neville, 1st Marquess of 345, 426
Margaret (de Monthermer) 565
Mary 105, 346
Mary (Lumley) 105
Maud (Francis) 565
Robert, 3rd Duke of Manchester 135
Robert, 3rd Earl of Manchester 135
Susan 67
Susan (Gordon) 67
Sybil 508, 514, 547, 584, 594, 607
Tanis Eva Bulkeley (Guinness) 124, 481
Theodosia 121
Thomas Browne, 3rd Viscount 109
William, 5th Duke of Manchester 67

William Drogo Sturgis (Hon.) 124
MONTAGU-DOUGLAS-SCOTT
Alice, Princess of Great Britain, Duchess of Gloucester 25, 28
Charmian Rachel 23
William Henry, 6th Duke of Buccleuch 28
MONTAGUE-SMITH
Patrick W. xxix, lxi
MONTAIGU (DE)
Jacqueline 961
MONTAL (DE)
Françoise 200
MONTALTO
Cobella Ruffo, Countess of 205
MONTALVO y RODRÍGUEZ
Matilde-Ignacia de la Caridad 443
MONTAUBAN (DE)
Marie 455
MONTDIDIER
Adelaide of 872
counts of 725
Hildouin IV, Count of 866, 868, 870, 872
Margaret of 866, 870
MONTEFELTRO DELLA ROVERE
Marianita 21
MONTEIL (DE)
Lambert III Adhémar, Seigneur 735

Louis Adhémar,
co-Seigneur 735
MONTEITH. *see also*
MENTEITH/
MONTEITH [later
DALYELL];
MENTEITH/MON-
TEITH/MENTETH
MONTELEÓN
Antonio Casado de
Acevedo y Velasco,
3rd Marquess of
140
Isidro Casado de
Acevedo y del Mazo,
1st Marquess of 140
MONTENUOVO
Albertine Leopoldine
Wilhelmine Julia
Maria, Princess of
11
Alfred, 2nd Prince
of 11
Franziska, Princess
of 11
Juliana (Batthyány
Német-Ujvár),
Countess 11
William Albert, 1st
Prince of 11
MONTESARCHIO
Alfonso II Felice
d'Avalos, Prince of
Francavilla and
186, 189
Ferdinando Fran-
cesco II d'Avalos,
Prince of Franca-
villa and 186, 189

Nicolo d'Avalos,
Prince of Troia and
189
MONTESPAN (DE)
Françoise-Athénaïs
de Rochechouart,
Marquise 287, 289
MONTFERRAT
Frederick II Gonzaga,
Duke of Mantua,
Marquess of 186,
189
Margaret
Palaeologina of
186, 189
MONTFICHET (DE)
Eleanor 843
MONTFORT (DE)
Alice 861, 862
Alice (de Audley)
861
Alice (de la
Plaunche) 861
Alix (de
Montmorency)
954, 959
Amicie 954
Baldwin (Sir) 687
Bertrade 778, 780,
785, 787, 789, 806,
813, 815, 817, 819,
821, 822, 824, 826
Clarissa 474, 729
Eleanor 697
Eleanor (de
Courtenay) 965
Elizabeth (Gresley)
697
Elizabeth of 832

family 956
Geoffrey I de
Sallmard, Seigneur
de Ressiz, de la
Fay, and 638
Guy, Count of
Bigorre 959
Hugh I, Count of
Bregenz, Count of
832
Jean de Sallmard,
Seigneur 638
Jeanne (de Levis)
965
Jérôme Bonaparte,
King of Westphalia,
Prince of xl, 858
Joan (Vernon) 687
John de Montfort,
1st Baron 861
Katharina 895
Katherine 687
Louis de Sallmard,
Seigneur 638
Margaret (de
Clinton) 687
Margaret (Pecche)
687, 688
Mary (Stapleton)
687, 688
Maud (de la Mare)
861
Peter (Sir) 861
Peter/Piers, 3rd
Baron Montfort
861
Pétronille 959
Pétronille (de
Comminges) 959

1401

Philip I, Seigneur de
La Ferté-Alais 965
Philip II, Seigneur
de La Ferté-Alais
965
Philippe-Guillaume de
Sallmard, Seigneur
de Ressiz, Roche-
Pingolet, and 638
Raymond I de
Sallmard, Seigneur
de Ressiz, Roche-
Pingolet and 638
Robert 687
Simon III, Earl of
Leicester 954, 959
Thomas 697
William (Sir) 687
**MONTFORT-
L'AMAURY (DE)**
Jeanne 965
**MONTFORT-
PFANNBERG**
George II, Count of
895
James, Count of 895
**MONTFORT-
TETTNANG**
Clara of 617
**MONTGOMERY/
MONTGOMERIE**
Agnes 173
Agnes (Drummond)
143, 173
Alexander 243
Alexander, 6th Earl
of Eglinton 143
Alexander, 8th Earl
of Eglinton 143

Alexander, 9th Earl of
Eglinton 143, 144
Anne (Livingston)
143
Catherine (Kennedy)
243
Elizabeth 239, 253
Elizabeth (Baxter)
269
Elizabeth (Crichton)
143
Elizabeth (Cunyng-
ham) 269
Ellen 687
Euphemia 143, 243,
933
Helen (Campbell)
269, 270, 271
Hugh, 1st Earl of
Eglinton 243,
269, 270, 271
Hugh, 2nd Earl of
Eglinton 173
Hugh, 3rd Earl of
Eglinton 143, 173
Hugh, 7th Earl of
Eglinton 143
Hugh, of Brigend
269
Isabel (Burnett)
clxiv, clxxi, 250,
269
Isabella (Vernon)
723, 724
Jane 269
Janet 271
Jean (Lyle) 269
Jean (Montgomery)
269

Joan (Delves) 721,
723
John, of Brigend 269
Katharine (Scott)
269
Margaret 90, 143,
150, 269, 723
Margaret (Cochrane)
143
Margaret (Mure)
269
Mariot (Seton) 173
Mary 144, 732
Mary (Leslie) 143
Maud 721
Neil (Sir), of
Lainshaw 269
Nicholas 723, 724
Nicholas (Sir) 721,
723
William clxiv, 250,
269
William, of Brigend
269
_____ 898
**MONTHERMER
(DE)**
Joan (Plantagenet) (de
Clare) of Acre,
Princess of England
xxxix, 466, 483, 489,
491, 495, 505, 508,
514, 528, 536, 547,
565, 567, 575, 577,
584, 587, 590, 592,
594, 606, 607, 615
Margaret 565
Margaret (____) 565

1402

Ralph de Monthermer, 1st Baron 565
Thomas de Monthermer, 2nd Baron 565
MONTIJO (DE)
Cipriano de Palafox y Portocarrero, Count 292
Eugénie (Eugenia María Ignace Augustine de Portocarrero de Guzmán y Kirkpatrick), Empress of the French 291, 292
María Francisca (de Sales de Portocarrero de Guzmán), Countess of 292
MONTLUEL (DE)
Béatrix 911
Guy, Seigneur de Châtillon 911
Marguerite (Alleman) 911
MONTMIREL (DE)
Adrien de Méhérenc, Seigneur, Seigneur de La Conseillère 946
Jean de Méhérenc, Seigneur, Seigneur de la Conseillère 946
Raoul de Coucy, Seigneur 944

MONTMORENCY (DE)
Aiglantine (de Vendôme) 943
Alix 954, 959
Anne de Montmorency, Duc 637
Bouchard IV, Seigneur 959
Charles, Count de Richemont, Constable of France 943
family 294
Guy VII, Sire de Laval 964
Hippolite 287
Jacqueline 943
Jean I, Seigneur 943
Jeanne 637
Jeanne (Bracque) 943
Jeanne (de Brienne) 943, 964
Jeanne (de Calletort) 943
Jeanne (de Lévis) 943
Jeanne (Rataut) 943
Mathieu, Constable of France 959
Mathieu, Seigneur d'Auvraymesnil 943
Mathieu II, Seigneur d'Auvraymesnil 943
Mathieu III, Seigneur 943

Mathieu IV, Seigneur, Admiral and Grand Chamberlain of France 943
Philippa 964
MONTMORILLON (DE)
Louise 293
MONTMORON (DE)
Charlotte 943
Renaud de Sévigné, Sieur 942, 943
MONTPERNY (DE)
Amalie, Marquise 641
MONTRÉSOR
Frances (Tucker) 368, 464
Henrietta (Fielding) clxxii, 368
James Gabriel 368, 464
John (Col.) 368, 464
Mary (Haswell) 368, 464
MONTROSE
James Graham, 1st Marquess of 161
James Graham, 2nd Marquess of 161
John Graham, 3rd Earl of 151, 152, 161, 170
John Graham, 4th Earl of 151, 161
William Graham, 1st Earl of 258, 940

1403

MONTVUAGNARD (DE)
Guillauma 872
MONTZ (DE)
Eleanor 826
MONYPENNY
Katherine 260
MOODIE
Barbara 85
Francis, of Breckness 85
Margaret (Stewart) 85
MOODY
Ceil 136
Deborah (Dunch) [Lady Deborah Moody] clxxvi, 738, 740
Henry (Sir), 1st Bt. 738
MOOR
Abigail (Franklin) 747, 758
Hiram D. 747, 758
John 747, 758
Mary (Davis) 747, 758
Victoria Josephine 342, 526, 747, 758, 814, 882
MOORE
Alice (Spencer) 137
Catherine Maria (Long) 346
Cecily (Bonville) 743
Dorothy 434

Eleanor (Milborne) 296
Elizabeth 137, 151, 296, 558
Elizabeth (Selwood) lxiii
Ellen 743
family 742
George 772, 773
Hannah (___) 106
Henry (Sir), 1st Bt. (Gov.) 346
Henry, 1st Earl of Drogheda 137
Henry, 3rd Earl of Drogheda 137
Jane 601
Jane (Barcroft) 772, 773
Jean 77
Joan 233
John 296, 601, 742
John, Archbishop of Canterbury 100
Katherine (Selwood) cxlv, cli, 742
Magdalene 772, 773
Mallie clxxxiv
Margery 507
Mary 629
Mary (Burke) 601
Mary (Cole) 137
Mary (Eden) 100
Mary Elsie 18
Morris 743
Rebecca (Axtell) 742
Susan 415

MORANT
Marie 950
MORAWETZ
Cathleen (Synge) clvi, 254
Herbert 254
MORAY
James Stewart, 1st Earl of 93, 95, 97
James Stewart, 2nd Earl of 93, 95, 97
James Stewart, 3rd Earl of 93, 97
James Stewart, 4th Earl of 93, 893
John Dunbar, 1st Earl of 219, 281
Margaret 789
Thomas Dunbar, 2nd Earl of 219
MORDAUNT
Anne 614, 826
Barbara (le Strange) 826
Robert 826
MORE
Anne 426
Anne (Poynings) 426
Christian (Hunter) 319
Elizabeth (Smalley) 319
Elizabeth (Woolnaugh) 319
Ellen 319
George (Sir) 426
Jane (___) (Crumpton) 319
Jasper 319

Joan 320
Katherine (More) 319
Mallie clxxxiv
Margaret 426, 526
Margaret (Cresset) 319
Mary 319
Richard lxv, lxix, clxxii, 319, 322
Samuel 319
Sarah 82
Thomas 319
MOREAU
Gail F. 939, 951
Marie-Jeanne 989
MORÉEN
Magdalena Dorothea 893
MOREHOUSE
Trial 924
MOREIRA DA SILVA-BURKE
Adrian Benjamin l, liii, lxiv, lxx, clxxxv, 248, 922
MOREL
Sybil 857, 861, 864
MORESBY
Anne 909
Christopher (Sir) 909
Elizabeth (Parr) 909
MORETON
Frances (Herbert) 77
Mary Elizabeth
Kitty 77

Thomas Reynolds, 1st Earl of Ducie 77
MORFUDD
ferch Gruffudd ap Llywelyn Fychan 686
ferch Ieuan Goch 659, 694
ferch Mathew ap Llywarch 650
MORGAN
ab Edward 555
Anna 923
Anna (Tucker) cxlix, 463, 465
Anne (Gosse) 401
Anne Gosse 401
ap Dafydd 810
Barbara 307
Cadwalader 658
Dorothy 859
Dorothy (Parke) 858, 932
Edmund 338
Elizabeth (Robert) 652
Elizabeth (Stradling) 338
Elizabeth (Vaughan) 338
Elizabeth Anne 362
James 555
Jane (____) 555
Jane (Price) 658
John l, liv, lv, 401, 555
Joseph 858, 932
Joseph, Jr. 859

Kathleen Helen (MacCarthy-Morrogh) (Summersby) [Kay Summersby] 546
Lewis 555
Margaret 548, 932
Mary 338
Nathaniel 463
Reginald Heber 546
Sarah 463
Sarah (Emmons) 859
Sarah (Jones) 555
Susanna (Woodhouse) 401
Ted [Sanche-Armand-Gabriel de Gramont] vi, xviii, liii, clxx, 49
Thomas 338
William 401, 652
MORHIER
Isabeau 950
MORIARTY
George Andrews, Jr. xxviii, lvi, lviii, lxi, lxii, lxvii, lxix, lxxi, clxxxi, 398
MORIN
Marion 211
MORISON
Katherine 98
MORLEY
Anne xxv, 317, 342, 343, 577
Eleanor 596
Elizabeth 588
Elizabeth (de Ros) 596

Elizabeth (Drake)
   419
Henry Parker, 1st
   Baron 596
Henry Parker, 2nd
   Baron 355
Isabel (de la Pole)
   577, 588, 596
James 419
Robert Morley, 6th
   Baron 596
Thomas Morley, 5th
   Baron 577, 588,
   596
ORLHON (DE)
François, Seigneur
   d'Asprières 634
Marguerite 634
Marguerite (de
   Senneterre) 634
MÖRNER
Carl Mörner, Baron
   457
Christina Maria 457
Maria (Ribbing) 457
MORNINGTON
Garret Wesley, 1st
   Earl of 340
MOROSOV
Xenia 799
MORRIS
Anna Maria 324
Catherine (Griffith)
   652, 693
Charlotte Augusta
   805
Eleanor (Williams)
   660

Elizabeth (Almy)
   764
Ellen 651, 660
family 652
Jane 740
Job 764
John 660
Lewis 764
Lydia 764
Magdalen 165
Mary (Ansley) 764
Mary Elizabeth
   800
Maud 380
Richard 764
Robert Thomas
   692
Sarah 764
____ 652
MORRISETTE
Alan 978
Alan-Joseph 978
Alanis Nadine 967,
   978
Georgia Mary Anne
   (Feuerstein) 978
Joseph 978
Joseph-Hillaire 978
Lucille (Hunault)
   978
Marie (Mercier) 978
Noelia Gertrude
   (McConnell) 978
MORRISON
Alexander, of
   Prestongrange 278
Bethia 278
Bridget (Hussey)
   351

Eleanor (Maule) 278
Elizabeth 121, 351
Richard (Sir) 351
MORROGH
Helen (MacCarthy)
   546
James 546
**MÖRS AND
SAARWERDEN**
Frederick IV, Count
   of 459
Walpurga of 459
MORSELEY
Judith 856
MORSTYN
John Andrew, Count,
   Great Treasurer of
   Poland 154
MORTEYN (DE)
Joan (de Rothwell)
   857, 861
Joan (Gobion) 857,
   861
John 857, 861
John (Sir) 857, 861
Lucy 857, 861
MORTIMER
Anne 107, 114,
   119, 126, 133, 134
Edmund, 3rd Earl of
   March 107, 114,
   119, 126, 133, 134,
   305, 310, 317, 319,
   327, 333, 342, 347,
   349, 351, 355, 359,
   361, 363, 374, 379,
   384, 385, 389, 399,
   401, 414, 418, 425,
   431, 901, 904, 905

Edmund Mortimer,
  1st Baron 647, 909
Eleanor (Cornwall)
  603
Eleanor (Holand)
  107, 114, 119, 126,
  133, 134
Elizabeth xxxiv,
  305, 310, 317, 319,
  327, 333, 342, 347,
  349, 351, 355, 359,
  361, 363, 374, 379,
  384, 385, 389, 399,
  401, 414, 418, 425,
  426, 431, 469, 473,
  477, 492, 552, 603,
  737, 901, 904, 905
family xli, 416
Hugh (Sir) 603
Isabel (Howard)
  473, 477
Isolde 761
Katherine 255
Margaret 541, 680
Margaret (de
  Fienes) 647, 909
Maud 647, 909
Maud (de Braose)
  680
Philippa (Plantagenet)
  107, 114, 119, 126,
  133, 134, 305, 310,
  317, 319, 327, 333,
  342, 347, 349, 351,
  355, 359, 361, 363,
  374, 379, 384, 385,
  389, 399, 401, 414,
  418, 425, 431, 901,
  904, 905
Ralph 680
Robert 473, 477
Roger (Sir) 680
Roger, 4th Earl of
  March 107, 114,
  119, 126, 133, 134
MORTON
Catherine 879, 919
Cecily (Charlton)
  697
Charles (Rev.) 836
Elizabeth 475
family 373
Frances (Kestell) 836
James Douglas, 1st
  Earl of 173, 222,
  223, 225, 898
James Douglas, 3rd
  Earl of 154, 157,
  167, 168, 179
Joan (___) 836
John Douglas, 2nd
  Earl of 160, 223,
  898
Margery 697
Nicholas 836
Richard 697
Sarah Copeland 858
MORUS
ap Gruffudd ab
  Ieuan 692
ap John 694
MORYSON
Elizabeth
  (Harington) 517
Francis (Dep. and
  Act. Gov.) 517,
  518
Fynes 518

Jane (Eltonhead)
  clxxiii, 498, 599
Richard 517
Richard (Sir) 517,
  518
Robert 498, 517
Winifred (___) 517
MOSBACH
Otto of Bavaria,
  Count Palatine of
  237
MOSCOW
Anastasia, Princess
  of 621
Anna of 797
Basil II, Grand Prince
  of 621, 797
Basil III, Grand
  Prince of 797
Dimitri IV, Grand
  Prince of 621, 797
Ivan I, Grand Prince
  of 791, 797
Ivan II, Grand
  Prince of 797
Maria of 791, 797
Michel Ney,
  Napoleonic
  Marshal, Duke
  d'Elchingen,
  Prince of 83
MOSELEY
Abigail 673
Abigail (Root) 673
Diana (Freeman-
  Mitford) (Guinness)
  (Hon.) [Diana
  Mitford] 23
John 673

1407

Joseph 673
Mary 389, 673
Mary (Newberry) 673
Oswald Ernald, Sir, 6th Baronet 23
MOSES
Amy 867
Sarah (Alderman) 867
Thomas 867
MOSLE
Alexander Samuel 440
Caroline Durnford (Dunscomb) vi, lxx, clvi, 440, 626
Charlotte Amalia (Schultze) 440
Dorothea Catharina (Rendorff) 440
Georg Rudolf 440
George vi, lxx, 440, 626
Marie Caroline 440, 626
MOSLEY
Charles ix, xxix, lxii
Frances 117
MOSTYN
Catherine 235
Elsbeth 657
MOSTYN-OWEN
Allegra G. A. 12
MOTIER DE CHAMPETIÈRES
Charles, Baron de Vissac 200

Marie (de Pons) 200
MOTIER/MOTIER DE LA FAYETTE. see also LA FAYETTE (DE)
Anastasie-Louise-Pauline 201
Édouard, Baron de Vissac 201
Marie-Adrienne-Françoise (de Noailles) l, clxxii, 201, 203, 288, 291
Marie-Catharine (de Chavaniac) 201
Marie-Joseph-Paul-Yves- Roch-Gilbert, Marquis de La Fayette [Lafayette] xvi, xxvi, xl, l, liii, clxx, 201, 203, 288, 291
Marie-Louise-Julie (de la Rivière) 201, 203
Michel-Louis-Christophe-Roch-Gilbert, Marquis de La Fayette 201, 203
MOTIN (DE)
family 952
Jeanne-Marie 939, 952, 953
Louis, Seigneur de Roeux-Corcelles 952
Marie (de Salins) 952

MOTON
family 697
MOTTA SAN GIOVANNI
Francesco Ruffo, Duke of Bagnara, Prince of 189
MOTTE
Anne (le Brassieur) (Pinckney) 311
Jacob 312
MOTTISTONE
John Edward Bernard Seely, 1st Baron 179
MOTTLEY
Mary 294
MOTTROM
Anne 348, 785
Frances 306
MOUCHY (DE)
Philippe de Noailles, Duc 200, 288
MOULSON
Catherine 367
MOUNT
Mary Fleur 10
MOUNT EDGCUMBE
William Henry Edgcumbe, 4th Earl of 28
MOUNTBATTEN
Edwina Cynthia Annette (Ashley) 299
Louis Francis Albert Victor Nicholas, 1st Earl Mountbatten of Burma 41, 299

Louise, Queen of
  Sweden 41
MOUNTJOY
  William Blount, 4th
    Baron 340
MOUNTSTEPHEN
  Joan (Christopher)
    754
MOUSÉ (DE)
  Guillaume le Voyer,
    Seigneur 964
MOWAT
  Christian (Stewart)
    87
  Jean 87
  John 87
MOWBRAY
  Christiana lvii,
    700, 703
  Eleanor xxv, 462,
    470, 473, 486, 526,
    539, 545, 579, 580,
    604, 609, 623
  Elizabeth (de
    Segrave) 462,
    470, 473, 486, 493,
    519, 522, 526, 534,
    539, 541, 545, 557,
    579, 580, 598, 599,
    604, 605, 609
  Elizabeth (FitzAlan)
    xxiii, xxiv, xxv,
    xxvi, xxxi, xxxii,
    473, 493, 497, 510,
    517, 522, 524, 532,
    541, 554, 557, 558,
    560, 563, 565, 571,
    574, 598, 605, 611

family xiii, xxvi,
  xxxi, xxxii, xxxiv,
  xli, 564
Isabel 295, 541,
  557, 598
Joan (Plantagenet)
  623
Joan/Genet xxv,
  425, 519, 599
John 703
John Mowbray, 3rd
  Baron 623
John Mowbray, 4th
  Baron 462, 470,
  473, 486, 493, 519,
  522, 526, 534, 539,
  541, 545, 557, 579,
  580, 598, 599, 604,
  605, 609
Margaret xxv, 314,
  473, 493, 522, 534,
  605, 661
Thomas, 1st Duke of
  Norfolk xiii, xxiii,
  xxiv, xxv, xxvi,
  xxxi, xxxii, clxxii,
  473, 493, 522, 541,
  557, 598, 605
MOYER
  Anna-Hélène
    (Paquin) [Anna
    Paquin] 967, 968,
    980
  Stephen 980
MOYLE
  Amy 491
  Loveday 400
  Mary (Kendall) 400
  Richard 400

MOYNE
  Bryan Walter
    Guinness, 2nd
    Baron 23
  Jonathan Bryan
    Guinness, 3rd
    Baron 23
  Walter Edward
    Guinness, 1st
    Baron 23
MOYNS
  Joan 491
MOYRIA (DE)
  Claude 952
  Irené, Seigneur
    Mailla 952
  Louise (de Chevron)
    952
MSCISŁAWSKA
  Anastasia, Princess
    621
MUDGETT
  Mary 344
MUDIE
  Janet 250
MUHLINEN/
MÜLINEN (VON)
  Anna 832
MUIR
  Alice 128
  Caroline Charlotte 98
  Elizabeth Huntly
    (Wemyss) 98
  William (Sir) 98
MUIRHEAD
  Rebecca 244
MUIRSON
  Louise Caroline
    Tobin 130

MULCASTER
Anne 130
MULGRAVE
Constantine Phipps,
1st Baron 22
Edmund Sheffield,
1st Earl of 327
MULLET
William (Rev.) 676
Winifred (Wolseley)
676
MULLOIS
Marie 965
MULTNEY
Margaret 845
MUMFORD
Catherine 464
Elizabeth (Bolling)
729
James 729
MUNCHENSY
Joan 785
MUNDAY
Elizabeth 543
Katherine 400
MUNDY
Richard 626, 860
MUNFORD/
MONTFORT
Anne (Brodnax)
474, 729
Robert 474, 729
MUNK
Christine (morganatic wife of Christian IV, King of Denmark)
35, 37
MUNNINGS
Anne 579

MUNRO
R. W. lvi, lvii, lix, lxii
MUNRO/MUNROE.
see also MONROE
Agnes (Munro), of Durness 260
Andrew 260
Andrew (Rev.) 260
Anne 276
Christian 283
Christian (Blair) 260
David, of Katewell 260
Euphemia (Munro), of Pittonachy 260
family 260
family, of Foulis clxxxiii
George, of Katewell 260
John clxxxiii
John (Rev.) lvi, lvii, lix, clxvii, clxxi, 240, 260
Margaret (Dunbar) 260
Mary 260
Robert, 14th Baron of Foulis 260
Sarah (Smith) (Pitt) 260
William lix, clxxxiii
MÜNSTERBERG
Bolko II of Schliesen-Liegnitz, Duke of, Duke of Fürstenberg 640

Nicholas IV of Schliesen-Münsterberg, Duke of 640
MUNTZ
Hope 879, 919
MURAT
Alexandre-Michel-Eugène-Joachim-Napoléon, Prince 83
Caroline (Marie-Annonciade-Caroline) (Bonaparte), Queen of Naples 82
Caroline Georgina (Fraser) 82
Caroline-Cécile-Alexandrine-Jeanne, Princess 63, 83
Cécile (Marie-Cécile-Michèle) (Ney) 83
Eudoxia (Somov) 83
Helen McDonald (Stallo) 83
Joachim Murat, 1st Prince, King of Naples 82
Joachim-Joseph-Napoléon Murat, 4th Prince 83
Joachim-Napoléon Murat, 5th Prince 83
Laure-Louise-Napoléone-Eugénie-Caroline Murat, Princess clii, 83, 635

Louis-Napoléon,
    Prince 83
Lucien-Charles-
    Joseph- Napoléon
    Murat, 3rd Prince
    xviii, 82
Malcy-Louise-
    Caroline-Frédérique
    (Berthier) 83
Michel-Anne-Charles-
    Joachim-Napoléon,
    Prince 83
Yvonne-Noele-Marie
    (Gillois) 83
MURDOCH
    Jean 732
MURE
    Agnes 732
    Elizabeth, first wife
        of Robert II, King
        of Scotland 219,
        269, 272, 273, 280,
        281, 283
    Margaret 269
MUROM
    Maria of 791, 797
MURPHY
    Nathan W. xlvii,
        lxii, lxiv, clxxxviii,
        562, 603, 729, 905
MURRAY
    Adam, of Cardon
        152
    Amelia 67
    Amelia Ann Sophia
        (Stanley) 62, 68,
        637
    Anne 62, 151
    Anne (Bennet) 210

Anne (Mackenzie)
    (Atkins), Lady 92
Anne Charlotte
    (Grant) 66
Archibald, of
    Murrayfield 177
Aurora 584, 648
Barbara clxix, 211
Barbara (Bennet)
    xxxiii, xxxv, clxviii,
    210, 211, 790, 923
Barbara, of
    Pennyland 82
Caroline Leonora 66
Catherine 65, 67
Catherine (Fraser)
    67
Catherine (Hamilton)
    66
Catherine (Murray)
    62
Charles, 1st Earl of
    Dunmore 62, 66, 67
Charlotte (Murray),
    Baroness Strange,
    Lady of the Isle of
    Man 66
Charlotte (Stewart)
    62
Christian 152
Christian (Veitch)
    152
Dorothy 790, 923
Elizabeth 210, 479,
    715
Emilia (Murray) 66
family xxxiv
Frances Allethea
    696

George, Lord 66, 67
Helen 152
James xxxiii, xxxv,
    clxi, 210, 211, 790,
    923
Jean (Fleming) 152
Jean (Hay) 177
John 92, 211
John (Gov.), 4th
    Earl of Dunmore
    62, 933
John, 1st Duke of
    Atholl 66, 67
John, 1st Marquess
    of Atholl 62, 637
John, 3rd Duke of
    Atholl 66
John, 4th Duke of
    Atholl 66
John, of Abercairney
    940
John, of Bowhill
    210
John, of Polmais
    151
John, of Unthank
    210
John Boyles 211
Katherine 218
Lilias (Stirling) 151
Lillias 266
Margaret 65, 90,
    241, 285
Margaret (Fleming)
    218
Margaret (Nairne)
    62
Margaret (Scott), of
    Ancrum 210, 211

1411

Marion 940
Martha
 (McClenachan) 211
Mary 92
Mary (Boyles) 211
Mary Caroline 285
Nicole (Graham)
 940
Patrick, of
 Philiphaugh 218
Rosalind 299
Susan 31, 67
Susan Mary 177
William (Sir), 3rd
 Bt. 67
William, 2nd Baron
 Nairne 62, 66, 67
William, 3rd Earl of
 Dunmore 62
William, of Cardon
 152
MURREY
Ann 779
MUSCOTE
Cecily 495
MUSGRAVE
Anne 361
Christopher (Sir),
 4th Bt. 361
Christopher (Sir),
 5th Bt. 361
Dorothy 361
Eleanor 363
Frances (Wharton)
 361
Julia (Chardin) 361
Juliana (Hutton) 361
Mary (Cogan) 361
Mary (Legge) 361

Philip 361
Philip (Sir), 2nd Bt.
 361
Richard (Sir), 1st Bt.
 361
MUSGROVE
Martha 320
MUSHAM
Leila Eliott (Burton)
 (Hadley) (Smitter)
 90
William C. 90
MUSKETT
James Joseph lii, liv,
 lv, lvi, lxii, lxvi, lxxi
MUSSAM
___ 253
MUSTON
Elizabeth 813
MUTH
Albert H. ix, lxii,
 lxvi, 589
MYFANWY
ferch Gruffudd 689
ferch Hwfa ab
 Iorwerth 689
MYLES
Anne (Humphrey)
 (Palmes) clxi,
 301, 304, 501
Edith Bradford 227
John (Rev.) 301
Katherine 375, 701
MYLNE
Christian 171
MYNNE
Anne 739
Elizabeth (Wroth)
 738, 739

George 738
MYRICK-BENNETT
Belinda 330
NABOKOV
Dimitri 618
Elena (Roukavish-
 nikov) 618
family 618
Maria (Korff),
 Baroness 618
Vera (Slonin) 618
Vladimir xii, xviii,
 xxvi, liii, clvi, 618
NAESETH
family xxii
Gerhard Brandt xxii
NAGLE
Mary 545
**NAHARRO DE
 HUMANES**
Isabel 995
NAINTRÉ (DE)
Charles Levrault,
 Seigneur 941
NAIRNE
Margaret 62
William Murray, 2nd
 Baron 62, 66, 67
NAMUR
Albert I, Count of
 874, 877
Albert II, Count of
 874, 877
Albert III, Count of
 874, 877
Elizabeth of 874, 877
family lxii
Godfrey, Count of
 874, 877

John of Flanders,
  Count of 944
Marie of 944
NANE
  Nina Maria viii
NANFAN
  Bridges 107
  Catherine 107, 462
  Catherine (Hastings)
    107
NANGLE
  Amy 545
  Catherine 488
  Eleanor (Dowdall)
    545
  Ismay (de Welles)
    545
  John 545
  Thomas 545
NANNAU
  Catherine 229
NANSEGLOS
  Mary 857
NAPIER
  Ann (Chisolm) 214
  Elizabeth 214
  John 214
  John, of Kilmahew
    170
  Katherine 170
  Lilias (Colquhoun)
    170
NAPLES
  Alfonso V, King of
    186, 189
  Beatrix, Princess of,
    Empress of
    Constantinople
    961

Beatrix, Princess of
  Provence, Queen
  of, Queen of Sicily
  965
Caroline (Marie-
  Annonciade-
  Caroline)
  (Bonaparte) Murat,
  Queen of 82
Charles I of Anjou,
  King of, King of
  Sicily 965
Charles II, Prince of
  Anjou and France,
  King of, King of
  Sicily 459
Eleanor of 186, 189
Ferdinand I, King of
  186, 189
Isabella of
  Clermont, Queen
  of 186, 189
Joachim Murat, 1st
  Prince Murat, King
  of 82
Joanna, Princess of
  Aragón, Queen of
  186, 189
Louis II, King of
  Sicily, Jerusalem,
  Aragón and 205
Marie, Princess of
  Hungary, Queen
  of, Queen of Sicily
  459
Marie of
  Châtillon-Blois,
  Queen of, Queen
  of Sicily,

Jerusalem, and
  Aragón 205
NAPOLÉON
  princes 288
NAPOLÉON I
  (Bonaparte),
  Emperor of the
  French 11, 157,
  292, 442, 858
NAPOLÉON III
  (Louis Napoléon
  Bonaparte),
  Emperor of the
  French 49, 291,
  292
NAPTON
  family clxxxvi
NARIMOND
  Prince of Pinsk 797
NARYSHKIN
  Alexandra 795
  Anna (Naryshkin)
    799
  Dimitri 799
  Konstantin 799
  Kyrill 795
  Maria 799
  Marie (Lobanovsky-
    Rostovsky),
    Princess 795
  Paul (Pavel) 799
  Praskovya
    (Dolgoruki),
    Princess 799
  Sophia (Uschakov)
    799
NASON
  Joyce 728

NASSAU-DILLENBURG
Anna of 184
Charlotte of 62, 637
George, Count of 194
John I, Count of 194
Juliana of 182, 196
Margaret of 194
NASSAU-HADAMAR
Albertine Johanette of 38
Claudia of 35
NASSAU-SAARBRÜCKEN
Anna Juliane, Princess of 56
Louise, Princess of 47
NASSAU-SIEGEN
Amalia Magdalena of 889
Elizabeth of 141, 181
John I, Count of 181
John II, Count of 181
John III, Count of 889
Sophia Amalia of 56
NASSAU-WEILBERG
Albert, Count of 184
Anna Eleanor of 184
John Casimir, Count of 184

NASSAU-WIESBADEN
Adolf I of, Holy Roman Emperor 617
Elisabeth of 617
Gerlach I, Count of 617
NAUNTON (DE)
Bridget 680
Eleanor (Boville) 680
Eleanor (de Vere) 680, 681
Hugh 680
Margaret (Barney) 680
Margaret (d'Oyley) 680
Margery (Brusyard) 680
Peter 680
Robert 680
Robert (Sir) 139
Thomas 680
___ (Tymberley) 680
NAVAILLES (DE)
Girarde 963
NAVARRE
Charles II, King of 287, 290, 293
Henry IV, King of, King of France 293, 615, 637
Jean d'Albret, King of 287, 293
Jeanne, Princess of 963

Joanna, Princess of 455
Joanna, Princess of, Duchess of Brittany, Queen of England 226, 229, 231, 233, 235, 287, 293
Joanna, Princess of France, Queen of 293, 455
Margaret, Princess and Queen of France and 637
Marguerite of 993
Philip III, King of 455
Sancha, Princess of 993
Theobald I, King of 993
NAVARRO
Lucia (Richardson Ojeda) 520
Perla (Amador Pineda) 521
NAVARRO LUGO
Francisco (Vice Pres.) 521
NAVARRO RICHARDSON
Ernesto "Tito" 521
Lucia 521
NAVILLE
Cécile 634
NAYLOR
Mary (Underhill) lx, cxlvi, clxxxi, 875, 1025
Thomas 875

NEAHR
 Anna Maria
  (Halladay) 867
 Anna Serepta
  (Wells) 867
 Henry Clay 867
 Hortense 867
 Jacob Robert 867
NEAL
 Anne 500
 Simon xx
NEALE
 Anna Maria (Gill)
  512, 558, 559, 676,
  875
 Dorothy 676
 Ellen 478
 family xxiv
 Goditha (Throck-
  morton) 874
 Grace (Butler) 478,
  874, 875
 Henrietta Maria 512
 James viii, li, lix,
  clxvi, clxxviii,
  clxxxi, 512, 558,
  676, 875, 1025
 Jane 311, 747
 Jane (Baker) 875
 John 478, 874
 Raphael 875
 Thomas 874
NEAVE
 Catherine Mary 127
NEED
 Anne (___) 384
 Dorothy (___)
  384
 Humphrey 384
 Joseph lxi, cxlix,
  384
 Mary 384
 Mary (Melford) 384
 Nathaniel 384
 Rebecca (___) 384
NEEDHAM
 Anne (Talbot) 574
 Barbara 833
 Dorothy 574
 Eleanor 561
 Frances (Aston)
  561, 574
 Joan (Lacy) 561
 Robert 574
 Robert (Sir) 561
 Robert, 1st Viscount
  Kilmorey 561
 Thomas 574
NEERWINDE
 Jean-Baptiste de la
  Bistrate, Seigneur
  of Laer and 804
NEESON
 Liam John xvii, 246
 Natasha (Richard-
  son) (Fox) xi,
  xvii, xlii, clvii, 246
NEGROPONTE
 Diana Mary (Villiers)
  xi, xlix, clvii, 122,
  125
 John Dimitri 122
 Marie 49
NEGUS
 Jane (Deighton)
  (Lugg) lxviii,
  clxi, clxxii, 297
 Jonathan 297
NEIPPERG (VON)
 Adam Adalbert,
  Count 11
 Maria Anna Bertha,
  Countess 19
NELIDOV
 Alexandra 793
NELLENBURG
 Agnes (von
  Eschenburg) 832
 Eberhard III, Count
  of 832
 Manegold I, Count
  of 832
 Manegold II, Count
  of 832
 Margareta of 832
NELSON
 Anne (Lambert) 126
 Dorothy (Stapleton)
  126
 Elizabeth (Lowell)
  126
 Elizabeth (Tailer/
  Taylor) 355, 921,
  924
 family vii, l, lvii,
  lxviii
 Glade Ian lvi, lxii,
  lxvi
 John xxiv, xxxv,
  lvii, clxi, 355, 356,
  921, 923, 925
 Jonathan Banks 690
 Margaret lvii, clxxix,
  clxxxviii, 356
 Mary (___) (Lunt)
  126

Mary (Temple)
355, 356
Matthew Sherwood
690
Mehitable 923
Philip lxv, cxlv,
clxi, 126
Philippa (Andrews)
(Felt) (Platts) 126
Rebecca 355
Robert 355
Sarah (Jewett) 126
Selma Amanda 662
Thomas lxiii, 126
Thomas, Jr. lxv,
cxlv, 126
NEMOURS
Louis-Charles-
Philippe-Raphael
of Orléans, Duke
of 290
NEPEAN
Emily Margaret 65
NERO
Carlo Gabriel
Redgrave 247
Franco [Francesco
Sparanero] 246
Vanessa (Redgrave)
(Richardson) 246
NESBIT
Mary 219
NESLE (DE)
Eleanor 954
Pierre de Vendôme,
Seigneur de Segré
and 946
Raoul III, Count of
Soissons 954

NEST
ferch Hywel Felyn
810
ferch Lles 886
ferch Rhun ap
Gronwy Fychan
810
**NETHERLANDS
(THE)**
Bernhard Leopold
Friedrich Eberhard
Julius Kurt Karl
Gottfried Peter,
Prince of Lippe-
Biesterfeld, Prince
Consort of 1, 47
Henry, Duke of
Mecklenburg,
Prince Consort of 8
Juliana, Queen of
1, 47, 907, 908
Maria Cristina,
Princess of 1
Marianne, Princess
of 8
Maxima (Zorriguieta
y Cerruti), Queen of
991
monarchs of 141,
615
Wilhelmina, Queen
of 8
Wilhelmine,
Princess of Prussia,
Queen of 8
William I, King of 8
William III "the
Silent," Prince of
Orange, Stadholder

of 62, 141, 181,
182, 184, 194, 196
William IV of
Orange, Stadholder
of 8
William V of Orange,
Stadholder of 8
NETTERVILLE
Alison 486
Alison (St.
Lawrence) 486
John 486
Lucas 486
Margaret (Luttrell)
486
Margaret
(Netterville) 486
NEUCHÂTEL
Louis-Alexandre
Berthier, Prince of,
Prince de Wagram,
Napoleonic
Marshal 83
**NEUF (LE) DE LA
VALLIÈRE**
Marguerite 964
NEUHAUS (VON)
Adam 895
Lucia Ottilia 895
NEVERS
family 945
**NEVERS and
MANTUA**
Anna Gonzaga of
38
NEVET
Elizabeth 366, 367
Priscilla (Fenwick)
366, 367

1416

Roland (Rev.) 366, 367
NEVILLE
Alice 324, 368, 419, 425, 434
Alice (de Audley) 761
Alice (Longford) 754
Alice (Montagu) 324, 339, 345, 368, 370, 397, 419, 426, 433, 434, 902
Alice (Wauton) 754
Amphyllis 717
Anne 123, 393, 403, 754
Anne, Queen of England 118
Anne (Beauchamp) 118, 419
Anne (Killigrew) 417, 427
Anne (Manners) 123
Anne (Maplethorpe) 717
Anne (Stafford) 331, 421
Anne (Warde) 398
Barbara (Hercy) 781
Bridget 115
Bridget (Saville) 781
Catherine 339, 370, 387
Catherine (Grenville) 77
Catherine (Howard) 314, 387
Cecily 107, 114, 119, 126, 133, 134, 405
Charles, 6th Earl of Westmoreland 123
Dorothy 334, 345, 346, 421, 482
Edward 781
Edward (Sir) 324, 405, 417
Edward, 1st Baron Abergavenny xxv, 314, 324, 357, 387, 405, 417, 429
Edward, 5th Baron Abergavenny 405
Edward, 6th Baron Abergavenny 405
Eleanor 310, 327, 333, 347, 351, 355, 361, 374, 379, 389, 397, 399, 401, 414, 418, 425, 431, 433, 761, 901, 902, 904, 905
Eleanor (Windsor) 324, 405, 417
Elizabeth 346, 357, 429
Elizabeth (Babington) 717, 754
Elizabeth (Beauchamp) xxv, 324, 331, 357, 405, 417, 421, 429
Elizabeth (Gresham) 417
Elizabeth (Newmarch) 398, 413
Elizabeth (Smythe) 417
Ellen clxxxiii, 755
family xxxii, 347
Frances (Manners) 122, 123
Geoffrey (Sir) 841
George 781
George, 1st Baron Latymer 331, 421
George, 2nd Baron Abergavenny 118, 324, 347, 357, 405, 417, 429
George, 3rd Baron Abergavenny 122, 347
Gertrude (Whalley) 781
Gilbert 781
Henry (Sir) clxxxiii, 331, 417, 421, 427
Henry, 4th Baron Abergavenny 122
Henry, 5th Earl of Westmoreland 123
Henry, 7th Baron Abergavenny 405
Hercy 781
Isabel 107, 114, 118, 426
Isabel (de Byron) 841
Isabel (Griffin) 754
Isabel (Ingoldsthorpe) 345, 426

Isabel (Waleran) 855
Jane 398, 413
Jane (Howard) 123
Joan 107, 114, 402, 855
Joan (Beaufort) (Ferrers) xxxiv, 107. 114, 119, 126, 133, 314, 324, 331, 339, 357, 366, 368, 370, 387, 393, 395, 397, 398, 403, 405, 413, 417, 418, 419, 426, 429, 433, 434, 902
Joan (Bourchier) clxxxiii, 331, 421
Joan (de Atherton) 841
Joan (Warde) 402
John 398, 413, 717, 781
John, 1st Marquess of Montagu 345, 426
John, 4th Baron Latymer 345, 418
John Neville, 3rd Baron 314, 761
Katherine cxlv, 324, 398, 417, 418, 427, 551, 552
Katherine (Brome) 405
Katherine (Palmer) 754
Lettice (Harcourt) clxxxiii

Lucy 340, 345
Lucy (Somerset) 345, 418
Margaret 314, 331, 495, 590, 841, 842
Margaret (Bland) 781
Margaret (de la Pole) 841
Margaret (de Lungviliers) 841
Margaret (Fenne) 118, 324, 347, 357, 405, 417, 429
Margaret (Stafford) 318, 425, 495, 590
Mary 77, 413, 781
Mary (Ferrers) 398, 413
Mary (Sackville) 405
Mary (Scott) 781
Mary (Stafford) 122, 347
Mary, Baroness le Despencer 122
Maud (Percy) xxx, 314, 761
Philippa 318
Rachel (Lennard) 405
Ralph 398, 402
Ralph (Sir) 413
Ralph, 1st Earl of Westmoreland xxxiv, 107, 114, 119, 126, 133, 314, 318, 324, 331, 339, 357, 368, 370, 387, 393, 397, 403, 405, 417,

418, 419, 425, 426, 429, 433, 434, 495, 590, 902
Ralph Neville, 2nd Baron 761
Richard, 1st Earl of Salisbury 324, 339, 345, 368, 370, 397, 419, 426, 433, 434, 902
Richard, 2nd Baron Latymer 331, 421
Richard, "the Kingmaker," Earl of Warwick and Salisbury 118, 419
Richard Aldworth, 2nd Baron Braybrooke 77
Robert 841
Robert (Sir) 754, 841
Sarah 366
Thomas clxxxiii, 717, 754
Ursula 347
William 754, 755, 855

NEVIN
Isabella (Cuming) 272
James 272
Jane 308

NEVSKY
Alexander, Grand Prince of Kiev and Vladimir 791, 797

NEWARK
David Leslie, 1st
Baron 92
NEWBERRY
Benjamin 673
family clxxxiv
Mary 673
Mary (Allyn) 673
Thomas lxix,
clxxxiv, 842
NEWBURY
Anne 223
NEWBY
Mary 473
NEWCOMB
Judith 243
NEWCOMEN
Eleanor 343
John 343
Mary (Skipwith)
343
NEWDIGATE
Amphyllis (Neville)
717
Grizel 717
Joan 653, 738
John 717
Juliana (Leigh)
517
Martha (Cave) 717
Mary 517, 518
Mary (Bagot) 517
Mary (Cheyney)
717
Mary (Hylton) 717
Richard (Sir), 1st Bt.
517
Richard (Sir), 2nd
Bt. 517

NEWENHAM
Anne 768
NEWGATE
Hannah 357, 749,
924
NEWLIN
Elizabeth 230
NEWMAN
Harry Wright
(H.W.) clxxxvi
John Henry, Cardinal
71
Mary 854
NEWMARCH
Elizabeth 398, 413
NEWPORT
Anna (Corbet) 412
Francis 412
Thomas 412
NEWTON
Anne 407, 408
Clere (Gilbert) 589
Ellen lviii, lxi, lxvii,
clx, 398, 667, 668
Ethel 335
Frances 315
Hester cxlvi, 413,
598
Isaac (Sir) 628
Isabel 761
John 667
John (Sir), 2nd Bt.
413
Juanita 545
Katherine
(Mainwaring) 407
Lancelot 667
Margaret 222

Margaret (Grimston)
667
Margaret (Mere) 407
Margaret (Thorpe)
667
Margery (Wright)
407
Mary (___) 667
Mary (Eyre) 413
Mary (Lee) 667
Nancy 925
Parnell (Davenport)
407
Robert 589
William 407
NEX 125
Lucinda Claire 125
NEY
Cécile (Marie-
Cécile-Michèle) 83
Michel, Napoleonic
Marshal, Duke
d'Elchingen, Prince
of Moscow 83
NEYRIEU (DE)
Guillaume de
Grolée, Seigneur
952
Guy de Grolée,
Seigneur 911
NIARCHOS
Daphne Suzannah
Diana Joan
(Guinness) (Hon.)
clv, 23
Eugenia (Livanos)
23
Nicolas Stavros 23
Spyros Stavros 23

Stavros 23
NICHOL
  Brom 531
NICHOLAS
  Charlotte
    (Frankland) 130
  Harriet 130
  Prince of Greece
    and Denmark 3, 4
  Robert 130
NICHOLAS I
  Czar of Russia 5, 7
  Duke of Troppau
    621
NICHOLAS II
  Czar of Russia 5,
    453
  Duke of Troppau
    621
NICHOLAS IV
  of Schliesen-
    Münsterberg, Duke
    of Münsterberg 640
NICHOLL
  Mary 867
NICHOLS/NICOLLS
  Dorothy 705
  Elizabeth 852
  Francis 456
  Margaret (Bruce)
    456
  Mary 464
  Richard (Gov.) 456
NICHOLSON
  Hannah 912
  Mary Ann 884
  Victoria Mary "Vita"
    (Sackville-West)
    299

NICKERSON
  Herman, Jr. (Lieut.
    Gen.) ix, xlvi,
    lxii, cxci, 583, 812
NICKLIN
  J. B. Calvert lxii
NICOLA/NICHOLAS
  Charles 736
  Charlotte (des
    Vignolles) 736
  Christiana (D'Oyly)
    736
  Jane (Bishop) 736
  Louis vii, lxiv, 736
NICOLL
  Gloriana Margaret
    128
NICOLLS. see
  NICHOLS/NICOLLS
NIEBLA
  Juan Carlos de
    Guzmán, Count of
    140
NIKITA
  Grand Duke of
    Russia 5
  Grand Duke of
    Russia [Nikita
    Romanoff] clvii,
    5
NIKONOWA
  Maria 14
NILSDOTTER
  Elsa 452
NINA
  Grand Duchess of
    Russia 4
NIOUSQUÉ (DE)
  Mechtilde 963, 990

NITHSDALE
  Robert Maxwell, 4th
    Earl of 155
NITSCHMANN
  Anne 237, 239
NIVEN
  David (James David
    Graham) xvii, 70
  Primula Susan
    (Rollo) cxlv, 70
NIXON
  Francis Anthony
    764
  Hannah (Milhous)
    764
  Jane 245
  Richard Milhous, 37th
    U.S. President 764
  Thelma Catherine
    "Pat" (Ryan) 764
NOAILLES (DE)
  Adrien-Maurice de
    Noailles, Duc
    288, 289
  Anne-Claudine-
    Louise (d'Arpajon)
    200, 288
  Anne-Jeanne-
    Baptiste-Adrienne-
    Louise-Catherine-
    Dominique (de
    Noailles) l, clxxii,
    200, 288
  Anne-Jules de
    Noailles, Duc 287
  Arthur-Anne-Marie-
    Charles de Noailles,
    Vicomte 227
  family 291

Françoise-Charlotte-
 Amable
 (d'Aubigné) 288
Jean-Louis-François-
 Paul de Noailles,
 Duc 288
Louis de Noailles,
 Duc 288
Louis-Marie de
 Noailles, Vicomte
 xvi, xxvi, l, liii,
 clxx, 200, 288
Marie-Adrienne-
 Françoise l, clxxii,
 201, 203, 288, 291
Marie-Françoise (de
 Bournonville) 287
Marie-Laure-
 Henriette-Anne
 (Bischoffsheim)
 227
Marie-Victoire-
 Sophie 287, 290
Philippe, Duc de
 Mouchy 200, 288
NOBLE
 Catherine (Van
 Brugh) 898
NOEL
 Andrew (Sir) 416
 Catherine 119
 Dorothy 819
 Elizabeth (___)
 819
 James 819
 Jane (Draycote)
 819
 Juliana 431
 Lucy 414, 416

Mabel (Harington)
 416
Mary 112, 345
Matilda (Brereton)
 819
Robert 819
Thomas 819
NOLA
 Ettore Pignatelli,
 Prince of 192
NOLLENT (DE)
 Blanche (Varin) 957
 Christine (du Bose)
 957
 Françoise 957
 Guillaume 957
 Jean 957
 Marie (Lhermitte)
 957
 Michel 957
NONANT (DE)
 Joan 674, 866
NORBORNE
 Elizabeth 345, 346
 Frances (Bacon) 345
 Walter 345
NORCLIFFE
 Antonia 401
 Dorothy (Fairfax)
 401
 Frances Fairfax
 116
 Thomas (Sir) 401
NORFLEET
 Sarah 170
NORFOLK
 Henry Charles
 Fitzalan-Howard,
 13th Duke of 71

Henry Granville
 Fitzalan-Howard,
 14th Duke of 71,
 72
Hugh Bigod, 3rd
 Earl of 806, 821,
 845, 846
John Howard, 1st
 Duke of 353, 473,
 493, 522, 605, 661
Margaret Plantagenet,
 Duchess of 462,
 470, 473, 486, 493,
 519, 522, 526, 534,
 539, 541, 545, 557,
 579, 580, 598, 599,
 604, 605, 609, 1024
Miles Francis
 Fitzalan-Howard,
 17th Duke of 72, 75
Roger Bigod, 1st
 Earl of 845
Roger Bigod, 2nd
 Earl of 737, 742,
 746, 749, 752, 754,
 757, 760, 761, 763,
 766, 768, 770, 772,
 845
Roger Bigod, 4th
 Earl of 845, 846
Roger Bigod, 5th
 Earl of 845, 846
Thomas Howard,
 2nd Duke of 300,
 333, 353, 355, 605,
 705, 904
Thomas Howard,
 3rd Duke of 333,
 431

Thomas Howard,
4th Duke of 334
Thomas Mowbray, 1st
Duke of xiii, xxiii,
xxiv, xxv, xxvi, xxxi,
xxxii, clxxii, 473,
493, 522, 541, 557,
598, 605
Thomas Plantagenet
of Brotherton,
Prince of England,
Earl of xxxix,
462, 470, 473, 486,
493, 519, 522, 526,
534, 539, 541, 545,
557, 564, 579, 580,
598, 599, 604, 605,
609
NORLIN
Sofia Matilda 60
NORMAN
Charlotte (Beadon)
306
George 306
George Warde 306
Henrietta (Wroughton)
306, 309
James 306, 309
Sibella (Stone) 306
Sibella Charlotte 306
**NORMAND DE
MORA (LE)**
Caroline-Josephine
289
NORMANDY
Adela of, Princess
of England 642,
911
Adelaide of 879, 919

Gunnora, Duchess
of 861
Judith of 861
Matilda of Flanders,
Duchess of, Queen
of England 642,
830, 851, 911, 1024
Richard I, Duke of
861
Richard II, Duke of
879, 919
Robert I, Duke of
879, 919
William I "the
Conqueror," Duke
of, King of England
xx, 642, 830, 851,
861, 879, 911, 919,
1024
NORRIS
Anne 670
Edward 492
Edward (Rev.)
xlix, lxi, cli, 492
Eleanor 743
Kathleen 5
Mary 33
Silvester (Poyntz)
492
NORRIS/NORREYS
Bridget (Kingsmill)
428
Elizabeth 428
Henry 428
Henry, 1st Baron
Norris/Norreys of
Rycote 428
Joan (de Vere)
428, 584

Margaret 584
Margaret (Williams)
428
Mary (Fiennes)
428
Richard 428
Thomas (Sir) 428
William (Sir) 428,
584
NORTH
Peregrine 235
NORTH WALES
David [Dafydd ap
Llywelyn Fawr],
Prince of xxxii,
650, 652, 657, 659,
686, 689, 692, 693,
694
Llywelyn Fawr ab
Iorwerth, Prince of
650, 657, 659, 680,
682, 686, 689, 692,
693, 694, 813, 824
Owain Gwynedd,
King of 815
NORTHAMPTON
George Compton,
4th Earl of 112
James Compton, 3rd
Earl of 112
James Compton, 5th
Earl of 112
Simon de St. Liz,
Earl of Huntingdon
and 778, 779,
780, 783, 785, 787,
789, 879, 919
Spencer Compton,
2nd Earl of 111

Waltheof II, Earl of,
 Earl of Huntingdon
 and Northumber-
 land 779, 879, 919
William Compton,
 1st Earl of 111
William de Bohun,
 1st Earl of xxxix,
 497, 500, 510, 517,
 524, 532, 551, 554,
 558, 560, 563, 565,
 571, 574, 588, 596,
 611, 613
NORTHCOTT
 Katherine (Gale) 745
 Walter 745
NORTHUMBERLAND
 Henry Percy, 2nd
  Earl of 310, 327,
  328, 333, 347, 351,
  355, 361, 374, 379,
  389, 399, 401, 414,
  418, 425, 431, 901,
  904, 905
 Henry Percy, 3rd
  Earl of 310, 327,
  333, 347, 361, 374,
  379, 389, 399, 401,
  402, 414, 418, 431
 Henry Percy, 4th
  Earl of lxvi, 333,
  347, 361, 389, 401,
  418, 431
 Henry Percy, 8th
  Earl of 418
 Henry Algernon
  Percy, 5th Earl of
  361, 389, 401,
  418, 431

John Dudley, 1st
 Duke of 477
Matilda of, Queen
 of Scotland 778,
 780, 783, 785, 787,
 789, 879, 919
Waltheof II, Earl of
 Huntingdon,
 Northampton and
 779, 879, 919
NORTHUMBRIA
 Edith of 857, 861,
  864
 Gospatrick I, Earl
  of, Earl of Dunbar
  857, 861, 864
 Uchtred, Earl
  (Ealdorman) of
  857, 861, 864
NORTON
 Anne 698, 778
 Courtenay (Walker)
  467
 Daniel 467
 Elizabeth 375, 393
 Fortune 295
 Henry lxii, cxci
 Jane 132, 337, 668
 Jane (Hatley) 467
 John xlix, cxlix,
  467, 469
 John (Sir) 698
 Margaret 870
 Margaret (Warde)
  698
 Walter lxii, cxci
NORVELL
 Mary 257

NORWAY
 Agnes Haakonsdotter
  of 452, 457
 Euphemia of Rügen,
  Queen of 452, 457
 Haakon V, King of
  452, 457
 Isabel (de Joigny),
  Queen of 452, 457
 monarchs of 45,
  444, 453, 615
 Sonja (Haraldsen),
  Queen of xxii
NORWICH
 Duff (Alfred Duff)
  Cooper, 1st
  Viscount 9
 John Julius Cooper,
  2nd Viscount 9
NORWOOD
 Charles 296
 Elizabeth (Lygon)
  296
 Elizabeth (Rodney)
  296
 Henry 296
 Henry (Lt. Gov.),
  M.P. lx, cxlv,
  clxxii, 296
 William 296
NOTBEAM
 Katherine (Pecche)
  880
 Margaret 880
 Thomas (Sir) 880
NOTT
 Anne (Thynne) 335
 Edward (Gov.)
  317, 335

1423

Margaret
  (Blakiston) 317,
  335
Thomas (Sir) 335
NOTTINGHAM
Charles Howard, 1st
  Earl of 605
NOTTINGHAM (DE)
Margery 877
NOURSE
Apollonia 131, 335
Elizabeth (Gregory)
  123
James 123
John 123
Sarah (Fouace)
  123
NOVA SCOTIA
Mary (Witham)
  Bolles, Baronetess
  of 471
NOVAK
Vera Chochroska
  973
NOVELLARA
Camillo Gonzaga,
  Count of 186
NOWELL
Alexander 701
Alexander, Dean of
  St. Paul's 703
Elizabeth 701
Elizabeth (Kay)
  701
family xxxiv, 704
Grace (Towneley)
  701
Increase vii, xlv, l,
  cxlv, clxi, 701,

703, 704
John 701
Laurence, Dean of
  Lichfield 369,
  701, 703
Mary (____) 369,
  701
Parnell (Gray)
  (Parker) 701
Roger 701
Sarah 369
Sarah (Smyth) 701
NOYELLE(S) (DE)
Alexandre de
  Carondelet, Baron,
  Vicomte de La
  Hestre 438
Antoine de
  Carondelet, Baron,
  Vicomte de La
  Hestre 438
Antoinette (de
  Mailly) 633
Elisabeth 445
François-Louis-Hect
  or de Carondelet
  (Gov.), Baron,
  Vicomte de La
  Hestre and du
  Langue liii,
  clxxiii, 438
Guillaume 445
Jean-Louis de
  Carondelet, Baron,
  Vicomte de La
  Hestre and du
  Langue 438
Magdalena (van
  Culemborg) 445

Nicole 633
Philippe, Vicomte
  de Langle 633
NOYES
Elizabeth 654
John 654
John, Jr. 654
Mary (Cutting) 654
Mary (Poor) 654
Mary (Thurlo) 654
Nicholas 654
NUGENT
Anne 739
Christopher, 3rd
  Baron Delvin 340
Mabel 340
NÜRNBERG
Elizabeth of (wife of
  Rupert III, Holy
  Roman Emperor)
  237, 291
NUTTAL
Olive 882
NYS
Maria 436
O (D')
Alix (de Vendôme)
  946
Isabelle 946
Robert IV, Seigneur
  946
OBAMA
Barack Hussein
  498, 726
Barack Hussein, Jr.,
  44th U.S. President
  498, 726, 923
family xxxvii

Michelle LaVaughn
  (Robinson) 498,
  726
Stanley Ann
  (Dunham) 498, 726
**OBOLENSKY
(-NELEDINSKY-
MELETZKY)**
  (Ava) Alice Muriel
    (Astor) 799, 800
  Claire (McGinnis)
    800
  Daria (Troubetskoy),
    Princess 793
  Dimitri, Prince 793
  family xxii
  Ivan, Prince 800
  Katharina
    (Yourievsky)
    (Bariatinski),
    Princess 799
  Maria (Naryshkin)
    799
  Maria, Princess 793
  Mary Elizabeth
    (Morris) 800
  Marylin (____)
    (Fraser-Wall) 799
  Platon, Prince 799
  Praskovia, Princess
    195
  Serge(i), Prince
    clvii, 799, 800
O'BRIEN
  Anne (O'Brien)
    122
  Catherine (Stuart),
    Baroness Clifton
    122

Catherine, Baroness
  Clifton 122
Dermod, 5th Baron
  Inchiquin 340
Donough, 2nd Earl
  of Thomond 601
Ellen (Butler) 601,
  602
Ellen (FitzGerald)
  340
Henry, 4th Earl of
  Thomond 122
Henry, 6th Earl of
  Thomond 122
Henry, Lord
  Ibrackan 122
Mabel (Nugent)
  340
Margaret 601
Mary 340
Mary (Brereton)
  122
Murrough, 4th
  Baron Inchiquin
  340
O'CALLAGHAN
  Mary 108
O'CARROLL
  Bibiana (O'Dempsey)
    601
  Charles 602
  Clare (Dunne/
    O'Doyne) 602
  Ferganainm 601
  Joan (Butler) 601,
    602
  John 601
  Margaret (O'Doyne)
    601

Mary (Dillon) 601
Mulrony 601
Sadhbh ní Giolla
  Phadraig (MacGilla-
  patrick/ Fitzpatrick)
  601
Shile 601
Teige 601, 602
William (Sir) 601
____ MacMorough
  Kavanagh 601
____ O'Kennedy
  Finn 601
OCHTERLONEY
  Elizabeth 251
**O'CONNOR/
O'CONOR**
  Anne (O'Molloy), of
    Aughtertire 885
  Cathal 885
  Catherine 885
  Catherine (O'Fagan)
    885
  Cecilia (O'Flynn),
    of Ballinlough
    885
  Charles 885
  Charles Oge 885
  Cornelia
    (Livingston)
    (McCracken) 885
  Denis 885
  Jane 405
  Margaret
    (O'Connor) 885
  Robert 863, 876
  Thomas xl, clvii,
    885
  ____ (Dillon) 885

1425

O'CONOR DON
Carbery 885
Dermot 885
Devorgilla (O'Conor Roe) 885
Dorothy (O'Conor Roe) 885
Edwina (O'Conor Sligo) 885
Evaine (O'Kelly) 885
Felim Geancach 885
Hugh (Sir) 885
Mary (O'Rourke), of Breffney 885
Owen Caech 885
Turlough Oge, King of Connaught 885
O'CONOR ROE
Devorgilla 885
Dorothy 885
O'CONOR SLIGO
Edwina 885
O'DANIEL
V. F. (Rev.) lxii
ODELL
Anne (Prather) 695
Eleanor 695
Henry 695
Keziah (Offutt) 695
Thomas 695
O'DEMPSEY
Bibiana 601
ODIM
Anne 830
ODINGSELLES (DE)
Ela (FitzRobert) 687, 749, 754, 757
Ida 687, 749, 754, 757
William (Sir) 687, 749, 754, 757
ODO
Duke of Burgundy 911
ODOEVSKY
Anastasia (Khvorostinine), Princess 794
Ivan, Prince 794
Maria (Lobanov-Rostovsky), Princess 794
Maria, Princess 791
Praskovia (Tolstoy), Countess 794
Varvara, Princess 794
Vassili, Prince 794
Youri, Prince 794
O'DOYNE
Margaret 601
ODROWAZ/ODROWAZNA
Sophia 621
Stanislaus 621
OETTINGEN
Anna of 640
Elisabeth of 617
OETTINGEN-FLOCHBERG
Beatrice (della Scala), of Verona 640
William I, Count of 640
OETTINGEN-SPIELBERG
Maria Josepha (Josephine) Theresia of 208
OETTINGEN-WALLERSTEIN
Euphemia (of Schliesen-Münsterberg) 640
Frederick III, Count of 640
Marie Anna, Princess of 19
OEVER (VAN)
Marijke Otten 776
O'FAGAN
Catherine 885
OFFLEY
Amelia xlviii, lvii, clxxiv, 495, 531, 684
Anne (Shute) 531, 684
Catherine 349
Margaret 625
Mary (Burton) 530
Robert 530
Stephen 530, 531, 684
Ursula (Clarke) 530
OFFUTT
Keziah 695
O'FLYNN
Cecilia, of Ballinlough 885
OGDEN
Malvina Belle 794
OGILVY/OGILVIE
Anne (Cabot) 97
Beatrix (Seton) 225
Clementina Gertrude Helen 22
David Graham Drummond, 7th Earl of Airlie 22

David Mackenzie
  xviii, cxlv, 97
Dorothy (Fairfield)
  97
Eila 97
Elizabeth
  (Scrymgeour) 257
Emily Charlotte 33
Francis John
  Longley 97
Francis Mackenzie
  97
George (Sir), of
  Dunlugas 225
Gilbert, of that Ilk
  257
Helen 261
Helen (Sinclair) 256
Henrietta Blanche
  (Stanley) 22
Herta (Lans) 97
Isabel 266
Isabel (Lindsay)
  256
James, 3rd Baron
  Ogilvy of Airlie
  256
James, 4th Baron
  Ogilvy of Airlie
  256
Janet 225
Janet (Beaton) 257
Jean (Graham) 256
John, 2nd Baron
  Ogilvy of Airlie
  256
John, of Powrie 257
Kythé Caroline
  (Mackenzie) 97

Margaret 223, 241,
  273
Margaret, of
  Deskford 239
Marion 99, 256
Mariota 789
Marjory 282
Marjory (Ogilvy)
  282
Melinda (Street)
  97
Sybilla 256, 257
Sybilla (Drummond)
  257
OGLANDER
Anne 475, 476
Mary 491
OGLE
Anne 519
Anne (Tasker) 327,
  328
Barbara 366
Catherine Meade
  535
Dorothy 328
Isabel (Craster) 328
Katherine (Graham)
  328
Luke 328
Margaret 599
Margaret
  (Gascoigne) 328
Maud (Grey) 519,
  599
Nicholas 328
Ralph Ogle, 3rd
  Baron 328
Robert (Sir) 519, 599
Samuel 328, 329

Samuel (Gov.)
  327, 328
Ursula (Markham)
  328, 329
OGLETHORPE
Eleanor xl, 613
Eleanor (Wall) 613
Elizabeth (Wright)
  613
family 614
Frances (Mathews)
  613
James Edward
  xxiv, xl, lxv, 613,
  614
Susan (Sutton) 613
Sutton 613
Theophilus (Sir)
  613, 614
William 613
O'GRADY
Charlotte Isabella
  145
OINGT (D')
family 952
OJEDA MEDERO
Rosaura 520
O'KELLY
Evaine 885
____ 433
OKEOVER
Catherine 134
OLDFIELD
Margaret 321
Mary 668
OLELKO
Alexander, Prince of
  Kiev 621

1427

OLELKOWICZ-SLUCKY
Anastasia (Mscislawska), Princess 621
Anna (___) 621
Michael, Prince 621
Siemion, Prince 621

OLGA
Grand Duchess of Russia, Queen of Greece 3
Princess of Greece 3

OLIPHANT
Jean 152
Lawrence Oliphant, 4th Baron 152
Margaret (Hay) 152

OLIVARES
Gaspar Philip de Guzmán, Count-Duke of 191

OLIVER
Eleanor 165
Jane (Rutherford) 165
Sybil 870
William, of Dinlabrye 165

OLNEY
Margaret 508, 721, 874

OLSSON
Nils W. 53

O'MOLLOY
Anne, of Aughtertire 885

ONANO
Francesco Sforza, Duke of 192

ONASSIS
Aristotle Socrates 16, 915
Jacqueline Lee (Bouvier) (Kennedy) [Jackie Kennedy Onassis] xl, xlii, xliii, xlvi, 16, 74, 914, 915

O'NEILL
Terri Bradshaw lxiii, 744

ONNEN
Ferdinand Henry, III 415

ONORATO II
(Grimaldi), Prince of Monaco 190

ONSLOW
Anne (Houghton) 534
Catherine (Corbet) 534
Catherine (Harding) 534
Cecily 534
Edward 534
Margaret (Poyner) 534
Richard 534
Robert 534
Roger 534

OOSTERVEEN
August Leopold van Pallandt, Heer van Eerde, Beerse and 445

OOSTERWIJK (VAN)
Ida 774

OPLOO (VAN)
Alexander Tengnagell, Heer 447

OPPENHEIM
Jill [Jill St. John] 44

ORADEUR (D')
Guyon de Belvezer, Baron, Baron de Jalavoux, Seigneur de Joncheres 200

ORANGE
William III, Prince of, King of England and Scotland 615
William III "the Silent," Prince of, Stadholder of The Netherlands 62, 141, 181, 182, 184, 194, 196
William IV, Prince of, Stadholder of The Netherlands 8
William V, Prince of, Stadholder of The Netherlands 8

ORANGE (D')
Guyonne 942

ORBY
 Elizabeth 214
ORCHARD
 family 248
 Janet/Jannette (Duncanson) (Aerdes) (Powell) 248
 Joan 870
 Robert 248
ORDE
 Leonora Louisa Isabella 34
O'REILLY
 Agnes Jane 161, 924
 Catherine 601
ORESTEN
 Gustaf Stenbock, Baron of Kronobäck and 452, 453
ORFORD
 Horace Walpole, 4th Earl of 482
 Robert Walpole, 1st Earl of 482
ORKNEY
 Henry Sinclair, 2nd Earl of 278
 Robert Stewart, 1st Earl of 82, 84, 85, 87, 89, 92, 98, 897
 William Sinclair, 3rd Earl of, 1st Earl of Caithness 278
ORLAMÜNDE
 Kunigunde of 849

ORLÉANS (D')
 Anne-Marie, Princess of, Queen of Sardinia 18
 Louis-Charles-Philippe-Raphael, Duke of Nemours 290
 Louis-Philippe-Joseph "Égalité" de Bourbon, Duke of 287, 288
 Marguerite-Adélaïde (Marie) of 290
ORLOV
 Grigori, Count, later Prince 14
 Varvara 795
ORMEROD
 George 815
ORMONDE
 James Butler, 1st Earl of 478, 512, 530, 553, 555, 582, 601, 603
 James Butler, 2nd Earl of 582, 601, 602
 James Butler, 3rd Earl of 500, 582, 583, 601
 James Butler, 4th Earl of 500, 502, 551, 553, 555, 574, 588, 596, 601
 James Butler, 9th Earl of 382
 Piers Butler, 8th Earl of 382, 601

 Thomas Boleyn, 1st Earl of Wiltshire, Earl of 300, 588
 Thomas Butler, 7th Earl of 392, 551, 588, 596, 1025
ORMSBY
 Mary Alice 115
ORON (D')
 Aymon, Seigneur de Bossonens and d'Attalens 911
 Catherine 911
 Philippine (de Chevron-Villette) 911
O'ROURKE
 Mary, of Breffney 885
ORR
 Agnes (Dalrymple) 173
 Alexander 173
 Alexander, of Hazelside 173
 Barbara (Crauford) 173
 John 173
 Susannah Monroe (Grayson) 173
ORRERY
 Charles Boyle, 4th Earl of 73
ORSAY (D')
 Anna-Quintana-Albertine-Ida Grimaud, Comtesse 49

Jean-François-Louis-
 Marie-Albert-
 Gaspard Grimaud,
 Count 49
ORSINI
 Eleanora 192
 Isabella (de' Medici)
 192
 Paolo Giordano, Duke
 of Bracciano 192
 Teresa of Gravina 18
ORTENBERG
 Anna Maria of 237
 Charles I, Count of
 237
ORTHWEIN
 Adolphus Busch, Jr.
 136
 Judith A. (Baring-
 Gould) 136
ORTÍZ ALFARO
 Eloïsa 996, 997
ORWELL
 George [Eric Arthur
 Blair] 122
OSBALDESTON
 Deborah 433
 Edward 433
 Geoffrey, Chief
 Justice of
 Connaught 433
 John (Sir) 433
 Lucy (Warren) 433
 Margaret (Stanley)
 433
 Maud (Halsall) 433
OSBORN(E)
 Abigail (Atkinson)
 (Winslow) 836

Danvers (Sir), 3rd
 Bt. (Gov.) 105,
 346
 Dorothy (Danvers)
 346
 Eleanor (Danvers)
 346
 Elizabeth (Strode)
 346
 Fanny (Van de
 Grift) 270
 John 346
 John (Sir), 1st Bt.
 346
 John (Sir), 2nd Bt.
 346
 Mary (Montagu)
 105, 346
 Peter (Sir) 346
 Sarah (Byng) 346
OSCAR II
 King of Sweden
 615
OSTENDORF
 Johann III van
 Raesfeld, Heer
 445
**OSTEN-SACKEN
 (VON DER)**
 Benigna 617
 Carl 617
 Christoph Friedrich
 617
 Eleanore
 Margarethe 618
 family 618
 Fromhold 617
 Katherina (von
 Korff) 617

Maria Elisabeth
 (von Fircks) 617
 Maria Elisabeth
 (von Polenz zu
 Schönberg) 617
ÖSTFRIESLAND
 Counts of 198
**OSTROGSKI/
 OSTROGSKA**
 Alexander, Prince
 621
 Alexandra (Sluka),
 Princess 621
 Anna (Kostczanka)
 621
 Constantine, Prince
 621
 Constantine Basil,
 Prince 621
 Sophia (Tarnowska),
 Countess 621
 Sophia, Princess 621
OSWALD
 Anne (Carter) 470
 Joseph, Jr. 470
 Susannah 470
OTIS/HOTESSE
 Cecile (Poulin) 623
 Elizabeth/Marie-
 Élisabeth (Wabert/
 Ouabard/Hubbard)
 623
 family clxix, clxxv,
 624, 945, 967
 John/Jean-Baptiste
 623
 Louise-Arel (Wabert/
 Ouabard/Hubbard)
 623

Marie-Anne
  (Perthius) (Caron)
  623
Marie-Françoise
  (Gagné) 623
Marie-Madeleine
  (Toupin) 623
Mary (Pitman) 623
Nathaniel/Paul 623
Richard 623
Rose (Stoughton)
  lviii, lxv, cxlv, clxix,
  clxxv, 623, 945
Rose/Françoise
  623
Stephen 623
Stephen, Jr./Joseph-
  Marie 623
Susanna (Hussey)
  623
OTLEY/OTTLEY
Adam 301
Elizabeth
  (Humphrey?) 301
OTTO
of Bavaria, Count
  Palatine of Mosbach
  237
Count of Lippe-
  Brake 194
Ernst (Theodor
  Ernst Heinrich)
  (Dr.) 321
Gerald Godfrey
  [Gerhard Gottfried]
  321
Hilda Margaret
  Rose (Thomas)
  lxiii, 321, 322

of Hohenstaufen,
  Count Palatine of
  Burgundy 735
Jean (Blackman)
  321
Julie Helen v, vi, ix,
  xxvi, xliii, l, lv, lxiii,
  lxvii, lxxi, 86, 113,
  131, 132, 141, 145,
  160, 174, 321, 322,
  323, 365, 968, 976
Rudolf (Karl Louis
  Rudolf) (Prof.) 321
OTTO I
Duke of Brunswick-
  Lüneburg 451
Duke of Meran,
  Count Palatine of
  Burgundy 735, 952
OTTO II
Duke of Brunswick-
  Göttingen 451
Duke of Brunswick-
  Lüneburg 452
Holy Roman
  Emperor 849
OTTO III
Margrave of
  Brandenburg 640
OTTO V
Margrave of
  Brandenburg 640
OTTWEIN
Susanna 619
OUABARD. see
  HUBBARD
OUELLET
Brigitte-Josèphe
  970

François-Germain
  971
Joseph 970
Marie-Françoise
  (Miville) 971
Marie-Josèphe
  (Lizot) 970
Marie-Théodiste
  971
OUESSEY (D')
Jeanne 956
OURROSSOV
Anastasia, Princess
  795, 796
Eudoxia
  (Sokovnine) 795
Feodosia (Lykov-
  Obolensky),
  Princess 795
Petr, Prince 795
Semen, Prince 795
OUVILLE (D')
Michel d'Aigneaux
  960
Olivier d'Aigneaux,
  Seigneur, Seigneur
  de La Chesnée 956
OVALLE
Arlene 991
OVERALL
Anne (Browning)
  498
George Washington
  498
Louisiana (Duvall)
  498
Robert 498
Susan Catherine 498

OWAIN
   ap Gruffudd 582, 810
   ap Gruffudd Fychan [Owen Glendower] 657, 813, 824
   ap Jenkin 811
   ap John 689
   ap Lewys 229
   ap Rheinallt 886
OWAIN GWYNEDD
   King of North Wales 815
OWEN
   ab Evan 651
   Agnes (Edwards) 660
   Alice (Gerard) 561
   Anne 560, 561
   ap Hugh 510
   ap Huw 809
   David (Sir) 603
   Dorothy (West) 603
   Edward 229
   Eleanor (Needham) 561
   Elen (Wen/Wynn) 690
   Elen Llwyd (ferch Robert ap Morgan) 229
   Elizabeth 510, 603, 690, 809
   Ellen 651, 809
   Elsbeth (ferch Robert ap Morgan) 770
   Henry (Sir) 603
   Humphrey 770
   Jane 510, 651, 660, 809
   Jane (Vaughan) lxvii, clxxi, 229, 230, 770
   John 510
   Joshua clxxiv, clxxxii, 510
   Lewis 229
   Lewys 770
   Lucy (Blaeney) 689
   Mably 658, 809
   Margaret 229
   Margaret (Puleston) 229, 770
   Martha (Shinn) 510
   Mary 307
   Mary (Bohun) 603
   Mary (Vaughan) 689
   Maurice 689
   Maurice/Morris 689
   Nancy 74
   Rebecca (Owen or Humphrey[s]) xxiv, clxv, clxxiv, clxxxii, 510, 651
   Robert clxv, clxxvii, 229, 510, 651, 770
   Roger 561
   Rondle/Randle 690
   William 660
   William (Sir) 561
OWEN/ HUMPHREY(S)
   Rebecca xxiv, clxv, clxxiv, clxxxii, 510, 651
OWENS
   Charles R. lvi, lxiii, lxvii, 257
OWSLEY
   Anne (___) 423
   Dorothea (Poyntz) xlviii, lxvii, 423, 598, 674
   John 423
   John (Rev.) xlviii, lxvii, 598, 674
   Mary (David/Davis) 423
   Poyntz 423
   Thomas xlviii, lxvii, clviii, clxxiii, 423
OXENBERG
   Catherine xvii, xlv, liv, 3
   Elizabeth (Karadjorjevic), Princess of Yugoslavia 3
   Howard 3
OXENBRIDGE
   Bathshua 933
   Daniel 324
   Elizabeth 324, 326, 327
   family xxxiv
   Frances (Woodward) lxx, cxlv, clxi, 324, 647, 649
   Jane (Butler) 324, 933
   John (Rev.) xl, li, cxlv, clxi, clxxii, 324, 325, 647, 933
   Katherine (Harby) 324

Malyn 420, 462
Mary (Hackshaw)
  324
Susanna (Parris)
  (Abbott) 324
Theodora 324
OXENDEN
Elizabeth 755
OXENHAM
Anne (___) 744
James 744
OXENSTIERNA
Anna (Banér) 452
Anna, Countess 452
Axel (Gustafson),
  Count 452
Barbro (Bielke)
  452
Beata (Trolle) 452
Bengt, Baron 452
Bengt, Count 452,
  453
Eva Magdalena,
  Countess 453
Gabriel, Baron 452
Gabriel, Count
  452, 454
Gustav, Baron 452
Magdalena
  (Stenbock),
  Countess 453
Sigrid (Tre Resor)
  452
OXFORD
Aubrey de Vere, 1st
  Earl of 680
Edward de Vere,
  17th Earl of 68,
  766

Hugh de Vere, 4th
  Earl of 680
John de Vere, 12th
  Earl of 584
John de Vere, 16th
  Earl of 68, 766
Richard de Vere,
  11th Earl of 584
Robert de Vere, 3rd
  Earl of 680
Robert de Vere, 5th
  Earl of 680, 681
Robert de Vere, 6th
  Earl of 680, 681
**OXFORD and
ASQUITH**
Herbert Henry
  Asquith, 1st Earl of
  306
OXLEY
Anne (Skipwith)
  (Goforth) lviii,
  cxlix, cli, 409
William 409
**OYEN en DIEDEN
(VAN)**
Johan Gerard van
  Gendt, Heer 907
Walraven van
  Gendt, Heer 907
Willem van Gendt,
  Heer 907
OZIEBLOWSKA
Christina 802
PABENHAM
Elizabeth (Engaine)
  705
Katherine 705, 763
Laurence (Sir) 705

**PACHECO DE
MIRANDA**
Juana 140
PACKNAM
Elizabeth 357
PAGE
Elizabeth 347, 409,
  472
Elizabeth (Bourchier)
  409
Marie Esther 92
Richard (Sir) 409
PAGENHAM
Anne 477, 517
**PAGENHARDT
(VON)**
Heidi (Schweiger) 13
Hope (Allen) 13
Marie Dupuy
  (Adams) 13
Maximilian
  Ferdinand Robert,
  Baron 13
Maximilian Hugo,
  Baron clvii, 13
Robert, Baron 13
Sylvia (Hommel) 13
PAGERIE (DE LA)
Gaspard de Tascher,
  Seigneur 442
Gaspard-Joseph de
  Tascher, Seigneur
  442
Joseph-Gaspard de
  Tascher, Seigneur
  442
PAGET
Frances 135
Frances (Rich) 135

1433

Gerald lxiii
Jane 63
William Paget, 6th
  Baron 135
PAGRAVE. see
  PALGRAVE/
  PAGRAVE
PAINEL
  Jeanne 957
PAISLEY
  Claud Hamilton, 1st
    Baron 156, 167, 179
PAKENHAM
  Antonia Margaret
    Caroline [Lady
    Antonia Fraser]
    xxxviii, 73, 122, 299
  Catherine 74
  family xxxviii
  Georgina Sophia 73
  William Lygon, 4th
    Earl of Longford 73
PALAEOLOGINA
  Margaret, of Mont-
    ferrat 186, 189
  Maria 797
PALAFOX (DE)
  Joachim-Antoine
    Ximeniz, 6th
    Marquis of Arriza
    292
PALAFOX Y CROY-
  HAVRE
  Philip Antoine 292
PALAFOX Y
  PORTOCARRERO
  (DE)
  Cipriano, Count of
    Montijo 292

PALATINATE
  (THE)
  Edward of 38
  Elizabeth Charlotte,
    Princess of 54
  Frederick V of,
    Elector Palatine of
    the Rhine, King of
    Bohemia ("the
    Winter King") 38
  Louise-Marie of 38
  Sophie, Princess of
    58, 432
PALBITSKI
  Adam, Baron 893
  Anna, Baroness 893
  Anne (Sutherland)
    893
  Ebba Margaretha,
    Baroness 893
  Magdalena
    Dorothea (Moréen)
    893
  Ulric Adolf, Baron
    893
PALGRAVE/
  PAGRAVE
  Alice (Gunton) 571
  Anna (___) 571
  Anne (Glemham)
    571
  Edward 571
  John 571
  Mary 571
  Richard (Dr.) xix,
    xxiv, xxxv, lxi, clxi,
    571
  Sarah 571
  Thomas 571

PALLANDT (VAN)
  Adolf Werner I,
    Heer van
    Bovenholt and
    Griethuysen 445
  Adolf Werner II,
    Heer van Zuthem
    and Egede 445
  Adolph Werner van
    Pallandt, Baron
    445
  Agnes Amalia (van
    Pallandt) 445
  Anna Elisabeth
    (Schimmelpenninck
    van der Oye) 445
  Anna Elisabeth (van
    Haersolte) 445
  August Leopold,
    Heer van Eerde,
    Beerse, and
    Oosterveen 445
  Cornelia Martina (van
    der Goes) 445
  Elisabeth (van
    Raesfeld) 445
  Guisbert Jan Anne
    Adolph, Baron 445
  Henrietta Philippina
    Jacoba, Baroness
    445
  Ida Margaretha (van
    Bottlenberg
    genaamd von
    Schirp) 445
  Johan II, Heer van
    Voorst 445
PALMER
  Anne 109

Barbara (Villiers),
　Duchess of
　Cleveland 22, 29,
　33, 34, 109
Gillian 531
Job 463
Katherine 754
Roger, 1st Earl of
　Castlemaine 109
Sarah (Morgan)
　463
Sarah Anne 463
PALMES
Anne 304
Anne (Humphrey)
　clxi, 301, 304, 501
Bryan 501
Edward clxxiv, 501
Elizabeth 501
family 501, 502
Francis (Sir) 301,
　501, 502
Isabel (Linley) 501
Jane 327, 401, 501
Lucy (Winthrop)
　501
Margaret (Corbet)
　501
Mary (Hadnall)
　301, 501, 502
Sarah (Farmer)
　(Davis) 501
Stephen 301, 501,
　502
Susanna xxiv, 304
William 301, 501,
　502
PANMURE
earls of 279

PANNILL
　Elizabeth 470
PANTON
Alice (Booth) 561
Elinor 561
Elizabeth 110
John 561
PAOLA [PAOLA
MARGHERITA
GIUSEPPINA
CONSIGLIA]
(Ruffo di Calabria),
　Queen of the
　Belgians xl, 201,
　204
PAPINEAU
Marie-Françoise
　979
PAPPENHEIM (ZU)
Adelaide, Countess
　43
Charles Frederick
　Theodore, Count
　43
Frederica Joanna
　(von Seckendorff),
　Baroness 43
Frederick Ferdinand,
　Count 43
Frederick William,
　Count 43
Lucie (von
　Hardenburg-
　Reventlow),
　Countess 43
PAQUIN
Adélard 980
Agnes (Jansen)
　980

Albert-Joseph 980
Anna-Hélène [Anna
　Paquin] 967, 968,
　980
Brian 980
Marcelline (Phaneuf)
　980
Marie (Allaire) 980
Mary (Brophy)
　980
Paul 980
Paul-Jean 980
Thérèse (Larue) 980
PARAMO(U)R
Ann (Scott) 316
Mary 316
PARGITER
Amy 864
PARKE
Alice (Freeman)
　(Thompson) xix,
　xxxvii, xl, lvi, lxi,
　lxviii, lxix, lxxi,
　clxiii, clxxviii,
　858, 859, 932
Dorothy 858, 860,
　932
Dorothy (Thompson)
　858, 860, 932
Lucy 348
Martha (Chaplin)
　858
Robert 858, 932
Thomas 858, 932
PARKER
Alice (Lovell) 596
Alice (St. John) 596
Catherine (Buller)
　550

Catherine (Goodwin) 596
Edie 971
Elizabeth 596
Elizabeth (Calthorpe) 596
Elizabeth (Stanley) 355
Ellen 397
George 550
Henry (Sir) 596
Henry, 1st Baron Morley 596
Henry, 2nd Baron Morley 355
James 550
John, 1st Baron Barrington 121
Mary 580
Mary (___) (Perkins) 550
Mary Elizabeth 116
Parnell (Gray) 701
Philip (Sir) 596
Richard lxv, 550
Theresa 121
Theresa (Robinson) 121
William 596

PARKER/PACKER
Elizabeth (Sharp) 642

PARKER BOWLES
Camilla Rosemary (Shand) [H.R.H. The Duchess of Cornwall] 655, 656, 930

PARKHURST
George clxxxvi
Phebe (Leete) clxxxvi

PARKINSON
Amber Mary 63

PARKMAN
Abigail (Fairfield) 342
Esther 342
John 342

PARKS
Margaret Mather (Merriman) 540
Wilbur George 540

PARKYNS
Mary Charlotte 289

PARMA
Cunigunde of, Queen of Italy 879, 919

PARR
Agnes (Crophull) (Devereux) 909
Agnes (Tunstall) 909
Anne 403
Constance (Tildesley) 815
Dorothy 815
Elizabeth 368, 909
Elizabeth (FitzHugh) 368
Elizabeth (Travers) 815
Emma (Hulton) 815
Hugh 815
Isabel (Dychefield) 815

John (Sir) 909
Mary (Salisbury) 368, 403
Maud 368
Richard 815
Thomas (Sir) 909
William (Sir) 368
William Parr, 1st Baron 368, 403

PARRIS
Susanna 324

PARRY
Elizabeth 505
family 507
George 505
Isabel (Vaughan) 505
Mary (Crosley) 505
Muriel 403
Roger 505

PARSONS
Audrey Divett (Buller) xlv, lxi, cxlv, 305
Audrey Jane Penelope 305, 306
Catherine (Clifton) 362
Christian Jeannette Paton (Thomas) 323
Cunliffe McNeile 323
Elizabeth 730
Frances (Dutton) 362
Grace 362

John (Sir), 2nd Bt. 362
Lloyd Halman 305
Mary 541
Nancy Jacqueline 323
Virginia Penelope 78
William (Sir), 3rd Bt. 362
PARTHIA
monarchs of xv
PASCOE
___ 595
PASHLEY
Anne 508
Elizabeth 514
Elizabeth (Woodville) 514
John (Sir) 514
Lowys (Gower) 514
Philippa (Sergeaux) 508, 514
Robert (Sir) 508, 514
PASSINS (DE)
Guy de Grolée, Seigneur 911
PASTON
Anne 407
Anne (Beaufort) 407
Eleanor 119
Elizabeth 491
Erasmus 494
Frances 494
Mary (Wyndham) 494

William (Sir) 407
PATCH
Mary 924
PATEFIELD
Rebecca 501
PATEY
Sarah 366
PATRICK
Prince of Pinsk 797
PATRIKEEV
Eudoxia (Khovrine) 797
Irina 798
Ivan Boulgak 798, 800
Ivan Grozdj 797
Maria (___) 797
Vassili 797
Xenia (Vsevoloje), Princess 798
PATSHULL
family 1025
Sybil 547
PATTEN
Jane 325
PATTERSON
Elizabeth 858
PAU (DE)
François 616
Sylvie (de Grasse) 616
PAUL
Beatrix Elinor 121
Czar of Russia 792
Grand Duke of Russia 3
James Balfour (Sir) xxvii, lxiii

Prince of Württemberg 12
Prince Romanovsky-Ilyinski [Paul R. Ilyinski] 4
PAUL III
Pope [Alessandro Farnese] 186, 188, 189, 192
PAUL FREDERICK
Grand Duke of Mecklenburg-Schwerin 8
PAULET/POULETT/ POWLETT
Alice (Galvington) 609
Alice (Paulet) 526, 905
Anne 598
Barbara (Hamden) 526
Constance (Poynings) 526, 609
Dorothy (Worth) 609
Edward 609, 610
Eleanor 526
Eleanor (Ros) 526
Elizabeth 527
Elizabeth (Paulet) 609
Elizabeth (Waller) 609
Elizabeth (Willoughby) 905
family 564
George 868
George (Sir) 526, 609, 610

Hamden (Sir) 526, 527
Hugh (Sir) 868
Isabel (Rodney) 609
Jane 70
John 526, 609
John (Sir) 526, 609, 905
Margaret (More) 526
Margery 905
Mary 307, 349, 609, 610
Philippa (Pollard) 868
Rachel 868
William 609
William, 1st Marquess of Winchester 905
Ysabel (Perrin) 868
___ (Rawlings?) 609

PAULMY (DE)
Charles-Yves-Jacques de La Rivière, Marquis, Count de La Rivière 203
Jacques de Voyer, Vicomte 202
Jean de Voyer, Seigneur 964
Jean-Armand de Voyer, Marquis 202
Philippon de Voyer, Seigneur 964
Pierre de Voyer, Seigneur 964
Renaud de Voyer, Seigneur 964

PAUNCEFOOT
Joan 351, 429

PAVER
Agnes 359

PAVSIC
Janko 953

PAXTON
Frances 643

PAYER
Jeanne 941

PAYNE
Anna 854
Archibald 278, 301
Catherine 278, 301, 387, 711, 823
Dorothea "Dolly" 497, 532
Elizabeth (Boleyn) 539
Madelyn Lee 498, 726
Martha (Dandridge) 278, 301
Mary 539
Thomas 539

PEABODY
family xxxvi

PEACOCK
Richarda 112

PEARCE
Mary (Giddings) 682
Samuel 682

PEARSON
Agnes Beryl (Spencer-Churchill) 80
Anne 374
Beryl Nancy 80
Weetman Harold Miller, 2nd Viscount Cowdray 80

PECCHE
Agnes (Holme) 881
Alice (FitzWalter) 880
Eve (___) 880
Gilbert 880
Gilbert Pecche, 1st Baron 880, 883, 884
Gilbert Pecche, 2nd Baron 880, 881
Hamon 880
Iseult (___) 880, 884
Joan (___) 880
Joan (de Creye) 880
Katherine 682, 880
Margaret 687, 688, 881
Margery 883
Simon 884
Simon (Sir) 881, 884

PEECK
Anna 914

PEEL
Beatrice Gladys "Bea" (Lillie) xvii, cxlv, 67
Elise 66

Emily (Hay) 67
Julia (Floyd) 66, 67
Mercedes (de
  Graffenried) 67
Robert (Sir), 2nd Bt.
  66, 67
Robert (Sir), 3rd Bt.
  67
Robert (Sir), 4th Bt.
  67
Robert (Sir), 5th Bt.
  cxlv, 67
PEET
  Abigail 589
PEETERS
  Marie-Louise 804
PEEVEY
  Mary Lucy Wade
    xiv
PEGAZE
  Jeanne 948
PELHAM
  Catherine (Thatcher)
    301
  Elizabeth 105, 108,
    115, 301
  Elizabeth (Bosvile)
    (Harlakenden)
    291, 301, 339, 807
  Elizabeth (West)
    (Hon.) 301
  family xxiv, li,
    lviii, lx, 576
  Herbert lx, clxi,
    291, 301, 304, 339,
    661, 807
  Herbert, Jr. 301
  Jemima (Waldegrave)
    clxi, 301, 661

John 301
Margaret (Vane)
  315
Penelope 301, 528,
  576
Penelope (West)
  (Hon.) 301
Philadelphia 315,
  605
Thomas (Sir), 2nd
  Bt. 315
William 301
PELISSON (DE)
  Jeanne 634
PELL
  Helen 750
PELLERIN
  Geneviève (Huard)
    978
  Louis 978
  Marie-Anne 978
PELLETIER
  Alma 977, 989
  Amable 989
  Célina (Beaulieu)
    989
  François 989
  Marguerite
    (Desrosiers) 989
PELLEW
  Augusta (Jay) 865
  Eliza (Jay) 865
  Frances (Addington)
    865
  George 865
  Henry Edward, 6th
    Viscount Exmouth
    lxx, 865

PELT
  Charles Penrose 27
PELTIER (LE)
  Louis V, Marquis de
    Rosambo 293
  Louise-Madeleine
    293
  Marie-Thérèse (de
    Lamoignon) 293
PEMBROKE
  Gilbert de Clare, 1st
    Earl of 837, 839,
    847
  Philip Herbert, 7th
    Earl of 226
  Richard de Clare
    ("Strongbow"),
    2nd Earl of 837,
    839, 847
  William de Valence,
    Earl of 785
  William Herbert, 1st
    Earl of (1st
    creation) 346,
    352, 808
  William Herbert,
    2nd Earl of (1st
    creation), Earl of
    Huntingdon 346
  William Marshall,
    1st Earl of 837,
    839, 845, 847
PEÑAFIEL
  Joanna of 190
PENANCOËT (DE)
  Guillaume, Seigneur
    de Kéroualle 226
  Marie (de Ploëuc)
    226

PENANCOËT DE KÉROUALLE (DE)
Henriette-Mauricette 226
Louise-Renée, Duchess of Portsmouth 25, 31, 226
PENDLETON
Virginia Philo 662, 664
PENESHURST
Alice 695
PENFOUND
Honor 744
PENHALLOW
Abigail (Atkinson) (Winslow) (Osborn) 836
Anne (Tamlyn) 836
Chamond 836
Mary (Cutts) 836
Mary (Porter) 835
Richard 835
Samuel 836
PENHOËT (DE)
Françoise 455
PENISTON
Katherine 326
PENN
Christian (Forbes) 149
Christiana Gulielma 149
Gulielma Maria (Springett) 149
Hannah (Callowhill) 226

Juliana (Fermor), Lady xvii, 226
Madonna Louise Veronica (Ciccone) [Madonna] xvii, cxlvi, 63, 967, 969, 975, 988
Mary (Jones) 149
Sean 63, 975, 988
Thomas xvii, 226
William 149, 226
William, Jr. 149
William (III) 149
PENN-GASKELL
Elizabeth (Edwards) 149
Peter lxv, 149
PENNEFATHER
Charity (Graham) 480
Elizabeth (Bolton) 480
Kingsmill 480
Levina (Kingsmill) 480
Mary 480
Matthew 480
Richard 480
PENNISTON
Susan 108
PENRHYN
Alice (Salway) 233
Gainor 233
William 233
PENROSE
Elizabeth (Vinicombe) 436
Jane (Trevenen) 436

John 436
Mary 436
PENTERS
Margareta 267
PENTHIÈVRE (DE)
Jean III de Brosse, Count 226
Louis-Jean-Marie de Bourbon, Duke 287
PENTZ (VON)
Armgaard Agnes, Countess 37
Christian, Count 37
PENZLIN
Johann Bernard II, Baron of Wartenburg and 195
PEPIN
King of Italy 879, 919
PEPYS
Elizabeth (Marchant) 480
Samuel 480
PERALTA
Luís María 997
María Josefa (Alviso) 997
María Luisa Bárbara Guadelupe 997
PERALTA ALVISO
María Luisa Bárbara Guadelupe 948
PERCEHAY/ PERESHAY
___ 708

PERCIVAL
  Christian 569
  Edmund 569
  Elizabeth (Yorke)
    569
  John, 1st Earl of
    Egmont 430
  Rebecca 750
PERCY
  Anne 355, 904, 905
  Catherine 351, 414,
    901
  Catherine (Spencer)
    361, 389, 401, 418,
    431
  Constance (___)
    425
  Eleanor 333, 347,
    431
  Eleanor (Acton) 425
  Eleanor (Harbottle)
    389, 418
  Eleanor (Neville)
    310, 327, 333, 347,
    351, 355, 361, 374,
    379, 389, 399, 401,
    414, 418, 425, 431,
    901, 904, 905
  Eleanor (Poynings)
    310, 327, 333, 347,
    361, 374, 379, 389,
    399, 401, 402, 414,
    418, 431
  Elizabeth 76, 121,
    305, 317, 319, 328,
    342, 349, 359, 363,
    384, 385, 402, 469
  Elizabeth (Mortimer)
    xxxiv, 305, 310,
    317, 319, 327, 333,
    342, 347, 349, 351,
    355, 359, 361, 363,
    374, 379, 384, 385,
    389, 399, 401, 414,
    418, 425, 431, 737,
    901, 904, 905
  family 416, 549
  George (Hon.) (Gov.)
    418
  Henrietta 382
  Henry "Hotspur"
    (Sir) [Lord Percy]
    xxxii, xxxiv, 305,
    310, 317, 319, 327,
    333, 342, 347, 349,
    351, 355, 359, 361,
    363, 374, 379, 384,
    385, 389, 399, 401,
    414, 418, 425, 431,
    737, 901, 904, 905
  Henry (Sir) 425
  Henry, 2nd Earl of
    Northumberland
    310, 327, 328, 333,
    347, 351, 355, 361,
    374, 379, 389, 399,
    401, 414, 418, 425,
    431, 901, 904, 905
  Henry, 3rd Earl of
    Northumberland
    310, 327, 333, 347,
    361, 374, 379, 389,
    399, 401, 402, 414,
    418, 431
  Henry, 4th Earl of
    Northumberland
    lxvi, 333, 347, 361,
    389, 401, 418, 431
  Henry, 8th Earl of
    Northumberland
    418
  Henry Algernon, 5th
    Earl of Northumber-
    land 361, 389, 401,
    418, 431
  Katherine (Neville)
    418
  Margaret 75, 310,
    327, 361, 374, 379,
    389, 399, 401, 414,
    431
  Margery 425
  Mary 389
  Maud xxx, 314, 761
  Maud (Herbert)
    333, 347, 361, 389,
    401, 418, 431
  Ralph (Sir) 425
  Susan 837
  Thomas (Sir) 389,
    418
PEREJASLAVL
  Daniel, Prince of
    791, 797
**PÉREZ DE
  GUZMÁN Y
  SOTOMAYOR**
  Alfonso (Adm.), 7th
    Duke of
    Medina-Sidonia
    191
**PÉREZ DE GUZMÁN
  Y ZUÑIGA**
  Juan Alonso Pérez,
    6th Duke of
    Medina-Sidonia
    140

PERGEN (VON)
  Maria Anna Josefa
    Franziska
    Walpurgis,
    Countess 187
PERIHAM
  Mary 337
PERIMAN/PERYAM
  Wilmot 594
PERKINS
  Eileen vi
  Elizabeth 471
  Elliot 120
  Hannah 921
  Hannah (Lathrop)
    921
  Jabez 921
  Mary 579, 838, 878
  Mary (___) 550
  Mary Frances Baker
    Wilbraham 120
PERONNE
  Pepin, lord of, lord
    of St. Quentin near
    Paris 879, 919
PERONNEAU
  Sarah Anne
    (Tatnall) 743
PERRAULT
  Marie-Anne 974
PERRIN
  Mary (Allen)
    (Clagett) 127
  Ysabel 868
**PERRONE DE SAN
    MARTINO**
  Adrienne-Jenny-
    Florimonde (de
    Fay) 201

  Charles-Joseph-
    Maurice-Hector,
    Count 201
  Louise 201
PERROT(T)
  Anne (Cheyney)
    136
  Dorothy (Devereux)
    136
  family 875
  John (Sir) 136,
    139, 232, 465
  Mary (Berkeley)
    136, 232
  Penelope 136
  Sined/Jenet 874
  Thomas (Sir) 136
PERRY
  Deborah 571
  family clxxxii
  Matthew Galbraith
    174
  Oliver Hazard (Com-
    modore) 174
  Ruth 924
PERSDOTTER
  Agda 51, 53, 889
PERSIA
  monarchs of xv
PERSSE
  Sarah 464
PERTH
  James Eric
    Drummond, 16th
    Earl of [Sir Eric
    Drummond] 72
  Matilda 837
PERTHIUS
  Marie-Anne 623

PERY
  Annabella
    (Edwards) 115
  Caroline Maria
    (Gray) 115
  Edmund Henry, 1st
    Earl of Limerick
    115
  Emilie Caroline 115
  Henry Hartstonge,
    Viscount
    Glentworth 115
  Jane (Twigge) 115
  Jane (Walcot) 115
  Mary Alice
    (Ormsby) 115
  May Imelda
    Josephine (Irwin)
    116
  Stackpole 115
  Susannah (Sheaffe)
    115
  Victoria May 116
  William Cecil, 1st
    Baron Glentworth
    115
  William Hale John
    Charles, 3rd Earl
    of Limerick 115
  William Henry
    Edmond de Vere
    Sheaffe, 4th Earl of
    Limerick 116
  William Henry
    Tennison, 2nd Earl
    of Limerick 115
PESHALL
  Adam (Sir) 506
  Eleanor 670

Humphrey 670, 671
Joyce (de Botetourte) (Freville) 506
Katherine 530
Lettice (Harcourt) 670, 671
Margaret 506

PESTER
Dorothy (Stratton) 706
William 706

PETAU
Geneviève 148, 940

PETER
America Pinckney 170
Elizabeth (Cocke) 170
Elizabeth (Scott) 170
Jean (Dunlop) 170
John 170
Katherine (Cocke) 170
Martha Parke (Custis) 170
Prince of France, Seigneur de Courtenay 965
Robert cxlv, 170
Sarah (Norfleet) 170
Thomas 170
Walter 170

PETER I
Duke of Bourbon 941
King of Constantinople 965

PETER I "the GREAT"
Czar of Russia 792

PETER II
King of Aragón 51
King of Portugal 615

PETER III
Czar of Russia 14, 615, 796
King of Aragón 642

PETER(S)
Anne (Rawe) 665
Deliverance (Sheffield) xlix, cxlv, clxxix, 577, 578, 665
Elizabeth 578
Elizabeth (Cooke) (Reade) 665
Hugh (Rev.) 577, 578, 665, 666
Thomas (Rev.) xlix, cli, 665, 666

PETIT
Amicia (Bloyou) 665
Isabel (Heligan) 665
Jane 665
Jane (Anthorne) 665
Joanna (Carminow) 665
John 665
John (Sir) 665
Margaret (Roscarrock) 665

Margaret (Trenowith) 665
Michael 665
Renée 941

PETIT dit ST.-MICHEL
Antoine 960
Josette (de Saint-Paul) 960

PETRE
Anna Maria Barbara (Radcliffe) 30
Catherine 30
Robert James Petre, 8th Baron 30

PETRIE
Isabel 219

PETRVALDSKÁ DE PETRVALDU
Marie Teresa Eleanora 220

PETTIT
Elizabeth L. cxcii

PETTY
Louise (FitzPatrick), Lady 299
Sophia (Carteret) 226
William, 1st Marquess of Lansdowne, 2nd Earl of Shelburne, Prime Minister 226, 299

PETTY-FITZMAURICE
Evelyn 25
Henry Charles Keith, 5th Marquess of Lansdowne 25, 28

Maud Evelyn
 (Hamilton) 25, 28
PEVERAL
 Joan 705
PEVERELL
 Catherine 570, 824
 Margaret (Courtenay)
  824
 Thomas (Sir) 824
PEYTO
 Audrey 722
 Edward 721
 Eleanor (Manfield)
  721
 family 722
 Goditha (Throck-
  morton) 721
 John 721
 Katherine (Gresley)
  721
 Margaret
  (Baynham) 721
 William 721
PEYTON
 Elizabeth (Yelverton)
  360
 family lxiii, lxviii,
  854
 Frances (Gerard)
  (Speake) 515
 Mariana 331
 Mary (___) 360
 Robert xxxv,
  clxvii, clxxii, 360
 Rose 854
 Thomas 360
PFALZ
 Louise Juliane,
  Princess of 56

Margaret of 291
PFEFFEL (VON)
 Adelaide Pauline
  (von Rothenburg)
  12
 family 12
 Helene (von Rivière),
  Baroness 12
 Hubert, Baron 12
 Karl, Baron 12
 Marie Luise,
  Baroness 12
PHANEUF
 Marcelline 980
PHELIPS
 Bridget (Gorges)
  457
 Clare Louisa 64
 Robert (Sir) 457
PHELPS
 Ann Naile lxiii,
  lxvi, 275
PHILIP
 de Courtenay,
  Emperor of
  Constantinople
  952, 961, 965
 Prince of Greece
  and Denmark,
  Prince of Great
  Britain, Duke of
  Edinburgh 3, 41,
  930
 of Savoy-Piemont,
  Prince of Achaya
  952
 of Swabia, King of
  the Romans lxiii,
  lxvii, 640, 733

PHILIP I
 Duke of Savoy 442
PHILIP II
 Duke of Burgundy
  438, 442, 445
 King of Spain 18,
  615
PHILIP II
AUGUSTUS
 King of France 950
PHILIP III
 Duke of Burgundy
  445
 King of France
  459, 941, 961
 King of Navarre
  455
PHILIP IV
 King of Spain 140,
  191
PHILIP VI
 King of France 459
PHILIPPA
 of Hainault, Queen
  of England 107,
  114, 119, 126, 133,
  134, 295, 300, 305,
  310, 314, 317, 319,
  324, 327, 331, 333,
  337, 339, 342, 345,
  347, 349, 351, 353,
  355, 357, 359, 361,
  363, 366, 368, 370,
  374, 375, 377, 379,
  382, 384, 385, 387,
  389, 392, 393, 395,
  396, 397, 398, 399,
  400, 401, 403, 405,
  407, 409, 410, 411,

413, 414, 417, 418,
419, 420, 421, 423,
425, 426, 427, 428,
429, 431, 433, 434,
436, 459, 774, 775,
776, 900, 901, 902,
904, 905
of Luxembourg
459
PHILIPPE I
King of the Belgians
xl, 201, 204
PHILIPPES
Élisabeth (Hanot)
950
Pierre 950
PHILIPS
Elen 555
PHILIPSON
Anne 109, 339,
905
PHILLIPS
Anne 778
Anne Patricia
(Tiarks) 321
Charles Edward
Harold John 124,
481
Elizabeth 329, 482
Elizabeth (Dryden)
482
Erasmus (Sir), 3rd
Bt. 482
Joanna 572
Katherine (Darcy)
482
Mark Anthony Peter
(Capt.) 321, 322
Owen 555

Peter Mark Andrew
323
Peter William
Garside 321
Richard (Sir), 2nd
Bt. 482
Tanis Eva Bulkeley
(Guinness)
(Montagu) (Dietz)
124, 481
Zara Anne Elizabeth
(wife of rugby
champion Mike
Tindall) 323
PHIPPS
Amy 63
Catherine
(Annesley) 22
Constantine, 1st
Baron Mulgrave
22
Henrietta Maria 22
Lepell (Hervey)
22, 23
William 22
**PHIQUEPAL
D'ARUSMONT**
Frances "Fanny"
(Wright) xi, clix,
390, 391
Guillaume Sylvan
390
PICKERING
Anne 909, 910
Anne (Moresby)
909, 910
Elizabeth 719, 923,
924
family 720

Grace (Sylvester)
386
Henry 481
Henry (Sir), 2nd Bt.
386
Isabel (Smith) 481
James (Sir) 909,
910
John 481, 719
Lucy (Kaye) 481,
719, 720
Mary 481
Mary (Wingate)
924
Sarah 923, 924
Timothy 924
Timothy, Jr. 924
PICQUIGNY (DE)
Catherine (de
Châtillon) 733
Jean, Seigneur
d'Ailly 733
Marguerite 733
PIDIWAMISKWA
Marie 963, 990
PIEN (DE)
Catherine 616
PIENCOURT (DE)
Mathieu de Bailleul,
Seigneur, Seigneur
de Canthelou 957
PIERCE
Agnes 623
Anna (Kendrick)
582, 811
Barbara xlii, xliii,
243, 474, 479, 572,
585, 632, 688, 703,
716, 729, 747, 769

1445

Benjamin, Jr. 582, 811
Chloe (Holbrook) 632
Elizabeth Slade 243
Franklin, 14th U.S. President 582, 812
James 632
James, Jr. 632
Jane Means (Appleton) xliii, 582, 812
Jonas James 632
Kate (Pritzel) 632
Lucy 925
Mabel (Marvin) 632, 688
Marvin 632, 688, 769
Mary (Stacy) 632
Pauline (Robinson) 632, 688, 769
Sarah (Richardson) 925, 927
Scott 632, 688
Thomas 927
William 925
PIERPONT
Grace 119
PIERREFEU (DE)
Louis-Dolorès-Emmanuel-Alphonse Dedons, Count 184
Louis-Joseph-Léonce Dedons, Marquis 184

PIERREPONT
Augusta Sophia Anne 74
Evelyn 33, 62, 64, 299
Evelyn, 1st Duke of Kingston-upon-Hull 64
Henry Manvers (Hon.) 74
Marguerite 961
Mary 64
Mary [Lady Mary Wortley-Montagu] 299
Sophia (Cecil) 74
Thibaut de Bar, Seigneur 944
PIGNATELLI
Ettore, Prince of Nola 192
Geronima 189, 192
Giovanna (Tagliava d'Aragona), Duchess of Terranova 192
PIGOT(T)
Caroline 33
Elizabeth 307, 657
PIJPE alias PIJPELINCKX
Clara (de Thovion) 804
Hendrik 804
PIJPELINCKX
Jan 804
Maria 804
Maria (Typoets) 804

PIKE
Sarah 476
PILFORD
Elizabeth 474
PILIEMANOV-SABOUROV
Euphemia 798
PILKINGTON
Alice (Kingsmill) 738
Catherine 512
Deborah 738
James, Bishop of Durham 738
Margaret 780
Ruth 517
PILLOT (DE)
Anna Elizabeth (de Sandersleben), Countess of Coligny 184
Charles-François-Emanuel-Edwige, Marquis de Coligny 184
Charles-Ignace, Marquis de Coligny 184
Charlotte-Victorine-Clémentine-Angélique (de Messey-Beaupré) 184
Marie-Anne-Claude (de Bernard de Sassenay) 184
Marie-Simone-Léopoldine 184
Thomas, Seigneur de Chenecey,

Marquis de
  Coligny 184
PIMENTEL
  Leonor 191
PIMENTEL Y
PACHECO
  Beatrix 191
PINCHBECK
  Anne (Greene)
    512, 513, 731
  Elizabeth 513
  family 731
  Grace 730, 731
  John 730, 731
  John (Sir) 731
  Margaret (Talboys)
    512, 730
  Richard 512, 513,
    730
  Thomas (Sir) 512,
    513, 731
PINCKNEY
  Anne (le Brassieur)
    311
  Joseph 312
PINDER
  Anne 925
PINKNEY (DE)
  family 768
PINNOCK
  Anne 464
PINSK
  Narimond, Prince of
    797
  Patrick, Prince of 797
  Youri, Prince of 797
PINTER
  Antonia Margaret
    Caroline (Pakenham)

(Fraser) [Lady
  Antonia Fraser]
  xxxviii, 73, 122, 299
  Harold 73, 122, 299
PIPE (DE)
  Margaret 723
PIPER
  Ulrika Eleanora,
    Countess 457
PISTOR
  Margaret 310
PITCAIRN
  David 215
  Eleanor 219
  Elizabeth
    (Dalrymple) 215
  John 215
  Katherine (Hamilton)
    215
PITMAN
  Mary 623
PITRE
  Angélique 981
PITT
  Angelina Jolie
    (Voight) (Miller)
    (Thornton)
    [Angelina Jolie]
    967, 974
  family xi
  Jennifer Joanna
    (Aniston) [Jennifer
    Aniston] 974, 985,
    986
  Sarah (Smith) 260
  William Bradley
    "Brad" 974, 985,
    986

PITTS
  Isabella (Wright)
    350
PIZARJEWA
  Alexandra 14
PIZARRO
  Francisco 191
PLACE
  Julia Anne 688
PLAINES (DE)
  Philippote 638
PLANTAGENET
  Alice (de Hales)
    lxix, 462, 470, 473,
    486, 493, 519, 522,
    526, 534, 539, 541,
    545, 557, 564, 579,
    580, 598, 599, 604,
    605, 609
  Anne xl, 119, 126,
    133, 134, 331, 353,
    392, 393, 403, 409,
    420, 421, 428, 436
  Anne (Mortimer)
    107, 114, 119, 126,
    133, 134
  Antigone 229, 231,
    233, 235, 377, 411
  Arthur, 1st Viscount
    Lisle 103
  Beatrix (de Falken-
    burg) 653, 661,
    672
  Beatrix, Princess of
    England 442,
    633, 942, 946, 963
  Blanche (of Artois)
    623, 625, 628, 630,
    632

Blanche, Duchess of
Lancaster 400
Catherine (Roët)
(Swynford) 295,
300, 314, 324, 331,
337, 339, 345, 357,
366, 368, 370, 375,
382, 387, 393, 395,
396, 397, 398, 403,
405, 407, 413, 417,
419, 421, 426, 427,
429, 433, 434, 900,
902
Cecily (Neville) 107,
114, 119, 126, 133
Constance 377, 410,
417, 423
Edmund, Prince of
England, 1st Earl
of Lancaster xxvi,
623, 625, 628, 630,
632
Edmund of Langley,
Prince of England,
1st Duke of York
xxxix, 107, 114,
119, 126, 133, 134,
377, 410, 411, 423
Edmund of Woodstock, Prince of
England, 1st Earl of
Kent 515, 600
Edward "the Black
Prince," Prince of
England, Prince of
Wales 600
Eleanor 625, 628,
630, 632, 642

Eleanor (Bohun)
331, 353, 392, 393,
409, 420, 421, 428,
436
Eleanor (Cobham)
229, 231, 233, 235
Eleanor, Princess of
England, Queen of
Castile 647, 909,
948, 964
Elizabeth 352, 400
Elizabeth (de Burgh)
107, 114, 119, 126,
133, 134, 305, 310,
317, 319, 327, 333,
342, 347, 349, 351,
355, 359, 361, 363,
374, 379, 384, 385,
389, 399, 401, 414,
418, 425, 431, 901,
904, 905
Elizabeth (Woodville)
(Grey), Queen of
England 100, 103,
105, 106, 134, 208,
323, 333, 339, 346,
347, 370, 397, 412,
431, 433, 514, 902
Elizabeth, Princess
of England xxxix,
478, 497, 500, 503,
510, 512, 517, 524,
530, 532, 543, 551,
553, 554, 555, 558,
560, 563, 565, 569,
571, 573, 574, 582,
588, 595, 596, 601,
603, 608, 611, 613

Elizabeth (of York),
Queen of England
62, 69, 76, 79, 80,
347, 348
Elizabeth of
Lancaster, Princess
of England 400
family 561, 939
Frances 103
Geoffrey, Count of
Anjou 841, 1025
George, 1st Duke of
Clarence xl, lxvi,
107, 114
Hamelin, Earl of
Surrey x, 841, 1025
Henry, 3rd Earl of
Lancaster 623,
625, 628, 630, 632
Humphrey, Duke of
Gloucester 229,
231, 233, 235
Isabel xl, 134
Isabel (Marshall)
653, 661, 672
Isabel (Neville)
107, 114, 118
Joan vii, lxviii, 623,
650, 652, 657, 659,
680, 682, 686, 689,
692, 693, 694, 813,
824
Joan, "The Fair
Maid of Kent,"
Princess Dowager
of Wales 107,
400, 515, 600
Joan of Acre, Princess
of England xxxix,

1448

466, 483, 489, 491,
  495, 505, 508, 514,
  528, 536, 547, 565,
  567, 575, 577, 584,
  587, 590, 592, 594,
  606, 607, 615
John of Gaunt,
  Prince of England,
  Duke of Lancaster
  xxxix, 295, 300,
  314, 324, 331, 337,
  339, 345, 357, 366,
  368, 370, 375, 382,
  387, 393, 395, 396,
  397, 398, 400, 403,
  405, 407, 413, 417,
  419, 421, 426, 427,
  429, 433, 434, 900,
  902
Lionel of Antwerp,
  Prince of England,
  Duke of Clarence
  xxxix, 107, 114,
  119, 126, 133, 134,
  305, 310, 317, 319,
  327, 333, 342, 347,
  349, 351, 355, 359,
  361, 363, 374, 379,
  384, 385, 389, 399,
  401, 414, 418, 425,
  431, 901, 904, 905
Margaret (not
  Elizabeth)
  clxxxv, clxxxvi,
  100, 105, 106
Margaret (Wake)
  515, 600
Margaret, Countess of
  Salisbury 107, 114

Margaret, Duchess of
  Norfolk 462, 470,
  473, 486, 493, 519,
  522, 526, 534, 539,
  541, 545, 557, 579,
  580, 598, 599, 604,
  605, 609, 1024
Mary (Bohun) xxv,
  229, 231, 233, 235,
  378, 412
Matilda, of Lancaster
  907
Maud (Chaworth)
  623, 625, 628, 630,
  632
Philippa 107, 114,
  119, 126, 133, 134,
  305, 310, 317, 319,
  327, 333, 342, 347,
  349, 351, 355, 359,
  361, 363, 374, 379,
  384, 385, 389, 399,
  401, 414, 418, 425,
  431, 901, 904, 905
Richard, 3rd Duke
  of York 107, 114,
  119, 126, 133
Richard, Earl of
  Cambridge 107,
  114, 119, 126, 133,
  134
Richard, Earl of
  Cornwall, King of
  the Romans
  xxxix, 652, 653,
  661, 672, 965
Thomas of Brother-
  ton, Prince of
  England, Earl of

Norfolk xxxix,
  462, 470, 473, 486,
  493, 519, 522, 526,
  534, 539, 541, 545,
  557, 564, 579, 580,
  598, 599, 604, 605,
  609
Thomas of Wood-
  stock, Prince of
  England, 1st Duke
  of Gloucester
  xxv, xxxix, 331,
  353, 392, 393, 409,
  420, 421, 428, 436
PLASENCIA
  Álvaro de Zuñiga,
  Duke of Arévalo,
  Béjar and 191
**PLATEN AND
HALLERMUND
(VON)**
  Franz Ernst, Count
  58, 432
  Klara Elisabeth (von
  Meysenburg) 432
  Sophia Charlotte,
  Countess, Countess
  of Leinster and
  Darlington 58,
  432
PLATER
  Anne 602
PLATER (VON)
  Maria 849
PLATER-ZYBERK
  Elizabeth [Elzbieta]
  Maria 11
  family 11
  Józafat, Count 11

Maria (Meysztowicz) 11
Maria Malgorzata Paulina Wilhelmina Róza Leopoldyna Julia (Wielopolska) lii, cxlvi, 11
PLATT
Nicholas 378
Oliver 378
Sheila (Maynard) 378
Theodora 14
PLATTS
Philippa (Andrews) (Felt) 126
PLAUNCHE (DE LA)
Alice 861
PLAUZET (DE)
Catherine (du Bourg) 202
Jacques d'Estaing, Baron 202
PLEASANTS
J. Hall lxiii
PLESSIS (DU)
Agatha (de Thiene) 442
Edmée-Henriette-Madeleine 442
Henri I, Seigneur de Savonnières 442
PLEYDELL-BOUVERIE
Alice Muriel (Astor) (Obolensky-Neledinsky- Meletzky) (von Hoffmansthal) (Harding) 799, 800

Audrey Evelyn (James) (Coats) (Field) 68
David 800
Peter 68
PLOËUC (DE)
Marie 226
Marie (de Rieux) 226
Mauricette 226
Sébastien, Marquis de Timeur 226
PLOUF
Josèphe/Josephte 972
PLUM(B)
Joanna 474
PLUMMER
John M. ix, lxiii, 810
PLUMPTON
Agnes 413
Agnes (Gascoigne) 413
Alice 700
Christiana (Mowbray) 700, 703
Elizabeth 359, 709
Elizabeth (Clifford) 359, 413
Lucy (de Ros) 700
Robert (Sir) 413, 700
William (Sir) 359, 413, 700
PLUNKETT
Christopher, 2nd Baron Killeen 486

Elizabeth (de Welles) 486
Frances (Bagenall) 900
Genet 486
Margaret 487, 900
Mary (FitzWilliam) 900
Matthew, 5th Baron Louth 900
Oliver, 4th Baron Louth 900
POCAHONTAS [MATAOKA] [REBECCA]
wife of John Rolfe 387, 711, 823
POCIEJOWNA
Louisa Honorata 622
POITEVIN
Jean 623
Rose/Françoise (Otis) 623
POITIERS (DE)
Agatha 965
Amé, Seigneur de St.-Vallier 952
Aymar III de Poitiers, Count 735
Constance 735
Diane, Duchess de Valentinois 202, 735
Marguerite 947, 952
POITOU
Adelaide of, Queen of France 866, 870, 872, 879, 919

POLAND
Barbara (Zápolya), Queen of 895
Boleslaw III, King of 791, 797, 802
Bona (Sforza), Queen of 895
Casimir IV, King of 194, 195, 196, 198, 895
Elizabeth, Archduchess of Austria, Queen of 194, 195, 196, 198, 895
Frederick Augustus II, Elector of Saxony, King of 20
Gertrude, Princess of 849
Judith of Bohemia, Queen of 791, 797, 802
Katarzyna of 895
Maria Josepha, Archduchess of Austria, Electress of Saxony, Queen of Poland 20
Mieszko II Lambert, King of 849
Richeza of, Queen of Hungary 832, 833
Salome of Berg-Schelklingen, Queen of 791, 797, 802
Sigismund I, King of 895
Sophie, Princess of 194, 196, 198
Stanislaus II August Poniatowski, King of 154
Wladislaw I, King of 791, 797, 802
____ of 791, 797, 802

POLASTRON (DE)
Gabrielle-Yolande-Claude-Martine 49, 289

POLE (DE LA POLE)
Agnes (Plumpton) 413
Alice (Langford) (Stradling) 716
Catherine 483, 489, 536, 606
Catherine (Popham) 337
Elizabeth 413, 615
family 291, 327, 329, 349
German 413
Henry, 1st Baron Montagu 107, 114
Isabel 577, 588, 596
Joan 353
Joan (Cobham) 543, 595
Joan (Neville) 107, 114
Joan, Baroness Cobham 543, 595
John (Sir) 543, 595
Katherine 107
Katherine (Stafford) 353, 577, 615
Margaret 841
Margaret (Plantagenet), Countess of Salisbury 107, 114, 716
Mary (Periham) 337
Michael, 2nd Earl of Suffolk 353, 577, 615
Richard (Sir) 107, 114, 716
Ursula 114
William (Sir) 337
William, 1st Duke of Suffolk 353
Winifred 114

POLENZ ZU SCHÖNBERG (VON)
Albert 617, 618
Anna (zu Heideck) 617
Barbara (von Eulenburg) 617
Christoph 617
Elisabeth (von Zehmen) 617, 618
family 618
Georg 617
Gottliebe (von Bredow) 617
Maria Elisabeth 617
Theophil 617

POLEY
Anne (Wentworth) 349

Constance
 (Gedding) 682
Edmund 682
Henry 682
John 349
Margaret 682
Mirabel 349
Mirabel (Garneys) 682
POLI AND GUADAGNOLO
Giulio Torlonia, 2nd Duke of 18
POLIGNAC (DE)
Auguste-Jules-Armand-Marie de Polignac, Prince 289
Barbara (Campbell) 289
Camille-Armand-Jules-Marie de Polignac, Prince clvii, 289, 290
Camille-Henri-Melchior de Polignac, Count 289
Caroline-Joséphine (le Normand de Mora) 289
Charles-Marie-Thomas de Polignac, Count 289
Charlotte-Louise-Juliette (Grimaldi), Hereditary Princess of Monaco, Duchess of Valentinois 289
Diane-Adélaïde-Zéphirine (Mancini-Mazarini) 289
 family 291
Gabrielle-Yolande-Claude-Martine (de Polastron) 49, 289
Jules-François-Armand de Polignac, 1st Duc 49, 289
Louise-Gabrielle-Renée-Aglaë 49
Louis-Melchior-Armand, Marquis de Chalencon 289
Margaret Elizabeth (Knight) 289
Marie Adolfine (Langenberger) 289
Marie-Charlotte-Calixte-Alphonsine (le Vassor de la Touche) 289
Mary Charlotte (Parkyns) 289
Maxence-Melchior-Édouard-Marie-Louis de Polignac, Count 289
Pierre-Marie-Xavier-Raphaël-Antoine-Melchior de Polignac, Count 289, 933
Suzanne-Marie-Stéphanie-Anne-Françoise (de la Torre y Mier) 289

POLK
Elizabeth Sturgis 63
James Knox, 11th U.S. President 666
POLKINGHORNE
Sarah (Mrs. Gerald) ix, lxiii, lxviii, 854
POLLARD
Agnes (Hext) 868
Anthony 674, 675
Elizabeth 665
Emote 841
F. H. ix, lxiii, 83
Lewis (Sir) 868
Mary 674
Petronell (Chudleigh) 674, 675
Philippa 868
POLLE
Ursula 56
POLLOK
Elizabeth 214
POLOTSK
Praskovya of 791, 797
POLSTEAD
Anne 567
POMERELIA/ POMERANIA
___ of 644
POMEROY
Andriah (Towgood) 594
Arthur, 1st Viscount Harberton 157
Ebenezer (III) 673
Edward 594
Esther (Spencer) 157

Eunice 673
George Holmes
    liv, clxxv, 594
Honor (Rolle) 594
Joan (Edgcombe)
    594
John, 4th Viscount
    Harberton 157
Margaret (___) 594
Martha 594
Martha (Smith) 594
Mary (Colley) 157
Mindwell (Lyman)
    673
Samuel 594
Thomas 594
Thomas (Sir) 594
Thomas Holmes 594
Wilmot (Periman/
    Peryam) 594
POMFRET
    Thomas Fermor, 1st
      Earl of 226
POMFRETT
    Mary cxcii
PONCE DE LEÓN
    Beatríz (de Xérica)
      993
    Catalina (de Vera
      Zurita) 994
    Eutropio 994
    family 991
    Juan 991, 994
    Juan, Conde de
      Arcos 994
    María (de Ayala)
      994
    Pedro, II Señor de
      Marchena 190, 993

Pedro, IV Señor de
    Marchena 994
Pedro, V Señor,
    Conde de Arcos
    994
Sancha (de Haro)
    994
Violante 995
PONCE DE LEÓN Y NAVARRO
    María 995
PONCE DE LEÓN Y XÉRICA
    Beatríz 190
PONCHON (DE)
    Marie-Jeanne-Franç
      oise 638
PONIATOWSKI
    princes or counts
      155
    Stanislaus II August,
      King of Poland
      154
PONS (DE)
    François, Seigneur
      de la Grange de
      Bart du Bou[s]chet
      200
    Françoise (de
      Douhet de Marlat)
      200, 203
    Marie 200
PONTE CARAFFA TOVAR (DE)
    Cecilia 192
PONTHIEU
    Ela of 841
    Enguerrand I, Count
      of 879, 919

Enguerrand II,
    Count of 879, 919
Guy II, Count of
    853
Hélène of 853
Hugh I, Count of
    879, 919
Hugh III, Count of
    879, 919
Joan of Dammartin,
    Countess of,
    Queen of Castile
    951
John I, Count of
    853
William III Talvas,
    Count of Alençon
    and 737, 853, 855
PONTHIEU or LENS
    Judith of 879, 919
PONTVERRE (DE)
    Isabelle 872
POOL
    Caroline xiv
POOLE
    Elizabeth 337
    Elizabeth (Brenton)
      924
    Jane 923
    Jane (Greene) xi,
      xlix, lxv, cxlvi,
      clxi, 337, 647, 743,
      745, 924
    John 924
    Margaret 752
    Mary 647
    Theophilus 745
    William clxi,
      clxxii, 337, 338,

647, 743, 924
POOR
  Mary 654
POPE
  Anne 515
  Elizabeth (Hunt)
    571
  Joanna clxxxv
  Lemuel 571
  Mercy 571
POPHAM
  Alexander 337
  Amy (Adams) 337
  Catherine 337
  Edward 337
  George 337
  Jane 337
  Jane (Norton) 337
  Jane (Stradling)
    337, 338
  John (Sir) 337
POPLEY
  Grace 855
PORCH
  Jennie (Jerome)
    (Spencer-Churchill)
    (Cornwallis-West)
    584, 585, 648
  Montagu Phippen
    585, 648
PORDAGE
  Anne (Mellish)
    357, 358
  Dorothy (St.
    Nicholas) 357
  Edward 357
  Elizabeth (Lynde)
    357, 924
  family xi

  George xlix, cl,
    357, 358, 924
  Hannah 924
  Joan 840
  Joshua 357, 358
PORGÈS
  Isabel-Fanny-Louise
    24
PORT
  Dorothy 107
PORTA-RADIANI (DELLA)
  Giacinta 20
PORTEOUS
  Judith (Cockayne)
    930
  Mildred 930
  Mildred (Smith) 930
  Robert 930
PORTER
  Alice (Arnold) 557
  Anne 467
  Arthur 557
  Augustine 917, 918
  Ellen (Smith) 917
  Gertrude (Chamond)
    835
  Isabel 557
  Jamie 793
  Jane 654
  Katherine 917
  Margaret (Arthur)
    557
  Mary 835
  Mary (Savill) 719
  Roger 557
  Walter 835
  ____ (Bellingham)
    917

PORTH
  Friederike
    Margarethe 12
PORTINGTON
  Anne 409
  Anne (Langton) 409
  Elizabeth (Skipwith)
    409
  Henry 409
  John 409
  Maud (Tyrwhit) 409
  Thomas 409
PORTLAND
  Hans William Bentinck, 1st Earl of 54
  Richard Weston, 1st
    Earl of 467
PORTMAN
  Elizabeth 340
PORTOCARRERO DE GUZMÁN Y KIRKPATRICK (DE)
  Eugenia María
    Ignace Augustine
    [Eugénie de Montijo, Empress of the
    French] 291, 292
PORTONERIA
  Libera 442
PORTSMOUTH
  Isaac Newton Wallop,
    5th Earl of 76, 77
  Louise-Renée de
    Penancoët de
    Kéroualle, Duchess
    of 25, 31, 226
  Newton Fellowes
    Wallop, 4th Earl of
    77

Oliver Henry Wallop,
  8th Earl of   76
PORTUGAL
  Alphonso III, King
    of   619
  Beatrice of   400
  Beatrix of Castile,
    Queen of   619
  Berengaria, Princess
    of, Queen of
    Denmark   644
  Catherine of
    Braganza, Princess
    of, Queen of
    England and Scot-
    land   22, 25, 29,
    30, 31, 33, 34
  Edward I, King of   190
  Fernando
    (Ferdinand) II,
    King of   290
  Isabella, Princess of
    438, 445
  John IV, King of   140
  Luisa Francisca de
    Guzmán, Queen of
    140, 142
  Matilda of
    Dammartin, Queen
    of   619
  monarchs of   45,
    142, 614, 615
  Peter II, King of
    615
POSSE
  Axel, Lord of
    Saatenes and Tun
    452
  Elsa   452

Elsa (Nilsdotter)
  452
POST
  Margaret   500
  Marjorie
    Merriweather   44
POTIER
  family   294
POTOCKI
  counts   155
POTTER
  Shawn H.   lxiii,
    clxxxvi, 245, 862
**POUILLY-LE-FORT
  (DE)**
  Jean I de Vaudétar,
    Seigneur   954
  Jean II de Vaudétar,
    Seigneur   954
  Pierre I de Vaudétar,
    Seigneur   954
  Pierre II de Vaudétar,
    Seigneur   954
POULETT. see
  PAULET/POULETT/
  POWLETT
POULIN
  Cecile   623
POULSON
  Fanny Frederikke
    Augusta   645
POUND
  Dorothy (Shakespear)
    lxvi, clvii, 131
  Ezra Loomis   xviii,
    131
POWELL
  Ann/Annette
    (Duncanson)   248

Anne (Seymour)
  598
Elizabeth   510
family   248
Janet/Jannette
  (Duncanson)
  (Aerdes)   248
John   510
Mary   695
Richard   598
Sybil (Gwyn)   510
Thomas   248
POWER
  Catherine   325
POWLETT. see
  PAULET/POULETT/
  POWLETT
POWNALL
  Alan   75
  Gabriella Zanna
    Vanessa (Anstruther-
    Gough-Calthorpe)
    [Gabriella Wilde]
    75
  Harriet (Churchill)
    (Fawkener)   xlvi,
    lii, 536, 537
  Thomas (Gov.)
    536, 537
POWYS
  Angharad, Queen
    of, Queen of South
    Wales   815, 886
  Cynfyn ap
    Gwerystan, lord of
    815, 886
  Rhywallon, Prince
    of   886
  Sionet of   886

1455

POWYS FADOG
Gruffudd ap Madog, Prince of 815, 822, 823
Madog ap Gruffudd Maelawr, Prince of 815
POYNER
Margaret 534
POYNINGS
Adrian (Sir) 426
Agnes 483, 489, 536, 587, 606
Anne 426
Constance 526, 609
Eleanor 310, 327, 333, 347, 361, 374, 379, 389, 399, 401, 402, 414, 418, 431
Eleanor (de Welles) 526, 609
family 564
Hugh (Sir) 526, 609
Isabel (FitzPayn) 737
Joan 466, 567, 592, 737, 740
Mary (West) 426
Richard Poynings, 3rd Baron 737
POYNTZ
Anne (Calva) 837
Anne (Sydenham) 423
Anne (Verney) 423
Catherine (Browne) 492
Dorothea xlviii, lxvii, 423, 598, 674
Edward 839
Eleanor (Baldwin) 837
Elizabeth 423, 424
Elizabeth (la Zouche) 837, 839
Elizabeth (Shaw) 837
Elizabeth Sophia 371
family xlv, 412, 598
Georgiana Anne 112
Isabella 73
Jane 598
Joan (Berkeley) 423, 598
John 423, 492, 837
John (Sir) 837
Margaret 838
Margaret Georgiana 69, 74
Mary 423, 522
Matilda (Perth) 837
Matthew 492
Maud 839
Newdigate 423
Nicholas 837, 839
Nicholas (Sir) 423, 598, 837, 839
Pontius 837
Sarah (Foxley) 423
Silvester 492
Susanna 837
Thomas 837
William 837
Wilmot 866
Winifred (Wilde) 492
POYPON (DE)
François, Seigneur de Chanay 912
Jeanne 912
Mye (de Belletruche) 912
PRACOMTAL (DE)
Antoine, Baron de Soussey 293
Louise 293
PRADES (DE)
Charles des Vignolles, Seigneur 736
Jacques des Vignolles, Seigneur 735
PRAET (VAN)
Catharina (van Egmond) 459
Françoise/Francina 459
Lodewijk, Heer van Moerkerke 459
PRAETORIUS
Ane Marie 645
PRATER/PRATHER
Anne 695
Anthony 695, 696
Elizabeth (Bigger) 695
family 696
Jane (MacKay?) 695
Jonathan 695
Jonathan, Jr. 695
Judith (Ivye) 695, 696

Margaret (Quintyne) 695
Mary (Powell?) 695
Thomas lvii, cl, cli, clxviii, clxxx, 695
PRATT
  Anna Joanna Dorothea (Wilcken) 924
  Anne Amelia 924
  Charity (Dickinson) 925
  Elizabeth 295
  Helemon 924
  James E. 422
  Jared 925
  John 422
  Mary (Kay) 422
  Mary (Woods) 925
  Nina 422, 764, 773
  Parley Parker 924
  Sarah 935
  Sophronia C. (Cowan) 422
PRAZMOVÁ DE BILKOVA
  Esther Elisabeth 220
PRENDERGAST
  Jonathan Barry [John Barry] xvii, clii, 27, 28
PRENDRETH
  Anne 358
  Elizabeth (Lowin) 358
  Milo 358

PRENTISS
  Mehitable Spencer 520
PRESCOTT
  Abel 702, 747
  Abigail (Brigham) 702, 747
  Helen M. 531
  James 842
  John 842
  Jonathan, Jr. 702, 746
  Lucy 572, 702, 747
  Rebecca (Bulkeley) 702, 746
  Samuel (Dr.) 702, 747
PRESLES (DE)
  Jeanne 438, 445
PRESSIGNY (DE)
  Nicole 964
PRESTON
  Barbara 173
  Barbara Gay (Hess) 371
  Frederick Augustus 371
  Frederick Willard (Dr.) 371
  Gertrude Eldred (Bradford) 371
  Margaret (Atwater) 371
PRESTWICHE/ PERWYCHE
  Rose 749
PRICE/PRYCE
  Anne (Humphrey) 229, 511

  Edward 658, 809
  Ellen Frances 254
  Ellis [Ellis ap Rees] 229, 511
  Florence (Clunn) 810
  Hannah 651, 658
  Jane 658
  Joan lxiii
  Joan (___) 810
  Joan(na) cxliii, clxii, 810
  John 810
  Mably (Owen) 658, 809
  Prentiss liii
  Richard 658
  Thomas 810
PRICKMAN
  Martha 743
PRIDE
  Elizabeth 1, cl, 103, 104
  Elizabeth (Monck) 103
  Thomas 103
  Thomas (Sir) 103
PRIDEAUX
  Magdalen 493
  Margaret 665
PRIEGO
  Pedro de Mendoza Carrillo de Albornoz, Count of 191
PRIEST
  Hannah 526
PRILLWITZ (VON)
  Auguste Arend 16

Friedrich Wilhelm
  August Ludwig 16
Georgine Marie
  Elizabeth Eugenie
  (von Moltke),
  Countess 16
PRIME
Elizabeth Thornton
  (Kemeys) 548
family 132
Pamela Dutton 129
Ruth Melville
  (Shaw Kennedy)
  129
Samuel Irenaeus
  (Rev.) 548, 549
Temple 356
William Albert, Jr.
  129
PRIMROSE
Archibald (Sir), 1st
  Bt. 223
Elizabeth (Keith)
  223
Margaret 223, 456
Sibella 85
PRINCE
Mary Evelyn 4
Philippe 953
PRINZ-VALDES
Eva 1
PRIOR/PRYOR
Eleanor 302
Elizabeth 717
PRITZEL
Kate 632
PROCENA
Paolo II Sforza,
  Marquess of 192

PROCTOR
Elizabeth 90
PROFFIT
Elizabeth 806
PROMNITZ (VON)
Benigna 196
Eleanor 195
Heinrich Anselm,
  Herr 195, 196
Sigismund Siegfried,
  Count 196
Sophia (von Kurz-
  bach) 195, 196
PROUDLER
Karen 1, 104
PROUST
Marcel 227
PROVENCE
Beatrix, Princess of,
  Queen of Naples
  and Sicily 965
Constance of, Queen
  of France 851,
  853, 855
Eleanor, Princess of,
  Queen of England
  623, 625, 628, 630,
  632, 633, 942, 944,
  945, 946, 963, 965
Margaret, Princess of,
  Queen of France
  634, 638, 965
Raymond Berenger
  V, Count of 965
Sancha, Princess of
  653, 672, 965
PROWSE
Agnes 870

Agnes (Bampfield)
  870
Alice (White) 870
Elizabeth (Collack
  alias Colwyck)
  870
Joan (Baynton)
  632
Joan (Orchard) 870
John 870
Margaret (Norton)
  870
Mary 632
Richard 870
Robert 870
Thomas 632
PROZOROVSKY
Anastasia 798
PRUNELÉ (DE)
Gilles, Seigneur de
  La Porte 948
Jacqueline 948
Jacqueline (de
  Graffart) 948
Jacques, Baron de
  Saint-Germain-le-
  Désirée 948
Renée (de Mésenge/
  Mazange) 948
PRUSSIA
Albert, Prince of 8
Albert Frederick,
  Duke of 47, 54,
  56, 891
Alexandrine,
  Princess of 8
Anna, Princess of 54
August, Prince of
  16

Augusta, Princess of 13
Charlotte Louise, Princess of, Empress of Russia 5, 7
Elizabeth Christina, Princess of Brunswick-Wolfenbüttel, Queen of 13
Ferdinand, Prince of 16
Frederica, Princess of Hesse-Darmstadt, Queen of 13
Frederick I, King of 56, 58, 432
Frederick William I, King of 16
Frederick William II, King of 8, 13
Frederick William III, King of 8, 40
Louise (Frederica Dorothea Louise Philippine), Princess of 16
Louise, Princess of Mecklenburg-Strelitz, Queen of 8, 40
Magdalen Sybilla, Princess of 47
monarchs of 52, 615
Sophie, Princess of 16, 54, 56
Sophie Charlotte, Princess of Hanover and Great Britain, Queen of 58, 432
Sophie Dorothea, Princess of Great Britain, Queen of 16
Wilhelmine, Princess of, Queen of The Netherlands 8
Wilhelmine, Princess of, wife of William V of Orange, Stadholder of The Netherlands 8

PRUTTESTON
Joan 672, 866

PRYCE. *see* PRICE/PRYCE

PRYCE-JONES
Alan Payan clvii, 73
Henry Morris 72
Marion Vere (Dawnay) 72
Mary Jean (Thorne) 73
Thérèse Carmen May (Poppy), Baroness Fould-Springer 73

PRYNNE
Frances 76
Seymour 107

PRYTZ
Anna Vendela 889

PRZEMYSL I NOSAK
Duke of Teschen and Glogau 713

PRZEMYSL OTTOKAR II
King of Bohemia 621

PRZEZDZIECKA
Maria, Countess 35

PUDSEY
Dorothy 697
Edith (Hore) 697
Eleanor (Harman) 697
Eleanor (Montfort) 697
Florence 363
George 697
Grace (Hamerton) 697
Henry 697
John (Sir) 697
Margaret 698
Margaret (Conyers) 697
Margaret (Eure) 697
Margaret (Tunstall) 697
Maud (Cotton) 697
Ralph (Sir) 697
Robert 652, 697
Rowland 697, 698
William 697

PUGH
Elizabeth (Williams) 650, 651, 660
Ellis 660
Evan 652
family 652
Gainor 809
Robert 650, 652, 660

Sarah (Evans) 652
Sina (___) 660
PUGH or HUGHES
Jane 652, 660
PULESTON
Angharad 813
Edward (Sir) 235
Eleanor (Whitney) 770
Ermin (Hanmer) 235
Jane 382, 510, 563, 900
John 770
Lowri (ferch Gruffudd Fychan) 813
Madog 770
Margaret 229, 235, 770
Robert 770, 813
Robert (Sir) 770
PULTENEY
Anne 34
PUREFOY
Anne (Fettiplace) 373
Edward 373
Jane 383
Magdalen 901
Mary 373
PURY
Joanna 299
PURYEAR
Mary (Ligon) xiii
Mary Stovall xiii
William xiii
PUTNAM
Priscilla 342, 814, 882

Priscilla (Baker) 814, 882
Tarrant, Jr. 814, 882
PYLE
Jane 503
PYMPE
Anne 469, 477, 514
Elizabeth (Pashley) 514
Reginald 514
PYNCHON
Amy (Wyllys) xlviii, lv, clxi, 533
Anne (Andrew) 533
family xxiv
John 533
William 533
PYNE
Albertina Shelton (Taylor) 165
Alice (___) 744
Anna (Rivington) 165, 744
Anne (___) (Oxenham) 744
Anstice (Rich) 744
Charity (White) 744
Christian (Heydon) 744
Cornelius 744
Elizabeth (Chichester) 744
Frederick Wallace (F. W.) lxiii
George 744
Honor (Penfound) 744

Honora (Smith) 744
Isabella (Pyne) 744
Joan (Darte) 744
John lxiii, 744
Josias 744
M. Taylor lxiii
Margaret (Markham) 744
Mary (Craze) 744
Mary (Hammett) 744
Nicholas 744
Percy Rivington 165
Philip 744
Robertina Rivington 165
Sarah (Gainesford) 744
Thomas lxiii, 165, 744
QUARE
Anna 256
QUARLES
Margery 554
QUARRELL
Mary 376
QUEENSBERRY
William Douglas, 1st Earl of 166
QUEILLE (DE LA)
Anne 215
QUEKE
Agnes 778
QUÉRANGAL (DE)
Aline-Anne 184
QUINCY
Anna (Shepard) 375, 393
Daniel 375, 393
Elizabeth 375, 393

Elizabeth (Norton) 375, 393
John 375, 393
QUINCY (DE)
Elizabeth 843
Hawise 680, 682
Margaret (de Beaumont) 680, 681, 682, 843
Matilda (de St. Liz) (de Clare) 851, 920
Robert (Sir) 682
Roger, 2nd Earl of Winchester 843
Saire 851, 920
Saire, 1st Earl of Winchester 680, 682, 843
QUINNELL
Ellen 837
QUINTEN
John 369
Mary (Bull) (Webb) (Limbrey) 369
QUINTYNE
Margaret 695
QUISTORP (VON)
Alexander August Gustav Henrik Achim Albrecht 58, 224
Emmy Melitta Cécile xviii
Maria Irmengard Emmy Luise Gisela liii, clxx, 59, 224
Marie Eleonore Dorothea (von Below) 58, 224

Theda Elisabeth Klementine Franziska (von Falkenhayn) 58, 224
Wernher Theodor August Friedrich Wilhelm 58, 224
R___SKY
Zinaïde (pseudonym of Elena [Fadeev] Hahn von Rotherhahn) 792
RÄÄF i SMALAND
Charlotta Eleonora 51
RABAN
Catherine Charlotte 401
RABESTAN (DE)
Patri/Patry de Chourses, Seigneur 948
RACAN-BASTIEN
Paul-Émile 970
RADCLIFFE 30
Anna Maria Barbara 30
Anna Maria (Webb) 30
Anne 399
Edward, 2nd Earl of Derwentwater 30
Isabel 100
James, 3rd Earl of Derwentwater 30
Jane 355, 905
Katherine 752
Margaret 123, 701

Margaret (Stanley) 355, 905
Mary (Tudor) 30
Robert, 1st Earl of Sussex 355, 905
RADMYLDE
Elizabeth 738
Margaret 737, 738
Margaret (Camoys) 737, 738
Ralph 737
RADZIWILL
Anna (Lubomirska), Princess 16
Anna, Princess 621
Anthony Henry, Prince 16
Anthony Stanislaus Albert, Prince 17, 914
Boguslav (Frederick William Louis Maria Ferdinand Henry August Boguslav), Prince 16
Carole (Di Falco) [Carole Radziwill] 17, 914
Caroline Lee (Bouvier) (Canfield) [Lee Radziwill] xviii, xlv, 16, 17, 74, 914
Ferdinand Frederick William Alexander, Prince 16
Grace (Kolin) 16
Janusz Francis Xavier Joseph

1461

Labre Bonislaus
Maria, Prince 16
Leontine (von Clary
und Aldringen),
Countess 16
Pelagia (Sapieha),
Princess 16
Rose (de Monléon)
16
Stanislaus Albert,
Prince xlv, cxlvi,
16, 17, 914
RAE
Margaret 251
RAESFELD (VAN)
Elisabeth 445
Elisabeth (van
Bronckhorst-
Batenburg) 445
Johann III, Heer van
Ostendorf 445
RAESFELD (VON)
Elisabeth 907
RAGDALE
Alice 819
RAGLAN
Alice 338
Anne (Dennis) 338
John (Sir) 338
RAGLAND
Charles J., Jr.
 clxxxvii
Doria Loyce 344
Evan clxxxvii
family clxxxvii
RAINBOW
Frances 882
RAINEY
Shelagh Ann 78

RAINIER
Archduke of Austria
 614
**RAINIER III LOUIS-
HENRY-MAXENCE-
BERTRAND**
Grimaldi, Sovereign
Prince of Monaco
xl, 289, 290, 934
RAINSBOROUGH
Martha 375
RAITT
Bonnie 64
RALEIGH
Anne (Chamber-
layne) 478
Bridget 428, 478,
480
Edward 478
Edward (Sir) 478
Elizabeth (Greene)
478
George 480
Margaret (Verney)
478
William 478
____ (____)
(Fitzgerald) 480
RAMBURES (DE)
Charles I, Seigneur
205
Charlotte 205
Claude (de Bourbon)
205
Françoise (d'Anjou)
205
Jean III, Seigneur,
Count of Dammartin
and Guînes 205

Jean IV, Seigneur
205
Renée (de Boulain-
villiers) 205
RAMERU (DE)
Érard de Brienne,
Seigneur 943
RAMEYEN
Nicolas Rubens,
Seigneur of 804
**RAMÍREZ DE
ARELLANO**
Ana 191
Juana 191
Pedro 191
RAMSAY/RAMSEY
Elizabeth 67
Isabel(la) 251, 285
Janet 278, 282
Jean 225
Lucy Booker 935
RAMSDEN
Margaret 472
RAND
Mary 632
RANDALL
Anne (Hynson)
348
RANDES
Mary 785
Mary (Yorke) 785
Thomas 785
RANDLE
Elizabeth 648
RANDOLPH
Catherine Elizabeth
(Drummond) 65
Cyril 65
Dorothy (Lane) 387

Elizabeth (___) 387
Elizabeth (Ryland) 387
Emily Margaret (Nepean) 65
family xxiv, xlviii
Felton George 65
Frances Selina (Hervey) 65
George 65
Henry 387
Isabel(la) 281, 732
Isham 387
Jane 387, 711, 822
Jane (Rogers) 387, 711
Judith (Soane) 387
Margaret Isobel 65
Mary (Isham) 387, 710
Richard 387
William xix, xxxiv, xxxvii, clxvii, 387, 710
RANDYLL
Mary 34
RANKIN
Elizabeth 379
RANTOUL
Augustus Neal 137
Matilda Charlotte Palgrave (Chetwynd-Talbot) clvii, 137
RANTZAU
Mette 644
RANTZOW (VON)
Christoph Ferdinand Anton, Count 891

Elizabeth (de Windt) 891
Juliette Marie Elizabeth, Countess 891
Julius Friedrich Ludwig, Count 891
Louise Henrietta (von Brockenburgh), Baroness 891
RAPIN (DE)
Jacob, Seigneur de Thoyras 634
Jeanne (de Pelisson) 634
Marie 635
Marie-Anne (Testard) 634
Paul, Seigneur de Thoyras 634, 636
Percide (de Lupé) 634
Pierre II, Baron de Maivers 634
Susanne-Esther 634
RASMUSSEN
James A. lxiv
RASOIR (DE)
Marie-Angélique-Bernard 438
RATAUT
Jeanne 943
RATCHITCH
Ekaterina 7
RATTRAY
Elizabeth 159, 160
Grizel 261, 266

RAUGLAUDRE (DE)
Daniel xii, lxxi, clxx
RAVENSBERG
Margaret of 459
RAVENSCROFT
Anne (Goodfellow) 518
Anne (Stanley) 517
Arthur 518
Eleanor (ferch Richard ap Howell) 518
Elizabeth 518
Elizabeth (___) 518
Frances xlviii, cxlviii, 518
George 518
John 518
Katherine (Grosvenor) 518
Margaret (Dod) 518
Margaret (Greenstreet) 518
Martyn 518
Maud 235
Ralph 517
Samuel 518
Thomas 518
William 518
RAVIER
Louise 965
RAVILIOUS
John P. 244, 709
RAWE
Anne 665
RAWLINGS
Margaret 877

____ 609
RAWLINS
 Ruth 752
RAWSON
 Abner 318
 Edmund 318
 Elizabeth (Hayward) 318
 Grindall 318
 Mary (Allen) 318
 Rhoda 318
 Susanna (Wilson) 318
RAY
 Anthony 362
 Gloria (Hallward) (Clements) (Ray) (Howard) [Gloria Grahame] (wife of both Nicholas and Anthony) xviii, 362
 Nicholas 362
RAYMOND
 Anne (Warkham) 548
 Frances (Harris) 548
 Hannah 400
 Isabella 548
 Isabella (Child) 548
 Margaretta (Bridges) 548
 Oliver 548
 Samuel 548
 St. Clere 548
 William 548
RAYNSFORD
 Alice (Anne) 861

 Edward lxiv, lxv, clxi, clxxv, 625
 Elizabeth 862
 Elizabeth (___) 625
 Juliana 483
 Mary (Kirton) 625
 Robert 625
 William 861
RAZAY (DE)
 Edmé de Thiene, Seigneur 442
 Henry de Thiene, Seigneur 442
 Nicolas de Thiene, Seigneur 442
READ
 Bridget clxxxvii
 Eleanor 852
 George (Sen.) 828
 Gertrude (Ross) (Till) 828
 Harmon Pumpelly lvii, lxiv
READ(E)
 Anne 489, 506, 882
 Anne (Windebank) 310
 Charles xxiv
 Elizabeth 297, 298, 501, 747, 758
 Elizabeth (Cooke) 665
 Elizabeth (Martiau) 310, 930
 Frances 310
 Frances (Shelley) 310
 Francis 310

 George (Col.) xix, xl, xlvii, liii, lxx, clxvii, 310, 930
 Henry 310
 Jane (Rudhall) 506
 Margaret 607
 Margaret (Beauchamp) 506
 Mary 239, 348, 353
 Mildred 310, 700, 930
 Mildred (Windebank) 310
 Richard 506
 Robert 310
 Sarah 279
 William 506
READING
 Elizabeth 157
REAGAN
 Anne Francis (Robbins) [Nancy Davis] xlii, xliii, 673
 Ronald Wilson, 40th U.S. President xlii, 673
RECUM
 Franz V. lxiv
REDDAWAY
 Elizabeth (Fraiswell) 590
REDDICH
 Euphemia 264
REDE
 Cecilia (Harlyngrugge) 877
 Joan clxxxiv, 877
 John 877

REDESDALE
 Algernon Bertram
  Freeman-Mitford,
  1st Baron 22
 David Bertram
  Ogilvy
  Freeman-Mitford,
  2nd Baron 22
REDGRAVE
 Corin William 246, 247
 Deirdre (Hamilton-Hill) 246, 247
 family xxxviii, xlix, lix, 240, 247
 Jemma Rebecca 247
 Kika (Markham) 246
 Lynn Rachel xi, xvii, xlii, clvii, 246
 Michael Scudamore (Sir) 246
 Rachel (Kempson) 246
 Vanessa xi, 246
REDLICH
 Leslie Corkill 94
REDLICH (VON)
 Marcellus Donald Arthur xx
REDMAN
 Randall R. M. 902, 909
REDMAN/ REDMAYNE
 Anne (Scrope) 698
 Elizabeth 698
 Thomas 698

REED
 Elizabeth 331
 family clxxxii
 Giles 331
 Katherine (Grevile) 331
 Paul C. viii, ix, xlv, xlvii, xlix, li, lvi, lviii, lxii, lxiv, lxviii, lxxi, clxxxv, cxc, 153, 217, 236, 476, 509, 527, 535, 553, 581, 708, 720, 729, 740
REES
 David 809
 Edward 510, 511
 Elizabeth 510
 Evan 809
 Helene Gertrude 101
 Rebecca (Humphrey) 510
 Sidney lvi, clxv, clxxx, 809
REES LEWYS
 ap John Gruffudd 229
REID
 Alison 456
 Janet 219
 Mary 464
REITWIESNER
 William Addams vii, viii, xlii, xlvi, xlvii, xlix, l, liii, lxiii, lxiv, lxv, lxvii, lxxi, clxxxix, 17, 61, 446, 458, 469, 520, 521, 583, 663, 669, 736, 803, 812, 833, 926, 991

RELTZENSTEIN (VON)
 Hedwig Florentine Louisa Friederike 641
REMINGTON
 Gordon Lewis l, lxiv, 248
REMPSTON
 Elizabeth 667
RENDEL
 Emily Catherine 117
RENDORFF
 Dorothea Catharina 440
RENWICK
 Jane Jeffrey 222
REPPES
 John 394
 Rachel (FitzWilliam) (Huddleston) (Hall) 394
REPPS
 Anne 846
 Elizabeth (Grimstone) 845
 Elizabeth (Jermy) 845
 Henry 845
REPSCH
 Janette 458
RERESBY
 Elizabeth 413, 528, 529
 Isabel 528, 529

Margaret
 (FitzWilliam) 528
 Ralph 528, 529
RESCARRICK
 Katherine 148
RESSIZ (DE)
 Bertrand de
  Sallmard, Seigneur
  de la Fay and 638
 Claude I de
  Sallmard, Seigneur
  de la Fay and 638
 Claude II de
  Sallmard, Seigneur
  de la Fay and 638
 Geoffrey I de
  Sallmard, Seigneur
  de la Fay, Montfort,
  and 638
 Geoffrey II de
  Sallmard, Seigneur
  de la Fay and 638
 Philippe-Guillaume
  de Sallmard,
  Seigneur de
  Montfort, Roche-
  Pingolet, and 638
 Raymond I,
  Seigneur de
  Montfort, Roche-
  Pingolet, and 638
 Raymond II de Sall-
  mard, Vicomte 638
RETHEL
 family lxii
 Gervais, Count of
  874, 877
 Millicent of clxxxi,
  874, 877

REUSS-EBERSDORF
 Augusta Caroline
  Sophia, Countess
  45, 46, 182
 Erdmuthe Dorothea,
  Countess liii, 196,
  237, 238
 Henry X, Count
  182, 196
 Henry XXIV, Count
  182
 Henry XXIX, Count
  182
 Joanna Dorothea,
  Countess 182
REUSS-GERA
 Henry II, Count
  182, 196
REUSS-KÖSTRITZ
 Anna Christa
  Stefanie (Clemm
  von Hohenberg) 8
 Enriqueta (Henrietta)
  Juana Francisca
  Susanna (de Casado
  y Huguetan) 141,
  142
 Ernestine Adelaide,
  Countess 141
 Friederike Luise
  Sophie, Countess
  141
 Henry II, Prince 8
 Henry VI, Count
  141, 142
 Henry XVIII, Prince
  8
 Henry XXXVII,
  Prince 8

Henry XLVIII,
  Count 141, 142
 Henry LV, Count 8
 Marianne Charlotte
  Katharina Stefanie,
  Princess xlv, 8
 Mary Justina (von
  Watteville),
  Baroness 8
**REUSS-
 LOBENSTEIN**
 Henry X, Count
  182, 196
**REUSS-
 OBERGREITZ**
 Marie Sybil,
  Countess 182,
  196
REVELL
 Anne lxx, cxlviii,
  757, 758
 Anne (Eyre) 528
 Anne (Knowles)
  757
 John 757, 758
 Margaret (Beighton)
  757
 Mary 528, 529
 Mary (Comerford)
  757
 Robert 757
 Thomas 528
REVENTLOW. *see*
 HAUGWITZ-
 HARDENBURG-
 REVENTLOW
REVERE
 Paul 702, 747

REYGATE
  Elizabeth 721
REYMES
  Anne 539
  Anne (Evans) 539
  Frances (___) 539
  John 539
  Mary (Payne) 539
  William 539
  ___ 539
REYNELL
  Elizabeth 672
REYNOR
  Elizabeth 524
RHEINALLT
  ap Gruffudd ap
    Rhys 658
  ap Madog Foel 886
RHETT
  Sarah 130
RHINE (THE)
  Frederick V, Elector
    Palatine of
    [Frederick I, King
    of Bohemia, the
    "Winter King"]
    38, 56
RHUDDLAU
  Llywelyn ap
    Dafydd, Constable
    of 650, 659, 686,
    694
RHYS
  ab Einion Sais ap
    Hywel Felyn ap
    Gruffudd 811
  ab Ieuan Goch 808
  ab Ifor Hael 810
  ap David Lloyd 810
  ap Griffith (Sir)
    723
  ap Richard 658
  (ap Rhys) ap
    Griffith 723
RHYS GOCH
  ap Tudur 809
RHYS LLWYD
  ap Adam ap Rhys ab
    Einion Sais ap
    Hywel Felyn ap
    Gruffudd 811
RHYS SAIS
  ab Ednyfed 886
RHYS-JONES
  Sophie Helen,
    Countess of
    Wessex 465
RHYWALLON
  Prince of Powys
    886
RIAPOLOVSKY
  Fedor, Prince 798
  Irina (Patrikeev) 798
  Ivan Khrilek, Prince
    798
  Semen Khripoun,
    Prince 798
RIBBING
  Anna 663
  Bengt, Baron 457
  Christina Maria
    (Mörner) 457
  Hedvig Juliana
    (Roos), Countess
    457
  Johan 457
  Juliana, Baroness
    457
  Lindorm, Lord of
    Boxholm 457
  Maria 457
  Mårta (Bonde) 457
  Ture, Baron 457
  Ulrika Eleanora
    (Piper), Countess
    457
RIBEIRA
  María Pais, 15th
    Senhora da Casa
    de Sousa 619
RIBERO
  Leonor 619
RICE
  Anne (Gibbs) 103,
    104
  Frances Emma 111
  Nathaniel (Gov.)
    103, 104
RICH
  Ada May 424
  Anne lix, clxviii,
    135, 653, 838
  Anne (Bourchier)
    883
  Anne (Evans) 837
  Anstice 744
  Audrey 359
  Charles Coulson, II
    424
  Edward 837, 838
  Frances 135
  Frances (Hatton)
    135
  Henry, 1st Earl of
    Holland 135
  Isabel (Cope) 135

Jane Susanne
  (Stock) 424
Judith (Saltonstall)
  837
Mary 509, 738
Penelope
  (Devereux) 135,
  136
Peter (Sir) 837
Robert, 1st Earl of
  Warwick 135
Robert, 2nd Earl of
  Warwick 135
Susan 883
Susan (Percy) 837
Thomas 883
RICHARD
  ab Ieuan 410
  Catherine 990
  Felicité 987
  Plantagenet, Earl of
    Cornwall, King of
    the Romans
    xxxix, 652, 653,
    661, 672, 965
  Prince of Great
    Britain, 2nd Duke
    of Gloucester 25
  of Tyddin Tyfod
    658
RICHARD I
  Duke of Normandy
    861
RICHARD II
  Duke of Normandy
    879, 919
  King of England
    xxiv, xxv, 714

RICHARD III
  King of England
    cxxvi, 107, 114,
    118, 119, 126, 133
RICHARDIE (DE LA)
  Gilbert de Besse,
    Seigneur 440
RICHARDS
  Anne Catherine
    120
  Edward 120
  Elizabeth 138
  Emily (Saurin) 120
  Jane 410
  Sarah (Gibbon)
    308
RICHARDSON
  Abigail 585
  Anne lxvii
  Barbara (Flavin) 521
  Cecil Antonio
    "Tony" xvii, 246
  Douglas vii, ix, x, xi,
    xix, xxvii, xlvi,
    xlviii, xlix, lii, liv, lv,
    lvi, lxiv, lxvi, clxxxi,
    clxxxii, clxxxiv,
    clxxxv, clxxxviii,
    cxci, 101, 105, 106,
    131, 298, 338, 372,
    394, 470, 477, 562,
    569, 583, 586, 587,
    624, 656, 675, 681,
    683, 714, 722, 745,
    836, 852, 868, 879,
    906, 919, 1024,
    1025, 1026
  Elizabeth (Bates)
    925

Esther (Joslin) 520
family xxxviii,
  xlix, lix, 240, 247
Frances (Mall) 307
Joely 247
Jonathan 925
Lucy (Merrick) 520
María Luisa (López
  Collada) 521
Mehitable Spencer
  (Prentiss) 520
Muriel Elsa
  Florence (Forbes-
  Robertson) [Muriel
  Forbes] clvii, 268
Natasha xi, xvii,
  xlii, clvii, 246
Peter 520
Ralph David (Sir)
  xvii, clvii, 268
Rosaura (Ojeda
  Medero) 520
Samuel 520
Sarah 925, 927
Sarah (____)
  (Edwards) 730
Susannah 519
Ursula 359
Vanessa (Redgrave)
  xi, 246
Vesta (Hodsdon)
  520
William 520
William Blaine, Jr.
  (Gov.) 521
William Blaney
  520
William Blaney/
  Blaine, Jr. 521

William Everett
  520, 521
**RICHARDSON
OJEDA**
  Lucia 520
RICHEMONT (DE)
  Charles de Mons,
    Seigneur de
    Beaulieu and 941
  Charles de
    Montmorency,
    Count, Constable
    of France 943
RICHERS
  Cecily (Tillys) 587
  Elizabeth (Batchcroft) 587
  Elizabeth (Stapleton) 587
  Frances 587
  Henry 587
  John 587
RICHEZA
  of Lorraine, Queen of Poland 849
  of Poland, Queen of Hungary 832, 833
RICHMOND
  Edmund Tudor, 1st Earl of 547
RICHMOND and LENNOX
  Charles Lennox, 1st Duke of 25, 31
  Charles Lennox, 2nd Duke of 31
  Charles Lennox, 4th Duke of 31

RIDDELL
  Helen 250
  Marion 210
  Susanna 211
RIDDLEFORD (DE)
  Emmeline 742, 746, 752, 760, 772
RIDLEY
  Edward 133
  Elizabeth 514
RIENECK
  Dorothea of 237
  Philip I, Count of 237
RIEUX (DE)
  Béatrix (de Jonchères) 226
  Isabel (de Brosse) 226
  Jean, Seigneur de Châteauneuf 226
  Jean IV, Sire, Sire de Rochefort, Count of Harcourt 226
  Marie 226
  René, Seigneur de Sourdéac 226
  Susanne (de Sainte-Melaine) 226
RIGBY
  Dorothy (Anderton) 611
  Edward 611
  Jane 611
  Katherine 427
RIGG
  Bethia (Carstairs) 276

  Catherine (Row) 276
  Diana, Dame 23
  Margaret 276
  Sarah (Inglis) 276
  Thomas, of Aithernie 276
  William 276
  William, of Aithernie 276
RIGGS
  Abigail (Peet) 589
  Cecilia Dowdall 127
  Ebenezer 589
  George 589
  George Washington 127, 488
  Hannah (Johnson) 589
  James 589
  Janet Madeleine Cecilia (Shedden) 127, 488
  John 589
  John, Jr. 589
  Lois (Hawkins) 589
  Maria 589
  Phebe (Caniff) 589
  Samuel 589
  Sarah (Baldwin) 589
  Sarah (Clark) 589
RIGLOS (DE)
  Francisca Javiera (de San Martín) 996
  Marcos José 996

RIGLOS y SAN MARTÍN (DE)
María Jacinta 996
Miguel Fermín 996
RIGNON
Félix-Henri-Victor-Gaspard-Édouard-Alexandre, Count 201
Louise (Perrone de San Martino) 201
Maria Cristina Giovanna Luigia 201
RIJCK (VAN)
Ambrosia Wilhelmina 460
RIJSWICK (VAN)
Elisabeth 776
RILEY-SMITH
Anne Elizabeth 135
RINDGE
Susanna 880
RIOUX
Catherine 987
Catherine (Leblond) 987, 988
Esther 977
Felicité 988
Jean, Seigneur de Trois-Pistoles 987, 988
Juliette (Drouin) 988
Louise (Asselin) 987
Marie-Catherine (Côté) 988
Marie-Josèphe (Sirois) 988
Nicolas, Seigneur de Trois-Pistoles 987, 988
Vincent 988
RIPLEY
George 155
Sophia Willard (Dana) 155
RIQUELME DE GUZMÁN
Alonso 995
Ursula (de Irala) 995
RISBY
Elizabeth 565
RISCOE
Anna (Willix) 530
Robert 359
RISHEL
Anne Julie (d'Harnoncourt) 221, 896
Joseph 221, 896
RITCHIE
Amber Mary (Parkinson) 63
Doris Margaretta (McLaughlin) 63
Guy Stuart lx, cxlvi, 63, 380, 975, 988
Jacqui (Ainsley) 63
John Vivian 63
Madonna Louise Veronica (Ciccone) (Penn) [Madonna] xvii, cxlvi, 63, 380, 967, 969, 975, 988
Stewart John 63
Susan 53
RITSCHEL
Eileen 112
RIVARD
Marie-Josephte 989
RIVARD dit LAVIGNE
François 989
Marie-Madeleine (Turcot) 988, 989
RIVAU (DE)
Jacques de Beauvau, Seigneur 202
RIVERS
Anthony Woodville, 2nd Earl 412
Elizabeth (Mallory) viii, li, cxlvi, 847, 1025
Richard Woodville, 1st Earl 208, 514
William 847
RIVES
Amélie Louise 194
Caroline Maria (King) 144
Francis Robert 144
George Lockhart 144
Matilda Antonia (Barclay) 144
Sara (Whiting) (Belmont) 144
RIVIÈRE (VON)
Helene 12
RIVINGTON
Anna 165, 744

ROACH
Hannah Benner lxv
ROBARTS
Marianne Jane 108
ROBBINS
Anne Ayers
 (Francis) 673
Anne Francis
 [Nancy (Davis)
 Reagan] xlii, xliii,
 673
Anne Jean 210,
 479, 716
Edith (Luckett)
 673
Edward Hutchinson
 210, 479, 715
Elizabeth
 (Hutchinson) 479,
 715
Elizabeth (Murray)
 210, 479, 715
John Newell 673
Kenneth Seymour
 673
Nathaniel 479, 715
ROBERDEAU
Daniel clxxi, 240,
 244
family 214
Isaac 244
Jane (Milligan)
 244
Mary (Bostwick)
 244
Mary (Cunyngham)
 244
ROBERT
ab Owain 229, 886
ap Dafydd Llwyd
 658
ap Hywel 694
ap Thomas 230
Elizabeth 652
Katherine 809
Prince of France,
 Count of Clermont
 634, 638
ROBERT dit LAFONTAINE
Charles 987
Marie-Anne
 (Menard) 987
Marie-Josèphe 987
ROBERT I
Duke of Burgundy
 853, 855
Duke of Normandy
 879, 919
King of France
 879, 919
ROBERT I "the BRUCE"
King of Scotland
 456, 787, 789
ROBERT II
King of France
 xxvi, 851, 853, 855
King of Scotland
 219, 269, 272, 273,
 275, 276, 278, 280,
 281, 282, 283, 285
ROBERT III
King of Scotland
 239, 240, 241, 243,
 245, 248, 249, 250,
 251, 252, 253, 254,
 255, 256, 257, 258,
 260, 261, 263, 264,
 266, 267, 268, 940
ROBERTON
Elizabeth 170, 218
James, of Bedlay
 218
Jean (Cunyngham)
 218
ROBERTS
Alice (___) 230
Anne 563
Anne (Humphrey)
 511
Augusta 138
Clarence Vernon lxv
Edward 511
Elizabeth (Owen)
 510
family xiii, xxxiv,
 clxv, 651, 694
Gainor (Pugh) 809
Gainor (Roberts)
 clxv, 660, 692
Gary Boyd v, vi, x,
 xiii, xviii, xix, xx,
 xxii, xxiii, xxvi,
 xxvii, xxviii, xxx,
 xxxi, xli, xlii, xliii,
 xliv, xlv, xlvi, xlvii,
 li, lii, liv, lvii, lx, lxi,
 lxv, lxviii, lxxi, clxx,
 clxxxviii, clxxxix,
 cxc, cxcii, 136, 155,
 298, 303, 323, 542,
 779, 967, 968, 976,
 991, 1024
George Blakemore
 Bayfield John
 363

Hugh 650, 651,
660, 809
Ida Catherine Villiers
(Law) 363
Isabel (Colepepper/
Culpeper) 920
Jack Carl xiii
Jane (Owen) 651,
660, 809
Joan 920
John clxv, 510,
660, 692, 809
John, of Pencoyd
lvi, clxxx
John St. Clair [St.
Clair Bayfield]
clii, 364, 365
Katherine (Jones)
809
Kathleen (Norris) 5
Kathleen
(Weatherley) 364
Margaret 229, 230
Margaret (Evans)
692
Mary Elizabeth
"Betty" (Boyd)
xiii
Richard 692
Robert 809
Sidney (Rees) lvi,
clxv, clxxx, 809
Thomas 230
Walter 920
ROBERTSON
Alexander, of Struan
219
Anne 393, 394
Bryan 393

Clifford Parker, III
("Cliff") 44
David, of Muirton
219
Eleanor (Pitcairn)
219
Elizabeth (Stewart)
219
Gilbert, of Muirton
219
Isabel (Petrie) 219
Janet 159, 790
Janet (Reid) 219
Janet, of Struan 85
Jean 219
John 268, 394
John, of Muirton
219
Malcolm, of
Carwhin 940
Margaret 145, 152,
223
Margaret (Crichton)
219
Margaret
(FitzWilliam) 393
Margaret (Forbes)
268
Margaret (Mitchell)
219
Marion (Murray)
940
Mary 219, 270
Mary (Nesbit) 219
Nedenia (Hutton)
(Rumbrough)
[Dina Merrill] 44
William 219
William (IV) 219

William, of Gledney
219
William, of Muirton
219
___ 940
___ (Innes) 219
ROBESON-MILLER
Stephen lxiv, lxv,
21, 664
ROBIE
Elizabeth 325
ROBIN
ap Robert 689
ROBINS
Eileen (Burden)
(Maynard) 378
Thomas, Jr. 378
ROBINSON
Anne (Walters) 390
Bridget (White)
917
Corinne (Roosevelt)
164
Corinne Douglas
164
Douglas clxx, 163
Douglas, Jr. 163,
164
Edward Arlington
793
Elizabeth (Innes)
163
family 247, 918
Fanny (Monroe)
163
Frances (Worsley)
121
George, of Gask
163

1472

Grace 390
Grace (Stapleton)
  390
Isaac xl, l, cli, 917,
  918
James 245
James Edgar 769
Jane (Brereton)
  563
Jane (Buchanan)
  245
John (Rev.) 917,
  918
Lula Dell (Flickinger)
  769
Margaret (Hanford)
  917
Mary 342
Mary (___) 917
Mary (Douglas)
  163
Mary Ann 146
Matilda Sarah 146
Michelle LaVaughn
  498, 726
Nicholas, Bishop of
  Bangor 563
Pauline 632, 688,
  769
Richard, 1st Baron
  Rokeby,
  Archbishop of
  Armagh 390, 391
Sarah Jane 246
Theresa 121
Thomas 390
Thomas, 1st Baron
  Grantham 121
William 390

William Rose, of
  Clermiston 163
**ROBINSON alias
NORRIS**
Eleanor 563
Margaret (Fowke)
  563
Piers 563
ROBISON
Alma Luella 924
Charles Edward
  924
Clarissa Minerva
  (Duzette) 925
Lewis 925
Rosetta Mary
  (Berry) 925
ROCHAMBEAU (DE)
Jean-Baptiste-Donat
  ien de Vimeur,
  Count xvi, xxvi,
  267, 455
Joseph-Charles I de
  Vimeur, Seigneur
  455
Joseph-Charles II de
  Vimeur, Seigneur
  455
René IV de Vimeur,
  Seigneur 455
ROCHE
Ellen 505, 575
Grizel 536
ROCHE-PINGOLET
Philippe-Guillaume
  de Sallmard,
  Seigneur de
  Ressiz, Montfort,
  and 638

Raymond I de
  Sallmard, Seigneur
  de Ressiz,
  Montfort, and
  638
**ROCHE-TESSON
(DE LA)**
Raoul V, Seigneur
  959
**ROCHECHOUART
(DE)**
Françoise-Athénaïs,
  Marquise de
  Montespan 287,
  289
ROCHEFORT (DE)
Jean IV, Sire de
  Rieux and, Count
  of Harcourt 226
**ROCHEFOUCAULD
(DE LA).** *see* LA
ROCHEFOUCAULD
(DE)
ROCHEMORE (DE)
Anne 735
ROCHFORT
Elizabeth (Moore)
  137
George 137
Jane 486
Thomasina 137
ROCHON
Augustin 979
François 979
Jean-Baptiste 979
Marguerite
  (Beauchamp) 979
Marie (Lavergne
  LeBuis) 979

1473

Marie-Charlotte
  (Gingras) 979
Marie-Françoise
  (Papineau) 979
Marie-Louise 979
Nicolas 979
ROCKEFELLER
  family xxiv
RODD
  Gloria Ellinor 77
  Nancy (Freeman-
    Mitford) (Hon.)
    [Nancy Mitford]
    22, 26
  Peter Murray
    Rennell (Hon.) 22
RODDAM (DE)
  Joan 843
RODES
  Charles 343
  Elizabeth (Jason)
    343
  Elizabeth
    (Lascelles) 343
  Frances (____) 343
  Frances (Constable)
    343
  Francis (Sir), 1st Bt.
    343
  John 343
  John (Sir) 343
RODHAM
  Hillary Diane
    (Sen.), U.S.
    Secretary of State
    923, 969
RODNEY
  Agatha 825
  Alice (Caesar) 307

Anne 613, 614
Anne (____) 307
Anne (Croft) 614,
  824
Anne (Mordaunt)
  614
Caesar 307
Caesar, Jr. 307
Elizabeth 296
Elizabeth
  (Compton) 614
Elizabeth
  (Crawford) 307
Elizabeth (Kirton)
  307, 824
family 307
Frances (Mall)
  (Richardson) 307
George 307, 824
Isabel 609
Isabel (____) 824
Jane (Seymour)
  307
John 307, 614
John (Sir) 307,
  614, 824
Margaret
  (Hungerford) 824
Mary (Hollyman)
  307
Rachel (____) 307
Sarah (Jones) 307
Thomas 824
Walter 614
Walter (Sir) 824
William lxi, clxix,
  307
ROE
  Elizabeth 512

ROËT
  Catherine 295, 300,
    314, 324, 331, 337,
    339, 345, 357, 366,
    368, 370, 375, 382,
    387, 393, 395, 396,
    397, 398, 403, 405,
    407, 413, 417, 419,
    421, 426, 427, 429,
    433, 434, 900, 902
ROEUX-
  CORCELLES (DE)
  Louis de Motin,
    Seigneur 952
ROGENDORF
  (VON)
  Agnes (Streun zu
    Schwarzenau)
    619
  Elisabeth (de Tovar),
    Baroness 619
  Elisabeth, Baroness
    619
  Georg Ehrenreich,
    Baron auf Mollen-
    burg 619
  Wilhelm, Baron zu
    Mollenburg 619
ROGER
  ap John 811
ROGERS
  Anchoretta 383
  Daniel 371
  Eleanor 380
  Elizabeth (Denison)
    371
  Honora 69, 76, 80
  Jane 387, 711
  John (Rev.) 371

Mary 682
Priscilla 371
Sarah (Appleton) 371
William C. 812
ROGGENBACH (ZU)
Jakob von Rüssegg, Baron 832
ROHAN (DE)
Alain IX, Vicomte 287, 293
Catherine 287, 293
Catherine (de Guesclin) 455
Catherine (de Silly) 455
Catherine-Éléonore-Eugénie (de Béthisy) 613
Charles, Prince of Rohan-Montauban 613
Charles, Seigneur de Gié, Vicomte de Fronsac 455
Charles, Seigneur de Guémené 455
François, Seigneur de Gié, Baron de Château-du-Loir 455
Françoise (called Diane) 455
Françoise (de Penhoët) 455
Jean I, Vicomte 455
Jeanne (de Saint-Severin) 455
Louis I, Seigneur de Guémené 455
Louise-Julie-Constance 613
Marie (de Montauban) 455
Pierre, Seigneur de Gié, Count de Marle 455
ROHANT (DE)
Eleanor 672
ROIGNON dît LA ROCHE
Marguerite 942
ROISON (DE)
Marie 733
ROKEBY
Richard Robinson, 1st Baron, Archbishop of Armagh 390, 391
ROLAND
Hyacinthe-Gabrielle 545
Hyacinthe-Gabrielle (Varis) 545
Pierre 545
ROLAZ DU ROSEY
Sophie-Albertine 912
ROLFE
John 387, 711, 823
Rebecca [Pocahontas] xiv, 387, 711, 823
ROLLE
Bridget 901
Honor 594
Mary 436, 665
ROLLESTON
Eila (Ogilvy) 97
Ellen 725
Henry Davy (Sir), 1st Bt. 97
Henry Davy [Eila Ogilvy], Lady 97
ROLLO
Kathleen Nina (Hill) 70
Primula Susan cxlv, 70
William Hereward Charles 70
ROMANOV/ ROMANOFF
[Anna] Audrey (Emery) 3
Alexander, Grand Duke of Russia 5
Alexander II, Czar of Russia 2, 5
Alexander III, Czar of Russia 5
Alexandra (Galitzine), Princess xii, clii, 793, 796
Alexei, Grand Duke of Russia 5
Alice (Eilken) (Baker) 5
Anastasia 792
Anastasia, Czarina of Russia 14, 792
Andrew, Grand Duke of Russia clvii, 5
Andrew, Grand Duke of Russia [Andrew Romanoff] 5

Constantine, Grand
  Duke of Russia 7
Dimitri, Grand Duke
  of Russia 3
Elizabeth (Ruffo)
  5, 824
family xxii
Fedor 792
George, Grand Duke
  of Russia 4
Hedwig Maria
  Gertrud Eva (van
  Chappuis) (Gage)
  5
Helen (Dourneff) 5
Helen, Grand
  Duchess of Russia
  3
Inez (von Bachelin)
  (Storer) [Inez
  Storer] 5
Janet Anne
  (Schoenwald) 5
Kathleen (Norris)
  (Roberts) 5
Maria (Vorontzov-
  Dachkov), Countess
  5
Maria, Grand
  Duchess of Russia
  7
Marie, Grand Duchess
  of Russia 2
Michael, Grand
  Duke of Russia 5
Nicholas I, Czar of
  Russia 5, 7
Nicholas II, Czar of
  Russia 5, 453
Nikita 792
Nikita, Grand Duke
  of Russia 5
Nikita, Grand Duke
  of Russia [Nikita
  Romanoff] clvii, 5
Nina, Grand
  Duchess of cliii
Nina, Grand Duchess
  of Russia 4
Olga, Grand Duchess
  of Russia, Queen of
  Greece 3
Paul, Czar of Russia
  792
Paul, Grand Duke of
  Russia 3
Peter I "the Great,"
  Czar of Russia 792
Peter III, Czar of
  Russia 14, 615,
  796
Rostislav, Grand
  Duke of Russia 5,
  793
Rostislav, Grand Duke
  of Russia [Rostislav
  Romanoff] clvii, 5,
  793
Stephena Verdel
  (Cook) 5, 793
Tatiana, Grand
  Duchess of Russia
  7
Xenia (Chestov) 792
Xenia, Grand
  Duchess of Russia
  5

**ROMANOVSKY-
  ILYINSKI**
Angela Philippa
  (Kaufman) 4
family 4
Mary Evelyn
  (Prince) 4
Paul, Prince [Paul R.
  Ilyinski] clvii, 4
ROMANS (THE)
Philip of Swabia,
  King of lxiii, 640,
  733
Richard Plantagenet,
  Earl of Cornwall,
  King of xxxix, 652,
  653, 661, 672, 965
ROMILLY
Esmond Marcus
  David 23
Jessica Lucy
  (Freeman-
  Mitford) (Hon.)
  [Jessica Mitford]
  xvii, 23, 26
ROMNEY
Anne Amelia (Pratt)
  924
Gaskell 924
George Wilcken
  (Sen.) 924, 926
Lenore Emily
  (LaFaunt) 924, 927
Willard Mitt (Gov.)
  xli, 923, 924
ROMODANOVSKY
Anastasia (Golitsyn),
  Princess 792
Andrei, Prince 792

Ekaterina, Princess 792
RØNNOW
  Margrethe 646
RONSTADT
  Linda 64
ROODENBURGH
  Lucretia 774
ROOKES
  Elizabeth 554
ROOS
  Hedvig Juliana, Countess 457
ROOSEVELT
  Alice Hathaway (Lee) xliii, 225, 283, 471
  Corinne 164
  Edith Kermit (Carow) xliii, 225, 283, 471
  Eleanor (Anna Eleanor) (Roosevelt) xxxv, xliii, 211, 356, 376, 394, 479, 524, 571, 716, 881, 921
  family xxxv, 591
  Franklin Delano, 32nd U.S. President xxxv, 49, 211, 356, 376, 394, 479, 524, 571, 716, 881, 921, 967
  Isaac 356, 376, 394, 524, 881, 921
  James 211, 356, 376, 394, 479, 524, 571, 716, 881, 921
  Lydia M. (Latrobe) viii, lvii, cxlvi, 590
  Maria Eliza (Walton) 881
  Martha (Bulloch) 225, 283, 471
  Mary Rebecca (Aspinwall) 356, 376, 394, 524, 881, 921
  Nicholas J. 590
  Sara (Delano) 211, 356, 376, 394, 479, 524, 571, 716, 881, 921
  Theodore 225, 283, 471
  Theodore, Jr., 26th U.S. President xliii, 164, 225, 283, 471, 858
ROOT
  Abigail 673
  Caroline (Pool) xiv
  Charles Mitchell xiv
  Elizabeth Robbins 673
  Ephraim Hough xiv
  Fannie Kate xiii, xiv
  Judah xiv
  Mary Lucy Wade (Peevey) xiv
  Sarah (Hough) xiv
ROPER
  Agnes 920, 922
  Alice (___) 922
  Alice (___) (Kemp) 922
  Anne 123
  Anne (Lennard), Baroness Dacre 109
  Beatrix (Lewknor) (Kemp) 920, 922
  Christopher, 5th Baron Teynham 109
  Edmund 920, 922
  Eliza 109
  Elizabeth (Browne) 109
  Elizabeth (Fish) 109
  Henry, 6th Baron Teynham 109
  Henry Richard 109
  John 922
  Margaret 607
  Mary (Tenison) 109
  Ralph 920, 922
  William 109
ROS (DE)
  Agnes 710, 719
  Alice 721, 725
  Eleanor 119, 526, 600
  Elizabeth 469, 596, 713, 727
  Eustache (FitzHugh) 700, 725
  George Manners, Baron 119, 121, 123, 126, 133
  Isabel 705, 723
  Isabel (d'Aubigny) 653, 705, 710, 713, 715, 719, 727, 728
  Laura (___) 708

Lucy 700, 730
Lucy (FitzPiers)
  700, 705, 710, 713,
  715, 719, 721, 725,
  727, 728, 730
Margaret 708
Margaret (de Brus)
  708
Margery (de
  Badlesmere) 713,
  715, 727, 728
Mary 653
Maud 462, 582,
  715, 728
Maud (Vaux) 710,
  713, 715, 719, 727,
  728
Philippa (Tiptoft)
  600
Robert 700, 705,
  708, 710, 713, 715,
  719, 721, 723, 725,
  727, 728, 730
Robert (Sir) 653,
  705, 710, 713, 715,
  719, 727, 728
Robert (Sir), of
  Wark 708, 723
Robert, of Wark 708
Thomas de Ros,
  Baron 600
William (Sir) 700,
  705, 710, 713, 715,
  719, 721, 725, 727,
  728, 730
William, 1st Baron
  Ros of Helmsley
  710, 713, 715, 719,
  727, 728

William, 2nd Baron
  Ros of Helmsley
  713, 715, 727, 728
ROSAMBO (DE)
Louis V le Peltier,
  Marquis 293
ROSCARROCK
Margaret 665
ROŚCISZEWSKI
Louise 793
ROSE
Alexander 261
Alexander, of Clava
  95
Anne (Cuming/
  Cumming) 261, 262
Anne (Fitzhugh) 261
Catharine (Brooke)
  261
Catherine (Thomas)
  983
Charles (Rev.) 261
Christine lx, lxv
Elizabeth 95
Étienne/Stephen 983
Eva Marie 983
family 262, 967
Hugh, of Kilvarock
  281
Janet (Urquhart), of
  Burdsymonds
  281
Jean 281
Jean (Innes) 95
Jean-Baptiste 983
John 261, 262
John, of Bellivat
  281

John, of Lochiehills
  261
Joseph 983
Margaret (Gordon)
  281
Margaret (Grant)
  261, 262
Marie-Louise
  (Mercereau) 983
Marjorie (Dunbar),
  of Conzie and
  Kilbuick 281
Mary (Burt) 983
Mary (Tarent) 261
Mary (Vaulx) 926
Nelly (Grant) 261
Robert (Rev.) lx,
  lxv, clxxi, 240, 261
Rose-Hermine 983
William, of
  Montcoffer 262
ROSEN (VON)
Anna 849
Gertrude 849
ROSENBERGER
Siga 37
ROSENKRANTZ
Folmer 644
Margrethe (Gylden-
  stierne) 644
Regitze 644
ROSENSPARRE
Brigitte 644
Jens 644
Maeritslef (Bille)
  644
ROSIERS (DES)
Anne (de Bonnet de
  la Chabanne) 440

Charles-Annet,
 Seigneur de
 Moncelet   440
François, Seigneur
 de Moncelet   440
Louise (de Saignes)
 440
ROSS
Alicia (Arnold)
 xxiv, liii, lxi, lxviii,
 clxvi, 333
Andrew, of Balbair
 828
Anne Arnold   333
Caroline Lee
 (Bouvier) (Canfield)
 (Radziwill) [Lee
 Radziwill]   xviii,
 xlv, 16, 74, 914
Catherine (Van
 Gezel)   828
Christian
 (Livingston?)   828
David, of Balbair
 828
David Lindsay,
 Bishop of   278
Donald, of
 Balmachy   828
Elizabeth   152, 163,
 166
Eupheme (__)   828
Euphemia   131
Euphemia of, Queen
 of Scotland   275,
 276, 278, 282, 285
family   1025
George (Rev.)   lvii,
 lxiv, clxv, 828

George, Jr.   828
George, of
 Balmachy   828
Gertrude   828
Grizel (McDonald)
 828
Herbert David   16,
 914
Hugh, of Balmachy
 828
Hugh, of Balnagown
 828
Hugh Ross, 4th Earl
 of   789, 828
Janet (Tulloch)   828
Jean   95
Jean (Comyn)   828
Jean (Douglas)   828
Joanna   789
Joanna (Williams)
 828
John   333
Katherine (Macleod)
 828
Katherine (McTyre)
 828
Margaret (de
 Barclay)   828
Margaret (Graham)
 789, 828
Margaret (Innes)
 828
Margaret
 (McCulloch)   828
Margaret (Stronach)
 828
Maud (Bruce)   789
Walter, of Balmachy
 828

Walter, of Balnagown
 828
Walter, of
 Shandwick   828
William, of
 Balnagown   828
William, of Little
 Allan   828
William Ross, 2nd
 Earl of   828
William Ross, 3rd
 Earl of   828
William Ross, 5th
 Earl of   789
ROSSE
Eleanor   825
ROSSEM (VAN)
Beatrix (van
 Haeften)   907
Joanna   447
Johan, Heer   907
Meralda   907
ROSSI (DI)
Flaminia   38
ROSSLYN
Robert Francis
 St. Clair-Erskine,
 4th Earl of   33
ROSTISLAV
Grand Duke of
 Russia   5, 793
Grand Duke of
 Russia [Rostislav
 Romanoff]   clvii,
 5, 793
ROSTOV
Anna of   791, 797
Boris, Prince of   797

1479

Constantine II,
  Prince of, Prince of
  Uglich 791, 797
Constantine III,
  Prince of 791, 797
Vassili, Prince of
  791, 797
Vassilko, Prince of
  791, 797
ROSWELL
  Roberta Brooke
  [Brooke Astor] 86
ROTH
  Mary 450
ROTHE
  Anne 308
**ROTHENBURG
(VON)**
  Karoline Adelheid
  Pauline 12
ROTHSCHILD (DE)
  Betty Caroline 65
  family xxxviii
ROTHWELL (DE)
  Joan 857, 861
ROTSY
  Mary 351
ROTTAL (VON)
  Johann Joseph von
  Rottal, Reichsgraf
  186
  Maria Antonia Cäcilia
  (Enkevoirth),
  Countess 186
  Maria Franziska
  Emanuela 186
ROUBANIS
  Sarah Consuelo
  (Spencer-Churchill)

(Russell) (Burgos)
  clvii, 27
  Theodorus 27
ROUCY (DE)
  Alice 866, 868,
  870, 872
  counts of 725
  Ebles I, Count 866,
  870, 872
  Hugh II, Count of,
  Count of Braine
  944
  Jean VI, Count of,
  Count of Braine
  944
  Jeanne, Countess of,
  Countess of Braine
  944
ROUELLÉ (DE)
  Jeanne 959
ROUKAVISHNIKOV
  Elena 618
**ROUMANIA/
RUMANIA**
  Ferdinand I, King of
  2
  Ileana, Princess of
  (Mother Abbess
  Alexandra) xviii,
  2, 6
  Marie of Edinburgh,
  Princess of Great
  Britain, Queen of
  2
  Michael I, King of,
  Prime Minister of
  288
  monarchs of 45, 81

ROUND
  John Horace xxiv,
  lxxi
ROUS
  Anne (Wood) 403
  Elizabeth (Knevet)
  403
  Elizabeth (Yelverton)
  403, 404
  Jane 400
  John (Sir) 403
  John (Sir), 1st Bt.
  403
  John (Sir), 2nd Bt.
  403
  John (Sir), 5th Bt.
  403
  Judith (Bedingfield)
  403
  Louisa Judith 403
  Lydia (Smith) 403
  Robert (Sir), 4th Bt.
  403
ROUSÉE
  Jeanne (de Vassy)
  959
  Perlette 959
  Raoul, Seigneur de
  La Nocherie 959
ROUSSEL (DE)
  Perrette 959
**ROUSSELET DE
CHÂTEAU-
RENAULT**
  Marie-Sophie 202
ROUSSILLON
  Louis de Bourbon,
  Count of 200, 205

1480

ROUSSILLON (DE)
  family 952
ROUX
  Carole 982
ROUX (LE)
  Anne 941
ROUXEL (DE)
  Angélique 616
ROVERE. *see*
  DELLA ROVERE
ROVÉRÉAZ (DE)
  Claudia Antonia
    872
  Guigues 872
ROVORÉE (DE)
  Guigues,
    co-Seigneur de
    Saint-Triphon and
    des Ormonts 872
  Guillauma (de
    Montvuagnard)
    872
  Isabelle (de
    Dompierre) 872
  Jean, co-Seigneur de
    Saint-Triphon and
    des Ormonts 872
  Jean, Seigneur de
    Bonneveaux 872
  Jean, Seigneur du
    Crest and La Roche
    d'Ollon 872
  Marguerite (de
    Greysier) 872
  Marie (de
    Confignon) 872
  Pierre, Seigneur des
    Granges (in Valais)
    872

ROW
  Catherine 276
  Elspeth (Gillespie)
    276
  Grizel (Ferguson)
    276
  John (Rev.) 276
  Lilias 276
  Margaret (Bethune)
    276
ROWAN
  Arabella 97, 405,
    406
  family 406
  George 405
  Mary (Blenner-
    hasset) 405
  Mary (Gorham)
    405
  Mary Anne 564
  William 405, 406
  ____ (Chute) 405
ROWLAND
  Dunbar (Mrs.) lxv
  Elizabeth (____) 831
ROWLAND alias
STEYNER
  Anne 541
ROWLEY
  Ethel (Newton) 335
ROWSON
  Constance 558
ROY
  Angélique 980
  Elizabeth (Brooke)
    137
  François-Nicolas 984
  Geneviève
    (Couture) 973

  Guillaume 973
  Harry 137
  Marie-Françoise 984
  Marie-Louise 973
  Marie-Madeleine
    (Leblond) 984
  Marie-Thérèse
    (Allard) 984
  Nicolas 984
  Thérèse 978
ROYALL
  Katherine (Banks)
    387, 710
ROYCE
  Elizabeth (Lathrop)
    xiv
  Esther xiv
  Hannah xiv
  Isaac xiv
  Joanna (Gaylord) xiv
  Robert xiv
ROYDON
  Elizabeth 358, 772
  Elizabeth (Wheten-
    hall) 358
  Margaret (Wheten-
    hall) 721
  Mary 721
  Thomas 358, 721
  Ursula 766
ROYDS
  Minna Mary Jessica
    383
ROYE (DE)
  family 951
ROYNON
  Joan 695
  Joan (Longland) 695
  John 695

ROYSTON
Ursula 706, 707
ROZER/ROZIER
Elizabeth
 (Whetenhall) lxii,
 cl, 905
Notley 905
RUBENS
Constance (Helman)
 804
Hélène 804
Hélène (Fourment)
 804
Isabelle (Brant) 804
Jan 804
Maria (Pijpelinckx)
 804
Nicolas, Seigneur of
 Rameyen 804
Peter Paul vi, vii,
 804, 805
RUBINCAM
Milton L. xxviii,
 lv, lvi, lxiv, lxv,
 lxvii, lxviii
RUBIROSA
Barbara Woolworth
 (Hutton) (Mdivani)
 (Haugwitz- Harden-
 berg-Reventlow)
 (Grant) (Troubetz-
 koy) xviii, 44, 46,
 63
Porfirio 44
RUCK
Hannah 479, 716
Hannah (Hutchinson)
 479, 716
John 479, 716

Sarah 484
RUDGERS
Daniel Wood lxvi
RUDHALL
Anne (Milborne)
 506, 647
Elizabeth 648
Frances 647
Isabella (Whittington)
 647
Jane 506
John 647, 648
Mary (Fettiplace)
 647
William 506, 647
RUDKIN
Alice 830
RUDOLF I
Holy Roman
 Emperor 449,
 451, 617
RUDOLF FRANZ KARL JOSEPH
Crown Prince of
 Austria 288
RUDOLF SYRINGUS PETER KARL FRANZ JOSEPH ROBERT OTTO ANTONIUS MARIA PIUS BENEDIKT IGNATIUS LAURENTINUS JUSTINIANI MARKUS D'DAVIANO
Archduke of Austria
 800

RUDOLPH
Arabella (Mason)
 480
Lucretia xlii, 480
Zebulon 480
RUDYARD
Alice (Boscawen)
 407
Anne (James) 407
Anne (Newton)
 407, 408
Anthony 407
family vii, xxiv, 408
Thomas 407
Thomas (Dep. Gov.)
 xlviii, lxvi, clxxiii,
 407, 408
RUE/RHUE
Eleanor (Tytler)
 159
family 160
William 159
RÜESCH
family ix, lxi
Hans 190
Maria Luisa (de la
 Feld), Countess
 190
Vivian lx, lxi, cxlv,
 clxx, 190
RUFFELL
Arthur W. 591
RUFFO
Anna Giuseppa
 (Cavaniglia) 189,
 192
Carlo, Prince of
 Sant'Antimo 189,
 192

Cecilia 189
Cobella, Countess of
  Montalto 205
Elizabeth 5, 824
Francesco, Duke of
  Bagnara, Prince of
  Motta San
  Giovanni 189
Ippolita (d'Avalos)
  189
**RUFFO DI
CALABRIA**
  Fulco Antonio
    Francesco
    Benjamino, 1st
    Prince 201
  Luisa Albertina
    Cristina Giovanni
    (Gazelli de
    Rossana) 201
  Paola Margherita
    Giuseppina
    Consiglia, Queen
    of the Belgians
    [Paola, Queen of
    the Belgians] xl,
    201, 204
RUGELEY
  Lettice (Knollys)
    302
  Mary 302, 303
  Rowland (Sir) 302
RÜGEN
  Euphemia of, Queen
    of Norway 452,
    457
RUGGE
  Frances 307
  Jane 611

RUÍZ DE ALEMANY
  Aldonza 140
RUMANIA. *see*
  ROUMANIA/
  RUMANIA
RUMBROUGH
  Nedenia (Hutton)
    [Dina Merrill] 44
RUNKEL (VON)
  George Hermann
    Reinhard, Count of
    Wied 142
RUPERT III
  of Wittelsbach, Holy
    Roman Emperor
    237, 291
RURIK
  Lord of Kiev 795
RUSE
  Lilian Augusta 462
RUSHTON/RISHTON
  Agnes 701
  Agnes (Sherburne)
    701, 703
  Henry 701
  Margaret (Radcliffe)
    701
  Nicholas 701
RUSPOLI
  Aileen (Getty)
    (Wilding) 21
  Alessandro "Dado,"
    Prince of Cerveteri
    21
  Barbara (Mossimo)
    21
  Bartolomeo liii,
    clvii, 21

Claudia (Matarazzo)
  21
Egle (Franchese) 21
Francesco Maria,
  Prince of Cerveteri
  21
Francesco Maria
  Quinto, Prince of
  Cerveteri 21
Giovanni, Prince of
  Cerveteri 21
Maria 49
Marianita
  (Montefeltro della
  Rovere) 21
Olivia Jane
  (Cockburn) [Olivia
  Wilde] xi, xviii,
  xlv, xlvi, xlviii,
  cliii, 21, 94
Tao liii, clvii, 21,
  94
RÜSSEGG (VON)
  Anfelisa (von
    Arburg) 832
  Apollonia 832
  Barbara (von
    Wineck), Baroness
    832
  Henman (Hans) II
    832
  Jakob, Baron zu
    Roggenbach 832
RUSSELL
  Anna (Trowbridge)
    870
  Anne 109
  Archibald lxvi,
    165, 211

Archibald Douglas 165
Bertrand Arthur William, 3rd Earl xxiv, 22, 25
Caroline 62, 299
Catherine 119
Charles James Fox, Lord 27
Constance Charlotte Elisa (Lennox) 31
Constance Rivington 165
Cynthia (Cary) (Van Pelt) 27
Donna Valley x
Edwin Fairman 27
Eleanor (de Gorges) 835
Eleanor (Oliver) 165
Elizabeth 121, 130
Elizabeth (Keppel) 25
Ellis 925
Ethelberta Pyne 165 family 298
Frances Anna Maria (Elliot) 22
Francis, Marquess of Tavistock 25
George, Sir, 4th Bt. 31
George Ely x, lvi, lxii, lxvi
Georgiana (Gordon) 25, 28
Georgiana Elizabeth (Byng) 25

Gertrude (Leveson-Gower) 25, 62, 75
Hannah (___) 151
Helen Rutherford (Watts) 165, 211
Henry Charles 27
Isabella Clara (Davies) 27
James 165, 166
Jane 245
Jane Catherine (Wolcott) 925
John 870
John, 1st Earl Russell, Prime Minister 22, 25
John, 4th Duke of Bedford 25, 62, 75
John, 6th Duke of Bedford 25, 28
John, Viscount Amberley 22
Katherine Louisa (Stanley) 22
Lelia Louisa Millicent (Willoughby) 27
Louisa Jane 25, 27, 28
Marie Clotilde 31
Mary 90, 925
Nancy 925, 927
Nancy (Newton) 925
Olive Isobel 27
Oliver 925
Rachel 71, 75
Rebecca 871

Robertina Rivington (Pyne) 165
Sarah (Trowbridge) 870
Sarah Consuelo (Spencer-Churchill) clvii, 27
Theobald (Sir) 835
William 927

RUSSIA
Alexander, Grand Duke of 5
Alexander II, Czar of 2, 5, 799
Alexander III, Czar of 5
Alexei, Grand Duke of 5
Anastasia (Romanov), Czarina of 14, 792
Andrew, Grand Duke of clvii, 5
Andrew, Grand Duke of [Andrew Romanoff] 5
Catherine II "the Great" [Sophie, Princess of Anhalt-Zerbst], Empress of 14, 615, 792
Charlotte Louise, Princess of Prussia, Empress of 5, 7
Constantine, Grand Duke of 7
czars of xv, 615
Dimitri, Grand Duke of 3

1484

George, Grand Duke of 4
Helen, Grand Duchess of 3
Ivan I, Czar of xxii
Ivan III, "first" Czar of 797
Ivan IV "the Terrible," Czar of 792
Ivan VI, Czar of 615
Maria, Grand Duchess of 7
Maria Feodorovna (Marie Sophie Frederikke Dagmar), Princess of Denmark, Empress of 5
Marie, Grand Duchess of 2
Marie of Hesse, Empress of 2, 3, 5
Michael, Grand Duke of 5
Michael III, Czar of 792
monarchs of 45
Nicholas I, Czar of 5, 7
Nicholas II, Czar of 5, 453
Nikita, Grand Duke of 5
Nikita, Grand Duke of [Nikita Romanoff] cliii, 5
Nina, Grand Duchess of 4
Olga, Grand Duchess of, Queen of Greece 3
Paul, Czar of 792
Paul, Grand Duke of 3
Peter I "the Great," Czar of 792
Peter III, Czar of 14, 615, 796
Rostislav, Grand Duke of 5, 793
Rostislav, Grand Duke of [Rostislav Romanoff] clvii, 5, 793
Tatiana, Grand Duchess of 7
Xenia, Grand Duchess of 5

RUTGERS
Helena 211

RUTHER
Anne 548

RUTHERFORD
Anna Clay (Zimmerman) lxiii, lxvi
Anne 165
Barbara 210, 211
Barbara (Abernethy) 210
Catherine 241
Catherine (Alexander) 165, 211
Eleanor (Elliot) 165, 211
Elizabeth (Cairncross) 211
family xxxiv
Jane 165
Jean (Eliot) 210
John 165
John (Sir), of Edgerston 211
John, of Edgerston 210
John, of Edgerston and N.Y. 165, 211
Magdalen (Morris) 165
Marion (Riddell) 210
Robert, of Edgerston 210
Sarah 854, 870
Susanna (Riddell) 211
Thomas, of Edgerston 210, 211
Walter lxvi, clxiv, 165, 211
William Kenneth lxiii, lxvi

RUTHVEN
Barbara 99
Dorothea (Stewart) 151, 170
Janet 88
Lilias 151, 170, 258
Margaret 151, 161, 170
William, 1st Earl of Gowrie 151, 170

RUTLAND
John Manners, 1st Duke of 119, 120

1485

John Manners, 2nd
 Duke of 119
John Manners, 3rd
 Duke of 119
John Manners, 8th
 Earl of 119
Thomas Manners,
 1st Earl of 119
**RUVIGNY and
RAINEVAL**
 Marquis of xxi,
  xxix, lxvi
RUYSCH
 Paschina 733
RUYVEN (VAN)
 Jacomina Jacob
  Claesdr. 774
RYAN
 Mary Lee 74
 Nancy 49
 Thelma Catherine
  "Pat" 764
RYCE
 Mary 493
RYDER
 Helen Jane 458
RYE
 Walter 762
RYLAND
 Elizabeth 387
RYLEY
 Anne 841
RYMER
 Elizabeth (Gerard)
  (Blakiston) 317
 Ralph 317
RYTHE
 Elizabeth 625

RYTHER
 Eleanor 328
RYTTER
 Catherina (Hand)
  53, 889
 Johan 889
 Johann 53
 Sofia 889
 Virginia 53
RYVES
 Alice 364
 Anne (Maude) 364
 Jerome (Rev.). Dean
  of St. Patrick's 364
SAARWERDEN
 Frederick IV, Count
  of Mörs and 459
 Walpurga of Mörs
  and 459
SAATENES
 Axel Posse, Lord of,
  Lord of Tun 452
SABINA
 of Simmern 291
SABINE
 Diana Amelia 136
 Joseph 136
 Sarah (Hunt) 136
SACAZE (DE)
 Marie 963
SACHEVERELL
 Millicent 377
SACKETT
 Daniel 673
 Daniel, Jr. 673
 Mary (Weller) 673
 Mehitable 673
 Mehitable (Cadwell)
  673

SACKVILLE
 Christopher 551,
  552
 Constance (Cole-
  pepper/Culpeper)
  551
 Isabel 429
 Jane 109, 905
 Joan (Downton)
  551
 John 429, 551, 552
 Margaret (Boleyn)
  429, 551
 Mary 405, 551, 552
SACKVILLE-WEST
 Victoria Mary
  "Vita" (Hon.) 299
SADE (DE)
 Charlotte-Germaine
  (de Maussion) 227
 Donatien-Alphonso-
  François de Sade,
  Count [the Marquis
  de Sade] 227
 Donatien-Claude-
  Armand de Sade,
  Count 227
 Jean-Baptiste-
  François- Joseph
  de Sade, Count
  227
 Laure-Marie-
  Charlotte 228
 Louise-Gabrielle-
  Laure (de Sade)
  227
 Marie-Antoine-
  Auguste de Sade,
  Count 227

Marie-Eléonore (de
  Maillé) 227
Renée-Pélagie
  (Cordier de Launay
  de Montreuil) 227
SADINGTON
  Isabel 830
SADLER
  Mary 625
SAEBY
  Ulv Jonson, Lord of
  Ervalla, Faanoe,
  Vreta, Huseby and
  452, 457
SAGE
  Kay Linn xviii,
  cliii, 20
SAIGNES (DE)
  Jean-Baptiste,
  Seigneur de
  Grizols 440
  Louise 440
  Louise (de Laizer)
  440
SAILLANS (DE)
  Charles-François
  d'Estaing, Marquis
  202
  Gaspard d'Estaing,
  Baron 202
  Jean d'Estaing,
  Baron 202
SAINT-ALLAIS (DE)
  Nicolas Viton
  xxvii
SAINT-ANDRÉE-DE-BRIOR (DE)
  Guy de Grolée,
  Seigneur 911

SAINT-AUBIN (DE)
  Patri/Patry (II) de
  Chourses, Seigneur
  948, 949
SAINT-CASTIN (DE)
  Jean-Jacques
  l'Abbadie, Baron
  963
  Jean-Vincent
  l'Abbadie, Baron
  961, 963, 990
SAINT-DIDIER (DE)
  Gilles de Sévigné,
  Sieur 943
SAINT-ESTÈVE (DE)
  Balthazard de
  Baschi, Seigneur
  735
  Louis de Baschi,
  Seigneur 735
  Thadée de Baschi,
  Seigneur 735
**SAINT-ÉTIENNE
  DE LA TOUR (DE).**
  see also TURGIS DE
  SAINT-ÉTIENNE
  Anne (Melanson)
  953
  Jacques 953
  Marie-Agathe 953
**SAINT-GERMAIN
  (DE)**
  François, Sieur du
  Post 959
  Françoise (de Breul)
  959
  Hélène (de Corday)
  959
  Jean 959

Jeanne (de La
  Poterie) 959
Jeanne (de Rouellé)
  959
Olivier, Sieur du
  Post 959
Stévenotte 959
**SAINT-GERMAIN-
  LE-DÉSIRÉE**
  Jacques de Prunelé,
  Baron 948
SAINT-GILLES (DE)
  Bonaventure,
  Seigneur 961
  Catherine-Bonne
  962
  Françoise (Bouhier)
  961
  Guillaume, Seigneur
  961
  Jacqueline (de
  Montaigu) 961
  Jacques, Seigneur
  961
  Jean, Seigneur 961
  Jeanne (de
  Betheville) 961
  Joachine (de Thère)
  961
  Marguerite (de
  Pierrepont) 961
SAINT-JUST (DE)
  Hector de Salazar,
  Baron 953
  Jean de Salazar(t),
  Seigneur, Seigneur
  of Marcilly and
  Montagu 953

SAINT-MICHEL DES DÉSERTS (DE)
Pierre Bonivard, Seigneur 911
SAINT-NECTAIRE (DE)
Nectaire Senneterre, Seigneur 634
SAINT-OURS (DE)
Henri 965
Jeanne (de Calignon) 965
Marguerite (Legardeur de Tilly) (Legouès) 962, 964, 965
Marie (Mullois) 965
Pierre de Saint-Ours, Seigneur, Seigneur de Deschaillons 962, 965
SAINT-PAUL (DE)
Josette 939, 960
SAINT-PAUL- LE-GAUTIER (DE)
Christophe de Mésenge (Mazange), Seigneur 948
SAINT-PIERRE
Hannah (England) 970
Julie 970
Michel 970
SAINT-PIERRE dit DESSAINT
Brigitte-Josèphe (Ouellet) 970

Marie-Josèphe 970
Michel 970
SAINT-QUENTIN (DE)
Ennemond de Beaumont, Seigneur 965
Roland de Beaumont, Seigneur 965
SAINT-SEVERIN (DE)
Jeanne 455
SAINT-TRIPHON (DE)
Guigues de Rovorée, Seigneur, Seigneur des Ormonts 872
Jean de Rovorée, Seigneur, Seigneur des Ormonts 872
SAINTE-MAURE (DE)
Charlotte 942
SAINTE-MAURE MONTGAUGIER (DE)
Marguerite (d'Amboise) 942
Pierre II, Vicomte de Bridiers 942
SAINTE-MAURE NEVELE (DE)
Jean, Count of Benaon 942
Jeanne (des Roches) 942

SAINTE-MELAINE (DE)
Susanne 226
SALAZAR(T) (DE)
Antoinette (de Courselles) 953
family 953
Hector 953
Hector, Baron de Saint-Just 953
Hélène (de Chastellux) 953
Jean, Seigneur de Saint-Just, Marcilly and Montagu 953
Marie 953
Marie (de La Trémouille) 953
SALES DE PORTOCARRERO DE GUZMÁN (DE)
María Francisca, Countess of Montijo 292
SALINGER
Claire Alison (Douglas) 166
Jerome David (J. D.) xviii, 166
SALINS (DE)
Anne (de Chantepinot) 952
Antoinette (de Seyturier) 952
Claude, Seigneur Charmée and Vincelles 952

Claude de Salins,
Seigneur Vincelles 952
Marie 952
SALIS-ZIZERS (VON)
Julie 895
SALISBURY
Ela, Countess of 687, 737, 742, 746, 749, 752, 754, 757, 760, 761, 763, 766, 768, 770, 772, 841, 856
Elizabeth 772
Elizabeth Parker Clark 334
Gilbert Burnet, Bishop of 273
John Montagu, 1st Earl of 565
Margaret Plantagenet, Countess of 107, 114, 716
Mary 368, 403
Patrick, Earl of 737, 841, 855
Richard Neville, 1st Earl of 324, 339, 345, 368, 370, 397, 419, 426, 433, 434, 902
Richard Neville, "the Kingmaker," Earl of Warwick and 118, 419
Robert Arthur Talbot Gascoyne- Cecil, 3rd Marquess of, Prime Minister xxxviii

Robert Cecil, 1st Earl of, Lord Treasurer 315, 336
William Cecil, 2nd Earl of 334, 336
William FitzPatrick, Earl of 737
William Longespee, 1st Earl of vii, 658, 687, 737, 741, 742, 746, 749, 752, 754, 757, 760, 761, 763, 766, 768, 770, 772, 841, 845
SALKELD
Isabella 909
SALLMARD (DE)
Bertrand, Seigneur de Ressiz and de la Fay 638
Charlotte (de Sarron) 638
Claude (de Virieux) 638
Claude I, Seigneur de Ressiz and de la Fay 638
Claude II, Seigneur de Ressiz and de la Fay 638
Eléonore (de Guillens) 638
Françoise (de Guillet) 638
Geoffrey I, Seigneur de Ressiz, de la Fay, and Montfort 638

Geoffrey II, Seigneur de Ressiz and de la Fay 638
Isabeau (de Vangelet) 638
Jean, Seigneur de Montfort 638
Jeanne-Catherine (de Bourbon) 638
Just-Madeleine (de Grammont) 638
Louis, Seigneur de Montfort 638
Madeleine (de Foudras) 638
Marguerite (de Tenay) 638
Marie-Anne (de Chabrières) 638
Marie-Jeanne-Françoise (de Ponchon) 638
Pauline 639
Philippe-Guillaume, Seigneur de Ressiz, Montfort, and Roche- Pingolet 638
Raymond I, Seigneur de Ressiz, Montfort, and Roche- Pingolet 638
Raymond II, Vicomte de Ressiz 638
SALM-NEUFVILLE
Charles Theodore, Prince of 38

Christina of 38
Dorothea Francisca
  of 38
Louis Otto, Prince
  of 38
SALM-SALM
  Agnes Elizabeth
    Winona Leclerq
    (Joy), Princess of
    xlv, 30, 38
  Constantin, Prince
    of 38
  Eleanore Wilhelmine
    Louise of 38
  Felix Constantin
    Alexander Johann
    Nepomuk, Prince
    of xlv, 30, 38
  Florentin, Prince of
    38
  Maximilian Friedrich,
    Prince of, Duke of
    Hoogstraeten 38
  Nicholas Leopold,
    Prince of 38
SALTER
  Anne 543
  Anne (Brooke) 543
  Catherine 235
  Jane 323, 592
  Nicholas (Sir) 543,
    544
SALTONSTALL
  Elizabeth 837
  family xxiv, 374
  Grace 374
  Grace (Kaye) 374,
    837
  Henry 374

Judith 837
Muriel (Gurdon)
  xlvi, lxii, lxxi, clxi,
  291, 353, 374
Nathaniel (Dr.)
  374, 838
Richard lxiii, clxi,
  291, 353, 374
Richard (Sir) lxvii,
  374, 837
Robert 374
Rosamond 374
Samuel 374
Susanna (Poyntz)
  837
SALTOUN of
ABERNETHY
  Alexander
    Abernethy, 4th
    Baron 273
  James Abernethy,
    3rd Baron 273
  Laurence Abernethy,
    1st Baron 273
SALTYKOV
  Alexandra 795
  Maria (Golitsyn),
    Princess 792
  Sergei, Count 792,
    796
  Vassili, Count 792
SALUSBURY
  Jane 235
SALUZZO
  Alasia of 642
  Manfred III,
    Marquess of 642
  Thomas, Marquess
    of 642

SALVAIN
  Margery 901
SALVATIERRA
  senhores of 190
SALVAYN
  Agnes (Mauleverer)
    708
  Alice (___) 708
  Gerard (Sir) 708
  John 708
  Margaret (de Ros)
    708
  Muriel 708
SALVIATI
  Francesca 24
  Scipione Borghese,
    Prince, Duca 24
SALVIN
  Mary (Talbot) 125
SALVO (DE)
  Frances Bruster 98
SALWAY
  Alice 233
  Anne (Vaughan)
    233
  Richard 233
SAMPAS
  Stella 971
SAMPSON
  Elizabeth (Say)
    705
  George clxxxiv
  Katherine clxxxiv
  Margery 705
  Thomas 705
SAMWELL
  Amy (Giffard) 857
  Richard 857
  Susanna 858

SAN FAUSTINO
Carlo Bourbon del
 Monte Santa Maria,
 Prince of 20
Ranieri Bourbon del
 Monte Santa Maria,
 Prince of cliii, 20
SAN GIOVANNI
Carlo Onero
 Cavaniglia, Duke
 of 192
SAN MARCO
Troiano Cavaniglia,
 Marquess of 192
SAN MARTÍN (DE)
Francisca Javiera
 996
Juan 996
María Rosa (de
 Avellaneda) 996
SANCERRE (DE)
Comtesse 954
Eleanor (de Nesle)
 954
Étienne II, Seigneur
 de Châtillon-
 sur-Loing 954
SANCHA
Princess of Navarre
 993
Princess of
 Provence 653,
 661, 965
SANDDE
ab Elidir 886
SANDELIN
Anna 774
SANDEMAN
Sibella 150

SANDERS
Amyas 358
Anna 358
Anna (Whetenhall)
 358
Anne (Prendreth)
 358
Charles Richard
 xxix, lxvi
Doris May 344
Edward 358
Frederick George
 344
Gertrude May
 (Merrill) 344
Henry Nevill (Prof.)
 308
John 358
Lilian May
 (Caulfield) clvii,
 308
____ (Austen) 358
**SANDERSLEBEN
(DE)**
Anna Elizabeth,
 Countess of
 Coligny 184
SANDES
Elizabeth 434
SANDFORD
Grace 322
Mildred 611
SANDILANDS
Margaret 171
SANDMIRE
David A. (Dr.) ix,
 xlvi, xlviii, lxvi,
 lxvii, 707

SANDOMIR
Casimir II, Prince
 of, Prince of
 Krakow, Kujamien
 and Mazovia 791,
 797, 802
**SÁNDOVAL Y DE
LA CERDA**
Juana 140
**SÁNDOVAL Y
ROJAS (DE)**
Juana 140
**SANDRECZKY VON
SANDRASCHÜTZ**
Eleanor Charlotte
 (von Heugel und
 Pollogwitz) 619
Friederike
 Konstantine
 Henriette,
 Countess 619
Hans Ferdinand,
 Count 619
Hans Friedrich,
 Baron 619
Juliane Elisabeth
 (von Haugwitz)
 619
SANDRET (DE)
Marguerite 946
SANDYS
Anne 509
Cecily (Wilsford)
 509, 783
Edwin (Sir) 396
Edwin, Archbishop
 of York 509, 783
George clxxvii,
 779, 783

Katherine (Bulkeley)
396
Margaret clxxvii,
314, 779, 783
Mercy (Colepepper/
Culpeper) 396, 783
Penelope 396
Samuel (Sir) 396,
783
SANFORD
Anne 480
Bridget (Hutchinson)
480
Dorothy 321
Helen Jefferson ix,
lxvi, 364, 434
John (Act. Gov.) 480
Mary 522
Mary (Coddington)
480
Peleg (Gov.) 480
SANFORD (DE)
Alice 680
SANGRO
dukes of 190
SANGRO (DI)
Maria Margherita
190
SANT'ANTIMO
Carlo Ruffo, Prince
of 189, 192
SANTVOORT
Mary 881
SAPCOTT(S)
Elizabeth 368
Winifred 471
SAPIEHA
Katherine Anne,
Princess 621

Pelagia, Princess 16
princes or counts
155
SARAWAK
Charles Vyner
Brooke (Sir), H.H.
Rajah of 137
Sylvia Leonora
(Brett) Brooke
(Hon.), H.H. Ranee
of 137
SARDINIA
Adelaide,
Archduchess of
Austria, Queen of,
Queen of Italy
614
Anne-Marie, Princess
of Orléans, Queen of
18
Charles Albert, King
of 18, 614
Maria Cristina,
Princess of, Queen
of the Two Sicilies
6
Maria Teresa of
Tuscany, Arch-
duchess of Austria,
Queen of 614
monarchs of 615
Victor Amadeus II,
King of 18
Victor Emanuel II,
King of, King of
Italy 18, 614
SARG
Anthony Frederick
"Tony" clvii, 116

Bertha Eleanor
(McGowan) 116
Francis Charles
Anthony 116
Johann Philip Anton
116
Mary Elizabeth
(Parker) 116
Mary Ellen (Best)
116
SARGEANT
Emma 290
SARGENT
Ellen (Makerness)
857
Hannah (___) 857
Hugh 857
John 983
Lydia (Chipman)
983
Margaret (Giffard)
857
Mary (___) 857
Mary (Lewis) 983
Roger 857
Sarah (___)
(Minshall) 857,
983
William 983
William (Rev.) lxi,
clxi, clxxviii, 857,
968, 983
Zathiah 983
SARRAZ (DE LA)
Barthélemy de
Grandson,
Seigneur, Seigneur
de Belmont 872

SARRAZIN
  Alphonse 987
  Bernard-Alphonse 987
  Joseph 987
  Laby (Logan) 987
  Léocadie (Marineau dite Hostin) 987
  Michael [Jacques-Michel-André] 968, 987, 988

SARREBRUCHE (DE)
  Aimé, Seigneur de Commercy 944
  Jeanne 944
  Robert, Seigneur de Commercy 944

SARRON (DE)
  Charlotte 638

SARSGAARD
  John Peter 663
  Maggie Ruth (Gyllenhaal) 663

SASSENAGE (DE)
  Marguerite 200, 205

SASSOON
  Betty Caroline (de Rothschild) 65
  Betty Cecile 65
  Richard (Sir), 2nd Bt. 65

SATZGER DE BÁLVÁNYOS
  Christa 6

SAUNDERS
  Anne 429
  Clement 758

  Dorothy (Belgrave) 757
  Elizabeth 144
  Honora 409
  Isabel (Carew) 420
  Margery 476
  Mary 420, 757
  Miriam 567
  Nicholas 420
  William 757

SAURIN
  Elizabeth (Lyster) 120
  Emily 120
  James, Bishop of Dromore 120

SAUVAGE de BRANTES
  Anne-Aymone 185

SAVAGE
  Alice 532
  Anne 336
  Anne (Bostock) 336, 396
  Anne (Lygon) 532
  Anne (Sheldon) 532
  Anne (Stanley) 532
  Anthony xi, xix, xxiv, li, lxviii, clxvii, clxxix, clxxxviii, 532, 1025
  Bridget 533
  Catherine 561
  Catherine (Stanley) 396, 407, 497, 532, 558, 560

  Christopher 532
  Dorothy (Vernon) 396
  Dulcia/Dulce 497, 498, 902
  Eleanor/Elizabeth (Brereton) 497, 752, 753
  Elizabeth (Hall) 532
  Elizabeth (Manners) 122, 123
  Elizabeth (Somerset) 396
  Ellen 558
  family lx, 533
  Francis 532, 533
  John (Sir) 122, 336, 396, 407, 497, 499, 532, 558, 560, 687, 752, 753
  Margaret 122, 396, 407, 558, 560, 561, 687, 746, 752, 753
  Mary 497, 653
  Maud (Swinnerton) 497, 687, 752
  Ralph 532
  Sarah 376
  Sarah (Constable) 532
  Walter 532

SAVARY (DE)
  counts 949

SAVILLE/SAVIL/SAVILE/SAVILL
  Agnes 343
  Bridget 781
  Mary 719

SAVOIE (DE)
  Honorat II, Count of Villars-en-Bresse 442
SAVONNIÈRES (DE)
  Henri I du Plessis, Seigneur 442
SAVOY
  Adela of, Queen of France 804, 954, 956, 965
  Amadeus I of, Prince of Carignan 18
  Amadeus IV, Count of, ruler of Milan 642
  Amadeus VIII, Duke of 442
  Beatrix, Princess of, Queen of Sicily 642
  Beatrix of, Queen of Sicily 642, 965
  Cecilia (de Baux) 642
  Charles-Emanuel I, Duke of 18
  Charles-Emanuel of, Prince of Carignan 613
  Charlotte, Princess of, Queen of France 200, 205
  counts of 186
  Elizabeth, Princess of 614
  Emanuel-Philibert of, Prince of Carignan 18
  Eugène, Prince of 289
  Louis I, Duke of 442
  Louis I of, Baron de Vaud 965
  Louis-Victor of, Prince of Carignan 18
  Madeleine of 637
  Margaret (of Burgundy) (wife of Amadeus IV, Count of) 642
  Philip I, Duke of 442
  René of, Count de Villars-en-Bresse 442
  Thomas II, Count of 965
  Thomas of, Prince of Carignan 18
  Victor Amadeus I of, Prince of Carignan 18
  Victor Amadeus II of, Prince of Carignan 613
  Victoria Francesca of, Madamigella di Susa 18
SAVOY-CARIGNAN
  Gabriella, Princess of 18
  Leopolda, Princess of 18
SAVOY-PIEMONT
  Jeanne of 952
  Philip of, Prince of Achaya 952
  Thomas III, Count of 952
SAVOY-VAUD
  Beatrix of 965
  Bonne of 640
SAWLE
  Elizabeth 665
SAWYER
  Susan Anne 34
SAXBY
  Mary 467
SAXE-ALTENBURG
  Alexandra of 7
  Elizabeth of 7
SAXE-COBURG-GOTHA
  Albert, Prince of, Prince Consort of Great Britain 2, 45, 290
  Ernest I, Duke of 45
  Victoire-Françoise-Antoinette-Julienne- Louise of 290
SAXE-COBURG-SAALFELD
  Ernest Frederick II, Duke of 44
  Francis, Duke of 45, 46, 182
  Sophie Frederica, Princess of 45
  Victoria, Princess of, Duchess of Kent 45
SAXE-EISENACH
  Caroline Christine, Princess of 43

John William, Duke
of 43
SAXE-GOTHA
Anna Sophia of
891, 892
Augusta, Princess
of, Princess of
Wales 12, 27
Frederick II, Duke
of 891
Louise Dorothea,
Princess of 45
**SAXE-HILDEBURG-
HAUSEN**
Charlotte, Princess
of 12
SAXE-LAUENBURG
Dorothea, Princess of,
Queen of Denmark
52, 58, 60, 432, 889,
891, 893
John V, Duke of 52
Katherine, Princess of,
Queen of Sweden
51, 52, 53, 889
Magnus II, Duke of
52
SAXE-MEININGEN
Adelaide, Princess
of, Queen of Great
Britain 9
Amelia Augusta,
Princess of 43
Anthony Ulrich,
Duke of 43, 46
**SAXE-
WEISSENFELS**
Augustus, Duke of
891

Magdalen Sybil of
891
SAXONY
Anna of 449
Augustus, Elector of
891
Christian I, Elector
of 891
Christine, Princess
of, Queen of
Denmark 181,
182, 184
Ernest, Elector of
451
Francis Xavier,
Prince of 20
Frederick Augustus
II, Elector of, King
of Poland 20
Frederick I, Elector
of 52, 449, 451
Frederick II, Elector
of 451
Ida of 874, 877
John George I,
Elector of 47, 891
Katherine, Princess
of 52
Magnus, Duke of
832
Margaret, Princess
of 220, 451, 454
Margaret, Princess
of, Queen of
Denmark 141
Maria Christina
Sabina, Princess
of, Countess von
der Lausitz 20

Maria Josepha,
Archduchess of
Austria, Electress of,
Queen of Poland 20
Marie, Princess of
613
Marie Elizabeth,
Princess of 47
Matilda of 849
monarchs of 45
William, Duke of,
Landgrave of
Thuringia 220
Wulfhilde of 832
SAY(E) (DE)
Anne 305, 309,
349, 385, 705
Elizabeth 705
Elizabeth (Cheney)
(Tilney) 309, 705
Emma (____) 853
family 854
Geoffrey, 2nd Baron
Say 783
Idonea 687
Isabel (____) 853
Joan 783
John (Sir) 309, 705
Mary 596
Maud (de
Beauchamp) 783
Robert 853
Sybil 853
Sybil (____) 853
Thomas (Sir) 853
William (Sir) 853
SAYE AND SELE
James Fiennes, 1st
Baron 783

1495

SAYN-WITTGENSTEIN
Amelia of 194
Peter (Ludwig Adolf Peter), Prince of, Marshal of Russia 194

SAYN-WITTGENSTEIN-BERLEBURG
Christian Ludwig Casimir, Count of 194
Ludwig Franz, Count of 194, 195

SAYN-WITTGENSTEIN-HOMBURG
Anna Amelia of 194

SCALA. see **DELLA SCALA**

SCALES
Egeline (de Courtenay) 713
Elizabeth 713
Katherine (de Ufford) 713
Margery 661
Robert Scales, 2nd Baron 713
Robert Scales, 3rd Baron 713

SCARBROUGH
Richard Lumley, 1st Earl of 105

SCARFE
Gerald 64
Jane (Asher) 64

SCHADE VAN WESTRUM
Josina 907

SCHADEE
Mathilda Petronella Hermanna 734

SCHAFER
Edwin George 567
Ella Frances (Miles) 567

SCHAUMBURG (VON)
Augusta Maria Gertrude, Princess von Hanau und zu Horowitz, Countess 13
Gertrude (Falkenstein), Princess von Hanau und zu Horowitz, Countess 13

SCHEIBLER
Anna dei Conti 24

SCHENK VON LIMPURG
Elizabeth (of Hohenlohe-Speckfeld) 617
Frederick III 617
Frederick IV 617

SCHENK VON LIMPURG-GAILDORF
Albert II 617
Conrad IV 617
Elisabeth (of Oettingen) 617

Ottilia [Schenk(in)] 617

SCHENKENBERG VAN MIEROP
Jannetje Gijsbertje Pijnacker (Hordijk) 907
Johan Hendrik Daniel 907
Johanna Elisabeth (Beelaerts) 907
Johanna Louisa (Thies) 908
Lodewijk Hendrik 907, 908
Marcus Ivan 448
Marcus Lodewijk [Marcus Schenkenberg] xii, lviii, lxix, clvii, 448, 908
Marianne Yvonne (Wientjes) 908
Marie Constance (Legrand) 908
Robert Lodewijk 908

SCHERER
John L. ix, lxii, lxvi, 96, 218, 589

SCHERMERHORN
Caroline Webster 44, 799

SCHERPENBERG (VAN)
Anna 460

SCHERTEL VON BURTENBACH
Anna Maria 640

1496

SCHIEFFELIN
  Elizabeth Wellborn lxvi
SCHILLING VON CANSTATT
  Karl Wilhelm Friedrich, Baron 57
  Lilli (Kann) 57
  Susanna, Baroness cliv, 57
  Victor Georg Wilhelm Friedrich Ödön Arpad, Baron 57
SCHIMMELPEN-NINCK VAN DER OYE
  Anna Elisabeth 445
SCHIRP (VON). see BOTTLENBERG (VAN) genaamd VON SCHIRP
SCHLENLEY
  Elizabeth Pole 135
SCHLESINGER
  Alexandra Temple (Emmet) 406
  Arthur Meier, Jr. 406
SCHLESWIG-HOLSTEIN
  Leonora Christina, Countess of 35
  Sofie Elisabeth, Countess of 37
SCHLESWIG-HOLSTEIN-SONDERBURG
  Margaret of 889

SCHLIEBEN (VON)
  Albert Frederick 640
  Euphrosine (Truchsess von Waldburg) 640
  Hedwig 640
SCHLIESEN-BEUTHEN
  Wratislaw, Duke of, Duke of Kosul 640
SCHLIESEN-LIEGNITZ
  Bolko I of, Duke of Schweidnitz 640
  Bolko II of, Duke of Fürstenburg and Münsterburg 640
SCHLIESEN-MÜNSTERBERG
  Bolko III of 640
  Euphemia of 640
  Nicholas IV of, Duke of Münsterburg 640
SCHLOSSBERG
  Caroline Bouvier (Kennedy) 915
  Edwin Arthur 915
SCHMETTAU (VON)
  Adelaide Amalia, Countess 798
SCHMON
  Teri 18
SCHNEIDER
  Gabrielle 44
SCHOENWALD
  Janet Anne 5

SCHÖNBERG (VON)
  Wilhelmine Maximiliane Luise Marina 182
SCHÖNBURG-HARTENSTEIN
  George Albert, Count of 142
  Joanna Sophie Elizabeth of 142
  Otto Louis, Count of 142
SCHÖNBURG-LICHTENSTEIN
  Catherine Elizabeth of 196
SCHÖNBURG-WECHSELBURG
  Charles Henry, Count of 142
  Christiane Henriette Antonie of 141, 142
  Francis Henry, Count of 142
SCHRATTENBACH (VON)
  Eleonora (Kolowrat-Liebsteinsky) 895
  Franz Ferdinand 895
  Maria Johanna Josefa Franziska Klara Serafina 895
  Marie Elisabeth 198
SCHREIBER
  family 132
  Heather (Milgram) 129

Liev (Isaac Liev) 129
Naomi (Watts) 129
Pamela Dutton (Prime) 129
Tell Carroll 129
Tell Carroll, Jr. 129
SCHREIBER (VON)
Adelaide (Frohne) 37
Anna Charlotte Elisabeth (Beinroth) 37
Emanuel Sigismund 37
George Adolf Carl 37
Luise (Studemund) 37
Sigismund 37
SCHRÖFL VON MANNSPERG
Marie Josephine, Baroness 895
SCHULENBERG (VON DER)
Marie Ernestine 127
SCHULTZE
Charlotte Amalia 440
SCHUMAN
Margaret 96
SCHUTZ
John A. (Prof.) 476
SCHUYLER
Alida 243
Elizabeth 214
Margareta 244
Mary (Walter) 253
SCHWAB
Maud (Morris) 380
SCHWARZBURG-LEUTENBERG
Margaret of 452
SCHWARZBURG-RUDOLSTADT
Albert VII, Count of 182, 196
Louis Frederick I, Prince of 891, 892
Magdalena of 182, 196
William Henry, Prince of 891
SCHWARZBURG-SONDERSHAUSEN
Augusta, Princess of 56
Augustus I, Prince of 56
Augustus II, Prince of 56
SCHWARZENBERG (VON/ZU)
Franz Friedrich, Prince 11
Ludmilla Maria, Princess clv, 11
Marie Caroline, Princess 18
SCHWARZENEGGER
Arnold Alois (Gov.) 26, 564, 914
Maria Owings (Shriver) 26, 564, 914
SCHWEIDNITZ
Bolko I of Schliesen-Liegnitz, Duke of 640
SCHWEIGER
Heidi 13
SCHWEINICHEN (VON)
Eva 619
SCHWEINITZ (DE) (VON)
Amalie Joanna Lydia (von Tschirsky und Bögendorff) clxx, 183, 197
Anna Dorothea Elizabeth (von Watteville), Baroness xxvi, clxx, 196
Edmund Alexander (Rev.) 183, 197
family xl, liii, lxi
Hans Christian Alexander 196
Isabel Allen (Bogge) 197
Lewis David 197
Louise Amalia (Ledoux) 197
SCHWENNICKE
Detlev lxvi
SCHWERIN (VON)
Katharina 452
SCOTLAND (SCOTS)
Ada of 732, 778, 780, 785

Annabella (Drummond), Queen of 239, 241, 243, 245, 248, 249, 250, 251, 252, 253, 254, 255, 256, 257, 258, 260, 261, 263, 264, 266, 267, 268, 940

Annabella (Stewart), Princess of viii, 176

Anne, Princess of Denmark, Queen of England and 35, 38, 47, 49, 52, 785

Bethoc of 828

Catherine of Braganza, Princess of Portugal, Queen of England and 22, 25, 29, 30, 31, 33, 34

Charles I, King of England and 430, 467

Charles II, King of England and xii, xxv, lvii, lxviii, 22, 25, 29, 30, 31, 33, 34, 103, 109, 615, 627

David, Prince of, Earl of Huntingdon 768, 778, 779, 780, 785, 787, 789

David I, King of xxvi, 778, 779, 780, 783, 785, 787, 789, 879, 919

Donald III Bane, King of 828

Duncan II, King of 828

Elizabeth (de Burgh), Queen of 456

Elizabeth (Mure) (first wife of Robert II, King of) 219, 269, 272, 273, 280, 281, 283

Elizabeth, Princess of England and, Queen of Bohemia 38

Ermengarde (de Beaumont), Queen of 700, 705, 708, 710, 713, 715, 719, 721, 723, 725, 727, 728, 730, 732

Euphemia of Ross, Queen of 275, 276, 278, 282, 285

Giles/Egidia (Stewart), Princess of 275, 278

Henry, Prince of, Earl of Huntingdon 774, 776, 778, 779, 780, 783, 785, 787, 789

Isabel, Princess of 845

Isabel of 700, 705, 708, 710, 713, 715, 719, 721, 723, 725, 727, 728, 730, 787, 789

James I, King of viii, 145, 152, 160, 173, 176, 222, 223, 225, 898

James II, King of xxv, 145, 148, 154, 157, 167, 168, 174, 179, 210, 213, 214, 215, 216, 218, 219, 459

James II, King of England, VII of clxxxix, 22, 24, 122, 536, 615, 627, 678, 727, 781

James IV, King of xxv, xxxix, xl, 128, 143, 146, 148, 150, 151, 152, 154, 157, 159, 161, 163, 165, 166, 167, 168, 170, 171, 173, 174, 176, 177, 179, 940

James V, King of xxv, xxxix, xl, 82, 85, 87, 88, 90, 92, 93, 95, 96, 97, 98, 893, 897

James VI, King of, I of England xxv, xlv, 35, 38, 47, 49, 52, 69, 76, 80, 430, 536, 785

Joan (Stewart), Princess of, "the dumb lady" 173, 222, 223, 225, 898

1499

Joan (Beaufort),
  Queen of xxv,
  152, 160, 173, 176,
  219, 222, 223, 225,
  241, 249, 256, 261,
  273, 278, 280, 283,
  898
John Baliol, King of
  780
Katherine/Jean/
  Elizabeth
  (Stewart), Princess
  of 275, 276, 282,
  285
lairds in xv
Madeleine, Princess
  of France, Queen
  of 82, 85, 87, 88,
  90, 92, 93, 95, 96,
  97, 98, 897
Malcolm IV, King
  of 778, 780, 785,
  787, 789
Margaret (Stewart),
  Princess of 219,
  249, 256
Margaret (Stewart),
  Princess of, Queen
  of France 200,
  205
Margaret (Tudor),
  Princess of England,
  Queen of 143, 146,
  148, 150, 151, 152,
  154, 157, 159, 161,
  163, 165, 166, 167,
  168, 170, 171, 173,
  174, 176, 177, 179
Margaret of 780,
  783
Marjorie (Stewart),
  Princess of 219,
  281
Mary (Stewart),
  Princess of 148,
  154, 157, 167, 168,
  179, 210, 213, 214,
  215, 216, 218, 239,
  240, 241, 243, 245,
  248, 250, 251, 252,
  253, 254, 255, 257,
  258, 260, 261, 266,
  267, 268, 940
Mary, Queen of
  xii, xl, 90
Mary Beatrice,
  Princess of
  Modena, Queen of
  England and 22,
  24
Mary II, Queen of
  England and 122,
  615, 678, 679, 781
Mary of Guelders,
  Queen of 148,
  154, 157, 167, 168,
  174, 179, 210, 213,
  214, 215, 216, 218,
  219, 459
Mary of Guise,
  Queen of 82, 85,
  87, 88, 90, 92, 93,
  95, 96, 97, 98, 897
Matilda, Princess of,
  Queen of England
  739, 806, 808, 810,
  811, 813, 815, 817,
819, 821, 822, 824,
  826, 957, 959
Matilda of
  Northumberland,
  Queen of 778,
  780, 783, 785, 787,
  789, 879, 919
monarchs of xv
Robert I "the
  Bruce," King of
  456, 787, 789
Robert II, King of
  219, 269, 272, 273,
  275, 276, 278, 280,
  281, 282, 283, 285
Robert III, King of
  239, 240, 241, 243,
  245, 248, 249, 250,
  251, 252, 253, 254,
  255, 256, 257, 258,
  260, 261, 263, 264,
  266, 267, 268, 940
William I "the
  Lion," King of
  xxvi, xxxix, 652,
  700, 705, 708, 710,
  713, 715, 719, 721,
  723, 725, 727, 728,
  730, 732, 778, 780,
  785, 787, 789
William III, Prince
  of Orange, King of
  England and 615
SCOTT
Ann 316
Anne (Pympe) 514
Bathshua 933
Bathshua
  (Oxenbridge) 933

Caroline 136
Caroline Lavinia
  496, 503, 731, 867,
  878
Catherine 316
Charles 314, 316
Deborah 314
Dorothea xlviii, lii,
  cxliv, 314, 316
Elizabeth 170
Elizabeth (Hussey)
  xlix, lxi, cl, 739,
  741
Elizabeth (Scott)
  210
Euphan clxiv,
  clxxix, 276
family x
Francis, of
  Mangerton 210
George, of Pitlochie
  276
Helena (Rutgers) 211
Irene Florence
  (Seely) 179
Jane (Wyatt) 314
Jane Emily 179
Janet 96
Janet (Eliot) 96
Jean (Scott), of
  Oakwood 96
John 211
John (Sir) 514
John (Sir), 1st Bt.
  210
John, Jr. 211
John Morin 211
Judith (Thomson)
  314, 316

Katharine 269
Katherine (Marbury)
  xlviii, clxiii, clxxiii,
  478, 926
Magdalen (Vincent)
  211
Margaret 241, 285
Margaret, of Ancrum
  210, 211
Margaret (Douglas)
  210
Margaret (Kerr) 210
Margaret (Rigg)
  276
Marion (Morin)
  211
Mary 210, 273,
  316, 347, 514, 781
Mary (Hay) 210
Mary (Knatchbull)
  314, 316
Mary (Tuke) 314,
  514
Mason Hogarth
  179
Reginald (Sir) 314,
  514
Richard 478, 933
Robert 739
Thomas 314, 316
Thomas (Junior)
  316
Walter (Sir), of
  Buccleuch 210
Walter, 1st Baron
  Scott of Buccleuch
  210
Walter, 1st Earl of
  Buccleuch 210

Walter, of Girnwood
  96
William, of
  Milsington 96
SCROPE (LE)
Annabella 431
Anne 698
Catherine (Clifford)
  401, 431
Eleanor 385, 395,
  493, 494
Eleanor (Washburne)
  494
Elizabeth 528
Elizabeth (Manners)
  431
Elizabeth (Percy)
  402
Elizabeth (Scrope)
  494, 495, 590, 698
Elizabeth
  (Strathbogie) 528
Emanuel, 1st Earl of
  Sunderland 431
family 699
Henry, 4th Baron
  Scrope of Bolton
  494, 495, 590, 698
Henry, 6th Baron
  Scrope of Bolton
  402
Henry, 7th Baron
  Scrope of Bolton
  402
Henry, 9th Baron
  Scrope of Bolton
  431
John (Sir) 528

1501

John, 8th Baron
  Scrope of Bolton
  401, 402, 431
Katherine (Zouche)
  698
Mabel (Dacre) 402
Margaret 401, 495
Margaret (Howard)
  431
Margaret (Neville)
  495, 590
Margery (de Welles)
  715, 728
Maud 466, 715,
  728
Philadelphia (Carey)
  431
Richard 494
Richard, 3rd Baron
  Scrope of Bolton
  495, 590
Robert (Hon.) 698
Stephen, 2nd Baron
  Scrope of Masham
  715, 728
Thomas, 10th Baron
  Scrope of Bolton
  431
**SCROPE of
  BOLTON.** see
  SCROPE (LE)
**SCROPE of
  MASHAM.** see
  SCROPE (LE)
SCRYMGEOUR
  Elizabeth 257
SCUDAMORE
  Jane 111, 137

SCUDDER
  Elizabeth xiv, 921
  Elizabeth
    (Stoughton) xiv,
    921
  John xiv, 921
SEABROOK
  Rebecca 726
SEAFORTH
  earls of 284
SEALE
  Anne 527
SEALS
  Mary Ann Diligent
    764, 773
SEAMAN
  Grace 385
SEATON
  Patricia 564
SEBRIGHT
  Giles Edward (Sir),
    13th Bt. 341
  Margery Hilda
    (Fremantle)
    (Massey) clvi,
    341
**SECKENDORFF
  (VON)**
  Frederica Joanna,
    Baroness 43, 292
SECKESTAD
  Filip Bonde, Lord of
    Bordsjoe and 457
SECKFORD
  Cecily 705
SEDLEY
  Abigail (Knevet)
    353
  Martin (Sir) 353

Muriel 353, 661
SEDLINGTON
  Isabel 830
SEELEY
  Sarah 688
SEELY
  Emily Florence
    (Crichton) 179
  Irene Florence 179
  John Edward
    Bernard, 1st Baron
    Mottistone 179
SEGAR
  Simon 843
SEGNI
  Alessandro Sforza,
    Duke of 192
SEGRAVE (DE)
  Eleanor 742, 746,
    752, 760, 772
  Elizabeth 462, 470,
    473, 486, 493, 519,
    522, 526, 534, 539,
    541, 545, 557, 579,
    580, 598, 599, 604,
    605, 609
  family 564
  John de Segrave, 4th
    Baron 462, 470,
    473, 486, 493, 519,
    522, 526, 534, 539,
    541, 545, 557, 579,
    580, 598, 599, 604,
    605, 609
  Margaret (Planta-
    genet), Duchess of
    Norfolk 462, 470,
    473, 486, 493, 519,
    522, 526, 534, 539,

541, 545, 557, 579,
580, 598, 599, 604,
605, 609, 1024
SEGRÉ (DE)
  Bouchard de
    Vendôme,
    Seigneur, Seigneur
    de Feuillet 946
  Pierre de Vendôme,
    Seigneur, Seigneur
    de Nesle 946
SÉGRIE (DE)
  Guillemette 956
SEGUIN
  Mathilda 979
SEIGNELAY (DE)
  Jean-Baptiste de
    Colbert, Marquis
    202
SELBY
  Angelica Mary 145
  Isabel 106, 599
SELDEN
  Sarah 630, 886
SELLERS
  Edwin Jaquett li,
    lxvi
SELLON
  Elizabeth
    (Fraiswell)
    (Reddaway) 590
  family 590, 591
  John 590
  Lydia 590
  Mary (Hunt) 590
  Samuel 590
  Sarah (Butler) 590
  Sarah (Harman) 590

Sarah (Littlehales)
    590, 591
William 590
William (Rev.)
    590, 591
SELWOOD
  Anne (Colleton)
    742, 743
  Elizabeth lxiii
  Humphrey 742
  Katherine cxlv, cli,
    742
SEMPHILL
  Agnes (Montgomery)
    173
  Barbara 173
  Barbara (Preston)
    173
  Isabel (Hamilton)
    173, 269
  Margaret 269
  Margaret (Mont-
    gomery) 269
  Robert (Hon.) 173
  Robert Semphill, 3rd
    Baron 173, 269
  Robert Semphill, 4th
    Baron 173
  William Semphill,
    2nd Baron 269
SEMUR-EN-AUXOIS
  Hélie of 853, 855
SEMYON
  Prince of Vladimir
    791
SENHOUSE
  Bridget 363
  Eleanor (Kirkby)
    363

Humphrey 363
SENI
  Anita 951
SENLIS (DE). see
  also ST. LIZ (DE)
SENNETERRE (DE)
  Marguerite 634
  Marguerite
    (d'Estampes) 634
  Nectaire, Seigneur de
    Saint-Nectaire 634
SERGEANT
  Margaretta 385
  Maude Frances
    914
SERGEAUX
  Alice 584
  Elizabeth 607
  Philippa 508, 514
  Philippa (FitzAlan)
    508, 514, 584, 607
  Richard (Sir) 508,
    514, 584, 607
**SERNA LLOSA (DE
  LA)**
  Celia 997
SERRACAPRIOLA
  Nicola Maresca
    Donnorso, 3rd
    Duke of 190
SETON
  Andrew, of Barnes
    222
  Anna Maria
    (Curson) 222
  Beatrix 225
  Cecilia
    (Kynnynmond)
    222

1503

Elizabeth 143
Elizabeth (Hay)
  222, 225
Elizabeth (Seton), of
  Belsies 222
Elizabeth Ann
  (Bayley) [Mother,
  later Saint, Eliza-
  beth Ann Seton]
  222
George (Sir), of
  Parbroath 222
George, of Cariston
  222
George Seton, 3rd
  Baron 173, 222,
  225
George Seton, 4th
  Baron 222, 225
Isabel 177
Isabel (Balfour)
  222
Isabella (Seton)
  222
James 222
Janet (Hepburn)
  173, 222, 225
John 222
John, of Cariston
  222
Margaret 157, 167,
  179, 219
Margaret (Ayton)
  222
Margaret (Mont-
  gomery) 143
Margaret (Newton)
  222
Margaret (Seton) 222

Mariot 173
Mary 222
Rebecca (Curson)
  222
Robert 222
Robert, 1st Earl of
  Winton 143
William 222
William Magee
  222
SEVENOAKS
  Joan 778
SEVERAC
  Jean-Louis
  d'Arpajon,
  Marquis de 200
SEVERSMITH
  Herbert Furman li,
  lxvi
SÉVIGNÉ (DE)
  Bertrand, Sieur des
  Tresmes 943
  Catherine (de la
  Charonière) 943
  Charlotte (de
  Montmoron) 943
  François, Seigneur du
  Plexis-Olivet 943
  Gabrielle (du
  Bellay) 942, 943
  Gilles 942, 943
  Gilles, Sieur de
  Saint-Didier 943
  Gillette (de Foy)
  942, 943
  Guillaume VI,
  Seigneur 943
  Jacqueline (de
  Montmorency) 943

Marguerite (de
  Champaigné) 943
Marie (de
  Keraldanet) 943
Renaud, Sieur de
  Montmoron 942,
  943
**SÉVIGNÉ/SÉVIGNY
dit LA FLEUR**
  Julien-Charles 939,
  942, 943
  Marguerite
  (Roignon dît la
  Roche) 942
SÉVIGNY
  Charles-Eusèbe 989
  Chloë Stevens 968,
  989
  Harold David 989
  Harold Sweet 989
  Janine (Malinowski)
  989
  Marie-Louise
  (Brisson) 989
  Mary Ernestine
  (Stevens) 989
  Rose (Marois) 989
  Wilfred 989
SEWALL
  family xxiv
  Henry viii, li,
  cxlvi, clxvi, 332,
  512, 819
  Jane (Lowe) xxxv,
  clxv, clxxiv, 332,
  339, 512, 819
  Mary 332
  Mary (Dugdale) 819
  Richard 819

SEYBORNE
  Winifred 721
SEYLIARD
  Dorothy (Cromer)
    474, 477
  Elizabeth 474
  William 474, 477
SEYMOUR
  Anne 306, 307, 598
  Anne (Delmé) 27
  Anne (Paulet) 598
  Anne (Stanhope) 305
  Barbara (Morgan)
    307
  Catherine 76
  Catherine (Filliol)
    305
  Cecily (Beauchamp)
    740
  Charles, 2nd Baron
    Seymour of
    Trowbridge 76
  Charles, 6th Duke of
    Somerset 76
  Dorothy (Killigrew)
    305
  Edward (Sir), 1st Bt.
    305
  Edward (Sir), 2nd
    Bt. 305, 306
  Edward (Sir) (Lord)
    305
  Edward, 1st Duke of
    Somerset, Lord
    Protector 305,
    307
  Edward, 1st Earl of
    Hertford 69, 76,
    80
  Edward, Baron
    Beauchamp 69,
    76, 80
  Elizabeth 27, 80,
    81, 307
  Elizabeth (Alington)
    76
  Elizabeth
    (Champernowne)
    305
  Elizabeth (Coker)
    741
  Elizabeth (Darrell)
    741, 855
  Elizabeth (Lyte)
    598
  Elizabeth (Percy)
    76
  Elizabeth (Webb)
    598
  family xxxii
  Frances 119
  Frances (Devereux)
    69, 75, 80
  Frances (Prynne)
    76
  Francis, 1st Baron
    Seymour of
    Trowbridge 76
  Francis, 1st
    Marquess of
    Hertford 27
  Henry (Sir) 307
  Henry, Baron
    Beauchamp 80
  Hester (Newton)
    cxlvi, 413, 598
  Honora (Rogers)
    69, 76, 80
  Isabel (William)
    740
  Isabella (FitzRoy)
    27
  Jane 307, 740
  Jane (Poyntz) 598
  Jane, Queen of
    England 305,
    705, 741, 855
  John 598, 741, 855
  John (Gov.) lxviii,
    cxlvi, 413, 598
  John (Sir) 305,
    598, 705, 740, 855
  Katherine (Grey)
    69, 76, 80
  Margaret (Bowles)
    598
  Margaret
    (Brockbury) 740
  Margaret (Walsh)
    305
  Margery
    (Wentworth) 305,
    705, 855
  Mary 69, 305, 306,
    307
  Mary (Capell) 80
  Maud (Estumy)
    740
  Robert, Lord 27
  Roger 740, 741
  Roger (Sir) 740
  Sybil (Harden) 740
  Thomas 598
  Thomas (Sir) 598
  William 740
  William, 2nd Duke of
    Somerset 69, 80

1505

SEYTURIER (DE)
  Antoinette 952
  Claude (de Moyria) 952
  Claude, Seigneur Cornod 952
SFORZA
  Alessandro, Duke of Segni 192
  Bona, Queen of Poland 895
  Dorotea (di Tocco) 192
  Eleanora 192
  Eleanora (Orsini) 192
  Francesco, Duke of Onano 192
  Olympia (Cesi) 192
  Paolo II, Marquess of Procena 192
SHAFFER
  Anna (Wintour), Dame xviii, clix, 117
  David 117
SHAFTESBURY
  Anthony Ashley Cooper, 7th Earl of 299
  Cropley Ashley Cooper, 6th Earl of 299
SHAFTO
  Catherine 100
  Catherine (Widdrington) 100

  Margaret (Ingleby) 100
  Mark 100
  Robert (Sir) 100
SHAKESPEAR
  Alexander 130
  Catherine Mary (Tayler) 130
  Dorothy lxvi, clvii, 131
  Henry Davenport 130
  Henry Hope 130
  John 130, 592
  Louise Caroline Tobin (Muirson) 130
  Martha 592
  Mary (Davenport) 130, 592
  Olivia (Tucker) 130
SHAKESPEARE
  John lxvi
  William xxiv
SHAND
  Bruce Middleton Hope 655
  Camilla Rosemary [H.R.H. The Duchess of Cornwall] 655, 656, 930
  Rosalind Maud (Cubitt) (Hon.) 655
SHANDS
  Carey 458
SHAPERA
  Robert J. [Robert J. Evans] 3

SHAPOV
  Varvara 798
SHARD
  Mary 318
SHARP
  Elizabeth 642
  J. C. B. cxc
SHARPE
  Bridget 757, 758
  Dorothy 758
  John 757
  Mary (Saunders) 757
  Nicholas 758
SHATTUCK
  family 155
  Howard Francis III [John Shattuck] 155
SHAW
  Agnes 271
  Elizabeth 837
  Euphemia 254
  Janet 245
  John 128
  T. E. [Thomas Edward Lawrence, "of Arabia"] xxiv, 101
  Wilhelmina Hannah (McAdam) 128
SHAW KENNEDY
  Eleanor Green (Wilkinson) 129
  family 132
  Grace Dunlop (Cummings) 129
  James (Sir) 128
  John 129

Mary Primrose
  (Kennedy) 128
Ruth Melville 129
Vernon Hew
  Primrose xlix,
  lxiii, clv, 129, 132
SHEAFE/SHEAFFE
Dorothy clxxxiii
Elizabeth 738
Susannah 115
SHEDDEN
family lxiv
Janet Madeleine
  Cecilia 127, 488
Matilda Cecilia
  (Dowdall) xl, liii,
  clxxiii, 488, 900
Thomas 488
SHEED
Francis Joseph 71
Mary Josephine
  "Maisie" (Ward)
  cxlvii, 71
SHEFFIELD
Deliverance xlix,
  cxlv, clxxix, 577,
  578, 665
Edmund, 1st Earl of
  Mulgrave 327
Eleanor 752
Elizabeth
  (Woodroffe/Woodr
  ove) 577
Frances 327, 329
Mary 329
Samantha
  Gwendoline 10
Sampson 577
Sampson (Col.) 578

Ursula (Tyrwhitt)
  327
SHELBURNE
William Petty, 2nd
  Earl of, 1st
  Marquess of
  Lansdowne, Prime
  Minister 226, 299
SHELDON
Anne 532
Flora 243, 474,
  479, 572, 585, 703,
  716, 729, 747
Mary Cornelia 589
Mary Elizabeth
  (Butler) 243
Robert Emmet 243
SHELLEY
Barbara (Cromer)
  474
Bridget (Eversfield)
  474
Bysshe (Sir), 1st Bt.
  474
Catherine (Michell)
  474
Elizabeth (Pilford)
  474
Frances 105, 136,
  310
Helen (Bysshe)
  474
Henry 474
Joan (Fuste) 474
Joanna (Plum[b])
  474
John 474
John (Sir), 3rd Bt.
  136

Mary (Fleetwood)
  136
Mary (Gage) 136
Mary Catherine
  (Michell) 474
Mary Wollstonecraft
  (Godwin) [Mary
  Shelley] 474
Percy Bysshe xxiv,
  474
Richard 136, 474
Timothy 474
Timothy (Sir), 2nd
  Bt. 474
SHELLMAN
Clarissa (Montfort)
  474, 729
John, Jr. 474, 729
Susan 474, 479,
  572, 585, 703, 716,
  729, 747
SHELTON
Grace 606
Prudence
  (Calthorpe) 606
Ralph 606
Sarah 219, 534
Violet Pauline
  [Violet Campbell]
  145
**SHEPARD/
  SHEPHERD**
Amphyllis
  (Chamberlain alias
  Spicer) 670
Anna 375, 393
Anna (Tyng) 375,
  393
Constance 670

Constance (Hawes) 670
Margaret (Estouteville/ Touteville) xxxv, lxv, cxlvi, clxi, 393
Mary (Anderson) 375, 393
Thomas 670
Thomas, Jr. 375, 393
Thomas (III) 375, 393
Thomas (Rev.) 393
Thomasine 359
SHEPPARD
Diane Wolford xii, 967, 968, 969, 972, 973, 974, 975, 976, 977, 978, 981, 982, 983
Henrietta Dawson Ayres xlvi, xlix, lxvi
Walter Lee, Jr. ix, xix, xxii, xxvii, xlvi, lvi, lviii, lxi, lxv, lxvii, 398
SHERARD
Anne 727
SHERBORNE
Anne 123
SHERBURNE
Agnes 701, 703
Alice (Plumpton) 700
family lvii
Isabel 700, 701, 703

Margaret 700
Matilda (Hamerton) 700
Richard 700
Richard (Sir) 700
SHERINGTON
Ursula 354, 470
SHERMAN
John (Rev.) 395
Mary (Launce) xxiv, lix, clxii, 395
Mildred 66
SHERWIN
Elizabeth (Pride) (Gibbs) l, cl, 103, 104
William 103, 104
SHERWOOD
Endymia (Winn) 370
George xxix
Lucinda 370
Thomas 370
SHIELDS
Brooke (Christa Brooke Camilla) xviii, 18
Francis Alexander 18
Francis Xavier 18, 19
Marina (Torlonia) xviii, lx, 18, 19
Teri (Schmon) 18
SHILLINGFORD alias ISODE/ IZARD. *see* IZARD
SHINN
Martha 510

SHIPP
Elizabeth (Doniphan) 171, 258
Emma Grant 171, 258
Richard 171, 258
SHIPPEN
Anne 411, 557
Sarah 275
SHIRLEY
Amee (Lolle) 653
Anne (Hevyn) 653
Anne (Kempe) 475, 491
Anne (Oglander) 475, 476
Anthony 475
Barbara (Walsingham) 475
Beatrix 654
Beatrix (de Braose) 653
Catherine (Okeover) 134
Cecily 300, 491
Dorothy (Devereux) 134
Eleanor 653
Eleanor (Willoughby) 653
Elizabeth 475
Elizabeth (Godman) 475
Elizabeth (Stapley) 475
Elizabeth, Baroness Ferrers of Chartley 112

Emily Harriet 135
Evelyn 135
family clxii
Frances (Barker) 475
George 135
Henry (Sir), 2nd Bt. 134
Hugh 653
Hugh (Sir) 653
Jane (Essex) 475
Joan (Basset) 653
John 653
Joyce 653
Margaret (Staunton) 653
Margaret (Wroth) 653, 656
Mary 134, 135
Mary (Sturt) 135
Phyllis Byam (Wollaston) 135
Ralph 653, 654
Ralph (Sir) 653
Robert 653
Robert (Sir), 4th Bt. 134
Robert, 1st Earl Ferrers 134
Selina (Finch) 134
Thomas 475
Thomas (Sir) 475, 491
William 475
William (Gov.) clxii, 32, 475, 476
SHISHKOV
Nina 618
SHORT
Marie (____) 320

____ 320
SHORTER
Charlotte 482
Elizabeth (Phillips) 482
family 482
John 482
SHOTBOLT
Jane (Tony) 537
John 537
Mary 537
Mary (Boteler) 536
Thomas 536
SHREWSBURY
Charles Talbot, 1st Duke of 125
George Talbot, "Earl of" 125
Gilbert Talbot, 13th Earl of 125
John Talbot, 2nd Earl of 500, 574
John Talbot, 10th Earl of 120, 125
SHRIVER
Eunice Mary (Kennedy) 26, 564, 914
Maria Owings 26, 564, 914
Robert Sargent, Jr. 26, 564, 914
SHUISKY
Vassili, Prince 791
SHUTE
Anne 531, 684, 853
Benjamin 531, 684
Frances (Meautys) 684

Francis 684
Patience/Anne (Caryl) 531, 684
Robert 684, 853
Samuel (Gov.) 531, 684
Thomasine (Burgoyne) 684, 853
SHUVALOV
Elizabeth, Princess 795
Praskovya 798
SIBBALD
Isabel 250, 251, 252
SIBOUR (DE)
Jean-Antonin-Gabriel, Count li, 639
Jean-Baptiste-Joseph, Count 639
Jules-Gabriel-Henri 639
Margaret Marie (Clagett) 639
Mary Louisa (Johnson) 639
Pauline (de Sallmard) 639
SIBYL. *see* SYBIL
SICILY
Beatrix, Princess of Provence, Queen of Naples and 965
Beatrix of Savoy, Queen of 642
Charles I of Anjou, King of Naples and 965

1509

Charles II, Prince of
Anjou and France,
King of Naples and 459
Constance, Princess of, Queen of Aragón 51, 642
Eleanor, Princess of Anjou, Princess and Queen of 51, 451
Elizabeth, Princess of Aragón and 51, 451
Frederick II, King of 51, 451
Louis II, King of Naples, Jerusalem, Aragón and 205
Manfred, King of 642
Marie, Princess of Hungary, Queen of Naples and 459
Marie of Châtillon-Blois, Queen of Naples, Jerusalem, Aragón, and 205

SIDLEY
Catherine, Countess of Dorchester 22
Elizabeth 839

SIDMOUTH
Henry Addington, 1st Viscount, Prime Minister 865

SIDNEY
Anne (Brandon) 517
Anne (Pagenham) 477, 517
Dorcas 307
Henry (Sir) 477, 518
Lucy 416, 517
Mary (Dudley) 477
Nicholas 517
Philip (Sir) 477
William (Sir) 477, 517

SIGISMUND I
King of Poland 895

SIGOUIN
Joseph 976
Julienne 976
Marie-Archange (Grignon) 976

SILESIA-RATIBOR
Anna of 621

SILFVERSCHIÖLD
Augusta Charlotta 60

SILFVERSWÅRD
Bengt 53
Catharina (Hierta) 53
Eva Sofia 53
Hans 53
Margareta Maria (Klingspor) 53

SILLY (DE)
Catherine 455

SILVA Y MENDOZA (DE)
Ana 140

SILVER
Sharon Helene 23

SILVERTOP
Mary 123

SILVIA
(Sommerlath), Queen of Sweden 991

SIMMERN
Anna Maria of, Queen of Sweden 40, 43
John II, Count Palatine of 291
Sabina of 291

SIMON VII
Count of Lippe-Detmold 141

SIMONS
D. Brenton v, vi, ix, lxvii, 430

SIMPSON
Hannah 921
Isaac (Capt.) 629
Jacob Williams 629
Jayne (Sarah Jayne) ix, lviii, 629
Lillie Boyce (Chambers) 629
Margaret 275
Mary Emma (Danvers) 629

SIMS
Tara 458

SINCLAIR
Agnes 82
Anna (Sinclair) 88
Anne 92, 897
Eleanor 219, 261, 278, 283
Elizabeth 98

Elizabeth, of Brims 82
Elizabeth (Leslie) 92, 897
Elizabeth (Stewart) 82
family xlix
Giles/Egidia (Douglas) 278
Helen 256
Henrietta 82
Henry, 2nd Earl of Orkney 278
Isabel (Boyd) 165
James (Sir) 82
James (Sir), 1st Bt. 92, 897
James, of Kirkwall 88
Jane, of Ulbster 82
Joanna (Gordon), of Cairston 88
John, of Stevenson 165
John, of Toab 88
Magnus 88
Margaret Joan 969
Maria (Duyckinck) 88
Marion 165
Marjory (Sutherland) 278
Mary (Stewart) 88
Robert xxxv, xlix, clxiv, clxx, 88
William 88
William, 3rd Earl of Orkney, 1st Earl of Caithness 278

SINGLETON
Elizabeth clxxxvii
Elizabeth (Cornwallis) clxxxvii
family clxxxvii
William clxxxvii
SINKEY
Bruce Harris ix, lxvii, 472
SIONET
of Powys 886
SIOUGEAT (DE)
Jérôme de Laizer, Seigneur 440
SIROIS
Marie-Josèphe 988
SITWELL
Edith Louisa, Dame 177
family xxiv, 177, 299
George (Sir), 2nd Bt. 177
George Reresby (Sir), 4th Bt. 177
Georgiana Caroline 177
Ida Emily Augusta (Denison) 177
Louisa Lucy (Hely-Hutchinson) 177
Osbert (Francis Osbert Sacheverell) (Sir), 5th Bt. 177
Sacheverell (Sir), 6th Bt. 177
Sitwell Reresby (Sir), 3rd Bt. 177
Susan Murray (Tait) 177

SJÖBARD
Charlotte Christina, Baroness 893
SKARSHOLM-SLÆGTEN
Barnim 644
Christine 644
Elisabeth (___) 644
Erik (knight) 644
Erik, Duke of Sønder-Holland 644
Gjertrud (Grubbe) 644
Knud, Duke of Estonia 644
SKELTON
Bathurst 711
Elizabeth 359
Martha (Wayles) xliii, 387, 711, 823
SKENARD
Joan 755
SKENE
Alison 272
Barbara 159
Elizabeth/Elspeth (Forbes) 159
James, of Skene 159
Jean (Burnett) 159
John, of Skene 159
SKEPPER/SKIPPER
Edward 342
Jane 344, 924
Jane (___) 342, 924
Joan (Legard) 342
Mary (Robinson) 342

1511

Richard 342
Sarah 342
Sarah (Fisher) 342
William (Rev.)
  lvii, cxlvi, clxii,
  342, 344, 924
SKERME
Mary 474
SKERNE
Thomasine 343
SKINNER
Anne (Storer)
  (Truman) cxlvi,
  628
Isabel 642
Margaret 137
Margaret (Littleton)
  137
Richard 137
Robert 628
SKIPWITH
Alice (Dymoke)
  343, 470, 471
Amy (Kempe) 470
Anne lviii, cxlix,
  cli, 409
Anne (Portington)
  409
Diana xxxv, lviii,
  clxvi, 470
Dorothy 471
Eleanor (Kingston)
  343, 409
Elizabeth 409
Elizabeth (___) 470
Elizabeth (Page)
  409, 472
Elizabeth (Tyrwhit)
  472

Grey (Sir), 3rd Bt.
  lviii, clxvii, 470
Henry 409, 470,
  471
Henry (Sir), 1st Bt.
  470
Honora (Saunders)
  409
Jane (Hall) 409,
  470
John 343, 409
Lelia 464
Margaret (Cave)
  470
Mary 343, 471
Mary (Chamberlain)
  409
Richard (Sir) 409
William 409
William (Sir) 343,
  409, 470, 472
Willoughby 409
SKLEROS
Theophano (wife of
  Otto II, Holy
  Roman Emperor)
  849
SKOVGAARD
Anne 644
SKRIMSHIRE
Anna 630
SKULL
Joyce 555
SKUNKBERG
Karl Hans
  Wachtmeister, 2nd
  Count of 453
SLANEY
Anne 840

**SLATER/
SLAUGHTER**
Edward W. 18
Elizabeth 706
Margaret (Leech)
  706
Marina (Torlonia)
  (Shields) xviii, lx,
  18
Mary 883
Richard 706, 707
SLAWATA
Franziska (von
  Meggau) 895
Joachim Ulrich 895
Johann Georg
  Joachim, Baron
  Slawata 895
Lucia Ottilia (von
  Neuhaus) 895
Maria Magdalena
  895
Maria Margareta
  (Trautson) 895
Wilhelm 895
**SLETTENGREN
(later SWAIN)**
Betsy Miller
  (Chase) 53
Caroline
  Wilhelmina
  (Fogelberg) 53
Christian 53
Christina
  Margaretha
  (Bråkenhielm) 53
Esais Reinhold
  clviii, 53
Per Gustav 53

1512

SLICER
  Catherine 714
SLINGSBY
  Barbara 130
  Barbara (Belasyse) 130
  Eleanor 389, 390
  Elizabeth (Vavasour) 389
  Frances 390
  Francis (Sir) 389
  Henry (Sir) 389
  Henry (Sir), 1st Bt. 130
  Mary (Percy) 389
SLOCUM
  Joanna 763
  Joseph 764
  Patience (Carr) 764
  Sarah 764
SLONIN
  Vera 618
SLUKA
  Alexandra, Princess 621
SMALLEY
  Elizabeth 319
SMEAD
  Judith (Stoughton) (Denman) cli, 921
  ___ 921
SMEDAL
  Erling Arnold xxii
  family xxii
SMITH/SMYTH/ SMYTHE
  Abigail xi, xlii, xlix, liii, lxix, cxlii, clxvi, clxxxi, 375, 393, 878, 1025
  Abigail (Chandler) 656
  Alva Erskine 26, 174, 175
  Anna 723
  Anna (Shepard) 375, 393
  Anne 535, 587
  Anne (Bassett) 878
  Anne (Bernard) 930
  Anne (Clarke) 535
  Anne Laughton 82
  Anthony 878
  Arabella (Barlow) 666
  Arabella Maria clxv, clxxv, 666
  Arthur, Archbishop of Dublin 480
  Barbara (Ingoldsby) 535
  Catherine Meade (Ogle) 535
  Charles Mayvore 361
  Chloe 656, 871
  Christopher 701
  Daniel 990
  Delia Stirling (Forbes) 174
  Dorothea (Burgh) 480
  Dorothy (___) 717
  Eleanor 917
  Eleanor Rosalynn [Rosalynn Carter] xlii, xliii, 422, 696, 765, 773
  Elizabeth 103, 351, 417, 552, 868, 881
  Elizabeth (Godson?) 467
  Elizabeth (Gorges) liii, clxxiii, 296, 457, 522
  Elizabeth (Quincy) 375, 393
  Elizabeth (Towneley) 701
  Elizabeth (Wormeley) (Kempe) (Lunsford) 483
  Elizabeth Frances (Turnor) 334
  Ellen 917
  Emily Smythies (Greene) 548
  Eric Carrington 121
  family 123, 362
  Frances 123
  Frances Allethea (Murray) 696
  Frances Dora 101, 930
  Frederic Machell 548
  George 174, 666
  Grace Matilda (Wroughton) 361
  Helen cxci
  Henrietta Mildred (Hodgson) 121, 930
  Henrietta Scott 270, 549

1513

Henry 375, 393
Honora 744
Hugh (Sir) 457, 522
Isabel 276, 481
Israel 656
James 54
Jean 223
Jean Ann (Kennedy) 26, 564, 914
John 344, 481, 930
John, Jr. 344, 930
Jonathan 539
Judith 764
Katherine (Porter) 917
Kathleen Machell 548
Lawrence xlvi, lxi, clxvii, clxxx, clxxxviii, 701
Lydia 403
Margaret (Lloyd) 355, 375, 394
Margaret Mackall 421, 533
Maria Jo(h)anna (Somerset) (Lowther) xlvi, cxlvi, 109
Martha 340, 594
Martha (Bacon) 878
Martha (Drake) 344
Mary 643, 725
Mary (___) 93, 344, 717
Mary (Debnam) 701
Mary (Maberly) 121
Mary (Mudgett) 344
Mary (Warner) 930
Mary Anne [Mrs. Maria FitzHerbert] 123
Mildred 930
Murray Forbes 174
Nathaniel 643
Oswald 121, 930
Phebe (Howell) 643
Phoebe Ann (Desha) 174
Prudence (FitzRandolph) 725
Ralph 535
Rebecca 355, 375, 394
Richard 109
Robert 483
Rosa(linde) Zeiman 361, 362
Samuel 334
Sarah 701
Sarah (___) 875
Sarah (Brewster?) clxiv, 539
Sarah Eleanor (Bell) 696
Sheila V. Mallory 848
Shubael 725
Solange (Knowles) (Ferguson) 990
Sophia 334
Susanna 481
Thomas, Bishop of Limerick 480
Virginia Katharine 121, 125
Wilburn Edgar 696
Wilhelmine Auguste Friederike (Bentinck) 54
William 535, 917
William, Jr. 375, 393
William Henry 355, 375, 394
William Juriston 696

SMITT (DE SMITT)
Eugenie 4

SMITTER
Leila Eliott (Burton) (Hadley) 90
Yvor Hyatt 90

SMYTHIES
Emily 548, 549
Frances Enid 108
Henry Yeats 548
Isabella (Raymond) 548
Margaretta 549

SNAKENBORG
Helena Bååt 457, 458, 522
Karin 457

SNARSKA
Antonia 194

SNELLING
Frances (Hele) 573
Jane (Specott) 835
Joan (Elford) 573, 835
John clxxix, 573
Margery/Margaret (Stagg) 835

Sarah (____) 573
Thomas 573, 835
William lxvii, cxlvi,
  573, 835
SNEYD(E)
Elizabeth 427, 592
Elizabeth (Audeley)
  592
Elizabeth (Bowyer)
  592
Felicia (Archbold)
  592
Margaret 560
Mary (Chetwynd)
  592
Phillis 427
Ralph 592
Sarah (Wettenhall)
  592
Susanna (Edmonds)
  592
William 592
SNOILSKY
Hedvig, Baroness
  889
SNOW
Susannah 29, 317,
  478, 515, 558
SOANE
Judith 387
SOCKWELL
Joanna (Lawson)
  490
SOISSONS
Raoul III de Nesle,
  Count of 954
SOKOVNINE
Eudoxia 795

SOLMS-BARUTH
Amalie Henriette
  Charlotte,
  Countess of 47,
  141
Helena Amelia of
  194, 195
John Christian I,
  Count of 195
John Christian II,
  Count of 141
SOLMS-BRAUNFELS
Frederick, Prince of
  40
Frederick William
Charles Louis
George Alfred
Alexander, Prince
  of [Prince Carl of
  Solms-Braunfels]
  xvii, clxx, 40, 41
SOLMS-LAUBACH
Erdmuthe Benigna
  of 182, 196
John Frederick,
  Count of 196
SOLMS-SONNENWALDE
Sophie Albertine of
  56
SOLNEY
family 1025
Margery/Margaret
  754
SOLON
Dorothy 112
SOMA
Enrica "Ricki" 9,
  65

SOMBREFFE (DE) (VON)
Jean I 804
Jean II de Mareau,
  Sire 804
Johann III, Sire 804
Jutta (von Weveling-
  hoven) 804
Margarethe (von
  Kerpen) 804
Maria 804
Wilhelm I 804
____ (de Beaumez)
  804
SOMERBY
Horatio Gates
  clxxxiv, 579
SOMERSET
Anne 110
Anne (Russell) 109
Blanche 110
Catherine
  (Baskerville) 109
Charles 109
Charles, 1st Earl of
  Worcester 345,
  396
Charles Seymour,
  6th Duke of 76
Charlotte Sophia
  (Leveson-Gower)
  64
Edmund Beaufort,
  1st Duke of 300,
  345, 396, 407, 427
Edward, 4th Earl of
  Worcester 109
Edward Seymour,
  1st Duke of, Lord

1515

Protector 305, 307
Eleanor 410
Elizabeth 109, 396
Elizabeth (Browne) 345
Elizabeth (Hastings) 109, 111
Elizabeth (Herbert) 345, 346, 396
Henrietta 27, 33
Henry, 1st Marquess of Worcester 109, 110
Henry, 2nd Earl of Worcester 345
Henry Beaufort, 2nd Duke of 345, 396
Henry Charles, 6th Duke of Beaufort 64
Isabella Frances Anne 64
John (Lord) 109
John Beaufort, 1st Duke of 547
John Beaufort, Marquess of, Marquess of Dorset xxv, 222, 300, 345, 396, 407, 427, 547, 898
Lucy 345, 418
Maria Jo(h)anna xlvi, cxlvi, 109
Mary (Arundell) 109
William Seymour, 2nd Duke of 69, 80

SOMERVILLE
Elizabeth 269, 280, 283
Gillian Margaret Hope 19
Jean 218
John, of Cambusnethan 218
Katherine (Murray) 218
SOMERVILLE (DE)
Isabel (de Merlay) 723
Joan 723
Margaret (de Pipe) 723
Philip (Sir) 723
Robert (Sir) 723
SOMERY (DE)
Joan 715, 728, 813, 824, 826
Margaret 819
Nicole (d'Aubigny) 813, 819, 824, 826
Roger 813, 819, 824, 826
SOMESTER
___ 905
SOMMERIVE
Honorat II de Savoie, Count of Tenbe and 442
SOMMERLATH
Silvia Renate, Queen of Sweden 991
SOMOV
Eudoxia 83

SOMOZA DEBAYLE
Anastasio (Pres.) 521
Luís (Pres.) 521
SOMOZA GARCÍA
Anastasio (Pres.) 521
SOMOZA URCUYO
Salvadora 521
SON
Sarah 985
SON (VAN)
Hendrik Jan Abraham 460
Louise Dorothea Adrienne 460
Wilhelmina Vincentia Maria (Baud) 460
SØNDER-HALLAND
Erik Skarsholmslægten, Duke of 644
SONDES
Frances 315
Margaret (Brooke) 315
Thomas (Sir) 315
SONJA
(Haraldsen), Queen of Norway xxii
SOPER
Mary Jerrine 2
SOPHIA
of Mecklenburg-Schwerin 220
SOPHIA AMALIA
of Nassau-Siegen 56

SOPHIA
ANTOINETTE
  Princess of
    Brunswick-
    Wolfenbüttel 44
SOPHIA HEDWIG
  of Lippe-Brake 194
SOPHIE
  Princess of Anhalt-
    Zerbst [Catherine II
    "the Great,"
    Empress of Russia]
    14, 615, 792
  Princess of Hungary
    832
  Princess of
    Mecklenburg-
    Güstrow, Queen of
    Denmark 47, 49,
    52
  Princess of Poland
    194, 196, 198
  Princess of Prussia
    16, 54, 56
  Princess of the
    Palatinate 58
  of Zweibrücken-
    Birkenfeld 60
SOPHIE
  CHARLOTTE
  Princess of Hanover
    and Great Britain,
    Queen of Prussia
    58, 432
SOPHIE
  DOROTHEA
  Princess of Great
    Britain, Queen of
    Prussia 16

SOPHIE
  ELISABETH
  Countess of
    Schleswig-Holstein
    37
SOPHIE
  FREDERICA
  Princess of Saxe-
    Coburg-Saalfeld
    45
SORE (LE)
  Sara 810, 811
SOREL
  Agnès 202, 208, 209
SORELL
  Julia 436
SORENSEN
  Virginia (Eggertsen)
    402
SOSNOWSKA
  Louisa 622
SOTEHILL/
  SOUTHILL
  Agnes (___) 708
  Agnes (Paver) 359
  Anna (Willix)
    (Riscoe) (Blount)
    359, 530
  Arthur 359
  Dorothy (___)
    359
  Elizabeth 359
  Elizabeth (Middleton)
    359
  Elizabeth (Plumpton)
    359, 709
  Elizabeth (Skelton)
    359
  family 360, 709

  Gerard (Sir) 708,
    709
  Henry 359, 709
  Isabel 708
  Joan (Empson) 359
  John 359
  Muriel (Salvayn)
    708
  Richard 708
  Robert 359
  Seth (Gov.) xlix,
    clxvi, 359, 360, 530
  Susan (Whitfield)
    359
  William 359, 360
  ___ (Foster) 359
  ___ (Percehay/
    Pereshay) 708
SOTEROS
  Stanley Ann
    (Dunham)
    (Obama) 726
SOTHEN (VON)
  Anna Margaretha
    449
  Barthold 449
  Catharina (Hartung)
    449
  David 449
  Ilsabe (Stockeleff)
    449
  ___ (von Sothen)
    449
SOTHREN
  Mary 846
SOUCY
  Marie-Françoise 971
SOUKINE
  Anna 792

SOULDET (DE)
Jeanne 440
SOURDÉAC (DE)
René de Rieux,
  Seigneur 226
SOUSA (DE)
Alvaro Dias, Senhor
  de Mafra e Ericeira
  619
Branca 619
Diogo Afonso,
  Senhor de Mafra e
  Ericeira 619
Isabel 619
Leonor (Ribero)
  619
Lope Dias, Senhor
  de Mafra e Ericeira
  619
María (Teles de
  Menezes) 619
Violante (Lopes
  Pacheco) 619
SOUSA Y CABEZA
DE VACA (DE)
Álvaro 619
Ana (de Tovar y
  Castilla) 619
SOUSSEY
Antoine de
  Pracomtal, Baron
  293
SOUTH CAROLINA
Thomas Colleton,
  Landgrave of 743
SOUTH WALES
Angharad, Queen of
  Powys and 815,
  886

SOUTHALL
Jane 806
SOUTHAMPTON
Charles Fitzroy, 2nd
  Duke of Cleveland,
  1st Duke of 34
Henry Wriothesley,
  2nd Earl of
  Southampton 905
Henry Wriothesley,
  3rd Earl of 137
SOUTHCOTT
Mary 308
SOUTH(E)Y
Anne 233, 311
SOUTHILL. *see*
SOTEHILL/
SOUTHILL
SOUTHWORTH
Alice (Carpenter)
  524
Christopher 525
Constant xix, clxii,
  clxxiv, clxxix, 524,
  525, 1025
Edward 524, 525
Elizabeth 524, 525
Elizabeth (Collier)
  524
Elizabeth (Reynor)
  524
Emma (Levesey) 525
family xxiv, lxx,
  clxxxviii
Immyn (Aston) 525
John 525
John (Sir) 524, 525
Margery (Boteler)
  524, 525

Mary (Ashton) 524,
  525
Richard 525
Rosamond (Lister)
  524
Thomas xxxv, clxii,
  clxxiv, clxxix, 524,
  525, 1025
Thomas (Sir) 524
SPAIN
Blanca, Princess of
  6
Catherine, Princess
  of 18
Elizabeth, Princess
  of France, Queen
  of 637
Ferdinand I, King of,
  II of Aragón, V of
  Castile 46, 140,
  186, 189, 615, 717
Isabella I, Queen of, I
  of Castile 46, 140
Joseph Bonaparte,
  King of 83
Julie (Marie-Julie)
  (Clary), Queen of
  83
monarchs of xiv,
  xv, 45, 141, 288
Philip II, King of
  18, 615
Philip IV, King of
  140, 191
SPALDING
Margaret 214
SPARANERO
Francesco [Franco
  Nero] 246

SPARKES
　Valentia 822
SPARROW
　Frances 484
SPATHIS
　Penelope Helen 593
SPAULDING
　Thomas W., Jr. xlviii, lxvii
SPEAKE
　Frances (Gerard) 515
SPEAR
　Elizabeth 245
SPECCOT/ SPECOTT
　Edmund 835
　Jane 835
　Jane (Grenville) 835
　Mary 436
SPEKE
　Dorothy 296
SPELMAN
　Ela 489
SPENCE
　family xi
　Harriet Brackett 86
　James 86
　Janet (Blaw) 86
　Keith xlix, cl, clxiii, 86
　Mary (Traill) 86
SPENCER
　Agnes (Harris) xix, lxiv, clxiii, 867, 924
　Alice 70, 79, 137
　Anne 302, 596

　Anne, Lady 299
　Anne (Churchill) 75
　Caroline (Russell) 62, 299
　Catherine 361, 389, 401, 418, 431
　Diana 33
　Diana Frances, Princess of Wales viii, xviii, xl, xlii, xliii, liv, 25, 32, 101, 306, 377, 380, 416, 417, 432, 482, 492, 543, 552, 576, 755, 858, 859, 930, 932
　Edward John Spencer, 8th Earl 932
　Eleanor (Beaufort) 300, 418
　Elizabeth 111
　Esther 157
　Frances (Mottrom) 306
　Frances Ruth (Burke Roche) 932
　George, 4th Duke of Marlborough 62, 299
　George John Spencer, 2nd Earl 551
　Georgiana 69, 75
　Georgiana Caroline (Carteret) 69, 70
　John 489
　John (Hon.) 69, 75
　John Spencer, 1st Earl 69, 74

　Margaret 110, 300
　Margaret Georgiana (Poyntz) 69, 74
　Mary 755
　Mary (Gostwick) 306
　Nicholas 306
　Nicholas (Act. Gov.) 306
　Penelope xlix, lxi, cl, 489, 490
　Penelope (Jernegan) 489
　Penelope (Wriothesley) 137
　Robert (Sir) 300, 418
　Robert, 3rd Earl of Sunderland 75
　Sarah 867, 924
　Susan (Knightley) 596, 755
　Thomas 489
　William 867, 924
　William (Sir) 596, 755
　William Spencer, 2nd Baron 137
SPENCER-CHURCHILL
　Agnes Beryl 80
　Albertha Frances Anne (Hamilton) 26, 28
　Alexandra Mary (Cadogan) 27
　Anne Clarissa 585, 648

1519

Augusta (Warburton) 80
Charles Richard John, 9th Duke of Marlborough 26
Clementine Ogilvy (Hozier) 67, 585, 648
Consuelo (Vanderbilt) 26
Cornelia Henrietta Maria 63
Edward, Lord 80
Frances Anne Emily (Vane-Stewart) 26, 63
George, 5th Duke of Marlborough 62
George, 6th Duke of Marlborough 63, 80
George Charles, 8th Duke of Marlborough 26, 28
Gwendoline Theresa Mary (Bertie) 585, 648
Jane Frances Clinton (Stewart) 63, 80
Jennie (Jerome) 63, 584, 585, 648
John Robert Edward, 10th Duke of Marlborough 27
John Strange 585, 648
John Winston, 7th Duke of Marlborough 26, 63
Pamela Beryl (Digby) (Hon.) 67
Randolph Frederick Edward 67
Randolph Henry [Lord Randolph Churchill] 63, 584, 648
Sarah Consuelo, Lady clvii, 27
Susan (Stewart) 62
Winston Leonard (Sir) (Prime Minister) [Sir Winston Churchill] 49, 63, 67, 371, 585, 648, 755, 967

SPENDLY
Joan (___) 727

SPENS
Agnes 252
Axel, Baron 889
Sofia (Rytter) 889
Virginia, Baroness 889

SPENSER
Edmund 478
Elizabeth (Boyle) 478

SPERANDIEU (DE)
Gabrielle 736

SPIER
Anthony 590
Barbara (Castillion) 590
Margaret 590

SPIGNO
Anna Teresa Canali, Marchesa di 18

SPINE (DE LA)/ SPINNEY
Alice (de Bruley) 874
Eleanor 755, 857, 874
Guy (Sir) 874
Katherine (___) 874
Margery (Durvassal) 874
William 874

SPINUCCI
Clara, Countess von der Lausitz 20

SPLATT
Anne (Mellish) cxlviii, 311
Mary 311
Richard 311

SPOFFORD
Hannah (Tyler) 370
John (IV) 370
Phoebe 370
Sarah (___) 898

SPONECK (VON)
Anna Sabina von Hedwiger, Countess 184
Leopoldine Eberhardine, Countess 184

SPOONER
Amy xiii
Hannah (Stanton) xiii

John xiii
SPÖRCKEN (VON)
 Charlotte Wilhelmine Hedwig, Baroness 58
 Melusina Agnes, Baroness 58
SPOTSWOOD
 Alexander (Lieut. Gov.) xxxv, clxvii, clxxi, 278
 Anne Butler (Brayne) 278
 Barbara 285
 Bethia (Morrison) 278
 Catherine (___) 278
 Dorothea 278, 301
 family lv
 John, Archbishop of St. Andrews 278
 Rachel (Lindsay) 278
 Robert 278
 Robert (Sir), of Dunipage 278
SPRAGUE
 Mary Jane 769
SPRIGGS
 Elizabeth (Poyntz) (Watts) 423, 424
 ___ 424
SPRING
 Dorothy (Waldegrave) 661, 662
 Frances 661
 John (Sir) 661

SPRINGER
 Bridget 379, 381
SPRINGETT
 Gulielma Maria 149
SPROULE
 Sarah 245
SQUIBB
 G. D. lxvii
SQUIERS
 Helen Fargo 44
SQUILACCE-CALABRIA
 Robert I of Dreux, Count of 956
ST. ALBANS
 Charles Beauclerk, 1st Duke of 33
 Francis Bacon, 1st Viscount [Sir Francis Bacon] 684, 846
ST. ANDREWS
 John Spotswood, Archbishop of 278
ST. AUBIN
 Isabel 845, 846
ST. BARBE
 Alice 678
 Jane (Harcourt) 678
 Joan (___) 678
 Joan (Sydenham) 678
 John 678
 Margery (Grey) 678
 Mary 678

 Richard 678
 Thomas 678
ST. CLAIR
 Edith 372
ST. CLAIR-ERSKINE
 Blanche Adeliza (Fitzroy) 33
 Millicent Fanny 33
 Robert Francis, 4th Earl of Rosslyn 33
ST. GEORGE
 Anne (Hatfield) 464
 Anne (Pinnock) 464
 Bridget (Blakeney) 465
 Catherine (Gifford) 462
 Elizabeth (Bligh) 464
 Elizabeth (St. John) 462
 family xxxiv
 Florence Evelyn (Baker) 465
 Frances 463
 George 464
 George (Sir) 462, 463, 464
 George Baker Bligh 465
 Henry 464
 Henry (Sir) 463, 464
 Howard Bligh 465
 Katherine Delano Price (Collier) 465

Mary 462
Mary (Dayrell) 463
Richard 464
Richard (Sir) 462
Richard (Sir), 1st Bt. 464
Richard Bligh (Sir), 2nd Bt. 465
Robert 465
Sarah (Persse) 464
Sophia Madelina Olivia (Mahon) 465

ST. GERMANS
Edward Granville Eliot, 3rd Earl of 64
William Eliot, 2nd Earl of 64

ST. HILAIRE (DE)
Maud 866, 870

ST. JOHN
Agnes 824
Agnes (Fisher) 662
Alexander 747
Alice 596, 662
Alice (Bradshaw) 318, 547
Anne 317, 318, 361, 384, 431
Barbara (Bladen) 313
Barbara (Gore) 590
Cresset 754
Dorothy 560
Elizabeth clxii, clxxvi, 462, 590, 747, 924

Elizabeth (Blount) 462
Elizabeth (Oxenbridge) (Cockcroft) 324, 326
Elizabeth (Scrope) 590
Elizabeth (Whetehill) 590
family xxxii
Henry 747
Henry (Hon.) 313
Isabel (Courtenay) 739
Jane (Dalison) 747
Jane (Iwardby) 590
Jane (Neale) 747
Jill [Jill Oppenheim] 44
John 462, 590
John (Sir) 318, 547, 590, 596, 662, 747, 754
John St. John, 1st Baron 739
Margaret 547, 662, 740
Margaret (Beauchamp) 547, 590
Margaret (Carew) 462, 465
Margaret (Waldegrave) 662, 754
Nicholas 462
Oliver 590, 747
Oliver (Sir) 547, 590

Oliver, 1st Baron St. John of Bletso 662
Sarah (Bulkeley) 747
Sybil (ferch Morgan ap Jenkin) 547, 596, 747
William 590

ST. LAWRENCE
Alison 486
Genet (Plunkett) 486
Henriétta Eliza 308
Henrietta Elizabeth Digby (Barfoot) 308
Isabella (King) 308
Margaret (Burke) 308
Nicholas, 16th Baron Howth 486
Thomas, 1st Earl of Howth 308
Thomas, 3rd Earl of Howth 308
William, 2nd Earl of Howth 308

ST. LEGER
Anne lxvi, 119, 121, 123, 126, 133, 347, 467
Anne (Plantagenet) (Holand) xl, 119, 126, 133
Anthony (Sir) 347
Dorothy 480
family liii
Jacquetta 743

Katherine liii, 296, 347, 839
Mary liii, 348
Mary (Heyward) 347
Mary (Scott) 347
Thomas (Sir) xl, 119, 126, 133
Ursula liii, 348
Ursula (Neville) 347
Warham (Sir) 347, 348

ST. LIZ (SENLIS) (DE)
Alice 851, 920
Matilda 851, 879, 920
Simon, Earl of Huntingdon and Northampton 778, 779, 780, 783, 785, 787, 789, 879, 919

ST. LO
Elizabeth 626
Elizabeth (Chiffinch) 626
family 627
George 626

ST. LOE
Elizabeth (Hardwick) (Barlow) (Cavendish) ["Bess of Hardwick"] 468, 512, 706

ST. MARTIN
Christiana (___) 855
Eva (___) 855
family 856
Joan 855

Joan (de Neville) 855
Jordan 855
Lawrence (Sir) 855, 856
Reynold/Reginald (Sir) 855, 856
Sybil (Lorti) 855
William (Sir) 855, 856

ST. MAURE
Elizabeth (Brooke) 595
Joan 595
John 595

ST. NICHOLAS
Deborah 358
Dorothy 357
Dorothy (Tilghman) 357
John 358
Marion (Brockhull) (Harfleet) 357
Thomas 357, 358
Vincent 357

ST. PAUL
Ellen (Neville) 755
Jane 343
John 755
Joyce 755
William 755
___ (Tyrwhitt) 755

ST. PAUL(E) (DE)
Aymon de Blonay, Seigneur 872
Jean de Blonay, Seigneur 911
Marie 285

ST. PHILIBERT (DE)
Ada (de Botetourte) 763, 768, 770
John (Sir) 763, 768, 770
Maud 763, 768, 770

ST. POL
Guy II de Châtillon, Count of 733
Guy III de Châtillon, Count of 633, 942, 944

ST. QUENTIN near PARIS
Pepin, lord of Peronne and, Count 879, 919

ST. QUINTIN
Agnes (Herbert) 725
Alice (de Ros) 725
Anthony 725
Elizabeth (Gascoigne) 725
family clxxxii, 726
Geoffrey 725
Geoffrey (Sir) 725
Joan/Elizabeth (de Thwenge) 725
John (Sir) 725, 726
Lora 667, 917
Margaret 725
Margery (Constable) 725
William (Sir) 725

STAATEN
Roger de Ghistelles, Seigneur de Dudzeele and 950

**STACKELBURG
(VON)**
  Anna 849
STACKPOLE (DE)
  Isabel 723
STACY
  Hannah (Littlehale) 632
  John 632
  Mary 632
  Mary (Clarke) 632
  Mary (Rand) 632
  Nymphas 632
  Philemon 632
STAFFORD
  Anne 331, 340, 400, 403, 421
  Anne (Neville) 393, 403
  Anne (Plantagenet) 393, 403, 409, 420, 421, 428, 436
  Anne (Tyler) 145
  Bulkeley Buckingham 145
  Catherine (Woodville) 333, 347, 431
  Dorothy (Stafford) 114
  Edmund Stafford, 1st Baron 819
  Edmund Stafford, 6th Earl of 393, 403
  Edward 145
  Edward, 3rd Duke of Buckingham 333, 347, 431
  Edward William (Sir), P.M. of New Zealand 145
  Eleanor (Aylesbury) 506, 532, 575, 763
  Eleanor (Percy) 333, 347, 431
  Elizabeth 114, 332, 333, 431, 482, 505, 506, 532, 575
  Elizabeth (Burdet) 763
  Ellen 763
  family xli, 327, 329, 349
  George William Jerningham, 2nd Baron 23
  Granville Leveson-Gower, 1st Marquess of 64, 71, 75
  Henry, 2nd Duke of Buckingham 333, 347, 431
  Henry Stafford, Baron 114
  Hugh Stafford, 2nd Earl of 495, 577, 590, 615
  Humphrey 331, 763
  Humphrey (Sir) 506, 532, 575, 763
  Humphrey, 1st Duke of Buckingham 393, 403
  Joan 393, 819, 820
  John (Sir) 819, 820
  Katherine 353, 577, 615, 677
  Katherine (Fray) 331, 763
  Katherine (Hastang) 819
  Margaret 318, 425, 495, 565, 590
  Margaret (Basset) 819
  Margaret (de Audley) 495, 505, 575, 577, 590, 615, 819
  Margaret (Stafford) 819, 820
  Margaret (Tame) 763
  Mary 122, 347
  Mary (Agnew) 145
  Maud (Hastang) 763
  Philippa (Beauchamp) 495, 577, 590, 615
  Ralph 763
  Ralph Stafford, 1st Earl of 495, 505, 575, 577, 590, 615, 819
  Ursula (Pole) 114
  William (Sir) 114
  William Jerningham, 1st Baron 23
STAGG
  Margery/Margaret 835
STAINES
  Mary 424

STAKE
  Märta 662
STALLO
  Helen McDonald 83
STAMP
  Marion Ellina 108
STANDISH
  Alexander 611
  Alexander (Sir)
    clxxxiv, 702
  Alice 611
  Anne (Molyneux)
    611
  Christian (Lace)
    clxxxiv
  Constance (Gerard)
    clxxxiv, 702
  Elizabeth 127
  family clxxxiv
  Gilbert clxxxiv
  Grace 702
  Huan clxxxiv
  Hugh, of Ormskirk
    clxxxiv
  John clxxxiv
  Mallie (Moore)
    clxxxiv
  Margaret (Croft)
    clxxxiv
  Myles (Capt.)
    clxxxiv
  Oliver 702
  Robert clxxxiv
STANFORD
  Elizabeth clxxxvii,
    508
STANHOPE
  Anne 305
  Bridget 368
  Elizabeth 350, 432
  Katherine (Hastings)
    107
  Maria 273
  Philip, 1st Earl of
    Chesterfield 107,
    109
  Philip Dormer, 4th
    Earl of
    Chesterfield 107
  Sarah 107
STANISLAUS II
AUGUST
  (Poniatowski), King
    of Poland 154
STANLEY
  Alice (Grosvenor)
    497
  Alice (Houghton)
    497
  Alice (Spencer) 70,
    79
  Alice Caroline
    xviii, 364, 434
  Amelia Ann Sophia
    62, 68, 637
  Anne 497, 499,
    517, 532, 676, 677,
    697, 721
  Anne (Harington)
    497
  Anne (Hart) 397,
    902
  Anne (Hastings)
    355, 904, 905
  Bridget (Broome)
    (Blount) 531
  Catherine 396, 407,
    497, 532, 558, 560
  Cecily (Freebody)
    407
  Cecily (Tarleton)
    497
  Charlotte (de La
    Trémouille) 62,
    637
  Dorothy 904
  Dorothy (Howard)
    75, 355, 904
  Dorothy (Tennant)
    130
  Edward 397
  Edward, 3rd Earl of
    Derby 75, 355,
    904
  Edward John, 2nd
    Baron Stanley of
    Alderley 22
  Eleanor 902
  Eleanor (Neville)
    355, 397, 433, 902
  Eleanor (Sutton)
    (Beaumont) 407,
    676
  Elizabeth 79, 231,
    355, 407, 611
  Elizabeth (de Vere)
    62, 68
  Elizabeth (Hopton)
    560
  Elizabeth (Weever)
    517, 558
  family 397, 561, 564
  Ferdinando, 5th Earl
    of Derby 70, 79
  Frances 70, 110,
    389, 755
  George 407, 676

George, Baron
 Strange 355, 397,
 433
Gwenhwyfar 689
Henrietta Blanche 22
Henrietta Maria
 (Dillon-Lee) 22
Henry 397
Henry, 4th Earl of
 Derby 62, 70, 75,
 79, 904
Henry Morton (Sir)
 xvii, 130
James 397
James (Sir) 397,
 902
James, 7th Earl of
 Derby 62, 637
Jane Caroline
 (Mahon) 364, 434
Joan 560
Joan (Beaumont)
 560
Joan (Goushill)
 397, 497, 510, 517,
 524, 532, 558, 560,
 563, 574, 611
Joan (Strange) 397,
 433, 902
John 407
John (Sir) 517, 558
Katherine Louisa 22
Louis Crandall
 364, 434
Margaret 355, 397,
 433, 510, 524, 563,
 574, 905
Margaret (Clifford)
 62, 70, 79, 904

Margaret (Stanley)
 397
Margery 558
Mary (Savage) 497
Maud 592
Peter 497, 499
Thomas, 1st Earl of
 Derby 397, 433,
 902
Thomas, 2nd Earl of
 Derby 355, 904,
 905
Thomas Stanley, 1st
 Baron 397, 497,
 510, 517, 524, 532,
 558, 560, 563, 574,
 611
William 397, 497
William (Sir) 497,
 560
William, 6th Earl of
 Derby 62
**STANLEY
ERRINGTON**
Ethel 123
Julia (MacDonald)
 123
Rowland (Sir), 11th
 Bt. 123
**STANLEY-MASSEY-
STANLEY**
Maria Frances 124
Mary (Haggerston)
 123
Thomas (Sir), 9th
 Bt. 123
STANSBY
family clxxxvi

STANTON
Hannah xiii
Henry xiii
John xiii, 468
Mary 480
Mary (Clarke)
 (Cranston) (Jones)
 xiii, 468
Mary (Hull) xiii
Permelia 925
STAPLES
Elizabeth 321
STAPLETON
Brian (Sir) 483,
 489, 536, 587, 606
Brian/Bryan 390,
 587
Catherine (de la Pole)
 483, 489, 536, 606
Cecily (Bardolf)
 483, 489, 536, 587,
 606
Dorothy 126
Dorothy (Hill) 126
Elizabeth 483, 489,
 536, 587, 606
Elizabeth (Darcy)
 390
Frances (Slingsby)
 390
Grace 390
Henry (Sir), 1st Bt.
 390
Isabel/Elizabeth
 (___) 587
Jane 126, 401
John 687
Katherine
 (Constable) 126

Margaret 687
Margaret (Deviock) 687
Margaret (Stapleton) 687
Mary 687, 688
Miles (Sir) 483, 489, 536, 606
Mona Josephine, Baroness Beaumont 72
Philip 126, 132
Robert (Sir) 126
STAPLEY
Elizabeth 475
STARHEMBERG (VON)
Anna (von Zinzendorf and Pottendorf), Baroness 237
Conrad, Count 237
Heinrich Ernst Rüdiger, Count 237
STARZHAUSEN (VON)
Joanna 622
STAUNTON
Elizabeth 830
Margaret 653
STAVELY
Isabel 387
STAVENISSE (VAN)
Brustijn van Herwijnen, Heer 447, 907
STAVERTON
Elizabeth 853

Elizabeth (Dabridgecourt) 853, 854
family clxxxvi
Ralph 853, 854
William 854
STAWELL
Eleanor (Merton) 695
Geoffrey 695
Joan (de Columbiers) 695
Juliana (Gastelin) 695
Margery 695
Matthew 695
STEBBINS
Josephine Vail 77
STEDMAN
Mary 345
Murray Salisbury, Jr. 626
Susan (Winter) 626
STEEN
Margaret 817
STEFAN
Archduke of Austria, Prince of Tuscany [Stefan Habsburg-Lothringen] 2
STEIN
Margaret 285
STEINBERG
Judith 162
STENBOCK
Beata Margareta (Brahe), Countess 452, 453
Eric, Count of Bogesund 452

Eva Magdalena (Oxenstierna), Countess 453
Gustaf, Baron of Kronobäck and Oresten 452, 453
Gustav Otto, Count 453
Katharina (von Schwerin) 452
Magdalena, Countess 452, 453
Magnus, Count 453
Ulrika Magdalena, Countess 453
STÉPHANIE-CLOTILDE-LOUISE-HERMINE-MARIA-CHARLOTTE
Princess of the Belgians, Crown Princess of Austria 204, 288
STÉPHANIE-MARIE-ÉLISABETH
Grimaldi, Princess of Monaco 934
STEPHEN
(Adeline) Virginia 611
family xxxvii
King of England 642, 774, 776, 830, 911
Leslie (Sir) 611
STEPHEN II
Duke of Bavaria-Landshut 451

1527

STEPHEN V
  King of Hungary 459
STEPHENS/
  STEVENS
  Abigail 138
  Ann (___) 82
  Anne (Stratton)
    (Lake) 706
  Dorothy 625
  Elizabeth 377
  family 323
  Frances (Cole-
    pepper/Culpeper)
    296, 347, 839, 856
  Jessie Anne 673
  Judith (Morseley)
    856
  Martha (Timbrell)
    507
  Mary 322, 323
  Mary Ernestine 989
  Mary (Newdigate)
    517, 518
  Mary Gill Caldwell
    148, 149
  Samuel (Gov.)
    347, 839
  Sarah 350
  William 706
  William (Gov.)
    517, 518
STEPLE/STAPYLLES
  Eleanor 506
STERNBERG (VON)
  Margaret 640
STERNBURG-
  MANDERSCHEID
  Maria Walpurga of
    38

STEUART
  Gladys Virginia 935
  Helen 165
  Helen (Cockburn)
    165
  John Henry 935
  Mary Virginia
    Ramsay (Harding)
    935
  Robert (Sir), 1st Bt.
    165
STEUBEN (VON)
  Augustin 181
  Charlotte Dorothea
    (von Effern),
    Countess 181
  Friedrich Wilhelm
    Ludolf Gerhard
    Augustin, Baron
    xvi, xxvi, liii, 141,
    181
  Maria Justina
    Dorothea (von
    Jagow) 181
  Wilhelm Augustin
    181
STEVENS. see
  STEPHENS/
  STEVENS
STEVENSON
  Fanny (Van de Grift)
    (Osborne) 270
  Margaret Isabella
    (Balfour) 270
  Robert Louis xvii,
    cxlvi, 270
  Thomas 270
STEVENTON
  Anne 411

Elizabeth (Vernon)
    411, 412
  John 411
STEWARD
  Scott Campbell ix,
    xlii, l, lxiii, lxiv,
    lxvii, lxxi, 374, 570
STEWART. see also
  STUART
  Adam, Lord 88
  Agnes (Keith) 93,
    95, 97
  Agnes, Countess of
    Bothwell 128,
    143, 146, 150, 151,
    152, 159, 161, 163,
    165, 166, 170, 177
  Alexander 264
  Alexander, 6th Earl of
    Galloway 62, 933
  Alexander, of
    Ardvorlich 264
  Alexander, of
    Ledcreish 264
  Alice (Cockburn)
    241
  Annabel (Buchanan)
    264
  Annabella, Princess
    of Scotland viii,
    176, 223
  Anne (Dashwood)
    62, 80
  Anne (de la Queuille)
    215
  Anne (Gordon) 93,
    97
  Anne (Stewart)
    145, 215

Barbara 85, 88
Catherine 154,
  157, 167, 168, 179,
  261, 264, 265
Catherine
  (Cochrane) 62,
  933
Catherine (de
  Balsac) 154, 215
Catherine
  (Drummond), of
  Logie Almond 897
Catherine
  (Rutherford) 241
Catherine (Stewart)
  264
Charlotte 62
Christian 87, 241,
  276
Christian (Erskine)
  276
Christian (Hay) 241
Christian Mary
  897
Clementina
  (Stewart), of
  Ballechin 897
Daniel (Gen.) 470
David, of Rosyth
  276, 277
Dorothea 151, 170
Duncan (Lieut.
  Gov.) 264, 265
Duncan, of Glenogle
  264
Edward Richard
  (Hon.) 80
Eleanor (Sinclair)
  219, 261, 278, 283

Elizabeth 82, 88,
  90, 93, 95, 97, 176,
  214, 218, 219, 239,
  256, 280, 283, 285,
  456, 805
Elizabeth (Gordon)
  176
Elizabeth
  (Hamilton) 148,
  215, 218
Elizabeth
  (Mackenzie) 897
Elizabeth (Menzie)
  264
Elizabeth (Stewart)
  88, 93, 95, 97, 148
Elizabeth, Princess
  of England and
  Scotland, Queen of
  Bohemia 38
Esmé, 1st Duke of
  Lennox 154, 215
Euphemia (Reddich)
  264
family 264, 265
Francis, 1st Earl of
  Bothwell 90, 96
George (Sir), 5th Bt.
  897
George, 8th Earl of
  Galloway 63
Giles/Egidia,
  Princess of
  Scotland 275, 278
Grizel 95
Grizel (Rattray)
  261, 266
Grizel/Elizabeth, of
  Kildon[n]an 263

Harriet 933
Harry, of Graemsay
  85
Helen 88, 145, 148
Helen (Menteith)
  85
Henrietta 93, 97,
  154, 161
Henry 88
Henry, 1st Baron
  Methven 151, 170
Henry, Lord
  Darnley xii
Isabel 269, 280,
  283
Isabel (de Ergadia)
  456
James (Sir), of
  Baldoran 264
James (Sir), "The
  Black Knight of
  Lorne" 241, 249,
  256, 261, 273, 278,
  280, 283
James, 1st Earl of
  Arran 88
James, 1st Earl of
  Buchan 241, 273,
  285
James, 1st Earl of
  Moray 93, 95, 97
James, 2nd Earl of
  Moray 93, 95, 97
James, 3rd Earl of
  Moray 93, 97
James, 4th Earl of
  Moray 93, 893
James, of Baldoran
  264

James, of Graemsay 85
James, of Traquair 241
Jane (Paget) 63
Jane Frances Clinton 63, 80
Janet 151, 176, 241, 249, 264
Janet (Campbell) 261, 266, 283
Janet (Kennedy) 82, 84, 85, 87, 92, 98, 151, 170, 897
Janet (McDougal) (Williamson) 264
Janet (Ruthven) 88
Janet (Stewart) 151, 170, 264
Jean 88, 92, 96, 146, 166, 176, 278, 456, 897
Jean (Hepburn) 90, 96
Jean (Mackenzie) 897
Joan 143, 146, 150, 151, 152, 159, 161, 163, 165, 166, 170, 177
Joan (Stewart) 280, 283
Joan, Princess of Scotland, "the dumb lady" 173, 222, 223, 225, 898
John (Sir), 3rd Bt. 897

John (Sir), 4th Bt. 897
John (Sir), of Ardgowan, Blackhall, and Auchingoun 263, 264
John (Sir), of Innermeath and Lorne 456
John, 1st Earl of Atholl 249, 256, 261, 278, 283
John, 2nd Baron Lorne 269, 270, 280, 283, 284
John, 2nd Earl of Atholl 151, 170, 261, 283
John, 3rd Earl of Atholl 261, 266
John, 3rd Earl of Lennox 145, 148, 215
John, 4th Earl of Atholl 88, 146, 176
John, 7th Earl of Galloway 62, 63, 64, 80
John, lord of Aubigny 215
John, Prior of Coldingham 90, 96
John Stewart, 1st Earl of 219
Katherine (Charteris-Wemyss) 80
Katherine (Kerr) 241

Katherine/Jean/Elizabeth, Princess of Scotland 275, 276, 282, 285
Margaret 85, 90, 143, 148, 154, 157, 159, 163, 165, 168, 171, 173, 174, 176, 218, 219, 261, 263, 264, 266, 272, 893, 933
Margaret, Princess of Scotland 219, 249, 256
Margaret (Douglas) 90, 96, 249, 256
Margaret (Drummond), of Drummonderinoch 264
Margaret (Fleming) 88, 146
Margaret (Graham), Countess of Menteith 264, 269, 272, 273, 280, 283
Margaret (Home) 90, 93, 893
Margaret (Ogilvy) 241, 273
Margaret (Urie) 88
Mariot (Campbell) 264
Marjorie, Princess of Scotland 219, 281
Marjory 269, 280, 283

Martha 225, 283, 471
Mary 88, 97, 98, 215, 216
Mary, Princess of Scotland 148, 154, 157, 167, 168, 179, 210, 213, 214, 215, 216, 218, 239, 240, 241, 243, 245, 248, 250, 251, 252, 253, 254, 255, 257, 258, 260, 261, 266, 267, 268, 940
Mary, Queen of Scots xii, xl, 90
Matilda 245
Matthew, 2nd Earl of Lennox 148, 215, 218
Murdoch, 2nd Duke of Albany 264
Octavia Catherine 363
Patrick 264
Penelope (Jones) 264
Robert (Sir), of Schillinglaw 241
Robert, 1st Baron Lorne 269, 280, 283
Robert, 1st Duke of Albany 264, 269, 272, 273, 280, 283
Robert, 1st Earl of Orkney 82, 84, 85, 87, 89, 92, 98, 897
Sibella (Primrose) 85

Susan 62
Susannah 64
Susannah (Oswald) 470
Thomas (Sir), 1st Bt. 897
Walter, of Baldoran 264
William lxx, cl, 240, 264
William, of Baldoran 264
William, of Traquair 241
___ (Colvin) 264
___ (Stewart), of Glenbuckie 264
___ [Mary?] 273

STEWART/STUART
Estelle 138
Thomas 138

STIER
Albert-Jean 804
Henri-Joseph, Seigneur of Aertselaer vii, liv, lxviii, 804, 805
Isabelle-Hélène (de la Bistrate) 804
Marie-Louise (Peeters) 804
Rosalie Eugenia 804

STIERNA
Christina 53
Göran 53
Virginia (Rytter) 53

STIGLIANO
Andrea Colonna, Prince of 189

STILLMAN
Hannah 213

STIRLING
Archibald (Sir), of Keir 258
Archibald Hugh 23
Charmian Rachel (Montagu-Douglas-Scott) 23
Christian 174, 275
Diana (Rigg) (Gueffen) [Dame Diana Rigg] 23
George 174, 175
James (Sir), of Keir 258
Jean 258, 259
Jean (Chisholm) 258
Jean (Stirling) 175
John (Sir), of Keir 151, 258
John, of Herbertshire 174
Lilias 151
Lilias (Colquhoun) 151
Margaret vi, lxiii, lxvii, clxvii, 174, 175, 264
Margaret (Forrester) 258
Mary (Drummond) 258
Mary (Erskine) 174
Sharon Helene (Silver) 23
Susan Rachel (Bligh) 23

1531

William (Sir), 2nd Bt. 174
William (Sir), 3rd Bt., of Glorat 175
William Joseph 23
____ (wife or mistress of George Stirling) 174
STIRLING-MAXWELL
Archibald 23
Margaret Mary (Fraser) 23
STITES
Mary (Underhill) (Naylor) lx, cxlvi, clxxxi, 875, 1025
Richard 875
STOBO
Patience 176
STOCK
Jane (Adams) clviii, 424
Jane Susanne 424
John 424
STOCKBRIDGE
Katherine 749
STOCKELEFF
Anna (von Medehem/ Medem) 449
Ilsabe 449
Marcus 449
STOCKETT
Mary (Wells) 625
STOCKMAN
Anne (Leigh) 476
John lii, 476
Joseph 476

Sarah (Pike) (Bradbury) 476
STOCKTON
Harold [Maurice Harold] Macmillan, Prime Minister, 1st Earl of 26
STOKES
Elizabeth 344
Martha Anne 688
STOLBERG-GEDERN
Caroline, Princess of 47
Frederick Carl, Prince of 47
Louis Christian I, Count of 47
STONARD
Helen 489
STONE
Ann 463
Don Charles ix, xlviii, xlix, lxiii, lxvii, lxviii, lxix, lxxi, clxxxv, clxxxviii, 230, 412, 759
Sibella 306
STONOR
Elise (Peel) 66
Frances (Towneley) 66
Francis 66
Francis Robert, 4th Baron Camoys 66
Jessica (Jessie)
Philippa (Carew) 66

Joan (de la Pole) 353
Mary 353
Mildred (Sherman) 66
Noreen (Mildred Sophia Noreen) (Hon.) [Hon. Mrs. Drexel] cliii, 66
Ralph Francis Julian, 5th Baron Camoys 66
Thomas 353
Thomas, 3rd Baron Camoys 66
STORER
Anne cxlvi, 628
Arthur cxlvi, 628, 629
Catherine (Babington) 628
Edward 628
family 155
Inez (von Bachelin) [Inez Storer] 5
STORRS
Martha (Burgess) 702
Mary 702
Samuel, Jr. 702
STORY
Elizabeth 710
Patience (Gardiner) 231
STOTEVILLE (DE). *see* ESTOUTEVILLE (D')/TOUTEVILLE/ DE STUTEVILLE
STOTT
Clifford L. clxxxiv

STOUGHTON
Agnes (___) 920
Agnes (Pierce) 623
Anthony 623
Edward 920
Elizabeth xiv, cli, 921
Elizabeth (Knight) 920
Elizabeth (Lewknor) 623, 624
Elizabeth (Thomson) 920
family xl, l, liii, lxx, 624, 922
Francis 920
Israel cli, 916, 920
Judith cli, 921
Katherine (___) 920
Lawrence (Sir) 623, 624
Margaret (Barrett) (Huntington) 920
Mary (Exhurst) 920
Rebecca 921
Rose lviii, lxv, cxlv, clxix, clxxv, 623, 945
Rose (Ive) 623
Thomas cli, 623, 624, 920, 922
William (Gov.) 920, 921

STOURTON
Edith 547
Margaret 855
Margaret (or Mary) 674

STOUT
Alice 508

STOWE
Eliakim 584, 647
Lydia (Miller) 584, 647
Nathaniel 584, 647
Sarah (Sumner) 584, 647
Thankful 584, 647

STRACHEN
Helen 163

STRACHEY
Eleanor (Read) 852
Elizabeth (Cross) 825, 852
Elizabeth (Elletson) 825
Elizabeth (Vernon) 825
family xxxvii, xxxviii, liii, lxvi
Frances (Forster) 825, 852
Helen (Clark) 825
Henry 825
Henry (Sir), 1st Bt. 825
Jane (Hodges) 825, 852
John 825, 852
Lytton (Giles Lytton) 825
Martha (___) 852
Mary (___) 825
Mary (Cooke) 852
Mary (Miller) 852
William clxxvii, clxxx, 825, 852

STRACHWITZ VON GROSS-ZAUCHE UND KAMMINETZ
Alexander Maria Hubertus Hyacinthus, Count clviii, 39
Christian Alexander Maria [Chris Strachwitz] 39
Emma (von Landsberg-Velen), Baroness 39
Friederike Frances Adelheid (von Bredow) 39
Hermann Franz Arthur 39

STRADLING
Alice (Langford) 716
Anna 716
Edward (Sir) 295, 298, 337, 375, 382, 900
Elizabeth 338
Elizabeth (Arundell) 337
Elizabeth (Herbert) 337, 375, 382, 900
family 298, 717
Henry (Sir) 337, 375, 382, 900
Jane 337, 338, 375, 382, 396, 510, 563, 900
Jane (Beaufort) 295, 337, 375, 382, 900
Janet (Mathew) 337, 375, 382, 900

John 716
Katherine (or Joan) 295, 298
Thomas 337, 375, 382, 900
STRANG
Nancy 985
STRANGE
Charlotte Murray, Baroness, Lady of the Isle of Man 66
Elizabeth 475
George Stanley, Baron 355, 397, 433, 902
Jacquetta (Woodville) 397, 433, 902
Joan 355, 397, 433, 902
John, 8th Baron Strange of Knokyn 397, 433, 902
STRANGEWAYS/ STRANGWAYS
Catherine (Neville) 370
Dorothy (Thynne) 133
Giles (Sir) 133
Grace 133
Henry (Sir) 133
Joan 370, 372
Joan (Wadham) 133
John 133
Margaret (Manners) 133
Thomas (Sir) 370

STRANGMAN
Josephine 308
STRATFIELD
Alice of 853
STRATFORD
Arundel 345
STRATHALLAN
William Drummond, 4th Viscount 65
STRATHBOGIE
David, 2nd Earl of Atholl 528
David, 8th Earl of Atholl 697
David, 10th Earl of Atholl 697
Elizabeth 528
Elizabeth (Ferrers) 528
Isabel (de Dover/de Chilham) 697
Joan (Comyn) 697
John, 9th Earl of Atholl 697
STRATHMORE
Claude Bowes-Lyon, 13th Earl of, Earl of Kinghorne 101, 930
Claude George Bowes-Lyon, 14th Earl of, Earl of Kinghorne 930
John Bowes-Lyon, 9th Earl of 101
Thomas Bowes-Lyon, 11th Earl of 101

STRATHNAVER
William Gordon [later Sutherland], Lord 98
STRATI
Patricia Wright ix, lxvii
STRATTON
Anne 706
Anne (Derehaugh) xlvi, cxlvi, clxii, 661, 706, 924
Cecily (Felton) 705
Dorothy 661, 706
Dorothy (Nicolls) 705
Edward 705
Elizabeth lxvii, clxii, clxxvi, 133, 503, 608, 661, 706, 924
Elizabeth (Luttrell) 503, 608
Eugene Aubrey xx, xlvi, xlvii, xlviii, lii, lvi, lxiii, lxiv, lxvi, lxvii, lxviii
family xlviii, lxvi, lxvii, 705
Joan (___) 705
John clxxvi, 503, 608, 661, 705, 706, 924
Joseph 705
Keziah 520
Thomas 705
STREET
Mary (Newman) 854

Melinda 97
STRETLE
  Isabel 857
STREUN ZU
  SCHWARZENAU
  Agnes 619
STREZEW
  Vsevolod III, Prince
    of 849
STRICKLAND (DE)
  Agnes (Hamerton?)
    398
  Alice (Tempest)
    398
  Ellen 398
  Elizabeth
    (d'Eyncourt) 864
  Joan 864
  Katherine (Neville)
    398
  Margaret 128
  Margaret
    (Cholmley) 127
  Walter 398
  Walter (Sir) 398,
    864
  William (Sir), 1st
    Bt. 127
STRODE
  Anne 308
  Elizabeth 346, 573
  Elizabeth
    (Courtenay) 573
  Frances (Cromwell)
    308
  Juliana 308
  Mary (Southcott)
    308
  Richard 308

Susannah (___)
  92
William 573
William (Sir) 308
STROGANOV
  Elena, Countess 7
  Grigori, Count 7
STROMBERG
  Anna Catharina 51
STRONACH
  Margaret 828
STRONG
  Benajah 932
  Eleanor 932
  Joseph (Dr.) 932
  Lucy (Bishop) 932
  Rebecca (Young)
    932
STROTHER
  Dorothy (___) 421
  Eleanor (Conyers)
    421
  Elizabeth 421
  Elizabeth (___)
    421
  Elizabeth (Berry)
    421
  family xxiv, 422
  Francis 421, 533
  Lancelot 421
  Margaret (Thornton)
    421, 532
  Robert 421
  Sarah (Bayly) 421,
    533
  Sarah Dabney 421,
    533
  Susannah (Dabney)
    421, 533

William xlvii, lxii,
  clxvii, clxxix,
  clxxxviii, 421, 422,
  533, 1025
William, Jr. 421, 532
STROUP
  Louise Eliza 726
STUART. *see also*
  STEWART
  Catherine, Baroness
    Clifton 122
  Charles, 4th Earl of
    Traquair 155
  Christian li
  Christian (Anstruther)
    155
  Christian, Lady 155
  family xlv, lxx
  Harriet R. 136, 138
  Jane 128
  John, 3rd Earl of
    Bute 299
  John, 6th Earl of
    Traquair 155
  John, Jr. 655
  Margaret xxviii
  Mary 655
  Mary (Maxwell)
    155
  Mary (Wortley-
    Montagu) 299
  Sophia (Jones) 655
STUART-MENTETH
  Catherine Maria
    (Wheeler) 79
  Charles Granville
    (Sir), 1st Bt. 79
  Isabella Maria
    (Tobin) 79

James 79
Ludivina
  (Loughnan) 79
Philadelphia 79
Thomas Loughnan
  xlvi, 79
STUBBMAN
Anne 546
STUBBS
Dionysia 359
STUDEMUND
Auguste Friederike
  (von Bernstorff)
  37
Friedrich 37
Luise 37
STUKELEY
Alice 744
Anne (Wood) 632
Elizabeth
  (FitzRoger)
  (Bonville) 742
Hugh 743
Joan 743
Katherine (de
  Affeton) 743
Margery 632
Nicholas 632, 743,
  744
Richard 742
Thomas (Sir) 632
Thomasine
  (Cockworthy)
  632, 743
STURGES
Hannah 901
STURT
Mary 135

**STUTEVILLE/
TOUTEVILLE
(DE).** *see*
ESTOUTEVILLE
(D')/TOUTEVILLE/
DE STUTEVILLE
ST.-VALÉRY (DE)
Eleanor 956
Laure 853
ST.-VALLIER (DE)
Aimé de Poitiers,
  Seigneur 952
STYLE
Elizabeth (Airmine)
  389
Rebecca 484
Susan 389
Thomas (Sir), 2nd
  Bt. 389
SUBLIGNY (DE)
Jean I Tesson,
  Seigneur 959
Jean II Tesson,
  Seigneur 959
SUFFIELD
Edward Harbord,
  2nd Baron 135
SUFFOLK
Charles Brandon,
  1st Duke of
  clxxxiii, 62, 69, 76,
  79, 80
Henry Brandon, 2nd
  Duke of clxxxviii
Henry Grey, 1st Duke
  of 69, 76, 80
Mary (Tudor),
  Princess of England,
  Queen of France,

  Duchess of xxxix,
  clxxxiii, clxxxviii,
  62, 69, 76, 79, 80
Michael de la Pole,
  2nd Earl of 353,
  577, 615
Theophilus Howard,
  2nd Earl of 334
Thomas Howard, 1st
  Earl of 334, 335,
  482
William de la Pole,
  1st Duke of 353
SULLIVAN
Jeanet Ellinwood
  542
SULLY (DE)
Agnes 830
family 442
Henri II, Sire 954
Isabel (de Craon)
  634
Jean II, Sire 634
Jeanne 954
Louis, Sire 634
Marie 634
Pernelle (de Joigny)
  954
William of
  Champagne,
  Seigneur 830
SULYARD(E)
Anne 607, 608
Anne (Andrews)
  608
Frances Henrietta
  23
John (Sir) 608
Mary 508, 596

SULZBACH
Augusta Sophie,
  Princess of 35, 49
Augustus, Count
  Palatine of 35, 49
SUMMERSBY
Gordon Thomas
  546
Kathleen Helen
  (MacCarthy-
  Morrogh) [Kay
  Summersby]
  xviii, cxlvi, 546
SUMNER
Elizabeth 397
Elizabeth
  (Clements) 584
family 585, 648
Hannah 585
Hannah (Henchman)
  584, 647
Sarah 584, 647
William 585
William, Jr. 584
William (III) 584,
  585, 647
SUNDERLAND
Alexander, 1st
  Baron Duffus 893
Anna (Hon.) 893
Charlotte Christina
  (Sjöbard),
  Baroness 893
Emanuel Scrope, 1st
  Earl of 431
James, 2nd Baron
  Duffus 893
Kenneth, 3rd Baron
  Duffus 893

Margaret
  (Mackenzie) 893
Margaret (Stewart)
  893
Robert Spencer, 3rd
  Earl of 75
SUNDSTRÖM
Elin 194
SURREY
Hamelin Plantagenet,
  Earl of x, 841,
  1025
Henry Howard, Earl
  of 62, 333, 335,
  431
William de Warren,
  2nd Earl of 841
William de Warren,
  3rd Earl of 841
SURRIAGE
Agnes 130
SURTEES
Bertha (Chauncey)
  100
Bertha Etelka 100
Charles Freville
  100
Crosier 100
Dorothy (Lambton)
  100
Elizabeth (Cookson)
  100
Herbert Conyers
  (Sir) 100
Jane (Surtees) 100
Madeleine Augusta
  (Crabbe) 100
Robert 100, 844

SUSA (DI)
Victoria Francesca
  of Savoy,
  Madamigella 18
SUSANNA
ferch Gruffudd ap
  Cynan ab Iago 815
SUSSEX
Robert Radcliffe, 1st
  Earl of 355, 905
Thomas Lennard,
  1st Earl of 109
SUTCLIFFE
Elizabeth 483
SUTHERLAND
Alexander Gordon,
  12th Earl of 82,
  148
Anne 893
Cromartie Leveson-
  Gower, 4th Duke
  of 33
Elizabeth 98
Elizabeth (Wemyss)
  98
Elizabeth Gordon,
  Countess of 71
George Gordon,
  15th Earl of
  Sutherland 98
George Granville
  Leveson-Gower,
  1st Duke of 71
George Granville
  William Leveson-
  Gower, 3rd Duke
  of 33
John Gordon, 11th
  Earl of 88, 148

1537

John Gordon, 16th
   Earl of 98
Katherine (Morison)
   98
Marjory 278
William Gordon,
   later Lord
   Strathnaver 98
William Sutherland,
   17th Earl of 98
**SUTHERLAND-
   LEVESON-GOWER**
Charlotte Sophia 71
Elizabeth Georgiana
   69, 75
George Granville,
   2nd Duke of
   Sutherland 33,
   69, 71
Harriet Elizabeth
   Georgiana (Howard)
   33, 69, 71
SUTHERST
Gladys Ethel
   Gwendolen
   Eugenie 9
SUTLIFF
Henry (III) ix,
   lxviii, 598
SUTTON. *see also*
   DUDLEY, SUTTON
   alias DUDLEY
Alice (Hall) 613
Anne 328, 497
Anne (Clarell) 515
Anne (Rodney)
   613, 614
Anne (Stanley)
   497, 499

Bridget 119
Catherine (Bassett)
   614
Constance (Blount)
   676, 677
Dorothy 319, 321
Edward 497
Eleanor 407, 628,
   630, 676
Elizabeth 426
Elizabeth (Berkeley)
   676, 691
Emeline (Disney)
   785
Hamon 785
Henry (Sir) 613, 614
Joan (___) 677
Joan (Clinton) 677
John 515
John (Sir) 676, 677
John, 1st Baron
   Dudley 676, 691
Katherine (Stafford)
   677
Margaret 515
Mary 785
Mary Georgiana
   (Manners-Sutton)
   120
Mary Isabella 120
Robert Nassau 120
Susan 613
Susan (Cony) 613
Thomas (Sir) 614
William 613
William (Sir) 613
**SUTTON alias
   DUDLEY.** *see also*
   DUDLEY; SUTTON

Cecily (Grey) 370
Cecily (Willoughby)
   370, 426
Edmund (Sir) 319,
   515
Edward, 2nd Baron
   Dudley 370, 426
John, 3rd Baron
   Dudley 370
Joyce (Tiptoft)
   319, 515
Matilda (Clifford)
   319
SUZDAL
Dimitri IV, Prince of,
   Prince of Vladimir
   791, 797
Eudoxia of 621,
   797
Maria of 791, 795
Semyon, Prince of
   791
SWABIA
Marie of 733
Philip of, King of
   the Romans lxiii,
   lxvii, 640, 733
SWAIN. *see also*
   SLETTENGREN
   (later changed to
   SWAIN)
Susan Wilhelmina
   53
SWEDEN
Anna Maria of
   Simmern, Queen
   of 40, 43
Brigitta (Bielke),
   Queen of 663

1538

Catherine, Princess
of 40, 43
Cecily, Princess of
208
Charles VIII
(Bonde), King of
457, 663, 664
Charles IX, King of
40, 43
Charles XIII, King
of 615
Charles XIV John
[Jean-Baptiste
Bernadotte], King
of 83
Christina, Queen of
615
Désirée [Desideria]
(Clary), Queen of
83
Eric XIV, King of
51, 53, 889
Gustav I (Vasa),
King of 40, 43,
51, 52, 53, 198,
199, 208, 267, 453,
889, 890, 893
Gustav VI Adolf,
King of 41
John III, King of
267, 453, 889, 890,
893
Katherine, Princess of
Saxe-Lauenburg,
Queen of 51, 52,
53, 889
Louise, Princess of
Battenberg, Queen
of 41

Margareta
(Leijonhufvud),
Queen of 40, 43,
198, 208, 267, 453
monarchs of xv,
45, 141, 444, 615
Oscar II, King of
615
Silvia Renate
(Sommerlath),
Queen of 991
SWEETMAN
Elizabeth 571
SWIFT
Elizabeth 143
Elizabeth (Dryden)
481
family lvi
Jonathan 481, 482
Jonathan, Dean of
St. Patrick's 482
Mary (Erick) 482
Thomas 481
SWINBORNE
Alice 766, 767
Joan (Botetourte)
766
Robert (Sir) 766
SWINBURNE
Algernon Charles
xxiv
SWINFEN
Alice (Ragdale)
819
Arthur 819
Dorothy (Noel)
819
Elizabeth 819
William 819

SWING
Laura Sparkes 548
SWINNERTON
Elizabeth (Beke)
752, 760, 772
family vii
Maud 497, 687,
752, 760, 772
Maud (Holand)
752, 760, 772
Robert (Sir) 752,
760, 772
Thomas (Sir) 752,
760, 772
SWINNOE
Ursula 821
SWINTON
Alan Henry
Campbell 177
Alexander (Sir), of
Mersington 272
Alexander (Sir), of
that Ilk 272
Alison (Skene) 272
Archibald Campbell
177
Elizabeth 272
Elizabeth
(Ebsworth) 177
George Sitwell
Campbell 177
Georgiana Caroline
(Sitwell) 177
Jean (Hepburn) 272
John (Sir) 177
John (Sir), of that
Ilk 272
John, of that Ilk
272

Judith Balfour
  (Killen) 177
Katherine (Lauder)
  272
Margaret (Home)
  272
Margaret (Stewart)
  272
Marion (Home) 272
Mariora Beatrice
  Evelyn Rochfort
  (Hankey) 177
Marjory (Dunbar)
  272
Robert, of that Ilk
  272
Tilda (Katherine
  Matilda) xvii,
  clviii, 177
SWYNFORD
Catherine (Roët)
  295, 300, 314, 324,
  331, 337, 339, 345,
  357, 366, 368, 370,
  375, 382, 387, 393,
  395, 396, 397, 398,
  403, 405, 407, 413,
  417, 419, 421, 426,
  427, 429, 433, 434,
  900, 902
SWYNHO
Margaret 725
SYBIL. *see also*
  SIBYL
  of Anhalt-Zerbst
  184
  ferch Morgan ap
  Jenkin 547, 596,
  747

SYDENHAM
Anne 423
Elizabeth 493
Elizabeth (Audley)
  423
Joan 678
John 423
John (Sir) 423
Mary (Poyntz) 423
Maud 835
Ursula (Bridges) 423
SYDNOR
Bridget (Jernegan)
  490
family 490
Fortunatus xlix,
  lxix, cxlvi, clxxix,
  490
Hester (Catelyn/
  Catlin) 490
Joan (Acton) 490
Joanna (Lawson)
  (Sockwell) 490
Paul 490
William 490
SYLVESTER
Constant 385, 386
Grace (Walrond)
  385, 386
Mary 385, 386
SYMES/SYME/SIMS
Abraham 364
Adam 338
Amy (Bridges) 337
Amy (Horner) 337
Anne 364
Anne (Le Hunte) 364
Dorothy (Everard)
  337

Edward 337
family 337, 338
George xlix, lxv,
  cl, 337, 338
John 337
Matthew 337
Sarah (Winston) 219
Thomas 337
SYMMES
Alice 343
Anna (Tuthill) 867
Anna Tuthill xlii,
  496, 503, 731, 867,
  878
Elizabeth (Collamore)
  867
family 344
John Cleves 867
Margaret (Bosvile)
  343
Mary (Cleves) 867
Timothy 867
Timothy, Jr. 867
William 343
SYMONDS
Davida E. ix,
  lxviii, 396
Isabel 377
SYNCH
Mary Kathleen 242
SYNGE
Cathleen clvi, 254
Edmund John
  Millington 254
Edward 254
Elizabeth Eleanor
  Mabel (Allen) 254
Ellen Frances
  (Price) 254

1540

John Hatch 254
John Lighton 254
Kathleen (Trail[l]) 254
SYPHER
Francis S. 734
SYRIA
monarchs of xv
SZÁPÁRY
Anton, Count 35
Anton Carl
  Sylvester, Count
  xviii, clviii, 35, 36, 209
Augusta (Keglevich
  von Buzin),
  Countess 35
Geza, Count 35
Maria (Gvöry von
  Radvány),
  Countess 35
Maria
  (Przezdziecka),
  Countess 35
Paul Anton
  Ladislaus Agoston
  Maria, Count 35
Sylvia (Széchényi),
  Countess 35
SZCZUCZANKA
Sophia 802
SZÉCHÉNYI (VON SÁRVÁR FELSŐVIDEK)
Alexandra (Sztáray-Szirnay), Countess 209
Emmerich (Irme), Count 209

Francizka de Paula
  (von Wurmbrand-Stuppach),
  Countess 209
Gladys Moore
  (Vanderbilt) 35, 209
Ladislaus (László),
  Count xviii, clviii, 35, 209
Ludwig Maria
  Alois, Count 209
Maria Agatha
  Franziska
  Ludovica
  Stephanie,
  Countess 187
Sylvia, Countess
  35, 209
SZEMIOTOWNA
Cunegonda 802
SZTÁRAY-SZIRNAY
Alexandra, Countess 209
TAFT
Aaron 318
Alphonso 318, 881
Helen (Herron)
  xliii, 318, 881
Louisa Maria
  (Torrey) 318, 881
Peter Rawson 318
Rhoda (Rawson) 318
Sylvia (Howard) 318
William Howard,
  27th U.S. President 291, 318, 881

TAGLIAVIA d'ARAGONA
Diego, Duke of
  Terranova 192
Giovanna, Duchess
  of Terranova 192
Juana Estefanía
  (Cortés), Marquesa
  del Valle de
  Oaxaca 192
TAILER/TAYLOR
Elizabeth 329, 355, 921, 924
Rebecca (Stoughton) 921
William 921
TAILLEBOURG (DE)
Charles de La
  Trémouille, Count 636
Olivier de Coëtivy,
  Seigneur 208
TAIT
Archibald Campbell, Archbishop of
  Canterbury 177
Crawford, of
  Harviestown 177
Susan (Campbell) 177
Susan Murray 177
TALBOT
Alice 530, 553, 555, 603
Alison (Netterville) 486
Ankaret (le Strange) 478, 512, 530, 553, 555, 603

1541

Anne lxix, cxlviii, cli, clxv, 120, 124, 125, 130, 339, 377, 500, 574
Anne (___) (Herbert) 711
Anne (Nugent) 739
Anne (Paston) 407
Anne (Ryley) 841
Anne (Talbot) 120, 125
Anne (Yate) 125
Audrey (Cotton) 574
Augusta 72
Barbara (Slingsby) 130
Charles, 1st Duke of Shrewsbury 125
Charles Talbot, 2nd Earl 137
Dorothy (Braddyll) 841
Edward 120, 125
Elizabeth 407, 414
Elizabeth (Butler) 500, 574
Elizabeth (Greystock) 407
Elizabeth (Hardwick) (Barlow) (Cavendish) (St. Loe), Countess of Shrewsbury ["Bess of Hardwick"] 468, 512, 706
family 124, 739
Frances (Arundell) 125

Frances Thomasine (Lambart) 137
George 739, 841
George, "Earl of Shrewsbury" 125
George, Jr. *see* Peter Talbot below
Gilbert (Hon.) 120
Gilbert (Sir) 407, 574
Gilbert, 13th Earl of Shrewsbury 125
Gilbert Talbot, 3rd Baron 478, 512, 530, 553, 555, 603
Grace 512
Grace (Calvert) (Hon.) 739
Hannah (Clarke) (Frizzell) 841
Helen/Ellen (Calvert) (Hon.) 739
Isabel (Jenney) 489, 711
James 739
Jane (Flatsbury) 120
Jane (Mede) 711
Joan Ankaret 125
John 125, 841
John (Rev.) 489, 711, 712
John (Sir) 130, 574
John, 2nd Earl of Shrewsbury 500, 574
John, 10th Earl of Shrewsbury 120, 125

John Ivory 130
Mabel (Carleton) 841
Margaret (Troutbeck) 574
Martha 130
Mary 125, 478, 486, 512
Mary (Fortescue) 120
Mary (Gold) (Wodell) 841
Mary (Mansel) 130
Mary (Talbot) 120
Peter xlvi, clxii, clxxvii, clxxx, clxxxv, clxxxviii
Peter [George, Jr.] 841, 842
Petronilla (Butler) 478, 512, 530, 553, 555, 603
Philippa (Ferrers) 512
Richard Talbot, 4th Baron 478, 512, 530, 553, 555, 603
Robert (Sir), 2nd Bt. 739
Sarah (___) 739
Thomas 125, 711
William (Sir), 1st Bt. 486
William (Sir), 3rd Bt. 739
___ 486

TALBOYS
Anne 310, 311, 389, 399, 414

Eleanor (de
 Burradon/de
 Boroughdon) 730
Elizabeth 311
Elizabeth
 (Gascoigne) 310,
 389, 399, 414
Elizabeth (Heron)
 310, 519
Elizabeth "Bessy"
 (Blount) 530
family 1025
George (Sir) 310,
 389, 399, 414
Gilbert, 1st Baron
 Talboys of Kyme
 530
Henry (Sir) 730
Margaret 512, 730
Margaret
 (Deincourt?) 730
Maud 327, 409,
 519, 719, 720
Robert (Sir) 310,
 519
Walter (Sir) 730
TALVAS
Ela 737, 855
William III, Count
 of Alençon and
 Ponthieu 737,
 853, 855
TAME
Margaret 763
TAMLYN
Anne 836
TAMWORTH
Catherine cxci

TANEY
Anne Phoebe
 Charlton (Key)
 333
Roger Brooke (Atty.
 Gen., Chief
 Justice) 333
TANFIELD
Anne 387
Bridget (Cave)
 387, 717
Catherine (Neville)
 387
Francis 387, 717
Isabel (Stavely) 387
Robert 387
William 387
TANGUAY
Marie-Thérèse 977
TANGUY
Kay Linn (Sage)
 (Bourbon del
 Monte Santa
 Maria) xviii, 20
Yves 20
TANGWYSTL
ferch Rhydderch ab
 Ieuan Llwyd 657,
 692
ferch Rhys ap
 Hywel Sais 810
TANKERVILLE
Henry Grey, 2nd
 Earl of 229, 231,
 233, 235, 377, 411
TANNER
Beatrice Stella [Mrs.
 Patrick Campbell]
 585, 648

TANNET
Dorothy 626
TANTON
Dorothea 322
TAPLIN
Catherine (Lovewell)
 519, 520
Henry 519, 520
John, Jr. 519
Lucinda 520
Melinda (Huntley)
 519, 520
Mortimer Mason
 520
TAPPEN
Helen 924
Peter Crannel 924
Sarah Lorania
 (Trowbridge) 924
TARDIF
Anne 946
Sophie 977
TARENT
Mary 261
TARLETON
Cecily 497
TARNOWSKA
Sophia, Countess
 621
TARONITES
family lxiii, lxvii
___ 640, 733
TARRAGON (DE)
Anne-Élisabeth
 939, 948, 985
Élisabeth/Isabelle
 (de Merlin) 948
Loup, Seigneur de
 Juvainville 948

Roland 939, 949
TARTAS (DE)
  Jean d'Albret,
    Vicomte 287, 293
TASBURGH
  Frances 30
TASCHER (DE)
  Edmée-Henriette-
    Madeleine (du
    Plessis) 442
  Gaspard, Seigneur
    de la Pagerie 442
  Gaspard-Joseph,
    Seigneur de la
    Pagerie 442
  Joseph-Gaspard,
    Seigneur de la
    Pagerie 442
  Marie-Françoise
    (Boureau
    [Bourreau] de la
    Chevalerie) 442
  Rose-Claire (des
    Vergers de
    Sannois) 442
TASCHER DE LA
PAGERIE (DE)
  Marie-Josèphe-Rose
    [Joséphine,
    Empress of the
    French] 292, 442,
    443, 444
TASCHEREAU
  Gabriel-Elzéar 951
  Marie-Louise-
    Élisabeth (Bazin)
    (Amiot) 951
TASKER
  Anne 327, 328

  Anne (Bladen)
    327, 752
  Benjamin (Act.
    Gov.) 327, 752
  Elizabeth 752
TASSELL
  Anne 490
TATE
  Arundel (Stratford)
    345
  Bartholomew 345
  Elizabeth xlviii,
    cxliv, 346
  Isabella (Traill) 88
  Katherine
    (Alington) 345
  Mary 346
  Mary (Noel) 345
  Mary (Stedman)
    345
  William 88, 345
  Zouche 345
TATHAM
  Barbara (Fleming)
    611
  Charles 611
  Elizabeth (Marsden)
    611
  John 611
  Mildred (Sandford)
    611
  Sandford 611
  William xlix, cli,
    611, 612
TATIANA
  Grand Duchess of
    Russia 7
TATISTCHEV
  Daria 794

TATTERSHALL
  Mary 625
TAVISTOCK
  Francis Russell,
    Marquess of 25
TAYLER
  Alistair xxix, lxviii
  Catherine Mary 130
  Henrietta xxix, lxviii
TAYLOE
  Elizabeth (Kingsmill)
    878
TAYLOR
  Albertina Shelton
    165
  Alice Eleanor 567
  Anne (Winslow)
    479
  Barbara (Hanbury)
    537
  Christopher 670,
    671
  Elizabeth xlix, cli,
    clxxix, 479, 537
  Elizabeth (Fuller?)
    670
  Elizabeth Dawson
    609
  Elizabeth Rosemond
    [Elizabeth Taylor]
    21, 190
  Frances Margaret
    (Kenyon) 592
  Geoffrey Fausit 592
  Grace 136
  Humphrey John
    Fausit clviii, 593
  James lii, lxv, cxlvi,
    clxii, 64, 670, 671

John 479
Margaret Mackall
  (Smith) 421, 533
Maria 348
Mary (Foxall) 670,
  671
Mary (Shotbolt) 537
Nathaniel Lane ix,
  xlvii, xlix, lv, lvi,
  lxiv, lxvi, lxvii,
  lxviii, lxix, 399,
  412, 531, 696, 709
Penelope Helen
  (Spathis) 593
Rebecca (Clark)
  670
Richard 421, 533
Sarah Dabney
  (Strother) 421,
  533
Sarah Knox 421,
  533
Thomas 537
William 537
Zachary, 12th U.S.
  President 421,
  533
TAZEWELL
  Anne (Kingsmill)
    310
  James 310
  Sophia (Harmanson)
    310
  William xlviii, cl,
    310
TEACKLE
  Margaret (Nelson)
    lvii, clxxix,
    clxxxviii, 356

Thomas (Rev.) 356
**TELES DE
MENEZES**
  María 619
TELLER/TAILLIER
  Margaret/Margret
    (Duncanson) cl,
    cli, clxviii, 248
  William 248
**TELLEZ
D'ACOSTA**
  Jeanne-Thérèse
    455
TELNICZANKA
  Katarzyna 895
TEMPEST
  Alice 398
  Anne 539, 540
  Dowsabel 395
  Eleanor 100
  John 539
  Katherine (de
    Welles) 539
  Robert 539
TEMPLE
  Christian 315
  Christian (Leveson)
    315
  Dorothy 356, 827
  Dorothy (Lee) 355
  Elizabeth 738
  Elizabeth (Bowdoin)
    923
  Elizabeth Bowdoin
    923
  family 356
  Harriet Penelope
    541
  Jane Martha 54

John (Sir) 355
John (Sir), 8th Bt.
  923
John Alexander 356
Mary 355, 356
Mary (Knapp) 315
Mehitable (Nelson)
  923
Peter (Sir), 2nd Bt.
  315
Richard (Sir), 3rd
  Bt. 315
Robert 923
Thomas (Sir), 1st
  Bt. (Gov.) 356
**TEMPLE-
BLACKWOOD**
  Frederick, 1st
    Marquess of
    Dufferin and Ava
    32
TEMPSKI (VON)
  Amy Dulcibella
    (Wodehouse)
    clviii, 131
  Armine 131, 132
  Louis 131, 132
TENAY (DE)
  Marguerite 638
**TENBE AND
SOMMERIVE**
  Honorat II de
    Savoie, Count of
    442
**TENDERYNG/
TENDRING**
  Alice
  family 1025
  Joan 806

1545

TENGNAGELL
  Alexander, Heer van
    Oploo 447
  Josina (van Dorth)
    447
  Maria 447
TENISON
  Mary 109
TENNANT
  Charles 130
  David Francis (Hon.)
    78, 109, 113
  Dorothy 130
  Edward Priaulx, 1st
    Baron Glenconner
    78
  Gertrude Barbara
    Rich (Collier) 130
  Hermione Youlanda
    Ruby (Clinton-
    Baddeley)
    [Hermione
    Baddeley] xvii,
    lxiii, clii, 78, 109,
    113
  Pamela Adelaide
    Genevieve
    (Wyndham) 78
  Shelagh Ann
    (Rainey) 78
  Virginia Penelope
    (Parsons) 78
TENNENT
  Catherine (Kennedy)
    xii, lvii, cl, 898
  Catherine (Van
    Brugh) (Noble)
    898
  Cornelia (De Peyster)
    (Clarkson) 898
  Gilbert (Rev.) 898
  Sarah (___)
    (Spofford) 898
  Suzanne (Vergereau)
    898
  William, Jr. (Rev.)
    898
  William (III) (Rev.)
    898
  William (Rev.) 898
TENNYSON
  Alfred Tennyson,
    1st Baron [Alfred,
    Lord Tennyson]
    xxiv, 355
TENREMONDE (DE)
  Antoinette 733
**TEODOSIO
  (THEODORE) II**
  Duke of Braganza
    140
TEPPER
  Michael v, vi, viii
TERNAY (DE)
  Jacques de Beauvau,
    Seigneur de Tigny
    and 941
TERNEY (DE)
  Jeanne 941
TERRANOVA
  Diego Tagliavia
    d'Aragona, Duke
    of 192
  Francesco Maria
    Correale, Count of
    190
  Giovanna Tagliavia
    d'Aragona, Duchess
    of 192
TERRY
  Ellen (Dame) 803
  Fred 803
  Kate 803
  Marion 803
TERVES (DE)
  Marie 964
TESCHEN
  Margaret of liv,
    lvii, 713, 714
  Przemysl I Nosak,
    Duke of, Duke of
    Glogau 713
TESSIER
  Anne-Marie 969,
    981, 982
  Élisabeth 954, 955
  Jeanne-Anne-Marie
    (Amiot) 969, 975,
    981, 982
  Marie-Catherine 975
  Paul 969, 975, 981,
    982
TESSON
  Isabelle 959
  Jean I, Seigneur de
    Subligny 959
  Jean II, Seigneur de
    Subligny 959
  Pétronille (de
    Montfort) 959
  Raoul V, Seigneur de
    la Roche-Tesson
    959
  Thomasse (___)
    959

TESTARD (DE)
  Marie-Anne 634
TEYNHAM
  Christopher Roper,
    5th Baron 109
  Henry Roper, 6th
    Baron 109
THACHER
  Peter (Rev.) 324
  Theodora
    (Oxenbridge) 324
THACKER
  Eltonhead (Conway)
    497
  Henry 497
  Martha 497
THATCHER
  Catherine 301
THEOBALD I
  King of Navarre
    993
**THEOPHANO
(SKLEROS)**
  wife of Otto II, Holy
    Roman Emperor
    849
THÈRE (DE)
  Joachine 961
THERMO
  Else 645
**THÉROUX/
THEROUX**
  Albert-Eugène 985
  Alexander Louis
    985, 986
  Anne (Castle) 985
  Anne Francesca
    (Dittami) 985
  Eugène-Albert 985

  Eva (Brousseau)
    985
  Geneviève
    (Badayac) 985
  Jean-Baptiste 985
  Jennifer Joanna
    (Aniston) (Pitt)
    [Jennifer Aniston]
    985, 986
  Joseph-Louis-Eugène
    985
  Justin Paul 985, 986
  Louis Sebastian
    985, 986
  Marcel Raymond
    985, 986
  Marie-Eugénie
    (Loiseau dit
    Cardin) 985
  Nancy (Strang)
    985
  Paul Edward 968,
    985, 986
  Peter Christopher
    Sebastian 985,
    986
  Phyllis (Grissim)
    985
  Pierre 985
  Sarah (Son) 985
  Sheila (Donnelly)
    985
  Susanna (Kleeman)
    985
THIARD (DE)
  Marie-Claudine-
    Silvie 24
THICKNESSE
  Mary (Touchet) 110

  Philip 110
**THICKNESSE-
TOUCHET**
  Elizabeth (Delaval)
    111
  Elizabeth Susanna
    111
  George, 19th Baron
    Audley 111
THIENE (DE)
  Agathe 442
  Bonne (de Burgat)
    442
  Edmé, Seigneur de
    Razay 442
  Henry, Seigneur de
    Razay 442
  Jacqueline (de
    Carnazet) 442
  Jeanne (de Villars)
    442
  Nicolas, Seigneur de
    Razay 442
THIERSTEIN
  Susanna of 617
THIES
  Johanna Louisa 908
THILL
  Becky (Mrs.) cxcii
THIMBLEBY
  Anne 715
  Elizabeth 519
  Elizabeth (Hilton)
    521, 715
  John 521
  Katherine (Tyrwhit)
    519
  Margaret (Boys)
    521

1547

Richard 521, 715
Richard (Sir) 521, 715
THION DE LA CHAUME
Jacqueline 227
THIRLESTANE
John Maitland, 1st Baron 177
THOMAS
ab Ieuan 658
Alice 548
Anna Lloyd (Braithwaite) 231, 232, 378
Anne (Griffith) 809
Anne (Lloyd) 809
ap Dafydd 693
ap Dafydd Gam 808, 809
ap Humphrey 689
ap Huw 809
ap John ap Morgan ap Gwilym 690
ap Morus 692
ap Robert 230, 658
ap Thomas ap John Wyn cxcii
of Brotherton, Prince of England, Earl of Norfolk xxxix, 462, 470, 473, 486, 493, 519, 522, 526, 534, 539, 541, 545, 557, 564, 579, 580, 598, 599, 604, 605, 609
Cadwalader 651, 809

Catherine 983
Christian Jean (Wallace) 321, 323
Christian Jeannette Paton 323
Dorothy (Carew) 338
Edgar Hastings 321, 322, 323
Elizabeth 338, 510
Elizabeth (King) 714
Ellen (Owen) 651, 809
Emmot 674
George 714
George (Sir) (Gov.), 1st Bt. clxxvi, 714
George Hudleston 321
Hilda Margaret Rose lxiii, 321, 322
Hugh Swynnerton, Baron Thomas of Swynnerton 994
Jane Ann 320
Joan (Lewis) 338
John 338, 809
Josiah (Ven.), Archdeacon of Bath 320
Katherine (Robert) 809
Lydia 302
Marquess of Saluzzo 642

Mary (Morgan) 338
Mary Anne (Broadhurst) 321
Prince of Carignan 18
Richard Henry (Dr.) 231
Sarah (Winthrop) 714
Susanna Isabella (Harington) 320
Thomas 338
William 338
of Woodstock, Prince of England, 1st Duke of Gloucester xxv, xxxix, 331, 353, 392, 393, 409, 420, 421, 428, 436
THOMAS GETHIN
ap Hywel Llwyd 659, 660
THOMOND
Donough O'Brien, 2nd Earl of 601
Henry O'Brien, 4th Earl of 122
Henry O'Brien, 6th Earl of 122
THOMPSON
Alice (Freeman) xix, xxxvii, xl, lvi, lxi, lxviii, lxix, lxxi, clxiii, clxxviii, 858, 859, 932
Dorothea (Tanton) 322

1548

Dorothy 347, 470, 491, 858, 860, 932
Elizabeth 489
Elizabeth (Blencowe) 322
Henry 322
Isabel 77
John 858, 932
Mary 858
Mary (Stephens/ Stevens) 322, 323
Neil D. ix, xii, xxv, xlvii, xlviii, xlix, li, lvii, lviii, lx, lxv, lxviii, lxxi, clxxxvi, cxc, cxci, 481, 490, 533, 680, 699, 884
Sarah 526
Stephens/Stevens xi, xlix, cxlvi, clxviii, 322, 323
Sydnor lxix
Thomasine (Ward) vii, lii, lxxi, clx, clxxvii, clxxx, clxxxviii, 741, 761, 762
William (Sir) 322, 323
Winifred 65

THOMSON
Elizabeth 920
Esther 88
Judith 314, 316

THOREAU
Cynthia (Dunbar) 655
Henry David 655

John 655

THORLEY
Margaret 623

THORNBOROUGH/ THORNBURG(H)
Alice (Lane) 909
Catherine (Langtree) 902
Charles 902
Charles C. (III) clxxxii
Edward cl, clxxxii, 902
Elizabeth (Leybourne) 902
Ethelred (Carus) 902
family clxxxii
Isabella (Salkeld) 909
Jane (Dalton) 902
Margaret 131
Margaret (___) 902
Mary (___) 902
Nicholas 909
Robert 902, 903
Rowland 902
Sarah (Jackson) 902, 903
Thomas cl, clxxxii, 902, 909
Thomasine (Bellingham) 902, 909
Walter 902
William 902
William (Sir) 902, 909

THORNDIKE
Andrew 923
Anna (Morgan) 923
Elizabeth 923
Elizabeth (Stratton) lxvii, clxii, clxxvi, 661, 706, 924
Israel 923
John lxvii, 706, 924
Mary (Bachelder) 924
Mary (Patch) 924
Mercy (Trask) 923
Paul 924
Paul, Jr. 924

THORNE
Mary (Purefoy) 373
Mary Jean 73
Susanna 370, 372, 373
Thomas 373

THORNES
Alice 233
Elizabeth (Astley) 233
Jane (Kynaston) 233
Joan (ferch Evan Lloyd Fychan) 233
John 233
Margaret (___) 233
Mary (Corbet) 233
Richard 233
Roger 233
Thomas 233

THORNTON
Alice (Savage) 532

Angelina Jolie
  (Voight) (Miller)
  [Angelina Jolie]
  967, 974
Anne (Smith) 587
Elizabeth 497, 532,
  548
Elizabeth (Cushin)
  587
family xxiv
Francis 532
Margaret 421, 532
Mary 587
Robert 587
Sydney 268
William 587
William Robert
  "Billy Bob" 974
THOROUGHGOOD/
THOROWGOOD
Anne 722
Elizabeth 471
THORPE
Isabel (Constable)
  667, 668
Margaret 667
Mary (Banks) 339
Stephen 667
THOUARS (DE)
Claude de La
  Trémouille, Duc
  62, 637
François de La
  Trémouille,
  Vicomte 636
Louis I de La
  Trémouille,
  Vicomte 634, 637

Louis III de La
  Trémouille, Duc
  637
THOVION (DE)
Clara 804
THOYRAS (DE)
Jacob de Rapin,
  Seigneur 634
Paul de Rapin,
  Seigneur 634
THRELFALL
John Brooks xlv,
  lix, lxix, clxxxiii,
  clxxxvi, clxxxviii
THRELKELD
Grace 321
THRIFT
Jane 875
THROCKMORTON
Agnes 857
Alice (Bedell) 720
Alice (Stout) 508
Anne (Chare/Chaire)
  720
Bassingborne 508
Catherine (Marrow)
  874
Clement 324
Eleanor 755
Eleanor (Spinney)
  755, 857, 874
Elizabeth 297
Elizabeth (Berkeley)
  297
Elizabeth (Blenner-
  hasset) 508
Elizabeth (Hussey)
  414, 416

Elizabeth (Pickering)
  719
Emma (Lawrence)
  719
family lxii, clxxxii,
  509, 862
Gabriel 719
George (Sir) 324,
  416
Goditha 721, 874
Jane (Baynard) 508
Jane (Beaufoe)
  719, 874
John lxii, lxiv,
  clxiii, clxxiv,
  clxxxii, 508, 509
John (Sir) 755,
  857, 874
John, Jr. 508
Judith (Hetley) 720
Katherine 324, 325
Katherine (Neville)
  324
Katherine (Vaux)
  324, 416
Lionel 508
Margaret (Olney)
  508, 721, 874
Margery 862, 875
Martha 325
Mary (Hill) 508
Muriel 414, 415
Patience 508
Rebecca (Farrand)
  508
Richard 719, 874
Robert lviii, lxiv,
  clxxx, 719, 720

Robert (Sir) 325, 414, 416, 874
Thomas (Sir) 297, 508, 721, 874

THURINGIA
Frederick II, Margrave of Meissen, Landgrave of 449, 451
William, Duke of Saxony, Landgrave of 220

THURLO
Mary 654

THURN UND TAXIS
Anselm Franz, Prince of 49
Maria Augusta, Princess of 49

THURTON
Grace (Shelton) 606
John 606
Maud 606

THWAITES
Anne 698
Elizabeth (Redman/Redmayne) 698
Isabel 600
Margaret 668
William 698

THWENGE (DE)
Joan/Elizabeth 725

THYNNE
Anne 335, 385
Catherine (Howard) 335
Dorothy 133
Elizabeth 70, 71

Elizabeth (Cavendish-Bentinck) 70
Frances 69
Frances (Finch) 69
Isabella Elizabeth (Byng) 70, 73
Louisa (Carteret) 70
Thomas (Sir) 335
Thomas, 1st Marquess of Bath 70
Thomas, 1st Viscount Weymouth 69, 70
Thomas, 2nd Marquess of Bath 70, 73
Thomas, 2nd Viscount Weymouth 70

TIARKS
Ada Constance Helen (Harington) 321
Anne Patricia 321
Evelyn Florence (Cripps) 321
John Gerhard 321
John Gerhard Edward 321

TIBETOT (DE)/TIPTOFT
Agnes (de Ros) 710, 719
Elizabeth 710, 719
family 1025
John de Tibetot/Tiptoft, 1st Baron 515, 600

John de Tibetot/Tiptoft, 2nd Baron 710, 719
Joyce 319, 515
Joyce (Cherleton) 515, 600
Margaret (Badlesmere) 710, 719
Margaret (Deincourt) 710, 719
Pain de Tibetot/Tiptoft, 1st Baron 710, 719
Philippa 600
Robert de Tibetot/Tiptoft, 3rd Baron 710, 719

TICHBORNE
Amphillis 626
Amphillis (Weston) 625
Anne (White) 625
Benjamin (Sir), 1st Bt. 625
Elizabeth (Rythe) 625
Ellen (White) 625
Henry (Sir), 3rd Bt. 905
Jane 625
Letitia 905
Mary (Arundell) 905
Nicholas 625
Richard (Sir), 2nd Bt. 625, 905
Susan (Waller) 905

TIGNY (DE)
Jacques de Beauvau, Seigneur, Seigneur de Ternay 941
TILDESLEY
Constance 815
TILGHMAN
Anna (Sanders) 358
Christopher cxci, 358
Dorothy 357
Elizabeth (Packnam) 357
family cxci, 358
Mary (Foxley) 357
Oswald 357
Richard lix, clxvi, 357
Ruth (Devonshire) 358
Susanna (Whetenhall) 357
William 357
TILL
Gertrude (Ross) 828
Isaac 828
TILLEY
Elizabeth 654, 983
TILLMAN
Elizabeth M. cxci
Stephen Frederick 358
TILLY (DE)
François-Joseph-Paul de Grasse, Count de Grasse, Marquis xvi, xxvi, lvii, 616
Jeanne 961

TILLYS
Cecily 587
TILNEY
Agnes 355, 605, 904
Elizabeth 300, 333, 353, 420, 428, 605, 705
Elizabeth (Cheney) 705
Frederick (Sir) 705
TIMBRELL
Martha 507
TIMBRUNE (DE)
Edmée-Nicole-Pulchérie (Brûlart) 206
Jean-Baptiste-Charles-Henri-Hector, Comte de Valence 206
Louise-Philippine-Séraphine-Félicité 206
TIMBRUNE DE VALENCE (DE)
Catherine-Jean-Emmanuel, Marquis de Valence 205
Émeric-Emmanuel, Marquis de Valence 205
Marie-Anne (du Breulh) 205
Marie-Louise (de Losse) 206
Renée-Charlotte (de La Roche) 205

Vincent-Sylvestre, Marquis de Ferrières 206
TIMEUR (DE)
Marie (de Rieux) 226
Sébastien de Ploëuc, Marquis 226
TINDALL
Zara Anne Elizabeth (Phillips) (wife of rugby champion Mike Tindall) 323
TIPTOFT. see TIBETOT (DE)/ TIPTOFT
TIROL
Elizabeth of (wife of Albert I, Holy Roman Emperor) 449, 451
TIRRELL
Jane 623
TISDALL
Mary 120
Mary (Brabazon) 120
William 120
TISENHUSEN (DE) (VON)
Anna (von Rosen) 849
Bartholomeus 849
Elsebe (Warendorp) 849
Fabian 849
Fromhold 849
Gertrude (von Rosen) 849

Johannes 849
Katherine (___)
  849
Madlena (von
  Kruse) 849
Madlena
  [Magdalena] 849
Peter 849
Sophia (von
  Kokenhusen) 849
TIZON (DE)
René du Bus,
  Seigneur 440
TOBIN
Isabella Maria 79
TOCCO (DI)
Dorotea 192
**TOCQUEVILLE
(DE)**
Alexis [Alexis-
  Henry de Clerel de
  Tocqueville] xvii,
  clviii, 294
Bernard-Bonaventure
  de Clerel, Count
  293
Hervé-Louis-
  François de Clerel,
  Count 293
Mary (Mottley) 294
TODD
Dorothea "Dolley"
  (Payne) 497, 532
Elizabeth Rosemond
  (Taylor) (Hilton)
  (Wilding)
  [Elizabeth Taylor]
  21, 190
Isabella 117

Mary 983
Sarah D. 673
TOENI (DE)
Alice 547, 783
Alice (de Bohun)
  547, 783
family 1025
Ida 737, 741, 742,
  746, 749, 752, 754,
  757, 760, 761, 763,
  766, 768, 770, 772,
  845
Margaret (de
  Beaumont) 845
Mary (___) 783
Ralph (Sir) 845
Ralph VII 783
Roger III 851
Roger V 547, 783
TOKTAI
Khan of the Golden
  Horde 797
TOLLEMACHE
Dorothy (Wentworth)
  349
Elizabeth 431, 432
Elizabeth (Cromwell)
  349
Elizabeth (Stanhope)
  350, 432
Lionel 349, 350
Lionel (Sir) 349
Lionel (Sir), 1st Bt.
  349
Lionel (Sir), 2nd Bt.
  350, 432
Mary 350
Susan 350
Susan (Jermyn) 349

TOLSON
Apollonia 321
TOLSTOY
Alexandra, Countess
  [Alexandra Leo
  Tolstoy] xviii,
  xxvi, clviii, 794,
  796
family xxii
Leo, Count xviii,
  xxvi, 193, 794
Maria (Volkonsky),
  Princess 794
Nicholas, Count
  794
Praskovia, Countess
  794
Sophia A. (Behrs)
  794
TOMBE (DES)
Jeanne 907
TOMKYNS
Louise 462
TOMLINSON
Catherine 385
TOMPKINS
Matthew clxxxviii
TONNERRE (DE)
Charles de Husson,
  Count 634
Charles-Henri de
  Clermont, Count
  de Clermont and
  202
Henri de Clermont,
  Count 202
Jacques du Bellay,
  Count 942

1553

TONY
Jane 537
TOPPING
David xlix, lxvii, lxviii, lxix, 412
TORBOCK
Catherine (Gerard) 558
Elizabeth (Moore) 558
Margaret 400, 558
Margery (Stanley) 558
Thomas 558
William 558
William (Sir) 558
TORDSDOTTER
Marta 452, 454
TORLONIA
Giulio, 2nd Duke of Poli and Guadagnolo 18
Marina xviii, lx, 18, 19
Marino, 4th Prince of Civitella-Cesi 18
Mary Elsie (Moore) 18
Teresa (Chigi-Albani) 18
TORRE (DE LA)
María 140
TORRE Y MIER (DE LA)
Suzanne-Marie-Stéphanie-Anne-Françoise 289

TORRENCE
Clayton xlix, lxix
TORREY
Anna (Davenport) 880
Clarence Almon xxviii, l, lvi, lviii, lix, lxi, lxix, lxxi
Deborah (Holbrook) 880
Jane (Haviland) clxii, 351
Joseph 880
Louisa Maria 318, 881
Samuel Davenport 880
Susan Holman (Waters) 880
Susanna (Giddings) 880
William 351, 880
TORRI
Giada 622
TORRIGLIA
Giovanni Andrea, Prince Doria-Pamfili-Landi, 2nd Prince of 18
Luigi Andrea Doria-Pamfili-Landi, Prince of Valmontore, 3rd Prince of 18
TORRINGTON
George Byng, 4th Viscount 73
TOTTESHURST
Margery clxxxvii

TOUCHEPRÈS (DE)
Antoine Menard, Seigneur 941
David Menard, Seigneur 941
François Menard, Seigneur 941
TOUCHET (or AUDLEY)
Anne 427, 565
Constance 410
Eleanor (Holand) 377, 410, 411, 423
Elizabeth (Arundell) 110
Elizabeth (Sneyd) 427
Elizabeth (Tuke) 427
George, 9th Baron Audley 427
Henry, 10th Baron Audley 427
James, 2nd Baron Audley 377, 410, 411, 423
James, 6th Earl of Castlehaven 110
James, 7th Baron Audley 427
John, 8th Baron Audley 427
Margaret 377, 378, 411, 569
Margaret (Dayrell) 427
Mary 110
Mary (Griffin) 427

TOULOUSE
Louis-Alexandre de Bourbon, Count of 287
TOUPIN dit DUSSAULT
Jean-Baptiste 988
Madeleine-Jacquette (Turcot) 988
Marie-Madeleine 623, 988
TOUR (DE LA)
Antoine de Beaumont, Seigneur 965
Bertrand VI, Count of Auvergne and Boulogne 637
Charles-Amador Turgis de Saint-Étienne (Gov.), Sieur 953
Claude Turgis de Saint-Étienne, Sieur 953
Jean I, Count of Auvergne and Boulogne 637
Jeanne (of Bourbon-Vendôme) 637
Louise (de La Trémouille) 637
TOUR (DE LA) DE SAINT-VIDAL
Philiberte 202
TOUR DU PIN (DE LA)
Albert, Baron 911
Catherine 952

Marie (d'Auvergne) 911
Sibylle 911
TOUR-LANDRY (DE LA)
François de Maillé de la Tour-Landry, Baron, Count de Châteauroux 455
TOUR-MAUBOURG (DE LA)
Just-Charles-César de Fay, Count 201
TOURNAY
Alice (Blechynden) 778
Jane 778
Thomas 778
TOURNOR
Edward, 5th Earl of Winterton 28
Georgiana Susan (Hamilton) 28
TOURZEL (DE)
Marguerite 293
TOVAR (DE/VON)
Elisabeth, Baroness 619
Luís/Ludwig, Baron von Enzesfeld 619
Susanna (Ottwein) 619
TOVAR Y CASTILLA (DE)
Ana 619
TOWE
Elizabeth 766
TOWGOOD
Andriah 594

TOWNELEY
Alice (Calvert) 700
Anne (Elborough) 859
Catherine (Curson) 859
Catherine (Forster) 552, 859
Charlotte Theresa (Drummond) 66
Edmund 859, 860
Elizabeth 701
Elizabeth (Smith) (Lawrence) (de Carteret) 552, 868, 881
family xxxiv, lxi, 859
Frances 66
Frances (Andrews) 859
Francis 552, 859
Grace 701
Helen (Hesketh) 700
Henry 700
Isabel (Sherburne) 700, 701
Jane 112
Jane (Gildredge) 112
Jennet (Halstead) 700
Jeremiah 859
Joan (White) 112, 552
John 700
Lawrence xxxiv, lxi, clxvii, 700, 701

1555

Margaret (Hartley) 700
Margaret Frances clxxviii, 859, 860
Mary xix, xxxiv, xl, lxi, clxviii, 700, 701, 930
Nicholas 112, 552
Peregrine Edward 66
Richard xlix, clxxiv, 552, 868, 881
Sarah 487
Sarah (Warner) 701
TOWNSHEND
Alice Cahen (d'Anvers) 112
Anne Elizabeth Clementina (Duff) 9
Audrey Dorothy Louise 112
Carolyn Elizabeth Ann, Lady xlv, 9
Charles Thornton 112
Charles Vere Ferrers (Sir) 112
Charlotte (Compton), Baroness Ferrers of Chartley 112
Elizabeth Pamela Audrey (Luby) 9
Frances (Baldwin) xi, xlix, liii, liv, cxlvii, clxviii, clxxxii, 727

Francis 727
George, 1st Marquess Townshend 112
George John Patrick Dominic, 7th Marquess Townshend 9
George Osborne (Lord) 112
Georgiana Anne (Poyntz) 112
Gladys Ethel Gwendolen Eugenie (Sutherst) 9
Jessie Victoria (McKellar) 112
John (Lord) 112
John, 4th Marquess Townshend 112
John James Dudley Stuart, 6th Marquess Townshend 9
John Villiers Stuart, 5th Marquess Townshend 9
Louise (Graham) 112
Richard 727
Robert 727
TOWRY
Anne 363
TOXWERDT
Marie Elisabeth Wilhelmine "Mimi" (Harbou) 645

Marie Gabrielle 645
Nicolas Peter Didrik 645
TOYNBEE
Arnold Joseph 299
Rosalind (Murray) 299
TRABUE
James Duvall 629
TRACY
Margaret 506
TRAFFORD
Edmund 561
Edmund (Sir) 558, 560
Elizabeth 561
Elizabeth (Longford) 561
Margaret (Savage) 558, 560, 561
Margery 558, 902
TRAHAEARN
ap Morgan 582
TRAHAN
Adelina 984
TRAIL(L)
Agnes (Gayer) 254
Anna (Baikie) 85, 88
Anne (Hayes) 254
Anthony 254
Barbara (Balfour) 85, 89
Charles 86
Elizabeth (Grotz) 88
family xi
George, of Holland 85, 89

George, of Quendall 85, 88
George William 85, 86
Isabell (Fea) 85
Isabella 88
Jean (Haldane) 254
John 85
Kathleen 254
Mary 85, 86
Mary (Colebrook) 85
Mary (Dow) 254
Mary (Gale) 85
Mary (Graham) 85, 89
Mary (Whipple) 85, 86
Mary Colebrooke 85, 86
Robert xlix, lxv, cl, clxiii, clxx, 85, 86, 88, 254
Sibella (Grant) 88
Thomas 88
William, of Kirkwall 85
William, of Westness 85, 89

TRANT
Helena 546

TRAPP (VON)
Agatha (Whitehead) 187, 188
Agathe Johanna Erwina Gobertina clviii, 187, 188
Erika (Klambauer) 187
family xii, xviii, xxxiv, liii, 187, 188
Georg(e) Johannes, Ritter 187, 188
Hedwig Maria Adolphine Gobertina clviii, 187, 188
Henriette (Lajoie) 187
Janice (Tyre) 187
Johanna Karolina clviii, 187, 188
Maria Agathe Franziska Gobertina clviii, 187, 188
Maria Augusta (Kutschera) 187
Martina clviii, 187, 188
Rupert Georg (Dr.) clviii, 187, 188
Werner clviii, 187, 188

TRAQUAIR
Charles Stuart, 4th Earl of 155
John Stuart, 6th Earl of 155

TRASK
Mercy 923

TRAUTMAN
Elizabeth 450

TRAUTSON
Maria Margareta 895

TRAVENFERT
Justina Margaretha 893

TRAVERS
Anne 874
Elizabeth 815

TRAVIS
Rebecca (Champion) 474

TRE ROSOR
Sigrid 452

TREADWAY
Alanis Nadine (Morrisette) 978
Mario 978

TREFFRY
Elizabeth (Killigrew) 665
Emilyn (Tresithny) 665
Janet 665
John 665
Martha 665
Thomas 665

TREGION
Jane 595

TRELAWNY
Jonathan (Sir), 2nd Bt. 305
Jonathan (Sir), 3rd Bt., Bishop of Winchester 305
Mary (Seymour) 305
Rebecca 305
Rebecca (Hele) 305

TREMAYNE
Elizabeth (Carew) 594
Joan 594
Margaret 674

Thomas 594
TRÉMOUILLE (DE LA). *see* LA TRÉMOUILLE (DE)
TRENCH
 Frances 157
TRENOWITH
 Margaret 665
TRESHAM
 Anne (Parr) 403
 Catherine 414, 415, 416
 Isabel 403
 Lewis (Sir) 416
 Muriel (Throckmorton) 414, 415
 Thomas (Sir) 403, 404, 414, 415
TRESITHNY
 Emilyn 665
TRETHERFF
 Elizabeth (Courtenay) 550
 John 550
 Margaret 550
 Maud (Trevisa) 550
 Thomas 550
TREUFFEN genannt LOWENSPRUNG (VON)
 Lucas 832
 Marie 832
 Ursula (Herport) 832
TREUHAFT
 Jessica Lucy (Freeman-Mitford) (Romilly) (Hon.)

[Jessica Mitford] xvii, 23, 26
 Robert Edward 23
TREVANION
 Anne (Edgcombe) 665
 Arabella 666
 Elizabeth (Pollard) 665
 Elizabeth (Sawle) 665
 Elizabeth (Westlake) 666
 Hugh (Sir) 665
 Jane (Petit) 665
 Janet (Treffry) 665
 John 665
 Margaret (Chamond) 665
 Mary (Rolle) 665
 Nathaniel 665
 Nicholas (Sir) 666
 Richard 665
 Thomas 665
 William (Sir) 665
 ___ (Maunder) 665
TREVELYAN
 family xxiv, xxxvii
 George Macaulay 436
 Janet Penrose (Ward) 436
TREVENEN
 Jane 436
TREVENER
 Margaret 835
TREVIÑO
 Pedro Manrique de Lara y Mendoza,

Lord of Amusco and 191
TREVISA
 Maud 550
TREVOR
 Anne 340
 Dorothy 235
 Rose 419, 813, 814
TREWORGY(E)
 John (Gov.) 489, 490
 Penelope (Spencer) xlix, lxi, cl, 489, 490
TRIEST
 Anne (de Bourgogne) 438
 family 439
 Jacqueline 438
 Nicolas, Seigneur de l'Auwerghem 438
TRIPP
 Anstice 595
 Phoebe 764
 Sarah (Slocum) 764
 William 764
TRIPPLETT
 Julian 538
TROBRIAND (DE)
 François-Marie Denis de Kerendern, Baron 443
 Régis, Comte 443
TROIA
 Nicolo d'Avalos, Prince of Montesarchio and 189

TROIS-PISTOLES (DE)
Jean Rioux, Seigneur 987, 988
Nicolas Rioux, Seigneur 987, 988

TROJDEN
Duke of Mazovia 621

TROLLE
Arvid, Lord of Bergkvara and Bo 452
Beata 452
Erik, Lord of Faanoe and Lagnoe 452
Karin (Gyllenstierna) 452
Kristina (Gädda) 452
Margrethe 644, 646

TROLLOPE
Anthony 320
Frances (Milton) xvii, clviii, 320, 322
Louisa Ellen (Harris) 320
Rose (Heseltine) 320
Thomas Anthony 320

TRONCO
Giovanni Antonio Maresca Donnorso, Count of 190

TROPPAU
Euphemia of 621
Nicholas I, Duke of 621
Nicholas II, Duke of 621

TROTTA genannt TREYDEN (VON)
Christoph Friedrich Levin 182
Frederica Theodora Elizabeth 182
Joanna Dorothea (Reuss-Ebersdorf), Countess 182

TROTTIER
Aimé 955
Marguerite 941

TROUBETSKOY/ TROUBETZKOY
Ada (Winans/ Wynans) 194
Alexander, Prince 793
Alexandra (Nelidov) 793
Amélie Louise (Rives) (Chanler) 194
Anna (Ladyjensky) 792
Barbara Woolworth (Hutton) (Mdivani) (Haugwitz-Hardenberg-Reventlow) (Grant) xviii, 44, 46, 63
Daria (Gruzinski), Princess 793

Daria, Princess 793
Dimitri, Prince 794
Dorothy Livingston (Ulrich) [Ulrich Troubetzkoy] 793, 796
Ekaterina, Princess 793, 794, 796
Elin (Sundström) 194
Elisabeth (Bachmetev) 793
Elizabeth (Galitzine), Princess 195
Elizabeth (von Moeller) 793
family xxii, 193
Louise (Rościszewski) 793
Maria (Kromin) 793
Maria, Princess 5
Muriel Marie (Beddam) 194
Nicolas, Prince 194
Nikita, Prince 793
Nina (Gugajew) 195
Olga (Demidov) 793
Olga (Merzelikin) 195
Paul (Paolo), Prince 194
Petr, Prince 793
Pierre (Peter), Prince clviii, 194

1559

Praskovia
  (Obolensky),
  Princess 195
Sergei, Prince liii,
  clviii, 195, 792,
  793
Sophia (Lopuchin)
  194
Varvara (Odoevsky),
  Princess 794
Varvara, Princess
  194
Vladimir, Prince
  clviii, 195
TROUTBECK
Adam 574
Joan 510, 563
Margaret 574
Margaret (Boteler)
  574
Margaret (Stanley)
  510, 563, 574
William (Sir) 510,
  563, 574
TROWBRIDGE
Agnes (Prowse)
  870
Anna 870
Elizabeth 520, 935
Elizabeth
  (Lamberton) 924
Elizabeth (Marshall)
  520, 870, 924, 935
Hester (How) 924
Isaac 924
James 520, 924,
  935
John 870
Joseph 924

Joseph, Jr. 924
Margaret (Atherton)
  520, 935
Mary (Winston)
  870
Olive (Clark) 924
Ruth (Perry) 924
Sarah 870
Sarah (Rutherford)
  870
Sarah Lorania 924
Thomas xix, xl, lv,
  lix, lxviii, clxiii,
  520, 870, 924, 935
Thomas, Jr. 870
Thomas (III) 870
Trial (Morehouse)
  924
William 924
TROYES
Eudes II, Count of,
  Count of Aumale
  879, 919
Robert, Count of
  Meaux and 879,
  919
**TRUCHSESS VON
WALDBURG**
Anna (of Oettingen),
  Countess 640
Anna (von
  Falkenberg) 640
Euphrosine 640
Frederick I 640
John I 640
TRUDEAU
Charles-Émile 969
Grace (Elliot) 969
Joseph 969

Justin Pierre James
  (Prime Minister)
  969
Louis 969
Louise (Dupuis) 969
Malvina (Cardinal)
  969
Margaret Joan
  (Sinclair) 969
Marguerite (Gagné
  dit Belavance)
  969
Pierre Elliot (Prime
  Minister) 967,
  968, 969, 982
Sophie (Grégoire)
  969
TRUMAN
Anderson Shipp
  171, 258
Anne (Storer)
  cxlvi, 628
Elizabeth Virginia
  "Bess" (Wallace)
  xlii, 171, 259, 673
Emma Grant
  (Shipp) 171, 258
Harry S, 33rd U.S.
  President xlii,
  171, 259, 673
James 628
John Anderson
  171, 258
Martha Ellen
  (Young) 171, 258
Mary Jane (Holmes)
  171, 258
William, Jr. 171,
  258

TRUMBLE
  Anthony 112
  Jane (Towneley)
    (Wilson) 112
TRUSSELL
  Isabel 768
  Joan clxxxv, 770
  Lawrence 768, 770
  Margery (Ludlow)
    clxxxv, 768, 770
  Matilda (de
    Charnells) 768,
    770
  Matilda (de
    Mainwaring) 763,
    768, 770
  Maud 763
  Maud (de St.
    Philibert) 763,
    768, 770
  Warin (Sir) 763,
    768, 770
  William (Sir)
    clxxxv, 763, 768,
    770
TRUXTON
  Elizabeth 629
TRYE
  Anne (Baynham)
    295
  Edward 295
  Isabel (Berkeley)
    295
  Katherine 295
  Sybil (Monington)
    295
  William 295
TRYON
  Charles 134

  Mary (Shirley)
    134, 135
  William (Gov.) 134
TSCHARNER (VON)
  Regina 832, 833
**TSCHIRSCHKY UND
  BÖGENDORFF
  (VON)** 183
  Amalie Joanna
    Lydia clxx, 183,
    197
  Augusta Theodora
    183
  Franz Ludwig 182,
    183
  Frederica Theodora
    Elizabeth (von
    Trotta genannt
    Treyden) 182
  Friedrich Ludwig
    182
  Wilhelmine
    Maximiliane Luise
    Marina (von
    Schönberg) 182
TÜBINGEN
  Hugh II, Count
    Palatine of 832
TUCKER
  Ann (Stone) 463
  Anna cxlix, 463,
    465
  Anne (Butterfield)
    463
  Anne (Mulcaster)
    130
  Benjamin S(tone)
    463
  Charlotte Maria 464

  Eliza Jane (Tucker)
    464
  Elizabeth (___) 463
  Elizabeth (Bridger)
    463
  family xxxiii, xlvi,
    lxix, cxcii, 463
  Frances 368, 464,
    465
  Frances (Bland) 464
  Frances (Bruere)
    130, 464
  Frances (St. George)
    463
  Frances (Tucker)
    464
  Frances (Tudor) 463
  George 463
  Henry cxlvi, 463,
    464, 465
  Henry, Jr. 463
  Henry (III) 130,
    464
  Henry St. George
    464
  Henry Tod(d) 130
  Jane (Boswell) 464
  Jane (Hubbard) 463
  John 463
  John Coulston Price
    130
  John Henry 464
  Lelia (Skipwith) 464
  Love (Gibbs?) 463
  Mansfield 463
  Maria (Johnson)
    130
  Mary 463, 465, 930
  Mary (Nichols) 464

1561

Mary Byrd Farley 325, 464, 465
Olivia 130
Robert Dennard lxix, cxcii
Rose (___) 558
Sarah cxlviii, 463, 465
St. George clxviii, 463, 464, 465
Thomas 464
Thomas Tudor (Rear Adm.) 464
Wilhelmina (Douglas de Lautour) 464
William cxcii, 463
William Thornhill 464

TUDERT (DE)
Sarah 912

TUDOR
Edmund, 1st Earl of Richmond 547
Elsa 185
family xxxii, 555, 603, 813
Frances 463
Katherine (de Valois), Princess of France, Queen Dowager of England, wife of Owen 226, 603, 813, 824
Margaret (Beaufort) 547
Margaret, Princess of England, Queen of Scotland 143, 146, 148, 150, 151, 152, 154, 157, 159, 161, 163, 165, 166, 167, 168, 170, 171, 173, 174, 176, 177, 179
Mary 30
Mary, Princess of England, Queen of France, Duchess of Suffolk xxxix, clxxxiii, clxxxviii, 62, 69, 76, 79, 80
Owen 226, 603, 813, 824

TUDUR
ap Gronwy 693
ap Gruffudd 689
ap Gruffudd Fychan 657, 689
ap Rhys 808

TUFNELL
Alice Clara 108

TUFTON alias MASON
Elizabeth (Taylor) xlix, cli, clxxix, 537
Robert 537

TUKE
Elizabeth 427
Mary 314, 514

TULLINS (DE)
Béatrix (de Montluel) 911
Catherine 911
Guy II, Seigneur 911

TULLOCH
Anna 281
Janet 828

TUN
Axel Posse, Lord of Saatenes and 452

TUNSTALL
Agnes 909
Anne (Bold) 902
Eleanor (FitzHugh) 398, 917
Elizabeth 902, 917, 918
Francis 902
Joan 398
Margaret 697
Thomas (Sir) 398, 917

TURBERVILLE
family 875

TURBILLY (DE)
François de Menon, Seigneur 455
Urbain de Menon, Seigneur, Count de Brestau 455

TURCOT
Anne (Desrosiers) 988, 989
Jacques 988, 989
Madeleine-Jacquette 988
Marie-Madeleine 988, 989

TURGIS
Elizabeth 356
Mary 93

TURGIS DE SAINT-ÉTIENNE
Charles-Amador (Gov.), Sieur de La Tour 953

Claude, Sieur de La
 Tour 953
Jeanne-Marie (de
 Motin) (de Menou)
 939, 952, 953
Marie (de Salazar)
 953
TURLAND
Anne 862
**TURLOUGH OGE
 O'CONOR DON**
King of Connaught
 885
TURNER
Mary 657
Natalie Sudler 79
TURNOR
Diana (Cecil) 334
Edmund 334
Elizabeth (Ferne)
 334
Elizabeth Frances
 334
John 334
Mary (Disney) 334
TUROW
Anastasia of 849
Jaropolk, Prince of
 Vladimir and 849
TURQUOIS
Michel 953
TURVEY
R. K. 232
TUSCANY
Anton Maria Franz
 Leopold Blanka
 Karl Joseph Ignaz
 Raphael Michael
 Margareta Nicetas,
 Archduke of
 Austria, Prince of
 2, 6
Cosimo I de'
 Medici, Grand
 Duke of 191, 192
Francesco Maria de'
 Medici, Grand
 Duke of 192
Joanna, Archduchess
 of Austria, Grand
 Duchess of 192
Karl Pius Maria
 Adelgonde Blanka
 Leopold Ignaz
 Raphael Michael
 Salvator Kyrill
 Angelus Barbara,
 Archduke of
 Austria, Prince of
 6
Karl Salvator,
 Archduke of
 Austria, Prince of
 6
Leonor (Alvarez de
 Toledo), Grand
 Duchess of 191,
 192
Maria Teresa of,
 Archduchess of
 Austria, Queen of
 Sardinia 614
Stefan [Stefan
 Habsburg-Lothring
 en], Archduke of
 Austria, Prince of
 2
TUTHILL
Anna 867
TUTTLE
Joan (Antrobus)
 (Lawrence) 880
TUYL (VAN)
Geertruijt Jansdr.
 (van Lent) 776
Jan Otten viii,
 xxxii, lvii, cxlvii,
 clxxx, 776
Jan Sandersz. 776
Marijke Otten (van
 Oever) 776
Neelken Geerlof
 (Aertsdr.) 776
Ott Jansz. 776
Sander Reijnersz.
 776, 777
Willemke (van
 Goor) 776, 777
**TUYLL VAN
 SEROOSKERKEN
 (VAN)**
Mary Catherine 54
TWEEDDALE
George Hay, 8th
 Marquess of 67
John Hay, 2nd
 Marquess of 177
TWIGDEN
Amphyllis 515
TWIGGE
Diana (Wray) 115
Jane 115
William (Ven.),
 Archdeacon of
 Limerick 115

TWISDEN/TWYSDEN
Anne (Wyatt) 314
Elizabeth (Roydon) 358
Frances 72
Margaret 315, 357, 358, 429
Roger 314
William 358
TWISLETON-WYKEHAM-FIENNES
Alberic Arthur 158
Gertrude Theodosia (Colley) 158
Maurice Alberic (Sir) 158
Sylvia Joan (Finlay) 158
TWO SICILIES (THE)
Ferdinand II, King of 6
Maria Amelia Theresa, Princess of, Queen of the French 288, 290
Maria Christina, Princess of Sardinia, Queen of 6
Maria Immaculata, Princess of 6
Maria Theresa, Archduchess of Austria, Queen of 6
Maria Theresa, Princess of, Empress of Austria 11
monarchs of 615

TWYSDEN. *see* TWISDEN/TWYSDEN
TYLDESLEY
Margaret 558
TYLER
Anne 145
Hannah 370
Job 370
John (IV), 10th U.S. President xlii, 643
Julia (Gardiner) xlii, 643
Lyon Gardiner lxxi
Margaret (Bradstreet) 370
TYMBERLEY
___ 680
TYNDAL/TINDAL
Alana (de Felbrigg) 713
Amphyllis (Coningsby) 713
Anna (Egerton) 713
Anne (Fermor) 713
Arthur 713
family lxii
John 713, 714
John (Sir) 713
Katherine (la Zouche) 713, 714
Margaret liv, lvii, clxii, clxxvi, 483, 713
Margaret (Yelverton) 713
Mary (Mondeford) 713

Thomas (Sir) 713
William (Sir) 713
TYNEDALE
Hextilda of 828
Uchtred of 828
TYNG
Anna 375, 393
Elizabeth (Coytmore) xxxv, li, 375
family xxiv
Rebecca 923
William 375
TYPOETS
Beater (van Beele) 804
Heinrich 804
Maria 804
Maria (von Sombreffe) 804
Thonis 804
TYRE
Janice 187
TYRRELL
Alice 543, 544
Anne 349, 588, 607
Anne (Arundell) 349, 588
Anne (Pashley) 508
Christian (Hartshorn) 607
Edward 508
Elizabeth (Munday) 543
Emma (Marney) 607
family clxxxvii
Humphrey 607

Isabel (Helion) 607
James (Sir) 349, 588
John (Sir) 543
Joyce 607
Margaret (Willoughby) 543, 588
Philippa 508
Robert (Sir) 607
Thomas (Sir) 543, 588, 607
TYRWHIT(T)
Agnes 403
Anne 719, 720
Anne (Constable) 403, 719
Elizabeth 472
Elizabeth (Oxenbridge) 327
family 720
Isabel (Girlington) (Kelke) 327, 343
Katherine 519
Margaret 123
Maud 409
Maud (Talboys) 327, 409, 519, 719, 720
Robert (Sir) 327, 409, 519, 719, 720
Ursula 327
William (Sir) 327, 403, 719
___ 755
TYSZKIEWICZ
Eleanor, Countess 802
Emmanuel

Wladislaw (Ladislaus), Count 802
Evanor Anna (Billozorowna) 802
Helena (Bykowska) 802
Sophia (Weslawski) 802
Stanislaw Anthony, Count 802
Theodore (Fedor), Count 802
TYTLER
Barbara (Skene) 159
Eleanor 159
Elizabeth (Rattray) 159, 160
family vi
George 159
James vi, xlix, lxiii, clviii, 159, 160
Janet (Robertson) 159
Jean (Aikenhead) 159, 160
John 159
Margaret 159, 160
___ (Cairns) 159
UDEKEM D'ACOZ (D')
Mathilde-Marie-Christiane-Ghislaine, Queen of the Belgians [Mathilde, Queen of the

Belgians] 154, 155, 201, 203, 204
UEXKÜLL (VON)
Anna (von Rosen) 849
Anna Elisabeth 849
Anna Maria (von Uexküll) 849
Berend Johann 849
Hans Jürgen (Georg) 849
Johann 849
Jürgen (Georg) 849
Jürgen (Georg) Detlov 849
Madlena [Magdalena] (von Tisenhusen) 849
Magdalene (von Bremen) 849
Maria (von Plater) 849
Renata Helene (von Budberg) 849
UFFORD (DE)
Katherine 713
Margaret 466, 567, 592
UGGES
Margaret 761
UGGLA
Anna 662
Annie (Bass) 458
Arnold Helmfrid 458
Carl Fredrik 457
Carl Magnus Helmfrid clviii, 458

1565

Daniel Cooley
  "Dan" 458
Elizabeth Armistead
  (Cooley) 458
family 458
Helen Jane (Ryder)
  458
Janette (Repsch)
  458
John Carl 458
Julia Regina Turinna,
  Baroness 889
Juliana (Ribbing),
  Baroness 457
Malvina Sofia Ulrika
  (Berggren) 457
Maria Elisabet
  (Brockman) 457
Pontus Helmfrid
  457
Tara (Sims) 458
UGLICH
Constantine II,
  Prince of Rostov
  and 791, 797
ULFELD (VON)
Anna Elisabeth
  Maria, Countess 35
Anna Maria (von
  Zinzendorf),
  Countess 35
Corfitz, Count 35
Corfitz Anton,
  Count 35
Leo, Count 35
Maria Elisabeth (of
  Lobkowicz),
  Countess 35

ULFSDOTTER
Katarina 452
ULFSSON
Peder, Lord of
  Ervalla and
  Huseby 457
ULFSTAND
Anne (Skovgaard)
  644
Brigitte (Rosensparre)
  644
Else (Bille) 644
Gregers 644
Helle (Hak) 644
Holger 644
Holger (knight)
  644
Ingeborg 644
Jens 644
Jens (knight) 644,
  646
Lisbet 646
Lisbeth (Gylden-
  stierna) 644
Margrethe (Trolle)
  644, 646
Sidsel 644
ULLENHALL (DE)
Lora 861
ULLITHORNE
Isabella 116
ULLOA
Elizabeth
  (Karadjordjevic)
  (Oxenberg)
  (Balfour), Princess
  of Yugoslavia 3
ULLOA ELIAS
Manuel 3

ULRICH
Dorothy Livingston
  [Ulrich
  Troubetzkoy]
  793, 796
UMFREVILLE (DE)
Andrew 843
Eleanor (de
  Montfichet?) 843
Elizabeth clxxxix,
  730
Elizabeth (Comyn)
  843
Gervase/Jarvis 843
Gilbert, 1st Earl of
  Angus 843
Isabel (___) 843
Joan (de Roddam)
  843
John 843
Katherine (Digby)
  843
Lucy (de Kyme) 730
Robert (Sir) 843,
  844
Robert, 2nd Earl of
  Angus 730, 843
Roger 843
Thomas 843
William 843
___ (Luddington)
  843
**UMFREVILLE/
HUMPHREVILLE**
John xii, lviii, cxlvi,
  clxiii, clxx, 843
UNDERHILL
Anne 880
Carl J. cxci

Edward 875
Humphrey lx,
 cxlvii, clxxxi, 875,
 1025
Jane (Thrift) 875
John (Capt.) lxviii,
 cxci, 875
Margaret (Middle-
 more) 875
Margery (Wylmer)
 875
Mary lx, cxlvi,
 clxxxi, 875, 1025
Sarah (___)
 (Smith) 875
Thomas 880
Thomasine
 (Caldebeck) 880
___ (Hall) 875
UNDERWOOD
Mary (Butler) liv,
 clxxv, clxxx, 674
William, Jr. 674
**UNGERN-
 STERNBERG
 (VON)**
Anna Dorothea,
 Baroness 14
UNTON
Anne (Seymour)
 306, 307
Cecilia 306
Edward (Sir) 306
UPPER OSSORY
John FitzPatrick, 1st
 Earl 299
UPSHUR
John Henry 170

Katherine Alicia
 (Williams) 170
URBINO
Francesco Maria I
 della Rovere, Duke
 of 186, 189
Guidobaldo II della
 Rovere, Duke of
 186, 189
Lavinia Feltrina
 della Rovere of
 186, 189
Lorenzo II de' Medici,
 Duke of 637
URIAGE (D')
Guigues Alleman,
 Seigneur 965
URIE
Margaret 88
URQUHART
Helen 273
Janet, of Burd-
 symonds 281
Jean (Campbell) 93
Jean (Urquhart) 93
John, of Craigston
 93
John, of Meldrum
 93
Mary 93
Mary (Forbes), of
 Monymusk 93
William, of
 Meldrum 93
URSULA
Princess of
 Brandenburg 220
USCHAKOV
Sophia 799

USHER
Bridget (Lisle)
 (Hoar) clxxii,
 297, 298
Hezekiah 297
UTRECHT
Guy of Avesnes,
 Bishop of 774, 776
VACHELL
___ 859
VAIL
Kay (Boyle) xviii,
 xlv, cliv, 15
Laurence 15
Marguerite "Peggy"
 (Guggenheim) 15
VALBONNAIS (DE)
Guigues I Alleman,
 Seigneur de
 Champs and 911
Odon II Alleman,
 Seigneur de Champs
 and 911, 912
VALENCE (DE)
Adam Baillon,
 Seigneur 950
(Catherine-) Jean-
 Emmanuel de Tim-
 brune de Valence,
 Marquis 205
Émeric-Emmanuel
 de Timbrune de
 Valence, Marquis
 205
Isabel 785
Jean-Baptiste-
 Charles-Henri-
 Hector de Timbrune,
 Comte 206

1567

Joan (Munchensy) 785
William, Earl of Pembroke 785
VALENTINOIS (DE)
Aymar III de Poitiers, Count 735
Cesare Borgia, Duc, tyrant of Italy 287, 293
Charlotte-Louise-Juliette Grimaldi, Hereditary Princess of Monaco, Duchess 289, 933
Diane de Poitiers, Duchess 202, 735
VALETTE (DE)
François de Grasse-Rouville, Seigneur 616
Honoré de Grasse, Seigneur 615
Jean-Pierre-Charles de Grasse, Seigneur 616
VALLE DE OAXACA (DEL)
Hernán Cortés, 1st Marquess 191
Juana Estefanía Cortés, Marquesa 192
Martín Cortés de Monroy, 2nd Marquess 191
VALLES
Marguerite 977

VALLETORT/ VAUTORT (DE)
Elizabeth 672
Hugh 672
Joan 653, 661, 672
John (Sir) 672
Lucia (le Bret) 672
___ (de Columbers) 672
VALLETTE
Marie 634
VALMONTORE
Luigi Andrea Doria-Pamfili-Landi, 2nd Prince of 18, 652
VALOIS (DE) (OF)
Charles, Prince of France, Count 459, 941, 961
Charlotte 202
Claudia (Claude), Princess of France, Duchess of Lorraine 637
Elizabeth, Princess of France, Queen of Spain 637
Isabel 941
Jeanne 200, 205
Jeanne, Princess of France 459, 961
Katherine, Princess of France, Queen of England, wife of Owen Tudor 226, 603, 813, 824
Margaret, Princess of France, Queen

of France and Navarre 637
Marie-Marguerite 208
VAN ALENDORP
Johan 733
Louise 733
Marguerite (de Haynin) 733
VAN BRUGH
Catherine 898
VAN CHAPPUIS
Hedwig Maria Gertrud Eva 5
VAN DE GRIFT
Fanny 270
VAN DE PAS
Leo viii, xii, liii, lviii, lxix, lxxi, clxx, 46, 68, 290, 362, 446, 447, 448, 636, 908
VAN DE WEYER
Eleanor Frances Weston 137
VAN DER GOES
Cornelia Martina 14, 445
VAN DER MEER
Arend 774
Catryn (van Foreest) 774
Clara (van Berendrecht) 774
Frank 774
Jacomina Jacob Claesdr. (van Ruyven) 774

Liedewey (de Wilt van Bleyswyck) 774
Pieter 774
VAN DER MEER VAN BERENDRECHT
Anna (Campe) 774
Anna (Sandelin) 774
Cornelia 774
Joost 774
Machteld (van der Dussen) 774
Sophia 774
Willem 774
VAN DER NOOT
Anne 460
VAN DER POEL
Peter G. lii, lxix
VAN DER POT
Anna Josina 733
VAN DIEN
Casper Robert 3
Catherine (Oxenberg) (Evans) xvii, xlv, liv, 3
family 3
VAN GEZEL
Catherine 828
VAN HANGEST D'IVOY
Antonia Louise (de Leeuw) 733
Catharina Frederica Cornelia 733
Maximilian 733
VAN HECKE
Josina 633

VAN HORNE
Anna Maria 273
VAN JEVER
Margareta Helena 635
VAN KIRK
Charity Malvina 859
Deborah (Watters) 859
Dorothy (Morgan) 859
Henry 859
Henry, Jr. 859
William 859
VAN PELT
Cynthia (Cary) 27
VAN RENSSELAER
Alida (Schuyler) 243
VAN SCHAICK
Katherine 750
VAN SON. see SON (VAN)
VAN SWEARINGEN
Anne 312, 327, 753
VAN TUYL. see TUYL (VAN)
VAN TUYLL VAN SEROOSKERKEN. see TUYLL VAN SEROOSKERKEN (VAN)
VAN VOORHIS
Bartow White 924
Helen (Tappen) 924
Helen Abbie 161, 924

VAN WAGENEN
Louisa Goddard 28
VAN WEEDE
Cornelia Henriette 733
Johan, Heer van Groot Weede 733
Maria (de Gonnes) 733
VANDERBILT
Alice Claypoole (Gwynne) 35, 209
Alva Erskine (Smith) 26, 174, 175
Consuelo 26
Cornelia Stuyvesant 73, 74
Cornelius II 35, 209
Edith Stuyvesant (Dresser) 73, 74
family xviii, xxxvi, liv, lxvii, 35
George Washington 73
Gladys Moore 35, 209
William Kissam 26, 174
VANDORO
Catherine 7
VANE
Anne 34
Christopher, 1st Baron Barnard 34
Constance 716
Dorothy 357

Elizabeth (Holles) 34
Frances (Darcy) 315
Frances (Wray) 34, 115, 116, 117, 315
Gilbert, 2nd Baron Barnard 34
Grace (Fitzroy) 34
Henry 315
Henry (Sir) (English Sec. of State) 315
Henry (Sir) (Gov.) 34, 115, 315
Henry, 1st Earl of Darlington 34
Margaret 315
Margaret (Twisden) 315
Mary (Randyll) 34
VANE-STEWART
Frances Anne Emily 26, 63
VANGELET (DE)
Isabeau 638
VANLANDINGHAM
Kyle Samuel lxviii, lxix, 531
VANSITTART
Arthur 102
Caroline (Eden) 102
Louisa 102
VARAS (DE)
Louise 735
VARENNES (DE)
Élisabeth/Isabelle 948
Isaac, Seigneur de Villegruau 948
Jacqueline (de Hallot) 948

VAREY (DE)
Catherine 911
VARICK (VAN)
Hendrika 447, 448, 907
VARIN
Blanche 957
VARIS
Hyacinthe-Gabrielle 545
VASA
Gustav I, King of Sweden 40, 43, 51, 52, 53, 198, 199, 208, 267, 453, 889, 890, 893
VASS
Sarah 833
VASSILI
Prince of Rostov 791, 797
VASSILKO
Prince of Rostov 791, 797
VASSOR (LE)
Élisabeth-Alexandrine 24
VASSOR DE LA TOUCHE (LE)
Marie-Charlotte-Calixte-Alphonsine 289
VASSY (DE)
Isabelle (Tesson) 959
Jeanne 959
Roland III, Seigneur de La Forêt-Auvray 959

VAUD (DE)
Louis I of Savoy, Baron 965
VAUDENET
Louise-Susanne 912
VAUDÉTAR (DE)
Antoinette (Baillet) 954
Jean I, Seigneur de Pouilly-le-Fort 954
Jean II, Seigneur de Pouilly-le-Fort 954
Jeanne-Catherine 954
Marguerite (de Chanteprime) 954
Marguerite (de Claustre) 954
Pernelle (des Landes) 954
Pierre I, Seigneur de Pouilly-le-Fort 954
Pierre II, Seigneur de Pouilly-le-Fort 954
VAUGHAN
Anne 233
Catherine (Nannau) 229
Catrin 410
Eleanor (Cornewall) 233
Elizabeth clxxxv, 338, 410, 505, 668, 669, 770
Elizabeth (Croft) 505
Elsbeth 811
Frances 403

Frances (Latham)
  (Dungan) (Clarke)
  241, 468, 488
Howel 689
Isabel 505
James, of Hergest
  505
Jane lxvii, clxxi,
  229, 230, 383, 770
Joan (Whitney)
  338, 410
Margaret 510
Margaret (Touchet
  or Audley) 377,
  411
Mary 689
Maud (Lucy) 326
Robert 229
Roger 233
Roger (Sir) 338,
  377, 410, 411
Sidney 167
Sybil (Baskerville)
  505
Watkin, of Hergest
  505
Watkyn 410
William (Sir) 410
**VAUGHAN or
GREY**
  Elizabeth 377, 378,
  411, 412
**VAUGHAN
WILLIAMS**
  Alice Margaret 380
  Arthur Charles 117
  Margaret Susan
  (Wedgwood) 117
  Ralph xxiv, 117

VAULX
  Catherine/Katherine
  Daisy Davey 924,
  926
  Eliza Geddy
  (Fenner) 924, 926
  family 926
  Huetha Snowden
  926
  James 924, 926
  James Junius 924,
  926
  Margaret (Garside)
  924, 926
  Mary 926
  Mary (___) 523
VAUX
  Anne 434
  Eleanor 857
  Elizabeth (FitzHugh)
  324, 434
  Katherine 324, 416
  Katherine (Peniston)
  326
  Maud 710, 713,
  715, 719, 727, 728
  Maud (Lucy) 326
  Nicholas, 1st Baron
  Vaux of
  Harrowden 324,
  326, 434
  William (Sir) 326
VAVASOUR
  Elizabeth 389
VEATCH/VEITCH
  Alexander, of
  Manor 241
  Barbara (Ainslie)
  241

  Christian 152
  Henry 241
  Henry Gordon 242
  James lx, clxxi,
  240, 241
  Janet (Stewart) 241
  John, of Dawyck
  241
  John, of Selkirk
  241
  Malcolm, of
  Muirdeen 241
  Margaret (Harrison)
  241
  Margaret (Scott)
  241
  Mary (Gakerlin)
  241
  Mary Kathleen
  (Synch) 242
  Robert, of Bromley
  241
  Violet Agnes 242
  William, of Redpath
  241
VÉDRINE (DE)
  Antoine de Douhet
  de Marlat,
  Seigneur 200,
  203
VELASCO (DE)
  Francisco 140
  María Francisca
  140
**VELASCO Y
GIRÓN (DE)**
  Ana 140
VELÁZQUEZ
  Francisca 140

Juana (Pacheco de
  Miranda) 140
**VELÁZQUEZ (DE
  SILVA Y)**
  Diego Rodríguez
    140
VELIAMINOV
  Nicholas 791, 795
  Xenia 791
VENABLES
  Elizabeth 822
  Margery 817
VENDÔME (DE) (OF)
  Aiglantine 943
  Alix 946
  Bouchard, Seigneur
    de Segré and de
    Feuillet 946
  Bouchard VI, Count
    946
  Catherine 638
  counts 442
  Jeanne (de Chazé)
    946
  John I of Bourbon,
    Count of La
    Marche and 638
  John II, Count 205
  Marguerite (de
    Brienne) 946, 947
  Pierre, Seigneur de
    Segré and de Nesle
    946
  Yolande 956
VENDÔMOIS
  Jeanne 638
VENEUR (LE)
  Marguerite 961

VENN
  family 612
  John 611
  John Archibald 611
  William (Rev.) 612
VENTHAM
  Wanda 101
VERA ZURITA (DE)
  Catalina 994
VERCELLANA
  Rosa Teresa,
    Countess di Mira-
    fiori and Fontana-
    fredda 614
VERDUN (DE)
  Clemence (le
    Botiller) 650,
    652, 657, 659, 680,
    682, 686, 689, 692,
    693, 694
  Elizabeth (de Clare)
    466, 528, 567, 592
  Isabel 466, 528,
    567, 592
  Margery 647, 909
  Maud (Mortimer)
    647, 909
  Nicholas 650, 657,
    659, 680, 682, 686,
    689, 692, 693, 694
  Theobald (Sir)
    466, 528, 567, 592
  Theobald de Verdun,
    2nd Baron 647, 909
VERE (DE)
  Agnes (de Essex)
    680
  Alice (de Clare)
    680, 845

Alice (de Sanford)
  680
Alice (Sergeaux)
  584
Anna (Cecil) 68
Aubrey 680, 845
Aubrey, 1st Earl of
  Oxford 680
Diana 33
Edward, 17th Earl
  of Oxford 68, 766
Eleanor 680, 681
Elizabeth 62, 68, 565
Elizabeth (Howard)
  565, 584
family 725
Frances 62, 333, 431
George (Sir) 565
Hawise (de Quincy)
  680
Hugh, 4th Earl of
  Oxford 680
Isabel 739
Isabel (de Bolebec)
  680
Joan 428, 584
John, 12th Earl of
  Oxford 565, 584
John, 16th Earl of
  Oxford 68, 766
Juliana 845
Margaret 625, 628,
  630
Margaret (de
  Mortimer) 680
Margaret (Stafford)
  565
Margery (Golding)
  68, 766

Richard, 11th Earl
 of Oxford 584
Robert, 3rd Earl of
 Oxford 680
Robert, 5th Earl of
 Oxford 680, 681
Robert, 6th Earl of
 Oxford 680, 681
Thomas (Sir) 681
VERGEREAU
 Suzanne 898
**VERGERS (DES) de
 SANNOIS**
 Rose-Claire 442
VERHEECKE
 José 37
VERITY
 Brad lxix, 124,
 125, 234, 298
VERMANDOIS
 Adela of 879, 919
 Adelaide of 835,
 837, 839, 841, 843,
 845, 847
 Herbert I, Count of
 879, 919
 Herbert II, Count of
 879, 919
 Isabel of 835, 837,
 839, 841, 843, 845,
 847, 1025
VERMUYDEN
 Catherine 628
VERNÆUIL (DE)
 Jeanne 964
VERNEY
 Anne 423
 Elizabeth 354
 Margaret 478

VERNON (DE)
 Anne (Ludlow)
 377, 411
 Anne (Talbot) 377,
 500
 Benedicta (Ludlow)
 723
 Dorothy 110, 119,
 396
 Eleanor 377
 Elizabeth 137, 319,
 411, 412, 500, 825
 Elizabeth
 (Devereux) 137
 Francis 412
 Henry (Sir) 377,
 500
 Henry, Esq. 412
 Isabella 723, 724
 Joan (ferch Rhys ap
 Gruffudd) 687,
 723
 John 541
 John (Sir) 137
 Margaret 826
 Mary 672, 695,
 739
 Maud (de
 Beaumont) 739
 Richard (Sir) 687,
 723
 Sarah (Wylde) 541
 Susanna 541
 Theobald (Sir)
 1024
 Thomas 377, 411,
 412
 William, 5th Earl of
 Devon 739

**VERNOU DE LA
 RIVIÈRE-
 BONNEUIL (DE)**
 Charlotte 200
VERONA
 Beatrice (della
 Scala), of 640
VERSMANN
 Emilie 849
VESEY
 Mary (Reade) 348
VEZINA
 Clothilde 989
 Jean-Nicolas 989
 Marie-Josephte
 (Rivard) 989
 Zoë 975
**VICTOIRE-
 FRANÇOISE-
 ANTOINETTE-
 JULIENNE-
 LOUISE**
 of Saxe-Coburg-
 Gotha 290
VICTOR AMADEUS
 Prince of Anhalt-
 Bernberg 56
VICTOR AMADEUS I
 of Savoy, Prince of
 Carignan 18
VICTOR AMADEUS II
 King of Sardinia
 18
 of Savoy, Prince of
 Carignan 613
VICTOR EMANUEL II
 King of Sardinia,
 King of Italy 18,
 614

VICTOR FREDERICK
Prince of Anhalt-Bernberg 56
VICTORIA
Princess of Saxe-Coburg-Saalfeld, Duchess of Kent 45
Queen of Great Britain xl, liv, 2, 10, 41, 45, 75, 182, 196, 237, 290
VICTORIA FRANCESCA
of Savoy, Madamigella di Susa, Princess of Carignan 18
VIDMER
Elizabeth (Brooke) (Roy) 137
Richard 137
VIELLA (DE)
Catherine 963
VIERECK
Edwina 16
family 17
Franz Georg Edwin Louis Withold vii, lxiv, 16
George Sylvester 16
Laura (Viereck) 16
Margaret Edith (Hein) 16
VIEUVILLE (DE LA)/ VIÉVILLE (DE LA)
Lucrèce-Françoise 287

Marie 438, 445
VIEUXPONT (DE)
counts 949
Jeanne-Catherine 205
VIGNERON
Allen Henry, Archbishop of Detroit 967, 968, 983
Bernardine (Kott) 983
Elwin 983
Eva Marie (Rose) 983
Henry Joseph 983
VIGNOLLES (DES)
Charles, Seigneur de Prades 736
Charlotte 736
Gabrielle (de Sperandieu) 736
Jacques, Seigneur de Prades 735
Louise (de Baschi) 735
VIGOUREUX
Madeleine 946
VILLAFRANCA DEL BIERZO
María Osorio Pimentel, Marquesa of 191
Pedro Álvarez de Toledo, Marquess of 191
VILLARD
Alexandra D. 112
VILLARS (DE)
Jeanne 442

VILLARS-EN-BRESSE (DE)
René de Savoie, Count 442
VILLE (DE)
Claudia Antonia (de Rovéréaz) 872
Georges 872
Marie 873
VILLEBÉON (DE)
Isabelle 956
VILLEGRUAU (DE)
Isaac de Varenne(s), Seigneur 948
VILLENEUVE (DE)
Anne 615
Mathieu Amiot, Seigneur 969, 972, 973, 975, 976, 977, 978, 979, 980, 981, 982
VILLENEUVE-TRANS (DE)
Véronique 616
VILLERS (DE)
Françoise 944
Isabella 633
Jean 633
Nicole (de Noyelles) 633
VILLE-SAVOIR (DE)
Jeanne 633
VILLETTE (DE)
André de Chevron, Seigneur 952
Aymar de Beauvoir, Seigneur 952
Humbert IV de Chevron-Villette,

Seigneur de
  Chevron and   911
Humbert V de
  Chevron-Villette,
  Seigneur de
  Chevron and   911
Petremand de
  Chevron, Seigneur
  952
Philiberte   952
Urbain de Chevron,
  Seigneur   952
VILLIERS
Algernon Hyde
  121
Anne (Egerton)   72
Barbara   334
Barbara, Duchess of
  Cleveland   22, 29,
  33, 34, 109
Beatrix Elinor
  (Paul)   121
Blanche (de Dreux)
  956
Catherine   956
Catherine
  (Grimston)   121
Charles, Seigneur de
  Villiers-sur-Port
  956
Charles English
  Hyde   122
Charlotte (Capell)
  121
Diana Mary   xi,
  xlix, clvii, 122, 125
Elizabeth   536
Eric Hyde   125
family   430

Frances (Twysden)
  72
Francis Hyde (Sir)
  121, 125
George (Hon.)   121
George (Sir)   430
George, 1st Duke of
  Buckingham   430,
  536
George Bussy, 4th
  Earl of Jersey   72
George William, 4th
  Earl of Clarendon
  121
Guillaume, Seigneur
  de Villiers-sur-Port
  and des Deux-
  Jumeaux   956
Harriet   72
Helen   684
James Michael
  Hyde [James
  Villiers]   clix, 125
Jeanne (d'Ouessey)
  956
Joan Ankaret
  (Talbot)   125
Lucinda Claire
  (Nex)   125
Marie José (de La
  Barre
  d'Erquelinnes),
  Countess   122
Mary (Beaumont),
  Countess of
  Buckingham   430
Patricia (Donovan)
  125
Susan   368

Theresa (Parker)
  121
Thomas, 1st Earl of
  Clarendon   121
Virginia Katharine
  (Smith)   121, 125
William, 3rd Earl of
  Jersey   72
**VILLIERS-SUR-
  PORT (DE)**
Charles de Villiers,
  Seigneur   956
Guillaume de Villiers,
  Seigneur, Seigneur
  des Deux- Jumeaux
  956
**VILLIERS-TERRAGE
  (DE)**
Jeanne-Marie   622
VIMEUR (DE)
Elizabeth (de
  Menon)   455
Jean-Baptiste-
  Donatien, Count de
  Rochambeau   xvi,
  xxvi, 267, 455
Jeanne-Thérèse
  (Tellez d'Acosta)
  455
Joseph-Charles I,
  Seigneur de
  Rochambeau   455
Joseph-Charles II,
  Seigneur de
  Rochambeau   455
Marie-Claire-Thérèse
  (Bégon)   455
Marie-Madeleine
  (Brachet)   455

René IV, Seigneur
  de Rochambeau
  455
VINCELLES (DE)
  Claude de Salins,
    Seigneur 952
VINCENT
  Anne (Tanfield)
    387
  Catherine Maria
    (Long) (Moore)
    346
  Clement 387
  Elizabeth 387
  family 387, 697
  Magdalen 211
  Richard 346
VIND
  Anne Elisabeth
    645
  Holger (knight)
    645
  Ingeborg (Ulfstand)
    644
  Jørgen (Adm.) 644
  Margrethe (Giedde)
    645
VINICOMBE
  Elizabeth 436
  Elizabeth (Ford)
    436
  John 436
VINING
  Ann 732
VIRIEUX (DE)
  Claude 638
VIRKUS
  Frederick Adams
    xxviii

VISCHER (DE)
  Antoine-Philippe-
    Fiacre-Ghislain,
    Baron de Celles
    206
  Louise-Philippine-
    Séraphine-Félicité
    (de Timbrune)
    206
  Pulchérie-Félicité-
    Cyrette 206
VISCONTI
  Elizabeth 451
  Magdalena 51
VISINGSBORG
  Eric Brahe, Count of
    452
VISSAC (DE)
  Charles Motier de
    Champetières,
    Baron 200
  Édouard Motier de
    La Fayette, Baron
    201
VISTORP
  Anna 663
VITOZZO
  Berthold di Baschi,
    Seigneur en parti
    of 735
VITRÉ (DE)
  Eleanor 737
VLADIMIR
  Alexander Nevsky,
    Grand Prince of
    Kiev and 791, 797
  Dimitri IV, Prince
    of Suzdal and
    791, 797

Jaropolk, Prince of,
  Prince of Turow
  849
VOIGHT
  Angelina Jolie
    [Angelina Jolie]
    967, 974
  Jon 974
  Marcia Lynne
    (Bertrand)
    [Marguerite
    Bertrand] 974
VOLKONSKY
  Ekaterina
    (Troubetskoy),
    Princess 794, 796
  Irina, Princess 799
  Maria, Princess 794
  Nicholas, Prince
    794, 796
VOORST (VAN)
  Johan II van Pallandt,
    Heer 445
**VORONTZOV-
  DACHKOV**
  Alexandra
    (Naryshkin) 795
  Elizabeth (Shuvalov),
    Princess 795
  Hilarion, Count
    795
  Irina, Countess
    794, 795
  Ivan, Count 795
  Maria, Countess 5
  Sophia, Countess
    795
  Varvara (Orlov)
    795

VOYER (DE)
Alix (de Cluys) 964
Françoise (de Beauvau) 202
Guillaume, Seigneur de Mousé 964
Jacques, Vicomte de Paulmy 202
Jean, Seigneur de Paulmy 964
Jean-Armand, Marquis de Paulmy 202
Jeanne 964
Jeanne (de Vernæuil) 964
Marguerite (de Bez) 964
Marie-Françoise-Céleste 203
Nicole (de Pressigny) 964
Philippa (de Montmorency) 964
Philippon, Seigneur de Paulmy 964
Pierre, Sieur de Paulmy 964
Radegonde (de Mauroy) 202
Renaud, Seigneur de Paulmy 964
VRETA
Ulv Jonson, Lord of Ervalla, Faanoe, Saeby, Huseby and 452, 457

VSEVELOD
Prince of Strezew 849
VSEVELOD III
Grand Prince of Kiev 791, 797, 802
VSEVOLOJE
Ivan, Prince 791, 798, 800
Vassilissa, Princess 791
Xenia (Veliaminov) 791
Xenia, Princess 798
VUYLCOOP (VAN)
Adolf de Gonnes, Herr 733, 734
VYVYAN
Opre 34
WABARD/WABERT/ OUABARD/ HUBBARD. *see also* HUBBARD
Louise-Arel 623
Marie-Élisabeth [Elizabeth] 623
WACHTENDONK (VON)
Wilhelmina 907
WACHTMEISTER
Axel Gustaf, Baron 453
Hedwig Eleonora, Baroness 453
Karl Hans, 2nd Count of Skunkberg 453

Louisa Katherina, Countess 889
Magdalena Sophia (Wachtmeister), Baroness 453
Ulrika Magdalena (Stenbock), Countess 453
WADE
Anne (Smythe) 535
Emily 540
Laura 540
Laura (Carthew) 540
Mary 757
Searles 540
Thomas 535, 540
WADHAM
Joan 133, 695
WAGNER
Anthony Richard (Sir) ix, xxiii, xxviii, xxix, lxix, clxxxiv, 25
Gillian Mary Millicent (Graham) 25
WAGRAM (DE)
Napoléon Berthier, Prince and Duke 83
WAHLBERG
Alma Louise (Donnelly) 976
Donald Edmond "Donnie" 968, 976
Donald Edward 976

family 1, 967
Jenny (McCarthy) 976
Kimberly (Fey) 976
Mark Robert Michael "Marky Mark" 968, 976
Rhea (Durham) 976
WAHUL/ WODHULL
family 768
WAKE
Anne 569, 573
Baldwin (Sir) 682
Hawise (de Quincy) 682
Hugh (Sir) 682
Joan (de Belauney) 682
Margaret 515, 600
Mirabel 682
WAKEMAN
Mary 642
WALCOT
Jane 115
WALDBURG-ZEIL (VON)
Leopoldina, Countess 15
WALDECK
Augusta, Countess of 57
Frederick, Count of 57
Josias, Count of 181
Magdalena of 181

Ursula Polle, Countess of 56
WALDECK-PYRMONT
Frederick Louis, Prince of 56
George, Prince of 56
WALDECK-WILDUNGEN
Christian, Count of 141, 181
Louise Sybil of 181
Maria Magdalena of 141
WALDEGRAVE
Anne (Drury) 483
Anthony 661, 662
Dorothy 483, 484, 548, 661, 662
Edward 483, 484
Elizabeth (Gray) 661
Elizabeth (Gurdon) 661
George 483
Jemima clxi, 301, 661
Joan (Acworth) 483
Juliana (Raynsford) 483
Margaret 662, 754
Margaret (Holmstead) 661
Margery 483, 484
Margery (Wentworth) 483, 661
Phyllis 484
Thomas 661

William (Sir) 483, 484, 661
WALDEMAR II
King of Denmark 644
WALDEN
Agnes 881
WALDSTEIN-WARTENBURG
George Christian Anton Michael Joseph Paternus Franz de Paula, Count of 35
Maria Elisabeth Joanna Baptista, Countess of 35
WALERAN
family 1025
Isabel 855
Isabel (FitzPatrick) 855
Walter 855
WALES
Augusta, Princess of Saxe-Gotha, Princess of 12, 27
Charles Philip Arthur George, Prince of Great Britain, Prince of lxiii, 209, 380, 655, 832, 930, 932
Diana Frances (Spencer), Princess of viii, xviii, xl, xlii, xliii, liv, 25, 32, 101, 306, 377, 380, 416, 417, 432, 482, 492, 543, 552,

576, 755, 858, 859, 930, 932
Edward "the Black Prince," Prince of England, Prince of 600
Ellen of 682, 683
Frederick Louis, Prince of Great Britain, Prince of 12, 27
Gwladys Ddu of 680
Henry (Harry) Charles Albert David of, Prince of Great Britain xlii, 25, 344, 858, 931, 932
Joan (Plantagenet), "The Fair Maid of Kent," Princess Dowager of 107, 400, 515, 600
rulers of xl
William Arthur Philip Louis of, Prince of Great Britain, Duke of Cambridge xlii, 25, 380, 858, 931, 932

WALKER
Courtenay 467
Dorothy xi, xlix, cxliv, clxvii, clxxvi, 243, 474, 479, 572, 585, 703, 706, 716, 729, 747
Edward 399

Elizabeth (Digby) 706
Elizabeth Rosemond (Taylor) (Hilton) (Wilding) (Todd) (Fisher) (Burton) [Elizabeth Taylor] 21, 190
Felix (Rep.) 609
Frances lxviii, cxlviii, 399
Gregory/George 706
Jane 299
John 72, 706, 707
Katherine (Harborne) 399
Margaret Gwendolyn Mary (Drummond), Lady 72
Marguerite 76
Platt B. 138, 139
Sarah 129
Ursula (Royston) 706, 707

WALKFARE
Eleanor 826

WALL
Eleanor 613
Margaret (Grice) 702

WALLACE
Christian (Murray) 152
Christian Jean 321, 323
David Willick 673
Elizabeth Virginia "Bess" xlii, 171, 259, 673

family 152
Isabel 128, 150
John xlix, cl, 152
John William 153
Margaret 87
Margaret "Madge" (Gates) 673
Mary (Maddox) 152

WALLENBERG
Maria Sofia (Wising) 60
Raoul 60
Raoul (Jr.) 60

WALLER
Anne 466, 467
Anne (Hampden) 466, 467
Anne (Hughes) 467
Anne (Keate) cxci
Catherine 536
Edmund cxcii, 466
Elizabeth 609
family cxcii
Gordon [of "Peter and Gordon"] 64
Hannah 467
Hannah (Coddington) 467
John cxcii, 467
John (Col.) cxci, cxcii
Margery (Paulet) 905
Mary cxci, cxcii, 603
Mary (Pomfrett) cxcii
Richard (Sir) 905

1579

Robert 466, 467
Robert Thomas 467
Susan 905
Ursula 466, 467
William 905
____ (Bramhall?) 467
____ (Somester) 905
WALLOP
Catherine (Fortescue) 77
Eveline Alicia Juliana (Herbert) 76, 77
French Addison (Gamble) (Goodwyn) 77
Isaac Newton, 5th Earl of Portsmouth 76, 77
Isabel (Thompson) 77
Jean (Moore) 77
Josephine Vail (Stebbins) 77
Judith (Warren) 77
Malcolm (Sen.) xviii, 77
Marguerite (Walker) 76
Newton Fellowes, 4th Earl of Portsmouth 77
Oliver Henry, 8th Earl of Portsmouth 76
Oliver Malcolm (Hon.) xviii, 77

WALNE
Peter xxix, lxix, lxx
WALPOLE
Charlotte (Shorter) 482
family lvi
Horace, 4th Earl of Orford 482
Robert, 1st Earl of Orford 482
WALROND
Bridget 745
Cecily 743, 745
Elizabeth 526
Elizabeth (Colles) 385
Grace 385, 386
Grace (Seaman) 385
Henry 386
Humphrey 385
Humphrey (Gov.) 385, 386
Jane (Hatch) 743
John 743
WALSH
Anne 522
Margaret 305
Mary Seton 545
WALSINGHAM
Barbara 475
Dorothy (Guilford) 320, 475
Frances 75, 134
Katherine 320
Thomas (Sir) 320, 475
WALTER(S)
Anne 390
Friderica 645

Mary 233, 253
Sarah 901
Thomasine 654
WALTHALL
Anne 473
WALTON
Abraham 881
Grace (Williams) 881
Jacob 881
Joan 661
Maria (Beekman) 881
Maria Eliza 881
Mary (Lawrence) 881
Mary (Santvoort) 881
Thomas 881
William 881
WALWYN
Margaret 824
WANCKE
family 449
WANDESFORD
Anne (Norton) 698
Christopher 698
Christopher (Sir), 1st Bt. 364
Eleanor (Lowther) 364
Frances 364
Margaret (Pudsey) 698
Susan 698
Thomas 698
WANGEN (VON)
Mechtild (Matilda) 832

WARBURTON
  Augusta 80
  Elizabeth 560, 561
  Elizabeth
    (Winnington) 560
  Ellen 560
  Joan (Stanley) 560
  John (Sir) 560
  Mary (Brereton)
    560, 562
  Piers (Sir) 560
WARCOP
  Anne 310
WARD
  Azubah 479
  Claire Leonora
    (Baring) 33
  Dionis (Burrow) 761
  Edward 654
  family 656
  George 761, 762
  Henry 761
  Jane 135
  Janet Penrose 436
  Josephine Mary
    (Hope) 71
  Judith (Lukyn) 654
  Lydia 656
  Margaret (Capel)
    761
  Margaret (Ugges)
    761
  Mary lviii, lx,
    cxlviii, cli, clx,
    clxxix, 654, 655,
    656
  Mary Augusta 131
  Mary Augusta
    (Arnold) [Mrs.
  Humphrey Ward]
    436
  Mary Josephine
    "Maisie" cxlvii,
    71
  Peter Alistair (Hon.)
    33
  Rachel Claire xvii,
    33
  Rebecca lviii, lx,
    cxlviii, cli, clx,
    clxxix, 655, 656
  Robert 761
  Robert Leigh clxxxv
  Rosemary Millicent
    (Leveson-Gower)
    33
  Sarah (Hon.) [Lalla
    Ward] 108, 113
  Thomas Humphrey
    436
  Thomasine vii, lii,
    lxxi, clx, clxxvii,
    clxxx, clxxxviii,
    741, 761, 762
  Thomasine (Fisher)
    761
  Tobias 761
  Wilfred Philip 71
  William George
    (Rev.) 71
  William Humble
    Eric, 3rd Earl of
    Dudley 33
WARDE
  Anne 398
  Christopher (Sir)
    398
  Frisalina 600
  Joan 402
  Joan (Tunstall) 398
  Margaret 698
  Margaret (Gascoigne)
    398
  Roger (Sir) 398
WARDWELL
  Grace 880
WARENDORP
  Elsebe 849
WARENNE (DE)
  Ada 774, 776, 778,
    780, 783, 785, 787,
    789
  ____ 917
  ____, mistress of
    John, King of
    England 372,
    667, 670, 676, 678,
    684, 691, 697
WARHAM
  Abigail 672, 925
WARKHAM
  Anne 548
WARNER
  Andrew 927
  Augustine 700,
    701, 930
  Augustine, Jr. 310,
    700, 930
  Catherine Conover
    (Mellon) 190
  David C. 925
  Elizabeth 766
  Elizabeth (Helion)
    766, 767
  Elizabeth Rosemond
    (Taylor) (Hilton)
    (Wilding) (Todd)

(Fisher) (Burton)
[Elizabeth Taylor]
21, 190
Elnora Lucretia
925, 927
John 766, 767
John William, Jr.
(Sen.) 190
Luther 925, 927
Mary 930
Mary (Russell) 925
Mary (Towneley)
xix, xxxiv, xl, lxi,
clxviii, 700, 701,
930
Mildred 310, 515,
700, 787
Mildred (Reade)
310, 700, 930
Permelia (Stanton)
925
Sarah 701
WARRE. *see* **LA
WARR(E) (DE)
(DELAWARE)**
WARREN
Anne 487
Anne (Crayford)
778
Catherine (Aylmer)
487
Catherine (Gookin)
778
Elizabeth Ann
"Betty" (Bloomer)
[Betty Ford] xlii,
xliii, 631, 655,
867, 868, 887
Ellen 487

family xl, liii, lxiv,
1026
Humphrey clxxxvi
Jane (___) 778
John 778
Judith 77
Lucy 433
Michael 487
Peter (Sir) clxxiii,
487, 900
Susannah (De
Lancey) 487
Thomas xlvii, lii,
clxix, 778, 779, 1025
William 778
William G. 868
WARREN (DE)
Alice 642, 1024
Ela 841
family 1025
Isabel 841
William, 2nd Earl of
Surrey 841
William, 3rd Earl of
Surrey 841
WARRENER
Elizabeth 730
WARTENBURG
Johann Bernard II
von Maltzan,
Baron of Penzlin
and 195
**WARTENSLEBEN
(VON)**
Caroline Frederica,
Countess 47
WARWICK
Guy de Beauchamp,
10th Earl of 783

Richard Neville, "the
Kingmaker," Earl
of, Earl of Salisbury
118, 419
Robert Rich, 1st
Earl of 135
Robert Rich, 2nd
Earl of 135
WASHBURN(E) (DE)
Alice 506
Anne (Reade) 506
Anthony 506
Eleanor 494
Eleanor (Steple/
Stapylles) 506
Emma (___) 507
family clxxxiv, 507
Joan (___) 507
Joan (Mitton) 506,
507
Joan (Whitehead)
507
John clxxxiv, 506,
507
Joyce (Jones)
(Hoskins) (Fleming)
515
Margaret (Tracy)
506
Margery (Moore)
507
Martha (Timbrell)
(Stevens) 507
Mary (Heriott) 506
Robert 506
William clxxxiv, 507
WASHINGTON
Agnes (le Gentyl)
864

Amphyllis
  (Twigden) 515
Amy (Pargiter) 864
Anne (Gerard)
  (Broadhurst)
  (Brett) 515
Anne (Pope) 515
Augustine 310,
  515, 518, 700
Elizabeth (Light)
  864
family xlvii, lxx
Frances (Browne)
  515
Frances (Gerard)
  (Speake) (Peyton)
  (Appleton) 515
George (Gen.), 1st
  U.S. President 29,
  310, 365, 515, 518,
  611, 700, 787
George Sidney
  Horace Lee xlvii,
  lxix, lxx, clxxxix
Joan (de Croft) 864
Joan (de Strickland)
  864
John 864
John (Col.), of
  Westmoreland Co.,
  Va. lxix, clxviii,
  515
John, of Surry Co.,
  Va. clxviii,
  clxxix, clxxxviii,
  516
Joyce (Jones)
  (Hoskins)
  (Fleming) 515

Lawrence lxix,
  310, 515, 700, 864
Magdalen 864
Margaret (__) 864
Margaret (Butler)
  515, 864
Margaret (Kitson)
  864
Martha 515
Martha (Dandridge)
  (Custis) 29, 170,
  301, 310, 515, 700
Mary (Ball) 310,
  515, 518, 700
Mary (Flood) (Blunt)
  (Ford) 516
Mary (Jones) 515
Mildred (Warner)
  310, 515, 700, 787
Richard 515
Robert 864
Elizabeth (Westfield)
  864
WASLEY
Mary 370
WASTENAYS (DE)
Ellen 815
WATERS
family clxxxiii
Henry FitzGilbert
  xxix, lxx, clxxxviii
Richard clxxxiii
Susan Holman 880
WATERTON
Joan 462, 470,
  473, 539, 579, 580,
  588, 604
WATKINS
Elizabeth (__) 349

Margery 682
Walter Kendall lxx
WATKINSON
Samuel 150
Sarah (Blair) lxiii,
  150
WATKYN
ap Edward 660
WATSON
Marston x, 304
____ 166
WATTERS
Deborah 859
WATTEVILLE
(VON)
Anna Dorothea
  Elizabeth,
  Baroness xxvi,
  clxx, 196
Henrietta Benigna
  Justina (of
  Zinzendorf and
  Pottendorf),
  Countess 8, 196
Johann Michael,
  Baron 8, 196
Maria Justina,
  Baroness 8
WATTS
Agnes (Mackworth)
  319
Alice (Humphrey)
  864
Anne (Rutherford)
  165
Anthony 864
Catherine 62
Eleanor 653
Elizabeth 424, 864

Elizabeth (___) 864
Elizabeth (Poyntz) 423, 424
Helen Rutherford 165, 211
Joanna (Bennett) 864
John 165, 864
Naomi 129
Richard 319
Thomas 424, 864
WAUGH
Alexander 401
Alexander Raban "Alec" xvii, clix, 402
Anne Gosse (Morgan) 401
Arthur 401
Barbara Annis (Jacobs) 402
Catherine Charlotte (Raban) 401
Evelyn Arthur St. John 401
Evelyn Florence Margaret Winifred (Gardner) 401
family xxxvii
Joan (Chirnside) 402
Laura Letitia Gwendolyn Evelyn (Herbert) 401
Virginia (Eggertsen) (Sorensen) 402
WAUTON (DE)
Alice 754
Maud 813, 824

WAYLES
John 711
Martha xliii, 387, 711, 823
Martha (Epes) 711
WAYTE
Elizabeth clxxxvi, 100, 103, 105, 106
WCHINITZ UND TETTAU (VON)
Wilhelmina, Countess 45
WEARE alias BROWNE
Joan 468
WEATHERLEY
Kathleen 364
WEAVER
Elizabeth 723
WEBB
Anna Maria 30
Anne 522
Catherine (Tresham) 414, 415, 416
Elizabeth 598
Jane 654
Jeremiah 369
John (Sir) 414
John (Sir), 1st Bt. 414, 415, 416
Lucy Ware 656, 702, 871
Margaret 721
Mariana 415
Mary (Bull) 369
Mary (Caryll) 414, 416
Rebecca 335

WEBBE
Joan 680
WEBSTER
Elizabeth 656
WEDGWOOD
Caroline Sarah (Darwin) 117
Clement Francis 117
Dorothy Mary (Winser) 117
Elizabeth (Allen) 116
Emily Catherine (Rendel) 117
Emma 116
Ethel Kate (Bowen) 117
family xxxviii
Frances (Mosley) 117
Francis 116
Josiah 116, 117
Josiah Clement Wedgwood, 1st Baron 117
Josiah Ralph Patrick cxlvii, 117
Margaret Susan 117
Susanna 116
Virginia Lloyd (Hunt) 117
WEEVER
Elizabeth 517, 558
WEIS
Frederick Lewis (Rev.) xix, lxx
WEISENSTEIN
Ruth Elizabeth 567

**WEISSENBURG
(VON)**
 Catherine 487
 Katharina 832
WEISZ
 Rachel 362
WELBY
 Anne (King) 115
 Elizabeth
  (Thimbleby) 519
 Frances (Bulkeley)
  519
 Marianne 115
 Olive lix, clx,
  clxxiv, 519, 925
 Richard 115, 519
 Thomas 519
WELCH
 Harold Bruce 833
 Jenna Louise
  (Hawkins) 833
 Laura Lane xxxv,
  xlii, xliii, 243, 474,
  479, 572, 585, 632,
  688, 703, 716, 729,
  747, 769, 833, 834
 Marie Lula/Lula
  Marie (Lane) 833
 Mark Anthony 833
 Mark Lane 834
 Nancy Jane
  (Aldridge) 833
 William Franklin
  833
WELD
 Eleanor (Leversage)
  752
 Jane 752
 John 752

Margaret 543
Mary Anne
 (Smythe) [Mrs.
 Maria FitzHerbert]
 123
WELLER
 Eleazer, Jr. 673
 Mary 673
 Mary (Moseley)
  673
WELLES (DE)
 Anne 500, 582,
  583, 601
 Anne (Barnewall)
  486, 488, 545, 546
 Cecily 588
 Eleanor 462, 473,
  486, 526, 580, 609
 Eleanor (Mowbray)
  xxv, 462, 470, 473,
  486, 526, 539, 545,
  579, 580, 604, 609
 Elizabeth 486
 Eudo 462, 470,
  473, 486, 539, 545,
  579, 580, 604
 family 564
 Ismay 545
 Joan (Waterton)
  462, 470, 473, 539,
  579, 580, 588, 604
 John de Welles, 4th
  Baron 462, 582,
  715, 728
 John de Welles, 5th
  Baron xxv, 462,
  465, 470, 473, 486,
  526, 539, 545, 579,
  580, 604, 609

Katherine 539
Lionel de Welles, 6th
 Baron 462, 470,
 473, 488, 539, 546,
 579, 580, 588, 604
Margaret 470, 471,
 579, 604
Margery 715, 728
Maud (de Greystock)
 462, 470, 473, 486,
 539, 545, 579, 580,
 604
Maud (de Ros) 462,
 582, 715, 728
William (Sir), Lord
 Deputy of Ireland
 486, 488, 545, 546
WELLESLEY
 Arthur, 1st Duke of
  Wellington 74,
  157, 341, 545
 Arthur Charles, 4th
  Duke of Wellington
  74
 Augusta Sophia Anne
  (Pierrepont) 74
 Catherine
  (Pakenham) 74
 Charles, Lord 74
 Dorothy Violet
  (Ashton) 74
 Elizabeth 74
 Gerald, 7th Duke of
  Wellington 74
 Hyacinthe-Gabrielle
  (Roland) 545
 Kathleen Emily
  Bulkeley (Williams-
  Bulkeley) 74

Richard Wellesley,
  1st Marquess
  340, 545
WELLINGTON
Arthur Wellesley,
  1st Duke of 74,
  157, 341, 545
Arthur Charles
  Wellesley, 4th
  Duke of 74
Benjamin 571
Elizabeth 571
Elizabeth (Sweetman)
  571
family xxiv
Gerald Wellesley,
  7th Duke of 74
Mary (Palgrave) 571
Roger 571
WELLS
Anna Serepta 867
H. G. (Herbert
  George) 406
Mary 625
Susannah 65
WELSH
Anne 806
WELSTEAD
Frances 480
WEMYSS
Anna (Balfour) 98
Anne (Douglas) 98
Beatrix 176
Caroline Charlotte
  (Binfield) 98
David Wemyss, 2nd
  Earl of 98
David Wemyss, 4th
  Earl of 98

Elizabeth 98
Elizabeth (Sinclair)
  98
Elizabeth
  (Sutherland) 98
Elizabeth Huntly 98
James 98
James (Hon.) 98
James, 1st Baron
  Brantisland 98
James Wemyss, 5th
  Earl of 98
Janet (Charteris) 98
Jean 98
Jean (Gray) 98
John Wemyss, 1st
  Earl of 98
Margaret (Wemyss),
  Countess of 98
WENCESLAUS I
King of Bohemia
  640
WENMAN
Agnes (Fermor)
  475
Jane (West) 475
Mary 475
Richard Wenman,
  1st Viscount 475
Thomas (Sir) 475
WEN/WYNN
Elen 690
WENTWORTH
Agnes 719
Anne 306, 349,
  708
Anne (Holgate) 821
Anne (Saye) 305,
  309, 349, 385, 705

Anne (Tyrrell)
  349, 607
Catherine (Marbury)
  708
Cecilia (Unton) 306
Christopher 708
Dorothy 349
Elinor 489
Elizabeth 342, 385,
  596
Elizabeth (Corbett)
  349
Elizabeth (Flintell/
  Flinthill) 821
Elizabeth (Hodgson)
  821
Elizabeth (Howard)
  607, 661, 710
Elizabeth (Knight)
  708
Elizabeth
  (Wentworth) 821
Ellen (Gilby) 708
family xxxii, xlvii,
  710
Helen 710
Helen
  (Agmondesham)
  710
Henry 607, 661, 710
Henry (Sir) 305,
  349, 385, 705
Isabel (Sotehill) 708
Jane 349
Jane (FitzSimon) 710
Jane (Josselyn) 710
Jane (Mirfield) 821
Joan (Calverley) 821
John 306, 821

Margaret 710
Margaret
  (Fortescue) 349
Margery 305, 483,
  607, 661, 705, 855
Margery
  (Despencer) 309,
  596, 661, 710, 719
Margery (Hales)
  821
Mary (Clifford)
  305, 342, 349, 385
Nicholas (Sir) 710
Oliver 708
Paul 710
Peter 710
Philip 349
Philip (Sir) 305,
  309, 342, 349, 385
Richard 821
Richard (Sir) 349
Roger 821
Roger (Sir) 309,
  596, 607, 661, 710,
  719
Sarah (Joiner) 821
Susanna (Carter)
  708
Thomas cl, 821
Thomas Wentworth,
  1st Baron 349
Ursula (Swinnoe)
  821
William xlviii, lvi,
  lxiv, lxviii, clxiii,
  clxxvi, 708, 821
WERDENBERG
  George II, Count of
  291

Magdalena of 459
WERTH (VAN)
  Jasper van Culem-
    borg, Heer 445
WESKE
  Jacqueline Frances
    Strange 620
WESLAWSKI
  Samuel 802
  Sophia 802
  Sophia (Kozelak-
    Puzyna), Princess
    802
WESLEY
  Anne (Hill) 340
  Garret, 1st Earl of
    Mornington 340
WESSEX
  Edward, Prince of,
    Duke of Kent 45
  Sophie Helen
    (Rhys-Jones),
    Countess of 465
WESSON
  Abigail 272
WEST
  Anne (___) 300
  Anne (Knollys)
    300, 302
  Anthony xviii,
    cxlvii, 406
  Barbara 473, 475
  Cecily (Shirley)
    300, 491
  Dorothy 603
  Eleanor 469, 477,
    492
  Eleanor (Copley)
    426, 477, 603

Elizabeth 476
Elizabeth (Hon.)
  301
Elizabeth (Huttoft)
  476
Elizabeth (Mortimer)
  477, 603
Elizabeth (Morton)
  475
Elizabeth (Strange)
  475
family xxiv, li, liii,
  lviii, 441, 576
Frances (Greville)
  302
Francis (Hon.)
  (Gov.) 300, 301
George (Sir) 475
Jane 475
Jane (Davye) 300
Joan (La Warre)
  623
John (Hon.) (Gov.)
  clxviii, 300, 301,
  304
John, Jr. 300
Katherine (Church)
  406
Lily Dulany
  (Emmet) 406
Margaret (___)
  (Blayney) 300
Margaret (Thorley)
  623
Martha (Woodward)
  300
Mary 426, 623
Mary (Guilford)
  426

1587

Nathaniel   300
Owen (Sir)   426
Penelope (Hon.)   301
Rebecca, Dame
  [Cicely Isabel
  Fairfield]   406
Reynold, 6th Baron
  Delaware (de la
  Warr)   623
Temperance
  (Flowerdew)
  (Yeardley)   300
Thomas (Gov.), 3rd
  Baron Delaware
  (de la Warr)   300,
  301, 491
Thomas (Sir)   476,
  623
Thomas, 2nd Baron
  Delaware (de la
  Warr)   300, 301,
  302
Thomas, 8th Baron
  Delaware (de la
  Warr)   426, 473,
  477, 603
Unity   301
Unity (Croshaw)
  300
William, 10th Baron
  Delaware (de la
  Warr)   475, 476
WESTFIELD
Elizabeth   864
WESTFRIESLAND
Adela, possibly of
  879, 919
WESTLAKE
Elizabeth   666

WESTLING
Christina Lovisa
  662
WESTMORELAND
Charles Neville, 6th
  Earl of   123
Francis Fane, 1st
  Earl of   122
Henry Neville, 5th
  Earl of   123
Ralph Neville, 1st
  Earl of   xxxiv, 107,
  114, 119, 126, 133,
  314, 318, 324, 331,
  339, 357, 368, 370,
  387, 393, 397, 403,
  405, 417, 418, 419,
  425, 426, 429, 433,
  434, 495, 590, 902
Thomas Fane, 8th
  Earl of   122
WESTON
Amphillis   625
Anna (Smyth)   723
Barbara (Kniveton)
  723, 724
Elizabeth (Weaver)
  723
Jerome (Sir)   467,
  717
Mary   467
Mary (Cave)   467,
  717
Ralph   723, 724
Richard   723, 724
Richard, 1st Earl of
  Portland   467
Thomas   li, clxxvi,
  clxxx, 723

WESTOVER
Mary   924
**WESTPHALEN
(VON)**
Caroline (Heubel)
  147
Christian Heinrich
  Philip, Baron   147
Jane (Wishart), of
  Pittarow   147
Johann Ludwig,
  Baron   147
Johanna (Jenny)
  Bertha Julie   147
WESTPHALIA
Jérôme Bonaparte,
  King of, Prince of
  Montfort   xl, 858
**WEVELINGHOVEN
(VON)**
Jutta   804
WEYMARN (VON)
Marie, Baroness   850
WEYMOUTH
Thomas Thynne, 1st
  Viscount   69, 70
Thomas Thynne,
  2nd Viscount   70
WHALESBURGH
Margaret   866
WHALLEY
Edward   clxxvii,
  781
Elizabeth (Hatfield)
  781
Frances   781
Frances (Cromwell)
  781
Gertrude   781

Jane xlviii, 781
Judith (Duffell)
  781
Mary (Middleton)
  781
Richard 781
Thomas 781
WHARTON
  Florence 328
  Frances 361
  Frances (Clifford)
    361, 362
  Philip Wharton, 3rd
    Baron 361
WHEELER
  Catherine Maria 79
  Catherine Maria
    (Hastings) 79
  Granville 79
  Marina Claire 12
  Rebecca 702, 746
WHEELOCK
  Julia 85
WHETCOMBE. *see*
  WHITCOMB(E)/
  WHETCOMB(E)/
  WITDECOMBE
WHETEHILL
  Adrian 813
  Elizabeth 590
  Elizabeth (Muston)
    813
  Margaret (Worsley)
    813
  Margery 813
  Richard (Sir) 813
WHETENHALL
  Agnes (Arderne)
    822

Alice (Berkeley)
  357, 358
Anna/Anne 358
Anne (Cromer)
  357, 466, 721, 783
Dorothy (Vane)
  357
Elizabeth lxii, cl,
  358, 905
family 358
George 357, 358
Henry 905
Henry (Father)
  905, 906
John 905, 906
John (Sir) 822
Letitia (Tichborne)
  905
Margaret 721, 822
Margaret (Heckstall)
  466
Rose 466, 467, 783
Sarah 592
Susanna 357
Thomas 357
William 357, 466,
  721, 783
WHIPPLE
  Mary 85, 86
  William, Jr. 85
WHITAKER
  Alexander (Rev.)
    701
  Elizabeth (Nowell)
    701
  family xxxiv, xlv
  Hester/Esther 467
  Jabez 354, 701

Mary (Bourchier)
  354, 701
Thomas 701
William 701
____ (Culverwell)
  701
WHITCOMB
  Norman K. clxxxv
WHITCOMB(E)/
WHETCOMB(E)/
WITDECOMBE
  Elizabeth (____)
    clxxxv
  family clxxxv
  Frances (Cogan)
    clxxxv
  Jesper/Jasper
    clxxxv
  Joanna (Pope)
    clxxxv
  John lix, clxxxv
  Thomas clxxxv
  William clxxxv
WHITE
  Alexander 917
  Alice 870
  Alison (St.
    Lawrence)
    (Netterville) 486
  Anne 625
  Bridget 917
  Catherine xl, cli,
    916, 917
  Charity 744
  Eleanor
    (Hungerford) 625
  Eleanor (Smith) 917
  Elizabeth (Engle-
    field) 625, 626

Ellen 625
family 552
Joan 112, 383, 552
John 625
John (Sir) 625
Margaret 486, 625
Margaret (Gainsford) 625, 626
Mary 308
Mary (Forster) 625
Mary (Sackville) 552
Patrick 486
Rebecca Crenshaw 150
Robert 625
Sallie Spiers 278, 301, 387, 711, 823
Stephen A. 939
Sybil (White) 625
William 552
WHITEFORD
Adam (Sir), 1st Bt. 128
Alice (Muir) 128
Anne (Cartwright) 128
Henrietta 128
John (Sir), 2nd Bt. 128
John (Sir), 3rd Bt. 128
Margaret (Cathcart) 128
WHITEHALL
Amy 272
WHITEHEAD
Agatha 187, 188

Agathe Johanna Maria Gobertina (Breunner-Enkevoirth), Countess 187
Alfred North xviii, 535
Auguste Caroline (Lammer) 188
Daniel 507
Evelyn Ada Maud Rice (Willoughby-Wade) cxlvii, 535
family 188
Frank 188
Joan 507
John 187
Robert 187, 188
WHITFIELD
Dorothy (Sheafe) clxxxiii
Henry (Rev.) clxxxiii
Susan 359
WHITGIFT
Anne (Dyn[e]well) 579
Elizabeth 579
Henry 579
John, Archbishop of Canterbury 579
William 579
WHITGREAVES
Frances 331
WHITING
Charlotte Lydia 635
Dorcas (Chester) 747, 758

Elizabeth 543, 924
Elizabeth (Read) 747, 758
Elizabeth (St. John) clxii, clxxvi, 747, 924
Katherine 747, 758
Samuel, Jr. 747, 758
Samuel (III) 747, 758
Samuel (Rev.) 747, 924
Sara 144
WHITLEIGH
Margaret 835
WHITMORE
J. B. xxviii
WHITNEY
Blanche 331
Constance (Touchet or Audley) 410
Eleanor 770
Elizabeth (Vaughan) clxxxv, 410, 770
Eustace clxxxv, 770
family xxxvi, clxxxv
Joan 338, 410
Joan (Trussell) clxxxv, 770
John 1, clxxxv
Mary (Bray) clxxxv
Robert clxxxv, 410
Robert (Sir) 770
Thomas clxxxv
WHITTINGHAM
Elizabeth (Bulkeley) clxi, clxxvi, 747
Richard 747

WHITTINGTON
Isabella 647
WHORWOOD
Elizabeth 299
WHYTT/WHYTE
Donald xxix, lxi, lxx, 171, 259
Jean 270
Louisa (Balfour) 270, 549
Martha 549
Robert (Prof.), of Bennochy 270, 549
WIAZEMSKY
Anne-Françoise-Sophie, Princess 635, 795
Catherine, Princess 794
Ivan, Prince 795
Marie-Thérèse (Mauriac) 795
Sophia (Vorontzov-Dachkov), Countess 795
Vladimir, Prince 795
WICKES
Anne (Hynson) (Randall) 348
WICKLIFFE
Alice 768
WIDDRINGTON
Alice (Grey) 425
Catherine 100
Elizabeth (Boynton) 425

Felicia (Claxton) 425
Frances (Fairfax) 100, 329
Gerard (Sir) 425
Henry (Sir) 425
Margery (Percy) 425
Mary 329, 425
Ralph (Sir) 425
Roger 425
Thomas (Sir) 100, 329
WIED
George Hermann Reinhard von Runkel, Count of 142
Sophia Sabine of 142
WIELOPOLSKI/ WIELOPOLSKA
Maria Malgorzata Paulina Wilhelmina Róza Leopoldyna Julia lii, cxlvi, 11
Zygmunt, Count, Marquis Gonzaga-Myszkowski 11
WIENER DE CROISSET
Franz 227
Germaine 227
Jacqueline (Thion de la Chaume) 227
Marie-Thérèse-Anne-Josèphe-Germaine

(de Chévigné) (Bischoffsheim) 227
Philippe 227
WIENTJES
Marianne Yvonne 908
WIGG
Mary (Hazzard) 176
WIGGIN
Abigail Fiske (Merriam) 111
Ann E. (Loder) 111
Augustus 111
Augustus Holme 111
Catherine (Holme) 111
Christina (Ferguson) 111
Elizabeth Sumner (Gerard) 111
Frances Emma (Rice) 111
Frederick clix, 111
Frederick Holme 111
Hannah (Hansen) 111
Timothy 111
William 111
WIGGINTON
Anne E. 278, 301, 387, 711, 823
WIGGLESWORTH
Henry 924
Olive Gertrude (Belden) 924

Sylvia 161, 924
WIGHT
Anne (Fielder)
(Gantt) l, lxii,
cxlix, cli, clxviii,
603
John (Dr.) 603
WIGMAN
Alida Hendrika
Maria 460
WIGTOWN
John Fleming, 1st
Earl of 152
WILBERFORCE
family xxxvii
WILBRAHAM
Katherine Frances
120
WILBRAHAM BAKER
George Barrington
(Sir), 5th Bt. 120
Joyce Christabel
(Kennaway) 120
Mary Frances 120
Philip (Sir), 6th Bt.
120
WILCKEN
Anna Joanna
Dorothea 924
WILCOX
Wayne Howard
Miller ix, lxx,
717
WILDE
Olivia [Olivia Jane
Cockburn] xi,
xviii, xlvi, xlviii,
21, 94

Winifred 492
WILDENSTEIN (VON)
Maria Dorothea
640
WILDING
Aileen (Getty) 21
Christopher Edward
21
Elizabeth Rosemond
(Taylor) (Hilton)
[Elizabeth Taylor]
21, 190
Michael 21
WILHELMINA
Queen of The
Netherlands 8
WILHELMINA MARIE
of Hesse-Homburg
54
WILHELMINE
of Baden 41
Princess of Prussia,
Queen of The
Netherlands 8
Princess of Prussia,
wife of William V
of Orange,
Stadholder of The
Netherlands 8
WILHELMINE AMALIE
Princess of
Brunswick-
Lüneburg 20
WILKES
Charles 222
Frances 481, 482

Jane Jeffrey
(Renwick) 222
John de Ponthieu
222
Mary (Seton) 222
Mary H. (Lynch)
(Bolton) 222
WILKINSON
Anne 686
Eleanor Green 129
Elizabeth 144
WILLARD
family xxiv
WILLET
Susanna 148
WILLIAM
ap Edward/Bedward
660
ap Huw 659, 693
ap Thomas (Sir)
337, 352, 808
ap Walter 656
ap Walter Thomas
654
ap William 693
Count of Egmont
459
Count of Holland
447
Duke of Brunswick-
Lüneburg 58, 60,
432
Duke of Courland
54, 56
Duke of
Mecklenburg 8
Duke of Saxony,
Landgrave of
Thuringia 220

1592

Isabel 740
WILLIAM I
  Emperor of
  Germany 41
  King of The
  Netherlands 8
WILLIAM I "THE
CONQUEROR"
  Duke of Normandy,
  King of England
  xx, 642, 830, 851,
  861, 879, 911, 919,
  1024
WILLIAM I "THE
LION"
  King of Scotland
  xxvi, xxxix, 652,
  700, 705, 708, 710,
  713, 715, 719, 721,
  723, 725, 727, 728,
  730, 732, 778, 780,
  785, 787, 789
WILLIAM II
  Elector of Hesse 13
  Emperor of
  Germany 20
WILLIAM III
  Count of Holland
  and Hainault 459
  Duke of Cleves,
  Juliers and Berg
  43, 54, 56, 891
  Duke of Juliers 451
  Prince of Orange,
  King of England
  and Scotland 615
WILLIAM IV
  King of Great
  Britain 9

of Orange,
  Stadholder of The
  Netherlands 8
WILLIAM V
  Duke of Juliers
  459
  of Orange,
  Stadholder of The
  Netherlands 8
WILLIAM VI
  Duke of Juliers 459
WILLIAM "THE
SILENT"
  Prince of Orange,
  Stadholder of The
  Netherlands 62,
  141, 181, 182, 184,
  194, 196
WILLIAM ALBERT
  1st Prince of
  Montenuovo 11
WILLIAM ARTHUR
PHILIP LOUIS
  of Wales, Prince of
  Great Britain, Duke
  of Cambridge xlii,
  25, 380, 858, 931,
  932
WILLIAM HENRY
  Prince of Great
  Britain, Duke of
  Gloucester 27
  Prince of Schwarz-
  burg-Rudolstadt
  891
WILLIAMS
  Abigail 672
  Abigail (Allyn)
  672

Abigail (Davis) 858
Abigail (Williams)
  672
Alicia Crane v, vi
America Pinckney
  (Peter) 170
Benjamin 858
Carol Mary 362
Catherine (Griffith)
  (Morris) (Edwards)
  652, 693
Dorothy (Griffith)
  375
Eleanor 660
Elijah 672
Elizabeth 650, 651,
  660
Ellis [Ellis William
  ap Huw] 659, 660
family xi
Frances (Baldwin)
  (Townshend)
  (Jones) xi, xlix,
  liii, liv, cxlvii,
  clxviii, clxxxii, 727
Frances (Deighton)
  clxii, clxxii, 297
George 170
Grace 881
Gwen 659, 660
Irene 12
Jane 375
Joanna 828
John lvi, lxv, clxxx,
  652, 672, 693
John Savage 860
Joseph 858
Joseph (III) 858
Joseph, Jr. 858

1593

Katherine Alicia 170
Kelsey Jackson lxx
Lydia (Dwight) 672
Margaret 428
Margaret (John) 659
Margaret Elizabeth 124
Marie Luise (von Pfeffel) 12
Martha (Howell) 858
Mary 858
Mary (Capen) 858
Mary (Evans) 690, 693
Richard 297
Robert 727, 860
Samuel 690
Sarah (Wise) 858
Sarah Copeland (Morton) 858
Stanley Fred 12
Stephen 858
Stephen, Jr. 858
Susan May xl, 858
Susanna (May) 858
Thomas 672
Thomasine 550
William 375

WILLIAMS-BULKELEY
Bridget Henrietta Frances clv, 124, 481
Kathleen Emily Bulkeley 74
Margaret Elizabeth (Williams) 124
Maria Frances (Stanley-Massey-Stanley) 124
Richard (Sir), 10th Bt. 124
Richard Lewis Mostyn (Sir), 11th Bt. 124

WILLIAMSON
Arabella 470
David Geoffrey lxx
Janet (McDougal) 264

WILLING
Anne 412
Anne (Harrison) 411
Anne (Shippen) 411, 557
Ava (Lowle) 412
Ava Lowle 799
Blanche 412
Charles xi, xlix, lxvii, lxviii, lxix, cxlvii, clxv, clxxiii, 411, 412, 557
Charles, Jr. 557
Dorothy 411, 412
Elizabeth Hannah (Carrington) xlix, clxxix, 557
Joseph 412
Margaret 411
Thomas 411, 412
Thomas Mayne 411

WILLIS
Anne (Rich) lix, lxvii, clxviii, 838
Anne Susanna Kent (Bund) 541
Daniel A. xxi
Elizabeth 349
family clxxxvi
Francis 838
Hermione Youlanda Ruby (Clinton-Baddeley) (Tennant) [Hermione Baddeley] xvii, lxiii, clii, 78, 109, 113
J. H. "Dozey" (Maj.) 109
John Walpole 541

WILLIS (BREWER-WARD)
Daniel xlv, lxx

WILLIS-BUND
Alexander Joseph 542
Harriet Penelope (Temple) 541
John William 541
Mary Susanna 542

WILLIS/WYLLYS
Richard clxxxvi
Thomas clxxxvi

WILLIX
Anna 530

WILLOUGHBY
Anne 311
Anne (Grey) 339
Bridget (Read) clxxxvii

Catherine
  (Goldwell)
  clxxxvii
Catherine (Hart)
  clxxxvii
Cecily 370, 426
Cecily (de Welles)
  588
Christopher
  clxxxvii
Christopher (Sir)
  311
Christopher (Sir), *de jure* 10th Baron Willoughby d'Eresby
  clxxxvii, 588
Clemence
  (Willoughby)
  clxxxvii
Dorothy
  (Willoughby)
  clxxxvii
Edward 331, 332
Eleanor 653
Elizabeth 317, 331, 339, 628, 630, 905
Elizabeth
  (Beauchamp) 332
Elizabeth (Talboys)
  311
family clxxxvii
Henry (Sir) 339
Henry, 8th Baron Middleton 27
Hugh (Sir) 653, 715
Isabel 716
Joan 418
Joan (Strangeways)
  370, 372
Julia Louisa
  (Bosville) 27
Kenelm clxxxvii
Lelia Louisa
  Millicent 27
Lucy 851
Margaret 339, 543, 588
Margaret (Freville)
  653, 715
Margaret (Jenney)
  clxxxvii, 588
Margaret (Neville)
  331
Margery 369, 667, 715, 716
Margery (Totteshurst)
  clxxxvii
Richard, 2nd Baron Willoughby de Broke 332
Robert clxxxvii
Robert (Sir) 588
Thomas clxxxvii
Thomas (Sir)
  clxxxvii
William (Sir) 370, 372
WILLOUGHBY-WADE
Arthur Robert 535
Evelyn Ada Maud Rice cxlvii, 535
Lucy Maria
  (Harvey) 535
WILMER
Jane (Falconer) 256
Simon 256
WILMINGTON
Spencer Compton, 1st Earl of 112
WILMOT
Anne 541
Elizabeth 491
WILSFORD
Bridget 467
Cecily 509, 783
Elizabeth 467
Elizabeth (Colepepper/Culpeper) 467, 469
Mary 469
Rose (Whetenhall) 466, 467, 783
Thomas 467, 783
WILSON 378
Anna Mary
  (Braithwaite) 231
Anne cliv, 116, 886
Anne (Adams) 138
Anne Elizabeth 232, 378
Charles Braithwaite 231, 232
Donna 979
Edith (Bolling)
  (Galt) xlii, 278, 301, 387, 711, 823
Elizabeth xlviii, cli, 112, 113
Elizabeth
  (Mansfield)
  cxlvii, cxlii, 318
Ellen Blanch
  (Hargrove) 231

Ellen Louise
  (Axson) xlii, 463,
  465, 508, 673, 726
family 232
Henry Braithwaite
  232
James 549
Jane (Towneley)
  112
Jane Whytt
  Elizabeth Ann
  549
Janet 275
John (Rev.) 318
John, Jr. 318
John Alexander
  549
Joseph 138
Leighton viii, li,
  cxlvii, 138
Louise 268
Margarethe Agnes
  "Grete" (Bodden)
  232
Marion (Balfour)
  549
Martha (Whytt) 549
Mary (Wood) 138
Richarda (Peacock)
  112
Sarah (Adams) 138
Sarah (Hooker)
  318
Susanna 231, 318
Thomas Crewdson
  231
William 112
William (Sir), 2nd
  Bt. 112

Woodrow (Thomas
  Woodrow), 28th
  U.S. President
  xlii, 278, 301, 387,
  463, 465, 508, 673,
  711, 726, 823
York Lowry xlvii,
  lxx
WILT VAN
BLEYSWYCK (DE)
  Liedewey 774
WILTSHIRE
  Bridget 565
  Thomas Boleyn, 1st
  Earl of, Earl of
  Ormonde 300,
  588
WIMBORNE
  Ivor Bertie Guest,
  1st Baron 63, 64
WINANS/WYNANS
  Ada 194
WINANT
  Constance Riving-
  ton (Russell) 165
  John Gilbert (Gov.)
  165
WINCH
  Cecily (Onslow)
  534
  Humphrey (Sir) 534
  Humphrey (Sir), 1st
  Bt. 534
  Judith (Burgoyne)
  534
  Mary 534
  Onslow 534
  Rebecca (Browne)
  534

WINCHESTER
  Jonathan Trelawny
  (Sir), 3rd Bt.,
  Bishop of 305
  Roger de Quincy,
  2nd Earl of 843
  Saire de Quincy, 1st
  Earl of 680, 682,
  843
  William Paulet, 1st
  Marquess of 905
WINCHILSEA
  Heneage Finch, 3rd
  Earl of 69
WINDEBANK
  Anne 310
  Frances (Dymoke)
  310
  Mildred 310
  Thomas (Sir) 310
WINDHAM. *see also*
  WYNDHAM/
  WINDHAM
  Edward, of Virginia
  xlix, cxlvii, 385
WINDSOR
  Andrews Windsor,
  1st Baron 324, 405,
  417, 501, 503, 1024
  Anne 501
  Edith 503
  Eleanor 324, 405,
  417
  Elizabeth (Andrews)
  503
  Elizabeth (Blount)
  324, 405, 417, 501,
  503

Thomas 503
WINDT (DE)
Elizabeth 891
family 891
WINECK
Barbara, Baroness 832
WINGATE
Joshua 924
Mary 924
Mary (Lunt) 924
WINGFIELD
Anne (Cromwell) 307
Anne (Touchet) 565
Anthony (Sir) 565
Bridget (Wiltshire) 565
Dorothy 554
Edward 308
Edward (Sir) 307
Edward Maria 565
Eleanor (Gore) 308
Elizabeth clxxxiii, 311, 354, 470, 517, 571, 613
Elizabeth (Cecil) 554
Elizabeth (FitzLewis) 566
Elizabeth (Goushill) 517, 554, 565, 571, 613
Elizabeth (Risby) 565
Elizabeth (Rookes) 554
Elizabeth (Vere) 565
Elizabeth Isabella 158
family lvii
Frances (Cromwell) 307
Henry 565
Henry (Sir) 554
Isabella 179, 308
John 307
John (Sir) 307, 566, 613
Lewis 307
Margery (Quarles) 554
Mary 565
Mary (___) 307
Mary (Hardwick) 565, 706
Mary (Owen) 307
Richard 565, 706
Richard (Sir) 565
Robert 554
Robert (Sir) 517, 554, 565, 571, 613
Sidney (Gore) 307
Thomas xi, clxxix, 307, 1025
Thomas Maria 565
___ (Kerry) 565
WINN
Endymia 370
Jacob (III) 370
Phoebe (Grout) 370
WINNINGTON
Elizabeth 560
WINSER
Dorothy Mary 117
WINSLOW
Abigail (Atkinson) 836
Agnes 857
Agnes (Throckmorton) 857
Anne 479
Edward 479
Edward (Gov.) clxxxiii
Elizabeth (Hutchinson) 479
family vii, lv, lviii, lix, lx, clxxxiii
Gilbert clxxxiii
John clxxxiii
Josiah clxxxiii
Kenelm clxxxiii
Mary (Chilton) clxxxiii
Thomas 857
WINSLOWE
Margery 495
WINSTON
Mary 870
Sarah 219
WINTER
Anne 110
Anne (Somerset) 110
Edward (Sir) 110
Elizabeth Tatham (Dick) 440, 626
Ernst Florian 187
Henry Mosle (H. M.) West vi, lxx, 440, 441, 626
Johanna Karolina (von Trapp) clviii, 187
Keyes 440, 626
Marie Caroline (Mosle) 440, 626

1597

Susan 626
WINTERTON
 Edward Tournor,
  5th Earl of 28
WINTHROP
 Alice Woodward
  (Babcock) 925
 Anne 396
 Anne (Dudley) 923
 Catherine (Slicer)
  714
 Elizabeth (___)
  714
 Elizabeth (Mason)
  923
 Elizabeth (Reade)
  501
 Elizabeth Bowdoin
  (Temple) 923
 Elizabeth Cabot
  (Blanchard) 923
 family lxii, clxii
 Henry Rogers 925
 Jane (Borland) 923
 John 923
 John (Gov.) 483,
  501, 713, 714
 John, Jr. (Gov., Dr.)
  501
 John Still 923
 Joseph 714
 Lucy 396, 501
 Margaret (Tyndal/
  Tindal) liv, lvii,
  clxii, clxxvi, 483,
  713
 Margaret Tyndal
  923
 Mary (Browne) 396

Mary (Forth) 501
Robert Charles 923
Robert Charles, Jr.
 923
Samuel 714
Sarah 714
Thomas Lindall
 923
Thomasine (Clopton)
 liv, 483, 714
Waitstill 396
WINTON
 Robert Seton, 1st
  Earl of 143
WINTOUR
 Alice Jane Blanche
  (Foster) 117
 Anna (Dame) xviii,
  clix, 117
 Charles Vere 117
 Eleanor "Nonie"
  Trego (Baker)
  117
 Fitzgerald 117
WISE
 Joseph 858
 Mary (Thompson)
  858
 Sarah 858
 Thomasine 744
WISEMAN
 Alice (Miles) 484
 Anne (Capell) cl,
  121, 484
 Elizabeth 302, 626
 John 302, 484
 Margaret 882
 Margery
  (Waldegrave) 484

Mary (Rugeley)
 302, 303
Penelope 596
Robert cl, 121, 484
Thomas 484
WISHART
 Anne (Campbell), of
  Orchard 147
 Elizabeth 250
 Fergusia 144
 George 147
 Jane, of Pittarow
  147
WISING
 Maria Sofia 60
WISTER
 Mary Channing
  (Wister) 383
 Owen 382, 383
 Owen Jones 382
 Sarah (Butler) 382
WITDECOMBE. *see*
 WHITCOMB(E)/
 WHETCOMB(E)/
 WITDECOMBE
WITHAM
 Anne 127
 Anne (Lawson)
  127
 Catherine
  (Meaburne) 127
 Elizabeth (Standish)
  127
 George 127
 Grace (Wyvill)
  127
 Henry 127
 John 127
 William 127

WITHINGTON
 Gertrude Bradbury 649
 Lothrop xxix, lviii, lxi, lxx, 649
WITTE (VON)
 Ekaterina (Fadeev) 792
 Julius 792
 Sergei, Count 792, 795
WITTELSBACH
 Rupert III of, Holy Roman Emperor 237, 291
WITTER
 Thomas cxcii
WITTS
 Sarah 135
WITTSTOCK
 Charlene Lynette 934
WITTY
 Mary 548
WLADISLAW I
 King of Poland 791, 797, 802
WLAZKO
 Prince of Kukenois 849
WODDROP
 Helen 263
WODEHOUSE
 Amy Dulcibella clviii, 131
 Anne (Armine) 335
 Annette Fanny (Massey) 131
 Apollonia (Nourse) 131, 335
 Armine (Sir), 5th Bt. 335
 Charles Nourse 131
 Dulcibella Jane (Hay) 131
 Eleanor (Deane) 335
 Ernest Hay clix, 131
 Ethel (Newton) (Rowley) 335
 Henry Ernest 335
 James Hay 131
 John (Sir), 4th Bt. 335
 Letitia (Bacon) 335
 Lucy (Cotton) 335
 Lydia (Lea) 335
 Mary 577
 Mary (Fermor) 335
 Mary Augusta (Ward) 131
 Pelham Grenville (P. G.) (Sir) xlvi, cxlvii, 335, 336
 Philip 131, 335
 Philip (Sir), 3rd Bt. 335
 Thomas (Sir) 335
WODELL
 Mary (Gold) 841
WODHULL
 Alice 768
 Alice (Wickliffe) 768
 Anne (Newenham) 768
 Elizabeth (Hall) 768
 Fulk 768
 Isabel (Trussell) 768
 Joan (Etwell) 768
 John 768
 Lawrence 768
 Margaret (___) 768
 Thomas 768
WOGAN
 Anne (Butler) 582, 583
 Catherine 582
 family 875
 John 582, 583
 Margaret 582
WOLCOTT
 Catherine (Loomis) 925
 Henry 925
 Jane (Allyn) 925
 Jane Catherine 925
 Thomas 925
WOLFE
 Janet Paulette Chevalley l, liii, lxx, 87, 568, 759, 922
 Robert Allen lxx, 759
WOLLASTON
 Phyllis Byam 135
WOLLEY
 Alice 343
 Anne (Leming) 343

1599

William 343
WOLRICH
Eleanor (Peshall) 670
Elizabeth 670
Humphrey 670
WOLSELEY
Anne lxi, lxii, 333, 676, 699
Anne (Stanley) 676, 677
Anthony 676
Cassandra (Giffard) 676
Devereux 333
Elizabeth (Zouche) 333
Ellen 677
Ellen (Broughton) 333, 676
Erasmus 676
family lxviii
John 676, 677
Margaret (Blythe) 676
Mary lxi, clxxv, 676, 699
Mary (Beauchamp) 676
Thomas (Sir) 333, 676
Walter 676
Winifred 676
WOOD
Abigail (Leighton) 138
Anne 370, 403, 632
Basil 138

Dorothy (Brereton) 772, 773
Eleanor (Strong) 932
Elizabeth xlix, cxlii, 772, 773
Elizabeth (___) 138
Elizabeth (Richards) 138
Ellen 932
Frances (King) 308
Hans Wadman 308
John 932
Katherine 883
Leighton 138
Margaret 308
Mary 133, 138
Michael Johnson vi, vii, xxiii, xxix, xliii, xlvii, l, lii, liii, lx, lxii, lxiv, lxv, lxvii, lxviii, lxxi, 397, 520, 762
Peter 772, 773
Sarah (Bond) 138
WOODCOCK
Alice (Washburn) 506
Mary xlviii, cxlii, clxxxiv, 506, 507
Ursula 839
William 506
WOODHOUSE
Anne (Bacon) 846
Anne (Repps) 846
Dorothy (Hatfield) 401
Hannah (Dell) 401

Henry liii, clxxvii, clxxx, 846, 1025
Henry (Gov.) 846
John 401
Judith (Manby?) (Haen) 846
Mary (___) 846
Mary (Sothren?) 846
Susanna 401
William 401
William (Sir) 846
WOODHULL
Anne 368
Canning 138
Elizabeth (Parr) 368
Nicholas (Sir) 368
Victoria (Claflin) [Victoria C. Woodhull] xvii, 138
WOODLIFFE
Anne 538
Anne (Drury) 537
Drew 537
family 538
John liii, lxiv, 538
Katherine (Duncombe) 538
Robert 537
WOODROFFE/ WOODROVE
Dionysia (Calthorpe) 577
Elizabeth 577
Robert 577
WOODRUFF
Jane 580

WOODS
Alice 520
Hannah (Farwell) 520
Mary 925
Mary Lee 520
Samuel 520

WOODSTOCK
Edmund Plantagenet of, Prince of England, 1st Earl of Kent 515, 600
Thomas Plantagenet of, Prince of England, 1st Duke of Gloucester xxv, xxxix, 331, 353, 392, 393, 409, 420, 421, 428, 436

WOODVILLE
Anne 134
Anthony, 2nd Earl Rivers 412
Catherine 333, 347, 431
Elizabeth 514
Elizabeth, Queen of England 100, 103, 105, 106, 134, 208, 323, 333, 339, 346, 347, 370, 397, 412, 431, 433, 514, 902
family xxxii, lvii, lxviii
Jacquetta 397, 433, 902
Mary 346
Richard, 1st Earl Rivers 208, 514

WOODWARD
Ezekias/Hezekiah (Rev.) 647, 648
Frances lxx, cxlv, clxi, 324, 647, 649
Frances (___) 647
Frances (Rudhall) 647
Martha 300, 877
Richard 647, 649
Sarah lviii, lxi, lxx, cxliv, clxi, 647, 649

WOOLF
(Adeline) Virginia (Stephen) 611

WOOLHOUSE
Elizabeth 495
Mary 495

WOOLLEY
Adam 528
Edward 528
Elizabeth (___) 528
Emmanuel lviii, cxlvii, 528, 529
Grace (Heywood) 528
John 528
Mary (Fritchley) 528
Mary (Revell) 528, 529

WOOLNAUGH
Elizabeth 319

WOOLSON
Gertrude 924

WOOLSTON
Susanna 348

WOOLWORTH
Edna 44
Frank Winfield 44, 63
Jennie (Creighton) 44

WORCESTER
Charles Somerset, 1st Earl of 345, 396
Edward Somerset, 4th Earl of 109
Henry Somerset, 1st Marquess of 109, 110
Henry Somerset, 2nd Earl of 345
Richard Beauchamp, 1st Earl of xxv, 357, 405, 417, 429

WORDEN/WERDEN
Isabel (Worthington) 701
Margaret (Grice) (Wall) 702
Mary 702
Mary (___) 702
Peter liii, cxlvii, clxii, 702, 704
Peter, Jr. 702
Robert 701

WORDSWORTH
William 330

WORK
Ellen (Wood) 932
Frances Eleanor "Ellen" 378, 932

Franklin H. "Frank" 932
WORMELEY
  Agatha (Eltonhead) (Kellaway) clxvi, clxxiii, 484, 491, 498, 551
  Elizabeth 551
  family xxiv
  Ralph 483, 498, 551
WORSAM
  Catherine (Tomlinson) 385
  Constantia Richilinda 386
  Henrietta Constantia xi, xlix, cxlv, clxv, 385, 386
  Henrietta Maria 386
  Maria Richard 386
  Mary (Sylvester) 385, 386
  Richard 385, 386
WORSHAM
  Elizabeth xiv
  Mary xiii, xiv
WORSLEY
  Fanny 475
  Frances 69, 121
  Frances (Thynne) 69
  Isabel 468
  Joyce 419
  Margaret 813
  Mary (Frankland) 121
  Otewell (Sir) 419, 813
  Robert (Sir), 4th Bt. 69
  Rose (Trevor) 419, 813, 814
  Thomas 121
WORST
  Grace Maud 450
WORTH
  Dorothy 609
  Wendy 64
WORTHINGTON
  Agnes (Rushton) 701
  Isabel 701
  Isabel (Anderton) 701
  Peter 701
  Richard 701
WORTHY
  Elizabeth 766
  Elizabeth (Warner) 766
  John 766
WORTLEY-MONTAGU
  Edward 299
  Mary 299
  Mary (Pierrepont) [Lady Mary Wortley-Montagu] 64, 299
WOTTON
  Anne 474
  Margaret 339
WRANGEL
  Herman (Field Marshal) 889
  Maria Christina, Baroness 889
WRAY
  Albinia 117
  Albinia (Cecil) 115
  Anne (Casey) 115
  Cecil 116, 117
  Christopher (Sir) 115
  Diana 115
  Drury (Sir), 6th Bt. 115, 116, 117
  Frances 34, 115, 116, 117, 315
  Frances (Drury) (Clifford) 114
  Frances Fairfax (Norcliffe) 116
  Isabella 116
  Isabella (Ullithorne) 116
  John (Sir), 6th Bt. 116
  Susanna (Cressy) 116
  Theodosia 116, 117
  William 116
  William (Sir) 114
WREN
  Christopher (Sir) 350
  Susan 350
WRENSHALL
  Ellen Bray 722
WRIGHT
  Alfred, Jr. 463
  Anne 563
  Anne (Blatchford) 350
  Anne (Merriton) 785

Anne (Mottrom)
  348, 785
Camilla Elizabeth
  (Campbell) 390,
  391
Edmund 661
Elizabeth 613
Elizabeth (Maudit)
  563
family 1026
Frances (Spring)
  661
Frances "Fanny"
  xi, clix, 390, 391
Francis 785
Isabella (Wright)
  (Pitts) 350
James (Sir), 1st Bt.
  350
Jane (Jermyn) 350
Jermyn 350
Joan de Beauvoir
  (de Havilland)
  (Aherne) (Dozier)
  (Young) [Joan
  Fontaine] xvii,
  463
Margery 407
Mary 661
Rebecca 924
Richard xlvi, 785,
  786
Robert (Chief
  Justice) 350
Robert (Sir) 350
Sarah (Maidman)
  350
Susan (Wren) 350
Thomas 350, 563

WRIOTHESLEY
Elizabeth (Vernon)
  137
Henry, 2nd Earl of
  Southampton 905
Henry, 3rd Earl of
  Southampton 137
Mary 110, 905
Mary (Browne) 905
Penelope 137
WROTH
Dorothy 580
Elizabeth 738, 739,
  845
Elizabeth (Lewknor)
  738, 845
Joan (Hawte)
  (Goodere) 552, 738
Joan (Newdigate?)
  653, 738
John 653, 656,
  738, 845
Mabel 509
Margaret 653, 656
Mary 739, 741
Mary (Rich) 509,
  738
Robert 552, 738
Thomas (Sir) 509,
  738
WROTTESLEY
Dorothy (Sutton)
  319, 321
Eleanor 319, 320
Elizabeth 33
Isabella (Harcourt)
  319
Joan 319, 320
Richard 319

Richard (Sir), 7th
  Baronet 33
Walter 319, 320
WROUGHTON
Anna (Berwick) 738
Anne (Eyre) 306,
  309
Anne (Farwell) 306
Diana Elizabeth
  (Denton) 361
Dorothy (Musgrave)
  361
Eleanor (Lewknor)
  738
family 362
George 306, 309,
  361
Georgina Grace
  (Chamier) 361
Gertrude 738
Grace Matilda 361
Henrietta 306, 309
James 306, 309
John Chardin 361
Thomas (Sir) 738
William 361
William (Sir) 738
**WURMBRAND-
STUPPACH (VON)**
Francizka de Paula,
  Countess 209
Heinrich (Wilhelm)
  Gundaccar (Vincenz
  Ferrerius Franz
  Xavier Anton von
  Padua Joseph Alois
  Felix), Count 208
Maria Josepha (von
  Ledebur zu

Wicheln),
Baroness 208
WURTS
John Sparhawk
xxviii
WÜRTTEMBERG
Augusta, Princess of
Brunswick, Queen
of 12
Charlotte, Princess
Royal of Great
Britain, Queen of
12
Elizabeth, Princess
of, Empress of
Austria 11
Frederick Eugene,
Duke of 49
Frederick I, King of
12
Matilda of 449
Paul, Prince of 12
**WÜRTTEMBERG
(VON)**
Eleanor, Baroness
von Franquement
49
**WÜRTTEMBERG-
MÖMPELGARD**
George, Duke of
184
Leopold Eberhard,
Duke of 184, 185
Louis Frederick,
Duke of 184
**WÜRTTEMBERG-
STUTTGART**
Charles Alexander,
Duke of 49

WYATT
Anne 314
Anne (Cox) 314
Barbara (Mitford)
liv, cxlvii, clxxxii,
314, 425
Elizabeth (___) 314
Elizabeth (Brooke)
314, 315
family xxxiv
Frances (Chichester)
672
Francis (Sir) (Gov.)
314, 783
George 314
Hawte (Rev.) liv,
314, 425
Jane 314
Jane (Finch) 314
Jane (Hawte) 314,
551
John 672
Margaret xix, liv, lv,
lxiv, clxii, clxxv,
672, 674, 925
Margaret (Sandys)
clxxvii, 314, 779,
783
Thomas (Sir) 314,
551
WYCHE
Elizabeth (Saltonstall)
837
Ellen (Quinnell)
837
Henry lxvii, 837
Richard 837
WYGERSLEY
Margaret 471

WYKE
Agnes 835
WYKES
family 412
WYLDE
Anne (Rowland
alias Steyner) 541
Catherine 772
Dorothy (Berkeley)
541
Robert 541
Sarah 541
Thomas 541
WYLLYS. *see also*
WILLIS/WILLYS
Amy xlviii, lv,
clxi, 533
Bridget (Yonge)
533
George (Gov.)
clxxxvi, 533
WYLMER
Margery 875
WYN
Elsbeth (Mostyn)
657
John 657
**WYNDHAM/
WINDHAM**
Alicia Maria
(Carpenter) 76,
78
Bridget (Mannock)
385
Catherine (Seymour)
76
Charles, 1st Earl of
Egremont 76, 77,
78

1604

Edward xlix,
  cxlvii, 385
Eleanor (Scrope)
  385, 493, 494
Elizabeth 77
Elizabeth (Ilive/
  Iliffe) 78
Elizabeth
  (Sydenham) 493
Elizabeth
  (Wentworth) 385
Elizabeth Alicia
  Maria 76
George, 1st Baron
  Leconfield 78
George O'Brien,
  2nd Earl of
  Egremont 78
Henry (Sir) 385
John (Sir) 493, 494
Madeline Caroline
  Frances Eden
  (Campbell) 78
Margaret 493, 494
Margaret (Howard)
  493
Mary 494
Mary Fanny (Blunt)
  78
Pamela Adelaide
  Genevieve 78
Percy Scawen
  (Hon.) 78
Susan (Clere) 385
Thomas (Sir) 385,
  493
William (Sir), 3rd
  Bt. 76
___ (Colles) 385

WYNN
  Catrin 232
WYNN(E)
  Alice (Coytmore)
    376
  Anne cxcii
  Catrin 231, 232
  Edward cxcii
  Elizabeth (Herbert)
    689
  Hannah cxcii, 510
  Harrie cxcii
  Hugh 376
  Humphrey 231, 689
  John cxcii
  Jonathan cxcii
  Margaret 772
  Mary cxcii
  Maud (ferch Oliver
    ap Thomas Pryce)
    231
  Peter cxcii
  Rebecca cxcii
  Sarah 376
  Sidney cxcii
  Tabitha cxcii
  Thomas (Dr.) lxi,
    cxcii
  William 376
WYNSLADE
  Joanna 595
WYVILL
  Anne (Brooke) 126
  Christopher 126
  Christopher (Sir),
    3rd Bt. 126
  Darcy 126
  Elinor (Boyd) 127
  family 127

Grace 127
Isabel (Gascoigne)
  126
Jane (Hessell) 126
Jane (Stapleton) 126
Marmaduke (Sir),
  2nd Bt. 126
Mary 127
Ursula (Darcy) 126
William 126
William (Sir), 4th
  Bt. 126
XENIA
  Grand Duchess of
    Russia 5
**XÉRICA/JÉRICA
(DE)**
  Beatríz 190, 993
  Beatríz (de Lauria)
    993
  Jaime Fernández de
    Aragón, Baron 993
  Jaime II, Señor 993
YALE
  Anne 658
  Anne (Lloyd) xix,
    xxxvii, xlvi, lvii,
    clxiii, 252, 657,
    686
  David 657, 920
  Elihu 657
  family vii, lii, 658,
    686
  Frances (Lloyd) 657
  Mary (Turner) 657
  Thomas clxiii, 657,
    686
  Ursula (Knight)
    657, 920

YARNALL/
YARNOULD
  Alice (____) 553
  Dorothy (Baker) 553
  Eleanor (Gower) 553
  family cli
  Francis lxiv, lxxi, cl, clxix, 553
  Hannah (Baker) 553
  John 553
  Philip lxiv, lxxi, cl, 553
  Sarah (____) 553
YARNBURY
  Helen Violet (Asquith) Bonham Carter, Baroness Asquith of 306
YATE
  Anne 125
  Dorothy (Stephens) 625
  Francis 625
  George lviii, lxii, clxxv, 625
  Jane (Tichborne) 625
  John 625
  Mary (Tattershall) 625
  Mary (Wells) (Stockett) 625
  Thomas 625
YATES
  John 361
  John Orfeur 361

  Julia (Lovell) 361
  Mary (Aglionby) 361
YEARDLEY
  George (Sir) (Gov.) 300
  Temperance (Flowerdew) 300
YELVERTON
  Anne 135
  Bridget (Drury) 359
  Christopher (Sir) 403, 404
  Dionysia (Stubbs) 359
  Elizabeth 360, 403, 404
  family 404
  Henry 359
  Margaret 713
  Margaret (Catesby) 403
  Ursula (Richardson) 359
  William (Sir), 1st Bt. 359
  William (Sir), 2nd Bt. 359
YOLANDE
  of Hainault, Empress of Constantinople 965
  of Ligne 292
YONGE
  Anne (Archer) 475
  Bridget 533
  Dorothy (Hartopp) 475

  Edward li, lxxi
  Elizabeth (____) (Fletcher) 475
  Elizabeth (Elliott) (Butler) (D'Arques) 311
  family viii, li
  Francis (Chief Justice) li, lxiv, lxxi, cxlvii, 313, 475, 476
  Hannah (____) (Eve) 311
  Henry 476
  Lydia (____) 475
  Mackworth 311
  Margaret (Bourne) 311
  Margaret (Mackworth) 311, 475
  Mary (Bonner) 533
  Philip 311, 475
  Robert lxxi, cxlvii, 311, 312, 313
  William 475, 533
YORK
  Anne (Hyde), Duchess of 22, 24, 122, 678, 679, 727, 780, 781, 782
  Beatrice of, Princess of Great Britain 25
  Edmund Plantagenet of Langley, Prince of England, 1st Duke of xxxix, 107, 114, 119, 126, 133, 134, 377, 410, 411, 423

Edward Lee, Archbishop of 419
Edwin Sandys, Archbishop of 509, 783
Elizabeth Plantagenet of, Queen of England 62, 69, 76, 79, 80, 347, 348
Eugenie of, Princess of Great Britain 25
George Merriton/Meriton/Meryton, Dean of 785
Isabel, Princess of Castile, Duchess of 107, 114, 119, 126, 133, 134, 377, 410, 411, 412, 423
John Kemp, Archbishop of, Archbishop of Canterbury 920, 922
Richard Plantagenet, 3rd Duke of 107, 114, 119, 126, 133
Sarah Margaret (Ferguson), Duchess of 25
YORKE
Anne 106
Dorothy 370, 373
Eleanor (Luttrell) 569
Elizabeth 569
Joan 92
Mary 323, 785
Mary (Sutton) 785
Roger 569
Thomas 785
YOUNG
Alice 695
Collier 463
G. V. C. clxxxiv
Gary E. lxxi, 553
Henry James l, lvi, lvii, lviii, lix, lxi, lxv, lxix, lxxi
Joan de Beauvoir (de Havilland) (Aherne) (Dozier) [Joan Fontaine] xvii, 463
Martha Ellen 171, 258
Rebecca 932
YOURI
Prince of Pinsk 797
YOURI I
King of Galicia 621
YOURIEVSKY
Catherine, Princess Dolguruki, Princess [second wife of Alexander II, Czar of Russia] 5, 799
YSOTA
ferch Ithel 815
YUGOSLAVIA
Alexander I, King of 3
Elizabeth (Karadjordjevic), Princess of 3
monarchs of 45, 81
Paul (Karadjordjevic), Prince Regent of 3
ZAHARIA
Elia, Queen of the Albanians 935
ZAHRADECKY VON ZAHRADEK
Eva (von Schweinichen) 619
Heinrich, Baron 619
Sophie Elisabeth, Baroness 619
ZAHRADECKY VON ZAHRADEK UND WISCHENAU
Carl, Baron 619
Elisabeth (von Rogendorf), Baroness 619
ZALUSKA
Françoise, Countess 622
ZAMOYSKI
Adam Stefan, Count 290
Elizabeth [Bianca Maria Constance] (Czartoryski), Princess 290
Emma (Sargeant) 290
counts 155
Stefan Adam, Count 290
ZÁPOLYA
Barbara, Queen of Poland 895

ZAVALETA
María Jacinta (de Riglos y San Martín) 996
ZAVALETA ARAMBURU (DE)
Mariano José 996
ZAVALETA RIGLOS
María Isabel 996
ZEHMEN (VON)
Elisabeth 617, 618
ZELKING (VON)
Anna Apollonia 237
ZHUKOVSKY
Alexandra 5
Vassili 5
ZIEGLER (VON)
Margareta 198
ZIEMOWIT III
Duke of Mazovia 621
ZIEROTIN (VON)
Antonia, Duchess von Lilgenau 895, 896
Joseph Karl 895
Maria Johanna Josefa Franziska Klara Serafina (von Schrattenbach) 895
ZIMMERMAN
Anna Clay lxiii, lxvi
ZINZENDORF/ SINZENDORF (VON)
Anna Maria, Countess 35
family lxi

Marie Esther Elisabeth 220
ZINZENDORF AND POTTENDORF (VON)
Anna, Baroness 237
Anna Amelia (of Dietrichstein-Hollenburg) 182, 237
Anna Apollonia (von Zelking) 237
Anne (Nitschmann) 239
Carlotta Justina (von Gersdorff) 237
Dorothea Renata, Countess 182, 237
Erdmuthe Dorothea (Reuss-Ebersdorf), Countess 196, 237
George Louis, Count 237
Henrietta Benigna Justina, Countess 8, 196
Johann Joachim, Baron 237
Maximilian Erasmus, Count 182, 237
Nicholas Ludwig, Count xxvi, xl, liii, clxxi, 196, 237
Otto Henry, Baron 237
ZITA
of Bourbon-Parma, Empress of Austria 800

ZITZEWITZ (VON)
Annalise 45
ZNAIM
Helena of 791, 797, 802
ZOG I
King of the Albanians [Ahmed Bey Zogu] 935
ZORRIGUIETA Y CERRUTI
Maxima, Queen of The Netherlands 991
ZOUCHE
Elizabeth 333
Isabel (Lowe) 333
John (Sir) 333
Katherine 698
Mary (Berkeley) 333
ZOUCHE of ASHBY, ZOUCHE of HARYNGWORTH.
see LA ZOUCHE (DE)
ZU FÜRSTENBERG.
see FÜRSTENBERG (VON) (ZU)
ZUÑIGA (DE)
Álvaro, Duke of Plasencia, Arévalo and Bejar 191
Leonor (Manrique) 191
Leonor (Pimentel) 191
Teresa (de Guzmán) 191

**ZUÑIGA Y
ARELLANO (DE)**
  Juana 191
**ZUÑIGA Y
GUZMÁN (DE)**
  Leonor 191
**ZUÑIGA Y
MANRIQUE (DE)**
  Pedro, Count of
    Bañares 191
**ZUÑIGA Y
PIMENTEL (DE)**
  Isabel 191
**ZUÑIGA Y SOTO-
MAYOR (DE)**
  Eleanor 140
ZUTHEM
  Adolf Werner II van
    Pallandt, Heer van,
    Heer van Egede
    445
ZWEIBRÜCKEN
  Elizabeth, Princess
    of 56
  Frederick, Count
    Palatine of 56
  John I, Count
    Palatine of 40,
    43, 56
  John II, Count
    Palatine of 56
**ZWEIBRÜCKEN-
BIRKENFELD**
  Caroline Henrietta
    Christine, Princess
    of 41
  Charles I, Count
    Palatine of 60, 893
  Sophie of 60, 893

**ZWEIBRÜCKEN-
KLEEBERG**
  Christine Magdalen,
    Princess of 40,
    43, 44
  Eleanor Catherine,
    Princess of 44
  John Casimir, Count
    Palatine of 40, 43
ZYLL (VAN)
  Helena 774
NO GIVEN NAME
  ferch Dafydd Las ap
    Hywel Fychan 810
  ferch Gronwy 693
  ferch Ieuan 808
  ferch Ieuan ap Rhys
    810
  ferch Llywelyn
    657, 689, 692, 693
  ferch Thomas ap
    Robert ap
    Gruffudd 660
  Maelog 808
  of Poland 791,
    797, 802
  Princess of France
    879, 919
NO SURNAME
  Adelaide, wife of
    Charles, Duke of
    Lower Lorraine
    874, 877, 879, 919
  Adelaide, wife of
    Nicholas I, Duke
    of Troppau 621
  Ælfflæd, wife of
    Ethelred II, King
    of England 861

  Aelis, wife of
    Robert I, King of
    France 879
  Alexandra, wife of
    Ivan II, Grand
    Prince of Moscow
    797
  Alexandra, wife of
    Semyon, Prince of
    Suzdal 791
  Anna, daughter of
    Iain [John], son of
    Alan M'Cowle 263
  Anna, wife of
    Andrei, Prince
    Golitsyn 798
  Anna, wife of
    Michael, Prince
    Olelkowicz-
    Slucky 621
  Anselm le Fleming
    864
  Avelina, sister of
    Gunnora, Duchess
    of Normandy 861
  Azubah ____, creole
    of Barbados 88
  Barbara, wife of
    Boleslaw IV, Duke
    of Mazovia 621
  Catrin (____), wife
    of Robert ap
    Thomas 230
  Clemence ____,
    mistress of John,
    King of England
    650, 657, 659, 680,
    682, 686, 689, 692,
    693, 694

1609

"Countess Henrietta" clxxxix
Edmund, brother-in-law of Gospatrick I, Earl of Northumberland and Dunbar 857
Eleanor le Fleming 864
Elisabeth, wife of Erik Skarsholmslægten, Duke of Sønder-Halland 644
Ellen (Evans) 652
Eudoxia, wife of Ivan, Prince Golitsyn 798
Eva, wife of Gedymin, Grand Duke of Lithuania 797
Gwen (Jones) 652
Helena, wife of Patrick, Prince of Pinsk 797
Helene, wife of Ivan I, Grand Prince of Moscow 791, 797
Herlève of Falaise 879, 919
Ida, wife of Guy II, Count of Ponthieu 853
Isabel, dau. of Alice de la Mare 852
Isabel, granddau. and co-heiress of Ralph FitzWilliam, wife of Nicholas Martin 851, 852
Jack the Ripper 542
John, first husband of Gwen Jones 652
John, husband of Ellen Evans 652
Kittamaquund 331, 332
Margaret, mistress of Donald Campbell, Abbot of Coupar Angus 280
Maria, wife of Narimond, Prince of Pinsk 797
Mor Ua Tuathail 837, 839, 847
Pocahontas [Mataoka] [Rebecca, wife of John Rolfe] xiv, 387, 711, 823, 851
Richard of Tyddin Tyfod 658
Richilde, wife of Baldwin VI, Count of Flanders 851
"Susan" [online name] 316
Sybil (de Say) 853
Xenia, wife of Youri, Prince Golitsyn 798
____ (Taronites) 640
____, husband of Sybil de Say 853
____, "native unmarried woman of Kumaon" 86

CHARACTERS, FICTIONAL
Bond, James 362
Guermantes, Duchess of 227
Holmes, Sherlock 136

NAMES, PERSONAL
Christian 277

POSTSCRIPT

Shortly after this index was completed, the engagement was announced of H.R.H. Princess Eugenie Victoria Helena of York, b. 1990 (younger daughter of H.R.H. Prince Andrew Albert Christian Edward, Duke of York, and Sarah Margaret Ferguson, known as Sarah, Duchess of York, and granddaughter of H.M. Queen Elizabeth II of Great Britain and H.R.H. Prince Philip of Greece and Denmark, Duke of Edinburgh, see pp. 3, 25, 321, 323, 930) to Jack Christopher Stamp Brooksbank. His descent fom Hon. William Saunders Sebright Lascelles and Caroline Georgiana Howard (see pp. 25, 69, 71) and from William Anne Keppel, 2nd Earl of Albemarle, and Anne Lennox (p. 25, a granddaughter of Charles II, King of England, and Louse-Renée de Penancoët de Kéroualle, Duchess of Portsmouth) is as follows: Jack Christopher Stamp Brooksbank; George Edward Hugh Brooksbank and Nicola Newton; Stamp Godfrey Brooksbank and Celia Dorothy Coke; Hon. Sir John Spencer Coke and Dorothy Olive Levy-Lawson; Thomas William Coke, 2nd Earl of Leicester, and Georgiana Caroline Cavendish; Thomas William Coke, 1st Earl of Leicester, and Anne Amelia Keppel, William George Cavendish, 2nd Baron Chesham, and Henrietta Frances Lascelles, William Charles Keppel, 4th Earl of Albemarle, and Elizabeth Southwell; Hon. William Saunders Sebright Lascelles and Caroline Georgiana Howard, SETH, George Keppel, 3rd Earl of Albemarle, and Anne Miller; William Anne Keppel, 2nd Earl of Albemarle, and Anne Lennox, SETH. See *BP* (Brookbanks, baronets; Leicester, Albemarle, Richmond, Chesham, Harewood). Note that these Brooksbank-to-Lascelles and Brooksbank-to-Lennox descents are not indexed in the preceding pages.

CPSIA information can be obtained
at www.ICGtesting.com
Printed in the USA
BVHW041149190920
589200BV00020B/229

9 780806 320762